Sixth Edition

ART
A Brief History

Marilyn Stokstad

Judith Harris Murphy Distinguished Professor of Art History Emerita

The University of Kansas

Michael W. Cothren

Scheuer Family Professor of Humanities

Department of Art, Swarthmore College

PEARSON

Boston Columbus Indianapolis New York San Francisco
Amsterdam Cape Town Dubai London Madrid Milan Munich Paris Montréal Toronto
Delhi Mexico City São Paulo Sydney Hong Kong Seoul Singapore Taipei Tokyo

Editor-in-Chief: Sarah Touborg
Senior Sponsoring Editor: Helen Ronan
Editorial Assistant: Victoria Engros
Senior Digital Media Editor: David Alick
Senior Media Project Manager: Rich Barnes
Project Management Team Lead: Melissa Feimer
Project Manager: Marlene Gassler
Program Manager: Barbara Cappuccio
Senior Operations Specialist: Diane Peirano
Digital Imaging Specialist: Corin Skidds
Senior Art Director/Cover Designer: Kathryn Foot
Cover Printer: Phoenix Color
Printer/Binder: Courier/Kendallville

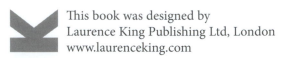

This book was designed by
Laurence King Publishing Ltd, London
www.laurenceking.com

Production Manager: Simon Walsh
Page Design: Ian Hunt
Photo Researcher: Evi Peroulaki
Copy Editor: Magda Nakassis

Cover photo and page iii: Pieter Bruegel the Elder, *Return of the Hunters*. 1565. Oil on wood panel, 3′10½″ × 5′3¾″ (1.18 × 1.61 m). Kunsthistorisches Museum, Vienna. Photo: akg-images/Erich Lessing.

Credits and acknowledgments borrowed from other sources and reproduced, with permission, in this textbook appear on the appropriate page within the text or on the credit pages in the back of this book.

Library of Congress Cataloging-in-Publication Data

Stokstad, Marilyn
    Art : a brief history / Marilyn Stokstad, Judith Harris Murphy Distinguished Professor of Art History Emerita, The University of Kansas; Michael W. Cothren, Scheuer Family Professor of Humanities, Department of Art, Swarthmore College. -- Sixth Edition.
        pages cm
    Abridgment of the author's Art history.
    Includes bibliographical references and index.
    ISBN 0-13-384375-0
    1. Art--History. I. Cothren, Michael Watt. II. Title.
    N5300.S923 2016
    709--dc23
                        2014028656

10 9 8 7 6 5 4 3 2 1

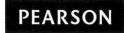

ISBN 10: 0-13-384375-0
ISBN 13: 978-0-13-384375-0
Instructor's Review Copy ISBN 10: 0-13-379007-X
ISBN 13: 978-0-13-379007-8
à la Carte ISBN 10: 0-13-378973-X
ISBN 13: 978-0-13-378973-7

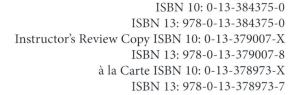

BRIEF CONTENTS

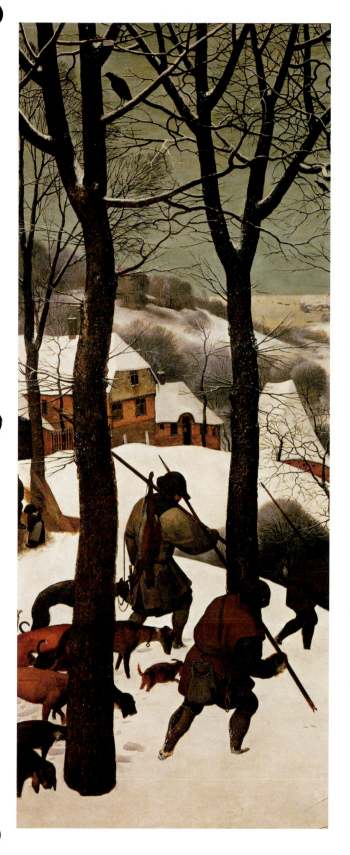

CONTENTS

6 ETRUSCAN AND ROMAN ART 128

7 JEWISH, EARLY CHRISTIAN, AND BYZANTINE ART 158

8 ISLAMIC ART 184

9 LATER ASIAN ART 204

10 EARLY MEDIEVAL AND ROMANESQUE ART 232

11 GOTHIC ART 260

12 EARLY RENAISSANCE ART 292

13 ART OF THE HIGH RENAISSANCE AND REFORMATION 324

This new edition of *Art: A Brief History* is the result of a continuing collaboration of two scholar-teachers who share a common vision. In certain ways, we also share a common history. Neither of us expected to become a professor of art history. Marilyn Stokstad took her first art history course as a requirement of her studio arts program. Michael Cothren discovered the discipline almost by chance during a semester abroad in Provence when a painting instructor sent him on a field trip to learn from the formal intricacies of Romanesque sculpture. Perhaps as a result of the unexpected delight we found in these formative experiences, we share a conviction that first courses in the history of art should be filled with as much enjoyment as erudition; that they should foster an enthusiastic, as well as an educated, public for the visual arts. With this end firmly in mind, we will continue to create books intended to help students relish learning the essentials of a vast and complex field of study. For millennia human beings have embodied their most cherished ideas and values in visual and tangible form. We have learned that by engaging with these works from the past, we can enrich our lives in the present, especially because we are living in a present when images have become an increasingly important aspect of how we communicate with each other.

Like its predecessors, this new edition seeks to balance formal and iconographic analysis with contextual art history in order to craft interpretations that will engage with a diverse student population. Throughout the text, the visual arts are treated as part of a larger world, in which geography, politics, religion, economics, philosophy, social life, and the other fine arts were related components of a vibrant cultural landscape. This is a daunting agenda for a "Brief" book. But we believe it is essential. Art and architecture have played a central role in human history, and they continue to do so today. Our book will fulfill its purpose if it introduces a broad spectrum of students to some of the richest human achievements created through the centuries and across the globe, and if it inspires those students both to respect and to cherish their historical legacy in the visual arts. Perhaps it will convince some to dedicate themselves to assuring that our own age leaves a comparable artistic legacy, thereby continuing the ever-evolving history of art.

So ... What's New in This Edition?

We believe that even an established introductory art history text should continually respond to the changing needs of its audience—both students and educators. In this way the art it introduces is more likely to challenge and nourish its readers' lives, both at the time of use and long into the future.

Our goal was to make this revised text an improvement over its earlier incarnations in sensitivity, readability, and accessibility without losing anything in comprehensiveness, in scholarly precision, or in its ability to engage the reader. As with past editions, thoughtful feedback from our many users and reviewers was critical in helping us meet this goal.

ART HISTORY REIMAGINED WITH REVEL

One of the most exciting developments that took place during this revision was the development and design of REVEL, a new digital format that makes *Art: A Brief History* excitingly interactive. We believe that REVEL presents the same material found in the printed version in a dynamic design that actually functions more like a classroom than a textbook. We are sure that this will make art history more engaging to the current generation of college students.

NEW LEARNING ARCHITECTURE

Throughout the text, we have rethought and expanded the learning architecture by coordinating the A-heads in the running text with both the learning objectives ("Learn About It") and the assessment questions ("Think About It"). These tools are rooted in four key outcomes that have helped steer and shape our revision since they emphasize the fundamental reasons we teach and study art history:

1. Identifying the hallmarks of regional and period styles in relation to their technical, formal, and expressive character
2. Understanding the principal themes, subjects, and symbols in the art of a variety of cultures, periods, and locations
3. Probing the relationship of works of art to human history by exploring their cultural, economic, political, social, spiritual, moral, and intellectual contexts
4. Recognizing and applying the critical thinking, creative inquiry, and disciplined reasoning that stand behind art historical interpretation, as well as the vocabulary and concepts used to describe and characterize works of art with clarity and power.

NEW SCHOLARSHIP, NEW IMAGES

Over the many years we have taught undergraduate beginners, we have always enjoyed sharing—both with our students and our fellow educators—the new discoveries and fresh interpretive perspectives that are constantly enriching the history of art. We relished the opportunity here to incorporate some of the latest thinking and most recent interpretations—whether this involved presenting a newly excavated example of a Han tomb model, including a more accurate reconstruction of the Akropolis, or featuring Raphael's newly restored *Madonna of the Goldfinch* in a discussion of his earlier devotional paintings. Indeed, changes have been made on many levels—from the introduction to the glossary, and from captions to chapter introductions and conclusions. Every change aims to make the text more useful to the instructors and students in today's art history classrooms.

IN GRATITUDE

As its predecessors did, this Sixth Edition of *Art: A Brief History* benefited from the reflections and assessments of a distinguished team of scholars and educators. We are grateful to the following academic reviewers for their numerous insights and suggestions for improvement:

Jacquelyn Coutre, Adelphi University
Bernadine Barnes, Wake Forest University
Marie Gasper-Hulvat, Kent State University Stark

Karen Goodchild, Wofford College
Roberta Hayes, Indiana Wesleyan University
Marian Hollinger, Fairmont State University
Maya Jimenez, Kingsborough Community College, CUNY
Mary Kilburn, Central Piedmont Community College
Ellen Konowitz, SUNY New Paltz
Diana McClintock, Kennesaw State University
Thomas Shillea, Northampton Community College
Rachelle Street, Borough of Manhattan Community College
Kenneth Wade, Champlain College
Bille Wickre, Albion College

WHAT'S NEW

Chapter by Chapter Revisions

Some of the key highlights of this new edition include the following:

Introduction
New images of flowers—a photograph of *Two Callas* by Imogen Cunningham and *Jack-in-the-Pulpit* painted by Georgia O'Keeffe—enrich the discussion of representational modes and present a productive opportunity for comparative analysis.

Chapter 1—Prehistoric Art in Europe
A new ground-level view of Stonehenge is coordinated with a better diagram of the whole site to clarify the presentation of this critical monument.

Chapter 2—Art of the Ancient Near East
The carved vessel from Warka is now illustrated with a double view showing two sides to enhance an understanding of the unfolding of the narrative, which is more fully explored in the text. A new Closer Look explores both sides of the Standard of Ur.

Chapter 3—Art of Ancient Egypt
A better image has been substituted for the Great Pyramids, and leader-line captions have been added to the reconstruction drawing.

Chapter 4—Early Asian Art
Better images were obtained to illustrate the lion capital of Ashokan pillar, the Gandhara Shakyamuni Buddha, the Mathura Buddha and attendants, Borobodur, Nanchan Temple, and the Great Wild Goose Pagoda. A more complex newly excavated example has been used to discuss Han tomb models.

Chapter 5—Art of Ancient Greece and the Aegean World
Better images were obtained to illustrate the *Riace Warriors*, the Parthenon, and the *Spear Bearer* (*Doryphoros*). The discussion of Mycenaen dagger blades centers on a new, more representa- tive example. Two critical reconstructions have been redrawn for greater clarity: the design scheme of a Cycladic figure, and a more accurate reconstruction of the Akropolis. Leader-line captions enrich the reconstruction drawings of Knossos and Mycenae. A new discussion of the temple from Aegina inte- grates the pediment sculpture with its architectural context.

Chapter 6 – Etruscan and Roman Art
Several new and improved drawings have been substituted for the reconstructions of an Etruscan temple and the Basilica of Maxentius and Constantine. A new figure of a detail has been added to the discussion of the Column of Trajan, and the Venice Tetrarchs now represent tetrarchic sculpture. The plan and reconstruction of the generic Roman house has been replaced with a plan of the House of the Vetii at Pompeii to create an integrated discussion of that house, including its architectural design as well as its wall paintings.

Chapter 7—Jewish, Early Christian, and Byzantine Art
Leader-line captions clarify the isometric drawing of Hagia Sophia. A plan has been added of the Hosios Lukas monastery complex, allowing an expanded discussion of the organization of monasteries within the text. Improved images illustrate the narthex mosaics of the Constantinopolitan monastic church of Christ in Chora.

Chapter 8—Islamic Art
We have reorganized the presentation of the monuments and works to clarify chronological relationships in the development of Islamic art. Better images illustrate the Dome of the Rock. To enrich the discussion of luxury arts, we have substituted Bihzad's "Yusuf Fleeing Zulayhka" for his "Turkish Bath." We have also added Sultan Muhammad's spectacular "Court of Gayumars," considered in its time as the greatest painting of the Persian narrative tradition.

Chapter 9—Later Asian Art
The chapter now features a woodblock print by Sharaku.

Chapter 10—Early Medieval and Romanesque Art

The Art and Its Contexts box on Hildegard of Bingen now includes an illustration of one of her visions as well as her author portrait. Better images have been found for the figures of the Moissac portal and the Bayeux Embroidery.

Chapter 11—Gothic Art

The interior of the abbey church of Saint-Denis, the Chartres Cathedral Royal Portal jamb statues, and the interior of the Sainte-Chapelle in Paris are captured better in a series of new images.

Chapter 12—Early Renaissance Art

There is a better image for the recently restored figure of Donatello's David. Giovanni Bellini's *St. Francis in Ecstasy* has been added to incorporate Venice into the discussion of the early Italian Renaissance.

Chapter 13—Art of the High Renaissance and Reformation

This chapter has a new opening focusing on Leonardo's *Mona Lisa*. Better images appear for the figures of Michelangelo's Vatican Pietà and Titan's *Pastoral Concert*. Raphael's newly restored *Madonna of the Goldfinch* has been used to discuss his early devotional paintings.

Chapter 14—Seventeenth-Century Art in Europe

A new Closer Look focuses on Rubens and Snyders's *Prometheus Bound*. A painting of the Immaculate Conception by Murillo has been added to coordinate with the newly included painting of the Virgin of Guadalupe in Chapter 17.

Chapter 15—Art of the Americas

Better images have been obtained for El Castillo and the chac-mool at Chichén Itzá. A reconstruction drawing has been added to the presentation of the Templo Mayor. A new Closer Look focuses on the Maya relief of Shield Jaguar and Lady Xok. The chapter now includes a discussion of a Mimbres painted bowl.

Chapter 17—European and American Art, 1715–1840

Fragonard's *The Swing*, Sebastian Salcedo's *Virgin of Guadalupe*, and Friedrich's *Abbey in an Oak Forest* have been added to this chapter.

Chapter 18—European and American Art, 1840–1910

The Life Line now represents the work of Winslow Homer. A re-written Art and Its Contexts box on "Japonisme" highlights prints by Suzuki Harunobu and Mary Cassatt.

Chapter 19—Modern Art in Europe and the Americas, 1900–1945

A glorious new color photograph captures Mary Colter's Lookout Studio at the Grand Canyon.

Chapter 20—Art since 1945

A new Art and Its Contexts box on "Controversies over Public Funding of the Arts" includes an illustration of Chris Ofili's *The Holy Virgin Mary*. A new painting is used in the discussion of Mark Rothko, and Jean-Michel Basquiat's *Horn Players* has been added to the chapter.

ACKNOWLEDGMENTS AND GRATITUDE

Art: A Brief History is a concise version of *Art History*, which was first published in 1995 by Harry N. Abrams, Inc. and Prentice Hall, Inc. Because this new edition builds on the revisions of previous editions of both *Art History* and *Art: A Brief History*, the work of many colleagues and friends who contributed to the original texts and their subsequent revisions is reflected here. We extend to them our long-term gratitude.

It was an absolute joy to work closely with two gifted and dedicated editors at Pearson, Sarah Touborg and Helen Ronan, in crafting a book that would incorporate effective pedagogical features into a shortened art historical narrative. We are continually bolstered by the warm and dedicated support of Marlene Gassler and Barbara Cappuccio in Pearson Project and Program Management. Cory Skidds and Victoria Engros facilitated our work in many ways. Much appreciation also goes to Maggie Moylan, Director of Product Marketing, and Wendy Albert, Executive Marketing Manager, as well as the entire Social Sciences and Arts team at Pearson. At Laurence King Publishing, Jodi Simpson, Kara Hattersley-Smith, Julia Ruxton, Evi Peroulaki, and Simon Walsh, along with designer Ian Hunt, oversaw the production of this new edition.

From Marilyn Stokstad:

I extend my thanks to Frederick M. Asher, Claudia Brown, Patricia J. Graham, and Robert D. Mowry for their contributions and assistance with Asian art; Joy Sperling for Modern art; D. Fairchild Ruggles for Islamic art, Sara E. Orel and Carol S. Ivory for art of the Pacific Islands; Douglass Bailey for Prehistoric art; Claudia L. Brittenham for the indigenous art of the Americas; and Patricia J. Darish and David A. Binkley for African art.

Of course, my very special thanks go to my sister, Karen Leider, and my niece, Anna Leider.

From Michael Cothren:

Words are barely adequate to express my gratitude to Marilyn Stokstad for welcoming me with such trust, enthusiasm, and warmth into the collaborative adventure of revising her path-breaking textbooks. Working alongside her—and our extraordinary editors Sarah Touborg and Helen Ronan—has been delightful and rewarding, enriching and challenging. I look forward to the continuing partnership.

I have been supported by a host of colleagues at Swarthmore College. Generations of students challenged me to hone my pedagogical skills and steady my focus on what is at stake in telling the history of art. Special thanks to List Gallery Director Andrea Packard, who brought the work of Hiroyuki Hamada to campus and set in motion my connection with him that led ultimately to his inclusion here. My colleagues in the Art Department—especially Stacy Bomento, June Cianfrana, Randall Exon, Constance Cain Hungerford, Patricia Reilly, and Tomoko Sakomura—have answered all sorts of questions, shared innumerable insights on works in their areas of expertise, and offered unending encouragement and support. I am so lucky to work with them.

Many art historians have generously provided assistance, and I am especially grateful to Claudia Brown, Cary Liu, Elizabeth Marlowe, Thomas Morton, Mary Shepard, Donna Sadler, David Shapiro, and Jeffrey Chipps Smith. This revision of *Art: A Brief History* was supported by the earlier work of Fletcher Coleman, Andrew Finegold, and especially Moses Hanson-Harding, three extraordinary research assistants involved in recent revisions of *Art History*.

I was fortunate to have the support of many friends. John Brendler, David Eldridge, Stephen Lehmann, Mary Marissen, Denis Ott, and Karen and Rick Taylor patiently listened and truly relished my enjoyment of this work. My extraordinary daughters Emma and Nora are a constant inspiration. I am so grateful for their delight in my passion for art's history, and for their dedication to keeping me from taking myself too seriously. My deepest gratitude is reserved for Susan Lowry, my wife and soulmate, who brings joy to every facet of my life. She was not only patient and supportive during the long distraction of my work on this book, she also provided help in so very many ways. The greatest accomplishment of my life in art history occurred on the day I met her at Columbia in 1973.

If the arts are ultimately an expression of human faith and integrity as well as human thought and creativity, then writing and producing books that introduce new viewers to the wonders of art's history, and to the courage and visions of the artists and art historians that stand behind it—remains a noble undertaking. We feel honored to be a part of such a worthy project.

Marilyn Stokstad
Lawrence, KS

Michael W. Cothren
Philadelphia, PA, and Sedona, AZ

Spring 2014

Give Your Students Choices for Learning with *Art: A Brief History*

Pearson arts titles are available in a variety of formats to give your students more choices—and more ways to save.

Explore REVEL—dynamic content matched to the way today's students read, think, and learn

Ideal for customers who want to experience Stokstad and Cothren's approach to art history in one highly interactive learning path, REVEL integrates:

- Spoken audio read by the author
- Pan/zoom and scale markers for nearly every image, along with perspective overlays
- Visual quizzes as well as content quizzing that allows students to check their understanding at regular intervals
- Media interactives including Closer Look tours, 360-degree architectural panoramas and simulations of major monuments, and videos
- Writing, journaling, and discussion prompts
- Image and term flashcards.

Fully mobile, REVEL enables students to interact with course material on the devices they use, anywhere and anytime.

REVEL's assignability and tracking tools help educators:

- Ensure that students are completing their reading and understanding core concepts
- Establish a clear, detailed schedule that helps students stay on task
- Monitor both class assignment completion and individual student achievement.

Support students with MyArtsLab—a robust companion study environment

For those customers who prefer companion study resources, MyArtsLab offers:

- Writing Space, providing a single place to create and evaluate graded writing assignments, featuring tools for developing and assessing concept mastery and critical thinking
- Media assignments such as Closer Look tours, panoramas, videos, and simulations
- Study resources such as flashcards
- Links to book specific test banks for quizzes.

Build your own Pearson Custom course material

For enrollments of at least 25, the Pearson Custom Library allows you to create your own textbook by:

- Combining chapters from best-selling Pearson textbooks in the sequence you want
- Adding your own content, such as a guide to a local art museum, a map of monuments in your area, your syllabus, or a study guide you've created.

A Pearson Custom Library book is priced according to the number of chapters and may even save your students money. To build your custom text, visit **www.pearsoncustomlibrary.com** or contact your Pearson representative.

Explore additional cost-saving options

The Books à la Carte edition offers a convenient, three-hole-punched, loose-leaf version of the traditional text at a discounted price—allowing students to take only what they need to class. *Students save 35% over the list price of the traditional book.* ISBN: 0-13-378973-X

The CourseSmart eTextbook offers the same content as the printed text in a convenient online format—with highlighting, online search, and printing capabilities. *Students save 60% over the list price of the traditional book.* **www.coursesmart.com** ISBN: 0-13-379005-3

To request an examination copy or for additional information on our extensive instructor resources, including image PowerPoints and Test Item Files, please visit us at **www.pearsonhighered.com/art**.

Art history focuses on the visual arts—painting, drawing, sculpture, prints, photography, ceramics, metalwork, architecture, and more. This Starter Kit contains basic information and addresses concepts that underlie and support the study of art history. It provides a quick reference guide to the vocabulary used to classify and describe art objects. Understanding these terms is indispensable because you will encounter them again and again in reading, talking, and writing about art.

Let us begin with the basic properties of art. A work of art is a material object having both **form** and **content**. It is often described and categorized according to its *style* and *medium*.

FORM

Referring to purely visual aspects of art and architecture, the term *form* encompasses qualities of LINE, SHAPE, COLOR, LIGHT, TEXTURE, SPACE, MASS, VOLUME, and COMPOSITION. These qualities are known as FORMAL ELEMENTS. When art historians use the term *formal*, they mean "relating to form."

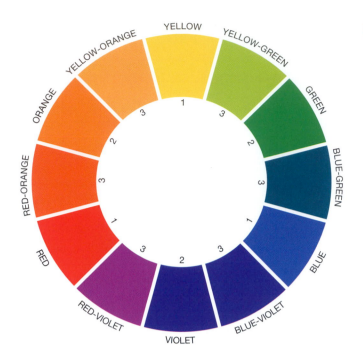

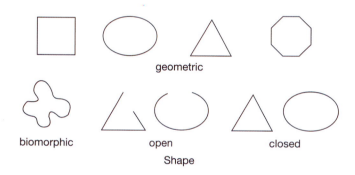

Shape

Line and **shape** are attributes of form. Line is an element—usually drawn or painted—the length of which is so much greater than the width that we perceive it as having only length. Line can be actual, as when the line is visible, or it can be implied, as when the movement of the viewer's eyes over the surface of a work follows a path determined by the artist. Shape, on the other hand, is the two-dimensional, or flat, area defined by the borders of an enclosing *outline* or *contour*. Shape can be *geometric*, **biomorphic** (suggesting living things; sometimes called *organic*), *closed*, or *open*. The *outline* or *contour* of a three-dimensional object can also be perceived as line.

Color has several attributes. These include HUE, VALUE, and SATURATION.

HUE is what we think of when we hear the word *color*, and the terms are interchangeable. We perceive hues as the result of differing wavelengths of electromagnetic energy. The visible spectrum, which can be seen in a rainbow, runs from red through violet. When the ends of the spectrum are connected through the hue red-violet, the result may be diagrammed as a color wheel. The **primary hues** (numbered 1) are red,

yellow, and blue. They are known as primaries because all other colors are made by combining these hues. Orange, green, and violet result from the mixture of two primaries and are known as secondary hues (numbered 2). Intermediate hues, or tertiaries (numbered 3), result from the mixture of a primary and a secondary. **Complementary colors** are the two colors directly opposite one another on the color wheel, such as red and green. Red, orange, and yellow are regarded as warm colors and appear to advance toward us. Blue, green, and violet, which seem to recede, are called cool colors. Black and white are not considered colors but neutrals; in terms of light, black is understood as the absence of color and white as the mixture of all colors.

VALUE is the relative degree of lightness or darkness of a given color and is created by the amount of light reflected from an object's surface. A dark green has a deeper value than a light green, for example. In black-and-white reproductions of colored objects, you see only value, and some artworks—for example, a drawing made with black ink—possess only value, not hue or saturation.

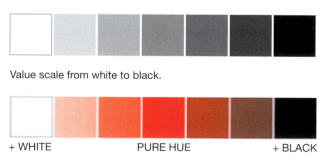

Value scale from white to black.

+ WHITE   PURE HUE   + BLACK

Value variation in red.

SATURATION, also sometimes referred to as *intensity*, is a color's quality of brightness or dullness. A color described as highly saturated looks vivid and pure; a hue of low saturation may or look a little muddy or grayed.

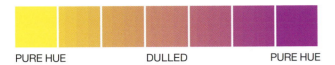

PURE HUE   DULLED   PURE HUE

Intensity scale from bright to dull.

Texture, another **attribute** of form, is the tactile (or touch-perceived) quality of a surface. It is described by words such as *smooth, polished, rough, prickly, grainy,* or *oily.* Texture takes two forms: the texture of the actual surface of the work of art and the implied (illusionistically described) surface of objects represented in the work of art.

Space is what contains forms. It may be actual and three-dimensional, as it is with sculpture and architecture, or it may be fictional, represented illusionistically in two dimensions, as when artists represent recession into the distance on a flat surface—such as a wall or a canvas—by using various systems of **perspective**.

Mass and **volume** are properties of three-dimensional things. Mass is solid matter—whether sculpture or architecture—that takes up space. Volume is enclosed or defined space, and may be either solid or hollow. Like space, mass and volume may be illusionistically represented on a two-dimensional surface, as in a painting or a photograph.

Composition is the organization, or arrangement, of forms in a work of art. Shapes and colors may be repeated or varied, balanced symmetrically or asymmetrically; they may be stable or dynamic. The possibilities are nearly endless, and artistic choice depends both on the time and place where the work was created as well as on the objectives of individual artists. PICTORIAL DEPTH (spatial recession) is a specialized aspect of composition in which the three-dimensional world is represented on a flat surface, or PICTURE PLANE. The area "behind" the picture plane is called the PICTURE SPACE and conventionally contains three "zones": FOREGROUND, MIDDLE GROUND, and BACKGROUND.

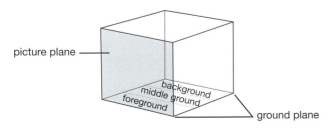

picture plane

background
middle ground
foreground

ground plane

Various techniques for conveying a sense of pictorial depth have been devised by artists in different cultures and at different times. A number of them are diagrammed here. In some European art, the use of various systems of PERSPECTIVE has sought to create highly convincing illusions of recession into space. At other times and in other cultures, indications of recession are actually suppressed or avoided to emphasize surface rather than space.

CONTENT

Content includes SUBJECT MATTER, but not all works of art have subject matter. Many buildings, paintings, sculptures, and other art objects include no recognizable references to things in nature nor to any story or historical situation, focusing instead on lines, colors, masses, volumes, and other formal elements. However, all works of art—even those without recognizable subject matter—have content, or meaning, insofar as they seek to communicate ideas, convey feelings, or affirm the beliefs and values of their makers, their **patrons**, and usually the people who originally viewed or used them.

Content may derive from the social, political, religious, and economic CONTEXTS in which a work was created, the INTENTION of the artist, and the RECEPTION of the work by beholders (the audience). Art historians, applying different methods of INTERPRETATION, often arrive at different conclusions regarding the content of a work of art, and single works of art can contain more than one meaning because they are occasionally directed at more than one audience.

The study of subject matter is called ICONOGRAPHY (literally, "the writing of images") and includes the identification of SYMBOLS—images that take on meaning through association, resemblance, or **convention**.

STYLE

Expressed very broadly, *style* is the combination of form and composition that makes a work distinctive. STYLISTIC ANALYSIS is one of art history's most developed practices, because it is how art historians recognize the work of an individual artist or the characteristic manner of groups of artists working in a particular time or place. Some of the most commonly used terms to discuss ARTISTIC STYLES include PERIOD STYLE, REGIONAL STYLE, REPRESENTATIONAL STYLE, ABSTRACT STYLE, LINEAR STYLE, and PAINTERLY STYLE.

Period style refers to the common traits detectable in works of art and architecture from a particular historical era. It is good practice not to use the words "style" and "period" interchangeably. Style is the sum of many influences and characteristics, including the period of its creation. An example of proper usage is "an American house from the Colonial period built in the Georgian style."

Regional style refers to stylistic traits that persist in a geographic region. An art historian whose specialty is medieval art can recognize Spanish style through many successive medieval periods and can distinguish individual objects created in medieval Spain from other medieval objects that were created in, for example, Italy.

Representational styles are those that describe the appearance of recognizable subject matter in ways that make it seem lifelike.

REALISM and NATURALISM are terms that some people used interchangeably to characterize artists' attempts to represent the observable world in a manner that appears to describe its visual appearance accurately. When capitalized, Realism refers to a specific period style discussed in Chapter 18.

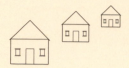

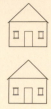

overlapping

In overlapping, partially covered elements are meant to be seen as located behind those covering them.

diminution

In diminution of scale, successively smaller elements are perceived as being progressively farther away than the largest ones.

vertical perspective

Vertical perspective stacks elements, with the higher ones intended to be perceived as deeper in space.

atmospheric perspective

Through atmospheric perspective, objects in the far distance (often in bluish-gray hues) have less clarity than nearer objects. The sky becomes paler as it approaches the horizon.

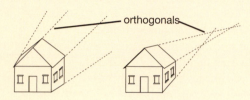

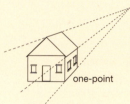

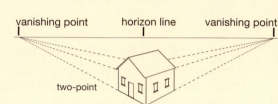

divergent perspective

In divergent or reverse perspective, forms widen slightly and imaginary lines called orthogonals diverge as they recede in space.

intuitive perspective

Intuitive perspective takes the opposite approach from divergent perspective. Forms become narrower and orthogonals converge the farther they are from the viewer, approximating the optical experience of spatial recession.

linear perspective

Linear perspective (also called scientific, mathematical, one-point, and Renaissance perspective) is a rationalization or standardization of intuitive perspective that was developed in fifteenth-century Italy. It uses mathematical formulas to construct images in which all elements are shaped by, or arranged along, orthogonals that converge in one or more vanishing points on a horizon line.

IDEALIZATION strives to create images of physical perfection according to the prevailing values or tastes of a culture. The artist may work in a representational style and idealize it to capture an underlying value or expressive effect.

ILLUSIONISM refers to a highly detailed style that seeks to create a convincing illusion of physical reality by describing its visual appearance meticulously.

Abstract styles depart from mimicking lifelike appearance to capture the essence of a form. An abstract artist may work from nature or from a memory image of nature's forms and colors, which are simplified, stylized, perfected, distorted, elaborated, or otherwise transformed to achieve a desired expressive effect.

NONREPRESENTATIONAL (or NONOBJECTIVE) ART is a term often used for works of art that do not aim to produce recognizable natural imagery.

EXPRESSIONISM refers to styles in which the artist exaggerates aspects of form to draw out the beholder's subjective response or to project the artist's own subjective feelings.

Linear describes both styles and techniques. In linear styles artists use line as the primary means of definition. But linear

paintings can also incorporate MODELING—creating an illusion of three-dimensional substance through shading, usually executed so that brushstrokes nearly disappear.

Painterly describes a style of representation in which vigorous, evident brushstrokes dominate, and outlines, shadows, and highlights are brushed in freely.

MEDIUM AND TECHNIQUE

Medium (plural, *media*) refers to the material or materials from which a work of art is made. Today, literally anything can be used to make a work of art, including not only traditional materials like paint, ink, and stone, but also rubbish, food, and the earth itself.

Technique is the process that transforms the medium into a work of art. Various techniques are explained throughout this book in Technique boxes. Two-dimensional media and techniques include painting, drawing, printing, and photography. Three-dimensional media and techniques are sculpture, architecture, and many small-scale arts (such as jewelry, containers, or vessels) in media such as ceramics, metal, or wood.

Painting includes wall painting and **fresco**, **illumination** (the decoration of books with paintings), **panel painting** (painting on wood panels), painting on canvas, and handscroll and **hanging scroll** painting. The paint in these examples is pigment mixed with a liquid vehicle, or binder. Some art historians also consider pictorial media such as **mosaic** and **stained glass**—where the pigment is arranged in solid form—also as a type of painting.

Graphic arts are those that involve the application of lines and strokes to a two-dimensional surface or support, most often paper. Drawing is a graphic art, as are the various forms of printmaking. Drawings may be sketches (quick visual notes, often made in preparation for larger drawings or paintings); studies (more carefully drawn analyses of details or entire compositions); **cartoons** (full-scale drawings made in preparation for work in another medium, such as fresco, stained glass, or **tapestry**); or complete artworks in themselves. Drawings can be made with ink, charcoal, crayon, or pencil. Prints, unlike drawings, are made in multiple copies. The various forms of printmaking include woodcut, the **intaglio** processes (**engraving**, **etching**, **drypoint**), and **lithography**.

Photography (literally, "light writing") is a medium that involves the rendering of optical images on light-sensitive surfaces. Photographic images are typically recorded by a camera.

Sculpture is three-dimensional art that is CARVED, MODELED, CAST, or ASSEMBLED. Carved sculpture is subtractive in the sense that the image is created by taking away material. Wood, stone, and ivory are common materials used to create carved sculptures. Modeled sculpture is considered additive, meaning that the object is built up from a material, such as clay, that is soft enough to be molded and shaped. Metal sculpture is usually cast or is assembled by welding or a similar means of permanent joining.

Sculpture is either free-standing (that is, surrounded by space) or in pictorial relief. **Relief sculpture** projects from the background surface of the same piece of material. **High-relief** sculpture projects far from its background; **low-relief** sculpture is only slightly raised; and **sunken relief**, found mainly in ancient Egyptian art, is carved into the surface, with the highest part of the relief being the flat surface.

Ephemeral arts include processions, ceremonies, or ritual dances (often with décor, costumes, or masks); **Performance Art**; **earthworks**; cinema and video art; and some forms of digital or computer art. All impose a temporal limitation—the artwork is viewable for a finite period of time and then disappears forever, is in a constant state of change, or must be replayed to be experienced again.

Architecture creates enclosures for human activity or habitation. It is three-dimensional, highly spatial, functional, and closely bound with developments in technology and materials. Since it is difficult to capture in a photograph, several types of schematic drawings are commonly used to enable the visualization of a building:

> PLANS depict a structure's masses and voids, presenting a view from above of the building's footprint or as if it had been sliced horizontally at about waist height.

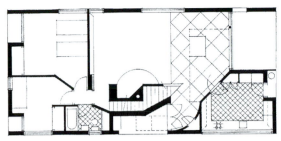

Plan: Philadelphia, Vanna Venturi House

SECTIONS reveal the interior of a building as if it had been cut vertically from top to bottom.

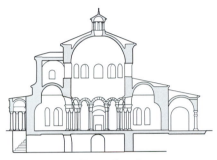

Section: Rome, Sta. Costanza

ISOMETRIC DRAWINGS show buildings from oblique angles either seen from above ("**bird's-eye view**") to reveal their basic three-dimensional forms (often cut away so we can peek inside) or from below ("worm's-eye view") to represent the arrangement of interior spaces and the upward projection of structural elements.

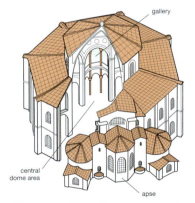

gallery

central dome area

apse

Isometric cutaway from above: Ravenna, San Vitale

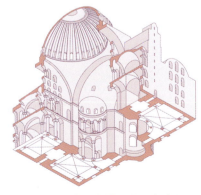

Isometric projection from below: Istanbul, Hagia Sophia

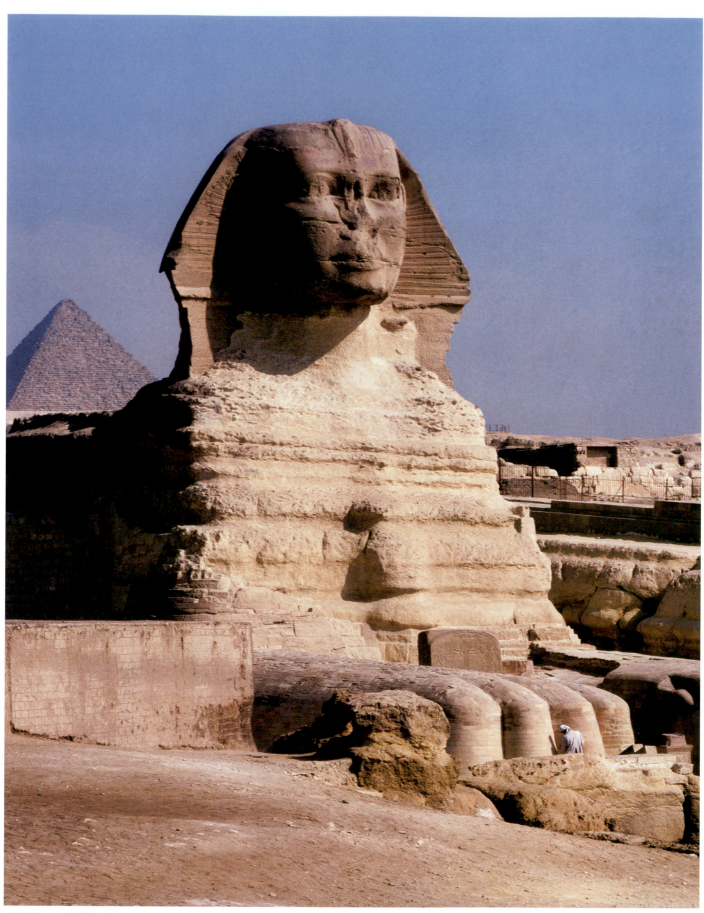

INTRO–1 • GREAT SPHINX, FUNERARY COMPLEX OF KHAFRE, GIZA, EGYPT
Old Kingdom, c. 2520–2494 BCE, Dynasty 4. Limestone, height approx. 65′ (19.8 m).

INTRODUCTION

Crouching in front of the pyramids and carved from the living rock of the Giza plateau in Egypt, the **GREAT SPHINX** is one of the world's best-known monuments (**FIG. INTRO-1**). By placing the head of the ancient Egyptian king Khafre on the body of a huge lion, the sculptors joined human intelligence and animal strength in a single image to evoke the superhuman power of a ruler. For nearly 4,600 years, the Sphinx has defied encroaching desert sands and other assaults of nature; today it also must withstand the human-driven sprawl of greater Cairo and the impact of air pollution. In its majesty, it symbolizes mysterious wisdom and dreams of permanence, of immortality. But is such a monument a work of art? Does it matter that the people who carved the Sphinx—unlike today's seemingly independent, individualistic, innovating artists—followed time-honored, formulaic conventions and the precise instructions of their **patrons**? Most people would answer, "Certainly, this is art. Human imagination conceived this amazing hybrid man-lion, and human skill gave material form to the concept behind it." Does the human combination of imagination and skill constitute a work of art?

What Is Art?

Answering this question was once easier than it is today. Most would agree that works of art demonstrate a combination of imagination, skill, training, and observation on the part of their human creators. They embody some of the most cherished beliefs of the culture that created them. If they appeal to our own taste for order and harmony, we may consider them beautiful. But now more than ever we realize that beauty lies in the eye of the beholder, and that our aesthetic responses may be inconsistent with the responses of those in the past who created and originally saw the works. Whether acquired at home, in classrooms, in museums, at the movies, or on the Internet, our responses to art—as well as our judgments about what constitutes art—are learned behaviors, influenced by class, gender, race, geography, and economic status, as well as by education.

Today, the definition of art can also incorporate notions about artists and patrons, who shared responsibility for the works. It relies, too, on the responses of viewers—both those today and those who saw the works when they were new. The role of art history is to probe these factors. Who are these artists and patrons? What were the ideas and expectations of the original viewers? Only after exploring such questions can we achieve a historical understanding and appreciation of those special artifacts we now consider works of art.

Modes of Representation

Not all cultures value the same qualities in works of art. The ancient Greeks admired the work of artists who were especially skillful at capturing the visual appearance of the natural world, as illustrated in a famous story about a competition between rival Greek painters named Zeuxis and Parrhasios held in the late fifth century BCE. Zeuxis painted a picture of grapes so detailed that birds flew down to peck at them. Then Parrhasios took his turn, and when Zeuxis asked his rival to remove the curtain hanging over the picture, Parrhasios gleefully pointed out that the curtain was his painting. Zeuxis agreed that Parrhasios had won the competition since he, Zeuxis, had fooled only birds, but Parrhasios had tricked an intelligent fellow artist.

In the seventeenth century, painters Adriaen van der Spelt (1630–1673) and Frans van Mieris (1635–1681) paid homage to the story of Parrhasios' curtain with their painting of blue satin drapery drawn aside to show a garland of flowers (**FIG. INTRO–2**).

More than a *tour-de-force* of **trompe l'oeil** painting (pictures that attempt to fool viewers into thinking what they are seeing is real, not a painted representation of the real), this work is an intellectual delight. The artists not only re-created Parrhasios' curtain illusion; they also included a reference to another Greek story that was popular in the fourth century BCE, the tale of Pausias, who depicted in a painting the exquisite floral garlands made by a young woman, Glykera. This second story raises the question of who was the true artist—the painter who copied nature in his art or the garland-maker who made works of art out of nature. The seventeenth-century collectors who bought such **still lifes** (pictures of inanimate objects and fruits or flowers taken out of their natural contexts) knew those stories and appreciated the artists' **Classical** references as well as their skills in drawing and manipulating colors.

Even today some people think that lifelike descriptions of the visual appearance of the natural world (sometimes referred to as **naturalism** or **realism**) represent the highest accomplishment in art. Not everyone agrees. The first European artist to argue persuasively that precise observation alone produced "mere likeness," not art, was the Italian master Leonardo da Vinci (1452–1519), who said that the painter who copied

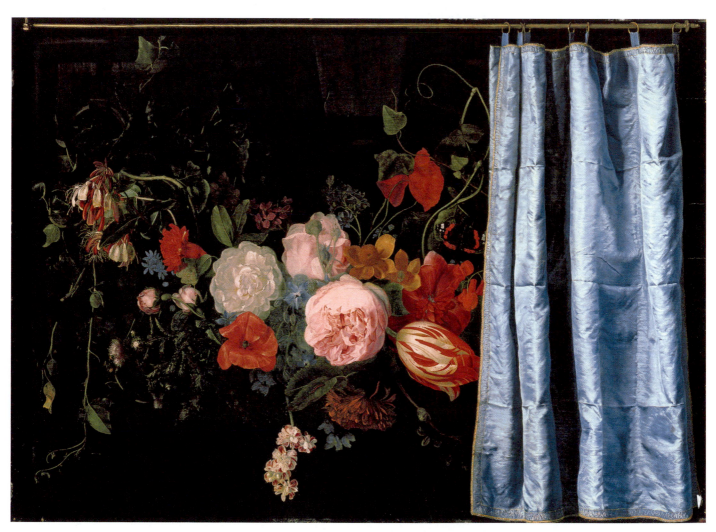

INTRO–2 • Adriaen van der Spelt and Frans van Mieris FLOWER PIECE WITH CURTAIN
1658. Oil on panel, 18¼″ × 25¼″ (46.5 × 64 cm). The Art Institute of Chicago. Wirt D. Walker Fund (1949.585).

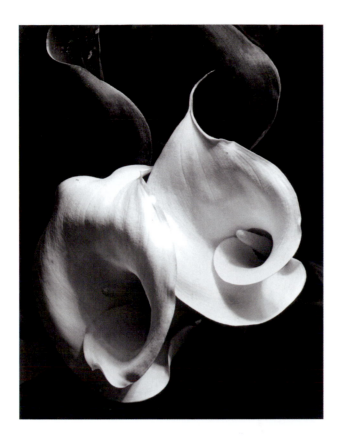

INTRO–3 • Imogen Cunningham **TWO CALLAS**
1929. Gelatin-silver print, 12″ × 9½″ (30.4 × 24.1 cm).
The Museum of Modern Art, New York. © 2014
Imogen Cunningham Trust.

the external forms of nature was acting only as a mirror. He believed that the true artist should engage in intellectual activity of a higher order and attempt to capture the inner life—the energy and power—rather than just the outward appearance of a subject.

Like Van der Spelt and Van Mieris, Imogen Cunningham (1883–1976) and Georgia O'Keeffe (1887–1986) created pictures of living plants. In her photograph **TWO CALLAS**, Cunningham used straightforward camera work to capture the forms and textures of her subject accurately, even if drained of its color (**FIG. INTRO–3**). But the artistic character of her photographic image depends not on the exacting detail recorded by the camera, but on the compositional choices and dramatic lighting controlled by the artist who used it. When Georgia O'Keeffe painted **JACK-IN-THE-PULPIT, NO. IV** (**FIG. INTRO–4**), she sought to capture the plant's essence, not merely its appearance, by concentrating its organic energy within a painted detail, rather than by describing the way the plant actually looked as a complete entity. She sought a new **abstract** beauty, conveying in

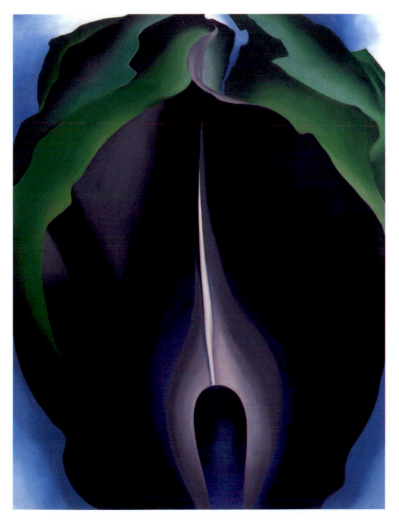

INTRO–4 • Georgia O'Keeffe
JACK-IN-THE-PULPIT, NO. IV
1930. Oil on canvas,
40″ × 30″ (101.6 × 76.2 cm). Alfred Steiglitz Collection, Bequest of Georgia O'Keeffe 1987.58.3. © 2015 National Gallery of Art, Washington, D.C.

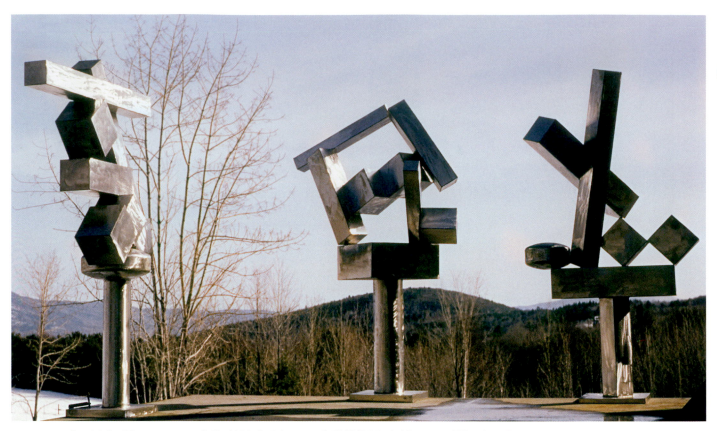

INTRO–5 • David Smith **CUBI XVIII** (*left*). 1964. Stainless steel, 9′ 8″ (2.94 m). Museum of Fine Arts, Boston. **CUBI XVII** (*center*). 1963. Stainless steel, 9′ 2″ (2.79 m). Dallas Museum of Fine Arts, Dallas. **CUBI XIX** (*right*). 1964. Stainless steel, 9′ 5⅜″ (2.88 m). Tate Gallery, London. Shown installed at Bolton Landing, New York, in 1965. Photo by David Smith.

paint the pure vigor of the flower's life force. We will encounter this move away from recording precise visual appearance and toward **abstraction** or **stylization**—in which artists transform recognizable natural subjects into patterns or make them conform to ideals—throughout the history of art. It is not unique to one time or place or culture.

Even further from the naturalistic mode of representation are the pure geometric creations of polished stainless steel made by David Smith (1906–1965). His **CUBI** (**FIG. INTRO–5**) are **nonrepresentational** (do not depict a recognizable natural subject). Stylized art like O'Keeffe's has both subject matter and content. Nonrepresentational art does not have subject matter, but it does have meaning, generated when the artist's intention and the viewer's interpretation interact. Some viewers may see the *Cubi* works as cubic plants sprung from the core of an unyielding earth, a reflection of a mechanistic society. For them, there is a reference here to nature, even if natural forms are not directly represented.

Because the meanings of works of art are complex, and can change over time, a central goal of art history is to explore the cultural factors that contributed to the production and initial reception of works of art—in other words to speculate on what they meant for the artists who made them and those who originally experienced them. But no art-historical explanation is definitive. The interpretation of works of art changes and develops through time as new evidence emerges and new approaches are established. Art history is a work continually in progress.

"Real" and "Ideal" Bodies

Ever since people first made what we call art, they have been fascinated with their own image and have used the human body to express ideas and ideals. Popular culture in the twenty-first century continues to be obsessed with notions of what constitutes a beautiful person. Today, the **MEDICI VENUS** (**FIG. INTRO–6**), with her plump arms and legs and sturdy body, would surely be expected to slim down. For generations, however, such a figure represented an ideal of female beauty. Such Classical figures inspired and guided artists and patrons from the fifteenth through the nineteenth century.

A very different notion of ideal beauty—also strictly regulated by **convention**—stands behind the stylized woman depicted in a **woodblock print** (**FIG. INTRO–7**) by Japanese artist Kitagawa Utamaro (1753–1806). Simplified shapes delineate the woman's garments and at the same time suggest the underlying form of her body. But the treatment of the rich textiles emphasizes surface pattern over bodily form, and the elaborate configuration of hair pins distracts us from the shape of her coiffure. Utamaro has rendered the decorative silks and carved pins meticulously, but only suggested the woman's face and hands with a few carefully chosen, sweeping lines.

A fifteenth-century **bronze** sculpture from India conforms to yet another ideal of female beauty, disquietingly distinct from those encountered thus far. Punitavati, a beautiful and generous woman who was deeply devoted to the Hindu god Shiva, was abandoned by her husband because she gave one of his

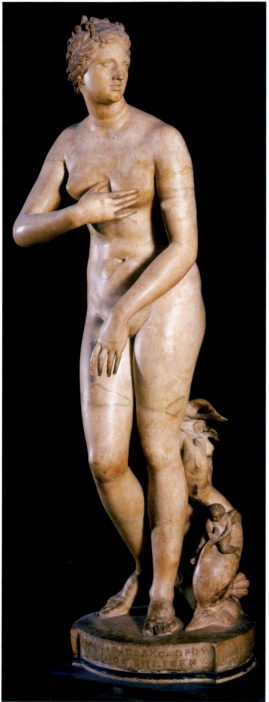

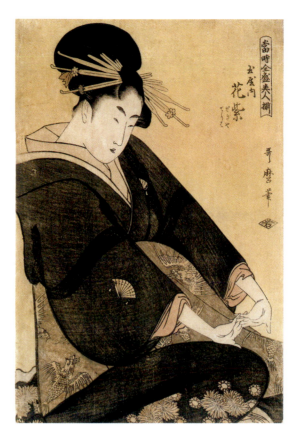

INTRO–7 •
Kitagawa Utamaro
**HANA-MURASAKI
OF THE TAMAYA**
From the series *Array
of Supreme Beauties
of the Present Day*.
Edo period, 1794.
Color woodblock print,
15⅛″ × 9¹⁵⁄₁₆″
(38.5 × 25.3 cm).
Spencer Museum of Art,
University of Kansas,
Lawrence. William
Bridges Thayer Memorial
(1928.7879).

INTRO–6 • **MEDICI VENUS**
Roman copy of a 1st-century BCE Greek statue. Marble,
height without base 5′ (1.53 m). Galleria degli Uffizi, Florence.

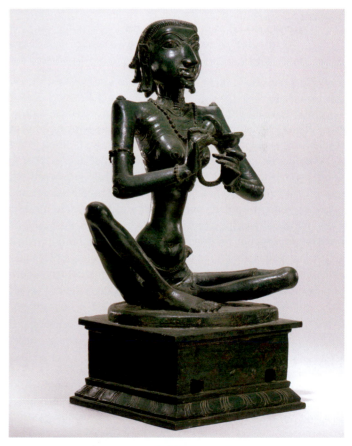

INTRO–8 • **PUNITAVATI (KARAIKKAL AMMAIYAR)**
A Shaiva saint, from Tamil Nadu, south India. Chola dynasty, c. 1050.
Bronze, height 19⅝″ (49.8 cm). The Nelson-Atkins Museum of Art,
Kansas City, Missouri. Purchase: William Rockhill Nelson Trust (33–533).

mangoes to a beggar. So Punitavati offered her beauty to Shiva,
and the god accepted the offering, and by taking her loveliness
away turned her into an emaciated, fanged hag (**FIG. INTRO–8**).
According to legend, Punitavati and her clanging cymbals
provide the music for Shiva as he keeps the universe in motion
by dancing the cosmic dance of destruction and creation
(SEE FIG. 9–4). The bronze sculpture, by depicting Punitavati's
hideous appearance, seeks to evoke the spiritual beauty of her
generosity and sacrifice.

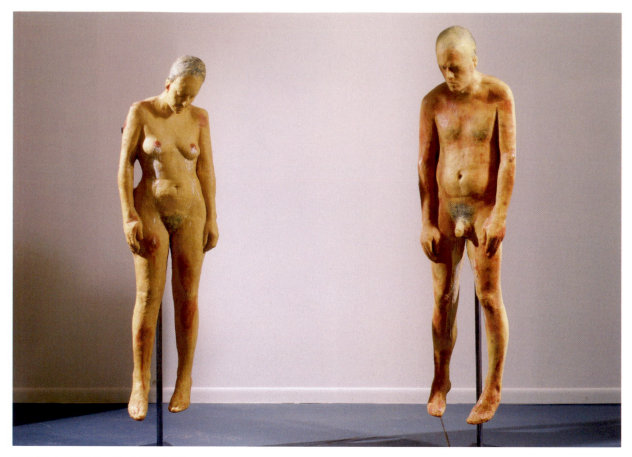

INTRO–9 • Kiki Smith UNTITLED
1990. Beeswax with microcrystalline wax figures on metal stands, female figure installed height 6′ 1½″ (1.87 m), male figure 6′ 4¹⁵⁄₁₆″ (1.95 m). Whitney Museum of American Art, New York. © Kiki Smith, courtesy Pace Gallery.

Sculptor Kiki Smith (b. 1954) uses the powerfully expressive subject of the human body not to engage with notions of ideal beauty—physical or spiritual—but to draw attention to the AIDS epidemic of the late twentieth century that claimed the life of her own sister. In her 1990 work **UNTITLED (FIG. INTRO–9)**, two life-size naked figures—made from flesh-colored painted beeswax—hang passively, but not quite lifelessly, side by side, a few inches above the ground. Milk drips from the woman's breasts and semen drips down the man's leg, as if both have lost control of bodily functions that were once a source of vitality and pleasure. Smith asks us to consider bodily control—both our own and the control that others exert on our body as we die—and suggests that relinquishing it may be as liberating as it is devastating.

How Do We Find the Meaning of Art?

As we have just seen, underlying our assumptions about works of art—whether in the past or in the present—is the belief that art carries a message, that it can inform, challenge, and/or persuade viewers, as well as give them pleasure or embody cherished cultural norms. But what gives a work of art meaning and expressive power? How do we discover its significance for the culture in which it was made and first experienced? How does it become meaningful to us?

On their own, exceptional works of art can speak to us with enduring eloquence over great expanses of time, but we usually need to understand a work's subject matter or **iconography** (conventional subjects and symbols and the study of them) before its deeper intended meanings become clear. For example, in *Flower Piece with Curtain* (SEE FIG. INTRO–2), the brilliant red and white tulip just to the left of the blue curtain was the most desirable and expensive flower in the seventeenth-century Netherlands; thus, it symbolizes wealth and power, not simply natural beauty. Yet insects creep out of it, and a butterfly—fragile and transitory—hovers above it. Consequently, these flowers also evoke the passage of time and the fleeting quality of human wealth and natural beauty. Once its subjects and symbols have been decoded, this painting becomes more than simply an exquisitely painted still life or a clever reference to an ancient Greek story. It begins to embody some of the central preoccupations of its cultural situation.

In "A Closer Look" (p. 7), the iconography of two other seventeenth-century still-life paintings—one by Chinese painter Zhu Da and the other by Netherlandish painter Clara Peeters—is identified and elucidated. To truly understand these works as bearers of cultural meaning, however, a deeper knowledge of the broader context and specific goals of artists and audiences is required. For example, the fact that Zhu Da became a painter is more about the political than the artistic

● **Iconography** ▶ The study and identification of conventional themes, motifs, and symbols to elucidate the subject matter of works of art.

These grapes sit on an imported, Italian silver tazza, a luxury object that recurs in several of Peeters's other still lifes and may commemorate Netherlandish prosperity and trade.

An image of the artist herself appears on the reflective surface of this pewter tankard, one of the ways that she signed her paintings and promoted her career.

Luscious fruits and flowers celebrate the abundance of nature, but because these fruits of the earth will eventually fade, even rot, they could be moralizing references to the transience of earthly existence.

These coins, including one minted in 1608–1609, help focus the dating of this painting. The highlighting of money within a still life could reference the wealth of the owner—or it could subtly allude to the value the artist has crafted here in paint.

Detailed renderings of insects showcased Peeters's virtuosity as a painter, but they also may have symbolized the vulnerability of the worldly beauty of flowers and fruit to destruction and decay.

This knife—which appears in several of Peeters's still lifes—is of a type that is associated with wedding gifts.

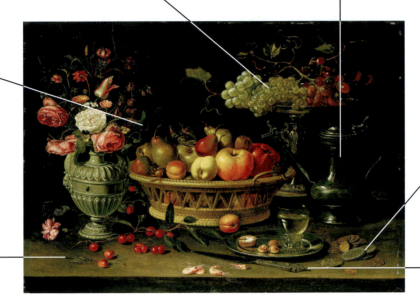

Clara Peeters. *Still Life with Fruit and Flowers*. c. 1612.
Oil on copper, 25⅕″ × 35″ (64 × 89 cm). Ashmolean Museum, Oxford.

Quince is an unusual subject in Chinese painting, but the fruit seems to have carried personal significance for Zhu Da. One of his friends was known as the Daoist of Quince Mountain, a site in Hunan Province that was also the subject of a work by one of his favorite authors, Tang dynasty poet Li Bai.

The artist's signature reads "Bada Shanren painted this," using his favorite pseudonym in a formula and calligraphic style that the artist ceased using in 1695.

This red block is a seal with an inscription drawn from a Confucian text: "teaching is half of learning." This was imprinted on the work by the artist as an aspect of his signature, just as the reflection and inscribed knife identify Clara Peeters as the painter of her still life.

Zhu Da (Bada Shanren).
***Quince (Mugua)*. 1690.**
Album leaf mounted as a hanging scroll; ink and colors on paper, 7⅞″ × 5¾″ (20 × 14.6 cm). Princeton University Art Museum.

● **View** the Closer Look for Iconography on **MyArtsLab**

history of China. As a member of the imperial family of the Ming dynasty, his life of privilege was disrupted when the Ming were overthrown during the Manchu conquest of China in 1644. Fleeing for his life, he sought refuge in a Buddhist monastery, where he wrote poetry and painted. Almost 40 years later, Zhu Da abandoned his monastic life and developed a career as a professional painter. His paintings are at times saturated with veiled political commentary; at times they seek to meet the expectations of collectors so they will buy them; and in paintings like the one illustrated here, the artist seems to hark back to the contemplative, abstract, and spontaneous paintings associated with great Zen Buddhist masters, whose calligraphic pictures of isolated fruits seem almost like acts of devotion or detached contemplations on natural forms, rather than the works of a professional painter.

Clara Peeters's still life, on the other hand, is the work of an established and successful professional, specializing in portrayals of food and flowers, fruit and reflective objects. In this tradition, still lifes could be celebrations of the abundance of the natural world and the wealth of luxury objects available in the prosperous mercantile society of the Netherlands. They could also be moralizing, warning of the ephemeral meaning of those worldly possessions, even of life itself. But this painting has also been interpreted as a more personal statement. Because the type of knife that sits in the **foreground** near the edge of

the table was a popular wedding gift, and since it is inscribed with the artist's own name, some have suggested that this still life could have celebrated Peeters's marriage. Or the knife could simply be a witty way to sign her picture. It certainly could be not only personal but also participate in the broader cultural meaning of still-life paintings at the same time. Mixtures of private and public meanings have been proposed for Zhu Da's paintings as well. The picture of quince illustrated here has been seen as one in a series of allegorical "self-portraits" that extend across his career as a painter. Art historians frequently reveal multiple meanings when interpreting a single work of art; these usually represent complex cultural and personal situations.

Art and Ritual

The paintings we have just examined were produced to be works of art. They were meant to be acquired and admired as such. But some works we now label as art were created for use in communal ritual as tools to establish ties to unseen powers, sometimes to connect the present with the past and the future. These special ritual objects—such as statues, masks, and vessels—may be valued as works of art by outsiders unaware of the circumstances and ceremonies that originally brought them to life, but that is not why they were made. Grasping their meaning requires us to understand the rituals that brought them to life.

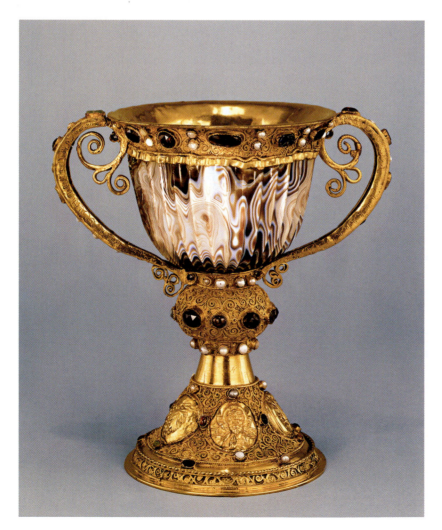

INTRO–10 • CHALICE OF ABBOT SUGER
From Abbey Church of Saint-Denis, France. Cup: Ptolemaic Egypt (2nd–1st century BCE) or Byzantine 11th century CE, sardonyx; mounts: France, 1137–1140 CE, silver gilt, adorned with filigree, semiprecious stones, pearls, glass insets, and opaque white glass with modern replacements, 7½″ × 4¼″ (19 × 10.8 cm). National Gallery of Art, Washington, D.C.

with gods **(FIG. INTRO–11)**. It once held the palm nuts offered at the beginning of ceremonies in which people call on the god Olodumare (or Olorun) to reveal their destiny. Created by master carver Olowe of Ise in about 1925, this sculpture appears to portray a woman with a child on her back holding an ornate, covered cup. Men and women underneath it help the woman support the bowl, and more women link arms in a ritual dance on the lid. The richly decorative and symbolic wood carving reminds us of all who sought to learn from Olodumare, the god of destiny, certainty, and order. But both Suger's chalice and Olowe's cup stand empty today. Encased in museum displays, these ritual vessels take on a new secular life, enshrined as precious works of art, serving a purpose very different from the original intention of their patrons and makers.

Art as Sociopolitical Commentary

As sophisticated forms of human communication, the visual arts shape, and are shaped by, their sociopolitical context. Powerful rulers and governments have used artworks throughout history to promote their political interests, and independent-minded artists have used, and continue to use, their art to critique the powers that be. A recent work with a challenging critical message recalls how American citizens of Japanese ancestry were removed from their homes and confined in internment camps during World War II. Roger Shimomura (b. 1939) painted **DIARY** in 1978 to visualize his grandmother's account of the family's experience in one such camp in Idaho **(FIG. INTRO–12)**. Shimomura has painted his grandmother in the close foreground, writing in her diary, while he (the toddler) and his mother stand farther back by an open door—not signifying freedom but opening onto a field bounded by barbed wire. In this commentary on discrimination and injustice, Shimomura cleverly refers to the traditional Japanese art of

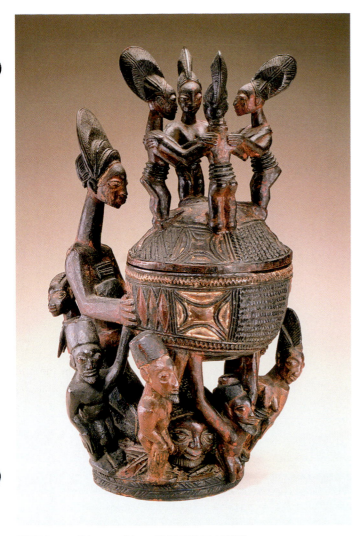

INTRO–11 • Olowe of Ise OFFERING BOWL
Nigeria. c. 1925. Wood and pigment, height 25¹⁄₁₆″ (63.7 cm). National Museum of African Art, Smithsonian Institution, Washington, D.C. Bequest of William A. McCarty-Cooper (95-10-1).

Two offering bowls—a European chalice and an African cup—are cases in point.

The **CHALICE OF ABBOT SUGER** was created in the middle of the twelfth century for what remains for many the central ritual of the Christian faith **(FIG. INTRO–10)**—the ceremonial commemoration of Jesus' Last Supper with his disciples, known as Holy Communion, the Mass, or the **Eucharist**. For Roman Catholics, during this ritual reenactment at a consecrated **altar**, ordinary wine becomes the blood of Christ, while for Protestants, the wine remains symbolic of that blood. But in both rites, the chalice (a vessel for the sacramental wine) plays a central role. Abbot Suger, head of the French monastery dedicated to St. Denis near Paris, found an antique agate cup in the storage chests of the abbey. He directed his goldsmiths to add a foot, a rim, and handles, embellished with semiprecious stones and medallions, transforming a secular object of prestige and delight into a sacred chalice to be used at the altar of his church in the celebration of the Eucharist.

The **OFFERING BOWL** created for the Yoruba people of West Africa also served in rituals designed to communicate

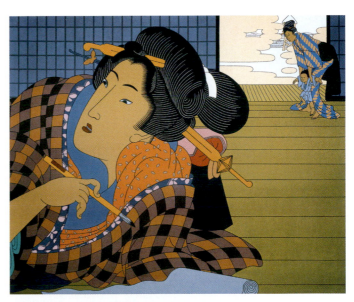

INTRO–12 • Roger Shimomura
DIARY (MINIDOKA SERIES #3)
1978. Acrylic on canvas, 4′ 11⁷⁄₈″ × 6′ ¹⁄₁₆″ (1.52 × 1.83 m). Spencer Museum of Art, University of Kansas, Lawrence. Museum purchase: State funds (1979.51).

color woodblock prints (SEE FIG. INTRO–7) but crafts a personal style that conveys his own dual cultural heritage. At the same time, his work recalls an ugly episode in American history in terms that will, by making it memorable, encourage viewers in the present neither to forget nor repeat it.

Who Are the Artists and Patrons?

Who are the artists who make works of art? Who are the patrons who commission and pay the artists to create those works? How artists have viewed themselves and how they have been viewed by those around them—especially their patrons—has changed dramatically over time.

Artists

In the ancient world, painters and sculptors were considered artisans—in other words, laborers. The ancient Greeks and Romans ranked painters and sculptors among skilled workers, admiring the creations more than their creators. The Greek word for art, *tekne*, is the source for the English word "technique," and the English words "art" and "artist" come from the Latin word *ars*, which means "skill." During the Middle Ages, whereas some artists continued to be seen as craftspeople, others began to be

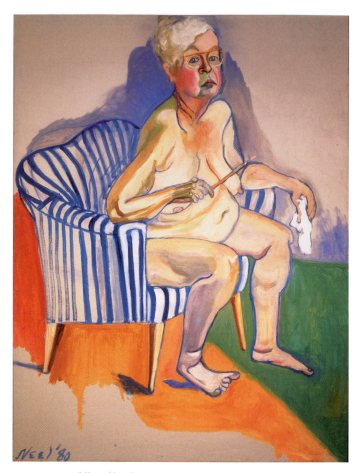

INTRO–14 • Alice Neel **SELF-PORTRAIT**
1980. Oil on canvas, 54″ × 40″ (1.37 × 1 m). National Portrait Gallery, Washington, D.C. © The Estate of Alice Neel. Courtesy David Zwirner, New York/London.

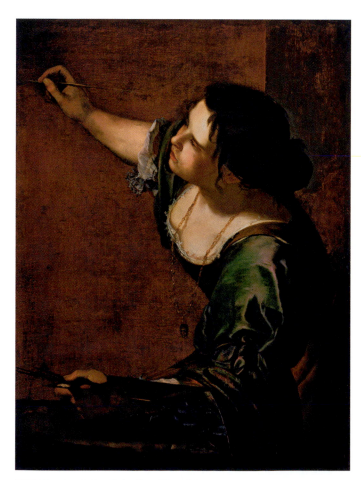

INTRO–13 • Artemisia Gentileschi
SELF-PORTRAIT AS THE ALLEGORY OF PAINTING
1630. Oil on canvas, 38″ × 29″ (96.5 × 73.7 cm).
The Royal Collection, England.

designated as "masters" in recognition of the esteem that was accorded their special creative skills. But not until the Renaissance did artists such as Leonardo da Vinci proclaim themselves to be geniuses with unique God-given abilities.

In their **SELF-PORTRAITS** artists often express how they—or those in their culture—conceive their role in society. In 1630, well after Leonardo and his peers had staked a claim for artists as men [*sic*] of genius endowed with special gifts, Artemisia Gentileschi (1593–c. 1652) painted a picture of herself as an allegorical personification of the art of painting, caught in a moment of inspiration during the act of creation (**FIG. INTRO–13**). She is richly dressed, with palette and brushes in hand, but the painting spotlights not her tools but her forehead, implying that the art of painting involves the mind more than the hand, conception over execution. By placing her own features on a personification of Painting, Gentileschi not only commemorates her profession but also claims her own place within it.

Compared with Gentileschi's graceful grandeur, the self-presentation of twentieth-century American artist Alice Neel (1900–1984) is something of a shock (**FIG. INTRO–14**). Both painters hold the tools of their trade; both are obliquely posed in relation to an unseen canvas on which they are working. But Neel replaces Gentileschi's allegorical eloquence and

Art and Architecture

This book contains much more than paintings, photographs, prints, vessels, and sculptures. Within these pages you will also encounter books, jewelry, tombs, chairs, architecture, and more. But as with the Great Sphinx (SEE FIG. INTRO–1) and Van der Spelt and Van Mieris's *Flower Piece with Curtain* (SEE FIG. INTRO–2), criteria have been used to determine which works are selected for inclusion in a book titled *Art: A Brief History*. Architecture presents an interesting case.

Buildings meet functional human needs by enclosing human habitation or activity. Many works of architecture, however, are considered "exceptional" because they transcend functional demands through distinguished architectural design or because they embody in important ways the values and goals of the culture that built them. Such buildings are usually produced by architects influenced, like painters, by great works and traditions from the past. In some cases they harmonize with, or react to, their natural or urban surroundings. For such reasons, they are discussed in books on the history of art.

Typical of such buildings is the church of Notre-Dame-du-Haut in Ronchamp, France, designed and constructed between 1950 and 1955 by Swiss architect Charles-Edouard Jeanneret, better known by his pseudonym, Le Corbusier (FIG. INTRO–15). This building is the product of a significant historical moment, rich in global cultural meaning. A pilgrimage church on this site had been destroyed during World War II, and the creation here of a new church symbolized the end of a devastating war, embodying hopes for a brighter global future. Le Corbusier's design—drawing on sources that ranged from Algerian mosques to imperial Roman villas, from crab shells to airplane wings—is sculptural as well as architectural. It soars at the crest of a hill toward the sky but at the same time seems solidly anchored in the earth. And its coordination with the curves of the natural landscape complements the creation of an outdoor setting for religious ceremonies (to the right in the figure) to supplement the church interior that Le Corbusier characterized as a "container for intense concentration." In fact, this building is so renowned today as a monument of modern architecture that the busloads of pilgrims who arrive at the site are mainly architects and devotees of architectural history.

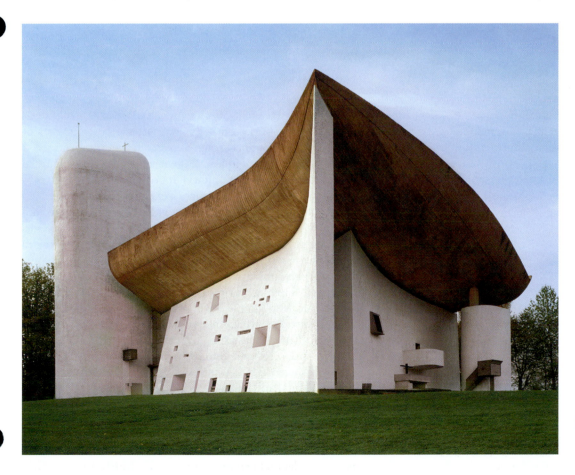

INTRO–15 • Le Corbusier
NOTRE-DAME-DU-HAUT
Ronchamp, France,
1950–1955.

🔍 **View** the Closer Look
for Notre-Dame-du-Haut
on **MyArtsLab**

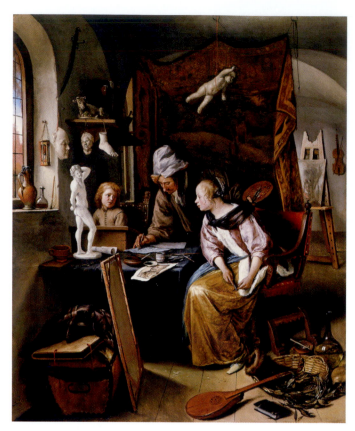

INTRO–16 • Jan Steen THE DRAWING LESSON
1665. Oil on wood, 19⅜″ × 16¼″ (49.3 × 41 cm). The J. Paul Getty Museum, Los Angeles, California.

detachment with a brutally forthright and psychologically rich engagement with the viewer, seemingly encouraging us to meet her unguarded honesty with our own. Neel—known for capturing the unvarnished individuality of her sitters, often exaggerating their physical peculiarities and emotional fragility—seems consciously to have contradicted idealized notions of female beauty cultivated in many portrayals of women (SEE FIGS. INTRO–6, INTRO–7) by shamelessly showcasing the sagging irregularities of her 80-year-old body. Like Gentileschi's self-portrait, the emphasis here is on the vibrant rendering of Neel's head. Its alertness almost eclipses the stark stylizations of her aging body.

All artists spend years in training and apprenticeship before they have mastered their craft. In his painting **THE DRAWING LESSON**, Dutch artist Jan Steen (1626–1679) takes us into an artist's studio where two people—a boy apprentice and a more mature young woman—are learning the foundations of their art from a master artist (FIG. INTRO–16). The older pupil has been drawing from sculpture and plaster casts because women were not permitted to work from male nude models. *The Drawing Lesson* seems to provide rare visual evidence of seventeenth-century educational practice and a valuable record of an artist's workplace.

Even mature artists learned from each other. Rembrandt van Rijn carefully studied Leonardo's late fifteenth-century painting of **THE LAST SUPPER** (FIG. INTRO–17). Leonardo had turned this traditional theme into a powerful human drama

by portraying the moment when Christ announced that one of the assembled apostles would betray him, and the men react with surprise and horror to this shocking news. Leonardo depicts the scene as a symmetrical **composition** with the apostles in balanced groups of three on each side of Christ, turning narrative chaos into compositional order. The regularly spaced tapestries and ceiling panels lead the viewers' eyes directly to Christ, who is silhouetted in front of an open window, as if framed by a natural **halo**.

Rembrandt, working 130 years later in the Netherlands, could only have known the Italian master's painting from a print, since he never went to Italy. Rembrandt "copied" **THE LAST SUPPER** in hard red chalk (FIG. INTRO–18). Then he reworked the drawing in a softer chalk, assimilating Leonardo's ideas but revising the composition and changing the mood of the original. With heavy overdrawing he reorganized the scene, shifting Jesus' position to the left, giving Judas more emphasis, and adding a dog at the right. Gone are the wall hangings and ceiling, replaced by a central canopy. The space is undetermined and expansive rather than constricted and focused. The artist must have been pleased with his version of Leonardo's masterpiece because he signed his drawing boldly in the lower right-hand corner to claim this composition for himself.

Patrons

The person or group who commissions or finances a work of art—the **patron**—can have a significant impact on it. The Great Sphinx (SEE FIG. INTRO–1) conforms to the conventions of pharaohs and priests in ancient Egypt; Suger's chalice was made following the design specifications laid down by this powerful monastic patron (SEE FIG. INTRO–10). Although some artists work speculatively, hoping to sell their work on the open art market, throughout history both individuals and institutions have commissioned works from specific artists. During periods of artistic efflorescence or major artistic developments or change, enlightened patronage has often been critical.

Individuals who collect art still constitute a very special audience for artists. Some collect out of a love of art—others to express or enhance their prestige, seeking an aura of power and importance by association. Private patronage can develop into cordial relationships between sponsors and artists, but this is not always the case. Patrons may change their minds and fail to pay their bills. Artists may ignore patrons' wishes or fail to complete commissions on schedule. In the late nineteenth century, Liverpool shipping magnate Frederick Leyland asked James Abbott McNeill Whistler (1834–1903), an American painter living in London, what color to paint the shutters in the dining room where he planned to hang Whistler's painting *Rose and Silver: The Princess from the Land of Porcelain*. The room had been decorated with antique embossed and gilded leather and finely crafted shelves to show off Leyland's collection of Chinese blue-and-white **porcelain**. Whistler, inspired by the Japanese theme of his own painting as well as by the porcelain, painted the window shutters with splendid turquoise, blue, and gold peacocks. But he did not stop there: While Leyland was away, Whistler painted the entire room, covering the expensive leather on the walls with painted turquoise peacock feathers

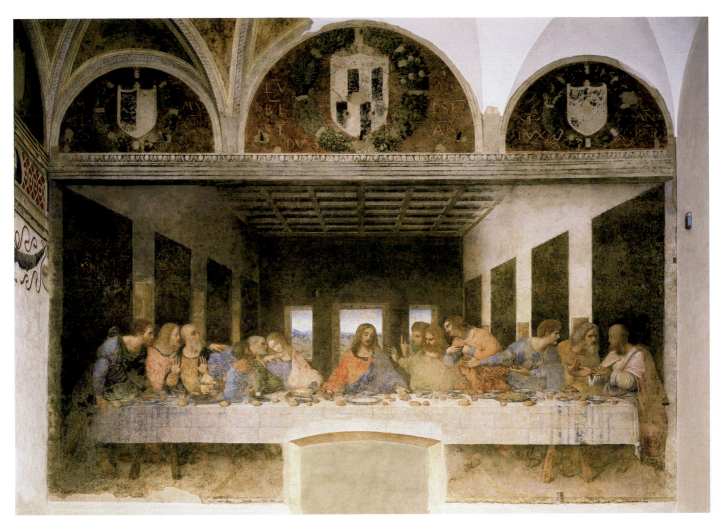

**INTRO–17 • Leonardo da Vinci
THE LAST SUPPER**
Wall painting in the refectory,
monastery of Sta. Maria delle Grazie,
Milan, Italy. 1495–1498. Tempera
and oil on plaster, 15′ 2″ × 28′ 10″
(4.6 × 8.8 m).

👁 **Watch** a video about
Leonardo's *The Last Supper*
on **MyArtsLab**

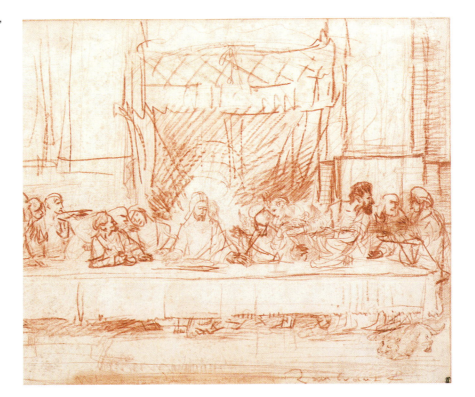

**INTRO–18 • Rembrandt van
Rijn THE LAST SUPPER**
After Leonardo da Vinci. Mid-1630s.
Drawing in red chalk, 14⅜″ × 18¾″
(36.5 × 47.5 cm). The Metropolitan
Museum of Art, New York. Robert
Lehman Collection, 1975 (1975.1.794).

(FIG. INTRO–19). Leyland, shocked and angry at what seemed to him to be wanton destruction of the room, paid Whistler less than half the agreed price. Luckily, he did not destroy Whistler's "Peacock Room." It was sold at Leyland's death to Charles Lang Freer (1854–1919), who installed it in his home in Detroit. When Freer died, the Peacock Room was moved to the Freer Gallery of Art in Washington, D.C.

From earliest times, people have gathered and preserved precious objects that embody cultural values or convey notions of power and prestige. Today, both private and public museums are major patrons, collectors, and preservers of art. Curators of such collections guide their museums in the acquisition of works of art and often assist patrons in obtaining especially fine pieces, although the idea of what is best and what is worth collecting and preserving changes from one generation to another. For example, the collection of abstract and nonrepresentational art formed by members of the Guggenheim family was once considered so radical that few people—and certainly no civic or governmental group—would have considered the art worth collecting at all. Today, the collection fills Guggenheim museums

that have become civic treasures and major tourist destinations (SEE FIG. 20–46).

Government sponsorship of art is epitomized by fifth-century BCE Athens, a Greek city-state whose citizens practiced an early form of democracy. Led by the statesman and general Perikles, the Athenians defeated the Persians, and then rebuilt Athens's civic and religious center, the **Akropolis**, as a tribute to the goddess Athena and a testament to the glory of Athens (SEE FIG. 5–25). Since Perikles led the Athenian government with a strong hand, his artistic policies for urban renewal were smoothly realized. This is not always the case. In the United States during the late twentieth century, the question of whether public money should be used to fund art sparked a political battle when the National Endowment for the Arts (NEA) sponsored works and exhibitions that many taxpayers found offensive, immoral, or indecent. The controversy centered on one work and one exhibition: *Piss Christ* by Andres Serrano (b. 1950)—a 1989 photograph that showed a plastic crucifix suspended in the artist's urine—and the homoerotic content of a traveling exhibition of photographs by Robert Mapplethorpe

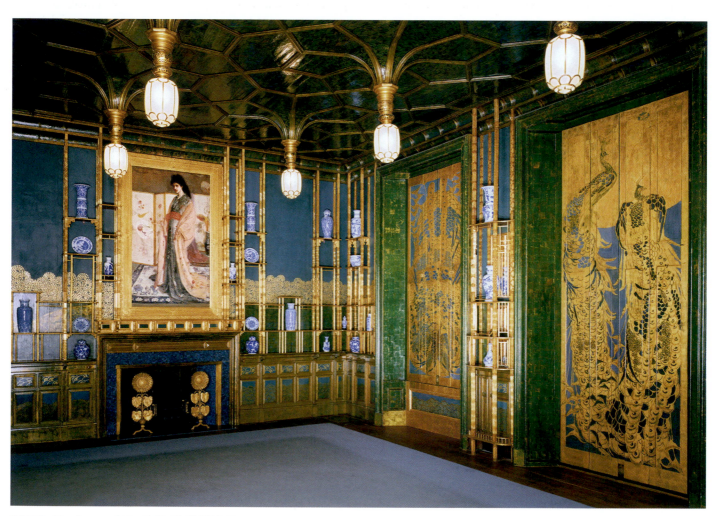

INTRO–19 • James Abbott McNeill Whistler HARMONY IN BLUE AND GOLD
The Peacock Room, northeast corner, from a house owned by Frederick Leyland, London. 1876–1877. Oil paint and metal leaf on canvas, leather, and wood, 13′ 11⅞″ × 33′ 2″ × 19′ 11½″ (4.26 × 10.11 × 6.83 m). Over the fireplace, Whistler's *Rose and Silver: The Princess from the Land of Porcelain*. Freer Gallery of Art, Smithsonian Institution, Washington, D.C. Gift of Charles Lang Freer (F1904.61).

(1946–1989). The ensuing debate pitted artists and museum administrators against political and religious figures, and the media had a field day. By 2000 the budget of the NEA had been cut by 45 percent.

What Is Art History?

Art history became an academic field of study in colleges and universities only relatively recently, but many art historians trace the discipline itself to the 1550 publication of *Lives of the Most Excellent Italian Architects, Painters, and Sculptors* by the Italian artist and writer Giorgio Vasari (1511–1574). Some would push the origins earlier, to the work of ancient Roman commentator Pliny the Elder (33–79), who recorded the story of the competition between Greek painters Zeuxis and Parrhasios that we have already explored. Others would prioritize the work of Johann Joachim Winckelmann (1717–1768), who redirected attention away from artists' lives and toward the primacy of artistic values, especially Classicism. But the pioneering example of sixth-century Chinese painter Xie He's "Six Laws of Painting" demonstrates that the development of art history extends beyond the Western world. There are many forebears.

As the term "art history" implies, this interpretive enterprise combines two distinct but ultimately interrelated aspects: the study of individual works of art outside time and place (formal analysis and certain types of critical theory) and the historical study of art as a product of its broad cultural context (iconography and **contextualism**). The scope of art history is immense, commensurate with the many and varied ways human beings have represented their world and expressed their ideas and ideals in visual form.

One method of scrutinizing individual art objects is known as **connoisseurship**. Through years of close contact with, and study of, the formal qualities that make up a work of art's style (such as design, composition, the manipulation of materials), connoisseurs categorize an undocumented and unidentified work by comparing it with related pieces, being in this way able to attribute it to a period, to a place, even to a specific artist. Today, such experts also make use of scientific testing—such as x-ray radiography, electron microscopy, infrared spectroscopy, and x-ray diffraction—but ultimately, connoisseurs depend on their visual memory as well as their skills in close formal analysis and the fine discernment of revealing details.

As a humanistic discipline, however, art history adds theoretical and contextual studies to the formal analysis of works of art and the identification of symbolism and subject matter through iconography. Art historians draw on biography to learn about artists' lives; on social history to evaluate the economic and political forces shaping not only artists, but also their patrons and their public; and on the history of ideas to gain an understanding of the intellectual currents infusing artists'

works and framing their reception. They also study the history of other arts, including music, drama, and literature, to gain a richer sense of the broader cultural context. Art-historical study is also enhanced by the work of anthropologists and archaeologists, who reconstruct the social context of newly discovered objects of material culture, not all of which are singled out as "works of art."

Today, however, art historians themselves study a wider range of works than ever before. Many reject altogether the idea of a fixed **canon** of superior masterpieces. The distinction between elite fine arts and popular utilitarian arts has become increasingly blurred, and the notion that some media, techniques, or subjects are better than others has almost disappeared.

Contemporary art historians are also concerned with natural and human threats to the very survival of works of art, and art historians face special challenges when interpreting works that have been damaged, transformed, or restored. As we try to understand such works of art, we must remain vigilant and flexible, recognizing, for example, that the legs of a marble figure may have been replaced (see "Restoring the Past: The *Laocoön*," p. 16), a section of a picture may have been repainted, and many important historical buildings may have been consolidated or transformed through continual use.

Such restorations are undertaken to conserve art, but throughout the world, people intentionally or mindlessly threaten the very survival of works of art and architecture. Centuries ago greedy thieves plundered and vandalized Egyptian tombs, and such theft continues to this day. Objects of cultural and artistic value in Iraq and Central America, for example, are being taken from official and unofficial excavation sites, then sold illegally. In industrialized regions of the world, emissions from cars, trucks, buses, and factories turn into corrosive rain that damages and sometimes literally destroys the works of art and architecture on which it falls. But war may be the most destructive of all human enterprises. History is filled with examples of plundered works of art that, as spoils of war, were wrenched from their original setting and relocated. Churches, synagogues, mosques, temples, and shrines have been burned, bombed, and denuded in the name of winning a war or confirming an ideology.

Nature, too, has played its part. Floods, hurricanes, tornadoes, avalanches, mudslides, and earthquakes all damage and destroy priceless treasures. For example, an earthquake on the morning of September 27, 1997, convulsed the small Italian town of Assisi, shaking the thirteenth-century Basilica of St. Francis of Assisi—a rich repository of wall painting—and causing great damage. Frescos crumbled from the vaults and fell to the floor, but with the help of documentary photographs, the generous support of donors, and the painstaking work of restorers, these fragments have been reassembled with such skill that visitors today would hardly guess that an earthquake had brought down the ceiling less than two decades ago.

Restoring the Past: The *Laocoön*

The challenges art historians face when studying works of art transformed by later restorations are clearly illustrated by comparing two reworkings, hundreds of years apart, of the renowned ancient Greek sculpture *Laocoön and His Sons*. Laocoön was a priest who warned the Trojans of an invasion by the Greeks in Homer's account of the Trojan War. Although Laocoön told the truth, the goddess Athena, who took the Greeks' side in the war, dispatched serpents to strangle him and his sons. A tragic hero, Laocoön represents a virtuous man destroyed by unjust forces. In this powerful sculpture, his features twist in agony, and the muscles of his and his sons' superhuman torsos and arms extend and knot as they struggle. When the sculpture was discovered in Rome in 1506, Michelangelo rushed to watch it being excavated, an astonishing validation of his own ideal, heroic style coming straight out of the earth. Pope Julius II acquired it for the papal collection, and it can still be seen in the Vatican Museums.

In piecing together the past of this one work, we know that mistakes were made during the initial restoration. The broken pieces of the *Laocoön* group were first reassembled with the figures flinging their arms out in the melodramatic fashion (**FIG. INTRO–20**, left). This would have been the sculpture seen by Renaissance and Baroque artists. Modern conservation methods, however, have produced a different image with a changed mood (**FIG. INTRO–20**, below). Missing pieces are not replaced, and Laocoön's right arm turns back upon his body, making a compact composition that internalizes the men's agony, perhaps speaking more directly to a self-centered twenty-first-century audience than the heroic struggle emphasized in the earlier reconstruction. We can only wonder what will be highlighted in the next transformation.

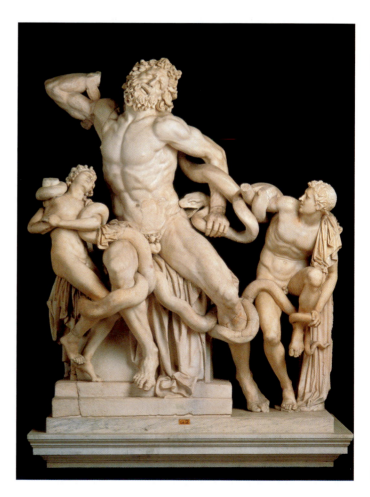

INTRO–20 • Hagesandros, Polydoros, and Athanodoros of Rhodes LAOCOÖN AND HIS SONS
An earlier restoration (left), and as restored today (right). Probably the original of the 1st century BCE or a Roman copy of the 1st century CE. Marble, height 8′ (2.44 m). Musei Vaticani, Museo Pio Clementino, Cortile Ottagono, Rome, Italy.

What are the Viewers' Roles, Responsibilities, and Rewards?

As viewers we enter into an engaging dialogue with artists across time and space. We re-create the works of art for ourselves as we bring to them our own experiences, our intelligence, and even our prejudices. Without our participation, artworks are only chunks of stone or smears of paint. But remember, all is change. From extreme lifelike description at one end of the spectrum to nonrepresentational abstraction at the other, artists have worked with varying degrees of naturalism, idealism, stylization, and even abstraction. The challenge for the student of art history is to discover not only how but also why those styles evolved, and ultimately what significance these changes hold for us, for our culture, for our future.

Our involvement with art may be casual or intense, naïve or sophisticated, self-contained or interactive. At first we may simply react instinctively to a painting or a building or a sculpture, but this level of "feeling" about art—"I know what I like"—can never be fully satisfying, because ultimately it is self-centered. The work of art becomes a mirror that reflects back to us only what we bring to it. Alternatively, like these late sixteenth-century awestruck visitors—friends of Dutch artist Hendrick Goltzius, whose **engraving** (FIG. INTRO-21) derives from a drawing he made while they all shared a visit to a gallery in Rome—we can admire and ponder ancient statues, like this one of Hercules, taking in their forms and ideas and returning our own questions and reflections in a virtual conversation of give and take that crosses over barriers of time and space. In this way, as viewers we participate in the continual re-creation of works of art, allowing their meanings to change and evolve from individual to individual, from era to era, and yet at the same time maintain their own integrity as bearers of meaning from the past. And in art history, our conversation opens to include friends and colleagues who, by sharing our interest in engaging with these cherished works from human history, enrich not only our communal understanding of the past, but can also refine our aspirations for the future.

For once we welcome works of art into our lives on their own terms, we have a ready source of sustenance and challenge that grows, changes, mellows, and deepens our daily experience. This book introduces us to works of art in their historical context, but no matter how much we study or read about art and artists, eventually we may return to the contemplation of an original work itself, the enduring tangible evidence of the ever-questing human spirit.

INTRO–21 • Hendrick Goltzius DUTCH VISITORS TO ROME LOOKING AT THE FARNESE HERCULES
c. 1592. Engraving, 16″ × 11½″ (40.5 × 29.4 cm).

After Goltzius returned from a trip to Italy in 1590–1591, he made engravings based on his drawings. These men have been identified as two of his Dutch friends.

THINK ABOUT IT

Intro.1 How would you define a work of art?

Intro.2 Identify the conventional subjects and symbolism of one specific painting in the Introduction and discuss how this subject matter takes on further meaning when understood in its cultural context.

Intro.3 What do the self-portraits of Artemisia Gentileschi and Alice Neel tell us about the way they conceived of themselves as artists? Compare what are they trying to accomplish in these paintings with Kiki Smith's goals in *Untitled*.

Intro.4 Compare the art-historical practice of interpreting and discussing works of art with the way that you usually think and talk about art.

✔ **Study** and **Review** on **MyArtsLab**

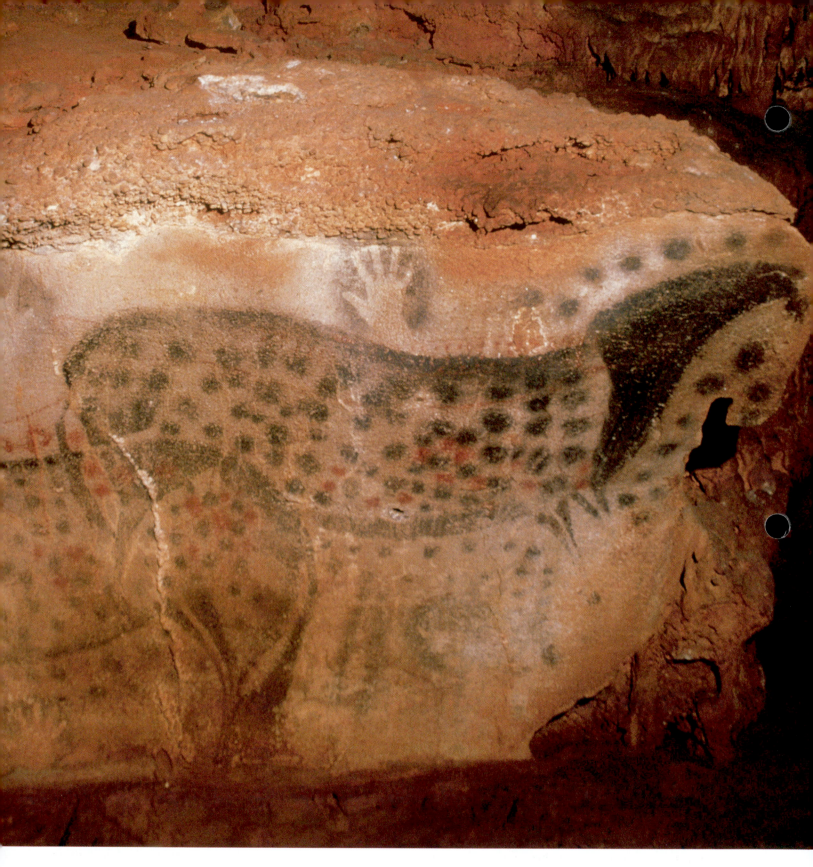

1–1 • SPOTTED HORSES AND HUMAN HANDS
Pech-Merle Cave, Lot, France. Horse on right 25,000–24,000 BCE; hands c. 15,000 BCE. Paint on limestone, height 5′ (1.5 m), length of horse on right 5′ (1.5 m).

View the Closer Look for Spotted Horses and Human Hands on **MyArtsLab**

PREHISTORIC ART IN EUROPE

1.1 Discuss whether the earliest representational images and shelters of the Paleolithic period can be considered works of art and architecture.

1.2 Summarize the diverse forms and potential meanings of Paleolithic cave paintings and sculptures.

1.3 Describe the changes in prehistoric art and architecture that resulted from the social and cultural changes of the Neolithic period.

1.4 Explain the construction and uses of megalithic architecture.

LOOKING FORWARD ▶

The first modern explorers of the painted caves of France and Spain entered an almost unimaginably ancient world. What they found in these deep recesses—hundreds of yards from entrances and accessed through long, narrow underground passages—astounded them then and still fascinates us now. At left is part of a **mural** from one chamber in the vast underground complex at Pech-Merle in southwestern France, portraying two overlapping horses, standing back to back (**FIG. 1–1**). The long, tapering neck of this horse follows the natural shape of the rock wall on which it is painted. Black dots surround portions of its contours and fill most of its body, a striking feature that was once believed to be decorative until DNA analysis of prehistoric horse remains, published in 2011, proved that one species flourishing at this time was actually spotted. Without written words and using only the essential design elements of line and color, these prehistoric painters communicate with arresting clarity across millennia.

But the most powerful and immediate human connections are embodied here in the handprints that appear in various locations within this cave. They are later additions made by artists who returned to the site 10,000 years after the horses were painted. Placing a hand against the stone surface as a stencil, the Paleolithic painters preserved its outline by spraying charcoal diluted with water and saliva directly from their mouths.

Thirty thousand years ago these ancestors of ours were not making "works of art." There were no "artists," as we use the term today. But painting on the walls of caves must have seemed vitally important to them, critical to their struggles for survival, not just a visual delight. Today, art historians, archaeologists, and anthropologists take these works as significant clues—along with fossils, pollen, and tools—for understanding early human life and culture. We may never know why they were made or precisely what they meant. Perhaps they meant different things to the various people who saw them, depending on their age and experience, their specific needs or desires. Our conclusions and interpretations about them are only hypotheses, and in the end, perhaps the greatest value of studying these mysterious images is their ability to lead us into our own speculations about why human beings create pictures.

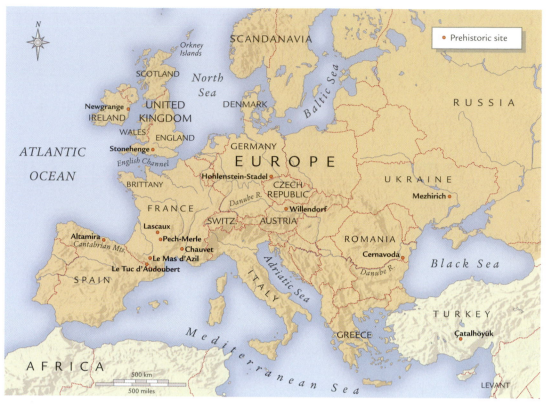

MAP 1–1 • PREHISTORIC EUROPE

As the Ice Age glaciers receded, Paleolithic, Neolithic, Bronze Age, and Iron Age settlements increased from south to north.

How and when modern humans evolved is the subject of ongoing debate, but anthropologists now agree that the species called *homo sapiens* ("wise human") appeared about 400,000 years ago, and that the subspecies to which we belong, *homo sapiens sapiens* (usually referred to as modern humans), evolved as early as 120,000 years ago. Based on archaeological evidence, it is now clear that modern humans spread from Africa across Asia, into Europe (**MAP 1–1**), and finally to Australia and the Americas. This vast movement of people took place between 100,000 and 35,000 years ago.

Scholars began the systematic study of prehistory—that is the thousands of years of human civilization before written historical records—less than 200 years ago. Nineteenth-century archaeologists, struck by the wealth of stone tools, weapons, and figures found at ancient sites, named the whole period of early human development the "Stone Age." Today's researchers further divide the time span into the Paleolithic, or Old Stone Age (from the Greek *paleo*, "old," and *lithos*, "stone")—which has Lower (earliest), Middle, and Upper phases—and the Neolithic, or New Stone Age (from the Greek *neo*, "new"). In this chapter we will consider the art of the Paleolithic and Neolithic periods in Europe. Later chapters will consider some prehistoric art on other continents and from other cultures.

The Upper Paleolithic Period (c. 42,000–8000 BCE)

Can we consider the earliest representational figures and built shelters as works of art and architecture?

Our hunter-gatherer ancestors lived in small nomadic groups and created figural representations and architecture as early as the Upper (later) Paleolithic period, when the glaciers of the last Ice Age still covered northern stretches of Europe, North America, and Asia. Representational images appear in the archaeological record beginning about 38,000 BCE in Australia, Africa, and Europe.

Artifacts or Works of Art?

As early as 30,000 BCE small figures, or figurines, of people and animals made of bone, ivory, stone, and clay appeared in Europe and Asia. Today, we interpret such self-contained, three-dimensional works as examples of **sculpture in the round** (statues that are carved free of any background or block), but we are not sure what they meant to those who made them. Whatever their original significance, Paleolithic sculptures exhibit a sense of the formal complexity that results when human beings attempt to pose and solve problems of visual design.

An early and puzzling example is a human figure—probably male—with a feline head (**FIG. 1–2**), made about 30,000–26,000 BCE. Archaeologists excavating at Hohlenstein-Stadel, Germany, found broken pieces of ivory (from the tusk of a now-extinct woolly mammoth) that they realized were parts of an entire figure. Nearly a foot tall, the remarkable statue that

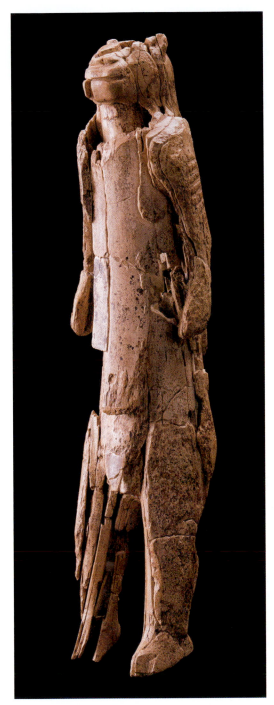

1–2 • LION-MAN STATUETTE
From Hohlenstein-Stadel cave, Germany. c. 40,000–
35,000 BCE. Mammoth ivory, height 12¼" (31.1 cm),
width 2⅞" (7.3 cm). Ulmer Museum, Germany.

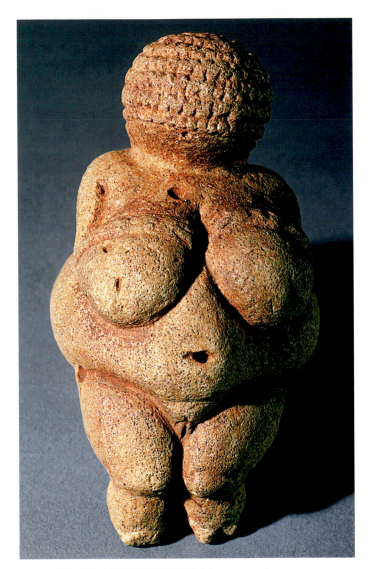

1–3 • WOMAN FROM WILLENDORF
Austria. c. 24,000 BCE. Limestone, height 4⅜" (11 cm).
Naturhistorisches Museum, Vienna, Austria.

they reconstructed from these fragments surpasses in size and complexity most early figurines. Instead of copying what he or she saw in nature, the carver created a unique creature, part human and part beast. Was the figure intended to represent a person wearing a ritual lion mask? Or has the man taken on the appearance and power of an animal? Archaeologists now think that the people who lived at this time held ideas very different from ours about what it meant to be human as distinct from animal. It is quite possible that they thought of animals

and humans as one common group of beings sharing the world. What is absolutely clear is that the *Lion-Man* shows complex thinking and creative imagination: the uniquely human ability to conceive and represent a creature never seen in nature.

Most carved human figures from the Upper Paleolithic period represent women, and the most famous female figurine is the **WOMAN FROM WILLENDORF (FIG. 1–3)**, found in Austria and dating from about 24,000 BCE (see "The Power of Naming," p. 22). Carved from limestone and originally colored with red ocher, the statuette's swelling, rounded forms make it seem much larger than its actual 4⅜-inch height. The sculptor exaggerated the figure's female **attributes** (features that identify a particular figure's identity) by giving it pendulous breasts, a bulging belly with a deep navel (actually a natural indentation in the stone), wide hips, dimpled knees and buttocks, and solid thighs. By carving a woman with a well-nourished body, the artist may be stressing her health and fertility, which would ensure the ability to produce strong children, thus guaranteeing the survival of the community.

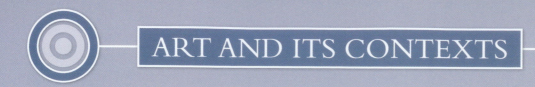

The Power of Naming

Our ideas about works of art are powerfully affected by the names we use to identify them, even in the captions of a textbook. Before the twentieth century, artists did not usually title their works. Titles were eventually supplied by owners or art historians, and they often carried the cultural prejudices of the times when they lived.

An excellent example of such distortion is provided by the names given to the hundreds of small prehistoric statues of women. For example, the sculpture in FIGURE 1–3 was originally labeled *Venus of Willendorf*, joining the name of the Roman goddess of love and beauty with the geographical location where the statuette had been found. The use of this name sent a message that the figure was associated with religious belief, that

it represented an ideal of womanhood, and that it initiated a long line of images of idealized feminine beauty.

Soon, similar works of Paleolithic sculpture came to be labeled as "Venuses." But there is no proof that any of these figures had religious associations. They have been interpreted as representations of actual women, fertility symbols, expressions of ideal beauty, erotic totems, ancestor figures, or even dolls meant to help young girls learn women's roles. They could have been any or all of these.

Our ability to understand and interpret works of art is compromised by distorting and limiting labels. Calling a prehistoric figure "woman" instead of "Venus" frees us to think about it in new and creative ways.

Shelter or Architecture?

The term "architecture" usually refers to spatial enclosures with aesthetic intentionality. Some people object to the use of this label for prehistoric structures, but building even a simple shelter requires a degree of imagination and planning, and some Paleolithic builders used great ingenuity in constructing enclosures that were far from simply utilitarian.

In the treeless grasslands of Russia and Ukraine, builders created settlements of up to ten houses using the bones of the woolly mammoth, whose long, curving tusks made excellent roof supports and arched door openings (**FIG. 1–4**). One such village, dating from about 16,000–10,000 BCE, was discovered near the Ukrainian village of Mezhirich. Its turf-and-hide-covered houses were cleverly constructed with dozens of skulls, shoulder blades, pelvis bones, jawbones, and tusks. Some floors were colored with powdered ocher in shades of yellow, red, or brown. The largest house is an impressive 24 by 33 feet; inside it, archaeologists found 15 small hearths containing ashes and charred bones left by its last occupants.

Cave Painting and Sculpture

What styles and meanings characterize the painted and sculpted images found in Paleolithic caves?

Art in Europe entered a rich and sophisticated phase after 30,000 BCE, when images were painted on the walls of caves in central and southern France and northern Spain. The existence of prehistoric cave paintings was only discovered in 1879, when a young girl, exploring with her father on the family estate in Altamira, crawled through a small opening in the ground and found herself in a cave chamber whose ceiling was covered with painted animals (SEE FIG. 1–8). Her father searched the rest of the cave, told authorities about the remarkable find, and published his discovery the following year. Few people believed that these amazing works could have been made by "primitive" people, and the scientific community declared the paintings a hoax. They were accepted as authentic only in 1902, after many other cave paintings, drawings, and engravings had been discovered elsewhere in Spain and France (SEE FIG. 1–1).

The site of the earliest-known prehistoric cave paintings is at Chauvet Cave in southeastern France, discovered only in 1994 (**FIG. 1–5**). These accomplished paintings of animals, whose forms seem to bulge from the wall as they shift and move, were made by artists in full command of their art. They have transformed their memories of active, three-dimensional creatures into two-dimensional representations by capturing the essence of well-observed animals—meat-bearing flanks, powerful legs, dangerous horns or tusks. The real significance of such cave

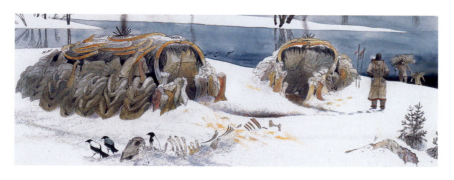

1–4 • RECONSTRUCTION DRAWING OF MAMMOTH-BONE HOUSES
Ukraine. c. 16,000–10,000 BCE.

ART AND ITS CONTEXTS

The Meaning(s) of Prehistoric Paintings

What caused people to paint such dramatic imagery on the walls of caves? In the nineteenth century, the idea that human beings inherently desire to decorate themselves and their surroundings—that an "aesthetic sense" is somehow innate to the human species—found ready acceptance. Many believed that prehistoric art was created out of the sheer love of beauty. The effort and organization required to accomplish the great cave paintings, however, suggest that their creators were motivated by more than pure aesthetics. Anthropologists and art historians have devised several hypotheses to explain cave art, but like the search for the meaning of prehistoric figurines, these explanations depend on the cultural views of those who advance them.

In the early twentieth century, scholars believed that art had a social function, and they proposed that cave paintings might be associated with prehistoric ceremonies performed to strengthen clan bonds or to enhance the fertility of animals used for food. In 1903, French archaeologist Salomon Reinach suggested that cave paintings were expressions of "sympathetic magic," that prehistoric painters may have produced pictures of reclining bison, for instance, to ensure that hunters found their prey asleep. Abbé Henri Breuil extended these ideas to claim that caves were used as places of worship and settings for initiation rites.

In the second half of the twentieth century, scholars rejected these ideas, basing their interpretations on timely scientific methods and current social theory. André Leroi-Gourhan and Annette Laming-Emperaire, for example, dismissed the sympathetic magic theory because debris from human settlements revealed that the animals used most frequently for food were not the ones traditionally portrayed in caves. These scholars discovered that cave images were often systematically organized, with different animals predominating in different areas of a cave. Leslie G. Freeman's study of the Altamira Cave in the 1980s concluded that the reclining bison are neither dead, asleep, nor disabled—as earlier thought—but dust-wallowing, common behavior during the mating season. A more recent interpretation by Steve Mithen argues that the paintings were used to teach novice hunters about animal behavior; they were situated deep within caves since this knowledge was intended only for a privileged group.

Although hypotheses that seek to explain cave art have changed, and will continue to change over time, there has been agreement that decorated caves must have had special meaning because people returned to them time after time over many generations, in some cases over thousands of years. Perhaps this art was the product of rituals intended to gain the favor of supernatural forces. Perhaps its significance had less to do with finished paintings than with the very act of creation. Artifacts and footprints suggest that the subterranean galleries, which were far from living quarters, had religious or magical functions. Perhaps the very experience of exploring the cave had significance for the image-makers. The discovery of musical instruments, such as bone flutes, may imply that even acoustical properties may have had a role to play, that caves were the site of performance as well as painting.

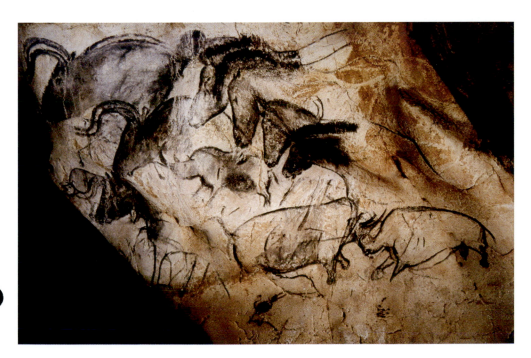

1-5 • WALL PAINTING WITH HORSES, AUROCHS (ANCIENT OXEN), AND RHINOCEROSES
Chauvet Cave, Vallon-Pont-d'Arc, Ardèche Gorge, France. c. 32,000–30,000 BCE. Paint on limestone.

In addition to animals, also included in the wall paintings of Chauvet Cave (named for one of the people who found it) are occasional humans (both male and female), many handprints, and hundreds of geometric designs. Footprints left in soft clay by a child go to a chamber containing bear skulls. According to radiocarbon dating, the charcoal used to depict the rhinos is 32,410 years old (give or take 720 years)!

👁 **Watch** a video about cave painting on **MyArtsLab**

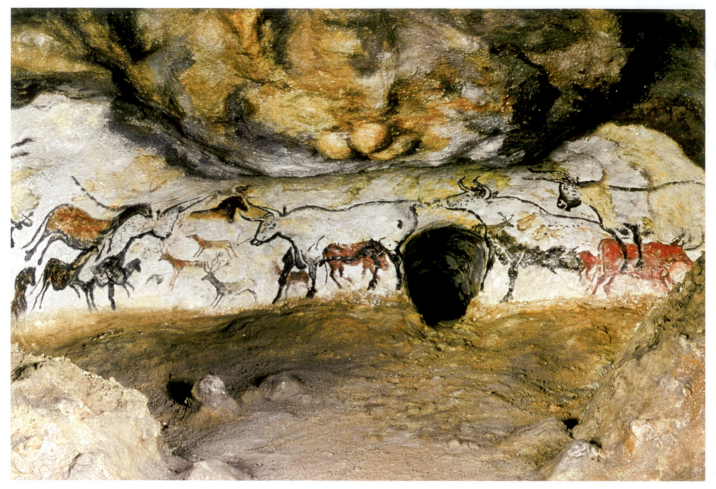

1-6 • HALL OF BULLS
Lascaux Caves. c. 15,000 BCE. Paint on limestone, length of largest auroch (bull) 18′ (5.5m).

Discovered in 1940 and opened to the public after World War II, the prehistoric "museum" at Lascaux soon became one of the most popular tourist sites in France—too popular, for the many visitors sowed the seeds of the paintings' destruction in the form of heat, humidity, exhaled carbon dioxide, and other contaminants. The cave was closed to the public in 1963 so that conservators might battle with an aggressive fungus that had attacked the paintings, and the authorities then created a facsimile of it. Visitors at what is called Lascaux II may now view copies of the painted images without harming the precious originals.

paintings is unknown, but many theories have been suggested (see "The Meaning(s) of Prehistoric Paintings," p. 23).

The best-known cave paintings are those found in 1940 at Lascaux, in southern France (**FIGS. 1-6, 1-7**), where remarkably lifelike and energetic images of cows, bulls, horses, and deer date from about 15,000 BCE. The animals appear singly, in rows, face to face, tail to tail, and even painted on top of one another. Their most characteristic features have been emphasized; horns, eyes, and hooves are shown as seen from the front, while heads and bodies are rendered in profile.

One scene at Lascaux is unusual not only because it includes a human figure but also because it is a rare example of a prehistoric painting that seems to tell a story (SEE FIG. 1–7). A figure appears to be lying on the ground. His greatly simplified form is recognizably male, with the head of a bird or wearing a bird's-head mask. A great bison looms over him. Below him lie a staff and a spear-thrower, an instrument that allowed hunters

to throw farther and with greater force, the outer end of which has been carved in the shape of a bird. The long diagonal line slanting across the bison's hindquarters may be a spear, and since he has been disemboweled, he will soon die. Why did the artist portray the man as only a sticklike figure when the bison was rendered with such accurate detail? Does the painting illustrate a myth regarding the death of a hero? Is it a record of an actual hunting event? Is it the vision of a shaman with the ability to foretell events and assist his people through contact with spirits in the form of animals or birds?

The cave paintings at Altamira, in northern Spain (**FIG. 1–8**)—the first to be discovered and identified with the Upper Paleolithic period—have recently been dated to about 12,000 BCE. The Altamira artists created sculptural effects by painting the bodies of their animals on natural protuberances in the cave's walls and ceilings. To produce the herd of bison on the ceiling of the main cavern, they used rich reds and browns to

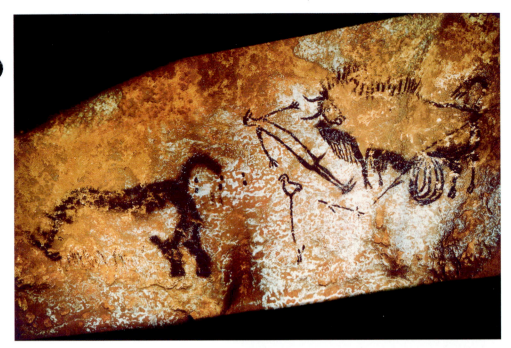

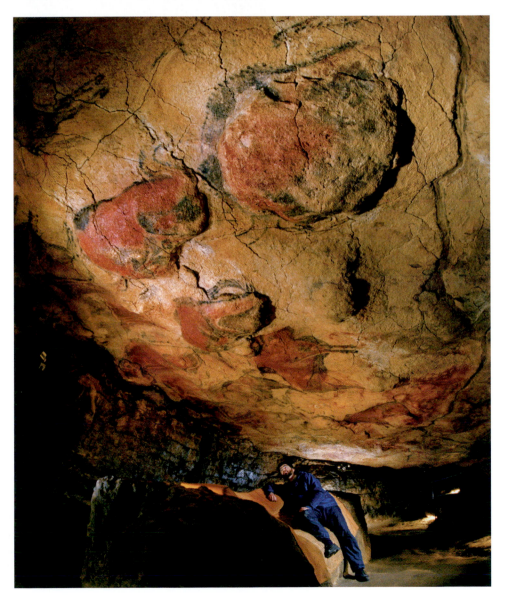

1–8 • BISON
On the ceiling of a cave at Altamira,
Spain. c. 12,000 BCE. Paint on limestone,
length approx. 8′ 3″ (2.5 m).

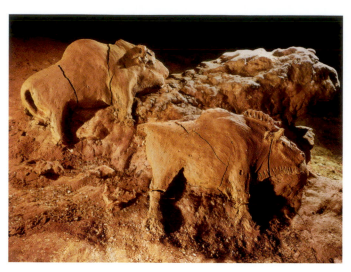

1–9 • BISON
Le Tuc d'Audoubert, France. c. 13,000 BCE. Unbaked clay, length 25″ (63.5 cm) and 24″ (60.9 cm).

paint the large areas of the animals' shoulders, backs, and flanks, then sharpened the contours of the rocks and added the details of the legs, tails, heads, and horns in black and brown. They mixed yellow and brown from iron-based ocher to make the red tones, and they derived black from manganese or charcoal.

In addition to paintings, caves sometimes contained relief sculptures created by **modeling**, or shaping, the damp clay of the cave's floor. An excellent example from about 13,000 BCE is preserved at Le Tuc d'Audoubert in southwest France. Here the sculptor created two **BISON** leaning against a ridge of rock (**FIG. 1–9**). Although these beasts are modeled in very high relief (they extend well forward from the background), they display the same conventions employed in cave paintings, with emphasis on the broad masses of the meat-bearing flanks and shoulders. To make the animals even more lifelike, their creator engraved short parallel lines below their necks to represent their shaggy coats. Numerous small footprints found in the clay floor of this cave suggest that important group rites took place here.

A CLOSER LOOK

A House in Çatalhöyük ▶ Çatalhöyük, Turkey, 7400–6200 BCE.

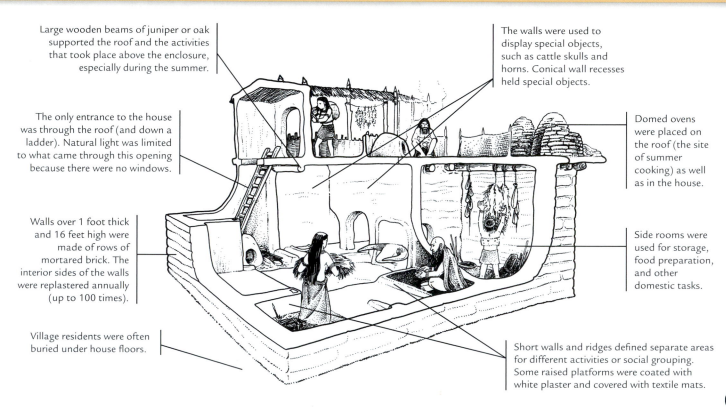

Large wooden beams of juniper or oak supported the roof and the activities that took place above the enclosure, especially during the summer.

The walls were used to display special objects, such as cattle skulls and horns. Conical wall recesses held special objects.

The only entrance to the house was through the roof (and down a ladder). Natural light was limited to what came through this opening because there were no windows.

Domed ovens were placed on the roof (the site of summer cooking) as well as in the house.

Walls over 1 foot thick and 16 feet high were made of rows of mortared brick. The interior sides of the walls were replastered annually (up to 100 times).

Side rooms were used for storage, food preparation, and other domestic tasks.

Village residents were often buried under house floors.

Short walls and ridges defined separate areas for different activities or social grouping. Some raised platforms were coated with white plaster and covered with textile mats.

View the Closer Look for a House in Çatalhöyük on **MyArtsLab**

The Neolithic Period
(c. 6500–3400/2300 BCE)

In what ways are the social and cultural changes brought by the Neolithic period expressed in prehistoric art and architecture?

Fundamental social and cultural changes mark the beginning of the Neolithic period around 6500 BCE. These include the development of organized agriculture, the maintenance of herds of domesticated animals, and the foundation of year-round settlements with houses and centers of ceramic production. The Neolithic period ended with the introduction of metalworking—the Bronze Age—around 3400 BCE in the Near East and about 2300 BCE in Europe.

Çatalhöyük

Much of what we know of daily life in Neolithic communities comes from material remains of art and architecture, and one of the richest archaeological sites is slightly east of the European heartland in the Konya plain of central Turkey at Çatalhöyük, where the first traces of a settlement date to 7400 BCE and where the continual building of house upon house in successive generations resulted in the rise of great mounds of villages. The oldest part of the site—home to as many as 3,000 people at any one time—consists of many densely clustered houses made of rectangular mud bricks held together with mortar. It provides us with a clear picture of the ways Neolithic architecture was used (see "A Closer Look," p. 26). Walls, floors, and ceilings were covered with plaster and lime-based paint. Frequent replastering and repainting, along with the mounding of house upon house, created a sense of historical continuity that outlasted any one human lifetime. The practice of burying the dead under the floors of many buildings rooted the site in the community's past as well as its future.

The houses of Çatalhöyük were powerful places not only because of the literal depths of their histories, but also because of the extraordinary art that decorated their interiors. Painted on the walls of some of the houses are violent and wild scenes. In some, humans are represented without heads as if they had been decapitated. Vultures or other birds of prey appear huge next to them, and narratives seem to highlight dangerous interactions between people and animals. In one painting (**FIG. 1–10**), a huge, horned deer is surrounded by small humans who are jumping or running; one of them is pulling something sticking out of the deer's mouth, perhaps its tongue. There is an emphasis on maleness: some of the human figures are bearded and the deer has an erect penis. Archaeologists have interpreted this scene as a dangerous game or ritual of baiting and taunting a wild animal. In other paintings, people hunt or tease boars or bulls.

Ceramics

Neolithic **ceramics**, or wares made of baked clay—whether vessels or figures of people and animals—display a high degree of technical skill and aesthetic imagination. Among the thousands of miniature figures of humans that have survived are a seated **WOMAN** and **MAN**, discovered at a pottery-production center in the Danube River valley at Cernavoda, Romania (**FIG. 1–11**). The artist who made them shaped their bodies out of simple cylinders of clay but posed them in ways that

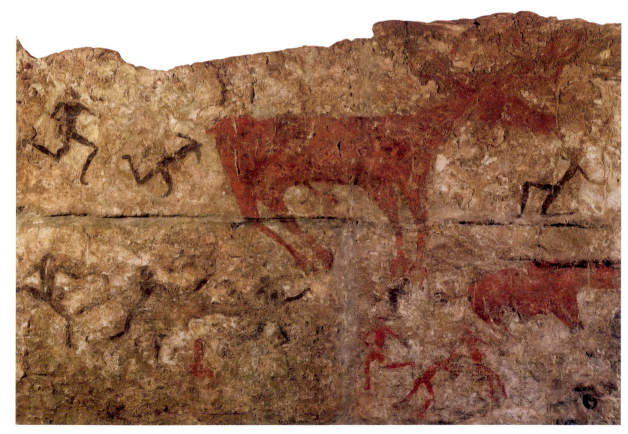

1–10 • MEN TAUNTING A DEER (?)
Detail of a wall painting from Çatalhöyük, Turkey.
c. 6000 BCE. Museum of Anatolian Civilization, Ankara, Turkey.

Neolithic Woman and Man

For all we know, the artist who created these figures almost 6,500 years ago had nothing particular in mind—people had been modeling clay figures in southeastern Europe for a long time. Perhaps a woman who was making cooking and storage pots amused herself by fashioning images of people she saw around her. But because these figures were found in a grave, they suggest an otherworldly message.

The woman, spread-hipped and big-bellied, sits directly on the ground. She exudes stability, and her ample figure seems to stress her fecundity, ensuring the continuity of her family. But in a lively, even elegant, gesture, she joins her hands coquettishly on one raised knee, curls up her toes, and tilts her head upward. Though earthbound, is she a spiritual figure communing with a celestial spirit world? Or does her upwardly tilted head suggest that she is watching smoke rise from the hearth, or worrying about holes in

the roof, or admiring hanging containers of laboriously gathered drying berries, or gazing adoringly at her partner? The man is comparatively slim, with massive legs and shoulders. He rests his head on his hands in a brooding, pensive posture, evoking thoughtfulness, even weariness or sorrow.

We can interpret the Cernavoda woman and man in many ways, but we cannot know what they meant to their makers or owners. Depending on how they are displayed, we spin out different stories about them. When set facing each other, side by side as they are in these photographs, we tend to see them as a couple—a woman and man in a relationship. In fact, we do not know whether the artist conceived of them in this way, or even made them at the same time. For all their visual eloquence, their significance remains secret.

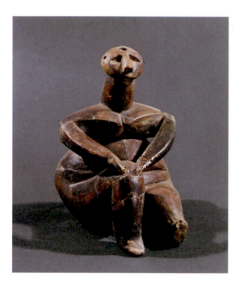
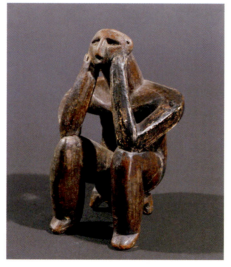

1–11 • WOMAN (LEFT) AND MAN (RIGHT)
From Cernavoda, Romania. c. 4500 BCE.
Ceramic, height 4½″ (11.5 cm). National
Historical Museum, Bucharest.

make them seem true to life. Archaeologists believe that such figures mark the emergence of the human body as the core location of human identity. The central role the body has played in the politics, philosophy, and art of historical and modern times seems to have begun around 6000 BCE with such Neolithic figurines.

Megalithic Monuments

How was monumental Neolithic architecture constructed and how was it used?

The massive tombs and ceremonial structures built from huge stones in the Neolithic period are known as megalithic architecture, from the Greek words for "large" (*megas*) and "stone"

(*lithos*). Archaeologists disagree about the nature of the societies that created them. Some believe megalithic monuments reflect complex, stratified societies in which powerful religious or political leaders dictated their design and commanded the large workforce necessary to accomplish these ambitious engineering projects. Other interpreters argue that these massive undertakings are clear evidence for cooperative collaboration within and among social groups, coalescing around a common project that fueled social cohesion without the controlling power of a ruling elite. Many megalithic structures are associated with death, and recent interpretations stress the fundamental role of death and burial as public theatrical performances in which individual and group identity, cohesion, and disputes were played out.

Of all the methods for spanning space, **post-and-lintel** construction is the simplest. At its most basic, two uprights (posts) support a horizontal element (**lintel**). There are countless variations, from the wood structures and underground burial chambers of prehistory, to Egyptian and Greek stone construction, to medieval timber-frame buildings, and even to present-day cast-iron and steel construction. Its limitation as a space spanner is the degree of tensile strength of the lintel material: the more flexible, the greater the possible span. Another early method for creating openings in walls and covering space is corbeling, in which rows or layers of stone are laid with the end of each row projecting beyond the row beneath, progressing until opposing layers almost meet and can then be capped with a stone (capstone) that rests across the tops of both layers.

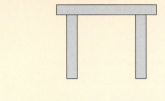

1. Post and lintel

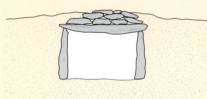

2. Cross section of post-and-lintel underground burial chamber

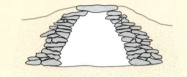

3. Cross section of corbeled underground burial chamber

👁 **Watch** an architectural simulation of post-and-lintel and corbel construction on **MyArtsLab**

Many megalithic tombs are preserved in Europe, where they were used for both single and multiple burials. In the simplest type, the **dolmen**, a tomb chamber was formed of huge upright stones supporting one or more table-like rocks, or **capstones**, in a post-and-lintel system. The structure was then mounded over with smaller rocks and dirt to form a **cairn** or artificial hill.

More elaborate burial sites—called **passage graves**—have corridors leading into a large burial chamber. At Newgrange in Ireland, a huge passage grave—originally 44 feet tall and 280 feet in diameter—was constructed about 3000–2500 BCE (**FIG. 1–12**). Its passageway, 62 feet long and lined with standing stones, leads into a three-part chamber with a **corbel vault** (an arched structure that spans an interior space). Some stones are engraved with **linear** designs, mainly rings, spirals, and diamond shapes. These patterns may have been marked out using strings or compasses, and then carved by picking at the rock surface with tools made of antlers. Recent analysis of such engraved designs suggest that we should understand them in terms of the neuropsychological effects—including hallucinations—they would have had on people visiting the tomb. They may have played important roles in ritual or political ceremonies that centered around death, burial, and the commemoration and visitation of the deceased by the living.

Of all the megalithic monuments of Europe, the one that has stirred the public imagination most strongly is **STONEHENGE** in southern England (**FIGS. 1–13, 1–14**). A **henge** is a circle of stones or posts, often surrounded by a ditch with built-up embankments. While Stonehenge is not the largest such

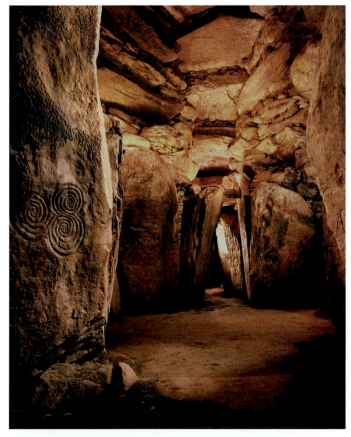

1–12 • TOMB INTERIOR WITH ENGRAVED STONES
Newgrange, Ireland. c. 3000–2500 BCE.

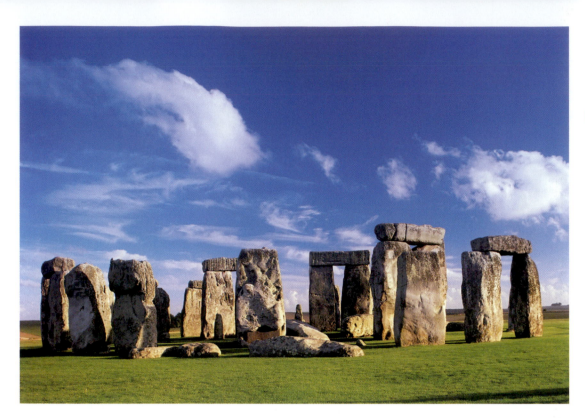

1–13 • STONEHENGE
Salisbury Plain, Wiltshire,
England. c. 3000–1500 BCE.

Watch the
Students on Site
video about
Stonehenge on
MyArtsLab

circle from the Neolithic period, it is one of the most complex, with eight different phases of construction and activity starting in about 3000 BCE and stretching over a millennium and a half through the Bronze Age.

The site started as a cemetery of cremation burials marked by a circle of bluestones, transported over 150 miles from the west, where they were quarried from a site in Wales that was also a prehistoric healing site. Through numerous sequences of alterations and rebuilding, Stonehenge continued to function as a place of the dead. Between 2900 and 2600 BCE, the bluestones were rearranged into an arc. Around 2500 BCE, a circle of huge sarsen stones—a gray sandstone—created the famous appearance of the site, with the bluestones rearranged within. The center of the site was now dominated by a horseshoe-shaped arrangement of five sarsen trilithons, or pairs of upright stones topped by lintels. The one at the middle rose taller than the others to a height of 24 feet, with a lintel over 15 feet long and 3 feet thick. This group was surrounded by the so-called sarsen circle, a ring of uprights weighing up to 26 tons each and averaging 13½ feet tall.

Many theories have been advanced to explain the meaning of Stonehenge. In the Middle Ages, people thought that Merlin, the legendary magician of King Arthur, had built it. Later, the complex was erroneously associated with the rituals of Celtic druids. Because its orientation is related to the position of the sun at the solstice, some have argued that it was an observatory to track cosmic events or a calendar for regulating agricultural schedules. None of these ideas is supported by current archaeologists and recent evidence. We now believe that Stonehenge was the site of ceremonies linked to death and burial, and that this complex can only be understood in relation to nearby prehistoric sites dating from the same period when it was in use.

The settlements built near Stonehenge also follow circular layouts, but they were built not of stone, but wood, and they

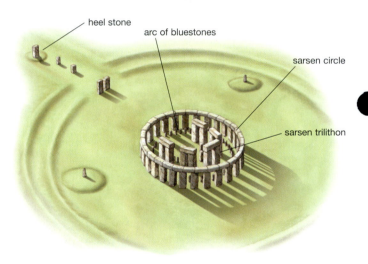

heel stone
arc of bluestones
sarsen circle
sarsen trilithon

1–14 • DIAGRAM OF STONEHENGE

were the site of human habitation rather than burial and ritual. A mile from Stonehenge is Durrington Walls, a large settlement (almost 1,500 feet across) surrounded by a ditch and containing a number of wooden circles and circular houses. Archaeological evidence demonstrates that some people who stayed here had traveled from regions far away from the site and may have been visiting as pilgrims. Stonehenge and Durrington Walls were connected to the Avon River by banked avenues, joining the world of the living (the wood settlement) with the world of the dead (the stone circle). Neolithic people would have moved between these worlds as they walked the avenues, sometimes to bring the dead for burial, sometimes to participate in ceremonies or rituals dedicated to the memory of ancestors. The meaning of Stonehenge, therefore, rests within an understanding of the larger landscape that contained habitations as well as ritual sites.

LOOKING BACK ◄

Long before men and women communicated with written words, they made images and objects. As early as 30,000 BCE, small figures of people and animals made of bone, ivory, stone, and clay appeared in Europe, and at about the same time images of animals, geometric figures, and human hands were applied to the walls of caves. Drawn, painted, and engraved— at times incorporating the natural formations and irregularities of the cave walls themselves—these images are remarkable for their descriptive realism and for their rich colors. But it is unlikely that these oldest-known artists were simply embellishing cave walls in the sense that we use the word "decorating." They may have believed that what they were doing was essential to their very existence and that of their fellow humans.

Our prehistoric ancestors also found ingenious and imaginative ways of providing themselves with shelters. As they adopted a settled, agricultural way of life, they began to build domestic structures clustered in villages and extensive tombs and ritual centers outside their settlements. As we stand awestruck in front of Stonehenge, we wonder how human beings could have imagined, planned, and then achieved such a marvelous and complicated creation, moving special stones from faraway sacred places to create and expand this exceptional site over more than a thousand years. We now understand this site as a funerary district, but it certainly holds additional secrets for future archaeologists to discover and future scholars to interpret. Writing the history of art is a continuing adventure. It is never complete.

THINK ABOUT IT

1.1 How can we gain an understanding of what the *Woman from Willendorf* meant to the person who made it or owned it? How would you interpret it?

1.2 What common motifs are found in the cave paintings of southern France and northern Spain? Summarize current theories about their meanings.

1.3 What do we learn about the life of Neolithic humans from the remains of their habitations at Çatalhöyük?

1.4 Discuss current theories on the purpose and use of Stonehenge.

| CROSSCURRENTS |

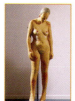
FIG. INTRO–9

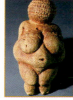
FIG. 1–3

We can be fairly certain concerning the meaning of Kiki Smith's female figure discussed in the Introduction, but little evidence survives to aid art historians in understanding the significance of prehistoric figures such as the *Woman from Willendorf*. Using only what you can see in this sculpture, what clues can you find that might help explain its meaning for those who made it and used it?

✓ **Study** and **Review** on **MyArtsLab**

IN PERSPECTIVE

42,000 BCE

Upper Paleolithic
c. 42,000–8000 BCE

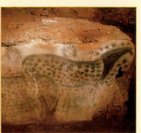
Spotted Horses and Human Hands, Pech-Merle Cave
c. 25,000–24,000 BCE

20,000

Last Ice Age
18,000–15,000 BCE

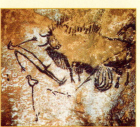
Bird-Headed Man with Bison, Lascaux Caves
c. 15,000 BCE

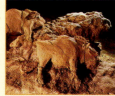
Bison, Le Tuc d'Audoubert
c. 13,000 BCE

10,000

Paleolithic–Neolithic Overlap
c. 9000–4000 BCE

Neolithic
c. 6500–3400/2300 BCE

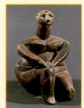 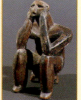
Woman and Man, Cernavoda
c. 4500 BCE

5000

Farming in Europe/Metallurgy
c. 5000 BCE

Domestication of Horses/Plow in Use
c. 4000 BCE

Potter's Wheel in Use c. 3250 BCE

Invention of Writing c. 3100 BCE

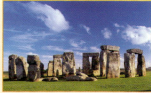
Stonehenge
c. 3000–1500 BCE

Bronze Age in Europe
c. 2300–1000 BCE

1000 BCE

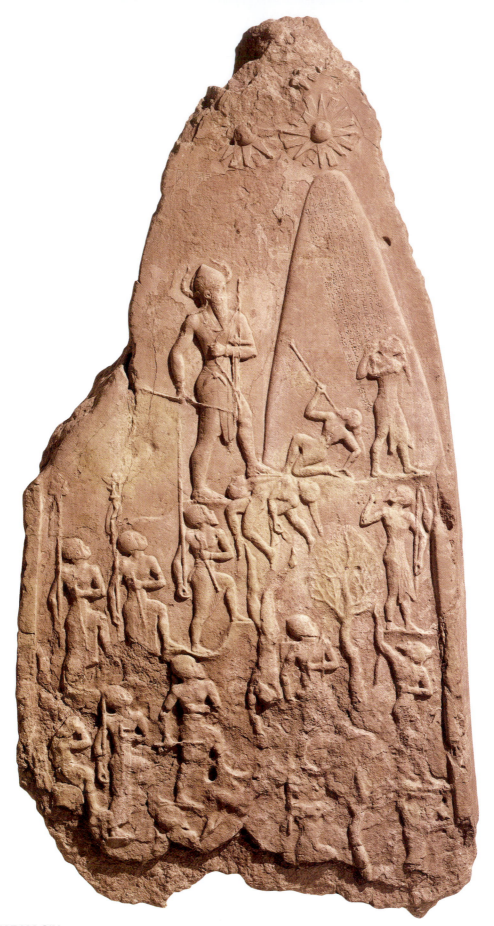

2–1 • STELE OF NARAM-SIN

From Sippar (found at Susa [present-day Shush, Iran]). c. 2254–2218 BCE. Limestone, height 6′ 6″ (1.98 m). Musée du Louvre, Paris.

View the Closer Look for the Stele of Naram-Sin on **MyArtsLab**

ART OF THE ANCIENT NEAR EAST

2.1 Discuss the early development of ancient Near Eastern art and architecture at Sumer.

2.2 Explain how the ancient art of Akkad, Ur, Lagash, and Babylon embodied the power, prestige, and achievements of a series of ancient Near Eastern rulers.

2.3 Characterize the design and meaning of the great palace complexes and urban development sponsored by Assyrian and Neo-Babylonian rulers.

2.4 Appraise the impact of the Persian conquest on the history of ancient Near Eastern architecture.

LOOKING FORWARD ▶

In public works such as this **stele** (upright stone slab), the artists of Mesopotamia developed a suave and sophisticated symbolic visual language—a kind of conceptual art—that both communicated and celebrated the political stratification that gave order and security to their world. Akkadian ruler Naram-Sin (ruled 2254–2218 BCE) is pictured proudly here (**FIG. 2–1**). His preeminence is signaled directly by size: He is by far the largest person in this scene of military triumph, conforming to an artistic practice we call **hierarchic scale**, where relative size indicates relative importance. He is also elevated well above the other figures, boldly silhouetted against blank ground; he strides toward a stylized peak that recalls his own shape, thus increasing the sense of his own grandeur by association. He clasps within his arms a veritable arsenal of weaponry—spear, battleaxe, bow and arrow—and the grand helmet that crowns his head sprouts horns, an **attribute** formerly restricted to representations of gods. By wearing it here, he is claiming divinity for himself. Art historian Irene Winter has gone even further, pointing to the eroticized pose and presentation of Naram-Sin, to the alluring display of a well-formed male body. In ancient Mesopotamia, male potency and vigor were directly related to mythical heroism and powerful kingship. Like the horns on his helmet, well-formed bodies were most frequently associated with gods. Thus every aspect of the representation

of this ruler speaks to his sacred and political authority as leader of the state.

But this stele is more than an emblem of Naram-Sin's divine right to rule. It also tells the story of one of his important military victories. The ruler stands above a crowded scene enacted by smaller figures. Those to the left, dressed and posed in a fashion similar to their ruler, represent his army, marching in diagonal bands up the hillside into battle. Identifiable native trees along the mountain pathway heighten the sense that this portrays an actual event, not a generic battle scene. Before Naram-Sin, both along the right side of the stele and smashed under his forward-striding leg, are representations of the enemy, in this case the Lullubi people from eastern Mesopotamia (in present-day Iran). One diminutive adversary has taken a fatal spear to the neck, while companions behind and below him beg for mercy.

Perhaps this ancient art, which combines symbols with stories, looks naïve or crude in relation to our own artistic standards, but we should avoid allowing such modern value judgments to block our appreciation of the artistic accomplishments of the ancient Near East—or, indeed, the art of any era or culture. For such ancient works of art maintain the power to communicate with us forcefully and directly, even across over four millennia of historical distance.

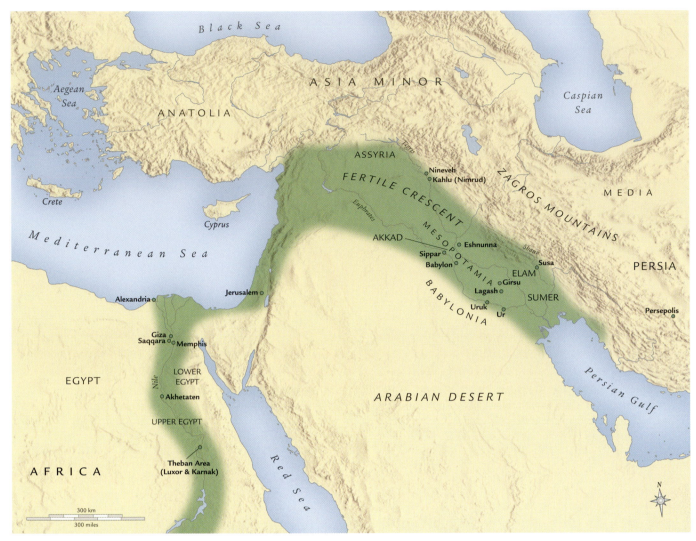

MAP 2–1 • THE ANCIENT NEAR EAST

The green areas represent fertile land that would support early agriculture, notably the area between the Tigris and Euphrates rivers and the strips of land on either side of the Nile in Egypt.

Well before farming communities appeared in Europe, people in Asia Minor and the ancient Near East domesticated grains in an area known today as the Fertile Crescent (**MAP 2–1**). A little later, in the sixth or fifth millennium BCE, agriculture developed in the alluvial plains between the Tigris and Euphrates rivers, which the Greeks called *Mesopotamia*, meaning the "land between the rivers," now in present-day Iraq. In a land prone to both drought and flood, there was a need for large-scale systems to control the water supply. Meeting this need may have contributed to the development of the first cities.

Between 4000 and 3000 BCE, a major cultural shift seems to have taken place. Agricultural villages evolved into cities simultaneously and independently in both northern and southern Mesopotamia. These prosperous cities joined with their surrounding territories to create what are known as city-states, each with its own gods and government. Social hierarchies—rulers and workers—emerged with the development of specialized skills beyond those needed for agricultural work. To grain mills and ovens were added brick and pottery kilns and textile and metal workshops. With extra goods and even modest affluence came increased trade and contact with other cultures.

Mesopotamia's wealth and agricultural resources, as well as its few natural defenses, made it vulnerable to political upheaval. Over the centuries, the balance of power shifted between north and south and between local powers and outside invaders. First the Sumerians controlled the south, but were eclipsed by the Akkadians, their neighbors to the north. When invaders from farther north conquered the Akkadians, the Sumerians regained power locally. The Babylonians next dominated the south. Later, the center of power shifted to the Assyrians in the north, then back again to the Babylonians (Neo-Babylonian period). Throughout this time, important cultural centers arose outside Mesopotamia, such as Elam on the plain between the Tigris River and the Zagros Mountains to the east, the Hittite kingdom in Anatolia (in present-day Turkey), and, beginning in the sixth century BCE, the land of the Achaemenid Persians in present-day Iran. The Persians eventually established an empire that included the entire ancient Near East.

Art as Spoils of War—Protection or Theft?

Art has always been a casualty in times of social unrest. One of the most recent examples is the looting of the head of a woman from Warka (Arabic for Uruk), when an angry mob in Baghdad looted the unguarded Iraq National Museum after the fall of Baghdad to U.S.-led coalition forces in April 2003. The delicate marble head (perhaps originally attached to a wooden statue of a goddess, c. 3300–3000 BCE) was later recovered, but not without significant damage. Also stolen was the Uruk vessel (SEE FIG. 2–3), eventually returned to the museum shattered into 14 pieces. The museum itself managed to reopen in 2009, but thousands of antiquities are still missing.

Some of the most bitter resentment spawned by war has involved the taking by the victors of art objects of great value to the conquered population. Two historically priceless objects unearthed in Elamite Susa, for example—the Akkadian Stele of Naram-Sin (SEE FIG. 2–1) and the Babylonian Stele of Hammurabi (SEE FIG. 2–9)—were not Elamite at all, but Mesopotamian. Both had been brought there as military trophies by an Elamite king, who added an inscription to the Stele of Naram-Sin explaining that he had merely "protected" it. The stele came originally from Sippar, an Akkadian city on the Euphrates River, in what is now Iraq. Raiders from Elam took it to Susa as booty in the twelfth century BCE. Uncovered in French excavations, both stelai were taken back to Paris at the turn of the twentieth century and are now displayed in the Louvre. Museums around the world contain such works, either acquired as a result of military conquest or modern archaeological discovery.

The Rosetta Stone, the key to deciphering Egyptian hieroglyphs, was discovered in Egypt by French troops in 1799, fell into British hands when they forced the French from Egypt, and ultimately ended up in the British Museum in London. In the early nineteenth century, the British Lord Elgin purchased and removed Classical Greek reliefs from the Parthenon in Athens with the permission of the Ottoman authorities who governed Greece

at the time (see pp. 114–15). Although his actions may have protected the reliefs from neglect and damage in later wars, they have remained installed in the British Museum, despite continuing protests from Greece. Many German collections include works that were similarly "protected" at the end of World War II and are surfacing now. In the United States, Native Americans are increasingly vocal in their demands that artifacts and human remains collected by anthropologists and archaeologists be returned to them.

"To the victor," it is said, "belong the spoils." But passionate and continuous debate surrounds the question of whether this notion is appropriate in the case of revered cultural artifacts.

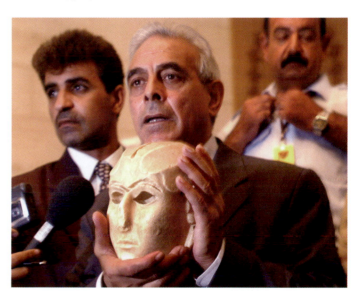

THE WARKA HEAD
Held in the hands of the Iraqi Minister of Culture, Mufeed Muhammad Jawad Al Jazairee, on its recovery in 2003 by the Iraq Museum, Baghdad. The Sumerian head is from Uruk (present-day Warka), c. 3300–3000 BCE. Marble, height approx. 8″ (20.3 cm).

Sumer

What were the principal characteristics of the early art and architecture of Sumer?

The cities and city-states that developed along the rivers of southern Mesopotamia between about 3500 and 2340 BCE are known collectively as Sumer. The Sumerians have been credited with many "firsts." They may have invented the wagon wheel, the plow, and copper and bronze casting. But perhaps their greatest contribution to later civilizations was the invention in about 3100 BCE of a form of writing on clay tablets, apparently as an accounting system for goods traded at the city of Uruk. Simple

pictures, or **pictographs**, were drawn in wet clay with a pointed tool, each representing a thing or a concept. Between 2900 and 2400 BCE, the pictographs evolved into phonograms—representations of syllable sounds—thus becoming a true writing system. Scribes (professionals who wrote and maintained records) developed a writing instrument called a **stylus**, with a triangular wedge at one end and point at the other. Mesopotamian writing is termed **cuneiform** (Latin for "wedge-shaped") after the shape of the marks made by this stylus.

In architecture, the Sumerians' most imposing buildings were **ziggurats**, stepped pyramidal structures with a temple

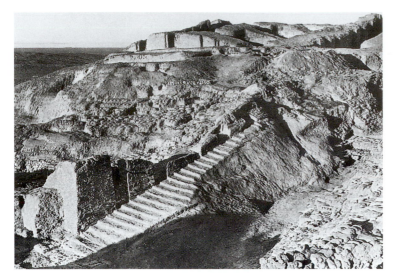

1. White Temple
2. altar
3. processional stairs
4. NW terrace

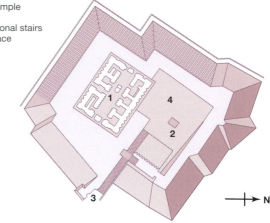

2–2 • RUINS AND RECONSTRUCTION DRAWING OF THE ANU ZIGGURAT AND WHITE TEMPLE
Uruk (present-day Warka, Iraq). c. 3300–3000 BCE.

or shrine on top. Towering over the flat plains, ziggurats proclaimed the wealth, prestige, and stability of a city's rulers and glorified its gods. They functioned as lofty bridges between the earth and the heavens, a meeting place for humans and their gods. The peoples of the ancient Near East were polytheistic; they worshiped many gods and goddesses, attributing to them power over human activities and the forces of nature. Each city had one special protective deity, and people believed that the fate of the city depended on the power of that deity. Religious specialists, eventually developing into a priest class, controlled rituals and sacred sites, ensuring that the gods were honored properly. Temple complexes—clusters of religious, administrative, and service buildings—stood in each city's center.

Two large temple complexes at Uruk (present-day Warka, Iraq)—one dedicated to the sky god Anu, the other to Inanna, goddess of love and war—mark the first independent Sumerian city-state. Anu's **ziggurat**, built up in stages over the centuries, ultimately rose to a height of about 40 feet. Around 3100 BCE, a whitewashed brick temple that modern archaeologists call the White Temple was erected on top (**FIG. 2–2**).

A tall vessel of carved **alabaster** (a soft white stone), found near Inanna's temple, shows how Mesopotamian sculptors told stories in stone—here and for the next 2,500 years—with great clarity and economy (**FIG. 2–3**). They organized this visual narrative into three **registers**, or horizontal bands, and condensed the story to its essential elements. The lower register shows the sources of life in the natural world, beginning with water and plants (variously identified as date palm and barley, wheat and flax) and continuing in the strip above them, where alternating rams and ewes march single file along a solid ground line. In the middle register, naked men carry baskets of foodstuffs, and in the top register, the goddess Inanna accepts an offering from two standing figures. Inanna stands in front of the gate of her shrine and storehouse, identified by two reed door-poles hung with banners. Facing her are two men, thought to be first a naked priest or acolyte presenting an offering-filled basket, followed by a ceremonially dressed figure of the priest-king, only

partially preserved. The scene may represent a reenactment of the ritual marriage between the goddess and Dumuzi, her consort—a role taken by the priest-king—that took place during the New Year's festival to ensure the fertility of crops, animals, and people, and thus the continued survival of Uruk.

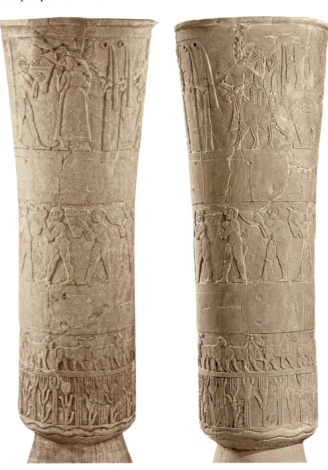

2–3 • CARVED VESSEL
From Uruk (present-day Warka, Iraq). c. 3300–3000 BCE. Alabaster, height 36″ (91 cm). Iraq Museum, Baghdad.

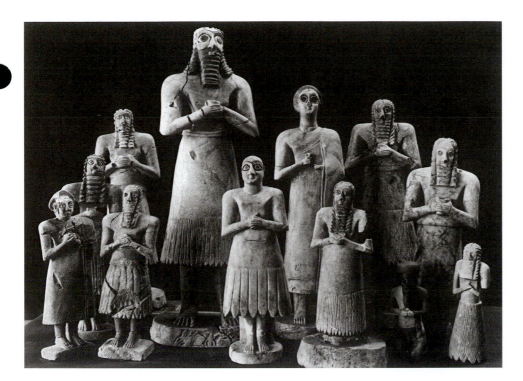

2–4 • VOTIVE STATUES
From the Square Temple, Eshnunna (present-day Tell Asmar, Iraq). c. 2900–2600 BCE. Limestone, alabaster, and gypsum, height of largest figure approx. 30″ (76.3 cm). The Oriental Institute Museum, University of Chicago.

Limestone statues dated to about 2900–2600 BCE from the Square Temple in Eshnunna (present-day Tell Asmar, Iraq) (**FIG. 2–4**) reveal another aspect of Sumerian religious art. These **votive figures** (images dedicated to the gods) are directly related to an ancient Near Eastern devotional practice in which wealthy worshipers would set up images of themselves in a shrine before a larger, more elaborate image of a god. A simple inscription might identify the figure as "one who offers prayers." Larger inscriptions might recount things donors had accomplished in the god's honor.

The carvers of these votive figures followed the **conventions** of Sumerian art—that is, the traditional ways of representing forms. The faces, bodies, and dress are stylized and streamlined to emphasize the cylindrical forms of the figures. Stocky, muscular, and bare-chested, the men in this group wear sheepskin kilts, and the female figures are as massive as the men. All stand solemnly, hands clasped in respect, perhaps a posture expected in devotional contexts. The bold, glaring, inlaid eyes may be related to statements in contemporary Sumerian texts that advise worshipers to approach their deities with an attentive gaze.

Sumerian artists worked in precious materials, as well as on stone sculpture and architecture. A superb example of their skill from c. 2600–2500 BCE is a lyre—a kind of harp—from a royal tomb in the city of Ur (present-day Muqaiyir, Iraq), which combines wood, gold, lapis lazuli, and shell (**FIG. 2–5**). Archaeologists

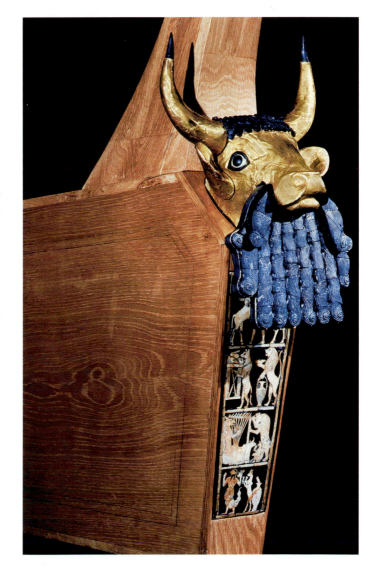

2–5 • LYRE WITH BULL'S HEAD
From a royal tomb, Ur (present-day Muqaiyir, Iraq). c. 2600–2500 BCE. Wood with gold, silver, lapis lazuli, bitumen, and shell, reassembled in modern wood support; height of head 14″ (35.6 cm); height of plaque 13″ (33 cm); maximum length of lyre 55½″ (140 cm). University of Pennsylvania Museum of Archaeology and Anthropology, Philadelphia.

A CLOSER LOOK

Scenes of War and the Celebration of Victory ▶

The front and back of a box known as the Standard of Ur. c. 2600–2500 BCE.
Shell, lapis lazuli, and red limestone inlaid in bitumen, originally attached to the large sides of a rectangular wooden box, 8″ × 19″ (20.3 × 48.3 cm). The British Museum, London.

The story begins with a battle scene, spread across the bottom register. The heat of the action increases in intensity from the calmly walking onagers (wild asses) at left toward the chariot animals' stances on the right. The animals progressively spread out and rise upward, trampling over the fallen enemy soldiers.

In the middle register, rows of Sumerian soldiers move in locked formation toward the center, removing the armor from enemy soldiers; the defeated shuffle toward the right, with conspicuously less order and disjointed postures.

The defeated army arrives from the right of the top register, moving toward the Sumerian ruler. He is easily recognized because hierarchic scale makes him the largest figure in the scene, as well as the central figure within the frieze.

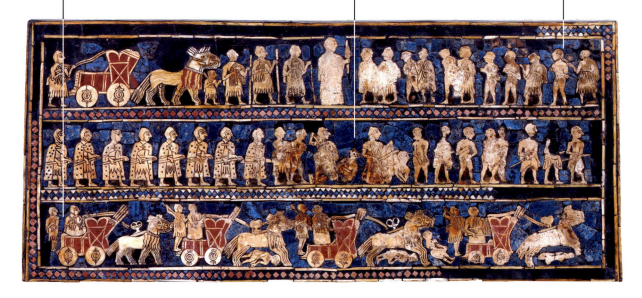

On the bottom two registers of the other side of the box, servants and royal stewards carry the provisions necessary for a large, celebratory feast.

The ruler presides over the banquet, this time placed off-center, but clearly singled out by hierarchic scale. He sits facing his distinguished guests, each of whom hoists a drinking cup in his right hand.

A woman sings to entertain the royal guests, accompanied by the playing of a bull's-head lyre similar to the one reconstructed from fragments (SEE FIG. 2–5).

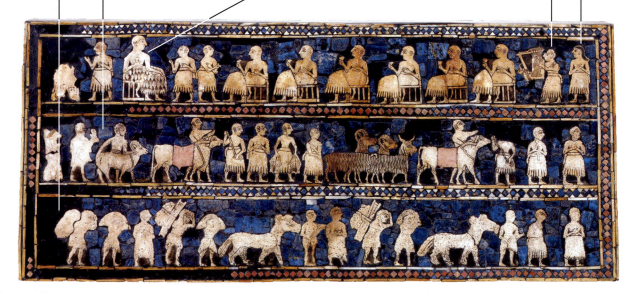

View the Closer Look for the Standard of Ur on **MyArtsLab**

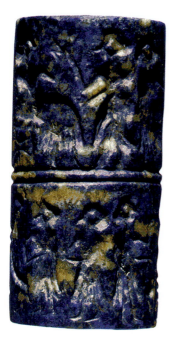

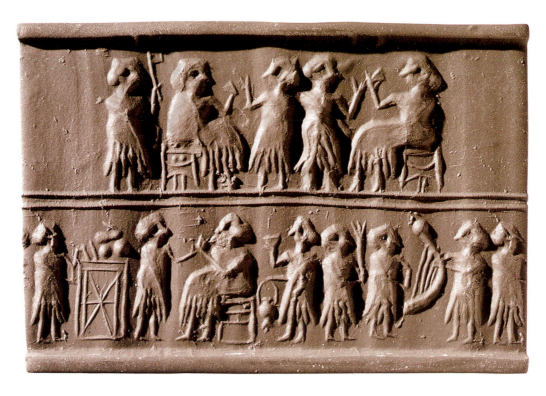

2–6 • CYLINDER SEAL AND ITS MODERN IMPRESSION
From the tomb of Queen Puabi, Ur (present-day Muqaiyir, Iraq). c. 2600–2500 BCE. Lapis lazuli, height 1⁹⁄₁₆″ (4 cm), diameter ²⁵⁄₃₂″ (2 cm). University of Pennsylvania Museum of Archaeology and Anthropology, Philadelphia.

have restored the lost wooden parts of the lyre and reassembled the surviving pieces. On one end of the sound box, surmounting a panel with inlaid shell images featuring animals behaving as humans, sits the gold, sculpted head of a magnificent bearded bull, intensely lifelike despite the decoratively patterned blue beard, created out of the semiprecious stone lapis lazuli. Since this material had to be imported from Afghanistan, it is enduring evidence of widespread trade in the region at this time. In the inlaid scene visible just under the lapis lazuli beard, a hyena and a lion deliver food and drink to a banquet, while in the scene just below, a musical ensemble of a donkey, a bear, and a fox provide the entertainment. The bottom scene portrays a scorpion-man associated with the Epic of Gilgamesh, a 3,000-line Sumerian poem about a hero who braves dangerous adventures in order to probe the question of immortality and the meaning of human existence.

Inlay is also used to create figural scenes on another spectacular object—a wooden box known at the Standard of Ur (see "A Closer Look," p. 38)—excavated from the royal tombs of Ur. Here the theme is success in battle on one side, and the subsequent banquet celebrating Sumerian victory on the other. The materials used are equally sumptuous, including blue lapis lazuli, red limestone, and shell. We are not sure of the function of this box, but its three registers of scenes are among the best surviving examples of the kind of pictorial narrative that captivated the Sumerian artistic imagination and conveyed their most important cultural messages.

In addition to inventing cuneiform writing, Sumerians developed seals to secure and identify documents and signify property ownership. **Cylinder seals**, usually less than 2 inches high, were made of hard and sometimes semiprecious stones with designs incised into the surface. Rolled across a damp clay surface, the seal leaves a mirror image of its design that cannot easily be altered once dry. The lapis lazuli cylinder seal in FIGURE 2–6 is one of over 400 that were found in excavations of the royal burials at Ur. It comes from the tomb of a royal woman known as Puabi, and was found leaning against the right arm of her body. The modern clay impression of its incised design shows two registers of a convivial banquet at which all the guests are women, with fringed skirts and long hair gathered up in buns behind their necks. Two seated women in the upper register raise their glasses, accompanied by standing servants, one of whom, at far left, holds a fan. The single seated figure in the lower register sits in front of a table piled with food, while a figure behind her offers a cup of drink, presumably drawn from the jar she carries in her other hand, reminiscent of the container held by the lion on the lyre plaque (SEE FIG. 2–5). Musical entertainment is provided by four women, standing to the far right.

Akkad, Ur, Lagash, and Babylon

How did the ancient art of Akkad, Ur, Lagash, and Babylon embody the power, prestige, and achievements of a series of ancient Near Eastern rulers?

During the Sumerian period, a people known as the Akkadians had settled north of Uruk. They adopted Sumerian culture, but unlike the Sumerians, the Akkadians spoke a Semitic language (the same family of languages that includes Arabic and Hebrew). Under the powerful military and political figure Sargon I (ruled

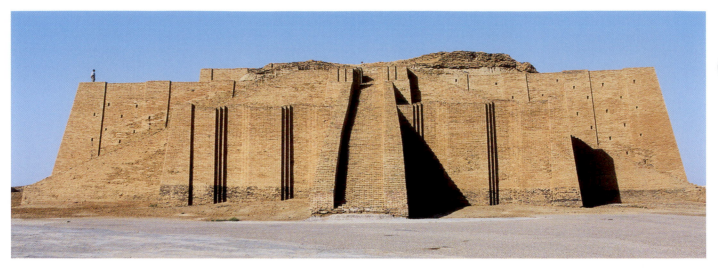

2-7 • NANNA ZIGGURAT
Ur (present-day Muqaiyir, Iraq). c. 2100–2050 BCE.

c. 2332–2279 BCE), they conquered most of Mesopotamia. For more than half a century, Sargon, "King of the Four Quarters of the World," ruled this empire from his capital at Akkad, the actual site of which is yet to be discovered.

The Stele of Naram-Sin, from about 2254–2218 BCE (SEE FIG. 2–1), commemorates a military victory of Sargon's grandson and successor Naram-Sin. Watched over by a cluster of solar deities, symbolized by the radiating suns at the top of the stele, the king, wearing the horned helmet-crown of a deity, stands above his soldiers and fallen foes near the top of the scene. The shape of the stele is used as a dynamic part of the composition. Its tapering top accommodates and emphasizes the carved mountain depicted within it, and Naram-Sin is posed to reflect the profile of both.

The Akkadian Empire fell around 2180 BCE to the Guti, a mountain people from the northeast. For a brief time the Guti controlled most of the Mesopotamian plain, but the Sumerians eventually regained control of the region in 2112 BCE under King Urnammu. He established his capital at Ur, where he built a mud-brick ziggurat dedicated to the moon god Nanna (FIG. 2–7). Three staircases converge at an imposing entrance gate atop the first platform. Each platform is angled outward from top to base, probably to prevent rainwater from forming puddles and eroding the pavement. The first two levels of the Nanna ziggurat and their retaining walls were reconstructed in recent times, and little remains of the upper level and temple.

The large Sumerian city-state of Lagash remained independent throughout this period under Gudea, who ruled from Girsu (present-day Telloh, Iraq) on the Tigris River. Gudea built and restored many temples, and within them, following a venerable

2-8 • VOTIVE STATUE OF GUDEA
From Girsu (present-day Telloh, Iraq). c. 2090 BCE. Diorite, height 29″ (73.7 cm). Musée du Louvre, Paris.

📖 **Read** the document related to the Votive Statue of Gudea on **MyArtsLab**

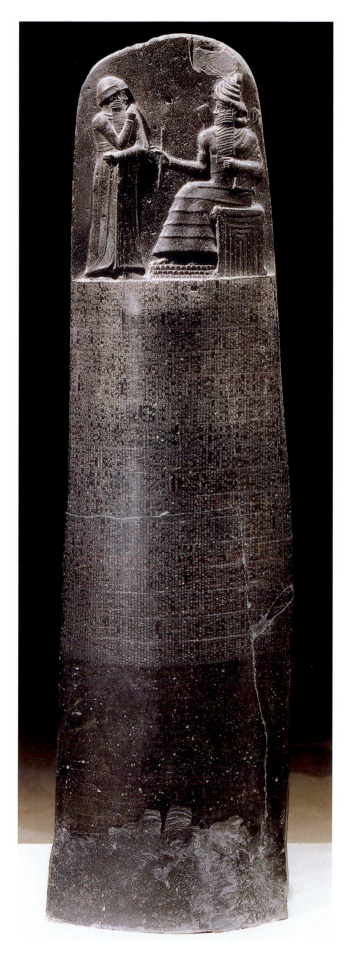

From Susa (present-day Shush, Iran). c. 1792–1750 BCE. Basalt, height of stele approx. 7′ (2.13 m), height of relief 28″ (71.1 cm). Musée du Louvre, Paris.

A prologue on the front of the stele and an epilogue on the back glorify Hammurabi and his accomplishments, but most of the inscription outlines laws guaranteeing uniform treatment of people throughout the Babylonian kingdom. Most famous are the instances when punishments are specifically tailored to fit specific crimes—an eye for an eye, a tooth for a tooth, a broken bone for a broken bone. The death penalty is imposed for crimes such as stealing from a temple or palace, helping a slave to escape, or insubordination in the army. Trial by water and fire could also be imposed, as when an adulterous woman and her lover were sentenced to be thrown into the water; if they did not drown, they were deemed innocent. Although some of the punishments seem excessive today, Hammurabi was breaking new ground by regulating laws and punishments rather than leaving them to the whims of rulers and officials.

Read the document related to Hammurabi on **MyArtsLab**

Mesopotamian tradition, he placed votive statues in diorite (a very hard imported stone) of himself as the embodiment of just rule. Twenty have survived, making Gudea's face a familiar one in the study of ancient Near Eastern art. In the cuneiform inscription on the statue shown here (FIG. 2–8), Gudea dedicates himself, the sculpture, and the temple in which the sculpture resided to the goddess Geshtinanna, the divine poet and interpreter of dreams. Gudea's prominent face, framed below a patterned wide-brimmed hat, is youthful and serene; his oversized, wide-open eyes perpetually confront the gaze of the deity. He holds in front of him a vessel from which life-giving water flows in two streams filled with leaping fish.

The land between the rivers remained a much-contested prize. Periods of political turmoil and stable government alternated until the Amorites, a Semitic-speaking people from the Arabian Desert to the west, moved into the area and reunited Sumer under Hammurabi (ruled 1792–1750 BCE). Their capital city was Babylon, and its residents were called Babylonians.

Among Hammurabi's achievements was a written legal code that recorded the laws of his realm and the penalties for breaking them. The code, incised in cuneiform script on a stele, appears under a portrait of the ruler standing before the enthroned supreme judge and sun god, Shamash, patron of law and justice (FIG. 2–9). In the introductory section of the stele's long inscription, Hammurabi declared that with this code of law he intended "to cause justice to prevail in the land to destroy the wicked and the evil, that the strong might not oppress the weak nor the weak the strong." Most of the 300 or so entries that follow deal with commercial and property matters. Only 68 relate to domestic life, and a mere 20 deal with physical assault. Punishments were based on the wealth, social standing, and gender of the offender. The rights of the wealthy are favored over the poor, citizens over slaves, men over women.

Assyrians and Neo-Babylonians

In what ways did the design and meaning of great palace complexes and urban development projects express the power of Assyrian and Neo-Babylonian rulers?

Around 1400 BCE the Assyrians rose to dominance in northern Mesopotamia. They controlled most of Mesopotamia by the end of the ninth century BCE, and by the early seventh century, they had extended their influence as far west as Egypt. Strongly influenced by Sumerian culture, the Assyrians adopted the ziggurat form and preserved Sumerian texts.

Assyrian rulers built fortified capital cities within which they constructed huge palaces decorated with wall paintings and stone reliefs of battle and hunting scenes, royal life or ceremonies, and religious imagery. During his reign (883–859 BCE), Assurnasirpal II established his capital at Kalhu (present-day Nimrud, Iraq), on the east bank of the Tigris, and undertook an ambitious building program, fortifying the

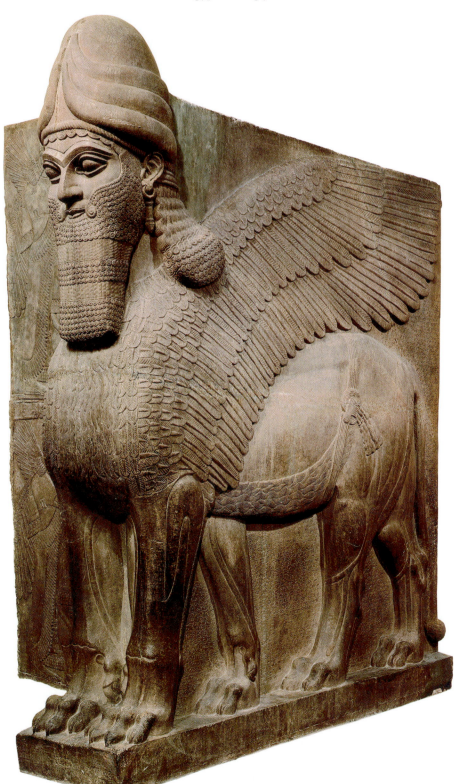

2–10 • HUMAN-HEADED WINGED LION (LAMASSU)
From the palace of Assurnasirpal II, Nimrud (Iraq). 883–859 BCE. Alabaster, height 10′ 2″ (3.11 m). The Metropolitan Museum of Art, New York. Gift of John D. Rockefeller, Jr. 1932 (32.143.2).

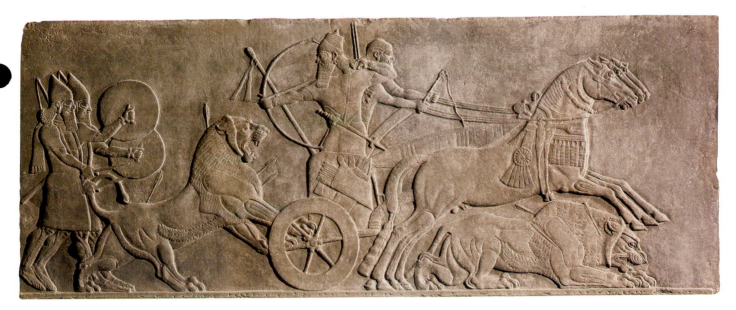

2–11 • ASSURNASIRPAL II KILLING LIONS
From the palace complex of Assurnasirpal II, Nimrud (Iraq). c. 875–860 BCE. Alabaster, height approx. 39″ (99.1 cm).
The British Museum, London.

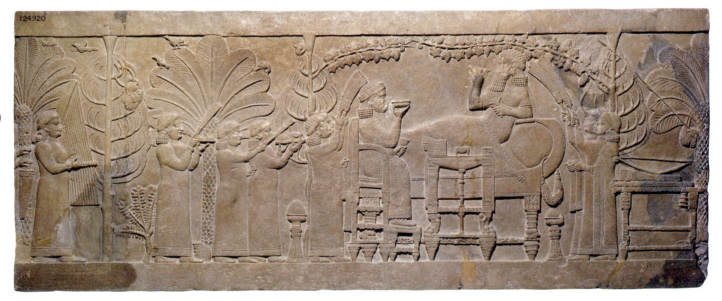

2–12 • ASSURBANIPAL AND HIS QUEEN IN THE GARDEN
From the palace at Nineveh (present-day Kuyunjik, Iraq). c. 647 BCE. Alabaster, height approx. 21″ (53.3 cm).
The British Museum, London.

👁 **Watch** a video about the process of sculpting in relief on **MyArtsLab**

new city with mud-brick walls 5 miles long and 42 feet high. Most of the buildings were also made of mud brick, but limestone and alabaster—more impressive and durable—were used to create a **veneer** of pictorial decoration. Colossal guardian figures, called lamassus, flanked the major portals (**FIG. 2–10**), and panels carved with scenes in low relief covered the walls. In a vivid lion-hunting scene (**FIG. 2–11**), Assurnasirpal II stands in a chariot pulled by galloping horses and draws his bow against an attacking lion, advancing from the rear with arrows already protruding from his body. Another expiring beast collapses on the ground under the horses. The immediacy of

this image marks a shift in Mesopotamian art, away from a sense of timeless solemnity and toward an engaging sense of visual narrative that draws the viewer into the drama and emotionalism of the event portrayed.

Assurbanipal, king of the Assyrians two centuries later, maintained his capital at Nineveh (present-day Kuyunjik, Iraq). He also had his palace decorated with panels of alabaster, carved with pictorial narratives in low relief. Most depict the king in battle or hunting, but one panel shows the king and queen relaxing in a pleasure garden (**FIG. 2–12**). The ruler, reclining on a couch, and his seated queen are surrounded

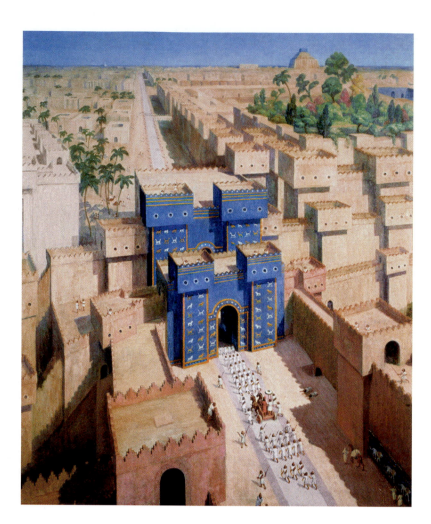

2–13 • RECONSTRUCTION DRAWING OF BABYLON

6th century BCE. The Oriental Institute Museum, University of Chicago.

In this view, the Ishtar Gate is in the center, and the palace of Nebuchadnezzar II, with its famous hanging gardens, can be seen just behind it to the right, west of the Processional Way. The Marduk ziggurat looms above the gardens in the far distance, on the east bank of the Euphrates.

by servants bringing trays of food and whisking away insects. The king has taken off his rich necklace and hung it on his couch, and he has laid aside his weapons, seen on the table behind him, but this tranquil domestic scene is actually a victory celebration. A grisly trophy, the upside-down severed head of his vanquished enemy, hangs from a tree at the far left.

At the end of the seventh century BCE, the Medes, a people from western Iran, allied with the Babylonians and the Scythians, a nomadic people from northern Asia (present-day Russia and the Ukraine), invaded Assyria. In 612 BCE, this army captured Nineveh. When the dust settled, Assyria was no more and the Neo-Babylonians—so named because they recaptured the splendor that had marked Babylon 12 centuries earlier under Hammurabi—controlled a region that stretched from present-day Turkey to northern Arabia and from Mesopotamia to the Mediterranean Sea.

The most famous Neo-Babylonian ruler was Nebuchadnezzar II (ruled 605–562 BCE), notorious today for his suppression of the Jews, as recorded in the book of Daniel in the Hebrew Bible. A great patron of architecture, he built temples throughout his realm and transformed Babylon—the cultural, political, and economic hub of his empire—into one of the most splendid cities of its day. A broad avenue, called the Processional Way because it was the route taken by religious processions honoring the city's patron god, Marduk, crossed the eastern sector of the city (FIG. 2–13). Up to 66 feet wide at points, the avenue was paved with large stone slabs. The Processional Way ended at the Ishtar Gate (FIG. 2–14), a main entrance to the city, faced with colorful glazed bricks. This decoration required careful planning and great technical skill. Each of the dragons on the gate, for example, required as many as 75 to 80 bricks. And since firing caused the bricks to shrink, each brick had to be slightly larger than its allotted space in the final design. With its four **crenellated** (notched) towers and its elaborate decoration, the Ishtar Gate symbolized Babylonian power.

Persia

What was the impact of the Persian conquest on the history of ancient Near Eastern architecture?

The Persians settled in southwestern Iran at the beginning of the first millennium BCE. Originally subservient to the Medes, the Persians obtained their independence in 549 BCE under Cyrus II "the Great," who ruled 559–530 BCE. He led the Persians in an astonishing series of conquests, creating an empire that included Babylonia (vanquished by Persia in 539 BCE), stretched from Iran into Anatolia, and would eventually include Egypt and Cyprus as well. By the time Darius I (ruled 521–486 BCE) took the throne, he could boast: "I am Darius, great King, King of Kings, King of countries, King of this earth." Darius and his successors were known as the Achaemenids, after

The Ishtar Gate and Nebuchadnezzar II's Palace

The Greeks told of the magnificent palaces, temples, and hanging gardens of ancient Babylon, and biblical accounts of the tyranny and decadence of Babylon's rulers still conjure up images of licentious splendor. The Jews had reason to record Babylonian faults. Twice—in 597 and 587 BCE—Babylonian armies destroyed Jerusalem and its temple and carried off the Jews into exile and captivity. In Babylon, one of these exiles, Daniel, survived an ordeal in the den of the king's lions, living to tell his story. The "Babylonian Captivity" became a turning point in Jewish history and prompted the poetic lamentations of the prophets Isaiah and Ezekiel.

Babylon was a huge city covering more than 3½ square miles on both sides of the Euphrates River in what is now Iraq. A wide Processional Way (SEE FIG. 2–13) running parallel to the river led to the northern palace complex. A moat, double walls, and gates with double towers defended the city. The northern gate in the royal sector was dedicated to Ishtar, goddess of love and war. Its deep-blue surfaces are decorated with alternating rows of bulls, associated with the storm god Adad, and dragons, sacred to the city god Marduk. Between 1905 and 1914, German archaeologists excavated the brilliant glazed-tile decoration of part of the Processional Way, the Ishtar Gate, and Nebuchadnezzar's throne room, much of which they shipped home to Germany.

Now reconstructed inside a Berlin museum, the Ishtar Gate sits next to a panel from the throne room in Nebuchadnezzar's nearby palace. In the portion seen here, an intricate design of striding lions (associated in the ancient Near East with royal power) and tall date-palm trees (associated with Ishtar) with blue fronds framed by white and yellow **rosettes** and **palmettes** are set against a deep-blue background.

2-14 • RECONSTRUCTED ISHTAR GATE AND THRONE ROOM WALL

Reconstructed in Berlin, but originally from Babylon (in present-day Iraq). c. 575 BCE. Glazed brick, height of gate originally 40′ (12.2 m) with towers rising 100′ (30.5 m). Vorderasiatisches Museum, Staatliche Museen zu Berlin, Preussischer Kulturbesitz.

In such a setting, described in the biblical book of Daniel, Nebuchadnezzar could have put up his golden idol, and Belshazzar, one of his successors, could have used gold and silver vessels stolen from the Jewish Temple to serve wine at his infamous feast, causing Daniel to proclaim, "You have been weighed in the balance and found wanting!" (Daniel 5:27). Indeed Belshazzar's feast was his last, for it was on that very night, in 539 BCE, that the Persians entered the gates—among them the Ishtar Gate—and destroyed Babylon.

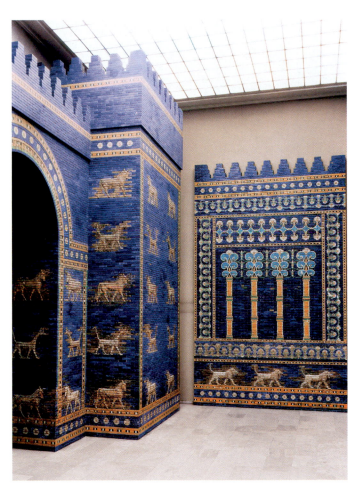

a semilegendary ancestor, Achaemenes. The dynasty ruled an expanding empire for nearly two centuries.

An able administrator, Darius organized the Persian lands into 20 tribute-paying areas under Persian governors, and he often left lesser local rulers in place. This practice, along with a tolerance for diverse native customs and religions, won the Persians the loyalty of many of their subjects. Darius also developed a system of fair taxation, issued a standardized currency, and improved communication throughout the empire. Like many powerful rulers, Darius created monuments to serve as visible symbols of his authority. About 515 BCE, he began building a new capital in the Persian homeland, today known by its Greek name: Persepolis. He imported materials, workers, and artists from across his empire. The result was a new multicultural style of art that combined many different traditions—Persian, Median, Mesopotamian, Egyptian, and Greek.

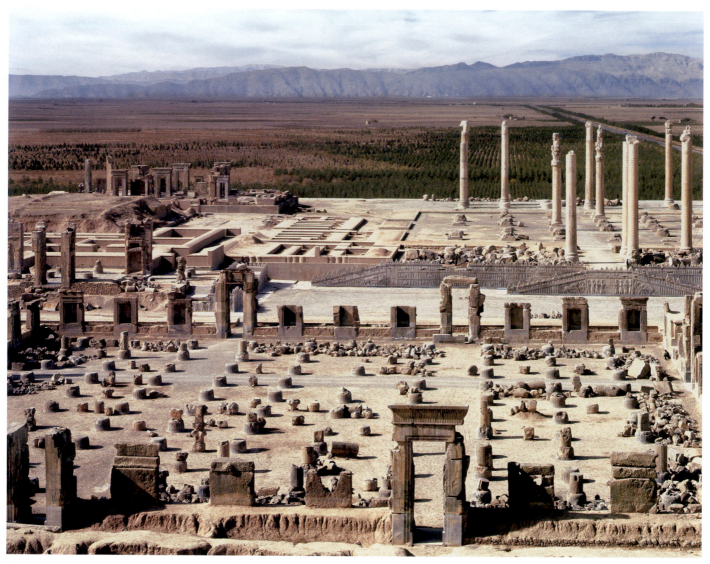

2–15 • AIR VIEW OF THE CEREMONIAL COMPLEX (INCLUDING AT RIGHT BACKGROUND THE APADANA [AUDIENCE HALL] OF DARIUS I AND XERXES I), PERSEPOLIS
Iran. 518–c. 460 BCE.

The historian Cleitarchus of Alexandria relates that Alexander the Great and his troops accidentally torched the royal compound at Persepolis during a wild banquet in celebration of their victory over the Persians. It is more probable that Alexander had it destroyed deliberately. The site was never rebuilt, and its ruins were never buried. Scholars have been measuring, mapping, and studying what remains of the complex for generations. Various pieces of architectural ornament have been stripped from Persepolis for display in museums around the world.

👁 **Watch** a video about Persepolis on **MyArtsLab**

In Assyrian fashion, the imperial complex at Persepolis was set on a raised platform, 40 feet high and measuring 1,500 by 900 feet, and like Egyptian and Greek cities, it was laid out on a rectangular **grid** (FIG. 2–15). The platform was accessible only from a single ramp made of wide, shallow steps that could be ascended on horseback. Construction extended over nearly 60 years, and Darius lived to see only the erection of a treasury, the Apadana (an audience hall that could hold several thousand people), and a small palace for himself. The Apadana was set above the rest of the complex on a second terrace covered with sculpture in low relief. On the walls, ranks of warriors seem ready to defend the palace, while

on the staircase, lions attack bulls at each side of the Persian generals. These animal combats (a popular theme throughout the Near East) emphasize the ferocity of the leaders and their men.

At its height, the Persian Empire ruled by Darius and his successors extended from Africa to India. Only mainland Greeks successfully resisted the armies of the Achaemenids, and it was a Greek who ultimately put an end to their rule. Alexander the Great of Macedonia crossed into Anatolia and swept through Mesopotamia in 334 BCE, subsequently defeating Darius III and sacking Persepolis in 330 BCE. Persia became part of the Hellenistic world.

LOOKING BACK ◄

Thousands of clay tablets covered with cuneiform writing document the evolution of writing in Mesopotamia, recording an organized system of justice and the world's first epic literature. Agricultural advances and control of the rivers increased food production and made urban life possible. The Sumerians built stepped ziggurats in their cities, and, by the ninth century, the Assyrians were building enormous palaces and fortresses. Sculpted figures stood guard at the gates, and walls were covered with relief sculptures, recounting in vivid detail the Assyrian rulers' prowess as warriors and hunters. Later, Babylon in the south became a luxurious city, whose palaces and ceremonial avenues were faced with brilliantly colored glazed bricks. Finally, the Achaemenid Persians formed a spectacularly rich empire, drawing from a series of cultural traditions to express its wealth and power in a huge palace complex at Persepolis.

We will turn next to another ancient river culture, established about the same time along the banks of the Nile. In Egypt, the early development of writing provides rich historical information, allowing us to understand much about the art and architecture it left behind. But in Egypt there will be a marked emphasis on stability rather than change.

THINK ABOUT IT

2.1 Discuss how precious materials are used in the Lyre with Bull's Head from Ur. How do the stories recalled by scenes on the lyre relate to the culture that produced it?

2.2 Explain how the design of the Stele of Naram-Sin makes claims about the special power of this Akkadian ruler.

2.3 How do the relief sculptures in FIGURES 2–11 and 2–12 characterize the two Assyrian rulers who built the palace complexes for which they were made?

2.4 Discuss the variety of sources drawn on in the design of the new city of Persepolis.

| CROSSCURRENTS |

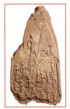
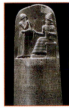

The ancient civilizations of Mesopotamia produced impressive works of art and architecture that expressed political power. Discuss how these two monuments proclaim the power of the two rulers represented on them.

FIG. 2–1   FIG. 2–9

✓ **Study** and **Review** on **MyArtsLab**

IN PERSPECTIVE

4000 BCE

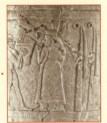

Sumer
c. 3500–2340 BCE

Goddess Inanna on Carved Vessel
c. 3300–3000 BCE

Potter's Wheel in Use
c. 3250 BCE

Invention of Writing
c. 3100 BCE

3000

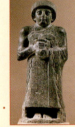

Akkad c. 2340–2180 BCE

Naram-Sin
ruled 2254–2218 BCE

Lagash
c. 2150–2046 BCE

Votive Statue of Gudea
c. 2090 BCE

2000

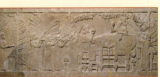

Hammurabi
ruled 1792–1750 BCE

Hittites (Anatolia)
c. 1600–1200 BCE

Stele of Hammurabi
c. 1792–1750 BCE

1000

Assyrian Empire
c. 1000–612 BCE

Assurnasirpal II
ruled 883–859 BCE

Assurbanipal and His Queen in the Garden
c. 647 BCE

Assurbanipal ruled 669–c. 627 BCE
Neo-Babylonia c. 612–539 BCE
Nebuchadnezzar II ruled 605–562 BCE
Persia 549–330 BCE

500 BCE

Darius I ruled 521–486 BCE

Alexander the Great Sweeps through Mesopotamia 334–330 BCE

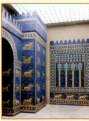

Ishtar Gate and Throne Room Wall
c. 575 BCE

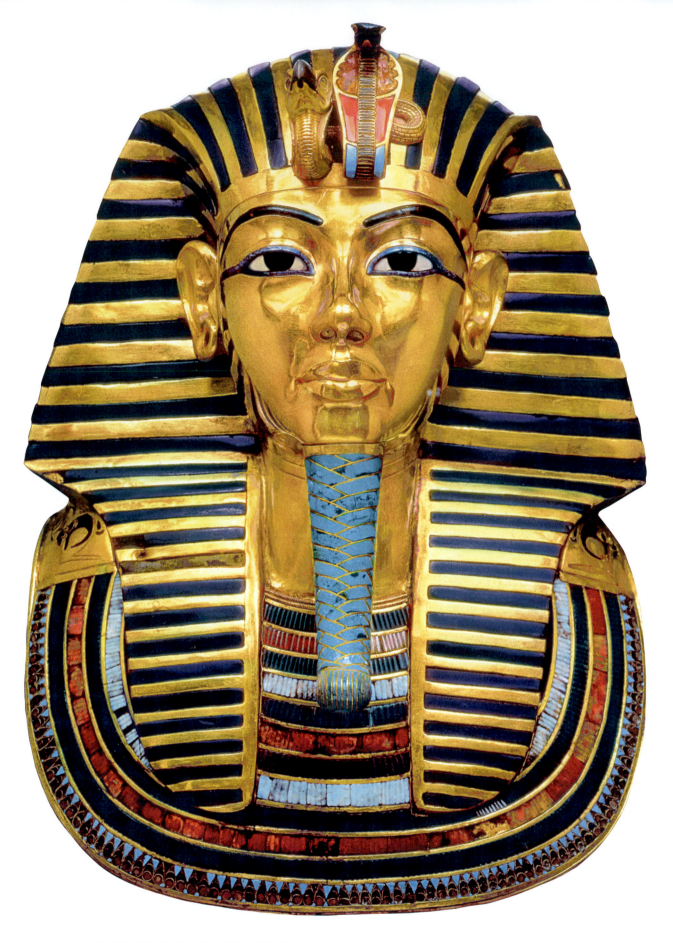

3–1 • FUNERARY MASK OF TUTANKHAMUN
(ruled 1332–1322 BCE, Dynasty 18). Gold inlaid with glass and semiprecious stones, height 21¼″ (54 cm),
weight 24 lb. (11 kg). Egyptian Museum, Cairo.

ART OF ANCIENT EGYPT

3.1 Define the pictorial and architectural conventions developed during the Early Dynastic and Old Kingdom periods in ancient Egyptian art.

3.2 Recognize the subtle changes to the conventions of ancient Egyptian art during the Middle Kingdom.

3.3 Distinguish the refinements and transformations that occurred in the New Kingdom.

3.4 Identify both traditional and new features seen in Late Egyptian art.

LOOKING FORWARD ▶

Singularly self-possessed and staring serenely, the funerary mask of the young Egyptian ruler Tutankhamun (FIG. 3–1) dazzles us with royal splendor, and its legendary relationship with its sensational discovery certainly adds to its appeal. British archaeologist Howard Carter's dramatic discovery of the king's tomb in 1922 established the "romance of archaeology" in the public mind. Now the more than 3,500 items from Tutankhamun's tomb are showcased in the Egyptian Museum in Cairo, and periodic blockbuster exhibitions of objects from the tomb keep its appeal fresh for successive generations of museum-goers.

Why are we so mesmerized by the art of Egypt? It may be simply the elegant style and exquisite craftsmanship. Or the reason may lie in our fascination with this ancient people's struggle to create an explanation for the transition between life and death and their belief in an eternal hereafter that allowed powerful people like Tutankhamun to carry their wealth with them into their new adventures in the other world.

As fragile humans, we observe nature's continuous cycle of birth, death, and rebirth, and we come to realize that for all our ingenuity, we cannot escape death. Yet our imaginations recoil at the idea of our own extinction. Through the centuries people have lived with the hope or expectation of a life after death. Ancient Egyptians, from their narrow river valley, observed the constant regeneration of the land through yearly floods. They could easily believe that such regeneration would be granted to human beings, or at least to their rulers, who became gods on earth. Ancient Egyptians conceived the afterlife as a continuation of the life they knew. Thus they made elaborate efforts to equip the dead magnificently for life in the hereafter.

But the enchantment of Egyptian art is also aesthetic. Look into Tutankhamun's eyes. They are beautifully formed, emphatic shapes—black disks set in white and energized by tiny touches of red at the corners, yet their dark outline avoids the natural detail of lashes. Capturing fleeting moments like the fluttering of lashes during the blink of an eye was of little interest to a people concerned with timeless and eternal visions. By emphasizing clarity of line and color, streamlined forms, and the distillation of nature to elemental geometric shapes, ancient Egyptian artists established a standard of technical and aesthetic excellence that we continue to revere to this day.

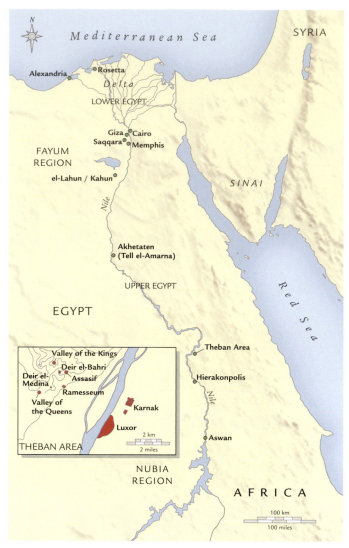

MAP 3–1 • ANCIENT EGYPT

Upper Egypt is below Lower Egypt on this map because the designations "Upper" and "Lower" refer to the directional flow of the Nile, not to our conventions for south and north in drawing maps. The two kingdoms were united c. 3000 BCE, just before the Early Dynastic period.

At the same time that city-states such as Sumer began to develop in Mesopotamia, a rich civilization arose in Egypt in the fertile valley and delta of the Nile (MAP 3–1). Around 5000 BCE, the valley's inhabitants adopted the agricultural village life associated with Neolithic culture. Farming communities along the Nile cooperated to control the river's flow, and, as in Mesopotamia, soon formed alliances. By about 3500 BCE, there were several larger chiefdoms in the lower Nile Valley. Soon, Egypt was politically unified under a succession of kings from powerful families or dynasties.

Early Dynastic and Old Kingdom Egypt (c. 2950–2150 BCE)

What characterizes the principal pictorial and architectural conventions that were developed during the Early Dynastic and Old Kingdom periods of ancient Egypt?

Around 3000 BCE, Egypt became a consolidated state along the banks of the River Nile. According to legend, the country had previously evolved into two kingdoms: Upper Egypt in the south and Lower Egypt in the north. ("Upper" and "Lower" refer to the flow of the Nile—upstream or downstream.) Since the works of art and architecture that survive from ancient Egypt come mainly from tombs and temples—the majority of which were located in secure places and built with the most durable materials—most of what we know about the ancient art of consolidated Egypt is rooted in religious beliefs and practices. Based on that knowledge, it is clear that the artistic **conventions** (established ways of representing things) that were developed during the Early Dynastic period would endure, with subtle but significant variations, over almost three millennia of Egyptian history. Stability and continuity would be valued more than innovation and change.

These artistic conventions are already established in a stone palette of about 2950 BCE found in the temple of Horus at Hierakonpolis and featuring representations of a king named Narmer. **Palettes** (flat stones with a circular depression carved on one side) were used to grind and prepare the makeup that was applied around the eyes to reduce the glare of the sun. The Palette of Narmer has the same form as these utilitarian objects but is much larger and must have had a ceremonial function.

On one side of the palette ("A Closer Look," p. 51, left), as in the Stele of Naram-Sin (SEE FIG. 2–1), hierarchic scale instantly signals the importance of Narmer by showing him overwhelmingly larger than the other figures around him. He is similarly silhouetted against a blank ground, distancing details of setting and story so they will not distract from his preeminence. He wears the White Crown of Upper Egypt (see "Egyptian Symbols," p. 58) and prepares to strike the enemy who kneels before him with an upraised mace. Above this foe, the god Horus—represented as a falcon with a human hand—holds a rope tied around the neck of a man whose head is attached to a block sprouting stylized papyrus, symbolizing Lower Egypt. This combination of symbols makes the central message clear: Narmer, ruler of Upper Egypt, is in firm control of Lower Egypt. He now rules both lands.

Many figures are shown here in composite poses that would be impossible to assume in real life. The artists chose a conceptual—rather than a perceptual—approach to the representation of the human figure. Heads are in profile, to capture most clearly their identifying features, while eyes, most recognizable and expressive when seen from the front, are rendered frontally. Shoulders and torso are also frontal, but hips, legs, and feet are shown in profile. These conventions of Egyptian painting and relief sculpture will endure for millennia when depicting royalty and other dignitaries. Persons of lesser social rank tended to be represented in ways that seem to us more lifelike.

Central to ancient Egyptian belief was the idea that every human being had a life force—the *ka*, or spirit—which lived on after the death of the body, forever engaged in the activities it had enjoyed during its earthly existence. Even after death, however, the *ka* needed a body to inhabit—either a carved likeness of the deceased or his or her actual corpse, preserved by mummification (see "Mummies," p. 65).

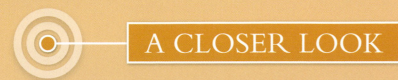
The Palette of Narmer ▶

From Hierakonpolis. Early Dynastic period, c. 2950 BCE.
Green schist, height 25″ (63.5 cm). Egyptian Museum, Cairo.

This figure, named by hieroglyphic inscription and standing on his own **ground line**, holds the king's sandals. Narmer is barefoot because he is standing on sacred ground, performing sacred acts. The same sandal-bearer, likewise labeled, follows Narmer on the other side of the palette.

Phonetic **hieroglyphs** centered at the top of each side of the palette name the king: a horizontal fish (*nar*) above a vertical chisel (*mer*). A depiction of the royal palace—seen simultaneously from above, as a ground plan, and frontally, as a **façade** (front wall of a building)—surrounds Narmer's name to signify that he is king.

Narmer here wears the Red Crown of Lower Egypt and is identified by the hieroglyph label next to his head, as well as by his larger size in relation to the other figures (hierarchic scale).

The royal procession inspects two rows of decapitated enemies, their heads neatly tucked between their feet.

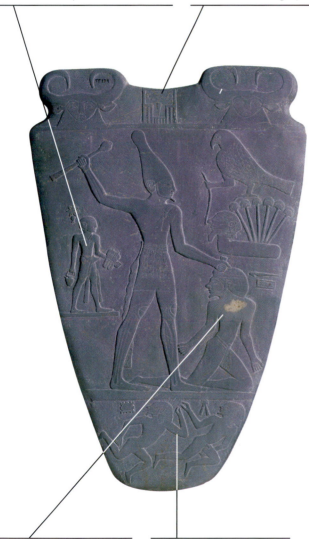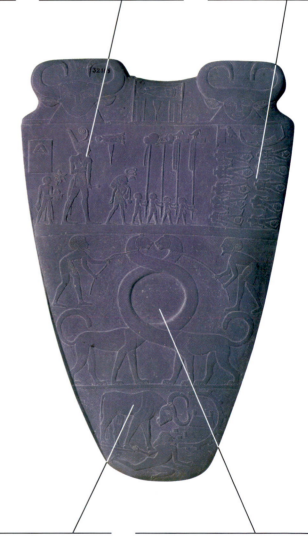

Narmer attacks a figure of comparable size, also identified by a hieroglyphic label, indicating that he is an enemy of real importance, likely the ruler of Lower Egypt.

Next to the heads of these two defeated enemies are, on the left, an aerial depiction of a fortified city, and on the right, a gazelle trap, perhaps indicating Narmer's dominion over both city and countryside.

A bull symbolizing the might of the king—he wears a bull's tail on both sides of the palette—tramples an enemy in front of a fortified city.

Palettes were tablets with circular depressions where eye makeup was ground and prepared. Although this example was undoubtedly ceremonial rather than functional, a mixing saucer is framed by the elongated, intertwined necks of lions, perhaps signifying the union of Upper and Lower Egypt.

View the Closer Look for the Palette of Narmer on **MyArtsLab**

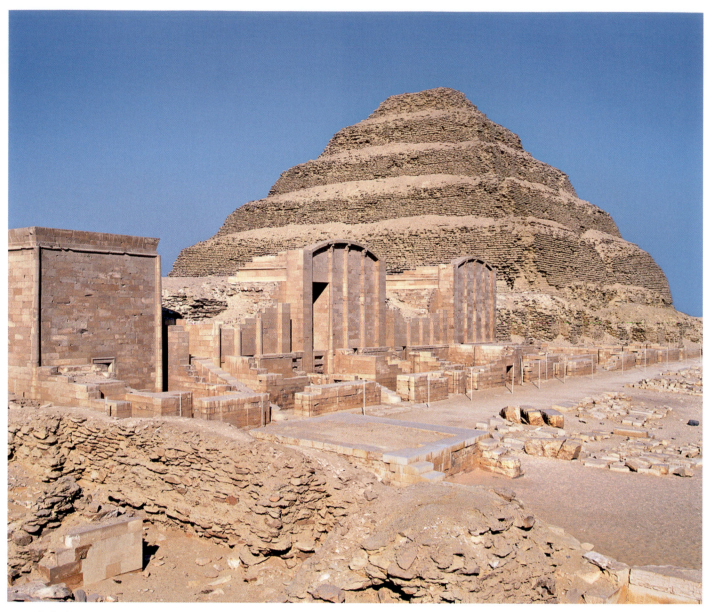

3–2 • Imhotep STEPPED PYRAMID AND SHAM BUILDINGS OF THE FUNERARY COMPLEX OF DJOSER
Saqqara. c. 2630–2575 BCE, Dynasty 3. Limestone, height of pyramid 204′ (62 m).

3–3 • RECONSTRUCTION DRAWING OF DJOSER'S FUNERARY COMPLEX
Saqqara.

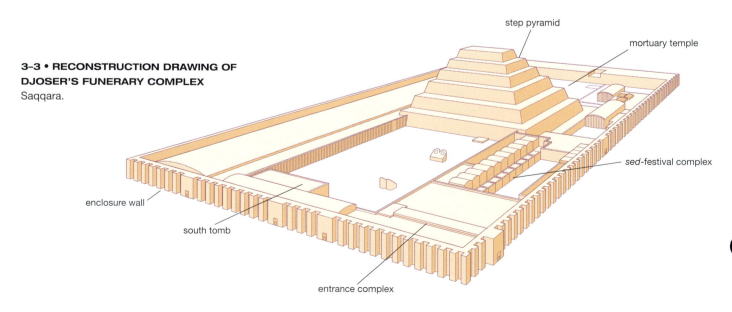

step pyramid

mortuary temple

sed-festival complex

enclosure wall

south tomb

entrance complex

The Egyptian burial structure—the gateway to the afterlife for kings and members of the royal court—began as a low rectangular mastaba with an internal room and chapel. Later, mastaba forms of decreasing size were stacked over underground burial chambers to form stepped pyramids. Eventually they developed into pyramids, housing an aboveground tomb and including false chambers, false doors, and confusing passageways to foil potential tomb robbers.

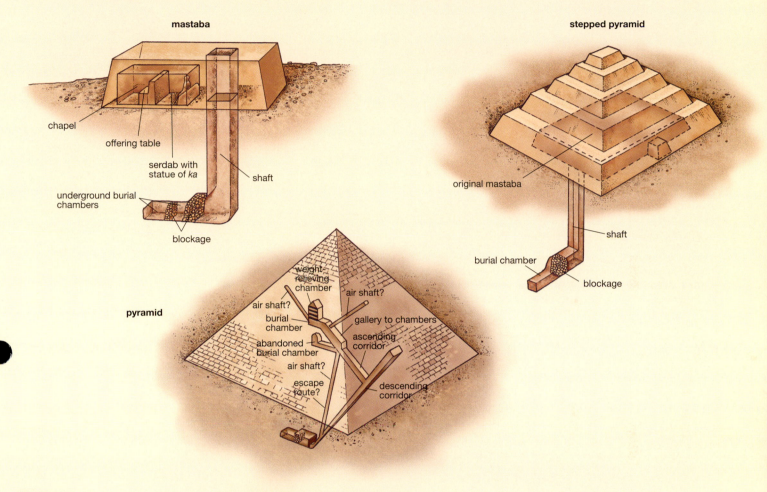

mastaba

chapel

offering table

serdab with statue of *ka*

shaft

underground burial chambers

blockage

stepped pyramid

original mastaba

shaft

burial chamber

blockage

pyramid

weight-relieving chamber

air shaft?

burial chamber

air shaft?

gallery to chambers

abandoned burial chamber

ascending corridor

air shaft?

escape route?

descending corridor

◉ Watch an architectural simulation about the pyramid on **MyArtsLab**

The need to fulfill the requirements of the *ka* led not only to the creation of statues as substitute bodies, but also to the development of elaborate funerary rites and tombs filled with supplies and furnishings that the *ka* might need throughout eternity. In the Early Dynastic period, the most common type of tomb structure in Egypt was the **mastaba**, a flat-topped, one-story structure with slanted walls erected above an underground burial chamber (see "Mastaba to Pyramid," above). These tended to be grouped together in a **necropolis**—literally, "city of the dead"—at the edge of the desert on the west bank of the Nile where the sun set.

Two of the most extensive of these early necropolises are at Saqqara and Giza, near present-day Cairo. For his tomb complex at Saqqara, the Third Dynasty King Djoser (ruled c. 2650–2631 BCE) commissioned the earliest-known **monumental** architecture in Egypt. The designer of the complex—Imhotep, prime minister and royal advisor—laid out Djoser's tomb as a stepped pyramid consisting of six mastaba-like elements stacked on top of each other and originally covered with a limestone facing, or veneer (**FIG. 3–2**). Although the final structure superficially resembles the ziggurats of Mesopotamia, it differs in both concept and purpose. It is built of finely cut stone, not mud brick; it rises in stages without ramps; and it signals a tomb, not a temple. From its top, a 92-foot shaft descends to a granite-lined burial vault. Adjacent to the stepped pyramid, a funerary temple was used for continuing worship of the dead king, and sham buildings—simple masonry shells filled with debris—reproduce the shrines, booths, and chapels Djoser had used during rituals associated with kingship, intended for the use of his *ka* in the afterlife (**FIG. 3–3**).

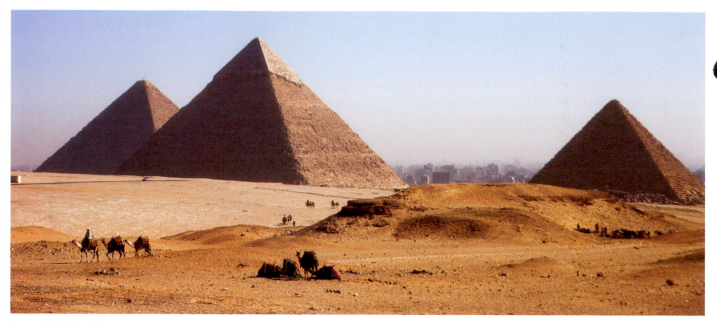

3-4 • GREAT PYRAMIDS

Giza. c. 2575–2450 BCE, Dynasty 4. Erected by (from left) Menkaure, Khafre, and Khufu. Granite and limestone, height of pyramid of Khufu 450′ (137 m).

The designers of the pyramids tried to ensure that the king and his tomb "home" would never be disturbed. Khufu's builders placed his tomb chamber in the very heart of the mountain of masonry, at the end of a long, narrow, steeply rising passageway, sealed off after the king's burial by a 50-ton stone block. Three false passageways, either deliberately meant to mislead or the result of changes in plan as construction progressed, obscured the location of the tomb. Despite such precautions, early looters managed to penetrate the tomb chamber and make off with Khufu's funeral treasure.

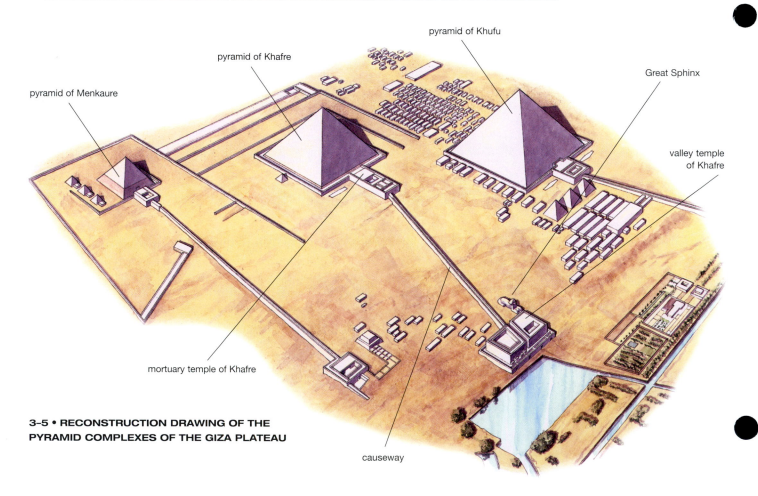

pyramid of Khufu

pyramid of Khafre

pyramid of Menkaure

Great Sphinx

valley temple of Khafre

mortuary temple of Khafre

causeway

3-5 • RECONSTRUCTION DRAWING OF THE PYRAMID COMPLEXES OF THE GIZA PLATEAU

The architectural form most closely identified with Egypt is the true pyramid with a square base and four sloping triangular sides. Most famous are the three **GREAT PYRAMIDS** at Giza (**FIG. 3–4**), part of tomb complexes built by three successive Fourth Dynasty kings—Khufu, Khafre, and Menkaure, whose reigns spanned c. 2551–2472 BCE. The oldest and largest of the Giza pyramids is that of Khufu, which covers 13 acres at its base and originally rose to a height of about 480 feet—some 30 feet above the current summit, which was once faced with a sheath of polished limestone. The complex of Khafre (ruled c. 2520–2494 BCE) is the best preserved. It is most famous for the colossal portrait of the king as a sphinx that combines his head with the body of a crouching lion (SEE FIG. INTRO–1).

Next to each of these pyramids was a funerary temple connected by an enclosed corridor, to a so-called valley temple on the bank of the Nile (**FIG. 3–5**). When a king died, his body was ferried across the Nile from the royal palace to his valley temple, where it was received with elaborate ceremony. It was then carried up the corridor to the funerary temple and placed in its chapel, where rites for the benefit of the king's spirit—meant to be continued for perpetuity—were initiated. Finally, the body was entombed in a well-hidden vault inside the pyramid.

In three-dimensional sculpture, a rigidly frontal, cubic conception of the figure continued for members of the royal family and high officials. The compact, rectilinear solidity of Egyptian forms—a striking contrast with the cylindrical shapes of early Mesopotamian sculpture—may derive from the desire to give these statues a sense of strength and permanence. An over-life-size statue of **KHAFRE** (**FIG. 3–6**) from the valley temple of his pyramid complex represents the ruler enthroned and protected by the falcon-god Horus, who perches behind the king's head, enfolding it in his wings. Khafre wears the traditional royal costume: a short kilt, a false beard symbolic of kingship, and a folded linen headdress. He conveys a strong sense of dignity, calm, and, above all, permanence. The statue's compactness—arms pressed tightly to the body, body firmly anchored in the block—projects a sense of unwavering power in an athletic body caught at the peak of perfection.

These same formal and expressive features characterize a double portrait of Khafre's son **MENKAURE** (ruled c. 2490–2472 BCE) **AND A QUEEN**, probably his principal

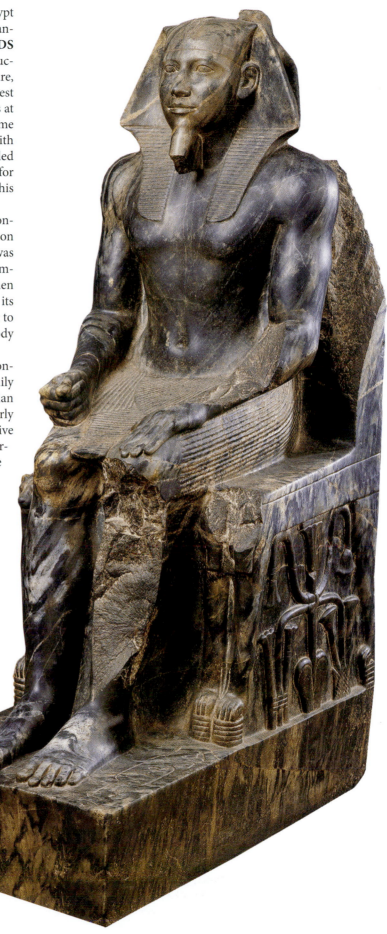

3–6 • KHAFRE
(ruled c. 2520–2494 BCE, Dynasty 4), from the valley temple of his pyramid complex, Giza. Gneiss, height 5′ 6⅛″ (1.68 m). Egyptian Museum, Cairo.

The statue was carved in an unusual material (imported from Nubia), which produces a rare optical effect in sunlight; it glows a deep blue, the celestial color of Horus. In its original location, the sun would have shown through clerestory windows, illuminating the alabaster floor and the figure, and creating a blue radiance around the figure.

wife Khamerernebty II (**FIG. 3–7**), discovered in his valley temple. The figures, carved from a single block of stone, are visually joined by the queen's symbolic embrace. The king, depicted in accordance with cultural and political ideals as an athletic, youthful figure nude to the waist, stands in a conventionally balanced pose with one foot extended, his arms straight at his sides, and his fists clenched over cylindrical objects. His equally youthful queen echoes his striding pose with a smaller step forward, and her sheer, tight-fitting garment reveals the soft curves of her body, a foil for the taut muscularity of the king.

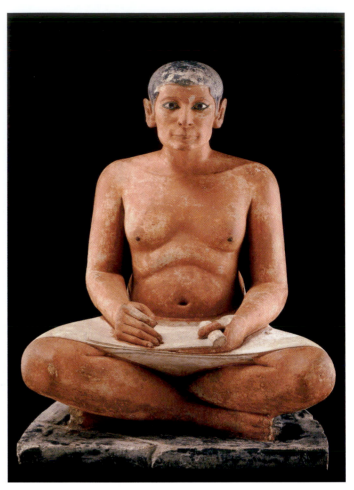

3–8 • SEATED SCRIBE
Found near the tomb of Kai, Saqqara. c. 2450–2325 BCE, Dynasty 5. Painted limestone with inlaid eyes of rock crystal, calcite, and magnesite mounted in copper, height 21″ (53 cm). Musée du Louvre, Paris.

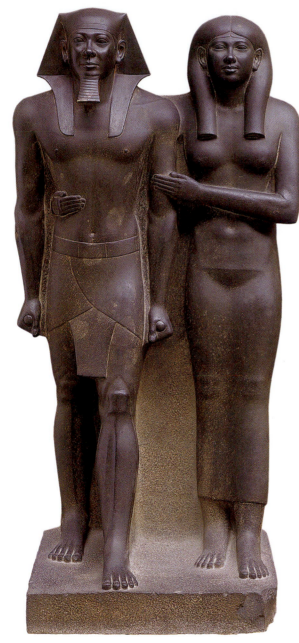

3–7 • MENKAURE (ruled 2490–2472 BCE, Dynasty 4)
**AND A QUEEN, PROBABLY HIS PRINCIPAL WIFE
KHAMERERNEBTY II**
From Menkaure Valley Temple, Giza, Egypt. Graywacke with traces of red and black paint, height 54½″ (142.3 cm). Museum of Fine Arts, Boston. Photograph © 2012 Museum of Fine Arts, Boston. Harvard University—Boston Museum of Fine Arts Expedition (11.1738).

Old Kingdom sculptors also produced statues of less prominent people, rendered in a more relaxed, lifelike fashion, as seen in a statue of a **SEATED SCRIBE** from early in the Fifth Dynasty (**FIG. 3–8**)—with round head, engaging and individualized face, and cap of close-cropped hair. The scribe's sedentary vocation has made his sagging body slightly flabby—advertising a life free from hard labor—and he sits holding a papyrus scroll partially unrolled on his lap, his right hand clasping a now-lost reed brush used in writing. The alert expression on his face reveals more than a lively intelligence. Because the pupils are slightly off-center in the irises, the eyes give the illusion of being in motion, as if they were seeking contact, and the reflective quality of the polished crystal **inlay** reproduces with eerie fidelity the contrast between the moist surface of eyes and the surrounding soft flesh in a living human face.

Elaborate paintings and reliefs often decorated the interiors of the tombs of royalty and wealthy individuals. These images frequently show the dead person going about the same duties and pleasures of earthly life, but they also had symbolic or religious meanings. A scene in the mastaba of a government official named Ti shows him supervising a hippopotamus hunt

Tomb of Ti, Saqqara.
c. 2450–2325 BCE,
Dynasty 5. Painted
limestone relief, height
approx. 45″ (114.3 cm).

Supervising
hippopotamus
hunts was a duty of
court officials like Ti.
It was believed that
Seth, the god of
darkness, disguised
himself as a hippo.
Hippos were thought
to be destructive since
they wandered into
fields, damaging crops.
Thus tomb depictions
of hippo hunts document
the valor of the deceased
and symbolize the
triumph of good
over evil.

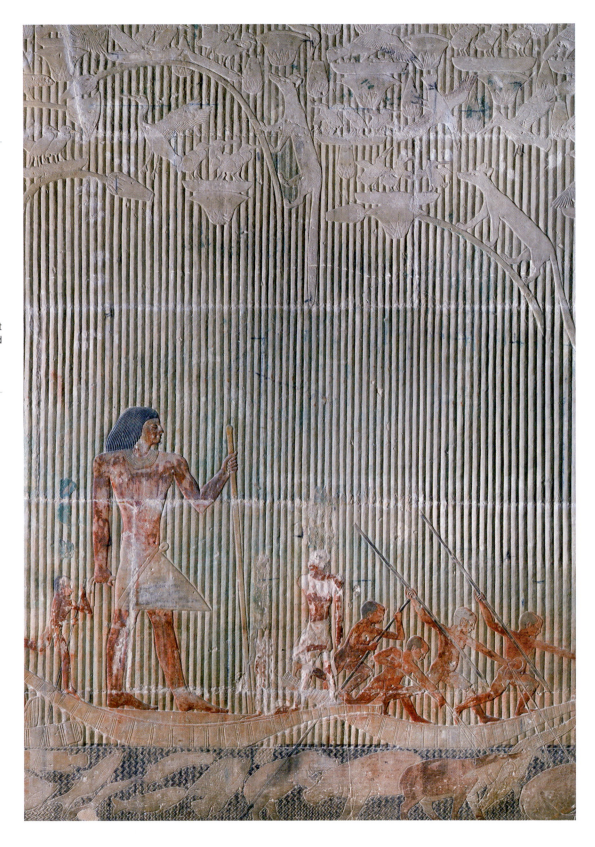

from a shallow boat (FIG. 3–9). The conventionally stylized, commanding figure of Ti looms over a vibrant Nile environment. The river itself is depicted as a series of wavy lines, as if seen from above, but like Ti and the other human figures in the boats, the creatures within are shown in profile to highlight their teeming activity, matched by the animals stalking birds within the papyrus at the top of the scene. In a separate boat ahead of Ti, the actual hunters, being of lesser rank and engaged in more strenuous activities, are rendered in a more lifelike and lively fashion than their master. They are captured at the charged moment of closing in on their prey, spears positioned at the ready, legs extended for the critical lunge forward.

Egyptian Symbols

Several crowns are used to symbolize kingship in Egyptian art. The false beard of a god or a god-king is long and braided, and it ends in a knob. A living king is portrayed with a shorter, squared-off beard (SEE FIG. 3–6). The upright form of the cobra, known as the *uraeus*, often appears at the front of the king's crown or headcloth.

The god Horus, king of the earth and a force for good, is represented most characteristically as a falcon. The eyes of Horus symbolize the sun and moon; the solar eye is called the *wedjat*. The *ankh* is symbolic of everlasting life, and the *scarab* (beetle) was associated with creation, resurrection, and the rising sun.

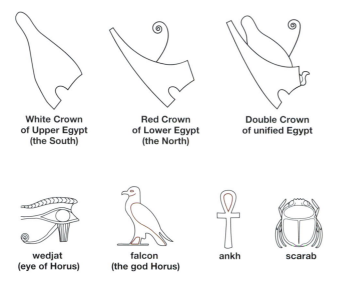

White Crown
of Upper Egypt
(the South)

Red Crown
of Lower Egypt
(the North)

Double Crown
of unified Egypt

wedjat
(eye of Horus)

falcon
(the god Horus)

ankh

scarab

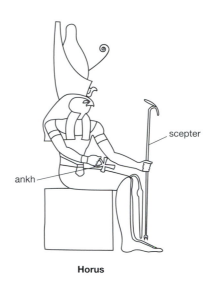

scepter

ankh

Horus

Middle Kingdom (c. 1975–1640 BCE)

What changes to ancient Egyptian artistic conventions occur during the Middle Kingdom?

About 2010 BCE, a series of kings named Mentuhotep (ruled c. 2010–c. 1938 BCE) reestablished royal power and reunited Egypt after several centuries of political disorganization. Under a stable, unified government, art and literature flourished in the Middle Kingdom, and they reflected a burgeoning awareness of the political upheaval of recent history.

Royal portraits of the Middle Kingdom do not always exhibit the self-confident formality of Old Kingdom examples. Some subjects appear to betray an unexpected awareness of the hardship and fragility of human existence. A statue of Twelfth Dynasty King Senusret III (ruled c. 1836–1818 BCE) reflects this new sensibility (**FIG. 3–10**). Senusret was a dynamic king and successful general who led four military expeditions into Nubia (Egypt's neighbor to the south), overhauled the central

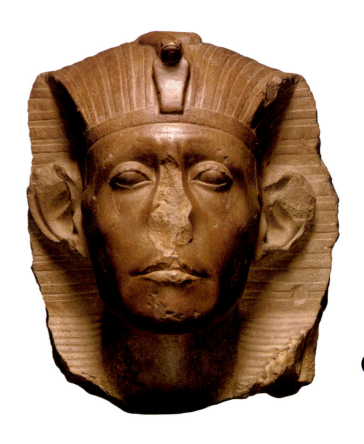

3–10 • HEAD OF SENUSRET III
(ruled c. 1836–1818 BCE, Dynasty 12). Yellow quartzite, 17¾″ × 13½″ × 17″ (45.1 × 34.3 × 43.2 cm). The Nelson-Atkins Museum of Art, Kansas City, Missouri. Purchase: William Rockhill Nelson Trust (62.11). Photograph Jamison Miller.

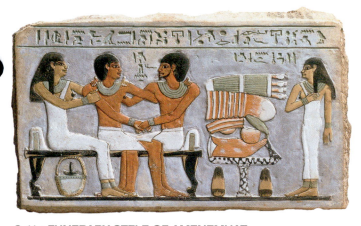

3–11 • FUNERARY STELE OF AMENEMHAT
From Assasif. c. 2000 BCE, late Dynasty 11. Painted limestone,
11″ × 15″ (30 × 50 cm). Egyptian Museum, Cairo.

administration at home, and was effective in regaining control over the country's increasingly independent nobles. But the sunken cheeks and drooping eyelids of his portrait statue seems to capture an emotionally drained monarch, with none of the bold self-confidence of his Old Kingdom forebears. Are we looking at the face of a man wise in the ways of the world but lonely, saddened, and burdened by the weight of his responsibilities? Or are we looking at a reassuring statement that in spite of troubled times—which have clearly left their mark on the face of the king himself—royal rule endured in Egypt?

In contrast, the family on a Middle Kingdom funeral stele (**FIG. 3–11**) presents a united and confident front. Underneath an inscription inviting food offerings for the deceased, Amenemhat sits on a lion-legged bench between his wife Iyi and their son Antef, embraced by both. Next to the trio is an offering table, heaped with meat, topped with onions. On the far right is his daughter Hapy, completing this touching tableau of family unity projected into their life after death. The painter of this relief follows an established Egyptian convention of differentiating gender by skin tonality: dark red-brown for men and lighter yellow-ocher for women.

There is little indication of how ancient Egyptians viewed the artists who created portraits of kings and nobles and recorded so many details of contemporary life, but artists must have been admired and respected. Some certainly had a high opinion of themselves. The tombstone of a Middle Kingdom sculptor claims, "I am an artist who excels in my art, a man above the common herd in knowledge. I know the proper attitude for a statue [of a man]; I know how a woman holds herself, [and how] a spearman lifts his arm.…There is no man famous for this knowledge other than I myself and my eldest son" (cited in Montet, p. 159).

New Kingdom (c. 1539–1075 BCE)

How is ancient Egyptian art refined, and in one dramatic instance transformed, during the New Kingdom?

During the New Kingdom, Egypt prospered both politically and economically. Its kings amassed great wealth and used their powerful army to surround the homeland with an empire. One of the most dynamic kings, Tutmose III of the Eighteenth

Dynasty (ruled 1479–1425 BCE), even extended Egypt's influence along the eastern Mediterranean coast as far as present-day Syria. Tutmose III was the first ruler to refer to himself as "pharaoh." The term means "great house" and was used the same way that people in the United States refer to the current president and his administration as "the White House." The successors of Tutmose III continued to call themselves pharaohs, and the title found its way into the Hebrew Bible and ultimately into modern usage.

One of the most intriguing political figures of the New Kingdom is Hatshepsut, wife of Tutmose II. At her husband's death in c. 1473, Hatshepsut became regent for his underage son, Tutmose III (born to one of his concubines), and within a few years she was declared "king" by the priests of Amun, making her coruler with Tutmose III for 20 years. There was no artistic formula for a woman ruler in Egyptian art, yet Hatshepsut had to be portrayed in her new role. What happened reveals something fundamental about the art of ancient Egypt. She was represented as a male king (**FIG. 3–12**), wearing a kilt and

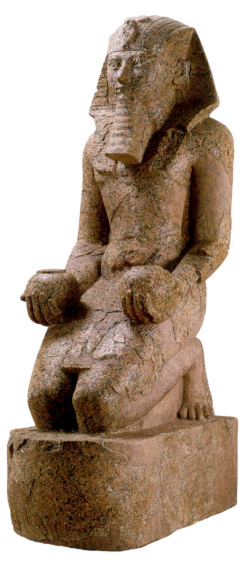

3–12 • KNEELING FIGURE OF HATSHEPSUT
(ruled c. 1473–1458 BCE, Dynasty 18), from Deir el-Bahri. Red granite, height 8′ 6″ (2.59 m). The Metropolitan Museum of Art, New York.
Rogers Fund, 1929 (29.31).

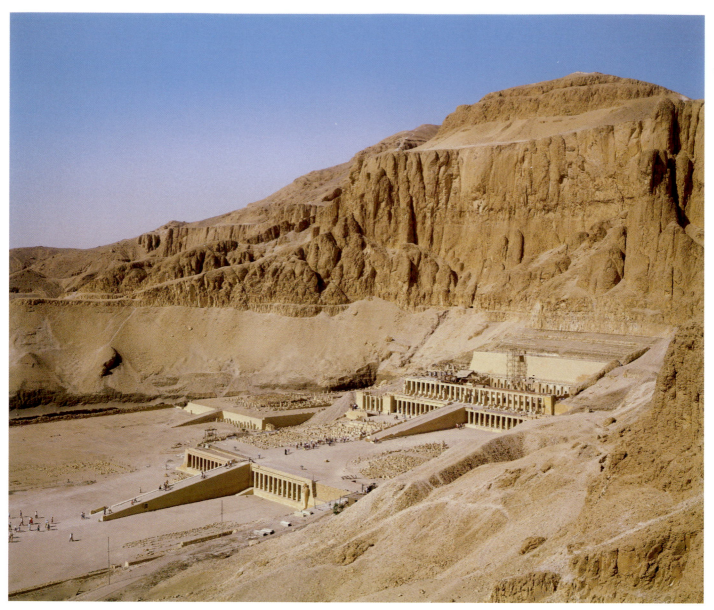

3-13 • FUNERARY TEMPLE OF HATSHEPSUT
(ruled c. 1473–1458 BCE, Dynasty 18), Deir el-Bahri.

View the Closer Look for the Funerary Temple of Hatshepsut on **MyArtsLab**

linen headdress, occasionally even a king's false beard. The formula was not adapted to suit one individual; she was adapted to conform to convention. What a powerful manifestation of the priority given to tradition and continuity in Egyptian royal art.

At the height of the New Kingdom, rulers again undertook extensive building programs, and Hatshepsut is responsible for one of the most spectacular: her imposing funerary temple located at Deir el-Bahri (FIG. 3–13) across the Nile from the New Kingdom religious center of Thebes and intended for funeral rites and commemorative ceremonies. Hatshepsut's actual tomb was small and hidden in the hills about a mile away, reversing the scale relationship familiar from the Old Kingdom pyramids of Giza. Here the temple is actually much larger and more prominent than the tomb itself.

Magnificently sited and sensitively reflecting the natural three-part layering in the rise of the landscape—from flat desert, through a sloping hillside, to the crescendo of sheer stone cliffs—Hatshepsut's temple was constructed on three levels connected by ramps and fronted by **colonnades** (rows of columns). The colonnade on the top level led to a **hypostyle hall**, a vast column-filled space, with chapels dedicated to Hatshepsut, her father Tutmose I, and the gods Amun and Ra-Horakhty. Rare myrrh trees decorated the temple's terraces, and a causeway lined with sphinxes connected the complex to a valley temple on the Nile.

Early in the New Kingdom, the priests of the god Amun in Thebes had gained such dominance that temples to the Theban triad of deities—Amun, his wife Mut, and their son

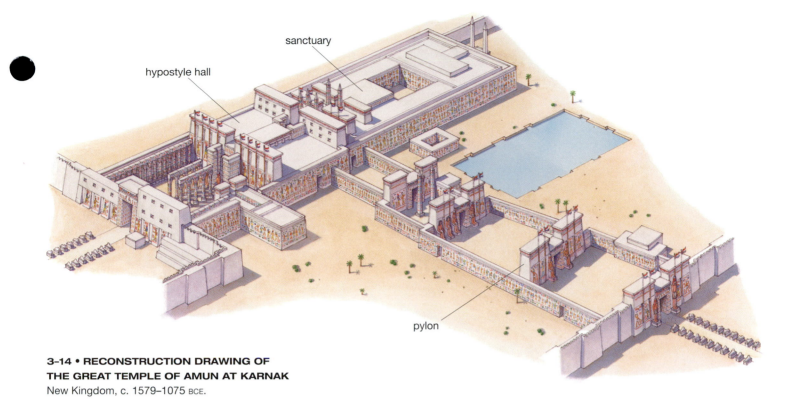

3-14 • RECONSTRUCTION DRAWING OF THE GREAT TEMPLE OF AMUN AT KARNAK New Kingdom, c. 1579–1075 BCE.

Khons—became a major focus of royal patronage, rivaling the tombs and temples erected to glorify the kings themselves. Two principal temple districts arose near Thebes—one at Karnak to the north and the other at Luxor to the south.

The heart of the **GREAT TEMPLE OF AMUN AT KAR-NAK (FIG. 3–14)** is a **sanctuary** containing the god's statue, accessed through a huge courtyard and a series of halls and courts, fronted by massive gateways called **pylons**. Only kings and priests were allowed to enter the sanctuary of Amun, where priests washed and dressed the god's statue every morning. Twice a day, they offered it tempting meals.

The dominant feature of the temple complex is an enormous hypostyle hall erected in the reigns of the Nineteenth Dynasty pharaohs Sety I (ruled c. 1290–1279 BCE) and his son Ramses II (ruled c. 1279–1213 BCE) **(FIG. 3–15)**. The hall, which may have been used for coronation ceremonies, is 340 feet wide and 170 feet long. Its 134 closely spaced columns supported a stepped roof of flat stones, the center section of which, resting on massive columns with papyrus **capitals** (sculpted blocks at the top of columns), rose some 30 feet above the flanking spaces **(FIG. 3–16)**. Smaller columns with bud capitals supported the roofs on each side. Piercing the side walls of the higher central

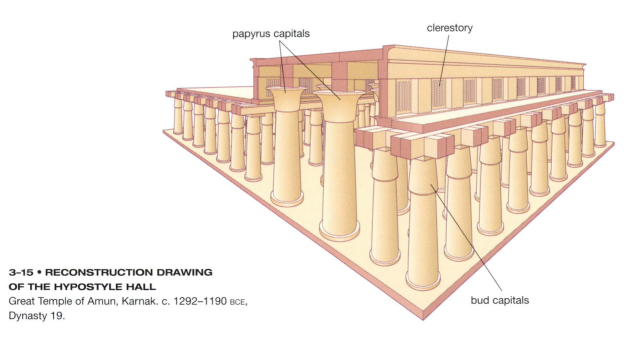

3-15 • RECONSTRUCTION DRAWING OF THE HYPOSTYLE HALL Great Temple of Amun, Karnak. c. 1292–1190 BCE, Dynasty 19.

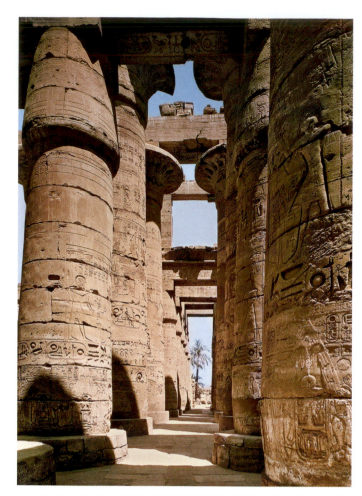

3–16 • COLUMNS WITH PAPYRIFORM AND BUD COLUMNS, HYPOSTYLE HALL
Great Temple of Amun, Karnak.

section was a long row of **clerestory** (top story) window openings, which may not have provided much light, but did permit a cooling flow of air through the hall. Despite the dimness of much of the interior, artists covered nearly every inch of the columns, walls, and crossbeams with carved and painted images and inscriptions.

The traditional figural arts of New Kingdom Egypt—using a representational system that had dominated Egyptian figural art since the time of Narmer—reached a pinnacle of aesthetic refinement and technical sophistication during the Eighteenth Dynasty reign of Amenhotep III (ruled c. 1390–1353 BCE), especially in the reliefs carved for the unfinished tomb of his vizier Ramose near Thebes (see "The Tomb of Ramose," p. 63). But in this refined world of stable convention, something very jarring took place during the reign of Amenhotep III's successor, Amenhotep IV (ruled c. 1353–1336 BCE). He radically transformed the political, spiritual, and cultural life of the country, founding a new religion honoring a single god, the life-giving sun disk Aten, and changing his own name to Akhenaten ("One Who Is Effective on Behalf of Aten"). Akhenaten built a new capital city well north of Thebes, naming it Akhetaten ("Horizon of the Aten"). Using the modern name for this site, Tell el-Amarna, historians refer to Akhenaten's reign as the Amarna period.

In addition to the creation of a new capital and the rise of a new religious focus, the Amarna period also saw radical changes in artistic conventions. Artists subjected royal representations to startling stylizations, even physical distortions. This new figure style can be seen in a colossal statue of **AKHENATEN** (FIG. 3–17), created for a new temple to the Aten that he built near the complex of Karnak. The pharaoh's strange, softly swelling form suggests androgyny to modern viewers. His sagging stomach and inflated thighs contrast with spindly arms, protruding clavicles, and an attenuated neck, on which sits a strikingly

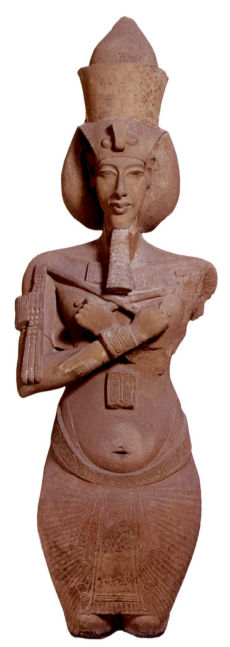

3–17 • COLOSSAL FIGURE OF AKHENATEN
From the temple known as the Gempaaten, built early in the reign of Akhenaten (ruled c. 1353–1336 BCE), just southeast of the temple of Karnak. Sandstone with traces of polychromy, height of remaining portion about 13′ (4 m). Egyptian Museum, Cairo.

📖 **Read** the document related to Akhenaten on **MyArtsLab**

ART AND ITS CONTEXTS

The Tomb of Ramose

As mayor of Thebes and vizier (principal royal advisor or minister) to both Amenhotep III (ruled c. 1390–1353 BCE) and Amenhotep IV (ruled 1353–c. 1336 BCE), Ramose was second only to the pharaoh himself in power and prestige. Soon after his ascent to political prominence, he began construction of an elaborate tomb composed of four rooms carved within living rock, including an imposing transverse hypostyle hall, 82 feet wide. Walls were covered with paintings or with shallow relief carvings, celebrating the accomplishments, affiliations, and lineage of Ramose and his wife Merytptah, or visualizing the funeral rites that would take place after their death. But the tomb was not used by Ramose. Decoration ceased in the fourth year of Amenhotep IV's reign, when he renamed himself Akhenaten and relocated the court to the new city of Akhetaten. Presumably Ramose moved with the court to the new capital, but neither his name nor a new tomb has been discovered there.

The tomb was abandoned in various stages of completion. The reliefs were never painted, and some walls preserve only preliminary sketches that would have guided the sculptors. But the works that were executed are among the most sophisticated relief carvings in the history of art. On one wall, Ramose and Merytptah appear, hosting a banquet for their family. All are portrayed at the same moment of youthful perfection, even though they represent two successive generations. Sophisticated carvers lavished their considerable technical virtuosity on the portrayal of these untroubled and majestic couples, creating dazzling textural differentiation of skin, hair, and cloth. The easy elegance of linear fluidity is not easy to obtain in this medium, and the convincing sense of three-dimensionality in forms and their placement is managed within an extraordinarily shallow depth of relief. In this detail of Ramose's brother and sister-in-law (**FIG. 3–18**), the traditional ancient Egyptian marital embrace (SEE FIGS. 3–7, 3–11) takes on a new tenderness, recalling—especially within the eternal stillness of a tomb—the words of a New Kingdom love poem:

> While unhurried days come and go,
> Let us turn to each other in quiet affection,
> Walk in peace to the edge of old age.
> (Foster, p. 18)

The conceptual conventions of Egyptian figural representation are rendered in these carvings with such warmth and refinement that they become almost believable. Our rational awareness of their artificiality is momentarily eclipsed by their sheer beauty.

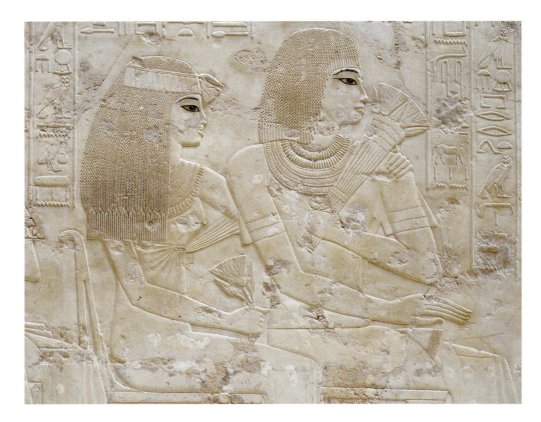

3–18 • RAMOSE'S BROTHER MAY AND HIS WIFE UREL
From the tomb of Ramose, Thebes.
c. 1375–1365 BCE, Dynasty 18.

 View the Closer Look for the Tomb of Ramose on **MyArtsLab**

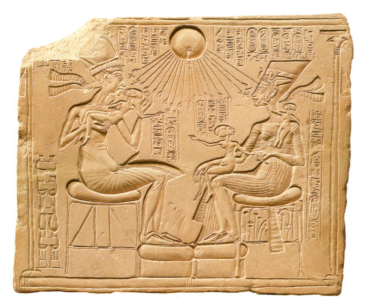

3–19 • AKHENATEN AND HIS FAMILY
From Akhetaten (present-day Tell el-Amarna). c. 1353–1336 BCE,
Dynasty 18. Painted limestone relief, 12¼″ × 15¼″ (31.1 × 38.7 cm).
Staatliche Museen zu Berlin, Preussischer Kulturbesitz,
Ägyptisches Museum.

Egyptian relief sculptors often employed the technique seen here,
called **sunken relief**. In ordinary reliefs, the background is carved
back so that the figures project out from the finished surface. In
sunken relief, the original flat surface of the stone is reserved as
background, and the outlines of the figures are deeply incised,
permitting the development of three-dimensional forms within the
stone block.

stylized head. Facial features are exaggerated, even distorted.
Slit-like eyes turn slightly downward, and the bulbous, sensuous lips are flanked by dimples that evoke the expression of
ephemeral human emotion. These stark deviations from convention are disquieting, especially since Akhenaten holds the
flail (a harvesting tool used to separate grain from its husks)
and shepherd's crook (a staff with a curved top), traditional
symbols of the pharaoh's sovereignty.

The new Amarna style characterizes not only official portraits, but also pictorial relief sculptures. In a scene portraying
royal family life (**FIG. 3–19**), Akhenaten and Queen Nefertiti sit
on cushioned thrones playing with their nude daughters, whose
elongated shaved heads conform to the newly minted figural
type. What a striking contrast with the relief from Ramose's
tomb! Rather than portraying composed serenity, this artist
described the fidgety, engaging behavior of children and the
loving involvement of their parents in a manner not even hinted
at in earlier royal portraiture. The couple receives the blessings
of the Aten, whose rays ending in hands penetrate the open
pavilion to offer *ankhs* before the royal nostrils, giving them the
"breath of life."

In a famous portrait of Nefertiti by the Akhetaten sculptor
Tutmose, her refined, regular features, long neck, and heavy-
lidded eyes seem almost too ideal to be human (**FIG. 3–20**),
but eerily consistent with standards of beauty in our own
culture. Part of the appeal of this head may be its dramatic use

of color. The **hues** of the blue headdress and its striped band
are repeated in the rich red, blue, green, and gold of the jeweled
necklace. The dark density of their patterns set off the sleek,
elegant contours of her revealed neck and head.

Akhenaten's new religion and revolutionary reconception
of pharaonic art outlived him by only a few years. The priesthood of Amun quickly regained its former power, and his son
Tutankhaten (ruled c. 1332–1322 BCE) returned to traditional
religious beliefs, changing his name to Tutankhamun, "Living
Image of Amun." Tutankhamun died young and was buried in
the Valley of the Kings, across the Nile from Thebes.

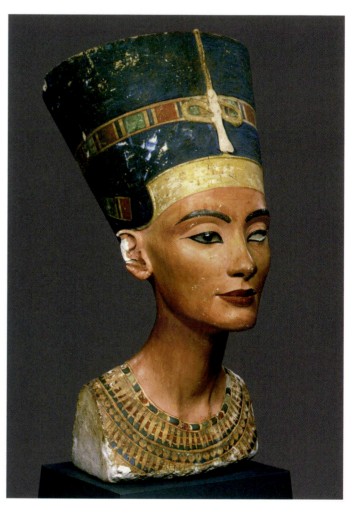

3–20 • Tutmose NEFERTITI
From Akhetaten (present-day Tell el-Amarna). c. 1353–1336 BCE,
Dynasty 18. Painted limestone, height 20″ (51 cm). Staatliche Museen
zu Berlin, Preussischer Kulturbesitz, Ägyptisches Museum.

This famous head was discovered in 1912 in the Akhetaten studio of
the sculptor Tutmose. It may have served as a model for full-length
sculptures or paintings of the queen. In 2007, a CT scan analysis
revealed the existence of a delicately carved limestone sculpture
underneath the modeled stucco of its outer surface. The faces of the
queen in the two likenesses differ slightly. In the outer stucco layer, the
sculptor seems to have smoothed out some of the facial irregularities
in the underlying limestone carving—including a bump on Nefertiti's
nose and creases around her mouth—and increased the prominence
of her cheekbones, probably to bring the queen's face into conformity
with contemporary notions of beauty, much in the way we would
retouch a photograph.

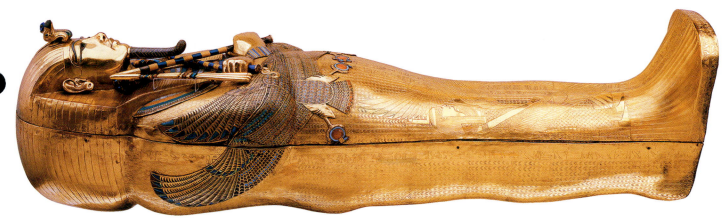

3–21 • INNER COFFIN OF TUTANKHAMUN
From the tomb of Tutankhamun (ruled 1332–1322 BCE, Dynasty 18), Valley of the Kings. Gold inlaid with glass and semiprecious stones, height 6′ ⅞″ (1.85 m), weight nearly 243 lb. (110.4 kg). Egyptian Museum, Cairo.

👁 **Watch** a video about Tutankhamun on **MyArtsLab**

Although some scholars doubted the royal lineage of the young pharaoh, recent DNA testing of a series of royal mummies from this period has confirmed that Tutankhamun was the son of Akhenaten and one of his sisters. And his death at such a young age seems not to have been the result of royal intrigue and assassination, but rather poor health and serious injury. The DNA analysis documented his struggles with malaria, and CT scans revealed a badly broken and seriously infected leg, as well as a series of birth defects that have been ascribed to royal inbreeding.

The undisturbed inner chambers of Tutankhamun's tomb, discovered in 1922, contained great treasures, including jewelry, textiles, furniture, and four gold chariots. The king's mummified body, crowned with a spectacular gold mask preserving his royal likeness (SEE FIG. 3–1), lay inside three nested coffins, the innermost (**FIG. 3–21**) made of over 240 pounds of solid gold,

decorated with colored **enamel**, semiprecious stones, and very finely incised linear designs. The king holds the crook and flail that symbolize his power as provider and protector to his people, and that associate him with Osiris, a fertility and vegetation god who presided over the dead and the underworld.

Egyptian funerary practices revolved around Osiris, his resurrection, and a belief in the continuity of life after death for the righteous. The dead were thought to undergo a last judgment consisting of two tests presided over by Osiris and supervised by the jackel-headed god Anubis. The deceased were first questioned by a delegation of deities about their behavior in life. Then their hearts, believed to be the seat of the soul, were weighed on a scale against an ostrich feather, the symbol of Ma'at, goddess of truth, order, and justice. A monster named Ammit, the "Eater of the Dead," waited beside the scale to devour those who tipped the balance.

TECHNIQUE | Mummies

Egyptians developed mummification techniques to ensure that the *ka* (soul or life force) could live on in the body after death. No recipes for preserving the dead have been discovered, but the basic process seems clear enough from images that have been found in tombs, the descriptions of later Greek writers, scientific analysis of mummies, and modern experiments.

By the time of the New Kingdom, the routine was roughly as follows. The body was taken to a mortuary, a special structure used exclusively for embalming. Under the supervision of a priest, workers removed the brain, generally through the nose, and emptied the body cavity—except for the heart—through an incision in the left side. They then covered the body with dry natron, a naturally

occurring salt, and placed it on a sloping surface to allow liquids to drain. This preservative caused the skin to blacken, so workers often used paint or powdered makeup to restore some color, using red ocher for a man, yellow ocher for a woman. They then packed the body cavity with clean linen soaked in various herbs and ointments. The major organs were wrapped in separate packets and stored in special containers called canopic jars, to be placed in the tomb chamber.

Workers next wound the trunk and each of the limbs separately with cloth strips, before wrapping the whole body in additional layers of cloth to produce the familiar mummy shape. The workers often inserted charms and other smaller objects among the wrappings.

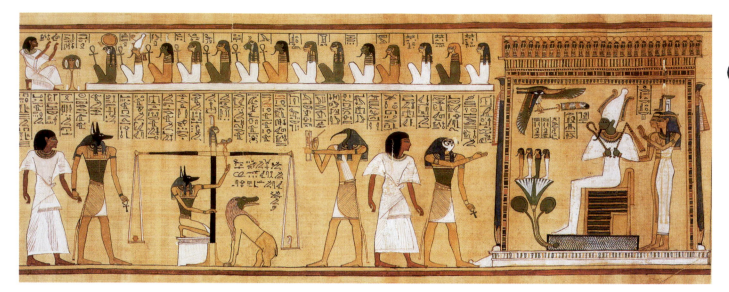

3–22 • JUDGMENT OF HUNEFER BEFORE OSIRIS
Illustration from a Book of the Dead. c. 1285 BCE, Dynasty 19.
Painted papyrus, height 15⅝″ (39.8 cm). The British Museum, London.

These beliefs gave rise to additional funerary practices especially popular among the nonroyal classes. Family members commissioned papyrus scrolls—"Books of the Dead"—containing magical texts or spells to help the dead survive and pass the tests. A scene from a Nineteenth Dynasty example, created for a man named Hunefer, shows three successive stages in his induction into the afterlife (**FIG. 3–22**). At the left, Anubis leads Hunefer to the spot where he will weigh the man's heart against the "feather of truth." After passing the test—recorded by the ibis-headed god, Thoth—Hunefer is presented by Horus to the enthroned Osiris, holding his usual crook and flail.

Late Egyptian Art

What traditional and new features are seen in Late Egyptian art?

In 332 BCE, the Macedonian Greeks, led by Alexander the Great, conquered Egypt. After Alexander's death in 323 BCE, his generals divided up his empire. Ptolemy took Egypt, declaring himself king in 305. The Ptolemaic dynasty ended with the death of Cleopatra VII (ruled 51–30 BCE), when Egypt became part of the Roman Empire.

Not surprisingly, works from this late period combined the conventions of Greco-Roman and Egyptian art. For example, the tradition of mummifying the dead continued well into Egypt's Roman period, and thousands of mummies from that time have been found in the Fayum region of Lower Egypt. Instead of a stylized mask (SEE FIG. 3–1), a Roman-style portrait (**FIG. 3–23**) painted on a wood panel in **encaustic** (hot, colored wax) is inserted over the face. Although great staring eyes invariably dominate such images—as they had in the funerary mask of Tutankhamun—their artists seem to have carefully recorded individual features of the deceased, providing a link between Egyptian art and emphasis on portrait likenesses that will characterize the art of ancient Rome.

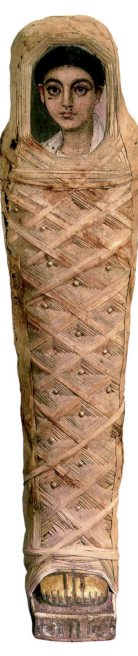

3–23 • MUMMY WRAPPING OF A YOUNG BOY
From Hawara. c. 100–120 CE, Roman period. Linen with gilded stucco buttons and inserted portrait in encaustic on wood; height of mummy 53⅜″ (133 cm); portrait 9½″ × 6½″ (24 × 16.5 cm). The British Museum, London.

All cultures have rules for representing people, things, and ideas, but Egyptian conventions are among the most distinctive and long-lived in the history of art. Everything is represented from its most characteristic viewpoint: profile heads sit on frontal shoulders and stare out at viewers with frontal eyes. And Egyptian art is geometrically conceived and sleekly stylized, often abstract and conceptual in design. Symbols were established early on and endured for almost two millennia. Stability was clearly valued over change.

Egyptian art and history has been divided into three principal periods known as the Old, Middle, and New Kingdoms. The Old Kingdom was a heroic age of funerary art and architecture whose most famous works—the pyramids and sphinx at Giza—define the essence of Egyptian art for most people. The Middle Kingdom saw an increase in sensitive and more personal art. In the New Kingdom, proud rulers focused extraordinary resources on building temples and expanding the Egyptian Empire. During the Eighteenth Dynasty, Akhenaten even attempted to redirect the course of history, religion, and art, but the powerful conventions he tried to replace returned in the rule of his successor, Tutankhamun. The discovery of this late, and relatively insignificant, pharaoh's tomb in 1922 ignited an international enthusiasm for Egyptian art that lasts to this day.

THINK ABOUT IT

3.1 Discuss the conventions for representing the human figure in ancient Egypt, using the Palette of Narmer as an example.

3.2 How would you characterize the expression on the face of the pharaoh in FIGURE 3–10? What aspects of this portrait adhere to principles established in the Old Kingdom?

3.3 Compare the subject, style, and technique of the reliefs from the tomb of Ramose in FIGURE 3–18 and the time of Akhenaten in FIGURE 3–19.

3.4 Discuss the debt to traditional Egyptian art and the innovations from the Greco-Roman tradition that are apparent in the mummy in FIGURE 3–23.

| CROSSCURRENTS |

FIG. 2–11

FIG. 3–9

What do these ancient scenes of hunting express about the wealthy and powerful people who commissioned them? How do the artists make their messages clear? How does the location of each relate to its meaning?

IN PERSPECTIVE

3500 BCE

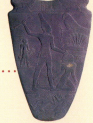

Palette of Narmer
c. 2950 BCE

3000

• **Early Dynastic Period** c. 2950–2575 BCE

• **Djoser** ruled c. 2650–2631 BCE
• **Old Kingdom** c. 2575–2150 BCE
• **Khafre** ruled c. 2520–2494 BCE

2500

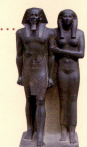

Menkaure and a Queen
ruled 2490–2472 BCE

• **First Intermediate Period** c. 2125–1975 BCE

2000

• **Middle Kingdom** c. 1975–1640 BCE

• **Senusret III** ruled c. 1836–1818 BCE

• **Second Intermediate Period** c. 1630–1520 BCE
• **New Kingdom** c. 1539–1075 BCE
• **Hatshepsut** ruled c. 1473–1458 BCE

1500

• **Akhenaten** ruled c. 1353–1336 BCE
• **Tutankhamun** ruled c. 1332–1322 BCE

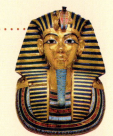

Funerary Temple of Hatshepsut
ruled c. 1473–1458 BCE

• **Third Intermediate Period** c. 1075–715 BCE

1000

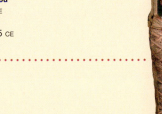

Funerary Mask of Tutankhamun
ruled 1332–1322 BCE

• **Late Period** c. 715–332 BCE

500

• **Conquest by Alexander the Great** 332 BCE
• **Ptolemaic Period** c. 323–30 BCE
• **Roman Period** c. 30 BCE–395 CE

1 CE

500

Mummy Wrapping of a Young Boy
c. 100–120 CE

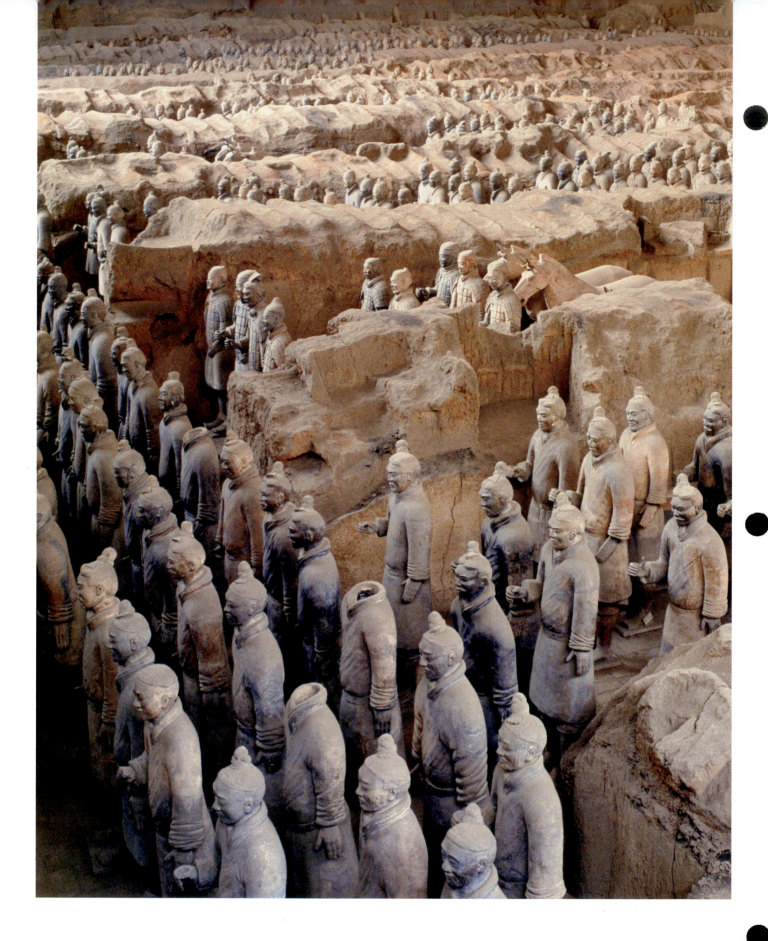

4–1 • SOLDIERS
From the mausoleum of Shihuangdi (the first emperor of Qin), Lintong, Shaanxi. Qin dynasty, c. 210 BCE.
Earthenware, life-size.

EARLY ASIAN ART

4.1 Discuss the early art of India and Southeast Asia from the early culture of the Indus Valley through the founding of Buddhism and Hinduism.

4.3 Explain the ancient native traditions of Japanese art that blossomed in Shinto and Buddhist art and architecture.

4.2 Trace the early development of art in China and Korea through a series of empires and the introduction of Buddhism.

LOOKING FORWARD ▶

How can we understand the fierce determination and driving will that could lead a single man to conceive of himself as ruler of the world, a man who believed that his right to reign was bestowed by supernatural powers and that he was the son of heaven? Between 221 BCE, when he brought the warring states under his control, until his death in 210 BCE, the first emperor of Qin, Shihuangdi, turned the vast lands of China into a unified state. His tremendous actions were simple, direct, and brilliant. To govern the Qin Empire, he created a bureaucracy—an intricate, hierarchical network—based on competence, not family heritage, and guided by a code of law. He united his lands with a common language and system of writing and more than 4,000 miles of roads. He brought prosperity by building canals and an irrigation system to increase agricultural production and by facilitating trade through uniform weights and measures. In fact, the name Qin (pronounced "chin") is the source of the name China.

During Emperor Shihuangdi's life, a huge army—historians write of 300,000 men—defended his empire. After his death, an underground army of thousands of disciplined and alert **terracotta** figures stood in battle array guarding his tomb, poised to defend their emperor throughout eternity (**FIG. 4–1**). These subterranean soldiers were hidden from view by mounds of earth that eventually blended into the local landscape. No one knew that an astonishing treasure lay beneath the surface until 1974, when peasants digging a well accidentally discovered the vault containing some 8,000 soldiers and 100 horses—life-size, standing in military formation, facing east, ready for battle.

How could such a vast project have been accomplished? The technical achievement of the artists and artisans is as amazing as the political organization that made the work possible and the worldview that inspired it. Perhaps as many as 1,000 potters molded and carved the clay, and 85 artists signed the figures. By using standardized molds, they mass-produced thousands of legs, torsos, arms, fingers, and heads. They joined the prefabricated parts and then modeled and carved them into individualized figures. After the firing of the clay, the artists painted the figures and supplied them with real weapons of bronze and wood. Just consider the size of the kilns and the quantity of wood necessary to fire such vast numbers of clay figures—let alone the organization of the skilled labor force. Yet we will find that comparably ambitious projects, focusing the resources and energy of sophisticated societies to express the power and prestige of the ruling elite, characterize early art and architecture across the Asian continent, from India through China to Japan.

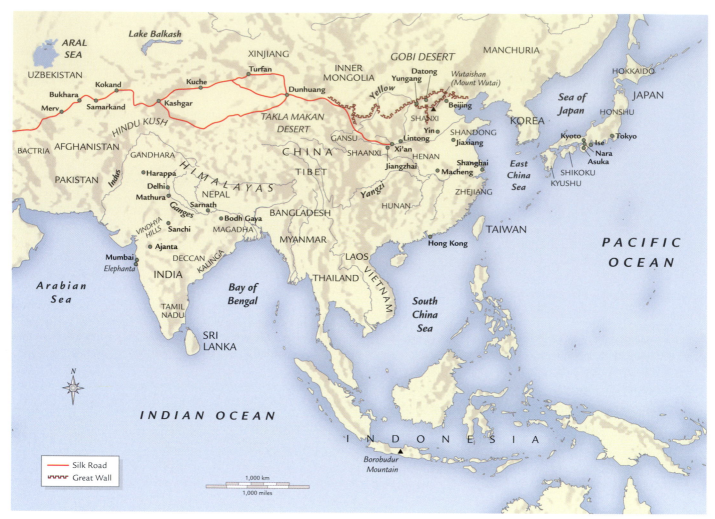

MAP 4–1 • EARLY ASIA

The vast continent of Asia was traversed as early as the second century CE by a flourishing trade route known as the Silk Road—a 5,000-mile network of caravan routes that brought luxury goods from the center of Han China all the way to Rome.

The civilizations of South and East Asia are among the world's oldest and rank among the most culturally rich. Together, the South Asian subcontinent and the East Asian lands of China and Japan (**MAP 4–1**) witnessed the birth of six great, still-active religions and/or philosophies: Buddhism, Hinduism, and Jainism in India; Confucianism and **Daoism** in China; and Shinto in Japan. The eastward spread of Buddhism—from the Indian subcontinent through Central Asia to the lands of present-day China, Korea, and Japan—united these regions philosophically and artistically. At the same time, the work of Indian, Chinese, and Japanese artists proudly reflects the profound differences between their aesthetic traditions.

The Indian Subcontinent and Southeast Asia

What characterizes the early art of India and Southeast Asia from the early culture of the Indus Valley through the founding of Buddhism and Hinduism?

The Indian or South Asian subcontinent includes present-day India, Afghanistan, Pakistan, Nepal, Bhutan, Bangladesh, and Sri Lanka. Throughout the history of the area, these places have been culturally linked. Differences in language, climate, and terrain within India have fostered distinct regional and cultural characteristics and artistic traditions. However, despite such regional diversity, several overarching traits tend to unite Indian art. Most evident is a distinctive sense of beauty, with voluptuous forms and a profusion of ornament, texture, and color. Visual abundance reflects a belief in the generosity and favor of the gods. Another characteristic is the pervasive symbolism that enriches all Indian arts with intellectual and emotional layers. Third, and perhaps most important, is an emphasis on capturing the vibrant quality of a world seen as infused with the dynamics of the divine. Gods and humans, ideas and abstractions, are given tactile, sensuous forms, radiant with inner spirit.

The Indus Civilization

The earliest civilization of South Asia was nurtured in the lower reaches of the Indus River (in present-day Pakistan and in northwestern India). Known as the Indus or Harappan civilization (after Harappa, the first site to be discovered), it flourished

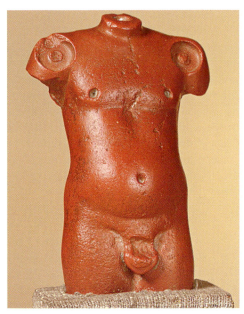

4–2 • TORSO
From Harappa. Indus civilization, c. 2600–1900 BCE. Red sandstone, height 3¾″ (9.5 cm). National Museum, New Delhi.

approximately 2600–1900 BCE, during roughly the same time as Egypt's Old Kingdom and the dynasties of Ur and Babylon in Mesopotamia. Indeed, it is considered along with them to be one of the world's earliest urban river valley civilizations.

A nude male **TORSO** found in Harappa exemplifies a naturalistic style that flourished in the Indus Valley (**FIG. 4–2**). Less than four inches tall, it is one of the most extraordinary portrayals of the human form to survive from any early civilization. In contrast to the tightly controlled athletic male ideal developed in ancient Egypt, this sculpture emphasizes the soft texture of the organic human body and the subtle nuances of muscular form. The abdomen is relaxed in the manner of a yogi able to control his breath. With these characteristics the Harappa torso forecasts the essential aesthetic attributes of later Indian sculpture.

For unknown reasons, the Indus civilization declined between 2000 and 1750 BCE, and seminomadic shepherds known as the Aryans entered India from Central Asia and the Russian steppes, bringing with them an Indo-European language called Sanskrit and a hierarchical social order. The Vedic period that followed (c. 1500 BCE until the late fourth century BCE) was named for the Vedas, their body of sacred writings.

ART AND ITS CONTEXTS

Buddhism

The Buddhist religion developed from the teachings of Shakyamuni Buddha (lifespan traditionally dated c. 563–483 BCE), who lived and taught in the present-day regions of Nepal and northern India. Born Prince Siddhartha Gautama, he left his family and home at age 29 to live as an ascetic in the wilderness. He was deeply troubled by the inevitable sufferings of the human condition—old age, sickness, and death—and the repetitions of these sufferings through the continual cycle of rebirth. But after six long years of meditation, while sitting under a pipal tree at Bodh Gaya, Siddhartha Gautama attained complete enlightenment, or understanding of true reality, becoming the Buddha (meaning "enlightened one").

In his teachings, Shakyamuni Buddha expounded the Four Noble Truths that are the foundation of Buddhism: (1) life is suffering; (2) this suffering has a cause, which is ignorance and desire; (3) ignorance and desire can be overcome and extinguished (4) by following the eightfold path of right view, right resolve, right speech, right action, right livelihood, right effort, right mindfulness, and right concentration. After the Buddha's death at age 80, his disciples developed his teachings and established the world's oldest monastic institutions.

The early form of Buddhism, known as Theravada, stresses self-cultivation for the purpose of attaining *nirvana*. In Mahayana Buddhism, which developed later and became popular in northern India, China, Korea, Japan, and Tibet, the goal was expanded from attaining *nirvana* for oneself to attaining buddhahood for all beings. A buddha is not a god but rather one who sees the ultimate nature of the world and is therefore no longer subject to the cycle of *samsara*—birth, death, and rebirth. Compassion for all became a primary motivating force of the religion.

Mahayana Buddhism recognizes not only Shakyamuni Buddha but also numerous other buddhas, such as Maitreya, the Buddha of the Future, and Amitabha (called Amida in Japan), the Buddha of Infinite Light and Infinite Life (that is, incorporating all space and time). Mahayana Buddhism developed the concept of **bodhisattvas**, saintly beings on the brink of buddhahood who have vowed to help others become buddhas before finally accomplishing it for themselves. The appearance of bodhisattvas in art is based on the princely image of Siddhartha Gautama before he became the Buddha. Their rich clothing, jewelry, and long hair make them easily distinguished in works of art from buddhas, who wear a monk's robe, no jewelry, and short hair.

The Vedic Period

The Vedic period is marked by the development of religiously sanctioned social classes or castes, which became hereditary, and by the beginnings of Buddhism, Hinduism, and Jainism—three of the four great religions of India. (The fourth is Islam.) The metaphysical texts known as the Upanishads were also written during this period. Examining the meaning of earlier, more cryptic Vedic hymns, the Upanishads focus on the relationship between the individual soul and the universal soul, or *Brahman*. The Upanishads advance concepts that became central to subsequent Indian philosophy, including the assertions that the material world is illusory and only the *Brahman* is real and eternal; that existence is cyclical; and that all beings are caught in *samsara*, which is a relentless cycle of birth, life, death, and rebirth. Believers aspire to attain *nirvana*—liberation from *samsara*—by uniting our individual souls with the eternal, universal *Brahman*. These philosophical ideas are expressed more accessibly in India's great literary epics, the *Mahabharata* and the *Ramayana*. Appearing toward the end of the Vedic period, these texts relate stories of gods and humans who later became immensely important in Hinduism.

In this stimulating religious, philosophical, and literary climate, numerous religious communities arose. The most influential teachers were Shakyamuni Buddha, whose teachings around 500 BCE are the basis of Buddhism (see "Buddhism," p. 71), and Mahavira (599–527 BCE), the founder of the Jain religion. Both espoused such basic Upanishadic tenets as the cyclical nature of existence and the desirability of escape from it. However, they rejected the authority of the Vedas and the hereditary class structure of Vedic society, with its powerful, exclusive priesthood. Buddhism and Jainism were open to all, regardless of social position.

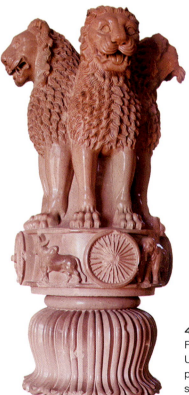

4–3 • LION CAPITAL
From Ashokan pillar at Sarnath, Uttar Pradesh, India. Maurya period, c. 250 BCE. Polished sandstone, height 7′ (2.13 m). Archaeological Museum, Sarnath.

The Rise of Buddhism

Buddhism provided the impetus for much of the major art created between the third century BCE and the fifth century CE. Under the Maurya Empire (c. 322–185 BCE), whose rule extended over all but the southernmost regions of the subcontinent, Buddhism became the state religion. For many centuries, the painting and sculpture of India were associated with imperial sponsorship of the religion. The Mauryan **LION CAPITAL** (**FIG. 4–3**), dated to about 250 BCE, is a prime example of one emperor's promotion of Buddhism. This capital once topped a 50-foot-high pillar of highly polished sandstone located in the grounds of the monastery at Sarnath, site of the Buddha's first teaching. One of many so-called Ashokan pillars, it was erected by Emperor Ashoka, who first established Buddhism as the major religion of his realm. The capital rises with a cushion of downturned lotus petals, on which rests a deep, round collar carved with four animals—lion, horse, bull, and elephant—alternating with four wheels called *chakra*s (see "Buddhist Symbols," p. 75). On top, four lions stand back to back facing the four cardinal directions, emblematic of the universal nature of Buddhism. Their heraldic stance and the strong stylization of elements such as leg tendons and veins, claws, manes, and toothy muzzles endow the lions with a powerful presence. When India gained its independence in 1947, this capital became the national emblem.

Between the second century BCE and the early first century CE, Buddhism remained the main inspiration for art in the region, and some of the most important and magnificent early Buddhist structures were created. In early Buddhist art, the Buddha himself is not shown in human form. Instead, he is represented by symbols such as his footprints, an empty "enlightenment" seat, or a **stupa** (see "Stupas," p. 73). Perhaps no early Indian monument is more famous than the **GREAT STUPA** at Sanchi in central India (**FIG. 4–4**). Stupas derive from burial mounds and their solid, **dome**-shaped earthen core contains **relics**, or material remains associated with a holy person. The first Buddhist stupas, holding the remains of the Buddha after his cremation, were venerated as his body and, by extension, his enlightenment and attainment of *nirvana*. Rituals of veneration at the stupa included circumambulation—walking around the stupa in a clockwise direction, following the sun's path across the sky.

Originally built during the time of Ashoka and enlarged between about 150 and 50 BCE, the Great Stupa at Sanchi was part of a large monastery complex crowning a hilltop. The stupa's brick dome, once covered with shining white plaster, is topped by a square stone railing symbolizing the domain of the gods atop the cosmic mountain. The railing encloses the top of a mast bearing three stone disks, or "umbrellas," of decreasing size. The mast itself is an ***axis mundi*** (axis of the world), connecting the cosmic waters below the earth with the celestial realm above it and anchoring everything in its proper place.

A 10-foot-high stone railing—punctuated by four stone gateways, or ***toranas***—rings the entire stupa. As in much religious architecture, the railing provides a physical and symbolic boundary between the inner, sacred area and the outer, profane world. Each gateway is decorated with a profusion of carved incidents from the Buddha's life and past lives, as well as figural

Stupas began in India as simple, solid dome-shaped structures containing Buddhist relics. Later, a multistoried form of the stupa developed in India's Gandhara region during the Kushan dynasty (c. 50–250 CE). As Buddhism spread northeastward along the Silk Road, the form of the multilevel stupa was merged with that of the watchtower of Han dynasty China, leading to the creation of multistoried masonry structures with projecting tiled roofs known as **pagodas**.

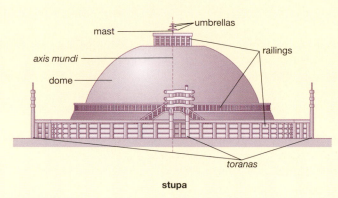

stupa

👁 **Watch** an architectural simulation of stupas and temples on **MyArtsLab**

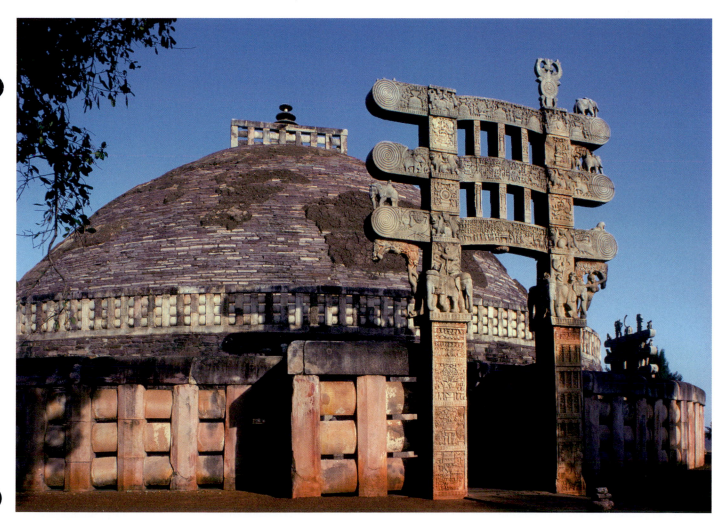

4–4 • GREAT STUPA
Sanchi, Madhya Pradesh, India. Founded 3rd century BCE; enlarged c. 150–50 BCE.

In all three regions and throughout Asian art, the Buddha is readily recognized by certain shared visual characteristics. He wears a simple monk's robe, and because he had been a prince in his youth and had worn the customary heavy earrings, his earlobes are distended. The top of his head has a protuberance (*ushnisha*), which in images often resembles a bun or topknot, a symbol of his enlightenment. Between his eyes is the *urna*, a tuft of white hair.

A typical image from Gandhara portrays the Buddha as more powerful and heroic than an ordinary human (**FIG. 4–6**). His robe is carved in tight, rib-like folds alternating with

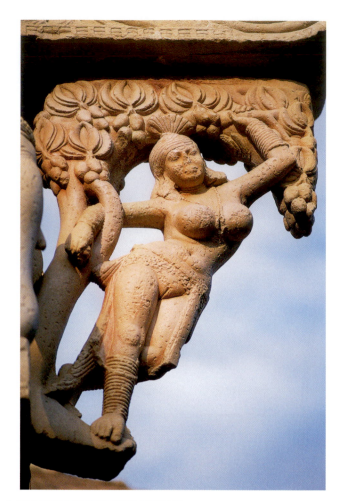

4–5 • YAKSHI BRACKET FIGURE
Detail of the east *torana*, Great Stupa, Sanchi. c. 150–50 BCE. Stone, height approx. 60″ (152.4 cm).

👁 **Watch** a video about the Great Stupa at Sanchi on **MyArtsLab**

sculpture depicting subjects such as *yakshi*s, figures that associate female beauty with the fertility of nature (**FIG. 4–5**). The swelling, arching curves of the *yakshi*'s body evoke her procreative and bountiful essence. Since her thin, diaphanous garment is noticeable only by its hems, she appears almost nude. As the personification of the waters, she is the source of life. Here she symbolizes the sap of the tree, which flowers at her touch.

Gandhara and Mathura Styles

Around the first century CE, the regions of present-day Afghanistan, Pakistan, and north India came under the control of the Kushans, a nomadic people from Central Asia. During this period Buddhism underwent profound change, resulting in the development of a form of Buddhism known as Mahayana (see "Buddhism," p. 71). Closely related to this new movement was the appearance of the first images of the Buddha himself. Distinctive styles of Buddha images arose in Kushan-ruled areas: Gandhara in the northwest (present-day Pakistan and Afghanistan) and Mathura in central India. About the same time, a third stylistic tradition evolved in the southeast under the Andhra dynasty.

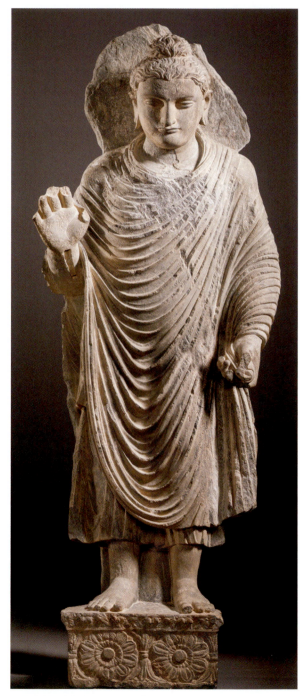

4–6 • SHAKYAMUNI BUDDHA
From Gandhara (Pakistan). c. 2nd–early 3rd century CE. Gray schist, height 47½″ (120.7 cm). Los Angeles County Museum of Art.

Buddhist Symbols

Buddhist symbols have myriad variations. A few of the most important are described here in their most generalized forms.

Lotus flower: Usually shown as a white water lily, the lotus (Sanskrit, *padma*) symbolizes spiritual purity, the wholeness of creation, and cosmic harmony.

Lotus throne: Buddhas are frequently shown seated on an open lotus, either single or double, which is a representation of *nirvana*.

Chakra: An ancient sun symbol, this wheel symbolizes both the various states of existence (the Wheel of Life) and the Buddhist doctrine (the Wheel of the Law). Its exact meaning depends on its number of spokes.

Attributes of a buddha: A buddha is distinguished by 32 physical attributes (*lakshana*s). Among them are a bulge on top of the head (*ushnisha*), a tuft of hair between the eyebrows (*urna*), elongated earlobes, and thousand-spoked circles (*chakra*s) on the soles of the feet.

Mudra: Ancient symbolic hand gestures that signify different states of being. In this diagram, the joined hands in the Buddha's lap form the Ohyana Mudra, a gesture of meditation and balance, symbolizing the path toward enlightenment. In FIGURE 4–7, Buddha's open-palmed gesture is the Abhaya Mudra ("have no fear"), conveying reassurance, blessing, and protection. The Vitarka Mudra of the bodhisattva in FIGURE 4–8 stands for intellectual debate.

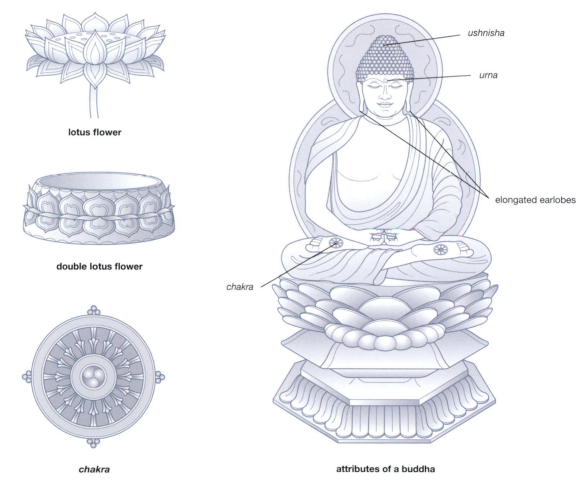

lotus flower

double lotus flower

chakra

attributes of a buddha

delicate creases, setting up a clear, rhythmic pattern of heavy and shallow lines. This complex pattern of folds resembles the treatment of togas in some ancient Roman sculptures (SEE FIGS. 6–9, 6–14), perhaps reflecting the region's long history of contact with the Hellenistic and Roman world. The Gandhara style, transmitted across Central Asia, also exerted a strong influence on portrayals of the Buddha in East Asia.

At Mathura, the image of Buddha developed not through contact with the Greco-Roman tradition but within the indigenous sculptural tradition as represented by statues of *yaksha*s,

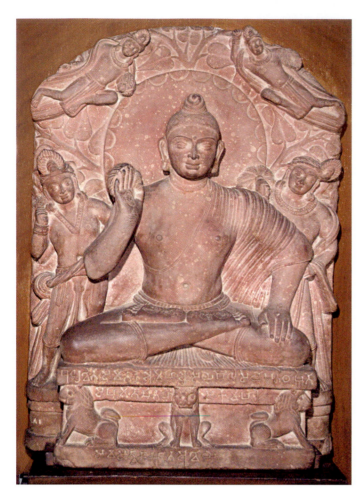

4-7 • BUDDHA AND ATTENDANTS
From Katra Keshavdev, Mathura, Madhya Pradesh, India. Kushan period, c. late 1st–early 2nd century CE. Red sandstone, height 27¼″ (69.2 cm). Government Museum, Mathura.

👁 **Watch** a video about the process of sculpting in relief on **MyArtsLab**

male nature deities. In one of the finest of the early Mathura images of Buddha (**FIG. 4-7**), the thin robe is pulled tightly over the body, allowing the fleshy form to be seen as almost nude. The Buddha is seated in a yogic posture, and his right hand is raised in a **mudra**, or symbolic gesture, meaning "have no fear." His distinctive features and the impressions of *chakra*s, or wheels, on his feet and right hand are all clearly visible (see "Buddhist Symbols," p. 75). In the background are the branches of the pipal tree, under which the Buddha was sitting when he achieved enlightenment.

Gupta Period

Buddhism reached its greatest influence in India during the Gupta period (c. 320–550 CE), named for the founders of a dynasty that ruled much of India at that time. Some of the finest surviving artworks of the Gupta period are **murals** (wall paintings) from the Buddhist rock-cut temples and halls of Ajanta, in western India. Since ancient times, caves, frequently the abode of holy people and ascetics, have been considered hallowed places in India. During the second century BCE, Buddhist

monks began to excavate two types of rock-cut halls from the plateaus of the Deccan region. The type known as the *vihara* was used for the living quarters of the monks, and that known as *chaitya*, meaning "sacred," usually enshrined a stupa. Cave I at Ajanta, carved around 475 CE, is a *vihara* with monks' chambers around the sides and a shrine chamber in the back. Flanking the entrance of the shrine are murals of two bodhisattvas dressed in lavishly adorned, princely garments and crowns festooned with pearls (**FIG. 4-8**). Their graceful bending postures convey their sympathetic attitudes, while their spiritual power is suggested by their large size in comparison with surrounding figures. In no other known example of Indian painting do bodhisattvas appear so magnanimous and graciously divine yet at the same time so human.

Even as Buddhism flourished, Hinduism, sponsored by Gupta monarchs, began the ascendancy that led to its eventual domination of Indian religious life (see "Hinduism," p. 77). Hindu temples—and sculpture of the Hindu gods—rose with increasing frequency during the Gupta period and the post-Gupta era of the sixth to mid seventh century.

In the mid sixth century, a rock-cut cave-temple devoted to the major Hindu god Shiva was carved on the island of Elephanta, off the coast of Mumbai in western India (**FIG. 4-9**).

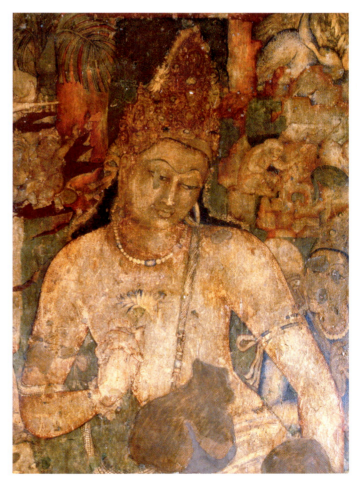

4-8 • BODHISATTVA
Detail of a wall painting in Cave I, Ajanta, Maharashtra, India. Gupta period, c. 475 CE. Visual Resources Collections, University of Michigan.

📷 **View** the Closer Look for this Bodhisattva on **MyArtsLab**

Hinduism

Hinduism is not one religion but many related beliefs and innumerable sects. It results from the mingling of Vedic beliefs with indigenous local beliefs and practices. All three major Hindu sects draw upon the texts of the Vedas, which are believed to be sacred revelations set down about 1200–800 BCE. The gods lie outside the finite world, but they can appear in visible form to believers. Each Hindu sect takes its particular deity as supreme. By worshiping gods with rituals, meditation, and intense love, individuals may be reborn into ever-higher positions until they escape *samsara*, the cycle of life, death, and rebirth. The most popular deities are Vishnu, Shiva, and the Great Goddess, Devi. Deities are revealed and depicted in multiple aspects.

Vishnu: A benevolent god who works for the order and well-being of the world. He is often represented lying in a trance or asleep on the Cosmic Waters, where he dreams the world into existence. His symbols are the wheel and a conch shell. He usually has four arms and wears a crown and lavish jewelry. He rides a man-bird, Garuda. Vishnu appears in ten different incarnations, including Rama and Krishna, who have their own sects. Rama embodies virtue, and—assisted by the monkey king—he fights the demon Ravana. As Krishna, Vishnu is a supremely beautiful, blue-skinned youth who lives with the cowherds, loves the maiden Radha, and battles the demon Kansa.

Shiva: Lord of Existence, both creative and destructive, light and dark, male and female. His symbol is the *linga*, an upright phallus, which is represented as a low pillar. As an expression of his power and creative energy, he is often represented as Lord of the Dance, whose Cosmic Dance within a ring of fire is the endless cycle of death and rebirth, destruction and creation (SEE FIG. 9–4). Shiva's animal is the bull. His consort is Parvati, and their sons are the elephant-headed Ganesha, overcomer of obstacles, and Karttikeya, associated with war.

Devi: The Great Goddess, controller of material riches and fertility. She has forms indicative of beauty, wealth, and auspiciousness, but also forms of wrath, pestilence, and power. As the embodiment of cosmic energy, she provides the vital force to all the male gods. Her symbol is an abstract depiction of female genitals, often associated with the *linga* of Shiva. When armed and riding a lion (as the goddess Durga), Devi personifies righteous fury. As the goddess Lakshmi, she is the goddess of wealth and beauty. She is often represented by the basic geometric forms of squares, circles, and triangles.

Brahma: The creator, who once had his own cult, embodies spiritual wisdom. His four heads symbolize the four cosmic cycles, four earthly directions, and four classes of society: priests (brahmins), warriors, merchants, and laborers.

There are countless other deities, but central to Hindu practice are *puja* (forms of worship) and **darshan** (beholding a deity), generally performed to obtain a deity's favor in the hope that this favor will lead to liberation from *samsara*. Because desire for the fruits of our actions traps us, the ideal is to consider all earthly endeavors as sacrificial offerings to the gods. Pleased with our devotion, a god may then grant us an eternal state of pure being, pure consciousness, and pure bliss.

Impressive in its size and layout, the cave-temple's interior is designed along two main axes, one running north–south, and the other east–west. The three entrances provide the only source of light, and the resulting cross- and backlighting effects add to the sense of the cave as a place of mysterious, almost confusing complexity, not unlike Shiva himself.

Shiva (meaning "the auspicious one") embodies the entire universe and exhibits a wide range of aspects or forms, both gentle and ferocious (see "Hinduism," above). He is the Great Yogi who dwells for vast periods of time in meditation in the Himalayas, the husband par excellence who makes love to the goddess Parvati for eons at a time, the Slayer of Demons, and the Cosmic Dancer who dances the destruction and re-creation of the world.

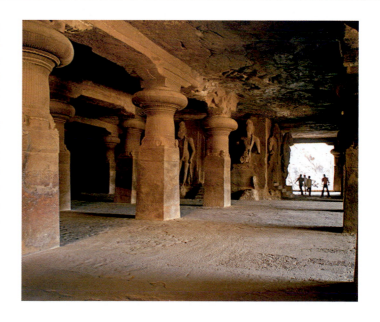

4–9 • CAVE-TEMPLE OF SHIVA
Elephanta, Maharashtra, India. Mid 6th century CE.
View along the east–west axis toward the *linga* shrine.

Many forms of Shiva appear in monumental relief panels adorning the cave-temple at Elephanta. A huge bust of the deity represents his Sadashiva, or **ETERNAL SHIVA**, aspect (**FIG. 4–10**). Carved out of the cave wall, three heads are shown in the photo resting upon the broad shoulders of the upper body, but five heads are implied: the fourth behind, facing the stone, and the fifth, never depicted, on top. The heads summarize Shiva's fivefold nature as creator (back), protector (left), destroyer (right), obscurer (front), and releaser (top). On his left shoulder, his protector nature is depicted as female, with curled hair and a pearl-festooned crown. On his right, his wrathful, destroyer nature wears a fierce expression, and in front, Shiva is in deep introspection, with the matted, piled-up hair of a yogi. The releaser contemplates the heavens. Indian artists often convey the many aspects or essential nature of a deity through multiple heads or arms—which they accomplish with such convincing naturalism that we readily accept the additions. Here, for example, the artist has united three heads onto a single body so skillfully that we still relate to the statue as an essentially human presence.

Southeast Asia

Buddhism spread rapidly across Asia. About 800 CE in Java, rulers of the Sailendra dynasty built a magnificent temple in the form of a sacred mountain at Borobudur (**FIG. 4–11**). The builders turned a natural hill into a three-step platform, measuring more than 400 feet across and oriented to the four cardinal directions. On this platform were erected five more platforms with walls covered in relief sculpture. At the top, three round terraces support 72 small stupas surrounding a

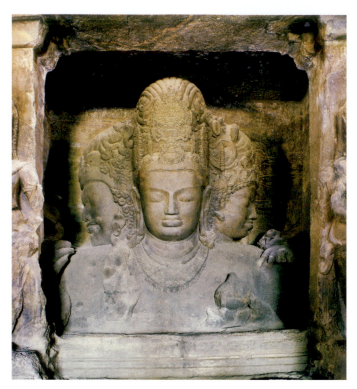

4–10 • ETERNAL SHIVA
Rock-cut relief in the cave-temple of Shiva at Elephanta. Mid 6th century CE. Height approx. 11′ (3.4 m).

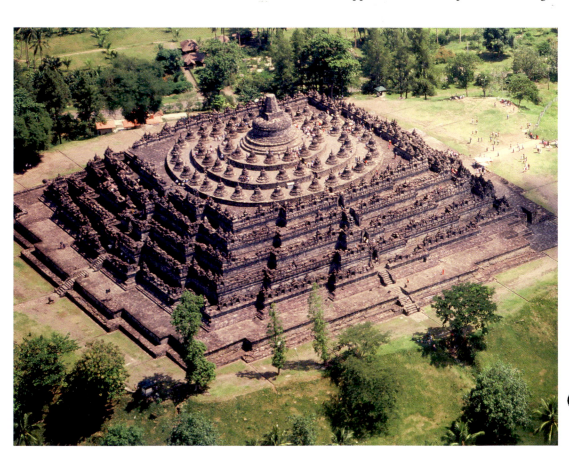

4–11 • BUDDHIST TEMPLE OF BOROBUDUR
Java, Indonesia. Sailendra dynasty, c. 800 CE. Lava stone, perimeter of lowest gallery 1,180′ (360 m); diameter of crowning stupa 52′ (16 m).

👁 **Watch** a video about Borobudur on **MyArtsLab**

large central stupa. The entire complex rises more than 100 feet above the ground. The stupas hold images of the Buddha, and the vertical walls of the three terraces are carved with the Wheel of Life—birth, life, death, and rebirth—the life and past lives of the Buddha, and the stages of enlightenment and paradise. The people who came to Borobudur followed the path established by these corridors of sculpture. Circling clockwise, they climbed the sacred mountain, hoping to achieve enlightenment when they reached the large stupa at the top.

China and Korea

How does art in China and Korea develop through a series of empires and the introduction of Buddhism?

Among the cultures of the world, China is distinguished by its long, uninterrupted development, which has been traced back some 8,000 years. Even more remarkably, while rulers have come and gone, the country has been, with only a few breaks, unified since 221 BCE. Geographically, China is notable for its size, occupying a landmass slightly larger than the continental United States.

The country's historical and cultural heart—sometimes called Inner China—is the land watered by its three great rivers, the Yellow (Huang He), the Yangzi, and the Xi (SEE MAP 4–1). Chinese towns and cities first emerged in the Neolithic period in fertile river valleys, especially around the deep southern bend of the Yellow River, nicknamed "China's Sorrow" because of its disastrous floods.

Agriculture based on rice and millet arose independently in East Asia before 5000 BCE. One of the clearest signs of Neolithic culture in China is the vigorous emergence of towns and cities. At Jiangzhai, near present-day Xi'an, the foundations of more than 100 dwellings have been discovered surrounding the remains of a community center, a cemetery, and a **kiln**. Dated to about 4000 BCE, the ruins point to the existence of a highly developed early society.

The Bronze Age

China entered its Bronze Age in the second millennium BCE. Traditional histories tell of three Bronze Age dynasties: the Xia, the Shang, and the Zhou. Experts at one time tended to dismiss the Xia and Shang as legendary, but twentieth-century archaeological discoveries fully established the historical existence of the Shang (c. 1700–1100 BCE) and point strongly to the historical existence of the Xia as well.

Shang kings ruled from a succession of capitals in the Yellow River valley, where archaeologists have found walled cities, palaces, and vast royal tombs. Society seems to have been highly stratified, with a ruling group that possessed the bronze technology needed to make weapons. They maintained their authority in part by claiming power as intermediaries between the supernatural and human realms. Nature and fertility spirits were also honored, and regular sacrifices were made to keep the spirits of dead ancestors vital so that they might help the living.

Bronze vessels are the most admired and studied of Shang artifacts. They were connected with ritual practices, serving as containers for offerings of food and wine. The bronze **FANG DING** illustrated here is a square vessel with four legs (FIG. 4–12), one of hundreds of vessels recovered from royal tombs near the last of the Shang capitals, Yin (present-day Anyang). In typical Shang style, its surface is decorated with a complex array of images based on animal forms. A large stylized, masklike face (*taotie*) adorns the center of each side; more appear on the legs; and the rest of the surface is filled with images resembling birds, dragons, and other fantastic creatures. The deeper significance of such motifs remains mysterious.

Around 1100 BCE, the Shang were conquered by the Zhou from western China. During the Zhou dynasty (1100–221 BCE), a feudal society developed, with nobles related to the king ruling over numerous small states. The supreme deity became known as Tian, or Heaven, and the king ruled as the Son of Heaven—that is, as the representative of Tian on earth. Later Chinese ruling dynasties continued to follow the belief that imperial rule emanated from a heavenly mandate.

Many of China's great philosophers lived during the Zhou dynasty, thinkers such as Confucius, Laozi, and Mozi. During the lifetime of Confucius (551–479 BCE)—a scholar born into an aristocratic family—warfare for supremacy among the various states of China had begun, and the traditional social fabric seemed to be breaking down. Looking back to the early Zhou dynasty as a golden age, Confucius thought about how a just and harmonious society could once again emerge (see "Confucianism," p. 80). He never found a ruler who would put his ideas into effect, but his philosophy, Confucianism, eventually became central to Chinese thought and culture.

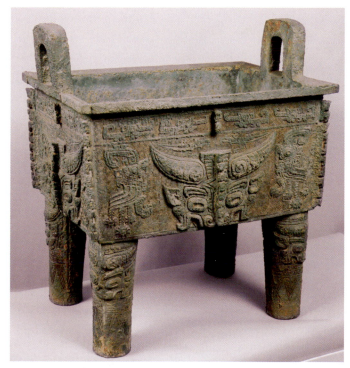

4–12 • FANG DING
From the tomb of Lady Hao, Anyang, Henan, People's Republic of China. Shang dynasty, c. 1200 BCE. Bronze, height 28⅞" (73.3 cm). Excavated from royal cemetery in 1935, tomb no. 1004.

Chinese Empires: Qin, Han, and Tang

Toward the middle of the third century BCE, the state of Qin launched military campaigns that led to its triumph over the other Chinese states by 221 BCE. For the first time, China was united under a single ruler, the powerful Shihuangdi (see "Looking Forward," p. 69). Intent on ensuring personal immortality, this first emperor of Qin built his own underground **mausoleum** (a building used as a tomb) at Lintong in Shaanxi Province. Archaeologists who began to excavate a pit near the tomb in 1974 were stunned to discover a vast subterranean army of thousands of terra-cotta soldiers and horses (SEE FIG. 4–1). Literary sources suggest that the tomb itself, which has not yet been opened, reproduces the world as it was known to the Qin, with stars overhead and rivers and mountains below. Thus did the tomb's architects try literally to ensure that the underworld—the world of souls and spirits—would match the human world on the earth's surface.

Although harsh and repressive as rulers, the Qin emperors established the mechanisms of centralized bureaucracy that molded China both politically and culturally into a single state, establishing an administrative framework still in use to this day. The country was divided into provinces and prefectures, the writing system and coinage were standardized, and forts on the northern frontier were connected to form the earliest Great Wall.

During the peaceful and prosperous Han dynasty that followed (206 BCE–220 CE), the country's borders were extended and secured. Chinese control over strategic stretches of Central Asia led to the opening of the famous Silk Road that linked China by trade all the way to Rome. The philosophies of Daoism and Confucianism flourished.

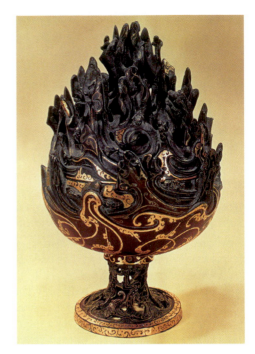

4–13 • INCENSE BURNER
From the tomb of Prince Liu Sheng, Mancheng, Hebei. Han dynasty, 113 BCE. Bronze with gold inlay, height 10½″ (26 cm). Hebei Provincial Museum, Shijiazhuang.

Daoism emphasizes the close relationship between humans and nature. It is concerned with bringing the quiet and humble individual life into harmony with the *Dao*, or Way, of the universe. On a popular level, Daoism developed into an organized

ART AND ITS CONTEXTS

Confucianism

Confucianism is based on the teachings of the Chinese scholar Confucius (551–479 BCE). His words have come down to us through a book known in English as the *Analects*, which records sayings of the philosopher collected by his disciples and their followers. At the heart of Confucian thought is the concept of *ren* (human-heartedness). *Ren* emphasizes morality and empathy as the basic standards for all human interactions, and is most fully realized in the Confucian ideal of the *junzi* (gentleman). Originally indicating noble birth, the term *junzi* was redirected to mean one who through education and self-cultivation becomes a superior person, right-thinking and right-acting in all situations.

Confucius also emphasized the importance of *li* (etiquette). The formalities of social interaction—scrupulous manners as well as ritual, ceremony, and protocol—choreographed life so that an entire society moved in harmony.

Both *ren* and *li* operated in the realm of the Five Constant Relationships defining Confucian society: ruler and subject, parent and child, husband and wife, elder sibling and younger sibling, and elder friend and younger friend. Deference based on age and sex is built into this view, as is the deference to authority that made Confucianism popular with emperors. Yet responsibilities also flow the other way: the duty of a ruler is to earn the loyalty of subjects, of a husband to earn the respect of his wife, and of age to guide youth wisely.

The Silk Road and the Making of Silk

The fabled trade links between East Asia and the West, collectively called the Silk Road, were a 5,000-mile-long network of caravan and sea routes stretching from Chang'an to the westernmost point of the Great Wall of China—then all the way to Rome. Caravans carried Chinese luxury goods to the West, and brought back gold in payment. They passed through some of the most hostile regions in Asia and the Middle East, although no one caravan had to make the entire trip; goods would be passed from trader to trader on both the overland and sea routes. The Silk Road's importance fluctuated with the politics of the various regions through which it passed, as did the level of safety for its travelers. Rarely in its long history was it entirely open and comparatively safe.

Among the many precious goods carried along the Silk Road were spices and other foodstuffs, horses for trade, metals, gems, and, of course, silk. The cultivation and weaving of silk had been a closely guarded secret in China since about 2640 BCE, and it was not until about 550 CE, when two Christian missionaries smuggled a few silkworm larvae to Constantinople, that the Chinese lost their virtual monopoly. However, from as early as the third century BCE, silk cloth had been exported to Europe. It was treasured in ancient Greece and Rome, and it became a protected palace industry in the Byzantine Empire. Eventually, sericulture (the cultivation of silkworms) and luxury textile weaving took hold in southern Europe. For this and many other reasons, the use of the Silk Road declined. By the sixteenth century, it was no longer in use.

---

religion, absorbing many traditional folk practices such as shamanism and the search for immortality. A popular Daoist legend, which tells of the Isles of the Immortals in the Eastern Sea, is depicted on a bronze **INCENSE BURNER** from the tomb of Prince Liu Sheng, who died in 113 BCE (**FIG. 4–13**). Around the bowl, gold inlay outlines the stylized waves of the sea. Above them rises the mountainous island, crowded with birds, animals, and people who have discovered the secret of immortality. This visionary world would have been shrouded in the shifting mist of incense when the burner was in use.

In contrast to the metaphysical focus of Daoism, Confucianism is concerned with the human world, and its goal is the attainment of equity. To this end, it proposes an ethical system based on reverence for ancestors and correct relationships among people (see "Confucianism," p. 80). Attracted by this emphasis on social order and respect for authority, the Han emperor Wudi (ruled 141–87 BCE) made Confucianism the official philosophy. It remained the state ideology of China until the end of imperial rule in the twentieth century and eventually assumed the form and force of a religion.

Confucian subjects appear frequently in Han art. Among the most famous examples are the low reliefs from the Wu family shrines built in 151 CE in Jiaxiang. Carved and engraved on stone slabs, the scenes were meant to teach such basic Confucian tenets as respect for the emperor, filial piety, and wifely devotion (see "A Closer Look," p. 82).

Contemporary literary sources are eloquent on the wonders of the Han capital, but nothing of Han architecture survives but ceramic models. One **MODEL OF A HOUSE** found in a tomb represents an elaborate seven-story dwelling, connected by a third-story passageway to a tower (**FIG. 4–14**). The entrance to the main house, flanked by short towers, opens into an enclosed

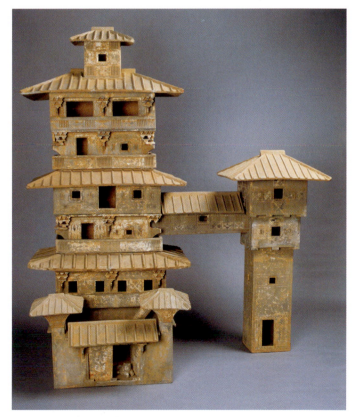

4–14 • TOMB MODEL OF A HOUSE AND TOWER
From Tomb 6, Baizhuang, Henan. Eastern Han dynasty, 1st century CE. Painted earthenware, height of main house 6′ 3½″ (1.92 m); height of tower 4′ 2½″ (1.28 m). Henan Museum.

The main house in this ceramic model is assembled from a stack of 13 individual components, their specific place in the assembly process at times indicated by hand-written inscriptions.

Rubbing of a Stone Relief ▶

Wu family shrine (Wuliangci), Jiaxiang, Shandong. Han dynasty, 151 CE. Stone, 27½" × 66½" (70 × 169 cm). Princeton University Art Museum, Princeton, New Jersey.

Birds and small figures, possibly alluding to mythical creatures or immortals.

A woman, possibly an empress, receiving visitors on the upper floor.

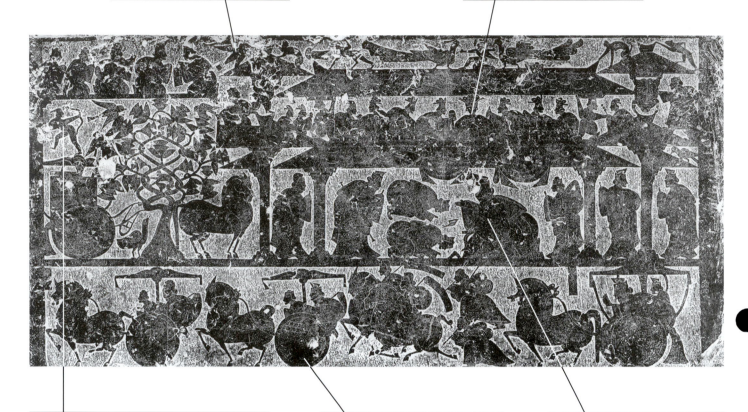

The legendary archer Yi saves the world from scorching by shooting all but one of the ten sun-crows.

Visitors arriving in horse-drawn chariots.

Possibly the first Han emperor receiving visitors on the ground floor.

🎧 **View** the Closer Look for Rubbing of a Stone Relief on **MyArtsLab**

courtyard, occupied here by a clay figure of the family dog. Pigs and oxen probably occupied the ground floor, with the second floor reserved for storage. The family lived in the upper stories, where larger windows raised above the street provided more light and air.

With the fall of the Han dynasty in 220 CE, China splintered into independent, warring kingdoms. This launched a period of almost constant turmoil, broadly known as the period of the Northern and Southern Dynasties (265–589 CE). Many intellectuals turned to Daoism, which contained a strong escapist element. Yet ultimately it was Buddhism that brought the greatest comfort to people of the time. First spreading from India into Central Asia, with the increased transportation of people, goods, and ideas along the Silk Road during the Han dynasty, Buddhism eventually reached China (see "The Silk Road and the Making of Silk," p. 81). To the Chinese of the post-Han period, beset by constant warfare and social devastation, Buddhism offered consolation in life and the promise of life after death.

The most impressive surviving works of Buddhist art from the period of the Northern and Southern Dynasties are hundreds of caves carved from the solid rock of cliffs. The caves at Yungang in Shanxi Province, for instance, contain many impressive examples of early Chinese Buddhist sculpture. The monumental **SEATED BUDDHA** illustrated here was carved in the latter half of the fifth century (**FIG. 4–15**). Because the front part of the cave has crumbled away, the 45-foot statue is now exposed to the open air. The overall effect of this colossus is remote and austere, less human than the more sensuous expression of earlier sculptures in India. The image of the Buddha became increasingly formal and unearthly as it traveled east from its homeland.

In 581 CE, a northern general reunified China and established the short-lived Sui dynasty, which paved the way for one of the greatest dynasties in Chinese history, the Tang (618–907 CE). Even today many Chinese living abroad call themselves "Tang people," emphasizing that part of the Chinese character that is strong and vigorous, noble and idealistic, but also realistic and pragmatic. Cosmopolitan and tolerant, too, the Tang were both self-confident and curious about the world. Many foreigners came to the splendid new capital, Chang'an (present-day Xi'an), and the Chinese depicted them in witty detail. A ceramic statue of a **CAMEL CARRYING A GROUP OF MUSICIANS** reflects the Tang fascination with the "exotic" Turkic cultures of Central Asia (**FIG. 4–16**).

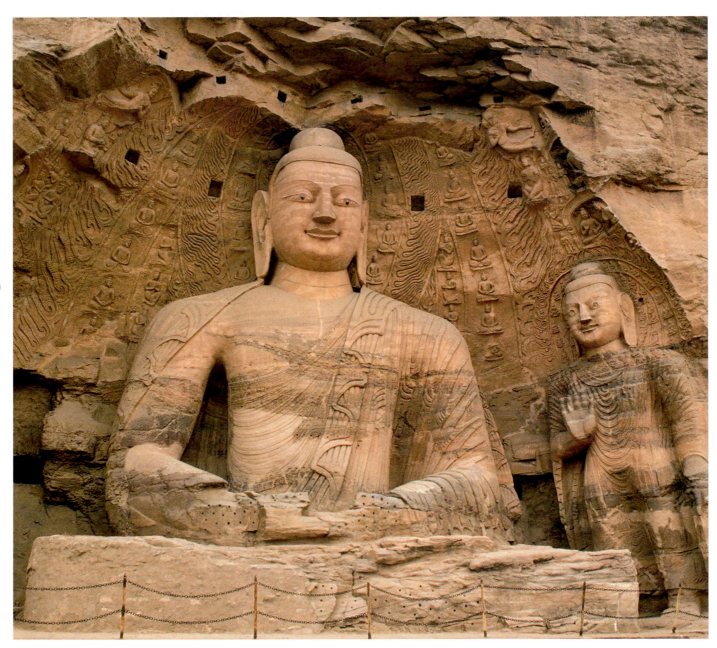

4–15 • SEATED BUDDHA
Cave 20, Yungang, Datong, Shanxi. Northern Wei dynasty, c. 460 CE. Stone, height 45′ (13.7 m).

The elongated ears, protuberance on the head (*ushnisha*), and monk's robe are traditional attributes of the Buddha. The masklike face, massive shoulders, and shallow, stylized drapery indicate a strong Central Asian influence.

View the Closer Look for the Seated Buddha on **MyArtsLab**

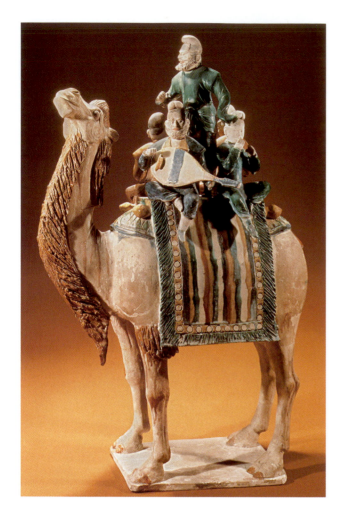

4–16 • CAMEL CARRYING A GROUP OF MUSICIANS
From a tomb near Xi'an, Shanxi. Tang dynasty, c. mid 8th century CE.
Earthenware with three-color glaze, height 26⅛" (66.5 cm).
National Museum, Beijing.

Such ceramic figurines, produced by the thousand for tombs, were decorated using a three-color-glaze technique that was a specialty of Tang ceramists. The glazes—usually chosen from a restricted palette of amber, yellow, green, and white—were splashed freely and allowed to run over the surface during firing to convey a feeling of spontaneity that complements the lively gestures and expressive faces of both camel and riders.

The early Tang emperors proclaimed a policy of religious tolerance, and virtually the entire country adopted the flourishing Buddhist faith. During the ninth century, however, a conservative reaction set in. Confucianism was reasserted and Buddhism was briefly persecuted as a "foreign" religion. Thousands of Buddhist temples, shrines, and monasteries were destroyed and innumerable bronze statues melted down. Fortunately, several Buddhist structures do survive from the Tang dynasty. One of them, the **NANCHAN TEMPLE**, located on Mount Wutai in the eastern part of Shanxi Province, is the first important surviving example of Chinese woodframe architecture (**FIG. 4–17**). Constructed in 782 CE, its curved and tiled roof has broad overhanging eaves supported by **brackets** (architectural supports projecting from the walls). Bracketing became a standard element of East Asian architecture, especially in

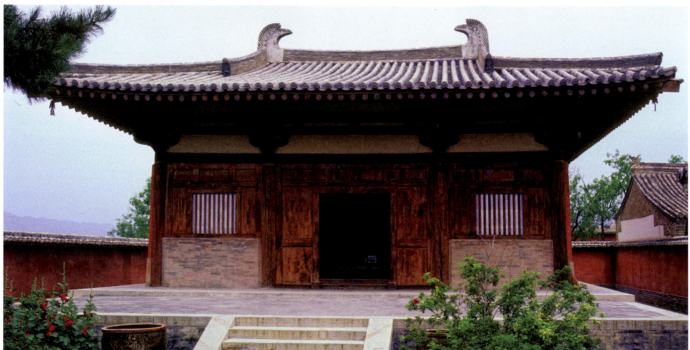

4–17 • NANCHAN TEMPLE
Mount Wutai (Wutaishan), Shanxi. Tang dynasty, 782 CE.

The tiled roof, first seen in the Han tomb model (SEE FIG. 4–14), has taken on a curved silhouette that becomes increasingly pronounced in later centuries. The very broad overhanging eaves are supported by a correspondingly elaborate bracketing system.

Calligraphy

The emphasis on expressiveness and structural importance of brushstrokes finds its purest embodiment in **calligraphy** (the word comes from the Greek meaning "beautiful writing"). In China, calligraphy is regarded as one of the highest forms of artistic expression. For more than 2,000 years, China's literati, all of them Confucian scholars, have enjoyed being connoisseurs and practitioners of this art form. During the fourth century, calligraphy came to full maturity. The most important early practitioner was Wang Xizhi (c. 307–365 CE), whose works have served as models of excellence for subsequent generations (FIG. 4–18).

Calligraphy is created by combining stylized strokes, executed with a brush and ink, to form the characters of Chinese writing. Chinese characters, unlike Western letterforms, evolved from pictographs, a picture or sign representing a thing or concept. Chinese calligraphic styles, from which Japanese and Korean calligraphy developed, are based on seven standard strokes, also known as the "Seven Mysteries": a horizontal line, a vertical line, a dot, sharp curves curling either to the left or right, and diagonal strokes executed at various angles, sweeping downward either toward the left or right.

Several styles of calligraphy developed in Asia over the centuries, each with its own unique traits and purpose. The characters in calligraphy used for meditation or poetry, for example, may appear far different from the characters seen in bureaucratic documents or official seals. Depending on the intent of the calligrapher, the width and length of strokes may vary between styles as may the sharpness of edges and corners and the concentration of ink on the page. Compare, for example, the uniformly placed, compact characters with sharp strokes in FIGURE 9-14 from China to the fluidity and wild curls that compose the elongated characters in FIGURE 9-22 from Japan.

The stamped characters that appear on Chinese artworks are seals, or personal emblems. The use of seals dates from the Zhou dynasty, and to this day seals traditionally employ the archaic characters, known appropriately as "seal script," of the Zhou or Qin. Cut in stone, a seal may state a formal, given name, or it may state any of the numerous personal names that China's painters and writers may have adopted throughout their lives. A treasured work of art often bears not only the seal of its maker but also those of collectors and admirers through the centuries. In the Chinese view, these do not disfigure the work but add another layer of interest and history. This sample of Wang Xizhi's calligraphy, for example, bears the seals of two Song dynasty emperors, a Song official, a famous collector of the sixteenth century, and two emperors of the Qing dynasty of the eighteenth and nineteenth centuries.

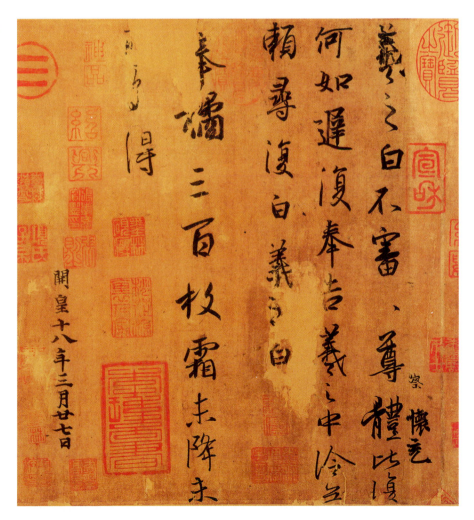

4-18 • Wang Xizhi PORTION OF A LETTER FROM THE FENG JU ALBUM
Northern and Southern Dynasties, mid 4th century CE. Ink on paper, 9¾″ × 18½″ (24.7 × 46.9 cm). National Palace Museum, Taipei, Taiwan, Republic of China.

The Ci'en Temple was constructed for the famous monk Xuanzang on his return from a 16-year pilgrimage to India. Here, he taught and translated the Sanskrit Buddhist scriptures that he had brought back with him. Over the years, when students passed their official examinations, they went to the temple and inscribed their names, creating a veritable history of Chinese calligraphy.

Pagodas—towers associated with East Asian Buddhist temples—originated in the Indian Buddhist stupas—elaborate, often multistory burial mounds that housed relics of the Buddha. In China this form blended with the earlier Han watchtowers to produce the pagoda, and multistoried wooden pagodas with upward-curving roofs supported by elaborate bracketing are much like these indigenous prototypes. Later pagodas often provided access to the ground floor and sometimes to the upper levels as well. Although modified and repaired in later years (its seven stories were originally five, and a new finial has been added), the Great Wild Goose Pagoda still preserves the essence of Tang architecture in its simplicity, symmetry, proportions, and grace.

Korea

Set between China and Japan, Korea occupies a peninsula in northeast Asia. Inhabited for millennia, the peninsula gave rise to a distinctively Korean culture during the Three Kingdoms period (57 BCE–668 CE), which saw the establishment of three

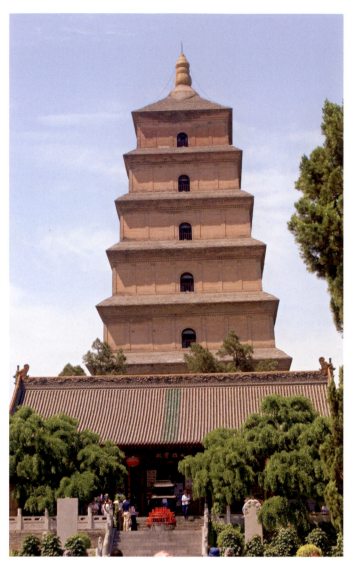

4–19 • GREAT WILD GOOSE PAGODA
Ci'en Temple, Chang'an (Xi'an), Shanxi. Tang dynasty, first erected 645 CE; rebuilt mid 8th century CE.

👁 **Watch** an architectural simulation about pagodas on **MyArtsLab**

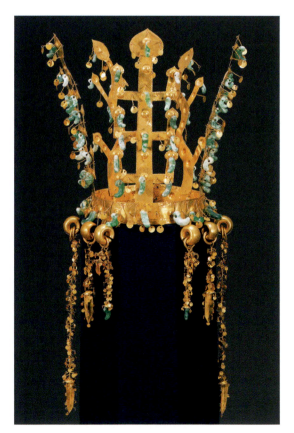

4–20 • CROWN
From the Gold Crown Tomb, Gyeongju, North Gyeongsang, Korea. Three Kingdoms period, Silla kingdom, probably 6th century CE. Gold with jadeite ornaments, height 17½″ (44.5 cm). National Museum of Korea, Seoul, Republic of Korea.

palaces and temples. Also typical is the **bay** system of construction, in which a cubic unit of space, a bay, is formed by four posts and their lintels. The bay functioned in Chinese architecture as a sort of **module**, a basic unit of construction. To create larger structures, an architect multiplied the number of bays. Thus the three-bayed Nanchan Temple, modest in scope, gives an idea of the vast splendor of the multistoried palaces of the Tang, now lost.

The **GREAT WILD GOOSE PAGODA** of the Ci'en Temple in the Tang capital of Chang'an also survives (**FIG. 4–19**). Originally built of mud bricks in 645 CE, and rebuilt in the mid eighth century of brick with wooden floors and steps, it imitates the forms of contemporary wooden architecture. The walls are decorated in low relief to resemble bays, and bracket systems are reproduced under the projecting roofs of each story.

independent nation-states: Silla in the southeast, Baekje in the southwest, and Goguryeo in the north. Large tomb mounds built during the fifth and sixth centuries are enduring monuments of this period.

Among the most impressive items recovered from these tombs is a spectacular headdress (FIG. 4–20). Made expressly for burial, it was assembled from cut pieces of thin gold sheet, held together by gold wire. Spangles of gold embellish the crown, as do comma-shaped ornaments of green and white jadeite. The tall, branching forms rising from the crown's periphery resemble trees and antlers. Within the crown is a conical cap woven of narrow strips of sheet gold and ornamented with appendages that suggest wings or feathers.

Buddhism was introduced into the Goguryeo kingdom from China in 372 CE, into Baekje by 384, and probably reached Silla in the second half of the fifth century. At first, Buddhist

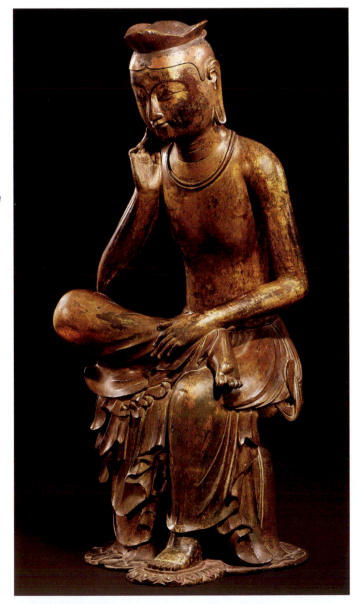

4–21 • BODHISATTVA SEATED IN MEDITATION
Korea. Three Kingdoms period, early 7th century CE. Gilt bronze, height 35⅞″ (91 cm). National Museum of Korea, Seoul, Republic of Korea.

art in Korea imitated Chinese examples. By the late sixth century, however, Korean sculptors had created a distinctive style, exemplified by a magnificent gilt bronze image of a seated bodhisattva from the early seventh century (FIG. 4–21). The slender figure leans on one knee, striking a graceful pose associated with meditation. The garment clings to his body, and the low relief of its folds forms linear patterns—repeated arcs over the legs and sharply pleated folds at the sides. Although the pose derives from late sixth-century Chinese sculpture, the slender body, elliptical face, elegant drapery folds, and trilobed crown are distinctly Korean, and this refined and courtly Korean style spread to Japan, where it became the basis for an international style of Buddhist art.

Japan

How do the ancient native traditions of Japanese art blossom in Shinto and Buddhist art and architecture?

From ancient times, indigenous Japanese taste has been distinguished by a respect for and a delight in natural materials. Wooden architecture was often left unpainted, and ceramics frequently are only partly glazed in order to display the clay bodies underneath. Japanese artists delighted in asymmetry, and a sense of humor and playfulness sometimes surfaces in unexpected contexts, even in religious art of great power and depth. Finally, the Japanese have preserved their cultural heritage while welcoming and creatively transforming foreign influences—first from China and Korea and more recently from Europe and North America.

Human habitation on the Japanese islands dates to around 30,000 years ago. During the Jomon period (c. 12,000–400 BCE), Neolithic hunter-gatherers developed the ability to make ceramics. Recent scientific study has dated some Japanese pottery to c. 12,000 BCE, making it the oldest now known.

Immigrants from Korea during the Yayoi period (c. 400 BCE–300 CE) helped to transform Japan into an agricultural nation, where rice cultivation became widespread. The emergence of a class structure can be dated to this time, as can the development of metal technology—first bronze and then iron.

The Kofun Period
During the ensuing Kofun, or "old tombs," period (c. 300–552 CE)—named for its large royal tombs—a pattern of venerating leaders grew into the beginnings of an imperial system. This system, still in existence today in Japan, eventually maintained that the emperor (or, very rarely, empress) descended directly from Shinto deities.

When a Kofun emperor died, chamber tombs furnished with pottery and other grave goods were constructed following Korean examples. Some tomb sites extend over more than 400 acres, with artificial hills built over the tombs themselves. On top of the hills were placed hollow ceramic works of sculpture called *haniwa*.

The first *haniwa* were simple cylinders that may have held jars with ceremonial offerings. By the fifth century CE, these cylinders came to be made in the shapes of ceremonial objects, houses, and boats, and later living creatures such as birds,

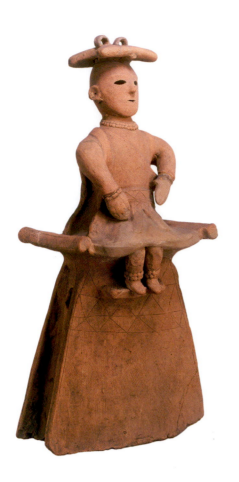

4-22 • HANIWA

from Kyoto. Kofun period, 6th century CE. Earthenware, height 27″ (68.5 cm). Tokyo National Museum.

There have been many theories concerning the function of *haniwa*. The figures seem to have served as some kind of link between the world of the dead, over which they were placed, and the world of the living, from which they could be viewed. This figure has been identified as a seated female shaman, wearing a robe, belt, and necklace and carrying a mirror at her waist. In early Japan, shamans acted as agents between the natural and the supernatural worlds, just as *haniwa* figures were links between the living and the dead.

deer, dogs, monkeys, cows, and horses. By the sixth century, **HANIWA** in human shapes were crafted, including females and males of various types, professions, and classes (**FIG. 4–22**). Unlike Chinese tomb ceramics, which concentrated on highly finished, glazed surfaces, the clay bodies of *haniwa* were left unglazed. Their makers explored instead the expressive potential of simple, bold forms, never perfectly symmetrical, charged with the idiosyncrasy of life and individuality.

Shinto is the indigenous religious belief system of Japan. It encompasses a variety of ritual practices that center around family, village, and national devotion to *kami* (Shinto deities). *Kami* were thought to inhabit many different aspects of nature, including particularly hoary and magnificent trees and rocks, as well as waterfalls, and living creatures such as deer. The term

4-23 • MAIN HALL, INNER SHRINE, ISE

Mie Prefecture. Photograph by Watanabe Yoshio (1907–2000), 1953.

Although Ise is visited by millions of pilgrims each year, only members of the Japanese imperial family and a few Shinto priests are allowed within the enclosure that surrounds its inner shrine. Detailed documents on its appearance date back to the tenth century—it was last rebuilt in 2013—but shrine authorities allowed photographers access to its inner compound only in 1953, when this iconic image was taken by a photographer officially engaged by a quasi-governmental cultural relations agency. The reluctance of shrine officials to permit photography even then may stem from beliefs that such intimate pictures would violate the privacy of the shrine's most sacred spaces.

👁 **Watch** a video about the rebuilding of the Ise Shrine on **MyArtsLab**

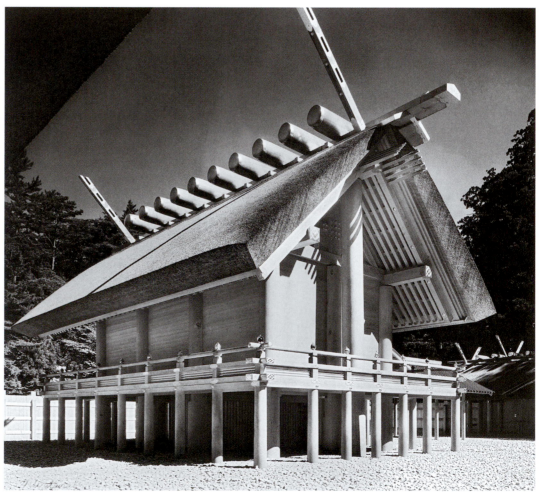

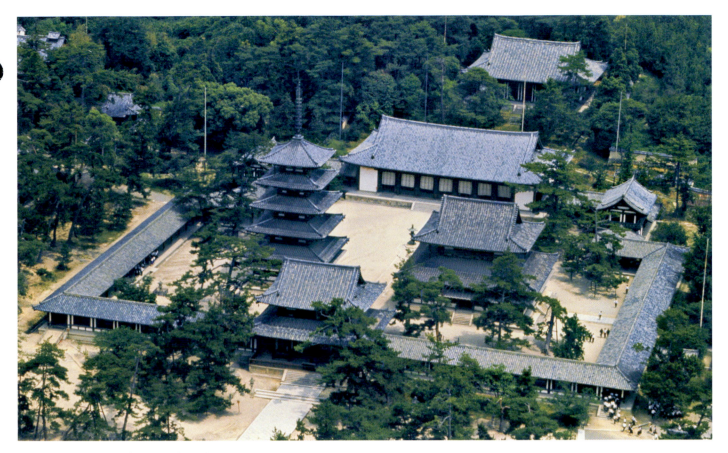

4–24 • MAIN COMPOUND, HORYU-JI
Nara Prefecture. Asuka period, 7th century CE.

"Shinto" was not coined until after the arrival of Buddhism in the sixth century CE, when under its influence *kami* worship became more systematized, with shrines, a hierarchy of deities, and more strictly regulated ceremonies.

One of the great Shinto monuments is the Grand Shrine at Ise, on the coast southwest of Tokyo (**FIG. 4–23**), where the main deity worshiped is the sun goddess Amaterasu-omikami, legendary progenitor of Japan's imperial family. Since at least 690 CE, the shrine has been ritually rebuilt, alternately on two adjoining sites, at 20-year intervals (most recently in 2013), by carpenters who train for the task from childhood. After the *kami* is ceremonially escorted to the freshly copied shrine, the old shrine is dismantled. Thus—like Japanese culture itself—this exquisite building is both ancient and constantly renewed. In this sense it embodies one of the most important aspects of the Shinto faith—ritual purification—derived from respect for the cycle of the seasons in which pure new life emerges in springtime and gives way to death in winter, yet is reborn again the following year.

Many aspects of the Ise Shrine are typical of Shinto architecture: the wooden piles that raise the building off the ground, the horizontal logs that hold a thatched roof in place, the unpainted cypress wood used prominently in construction—all of which impart an overall feeling of natural simplicity rather than imposing size and elaborate decoration. The building's shape derives from raised granaries used during the Yayoi period to store food. The sensitive use of wood and thatch in the

Ise Shrine suggests an early origin for the Japanese appreciation of natural materials that persists to this day.

The Asuka Period

During the single century of the Asuka period (552–645 CE), new forms of philosophy, medicine, music, food, clothing, agriculture, city planning, religion, visual art, and architecture entered Japan from Korea and China at an astonishing pace. Among the most significant imports were Buddhism, a centralized governmental structure, and a system of writing. Buddhism reached Japan in Mahayana form, with its many buddhas and bodhisattvas (see "Buddhism," p. 71), and soon became a state religion. The imported religion introduced different gods, with rich anthropomorphic iconography (*kami* were not portrayed in human form), and ceremonial worship focused in temples. Buddhism also offered a rich cosmology with profound teachings of meditation and enlightenment, and the protective power of deities that enabled ruling elites to justify their own power through religious association.

The most significant surviving early Japanese Buddhist temple is **HORYU-JI** (**FIG. 4–24**), located not far from Nara. Founded in 607 CE and rebuilt after a fire in 670, Horyu-ji is the oldest wooden temple in the world. The main compound consists of a rectangular courtyard surrounded by covered corridors. Within are two Chinese-style buildings, a large *kondo*, or golden hall, and a five-story pagoda. The *kondo* is filled with Buddhist images and is used for worship and ceremonies.

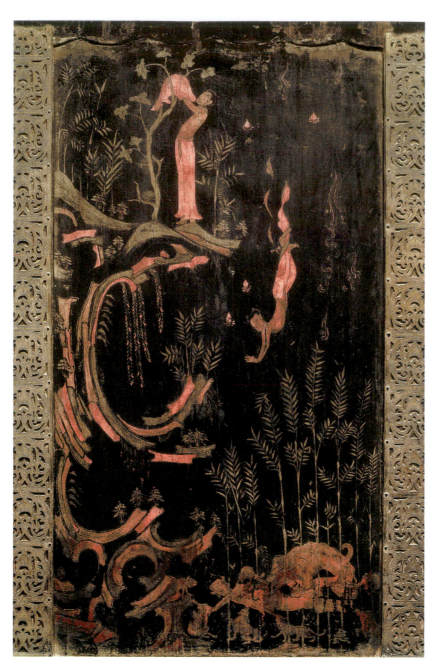

4–25 • HUNGRY TIGRESS JATAKA
Panel of the Tamamushi Shrine, Horyu-ji.
Asuka period, c. 650 CE. Lacquer on wood,
height of shrine 7′ 7¾″ (2.33 m). Horyu-ji
Treasure House.

The pagoda serves as a **reliquary** (a repository for sacred relics) and is not entered. Other monastery buildings, such as a repository for sacred texts and dormitories for monks, lie outside the main compound.

Among the many treasures preserved in Horyu-ji is a miniature shrine decorated with paintings in **lacquer** (a type of hard, glossy varnish). It is known as the Tamamushi Shrine after the tamamushi beetle, whose iridescent wings were originally affixed to the shrine to make it glitter.

The paintings on the side of the Tamamushi Shrine are among the few two-dimensional works of art to survive from the Asuka period. The painting in **FIGURE 4–25** tells a story from a former life of the Buddha, who is shown nobly sacrificing his life in order to feed his body to a starving tigress and her cubs. Since the tigers are at first too weak to eat him, he jumps off a cliff to break open his flesh. The Buddha appears three times in three sequential stages of the story, all contained within this single frame. The graceful, slender forms of the figures and the stylized treatment of the cliff, trees, and bamboo represent an international Buddhist style transmitted to Japan via China and Korea.

During the seventh and eighth centuries, Buddhism so thoroughly permeated the upper levels of society that an empress sought to cede her throne to a Buddhist monk. Her advisors intervened, but Buddhism remained the single most significant element in Japanese culture, comfortably coexisting with Shinto, just as it had with Hinduism in India and with Confucianism and Daoism in China.

The culturally rich civilizations of South and East Asia—including those that flourished in what are today India, China, Korea, Japan, and Indonesia—are among the world's oldest. Early Asian cultures evolved from simple societies into complex, highly organized political and economic systems. They were bolstered by belief systems and rituals that evolved into religions that are still widely practiced today. Indigenous beliefs such as Hinduism in India, Confucianism in China, and Shinto in Japan contributed to distinctive artistic styles and subjects in the locations where these religions proliferated. Buddhism, which originated in India, spread throughout the continent, making the Buddha a common subject throughout Asian art.

The rich philosophical and spiritual life of early Asian cultures was paralleled by increasing technical refinement and artistic skill in many media. Writing evolved into calligraphy, a complex and stylized pictographic script in which the image of every character is a miniature work of art. Ultimately, calligraphy came to be considered the highest form of art, a situation we will encounter again in the more recent art of Islam.

THINK ABOUT IT

4.1 Choose an early Indian image of the Buddha and discuss the specific features that allow you to identify him as the subject.

4.2 What is the relationship between early stupas in India and later pagodas in China? Build your answer on a discussion of two specific examples, a stupa and a pagoda.

4.3 Discuss those elements of the Ise Shrine that express indigenous Japanese artistic tendencies.

| CROSSCURRENTS |

These two imposing complexes from Egypt and China are royal tombs. Explain how they represent the political stature of the entombed and the beliefs of their cultures.

FIG. 3–2   FIG. 4–1

IN PERSPECTIVE

3000 BCE

2500

2000

1500

1000

500

0

500 CE

1000

Indus Civilization
c. 2600–1900 BCE

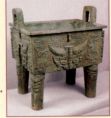

Fang Ding
c. 1200 BCE

Shang Dynasty in China
c. 1700–1100 BCE

Vedic Period in India
c. 1500–late
4th century BCE

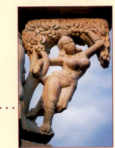

Yakshi Bracket Figure, Sanchi
c. 150–50 BCE

Shakyamuni Buddha
c. 563–483 BCE
Confucius 551–479 BCE

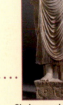

Shakyamuni Buddha
2nd–3rd century CE

Qin Dynasty in China
221–206 BCE
Han Dynasty in China
206 BCE–220 CE
Three Kingdoms Period in Korea
57 BCE–668 CE

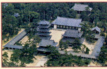

Main Compound, Horyu-ji
7th century CE

Kofun Period in Japan c. 300–552 CE
Gupta Period in India c. 320–550 CE

Asuka Period in Japan
552–645 CE
Tang Dynasty in China 618–907 CE

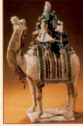

Camel Carrying a Group of Musicians
c. mid 8th century CE

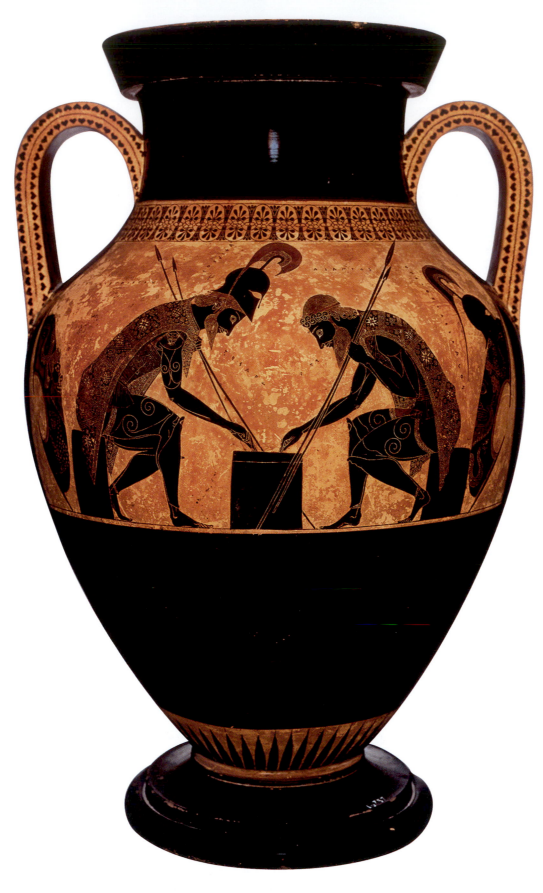

5–1 • Exekias (potter and painter) AJAX AND ACHILLES PLAYING A GAME
c. 540–530 BCE. Black-figure decoration on a ceramic amphora, height of amphora 24″ (61 cm).
Vatican Museums, Rome.

🔎 **View** the Closer Look for Exekias's amphora with Ajax and Achilles Playing a Game on **MyArtsLab**

ART OF ANCIENT GREECE AND THE AEGEAN WORLD

LEARNING OBJECTIVES

5.1 Identify the diverse forms of art and architecture surviving from the Bronze Age in the Aegean.

5.2 Describe the distinctive ideals of human representation and architectural design that emerged at the beginning of ancient Greek civilization.

5.3 Trace the developing features that characterize Classical Greek art and architecture.

5.4 Distinguish Hellenistic art from the Classical art that preceded it.

LOOKING FORWARD ▶

This elegantly contoured **amphora** (FIG. 5–1) was conceived and created to be more than the all-purpose storage jar indicated by its shape, substance, and size. A strip around the belly of its bulging form was reserved by Exekias—the mid-sixth-century BCE Athenian artist who signed it proudly as both potter and painter—for the presentation of a narrative episode from the Trojan War, one of the signal stories of the ancient Greeks' mythical conception of their past. Two heroic warriors, Achilles and Ajax, sit across from each other, supporting themselves on their spears as they lean in toward the block between them that serves as a makeshift board for their game of dice. Ajax, to the right, calls out "three"—the spoken word written out diagonally on the pot's surface as if issuing from his mouth. Achilles counters with "four," the winning number, his victory presaged by the visual prominence of the boldly silhou-etted helmet perched on his head. (Ajax's headgear has been set casually aside on his shield, leaning behind him.) Ancient Greek viewers, however, would have perceived the tragic irony of Achilles's victory. When these two warriors returned from this playful diversion into the serious contest of battle, Achilles would be killed. Soon afterward, Ajax would take his own life in despair.

The poignant narrative encounter portrayed on this amphora is also a masterful compositional design. Crisscross-ing diagonals and compressed overlapping of spears, bodies, and table describe spatial complexity as well as surface pat-tern. The varying textures of hair, armor, and clothing are daz-zlingly evoked by the alternation between expanses of unar-ticulated surface and the finely incised lines of dense pattern. Careful contours convey a sense of three-dimensional human form. And the arrangement coordinates with the very shape of the vessel itself, its curving outline matched by the warriors' bending backs, the line of its handles continued in the tilt of the leaning shields.

There is no hint here of gods or kings. Focus rests on the private diversions of heroic warriors as well as on the identity and personal style of the artist who portrayed them. Supremely self-aware and self-confident, the ancient Greeks developed a concept of human supremacy and responsibility that required a new visual expression. Their art was centered on the mate-rial world, but it also conformed to strict ideals of beauty and mathematical concepts of design, paralleling the philosophers' search for the human values of truth, virtue, and harmony, quali-ties that imbue both subject and style in this celebrated work.

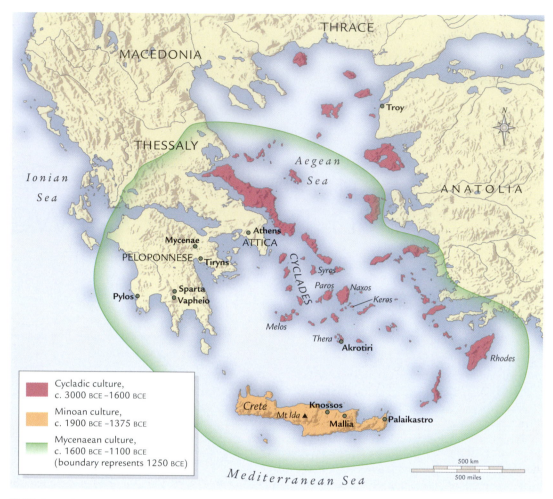

MAP 5–1 • THE AEGEAN WORLD

The three main cultures in the ancient Aegean were the Cycladic, in the Cyclades; the Minoan, on Thera and Crete; and the Helladic, including the Mycenaean, in mainland Greece but also encompassing the regions that had been the center of the two earlier cultures.

The Aegean region of Europe is an area composed of the Greek peninsula and a cluster of nearby islands in the Aegean Sea between the mainland and the large island of Crete. Living on rocky peninsulas and islands, the Aegeans became seafaring and adventurous by necessity. Unlike most of the early civilizations we have already considered, which arose in fertile river valleys, the people of Greece, the Cyclades, and Crete looked to the surrounding seas for both security and resources (MAP 5–1). And, from the third millennium BCE, through the Classical art of fifth-century BCE Athens, and extending into the broader development of the Hellenistic period beginning at the end of the next century, they created visual arts of arresting quality and originality.

At the start of the Aegean Bronze Age, about 3100 BCE, a culture marked by the use of bronze weapons and tools began to take shape on the island of Crete. By around 1900 BCE it developed into the culture modern archaeologists have called Minoan. Strategically located, Minoan Crete became a great sea power, reaching its height between 1700 and 1450 BCE, the so-called New Palace period. Excavations in and around immense

architectural complexes, dating from as early as 1900 BCE, have revealed the richness of Minoan art and ceremony and have uncovered ceramics, sculpture, wall paintings, and spectacular work in ivory and gold.

Minoan Crete declined after 1500 BCE, and dominance in the Aegean region shifted to a mainland Greek culture known as Mycenaean, after one of its major cities, Mycenae. The Mycenaeans, who spoke an early form of the Greek language, built fortified strongholds ruled by local princes or kings, warlords whose exploits were memorialized in later Greek epics such as the *Iliad* and the *Odyssey*.

The Aegean Bronze Age ended about 1100 BCE, when Mycenaean civilization collapsed for unknown reasons. Not until around 900 BCE did the inhabitants of the Aegean region begin to flourish again. These were the people who came to be called the Greeks. Linked by language, they lived in self-sufficient, close-knit communities scattered throughout the region, which eventually developed into independently governed city-states.

Over the ensuing 700 years, the Greeks were spectacularly creative. We still credit them with groundbreaking experiments in science, mathematics, and herbal medicine; with the implementation of a representative government that is a forerunner of modern democracy; and with an astounding legacy of art and architecture that continues to influence the Western world to this day. Admiration for the works of Greek poets, dramatists, and philosophers, including Homer, Aeschylus, Sophocles, Euripides, and Plato, has endured for more than two millennia.

Ancient Greek philosophers sought to define the ideal community, the actions of responsible citizenship, and the meaning of a good life by speculating on the nature of the Good, the True, the Beautiful. Artists responded by embodying such intangible concepts in the material forms of sculpture, architecture, and painting. "Know thyself" and "Nothing in excess" were maxims inscribed in the sanctuary of the sun god, Apollo, at Delphi in the mountains above the Gulf of Corinth. These words and the ideas they embody and inspire seem to have been imprinted on the heart and hands of every Greek artist: focus on human beings; study the variety found within the natural world in which we live; and strive to simplify and clarify these impressions in order to capture an ideal essence of life.

The Bronze Age in the Aegean

What diverse forms of art and architecture survive from the Bronze Age in the Aegean?

Human settlements were established in the Cyclades during the Neolithic period, as early as 6000 BCE, but since the inhabitants left no written records, the prosperous Bronze Age society that developed there about 3000 BCE remains a mystery. The art they left behind has become a principal source of information about them.

The Cycladic Islands

During the late Neolithic and early Bronze Age, the people who lived on the Cyclades—like their contemporaries in the ancient Near East and Egypt (see Chapters 2 and 3)—farmed, made utensils, and engaged in trade. Sleek, abstracted representations of human figures, carved from a fine white marble, abundant especially on the islands of Naxos and Paros, have been unearthed in and around Cycladic graves.

Most of these sculptures represent nude women (FIG. 5–2), posed in strict symmetry, with arms folded just under gently protruding breasts, as if they were clutching their abdomens. Necks are long, heads tilted back, and faces are featureless except for a prominent, elongated nose. The sculptors carefully designed these figures, laying them out with a compass in conformity to three evenly spaced and equally sized circles. For us, these elegant, pure stylizations recall the pristine forms of modern sculpture, but originally their smooth marble surfaces were enlivened by painted motifs in blue, red, and, more rarely, green paint, emphasizing their surfaces rather than their three-dimensional shapes. Today, evidence of such painting is extremely faint, but many patterns have been recovered using controlled lighting and microscopic investigation. Unlike the forms themselves, the painted features are often asymmetrical in organization. In the example illustrated here, wide-open eyes appear on forehead, cheeks, and thigh, as well as on either side of the nose.

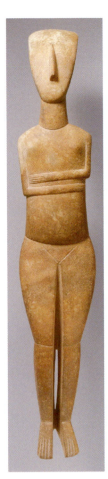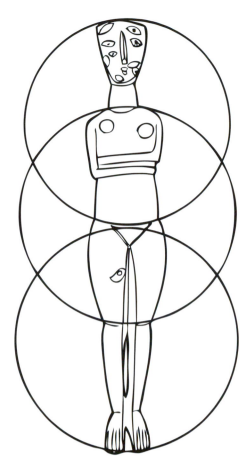

5–2 • FIGURE OF A WOMAN WITH A DRAWING SHOWING EVIDENCE OF ORIGINAL PAINTING AND OUTLINING DESIGN SCHEME
From the Cyclades. c. 2600–2400 BCE. Marble, height 24¾″ (62.8 cm).
Figure: The Metropolitan Museum of Art, New York.
Gift of Christos G. Bastis (68.148). Drawing: Elizabeth Hendrix.

Art historians have proposed a variety of explanations for the meaning of these painted motifs. The angled lines on some figures' bodies could bear witness to the way Cycladic peoples decorated their own bodies—whether permanently with tattoos or scarification, or temporarily with body paint, applied either during their lifetimes or to prepare their bodies for burial. The staring eyes, which seem to demand the viewer's return gaze, may have been a way of connecting these sculpted images to those who owned or used them. And eyes on locations other than faces may aim to draw viewers' attention—perhaps even healing powers—to a particular area of the body.

Minoan Crete

Crete is the largest of the Aegean islands: 155 miles long and 36 miles wide. The splendid culture that flourished there between c. 1900 and 1375 BCE is named "Minoan" after a Greek legend about King Minos of Crete, who was said to have kept a human-eating monster called a Minotaur (half human and half bull) at the center of a labyrinth, or maze. The earliest Minoans were self-sufficient agriculturally; they produced grain and

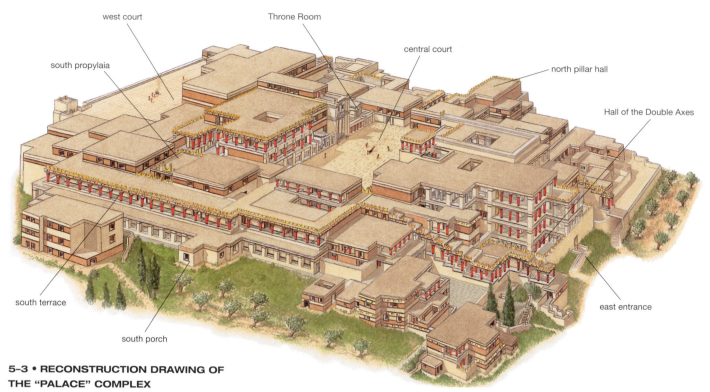

west court | Throne Room | central court | north pillar hall
south propylaia | | | Hall of the Double Axes
south terrace | | east entrance
south porch

5-3 • RECONSTRUCTION DRAWING OF THE "PALACE" COMPLEX

Knossos, Crete. Site occupied 2000–1375 BCE.

The architectural complex depicted in this drawing is the one built after destructive earthquakes and fires in about 1700 BCE. It would be destroyed again in about 1375 BCE. From the central courtyard, which may have been the focus of the complex, corridors and stairs led to several levels of rooms, additional smaller courtyards, and light-wells.

fruit and raised cattle and sheep, which they traded for various luxury goods and for the copper and tin ores they needed to make bronze. They must have been highly skilled sailors, for they traveled and traded to Egypt, the Near East, and Anatolia (western Turkey).

Relatively little is known about daily life during the Minoan period, although a number of written records have been found at archaeological sites. The two earliest forms of Minoan writing, a form of hieroglyphs and a script called Linear A, still defy translation, but surviving documents in a later script, Linear B, give insights into Minoan material culture.

Minoan civilization remained very much a mystery until 1900 CE, when British archaeologist Sir Arthur Evans (1851–1941) excavated the buried ruins of an extraordinary building complex at Knossos, near Crete's north coast. Evans called great complexes like Knossos "palaces" because he believed they were occupied by a succession of kings, but more recent scholars have proposed that Minoan society was not ruled by kings but by a fluid confederation of aristocrats. In that light, they interpret the complexes not primarily as residences, but as sites of periodic religious ceremony or ritual, perhaps enacted by a community that gathered in the courtyards that are their core architectural feature.

The builders of Knossos devised an almost earthquake-proof flexible wall system of timber supports and braces with light, mud-brick infill. Only façades and lower walls were faced with **dressed stone** (cut and highly finished masonry). Even so,

damage to several complexes, including Knossos, from a major earthquake in about 1700 BCE required repair, and in the process many were enlarged. The resulting "new palaces"—multi-storied, flat-roofed, and with many columns—were designed with staggered levels, open stairwells, and strategically placed air shafts and light-wells to maximize air and light, as well as to define access and circulation patterns.

During its heyday, the architectural complex at Knossos covered 6 acres (**FIG. 5–3**). Courtyards—not audience halls or temples—were the central and most prominent features; suites of rooms were arranged around them. Clusters of workshops formed commercial centers. The huge scale of the centralized management of trade in foodstuffs was demonstrated when excavators uncovered in a single storeroom enough large ceramic jars to hold 20,000 gallons of olive oil.

Minoan painters worked on a large scale, covering the walls of rooms with geometric borders, views of nature, and scenes of human activity. Elegantly drawn linear contours are filled with bright, unshaded fields of pure color. There is a preference for profile or full-faced views, and a love of stylization that turns natural forms into decorative patterns but at the same time captures the appearance of the human body in motion. These conventions can be seen in the vivid murals surviving at Akrotiri, an outpost of Minoan culture on the island of Thera, north of Crete. One of the houses at Akrotiri has rooms dedicated to young women's initiation ceremonies. In the detail shown here, a young woman harvests saffron from the purple flowers of the fall crocus (**FIG. 5–4**). Saffron was used as a yellow dye, as a flavoring for food, or as a medicinal herb to alleviate menstrual cramps. The girl wears the typically colorful Minoan flounced skirt with a short-sleeved, open-breasted bodice, large earrings, and bracelets. She still has the shaved head, fringed hair, and long ponytail of a child, but the light blue color of her

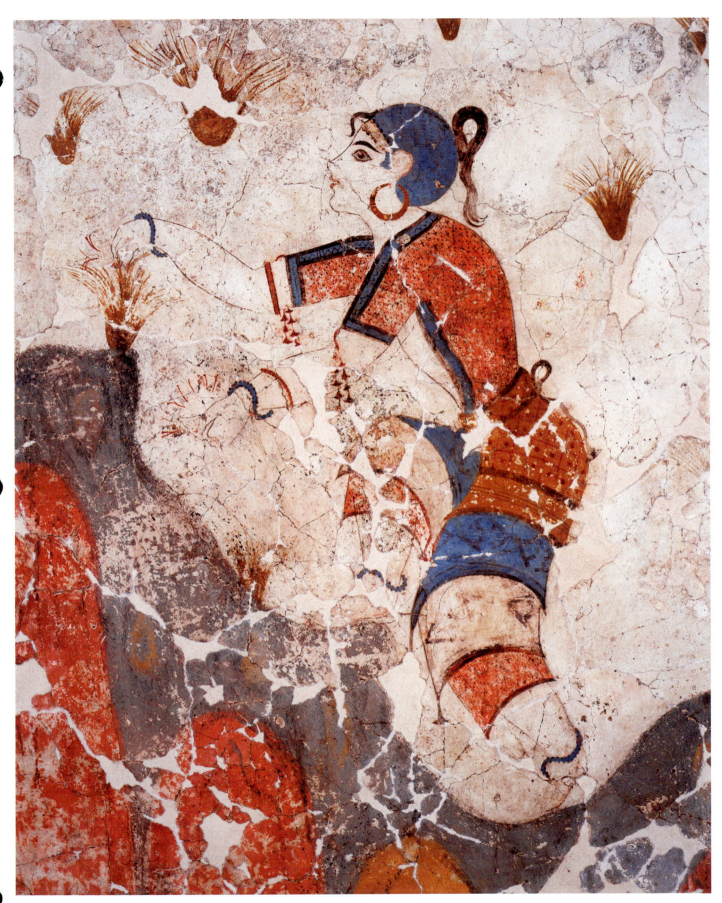

5–4 • YOUNG GIRL GATHERING SAFFRON CROCUS FLOWERS
Detail of wall painting, Room 3 of House Xeste, Akrotiri, Thera. Before 1630 BCE. Thera Foundation,
Petros M. Nomikos, Greece.

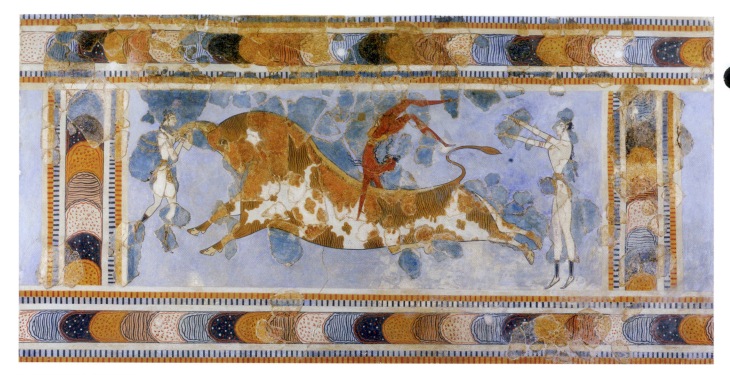

5–5 • BULL LEAPING

Wall painting with areas of modern reconstruction, from the "palace" complex, Knossos, Crete. Late Minoan period, c. 1550–1450 BCE. Height approx. 24½″ (62.3 cm). Archaeological Museum, Iraklion, Crete.

Careful sifting during excavation preserved many fragments of the paintings that once covered the walls at Knossos. The pieces were painstakingly sorted and cleaned by restorers and reassembled into puzzle pictures; more pieces were missing than found. Areas of color have been used in this reconstruction to fill the gaps, making it obvious which portions are restored, but allowing us to have a sense of the original image.

scalp indicates that hair is beginning to grow out, suggesting that she is entering adolescence.

One of the most famous paintings surviving from the palace at Knossos shows two women and a man engaging in the dangerous ritual of bull leaping (**FIG. 5–5**). (Minoan painters followed the convention of depicting women with pale skin and men with dark skin already seen in ancient Egypt; SEE FIG. 3–11.) The woman at right is prepared to catch the man who is in the midst of his leap, and the woman at left is grasping the bull by its horns, perhaps to help steady it, or perhaps preparing to begin her own vault.

Painting on a smaller scale decorated Minoan ceramics. A striking vessel from the east Cretan site of Palaikastro—a bottle known as the **OCTOPUS FLASK** and dating from about 1500–1450 BCE (**FIG. 5–6**)—is decorated with a dynamic arrangement of marine life, seemingly in celebration of Cretan maritime power. Like microscopic life teeming in a drop of seawater, sea creatures float among an octopus's curling, sucker-lined tentacles. The painter captures the grace and energy of natural forms while presenting them as a stylized design in conspicuous harmony with the vessel's bulging shape.

The skills of Minoan metalsmiths made their work highly sought after in mainland Greece. Jewelers developed an early sophistication in **granulation** (minute granules, or balls, of

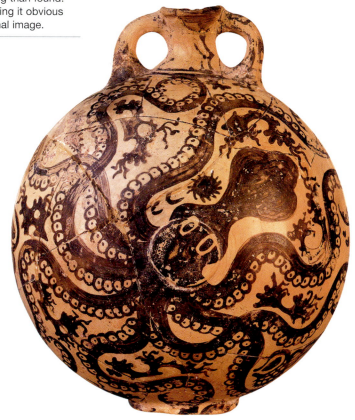

5–6 • OCTOPUS FLASK

From Palaikastro, Crete. c. 1500–1450 BCE. Ceramic, height 11″ (28 cm). Archaeological Museum, Iraklion, Crete.

Mythology and History

Human beings are storytellers, and virtually every society has created stories to give form to its religious beliefs and to attempt to explain the unexplained, including the origin of the universe, the meaning of birth and death, and the nature of good and evil. Throughout the world, mythological characters and their stories are among the most frequently represented subjects in the history of art. The main characters of Classical mythology—the traditional stories of Greek and Roman civilizations—are gods, demigods, heroes, and monsters. The behavior, relationships, and attitudes of such mythical characters mirror the beliefs and values of the society that created them.

Some myths seem to have originated in actual events. The Greek war against Troy in Asia Minor, for example, is now believed to have happened more than 300 years before it was mythologized in the *Iliad* and the *Odyssey*, by the poet known as

Homer, in the eighth century BCE. Homer tells of a Greek siege of the city of Troy, generally believed to have stood on the site of Hissarlik, in what is now Turkey. Paris, son of the Trojan king, abducted Helen, the most beautiful woman in the world and wife of King Menelaus of Sparta. Menelaus and his brother, King Agamemnon of Mycenae, the sons of Atreus, led the Greek troops in retaliation against Troy. Human warriors, gods, and goddesses took sides in the ten-year war.

It is not clear whether Helen, Menelaus, or Agamemnon existed, or even if the Trojan War actually took place, but the story probably had roots in a real battle or raid. Ancient Greek historians, accepting the Trojan War as history, dated it anywhere from 1334 BCE to 1150 BCE, certainly long before Homer turned it into a legendary combat.

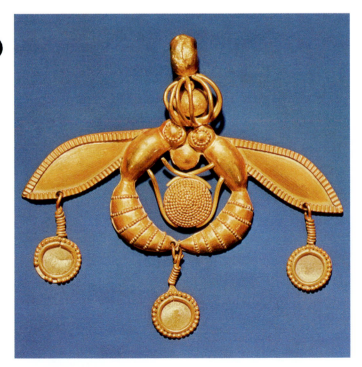

5–7 • PENDANT
In the form of two bees or wasps, from Chryssolakkos near Mallia, Crete. c. 1700–1550 BCE. Gold, height approx. 11³⁄₁₆″ (4.6 cm). Archaeological Museum, Iraklion, Crete.

precious metal fused to a surface). The use of this technique enlivens a **PENDANT** perhaps made for a necklace in about 1700–1550 BCE (**FIG. 5–7**). The artist arched a pair of bees or wasps around a circular drop of honey covered with granulation. Their sleek bodies, decorated with parallel rows of granules, are framed by a single pair of outspread wings.

The Mycenaeans

At some time about 3000 BCE, Greek-speaking peoples invaded the Greek peninsula. They brought advanced metalworking, ceramic, and architectural techniques and displaced the local Neolithic culture. Archaeologists use the term "Helladic" (from *Hellas*, the Greek name for Greece) to designate this Bronze Age period on mainland Greece. The Helladic period extends from about 3000 to 1000 BCE, concurrent with Cycladic and Minoan cultures. Later in the Aegean Bronze Age, the people of the mainland city of Mycenae rose to power and extended their influence into the Aegean islands as well.

Life in the fortified city of Mycenae and other mainland strongholds probably contrasted sharply with life in the open palace complexes on the island of Crete. Mycenaean communities were centered around strongholds controlled by local princes or kings. Evidence from shaft graves (deep vertical pits used for burial) dating from between 1600 and 1500 BCE suggests a society that became increasingly wealthy and stratified. Excavated by the German archaeologist Heinrich Schliemann (1822–1890) in 1876, the magnificent swords, daggers, scepters, jewelry, and drinking cups found in Mycenae graves mark the burials of an elite class of warriors.

Three bronze dagger blades found in one of these shaft graves are decorated with inlaid scenes. The artist cut shapes

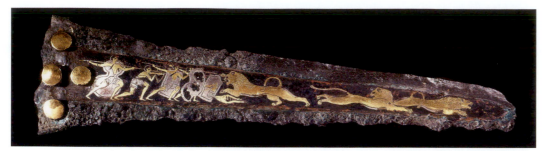

5–8 • DAGGER BLADE
From Shaft Grave IV,
Grave Circle A, Mycenae,
Greece. c. 1550–1500 BCE.
Bronze inlaid with gold, silver,
and niello, length 9⅜″ (23.8 cm).
National Archaeological
Museum, Athens.

out of different-colored metals—copper, silver, and gold—and inlaid them in the bronze blades, adding fine details in **niello** (a black sulfur alloy often inlaid into details incised into silver or gold). In the *Iliad*, Homer's epic poem about the Trojan War, the poet describes similar decoration on Agamemnon's armor and Achilles's shield. The blade shown here (**FIG. 5–8**) depicts four lunging hunters—Minoan in style—attacking a charging lion; the lion has already downed one of their companions, who lies under the animal's front legs. Two other lions retreat in full flight. Like the bull in FIGURE 5–5, these fleeing animals stretch out in the **flying gallop** pose to indicate speed and energy.

Other legends tell of a race of giants, the Cyclops, who moved huge stones and gave the name **cyclopean** to the large-stone masonry seen in Mycenaean citadels and tombs. By about 1600 BCE, members of the elite class on the mainland had begun building large aboveground burial places referred to as **tholos tombs**. More than 100 have been found on mainland Greece, nine of them in the vicinity of Mycenae. Possibly the most impressive is the so-called "Treasury of Atreus," built around 1300–1200 BCE (**FIG. 5–9**).

An uncovered, walled passageway about 114 feet long and 20 feet wide led to the door of a conical structure, the **beehive tomb**. The spacious circular main chamber—47½ feet in diameter and 43 feet high—is formed by a **corbeled vault**: a stone ceiling built up in regular **courses** (layers) of dressed stone in overlapping and ever-decreasing rings carefully calculated to

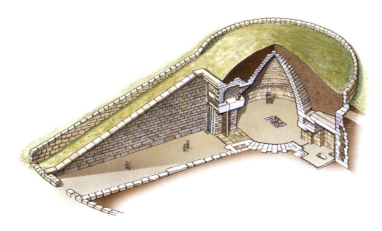

5–9 • CUTAWAY DRAWING OF THOLOS TOMB
(the so-called Treasury of Atreus), Mycenae, Greece.
c. 1300–1200 BCE.

5–10 • CORBELED VAULT
Interior of tholos tomb (the so-called Treasury of Atreus),
Mycenae, Greece. Limestone, height of vault approx. 43′ (13 m),
diameter 47′ 6″ (14.48 m).

For over a thousand years after it was constructed, this vast vaulted chamber remained the largest unobstructed interior space built in Europe. It was exceeded in size only by the Roman Pantheon (SEE FIG. 6–27), built 110–128 BCE.

👁 **Watch** an architectural simulation of a corbel vault construction on **MyArtsLab**

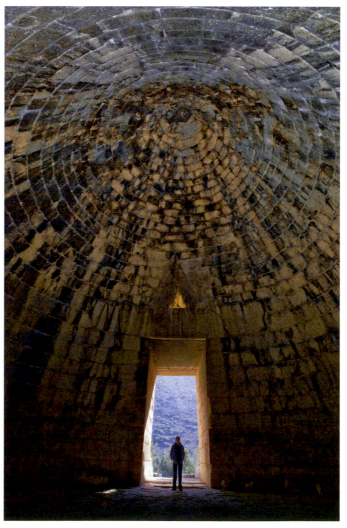

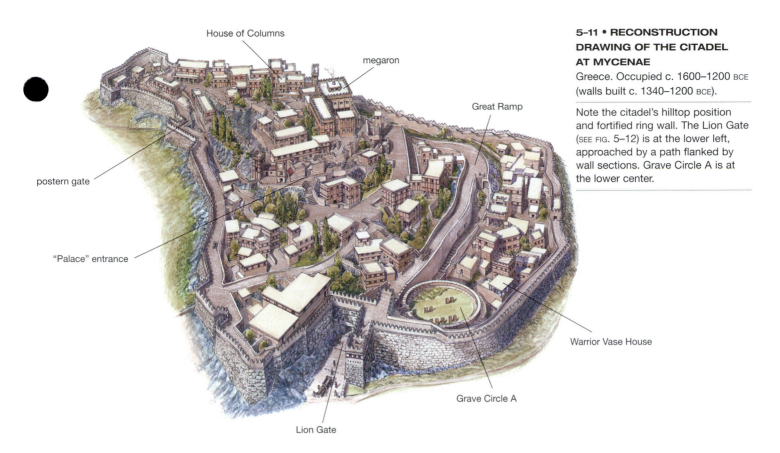

House of Columns

megaron

Great Ramp

postern gate

"Palace" entrance

Warrior Vase House

Grave Circle A

Lion Gate

5–11 • RECONSTRUCTION DRAWING OF THE CITADEL AT MYCENAE

Greece. Occupied c. 1600–1200 BCE (walls built c. 1340–1200 BCE).

Note the citadel's hilltop position and fortified ring wall. The Lion Gate (SEE FIG. 5–12) is at the lower left, approached by a path flanked by wall sections. Grave Circle A is at the lower center.

meet at the peak in a single **capstone** (topmost stone that joins the sides and completes a structure) (**FIG. 5–10**). Like Neolithic passage graves (SEE FIG. 1–12), the stone structure was covered by earth to form an artificial mound.

"Cyclopean" walls encircled the fortress of Mycenae (**FIG. 5–11**). A large building at the central and highest point may have been a ruler's residence. An entrance porch and vestibule led into a **megaron** (or "great room") where four large columns around a central hearth supported the ceiling. The roof section above the hearth was either raised or open to admit light and air and to permit smoke to escape. The imposing **LION GATE** (c. 1250 BCE) was the entrance to the citadel itself (**FIG. 5–12**). A post-and-lintel frame that once held massive wood and metal doors was crowned by a **relieving arch**, in this case, a **corbel arch** spanning the open space with layers of stones, each layer projecting over the preceding layer. In the opening over the door, a pair of lions nearly 9 feet tall flank a Minoan-style column that may symbolize the king's palace, and thus his royal power. The animals have lost their heads, but holes in the stones suggest that the heads were removable and probably fashioned of some precious material. If the lion heads were indeed made of bronze or gold, they must have created an imposing presence.

Mycenaean civilization does not have a long history. By 1200 BCE, invaders are believed to have crossed into mainland Greece and taken control of the major cities and citadels, precipitating a period of political and economic instability and upheaval. But by the middle of the eleventh century, a new culture was forming—one that looked back to the exploits of the Helladic warrior princes and the glories of a heroic age, while setting the stage for a truly new Greek civilization.

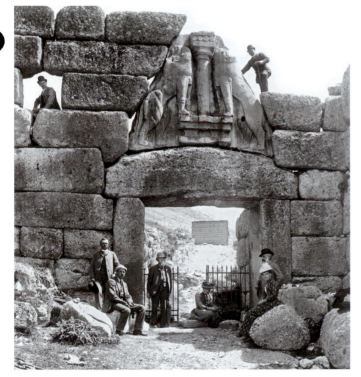

5–12 • LION GATE

Mycenae. c. 1250 BCE. Limestone relief, height of sculpture approx. 9′ 6″ (2.9 m).

In this historic photograph, Heinrich Schliemann, director of the excavation beginning in 1876, stands to the left of the gate, and his wife and partner in archaeology, Sophia, sits to the right.

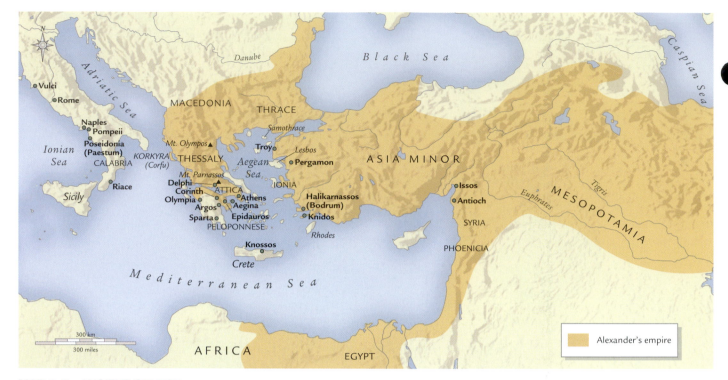

MAP 5-2 • ANCIENT GREECE

The cultural heartland of ancient Greece consisted of the Greek mainland, the islands of the Aegean, and the west coast of Asia Minor, but colonies on the Italic peninsula and the island of Sicily extended Greek cultural influence farther west into the Mediterranean. Alexander the Great created a Greek empire that extended from the Greek mainland and Egypt across Asia Minor and as far east as India.

The Emergence of Greek Civilization

What were the distinctive ideals of human representation and architectural design that emerged at the beginning of ancient Greek civilization?

Ancient Greece was a mountainous land of spectacular natural beauty, where olive trees and grapevines grew on steep hillsides, producing oil and wine. But with little good farmland, the Greeks turned to commerce and colonization to alleviate food shortages as the population grew. In towns, skilled artisans provided metal and ceramic wares to trade abroad for grain and raw materials. Greek merchant ships carried pots, olive oil, and bronzes around the Mediterranean Sea. Greek colonies in Italy, Sicily, and Asia Minor rapidly became powerful independent commercial and cultural centers, but they remained tied to the homeland by common language, traditions, religion, and history (MAP 5-2).

During the ninth and eighth centuries BCE, the Greeks began to form independently governed city-states—autonomous regions with a city such as Athens, Sparta, or Corinth, as its political, economic, religious, and cultural center—each with its own form of government and economy. By the sixth century, Athens began to assume cultural and commercial preeminence. Soon it had also established the notion that all citizens should share in the rights and responsibilities of government. This notion blossomed under Kleisthenes (d. 508 BCE, often called the father of democracy) into a system that was democratic in principle, but was in fact open only to Athenian men. Since they were not considered citizens, women took no official part in government, nor did slaves or men born outside Athens. The census of 309 BCE in Athens listed 21,000 citizens, 10,000 foreign residents, and 400,000 others—that is women, children, and slaves.

Within a remarkably brief time, Greek artists developed focused and distinctive ideals of human representation and architectural design that continue to exert a profound influence today. From about 900 BCE until about 100 BCE, they concentrated on a new, rather narrow range of subjects and produced an impressive body of work with clear stylistic aspirations in a variety of media. Greek artists were restless. They continually sought to change and improve existing artistic trends and fashions, effecting striking stylistic change over the course of a few centuries. This is in stark contrast to the situation we discovered in ancient Egypt, where a desire for permanence and continuity maintained stable artistic conventions for nearly 3,000 years. Art historians have named four of the successive stages in the development of ancient Greek art: Geometric, Archaic, Classical, and Hellenistic.

The Geometric Style

What we call the **Geometric** style flourished between about 900 and 700 BCE. One of a series of large Athenian ceramic vessels exemplifies the complex, linear, stylized decoration that gives this period its name (FIG. 5-13). Dated about 750–735 BCE, this huge pot was a grave marker, and funerary rituals are recorded in two bands, or registers, of decoration. In the top register, the body of the deceased lies on its side atop a funeral bier, perhaps awaiting the relatively new Greek practice of cremation.

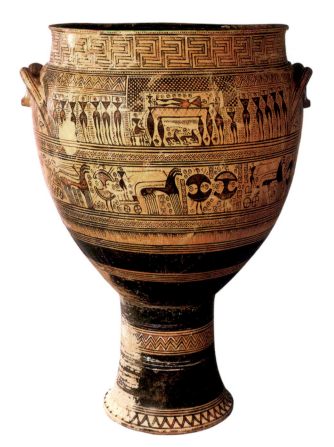

5–13 • FUNERARY VESSEL (KRATER)
From the Dipylon Cemetery, attributed to the Hirschfeld Workshop, Athens. c. 750–735 BCE. Ceramic, height 42⅝" (108 cm). The Metropolitan Museum of Art, New York. Rogers Fund, 1914 (14.130.14).

👁 **Watch** a video about the process of ceramics on **MyArtsLab**

Accompanying figures with their hands on their heads may be tearing their hair with grief. Triangles represent torsos; round dots stand for eyes in profile heads; lines depicting arms and legs swell into bulging thighs and calves. Below, a procession of horse-drawn chariots and foot soldiers, who look like walking shields, recall the athletic competitions or funeral games held to honor dead men. Figures are shown in either full-frontal or full-profile views. Any sense of three-dimensionality or receding space has been avoided to emphasize flat patterns and crisp outlines.

The Archaic Period

The Archaic period (c. 600–480 BCE) does not deserve its name. "Archaic" means "antiquated" or "old-fashioned," even "primitive," but this was a time of great new achievement. It was when Sappho wrote her inspired poetry on the island of Lesbos, when the legendary storyteller Aesop crafted his animal fables. Artists and architects shared in the growing prosperity as city councils and wealthy individuals sponsored the creation of sculpture, fine ceramics, and civic and religious buildings in cities and sanctuaries.

The earliest standing Greek temples date from the Archaic period. A temple was conceived both as earthly home and treasury for its honored god or goddess. Essentially, it is an idealized

shelter, built in conformity to a standard plan, a set of strict proportional relationships, and a regulated decorative system we call the Greek **orders** (see "The Greek Orders," p. 104).

Aegina. A fully developed and relatively well-preserved Archaic temple was built on the island of Aegina during the first quarter of the fifth century BCE (**FIG. 5–14**). The builders used the **Doric order**. Fluted **columns** without bases, resting directly on the **stylobate**, rise to unadorned, cushion-like **capitals**. The robust columns—each topped with a capital composed of a widely flaring **echinus** and a broad, blocky **abacus**—create a strong impression of permanence and stability. But because the columns swell in the middle and contract toward the top (a refinement known as **entasis**), the building retains a sense of energy and upward lift. Above the columns, a horizontal **entablature** (composed of **architrave**, **frieze**, and **cornice**) and the triangular **pediments** (forming the triangular **gable** ends) would have supported the temple's roof. In the Doric order, pediments and usually **metopes** were filled with sculpture.

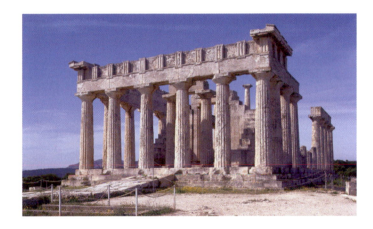

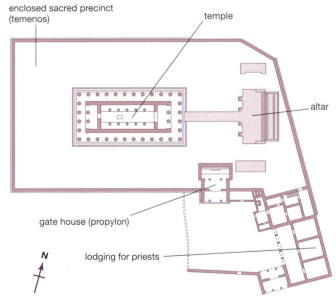

5–14 • EXTERIOR VIEW FROM THE EAST AND PLAN OF COMPLEX OF TEMPLE OF APHAIA
Aegina. c. 500 or 465 BCE. Column height about 17′ (5.18 m).

🔑 **View** the Closer Look for the Temple of Aphaia in Aegina on **MyArtsLab**

Orders

The three Greek architectural orders are **Doric**, **Ionic**, and **Corinthian**. Each order is composed of a system of interdependent parts whose proportions are based on mathematical ratios. No element of an order could be changed without producing a corresponding change in the other elements.

The basic components of each Greek order are the **column** and **entablature**, which function as the post and lintel of the structural system. All types of columns have a vertical **shaft** topped by a **capital**; some also have a base. The shafts are formed of round sections, or **drums**, which are joined inside by metal pegs. The **entablature** consists of an **architrave**, **frieze**, and **cornice**.

The Doric order is the oldest and plainest of the three. Shafts—**fluted**, or channeled, with sharp edges—rise directly from the stylobate without a base. Perhaps the most distinctive features are the **capitals**, where a cushion-like **echinus** signals the transition between **abacus** and shaft, and the frieze composed of the rhythmic alternation between projecting **triglyphs** and **metopes**, the latter sometimes filled with figural sculpture.

The Ionic order has more elongated proportions—the height of a column being about nine times its diameter. The flutes of the shafts are deeper and separated by flat surfaces called **fillets**, the capitals have distinctive scrolled **volutes**, and the frieze is a continuous strip.

The Corinthian order, initially a variation of the Ionic, was developed first for interiors, but by the Hellenistic period is common on exteriors as well. Its elaborate capitals are sheathed with stylized **acanthus** leaves below the volutes.

Beginning with the ancient Romans and continuing into the present, Western architects have invoked the Greek orders to express rationality and restraint, or to create playful variations on a traditional decorative system.

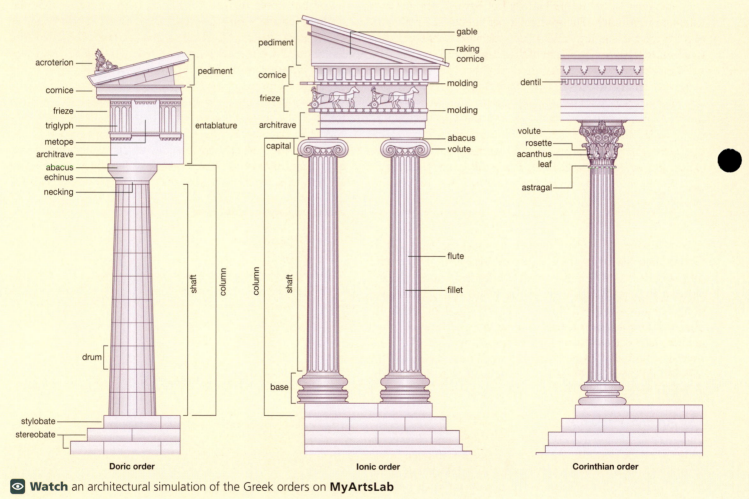

Doric order   Ionic order   Corinthian order

⊙ **Watch** an architectural simulation of the Greek orders on **MyArtsLab**

Like most Greek temples, this building was neither isolated nor situated in open space, but set in relation to an outside altar where religious ceremonies were focused. By enclosing the temple within a walled precinct or temenos, the designer could control the visitor's initial experience of the temple. As visitors entered the sacred space through a gatehouse, the temple would be seen at an oblique angle. Unlike ancient Egyptian temples, where long processional approaches led visitors directly to the flat entrance façade of a building (SEE FIGS. 3–13, 3–14), the Greek architect revealed the full shape of a closed, compact, sculptural mass from the outset, inviting visitors to walk around the exterior, exploring the rich sculptural embellishment on

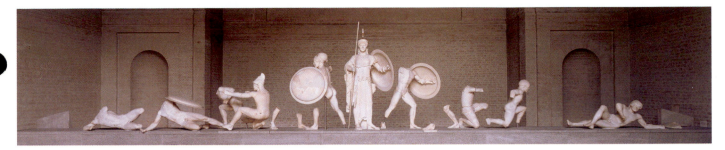

5–15 • SCULPTURE FROM THE WEST PEDIMENT OF THE TEMPLE OF APHAIA IN AEGINA
c. 500–490 or 470s BCE. Width about 49′ (15 m). Surviving fragments as assembled in the Staatliche Antikensammlungen und Glyptothek, Munich (early restorations removed).

pediments and friezes, rather than entering directly and seeking something within. Cult ceremonies, after all, took place at the altar outside temples.

Modern visitors, however, will not find exterior sculpture at Aegina. Nothing remains from the metopes, and substantial portions of the two pediments were purchased in the early nineteenth century by the future Ludwig I of Bavaria, and are now exhibited in Munich. The triangular pediments in Greek temples created challenging problems for sculptors intent on fitting figures into the tapering spaces of the outside corners. The scale of human figures could not change, only their poses. The west pediment at Aegina, traditionally dated about 500–490 BCE, before its eastern counterpart, represents a creative solution that became a design standard during the Classical period (**FIG. 5–15**). The subject, rendered in fully three-dimensional figures, is the participation of local warriors in the military expedition against Troy. Fallen warriors fill the angles at both ends of the pediment base, while others crouch and lunge, rising

in height toward an image of Athena as warrior goddess—who can fill the elevated pointed space at the center peak since she is allowed to be represented larger (hierarchic scale) than the humans who flank her.

Among the best-preserved fragments from Aegina is the **DYING WARRIOR** from the far right corner (**FIG. 5–16**). This tragic but noble figure struggles to raise himself, supported on bent leg and elbow. He rises to extract an arrow from his chest, even though his death seems certain. Originally the figure would have been painted and fitted with authentic bronze accessories, heightening the sense of reality (see "Color in Greek Sculpture," p. 106).

A similar figure appeared on the east pediment at Aegina, traditionally seen as postdating the west pediment by a decade or so (**FIG. 5–17**). The sculptor of this dying warrior also exploited the difficult framework of the pediment corner, only here, instead of an uplifted frontal form in profile, we see a twisted body capable of turning in space. The figure is

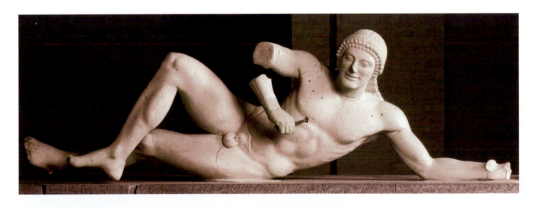

5–16 • DYING WARRIOR
From the right corner of the west pediment of the Temple of Aphaia, Aegina. c. 500–490 or 470s BCE. Marble, length 5′ 6″ (1.68 m). Staatliche Antikensammlungen und Glyptothek, Munich.

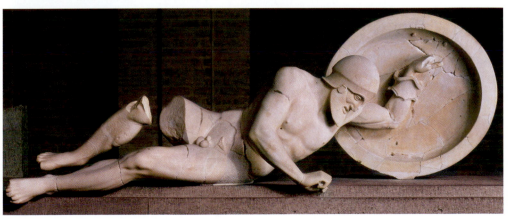

5–17 • DYING WARRIOR
From the left corner of the east pediment of the Temple of Aphaia, Aegina. c. 490–480 or 470s BCE. Marble, length 6′ (1.83 m). Staatliche Antikensammlungen und Glyptothek, Munich.

Color in Greek Sculpture

For many modern viewers, it comes as a real surprise, even a shock, that the stone sculptures of ancient Greece did not always have stark white, pure marble surfaces, comparable in appearance to—and consistent in taste with—the more recent but still classicizing sculptures of Michelangelo or Antonio Canova (SEE FIGS. 13–9, 17–12). But they were originally painted with brilliant colors. A close examination of Greek sculpture and architecture has long revealed evidence of polychromy, even to the unaided eye, but our understanding of the original appearance of these works has been greatly enhanced recently. Since the 1980s, German scholar Vinzenz Brinkmann has used extensive visual and scientific analysis to evaluate the traces of painting that remain on ancient Greek sculpture, employing tools such as ultraviolet and x-ray fluorescence, microscopy, and pigment analysis. Based on this research, he and his colleague Ulrike Koch-Brinkmann have fashioned reconstructions that allow us to imagine the exuberant effect these works would have had when they were new.

Illustrated here (FIG. 5–18) is their painted reconstruction of a kneeling archer from about 500 BCE that once formed part of the west pediment of the Temple of Aphaia at Aegina (SEE FIG. 5–15). To begin with they have replaced features of the sculpture—ringlet hair extensions, a bow, a quiver, and arrows—probably made of bronze or lead and attached to the stone after it was carved, using the holes still evident in the current state of the figure's hip and head (FIG. 5–19). Most stunning, however, is the diamond-shaped patterns that were painted on his leggings and sleeves, using pigments derived from malachite, azurite, arsenic, cinnabar, and charcoal. And the surfaces of such figures were not simply colored in. Artists created a sophisticated integration of three-dimensional form, color, and design. The patterning applied to this archer's leggings actually changes in size and shape in relation to the body beneath it, stretching out on expansive thighs and contracting on tapering ankles. Ancient authors indicate that sculpture was painted to make figures more lifelike, and these recent reconstructions certainly back them up.

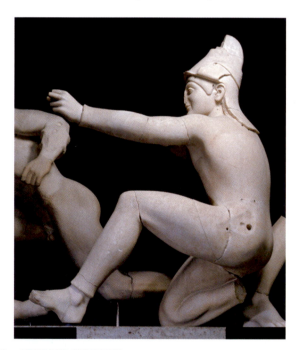

5–18 • Vinzenz Brinkmann and Ulrike Koch-Brinkmann
RECONSTRUCTION OF ARCHER
From the west pediment of the Temple of Aphaia, Aegina. 2004 CE. Staatliche Antikensammlungen und Glyptothek, Munich.

5–19 • **ARCHER ("PARIS")**
From the west pediment of the Temple of Aphaia, Aegina. c. 500–490 or 470s BCE. Marble. Staatliche Antikensammlungen und Glyptothek, Munich.

more precariously balanced on his shield, clearly about to collapse. There is an increased sense of softness in the portrayal of human flesh and a greater sophistication in tailoring bodily posture not only to the tapering shape of the pediment, but also to the expression of the warrior's own emotional involvement in the agony and vulnerability of his predicament, which in turn inspires a sense of pathos or empathy in the viewer. Over the course of a decade, the sculptors of Aegina allow us to trace the transition from Archaic toward Early Classical art.

Greek Gods and Goddesses	
Zeus	king of the gods
Hera	Zeus's wife and sister, queen of the gods
Athena	goddess of wisdom and civilization
Ares	god of war
Apollo	god of the sun, creativity, and the fine arts
Aphrodite	goddess of love and beauty
Artemis	goddess of the moon and hunting (twin sister of Apollo)
Hermes	god of commerce; also messenger of the gods
Hades	god of the underworld
Dionysos	god of wine
Hephaistos	god of fire and metalworking
Hestia	goddess of hearth and family
Demeter	goddess of crops and the harvest
Poseidon	god of the sea and earthquakes (brother of Zeus)
Eros	god of love (son of Aphrodite)
Although sometimes worshiped as a god, the hero Herakles, a son of Zeus, is a demigod, renowned for his physical strength.	

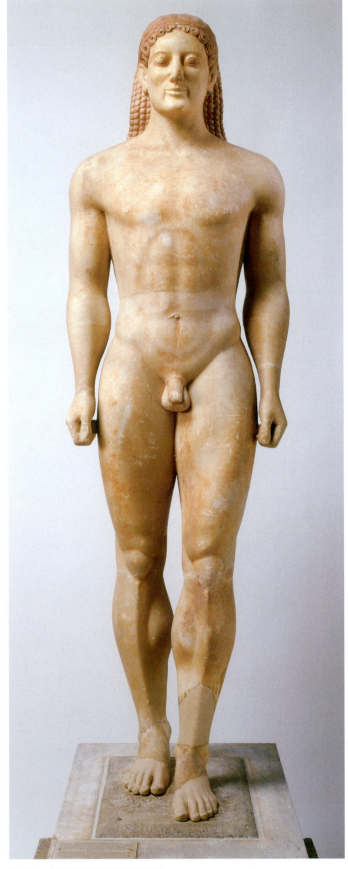

5–20 • ANAVYSOS KOUROS
From cemetery at Anavysos, near Athens. c. 530 BCE. Marble with remnants of paint, height 6′ 4″ (1.93 m). National Archaeological Museum, Athens.

Kouros and Kore. In addition to carving sculpture for temple exteriors, Archaic sculptors also created free-standing statues. Usually life-size or larger, most were made of white marble and, like the Aegina pediment, were originally painted in bright colors to enhance their lifelike qualities. Some bore inscriptions indicating that they had been commissioned by individual men or women for a commemorative purpose. While some marked graves, most stood in sanctuaries, where they lined the sacred way from the entrance to the main temple.

A female statue of this type is called a **kore** (plural, *korai*), Greek for "young woman," and a male statue is called a **kouros** (plural, *kouroi*), meaning "young man." The Archaic *korai*, always clothed, probably represented deities, priestesses, or nymphs. The *kouroi*, nearly always nude, have been variously identified as gods, warriors, and victorious athletes. Because the Greeks associated young athletic males with fertility and family continuity, the *kouroi* may have symbolized ancestors.

A statue known as the **ANAVYSOS KOUROS** dating from about 530 BCE (**FIG. 5–20**) exemplifies the Archaic Greek ideal. Reminiscent of standing males in Egyptian sculpture (SEE FIG. 3–7), this young Greek is shown frontally, arms at his sides, fists clenched, and one leg striding in front of the other. Unlike ancient Egyptian stone statuary, however, is the figure's rounded athletic body and the way the sculptor has freed the arms and legs from the block of stone to make the figure more free and energetic. The carefully rendered anatomy and bulging muscularity enhance this sense of lifelike power and presence. The eyes are unnaturally large and wide open, and the mouth forms a characteristic closed expression, known as the **Archaic smile**, apparently used to enliven the expressiveness

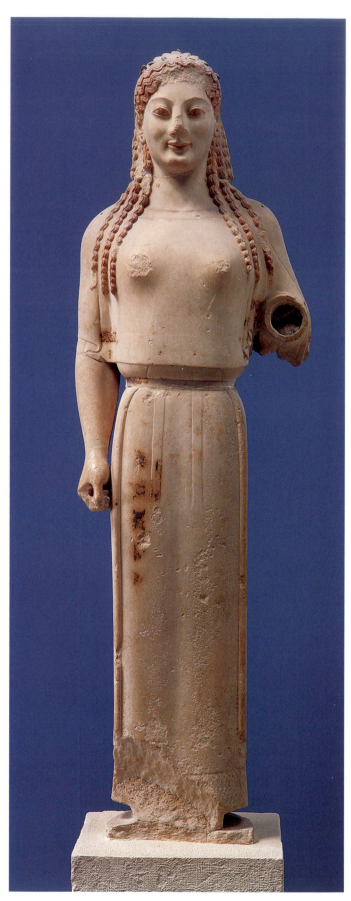

of the face. Unlike his partially clothed Egyptian counterpart, this young Greek's total nudity serves to remove the figure from a specific place, time, or social class. He is a symbol or type, not a specific individual.

The **"PEPLOS" KORE** (FIG. 5–21), dated about the same time as the *Anavysos Kouros* (though she is a votive rather than a funerary statue), exhibits comparably rounded body forms, even though she is clothed. Her arms and head convey a sense of soft flesh covering an anatomically correct bone structure, and the smooth, feminine curves of her body are apparent under her garment. The original painted colors on both body and clothing must have made her seem even more lifelike, and she also once wore a metal crown and jewelry. The name we use for this figure is based on an assessment of her clothing, but it has recently been shown that she is not wearing the simple *peplos* of a young girl but a sheath-like garment—originally painted with a frieze of animals—identifying her instead as a goddess, perhaps Athena or Artemis. Her missing left forearm—which was made of a separate piece of marble fitted into the still-visible socket—would have extended forward horizontally and may have held an attribute that provided the key to her identity.

Ceramic Painting. In the painting of Archaic ceramic vessels, artists presented not independent figures, but scenes evoking a story. Abandoning the narrow bands of decoration characteristic of the Geometric period (SEE FIG. 5–13), Athenian painters gradually increased the size of figures until one or two narrative scenes occupied the body of a vessel. An amphora—a large, all-purpose storage jar—contemporary with the *kouros* and *kore* just discussed illustrates well this development (SEE FIG. 5–1). One side shows the Trojan War heroes Ajax and Achilles in a rare moment of relaxation playing dice. This is an episode not included in any literary source, but for Greeks familiar with the story, this anecdotal portrayal of friendly play would have been a poignant reminder that before the end of the war, the heroes would both be dead, Achilles in battle and Ajax by suicide. Knowing the story was critical to engaging with such paintings, artists often included identifying labels beside the characters to guide viewers to the narrative source.

In painting this amphora, Exekias used a technique known as **black-figure**, the principal mode of ceramic painting in the sixth century BCE. **Slip** (a mixture of clay and water) is used to silhouette the shapes of figures against the unpainted clay of the background. Details were incised into the slip with a sharp tool inside the silhouetted shapes. The characteristic color contrast occurred only in the firing process when the slip emerged from the kiln as black and the body clay of the vessel turned red. On some pieces, touches of white and reddish-purple gloss, made of metallic pigments mixed with slip, enhanced the decorative effect.

Although painters were still creating handsome black-figure wares in the last third of the sixth century BCE, some turned away from this meticulous process to a new, more fluid **red-figure** technique—so called because red figures stand out against a black background. Painters first covered the pot with slip but left or "reserved" the shapes of the figures unpainted to reveal the underlying clay body. Instead of engraving details within a silhouetted area covered by slip, painters drew on the reserved areas with a fine brush dipped in liquid slip. As with

Krater with the Death of Sarpedon ▶

Euphronios (painter) and Euxitheos (potter). c. 515 BCE. Red-figure decoration on a calyx krater. Ceramic, height of krater 18″ (45.7 cm). Etruscan Museum, Villa Giulia, Rome.

Hypnos (Sleep) and Thanatos (Death), identified by inscriptions that seem to emerge from their mouths, face each other on either side of the fallen body of Sarpedon, gently raising the slain warrior.

The god Hermes is identified not only by inscription, but also by his caduceus (staff with coiled snakes) and winged headgear. The attention to contours, distribution of drapery folds, and overlapping of forms give the twisting figure a sense of three-dimensionality.

Euphronios makes it appear as if Sarpedon's left leg is projecting into the viewer's space through the technique of **foreshortening**.

The painting's field is framed by dense bands of detailed ornament, placed to highlight the contours of the krater.

Sarpedon's body is turned to face the viewer, allowing Euphronios to outline every muscle and ligament of the torso, showing off both his knowledge of anatomy and his virtuosity in using the newly developed red-figure technique.

Blood continues illogically to pour from the wounds in Sarpedon's corpse, not out of ignorance on the part of the artist but because of his determination to heighten the dramatic effect of the scene.

🔍 **View** the Closer Look for Euphronios's krater with the Death of Sarpedon on **MyArtsLab**

the black-figure technique, after firing, the slip turned black and the clay body red. But here the result was a lustrous dark vessel with red-colored figures articulated with black painted details. The greater ease, speed, and flexibility of this technique allowed artists to create more lively figures with a more developed sense of bodily form. Painters quickly adopted it as the preferred method of painting on ceramics.

One of the best-known red-figure artists was Euphronios. His rendering of the Death of Sarpedon, about 515 BCE (see "A Closer Look," above), is painted on a krater—a vessel used as a punch bowl during a symposium, a social gathering of rich and powerful men. According to Homer's *Iliad*, Sarpedon, a son of Zeus and a mortal woman, was killed by the Greek warrior Patroklus while fighting for the Trojans. Euphronios captures the scene in which the warrior is being carried off to the underworld, the land of the dead.

Euphronios has created a balanced composition of verticals and horizontals that takes the shape of the vessel into account. The bands of decoration above and below the scene echo the long horizontal of the dead fighter's body, which seems to levitate in the gentle grasp of its bearers, and the inward-curving lines of the handles mirror the arching backs and extended wings of Hypnos and Thanatos. The upright figures of the lance-bearers on each side and Hermes in the center counterbalance the horizontal and diagonal elements of the composition. While conveying a sense of the mass and energy of human subjects, Euphronios also portrayed the elaborate details of their clothing, musculature, and facial features with the fine tip of a brush. A palpable sense of pathos in the face of Sarpedon's fate seems to connect Euphronios's work with the dying warriors of the pediments at Aegina (SEE FIGS. 5–16, 5–17), which would be sculpted a little over a decade later.

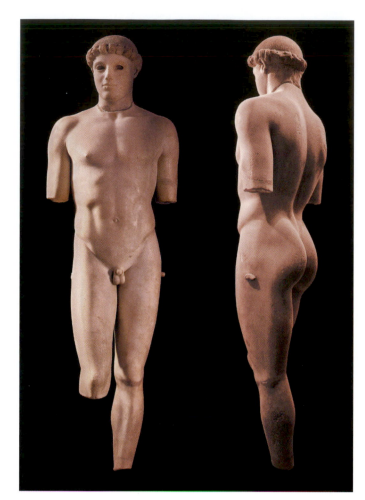

The Classical Period

What features define Classical Greek art and architecture? How did they develop through the fifth and fourth centuries BCE?

The early fifth century BCE was marked by a series of military invasions from Persia. Greek city-states banded together against their common foe, and in 480 BCE an alliance led by Athens and Sparta defeated the invaders. Perhaps this success against the Persians gave the Greeks a self-confidence that inspired and accelerated artistic development, for during the next two decades their art took a new stylistic direction, away from elegant stylization and toward a sense of greater faithfulness to the natural appearance of human beings and their world, initiating what art historians refer to as the Classical period of ancient Greek art. This period of marked change followed an evolution that scholars have subdivided into the Early Classical period (from the end of the Persian Wars to about 450 BCE), the "High" Classical period (c. 450–400 BCE), and the Late Classical period (400–323 BCE).

The Early Classical Period (c. 480–450 BCE)

In free-standing sculpture, the Greeks shifted in only a few generations from the stiff frontality of Archaic *kouroi* to more relaxed, lifelike figures such as the so-called **"KRITIOS" BOY** (**FIG. 5–22**). In contrast to the over-life-size *Anavysos Kouros* (SEE FIG. 5–20), the *"Kritios" Boy* originally stood only about 4 feet tall. The softly rounded body forms, broad facial features, and calm expression—lacking even a trace of the tight Archaic smile—give the figure an air of self-confident seriousness. The easy pose contrasts markedly with the more rigid bearing of Archaic *kouroi*. His weight rests on his left, "engaged" leg, while his relaxed right leg bends slightly at the knee. The curve in his spine counters the slight shifting of his hips and the subtle drop of one shoulder. We see here the beginnings of **contrapposto**, the convention (later developed in full by "High" Classical sculptors such as Polykleitos) of presenting standing figures with opposing alternations of tension and relaxation around a central axis, which will come to dominate Classical art.

5–22 • "KRITIOS" BOY
c. 480–475 BCE. Marble, height 3′ 10″ (1.17 m). Akropolis Museum, Athens.

When the *"Kritios" Boy* was excavated from debris at the Akropolis of Athens, the statue was thought by its finders to be by the Greek sculptor Kritios, whose work they knew only from Roman copies.

5–23 • Foundry Painter
A BRONZE FOUNDRY
Red-figure decoration on a kylix found in Vulci, Italy. 490–480 BCE. Ceramic, diameter of kylix 12″ (31 cm). Staatliche Museen zu Berlin, Preussischer Kulturbesitz, Antikensammlung.

The painter has masterfully organized his workshop scene within the flaring space that extends upward from the foot of the vessel and along its curving underside up to the lip, thereby using a constricted circle as the ground-line for the composition.

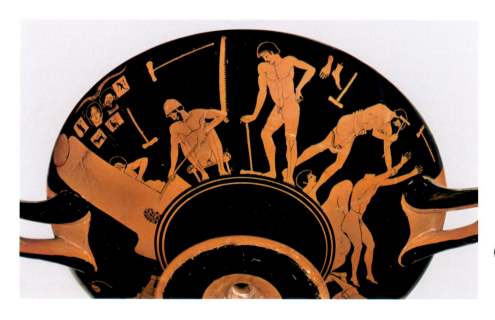

The technique of modeling and hollow-casting bronze was developed at the end of the Archaic period, making possible more complex action poses with outstretched arms and legs. These were very difficult to create in marble, since unbalanced figures might topple over and extended appendages might break off due to their unsupported weight. The painted underside of a red-figure **kylix** (a shallow, two-handled drinking cup) portrays work in a late Archaic foundry (**FIG. 5–23**) and shows that the Greeks were creating large bronze statues in active poses as early as the first decades of the fifth century BCE. On the walls of the workshop hang tools and other foundry paraphernalia—hammers, molds of a human foot and hand, and several sketches. One worker, wearing what looks like a present-day construction helmet, squats to tend the furnace at left, aided by an assistant who peeks from behind. The man in the center—perhaps the supervisor—leans on a staff, while a third worker assembles a leaping bronze figure braced against a molded support. The unattached head lies between the worker's feet.

A pair of over-life-size bronze figures known as the *Riace Warriors* (**FIG. 5–24**) illustrates the developing skill of ancient Greek sculptors in depicting the male nude figure. Found by

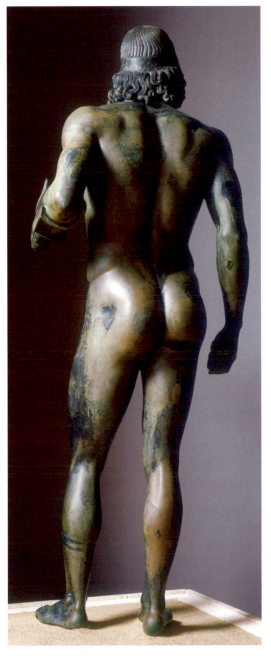
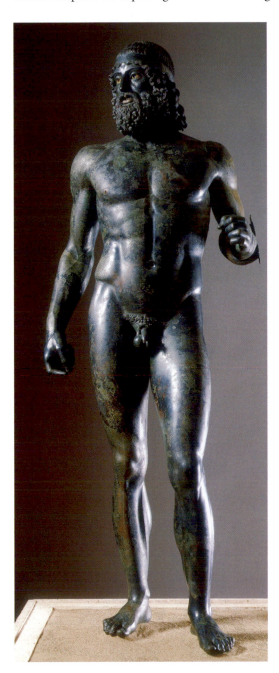

5–24 • WARRIOR
found in the sea off Riace, Italy. c. 460–450 BCE. Bronze with bone and glass eyes, silver teeth, and copper lips and nipples, height 6′ 9″ (2.05 m). Museo Archaeologico Nazionale, Reggio Calabria, Italy.

The man held a shield (parts are still visible) on his left arm and a spear in his right hand. He may have been part of a monument commemorating a military victory, perhaps against the Persians.

Classic and Classical

Our words "classic" and "classical" come from the Latin word *classis*, referring to the division of the people in a society into "classes" based on wealth. "Classic" has come to mean "first class" or "the standard of excellence." Greek artists in the fifth century BCE sought to create ideal images based on perfect mathematical proportions. Since Roman artists were also inspired by these ideals, the term "Classical" often refers to the cultures of ancient Greece and Rome. By extension, the word may also mean "in the style of ancient Greece and Rome," whenever or wherever that style is used. In the most general usage, a classic is something—whether a literary work, automobile, a film, even a soft drink—of lasting quality and universal esteem.

a diver on the seabed near Riace, a town on the southeastern coast of Calabria, Italy, the statues, dating from about 460–450 BCE, may have either been thrown from a sinking ship by sailors trying to lighten the load or been lost in a shipwreck. The figure illustrated here reveals a striking balance between the idealized smoothness of "perfected" anatomy conforming to Early Classical standards and the reproduction of details observed from nature, such as the swelling veins on the backs of the hands. *Contrapposto* is further developed here than in the "*Kritios*" *Boy*, with a more pronounced counterbalance between tension (right leg and left arm) and relaxation (left leg and right arm), introducing the prospect of a shift in posture and with it the possibility of movement and life. The lifelike quality of this bronze is further heightened by inserted eyeballs of bone and colored glass, silver plating on the teeth, copper inlays on lips and nipples, and attached eyelashes and eyebrows of separately cast strands of bronze. This accommodation of the intense study of the human figure with idealism that belies the irregularity of nature will be continued by artists in the "High" Classical period.

The "High" Classical Period (c. 450–400 BCE)

The use of the word "high" to qualify the art of this time reflects the value judgments of art historians who have considered this period a pinnacle of artistic refinement, producing works that set a standard of unsurpassed excellence. Some have even referred to this period as Greece's "Golden Age," although these decades were also marked by the turmoil and destruction of the Peloponnesian War. Without a common enemy, Sparta and Athens turned on each other. Sparta dominated the Peloponnese peninsula and much of the rest of mainland Greece, while Athens controlled the Aegean and became the wealthy and influential center of a maritime empire. Today we remember Athens more for its cultural and intellectual brilliance and its experiments with democratic government, which reached its zenith in the fifth century BCE under the charismatic leader Perikles (c. 495–429 BCE), than for the imperialistic tendencies of its considerable commercial power.

The Athenian Akropolis, the hill that formed the city's ceremonial center, visually expressed the city's values and its civic pride. The Persians had destroyed the site's earlier buildings and statues in 480 BCE, and Perikles promoted and organized the rebuilding of its monuments, beginning with the Parthenon in about 447 BCE. According to Greek mythology, Athena, goddess of wisdom and civilization, claimed Athens as her city, and this new temple, dedicated to the Virgin Athena (*Athena Parthenos* in Greek), would proclaim this association, rising triumphantly over the city. The Parthenon, designed and built by the architects Kallikrates and Iktinos, was meant to dominate the other structures on the hilltop site (FIG. 5–25). The builders used the finest white marble throughout—even on the roof, replacing the customary terra-cotta tiles. The renowned sculptor Phidias designed its sculptural decorations and supervised the entire Akropolis project. The building itself was completed in 438 BCE, and its sculpture, executed by Phidias and other sculptors in his workshop, was finished in 432 BCE.

In its structure and design, the Parthenon illustrates the refinement of ancient Greek architecture (FIG. 5–26). It follows the traditional cella and peristyle **plan**, and to counteract the optical illusions that would distort its appearance when seen from a distance, the architects made many subtle adjustments to strict regularity. Since long horizontal lines appear to sag in the center, the architects designed both the base of the temple and the entablature to curve slightly upward to correct this optical distortion. The columns have a subtle swelling (**entasis**) and tilt inward slightly toward the center of the building. In addition, the corners are strengthened visually by reducing the space between columns at the ends of the colonnades. These subtle refinements in the arrangement of seemingly regular elements give the Parthenon a buoyant organic appearance and prevent it from looking like a heavy, lifeless stone box.

As in most temples, sculpture in the round filled both pediments of the Parthenon, set on the projecting shelf of the cornice and secured to the wall with metal pins. The sculptors expertly rendered the human form beneath the clinging draperies that create curvilinear patterns rippling over torsos, breasts, and knees. Most of the works of sculpture from the Parthenon have been damaged or lost over the centuries, but using the locations of existing pinholes, scholars have determined the placement of the surviving statues and can speculate on the poses of the missing ones.

The statues of the east pediment above the entrance to the cella are the best preserved of the two groups (FIG. 5–27).

5-25 • RECONSTRUCTION DRAWING OF THE AKROPOLIS
Athens. c. 400 BCE.

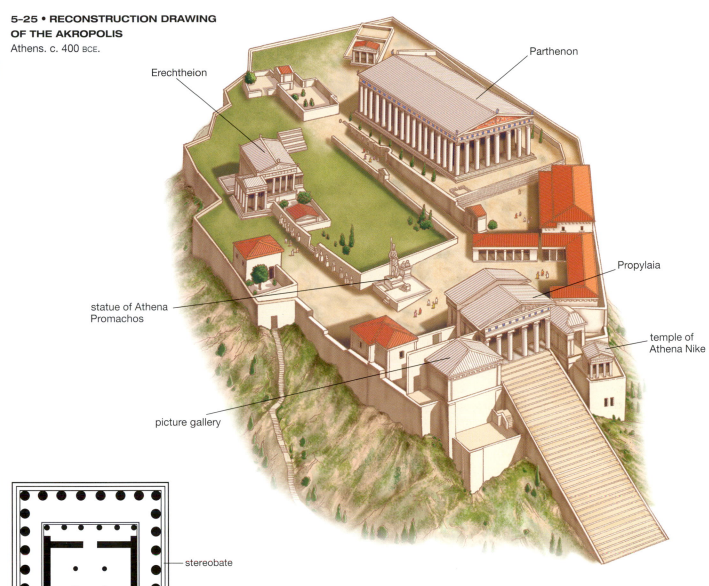

Erechtheion

Parthenon

statue of Athena Promachos

Propylaia

temple of Athena Nike

picture gallery

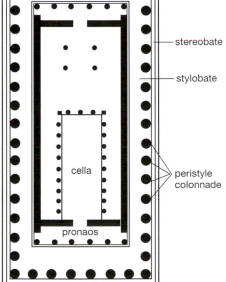

stereobate

stylobate

cella

peristyle colonnade

pronaos

5-26 • Kallikrates and Iktinos PLAN AND EXTERIOR VIEW FROM THE NORTHWEST OF THE PARTHENON
Akropolis, Athens. c. 447–432 BCE.

Explore the architectural panoramas of the Parthenon on **MyArtsLab**

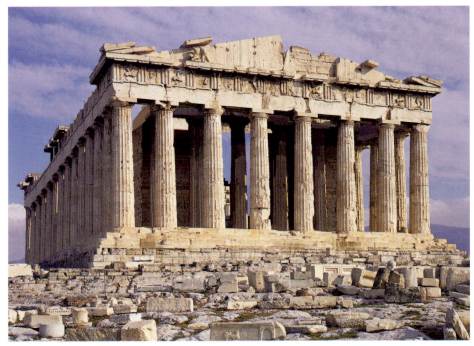

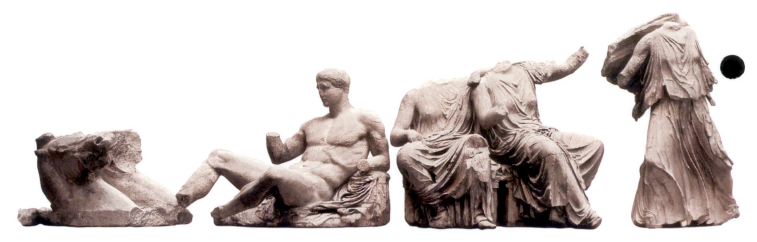

5-27 • PHOTOGRAPHIC MOCK-UP OF THE EAST PEDIMENT OF THE PARTHENON
(using photographs of the extant marble sculpture). c. 447–432 BCE. The British Museum, London.

At the beginning of the nineteenth century, Thomas Bruce, the Earl of Elgin and British ambassador to Constantinople, acquired much of the surviving sculpture from the Parthenon, which was being used by the Turks for military purposes at the time. He shipped the pieces back to London in 1801 to decorate his lavish mansion, but after a financial dispute and other difficulties, he sold them to the British government in 1816. Referred to as the Elgin Marbles, most of the sculpture is now in London's British Museum, including all the elements seen here. In recent times, the Greek government has tried unsuccessfully to have the Elgin Marbles returned.

Originally over 90 feet long, the pediment lacks its central part, amounting to about 40 feet, probably destroyed in the fifth century when Christians turned the Parthenon into a church and built an **apse** at the east end. The ensemble illustrated the birth of Athena. The missing statues in the center probably showed Zeus seated on a throne, and standing next to him, Athena, who according to mythology had emerged fully grown from his head. The male nude, who fits so easily into the sloping pediment toward the left, has been identified as the hero Herakles with his lion skin or the wine god Dionysos lying on a panther skin. The two seated women next to him may be the earth and grain goddesses, Demeter and Persephone. The running female figure just left of center is Iris, messenger of the gods, already spreading the news of Athena's birth. The three female figures on the right side are probably Hestia (a sister of Zeus and goddess of the hearth), Dione (one of Zeus's many consorts), and her daughter Aphrodite (goddess of love), who reclines like her male counterpart on the other side of the pediment to conform to its tapering triangular shape. The horses' heads represent (at far left) the ascending chariot of the sun god, Helios (Apollo), and (at far right) the descending moon goddess, Selene.

Originally, the Parthenon's white marble columns and inner walls supported bands of brightly painted low-relief sculpture. The exterior Doric frieze included 92 carved metopes with scenes of victory. On the south side, they depicted the fight between half-human centaurs and a legendary Greek tribe known as the Lapiths. The Lapith victory over the centaurs represented the triumph of reason over animal passions. In one relief (**FIG. 5–28**), what should be a death struggle seems more like a choreographed, athletic ballet, displaying the Lapith's muscles and graceful movements against the implausible backdrop of his carefully draped cloak.

Inside the Parthenon's Doric peristyle, an Ionic frieze (see "The Greek Orders," p. 104) decorated the upper temple wall

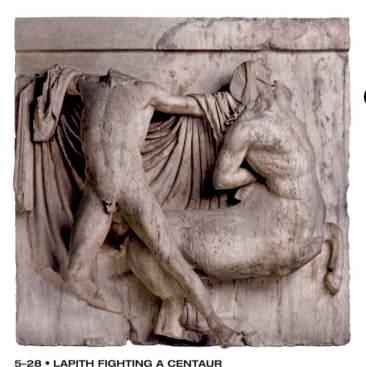

5-28 • LAPITH FIGHTING A CENTAUR
Metope relief from the Doric frieze on the south side of the Parthenon. c. 447–432 BCE. Marble, height 56″ (1.42 m). The British Museum, London.

(**FIG. 5–29**). Unlike the staccato alternation of metope and triglyph in the Doric frieze, the Ionic frieze consisted of a continuous band of sculpture. Here, along the 525-foot-long strip, a procession unfolds, traditionally interpreted as an evocation of the great Panathenaic festival when the women of Athens carried a new wool *peplos* to the Akropolis sanctuary to clothe an ancient wooden cult statue of Athena. Throughout the frieze,

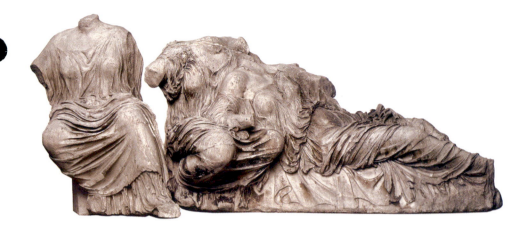

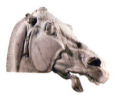

carefully planned rhythmic variations enliven the composition. Horses plunge ahead at full gallop; women proceed with a slow, stately step; parade marshals pause to look back at the progress of those behind; and gods and goddesses seated on benches await the arrival of the marchers.

The maidens in this detail, who walk with such grace and dignity, represent the Greek ideal of young womanhood, just as the muscular but poised marshals idealize manhood. The procession they participate in is an ideal one, outside time and place. The marble sculpture of the frieze was originally painted in dark blue, red, and ocher, and details such as the bridles and reins of the horses were added in bronze. To compensate for the dim lighting inside the peristyle, the top of the frieze band is carved in slightly higher relief than the lower part, tilting the figures outward to catch reflected light from the pavement. The procession of maidens attended by parade marshals, although only a fragment of the architectural decoration, epitomizes the extraordinary quality characterizing every detail of the temple.

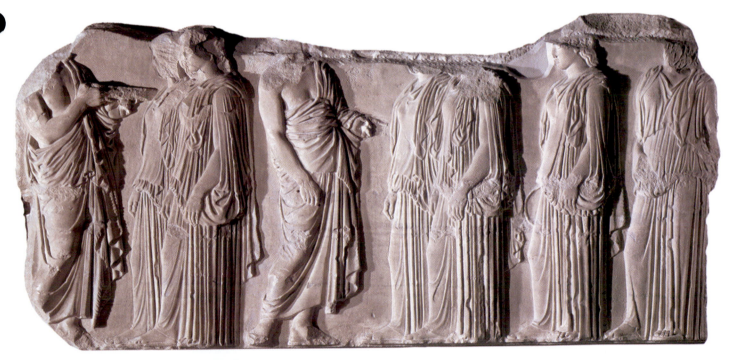

5-29 • MARSHALS AND YOUNG WOMEN
Detail of the Procession, from the Ionic frieze on the east side of the Parthenon. c. 447–432 BCE.
Marble, height 3′ 6″ (1.08 m). Musée du Louvre, Paris.

A recent interpretation by art historian Joan Connelly has challenged the traditional reading of the frieze as an ideal rendering of a contemporary event. She argues that—consistent with what we know of temple decoration elsewhere— what is portrayed here is not contemporary but mythological history: the legendary Athenian King Erechtheus, who sacrificed one of his own daughters to save the city of Athens from an external enemy. This theme, also incorporating a procession, would have had obvious resonance with the recent Athenian victory over the Persians.

The Canon of Polykleitos

Just as Greek architects defined and followed a set of strict standards for ideal temple design, Greek sculptors sought an ideal for representations of the human body. Studying human appearances closely, the sculptors of the Classical period selected those attributes they considered most desirable and beautiful, such as regular facial features, smooth skin, and particular body proportions, then combined them into a single ideal.

The best-known art theorist of the Classical period was the sculptor Polykleitos of Argos. About 450 BCE he developed a set of rules for constructing what he considered the ideal human figure, which he set down in a treatise called "The Canon" (*kanon* is Greek for "measure," "rule," or "law"). To illustrate his theory, Polykleitos created a larger-than-life bronze statue of a man carrying a spear—perhaps the hero Achilles **(FIG. 5–30)**. Neither the treatise nor the original statue has survived, but both were widely discussed in the writings of his contemporaries, and later Roman artists made marble copies of the *Spear Bearer* (*Doryphoros*). By studying these copies, scholars have tried to determine the set of measurements that defined the ideal proportions in Polykleitos's canon.

The canon included a system of ratios between a basic unit and the length of various body parts. Some studies suggest that his basic unit may have been the length of the figure's index finger or the width of its hand across the knuckles; others suggest that it was the height of the head from chin to hairline. The canon also included guidelines for *symmetria* ("commensurability"), by which Polykleitos meant the relationship of body parts to one another. In the *Spear Bearer*, he explored not only proportions but also the relationships between weight-bearing and relaxed legs and arms in a perfectly balanced figure. The cross-balancing of supporting and relaxed elements in a figure is sometimes referred to as *contrapposto*.

The Roman marble copy of the bronze *Spear Bearer* illustrated here shows a male athlete, perfectly balanced, with the whole weight of the upper body supported by the straight (engaged) right leg. The left leg is bent at the knee, with the left foot poised on the ball of the foot, suggesting the shift of weight involved in movement. The pattern of tension and relaxation is reversed in the arrangement of the arms, with the right relaxed on the engaged side and the left bent to support the weight of the (missing) spear. This dynamically balanced body pose— characteristic of Classical standing figure sculpture—evolves out of

the pose of the *"Kritios" Boy* (SEE FIG. 5–22) of a generation earlier. The tilt of the *Spear Bearer*'s hipline is a little more pronounced to accommodate the raising of the left foot onto its ball, and the head is turned toward the same side as the engaged leg.

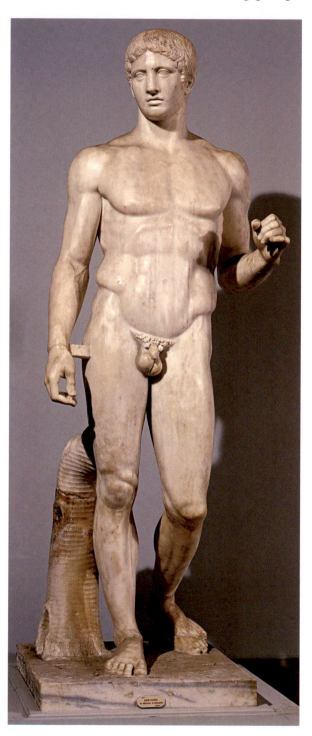

5–30 • Polykleitos SPEAR BEARER (DORYPHOROS)
Perhaps Achilles. Roman copy after the original bronze of c. 450–440 BCE (tree trunk and bracing strut are Roman additions). Marble, height 6′ 11″ (2.12 m). Museo Archaeologico Nazionale, Naples.

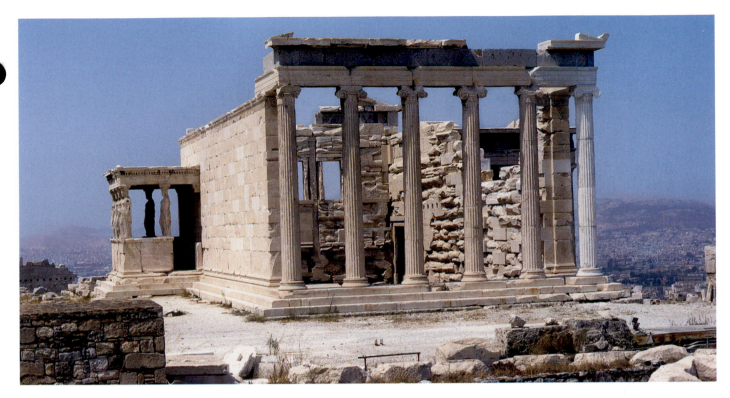

5-31 • ERECHTHEION
View from the east, porch of the maidens at left. Akropolis, Athens. 430s–406 BCE.

Upon completion of the Parthenon, Perikles commissioned a monumental gatehouse for the Akropolis, the Propylaia. Work began on it in 437 and stopped in 432, with the structure still incomplete. The Propylaia had no sculptural decoration, but its north wing eventually became the earliest known museum (meaning "home of the Muses"), a gallery built specifically to house a collection of paintings for public view.

Construction of the **ERECHTHEION**, the second important temple erected on the Akropolis under Perikles's building program (**FIG. 5–31**), began in the 430s and ended in 406 BCE, just before the fall of Athens to Sparta. The asymmetrical plan on several levels reflects the building's multiple functions in housing several shrines, and it also conforms to the sharply sloping terrain on which it is located. The Erechtheion stands on the site of the mythical contest between the sea god Poseidon and Athena for patronage of Athens. During this contest, Poseidon struck a rock with his trident (three-pronged harpoon), bringing forth a spout of water, but Athena gave an olive tree and won the contest. The Athenians enclosed what they believed to be this sacred rock, bearing the marks of the trident, in the Erechtheion's north porch. Another area housed a sacred spring dedicated to Erechtheus, a legendary king of Athens, during whose reign the goddess Demeter was said to have instructed the Athenians in the arts of growing crops and other plants. It also housed the venerable wooden cult statue of Athena that was the focus of the Panathenaic festival.

The north and east porches of the Erechtheion have come to epitomize the Ionic order, serving as an important model for European architects since the eighteenth century. Taller and more slender in proportion than the Doric, the Ionic order also has richer and more elaborately carved decoration (see "The Greek Orders," p. 104). The columns rise from molded bases and end in **volute** (spiral scroll) capitals; the frieze is continuous. At the west end of the south side, six **caryatids** (female figures acting as columns) support the entablature of yet another porch.

A second Ionic temple, dedicated to Athena Nike (Victory), stands near the entrance to the Akropolis precinct (SEE FIG. 5–25). Between 410 and 405 BCE, this temple was surrounded by a low wall faced with relief panels of Athena presiding over her winged attendants (known as Nikes or Victories) as they prepared for a victory celebration. One of the most admired panels depicts a Nike adjusting her sandal (**FIG. 5–32**). The figure bends forward gracefully, allowing her ample robe to slip off one shoulder. Her large overlapping wings effectively balance her unstable pose. Unlike the decorative swirls of heavy fabric covering the Parthenon goddesses or the weighty, pleated robes of the Erechtheion caryatids, the textile covering this Nike appears delicate and light, clinging to her body like wet silk. It is one of the most discreetly erotic images in ancient art. Artistic objectives have clearly changed dramatically since the creation of the "*Peplos*" *Kore* (SEE FIG. 5–21).

"High" Classical Greek sculptors sought to create timeless images of men and women by embodying within them an ideal notion of human appearance and deportment. They accomplished this by first observing, and then paring down, the irregularities they saw in nature, and by using their knowledge of geometry to find what they believed were perfect proportions (see "The Canon of Polykleitos," p. 116). And, to achieve the rhythmic harmony presented in narrative works such as the Parthenon's Procession frieze (SEE FIG. 5–29)—in which each form

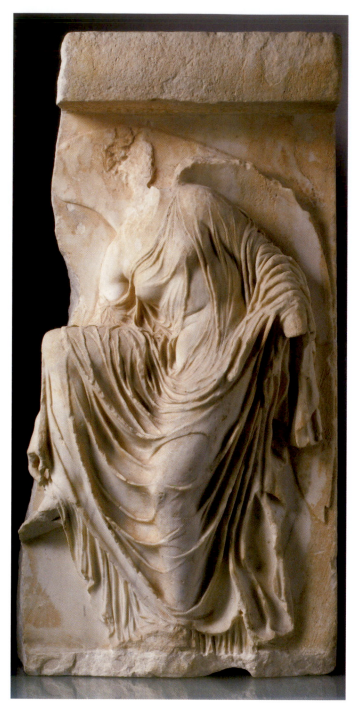

5–32 • NIKE (VICTORY) ADJUSTING HER SANDAL
Fragment of relief decoration from the parapet (now destroyed), Temple of Athena Nike, Akropolis, Athens. c. 410–405 BCE. Marble, height 3′ 6″ (1.06 m). Akropolis Museum, Athens.

is distinct and individual yet all are united into a balanced and interconnected whole—the artists must have carefully observed and distilled the incidents of many similar events. This quest to explore the relationship between the actual and the ideal was matched in the work of the Greek philosopher Socrates (c. 470–399 BCE) and his disciple Plato (c. 429–347 BCE), both of whom argued that all objects in the physical world were mere reflections of ideal forms that could be discovered through reason.

The Late Classical Period (400–323 BCE)

In 404 BCE, the Peloponnesian War concluded with the defeat of Athens by Sparta. Ancient Athens never regained its dominant political and military status, yet Sparta failed to establish a lasting preeminence over the other Greek lands. The quarreling city-states finally fell under the dominance of Philip II of Macedon in 338 BCE and, after Philip's assassination two years later, his 20-year-old son, Alexander the Great, incorporated the Greek city-states into an empire that extended from India to Egypt.

Praxiteles and Lysippos. Remarkably, Greek art continued to evolve during this turbulent period. In their restless search for an ideal human form, sculptors, most notably Praxiteles and Lysippos in the fourth century BCE, developed a new **canon of proportions** for figures. Polykleitos's fifth-century BCE canon called for figures 6½ or 7 times the height of the head. Praxiteles, who worked in Athens from about 370 to 335 BCE or later, created figures about 8 or more "heads" tall. A marble sculpture of **HERMES AND THE INFANT DIONYSOS (FIG. 5–33)**—probably a Hellenistic or Roman copy but so fine that generations of scholars believed it to be an original statue by Praxiteles—has a smaller head and a more sensual and sinuous body than Polykleitos's *Spear Bearer* (SEE FIG. 5–30). Its off-balance, S-curve pose contrasts sharply with that of the tenser earlier work. And the subject is less detached. Indeed, there is a hint of human narrative: Hermes teases the infant god of wine with a bunch of grapes. But the soft modulations in the musculature, the deep folds in the draperies, and the rough locks of hair create a sensuous play of light and shadow over the figure's surface, emphasizing textural distinctions found in nature.

Around 350 BCE, Praxiteles created a daring statue of Aphrodite, the goddess of love, for the city of Knidos in Asia Minor (FIG. 5–34). For the first time, a well-known Greek sculptor depicted a goddess as a completely nude woman. The original sculpture is lost, but many Roman copies survive. As with the statue of Hermes, Praxiteles has incorporated a sense of narrative. The goddess is preparing to take a bath. Her right hand is caught in a gesture of modesty that actually calls attention to her nudity. Her strong and well-toned body leans forward slightly with one knee bent in a seductive pose that emphasizes the swelling forms of her thighs and abdomen. According to an old legend, Aphrodite herself journeyed to Knidos to see Praxiteles's statue and cried out in shock, "Where did Praxiteles see me naked?"

The other major sculptor of the fourth century BCE whose name and fame come down to us is Lysippos. We know Alexander the Great commissioned an official portrait from Lysippos, who portrayed the ruler with head slightly turned and raised upward toward the sky, as if waiting to receive divine advice. But this sculpted portrait does not survive, nor do any of Lysippos's original statues. There are, however, Roman copies of his famous portrayal of a man scraping himself (*Apoxyomenos*) (FIG. 5–35). This typically Classical subject—a nude male athlete—recalls the work of Polykleitos (SEE FIG. 5–30), a sculptor Lysippos admired greatly. But Lysippos's figure reflects a different canon of proportions, and stands in a different posture, swaying with a pronounced curve. As in the contemporary work of Praxiteles,

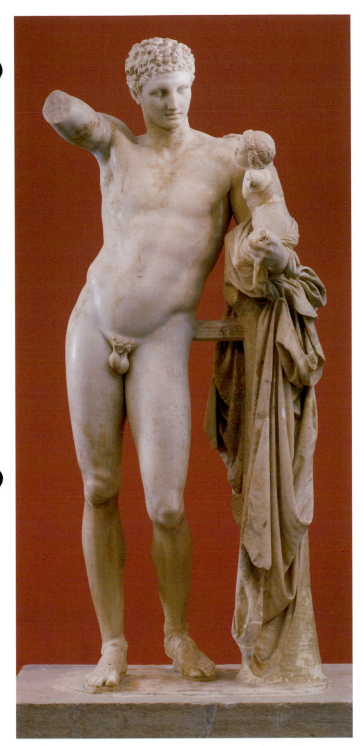

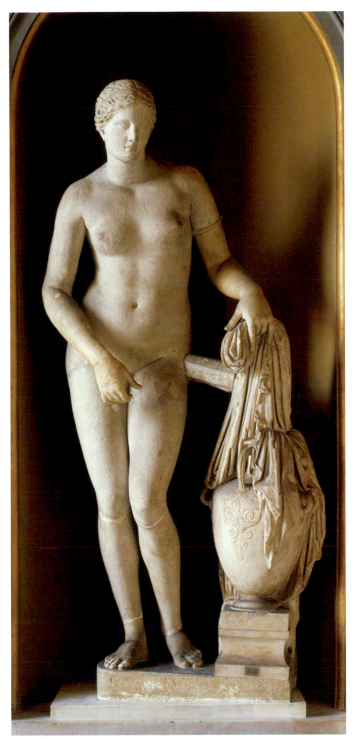

5–33 • Praxiteles or his followers
HERMES AND THE INFANT DIONYSOS
Probably a Hellenistic or Roman copy after a 4th-century BCE original. Marble, with remnants of red paint on the lips and hair, height 7′ 1″ (2.15 m). Archaeological Museum, Olympia.

Discovered in the rubble of the ruined Temple of Hera at Olympia in 1875, this statue is now widely accepted as an outstanding Roman or Hellenistic copy. Support for this conclusion comes from certain elements typical of Roman sculpture: Hermes's sandals, which recent studies suggest are not accurate for a fourth-century BCE date; the supporting element of crumpled fabric covering a tree stump; and the use of a reinforcing strut, or brace, between Hermes's hip and the tree stump.

5–34 • Praxiteles
APHRODITE OF KNIDOS
Composite of two similar Roman copies after the original marble of c. 350 BCE. Marble, height 6′ 8″ (2 m). Vatican Museums, Museo Pio Clementino, Gabinetto delle Maschere, Rome.

The head of this figure is from one Roman copy, the body from another. Seventeenth- and eighteenth-century CE restorers added the nose, the neck, the right forearm and hand, most of the left arm, and the feet and parts of the legs. This kind of restoration would rarely be undertaken today, but it was frequently done and considered quite acceptable in the past, when archaeologists were trying to put together a body of work documenting the appearances of lost Greek statues.

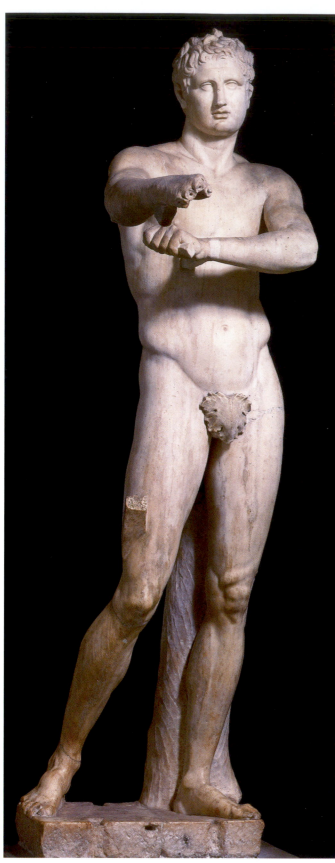

5-35 • Lysippos MAN SCRAPING HIMSELF (APOXYOMENOS)
Roman copy after the original bronze of c. 350–325 BCE. Marble, height 6′ 9″ (2.06 m). Vatican Museums, Museo Pio Clementino, Gabinetto dell'Apoxyomenos, Rome.

there is an implied narrative here—a young man caught cleaning up after his workout, removing oil and dirt from his body with a scraping tool called a *strigil*. Perhaps more significantly, in contrast to the compact frontal mass of Polykleitos's *Spear Bearer*, Lysippos's *Man Scraping Himself* reaches out into the surrounding space, inviting viewers to move around the statue in order to absorb its full impact.

Mosaics. Little remains of original Greek wall paintings from any period, but as with Greek sculpture, later Roman patrons, who greatly admired Greek murals, commissioned copies. A first-century BCE floor **mosaic** (a picture created from **tesserae**, small cubes of colored stone or marble) from Pompeii (**FIG. 5–36**), showing a battle between Alexander the Great and Darius III of Persia, is a Roman copy of a Late Classical Greek wall painting of about 310 BCE. The historian Pliny the Elder mentions a painting of this subject by the Greek painter Philoxenos of Eretria, but a recent theory claims this as a work of Helen of Egypt, one of a number of women painters recorded in ancient Greece.

The dramatic scene is one of violent action, diagonal disruption, and radical **foreshortening** (a technique that shows things as if they were receding or projecting forward within space), eliciting a strong response in the viewer. Astride a rearing horse at the left, his hair blowing free and his neck bare, Alexander challenges the helmeted and armored Persian leader, who stretches out his arm in a gesture of defeat and apprehension as his charioteer whisks him back toward safety within the Persian ranks. Presumably in close imitation of the original painting, the mosaicist created the illusion of solid figures through **modeling**, mimicking the play of light on three-dimensional surfaces by highlighting protruding areas and shading receding ones.

Hellenistic Art

How does Hellenistic art differ from the Classical art that preceded it?

After establishing an empire that stretched from Greece south to Egypt, and as far east as India, Alexander died of a fever in Babylon at age 33 in 323 BCE. His untimely end left his vast empire with no administrative structure and no appointed successor. Almost immediately, his generals turned against one another, and local leaders fought to regain their lost autonomy. By the early third century BCE, three of Alexander's generals—Antigonus, Ptolemy, and Seleucus—had carved out kingdoms. The Antigonids controlled Macedonia and mainland Greece; the Ptolemies ruled Egypt; and the Seleucids controlled Anatolia, Syria, Mesopotamia, and Persia. Each of these regions followed a different political course, but they were unified artistically and culturally by Greek ideas and Greek art. This Hellenistic world would last until the rise of Rome in the second and first centuries BCE.

Artists of the Hellenistic period developed visions discernibly distinct from those of their Classical Greek predecessors. Where earlier artists sought to codify a generalized artistic ideal, Hellenistic artists shifted focus to the individual and the specific. They turned increasingly from the heroic to the everyday, from

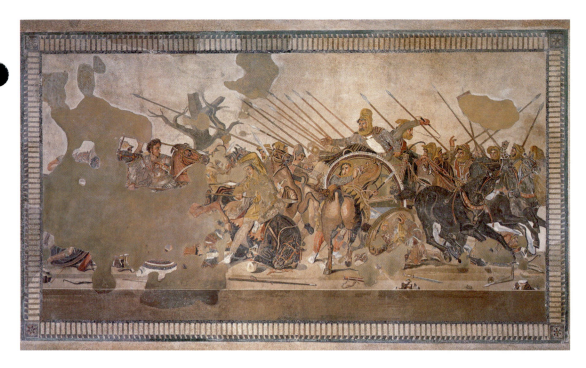

5-36 • ALEXANDER THE GREAT CONFRONTS DARIUS III AT THE BATTLE OF ISSOS
1st century BCE floor mosaic from Pompeii, Italy, copied after a Greek painting of c. 310 BCE, perhaps by Philoxenos or Helen of Egypt. Entire panel 8' 10" × 17' (2.7 × 5.2 m). Museo Archeologico Nazionale, Naples.

View the Closer Look for the Alexander mosaic on **MyArtsLab**

ART AND ITS CONTEXTS

Women Artists in Greece

Although comparatively few artists in ancient Greece were women, there is evidence that women artists worked in many media. Ancient writers noted women painters—Pliny the Elder, for example, listed Aristarete, Eirene, Iaia, Kalypso, Olympias, and Timarete. Helen, a painter from Egypt who had been taught by her father, is known to have worked in the fourth century BCE and may have been responsible for the original wall painting copied in the mosaic of *Alexander the Great Confronts Darius III at the Battle of Issos* (SEE FIG. 5-36). Greek women excelled in creating narrative or pictorial tapestries, and they also worked in pottery-making workshops.

The hydria shown here (FIG. 5-37), dating from about 450 BCE, shows a woman and three men painting in such a workshop. In the center Athena, patron of crafts and the arts, holds a wreath, and Nikes crown the men, symbolizing victory in an artistic competition. The woman sits on a raised dais at far left, painting the largest vase in the workshop but isolated from the other artists as well as the awards ceremony. Perhaps most women were excluded from public artistic competitions, as they were from athletic competitions. But could this woman be the head of this workshop? Secure in her own status,

she may have encouraged her assistants to enter contests to further their careers and bring glory to her enterprise.

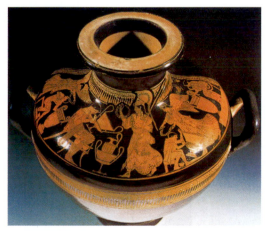

5-37 • The Leningrad Painter A CERAMIC PAINTER AND ASSISTANTS CROWNED BY ATHENA AND VICTORIES
Red-figure decoration on a hydria from Athens. c. 450 BCE. Private collection, Milan.

In ancient Greece, the theater offered more than entertainment; it was a vehicle for the communal expression of religious beliefs through music, poetry, and dance. During the fifth century BCE, the plays were primarily tragedies in verse based on popular myths and were performed at festivals dedicated to Dionysos. The three great Greek tragedians—Aeschylus, Sophocles, and Euripides—created works that defined tragedy for centuries.

Because ancient theaters were used continuously and frequently modified, none have survived in their original form. The largely intact theater at Epidauros, however, which dates from the fourth century BCE, is a characteristic early example (FIG. 5–38). A semicircle of tiered seats built into a hillside overlooked a circular performance area, called the orchestra (from the Greek *orkhestra*, meaning "to dance"), at the center of which was an altar to Dionysos. Rising behind the orchestra was a two-tiered stage structure made up of the vertical *skene* (scene)—an architectural backdrop for performances that also screened the backstage area from view—and the *proskenion* (proscenium), a raised platform in front of the *skene* that was increasingly used over time as an extension of the orchestra. Ramps connecting the *proskenion* with lateral passageways provided access to the stage for performers. Steps gave the audience access to the 55 rows of seats and divided the seating area into uniform wedge-shaped sections.

(At Epidauros, the tiers of seats above the wide corridor, or gangway, were added at a much later date.) This design provided uninterrupted sight lines and excellent acoustics, and allowed for the efficient entrance and exit of 12,000 spectators—a basic plan not greatly improved upon since.

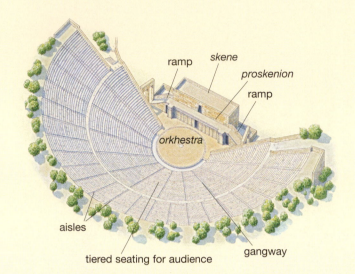

aisles · tiered seating for audience · gangway · ramp · *skene* · *proskenion* · ramp · *orkhestra*

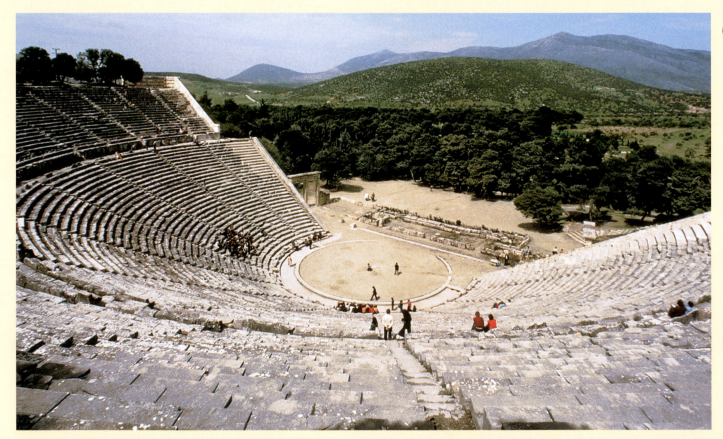

5–38 • RECONSTRUCTION DRAWING AND EXTERIOR VIEW OF THE THEATER OF EPIDAUROS
Greece. 4th century BCE and later.

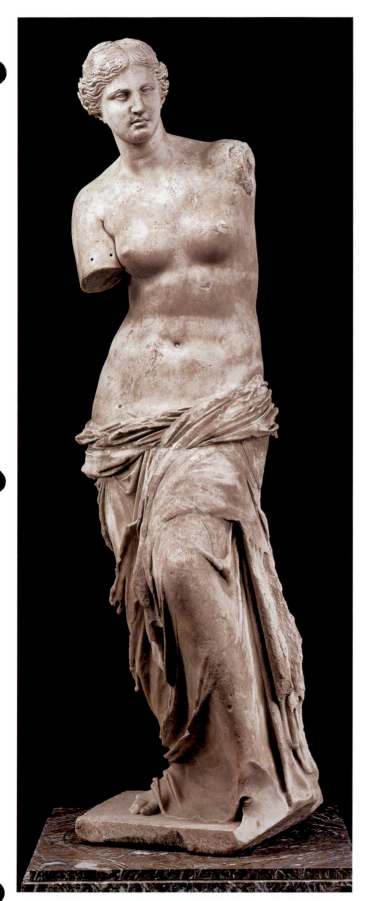

5-39 • Alexandros APHRODITE OF MELOS
Also called *Venus de Milo*. c. 150–100 BCE. Marble,
height 6′ 8″ (2.04 m). Musée du Louvre, Paris.

aloof serenity to individual emotion, and from decorous drama to emotional melodrama. Their works appeal to the senses through luscious or lustrous surface treatments and to our hearts as well as our intellects through expressive subjects and poses. Although such tendencies are already evident during the Late Classical period of the fourth century BCE, they became much more pronounced in Hellenistic art.

Hellenistic sculptors produced an enormous variety of work in a wide range of materials, techniques, and styles. The period was marked by two broad and contrasting trends. One (sometimes called anti-Classical) abandoned Classical strictures and experimented freely with new forms and subjects. This radical style was practiced in Pergamon and other eastern centers of Greek culture. The other trend emulated earlier Classical models. Sculptors selected aspects of favored works by fourth-century BCE sculptors—especially Praxiteles and Lysippos—and incorporated them into their own works.

This nostalgic interest in Late Classical style is exemplified by the **APHRODITE OF MELOS (FIG. 5–39)**, found on the Aegean island of Melos by French excavators in the early nineteenth century. This sculpture was intended by its maker Alexandros, son of Menides, to recall the *Aphrodite of Knidos* by Praxiteles (SEE FIG. 5–34), and indeed the head, with its dreamy gaze, suggests the lost Praxitelean work. But the twisting stance and strong projection of the knee, as well as the rich, three-dimensional quality of the drapery, are typical of Hellenistic art. Moreover, the juxtaposition of soft flesh with the crisper texture of drapery, especially since it seems to be slipping off the figure, adds an insistent note of erotic tension that is thoroughly Hellenistic.

The Late Classical normative beauty of the *Aphrodite of Melos* contrasts sharply with the seemingly unvarnished portrayal of an elderly woman carrying a basket of vegetables and a chicken, also carved in the second century BCE (FIG. 5–40). At first glance she seems to be simply an old peasant woman doing her marketing. However, the disarray of her elegantly designed dress and her unfocused stare suggest that she represents an aging, dissolute follower of the wine god Dionysos, struggling on her way to make an offering. Such representations of people from all levels of society, as well as a taste for unusual physical types, became popular during the Hellenistic period.

More dynamic in its depiction of action is the **NIKE (VICTORY) OF SAMOTHRACE (FIG. 5–41)**. The forward momentum of this 8-foot-high victory goddess is balanced by the powerful backward thrust of her enormous wings. She has just landed on the prow of the stone ship that formed the original base of the statue. The ensemble originally stood in a hillside niche high above the sanctuary of the Samothracian gods, perhaps drenched with spray from a fountain.

Some of the best-known examples of Hellenistic art were made in the third and second centuries BCE in the kingdom of Pergamon, a breakaway state within the Seleucid realm on the west coast of Asia Minor. After gaining independence in the early third century BCE, Pergamon quickly became a leading center of the arts and the hub of a new sculptural style that had far-reaching influence. This radical style characterized a monument with bronze figures mounted on a **pedestal** commemorating the victory in 230 BCE of Attalos I

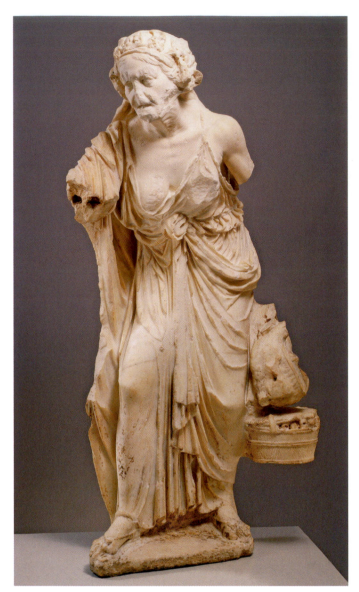

5–40 • MARKET WOMAN
Roman copy of 1st century CE. Marble, height 49½″ (1.25 m). The
Metropolitan Museum of Art, New York. Rogers Fund, 1909 (09.19).

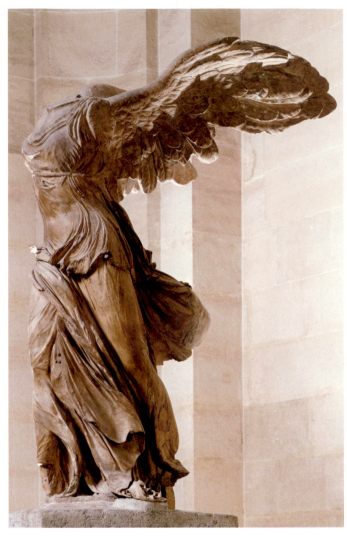

5–41 • NIKE (VICTORY) OF SAMOTHRACE
From the Sanctuary of the Great Gods, Samothrace. c. 180 BCE (?).
Marble, height 8′ 1″ (2.45 m). Musée du Louvre, Paris.

This work probably commemorated an important naval victory,
perhaps the Rhodian triumph over the Seleucid King Antiochus
III in 190 BCE. Along with a fragment of its stone ship base, it was
discovered by a French explorer in 1863 and soon after entered
the Louvre.

(ruled 241–197 BCE) over the Gauls, a Celtic people who
invaded from the north (see "The Celts," p. 125). The sculpture is known today only from Roman marble copies. One
figure, with the name Epigonos inscribed on its base, shows the
agonizing death of a wounded Celtic soldier-trumpeter **(FIG.
5–43)**. His wiry, lime-spiked hair, mustache, and neck ring or
torc (reputedly the only item of dress the Gauls wore in battle)
identify him as a "**barbarian**" (the ancient Greek term for all
foreigners, whom they considered uncivilized), and this portrayal conveys his dignity and heroism in defeat, inspiring in
viewers both admiration and pity for this fallen warrior. There
is a sense of arrested motion as the trumpeter supports himself on his right arm, struggling to remain upright. This kind

of deliberate attempt to elicit a specific emotional response in
the viewer is known as **expressionism**, another characteristic
of Hellenistic art.

The style and approach seen in the monument with the
defeated Gauls culminated in the celebrated frieze of the Pergamon Altar enclosure. Wrapped around the base of a huge Ionic
colonnade that enclosed an altar to Zeus on a mountainside
(FIG. 5–44), this over-7-foot-high frieze was probably carved
during the reign of Eumenes II (ruled 197–159 BCE). It depicts
the battle between the gods and the giants, a mythical struggle
that the Greeks saw as a metaphor for their conflicts with "barbarian" outsiders. In this case it evokes the Pergamenes' victory
over the Gauls.

The Celts

During the first millennium BCE, Celtic peoples inhabited most of central and western Europe. The Celtic Gauls portrayed in the Hellenistic Pergamene victory monument (SEE FIG. 5-44) moved into Asia Minor from Thrace during the third century BCE. The ancient Greeks referred to these neighbors, like all outsiders, as "barbarians." Pushed out by migrating people, attacked and defeated by challenged kingdoms like that at Pergamon, and then finally by the Roman armies of Julius Caesar, ultimately the Celts were driven into the northwesternmost parts of the continent: Ireland, Cornwall, and Brittany. Their wooden sculpture and dwellings and their colorful woven textiles have disintegrated, but spectacular funerary goods such as jewelry, weapons, and tableware have survived.

This golden torc (FIG. 5-42), dating sometime between the third and first centuries BCE, was excavated in 1866 from a Celtic tomb in northern France, but it is strikingly similar to the neck ring worn by the noble dying trumpeter illustrated in FIGURE 5-43. Torcs were worn by noblemen and were sometimes awarded to warriors for heroic performance in combat. Like all Celtic jewelry, the decorative design of this work consists not of natural forms but of completely abstract ornament, in this case created by the careful twisting and wrapping of strands of pure gold, resolved securely by the definitive bulges of two knobs. In Celtic hands,

pattern becomes an integral part of the object itself, not an applied decoration. In stark contrast to the culture of the ancient Greeks, where the human figure was at the heart of all artistic development, here it is abstract, nonrepresentational form and its continual refinement that is the central artistic preoccupation.

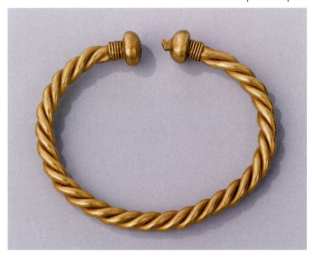

5-42 • TORC
Found at Soucy, France. Celtic Gaul, 3rd–1st century BCE. Gold. Musée Nationale du Moyen-Age, Paris.

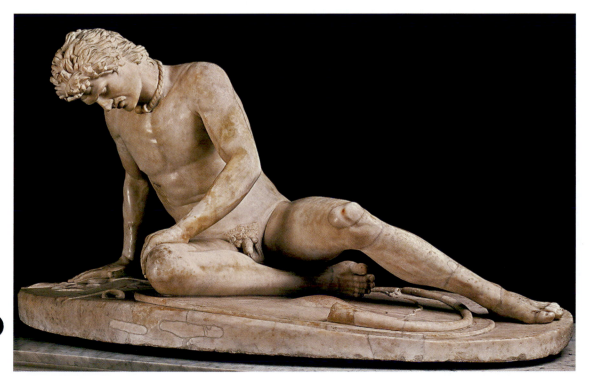

5-43 • Epigonos (?)
DYING GALLIC TRUMPETER
Roman copy after the original bronze of c. 220 BCE. Marble, life-size, height 36½″ (93 cm). Museo Capitolino, Rome.

Pliny the Elder described a work like the *Dying Gallic Trumpeter*, attributing it to an artist named Epigonos. Recent research indicates that Epigonos probably knew the early fifth-century BCE sculpture of the Temple of Aphaia at Aegina, which included the *Dying Warriors* (SEE FIGS. 5-16, 5-17), and could have had it in mind when he created this work.

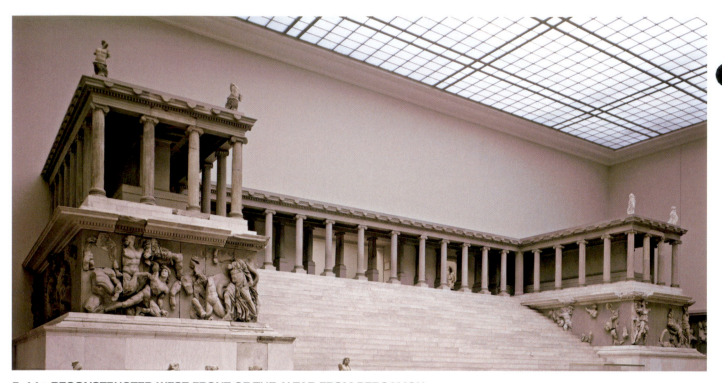

5–44 • RECONSTRUCTED WEST FRONT OF THE ALTAR FROM PERGAMON
Turkey. c. 175–150 BCE. Marble. Staatliche Museen zu Berlin, Pergamonmuseum, Preussischer Kulturbesitz, Antikensammlung.

The Greek gods fight here not only with giants, but also with grotesque hybrids emerging from the bowels of the earth. In one section, the goddess Athena has forced a winged monster to his knees (**FIG. 5–45**). Inscriptions along the base of the sculpture identify her foe as Alkyoneos, son of the earth goddess Ge, who rises from the ground on the right, pleading for her son's life. At upper right, a winged Victory reaches to crown the victorious Athena.

The Pergamon frieze is carved in high relief with deep **undercutting** that creates dramatic contrasts of light and shade, playing over the complex forms. Compositionally, the Pergamene sculptors sought to balance opposing forces in three-dimensional space along diagonal lines, whereas "High" Classical Greek artists had sought equilibrium and control on a grid of horizontals and verticals (compare **FIGS.** 5–28, 5–29). Some figures in the Pergamon frieze even extend beyond the architectural setting, crawling out onto the steps that visitors climbed on their way up to the altar. Many consider this theatrical interaction of deep space and complex form to be a benchmark of the Hellenistic style, just as they consider the controlled restraint of the Parthenon sculpture to epitomize "High" Classical style. Similarly, the detached composure admired in Classical art gives way in the Hellenistic period to extreme expressions: pain, stress, anger, fear, or despair. (See also the Hellenistic sculpture of *Laocoön and His Sons*, FIG. INTRO–20.) Whereas Classical artists asked only for an intellectual commitment, Hellenistic artists demanded that viewers also empathize.

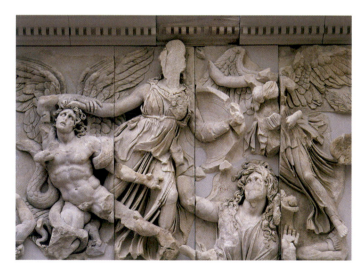

5–45 • ATHENA ATTACKING THE GIANTS
Detail of the frieze from the east front of the altar from Pergamon. Marble, frieze height 7′ 7″ (2.3 m). Staatliche Museen zu Berlin, Pergamonmuseum, Preussischer Kulturbesitz, Antikensammlung.

At one time "High" Classical Greek art and architecture were considered the pinnacle of artistic achievement. Today we also recognize the vibrant richness of earlier Aegean art, as well as the dramatic artistic intensity of the Hellenistic world, admiring the works of Minoan painters as early as the seventeenth century BCE as well as the dramatic virtuosity of the Hellenistic sculptors of Pergamon almost a millennium and a half later. Greek artists, early and late, studied their surroundings with an interest in describing its detail—from curling acanthus leaves, to the sleek tension of developed musculature, to the folds of draped clothing. But they tempered their depictions of the natural world to conform to a series of changing ideals of artistic perfection. Such idealized representations of the real world embodied the same ideas and values explored by contemporary philosophers, playwrights, and politicians.

And we are not the first to to be fascinated with the splendid works of art that emerged from this long period of Greek creativity and experimentation. We will find in the next chapter that the ancient Romans admired the artistic production of their Greek predecessors to such an extent that they emulated and copied it, making Greek art and architecture one of several foundations for the glories that were Rome.

THINK ABOUT IT

5.1 Choose one work from the ancient Aegean and explain how archaeologists and art historians have used it to understand the history and values of the culture that produced it.

5.2 Compare the approach to representing the male nude in the two dying warriors from the pediments of the Temple of Aphaia in Aegina (FIGS. 5–16, 5–17). How are they similar and how are they different?

5.3 Define the term "High" Classicism, discussing one building and one work of sculpture that exemplify it. What are the value judgments that underlie this art-historical category?

5.4 How do the relief sculptures from the altar to Zeus from Pergamon depart from Classical norms?

| CROSSCURRENTS |

FIG. 2–5

FIG. 5–28

What is the common theme found in the heroic contexts depicted on these two very different works? What does the specific function and location of each indicate about the importance of that theme in each culture?

✓ **Study** and **Review** on **MyArtsLab**

IN PERSPECTIVE

3500 BCE

2000

1000

500

400

300

200

100

0

Cycladic Culture
c. 3000–1600 BCE

Minoan Culture on Crete
c. 1900–1375 BCE

Mycenaean Culture
c. 1600–1100 BCE

Geometric Period
c. 900–700 BCE

Earliest Surviving List of Olympic
Games Winners c. 776 BCE

Archaic Period c. 600–480 BCE

Perikles c. 495–429 BCE
Early Classical Period c. 480–450 BCE
Athenian and Spartan Alliance Defeats
the Persians 480 BCE
Socrates c. 470–399 BCE

"High" Classical Period c. 450–400 BCE

Plato c. 429–347 BCE

Conclusion of Peloponnesian War
404 BCE
Late Classical Period
c. 400–323 BCE

Death of Alexander the Great
323 BCE
Hellenistic Period c. 323–31 BCE

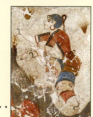
Young Girl, Akrotiri
before 1630 BCE

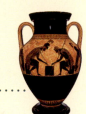
EXEKIAS,
Ajax and Achilles
c. 540–530 BCE

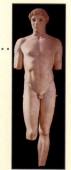
"Kritios" Boy
c. 480–475 BCE

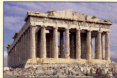
Parthenon, Athens
c. 447–432 BCE

ALEXANDROS,
Aphrodite of Melos
c. 150–100 BCE

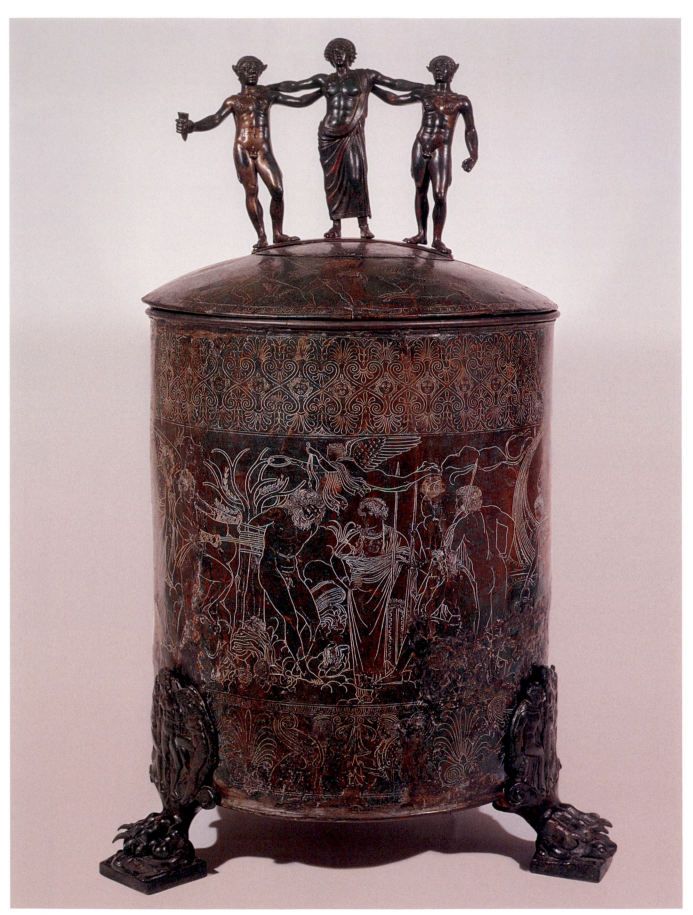

6–1 • Novios Plautios FICORONI CISTA
350–300 BCE. Bronze, 2′ 6¼″ (78.6 cm). Museo Nazionale di Villa Giulia, Rome.

View the Closer Look for the Ficoroni Cista on **MyArtsLab**

ETRUSCAN AND ROMAN ART

6.1 Characterize the ways in which Etruscan art celebrates the vitality of human existence.

6.2 Discuss the distinctive modes of human representation and architectural design that emerged during the Roman Republic and Early Empire.

6.3 Identify major trends and monuments of imperial Roman art and architecture.

6.4 Distinguish the continuities and changes in art and architecture during the Late Roman Empire.

LOOKING FORWARD ▶

Long before the Romans ruled the entire Italic peninsula as the center of an expanding empire, the Etruscans created a thriving culture in northern and central Italy. Etruscan artists were known throughout the Mediterranean world for their special sophistication in casting and engraving on bronze. Some of their most extraordinary works were created for domestic use, including a group of surviving **cistae**—cylindrical containers used by wealthy women as cases for toiletry articles such as mirrors, cosmetics, and perfume.

This exquisitely wrought and richly decorated example—the **FICORONI CISTA**, named after an eighteenth-century owner **(FIG. 6–1)**—was made in the second half of the fourth century BCE and excavated in Palestrina, southeast of Rome. It was commissioned by an Etruscan woman named Dindia Macolnia as a gift for her daughter, perhaps on the occasion of her marriage. The artist, Novios Plautios, signed the precisely engraved drawings around the cylinder, accomplished while the hammered bronze sheet from which it was constructed was still flat. First he incised lines in the metal and then filled them with a white substance to make them stand out. The cista's legs and handle—created by the figural group of Dionysos between two satyrs—were cast as separate pieces, attached during the assembly process.

The natural poses and individualization of these figures—both incised and cast—recalls the relaxed but lively naturalism

of Etruscan wall paintings, but the Classicizing **idealization** of bodies and poses seems to come directly from contemporary Greek art. And the use of broad foliate and ornamental bands to frame the frieze of figural narrative running around the cylinder also matches the practice of famous Greek ceramic painters like Euphronios (see "A Closer Look," p. 109). As with Greek pots, the most popular subject matter for the decoration of cistae were Greek myths. Here Novios has engraved sequential scenes drawn from an episode in the story of the Argonauts, when the sailors sought water in the land of the hostile king Amykos. The king would only give them water from his spring if they beat him in a boxing match. After the immortal Pollux defeated Amykos, the Argonauts tied the king to a tree, the episode highlighted on the side of the cista seen here.

Novios Plautios probably based this scene on a monumental, mid-fourth-century BCE Greek painting of the Argonauts by Kydias that seems to have been in Rome at this time—perhaps explaining why the artist tells us in his inscribed signature that he executed this work in Rome. The combination of cultural components coming together in the creation of this cista—Greek stylistic sources in the work of an Etruscan artist living in Rome—will continue as Roman art develops out of the native heritage of Etruria and the emulation of the imported Classical heritage of the Greeks.

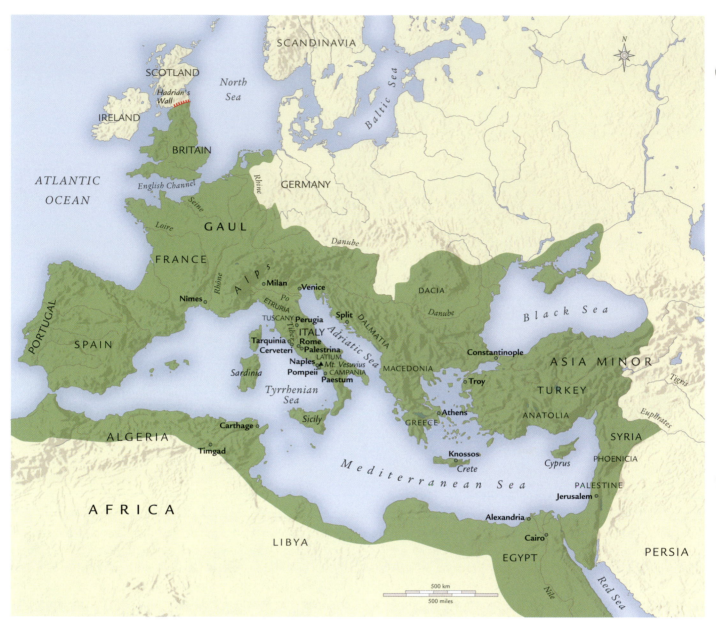

MAP 6–1 • THE ANCIENT ROMAN WORLD

This map shows the Roman Empire at its greatest extent, which was reached in 106 CE under the emperor Trajan.

The Etruscans

How does Etruscan art celebrate the vitality of human existence?

The ancient inhabitants of the boot-shaped Italian peninsula (**MAP 6–1**) were exposed through maritime trading and exploration to the rich cultural interplay among Near Eastern, Egyptian, and Greek civilizations. Etruscan society emerged in the seventh century BCE in Etruria (present-day Tuscany), perhaps descending from a people called the Villanovans, who had occupied the northern and western regions of Italy since the Bronze Age. The Etruscans reached the height of their power in the sixth century BCE, when they formed a loose federation of a dozen cities. The fertile soil of Etruria and its rich lodes of metal ore formed the basis of their wealth.

Etruscan artists excelled at making monumental sculpture not out of stone, but with terra cotta. It required great technical and physical skill to prevent these works from collapsing under their own weight while the raw clay was still heavy with moisture. It was also challenging to regulate kiln temperatures during the long firing process. This life-size terra-cotta figure of **APULU (APOLLO)** (**FIG. 6–2**) was made about 510–500 BCE. Its well-developed body and "Archaic smile" demonstrate that Etruscan sculptors knew the work of their Archaic Greek counterparts (**SEE FIG. 5–20**). But the Etruscans did not represent their gods in the nude; Apulu is partly concealed by a rippling robe. His dynamic stride imparts a vigor that contrasts with the rigid stance of Archaic Greek *kouroi*. The sense of purposeful movement that characterizes his pose is a prominent feature of Etruscan sculpture and painting. This Apulu was originally placed on the roof ridge of an Etruscan temple at Veii as

part of a four-figure narrative scene depicting a labor of Hercle (Hercules) that involved fighting with Apulu for possession of a sacred deer.

According to the first-century BCE Roman architect and theorist Vitruvius, in certain ways Etruscan temples resembled Greek temples. For example, Etruscan builders also used post-and-lintel structures and gable roofs. The bases, column shafts, and capitals recall those of either the Greek Doric or Ionic order, and some entablatures have a frieze. Vitruvius used the term "**Tuscan Order**" to describe the characteristic variation of an unfluted shaft with a simplified base, capital, and entablature (see "Roman Architectural Orders," p. 145). But although the Etruscans also built their temples on a high base, they had only one flight of stairs, leading to a columned porch on one short side of the rectangular temple, not the uniformly stepped stereobate and continuous peristyle colonnade surrounding Greek temples (SEE FIG. 5–26). The deep porch led in turn to a cella, which was divided into three parallel rooms (FIG. 6–3).

The typical Etruscan home was a rectangular mud-brick structure built either around a central courtyard or around an **atrium**, a room with a shallow indoor pool for drinking, cooking, and bathing, fed by rainwater through a large opening in the roof. The burial chamber of the third-century BCE **TOMB OF THE RELIEFS** at Cerveteri (near Rome) was carved to

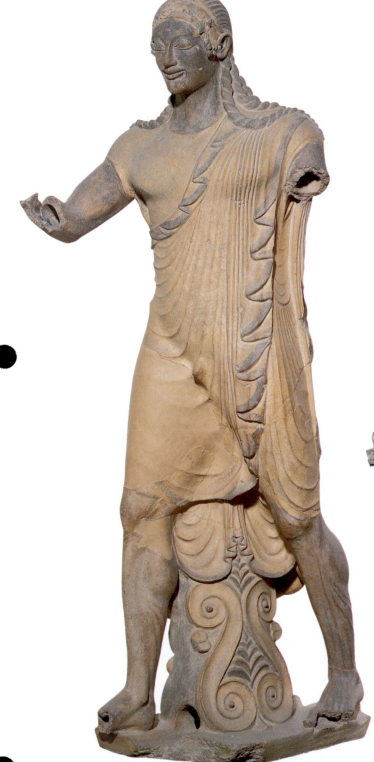

6–2 • Master Sculptor Vulca (?) APULU (APOLLO)
From the Temple of Minerva, Portonaccio, Veii. c. 510–500 BCE. Painted terra cotta, height 5′ 10″ (1.8 m). Museo Nazionale di Villa Giulia, Rome.

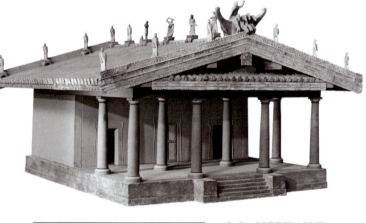

6–3 • MODEL AND PLAN OF ETRUSCAN TEMPLES
based on descriptions by Vitruvius. University of Rome, Istituto di Etruscologia e Antichità Italiche.

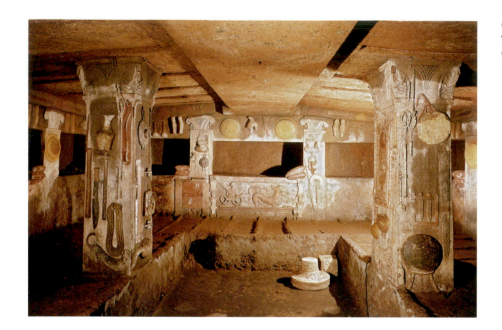

imitate such a house (**FIG. 6–4**). Its walls were plastered and painted, and it was provided with a full selection of furnishings, some carved, others formed of **stucco**, a slow-drying type of plaster that can easily be modeled or molded. Simulated pots, jugs, robes, axes, and other household items look like real objects hanging on hooks. Could the animal rendered in low relief at the bottom of the pillar left of center be the family pet?

Some tombs were painted, not carved. In the Tomb of the Triclinium at Tarquinia, dating from about 480–470 BCE, friezes of figural scenes surround a room whose ceiling is enlivened with colorful geometric decoration (**FIG. 6–5**). Energetic dancers—alternating between lighter-skinned women and their swarthy male partners, in conformity with a coloristic convention for gender differentiation already familiar from the ancient art of Egypt and Greece—line the side walls, and at the end of the room couples recline on couches enjoying a banquet while cats prowl underneath the table searching for scraps. The immediacy of this wall painting is striking. Both dancers and diners engage in the joyful diversions of human life as we know it.

Etruscan **sarcophagi** (large carved tomb chests) also reflected domestic life. The sculpted terra-cotta figures of a husband and wife who recline comfortably on the lid of a

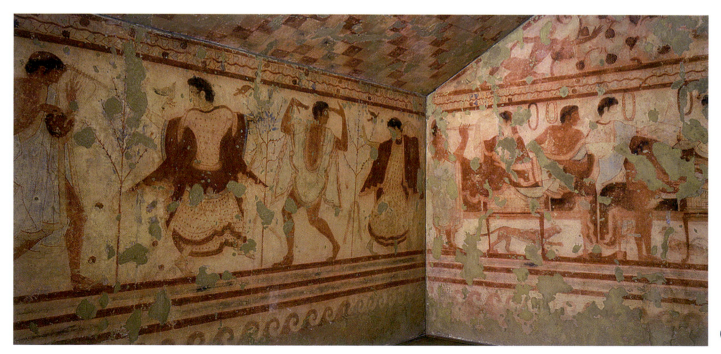

6–5 • DANCERS AND DINERS
Tomb of the Triclinium, Tarquinia. c. 480–470 BCE.

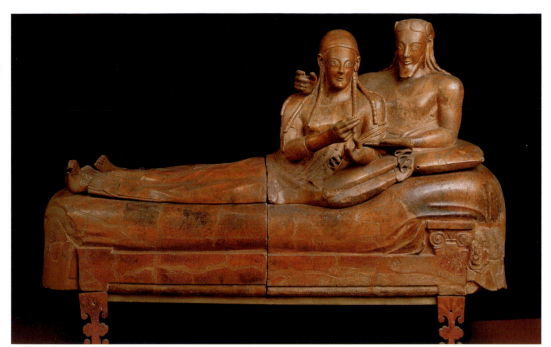

sarcophagus made to look like a couch (FIG. 6–6) do not constitute a cold, somber memorial to the dead. Two happy individuals with alert eyes and warm smiles greet us with lively gestures. The man once raised a drinking vessel, addressing the viewer with the lively and engaging gesture of a genial host, perhaps offering an invitation to dine with them for eternity or join them in the sort of convivial festivities recorded on the walls of Etruscan tombs.

Etruscan art and architectural forms left an indelible stamp on the art and architecture of early Rome, rivaled only by the influence of Greece. By 88 BCE, when the Etruscans were granted Roman citizenship, their art had already been absorbed into the developing Roman culture that would soon dominate the entire Mediterranean region and even beyond.

The Romans: From Republic to Empire

What were the distinctive modes of human representation and architectural design that emerged during the Roman Republic and Early Empire?

At the same time as Etruscan civilization was flourishing in Etruria and Greek culture was dominant farther south in the colony around Paestum, the Latin-speaking inhabitants of Rome began to develop into a formidable power. By the end of the third century BCE, the Etruscans themselves were absorbed into the Roman Republic, which was at that time expanding in many directions. At the height of their power—in the early second century CE—Romans would rule all the lands around the Mediterranean Sea, which they proudly referred to as *mare nostrum*, "our sea." Their empire stretched east to the Euphrates and northwest as far as Scotland.

To spur growth and to signify cohesion across this vast empire, the Roman government undertook building programs of staggering scale and complexity, constructing central administrative and commercial centers (**forums** with **basilicas**),

Roman Counterparts of Greek Gods	
ROMAN NAME	GREEK NAME
Jupiter	Zeus
Juno	Hera
Minerva	Athena
Mars	Ares
Apollo	Apollo
Venus	Aphrodite
Diana	Artemis
Mercury	Hermes
Pluto	Hades
Bacchus	Dionysos
Vulcan	Hephaistos
Vesta	Hestia
Ceres	Demeter
Neptune	Poseidon
Cupid (*or* Amor)	Eros
Hercules	Herakles (a demigod)

racetracks, theaters, public baths and water systems, apartment buildings, and even entire new cities. To facilitate commerce and the movement of troops, the Romans built a vast network of roads between their capital and the empire's farthest reaches. Many modern European highways still follow the routes laid down by ancient Roman engineers, and Roman-era foundations underlie the streets of many European cities.

Culturally, the Romans borrowed heavily from Greece and the larger Hellenistic world. They incorporated Greek orders into their architecture, imported and imitated Greek art, and employed Greek artists. Like the Etruscans, they also adopted Greek gods and heroes as their own, giving them Latin names (see "Roman Counterparts of Greek Gods," p. 133). In western Europe, the sophisticated legal, administrative, and cultural systems that the Romans imposed on the people they conquered endured for some 500 years. And in the eastern Mediterranean, the Classical traditions and styles of ancient Rome survived into the fifteenth century as Byzantine art.

The Republican Period

Early Rome was governed by a series of kings and an advisory body called the Senate, made up of patricians (wealthy, upper-class citizens). In 509 BCE, Romans overthrew the last king and established the Roman Republic as an oligarchy (government by patricians) that would last until 27 BCE. Rome's conquest of lands outside the Italian peninsula strained its political system, weakening the authority of the Senate and leading to a series of civil wars among powerful generals. In 49 BCE, Julius Caesar invaded Italy from his post in France, and three years later this general, who had ruled Rome with Pompey and Crassus in the First Triumvirate, emerged victorious over his rivals. He held power as dictator until his assassination in 44 BCE.

Artists of the Republican period sought to create lifelike images, seemingly based on careful observation of their subjects. Viewing a **PORTRAIT OF JULIUS CAESAR** on a *denarius* (silver coin) of 44 BCE (**FIG. 6–7**), we almost believe we know what he actually looked like. The tiny relief sculpture presents an elder ruler's careworn features and alert expression. This idea of placing a living ruler's portrait on one side of a coin, and on the other a symbol of the country or an image that recalls some important action or event, was adopted by Caesar's successors, allowing us to follow the progression of Roman history through imperial portraits, values, and accomplishments.

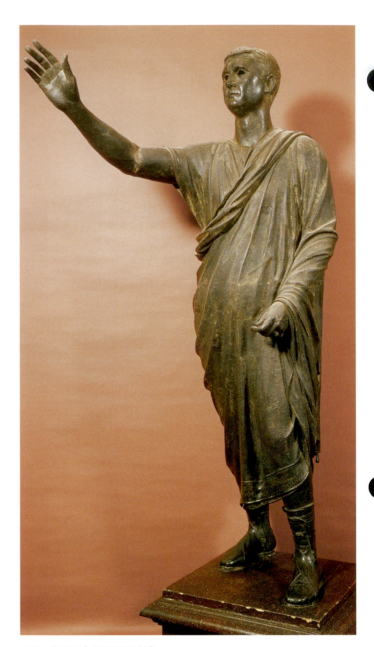

6–8 • AULUS METELLUS
found near Perugia. c. 80 BCE. Bronze, height 5′ 11″ (1.8 m). Museo Archeologico Nazionale, Florence.

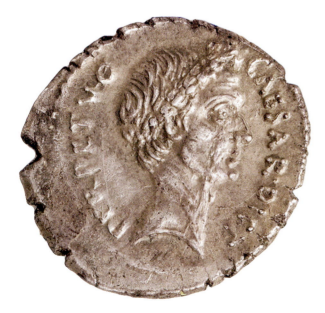

6–7 • DENARIUS WITH PORTRAIT OF JULIUS CAESAR
44 BCE. Silver, diameter approximately ¾″ (1.9 cm). American Numismatic Society, New York.

The convention of emphasizing the effects of aging in portraits that appear to be accurate and faithful descriptions of actual individuals may have derived from the practice of making and displaying death masks of deceased relatives (see "Roman Portraiture," p. 135). During the Republican period, patrons clearly admired such seemingly realistic portraits and often turned to skilled Etruscan artists to execute them. The life-size bronze portrait of **AULUS METELLUS (FIG. 6–8)**—the Roman official's name is inscribed on the hem of his garment in Etruscan letters—depicts the man addressing a gathering, his arm outstretched and slightly raised, a pose expressive of rhetorical persuasiveness. The orator wears sturdy, laced leather boots and a folded and draped toga, the characteristic garment of Roman senators. According to Pliny the Elder, large statues like this were often placed atop columns as memorials.

Roman Portraiture

The strong emphasis on portraiture in Roman art may stem from the early practice of creating likenesses—in some cases actual wax death masks—of revered figures and distinguished ancestors for display on public occasions, most notably funerals. Contemporary historians have left colorful evocations of this distinctively Roman custom. Polybius, a Greek exiled to Rome in the middle of the second century BCE, wrote home with the following description:

> ...after the interment [of the illustrious man] and the performance of the usual ceremonies, they place the image of the departed in the most conspicuous position in the house, enclosed in a wooden shrine. This image is a mask reproducing with remarkable fidelity both the features and the complexion of the deceased. On the occasion of public sacrifices, they display these images, and decorate them with much care, and when any distinguished member of the family dies they take them to the funeral, putting them on men who seem to bear the closest resemblance to the original in stature and carriage....There could not easily be a more ennobling spectacle for a young man who aspires to fame and virtue. For who would not be inspired by the sight of the images of men renowned for their excellence, all together and as if alive and breathing?...By this means, by the constant renewal of the good report of brave men, the celebrity of those who performed noble deeds is rendered immortal, while at the same time the fame of those who did good services to their country becomes known to the people and a heritage for future generations.
> (*Histories*, VI, pp. 53–54)

Growing out of this heritage, Roman Republican portraiture is frequently associated with the notion of **verism**—an interest in the faithful reproduction of the immediate visual and tactile appearance of subjects. Since we find in these portrait busts the same sorts of individualizing physiognomic features that allow us to differentiate among the people we know in our own world, it is easy to assume that they are exact reproductions of their subjects as they appeared during their lifetime. Of course, this is impossible to verify, but our strong desire to believe it must realize the intentions of the artists who made these portraits and the patrons for whom they were made.

A life-size marble statue of a Roman patrician (**FIG. 6–9**), dating from the period of the emperor Augustus, embodies the practices documented much earlier by Polybius and links the man portrayed with a revered tradition and its laudatory associations. The large marble format emulates a Greek notion of sculpture, and its use here signals not only this man's wealth but also his sophisticated artistic tastes, characteristics he shared with the emperor himself. His toga, however, is not Greek but indigenous and proclaims his respectability as a Roman citizen of some standing. The busts of ancestors that he holds in his hands document his distinguished lineage in the privileged upper class—there were laws regulating which members of society could own such collections—and the statue as a whole asserts his adherence to the family tradition by having his own portrait created.

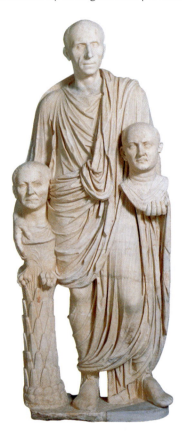

6–9 • PATRICIAN CARRYING PORTRAIT BUSTS OF TWO ANCESTORS (BARBERINI TOGATUS)
End of 1st century BCE or beginning of 1st century CE. Marble, height 5′ 5″ (1.65 m). Palazzo de Conservatori, Rome.

The head of this standing figure, though ancient Roman in origin, is a later replacement and not original to this statue. The separation of head and body in this work is understandable since in many instances the bodies of full-length portraits were produced in advance, waiting in the sculptor's workshop for a patron to commission a head with his or her own likeness that could be attached to it. Presumably the busts carried by this patrician were likewise only blocked out until they could be carved with the faces of the commissioner's ancestors. These faces share a striking family resemblance, and the stylistic difference between the two bust formats reveals that these men lived in successive generations. They could be the father and grandfather of the man who carries them.

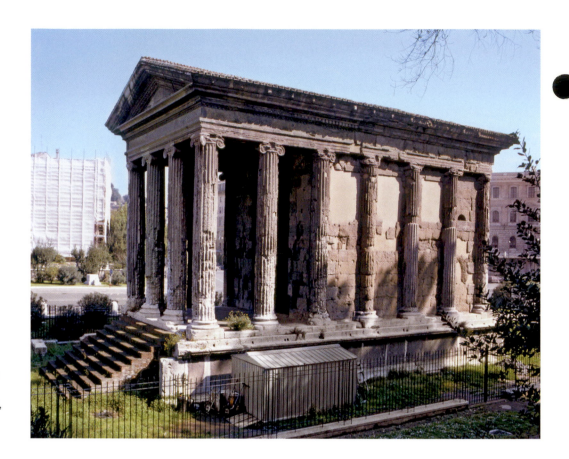

6–10 • EXTERIOR VIEW AND PLAN OF A TEMPLE
(perhaps dedicated to Portunus), Forum Boarium (Cattle Market), Rome. Late 2nd century BCE.

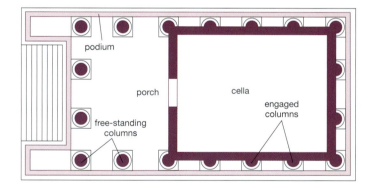

Architecture during the Republic reflected both Etruscan and Greek traditions. In religious architecture, the Romans favored urban temples set, in the Etruscan manner, in the midst of congested commercial centers, rather than isolated temples set within sacred precincts as preferred by the ancient Greeks. An early example is a small, rectangular temple on a **podium** (raised platform) built in Rome during the late second century BCE, perhaps dedicated to Portunus, the god of harbors and ports (**FIG. 6–10**). It uses the Etruscan system of a rectangular cella (interior room) and a colonnaded porch at one end reached by a broad, inviting staircase. The Romans adopted the Greek Ionic order here, but in contrast to Greek temples, only the columns on the porch are free-standing and structural. Around the cella, **engaged** half-columns were applied to articulate the load-bearing wall. In another departure from the Greek tradition—which had encouraged viewers to walk around temples, exploring their uniformly articulated sculptural mass—Roman temples are defined in relation to interior spaces, which viewers are invited to enter through one opening along the longitudinal axis of a symmetrical plan.

As city dwellers, Romans also devoted their ingenuity and resources to secular architecture. In fact, it was public building projects related to the transport and storage of food and water that made Roman cities viable. Many impressive examples of Roman engineering still stand. A stunning example is the **PONT DU GARD** in southern France (**FIG. 6–11**), designed to carry water over the Gard River to the Roman city of Nîmes. This **aqueduct**—a structure with water conduits—was part of a system that used gravity to transport water from springs 30 miles to the north, providing 100 gallons of water a day for every person in Nîmes.

The Pont du Gard was constructed of precisely cut stones from a nearby quarry. It consists of a stack of three **arcades**

6–11 • PONT DU GARD
Near Nîmes, France. Late 1st century BCE.

The three arcades of the aqueduct rise 160 feet (49 m) above the river. They exemplify the simplest use of the arch as a structural element. The thick base arcade supports a roadbed approximately 20 feet wide. The arches of the second arcade are narrower than the first and are set at one side of the roadbed. The narrow third arcade supports the water channel, 900 feet long on 35 arches, each of which is 23 feet high.

👁 **Watch** an architectural simulation of an arch on **MyArtsLab**

The round arch is a basic unit of Roman architecture. It is designed to displace most of the weight above it to its curving sides, and from there to the ground through supporting upright elements (**piers**, columns, or door or window jambs). Within a succession of arches, the unit made up of one arch and its supports is called a **bay**. Wall areas adjacent to curves of an arch are called **spandrels**. In the illustration, arrows indicate the outward thrust and downward gravity pull (weight) of the arch or vault.

A simple round arch can be lengthened to form a cylindrical **barrel vault**. In a barrel vault, however, the outward pressure exerted by its long curving sides usually requires added external support, called **buttressing**. When two barrel-vaulted spaces intersect each other at right angles, the result is a **groin vault**. The round arch and barrel vault were known and put to limited use by the ancient Mesopotamians, Egyptians, and Greeks. And they were employed more extensively by the Etruscans. But it was the Romans who realized the potential strength and versatility of these architectural elements and who exploited them to the fullest degree.

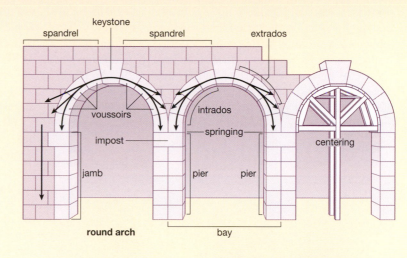

round arch

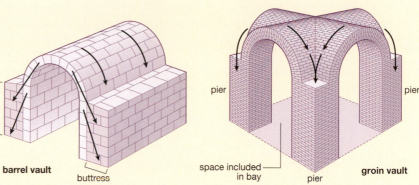

barrel vault

groin vault

Watch an architectural simulation of barrel and groin vaults on **MyArtsLab**

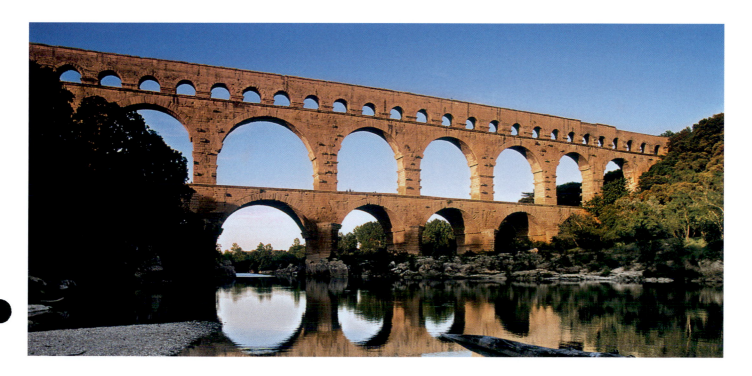

(series of regularly spaced arched openings) formed by fitting together wedge-shaped pieces, called **voussoirs**, which are locked together at the top center by a final piece, called a **keystone** (see "Arch and Vault," p. 137). A utilitarian structure, the aqueduct was left undecorated, and the projecting blocks that supported scaffolding during construction were left to provide easy access for repairs. Nevertheless, the Pont du Gard conveys a sense of balance, proportion, and rhythm, and although it harmonizes with its natural setting, it also makes a bold statement about Rome's ability to control nature in order to provide for its cities.

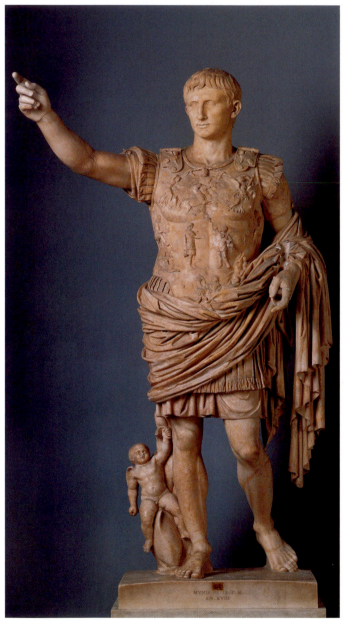

6–12 • AUGUSTUS OF PRIMAPORTA
Early 1st century CE (perhaps a copy of a bronze statue of c. 20 BCE). Marble, originally painted, height 6′ 8″ (2.03 m). Musei Vaticani, Braccio Nuovo, Rome.

The Age of Augustus

After Julius Caesar's death in 44 BCE and a period of renewed fighting, his 19-year-old great-nephew and adopted son, Octavian, assumed power. Although Octavian kept the forms of Republican government, he concentrated real authority in himself, and his accession marks the end of the Republic. By 27 BCE the Senate had conferred on him the title of "Augustus" (meaning "exalted," "sacred"), and as emperor, he began to use portraiture as political propaganda. An over-life-size statue discovered in the **villa** of his wife Livia, the **AUGUSTUS OF PRIMAPORTA** (**FIG. 6–12**), shows Augustus as he wanted to be seen and remembered. His image is inspired by heroic Greek figures such as Polykleitos's *Spear Bearer* (SEE FIG. 5–30) and portrays him in the physical prime of his youth rather than the advanced age idealized in the coin portrait of Julius Caesar. At the same time the emperor's head is rendered with sufficient naturalistic detail to make him easily recognizable. Augustus wears a cuirass (body armor) that portrays defeated barbarians and scenes of his military victories. His bare feet have led some scholars to propose that the work was made after his death to commemorate his **apotheosis**, or elevation to divine status.

On commemorative arches, columns, and tombs—often encrusted with sculpture—imperial Roman art celebrated not only emperors but contemporary events associated with them. The **ARA PACIS AUGUSTAE**, or **ALTAR OF AUGUSTAN PEACE** (**FIG. 6–13**), begun in 13 BCE and dedicated in 9 BCE, fuses Roman traditions and Greek Classicism to commemorate Augustus's triumphal return to Rome after establishing Roman rule in Gaul. The walled rectangular enclosure—the altar itself is inside and was approached by a flight of steep steps—was originally outdoors like Greek altars, not contained within a building as in more traditional Roman practice. Its sculpture is a creative union of portraiture and **allegory**, religion and politics, public and private. Relief panels along the exterior of the north and south sides depict senators and members of the imperial family who would have attended the victory celebrations (**FIG. 6–14**).

Unlike the Greek sculptors who created an ideal procession for the Parthenon frieze (SEE FIG. 5–29), the Roman sculptors of the *Ara Pacis* depicted actual individuals participating in a specific event at a specific time. To suggest a double line of marchers in space, they varied the depth of the carving, with the closest elements in higher relief and those farther back in increasingly lower relief. The design draws us, as spectators, into the event by making the feet of the nearest figures project into our space.

The marriage of Augustus and Livia was childless, so the emperor's successor was Tiberius, one of Livia's two sons by her first marriage, to Tiberius Claudius Nero. A large onyx **cameo** (a gemstone carved in low relief) known as *Gemma Augustea* evokes the apotheosis of Augustus after his death in 14 CE and the transfer of power to Tiberius (see "A Closer Look," p. 140). This work combines the idealized, heroic figures characteristic of Classical Greek art with recognizable portraits, the dramatic action of Hellenistic art, and a purely Roman penchant for portraying historical events as imperial propaganda.

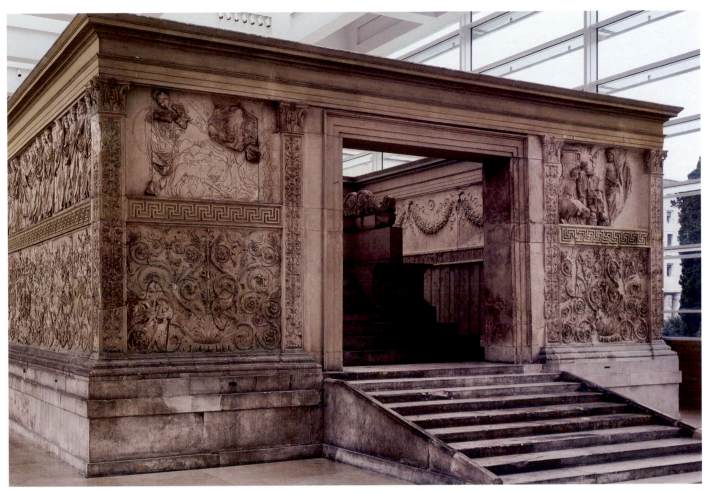

6–13 • ARA PACIS AUGUSTAE (ALTAR OF AUGUSTAN PEACE)
Rome. 13–9 BCE. Marble, approx. 34′ 5″ × 38′ (10.5 × 11.6 m).

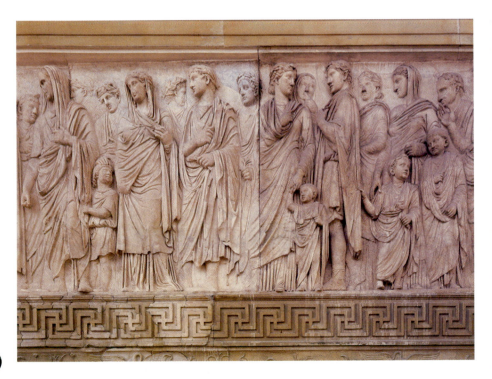

6–14 • IMPERIAL PROCESSION
Detail of a relief on the *Ara Pacis*.
Height 5′ 2″ (1.6 m).

The figures in this frieze represent members of Augustus's extended family, and scholars have proposed some specific identifications. The middle-aged man with the shrouded head at the far left may be Marcus Agrippa, who would have been Augustus's successor had he not predeceased him in 12 BCE. The bored but well-behaved youngster pulling at Agrippa's robe—and being restrained gently by the hand of the man behind him—is probably Agrippa's son, Gaius Caesar. The heavily swathed woman next to Agrippa on the right may be Augustus's wife, Livia, followed by the elder of her two sons, Tiberius, who would become the next emperor. Behind Tiberius could be Antonia, the niece of Augustus, looking back at her husband, Drusus, Livia's younger son. She may grasp the hand of Germanicus, one of her younger children. Behind their uncle Drusus seem to be Gnaeus and Domitia, children of Antonia's older sister, who would be standing quietly beside them. The depiction of children and real women in an official relief was new to the Augustan period and reflects Augustus's desire to promote private family life and proclaim dynastic succession.

Gemma Augustea ▶

Early 1st century CE. Onyx, 7½″ × 9″ (19 × 23 cm). Kunsthistorisches Museum, Vienna.

A personification of Rome (female since the word "Roma" is feminine in Latin), with the facial features of Augustus's wife Livia, looks admiringly over at the emperor, who is enthroned next to her.

The zodiac sign Capricorn refers either to the month in which Augustus was conceived or the date when the Senate conferred on him the title "Augustus" (January 16, 27 BCE).

Tiberius—Augustus's adopted son—steps out of his chariot, returning victorious from the German front prepared to assume the imperial throne as Augustus's chosen heir.

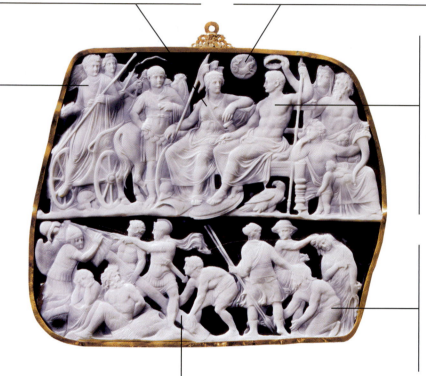

Augustus—crowned with a victor's wreath by Oikoumene, personification of the entire civilized world—assumes the pose and identity of the supreme god Jupiter (the eagle at his feet signifies Jupiter). The emperor's divine pretensions are not expressed overtly in public works such as the *Ara Pacis*, suggesting that this cameo was intended for a more private audience, drawn from his inner circle.

This cameo is carved from a piece of onyx with veins, or layers of color. The figures are carved within a layer of white, while the dark blue background is created by removing the white layer around them completely to reveal the vein of color underneath.

Below the realm of god-like rulers is a scene rooted not in allegory but public ritual, referring to Tiberius's victory over the Germans in 12 CE. Roman soldiers are raising a pole on which armor, captured from the defeated enemy, is displayed, while cowering, shackled barbarians wait to be tied to the pole as the trophy's base.

 View the Closer Look for the *Gemma Augustea* on **MyArtsLab**

The Roman House

In large cities, most Romans lived in multistory apartment buildings with shared walls, but the wealthiest citizens lived in gracious private residences with beautiful interior gardens. The affluent southern Italian city of Pompeii, a thriving center of between 10,000 and 20,000 inhabitants, gives a vivid picture of Roman city life. In 79 CE, Mount Vesuvius erupted, burying the city under more than 20 feet of volcanic ash and preserving it until its rediscovery and excavation, beginning in the eighteenth century.

Luxurious Pompeian townhouses usually consisted of small rooms laid out around one or two open courtyards, the atrium and the peristyle (**FIG. 6–15**). People entered the house from the street by stepping into the atrium, a large space with a centralized **impluvium** (pool for catching rainwater). Farther into the house was the peristyle, a planted courtyard enclosed by columns. Private areas—the family dining and sitting rooms, as well as bedrooms and service areas, such as the kitchen and servants' quarters—could be arranged around the peristyle or the atrium. Off the peristyle opened a formal reception room where the head of the household conferred with clients. The mild southern climate permitted gardens to flourish year-round in Pompeii, so the peristyle was often turned into an outdoor living room with painted walls, fountains, and sculpture, as in the House of the Vettii (**FIG. 6–16**), built by two brothers—wealthy freed slaves A. Vettius Conviva and A. Vettius Restitutus.

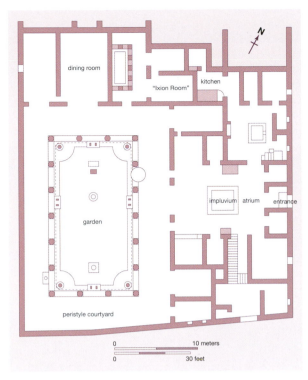

6–15 • PLAN OF THE HOUSE OF THE VETTII
Pompeii. Rebuilt 62–79 CE.

Mosaics were popular as decoration for the floors and fountains of Roman houses, where durability and waterproofing were desired (see "Roman Mosaics," p. 142). The interior walls were smooth plaster surfaces with few architectural moldings or projections. On these invitingly plain surfaces, artists painted decorations using pigment in a solution of lime and soap, sometimes with a little wax. After such paintings were finished, they were polished with a burnisher and buffed with a cloth. Many fine wall paintings have come to light through excavations, first in Pompeii and other communities surrounding Mount Vesuvius, and more recently in and around Rome.

In the earliest paintings, beginning about 200 BCE, artists created the illusion of thin slabs of colored marble covering the walls. They also modeled shallow architectural moldings and columns in plaster. By about 80 BCE, painters began to extend the space of a room visually with scenes of figures on a shallow platform or with a landscape or cityscape. Architectural details such as columns were painted rather than modeled from plaster. As time passed, such illusionistic architecture became increasingly fanciful. Solid colored walls were decorated with slender, whimsical architectural and floral details and small, delicate vignettes. The wall surfaces seem to recede or even disappear behind a maze of floating architectural forms.

Some of the finest surviving Roman wall paintings are found in the Pompeian House of the Vettii, whose plan and

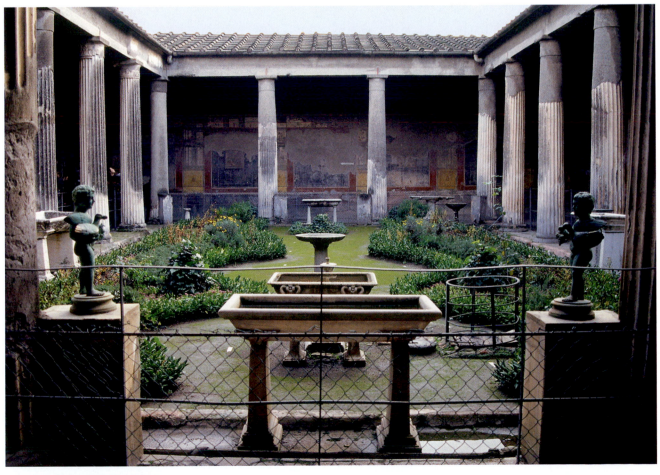

6–16 • PERISTYLE GARDEN
House of the Vettii, Pompeii. 62–79 CE.

Mosaics, already used widely in Hellenistic times, were popular in wealthy Romans' homes. Mosaic designs were created with pebbles or small cubes of colored stone or glass called tesserae, which were pressed into a soft cement called grout to hold them in place and fill the spaces between them.

Some highly skilled mosaicists copied well-known paintings, employing very small tesserae to create subtle shadings and color changes. The "Alexander mosaic" (SEE FIG. 5–36), once the floor of a house in Pompeii, is a superb example. And in an "unswept floor" mosaic (FIG. 6–17), Heraklitos adapted the *trompe l'oeil* ("fool the eye") representation of a floor littered with table debris by an earlier Hellenistic painter named Sosos. Heraklitos's mosaic version, made three centuries later—including a mouse among the table scraps—portrays the refuse of a lavish meal—bones of fish and fowl, shells and nuts, fruits and twigs—in meticulous detail, even showing the shadows these modeled, three-dimensional objects cast on the floor.

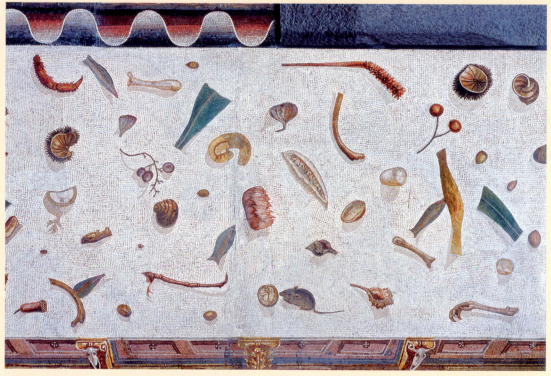

6–17 • Heraklitos THE UNSWEPT FLOOR
Mosaic version of a 2nd-century BCE painting by Sosos of Pergamon. 2nd century CE. 13′ 3½″ (4.05 m). Musei Vaticani, Museo Gregoriano Profano, Rome.

View the Closer Look for technique of mosaic on **MyArtsLab**

peristyle garden we have already seen (SEE FIGS. 6–15, 6–16). Between its damage during an earthquake in 62 CE and the eruption of Vesuvius in 79 CE, the walls of this house were repainted, and this spectacular decoration was uncovered in a splendid state of preservation during excavations at the end of the nineteenth century.

A complex combination of painted fantasies fills the walls of a reception room off the peristyle garden known as the "Ixion Room" (FIG. 6–18). At the base of the walls is a lavish simulated frieze of colored-marble revetment, imitating the actual stone veneers that are found in some Roman residences. Above this "marble" **dado** (the lower part of a wall) are broad areas of pure red or white, onto which are painted pictures resembling framed **panel paintings**, **swags** of floral garlands, or unframed

figural vignettes. The framed picture seen here portrays a Greek mythological scene from the story of Ixion, who was bound by Zeus to a spinning wheel as punishment for attempting to seduce Hera. Between these pictorial fields, and along a long strip above them that runs around the entire room, are fantastic architectural vistas with multicolored columns and undulating entablatures that recede into fictive space through the use of fanciful **linear perspective** (see "Starter Kit," p. xvi). The fact that these architectural renderings are occupied here and there by **volumetric** figures only enhances their sense of three-dimensionality.

One of the most famous painted rooms in Roman art is in the so-called **VILLA OF THE MYSTERIES** at Pompeii (FIG. 6–19). The rites of mystery religions were often performed in

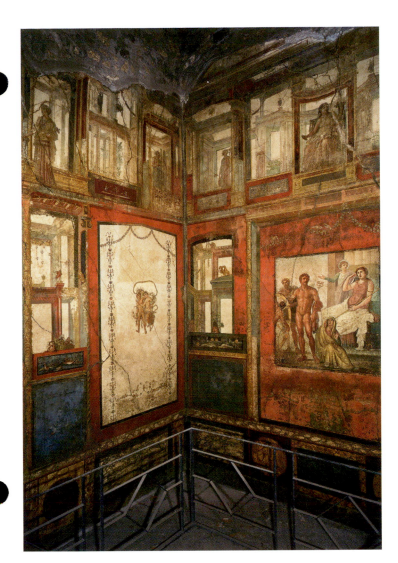

private homes as well as in special buildings or temples, and this room, at the corner of a suburban villa, may have been a shrine or a meeting place for such a cult. The murals may depict initiation rites into the cult of Bacchus, god of vegetation and fertility as well as wine, who was one of the most popular deities in Pompeii. The entirely painted architectural setting consists of a "marble" dado similar to that in FIGURE 6–18 and, around the top of the wall, an elegant frieze supported by **pilasters** (engaged strips). The action unfolds on a shallow "stage" running around the entire room above the dado, and against a background of a brilliant, deep red that was so popular with Pompeian painters that it has come to be called "Pompeian red."

Imperial Rome

What were some major trends and monuments of imperial Roman art and architecture?

The sequence of related Roman rulers that follows Augustus, beginning with Tiberius and ending with the reign of the despotic and capricious Nero, is known as the Julio-Claudian dynasty (14–68 CE). A powerful general named Vespasian seized control of the government after Nero's death to found the Flavian dynasty (69–98 CE). The Flavian emperors—Vespasian (ruled 69–79 CE), Titus (ruled 79–81 CE), and Domitian (ruled 81–96 CE)—restored imperial finances and stabilized the empire's frontiers. Five outstanding rulers followed the Flavians: Nerva (ruled 96–98 CE), Trajan (ruled 98–117 CE), Hadrian (ruled 117–138 CE), Antoninus Pius (ruled 138–161 CE), and Marcus

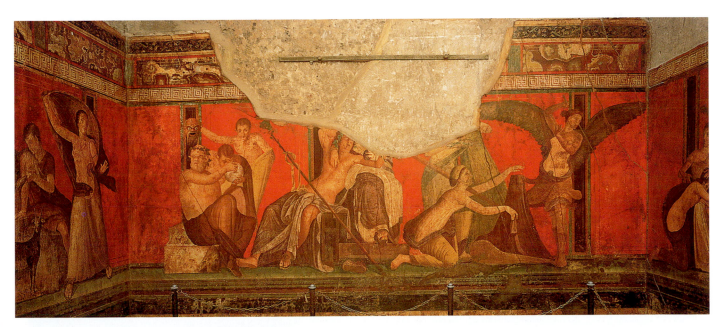

6–19 • WALL PAINTING, VILLA OF THE MYSTERIES
Pompeii. c. 60–50 BCE.

 Watch a video about Pompeii on **MyArtsLab**

Aurelius (ruled 161–180 CE). These "Five Good Emperors" oversaw a long period of stability and prosperity. Under Trajan, the Roman Empire reached its greatest extent, annexing Dacia (roughly, present-day Romania) in 106 CE and expanding the empire's boundaries in the Near East.

Imperial Art and Architecture

Romans were huge sports fans, and the Flavian emperors catered to their taste by building splendid facilities, notably the Flavian Amphitheater (FIG. 6–20), Rome's greatest arena, begun in 72 CE during the reign of Vespasian and dedicated by Titus in 80 CE. This building came to be known as the "Colosseum," because a gigantic statue of Nero, called the Colossus, stood next to it. The Flavians erected the arena to bolster their popularity in Rome, and in this enormous entertainment center, audiences watched blood sports and spectacles including animal hunts, fights to the death between gladiators or between gladiators and wild animals, and performances by trained animals and acrobats. The opening performance in 80 CE lasted 100 days, during which time, it was claimed, 9,000 wild animals and 2,000 gladiators died for the amusement of the spectators. For its ease of crowd movement and unobstructed views, the design of the Colosseum, which held about 50,000 spectators, has never been improved upon.

The Colosseum was built entirely of travertine and tufa blocks and of **concrete** faced with stone. Eighty barrel vaults built to cover corridors and stairs radiate from the arena's center, forming groin vaults where they intersect the barrel ring vaults that cover the passageways around the perimeter (see "Arch and Vault," p. 137). These complex curved shapes could be formed of concrete faster and more cheaply than from stone blocks, which had to be cut by trained masons. The concrete consisted of stone rubble (*caementa*) in a binder made from volcanic sand and water. This rough but strong core was faced on the outside of the building with finer, worked stone, creating a curving façade of three levels of arcades surmounted by a wall-like top, or **attic story**. Every arch is framed by **engaged columns**, which support friezes that mark the division between levels. Each level uses a different architectural order, and the levels become increasingly decorative as they rise. At ground level are columns in the Tuscan order (see "Roman Architectural Orders," p. 145); the Ionic order is used on the second level, the Corinthian on the third, and flat Corinthian pilasters adorn the fourth. These are purely decorative elements, serving no structural function.

When Domitian became emperor in 81 CE, he immediately commissioned a **triumphal arch** to commemorate the capture of Jerusalem in 70 CE by his brother and deified predecessor Titus (FIG. 6–21). The **ARCH OF TITUS**, constructed of concrete and faced with marble, is essentially a large free-standing gateway whose passageway is covered by a barrel vault. Applied to the faces of the arch are Composite columns (see "Roman Architectural Orders," p. 145). Originally the 50-foot-high arch served as a giant base for a monumental bronze statue of a four-horse chariot and driver, a typical Roman triumphal symbol.

Titus's capture of Jerusalem ended a fierce campaign to crush a revolt of the Jews in Palestine. The Romans looted and

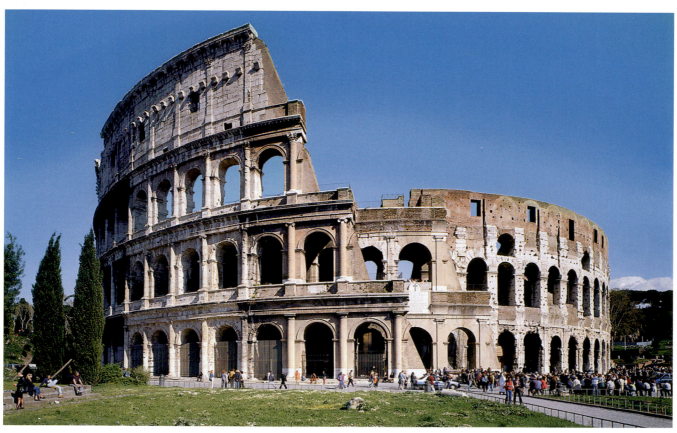

6-20 • COLOSSEUM
Rome. 72–80 CE.

The Etruscans and Romans adapted Greek architectural orders to their own tastes, often using them as applied decoration on walls. The Etruscans developed the sturdy Tuscan order by modifying the Greek Doric order, smoothing out the shafts and setting them on a base. The Romans created the **Composite order** by combining the volutes of the Greek Ionic capital with the acanthus leaves of the Corinthian order. In this diagram, the Roman orders are shown on pedestals, which consist of a **plinth**, a dado, and a cornice.

👁 **Watch** an architectural simulation of the Roman orders on **MyArtsLab**

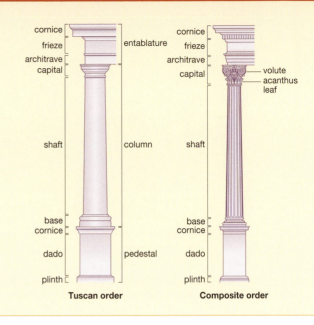

Tuscan order   Composite order

destroyed the Second Temple of Jerusalem and carted off its sacred treasures to display them in Rome during Titus's triumphal procession. A relief on the inside walls of the arch, capturing the drama of the occasion, depicts Titus's soldiers flaunting this booty—prominently a huge **menorah**, or seven-branched lamp holder—as they carry it through the streets of Rome (**FIG. 6–22**). Viewing this crowd as through a window, the observer can easily imagine the boisterous scene. The varying depth of relief sculpture creates the impression that the marchers are moving toward the viewer and then turning to move away at the right through a distant arch, producing a clear illusion of deeper and more complex space than that in the earlier reliefs of the *Ara Pacis* (SEE FIG. 6–13).

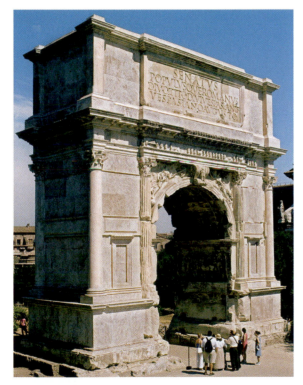

6–21 • ARCH OF TITUS

Rome. c. 81 CE (restored 1822–1824). Concrete and white marble, height 50′ (15 m).

The dedication inscribed across the tall attic story above the arch opening reads: "The Senate and the Roman People to the Deified Titus Flavius Vespasianus Augustus, son of the Deified Vespasian." The Romans typically recorded historic occasions and identified monuments with solemn prose and beautiful inscriptions in stone. The perfectly sized and spaced Roman capital letters—meant to be read from a distance and cut with sharp terminals (serifs) to catch the light—established a standard that calligraphers and font designers still follow.

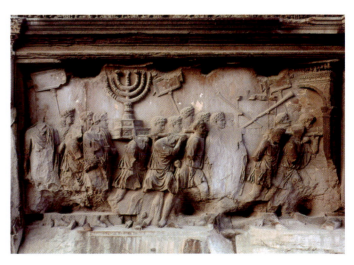

6–22 • SPOILS FROM THE TEMPLE OF SOLOMON IN JERUSALEM

Relief in the passageway of the Arch of Titus, Rome. Marble, height 6′ 8″ (2.03 m).

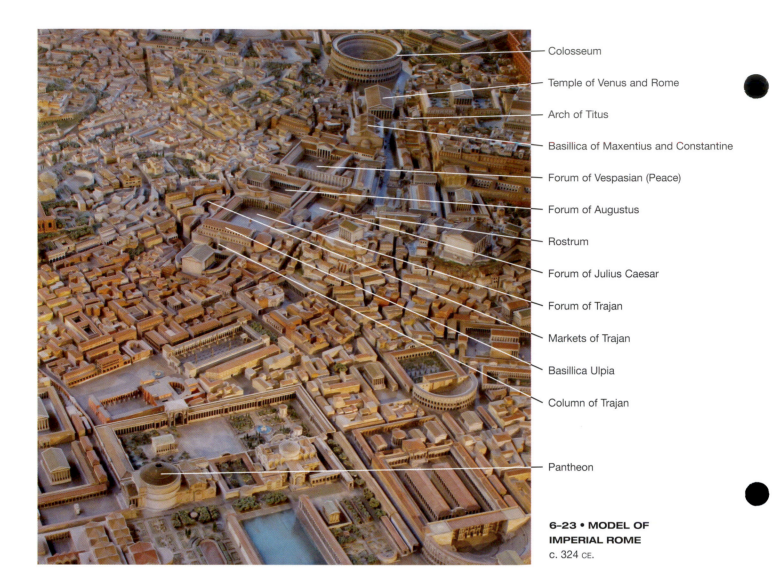

Colosseum

Temple of Venus and Rome

Arch of Titus

Basillica of Maxentius and Constantine

Forum of Vespasian (Peace)

Forum of Augustus

Rostrum

Forum of Julius Caesar

Forum of Trajan

Markets of Trajan

Basilica Ulpia

Column of Trajan

Pantheon

6–23 • MODEL OF IMPERIAL ROME
c. 324 CE.

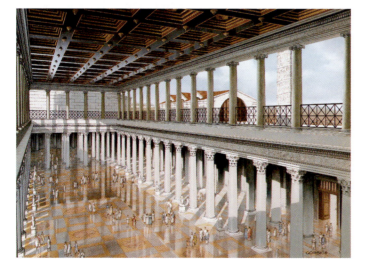

6–24 • INTERIOR VIEW AND PLAN OF THE BASILICA ULPIA

From the Forum of Trajan, Rome. c. 113 CE. Reconstruction drawn by Gilbert Gorski.

The building may have had clerestory windows instead of the gallery shown here. The Column of Trajan can be seen through the upper colonnade at the right.

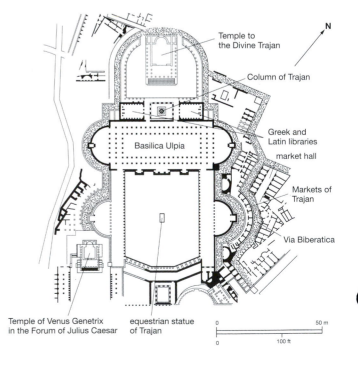

N

Temple to the Divine Trajan

Column of Trajan

Greek and Latin libraries

market hall

Basilica Ulpia

Markets of Trajan

Via Biberatica

Temple of Venus Genetrix in the Forum of Julius Caesar

equestrian statue of Trajan

0   50 m
0   100 ft

Emperors built not only in Rome, but throughout the empire. Projects such as the imperial **forums** (civic centers) of the capital (**FIG. 6–23**) were repeated elsewhere on a smaller scale. Forums consisted of a large open square or oblong space generally surrounded by colonnades leading to a temple. They sometimes included a **basilica**, a large rectangular building with an expansive interior space, adaptable for a variety of administrative functions. Basilicas could serve as imperial audience chambers, army drill halls, courts of law, or schools. These spacious and flexible interiors made the basilica attractive to Christians, who would later appropriate it as a design for churches.

The **BASILICA ULPIA**, one of the largest components of the Forum of Trajan (**FIG. 6–24**), was dedicated as a court of law in 113 CE. It was a grand, rectangular building partitioned into a large central area called a **nave**, flanked by two lower colonnaded **aisles** and entered through several doors on the long side of the building that faced the Forum's open square. **Apses** (rounded extensions) at each end provided imposing settings for judges when the court was in session.

Behind the Basilica Ulpia stood twin libraries built to house the emperor's collection of Latin and Greek texts. These buildings flanked an open court, the location of a grand column that became Trajan's tomb (**FIG. 6–25**). The **COLUMN OF TRAJAN**

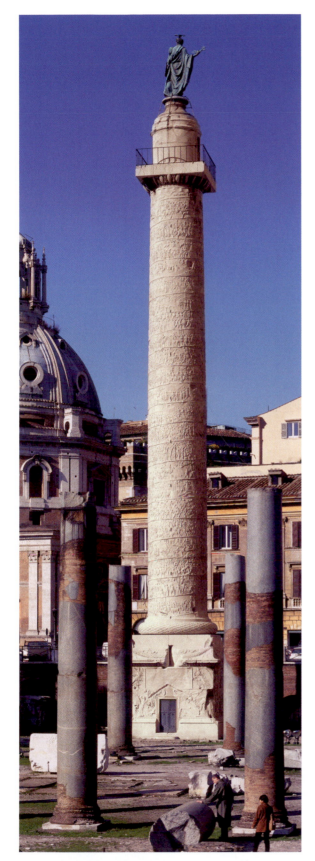

6–25 • COLUMN OF TRAJAN

Rome. 113–116 or after 117 CE. Marble, overall height with base 125′ (38 m), column alone 97′ 8″ (29.77 m); length of relief 625′ (190.5 m).

View the Closer Look for the Column of Trajan on **MyArtsLab**

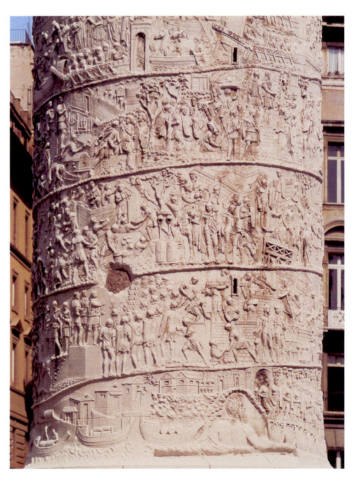

6–26 • ROMANS CROSSING THE DANUBE AND BUILDING A FORT

Detail of the lowest part of the Column of Trajan. 113–116 CE, or after 117 CE. Marble, height of the spiral band approx. 36″ (91 cm).

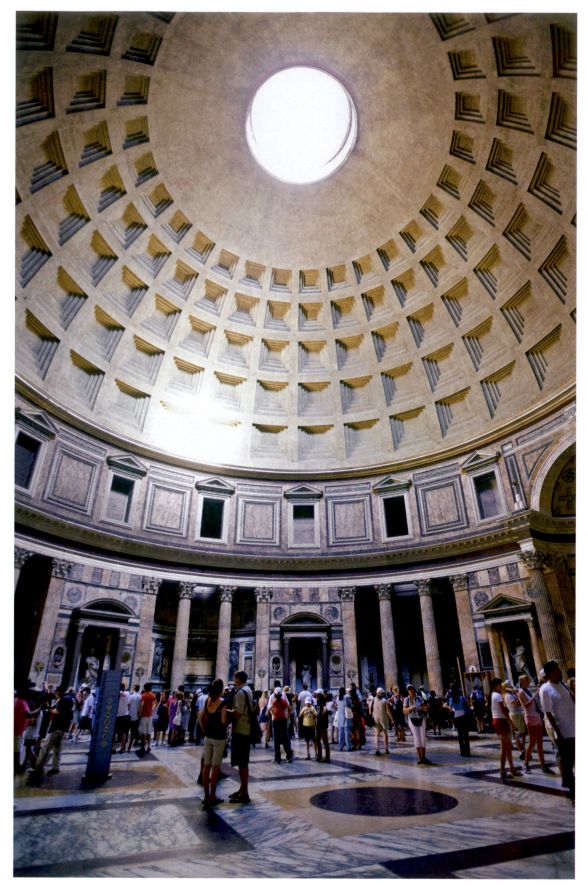

6–27 • DOME OF THE PANTHEON
Rome. 110–128 CE.

✳ **Explore** the architectural panoramas of the Pantheon on **MyArtsLab**

6–28 • EXTERIOR VIEW AND PLAN OF THE PANTHEON
Rome. 110–128 CE.

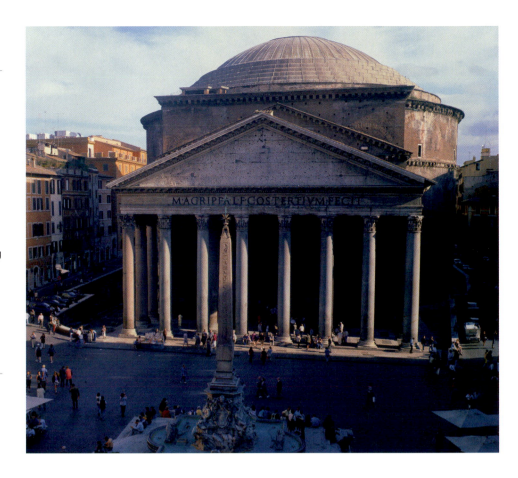

Although this magnificent monument was designed and constructed during the reigns of Emperors Trajan and Hadrian, the long inscription on the architrave states that it was built by "Marcus Agrippa, son of Lucius, who was consul three times." Agrippa, the son-in-law and valued advisor of Augustus, sponsored a building on this site in 27–25 BCE. After a fire in 80 CE, Domitian either restored the Pantheon or built a new temple, which burned again after being struck by lightning in 110 CE. Although there has been a strong scholarly consensus that it was Hadrian who reconstructed the building in its current state in 118–128 CE, a recent study of the brick stamps has argued convincingly that the Pantheon was begun soon after 110 under Trajan, but only completed during the reign of his successor, Hadrian.

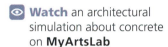

Watch an architectural simulation about concrete on **MyArtsLab**

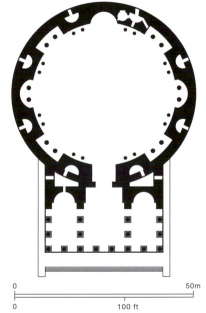

was carved with dense reliefs depicting his victorious campaign against the Dacians (102–106 CE). This long, spiraling narrative strip—almost 625 feet if laid out straight—includes more than 2,500 individual figures, linked by landscape and architecture, punctuated by the recurring figure of Trajan.

The scene at the beginning of the spiral, at the bottom of the column, shows Trajan's army crossing the Danube River on a pontoon bridge to launch the campaign (FIG. 6–26). Soldiers construct battlefield headquarters in Dacia from which the men on the frontiers will receive orders, food, and weapons. In this spectacular piece of imperial ideology or propaganda, Trajan is portrayed as a strong, stable, and efficient commander of a well-run army, and his barbarian enemies are shown as worthy opponents of Rome.

A handsome market was built into a hillside adjacent to Trajan's Forum to replace a commercial district that was razed to make room for the imperial complex. Comparable in size to a large modern shopping mall, it had more than 150 individual shops on several levels and included a large, groin-vaulted main hall. The collective structures and spaces that make up the Forum and Markets of Trajan exemplify the finest in imperial city planning, satisfying both the needs of the citizens and the desire of the emperor for impressive public works and memorializing propaganda.

Trajan, and his well-educated and widely traveled successor Hadrian, were responsible for the most remarkable ancient building surviving in Rome, one of the marvels of world architecture in any age. This temple to Mars, Venus, and the divine Julius Caesar, known as the **PANTHEON**, was built between 110 and 128 CE (FIGS. 6–27, 6–28). The entrance porch, made to resemble the façade of a typical rectangular Roman temple, was all that original viewers could see since their approach was controlled by an enclosed courtyard (SEE FIG. 6–23). The actual circular shape of the building was concealed. This theatrical presentation allowed the soaring and enclosing space of the giant **rotunda** (circular room) surmounted with a huge, bowl-shaped dome, 143 feet in diameter and 143 feet from the floor to its summit, to be a surprise encountered by viewers only

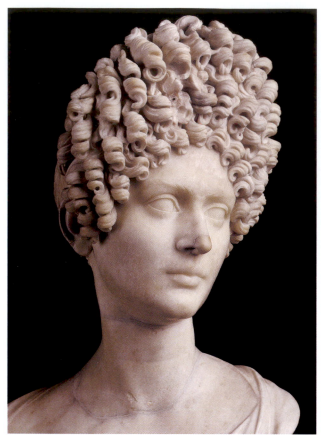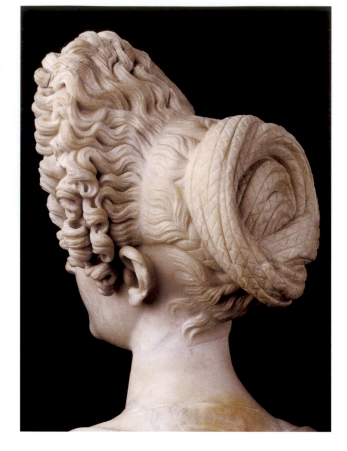

6–29 • YOUNG FLAVIAN WOMAN
c. 90 CE. Marble, height 25″ (65.5 cm). Museo Capitolino, Rome.

after they passed through the rectilinear and restricted aisles of the **portico** toward the huge main door. Even without the controlled courtyard approach, encountering this glorious space today is still an overwhelming experience—for many of us, one that is repeated even on successive visits to the rotunda.

The Pantheon is a prime example of the spatial experimentation and structural audacity that are hallmarks of Roman imperial architecture. The circular wall, or **drum**, of the rotunda, which supports and buttresses the dome, is formed of brick arches and concrete, in a honeycombed interior structural system that is concealed beneath the delicate architectonic patterns of marble veneer. Structurally, a dome works as an arch pivoted 360 degrees around the top of a drum. In the Pantheon, the usual keystone is replaced by a 29-foot-wide central circular opening, or **oculus**. The repetition of square against circle, established on a large scale by juxtaposing the rectilinear portico against the circular rotunda, dominates the building's ornamentation. Seven interior **niches**, rectangular alternating with semicircular, originally held statues of the gods. Inside the dome, square, boxlike **coffers** (recessed ceiling panels) help lighten the weight of the masonry and may once have contained gilded bronze rosettes or stars suggesting the heavens.

Inside, our eyes are drawn upward over the pattern made by the coffers to the light entering through the oculus (SEE FIG. 6–27), which creates a brilliant circle against the surface of the dome, a disk that moves around this microcosm throughout the day like a sun. Clouds can be seen traveling across the opening on some days; on others, rain falls through and drains through conduits planned by the original engineer. Occasionally, a bird flies in. This open, luminous space imparts the sense that one could rise buoyantly upward to escape the spherical hollow of the building and commune with the cosmos.

Portraits in Sculpture and Painting

The development of art in Rome depended on private as well as public patronage, and private Roman patrons continued to expect recognizable likenesses in their portraits. This did not preclude idealization. The portrait of an unidentified **YOUNG FLAVIAN WOMAN** (FIG. 6–29) is idealized in a manner similar to the *Augustus of Primaporta* (SEE FIG. 6–12). Her well-observed, recognizable features—strong nose and jaw, heavy brows, deep-set eyes, and long neck—contrast with the smoothly rendered flesh and soft, sensual lips. Her hair is piled high in an extraordinary mass of ringlets following the latest court fashion. Executing the head required skillful chiseling and **drillwork**, a technique for rapidly cutting deep grooves with straight sides used here to render the holes in the center of the curls. The overall effect, especially from a distance, is quite lifelike. The play of natural light over the more subtly sculpted marble surfaces simulates the textures of real skin and hair.

A contemporary bust of an older woman (FIG. 6–30) presents a strikingly different image of its subject. Although she also wears her hair in the latest fashion, it is less elaborate and less painstakingly confected than that of her more

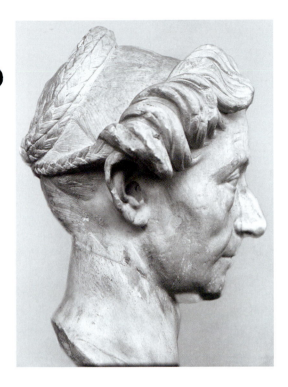

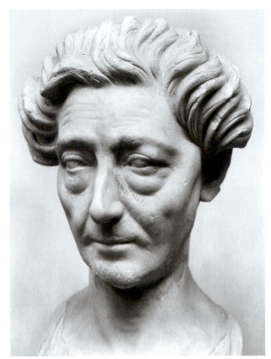

youthful counterpart. The portrait she commissioned emphasizes not the fresh sheen of an unblemished face, but a visage clearly marked by the passage of time during a life well lived. We may experience this portrait as less idealized and more naturalistic, but for a Roman viewer, it conformed to an ideal of age and accomplishment by showcasing signs of aging facial features cherished since the Republican period as reflections of virtue and venerability.

Portraits were also popular in wall painting. In this arresting double portrait of a young husband and wife from Pompeii (FIG. 6–31), the couple looks out from their simulated spatial world through the wall and into the viewers' space within the room. The swarthy, wispy-bearded man addresses us with a direct stare, holding a scroll in his left hand, a conventional attribute of educational achievement seen frequently in Roman portraits. Though his wife overlaps him to stake her claim to the foreground, her gaze out at us is less direct. Like him, she holds fashionable attributes of literacy—the stylus she elevates in front of her chin and the folding writing tablet on which she would use the stylus to inscribe words into a wax infill. This picture is comparable to a modern studio portrait— perhaps a wedding photograph—with its careful lighting and retouching, conventional poses and accoutrements. But the attention to physiognomic detail—note the differences in the spacing of their eyes and the shapes of

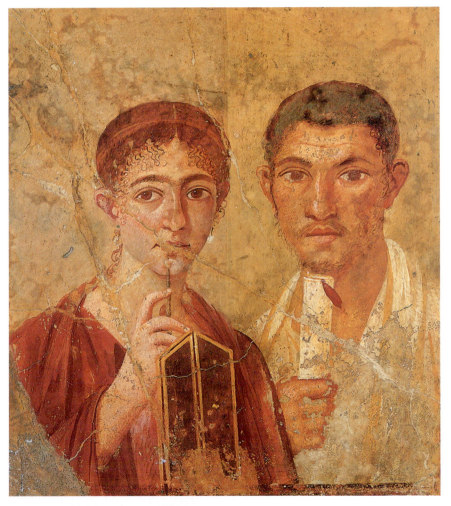

6–31 • PORTRAIT OF A MARRIED COUPLE
Wall painting from Pompeii. Mid 1st century CE. Height 25½″ (64.8 cm). Museo Archeologico Nazionale, Naples.

their noses, ears, and lips—makes it quite clear that we are in the presence of actual human likenesses.

Hadrian's successor, **MARCUS AURELIUS**, was renowned both for his intellectual and his military achievements. In a gilded bronze equestrian statue, the commanding emperor wears a tunic and short, heavy cloak (**FIG. 6–32**). The raised foreleg of his horse is poised to trample a defeated foe (now lost), but the emperor wears no armor and carries no weapons. Like Egyptian kings, he conquers effortlessly by divine will. And like his illustrious predecessor Augustus (SEE FIG. 6–12), he reaches out to those around him in a conventional rhetorical gesture of address. In a lucky error or twist of fate, this statue came mistakenly to be revered during the Middle Ages as a portrait of Constantine, the first Christian emperor. Consequently, it escaped being melted down, a fate that befell many other bronze statues from antiquity.

Marcus Aurelius was succeeded by his son Commodus, a man without political skill, administrative competence, or intellectual distinction. During his unfortunate reign (180–192 CE), Commodus devoted himself to luxury and frivolous pursuits. He did, however, sponsor some of the finest artists of the day. In a spectacular marble bust (**FIG. 6–33**), the emperor is presented as Hercules, adorned with references to the hero's

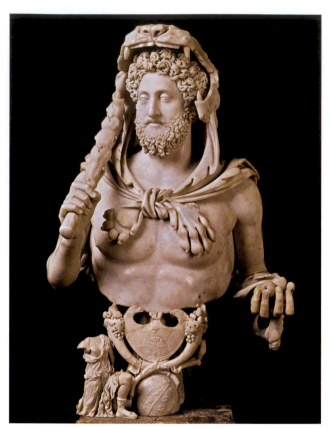

6-33 • COMMODUS AS HERCULES
From the Esquiline Hill, Rome. c. 191–192 CE. Marble, height 46½″ (118 cm). Palazzo dei Conservatori, Rome

legendary labors—his club, the skin and head of the Nemean lion, and the golden apples from the gardens of the Hesperides. Commodus's likeness emphasizes his family resemblance to his more illustrious and powerful father (SEE FIG. 6–32), but this portrait also captures well his vanity through the grand pretensions of his costume and the Classical idealization of his body type.

The Late Empire

What continues and what changes in art and architecture during the Late Roman Empire?

The reign of Commodus marked the beginning of a period of political and economic decline. During the rule of the succeeding Severan emperors (193–235 CE), migrating peoples from the north and east began to cross Rome's frontiers, disrupting provincial government. Imperial rule became increasingly autocratic, and soon the army controlled the government. Following the assassination of the last Severan emperor by one of his military commanders in 235 CE, Rome was plunged into a period of anarchy that lasted for half a century.

The anarchy of the mid third century ended with the rise to power of the emperor Diocletian (ruled 284–305 CE). This brilliant politician and general reversed the empire's declining fortunes, but he also initiated an increasingly dictatorial government, eventually dividing the empire among four rulers known as the tetrarchs. This political restructuring is paralleled

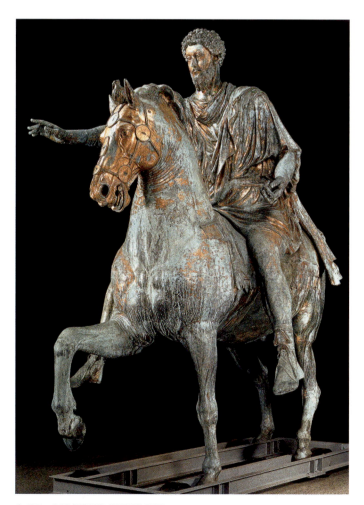

6-32 • MARCUS AURELIUS
c. 176 CE. Bronze, originally gilded, height of statue 11′ 6″ (3.5 m). Museo Capitolino, Rome.

Thereafter, two main contenders—both sons of tetrarchs—emerged in the western part of the empire: Maxentius, who controlled the Italian peninsula, and Constantine.

Although the city of Rome had declined in importance by this time, building did not end altogether. Maxentius (ruled 306–312 CE) ordered the repair of many buildings in Rome and

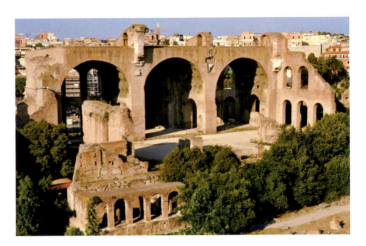

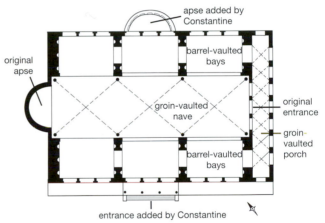

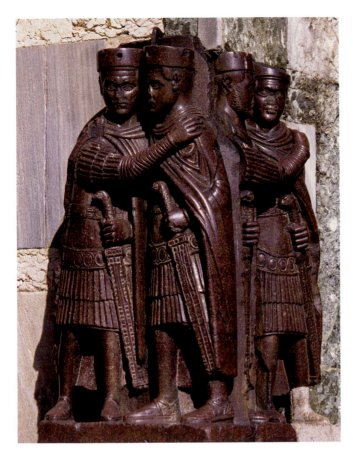

6-34 • THE TETRARCHS

c. 300 CE. Porphyry, height of figures 51″ (1.29 m). Cathedral of St. Mark, Venice.

This group of figures may have been sculpted in Egypt and moved to Constantinople after 330 CE. Christian crusaders who looted Constantinople in 1204 CE took the statue to Venice and cut it into two parts for installation on the corner of the façade of the cathedral of St. Mark.

by the introduction of a radically new, hard style of geometricized abstraction, especially notable in portraits of the tetrarchs themselves. In a surviving sculptural group, **THE TETRARCHS** are startlingly alert with searing eyes (**FIG. 6–34**), the stylistic antithesis of the suave Classicism seen in the portrait of Commodus as Hercules (**SEE FIG. 6–33**). There is no clear sense of likeness. Who these individuals are is less significant than the powerful position each holds. Some art historians have interpreted this change in style as a conscious embodiment of Diocletian's new abstract concept of government, while others have pointed to parallels with the provincial art of Diocletian's Dalmatian homeland or with the Neoplatonic aesthetics of idealized abstraction promoted by Plotinus, a third-century CE philosopher who was widely read in the late Roman world. In any event, these riveting works represent not a degeneration of the Classical tradition but its conscious replacement by a different aesthetic viewpoint—militaristic, severe, and abstract, rather than suave, slick, and classicizing.

The orderly succession that Diocletian had hoped for failed to occur. After his own abdication and retirement in 305 CE, a struggle for position and advantage ensued almost immediately.

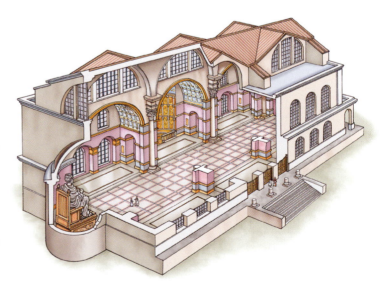

6-35 • EXTERIOR VIEW, PLAN, AND RECONSTRUCTION DRAWING OF THE BASILICA OF MAXENTIUS AND CONSTANTINE

Rome. 306–313 CE.

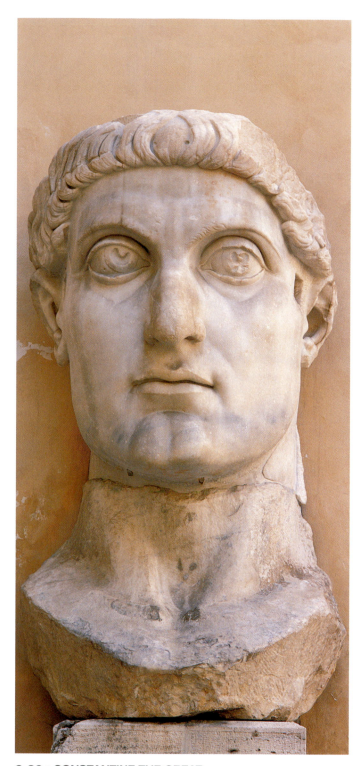

6–36 • CONSTANTINE THE GREAT
From the basilica of Maxentius and Constantine, Rome. 325–326 CE. Marble, height of head 8′ 6″ (2.6 m). Palazzo dei Conservatori, Rome.

This head came from a gigantic, awe-inspiring statue of the seated emperor. Only a few marble fragments survive—the head, a hand, a knee, an elbow, and a foot. The trunk of the body might have been made of colored stone or of a scaffold of wood and bricks sheathed in bronze.

had others built during his short reign. His most impressive undertaking was a huge new basilica called the Basilica Nova, or New Basilica (**FIG. 6–35**). Now known as the **BASILICA OF MAXENTIUS AND CONSTANTINE** (who modified and completed it), this was the last important imperial government building erected in Rome itself. It functioned as an administrative center and provided a magnificent setting for the emperor when he appeared as supreme judge. Three gigantic brick-and-concrete barrel vaults from one side aisle still loom over the streets of modern Rome. The central hall was covered with huge groin vaults (see "Arch and Vault," p. 137) buttressed by the barrel vaults of the side aisles. Such strong support for the central groin vaults allowed the opening of generous windows in the clerestory. A porch extended across one short side sheltering a triple entrance to the central hall. At the opposite end an apse acted as a focal point for the interior. The directional focus along a longitudinal axis from the entrance to the apse emphasized the presence of the emperor, or at least his statue. A monumental portrait of Constantine, found in the basilica, served as a stand-in for the emperor and a powerful reminder of his imperial power when he himself was unable to be present (**FIG. 6–36**).

After defeating Maxentius at the Battle of the Milvian Bridge in 312 CE, Constantine (ruled 307–337) became sole ruler in the west. According to tradition, the night before the battle Constantine had a vision of a flaming cross in the sky bearing these words: "In this sign you shall conquer" (*in hoc signo vinces*). The next morning he ordered that his army's shields and standards be inscribed with the monogram XP (the Greek letters *chi* and *rho* for *Christos*, or Christ), and they won the battle. In 313 CE, Constantine issued the Edict of Milan granting freedom to all religious groups, including Christians.

In Rome, next to the Colosseum, the Senate erected a triumphal arch to commemorate Constantine's victory over Maxentius (**FIG. 6–37**), a huge triple arch that dwarfs the nearby Arch of Titus (**SEE FIG. 6–21**). Three barrel-vaulted passageways are flanked by columns on high pedestals and surmounted by a large attic story with elaborate sculpture and a laudatory inscription—"To the Emperor Constantine from the Senate and the Roman People. Since through divine inspiration and great wisdom he has delivered the state from the tyrant and his party by his army and noble arms, [we] dedicate this arch, decorated with triumphal insignia." The "triumphal insignia" were in part appropriated from earlier monuments made for Constantine's illustrious predecessors—Trajan, Hadrian, and Marcus Aurelius. The reused items visually link the old Roman virtues of strength, courage, and piety associated with these exemplary emperors to Constantine himself. New reliefs made for the arch recount the story of Constantine's victory and proclaim his power and generosity. A rectangular panel above one side arch, below the two roundels in **FIGURE 6–38**, depicts Constantine's first public speech after defeating Maxentius. Toward the center of the panel, the emperor (his head is missing) stands at the rostrum, or speaker's platform, in the Roman Forum, flanked by standing officials and seated statues of Emperors Marcus Aurelius and Hadrian.

Although the new reliefs reflect the long-standing Roman fondness for depicting important events with recognizable

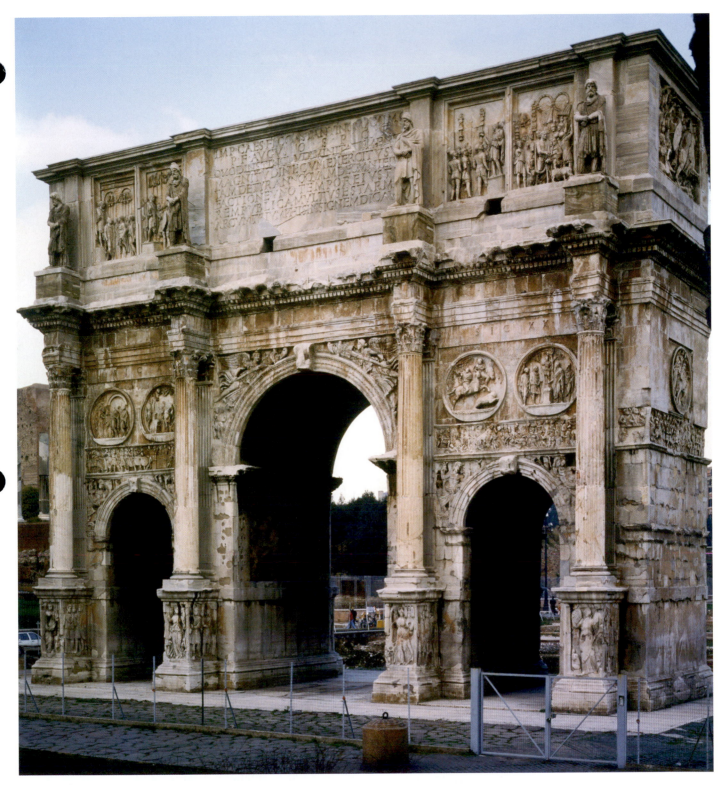

6–37 • ARCH OF CONSTANTINE
Rome. 312–315 CE (dedicated July 25, 315 CE). Height about 69′ (21 m).

This massive, triple-arched monument to Emperor Constantine's victory over Maxentius in 312 CE is a wonder of recycled sculpture. On the attic story, flanking the inscription over the central arch, are relief panels taken from a monument celebrating the victory of Marcus Aurelius over the Germans in 174 CE. On the attached piers framing these panels are large statues of prisoners made to celebrate Trajan's victory over the Dacians in the early second century CE. On the inner walls of the central arch are reliefs also commemorating Trajan's conquest of Dacia. Over each of the side arches are pairs of giant roundels taken from a monument to Hadrian. The rest of the decoration is contemporary with the arch.

View the Closer Look for the Arch of Constantine on **MyArtsLab**

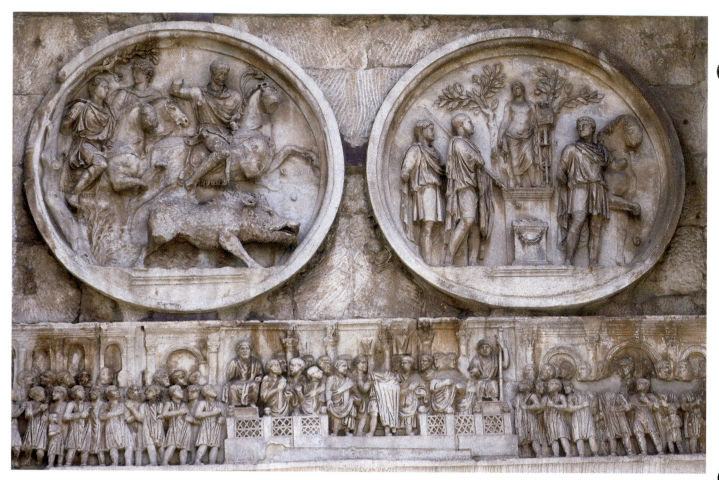

6-38 • HADRIAN HUNTING BOAR AND SACRIFICING TO APOLLO; CONSTANTINE ADDRESSING THE ROMAN PEOPLE IN THE ROMAN FORUM

Arch of Constantine, Rome. 312–315 CE. Two roundels made c. 130–138 CE for a monument to Hadrian and reused here. Marble, diameter about 6′ 6″ (2 m); frieze carved by Constantinian sculptors 312–315 CE. Marble, height 3′ 4″ (1 m).

The two circular reliefs (tondi) were originally part of a lost monument erected by the emperor Hadrian (ruled 117–138 CE). The boar hunt demonstrates his courage and physical prowess, and his sacrificial offering to Apollo shows his piety and gratitude to the gods for their support. The classicizing heads, form-enhancing drapery, and graceful poses of the figures betray a debt to the style of Late Classical Greek art. In the fourth century CE, Constantine had these roundels removed from the original monument, had Hadrian's head recarved with his own or his father's features, and incorporated them into his own triumphal arch (SEE FIG. 6–37) so that the power and piety of this predecessor could reflect on him and his reign. In a strip of relief underneath the roundels, sculptors from his own time portrayed a ceremony performed by Constantine during his celebration of the victory over his rival, Maxentius, at the Battle of the Milvian Bridge (312 CE). Rather than the Hellenizing mode popular during Hadrian's reign, the Constantinian sculptors employ the blocky and abstract stylizations that were fashionable during the Tetrarchy.

detail, in style they contrast with the arch's reused elements in their faithfulness to the avant-garde tetrarchic style. The forceful, blocky, mostly frontal figures are compressed into the foreground plane. The participants below the standing Constantine almost congeal into a uniformly patterned mass that isolates the new emperor and connects him visually with the statues of his illustrious predecessors on pedestals to each side. This two-dimensional, hierarchical approach, with its emphasis on authority and power rather than on individualized outward form, is far removed from the classicizing **illusionism** of earlier imperial reliefs.

After 324 CE, Constantine ruled as sole Roman emperor of the reunited empire until his death in 337. He founded a new capital at the port city of Byzantium and renamed it after himself—Constantinople (present-day Istanbul, Turkey). After Constantinople was dedicated in 330, Rome, which had already ceased to be the seat of government in the west, further declined in importance.

The ancient Romans conquered and controlled a vast territory around the Mediterranean Sea. As the empire absorbed the peoples it conquered, it imposed on them a legal, administrative, and cultural structure that endured for centuries, leaving a lasting mark on subsequent civilizations in this area.

As sophisticated visual propaganda, Roman art served the state and imperial authority. Representing both government officials and private individuals, Roman sculptors developed portraiture as a major art form. They recorded historical events on commemorative arches, columns, and mausoleums erected in public places. But perhaps the greatest Roman achievement was architectural: the development and exploitation of concrete as a building material. In contrast to stone, the components of concrete are cheap, light, and easily transported, and its use requires a semiskilled workforce directed by a few experienced supervisors following the plans of gifted designers. The use of concrete allowed ancient builders to move beyond the limitations of post-and-lintel architecture and enclose soaring architectural spaces with vast arching vaults.

The works of Roman artists and architects established enduring models of excellence, and as imperial authority ceded power to the migratory people the Romans called "barbarians," these newcomers continued to appreciate the artistic innovations the Romans left behind. They form the basis for medieval art and will be "revived" during the Italian Renaissance. We still draw heavily on them today.

THINK ABOUT IT

6.1 How do the subjects used in Etruscan tomb paintings and sarcophagi celebrate the vitality of human life in these monuments for the dead?

6.2 How did the Roman interest in portraiture grow out of early funeral rituals?

6.3 Discuss how Roman emperors used public monuments as imperial propaganda, focusing your discussion on two specific examples included in this chapter.

6.4 Characterize the nature of and reasons for a radical stylistic shift in human representation that took place in the Late Roman Empire.

| CROSSCURRENTS |

FIG. 5–26

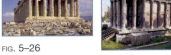

FIG. 6–10

Greek and Roman temples have features in common, but they are fundamentally different in important respects. Evaluate the significant similarities and dissimilarities by comparing these two buildings.

✓ **Study** and **Review** on **MyArtsLab**

IN PERSPECTIVE

700 BCE

Etruscan Supremacy c. 700–509 BCE

Persian Empire c. 549–330 BCE

500

Roman Republic 509–27 BCE
Classical Greek Culture 480–323 BCE

Conclusion of Peloponnesian War 404 BCE

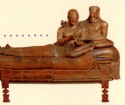

Reclining Couple, Etruscan Sarcaphagus c. 520 BCE

300

100

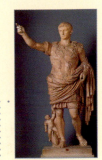

Julius Caesar Assassinated 44 BCE

Roman Empire Established 27 BCE–395 CE

Emperor Augustus ruled 27 BCE–14 CE

0

Augustus of Primaporta early 1st century CE

Emperor Nero ruled 54–68 CE
Flavian Dynasty 69–98 CE
Titus's Conquest of Jerusalem 70 CE
Eruption of Mount Vesuvius that Buried Pompeii 79 CE
Emperor Trajan ruled 98–117 CE
Emperor Hadrian ruled 117–138 CE

100 CE

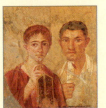

Married Couple from Pompeii mid 1st century CE

Emperor Marcus Aurelius ruled 161–180 CE

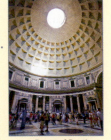

200

Dome of Pantheon 110–128 CE

Diocletian Establishes the Tetrarchy 284 CE

Emperor Constantine ruled 307–337 CE

300

Battle of Milvian Bridge 312 CE

Dedication of Constantinople as Eastern Capital 330 CE

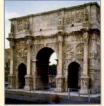

Arch of Constantine 312–315 CE

Division of Empire 395 CE

400

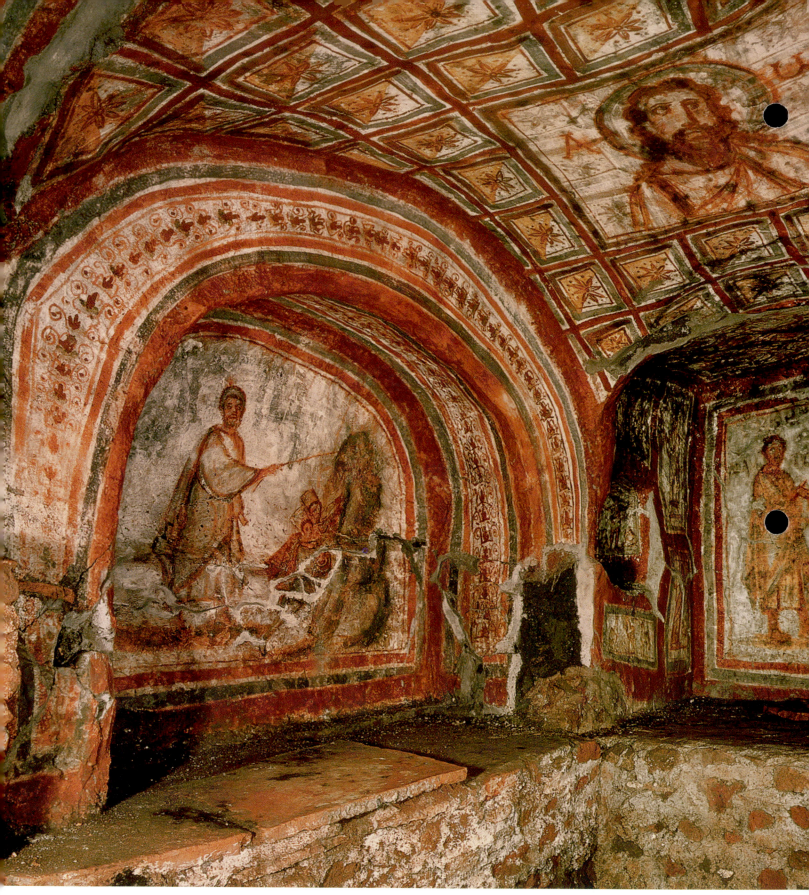

7–1 • CUBICULUM OF LEONIS, CATACOMB OF COMMODILLA
Near Rome. Late 4th century.

JEWISH, EARLY CHRISTIAN, AND BYZANTINE ART

7.1 Describe the early history of Jewish art.

7.2 Explain the origins and first flowering of Christian art and architecture within the conventions of late Roman art.

7.3 Characterize the early development of Byzantine art and architecture in the Eastern Roman Empire.

7.4 Identify the changes in Byzantine art during its middle and late periods.

LOOKING FORWARD ▶

In this Roman **catacomb** painting, St. Peter, like Moses before him, strikes a rock and water flows from it (**FIG. 7–1**, scene at left). Imprisoned in Rome at the end of his missionary journeys, Peter converted his fellow prisoners and jailers to Christianity, but he needed water with which to baptize them. Miraculously a spring gushed forth at the touch of his staff. In spite of his all too human frailty, Peter became the rock (Greek *petros*) on which Jesus founded the Church. He was the first bishop of Rome, considered the predecessor of today's pope. By including Peter in the chamber's decoration, the early Christians, who dug this catacomb as a place to bury their dead, may have sought to emphasize the importance of their own city in Christian history.

In the star-studded heavens painted on the vault of this chamber, floats the face of Christ, flanked by the first and last letters of the Greek alphabet, alpha and omega. Here Christ takes on the guise not of a youthful teacher or miracle worker seen so often in Early Christian art, but of a Greek philosopher, with long beard and hair. The **halo** (circle) of light around his head indicates his importance and his divinity, a symbol appropriated from the conventions of late Roman imperial art, where haloes often appeared around the heads of emperors.

These two catacomb paintings represent two major directions of Christian art—the narrative and the iconic. The **narrative image** recounts an event drawn from St. Peter's life—striking the rock for water—which in turn evokes the establishment of the Church as well as the essential Christian rite of baptism. The **iconic image**—Christ's face flanked by alpha and omega—offers a tangible expression of an intangible concept. The letters signify the beginning and end of time, and, combined with the image of Christ, symbolically represent not a story, but an idea—the everlasting dominion of the heavenly Christ.

Throughout the history of Christian art these two tendencies will be apparent—the narrative urge to tell a good story, whose moral or theological implications often have instructional value, and the desire to create iconic images that symbolize the core concepts and values of the developing religious tradition. In both cases, the works of art take on meaning only in relation to viewers' stored knowledge of Christian stories and beliefs. This art was made not to teach nonreaders new stories or concepts, as is so often claimed, but rather to remind faithful viewers of stories they had already heard—perhaps to draw specific lessons in their retelling—or to highlight ideas that were central to religious belief and would guide the religious devotional practice it inspired.

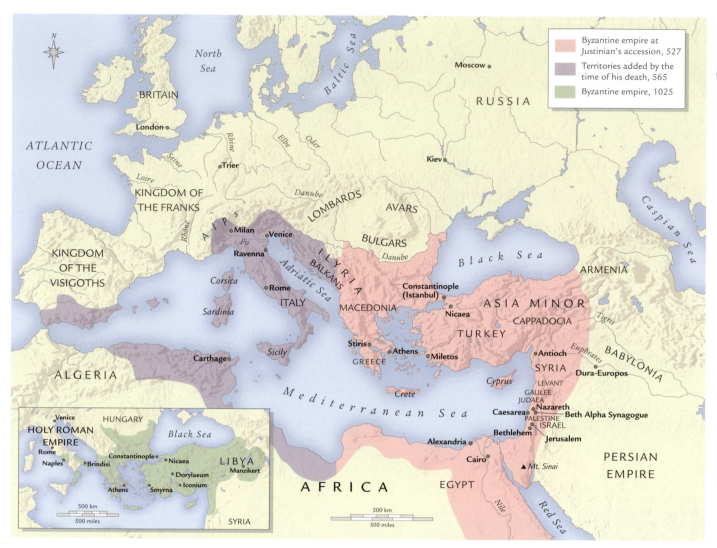

MAP 7-1 • THE LATE ROMAN AND BYZANTINE WORLD

The eastern shores of the Mediterranean, birthplace of Judaism and Christianity, was the heartland of the Byzantine Empire. It expanded farther west under the emperor Justinian, though by 1025 CE it had contracted again to its eastern core.

Three religions that arose in the Near East and flourished across the Mediterranean Roman world (MAP 7-1) still dominate the spiritual life of the Western world: Judaism and Christianity, discussed in this chapter, and Islam, treated in Chapter 8. All three are monotheistic, meaning that their followers believe that the same God of Abraham created and rules the universe. They are known as "religions of the book" because they have written records of what they believe are God's will and words: the Hebrew Bible; the Christian Bible, which includes both the Hebrew Bible as its "Old Testament" and the Christian New Testament; and the Muslim Qur'an (or Koran), revealed from God (Allah) through the angel Gabriel to the Prophet Muhammad. Each religion builds on the beliefs and traditions of the earlier one. Traditional Jews believe that God made a covenant, or pact, with their ancestors and that they are God's chosen people. They await the coming of a savior, the Messiah, "the anointed one." Christians maintain that Jesus of Nazareth was that Messiah (the title "Christ" is derived from a Greek word meaning "anointed"). They believe that, in Jesus, God took human form, preached among men and women, was executed on a cross, and then rose from the dead and ascended into heaven, having established the Christian Church under the leadership of the apostles (his closest disciples). The followers of Islam, called Muslims, while accepting the Hebrew prophets and Jesus as divinely inspired, believe Muhammad to be Allah's last and greatest prophet, through whom Islam was revealed some six centuries after Jesus's earthly lifetime.

Jewish, Christian, and Muslim art combine in varying degrees Greek, Roman, and Near Eastern themes and forms. Jews and Christians visualized in art their foundational stories and signified their core beliefs, using both narrative and iconic imagery for the ornamental enrichment of sacred buildings and books. Muslims also decorate buildings and books with ornamental forms and abstract styles but prefer to convey religious meaning through the artistic enhancement of words rather than through figural images.

Early Jewish Art

What do we know of the early history of Jewish art?

Although we will concentrate here on the art and architecture of the late Roman world, Jewish art has a much longer history. The Jewish people trace their ancestry to a Semitic people called the Hebrews, who lived in the land of Canaan. Canaan, known from the second century CE by the Roman name Palestine, was located along the eastern edge of the Mediterranean Sea. According to the Torah (the first five books of the Hebrew Bible), God promised the patriarch Abraham that Canaan would be a homeland for the Jewish people (Genesis 17:8), a belief that remains important for some Jews to this day.

Jewish settlement of Canaan probably began sometime in the second millennium BCE. According to Exodus, the second book of the Torah, the prophet Moses led the Hebrews out of slavery in Egypt to the promised land of Canaan. At one crucial point during the journey, Moses climbed alone to the top of Mount Sinai, where God gave him the Ten Commandments, the cornerstone of Jewish law. These commandments, inscribed on tablets, were kept in a gold-covered wooden box, the Ark of the Covenant.

In the tenth century BCE, King Solomon built a temple in Jerusalem to house the Ark of the Covenant. The Temple consisted of courtyards, a porch, a hall, and the Holy of Holies housing the Ark with its guardian **cherubim** (high-ranking angels closely associated with God). Solomon sent to nearby Phoenicia for cedar, cypress, and sandalwood, and for a master craftsman to supervise the Temple's construction (II Chronicles 2:3–16). This First Temple was the spiritual center of Jewish life.

In 587 BCE, the Neo-Babylonians, under King Nebuchadnezzar II, conquered Jerusalem (see Chapter 2). They destroyed the Temple, exiled the Jews, and carried off the Ark of the Covenant. When Cyrus the Great of Persia conquered Babylonia in 538 BCE, the Jews were permitted to return to Jerusalem and build the Second Temple, but from that time forward, Canaan existed primarily under foreign rule and eventually became part of the Roman Empire. In 70 CE, Roman forces led by the future emperor, Titus, destroyed the Second Temple and Jerusalem (SEE FIG. 6–22).

Jews continued to live in dispersed communities throughout the Roman Empire. Most of the earliest surviving examples of Jewish art date from the Hellenistic and Roman periods. Six Jewish **catacombs** (underground cemeteries), discovered just outside the city of Rome and in use from the first to the fourth century CE, display wall paintings with Jewish themes. In one example, from the third century CE, two **menorahs**, or seven-branched lamps, flank the long-lost **ARK OF THE COVENANT** (FIG. 7–2). The conspicuous representation on the Arch of Titus of the menorah looted from the Second Temple in Jerusalem kept the memory of these treasures alive in Rome.

Judaism has long emphasized religious learning. When Jews gather in synagogues to study the Torah, this is considered a form of worship. A synagogue can be any large room where the Torah scrolls are kept and read. Synagogues were also sites of communal social gatherings, and could be located either in private homes or in buildings originally constructed as homes.

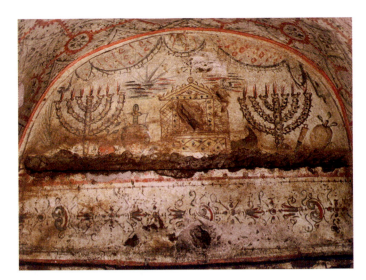

7-2 • MENORAHS AND ARK OF THE COVENANT
Wall painting in a Jewish catacomb, Villa Torlonia, Rome. 3rd century. 3′ 11″ × 5′ 9″ (1.19 × 1.8 m).

Far less early Jewish art than Early Christian or early Islamic art survives, but a number of synagogues have been discovered or excavated. Their architecture and ornament reflect late Roman artistic traditions but incorporate specifically Jewish symbols.

In the Roman city of Dura-Europos, in present-day Syria, excavators discovered a Jewish house-synagogue, or synagogue built within a private home (see also "Dura-Europos," p. 163). The first Dura-Europos synagogue consisted of an assembly hall, a separate alcove for women, and a courtyard. After a remodeling of the building, completed in 244–245 CE, men and women shared the hall, and residential rooms were added. Two architectural features distinguished the assembly hall: a bench along its walls and a **NICHE** for the Torah scrolls (FIG. 7–3). In paintings on the walls, the story of Moses unfolds in a continuous narrative around the room, employing the Roman tradition of epic historical representation. The frontal poses, strong outlines, and flat colors are pictorial devices associated with Near Eastern art.

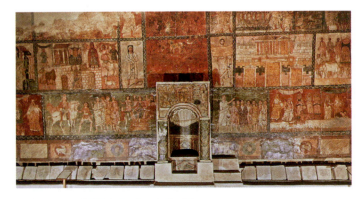

7-3 • WALL WITH TORAH NICHE
From a house-synagogue, Dura-Europos, Syria. 244–245. Tempera on plaster, section approx. 40′ (12.19 m). Reconstructed in the National Museum, Damascus, Syria.

The Mosaic Floor of the Beth Alpha Synagogue ▶

Marianos and Hanina. Ritual Objects, Celestial Diagram, and Sacrifice of Isaac. Galilee, Israel. 6th century.

The shrine that holds the Torah is flanked by menorahs and growling lions, perhaps there as a security system to protect such sacred objects.

The figures in the four corners are winged personifications of the seasons; this figure holding a shepherd's crook and accompanied by a bird is Spring

At the center of the zodiac wheel is a representation of the sun in a chariot set against a night sky studded with stars and a crescent moon.

The 12 signs of the zodiac appear in chronological order following a clockwise arrangement around the wheel of a year, implying perpetual continuity since the series has no set beginning and no end. This one is Scorpio.

The peaceful coexistence of the lion and the ox (predator and prey) may represent a golden age or peaceable kingdom (Isaiah 11:6–9; 65:25).

Torah shrine and ritual objects
•
The Metaphysical Realm

The sun, seasons, and signs of the zodiac
•
The Celestial Realm

The Sacrifice of Isaac (Genesis 22:1–19)
•
The Terrestrial Realm

This ram (identified by inscription) will ultimately take Isaac's place as sacrificial offering. Throughout the mosaic, animals are shown consistently in profile, human beings frontally.

These two texts—one in Aramaic and one in Greek—identify the artists of the mosaic as Marianos and his son Hanina, and date their work to the reign of Emperor Justin I (518–527) or that of Justin II (565–578).

Abraham, preparing to sacrifice Isaac, is interrupted by the hand of God rather than by the angel specified in the Bible. Both Abraham and Isaac are identified by inscription, but Abraham's advanced age is signaled pictorially by the streaks of gray in his beard.

🔍 **View** the Closer Look for the mosaic floor of the Beth Alpha Synagogue on **MyArtsLab**

Dura-Europos

Our understanding of buildings used for worship by third-century Jews and Christians was revolutionized by the spectacular discoveries made in the 1930s while excavating the Roman military garrison and border town of Dura-Europos (in present-day Syria). In 256, threatened by the Parthians attacking from the east, residents of Dura built a huge earthwork mound around their town in an attempt to protect themselves from the invading armies. In the process, since the houses used by Jews and Christians as places of worship were located on the city's margins right against its defensive stone wall, they were buried under the earthwork perimeter. In spite of this enhanced fortification, the Parthians conquered Dura-Europos. But since the victors never unearthed the submerged margins of the city, an intact Jewish house-synagogue and Christian house-church remained underground awaiting the explorations of modern archaeologists.

We have already seen the extensive strip narratives flanking the Torah shrine in the house-synagogue. The discovery of this expansive pictorial decoration contradicted a long-held scholarly belief that Jews of this period avoided figural decoration of any sort in conformity with Mosaic law (Exodus 20:4). And a few blocks down the street, a typical Roman house built around a central courtyard held another surprise. Only a discreet red cross above the door distinguished it from the other houses on its block, but the arrangement of the interior clearly documents its use as a Christian place of worship. A large assembly hall that could seat 60–70 people lies on one side of the courtyard, and across from it is a smaller but extensively decorated room with a water tank set aside for baptism, the central rite of Christian initiation (FIG. 7–4). Along the walls were scenes from Christ's miracles and a monumental portrayal of the women visiting his tomb about to discover his resurrection (right). Above the baptismal basin is a **lunette** (semicircular wall section) featuring the Good Shepherd with his flock, but also including at lower left (though difficult to see in this illustration) diminutive figures of Adam and Eve covering themselves in shame after their sinful disobedience. Even this early in Christian art, sacred spaces were decorated with pictures proclaiming the theological meaning of the rituals they housed. In this painting, Adam and Eve's fall from grace is juxtaposed with a larger image of the Good Shepherd (representing Jesus) who came to earth to care for and guide his sheep (Christian believers) toward redemption and eternal life—a message especially appropriate to the rite of Christian baptism, which signaled the converts' passage from sin to salvation.

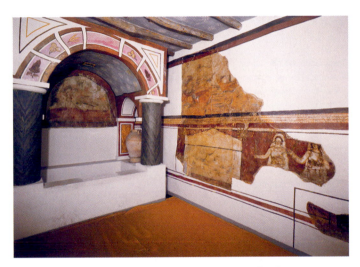

7–4 • MODEL OF WALLS AND BAPTISMAL FONT, WITH FRESCO DECORATION
From the baptistery of a Christian house-church, Dura-Europos, Syria. Before 256. Yale University Art Gallery, New Haven, Connecticut.

Other synagogues were designed on the model of Roman basilicas with a central nave flanked by aisles, a semicircular apse enclosing the Torah shrine, and sometimes an atrium (courtyard) in front of a porch or **narthex** (vestibule). Paintings and mosaics often decorated walls and floors. The fifth-century CE synagogue at Beth Alpha—discovered by farmers in 1928—follows this pattern. Its mosaic floor, added in a sixth-century remodeling, is primarily geometric in design, but in the central nave there are three complex panels full of figural compositions and symbols (see "A Closer Look," p. 162).

In 395, the Roman Empire split permanently in two, becoming the Western Empire, which collapsed in 476, and the Eastern, or Byzantine, Empire, which lasted until 1453, when it fell to the Ottoman Turks. By this time most Jews lived outside Palestine, in communities spread across the Near East, North Africa, and Europe. Because their religious practice set them apart, and their numbers made them a minority, they faced special taxes, restrictions on the professions they could enter, and sometimes violent suppression or forced exile. The history of Jewish art is fragmented because so many artworks vanished when Jewish homes and synagogues were wantonly destroyed during these periodic persecutions.

Early Christian Art

How does Christian art develop from the conventions of late Roman art and architecture?

Christianity began with the life and teachings of Jesus of Nazareth, a Jew born sometime between 8 and 4 BCE and crucified at age 33. Early Christians believed that Jesus was the Son of

The Life of Jesus and the Virgin Mary

Episodes from the life of Jesus in the Gospels form the principal subject matter of Christian visual art. What follows is a list of main events in his and his mother's life with parenthetical references when there are textual sources in the Gospel texts.

MATERNITY OF MARY AND CHILDHOOD OF JESUS

Annunciation: The archangel Gabriel informs the Virgin Mary that God has chosen her to bear his Son. A dove often represents the *Incarnation*, her miraculous conception of Jesus through the Holy Spirit. (Lk 1:26–28)

Visitation: The pregnant Mary visits her older cousin Elizabeth, pregnant with the future St. John the Baptist. (Lk 1:29–45)

Nativity: Jesus is born in Bethlehem. The Holy Family—Jesus, Mary, and her husband, Joseph—is usually portrayed in a stable, or, in Byzantine art, a cave. (Lk 2:4–7)

Annunciation to and Adoration of the Shepherds: Angels announce Jesus's birth to shepherds, who hurry to Bethlehem to honor him. (Lk 2:8–20)

Adoration of the Magi: Wise men from the East follow a star to Bethlehem to honor Jesus as King of the Jews, presenting him with precious gifts. Eventually these Magi became identified as three kings, often differentiated through facial type as young, middle-aged, and old. (Mat 2:1–12)

Presentation in the Temple: Mary and Joseph bring the infant Jesus to the Temple in Jerusalem. (Lk 2:25–35)

Flight into Egypt and Massacre of the Innocents: An angel warns Joseph that King Herod, to eliminate the threat of a newborn rival king, plans to murder all male babies in Bethlehem. The Holy Family flees to Egypt. (Mat 2:13–16)

JESUS'S MINISTRY

Baptism: At age 30, Jesus is baptized by John the Baptist in the River Jordan. The Holy Spirit appears in the form of a dove and a heavenly voice proclaims Jesus as God's Son. (Mat 3:13–17, Mk 1:9–11, Lk 3:21–22)

Marriage at Cana: At his mother's request, Jesus turns water into wine at a wedding feast, his first public miracle. (Jn 2:1–10)

Miracles of Healing: Throughout the Gospels, Jesus performs miracles of healing the blind, possessed (mentally ill), paralytic, and lepers; he also resurrects the dead.

Calling of Levi/Matthew: Jesus calls to Levi, a tax collector, "Follow me." Levi complies, becoming the disciple Matthew. (Mat 9:9, Mk 2:14)

Raising of Lazarus: Jesus brings his friend Lazarus back to life four days after death. (Jn 11:1–44)

Transfiguration: Jesus reveals his divinity in a dazzling vision on Mount Tabor as his closest disciples—Peter, James, and John—look on. (Mat 17:1–5, Mk 9:2–6, Lk 9:28–35)

Tribute Money: Challenged to pay the temple tax, Jesus sends Peter to catch a fish, which has the required coin in its mouth. (Mt 17:24–27, Lk 20:20–25)

JESUS'S PASSION, DEATH, AND RESURRECTION

Entry into Jerusalem: Jesus, riding an ass and accompanied by his disciples, enters Jerusalem, while crowds honor him, spreading clothes and palm fronds in their path. (Mat 21:1–11, Mk 11:1–11, Lk 19:30–44, Jn 12:12–15)

Last Supper: During the Jewish Passover *seder*, Jesus reveals his impending death to his disciples, instructing them to drink wine (his blood) and eat bread (his body) in remembrance of him, the foundation for the Christian Eucharist (Mass). (Mat 26:26–30, Mk 14:22–25)

Jesus Washing the Disciples' Feet: At the Last Supper, Jesus humbly washes the disciples' feet. (Jn 13:4–12)

Agony in the Garden: In the Garden of Gethsemane on the Mount of Olives, Jesus struggles between his human fears of pain and death and his divine strength to overcome them. The apostles sleep nearby, oblivious. (Lk 22:40–45)

Betrayal (Arrest): Judas Iscariot (a disciple) has accepted a bribe to betray Jesus to an armed band of his enemies, identifying him to them by kissing him. (Mat 26:46–49, Mk 14:43–46, Lk 22:47–48, Jn 18:3–5)

Jesus Before Pilate: Jesus is taken to Pontius Pilate, Roman governor of Judaea, and charged with treason. Pilate proposes freeing Jesus but the mob demands Jesus be crucified. (Mat 27:11–15, Mk 15:4–14, Lk 23:1–24, Jn 18:28–40)

Crucifixion: Jesus is executed on a cross between two crucified criminals, while the Virgin Mary, John the Evangelist, Mary Magdalen, and other followers stand at the foot of the cross; Roman soldiers torment Jesus, extending a sponge on a pole with vinegar for him to drink and stabbing him in the side with a spear. (Mat 27:35–50, Mk 15:23–37, Lk 23:38–49, Jn 19:18–30)

Descent from the Cross (Deposition): Jesus's followers take his body down from the cross. (Mat 27:55–59, Mk 15:40–46, Lk 23:50–56, Jn 19:38–40)

Lamentation/Pietà: Jesus's sorrowful followers gather around his body to mourn. An image of the grieving Virgin alone with Jesus across her lap is known as a **pietà** (from Latin *pietas*, "pity"). (Mat 27:60–61, Jn 19:41–42)

Resurrection/Holy Women at the Tomb: Three days after his entombment, Christ rises from the dead, and his female followers discover his empty tomb; an angel announces his resurrection. (Mat 28, Mk 16, Lk 24:1–35, Jn 20)

Descent into Limbo (Harrowing of Hell or Anastasis): The resurrected Jesus descends into limbo, or hell, to free deserving predecessors, among them Adam, Eve, David, and Moses. (Not in the Gospels)

Noli Me Tangere ("Do Not Touch Me"): Christ appears to Mary Magdalen as she weeps at his tomb. When she reaches out to him, he warns her not to touch him. (Lk 24:34–53, Jn 20:11–31)

Ascension: Christ's body ascends to heaven from the Mount of Olives, disappearing in a cloud, while his apostles watch. (Acts 1)

MARY'S DEATH

Dormition of the Virgin: Literally Mary's "falling asleep." She dies surrounded by the apostles, while her soul, in the form of a baby or child, appears above her in the arms of the risen Christ. (Not in the Gospels)

Assumption of the Virgin: Mary's body ascends to heaven. (Not in the Gospels)

God, born in a human body to a virgin woman, Mary, and resurrected after death. Christian doctrine proclaimed one God manifest in three Persons, a Trinity of Creator-Father (God), Son (Jesus Christ), and Holy Spirit. In later years Christians also began to acknowledge and venerate saints—devout individuals connected with verifiable miracles and canonized, or officially honored, by the Church for upholding and practicing Christian beliefs, often at the cost of martyrdom (execution).

The Christian New Testament describes the life of Jesus in its first four books, known as the Gospels (the Good News). Jesus is seen as a descendant of the Jewish royal house of King David, born in Bethlehem in Judaea, where his mother, Mary, and her husband, Joseph, had gone to be registered in the Roman census. He grew up in Nazareth in Galilee, where Joseph was a carpenter. At age 30, Jesus began his public ministry, gathering about him a group of disciples, male and female followers. He performed miracles of healing and preached love for God and neighbor, the sanctity of social justice, the forgiveness of sins, and the promise of life after death. From his followers, he chose 12 apostles to carry on his work after his crucifixion and resurrection.

Jesus focused his ministry on his Jewish community; it was his apostles, as well as later followers such as Paul, who took Jesus's teachings to gentiles (non-Jews). Despite sporadic persecution, Christianity persisted and spread throughout the Roman Empire. The Roman emperor Constantine (see Chapter 6) permitted Christians freedom of worship with the Edict of Milan in 313 CE. By the end of the fourth century, Christianity had become the official religion of the empire and it was non-Christians who became the targets of persecution.

Throughout the Roman Empire, even before their religion was recognized, Christians met in private houses for worship. In Rome itself, they also excavated underground cemeteries, or catacombs, consisting of narrow passages and small burial chambers lined with rectangular burial niches (SEE FIG. 7–1). These niches were filled with stone sarcophagi or sealed with tiles or stone slabs. The painted walls and ceilings of such catacombs provide some of the earliest surviving examples of Christian art. By the fourth century, pictorial programs included narrative scenes, pictures of individuals, and iconic symbols. But even earlier paintings, from the middle of the third century, were discovered on the fringes of the empire in a house-church excavated at Dura-Europos (see "Dura-Europos," p. 163), uncovered at the same time as the house-synagogue with Jewish narrative wall paintings (SEE FIG. 7–3).

Early Christian sculpture before the fourth century is even rarer than painting. What survives is mainly sarcophagi and small statues or reliefs, many of them featuring the Good Shepherd, a Greco-Roman pagan motif associated with notions of the afterlife as a pastoral idyll that became an allegorical representation of Jesus for Christians familiar with their oral traditions or scriptural heritage (e.g., Luke 15:3–7; John 10:11–18). A remarkable set of small marble statues discovered in Asia Minor during the 1960s includes a sensitive carving of **THE GOOD SHEPHERD** (FIG. 7–5) which must have been created for a Christian context since it was found with sculptures portraying the life of the prophet Jonah, another very popular theme in Early Christian art.

Religious toleration, which began with the Edict of Milan and Constantine's active support of Christianity, spurred the building of Christian churches and shrines on a much larger scale. Constantine ordered a monumental basilica constructed at the place where Christians believed St. Peter, the leader of the apostles, was buried. Peter (d. c. 64 CE) had led the first Christian community in Rome. As the city's first bishop (spiritual and administrative church leader), he was later recognized as the precursor of the popes (heads of the Christian Church in the West). The Constantinian Basilica of St. Peter (called "Old" St. Peter's because it was destroyed and replaced by a new building during the Renaissance) became the pope's church and came to signify his authority over all Christendom.

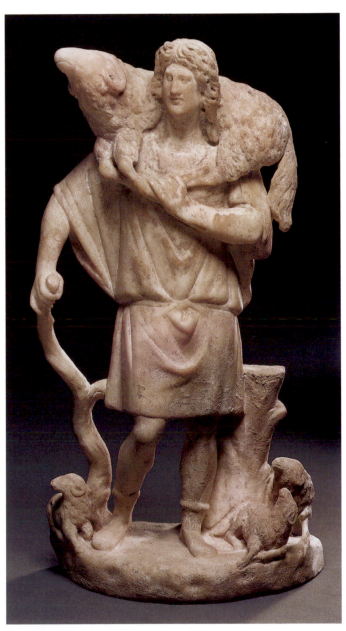

7–5 • THE GOOD SHEPHERD
Eastern Mediterranean, probably Anatolia (present-day Turkey). Second half of the 3rd century. Marble, height 19½" (49.5 cm), width 10" (26 cm), depth 6" (16.2 cm). The Cleveland Museum of Art. John L. Severance Fund (1965.241).

The forms of Early Christian buildings were based on two Roman prototypes: rectangular basilicas (SEE FIGS. 6–24, 6–35) and circular or squared structures, including rotundas like the Pantheon (SEE FIG. 6–28). As in the basilica of Old St. Peter's in Rome (FIG. 7–6), **longitudinal-plan** churches are characterized by a forecourt (the **atrium**) leading to an entrance porch (the **narthex**), which spans one of the building's short ends. Doorways—known collectively as the church's **portals**—lead from the narthex into a long, congregational area called a **nave**. Rows of columns separate the high-ceilinged nave from one or two lower **aisles** on either side. The nave can be lit by windows along its upper level just under the ceiling, called a **clerestory**, that rises above the side aisles' roofs. At the opposite end of the nave from the narthex is a semicircular projection, the **apse**. The apse functions as the building's focal point where the altar, raised on a platform, is located. Sometimes there is also a **transept**, a wing that crosses the nave in front of the apse, making the building T-shaped. When additional space comes between the transept and the apse (a liturgical **choir**), the plan is known as a Latin cross.

Central-plan buildings were first used by Christians, like their pagan Roman forebears, as tombs. Central planning was also employed for baptisteries (where Christians "died"—giving up their old life—and were reborn as believers) and for churches dedicated to martyrs (e.g., San Vitale, SEE FIG. 7–15), often built directly over their tombs. Like basilicas, central-plan churches can have an atrium, a narthex, and an apse. But instead of the longitudinal axis of basilican churches, which draws worshipers forward along a line from the entrance toward the apse, central-plan buildings, such as the mausoleum of Constantina—rededicated in 1256 as the church of Sta. Costanza (FIG. 7–7)—have a more vertical axis, from the center up through the dome, which may have functioned as a symbolic "vault of heaven."

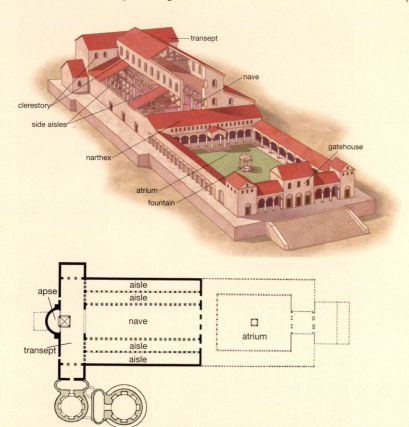

7–6 • RECONSTRUCTION DRAWING AND PLAN OF OLD ST. PETER'S BASILICA
Rome. c. 320–327; atrium added in later 4th century. Approx. 394′ (120 m) long and 210′ (64 m) wide.

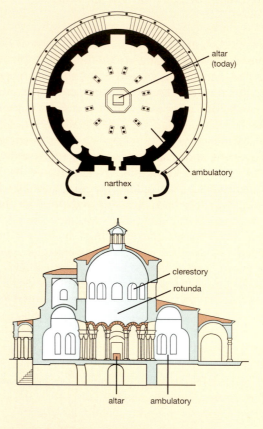

7–7 • PLAN AND SECTION DRAWING OF STA. COSTANZA
(originally mausoleum of Constantina, daughter of Constantine), Rome. c. 350.

Old St. Peter's (see "Longitudinal-Plan and Central-Plan Churches," above) included architectural elements arranged in a way that has characterized Christian basilica churches ever since it was built. **Transepts**—wings that intersected with the nave and aisles at a right angle—met the need for more space near the tomb of the saint, where a large number of clergy and pilgrims gathered for elaborate rituals. Christians believed St. Peter's bones lay beneath the high altar; indeed Early Christian and pagan tombs did lie under the church, and the interior of the church itself initially served as a funerary space, with

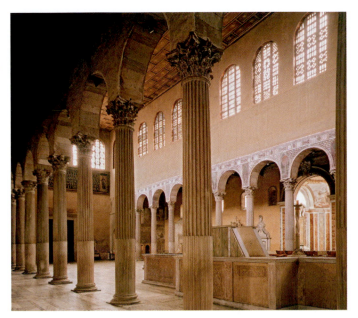

7-8 • INTERIOR, CHURCH OF STA. SABINA
Rome. 422–432.

sarcophagi lined up along the aisles. Thus Old St. Peter's served a variety of functions: as a burial place, as a pilgrimage shrine containing the relics of St. Peter, and as a congregational church that could hold at least 14,000 worshipers. It remained the largest church in Christendom until the eleventh century.

Old St. Peter's is gone, but some idea of a typical Early Christian basilica can be gained from the Roman **CHURCH OF STA. SABINA**. The interior, constructed by Peter of Illyria between 422 and 432, appears much as it did when first built (**FIG. 7–8**). The basic elements of the basilica church are clearly visible: a nave lit by clerestory windows, ending in a rounded apse and flanked by side aisles. Sta. Sabina's interior displays a wealth of marble veneer and 24 fluted marble columns with Corinthian capitals reused from a second-century pagan building. The columns support arches creating a **nave arcade** (series of arches). The **spandrels**, above the columns and between the arches are faced with marble images of the chalice (wine cup) and paten (bread plate)—the essential items for the **Eucharistic** (Mass or Holy Communion) rite that took place at the altar. In such basilicas, the expanse of wall between the arcade and the clerestory typically had paintings or mosaics with biblical scenes. Here, however, the upper-wall decoration is lost.

The beauty and richness of many Early Christian church interiors is best experienced in several fifth- and sixth-century buildings in Ravenna. By the fifth century, Rome had lost its political, although not its spiritual, importance. The capital of the Western Roman Empire was moved to Milan in the late third century and then to Ravenna at the beginning of the fifth century. Ravenna offered direct access by sea to Constantinople, the capital of the Eastern (Byzantine) Roman Empire.

One of the earliest surviving Christian structures in Ravenna is a small, cross-shaped **oratory** (chapel designated for prayer) attached about 425–426 to the church of the imperial palace. It is named after the remarkable Galla Placidia, daughter of Roman emperor Theodosius I, wife of Visigothic King Athaulf, sister of Emperors Honorius and Arcadius, and mother of Emperor Valentinian III. As regent for her son after 425, she ruled the Western Empire. The upper walls and vaults of the tiny chapel are richly decorated with mosaics; panels of veined marble cover the walls below (**FIG. 7–9**). Floral and geometric patterns decorate the four central arches and vaults, and the walls above them are filled with figures of standing apostles

7-9 • ORATORY OF GALLA PLACIDIA
Ravenna, Italy. c. 425–426. The three visible arms of the cross-shaped building hold sarcophagi. The lunette mosaic portrays the martyrdom of St. Lawrence; upper walls, apostles.

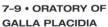 **Explore** the architectural panoramas of the oratory of Galla Placidia on **MyArtsLab**

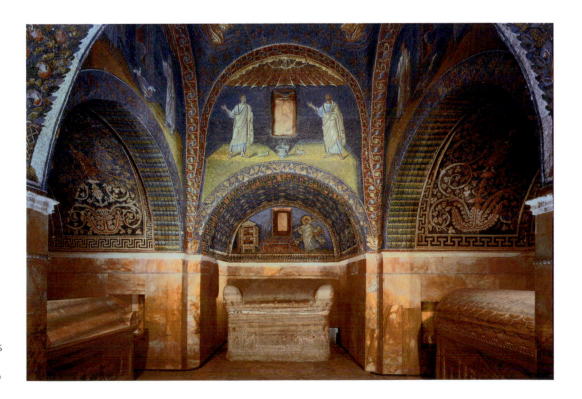

The Good Shepherd

Few images are as appealing as the Good Shepherd, with its associations of loving, caring, protectiveness, and strength (FIG. 7–10). Originating in agrarian societies, the theme of the shepherd watching over a flock of sheep or carrying home a weak or lost lamb became a powerful and positive image, even in urban cultures. Today the Good Shepherd may be thought of as a Christian symbol, but it was not conceived as such. Ancient Greeks and Romans sometimes represented Hermes as a shepherd carrying a lamb or calf, and Orpheus was believed to have charmed flocks with his music. Jewish patriarchs measured their wealth in herds of sheep and camels, and one of the best known of the songs of King David envisions God as an all-providing shepherd (Psalm 23). Not surprisingly, Christians adopted this imagery for Jesus as early as the third century (SEE FIGS. 7–4, 7–5). He had used it himself in parables as an effective way to make God's love understandable to his listeners (Luke 15:3–7 and Matthew 18:12–14). According to John (10:11–16), Jesus called himself the good shepherd who lays down his life for his sheep. As the motif was not exclusively Christian, it only took on Christian meaning through the Christian viewer who was beholding it, a convenient subtlety for a religious movement that was under threat of periodic persecution.

By the fifth century, however, Christianity had become the state religion in the Roman Empire—over a century had passed since the last official persecution—and artists and patrons were free to showcase specifically Christian symbols in works of art. The Good Shepherd, now manifestly Christian, remained popular but it was transformed. In this mosaic from Ravenna, Jesus sits with his sheep in a luxuriant landscape, but his shepherd's crook has become a golden cross standard. Indeed, Jesus is no longer the boy in a simple tunic featured in Early Christian works, but

a young emperor wearing purple and gold imperial robes. His imperial majesty is signaled by the golden halo surrounding his head. This mosaic asserts the glory of Jesus Christ in mosaic, the richest known medium of architectural decoration, using an imperial image, still imbued with pagan spirit, but now signaling the triumph of the new faith.

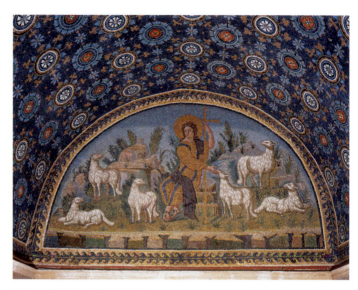

7–10 • GOOD SHEPHERD
Mosaic in the lunette over the west entrance, oratory of Galla Placidia, Ravenna, Italy. c. 425–426.

The rocky band at the bottom of the scene, resembling a cliff face riddled with clefts, separates the divine image from worshipers, as if it were taking place on a stage that extends above and beyond the oratory in which they stand.

gesturing like orators. St. Lawrence is represented in the central **lunette** (semicircular wall section under the vault) at the end of one arm of the building. The triumphant martyr carries a cross over his shoulder like a trophy and stands next to the fire-engulfed metal grill on which he was literally roasted to death. Left of the grill stands a tall cabinet containing the books of the Gospels, signifying the faith for which Lawrence gave his life. Opposite St. Lawrence, in a lunette over the entrance **portal**, is a mosaic of Jesus as the Good Shepherd (see "The Good Shepherd," above).

In sculpture, as in architecture, Christians adapted Roman forms for their own needs, especially monumental marble sarcophagi, like the one made for Roman official **JUNIUS BASSUS** (FIG. 7–11), who, as an inscription tells us, died on August 25, 359, at age 42, newly baptized. In the center of both

registers is a triumphant Christ. Above, he appears as a Roman emperor, distributing legal authority in the form of scrolls to flanking figures of SS. Peter and Paul, and resting his feet on the head of Coelus, the pagan god of the heavens, here representing the cosmos to identify Christ as Cosmocrator (ruler of the cosmos). In the bottom register, the earthly Jesus makes his triumphal entry into Jerusalem, like a Roman emperor entering a conquered city. Jesus, however, rides on a humble ass rather than a powerful steed.

Early Christian art uses stories from the Hebrew Bible as allegories, prefiguring important events in the New Testament. For example, in this sarcophagus, at top left, Abraham passes the test of faith and need not sacrifice his son Isaac. Christians believed this story foreshadowed God's sacrifice of his own Son, Jesus, which culminates not in Jesus's death, but

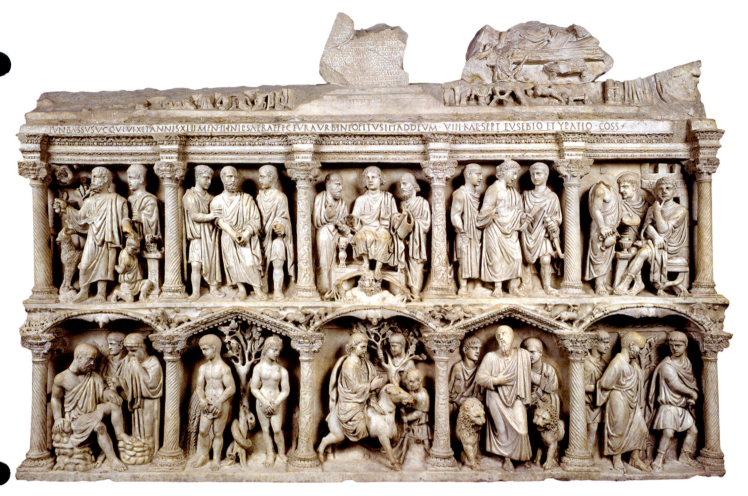

7–11 • SARCOPHAGUS OF JUNIUS BASSUS
Grottos of St. Peter, Vatican, Rome. c. 359. Marble, 4′ × 8′ (1.2 × 2.4 m).

At upper right, spread over two compartments, Jesus appears before Pontius Pilate, who is about to wash his hands, symbolizing that he denies responsibility for Jesus's death. Jesus's position here, held captive between two soldiers, recalls (and perhaps could also be read as) his arrest in Gethsemane, especially since the composition of this panel is reflected in the arrests of the apostles Peter (top, second frame from the left) and Paul (bottom, far right).

View the Closer Look for the sarcophagus of Junius Bassus on **MyArtsLab**

his resurrection. Under the triangular gable, second from the end at bottom right, the Hebrew Bible story of Daniel saved by God from the lions prefigures Christ's emergence alive from his tomb. At bottom far left, God tests the faith of Job, who provides a model for the sufferings of Christian martyrs. Next to Job, the sin of Adam and Eve sets in motion the entire Christian redemption story. Lured by the serpent, they have eaten the forbidden fruit and, conscious of their nakedness, are trying to hide their genitals with leaves.

Early Byzantine Art

How does early Byzantine art and architecture develop within the Eastern Roman Empire?

During the fifth and sixth centuries, the Italian peninsula was

invaded by the Visigoths, Vandals, and Ostrogoths—Germanic peoples from the north. Rome was sacked twice, in 410 and 455. When Italy fell to the Ostrogoths in 476, the Western Roman Empire collapsed.

During the same period, the Eastern Roman (or Byzantine) Empire and its capital city of Constantinople flourished. Byzantine political power, wealth, and culture peaked in the sixth century, under Emperor Justinian I (ruled 527–565), ably seconded by Empress Theodora (c. 500–548). At its most expansive under Justinian, the Byzantine Empire included the lands that are now Greece, the Balkans, and Turkey; the Levant from Syria south to Arabia; Egypt; part of Spain; and a long strip along the Mediterranean coast of Africa. Justinian also reconquered Italy and Sicily, establishing Ravenna as the administrative capital on the Italian peninsula.

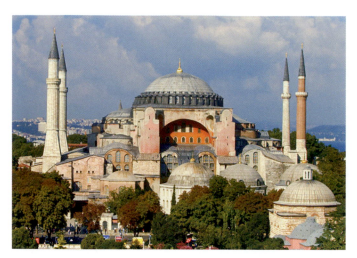

7-12 • Anthemius of Tralles and Isidorus of Miletus CHURCH OF HAGIA SOPHIA
Istanbul, Turkey. 532–537. View from the southwest.

The body of the original church is now surrounded by later additions, notably the slender minarets built after 1453 by the Ottoman Turks, who transformed Hagia Sophia into a mosque.

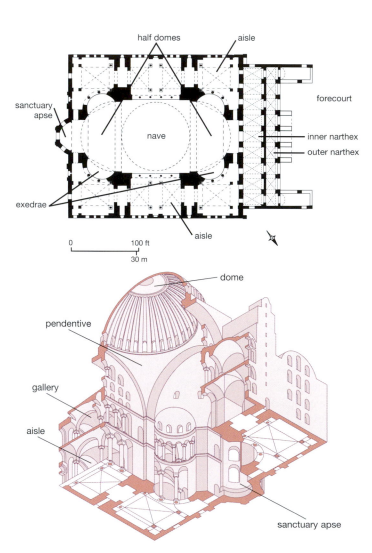

7-13 • PLAN AND ISOMETRIC DRAWING OF THE CHURCH OF HAGIA SOPHIA

The Golden Age of Justinian

In Constantinople, Justinian began a campaign of building and renovation in the wake of the devastating urban Nika Riots in 532, but little remains of his architectural projects or of the old imperial city. The **CHURCH OF HAGIA SOPHIA** (Holy Wisdom) is a spectacular exception (**FIGS. 7–12, 7–13, 7–14**). Designed by two scholar-theoreticians, Anthemius of Tralles and Isidorus of Miletus, it embodies both imperial power and Christian glory. Anthemius was a specialist in geometry and optics, and Isidorus was a specialist in physics who had studied vaulted construction. Their crowning achievement was the dome of Hagia Sophia, which provided a golden, light-filled canopy high above a processional space. Procopius of Caesarea, who chronicled Justinian's reign, claimed poetically that the dome seemed to hang suspended on a "golden chain from heaven." It was rumored that Hagia Sophia was constructed by angels; in fact, mortal builders achieved the feat in only five years (532–537).

Hagia Sophia is an innovative and audacious hybrid of longitudinal and central architectural planning. The building is clearly dominated by the hovering form of its gigantic dome (SEE FIG. 7–14). But flanking **conches** (semidomes) form a longitudinal nave that expands outward from the central dome to connect with the narthex on one end and the sanctuary apse on the other. This processional core is flanked by side aisles, and galleries above them overlook the nave space.

Since this idiosyncratic mixture of basilica and rotunda precludes a drum—the ring of masonry underneath a dome that provides support around its circumference (as in the Pantheon)—the main dome of Hagia Sophia rests instead on four **pendentives** (triangular curving wall sections) that connect the base of the dome with the huge supporting **piers** (large masonry supports) at the four corners of the square area beneath it (see "Pendentives and Squinches," p. 174). And since these piers are essentially submerged back into the aisles, rather than expressed within the nave space itself (SEE FIG. 7–13), the dome seems to float mysteriously over a void. The miraculous, weightless effect was reinforced by the light-reflecting gold mosaic that covered the surfaces of dome and pendentives alike, as well as the band of 40 windows that perforate the base of the dome where it meets its support. This daring move challenged architectural logic by seeming to weaken the integrity of the masonry at the very place where it needs to be strong, but the windows created the circle of light that helps the dome appear to hover, and a reinforcement of buttressing on the exterior made the solution sound as well as shimmering. The origin of the dome on pendentives is obscure, but its large-scale use at Hagia Sophia was totally unprecedented and represents one of the boldest architectural experiments in the history of architecture. It became the preferred method of supporting domes in Byzantine architecture.

Among the most important sixth-century Byzantine churches built outside Constantinople is the **CHURCH OF SAN VITALE** in Ravenna. It was commissioned by a local bishop, Ecclesius, when Italy was under Ostrogothic rule, but it was completed only after Justinian's conquest of Ravenna. The church was dedicated in 547 as a **martyrium** for the Early Christian martyr, St. Vitalis. Its design is basically a dome-covered

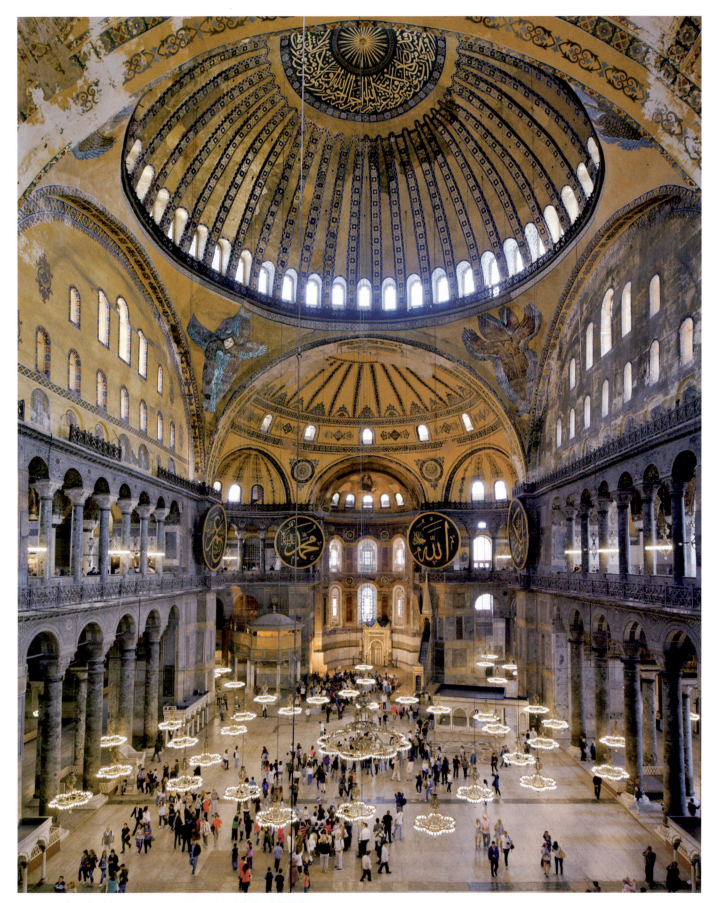

7-14 • INTERIOR OF THE CHURCH OF HAGIA SOPHIA

📖 **Read** the document related to the church of Hagia Sophia on **MyArtsLab**

Naming Christian Churches: Designation + Dedication + Location

Christian churches are identified by a three-part descriptive title combining (1) designation (or type), with (2) dedication (usually to a saint), and finally (3) geographical location, cited in that order.

Designation: There are various types of churches, fulfilling a variety of liturgical and administrative objectives, and the identification of a specific church often begins with an indication of its function within the system. For example, an *abbey or monastery church* is the place of worship within a monastery or convent; a *pilgrimage church* is a site that attracts visitors wishing to venerate **relics** (material remains or objects associated with a saint) as well as attend services. A *cathedral* is a bishop's primary church (the word derives from the Latin *cathedra*, meaning throne, since the throne of a bishop is contained within his cathedral). A bishop's domain is called a *diocese*, and there can be only one church in the diocese designated as its bishop's cathedral, but the diocese is full of *parish churches* where local residents attend regular services.

Dedication: Christian churches are always dedicated to Christ, the Virgin Mary, a saint, or a sacred concept or event, for example St. Peter's basilica or the church of Hagia Sophia (Christ as "divine wisdom"). In short-hand identification, when we omit the church designation at the beginning, we always add an apostrophe *s* to the saint's name, as when using "St. Peter's" to refer to the Vatican Basilica of St. Peter in Rome.

Location: The final piece of information that clearly pinpoints the specific church indicated in a title is its geographical location, as in church of San Vitale in Ravenna or the cathedral of Notre-Dame (French for "Our Lady," referring to the Virgin Mary) in Paris. "Notre-Dame" alone usually refers to this Parisian cathedral, in spite of the fact that many contemporary cathedrals (e.g., at Chartres and Reims) were also dedicated to "Notre-Dame." Similarly, "St. Peter's" usually means the Vatican church of the pope in Rome.

---

octagon surrounded by eight radiating **exedrae**, or semicircular niches (**FIG. 7–15**), one of which extends through the aisle to form the sanctuary.

The floor plan of San Vitale only begins to convey the effect of the complex, interpenetrating interior spaces of the church. The dome rests on eight large piers that frame the exedrae and the sanctuary. The undulating, two-story exedrae open through superimposed arcades into outer aisles on the ground floor and into galleries on the second floor. They billow out from the

cylindrical central space and create a swelling spatial sensation. The diaphanous quality of the walls is enhanced by the liberal use of reflective veined marble veneer and colored glass and gold mosaics in the surface decoration. In the conch of the sanctuary apse (**FIG. 7–16**), an image of Christ is imperially enthroned in paradise on a cosmic orb and flanked by archangels. St. Vitalis (on his far right) is receiving from Christ a crown of martyrdom and Bishop Ecclesius (on Christ's far left) presents to Christ a model of the church itself.

Justinian and Theodora may never have set foot in Ravenna, but two large mosaic panels that face each other

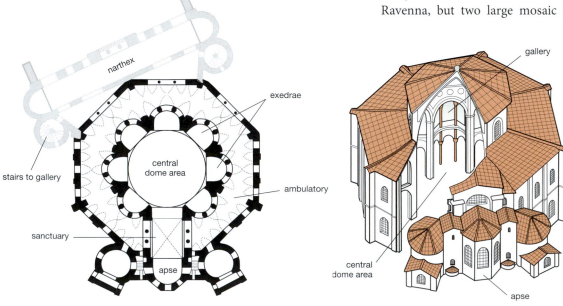

7–15 • PLAN AND CUTAWAY DRAWING OF THE CHURCH OF SAN VITALE
Ravenna, Italy. Under construction from c. 520; consecrated 547; mosaics c. 526–548.

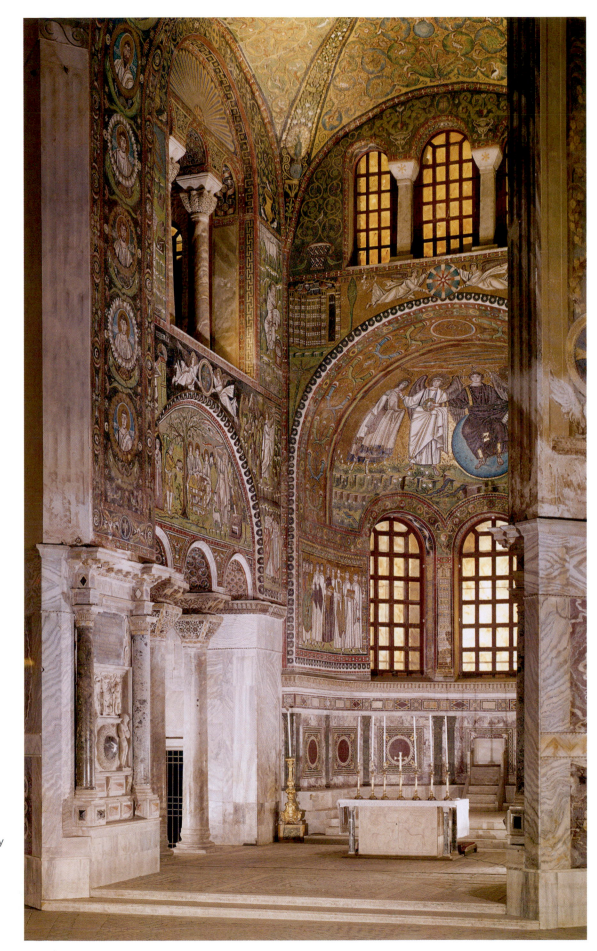

7–16 • CHURCH OF SAN VITALE
View into the sanctuary toward the northeast.

✳ **Explore** the architectural panoramas of San Vitale on **MyArtsLab**

Pendentives and **squinches** are two methods of supporting a round dome or its drum over a square space. Pendentives are spherical triangles between arches that rise upward and inward to form a circular opening on which the dome sits. Squinches are diagonal lintels supported on bracket-like constructions placed across the walls' upper corners. Because squinches create an octagon, which is close in shape to a circle, they provide a solid base around the perimeter of the dome, usually elevated on a drum, whereas pendentives project the dome inward, over the space it covers, making it seem to float over a void. Byzantine builders preferred pendentives (as at Hagia Sophia, SEE FIG. 7–13) and elaborate squinch-supported domes became a hallmark of Islamic architecture (SEE FIG. 8–12).

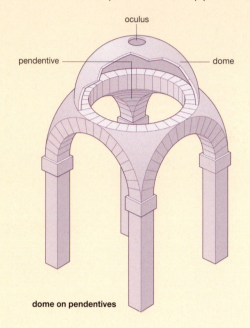

dome on pendentives

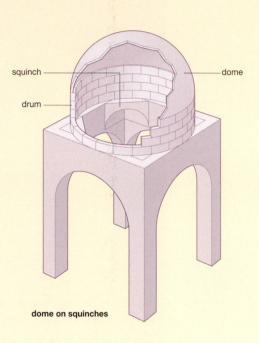

dome on squinches

⊙ **Watch** an architectural simulation of pendentives on **MyArtsLab**

across the sanctuary of San Vitale, below the scene of Christ holding court in paradise, picture their presence here for perpetuity. In one panel, **JUSTINIAN (FIG. 7–17)**, accompanied by Bishop Maximianus and leaders of church and state, presents a paten—the plate that will be used to hold the Eucharistic bread. In the other, **THEODORA (FIG. 7–18)**, followed by her sisters and ladies of the court, carries a huge, golden, jewel-encrusted chalice for Eucharistic wine. The rulers present these as precious offerings to Christ—emulating most immediately Bishop Ecclesius who offers a model of the church to Christ in the apse, as well as the Magi, wise men from the East, who brought valuable gifts to the infant Jesus, embroidered at the bottom of Theodora's purple cloak. In fact, the chalice and paten offered by the royal couple will be used by this church to offer Eucharistic bread and wine to the local Christian community during the liturgy. At the core of this central ceremony of Christian worship is the identification of the sacrificial body and blood of Christ with the substances of bread and wine, which Jesus had instructed his followers to eat and drink in remembrance of him, and which became emblematic of his offering of himself on the cross for their redemption. In this way the entire program of mosaic decoration revolves around the theme of offering, extended into the theme of the Eucharist itself.

Theodora's group stands beside a fountain, presumably at the entrance to the women's gallery. The open doorway and curtain are classical space-creating devices, but here the mosaicists have deliberately avoided allowing their illusionistic power to overwhelm their ability also to create flat surface patterns. Notice, too, that the figures cast no shadows, and though modeled, their outlines as silhouetted shapes are more prominent than their sense of three-dimensionality. Still, especially in Justinian's panel, a complex and carefully controlled system of overlapping allows us to see these figures situated clearly and logically within a shallow space, moving in a stately procession from left to right toward the entrance to the church and the beginning of the liturgy. So the scenes portrayed in these mosaic paintings are both flattened and three-dimensional, abstract and representational, patterned and individualized. Like Justinian and Theodora, they are both there and not there at the same time.

Illuminated Manuscripts

Christians also commissioned books for religious services and clerical instruction, for personal study and meditation, or as expressions of prestige by wealthy leaders of church and state. We have seen Gospel books in the cabinet on the St. Lawrence

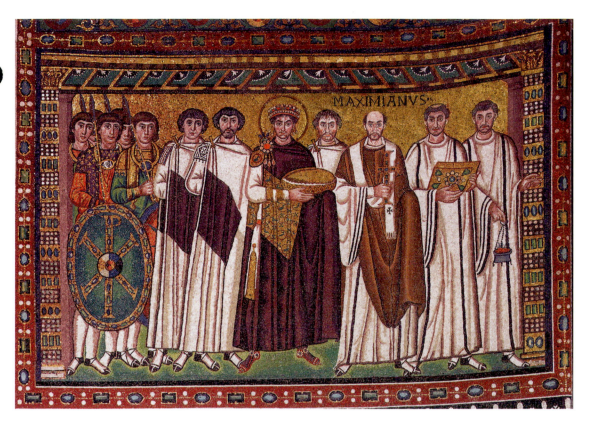

7–17 • EMPEROR JUSTINIAN AND HIS ATTENDANTS

North sanctuary wall of the church of San Vitale, Ravenna, Italy. c. 547. Mosaic, 8′ 8″ × 12′ (2.64 × 3.65 m).

As head of state, Justinian—nimbed (head surrounded by a **nimbus** or halo) and wearing a huge jeweled crown and a purple cloak—carries a large golden paten that he is donating to San Vitale for the celebration of the Mass. Bishop Maximianus at his left holds a jeweled cross and another churchman holds a jewel-covered book. Government officials stand at Justinian's right, followed by barbarian mercenary soldiers, one of whom wears a neck torc, another a classical cameo cloak clasp.

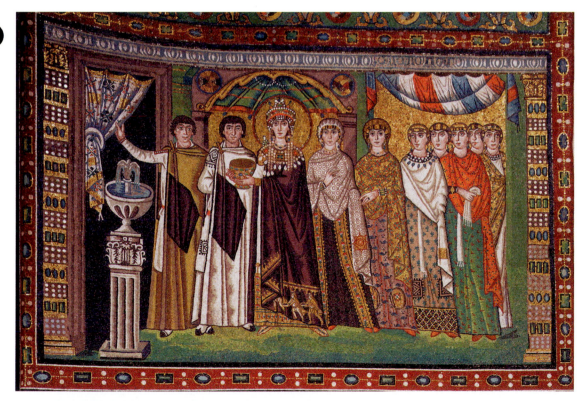

7–18 • EMPRESS THEODORA AND HER ATTENDANTS

South sanctuary wall of the church of San Vitale. c. 547. Mosaic, 8′ 8″ × 12′ (2.64 × 3.65 m).

Like Justinian, Theodora has a halo, wears imperial purple, and carries in her hands a liturgical vessel—the chalice that held the Eucharistic wine—that she will donate to the church. Her elaborate jewelry includes a wide collar of embroidered and jeweled cloth. A crown, hung with long strands of pearls (thought to protect the wearer from disease), frames her face. Her attendants also wear the rich textiles and jewelry of the Byzantine court.

lunette (SEE FIG. 7–9), and a book with a jeweled cover is carried by a deacon in Justinian's procession at San Vitale (SEE FIG. 7–17). Until the invention of printing, all European books were **manuscripts**—that is, they were written by hand on **parchment** (specially prepared animal skin). If they were decorated or illustrated, today we call them **illuminated**. During the Middle Ages, many illuminated manuscripts were made not only in professional workshops, but also in monasteries and convents, religious communities where monks and nuns withdrew from the secular world to devote their lives to study and prayer.

The **MANUSCRIPT PAGE** (called a **folio**) illustrated in FIGURE 7–19 comes from a **codex** (bound, rectangular book in the modern sense, rather than a scroll), written in Greek on purple **vellum** (fine animal skin prepared for writing). The purple color indicates that it may have been done for an imperial patron; the costly purple dye, made from the secretions of murex mollusks, was usually restricted to imperial use. Illustrations appear below the text at the bottom of the page. The story of Rebecca at the well (Genesis 24) on this leaf appears to be a single scene, but the painter—faithful to the continuous narrative tradition that had characterized the illustration of scrolls—combines events that take place at different times in the story within a single narrative space. Rebecca appears at the left walking away from the walled city of Nahor with a large jug on her shoulder, going to fetch water. A colonnaded road leads to a spring, personified by a reclining pagan water nymph holding a flowing jar. In the foreground, Rebecca appears again,

clearly identifiable by continuity of costume. Her jug now full, she encounters a thirsty camel driver and offers him a drink. Since he is Abraham's servant Eliezer, who is searching for a bride for Abraham's son, Isaac, Rebecca's generosity leads to her marriage. The lifelike poses and rounded, full-bodied figures of this narrative scene conform to the conventions of traditional Roman painting. The sumptuous purple of the background and the glittering metallic letters of the text situate the book within the world of the privileged and powerful in Byzantine society.

Icons and Iconoclasm

Christians in the Byzantine world prayed to Christ, the Virgin Mary, and the saints while looking at images of them in **manuscripts**, on the walls of churches, or on independent painted panels known as **icons** (not to be confused with the word **iconic** which refers in general to images that represent symbols or ideas). Church doctrine concerning the veneration of icons distinguished between idolatry—the worship of images—and the veneration of an idea or holy person depicted in a work of art. Icons were thus accepted as aids to meditation and prayer; the images were thought to act as intermediaries between worshipers and the holy personages they depicted, and honor showed to the image was believed to transfer directly to its spiritual prototype.

Surviving early icons are rare. Among the most representative is the **VIRGIN AND CHILD WITH SAINTS AND ANGELS** (FIG. 7–20). The Virgin Mary, as the earthly mother

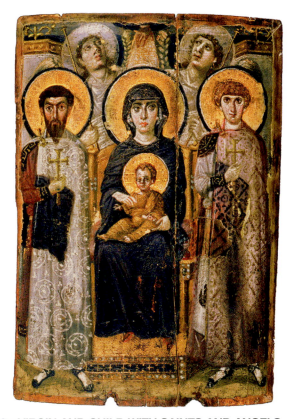

7-19 • MANUSCRIPT PAGE WITH REBECCA AT THE WELL
From the book of Genesis (known as the Vienna Genesis), probably made in Syria or Palestine. Early 6th century. Tempera, gold, and silver paint on purple-dyed vellum, 13½″ × 9⅞″ (33.7 × 25 cm). Österreichische Nationalbibliothek, Vienna.

7-20 • VIRGIN AND CHILD WITH SAINTS AND ANGELS
Icon in the monastery of St. Catherine, Mount Sinai, Egypt. Second half of 6th century. Encaustic on wood, 27″ × 18⅞″ (69 × 48 cm).

Iconoclasm

Iconoclasm (literally "image breaking," derived from the Greek words *eikon* for "image" and *klao* meaning "break" or "destroy") is the prohibition and destruction of works of visual art, usually because they are considered inappropriate in religious contexts.

During the eighth century, mounting discomfort with the place of icons in Christian devotion grew into a major controversy in the Byzantine world, and between 726 and 730, Emperor Leo III (ruled 717–741) initiated a policy of iconoclasm, systematically destroying images of saints and sacred stories on icons and in churches, as well as persecuting those who made them and defended their use. His successor Constantine V (ruled 741–775) enforced these policies with even greater fervor. But at the end of the reign of Leo IV (ruled 775–780), his widow, empress Irene, who ruled as regent for their son Constantine IV (ruled 780–797), put an end to iconoclasm in 787 through a church council held in Nicaea. Leo V (ruled 813–820) instituted a second phase of iconoclasm in 813, and it remained imperial policy until March 11, 843, when the widowed Empress Theodora reversed her husband Theophilus's policy and reinstated the central place of images in Byzantine devotional practice.

A number of explanations have been proposed for these two interludes of Byzantine iconoclasm. Some church leaders feared that the use of images in worship could lead to idolatry or at least distract worshipers from their spiritual exercises. Specifically, there were questions surrounding the relationship between images and the Eucharist, the latter considered by iconoclasts as sufficient representation of the presence of Christ in the church. But there was also anxiety in Byzantium about the weakening state of the empire, especially in relation to the advances of Arab armies into Byzantine territory. It was easy to pin these hard times on God's displeasure at the idolatrous use of images. Coincidentally, Leo III's success fighting the Arabs could be interpreted as divine sanction of his iconoclastic position, and its very adoption might appease the iconoclastic Islamic enemy itself. Finally, since the production and promotion of icons were centered in monasteries—at that time rivaling the state in strength and wealth—attacking the use of images might check their growing power. Perhaps all these factors played a part, but at the triumph of the iconophiles (literally "lovers of images") in 843, the place of images in worship was again secure: icons proclaimed Christ as God incarnate and facilitated Christian worship by acting as intermediaries between humans and saints. The suppressors of icons were designated heretics (FIG. 7–21).

But iconoclasm is not restricted to Byzantine history. It reappears from time to time through the history of art. Some Protestant reformers of sixteenth-century Europe adopted what they saw as the iconoclastic position of the Hebrew Bible

(Exodus 20:4), and many works of Catholic art were destroyed by zealous reformers and their followers. Even more recently, in 2001, the Taliban rulers of Afghanistan dynamited two gigantic sixth-century CE statues of the Buddha carved into the rock cliffs of the Bamiyan Valley, specifically because they believed such "idols" violated Islamic law.

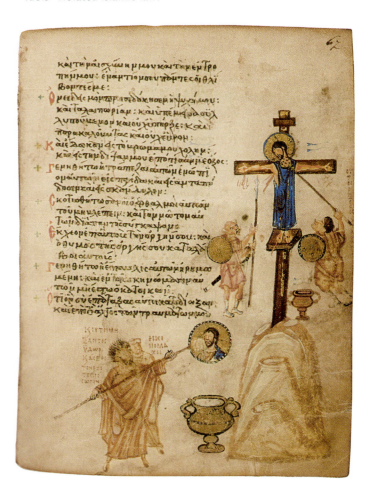

7–21 • CRUCIFIXION AND ICONOCLASTS

From the *Chludov Psalter*. Mid 9th century. Tempera on vellum, 7¾″ × 6″ (19.5 × 15 cm). State Historical Museum, Moscow (MS D.29, fol. 67r).

This page and its illustration of Psalm 21, made soon after the end of the iconoclastic controversy in 843, records the iconophiles' harsh judgment of the iconoclasts. Painted in the margin at the right, a scene of the Crucifixion shows a soldier tormenting Christ with a vinegar-soaked sponge. In a striking visual parallel, two named iconoclasts—identified by inscription—in the adjacent picture along the bottom margin employ a whitewash-soaked sponge to obliterate an icon portrait of Christ, thus linking their actions with those who had crucified him.

of Jesus (called in Greek *Theotokos*, bearer of God), was viewed as a powerful intercessor, or go-between, who could appeal to her divine Son for mercy on behalf of devout and repentant worshipers. She was also called the Seat of Wisdom, and like many images, this **icon** shows her holding Jesus on her lap in a way that suggests that she has become his imperial throne. Mother and child are flanked here by the Christian warrior-saints Theodore (left) and George (right). These two legendary figures said to have slain dragons represent the triumph of the Church over the "evil serpent" of paganism. The artist has painted the Christ Child, the Virgin, and the angels in an illusionistic, Roman manner that renders them lifelike in appearance. But the warrior-saints are more stylized; the artist barely hints at bodily form beneath the richly patterned textiles of their cloaks and their tense faces are frozen in frontal stares of gripping intensity, addressing viewers directly.

In the eighth century, in a reaction against the veneration of images, several emperors ordered the systematic destruction of icons and banned the use of images in Christian worship, a policy known as **iconoclasm** (see "Iconoclasm," p. 177). A few survived in isolated places such as Mount Sinai in Egypt, which was no longer part of the Byzantine Empire at this time. But iconoclasm did not last. In 787, iconoclasm was revoked at the instigation of Empress Irene, only to be reinstated in 813. Again it was an empress—Theodora, widow of Theophilus, last of the iconoclastic emperors—who reversed her husband's policy in 843, and from this moment onward icons would play an increasingly important role in the development of Byzantine art.

Middle and Late Byzantine Art

How did Byzantine art change during its middle and late periods?

After the defeat of the iconoclasts Byzantine art flourished again, especially after 867 under the leadership of an imperial dynasty from Macedonia. One of the most important developments during this middle period was the schism of 1054, which effectively divided Christianity into two parts: the Roman Catholic Church in Western Europe and the Eastern Orthodox Church of the Byzantine world centered in Constantinople. The Byzantine cultural revival continued until Christian crusaders from the West occupied Constantinople in 1204. When the occupation of the Western crusaders ended in 1261, Byzantine art blossomed once again, not only in Constantinople but in other Orthodox Christian kingdoms as well.

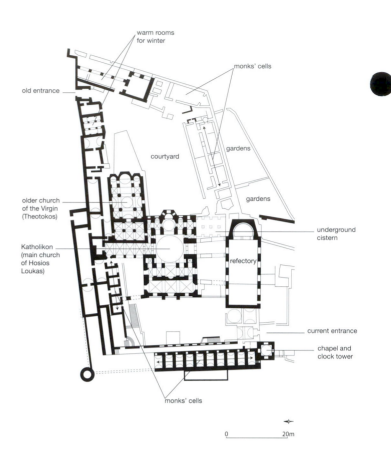

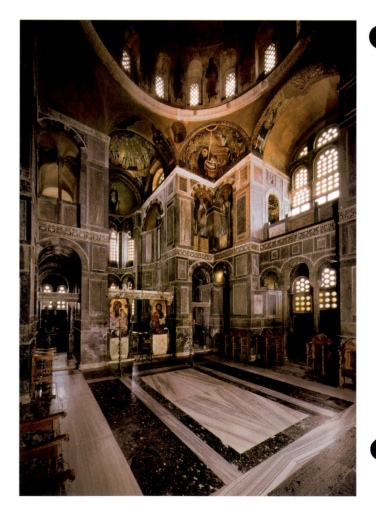

7–22 • PLAN OF MONASTERY AND CENTRAL DOMED SPACE AND SANCTUARY OF KATHOLIKON, HOSIOS LOUKAS

Near Stiris, Greece. Early 11th century and later.

※ **Explore** the architectural panoramas of the monastery churches at Hosios Loukas on **MyArtsLab**

Middle Byzantine Art (843–1204)

Little Middle Byzantine art survives from Constantinople, but many central-plan domed churches, favored by Byzantine architects, still exist in Greece and Ukraine, and they are reflected in Venetian architecture. Greece lay within the Byzantine Empire in the tenth and eleventh centuries, and the two churches of the monastery of Hosios Loukas (near Stiris) are excellent examples of Middle Byzantine architecture (FIG. 7–22). The church stood within the courtyard of the walled monastery enclosure, a complex that contained the life of the monks. The monks slept in individual rooms incorporated into the monastery walls and ate communally within a long, rectangular dining hall parallel to the main church.

The Katholikon (the major church) is a compact, central-plan structure, whose builders seems to have reveled in architectural complexity. The high central space carries the eye of the worshiper upward into the main dome soaring above a ring of tall arched openings. Single, double, and triple windows create intricate and unusual patterns of light. Curving surfaces are covered with a rich program of mosaics, and flat walls are sheathed in intricate marble veneers. Visible here are images of the Virgin and Child in the apse, Pentecost (the Lamb of God hovering over the twelve apostles) in the sanctuary dome, and the Nativity and standing saints in the vaults. (A mosaic of Christ Pantokrator [ruler of the universe] was once in the central dome.) An icon screen (**iconostasis**) separates the sanctuary from the congregation.

The northeastern Italian city of Venice holds many rich treasures of Middle and Late Byzantine art. At the end of the tenth century, Constantinople granted Venice a special trading status that allowed it to control much of the commercial exchange between Western Europe and the Eastern Empire. With untold wealth flowing into the city's coffers, Venice's ruler, the doge, in 1063 commissioned a splendid church to replace an older chapel holding the relics of the martyred patron saint of Venice, the apostle St. Mark. Venetian architects looked to Byzantine domed churches for inspiration, especially the church of the Holy Apostles in Constantinople. This important church—commemorating Constantine as well as the apostles—had a Greek cross plan of five square units, each surmounted by a dome on pendentives; this was adopted by the builders of **ST. MARK'S** (FIG. 7–23). Inside the church,

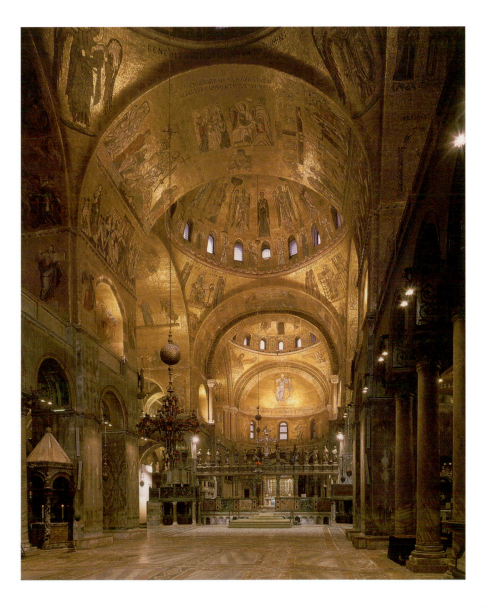

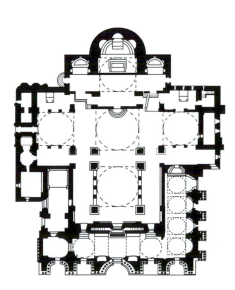

7-23 • PLAN AND INTERIOR VIEW OF THE CATHEDRAL OF ST. MARK
Venice. Begun 1063.

these domed compartments, separated by barrel vaults and lit by circles of windows, produce a complex space in which each individual dome vies for attention, unlike the powerful focus of Hagia Sophia, with its sweeping upward and forward movement focused by the unity of a single dome. Later Byzantine builders preferred intricate compartmentalization.

Late Byzantine Art (1261–1453)

A last great age of Byzantine art began after crusaders, who had occupied Constantinople in 1204, were expelled from the city in 1261. Byzantine culture blossomed in the fourteenth and early fifteenth centuries until the capital was conquered by Muslim Ottoman Turks in 1453, and Constantinople became Istanbul.

The patronage of emperors and wealthy courtiers was the stimulus for renewed church building and renovation. For example, in the early fourteenth century, Theodore Metochites (1270–1332)—poet, scientist, and imperial treasurer—funded an elaborate expansion and renovation of the Constantinopolitan church of the monastery of Christ in Chora, perhaps the most impressive interior architectural decorations that survive

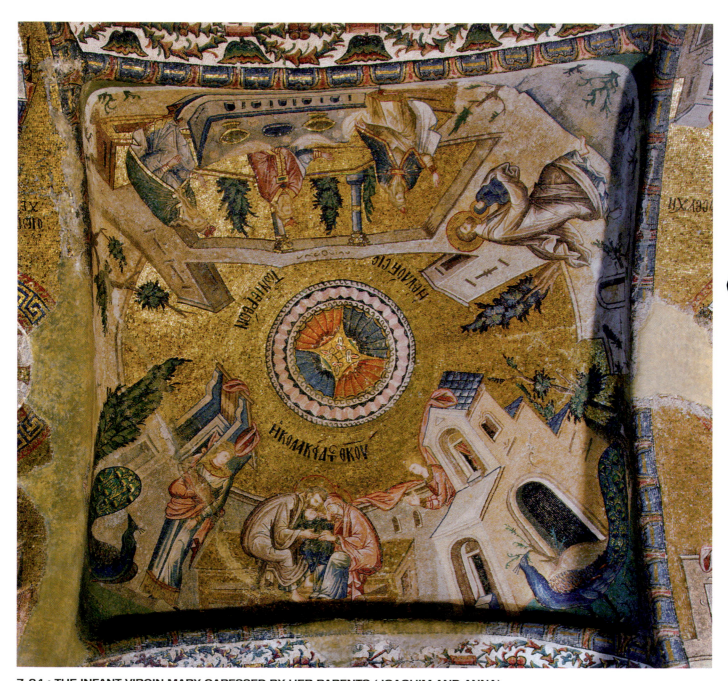

7–24 • THE INFANT VIRGIN MARY CARESSED BY HER PARENTS (JOACHIM AND ANNA)
Lower half of this mosaic in the inner narthex, church of the monastery of Christ in Chora, Constantinople (now Kariye Müzesi, Istanbul, Turkey). c. 1315–1321.

The Greek inscription placed over the family group identifies this scene as the fondling of the Theotokos (bearer of God).

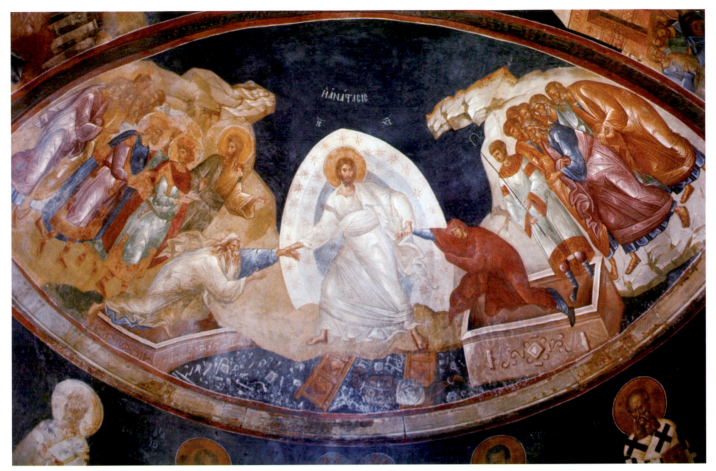

7–25 • ANASTASIS
Fresco in the apse of the funerary chapel, church of the monastery of Christ in Chora (now Kariye Müzesi, Istanbul, Turkey). c. 1315–1321.

✸ **Explore** the architectural panoramas of the monastery church of Christ in Chora on **MyArtsLab**

in the capital from the Late Byzantine period. They rival in splendor and technical sophistication the works of the age of Justinian, but on a more intimate scale. A scene of the infant Virgin Mary, cuddled between her adoring parents Joachim and Anna (**FIG. 7–24**), occupies half of the mosaic decoration covering a vault in the church's double narthex. Servants on either side of the family look on with gestures and expressions of admiration and approval, perhaps modeling the response that is expected from viewers within the narthex itself. The human interaction even extends to details, such as the nuzzling of Mary's head into the beard of her father as she leans back to look into his eyes, and her tentative reach toward her mother's face at the same time. In another scene, the young Jesus rides on the shoulders of Joseph, in a pose still familiar to fathers and children in our own time. The informality and believability that these anecdotal details bring to this sacred narrative recalls developments as far away as Italy, where near this same time Giotto and Duccio were using similar devices to bring their stories to life (see Chapter 11).

A painting of the Resurrection of Christ, known in Greek as the **ANASTASIS**, fills the apse in the new funeral chapel at the Chora church, which would be the site of the patron's own

funeral in 1332 (**FIG. 7–25**). Artists in Western Europe usually depicted the Resurrection as the triumphant Christ emerging in glory from his tomb, but in the Eastern Church Christ is shown descending into hell to rescue Adam and Eve and others among his devout Jewish ancestors from Satan's grip. Here a boldly striding Christ—brilliantly outfitted in a pure white that makes him the shining focus of the action—lunges to rescue Adam and Eve from their tombs, pulling them upward with such force that they seem to float airborne under the spell of his power. Satan lies tied into a helpless bundle at his feet, and patriarchs, kings, and prophets to either side look on in admiration, perhaps waiting for their own turn to be rescued.

The rulers of Rus—present-day Ukraine, Belarus, and Russia—had fallen under the spell of Constantinople and adopted Orthodox Christianity as early as the tenth century, when Princess Olga (c. 890–969) was baptized by the patriarch himself, with the Byzantine emperor as her godfather. Byzantine art flourished here in the Late Byzantine period, when the production of icons became a major artistic focus. A remarkable work from this time is **THREE ANGELS VISITING ABRAHAM (OLD TESTAMENT TRINITY)**, a large icon created between about 1410 and 1425 by the famed Russian artist-monk

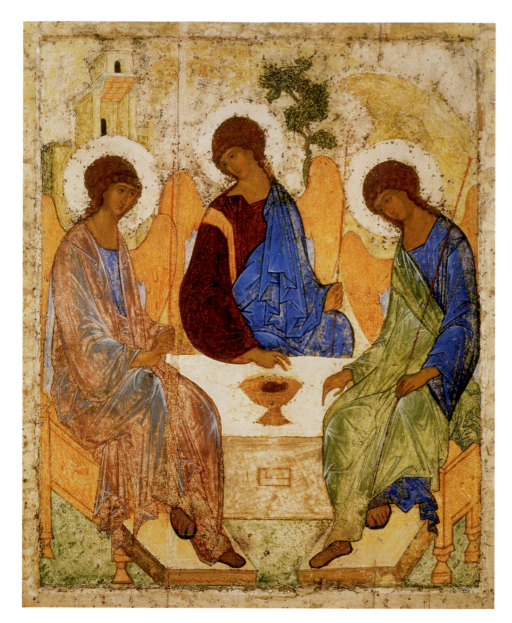

7–26 • Andrey Rublyov THREE ANGELS VISITING ABRAHAM (OLD TESTAMENT TRINITY)
Icon. c. 1410–1425. Tempera on panel, 55½″ × 44½″ (141 × 113 cm). Tretyakov Gallery, Moscow.

📖 **Read** the document about painting icons on **MyArtsLab**

Andrey Rublyov (FIG. 7–26). It was commissioned in honor of Abbot Sergius of the Trinity-Sergius Monastery, near Moscow. The theme of the Trinity is always a great challenge for artists. One late medieval solution was to show three identical divine individuals—here, three angels—to suggest the idea. Rublyov's composition was inspired by a story in the Hebrew Bible of the patriarch Abraham and his wife, Sarah, who entertained three strangers who were in fact God represented by three divine beings in human form (Genesis 18). Tiny images of Abraham and Sarah's home and the oak of Mamre can be seen above the angels; on the table, the food the couple offered to the strangers becomes a chalice on an altar-like table.

Rublyov's icon clearly illustrates how Late Byzantine artists relied on mathematical conventions to create ideal figures, as did the ancient Greeks, thus giving their work remarkable consistency. Unlike the Greeks, who based their formulas on close observation of nature, however, Byzantine artists invented an ideal geometry to evoke a heavenly realm and conformed their representations of human forms and features to it. Here, as elsewhere, the circle—most apparent in the haloes—forms the basic underlying structure for the composition. Despite their seemingly formulaic approach, talented artists like Rublyov created personal expressive styles. He relied on Byzantine conventions such as salient contours, elongation of the body, and a focus on a limited number of figures to capture the sense of the spiritual in his work, yet he distinguished his art by imbuing it with a sweet, poetic ambience. In his hands, the Byzantine style took on a graceful and eloquent new life.

The Byzantine tradition continues in the art of the Eastern Orthodox Church until today. But in Constantinople, Byzantine art—and the empire itself—came to a decisive end in 1453. When the forces of the Ottoman sultan Mehmed II overran the capital, the Eastern Empire became part of the Islamic world, which absorbed aspects of the Byzantine art tradition into a very rich aesthetic heritage of its own. Leadership of the Orthodox world shifted to Russia, whose rulers declared Moscow to be the third Rome and themselves the heirs of the Caesars (tsars).

Both Jews and Christians believe in a single god and seek to conform their lives and their societies to the will of that god as revealed and recorded in sacred Scripture. And they have expressed their aspirations and core beliefs in pictures as well as words. Even though strictures within Jewish law forbidding the creation and worship of idols made the representational arts suspect, artists working for Jewish patrons depicted both symbolic and narrative Jewish subjects.

Believing that God came to earth in human form—Jesus Christ—Christians also created a powerful figurative art using human beings as expressive symbols, creating a tradition that would extend beyond the collapse of the Western Roman Empire to flourish in the Byzantine East for a thousand years, until Constantinople fell to the Islamic Ottoman Turks in 1453.

But during the formative third and fourth centuries, both Jews and Christians had looked to Near Eastern and Roman art for inspiration. These same two sources will coalesce around different social and religious principles in the formation of Islamic art, the subject of the next chapter.

THINK ABOUT IT

7.1 What does the style and subject matter of the mosaic pavement of the Beth Alpha Synagogue tell us about the nature of early Jewish art?

7.2 Discuss the Roman foundations of Early Christian sculpture, focusing your answer on the Sarcophagus of Junius Bassus (FIG. 7–11).

7.3 How were images used in Byzantine worship? Why were images suppressed during iconoclasm?

7.4 Characterize the Late Byzantine style of the mosaics and frescos of the Constantinopolitan church of the monastery of Christ in Chora (FIGS. 7–24, 7–25). How is it different from the much earlier style at San Vitale (FIGS. 7–16 to 7–18)?

| CROSSCURRENTS |

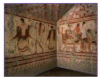
FIG. 6–5

FIG. 7–1

Both Etruscans and Early Christians often painted the interior walls of their tombs. Discuss the themes chosen for the murals in these two examples. Are the images related to life, to death, or to life after death? How are the styles and subjects related to these two cultures?

☑ **Study** and **Review** on MyArtsLab

IN PERSPECTIVE

100 CE

• Roman Destruction of the Temple in Jerusalem 70

• Parthians Conquer Dura-Europos 256

300

• Edict of Milan Legalizes Christianity in the Roman Empire 313

• Council of Nicaea 325

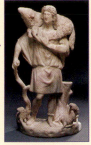
The Good Shepherd
2nd half of 3rd century

• End of the Western Roman Empire 476

500

• Justinian ruled 527–565

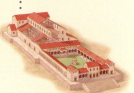
Old St. Peter's Basilica, Rome
c. 320–327

700

• Iconoclasm 726–843

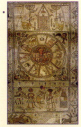
Mosaic Floor, Beth Alpha Synagogue
6th century

900

• Russia Becomes Christian 988

• Division of Church into Roman Catholic and Eastern Orthodox 1054

• First Crusade 1095–1099

1100

• Western Rule of Constantinople 1204–1261

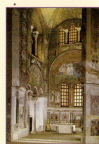
Church of San Vitale, Ravenna 547

1300

• Fall of Constantinople to the Ottoman Turks, Signaling the End of the Roman Empire 1453

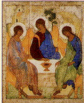
RUBLYOV, Old Testament Trinity
c. 1410–1425

1500

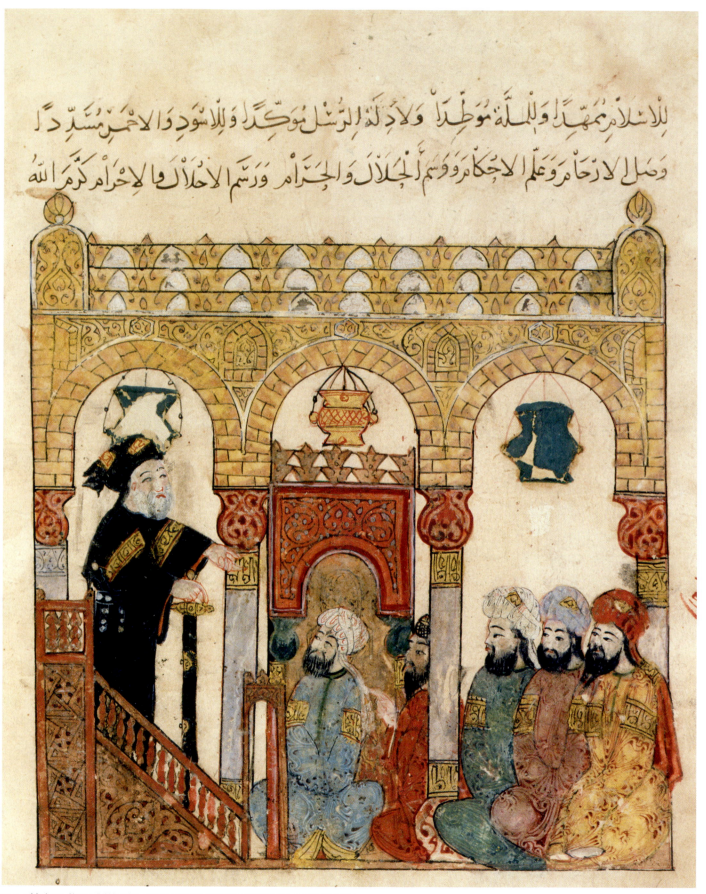

للاسلام ممهدا وللملة موطدا ولادلة الرسل موكدا وللاسود والاحمر مسددا

وصل الارحام وعلم الاحكام وسم الحلال والحرام ورسم الاحلال والاحرام كرم الله

8–1 • Yahya Ibn al-Wasiti ABU ZAYD PREACHING IN A MOSQUE

From an illustrated manuscript of the *Maqamat* of al-Hariri. Baghdad, Iraq. 1237. Ink, pigments, and gold on paper. Bibliothèque Nationale, Paris (MS arabe 5847, fol. 18v).

ISLAMIC ART

8.1 Describe the early formulation of Islamic art and architecture.

8.2 Recognize later developments in the Islamic art and architecture of Persia, Spain, and Turkey.

8.3 Interpret the diverse forms of luxury art produced in the Islamic world.

8.4 Identify the extension of Islamic art into the modern period.

LOOKING FORWARD ▶

The *Maqamat* (*The Assemblies*), by al-Hariri (1054–1122), belongs to a popular Islamic literary **genre** of cautionary tales. Al-Hariri's stories revolve around a silver-tongued scoundrel named Abu Zayd, whose cunning inevitably triumphs over other people's naivety. His exploits take place in a world of colorful settings—desert camps, ships, pilgrim caravans, apothecary shops, mosques, gardens, libraries, cemeteries, and courts of law. In such settings, these comic stories of trickery and theft would seem perfectly suited for illustration, and that is the case in this spectacular manuscript, made in Baghdad during the thirteenth century. Human activity permeates the compositions—pointing fingers, arguing with adversaries, riding horses, stirring pots, and strumming musical instruments. And these vivid visualizations of Abu Zayd's adventures provide us with rare windows into Muslim life, here prayer in the congregational **mosque (FIG. 8–1)**, a religious and social institution at the center of Islamic culture.

The congregation has gathered to hear a sermon preached by the deceitful Abu Zayd, who plans to leave with the alms collection. The men sit directly on the ground, as is customary not only in mosques, but in traditional dwellings. The listener in the front row tilts his chin upward to focus his gaze directly upon the speaker. He is framed and centered by the arch of the *mihrab* (the niche indicating the direction of Mecca) on the rear wall; his white turban contrasts noticeably with the darker gold background. Perhaps he stands in for the manuscript's reader who, perusing the illustrations of these captivating stories, pauses to project him- or herself into the scene.

The columns of the mosque's arcades have ornamental capitals from which spring half-round arches. Glass mosque lamps hang from the center of each arch. Figures wear turbans and flowing, loose-sleeved robes with epigraphic borders (*tiraz*) embroidered in gold. Abu Zayd delivers his sermon from the steps of a pulpit (*minbar*) with an arched gateway opening at the lowest level. This *minbar* and the arcades that form the backdrop of the scene are reduced in scale so the painter can describe the entire setting and still make the figures the main focus of the composition. Likewise, although in an actual mosque the *minbar* would share the same wall as the *mihrab*, here they have been separated, perhaps to keep the *minbar* from hiding the *mihrab*, and to rivet our focus on what is most important—the rapt attention Abu Zayd commands from his captive audience, a group we ourselves join as we relish the anecdotal and pictorial delights of this splendid example of Islamic visual narrative.

The religion called Islam (meaning "submission to [God's will]") originated in Arabia in the early seventh century. Under the leadership of its founder, the Prophet Muhammad (c. 570–632), and his successors, Islam spread rapidly, encompassing large areas of Africa, Europe, and Asia. Under four of Muhammad's closest associates, who assumed in turn the title of caliph (successor), Muslim armies conquered Persia (Iran), Egypt, and the Byzantine provinces of Syria and Palestine. The last of these caliphs, Ali (ruled 656–661), was succeeded by a rival, Muawiya (ruled 661–680), who founded the Umayyad dynasty. By the early eighth century, the aggressively expansionist Umayyads had reached India, conquered all of North Africa and Spain, and penetrated France to within 100 miles of Paris before being turned back (**MAP 8-1**). Today Islam is the world's fastest growing religion.

At first, Islamic art absorbed local traditions—as diverse as Roman, Byzantine, and Persian—in art and architecture. Because conservative Muslims discouraged, even prohibited, the representation of humans, especially in religious contexts, artists living in Islamic lands developed a particularly rich vocabulary of ornament, including complex geometric designs and the scrolling vines known outside the Islamic world as **arabesques**. Artists excelled in surface decoration, manipulating an infinite variety of highly controlled patterns, and often highlighting the interplay between pure abstraction, organic form, and script. For some people, such designs help free the mind from a focus on material form, opening it to contemplation of the enormity of divine presence.

Early Islamic Art

What characterizes the early formation of Islamic art and architecture?

The caliphs of the Umayyad dynasty (661–750) ruled from Damascus in Syria. Inspired by the Roman and Byzantine architecture of the eastern Mediterranean, the Umayyads became enthusiastic builders of shrines, mosques, and palaces throughout their empire. After Mecca and Medina—sites directly associated with the life of Muhammad—Jerusalem was the third most holy site in Islam. In the center of the city rises the Haram al-Sharif ("Noble Sanctuary"), a rocky outcrop that Muslims identify as the place from which Muhammad ascended to the presence of God on the "Night Journey" described in the Qur'an. The same rock is also associated with the creation of Adam; the place where the patriarch Abraham prepared to sacrifice his son, Isaac, at the command of God; and the site of the temple of Solomon, making it important to Jews and Christians, as well as Muslims.

In 691–692, the Umayyads constructed a shrine over the rock (**FIG. 8-2**) using Syrian artisans trained in the Byzantine tradition. The **DOME OF THE ROCK** is the first great monument of Islamic art, decorated on the interior with a mosaic frieze containing the earliest written text of the Qur'an. Its centralized octagonal plan derives from Early Christian and Byzantine **martyria** (SEE FIG. 7–15). By claiming a site holy to Jews and Christians and crowning it with an Islamic monument that incorporates aspects of those earlier artistic traditions,

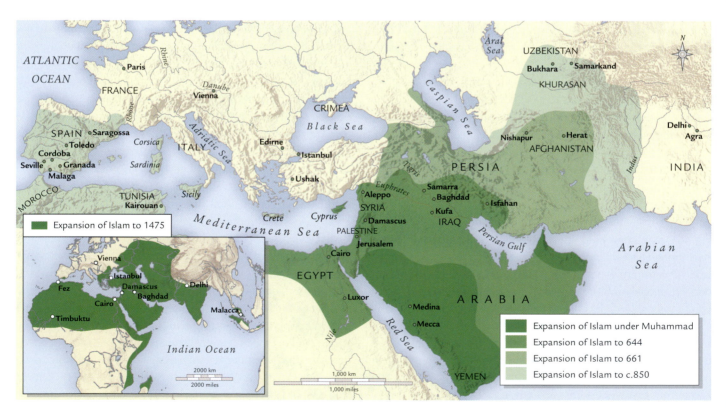

Map 8–1 • THE ISLAMIC WORLD

Within 200 years after 622, the Islamic world expanded from Mecca to India in the east, and to Morocco and Spain in the west.

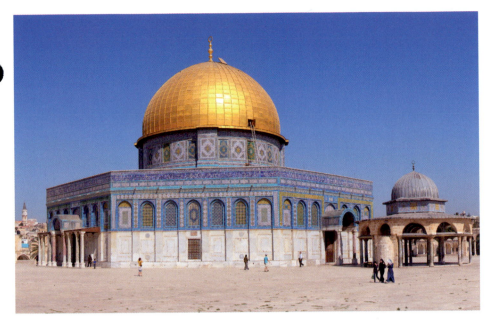

8-2 • EXTERIOR VIEW AND CUTAWAY DRAWING OF THE DOME OF THE ROCK
Jerusalem, Israel. Begun 691.

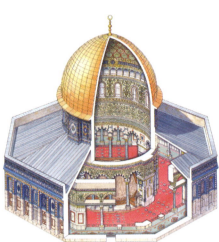

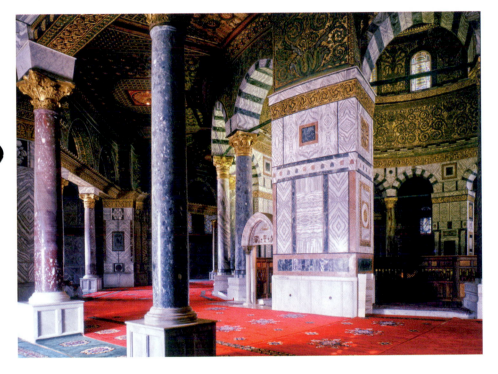

8-3 • INTERIOR, DOME OF THE ROCK
Jerusalem, Israel. Begun 691.

Concentric aisles (**ambulatories**) permit the devout visitor to circumambulate (walk around) the rock. Inscriptions from the Qur'an interspersed with passages from other texts and commentaries, including information about the building, form a frieze around the inner wall in gold mosaic on a turquoise-green ground. The pilgrim must walk around the central space first clockwise and then counterclockwise to read the inscriptions. The carpets and ceiling are modern but probably reflect the original intent.

🔍 **View** the Closer Look for the Dome of the Rock on **MyArtsLab**

the Dome of the Rock is the first architectural manifestation of Islam's view of itself as completing and superseding the prophesies of Judaism and Christianity.

The central space is covered by a dome on a tall drum supported by an arcade. Two concentric aisles enclose the rock. Marble veneer at ground level and glass mosaics above decorate the building's interior (**FIG. 8–3**). The mosaic frieze depicts thick, symmetrical vine scrolls and trees in turquoise, blue, and green, embellished with imitation jewels, over a gold ground, imagery variously interpreted as the gardens of Paradise and trophies of Muslim victories offered to God. The lower part of the exterior walls retains its original white marble facings, inset with patterns in colored stone, and originally, glass mosaics also covered the upper half of the octagon's outer walls, but they deteriorated over time. In the sixteenth century, the Ottoman sultan Suleyman ordered the mosaics replaced with magnificent, colorful ceramic tiles, specialties of Turkish builders of that time.

The focal point of the building, remarkably enough, is not the decorative program—nor even something that can initially be seen. From the entrance one sees only pure light streaming down to the unseen rock, surrounded by color and pattern. After penetrating the space, the viewer/worshiper realizes that the light falls on the precious rock, envisioning the very passage of Muhammad to the heavens.

The Dome of the Rock is a special shrine, and Muslim congregations gather on Fridays for regular public worship not in shrines but in **mosques**. The plans of mosques (in Arabic, *masjid*, a "place of prostration") vary in detail, but all are usually entered

Islam and the Prophet Muhammad

Islam originated in the Arabian peninsula in the seventh century. According to Islamic belief, God (Allah) transmitted revelations that would become the basis of Islam through the archangel Gabriel to an Arab merchant, Muhammad. Islamic believers (Muslims) submit to God and acknowledge Muhammad as their Prophet. Muslims also recognize earlier prophets—Moses, Abraham, Jesus—and share with Jews and Christians the belief in one God. Originally God's revelations were committed to memory and passed down orally, but after Muhammad's death the Qur'an was written down and assembled into 114 chapters, or surahs, to become the sacred Scripture of Islam.

The Prophet Muhammad was born about 570 in Mecca, a city in west-central Arabia that was home to the Kaaba, an ancient, cube-shaped stone building believed to be the house Abraham built for God. Muhammad received his first revelations in 610 and was soon accepted as God's Prophet by his friends and family. After failing to convert the local population, Muhammad and his companions were forced to flee in 622 to Medina. It is from this event, called the *hijira* (emigration), that Muslims date their history. Muhammad regained control of Mecca in 630, and

the inhabitants eventually accepted the new religion. The Kaaba became Islam's sacred center, toward which Muslims around the world still face when praying. Muhammad died in Medina in 632.

Muslims believe in a single, all-powerful God and in Muhammad as the last in the succession of true prophets. Islam also requires Muslims to follow the Five Pillars of Islam, sometimes symbolized by an open hand with five extended fingers. The first and most important pillar is the statement of faith: "There is no god but God and Muhammad is his messenger." The second pillar requires prayer five times a day facing Mecca. The remaining pillars are charity to the poor (*zakah*), the dawn-to-dusk fast (*sawm*) during the month of Ramadan, and, if possible, a pilgrimage to Mecca (*hajj*). Muslims participate in congregational worship and listen to a sermon at a mosque (prayer hall) on Fridays.

After Muhammad's death, his father-in-law Abu Bakr became the first caliph, or successor to the Prophet. Ali—the husband of Muhammad's daughter Fatima—was the fourth caliph. The power struggle that ended in Ali's death led to the division of Islamic communities into Sunni (traditional) and Shi'ite (followers of Ali).

through a courtyard, and each must have a large covered space to accommodate the entire worshiping community. All mosques are oriented in the direction of Mecca (**qibla**), and worshipers arrange themselves in rows to pray facing Mecca. A niche called a **mihrab** identifies the *qibla* wall, a practice deriving from a long tradition of using niches to signify holy places: the Torah shrine in a synagogue, the recessed frame for sculpture of gods and ancestors in Roman architecture, the apse in a Christian church. The **maqsura**, an enclosure in front of the *mihrab* for the ruler and other dignitaries, became a feature of the principal congregational mosque after an assassination attempt on an Umayyad ruler. The **minbar**, or pulpit, stands by the *mihrab* as a raised platform for the prayer leader and a symbol of his authority. The faithful gather for Friday prayers and listen to a sermon in a city's principal mosque, called the Great Mosque or Masjid-i Jami ("Friday" or "Congregational" Mosque).

The earliest mosques were very simple, modeled on Muhammad's house with its courtyard and porticoes, where early followers gathered for worship and to hear the Prophet speak from his raised seat. **THE GREAT MOSQUE** of Kairouan, Tunisia (**FIG. 8–4**), although built in the ninth century, reflects this early form of the mosque. Its large rectangular plan is divided between a courtyard and a hypostyle prayer hall with a flat roof. The system of repeated bays and aisles can easily be extended as the congregation grows in size. The huge **minaret** (a tower from which criers call the faithful to prayer) that rises

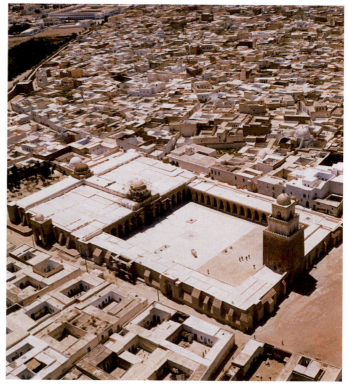

8–4 • THE GREAT MOSQUE
Kairouan, Tunisia. 836–875.

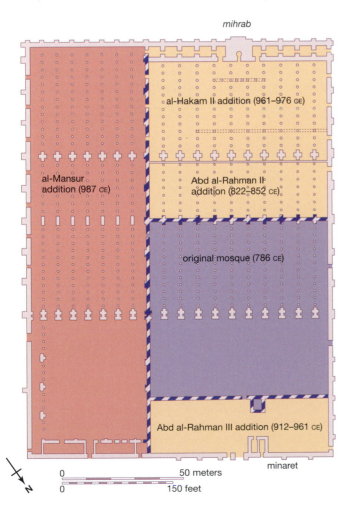

8–5 • PRAYER HALL AND PLAN

Great Mosque, Cordoba, Spain. Begun 785/786.

The plan shows the gradual growth of the original eighth-century mosque, which was expanded several times over the ninth and tenth centuries.

👁 **Watch** an architectural simulation of Islamic arches on **MyArtsLab**

mihrab

al-Hakam II addition (961–976 CE)

al-Mansur addition (987 CE)

Abd al-Rahman II addition (822–852 CE)

original mosque (786 CE)

Abd al-Rahman III addition (912–961 CE)

minaret

0   50 meters
0   150 feet

at one end of the courtyard will become a standard feature of mosques and a powerful sign of Islam's presence.

When the Abbasids overthrew the Umayyads in 750, Abbasid caliphs ruled the central and eastern lands of Islam from their capitals at Baghdad and Samarra (in present-day Iraq) until 1258. But the Umayyads maintained control in the far western lands of Islam. As the Abbasid caliphs took power, a survivor of the Umayyad dynasty, Abd al-Rahman I, fled across North Africa into southern Spain (al-Andalus in Arabic), establishing himself there as provincial ruler, or emir (ruled 756–788). From a new capital at Cordoba, the Umayyads governed al-Andalus until 1031, first as emirs and then, beginning with Abd al-Rahman III (ruled 912–961), as caliphs, setting themselves up as equals to the Abbasids. Their court at Cordoba became a renowned international center for scholars, scientists, poets, and musicians.

The finest surviving example of Spanish Umayyad architecture is the Great Mosque of Cordoba. This sprawling structure was begun in 785 by appropriating the site of a Christian church, and later rulers enlarged the building three times to meet the needs of an expanding urban population. Today the walls enclose an area of about 620 by 460 feet. The marble columns and capitals in the first hypostyle **PRAYER HALL** (**FIG. 8–5**) were recycled from the church and from local ruins of Classical buildings in this formerly wealthy Roman province. Two tiers of arches, one above the other, surmount the columns, increasing the height of the interior space. The distinctively shaped **horseshoe arches**—a form known from ancient Roman times—came to be closely associated with Islamic architecture

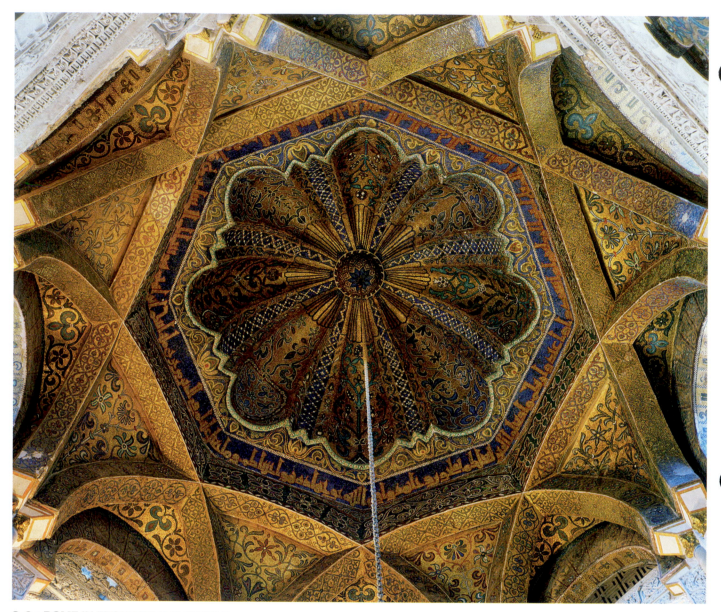

8–6 • DOME IN FRONT OF THE MIHRAB
Great Mosque, Cordoba. 965.

The costly and luxurious decoration of the additions that al-Hakam II (ruled 961–976) made to the Great Mosque disturbed many of his subjects. The caliph attempted to answer their objections with an inscription giving thanks to God, who "helped him in the building of this eternal place, with the goal of making this mosque more spacious for his subjects, something which both he and they greatly wanted" (Dodds, p. 23).

in the west. Another distinctive feature of these arches, inspired by Roman and Byzantine buildings, is the alternation of white stone and red brick voussoirs (wedge-shaped blocks) in the curving arches. While the alternating colors and textures are decorative, the use of contrasting materials adds strength to the arches, and the brick lends flexibility, which helps them withstand earthquakes.

In the final century of Umayyad rule, Cordoba emerged as a major commercial and intellectual hub and a flourishing center for the arts, surpassing Christian European cities economically and in science, literature, and philosophy. As a sign of this new prestige and power, Abd al-Rahman III boldly reclaimed the title of caliph in 929. He and his son al-Hakam II

(ruled 961–976) made the Great Mosque a focus of patronage, commissioning costly and luxurious renovations such as a new *mihrab* with three bays in front of it. Just in front of the *mihrab*, a melon-shaped, ribbed dome seems to float over a support of intersecting arches (**FIG. 8–6**). Lushly patterned mosaics with inscriptions, geometric motifs, and stylized vegetation clothe both this dome and the *mihrab* below in brilliant color and gold. These were installed by a Byzantine master who was sent by the emperor in Constantinople, bearing boxes of the small glazed ceramic and glass cubes (tesserae) used to create mosaics. Such artistic exchange is emblematic of the interconnectedness of the medieval Mediterranean—through trade, diplomacy, and competition.

Calligraphy

From the beginning, Arabic language and script have been revered in Islamic society. As the language of the Qur'an, Arabic is a powerful unifying force. From the eighth through the eleventh centuries, it was the universal scholarly language in Muslim lands. Reverence for the Qur'an as the word of God extends by association to the act of writing itself, and calligraphy—the art of fine hand lettering—becomes one of the glories of Islamic art.

Kufic, the earliest formal script, is blocky and angular and may have evolved from inscriptions on stone monuments. A page from a ninth-century Syrian Qur'an exemplifies a style of kufic common from the eighth to tenth century (**FIG. 8–7**). Red diacritical marks (pronunciation guides) accent the black ink. Horizontal strokes are elongated, and fat-bodied letters are emphasized. The surah ("chapter") title is embedded in the golden ornamental strip at the bottom of the page. The knob-like projection in the left-hand margin is a distinctive means of signaling chapter breaks in a book with no page numbers. This Qur'an is written on vellum, an especially fine parchment (prepared animal skin). Paper, a Chinese invention, was made in the Islamic world by the mid eighth century but did not fully replace parchment until after the year 1000.

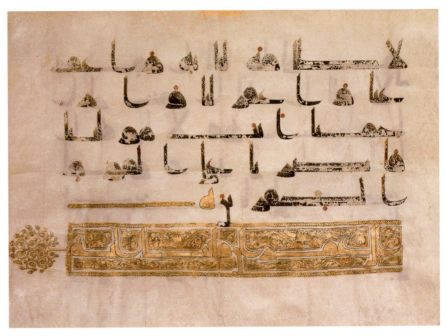

8–7 • PAGE FROM THE QUR'AN

Surah 2:286 and title for surah 3 in kufic script, from Syria. 9th century. Black ink, pigments, and gold on vellum, 8⅜" × 11⅛" (21.8 × 29.2 cm). The Metropolitan Museum of Art, New York. Rogers Fund, 1937 (37.99.2).

📖 **Read** the document with an excerpt from the Qur'an on **MyArtsLab**

Beautifully designed script was not limited to books and documents, however. It was also displayed on walls of buildings and on metalwork, textiles, glass, and ceramics. Kufic script was the sole decoration on a type of white pottery made from the tenth century onward in and around the region of Nishapur (in Khurasan, in present-day Iran) and Samarkand (in present-day Uzbekistan). These elegant earthenware bowls and plates are characterized by a clear lead glaze applied over a black inscription on a white, slip-painted ceramic ground (**FIG. 8–8**). Here the script has been elongated to fill the plate's rim, stressing the letters' verticality in such a way that they seem to radiate from the bold spot at the center of the circle. But this is not abstract decoration; the inscriptions on these plates provide a storehouse of popular sayings. This one translates, "Knowledge, the beginning of it is bitter to taste, but the end is sweeter than honey."

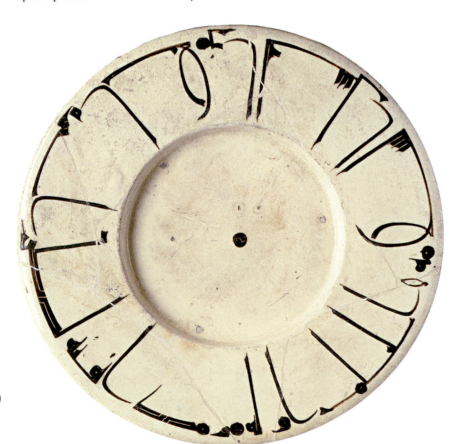

8–8 • PLATE WITH KUFIC BORDER

From Khurasan. 10th–12th century. Earthenware with white and black slip and lead glaze, diameter 14½" (33.8 cm). Musée du Louvre, Paris.

The white ground of this plate imitated prized Chinese porcelains made of fine white kaolin clay. Since Khurasan was connected to the Silk Road (see Chapter 4), the great caravan route to China, it was open to Chinese influence.

Later Islamic Art in Persia, Spain, and Turkey

What characterizes later developments in the Islamic art and architecture of Persia, Spain, and Turkey?

In the eleventh century, power in the Islamic world fell into the hands of more or less independent regional rulers. As the Abbasid caliphate disintegrated, the Saljuqs rose to power. A Turkic people from Central Asia who converted to Islam in the tenth century, the Saljuqs first conquered Persia in 1037–1040, establishing a dynasty that lasted until 1157.

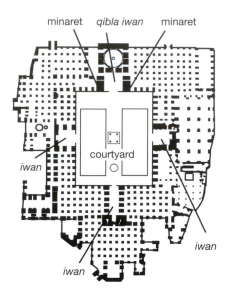

8–9 • PLAN AND COURTYARD VIEW TOWARD QIBLA IWAN, MASJID-I JAMI

(Congregational mosque), Isfahan, Iran. 11th–18th century.

👁 **Watch** a video about the Masjid-i Jami on **MyArtsLab**

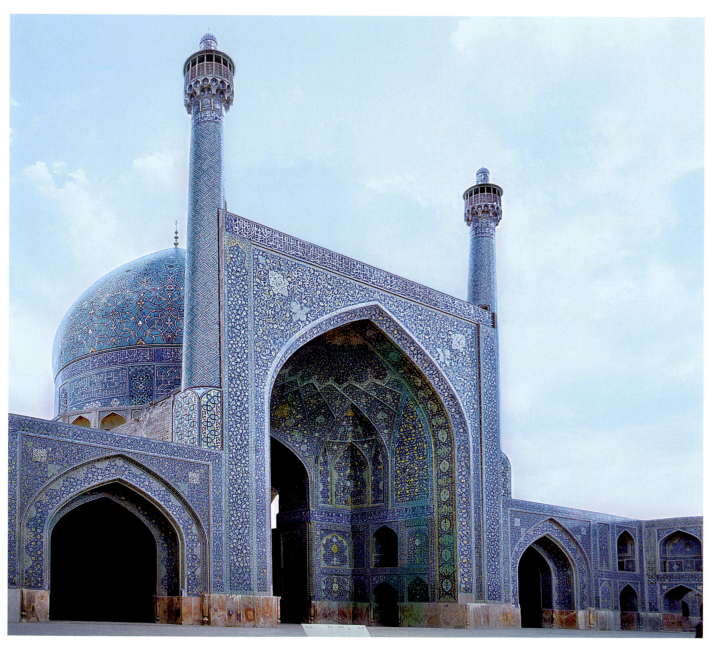

In 1055, they took over the Abbasid capital city of Baghdad, although the Abbasids survived as token rulers until 1258. In 1071, one branch of the Saljuqs defeated the Byzantine army and conquered most of the eastern Mediterranean including Anatolia (present-day Turkey), which they held until the fourteenth century. In the meantime, Mongols, led by Ghenghiz Khan (ruled 1206–1227) and his successors thundered into the region to capture a vast empire between northern China and Egypt. In the west, Umayyad Spain broke up into small kingdoms centered around major cities such as Saragossa, Málaga, Granada, and Seville. They engaged in constant warfare with Christian armies, who were determined to expel them from the Iberian peninsula. This military action (or Reconquest as the Christians called it) continued over a 400-year period, ending only in 1492 with the overthrow of the Nasrid dynasty in the Kingdom of Granada. Meanwhile, early in the fourteenth century, Ottoman Turks had replaced the Saljuqs as rulers of northwestern Anatolia, eventually conquering most of the eastern Mediterranean, Arabia, northern Africa (except Morocco), and part of eastern Europe, eventually taking in Constantinople in 1453.

The Saljuqs in Persia

The rulers of the Great Saljuq dynasty proved themselves enlightened patrons of the arts. They built on a grand scale—mosques, *madrasa*s (schools for advanced study), palaces, urban hostels, and remote caravanserais (inns) for traveling merchants to encourage long-distance trade. They adopted the Persian *iwan*, a vaulted open room, and they perfected a mosque/*madrasa* plan in which four *iwan*s are arranged around an internal courtyard. The Masjid-i Jami in the Saljuq capital of Isfahan (in present-day Iran) has a four-*iwan* plan (**FIG. 8–9**). The **QIBLA IWAN** on the south was vaulted with *muqarnas* (niche-like cells) in the fourteenth century. The tall, slender minarets and brilliant blue tiles were added in the seventeenth century.

Such tile work—one of the glories of Islamic art—can be seen in a fourteenth-century **TILE MOSAIC MIHRAB** originally from a *madrasa* in Isfahan (**FIG. 8–10**). More than 11 feet tall, the dazzling surface pattern was made by painstakingly cutting each piece of tile, including the pieces making up the calligraphy on the curving surface of the niche, and assembling them like a complicated puzzle set in mortar. The dense decoration includes regular organic and geometric forms that contrast

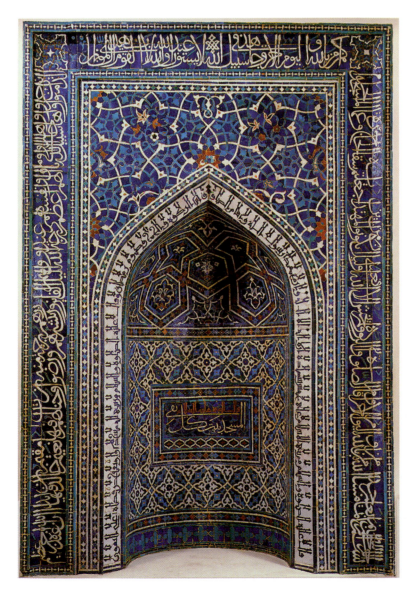

8–10 • TILE MOSAIC MIHRAB, FROM THE MADRASA IMAMI

From Isfahan, Iran. c. 1354. Glazed and cut ceramic tiles, 11′ 3″ × 9′ 5¹¹⁄₁₆″ (3.43 × 2.89 m). The Metropolitan Museum of Art, New York. Harris Brisbane Dick Fund (39.20). Photograph © 1982 The Metropolitan Museum of Art, New York.

One of the three Qur'anic inscriptions on this *mihrab* dates it to approximately 1354. Note the combination of decorated kufic (inner inscription) and cursive *muhaqqaq* (outer inscription) scripts. The outer inscription tells of the duties of believers and the heavenly rewards for the builders of mosques. The inner arch gives the Five Pillars of Islam in kufic. The framed center panel says: "The mosque is the house of every pious person."

View the Closer Look for the Tile Mosaic Mihrab on **MyArtsLab**

with the sinuous irregularity of the inscriptions. The colors—white against turquoise and cobalt blue with accents of dark yellow and green—are characteristic of Persian tile work.

The Nasrids in Spain

Muslim patrons spent lavishly on luxurious palaces set in beautiful gardens. The Alhambra in the southeastern Spanish capital of Granada is a splendid example. This fortified hilltop palace complex was the seat of the Nasrids, the last Spanish Muslim dynasty (1232–1492). The Alhambra gained its present form in the fourteenth century. The builders combined a fortress and royal residences with a small town, including mosques, baths, servants' quarters, barracks, stables, workshops, and a mint, that extends for about half a mile along the crest of a high hill overlooking the city of Granada.

An especially luxurious section of the complex is the Palace of the Lions, a private retreat built by Muhammad V (ruled 1354–1359 and 1362–1391). At its heart is the rectangular **COURT OF THE LIONS** (FIG. 8–11), named for a fountain whose basin is supported on the backs of 12 stylized stone lions. The courtyard is enclosed by an arcade of carved stucco arches supported by slender columns, often clustered in groups of two or three. Although it is filled with gravel today, the courtyard was originally a sunken garden with raised fountains and water channels. Aromatic shrubs, flowers, and small citrus trees were planted between the four radiating channels—evocative of the rivers of paradise—that divide the courtyard into quarters. The architectural focus of the Alhambra was largely directed inward, toward such lushly planted courtyards, which embody the Islamic vision of paradise as a well-watered, walled garden.

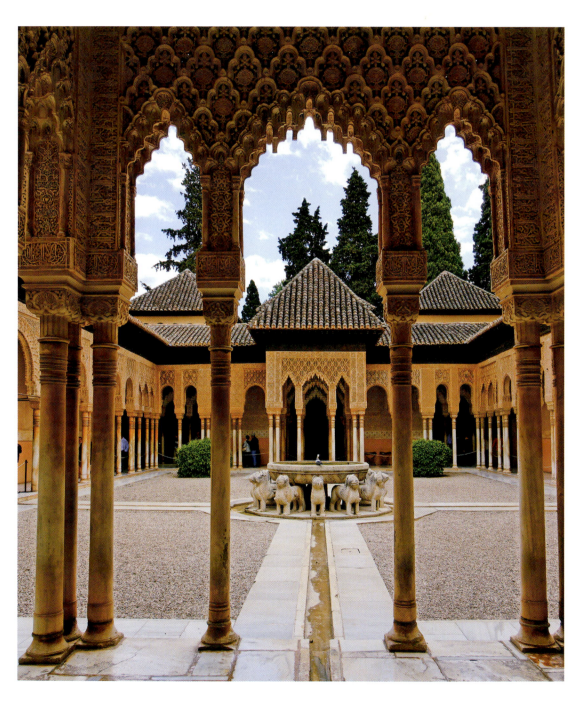

8–11 • COURT OF THE LIONS
Alhambra, Granada, Spain. 1354–1391.

Granada, with its ample water supply, had long been known as a city of gardens. The 12 stone lions of the fountain in the center of this court were salvaged from the ruins of an earlier palatial complex on the Alhambra hill. The earlier structure was begun in the late eleventh century by a high Granadan official of Jewish origin named Samuel ibn Naghralla and completed by his son Yusuf in the early twelfth century. Commentators of the time praised this complex, with its pools, fountains, and gardens.

✳ **Explore** the architectural panoramas of the Alhambra on **MyArtsLab**

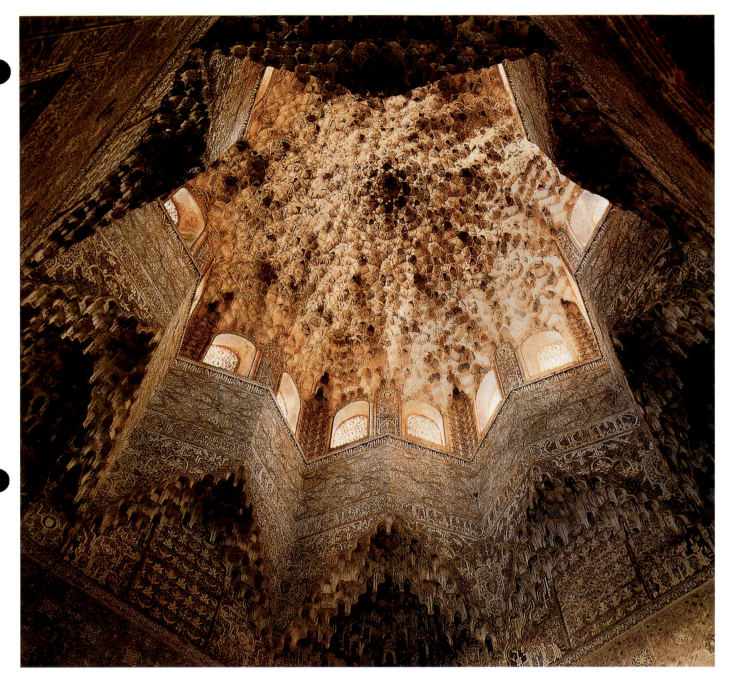

8-12 • MUQARNAS DOME
Hall of the Abencerrajes, Palace of the Lions, Alhambra, Granada, Spain. 1354–1391.

The stucco *muqarnas* decoration does not support the dome but is actually suspended from it, composed of some 5,000 individual pieces. Of mesmerizing complexity, the vault's effect can be perceived, but its structure cannot be fully comprehended.

Indeed, the English word *paradise* comes from *pairidiz*, the old Persian term for an enclosed park.

Pavilions used for dining and musical performances open off the Court of the Lions. One of these, the so-called Hall of the Abencerrajes, is covered by a spectacularly intricate ceiling of exquisitely carved stucco that also enhances its excellent acoustics (**FIG. 8–12**). The star-shaped dome is formed of a honeycomb of clustered *muqarnas* and supported by corner squinches and wall projections filled with more *muqarnas*.

The effect is a dematerialized architectural form, an ephemeral evocation of dazzling heavenly space. The experience is heightened by a ring of windows just under the springing of the dome itself, spotlighting it in splashes of light that vary in balance and intensity throughout the day.

The Ottomans in Turkey

In 1453, the Ottoman Turks, who had already created a vast empire, captured the Byzantine capital of Constantinople (ultimately renamed Istanbul), bringing the Byzantine (and thus Roman) Empire to an end. The church of Hagia Sophia (SEE FIGS. 7–12 TO 7–14) became a mosque framed by the addition of four graceful Ottoman minarets. The church's mosaics were destroyed or plastered over and huge calligraphic disks with the names of God, Muhammad, and the early caliphs were added over the pendentives in the mid nineteenth century.

Inspired by this great Byzantine structure, Ottoman architects built ever more ambitious, central-plan, domed mosques. The finest examples were designed by the architect Sinan (c. 1489–1588). In 1528, he became chief architect to Suleyman I, known as "the Magnificent," the tenth Ottoman sultan (ruled 1520–1566). Suleyman's reign marked the height of Ottoman power, and the sultan sponsored a building program on a scale not seen since the days of the Roman Empire. Serving Suleyman and his successor, Sinan is credited with more than 300 imperial commissions, including palaces, *madrasas* and Qur'an schools, tombs, public kitchens and hospitals, caravanserais, baths, bridges, viaducts, and 124 mosques.

Sinan's crowning accomplishment, completed about 1575, when he was over 80 years old, was a mosque he designed in the provincial capital of Edirne for Suleyman's son Selim II (ruled 1566–1574) (FIG. 8–13). The gigantic hemispheric dome that tops this structure is more than 102 feet in diameter, larger than the dome of Hagia Sophia, as Sinan proudly pointed out. The dome crowns a building of extraordinary architectural coherence. In addition to the mosque, the complex housed a *madrasa* and other educational buildings, a cemetery, a hospital, and

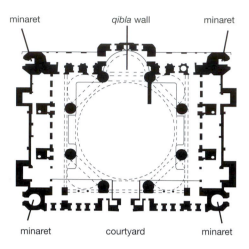

8–13 • Sinan PLAN AND EXTERIOR VIEW OF SULTAN SELIM MOSQUE
Edirne, Turkey. 1568–1575.

The minarets that pierce the sky around the prayer hall of this mosque, their sleek, fluted walls and needle-nosed spires soaring to more than 295 feet, are only 12½ feet in diameter at the base, an impressive feat of engineering.

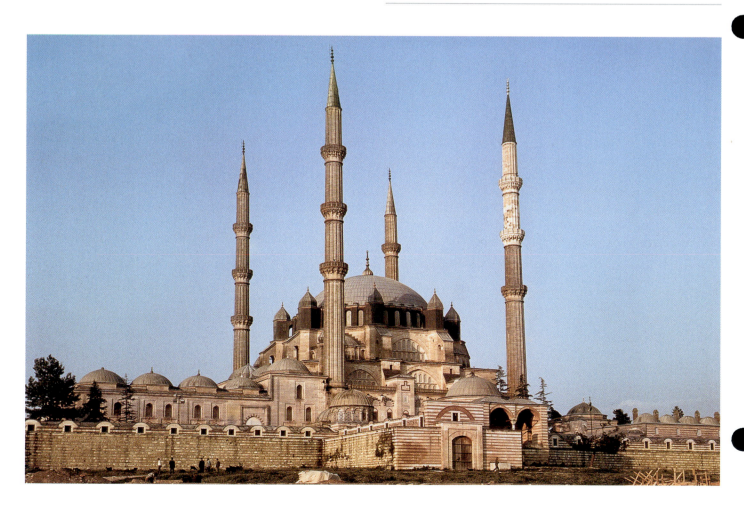

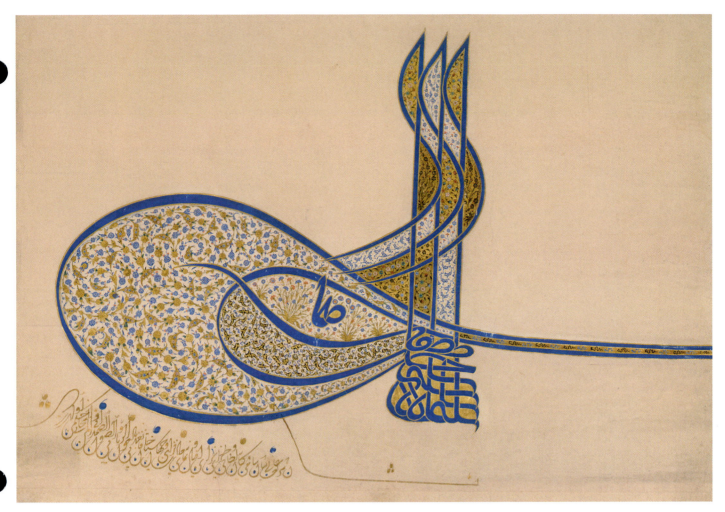

8–14 • ILLUMINATED TUGRA OF SULTAN SULEYMAN I
From Istanbul, Turkey. c. 1555–1560. Ink, paint, and gold on paper, removed from a *firman* (official document) and trimmed to 20½″ × 25⅜″ (52 × 64.5 cm). The Metropolitan Museum of Art, New York. Rogers Fund, 1938 (38.149.1).

charity kitchens, as well as the income-producing market and baths. Framed by the vertical lines of four minarets and raised on a platform at the city's edge, the mosque of Sultan Selim proudly dominates the skyline.

Following a practice begun by the Saljuqs and Mamluks, the Ottomans put calligraphy to political use, developing the design of imperial ciphers—*tugra*s—into a specialized art form. Ottoman *tugra*s combined the ruler's name and title with the motto "Eternally Victorious" into a monogram. Symbolizing the authority of the sultan, *tugra*s appeared on seals, coins, and buildings, as well as on official documents. Suleyman issued hundreds of edicts, and a high court official supervised specialist calligraphers and illuminators who produced documents that required particularly fancy *tugra*s. The **TUGRA** shown here (**FIG. 8–14**) is from a document endowing a charitable institution in Jerusalem that had been established by Suleyman's powerful wife, Hurrem.

*Tugra*s were drawn in black or blue ink with three long, vertical strokes to the right of two concentric, horizontal teardrops. Executing them required great skill. The sweeping, fluid lines had to be drawn with perfect control according to set proportions, and a mistake meant starting over. The color

scheme of the delicate floral **interlace** enclosed in the body of this *tugra* may have been inspired by Chinese blue-and-white ceramics, and similar designs appear on Ottoman ceramics and textiles. The Ottoman *tugra* is a sophisticated merging of stylization with naturalism, boldness with delicacy, political power with refined patronage, and function—both utilitarian and symbolic—with adornment.

Luxury Arts

What diverse forms of luxury art were produced in the Islamic world?

In cosmopolitan Islamic societies, exquisite artistry and luxurious expense was lavished not only on mosques and palaces but also on small, precious objects—highly valued for their beauty, for their costly materials, for their technical virtuosity, and for the status they bestowed on their owners. Glass, made with the most ordinary ingredients—sand and ash—becomes the most ethereal of materials, and enameled glass vessels were prized luxury objects across the Islamic world. The lamps that hung in mosques (SEE FIG. 8–1) were often made of enameled glass, especially in Egypt and Syria, where glass production flourished

A Mamluk Glass Oil Lamp ▶

Ali ibn Muhammad al-Barmaki, Cairo, Egypt. c. 1329–1335. Blown glass, polychrome enamel, and gold, diameter 9⅜″ (23.89 cm), height 14″ (35.56 cm). The Metropolitan Museum of Art, New York. Gift of J. Pierpont Morgan, 1917 (17.190.991).

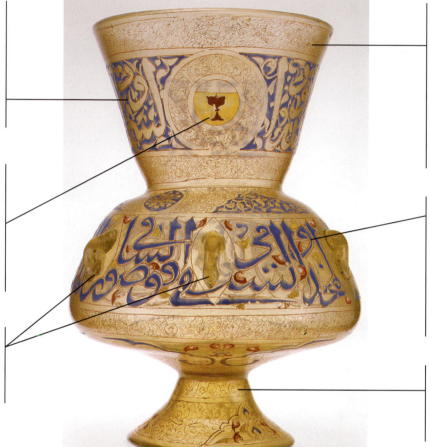

The inscription on the lamp's flared neck is a quotation from the Qur'an (surah 24:35): "God is the light of the heavens and the earth. His light might be compared to a niche that enshrines a lamp, the lamp within a crystal of star-like brilliance."

This emblem of a cup in a medallion is called a blazon. It identifies the commissioner of the lamp as a cup-bearer to the sultan. The use of blazons traveled to Western Europe during the crusades, where it evolved into the system we know as heraldry.

The lamp was suspended from chains attached to six handles formed of attached loops of glass, although it could also stand on its footed base.

During the thirteenth and fourteenth centuries, Mamluk glassmakers in Egypt and Syria imparted an elegant thinness to their vessels through refined glass-blowing and molding techniques. The blue, red, and gold enamel used to decorate the lamp was affixed to the glass surface by reheating the painted vessel.

This inscription around the body of the lamp identifies the patron, Sayf al-Din Qawsun (d. 1342), emir and cup-bearer of the Mamluk Sultan al-Nasir, Muhammad ibn Qalaun (ruled 1293–1341). It was probably intended for one of the patron's architectural commissions in Cairo.

The artist, Ali ibn Muhammad al-Barmaki, signed this work discreetly on the upper band of the foot, asking for God's protection.

🄠 **View** the Closer Look for a Mamluk Glass Oil Lamp on **MyArtsLab**

---

under the Mamluk dynasty (1250–1517). Sultans and their courtiers frequently commissioned lamps as donations to religious institutions, especially those they had founded or were supporting (see "A Closer Look," above).

Wealthy courtiers commissioned works in metal, ivory, and precious stones, as well as glass. Like glassmakers, metalworkers inherited the techniques of their Roman, Byzantine, and Sassanian Persian predecessors, employing established artistic traditions to create new forms. This basin (FIG. 8–15), made in the late thirteenth or early fourteenth century by Mamluk artist Muhammad ibn al-Zain (who signed it in six places), is among the finest works of metal produced in the Islamic world. The dynamic surface is crowded with overlapping figures, in vigorous poses, that nevertheless remain distinct by means of

hatching, modeling, and framing. The exterior face is divided into three bands. The upper and lower depict running animals, and the center shows scenes of horsemen flanked by attendants, soldiers, and falcons—scenes of the princely art of horsemanship and hunting. A severe silver shortage in the mid twelfth century may have prompted the development of inlaid brass pieces like this one that used the more precious metal sparingly.

Rugs and mats have long been used for Muslim prayer, which involves repeatedly prostrating oneself (kneeling and touching the forehead to the floor) before God. Many mosques were literally "carpeted" with wool-pile rugs received as pious donations. Since the late Middle Ages, carpets have been the Islamic art form best known in Europe. Rugs from Persia, Turkey, and elsewhere were highly prized among wealthy Westerners, who often

8–15 • Muhammad ibn al-Zain
BAPTISTERY OF ST. LOUIS
From Syria or Egypt. c. 1300. Brass inlaid with silver and gold, 8¾″ × 19¾″ (22.2 × 50.2 cm). Musée du Louvre, Paris.

This beautifully crafted basin, with its princely themes of hunting and horsemanship, was made for an unknown, aristocratic Mamluk patron, judging by its emblems and coats of arms. However, it became known as the *Baptistery of St. Louis*, because it was acquired by the French sometime before the end of the fourteenth century (long after the era of St. Louis [King Louis IX, ruled 1226–1270]) and used for royal baptisms.

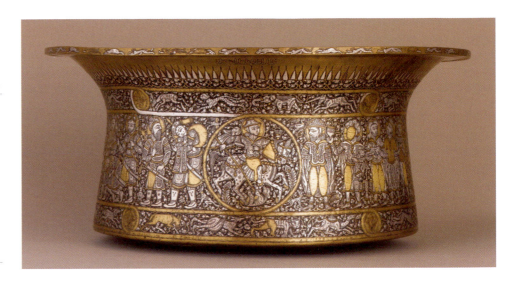

TECHNIQUE | Carpet Making

Knotted carpets are an ancient invention. The oldest known example, excavated in Siberia and dating to the fourth or fifth century BCE, has designs evocative of Achaemenid Persian art, suggesting that the technique may have originated in Central Asia. In knotted carpets, the pile—the plush, thickly tufted surface—is made by tying colored strands of yarn, usually wool but occasionally silk for deluxe carpets, onto the vertical elements (**warp**) of a yarn grid. These knotted loops are later trimmed and sheared to form the plush surface of the carpet. The **weft** strands (crosswise threads) are shot horizontally, usually twice, after each row of knots is tied, to hold the knots in place and to form the horizontal element common to all woven structures. The weft is usually an undyed yarn and is hidden by the colored knots of the warp. Two common tying techniques are the symmetrical knot, extensively used in Iran, Egypt, and Central Asia (formerly termed the Sehna knot) and the asymmetrical knot, used extensively in Turkey (formerly called the Gördes knot). The greater the number of knots, the shorter the pile. The finest carpets have up to 2,400 knots per square inch, each one tied separately by hand.

Although royal workshops produced the most luxurious carpets, most knotted rugs have traditionally been made in tents and homes. Carpets are woven by either women or men, depending on local custom. And often larger carpets are a collaboration of two or more weavers. Generally, an older weaver works with a younger one, who learns the art of carpet weaving at the loom and eventually passes it on to the next generation.

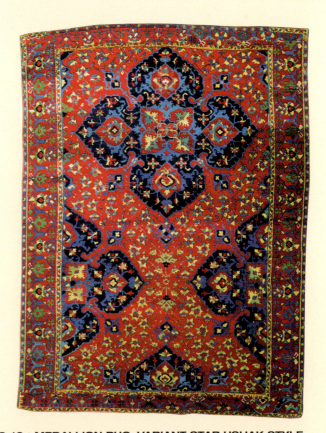

8–16 • MEDALLION RUG, VARIANT STAR USHAK STYLE
From Anatolia (present-day Turkey). 16th century. Wool, 10′ 3″ × 7′ 6¼″ (3.13 × 2.29 m). Saint Louis Art Museum, Gift of James F. Ballard.

Carpets were usually at least three times as long as they were wide; the asymmetry of this carpet may indicate that it has been shortened.

displayed them on tables rather than floors. A sixteenth-century carpet from Ushak in western Anatolia (present-day Turkey) retains its vibrant colors (FIG. 8–16). Large quatrefoil medallions establish a repeating pattern of bold blue stars, and vine-scrolls flow in every direction in the so-called "infinite **arabesque**" motif characteristic of Ushak carpets.

The art of book production also flourished throughout the Muslim world. An emphasis on the study of the Qur'an created a high level of literacy among both women and men in Islamic societies, and calligraphers were the first artists to emerge from anonymity and achieve individual distinction and recognition. Books on a wide range of secular as well as religious subjects were available, although hand-copied and illuminated books—even on paper—were costly. Libraries, often associated with *madrasa*s, were endowed by members of the educated elite. Books made for royal patrons had luxurious bindings and highly embellished pages, the result of workshop collaboration between noted calligraphers and painters.

In addition to religious works, scribes copied and recopied famous secular texts: scientific treatises, manuals of all

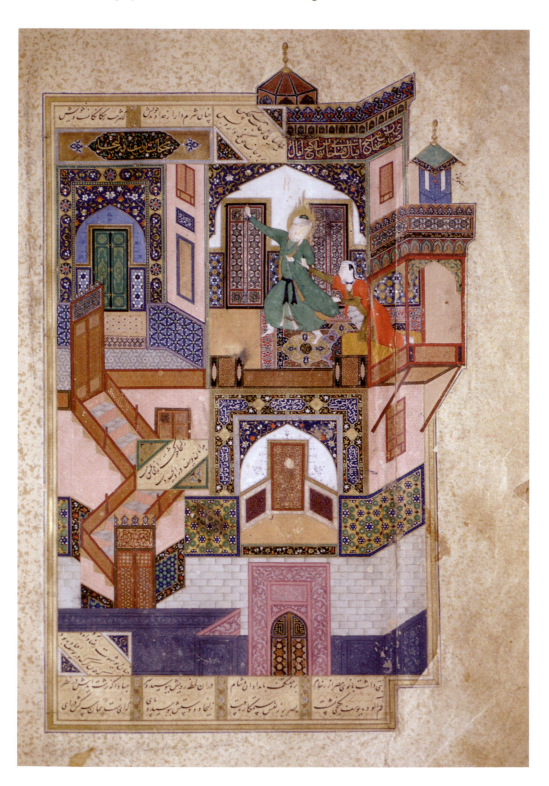

8–17 • Kamal al-Din Bihzad
YUSUF FLEEING ZULAYHKA
From a copy of the *Bustan* of Sa'di, from Herat, Afghanistan. 1488. Ink and pigments on paper, approx. 12″ × 8½″ (30.5 × 21.5 cm). Cairo, National Library, MS Adab Farsi 908, fol. 52v.

kinds, fiction, and especially poetry. Painters supplied dazzling illustrations for these books with extraordinary detail and gem-like colors. A great royal center of book production was founded at Herat (in western Afghanistan) in the early fifteenth century under the highly cultured patronage of the Persian Timurid dynasty (c. 1370–1507). In the second half of the fifteenth century, the workshop was led by Kamal al-Din Bihzad (c. 1450–1514), considered by many contemporaries as the greatest of Persian painters.

Bihzad's key paintings, including his only signed works,

appear in a manuscript of thirteenth-century Persian poet Sa'di's *Bustan* ("Orchard") that was made for the Timurid royal library in 1488. Sa'di's narrative anthology includes the story of Yusuf and Zulayhka—the biblical Joseph whose virtue was proven by resisting seduction by his master Potiphar's wife, named Zulayhka in the Islamic tradition (Genesis 39:6–12; surah 12:23–25). Following a more mystical version of this story by Timurid poet Jami, Bihzad sets Yusuf's flight from his seductress within a palace that Zulayhka had built specifically for this encounter, and into which she led Joseph ever inward from room to room, with entrance

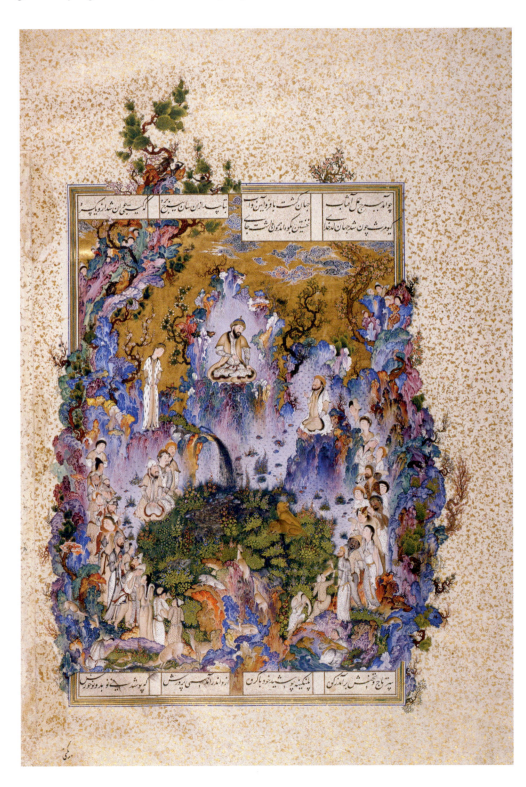

8–18 • Sultan Muhammad
THE COURT OF GAYUMARS
From the *Shahnama* of Shah Tahmasp (fol. 20v), from Tabriz, Iran. c. 1525–1535. Ink, pigments, and gold on paper, page size 18½" × 12½" (47 × 31.8 cm). Aga Khan Museum, Toronto (AKM 165).

View the Closer Look for Sultan Muhammad's "Court of Gayumars" on **MyArtsLab**

doors locked as they passed from one room to the next. But as Zulayhka lunges to possess him, Joseph flees her advances as the doors miraculously open before him.

Bihzad's visualization of this event (**FIG. 8–17**) is a masterpiece of Persian narrative painting. The brilliant, jewel-like color of the complex architectural forms, and the exquisite detail with which each is rendered, are salient characteristics of his style, as is the dramatic lunge of Zulayhka and Yusuf's balletic escape. The asymmetrical composition depends on a delicately balanced placement of flat screens of colorful ornament and two emphatically three-dimensional architectural features—a projecting balcony to the right and a zigzagging staircase to the left.

The Persian narrative painting tradition continued to flourish under the Safavid rulers who replaced the Timurids in 1501, moving their capital, and the royal manuscript workshop, to Tabriz. Among the most impressive paintings produced there—indeed, a work many consider the greatest of all Persian narrative paintings—is a rendering of **THE COURT OF GAYUMARS** (**FIG. 8–18**) from a spectacular copy of the *Shahnama* ("Book of Kings") commissioned for the youthful Shah Tahmasp and painted by Sultan Muhammad, the most renowned artist in the Safavid royal workshop. The scene portrays the idyllic reign of the legendary first Shah, Gayumars, who ruled from a mountaintop over a people who were the first to make clothing from leopard skins and develop the skill of cooking. The elevated and central figure of the king is surrounded by the members of his family and court, each rendered with individual facial features and varying body proportions to add a sense of naturalism to the unleashed fantasy characterizing the surrounding world. The landscape sparkles with brilliant color, encompassing the detailed delineation of lavish plant life as well as melting renderings of pastel rock formations, into which are tucked the faces of spirits and demons animating this primitive paradise. This is a painting meant to be savored slowly by an intimate, elite audience within the Safavid court. It is packed with surprises and unexpected delights.

Modern Islam

How does Islamic art extend into the modern period?

Islamic art is not restricted to the distant past. The twentieth century saw the dissolution of the great Islamic empires and the formation of smaller nation-states in their place. The question of identity and its expression in art changed significantly as Muslim artists and architects sought training abroad and participated in an international movement that swept away many of the visible signs that formerly expressed their cultural character and difference. Some architects, however, sought to reconcile modernity with an Islamic cultural identity that was distinct from the West. For example, the Iraqi architect Sami Mousawi and the Italian firm of Portoghesi-Gigliotti designed the **ISLAMIC MOSQUE AND CULTURAL CENTER** in Rome (completed 1992) with clean modern lines, exposing the structure while at the same time taking full advantage of opportunities for ornament (**FIG. 8–19**). The structural logic appears in the prayer hall's columns, made of concrete with an aggregate of crushed Carrara marble. These rise to meet abstract capitals in the form of plain rings, then spring upward to make a geometrically dazzling eight-pointed star supporting a dome of concentric circles. There are references here to the interlacing ribs of the *mihrab* dome in the Great Mosque of Cordoba (SEE FIG. 8–6), to the great domed spans of Sinan's prayer halls (SEE FIG. 8–13), and to the simple palm-tree trunks that supported the roof of the Mosque of the Prophet in Medina.

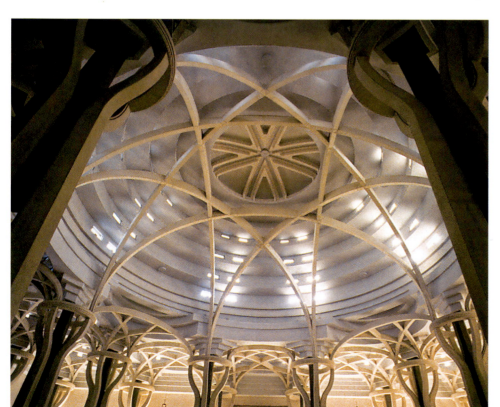

8-19 • Paolo Portoghesi, Vittorio Gigliotti, and Sami Mousawi **ISLAMIC MOSQUE AND CULTURAL CENTER** Rome. 1984–1992.

The prayer hall (197′ × 131′ [60 × 40 m]), which has an ablution area on the floor below, can accommodate a congregation of 2,500 on its main floor and balconies. The large central dome (65½′ [20 m] in diameter) is surrounded by 16 smaller domes, all similarly articulated with concrete ribs.

LOOKING BACK ◄

For Islam, God's word in the Qur'an, rather than any likeness in heaven or on earth, held a position of primary cultural importance. As a result, calligraphy emerged as the most highly valued form of art, and the written word was raised to a level of sophistication and expressiveness only matched in the neighboring cultures of East Asia. Islamic artists employed calligraphy everywhere, from monumental architectural inscriptions to the hand-written texts of luxury manuscripts (where those who penned the words were paid much more than those who painted the pictures), from clay plates to metalwork boxes, from luxurious silk fabrics to fragile glass bottles. Appearing in works of every medium, produced in every geographical location, the dominance of calligraphy, more than anything else, binds Islamic art into a cohesive cultural system across time and space, and even into the modern world.

THINK ABOUT IT

8.1 Select an Islamic building that is influenced by Roman or Byzantine art. Discuss which forms are borrowed from the earlier culture and how they are transformed in their new Islamic context.

8.2 Compare two mosques from two different parts of the Islamic world. What do they have in common and how do they vary? Why?

8.3 Choose a luxury work of art discussed in this chapter and identify and explain the materials and techniques with which it was made.

8.4 In what ways is the Islamic Mosque and Culture Center in Rome linked to traditional features of Islamic architecture?

| CROSSCURRENTS |

 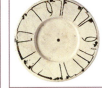

FIG. 5–6   FIG. 8–8

Throughout the history of art, the artists who painted on the surfaces of ceramic vessels and objects often composed their images in relation to the contours of the forms on which they worked. Evaluate how the motifs on this flask and plate are related to their shapes. What is the message conveyed by each work, and how does it relate to the cultures that produced it?

IN PERSPECTIVE

600

- **Founding of Islam** 622
- **Early Caliphs** 633–661
- **Umayyad Dynasty** c. 661–750
- **Abbasid Dynasty** c. 750–1258
- **Spanish Umayyad Dynasty** c. 756–1031

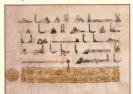

Dome of the Rock, Jerusalem begun 691

800

- **Fatimid Dynasty** c. 909–1171

1000

- **Great Saljuq Dynasty** c. 1037–1157

- **Saljuq Dynasty of Rum** late 11th–early 14th century

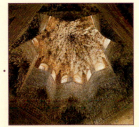

Page from the Qur'an 9th century

1200

- **Spanish Nasrid Dynasty** 1232–1492
- **Egyptian Mamluk Dynasty** 1250–1517
- **Ottoman Empire** c. 1281–1918

- **Timurid Dynasty** c. 1370–1507

1400

- **Fall of Constantinople to Ottoman Turks** 1453

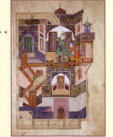

Muqarnas Dome, Alhambra 1354–1391

1600

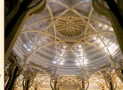

BIZHAD, Yusuf Fleeing Zulayhka 1488

1800

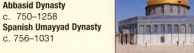

2000

Islamic Mosque and Cultural Center, Rome 1984–1992

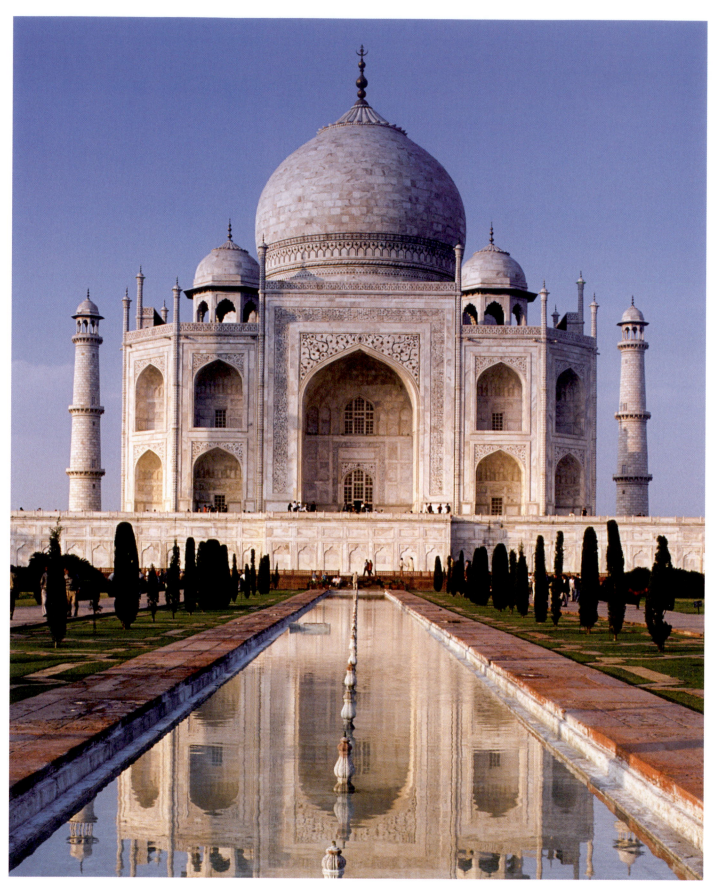

9–1 • TAJ MAHAL
Agra, India. Mughal period, reign of Shah Jahan, c. 1631–1648.

👁 **Watch** a video about the Taj Mahal on **MyArtsLab**

LATER ASIAN ART

LEARNING OBJECTIVES

9.1 Discuss the effects of evolving Hindu traditions and the Mughal conquest on the later art of India and Southeast Asia.

9.2 Trace the evolution of painting and ceramics in the later art of China and Korea.

9.3 Identify important monuments and developments in the later art of Japan.

LOOKING FORWARD ▶

Upon entering the gateway that today serves as the entrance to the complex surrounding the **TAJ MAHAL**, visitors behold the majestic white marble structure that is one of the world's best-known monuments **(FIG. 9–1)**. Its reflection shimmers in the pools of a garden meant to evoke a vision of paradise as described in the Qur'an, the holy book of Islam. The building's façades are delicately inlaid with inscriptions designed by India's foremost calligrapher of the time, Amanat Khan, and floral arabesques in semiprecious stones—carnelian, agate, coral, turquoise, garnet, lapis, and jasper. Above, its luminous, white marble dome reflects each shift in light, flushing rose at dawn, dissolving in its own brilliance in the noonday sun. This extraordinary building, originally and appropriately called the Illuminated Tomb and only from the nineteenth century known as the Taj Mahal, was built between 1631 and 1648 by the Mughal ruler Shah Jahan as a mausoleum for his favorite wife, Mumtaz Mahal, who died in childbirth, and likely as a tomb for himself.

Inside, the Taj Mahal invokes the *hasht behisht* ("eight paradises"), a plan named for the eight small chambers that ring the interior—one at each corner and one behind each *iwan*, a vaulted opening with an arched portal, that is a typical feature of eastern Islamic architecture. In two stories (giving a total of 16 chambers), the rooms ring the octagonal central area, which rises the full two stories to a domed ceiling that is lower than the outer dome. In this central chamber, surrounded by a finely carved octagonal openwork marble screen, are the exquisite inlaid **cenotaphs** (funerary monuments) of Shah Jahan and his wife, whose actual tombs lie in the crypt below.

The Taj Mahal complex includes much more than the white marble tomb. On one side is a mosque, while opposite and very similar in appearance is a building that may have served as a rest house. The enormous garden, both in front of the building and in its continuation on the opposite side of the Yamuna River, lends a lush setting consistent with Islamic notions of paradise. Both the side buildings and the two parts of the garden provide a sense of perfect symmetry to the entire complex.

A dynasty of Central Asian origin, the Mughals were the most successful of the many Islamic groups that established themselves in India, beginning in the twelfth century. Under their patronage, Persian and Central Asian influences mingled with the older traditions of the South Asian subcontinent, adding yet another dimension to the already complex artistic heritage of the art and architecture of Asia.

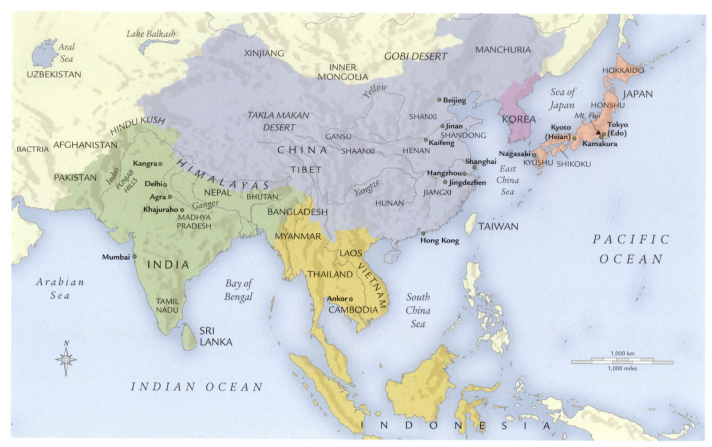

MAP 9–1 • ASIA

The color-coding on this map shows the division of the world of Asian art into the geographical regions of India, China, Korea, Japan, and Southeast Asia.

The long period between c. 650 and 1526 was a time of transition in India. Buddhism declined as a cultural force, while artistic achievements inspired by Hinduism soared. The monumental architecture of Hindu temples was rich in symbolism and ritual function, with each region of India developing its own variation. Later, Turkic people carried Islam to the South Asian subcontinent, and Muslim art expanded the already rich mix of styles, especially in the north, reaching its height under the Mughals (1526–1858).

During roughly the same period that Hinduism was displacing Buddhist primacy in India, Buddhism reached its height in China under the Tang dynasty (618–907) (see Chapter 4). But soon there was a reaction to this flowering of a foreign religion on Chinese soil. Under the Song dynasty (960–1279), openness to foreign influence gave way to greater cultivation of China's own traditions, including the revival of Confucianism. Landscape painting emerged as a way of expressing both philosophical and personal concerns.

Introduced from India by way of China and Korea, Buddhism was an important force in Japanese culture by the beginning of the Heian period (794–1185). New forms of Buddhism evolved: first Esoteric Buddhism and Pure Land Buddhism, and later, Zen. By the end of the fourteenth century, Zen Buddhism began to influence many aspects of Japanese life and culture, and soon

Zen beliefs were expressed in sophisticated painting, calligraphy, ceramics, and gardens (MAP 9–1).

India and Southeast Asia

What were the effects of evolving Hindu traditions and the Mughal conquest on the later art of India and Southeast Asia?

As Hinduism, with its many gods and varied sects, flourished in the Indian subcontinent, temple architecture developed rapidly. Local rulers rivaled each other in the building of temples to their favored deities—Shiva, Vishnu, and the Great Goddess Devi—until the middle of the thirteenth century when Hindu temples reached new levels of grandeur and complexity.

A Hindu temple of the so-called northern type (FIGS. 9–2, 9–3) is exemplified by the **KANDARIYA MAHADEVA TEMPLE** (c. 1000 CE) dedicated to the god Shiva, one of more than 80 temples at Khajuraho in central India. It is dominated by a superstructure called a *shikhara*, which rises as a solid mass above the flat stone ceiling of a windowless sanctuary housing an image of the temple's "resident" deity. Crowning the *shikhara* is a circular, cushion-like element, known as an *amalaka*. A **finial** (knob-like decoration at the top of an architectural form) leads the eye to the point where earthly and cosmic worlds are

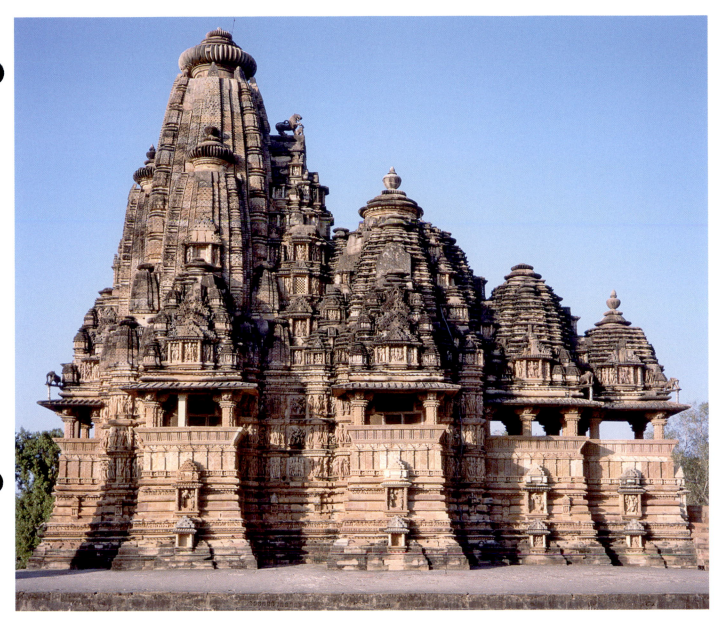

9–2 • KANDARIYA MAHADEVA TEMPLE
Khajuraho, Madhya Pradesh, India. Chandella dynasty, c. 1000 CE.

thought to join. An imaginary *axis mundi* (line connecting the center of the earth to the heavens) runs from the finial down the *shikhara* through the image of the deity into the ground below. In this way the temple becomes a conduit between celestial realms and the earth, a concept familiar from Buddhist stupas. At the Kandariya Mahadeva temple, the *shikhara* is bolstered by the clustering of many smaller *shikhara* motifs bundled around it. Below, porches surround the body of the temple, and at the front (to the right in FIG. 9–3), a steep flight of stairs leads into a series of three halls, known as *mandapas*, preceding the sanctuary and capped on the exterior with a sequence of projecting forms that step down to form a smooth diagonal in front of the tall *shikhara* as they progress toward the temple front. The halls serve as a place for rituals, such as dances performed for the deity, and for the presentation of offerings. The surface of the temple is encrusted with decorative architectural motifs (miniature *shikhara*s) and some 600 sculpted figures that both soften

and enrich the delineation of architectural form. Included among them are not only gods and goddesses, but also erotic couples in acrobatic postures. They are thought to express Shiva's divine bliss and the manifestation of his presence within, as well as a reminder that devotion to a god resembles the passion of love.

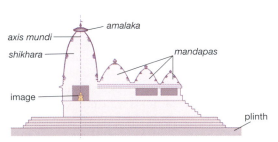

9–3 • SCHEMATIC DRAWING OF A TYPICAL NORTHERN INDIAN HINDU TEMPLE FORM

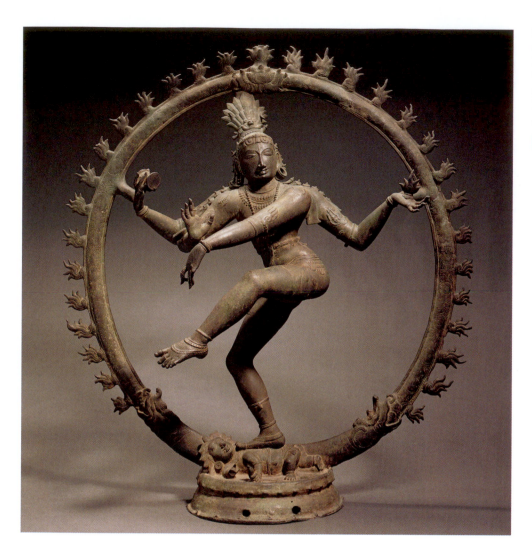

9–4 • SHIVA NATARAJA (SHIVA AS LORD OF THE DANCE)
From South India. Chola dynasty, 11th century CE. Bronze, 43⅞″ × 40″ (111.5 × 101.65 cm). Cleveland Museum of Art. Purchase from the J. H. Wade Fund, 1930.331.

View the Closer Look for *Shiva Nataraja* on **MyArtsLab**

At the time when this temple was built, two major religious developments affected Hindu practice and art: the Tantric, or Esoteric, movement primarily in the north and the *bhakti*, or devotional, movement primarily in the south. The *bhakti* movement—based on ideas expressed in ancient texts, especially the *Bhagavad-Gita*—seeks an ideal relationship between humans and deities, rooted in an intimate, personal, and loving connection with a god, involving complete devotion and surrender. This movement profoundly influenced the Chola dynasty, rulers in the far south of India from the mid ninth into the late thirteenth century, when southern artists produced some of India's most interesting works of sculpture, cast in bronze.

The bronze **SHIVA NATARAJA (FIG. 9–4)** embodies the *bhakti* movement at its most fervent. No longer does the deity appear self-absorbed and introspective (SEE FIG. 4–10). Instead, he generously displays himself to the devotee in full awareness of his benevolent powers. Dancing within a ring of fire, Shiva's extended left hand holds a spray of flames, emblematic of the destruction of the universe as well as of our ego-centeredness. Shiva's back right hand holds a drum, whose ceaseless beat represents the unstoppable rhythms of creation and destruction, birth and death. With his right front hand, he makes the "have no fear" gesture. His left front arm, gracefully stretched across his body with the hand pointing to his raised foot

and leg, signifies the promise of liberation. The earlier Hindu emphasis on ritual and the depiction of the gods' heroic feats are here subsumed into the humanizing factor of grace. (For another example of bronze sculpture from south India, see FIG. INTRO–8.)

The *bhakti* movement spread subsequently to north India and flourished in the courts of local Hindu princes such as the Rajputs. This period also witnessed the spread of Islam in India. The Muslim conquerors brought Islamic architectural design to the subcontinent, but it was the Mughal dynasty that made the most lasting Islamic contribution to the art and architecture of India.

The Mughal Empire

Islam first touched the Indian subcontinent in the eighth century, when Arab armies captured a small territory near the Indus River. In the eleventh century, Turks began a war of conquest from the north, and from 1193 Turkic and Afghan dynasties ruled portions of the subcontinent from the northern city of Delhi. Although these early dynasties left their mark, it was in the sixteenth and seventeenth centuries that the Mughals made a lasting impression on Indian art.

The Mughals, like the Turks, originated in Central Asia. The first Mughal emperor, Babur (ruled 1526–1530), conquered an empire stretching from Afghanistan to Delhi. Later Akbar (ruled 1556–1605) extended Mughal control over most of north India, and under his two successors, Jahangir and Shah Jahan, northern India became a unified Mughal Empire.

An interest in painting at the Mughal court was established early on by Akbar. He created an imperial **atelier** (workshop) of painters, placed under the direction of two artists from the Persian court. Learning from these masters, Mughal painters soon tempered idealized Persian lyricism with robust Indian naturalism. Jahangir (ruled 1605–1627), Akbar's son and successor, was also a connoisseur of painting; even before he became emperor he established his own workshop of painters. In his memoirs, he claimed:

> My liking for painting and my practice in judging it have arrived at such a point that when any work is brought before me, either of deceased artists or of those of the present day, without their names being

told me I say on the spur of the moment that it is the work of such and such a man, and if there be a picture containing many portraits, and each face be the work of a different master, I can discover which face is the work of each of them. And if any other person has put in the eye and eyebrow of a face, I can perceive whose work the original face is and who has painted the eye and eyebrows.

The double portrait Jahangir commissioned of himself leaning to embrace a contemporary Islamic ruler—the Safavid Persian emperor Shah Abbas (1588–1629)—asserts Jahangir's sense of his own superiority **(FIG. 9–5)**. He is depicted larger than Shah Abbas, who appears to bow deferentially to the Mughal emperor. Jahangir's head is centred in the halo behind them, and he stands on the dominant lion, whose body spans a vast territory, including Shah Abbas's own Persia. We can only speculate on the target audience for this painting. Because it

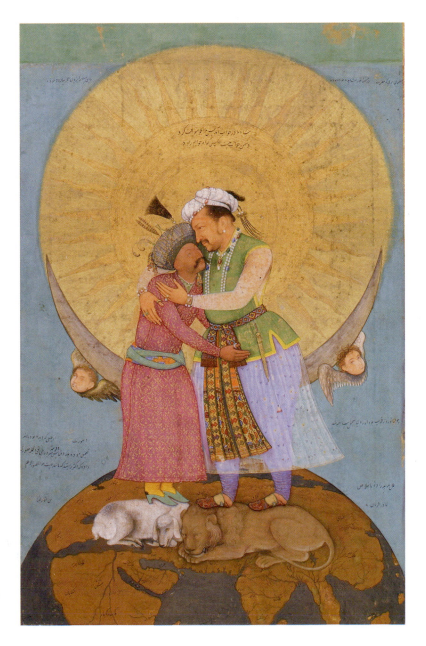

9–5 • Nadir al-Zaman (Abu'l Hassan)
JAHANGIR AND SHAH ABBAS
Mughal period, c. 1618. Opaque watercolor, gold, and ink on paper, 9⅜″ × 6″ (23.8 × 15.4 cm). Freer Gallery of Art, Smithsonian Institution, Washington, D.C. F1945.9.

Before the introduction of paper—about the same time in India as in Europe—most painting in India was on walls or palm leaves. For this new medium, artists adapted painting techniques from Persia and over the centuries produced jewel-toned paintings of arresting beauty.

Beginning their training early as apprentices, painters learned to make brushes from the curved hairs of a squirrel's tail, arranged to taper from a thick base to a few hairs at the tip, and to grind the mineral and vegetable pigments, bound with a solution of gum from the acacia plant, to produce paint. Paper was made by crushing fibers of cotton and jute to a pulp, pouring the mixture onto a woven mat, drying it, and then burnishing (rubbing) with a smooth stone to achieve a glossy finish.

Artists frequently worked from a collection of sketches in a master painter's studio. Sometimes, to transfer designs, sketches were pricked with small holes, and wet color was dabbed over the holes to transfer the drawing to a blank sheet beneath. The dots were connected into outlines, and the process of painting began. First, the painter applied a thin **wash** of chalk-based white, which sealed the surface of the paper while allowing the underlying sketch to show through. Next, the outlines were filled in with opaque color. When the colors were dry, the painting was laid face down on a smooth marble surface and burnished with a rounded agate stone. The indirect pressure against the marble polished the pigments to a high luster. Then outlines, details, and modeling were added with a fine brush. Raised details such as the pearls of a necklace were made with thick, chalk-based paint, each pearl a single droplet hardened into a tiny raised mound.

is small, it certainly was not intended for Jahangir's subjects; a painting of this size could not be publicly displayed. But paintings were commonly sent as diplomatic gifts from one kingdom to another, and this one may have been intended as a gift for Shah Abbas, conveying a message of clear strength and superiority cloaked in the diplomatic language of cordiality.

Mughal architects were the heirs to a 300-year-old tradition of Islamic construction using arches and domes and also benefited from indigenous virtuosity in stone carving. Perhaps the most famous of all Indian Islamic buildings, the Taj Mahal (SEE FIG. 9–1) stands on the bank of the Yamuna River at Agra in northern India. Built between 1631 and 1648, it was commissioned as a mausoleum for his wife by the emperor Shah Jahan (ruled 1628–1658), who is believed to have taken a major part in overseeing its design and construction.

As visitors enter through a monumental, hall-like gate, the tomb rises before them across a spacious garden—measuring some 1,000 by 1,900 feet—set with long reflecting pools. In Shah Jahan's time, fruit trees and cypresses—symbolic of life and death—lined the walkways, and fountains played in the shallow pools. Truly, the senses were beguiled in this earthly evocation of paradise as described in the Qur'an.

A lucid geometric symmetry pervades the entire design. Each façade of the tomb is identical, with a central *iwan* flanked by two stories of smaller *iwan*s. By creating voids in the façades, these *iwan*s contribute to the building's sense of weightlessness. The dome rises gracefully on its drum, allowing the swelling curves and lyrical lines of its beautifully proportioned, surprisingly large form to emerge with perfect clarity. Four minarets surround the central structure, each crowned with a pavilion. Traditional embellishments of Indian palaces, these pavilions quickly passed into the vocabulary of Islamic architecture in India. Four more pavilions, this time on the roof surrounding the dome, create a visual transition from the small caps of the minarets to the bulbous majesty of the dominating dome.

The pristine surfaces of the Taj Mahal are embellished with utmost subtlety. The sides of the platform are carved in relief with a blind arcade motif, and carved relief panels of flowers adorn the base of the building. The portals are framed with verses from the Qur'an inlaid in black marble, while the spandrels are decorated with floral arabesques inlaid in colored semiprecious stones. Not strong enough to detract from the overall purity of the white marble, the embellishments enliven the surfaces of this imposing yet delicate masterpiece.

Rajput Painting and the Luxury Arts

Outside the Mughal strongholds at Delhi and Agra, much of northern India was governed by local Hindu princes, descendants of the Rajput warrior clans, who were allowed to keep their lands in exchange for allegiance to the Mughals. Like the Mughals, Rajput rulers frequently established painting workshops at their courts. In Kangra, a large Rajput kingdom in the Punjab Hills (foothills of the Himalayas north of Delhi), a strong school of painting developed in the middle of the eighteenth century, influenced by Mughal naturalism.

Inspired by a revival of the emotional *bhakti* movement, poets wrote of the love of gods for humans, expressed metaphorically through the love of the young Krishna for the cow maiden Radha. In **THE HOUR OF COWDUST** (FIG. 9–6), painted around 1790, the subject is Krishna, who has been living among the cowherds. Wearing his peacock crown, garland of flowers, jewelry, and yellow garment, the god plays his flute as he returns to the village surrounded by cowherds and their cattle. Eyes are upon him as he plays his flute, said to enchant all who hear it. Women with water jugs on their heads turn to look; others lean from windows to watch and call out to him. We are drawn into this charming village scene by the diagonal movement of the cows as they surge through the gate and into the courtyard beyond. Pastel walls define receding space, and in the distance we glimpse other villagers going about their work or sitting within their houses. A rim of dark trees softens the

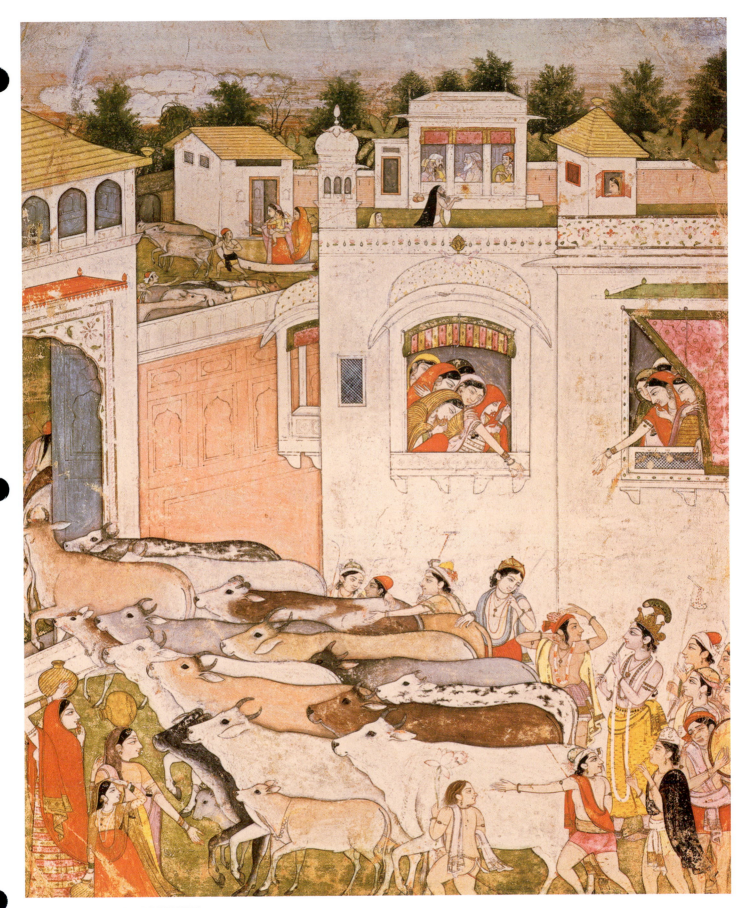

9–6 • THE HOUR OF COWDUST
from Punjab Hills, India. Kangra school, c. 1790. Gouache on paper, 14¹⁵⁄₁₆″ × 12⁹⁄₁₆″ (38 × 31.9 cm).
Museum of Fine Arts, Boston. Photograph © 2015 Museum of Fine Arts, Boston, Denman W. Ross Collection (22.683).

Panel from an Ivory Box

The decorative arts of India have represented the height of opulent luxury since the first century BCE. An Indian ivory carving was found at Pompeii, while other Indian works of this time have been discovered along the Silk Road connecting China with Rome. Technically superb and crafted from precious materials, tableware, jewelry, furniture, and containers enhance the prestige of their owners and give visual pleasure as well. Metalwork and work in rock crystal, agate, and jade, carving in ivory, and intricate jewelry are all characteristic Indian arts. Because of the intrinsic value of their materials, however, pieces have been disassembled, melted down, and reworked, making the study of Indian luxury arts very difficult. Many pieces, like the carved ivory panel illustrated here (FIG. 9–7), have no date or records of manufacture or ownership.

Frozen in timeless delight, carved in ivory against a golden ground, where openwork, stylized vines with spiky leaves weave an elegant arabesque, loving couples dally under the arcades of a palace courtyard, whose thin columns and cusped arches resemble the arcades of the palace of Tirumala Nayak (ruled 1622–1662) in Madurai (Tamil Nadu) where this ivory plaque was made. The Nayak rulers commissioned sculpture and painting, but wood and ivory carving ranks among their artists' highest achievements, hardly a minor art. This plaque must have decorated a container for precious objects—note the keyhole at top center and the small holes in the borders where nails would have attached it to the side of a wooden box—perhaps personal belongings such as jewelry, perfume, or cosmetics.

The huge eyes set under the figures' heavy brows suggest the intensity of their gaze, and the artist's choice of profile view shows off their long noses and sensuously thick lips. Their hair is tightly controlled; the men wear their uncut hair in huge knots, and the women have long braids hanging down their backs. Are they divine lovers? After all, Krishna lived and loved on earth among the cowherd maidens. Or are we observing scenes of courtly romance?

The rich jewelry and well-fed look of the couples indicate a high station in life. Men as well as women have voluptuous figures—rounded buttocks and thighs, ample tummies hanging over jeweled belts, sharply indented slim waists that emphasize seductive breasts. All this smooth flesh contrasts with diaphanous fabrics that swath their plump legs, and their long arms and elegant gestures seem designed to show off their rich jewelry—bracelets, armbands, necklaces, and huge earrings. Such amorous couples symbolize harmony as well as fertility, satisfaction as well as desire.

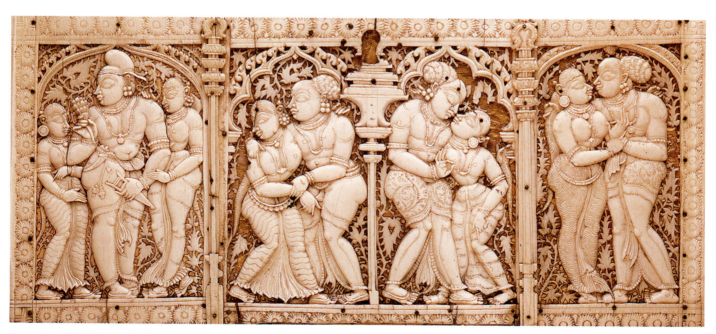

9–7 • PANEL FROM A BOX
From Tamil Nadu, India. Nayak dynasty, late 17th–18th century. Ivory backed with gilded paper, 6″ × 12⅜″ × ⅛″ (15.2 × 31.4 × 0.3 cm). Virginia Museum of Fine Arts. The Arthur and Margaret Glasgow Fund. 80.171.
Katherine Wetzel © Virginia Museum of Fine Arts, Richmond.

horizon, and a rose-tinted sky completes the aura of enchantment. The scene reflects the sublime purity and grace of the divine, which, as in so much Indian art, is evoked within our human world to coexist with us as one.

The high quality of luxury arts—work in rock crystal, ivory (SEE FIG. 9–7), mother-of-pearl, metalwork, and jewelry—from the southern Indian state of Tamil Nadu made them renowned even outside India, and, beginning in the sixteenth century, objects were made for export as well as for local sale. Sikhs took over the kingdom in 1826, and the British followed in 1846, effectively putting an end to the distinctive local styles.

Cambodia

Cambodia lies between India and China geographically and culturally. Buddhism and Hinduism supplanted local religions, and the indigenous Khmer people eventually developed a distinctive synthesis of beliefs that evolved into a state religion under a divine king who ruled at Angkor ("capital city")

from the ninth to the thirteenth century. Suryavarman II (ruled c. 1112–1153) began the royal complex known to us as ANGKOR WAT (FIG. 9–8). Dedicated to Vishnu, the vast array of structures is both a temple and a symbolic cosmic mountain, home to the deity and axis of the world. Originally, the visitor approached the building over a bridge across a wide moat and, after passing through a monumental gateway, continued up a long avenue between two water-filled tanks to the building itself. The building has a simple plan of squares within squares defined by galleries surrounding a tall central tower with four lesser towers. Additional towers at the outer corners define the extent of the huge complex.

Suryavarman's predecessors had already associated themselves with Hindu and Buddhist deities at Angkor by building sacred structures, and he pairs himself here with Vishnu to affirm his royal status and to claim his ultimate destiny of union with the Hindu god. Sculpture covers every possible surface, depicting the many incarnations of Vishnu in dizzying detail.

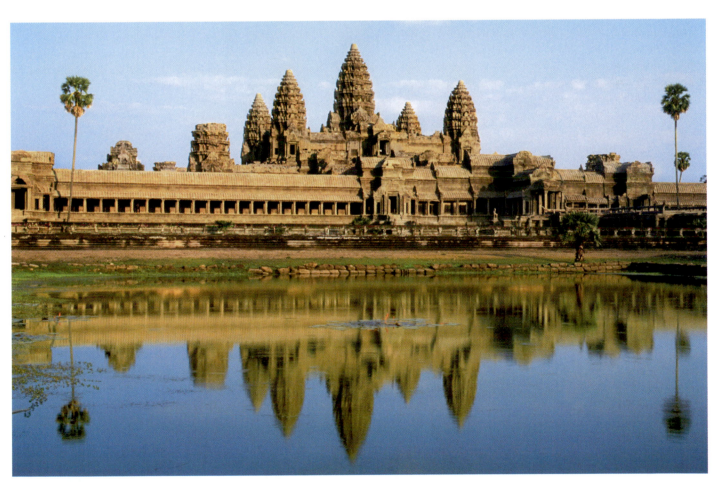

9–8 • ANGKOR WAT
Angkor, Cambodia, west entrance. 12th century. Temple wall 3,363′ × 2,625′ (1025 × 800 m); moat 623′ (190 m) wide.

After the Siamese conquered the Khmer kingdom in 1437, the buildings of Angkor fell into neglect. By the time they were rediscovered in the nineteenth century, the jungle had covered them. Although Angkor Wat is now under the protection of UNESCO, twentieth-century wars and twenty-first-century thieves continue to imperil the existence of the site.

View the Closer Look for Angkor Wat on **MyArtsLab**

China and Korea

How did the traditions of painting and ceramics evolve in the later art of China and Korea?

A brief period of disintegration followed the fall of the Tang dynasty in 907 before China was united again under the Song dynasty (960–1279). In 1126, invaders from Manchuria defeated the Song, sacking the capital Bianjing (present-day Kaifeng) and occupying much of the northern part of the country. Song forces withdrew south and established a new capital at Hangzhou. The dynasty from this point on is known as Southern Song (1127–1279), whereas the earlier years are called Northern Song (960–1126).

In spite of the changing political fortunes, patronage was plentiful and the arts flourished. No hint of disruption or despair intrudes on the sublime grace and beauty of this **SEATED**

GUANYIN BODHISATTVA (**FIG. 9–9**). Bodhisattvas—beings who, though close to enlightenment themselves, voluntarily remain on earth to help others achieve it—are represented as young princes wearing royal garments and jewelry, their finery indicative of their worldly but virtuous lives. Guanyin is the Bodhisattva of Infinite Compassion, who appears in many guises. Here, as the Water and Moon Guanyin, he sits on rocks by the sea, in the posture known as "royal ease." His right arm rests on his raised and bent right knee and his left arm and foot hang down, the foot touching a lotus blossom. The wooden figure was carved between the tenth and twelfth centuries, but the painting and **gilding** were restored in the sixteenth century.

During the Song period, the martial vigor of the Tang gave way to a culture of increasing refinement and scholarship. The study of history, literature, and philosophy flourished, while Song philosophers revived Confucianism. Drawing on both

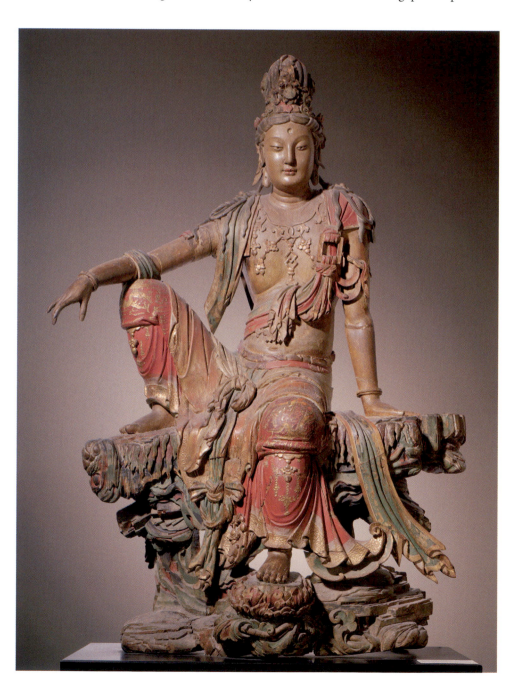

9–9 • SEATED GUANYIN BODHISATTVA
Liao dynasty, 10th–12th century CE. Wood with paint and gold, 95″ × 65″ (241.3 × 165.1 cm). The Nelson-Atkins Museum of Art, Kansas City, Missouri. Purchase: William Rockhill Nelson Trust (34-10). Photograph by Jamison Miller.

Buddhism and Daoism they provided Confucianism with a metaphysical basis, a systematic and comprehensive explanation of the universe called Neo-Confucianism. It teaches that the universe consists of two interacting forces known as *li* (principle or idea) and *qi* (matter). All pine trees, for instance, consist of an underlying *li* that we might call the "Pine Tree Idea," brought into the world through *qi*, the living tree. All the *li* of the universe, including humans, are but aspects of an eternal first principle known as the Great Ultimate. The task of humans is to purify their *qi* through education and self-cultivation so that their *li* may achieve union with the Great Ultimate.

Neo-Confucian ideas were visualized in landscape painting, which became the most highly esteemed subject for painters. Northern Song artists studied nature closely to master its varied appearances: the way each species of tree grew, the distinctive character of each rock formation, the signs of changing seasons, and the myriad birds, blossoms, and insects. This study was integral to the artist's self-cultivation—mastering outward forms showed an understanding of the principles behind them. Yet despite their faithful visual description of individual forms, Song paintings do not record a specific site. The artist's goal was to paint the eternal essence of "mountain-ness," for example, not to reproduce the appearance of a particular mountain. Thus landscape painting expressed the desire for spiritual communion with nature as a key to enlightenment. As the tradition progressed, landscape painting also became a vehicle for conveying human emotions, even for expressing profound personal feelings.

One of the first great masters of Song landscape was Fan Kuan (active c. 990–1030), whose monumental **TRAVELERS AMONG MOUNTAINS AND STREAMS** (mounted on a hanging scroll; see "Formats of Chinese Painting," p. 216) is regarded as one of the greatest achievements in the history of Chinese art (**FIG. 9–10**). The composition unfolds in three stages, comparable to the three acts of a drama, moving step by step as we explore the world of the painting from front to back, bottom to top. A low-lying group of rocks at the bottom establishes the extreme foreground. In anticipating, on a small scale, the shape and substance of the mountains to come, the rocks introduce the main theme of the work, much as the first act of a drama introduces the principal characters. In the **middle ground**, travelers and their mules enter from the right. Their size establishes our human scale—how small we are, how vast is nature. This middle ground, like the second act of a play, shows variation and development. Instead of a solid mass, the rocks are separated here into two groups by a waterfall. At right, the rooftops of a temple stand out above the trees.

Mist veils the transition to the background; the mountain seems to loom up suddenly. This background area, almost twice as large as the foreground and middle ground combined, is the climactic third act of the drama. As our eyes begin their ascent, the mountain solidifies. Its ponderous weight increases as it billows upward, finally bursting into sprays of energetic brushstrokes that describe the scrubby growth on top. To the right, a slender waterfall plummets, not to balance the powerful upward thrust of the sheer face of the mountain, but to enhance its monumentality through linear contrast. The painting as a whole summons up the feeling of climbing a high mountain,

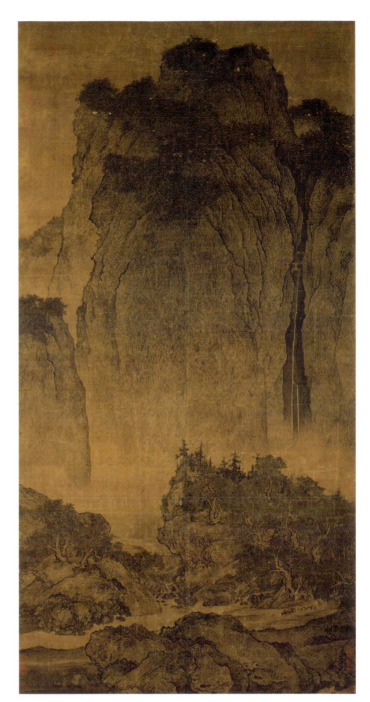

9–10 • Fan Kuan TRAVELERS AMONG MOUNTAINS AND STREAMS
Northern Song dynasty, early 11th century. Hanging scroll, ink and colors on silk, height 6′ 9¼″ (2.06 m). National Palace Museum, Taipei, Taiwan, Republic of China.

View the Closer Look for the technique of ink painting on **MyArtsLab**

leaving the human world behind to come face to face with the Great Ultimate in a spiritual communion.

The ability of Chinese landscape painters to take us out of ourselves and let us wander freely through their visions of the natural world is closely linked to the avoidance of **linear perspective** as used in European painting after fifteenth-century Florentine painters developed a "scientific" system for recording

Except for wall paintings in palaces, temples, and tombs, most Chinese paintings were done in ink and water-based colors on silk or paper. Finished works were usually mounted as **handscrolls**, hanging scrolls, or leaves in **albums**.

An album comprises a set of paintings of similar size, and usually related in subject, mounted in a book. Album-size paintings could also be mounted as a handscroll, a horizontal format generally about 12 inches high and anywhere from a few feet to dozens of feet long. More typically, however, a handscroll would be a single continuous painting, generally preceded by a panel giving the work's title and often followed by a long panel bearing **colophons**—inscriptions, such as poems, in praise of the work or comments by its owners over the centuries.

Seals of the maker and also those of collectors and admirers through the centuries added another layer of interest.

Handscrolls were not meant to be displayed all at once, the way they are commonly presented today in museums. Rather, they were kept rolled up and only occasionally taken out for viewing. The viewer would unroll the scroll gradually, moving slowly through its entire length from right to left, lingering over favorite details.

Like handscrolls, hanging scrolls were not displayed permanently but taken out for a limited time—a day, a week, or a season. Unlike handscrolls, however, the hanging scroll was viewed as a whole, unrolled and hung on a wall, with the wooden roller at the lower end acting as a weight to help the scroll hang flat.

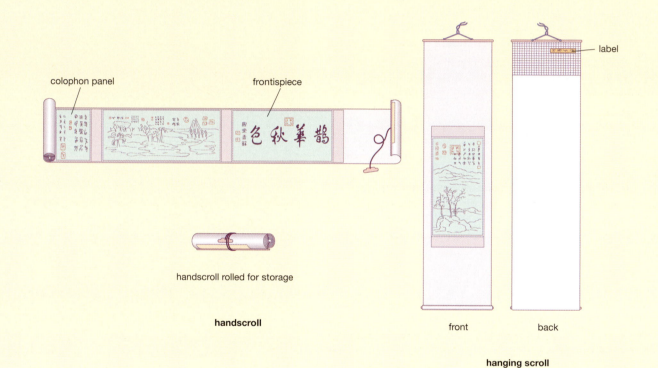

colophon panel

frontispiece

handscroll rolled for storage

handscroll

label

front   back

hanging scroll

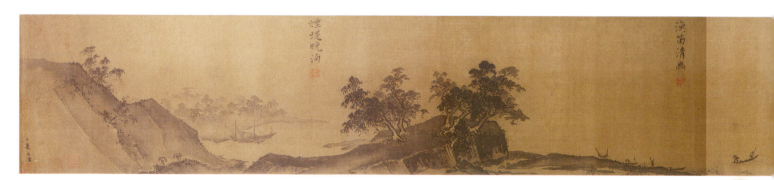

9–11 • Xia Gui TWELVE VIEWS OF LANDSCAPE
Two of surviving four views. Southern Song dynasty, early 13th century. Handscroll, ink on silk, height 11″ (28 cm), extant portion 11 × 90¾″ (28 × 230.5 cm). The Nelson-Atkins Museum of Art, Kansas City, Missouri. Purchase: William Rockhill Nelson Trust (32-159/2). Photograph by John Lamberton.

or imagining views of a world seen from a single, fixed vantage point (see "Linear Perspective," p. 314). The goal of Chinese painting is precisely to avoid such controlling limitations and instead show a panoramic totality that transcends any one single viewpoint to reveal the complexity of nature through multiple viewpoints—distant, all-seeing, and mobile.

Chinese landscape painting took a very different course after the fall of the Northern Song in 1126 and the removal of the court to Hangzhou. A new sensibility is reflected in the work of Xia Gui (flourished c. 1195–1235), a member of the newly established Academy of Painters. In contrast to the majestic, austere landscapes of the Northern Song painters, his **TWELVE VIEWS OF LANDSCAPE (FIG. 9–11)** presents an intimate and lyrical view of nature. In the surviving four of the twelve views that originally made up this long **handscroll** (narrow, horizontal, rolled painting), subtly modulated ink washes evoke a landscape veiled in mists. A few deft brushstrokes suffice to suggest details showing through—the grasses growing by the bank, the fishers at their work, the trees laden with moisture, the two bent-backed figures carrying heavy loads along the path that skirts the hill. Simplified forms, stark contrasts of light and dark, asymmetrical compositions, and great expanses of blank space suggest a fleeting, intangible world that can be grasped only in glimpses.

This development in Song painting from the rational and intellectual to the emotional and intuitive had a parallel in philosophy. During the late twelfth century, a new school of Neo-Confucianism called the School of the Mind insisted that self-cultivation could be achieved through contemplation, which might lead to sudden enlightenment. The idea of sudden enlightenment may have come from Chan Buddhism, better known in the West by its Japanese name, Zen. Chan Buddhists used meditation and techniques designed to "short-circuit" the rational mind. Xia Gui's painting seems also to suggest this intuitive approach.

The highly cultivated audience that appreciated subtle and sophisticated Song painting was equally discerning in other arts, such as ceramics. Of the many types of Song ceramics, one of the most prized was Guan ware, made mainly for imperial use (**FIG. 9–12**). The shape of this graceful vessel flows without interruption from base to lip, but the potter intentionally

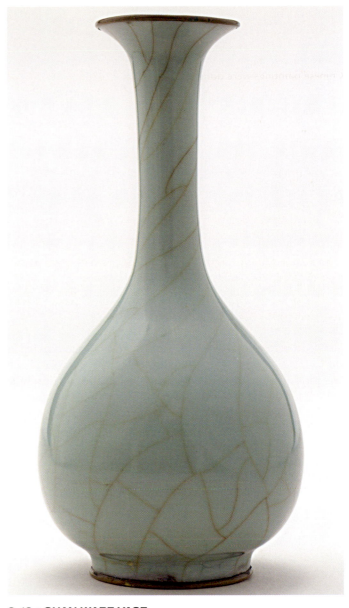

9–12 • GUAN WARE VASE
Southern Song dynasty, 13th century. Stoneware with crackled glaze, height 6⅝″ (18 cm). Percival David Foundation of Chinese Art, British Museum, London.

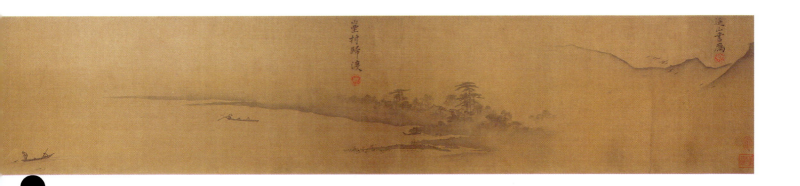

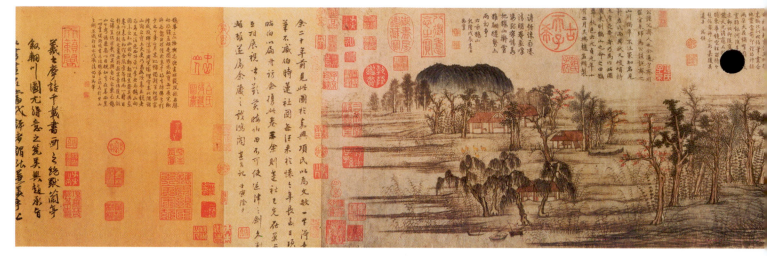

9–13 • Zhao Mengfu AUTUMN COLORS ON THE QIAO AND HUA MOUNTAINS
Yuan dynasty, 1296. Handscroll, ink and color on paper, 11¼″ × 36¾″ (28.6 × 93.3 cm).
National Palace Museum, Taipei, Taiwan, Republic of China.

allowed a pattern of irregular, spontaneous cracks to develop in the lustrous off-white glaze. This creates an interplay of ordered and unplanned elements, setting the controlled regularity of the vessel's form against the uncontrollable spontaneity of the linear network in the glaze. Such ceramics have an introspective quality as eloquent as the blank spaces and fugitive forms in Xia Gui's painting.

In 1279, the Southern Song dynasty fell to the armies of the Mongol leader Kublai Khan, and China became part of the vast Mongol Empire. Kublai Khan founded the Yuan dynasty (1279–1368), setting up his capital in the northeast, in what is now Beijing. The center of Chinese culture remained in the south, however, and southern Chinese scholars found themselves alienated from the Mongol court. Denied normal access

to the government positions for which they were educated, these scholars, the literati, retreated into alternative outlets for their talents, including the arts.

The southerner Zhao Mengfu (1254–1322), a descendant of the imperial line of Song, is typical in this regard; a painter, calligrapher, and poet, he produced works for an elite audience of cultivated southern literati. Unlike many other scholars, however, he eventually served the Yuan government in Beijing and was made a high official. Zhao painted **AUTUMN COLORS ON THE QIAO AND HUA MOUNTAINS** (FIG. **9–13**) for a friend living in the south, supposedly depicting the friend's ancestral home, Jinan, in the north. The mountains are not painted in the evocative, descriptive mode perfected by Song painters but rather in an archaic manner that recalls the

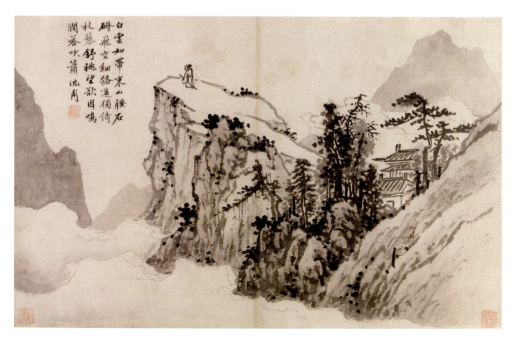

9–14 • Shen Zhou
POET ON A MOUNTAINTOP
Leaf from an album of landscape paintings, now mounted as part of a handscroll. Ming dynasty, c. 1500. Ink and color on paper, 15¼″ × 23¾″ (40 × 60.2 cm). The Nelson-Atkins Museum of Art, Kansas City, Missouri. Purchase: William Rockhill Nelson Trust (46–51/2).

The poem at the upper left reads:

> White clouds like a belt encircle the
> mountain's waist
> A stone ledge flying in space and
> the far thin road.
> I lean alone on my bramble staff
> and gazing contented into space
> Wish the sounding torrent would
> answer to your flute.

(translation by Richard Edwards, *Eight Dynasties of Chinese Paintings*, p. 185).

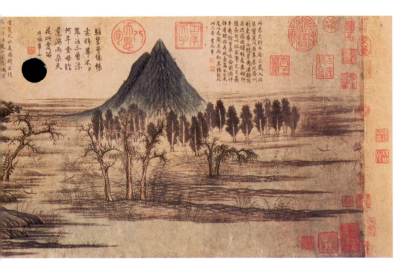

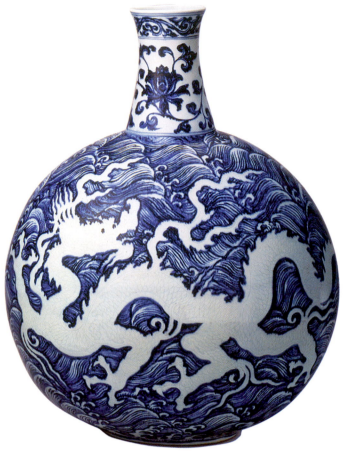

9-15 • PORCELAIN FLASK
With decoration in cobalt blue underglaze. Ming dynasty, c. 1425–1435. The Palace Museum, Beijing.

Dragons have featured prominently in Chinese folklore from earliest times—Neolithic examples have been found painted on pottery and carved in jade. In Bronze Age China, dragons came to be associated with powerful and sudden manifestations of nature, such as wind, thunder, and lightning. At the same time, dragons became associated with superior beings such as virtuous rulers and sages. With the emergence of China's first firmly established empire during the Han dynasty, the dragon was appropriated as an imperial symbol, and it remained so throughout Chinese history. Dragon sightings were duly recorded and considered auspicious. Yet even the Son of Heaven could not monopolize the dragon. During the Tang and Song dynasties the practice arose of painting pictures of dragons as a prayer for rain, and for Chan (Zen) Buddhists, the dragon was a symbol of enlightenment.

much earlier art of the Tang dynasty. In this way Zhao imbues his painting with a feeling of nostalgia, not only for his friend's distant homeland, but also for China's past.

This educated elite taste for antique styles became an enduring aspect of **literati painting**. Also typical of the tradition are the unassuming brushwork, the subtle colors sparingly used, and even the choice of audience—the literati painted not for public display but for each other. They favored handscrolls, hanging scrolls, or album leaves, which could easily be transported to show to friends or small gatherings (see "Formats of Chinese Painting," p. 216).

The contrast between the opulent display of the court and the austere aesthetic ideals of the literati is a defining feature of painting during the subsequent Ming dynasty (1368–1644). Whereas Ming court painters revived academic traditions of the Song, many literati painters built on the styles created by their Yuan predecessors. One of the major literati artists of the Ming period is Shen Zhou (1427–1509), who spent most of his life in the southern city of Suzhou, far from the court in Beijing. He studied Yuan painters avidly and tried to recapture their spirit in such works as **POET ON A MOUNTAINTOP** (**FIG. 9–14**). Here the poet has climbed a mountain and dominates the landscape. Before his gaze, a poem hangs in the air, like a projection of his thoughts. The poem, like the landscape painting, is a vehicle for Shen Zhou's self-expression, having more to do with the artist's response to nature than with the physical world itself. With its synthesis of poetry, calligraphy, and painting, and its harmony of mind and landscape, *Poet on a Mountaintop* represents the very essence of literati painting.

The prosperous Ming court patronized the arts on a lavish scale. Ming China became famous the world over for its exquisite ceramics, especially **porcelain**. Porcelain is made from kaolin, an extremely refined white clay, and petuntse, a variety of the mineral feldspar. When properly combined and fired at a high temperature, the two materials fuse into a glass-like, translucent ceramic that is far stronger than it looks. This **PORCELAIN FLASK** (**FIG. 9–15**) came from the imperial kilns in Jingdezhen, in Jiangxi Province, the most renowned center for porcelain in Ming China. The blue decoration—made from cobalt oxide, finely ground and mixed with water—was painted directly onto the unfired porcelain vessel in a technique known as **underglaze painting**. Next, the painter applied a clear glaze over the entire surface. After firing, the flask emerged from the kiln with its blue decoration set sharply against white. In this case a dragon is reserved in white against a background painted with blue patterning. The subtle shape, the refined yet vigorous decoration of dragons writhing in the sea, and the flawless **glazing** typify the high achievement of Ming potters.

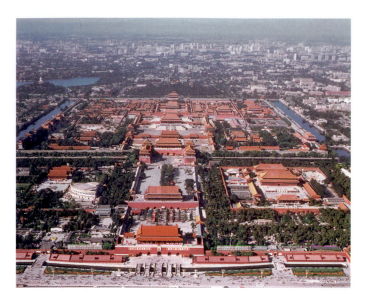

9–16 • THE FORBIDDEN CITY
Now the Palace Museum, Beijing, view from the southwest.
Mostly Ming dynasty.

Ming ceramists were not alone in their creativity and technical skill. Ming architects created the most important surviving example of traditional Chinese architecture: **THE FORBIDDEN CITY**, the imperial palace compound in Beijing (**FIG. 9–16**). The basic plan of Beijing was the work of the Mongols, who laid out their capital city according to Chinese principles, creating a walled rectangle with gates oriented to the four cardinal directions and streets running north–south and east–west arranged as a grid. The palace enclosure occupied the center of the northern part of the city. Under the third Ming emperor, Yongle (ruled 1403–1424), the Forbidden City was rebuilt as we see it today.

Visitors entered from the south and passed through the Meridian Gate, the monumental U-shaped complex near the middle of FIGURE 9–16. Inside the gate, a bow-shaped canal spanned by five arched marble bridges crosses a broad courtyard. On the north side of the courtyard is the Gate of Supreme Harmony, opening into the larger Outer Court. This area houses three ceremonial halls raised on a broad platform, classic examples of Chinese palace architecture, with brilliant terra-cotta-tile roofs and red lacquered columns. In the first and largest, the Hall of Supreme Harmony, the emperor sat on his throne during important state occasions. He faced south, looking out toward his city and, by extension, his realm. His back was to the north, the source of evil spirits, not to mention military threats from non-Chinese peoples beyond the Great Wall. Continuing on to the north in the Forbidden City, the visitor encounters the secluded and smaller Inner Court, which also has a progression of three buildings. This is where the emperor lived and conducted more private business affairs.

In its directional orientation and symmetrical arrangement, the plan of the Forbidden City reflects ancient Chinese beliefs about the harmony of the universe and emphasizes the emperor's role as the Son of Heaven, whose duty was to maintain the cosmic order from his throne in the middle of the world.

Korea

The Goryeo dynasty (918–1392) sponsored a period of courtly refinement in Korea best known for exquisite celadon—a high-fire transparent pale-green glaze, typically applied over a light gray stoneware body. Chinese potters invented celadon glazes as early as the first century CE, and Korean potters were using them by the eighth and ninth centuries. At first they emulated Chinese examples, but during the Goryeo dynasty potters developed distinctive forms, notably inlaid decoration, in which black and white slips were inlaid into lines incised or stamped in the clay body, creating underglaze designs in contrasting colors. The bottle in **FIGURE 9–17** displays such an inlaid pictorial scene. A clump of bamboo intertwines with the branches of a blossoming plum tree at the edge of a lake. Geese swim by and dragonflies flutter above.

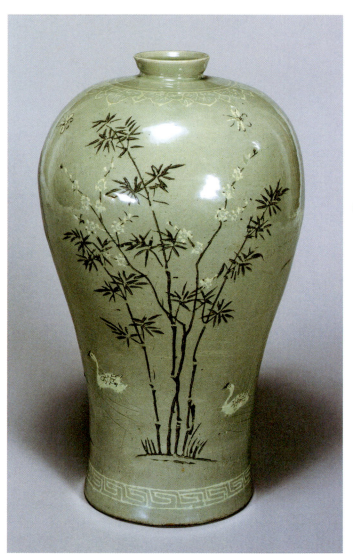

9–17 • MAEBYEONG BOTTLE WITH DECORATION OF BAMBOO AND BLOSSOMING PLUM TREE
Korea. Goryeo dynasty, late 12th–early 13th century. Celadon ware inlaid with black and white slip under the glaze, height 13¼″ (33.7 cm). Tokyo National Museum, Japan.

👁 **Watch** a video about the process of ceramics on **MyArtsLab**

9–18 • Jeong Seon PANORAMIC VIEW OF THE DIAMOND MOUNTAINS (GEUMGANG-SAN)
Korea. Joseon dynasty, 1734. Hanging scroll, ink and colors on paper, 40⅝″ × 37″ (130.1 × 94 cm). Lee'um, Samsung Museum, Seoul, Republic of Korea.

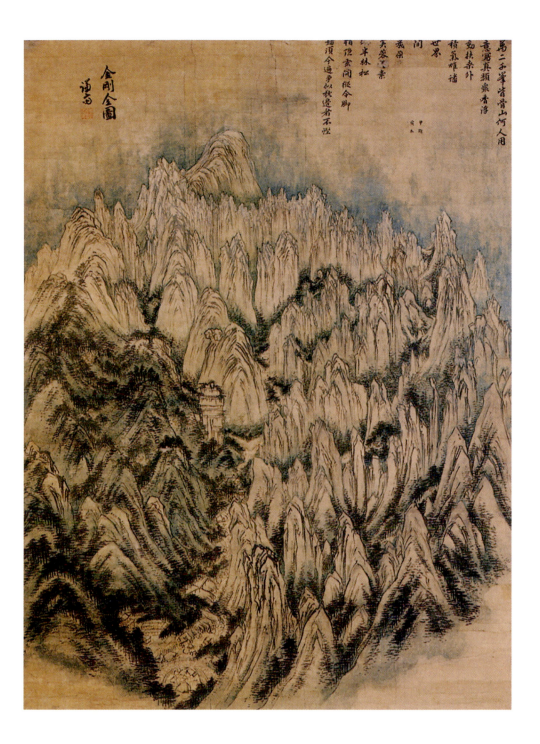

Such broad-shouldered bottles were used as storage jars for wine, vinegar, and other liquids, and a small, bell-shaped cover originally capped the vessel, protecting its contents and complementing its curves.

The long-lived Joseon dynasty (1392–1910) bridged the cultural change in Korea from domination by China to entry into the modern world. The seventeenth and eighteenth centuries were a time of intellectual revival, bringing a new creativity to the arts, especially literature and painting. Buddhism gave way to Confucian religious belief and practice. In Korea, as in Japan, an admiration for natural effects and practical solutions emerged. Korean painters turned to their own landscape for inspiration, and both writers and painters used Korean themes. **Genre paintings** were also popular at the time. With an energy and pride that recall the seventeenth-century Dutch Republic or nineteenth-century America, Korean artists found inspiration in their own lives and country.

Typical of this turn to Korean themes is the landscape painting of Jeong Seon (1676–1759), who chose well-known Korean vistas as the subjects of his paintings rather than the Chinese themes favored by earlier Korean artists. In this scroll (**FIG. 9–18**) painted in 1734, for example, he represents the Diamond Mountains, a celebrated range along Korea's east coast, aptly capturing its craggy, needle-like peaks emerging from the mist. The subject is Korean, and so is the energetic spirit and the intensely personal style, with its crystalline mountains, distant clouds of delicate ink wash, and individualistic brushwork.

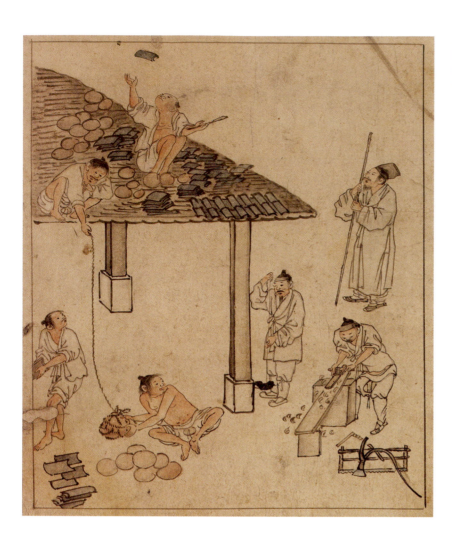

Other artists expanded the growing interest in Korean themes to different sorts of subject matter. Kim Hongdo (1745–1806) painted genre scenes that showcased the everyday lives and occupations, not of the nobility, but of commoners. His painting of **ROOF TILING** (FIG. 9–19)—one of a series of 25 album leaves portraying genre scenes—shows a team of six laborers engaged in various aspects of their roofing job. At lower right a carpenter smooths a propped-up board with his plane, while two colleagues perch on the roof itself, one about to hoist up a bundle of materials and the other catching a tile that has been heaved to him from below. The seventh man, leaning on his staff at upper right to survey the work, is presumably the roofers' supervisor. The circular figural composition animates the compressed, foreground tableau and organizes the viewers' patient examination of the carefully detailed workers, energized by their active postures and expressive faces. Kim Hongdo creates a strong sense of narrative; we seem to have happened upon the middle of an unfolding story.

Japan

What are the important monuments and developments in the later art of Japan?

The Japanese fully absorbed and transformed their cultural borrowings from China and Korea during the Heian period (794–1185). Generally peaceful conditions contributed to a new air of self-reliance. The imperial government severed ties with China in the ninth century, a time when the power of inter-related aristocratic families increased. An efficient method of writing the Japanese language was developed, and the rise of vernacular literature generated such prose masterpieces as Lady Murasaki's *Tale of Genji*. During these four centuries of splendor and refinement, two major streams of Buddhism emerged: first, esoteric sects and later, those espousing salvation in the Pure Land Western Paradise of the Buddha Amida.

Pure Land Buddhism came to prominence in the latter half of the Heian period, a time characterized by rising militarism, political turbulence, and the excesses of the imperial court. During such unsettled times, people turned increasingly to the promise of salvation after death through simple faith in the existence of a Buddhist realm known as the Western Paradise of the Pure Land, a resplendent place filled with divine flowers and music, where Amida and his attendant bodhisattvas presided as divine protectors of the faithful. Pure Land belief, which had spread to Japan from China and Korea, held that merely by chanting a mantra—the phrase *Namu Amida Butsu* ("Hail to Amida Buddha")—the faithful would be reborn into Amida's paradise.

One of the most beautiful expressions of Pure Land Buddhism is the Byodo-in temple complex, located in the Uji Mountains not far from Kyoto (FIG. 9–20). Originally a secular palace whose form was intended to suggest the appearance

Writing, Language, and Culture in Japan

Written Chinese was the international language of scholarship in East Asia, much as Latin was in medieval Europe. Educated Koreans, for example, wrote almost exclusively in Chinese until the fifteenth century. In Japan, Chinese continued to be used for certain kinds of writing, such as philosophical and legal texts, into the nineteenth century.

When the Japanese first began to write, they borrowed Chinese characters, which they refer to as *kanji*. However, differences between the Chinese and Japanese languages made this system extremely unwieldy, so during the ninth century the Japanese developed two syllabaries (*kana*), *katakana* and *hiragana*, to transcribe the sounds of their own language. (A syllabary is a system in which each symbol stands for a syllable.) *Katakana*, now generally used for writing foreign words, consists of mostly angular symbols, while *hiragana*, which is used for Japanese words, has graceful, cursive symbols.

A charming poem originated in Heian times to teach the new writing system. In two stanzas of four lines each, it uses almost all of the syllable sounds of spoken Japanese and thus almost every *kana* symbol. It was memorized as we would write our ABCs. The first stanza translates

Although flowers glow with color
They are quickly fallen,
And who in this world of ours
Is free from change?
(translation by Earl Miner)

Below is the stanza written three ways. At the right, it appears in *katakana* glossed with the original phonetic value of each symbol. (Modern pronunciation has shifted slightly.) In the center, the stanza appears in flowing *hiragana*. At left is the mixture of Chinese characters and *kana* that eventually became standard. This alternating rhythm of simple *kana* symbols and more complex Chinese characters gives a special flavor to Japanese calligraphy. In all three versions of the stanza, the text is written, like Chinese, in columns from top to bottom and across the page from right to left. Following this logic, Chinese and Japanese narrative paintings also read from right to left.

色は匂へど
散りぬるを
我世誰ぞ
常ならむ

いろはにほへと
ちりぬるを
わかよたれそ
つねならむ

イロハニホヘト
Chi-ri-nu-ru-wo
リヌルヲ
ワカヨタレソ
Wa-ka-yo-ta-re-so
ツネナラム
Tsu-ne-na-ra-mu
I-ro-ha-ni-ho-he-to

kanji and *kana*   *hiragana*   *katakana*

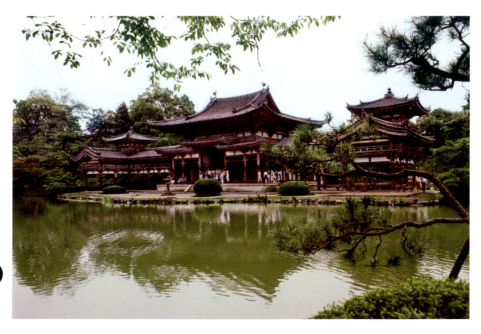

9–20 • PHOENIX HALL, BYODO-IN, UJI
Kyoto Prefecture. Heian period, c. 1053.

of the palatial residence of Amida in his Western Paradise, the Byodo-in was built for a member of the powerful Fujiwara family who served as principal advisor to the emperor. After his death in 1052, his family converted the palace into a memorial temple complex to honor his spirit. The principal building of the Byodo-in is often called the Phoenix Hall, not only for the pair of phoenix images on its roof, but also because the shape of the building itself suggests this mythical bird. Its thin columns give the Byodo-in Phoenix Hall a sense of airiness, as though the entire building could easily rise up through the sky to Amida's Western Paradise.

The Byodo-in's central image of Amida (**FIG. 9–21**), carved by the master sculptor Jocho (d. 1057), embodies the serenity and compassion of this Buddha. Reflected in the water of the pond in front of it, the Amida image, heightened with **gold leaf** and lacquer (a hard, glossy surface varnish), seems to shimmer in its private retreat. The figure was not created from a single block of wood like earlier sculpture but from several individually carved blocks in Jocho's innovative **joined-block** method of construction, which allowed sculptors to create larger but lighter statues. It also reflects the growing importance of wood as the medium of choice for Buddhist sculpture, reflecting a long-standing Japanese love for this natural material.

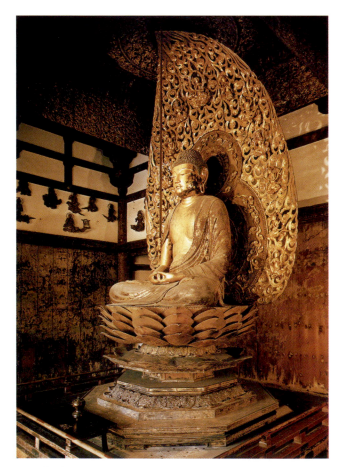

9–21 • Jocho AMIDA BUDDHA
Phoenix Hall, Byodo-in. Heian period, c. 1053. Gold leaf and lacquer on wood, height 9′ 8″ (2.95 m).

👁 **Watch** a video about Jocho's joined-block technique on **MyArtsLab**

Alongside this flourishing of Buddhist art, a singularly refined secular culture also arose at the Heian court. A new system of writing developed, known as *kana* script (see "Writing, Language, and Culture in Japan," p. 223). With its simple, flowing symbols interspersed with more complex Chinese characters, *kana* allowed Japanese writers to create a distinctive calligraphy quite unlike that of China.

Kana was used to write poetry, notably the most popular native poetic form—a 31-syllable format known as *waka*. During the Heian era, the finest *waka*s by various writers were collected into an anthology and hand-copied into albums. The most popular collection, compiled in the eleventh century, features writers known collectively as the Thirty-Six Immortal Poets and is still appreciated by educated Japanese today. The earliest surviving copy—the *Ishiyama-gire*—consists of 39 volumes of poems, elegantly written on high-quality papers decorated with painting, **block printing**, scattered gold and silver, and sometimes **collage** (pasted colored papers), over which the *waka*s themselves seems to float (**FIG. 9–22**). The wiry, flowing calligraphy and the patterning of papers match the elegance of the poetry, epitomizing courtly Japanese taste.

Considered by some to be the world's first known novel, *The Tale of Genji*, written at the beginning of the eleventh century by Lady Murasaki, transposed the lifestyle of Heian aristocrats into fiction for her fellow court ladies. Underlying the story of the love affairs of Prince Genji and his companions is the Japanese conception of fleeting pleasures and ultimate sadness in life, an echo of the Buddhist view of the vanity of earthly pleasures.

Among the earliest extant secular paintings in a new, native Japanese style known as *yamato-e* are scenes from *The Tale of Genji*, in a twelfth-century handscroll that alternates between sections of text and illustrated narrative episodes. This style is characterized by delicate lines and bold shapes in strong, if sometimes muted, colors. The asymmetrical compositions generally show courtiers in architectural settings. These figures do not express their emotions on their simply delineated faces. Instead their feelings are conveyed by colors, poses, and compositional arrangements.

One scene portrays Prince Genji viewed from behind while visiting his favorite consort, Murasaki (not the same person as the author of the novel), who faces him across the narrow interior space (see "A Closer Look," p. 226). Although Genji was especially fond of her, Murasaki could not become his principal wife because she was not from an aristocratic family. Here he comes to see her shortly before her death. One might expect the visualization of such a poignant moment to focus on the people involved. Instead the figures are relatively small and all but consumed by their clothing. The screens of the domestic interior dominate the scene, effectively squeezing Genji and Murasaki into a confined corridor. The composition, not the facial expressions or bodily postures, conveys the melancholy of this moment. The airy openness of the outdoor garden to the left—and the loose delicacy of the sketchily defined plants within it—heighten the sense of confinement and impending loss.

The courtiers of the Heian era became so engrossed in their own search for refinement that they neglected their responsibilities for governing the country. Clans of warriors outside

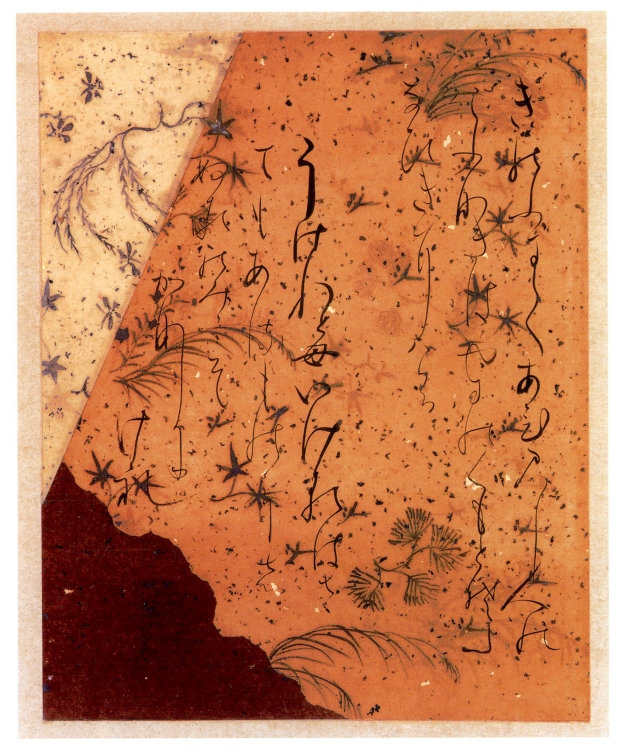

9–22 • ALBUM LEAF FROM THE ISHIYAMA-GIRE

(Dispersed volumes, once owned by the Ishiyama Temple, Anthology of the Thirty-Six Immortal Poets)
Heian period, early 12th century. Ink with gold and silver on decorated and collaged paper, 8″ × 6⅜″
(20.3 × 16.1 cm). Freer Gallery of Art, Smithsonian Institution, Washington, D.C. F1969.4.

*This page reproduces two verses by the courtier Ki no Tsurayuki, expressing sadness for the loss of a lover.
One reads:*

> Until yesterday
> I could meet her,
> But today she is gone—
> Like clouds over the mountain
> She has been wafted away.
>
> (translation by Stephen Addiss)

Scene from The Tale of Genji ▶ Heian period, 12th century. Handscroll, ink and colors on paper, 8⅝" × 18⅞" (21.9 × 47.9 cm). Gotoh Museum, Tokyo.

Only 19 illustrated scenes survive from this earliest known example of an illustrated handscroll of *The Tale of Genji*, created about 100 years after the novel was written. Scholars assume that it originally contained illustrations from the entire novel of 54 chapters, approximately 100 pictures in all. Each scroll seems to have been produced by a team of artists. One was the calligrapher, most likely a member of the nobility. Another was the master painter, who outlined two or three illustrations per chapter in fine brushstrokes and indicated the color scheme. Next, colorists went to work, applying layer after layer of color to build up patterns and textures. After they had finished, the master painter returned to reinforce outlines and apply the finishing touches, among them the details of the faces.

The roof has been removed so we can see what is happening inside the building.

Thickly applied mineral colors are now cracking and flaking.

Following courtly convention, Murasaki's body is concealed beneath voluminous robes; she holds a fan to shield her face; and her loosened hair cascades around her face and over her clothes.

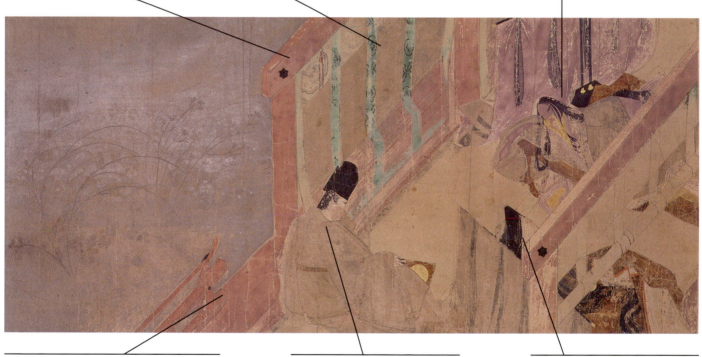

Wooden verandas surrounded Japanese houses, merging interior and exterior to provide vantage points for admiring the gardens.

The non-individualized faces of the prince and his consort betray none of the emotional content of the scene.

Murasaki's daughter is discreetly tucked between a "privacy" curtain and the wall.

🔍 **View** the Closer Look for the Scene from *The Tale of Genji* on **MyArtsLab**

the capital, known as samurai, grew increasingly strong, becoming the real powers in Japan. The Kamakura era (1185–1392) began when the samurai Minamoto Yoritomo (1147–1199) defeated his rival to assume power in Japan as shogun (general-in-chief). To resist the softening effects of courtly life in Kyoto, he established his military capital at the seaside town of Kamakura, leaving the emperor in Kyoto. As shogun, Yoritomo claimed both military and political power for himself, establishing a tradition of rule by shogun that lasted in various forms until 1868.

Toward the latter part of the Kamakura period, Zen Buddhism was introduced to Japan from China, where—known as Chan—it was already highly developed. In some ways, Zen resembles the original teachings of the historical Buddha in emphasizing individual enlightenment through meditation, without the help of deities or magical chants. Zen especially appealed to the self-disciplined spirit of the samurai, who associated earlier forms of Buddhism with the Japanese court.

An abbot named Kao at an early Zen temple was a pioneer in a kind of rough and simple painting in black ink that directly expresses the Zen spirit. A remarkable portrait of a **MONK SEWING** his robe (**FIG. 9–23**) draws us into the activity portrayed in the painting rather than distancing us from it as a work of art. The almost humorous compression of the monk's face, coupled with the position of the darker robe, focuses our attention on his eyes, which then lead us out to his hand pulling the needle, a compact rendering of intense concentration.

By the beginning of the Muromachi period (1392–1573), Zen dominated many aspects of Japanese culture. One of the most renowned Zen creations in Japan was built at this time: the dry landscape garden at the temple of Ryoan-ji in Kyoto (**FIG. 9–24**). A flat rectangle of raked gravel, about 29 by 70 feet, surrounds 15 stones of different sizes in islands of moss. The stones are set in asymmetrical groups of two, three, and five. Low walls establish the garden's boundaries, but beyond the perimeter wall maple, pine, and cherry trees add color and texture to the scene. Called "borrowed scenery," these elements are considered part of the design even though they grow outside the garden. This garden—celebrated for its severity and emptiness—has been interpreted as representing islands in the sea or mountain peaks rising above the clouds, a swimming tigress with her cubs or constellations of stars and planets. All or none of these interpretations may be equally satisfying—or irrelevant—to a monk seeking clarity of mind through contemplation.

During the Momoyama period (1573–1603), civil wars swept through Japan, fought among samurai loyal to their own feudal lords rather than to the central government. Portuguese explorers and traders arrived, and with them European muskets and cannon, which soon changed the nature of Japanese warfare. In response to the new weapons, monumental fortified castles were built in the early seventeenth century. Many were sumptuously decorated, offering artists new opportunities to work on a grand scale. Large murals on *fusuma* (paper-covered sliding doors) were particular features of Momoyama design, as were folding screens with gold-leaf backgrounds, whose glistening surfaces not only reflected light within castle rooms but also displayed the wealth of the warrior leaders. Temples, too, commissioned large-scale decorative paintings for grand reception rooms where monks met their wealthy warrior patrons.

Daitoku-ji, a celebrated Zen monastery in Kyoto, has a number of subtemples for which Momoyama painters created magnificent *fusuma*. One, the Juko-in, features *fusuma* by Kano Eitoku (1543–1590), one of the most brilliant painters from the hereditary lineage of professional artists known as the Kano school, which painted for the highest-ranking warriors from the sixteenth century through 1868. **FIGURE 9–25** shows two of three walls of **FUSUMA** panels painted by Eitoku when he was in his mid-twenties. To the left is the familiar Kano-school theme of cranes and pines, both symbols of long life; to the right is a great gnarled plum tree, symbol of spring and renewal. An island rounding both walls at the far corner provides a focus for the outreaching trees. Ingeniously, it belongs to both compositions at the same time, thus uniting them into a single organic whole.

Japanese art is never one-sided. Along with castles and their opulent interiors, there was an equal interest during the Momoyama period in the quiet, the restrained, and the natural. This was expressed primarily through the tea ceremony. The term "tea ceremony," a phrase now in common use, does not

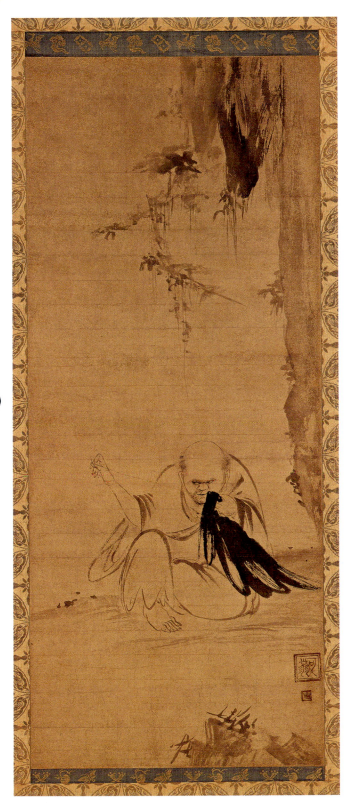

9–23 • Attributed to Kao Ninga MONK SEWING
Kamakura period, early 14th century. Ink on paper, 32⅞″ × 13¾″ (83.5 × 35.4 cm). The Cleveland Museum of Art.
John L. Severance Fund, 62.163.

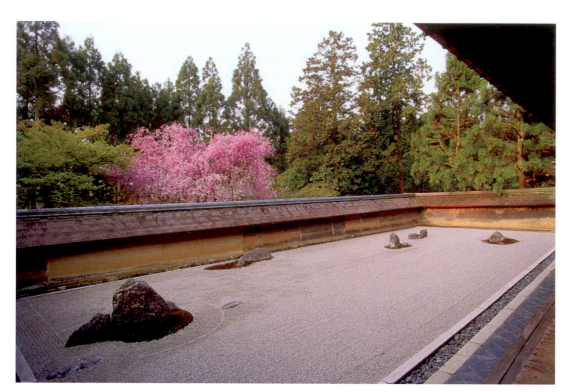

The American composer John Cage once exclaimed that every stone at Ryoan-ji was in just the right place. He then said, "And every other place would also be just right." His remark is thoroughly Zen in spirit. There are many ways to experience Ryoan-ji. For example, we can imagine the rocks as having different visual "pulls" that relate them to one another. Yet there is also enough space between them to give each one a sense of self-sufficiency and permanence.

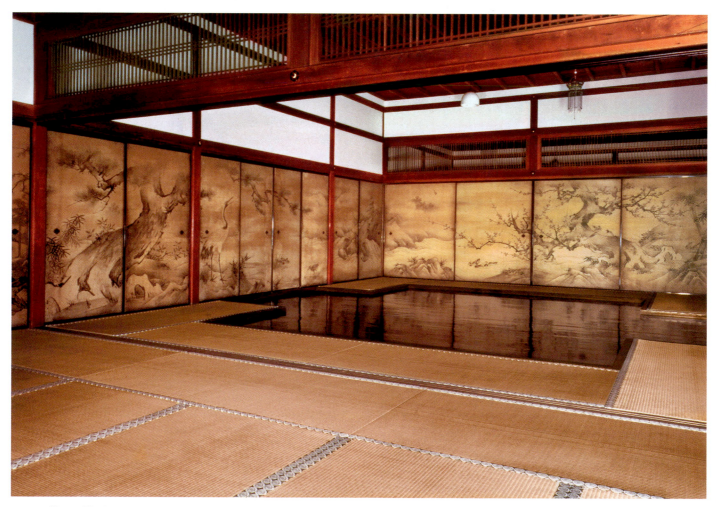

9-25 • Kano Eitoku **FUSUMA**
depicting a pine tree and a crane (left) and a plum tree (right), from the central room of the Jukoin, Daitoku-ji, Kyoto. Momoyama period, c. 1563–1573. Ink and gold on paper, height 5′ 9⅛″ (1.76 m).

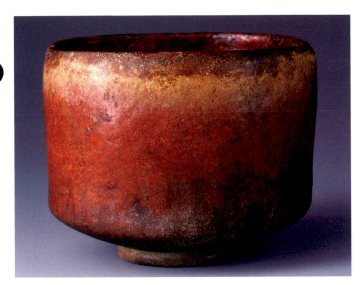

9–26 • Chojiro TEABOWL, CALLED YUGURE ("TWILIGHT")
Momoyama period, late 16th century. *Raku* ware, height 3½″ (9 cm).
The Gotoh Museum, Tokyo.

Connoisseurs developed a subtle vocabulary to discuss the aesthetics of tea. A favorite term was *sabi* ("loneliness"), which refers to the tranquility found when feeling alone. Other virtues were *wabi* ("poverty"), which suggests the artlessness of humble simplicity, and *shibui* ("bitter" or "astringent"), meaning elegant restraint. Teabowls such as this embody these aesthetics.

convey the full meaning of *chanoyu*, the Japanese ritual drinking of tea. There is no counterpart in Western culture. The most famous tea master in Japanese history, Sen no Rikyu (1522–1591), conceived of *chanoyu* as an intimate gathering in which a few people entered a small, rustic room, drank tea carefully prepared in front of them by their host, and quietly discussed the tea utensils or a Zen scroll hanging on the wall.

The age-old Japanese admiration for the natural and the asymmetrical found full expression in tea ceramics. A teabowl would be judged by such factors as how well it fitted into the hands, how subtly its shape and texture appealed to the eye, and who had previously used and admired it. If a bowl had been given a name by a leading tea master, it was especially treasured by later generations. One of the finest surviving early teabowls (**FIG. 9–26**) is attributed to Chojiro (1516–1592), the founder of the Raku family of potters. Named **YUGURE ("TWI-LIGHT")** by tea master Sen no Sotan (1578–1658), a grandson of Rikyu, this bowl is an exquisite example of red *raku* ware— a hand-built, low-fired ceramic of gritty red clay, developed especially for use in the tea ceremony. The effect created by the glaze-shaded red hue and lively surface texture evokes a gentle landscape illuminated by the setting sun. With its small foot, straight sides, irregular shape, and crackled texture, this bowl exemplifies tea taste at the beginning of its development.

Ukiyo-e: *Pictures of the Floating World*

During the Edo period (1603–1868), peace and prosperity came to Japan at the price of an increasingly rigid and often repressive form of government centered in a new capital—Edo (present-day Tokyo). Zen Buddhism was replaced as the prevailing intellectual force by a form of Neo-Confucianism, the philosophy formulated in Song dynasty China that emphasized loyalty to the state, though the popularity of Buddhism surged among commoners. The government discouraged foreign ideas and foreign contacts, forbidding Japanese from traveling abroad and barring outsiders from Japan, with the exception of small Chinese, Korean, and Dutch trading communities on an island off the southern port of Nagasaki.

In addition to serving as the shogun's capital, Edo was the center of a flourishing popular culture associated with tradespeople. Deeply Buddhist, these commoners were acutely aware of the transience of life and sought to live by the mantra: Let's enjoy it to the full as long as it lasts. This they did with abandon in the restaurants, theaters, bathhouses, and brothels of the city's pleasure district, named after the *ukiyo*— "floating world." Here heroes were not samurai or aristocratic poets, but famous actors and glamorous courtesans, paragons of pleasure and fashion who soon were memorialized in

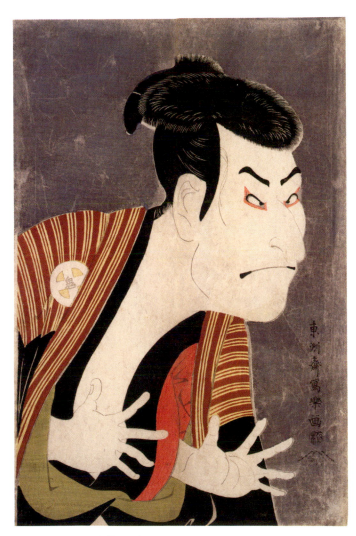

9–27 • Toshusai Sharaku OTANI ONIJI IN THE ROLE OF YAKKO EDOBE
Edo period, 1794. Polychrome woodblock print, ink, colors, and white mica on paper, 15″ × 9⅞″ (38.1 × 25.1 cm). The Metropolitan Museum of Art, New York.

🔍 **View** the Closer Look for Sharaku's print of Otani Oniji on **MyArtsLab** woodblock prints known as *ukiyo-e*—"pictures of the floating world"—produced by the hundreds for popular distribution (SEE FIGS. INTRO–7, 18–31).

These woodblock prints represent the combined expertise of four people: the publisher, the artist, the carver, and the printer. The publisher commissioned, coordinated, and funded the project and distributed the works to the stores or itinerant vendors who sold the prints. The artist supplied the master drawing for the print, executing its outlines in ink on tissue paper. The carver pasted the drawing face-down on a hardwood block and, always working in the same direction as the original brushstrokes, cut around the lines with a sharp knife. The rest of the block was chiseled away, leaving the outlines standing in relief. This block, which reproduced the master drawing, was called the **key block**. If the print was to have several colors, the carver made a separate block for each color. The printer brushed water-based ink or color over the blocks, beginning with the key block, placed a piece of paper on top, and then rubbed with a smooth, padded device called a *baren* to make an **impression**.

Toshusai Sharaku is one of the most mysterious, if today among the most admired, masters of *ukiyo-e*. He seems to have been active less than a year in 1794–1795, during which he produced 146 prints, of which all but ten are pictures of famous actors in a popular form of drama known as Kabuki. He was renowned for half-length portraits that captured the dramatic intensity of noted performers outfitted in the costumes and makeup of the characters they played on stage. Much as people today buy posters of their favorite sports, music, or movie

stars, so too in the Edo period people clamored for images of their Kabuki idols. The crossed eyes, craning neck, and stylized gestures of Sharaku's portrayal of actor Otani Oniji (FIG. 9–27) capture a frozen, tension-filled moment in an action-packed drama, precisely the sort of stylized intensity that was valued in Kabuki performance.

Beginning in the nineteenth century, woodblock prints of famous sites in Japan, such as *Thirty-Six Views of Mount Fuji* by Katsushika Hokusai (1760–1849), came into fashion. Hokusai's blocks were printed again and again until they were worn out. Then they were recarved and more copies printed. Thousands of prints from this series still survive. **THE GREAT WAVE** (FIG. 9–28) may be the most famous scene from the series. The great wave rears up like a dragon with claws of foam, ready to crash down on the figures huddled in the boats below. Exactly at the point of disaster, but far in the distance, rises Japan's most sacred peak, whose slopes, we suddenly realize, swing up like waves and whose snowy crown is like sea foam—associations the artist makes clear in the wave nearest us, caught just at the moment of greatest resemblance.

These prints were not considered fine art in Japan, but when they first appeared in Europe and America, they were immediately acclaimed and had a strong impact on late nineteenth- and early twentieth-century Western art (see "Japonisme," p. 500). Not only was the first book on Hokusai published in France, but the value of these prints as collectable works of art was recognized in the West before it was in Japan. Only within the past 50 years or so have Japanese museums and **connoisseurs** fully recognized the value of this originally "plebeian" form of art.

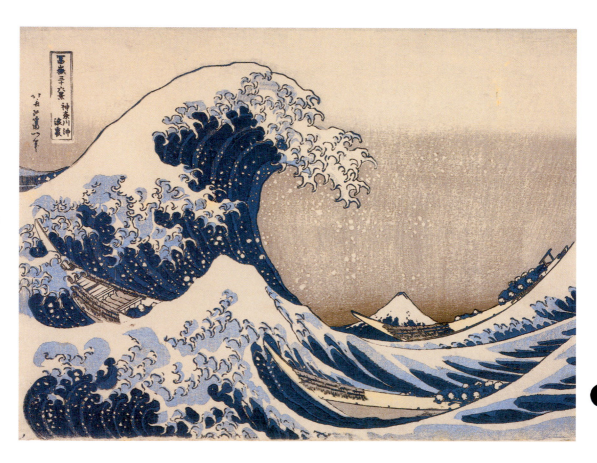

9–28 •
Katsushika Hokusai
THE GREAT WAVE
From *Thirty-Six Views of Mount Fuji*. Edo period, c. 1831. Polychrome woodblock print on paper, 9⅞" × 14⅝" (25 × 37.1 cm). Honolulu Academy of Arts, Hawaii. Gift of James A. Michener, 1955 (13695).

⊙ **Watch** a video on the printmaking process of woodcuts on **MyArtsLab**

Asian art combines material splendor and philosophical depth with an affinity for giving visual form to the spirituality of the natural world. Wealthy rulers devoted staggering resources to creating spectacular architectural complexes: temples in India, Angkor Wat in Cambodia, the Forbidden City in Beijing, samurai castles in Japan. Calligraphy continued to be refined into an ever more subtle and sophisticated art. But we usually associate the finest later Asian art with more intimate and intricate creations: album paintings and delicate ivory carvings in India; **ink painting** and ceramics in China, Korea, and Japan; or that most ephemeral of the arts, gardening.

THINK ABOUT IT

9.1 Which aspects of the Taj Mahal derive from the Islamic traditions introduced into India during the Mughal period?

9.2 Use a discussion of Fan Kuan's *Travelers Among Mountains and Streams* to outline the principal features of Song dynasty landscape painting, both its form and its meaning.

9.3 Compare the forms and objectives of the Japanese pictures represented in "A Closer Look" and FIGURE 9–27.

| CROSSCURRENTS |

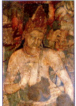 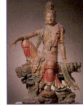

FIG. 4–8   FIG. 9–9

The theme of the bodhisattva can be traced through the history of Buddhist art across Asia. Use these two examples from India and China—separated by over five centuries in date—to characterize the appearance and describe the significance of such princely figures within the artistic and religious traditions of Buddhism.

IN PERSPECTIVE

1000

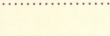
- Heian Period in Japan 794–1185
- Goryeo Dynasty in Korea 918–1392
- Song Dynasty in China 960–1279

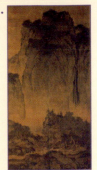

FAN KUAN, Travelers Among
Mountains and Streams
early 11th century

- Kamakura Era in Japan
  1185–1392

1200

- Yuan Dynasty in China
  1279–1368

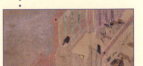

Scene from *The Tale of Genji*
12th century

- Ming Dynasty in China
  1368–1644
- Muromachi Period
  in Japan 1392–1573
- Joseon Dynasty in Korea
  1392–1910

1400

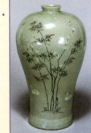

- Mughal Dynasty in India
  1526–1858

- Momoyama Period 1573–1603

- British East India Company Begins
  Activity in India c. 1600
- Edo Period in Japan
  1603–1868

Maebyeong Bottle
late 12th–early
13th century

1600

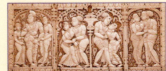

Rock Garden, Ryoan-ji
c. 1480

1800

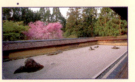

- Peak of British Imperial
  Power in India 1848–1947

Ivory Panel with
Loving Couples
late 17th–18th century

- Republic of China (Mainland) 1912–1949

- South Korea/North Korea 1945 to present
- Indian Independence 1947
- People's Republic of China
  1949 to present

2000

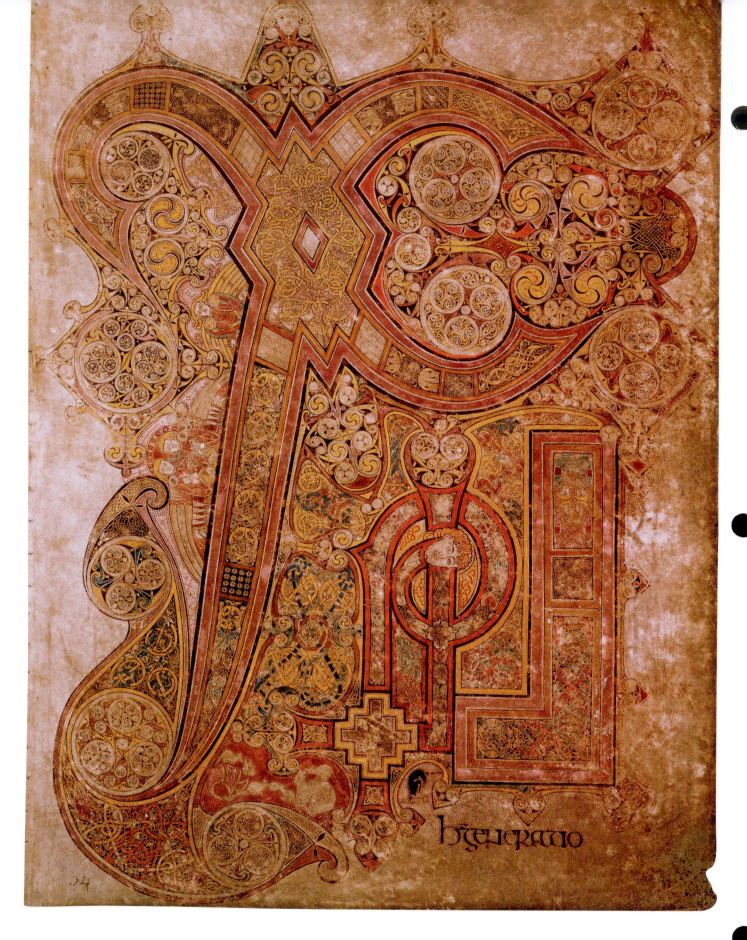

10–1 • CHI RHO PAGE
Gospel of Matthew, *Book of Kells*, probably made at Iona, Scotland. c. 800. Oxgall inks and pigments on vellum,
12¾″ × 9½″ (32.5 × 24 cm). The Board of Trinity College, Dublin (MS 58 [A.1.6.], fol. 34v).

EARLY MEDIEVAL AND ROMANESQUE ART

LOOKING FORWARD ▶

The explosion of ornament surrounding—almost suffocating—the words on this page from an early medieval manuscript clearly indicates the importance of what is being expressed (FIG. 10–1). The large Greek letters *chi rho iota* (*XPI*) abbreviate the word *Christi* that starts the Latin phrase "*Christi autem generatio*"—the last word is written out fully and legibly at bottom right, clear of the decorative expanse. These words begin Matthew 1:18: "Now the birth of Jesus the Messiah took place in this way." So what is signaled here—not with a picture of the event but with an ornamental celebration of its initial mention in the text—is Christ's first appearance within a Gospel book that not only contains the four biblical accounts of his life, but would also evoke his presence on the altar of the monastery church where this lavish book was once housed. It is precisely the sort of ceremonial book that is carried in the hands of a deacon in Justinian's procession into San Vitale in Ravenna to begin the Mass (SEE FIG. 7–17).

There is nothing explicitly Christian about the ornamental motifs celebrating the first mention of the birth of Christ in this manuscript—the *Book of Kells*, produced in Ireland or Scotland sometime around the year 800. The swirling spirals and interlaced tangles of stylized animal forms have their roots in jewelry created by the migrating, so-called barbarian tribes that formed the "other" of the Greco-Roman world. But by this time, this ornamental repertory had been subsumed into the flourishing art of Irish monasteries. And Irish monks became as famous for writing and copying books as for their intense spirituality and missionary fervor.

Wealthy, isolated, and undefended, Irish monasteries fell easy victims to Viking attacks. In 806, fleeing Viking raids on the island of Iona (off the coast of present-day Scotland), its monks established a refuge at Kells on the Irish mainland. They probably brought the *Book of Kells* with them. It was precious. Producing this illustrated version of the Gospels entailed lavish expenditure: four scribes and three major illuminators worked on it (modern scribes take about a month to complete such a page); 185 calves were slaughtered to make the vellum; and colors for some paintings came from as far away as Afghanistan.

Throughout the Middle Ages and across Europe, monasteries were principal centers of art and learning. While prayer and acts of mercy represented their primary vocation, some talented monks and nuns also worked as painters, jewelers, carvers, weavers, and embroiderers. Few, however, could claim a work of art as spectacular as this one.

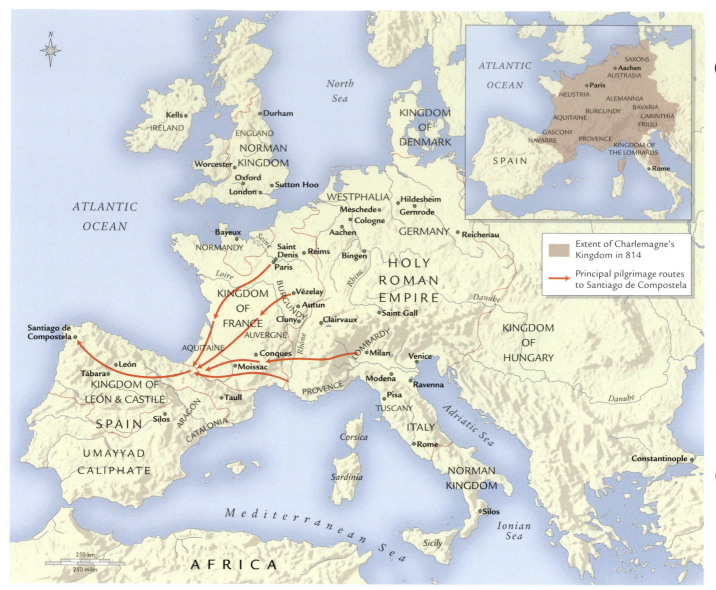

MAP 10–1 • MEDIEVAL EUROPE AROUND 1100

A series of well-traveled roads developed across France and into northern Spain to take pilgrims to the holy shrine of St. James at Compostela in Galicia.

The roughly 1,000 years of European history between the dissolution of the Western Roman Empire during the fifth century and the Florentine Renaissance in the fifteenth century are generally referred to as the Middle Ages, or the medieval period (from the Latin *medium aevum*, meaning "middle age"). These terms reflect the view of Renaissance Humanists who regarded the period that preceded theirs as a "dark age" of ignorance, decline, and barbarism, standing in the middle and separating their own "golden age" from the golden ages of ancient Greece and Rome. Although scholars now acknowledge the ridiculousness of this self-serving formulation and recognize the millennium of the "Middle Ages" as a period of great richness, complexity, creativity, and innovation, the terms endure.

As Roman authority crumbled at the dissolution of the Western Empire, Christianity gained steadily in strength, and political power in Western Europe passed to bishops as well as to secular lords. The Church helped unify Europe's heterogeneous population—now an amalgam of Romans and the people who moved in from outside the empire, whom the Romans called "barbarians." Christianity spread into lands far from its Mediterranean origins, as far away as Ireland and eventually Scandinavia, which had never been ruled by Rome. The result was a vibrant, if sometimes tense, multiculturalism in which a variety of traditions intermingled to form a new medieval culture (MAP 10–1).

The Christian Church, as the repository of Roman tradition and learning, provided intellectual and artistic as well as spiritual leadership. As patrons of the arts, the clergy sponsored the building of churches and the creation of equipment for use in rituals, including crosses, reliquaries (shrines containing holy relics), and copies of sacred books. Secular leaders—in the wake of the fifth century, mainly Germanic peoples, including Ostrogoths, Visigoths, Angles, Saxons, and Franks—built castles and commissioned the making of secular works of art such as jewelry, textiles, and armor, little of which survives. Stylistically, early medieval art reflects the fusion of the Germanic and late Roman traditions of the former Western Empire, as well as the influence of both pre-Christian art from northern Europe and the Islamic art of Spain.

Western Europeans in this early medieval period looked with dismay on the rapid advance of Islam. Also monotheistic "People of the Book," Muslims accepted Judaism and Christianity as forerunners of their own prophet, Muhammad, and they were often tolerant of Christians and Jews in their territories. But less broad-minded western and northern European leaders viewed Muslims not only as unwanted foreigners but also as dangerous infidels. The presence of Muslims in Spain from the eighth century on raised fears among Christians of further Islamic inroads into Europe. The Franks, however, checked the advancing Muslim armies in the eighth century, safeguarding the rest of Europe as Christian lands. By the end of the eleventh century, it was Christians who went on the crusading offensive, mounting holy wars against the Muslims to "free" what they considered their Holy Land.

The British Isles and Scandinavia

What characterizes the early medieval art of the British Isles and Scandinavia?

Another clash of cultures had occurred much earlier in the British Isles. The Romans subjugated the native Celtic inhabitants of Britain in 43 CE but did not invade Ireland. During the period of Roman rule, which lasted until the beginning of the fifth century, Christianity took root in Britain and spread to Ireland. After the collapse of the Western Roman Empire in the fifth

century, British chieftains took control, vying for dominance with the help of soldiers from continental Europe, thus giving rise to the legends of King Arthur and the Round Table. The Angles, Saxons, and Jutes from the Continent soon established kingdoms of their own, and the people under their rule adopted Anglo-Saxon speech and customs. Over the next 200 years, a new Anglo-Saxon and Hiberno-Saxon culture (*Hibernia* was the Roman name for Ireland) formed out of a fusion of Celtic, Germanic, and surviving Roman traditions.

Metalworking is one of the glories of Anglo-Saxon art. References to splendid jewelry and military equipment decorated with gold and silver fill Anglo-Saxon literature, such as the epic poem *Beowulf*. An early seventh-century burial mound, excavated in the English region of East Anglia at a site called Sutton Hoo (*hoo* means "hill"), concealed a hoard of such treasures, representing the broad cultural heritage that characterized the British Isles at this time—Celtic, Scandinavian, and Classical Roman, as well as Anglo-Saxon. There was even a Byzantine silver bowl. The grave's still unidentified occupant was buried in a 90-foot-long ship. The vessel held weapons, armor, and other equipment for the afterlife, and such luxury items as an exquisite clasp of pure gold that once secured over his shoulder the leather body armor of its wealthy and powerful owner (FIG. 10–2).

The two sides of the clasp—essentially identical in design—connected when a long gold pin, attached to one half by a delicate but strong gold chain, was inserted through a series of aligned channels on the back side of the inner edge of each. The exquisite decoration of this work is created by thin pieces of garnet and blue-checkered glass (known as **millefiori**, from the Italian for "a thousand flowers") cut into precisely stepped geometric shapes or to follow the sinuous contours of stylized animal forms. The cut shapes were then inserted into channels and supplemented by granulation (SEE FIG. 5–7). Under the stepped geometric pieces that form a rectangular patterned field on each side, jewelers placed gold foil stamped with incised motifs that reflect light back up through the transparent garnet to spectacular effect. Around these carpet-like

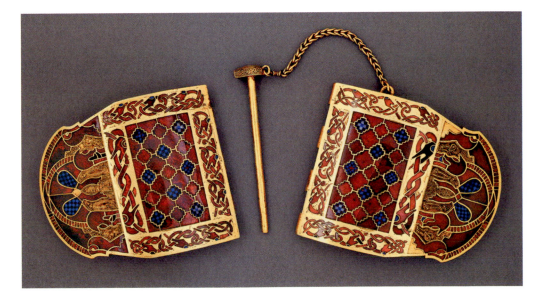

10–2 • HINGED CLASP

From the Sutton Hoo burial, Suffolk, England. First half of 7th century. Gold plaques with granulation and inlays of garnet and millefiori glass, length 5″ (12.7 cm). The British Museum, London.

The Medieval Scriptorium

Today, books are made with the aid of computer software that can set type, lay out pages, and insert and prepare illustrations. Modern presses can produce hundreds of thousands of identical copies. In medieval Europe, however, before the invention of printing from movable type in the mid-1400s, books were made by hand, one at a time, with pen, ink, brush, and paint. Each one was a time-consuming and expensive undertaking. No two were exactly the same.

Medieval books were first made by monks and nuns in a workshop called a **scriptorium** (plural, *scriptoria*) within the monastery. As the demand for books increased, rulers set up palace workshops employing both religious and lay scribes, supervised by scholars.

Books were written on carefully prepared animal skins—either **vellum**, which was fine and soft, or **parchment**, which was heavier and shinier. Ink and paint also required time and experience to prepare, and many pigments—particularly blues and greens—were made from costly semiprecious stones. In lavish manuscripts, artists also used gold leaf or gold paint.

Work on a book was often divided between scribes, who copied the text, and one or more artists, who created illustrations, large initials, and other decorations. Occasionally scribes and illustrators signed their work at the end of the manuscript, in what is called a colophon, also sometimes containing notes on the book's production. One scribe even took the opportunity to warn, "O reader, turn the leaves gently, and keep your fingers away from the letters, for, as the hailstorm ruins the harvest of the land, so does the injurious reader destroy the book and the writing" (cited in Dodwell, p. 247).

---

rectangles are borders of interlacing snakes, and in the curving compartments to the outside stand pairs of semitransparent, overlapping boars stylized in ways that reflect the traditions of Scandinavian jewelry. Their curly pig's tails overlap their strong rumps at the outer edges on each side of the clasp, and following the visible vertebrae along the arched forms of their backs, we arrive at their heads, with floppy ears and extended tusks. Boars represented strength and bravery, important virtues in warring Anglo-Saxon society.

Among the richest surviving works of Hiberno-Saxon Christian art were lavishly decorated Gospel books, essential not only for the spiritual life within established monasteries, but also critical for the missionary activities of the Irish Church since a Gospel book was required in each new foundation. Often bound in gold and jeweled covers, they were placed on the altars of churches, carried in procession, and even thought to protect the faithful from enemies, disease, and various misfortunes. Such sumptuous books were produced by monks in local monastic workshops called **scriptoria**.

One of the earliest Hiberno-Saxon Gospel books is the *Book of Durrow*, dating to the second half of the seventh century. The book's format reflects Roman Christian models, but its paintings are an encyclopedia of Hiberno-Saxon design. Each Gospel is introduced by a three-part decorative sequence:

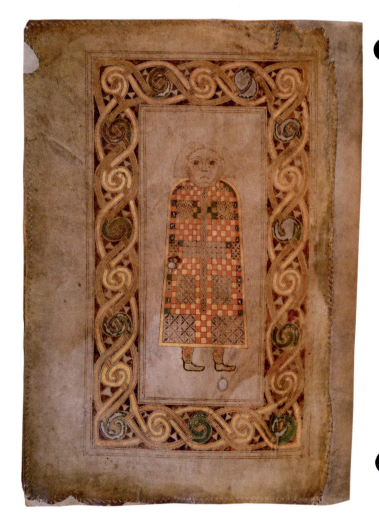

10–3 • MAN (SYMBOL OF ST. MATTHEW)

Gospel of Matthew, *Book of Durrow*. Hiberno-Saxon, second half of 7th century. Ink and tempera on parchment, 9⅝" × 6⅛" (24.4 × 15.5 cm). The Board of Trinity College Dublin (MS 57, fol. 21v).

a page with the symbol of its evangelist author, followed by a page of pure ornament, and finally elaborate decoration highlighting the initial words of the text. The Gospel of Matthew is preceded by his symbol, a man (**FIG. 10–3**). What a difference from the way humans were represented in the Greco-Roman tradition! The armless body is formed here by a colorful checkered pattern, recalling the rectangular panels on the Sutton Hoo clasp (SEE FIG. 10–2). A schematic, symmetrical, frontal face stares out at the viewer over the body's rounded shoulders, and the tiny feet that emerge at its other end are seen from contrasting profile view, as if to deny any hint of lifelike form or earthly spatial placement. Equally prominent is the bold band of complicated but coherent interlacing ornament that borders the figure's field.

Comparable priority of ornament over figure also characterizes the *Book of Kells*, one of the most spectacular and inventive of the surviving Hiberno-Saxon Gospels, probably made around 800 in an Irish monastery on Iona, an island off the west coast of Scotland. Its most celebrated page may be the one that begins the account of Jesus's birth in Matthew's Gospel (SEE FIG. 10–1). The Greek letters *chi*, *rho*, and *iota* create an irregular shape that resembles a cluster of gold and enamel brooches. At first glance, the page seems filled only with letters and abstract ornament, but hidden in the dense thicket of spirals and interlaces are human and animal forms. The spiral of the *rho* at the lower-right center of the page ends in the head of a red-headed youth, possibly Christ. At left center, three angels hold the edge of the plunging *chi*. At bottom center, just at right of the end of this longest stroke, two cats—with mice perched on their backs—each step on the tails of mice who hold in their mouths the Eucharistic host set between them. This cat-and-mouse scene may signal the triumph of good (represented by the cats) over evil (embodied by the mice who nibble at the host or the Communion wafer, the mystical body of Christ).

Even as monks finished the *Book of Kells*, Hiberno-Saxon culture came under threat from abroad. At the end of the eighth century, seafaring bands of western Scandinavians known as Vikings began to appear on the coasts of the British Isles, lured by the wealth of church treasuries and fertile land. Intermittently looting and destroying coastal and inland river communities, they were a terrifying presence throughout Europe for nearly 300 years, eventually settling in what is now Iceland, Greenland, Ireland, England, France, Scotland, and Russia. About the year 1000, they even established a short-lived outpost in eastern North America.

Scandinavia

The Scandinavian homeland of the Vikings was a vital artistic center long before their raiding explorations and continued to flourish long after they had resettled in their foreign homes. Since Scandinavia was never part of the Roman Empire, by the fifth century CE pure **animal style**, untouched by the Classical Mediterranean world, still dominated the arts. The **GUMMERSMARK BROOCH** (**FIG. 10–4**), a large silver-gilt pin made in Denmark during the sixth century, was probably one of a pair used to fasten a cloak around the owner's shoulders. The brooch displays an impressive array of generally symmetrical designs, seething with fantastic animal forms. Ribs

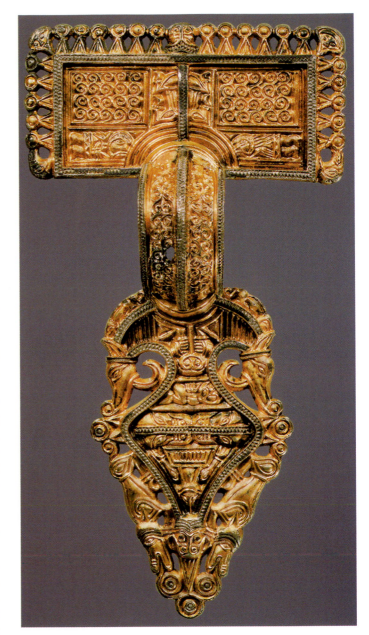

10–4 • GUMMERSMARK BROOCH
Denmark. 6th century. Silver gilt, height 5¾″ (14.6 cm). Nationalmuseet, Copenhagen.

and spinal columns are exposed as if they had been x-rayed; hip and shoulder joints are pear-shaped; tongues and jaws extend and curl, and legs end in long claws. The stylistic origins of the boars on the Sutton Hoo clasp are easily seen here.

The vast forests of Scandinavia provided the materials for timber buildings of many kinds, but, since they were subject to decay and fire, the earliest of these structures have disappeared, leaving few traces. In rural Norway, however, twelfth-century **stave churches**—named for the four huge timbers (staves) that form their structural core—have survived, and they seem to record the structure and appearance of timber architectural traditions that once predominated in the northern European landscape of the Middle Ages. Borgund church, built about

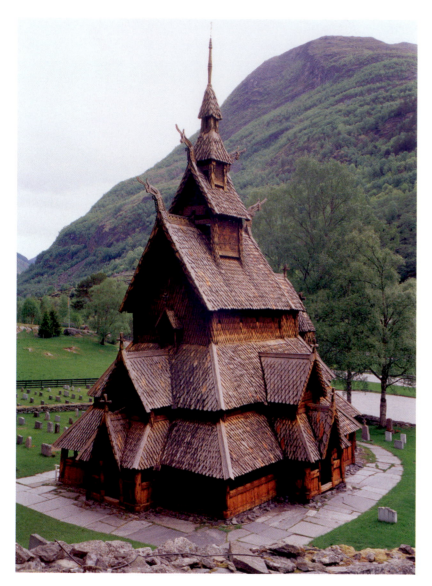

10-5 • EXTERIOR VIEW AND SECTION
DRAWING OF STAVE CHURCH
Borgund, Norway. c. 1125–1150.

👁 **Watch** an architectural simulation of
stave church construction on **MyArtsLab**

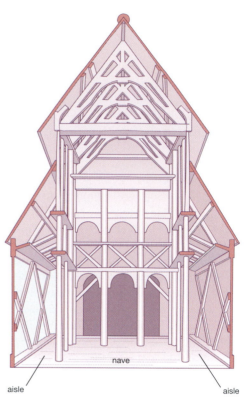

aisle

nave

aisle

1125–1150, is one of the finest (**FIG. 10–5**). Four corner staves support the central roof, with additional interior posts that create the effect of a nave and side aisles. A rounded apse covered with a timber tower is attached to the choir. The steeply pitched roofs protect the walls from the rain and snow. On all the gables, either crosses or dragon heads protect the church and its congregation from trolls and demons. The same basic wooden structure was used for almost all building types: on a large scale for palaces, assembly halls, and churches; on a small scale for domestic shelters which people shared with their animals.

The Carolingian Revival

What defines the Carolingian revival in architecture and the visual arts?

By the end of the fifth century, Frankish barbarians had settled in northern Gaul (present-day France), and it was Frankish warriors who in 732 turned back the Muslim invasion of Gaul. The leaders of the Franks established a dynasty of rulers known as the Carolingians, after their greatest member Charles the Great, called Charlemagne (ruled 768–814). Charlemagne's empire in continental Europe encompassed at its greatest extent present-day France, western Germany, Belgium, Holland, Luxembourg, and the Lombard kingdom in Italy. He imposed Christianity throughout this territory, and in 800 Pope Leo III (pontificate 795–816) granted Charlemagne the title of emperor, declaring him the rightful successor to the first Christian Roman emperor, Constantine. This endorsement reinforced Charlemagne's authority and strengthened the bonds between the papacy and secular government in the West.

The Carolingian rulers' ascent to the Roman imperium, and the political pretensions it implied, are clearly signaled in a small bronze equestrian statue—once thought to be a portrait of Charlemagne himself but now usually identified as his grandson, **CHARLES THE BALD** (**FIG. 10–6**). The idea of representing an emperor as a proud equestrian figure recalls the much larger image of Marcus Aurelius (SEE FIG. 6–32) that was believed during the Middle Ages to portray Constantine, the first Christian emperor and an ideal prototype for the ruler of the Franks, newly legitimized by the pope. But unlike the bearded Roman, this Carolingian king sports a mustache, a Frankish sign of nobility that had also been common among the

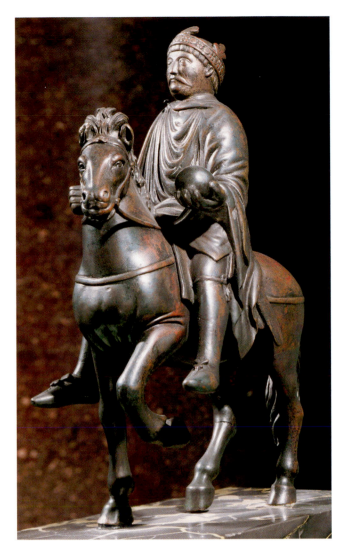

10–6 • EQUESTRIAN PORTRAIT OF CHARLES THE BALD (?)
9th century. Bronze, height 9½″ (24.4 cm). Musée du Louvre, Paris.

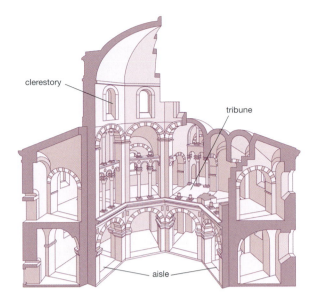

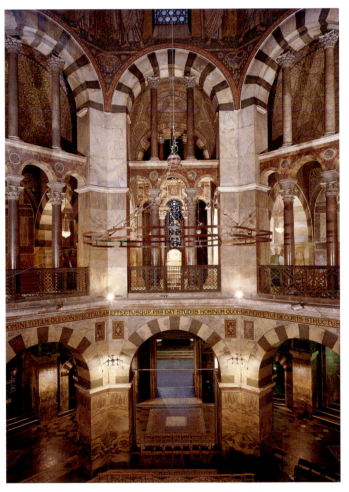

10–7 • SECTION DRAWING AND INTERIOR VIEW OF THE PALACE CHAPEL OF CHARLEMAGNE
Aachen, Germany. Constructed 792–805.

Extensive renovations took place here in the nineteenth century, when the chapel was reconsecrated as the cathedral of Aachen, and in the twentieth century, after it was damaged in World War II.

👁 **Watch** a video about the palace chapel of Charlemagne on **MyArtsLab**

Celts (SEE FIG. 5–43). Works of art such as this are not the result of a slavish mimicking of Roman prototypes, but the creative appropriation of Roman imperial typology to glorify manifestly Carolingian rulers.

To proclaim the glory of the new empire in monumental form, Charlemagne's architects turned to the two former Western imperial capitals, Rome and Ravenna, for inspiration. Charlemagne's biographer, Einhard, reported that the ruler, "beyond all sacred and venerable places…loved the church of the holy apostle Peter at Rome." Not surprisingly, Constantine's basilica of St. Peter, with its long nave and side aisles ending in a transept and projecting apse (SEE FIG. 7–6), served as a model for many important churches in Charlemagne's empire. The basilican plan, which had fallen out of favor since the Early Christian period, emerged again as the principal arrangement of large churches, and would remain so throughout the Middle Ages and beyond.

The **PALACE CHAPEL OF CHARLEMAGNE** at Aachen also has clear Italian roots (FIG. 10–7). This building functioned as the emperor's private chapel, the church of his imperial court, a place for precious relics of saints, and, after

Charlemagne's death, the imperial mausoleum. The central octagonal plan recalls the church of San Vitale in Ravenna (SEE FIG. 7–15), but at the front of the building is a new architectural feature—the **westwork**, or monumental entrance block that forms an imposing façade. The soaring core of the building is surrounded at ground level by an **ambulatory** (curving aisle passageway) and, on the second floor, is ringed by a **gallery** (a continuous upper-story platform overlooking the main space). Two tiers of columns and railings at gallery level form a screen that re-emphasizes the flat, pierced walls of the octagon and enhance the clarity and planar geometry of its design. The effect is quite different from the dynamic spatial play and undulating exedrae of San Vitale, but the veneer of richly patterned and multicolored stone—some imported from Italy—on the walls and the mosaics covering the vaults at Aachen were clearly inspired by Byzantine architecture.

Charlemagne turned to the Church to help stabilize his empire through religion and education. He looked most especially to Benedictine monks whom he called his "cultural army." Carolingian monks followed the *Rule for Monasteries*, written by St. Benedict of Nursia (c. 480–c. 547), a set of practical guidelines for secluded communal life that outlined monastic vocation as a combination of work and prayer (liturgical services as well as private devotion). While contemplating how best to house such a community, Abbot Haito of Reichenau developed, at the request of Abbot Gozbert of Saint Gall, a conceptual plan for the layout of monasteries. This extraordinary ninth-century drawing survives in the library of the abbey of St. Gall and is known as the **ST. GALL PLAN (FIG. 10–8)**. This is not a "blueprint" in the modern sense, prepared to guide the construction of an actual monastery, but an intellectual record of Carolingian meditations on the nature of monastic life. It does, however, reflect the basic design used in the layout of medieval monasteries, an efficient and functional arrangement that continues to be used by Benedictine monasteries to this day. At its center is the **cloister**, an enclosed courtyard from which open all the buildings that are most central to the life of the monk. Most prominent is a large basilican church with towers, multiple altars with relics, and, at the east end, a sanctuary where monks would gather for communal prayer throughout the day and night. The monks' quarters lie off the southern and eastern sides of the cloister, with dormitory, refectory (dining

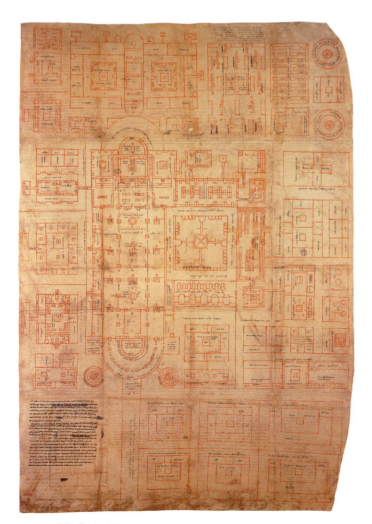

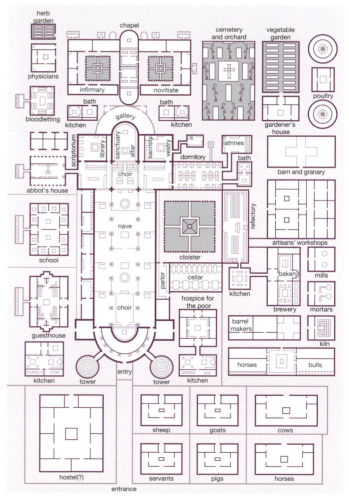

10–8 • ST. GALL PLAN
Original (left) and redrawn with captions (right). c. 817. Original in red ink on parchment, 28″ × 44½″ (71.1 × 112.1 cm). Stiftsbibliothek, St. Gallen, Switzerland (Cod. Sang. 1092).

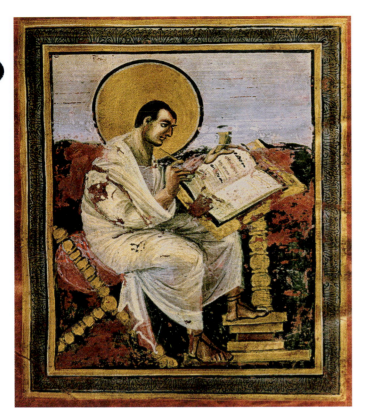

10–9 • PAGE WITH MATTHEW THE EVANGELIST

From the *Coronation Gospels*. Early 9th century. Ink and colors on vellum, 8¹¹⁄₁₆″ × 7½″ (22 × 19 cm). Kunsthistorisches Museum, Vienna.

Tradition holds that this Gospel book was buried with Charlemagne in 814, and that in the year 1000 Emperor Otto III removed it from his tomb. Its title derives from its use in the coronation ceremonies of later German emperors.

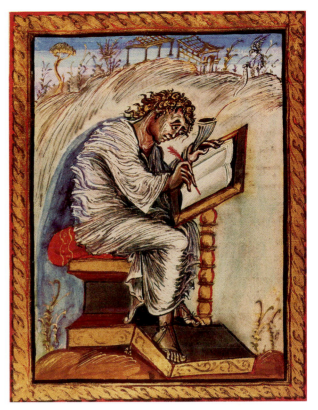

10–10 • PAGE WITH MATTHEW THE EVANGELIST

From the *Ebbo Gospels*. Second quarter of the 9th century. Ink and colors on vellum, 10¼″ × 8¾″ (26 × 22.2 cm). Bibliothèque Municipale, Epernay, France (MS 1, fol. 18v).

View the Closer Look comparison of the two Matthew portraits in the *Coronation* and *Ebbo Gospels* on **MyArtsLab**

---

room), and workrooms. Further east are the cemetery, hospital, and school for novices (monks in training). To the north stand the abbot's residence, guest quarters, and a hospice for the poor. Buildings for lay farmworkers and shelter for animals surround this central core.

As part of their monastic work life, some monks and nuns produced books—central components in the Carolingian renewal of learning. Charlemagne himself sponsored the scrupulous editing and copying of key ancient and religious texts, written in a new, clear script called Carolingian minuscule, based on ancient Roman forms but with a uniform lower-case alphabet that increased legibility and streamlined production. Like the builders and sculptors who transformed revived Roman types, such as basilicas, central-plan chapels, or equestrian imperial portraits, into creative new works, scribes and illuminators revived, reformed, and revitalized traditions of book production. Portraits of writing evangelists—rather than the symbols used to represent them in the *Book of Durrow* (SEE FIG. 10–3)—began to look like pictures of Roman authors.

The portrait of Matthew in the early ninth-century *Coronation Gospels* conforms to the principles of idealized, lifelike representation consistent with the Greco-Roman Classical tradition (**FIG. 10–9**). The full-bodied, white-robed figure is

modeled in brilliant white and subtle shading. He sits on the cushion of a folding chair set within a freely painted landscape. The way his foot lifts up to rest on the solid base of his writing desk emphasizes his three-dimensional placement within an outdoor setting. Conventions for creating the illusion of solid figures in space could have been learned from Byzantine manuscripts in a monastic library, or from Byzantine artists seeking refuge at the Carolingian court during the iconoclasm (726–843; see "Iconoclasm," p. 177).

As with architecture, the revival of the Roman tradition in manuscript painting became the basis for a series of creative Carolingian variations. One of the most innovative and engaging is a Gospel book made for Archbishop Ebbo of Reims (archbishop 816–835, 840–841) at the nearby abbey of Hautvillers (**FIG. 10–10**). The calm, carefully painted grandeur characterizing Matthew's portrait in the *Coronation Gospels* (SEE FIG. 10–9) has given way here to spontaneous, calligraphic painting suffused with energetic abandon. This may be most immediately apparent in the intensity of Matthew's gaze, but the whole composition is charged with energy, from the evangelist's wiry hairdo and rippling drapery, to the rapidly sketched landscape, and even extending into the windblown acanthus leaves of the frame. The picture's style is related to its meaning since the

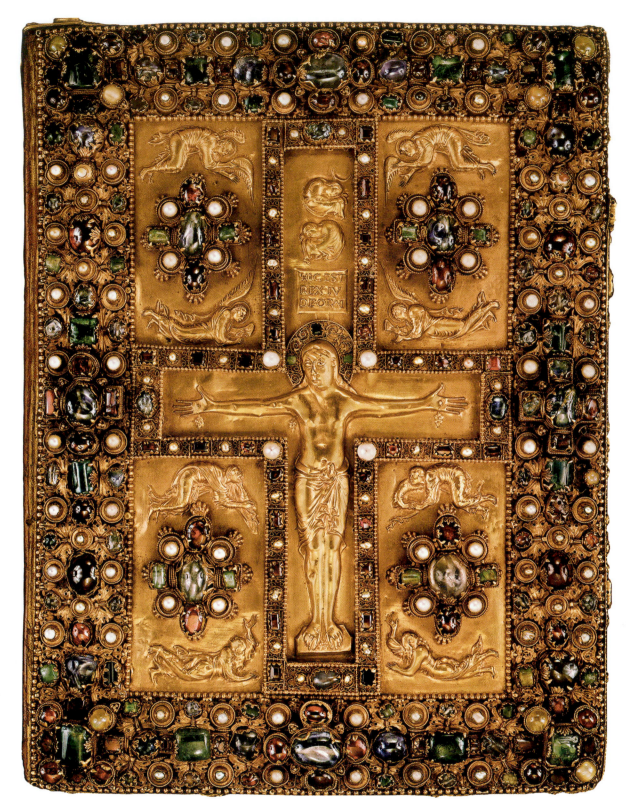

10–11 • CRUCIFIXION WITH ANGELS AND MOURNING FIGURES
Outer cover of the *Lindau Gospels*. c. 870–880. Gold, pearls, sapphires, garnets, and emeralds,
13¾″ × 10⅞″ (36.9 × 27.5 cm). The Pierpont Morgan Library, New York (MS M1).

marked expressionism evokes the evangelist's spiritual excitement as he hastens to transcribe the Word of God delivered by
the angel (also serving as Matthew's symbol), who is almost lost
in the upper-right corner. As if swept up in the saint's turbulent

emotions, the footstool tilts precariously, and the top of the desk
seems about to detach itself from the pedestal.

Sumptuous books such as these represent an enormous
investment of time, talent, and materials. They were protected

with heavy wooden covers that were sometimes sheathed in sheets of pure gold embellished with jeweled decoration. One of the richest of these (**FIG. 10–11**)—covering the *Lindau Gospels* and probably made between 870 and 880 in a workshop sponsored by Emperor Charles the Bald (ruled 840–877)—combines jewels and pearls with sculpture in gold. The Crucifixion is represented by figures formed from the gold background using the **repoussé** technique—pushing or hammering up from the back of a metal panel to produced raised forms on the front. Grieving angels hover above the arms of the cross, and earthbound mourners twist in agony below. Over Jesus's head personifications of the sun and moon hide their faces in anguish. In contrast to these gracefully agitated figures, the artist modeled a monumental Jesus in a more rounded, calmer, Classical style. He seems almost to be standing in front of the cross—straight, wide-eyed, with outstretched arms, as if to prefigure his ultimate triumph over death. The jewels, rounded to form cabochons (polished, not faceted, stones), are raised on tiny feet or architectural configurations so as to allow light to penetrate under them, thus enhancing their luster and reminding medieval believers of biblical descriptions of the heavenly Jerusalem.

The Tenth-Century Art of Spain and the Ottonian Empire

What developments characterize the tenth-century art of Spain and the Ottonian Empire?

Christian and Islamic worlds met in medieval Spain. When Muslim armies arrived in the early eighth century, Spain was governed by the Visigoths, a Germanic people who had ruled over the indigenous Spanish population since the fall of the

Western Roman Empire. The Islamic conquest of Spain in 711 ended Visigothic rule. With some exceptions, the Muslims allowed Christians and Jews to follow their own religious practices. In a rich exchange of artistic influences, Christian artists incorporated some features of Islamic art into a colorful new style known today as **Mozarabic**.

Antagonisms among Muslims, Orthodox Christians, and the followers of various heretical Christian beliefs provided fertile material for Spanish theologians, and writing biblical commentaries to refute heretical beliefs became a major task of the monasteries of northern Spain. Beatus (d. 798), the abbot of the monastery of Liébana near the north coast, compiled around 776 an influential commentary on the Apocalypse, describing the final and fiery destruction of the world before the Last Judgment and triumph of Christ. Illustrated manuscripts of this text are among the glories of early medieval art in Spain.

A particularly lavish copy was produced around 940–945, probably at the monastery of San Salvator at Tábara, by an artist named Maius (d. 968), who both wrote the text and painted the illustrations. His gripping portrayal of the **SEVEN-HEADED DRAGON AND WOMAN CLOTHED WITH THE SUN** (**FIG. 10–12**), based on the biblical text of Apocalypse (Revelation 12:1–18), extends over two pages to cover an entire opening of the book. Maius has stayed close to the text in composing his tableau, which is dominated by the long, seven-headed, red dragon that slithers across practically the entire width of the picture to threaten at top left the "woman clothed with the sun, with the moon under her feet, and on her head a crown of twelve stars" (12:1). With his tail, at upper right, he sweeps a third of heaven's stars toward the earth while the woman's male child appears before the throne of God. Maius presents this

10–12 • Maius SEVEN-HEADED DRAGON AND WOMAN CLOTHED WITH THE SUN
From the *Morgan Beatus*, probably made at San Salvator at Tábara, Spain. 940–945. Tempera on vellum, 15⅛″ × 22¹⁄₁₆″ (38.5 × 56 cm). The Pierpont Morgan Library, New York (MS M644, fols. 152v–153r).

When French painter Fernand Léger (1881–1955; SEE FIG. 19–11) was visiting the great art historian Meyer Schapiro (1904–1996) in New York during World War II, the artist asked the scholar to suggest the single work of art that was most important for him to see while there. Schapiro took him to the Morgan Library to leaf through this manuscript, and the strong impact it had on Léger can be clearly seen in his later paintings.

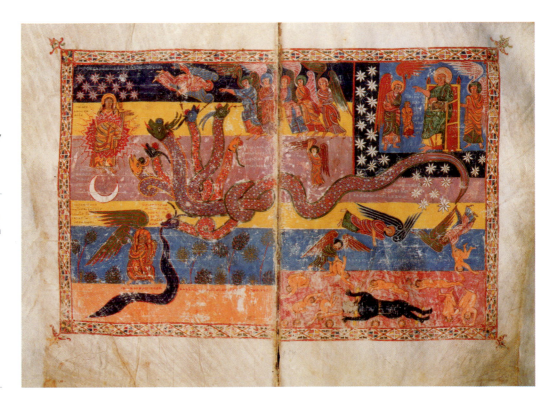

complex allegory of the triumph of the Church over its enemies with a forceful, abstract, ornamental style that accentuates the dramatic, nightmarish qualities of the events outlined in the text. The background has been distilled into horizontal strips of color; the figures become striped bundles of drapery capped with faces dominated by staring eyes and silhouetted, framing haloes. Momentous apocalyptic events have been transformed by Maius into exotic abstractions that still maintain their power to captivate our attention.

The Ottonian Empire

By the third generation of the Carolingian dynasty, the empire had been divided into three parts, setting the stage for the modern partitioning of Europe. The western portion eventually became France. In the tenth century, control of the eastern portion—corresponding roughly to present-day Germany, Switzerland, and Austria—passed to a dynasty of Saxon rulers known as the Ottonians, after its three principal figures: Otto I (ruled 936–973), Otto II (ruled 973–983), and Otto III (ruled 983–1002). Otto I gained control of Italy in 951, and the pope crowned him emperor in 962.

In the tenth and eleventh centuries, Ottonian artists in northern Europe, drawing on Roman, Byzantine, and Carolingian models, began a new tradition of large sculpture in wood and bronze that would have a significant influence on later medieval art. The **GERO CRUCIFIX** (**FIG. 10–13**) is one of the few large works of carved wood to survive. Archbishop Gero of Cologne (archbishop 969–976) commissioned the sculpture for his cathedral in about 970. The figure of Christ is life-size, and the focus is on his human suffering. He is shown as a tortured martyr, not as the triumphant hero of the *Lindau Gospels* cover (SEE FIG. 10–11). His broken body sags in death on the cross, head falling forward, eyes closed. The straight, linear fall of his golden drapery heightens the impact of his drawn face, emaciated arms and legs, sagging torso, and limp, bloodied hands. This is an image of distilled anguish, meant to inspire pity and awe in the empathetic responses of its viewers.

Late in the Ottonian period, Bishop Bernward of Hildesheim in Germany, who was himself a skilled goldsmith, emerged as an important patron. A pair of **BRONZE DOORS** made under his direction for his abbey church of St. Michael represents the most ambitious and complex bronze-casting project since antiquity (**FIG. 10–14**). Each door was cast as a single piece, and the inscription in the band running across the center of the doors states that Bishop Bernward installed them in 1015.

Standing more than 16 feet tall, the doors portray scenes from the Hebrew Bible on the left (read down from the Creation of Eve at the top to Cain's murder of Abel at the bottom) and from the New Testament on the right (read upward from the Annunciation at the bottom to the *Noli me tangere* at the top). In each pair of scenes, the event from the Hebrew Bible is meant to represent a prefiguration of or complement to the adjacent New Testament event. For instance, the third panel down on the left shows Adam and Eve picking the forbidden fruit of Knowledge in the Garden of Eden, an act believed by Christians to be the source of human sin, suffering, and death. This scene is paired on the right with the Crucifixion of Jesus,

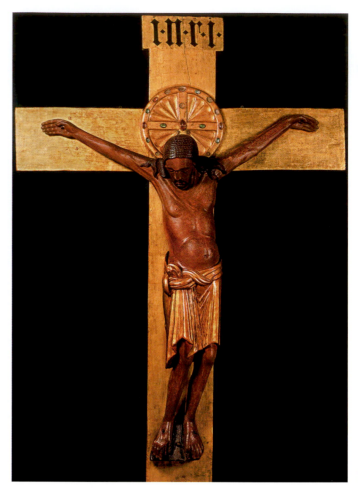

10-13 • GERO CRUCIFIX
Cologne Cathedral, Germany. c. 970. Painted and gilded wood, height of figure 6′ 2″ (1.88 m).

This life-size sculpture is both a crucifix to be suspended over an altar and a special kind of reliquary. A cavity in the back of the head was made to hold a piece of the Host, or Communion bread, already consecrated by the priest. Consequently, the figure not only represents the body of the dying Jesus but also contains within it the body of Christ obtained through the Eucharist.

whose sacrifice was believed to have atoned for Adam and Eve's Original Sin, bringing the promise of eternal life. At the center of the doors, six panels down—between the door pulls—Eve (left) and Mary (right) sit side by side, holding their sons: Cain (who murdered his brother) and Jesus (who was unjustly executed) signify the opposition of evil and good, damnation and salvation. Other telling pairs are the murder of Abel (the first sin) with the Annunciation (the advent of salvation) at the bottom, and fourth from the top, the passing of blame from Adam and Eve to the serpent paired with Pilate washing his hands of any responsibility for the execution of Jesus.

Aristocratic Ottonian women often held positions of authority, especially as leaders of religious communities. When the provincial military governor Gero founded the convent of

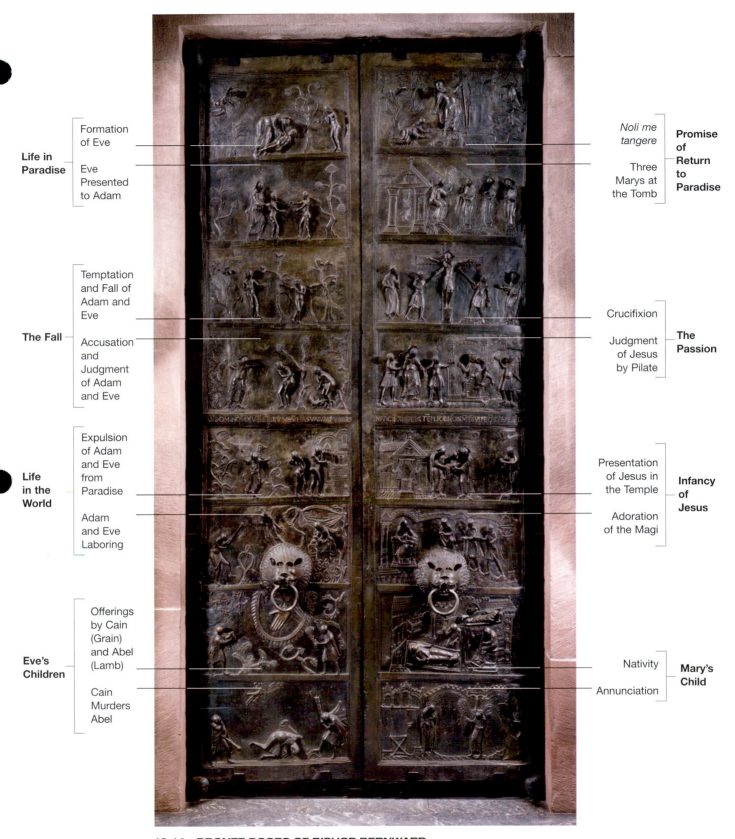

Life in Paradise
- Formation of Eve
- Eve Presented to Adam

The Fall
- Temptation and Fall of Adam and Eve
- Accusation and Judgment of Adam and Eve

Life in the World
- Expulsion of Adam and Eve from Paradise
- Adam and Eve Laboring

Eve's Children
- Offerings by Cain (Grain) and Abel (Lamb)
- Cain Murders Abel

Promise of Return to Paradise
- *Noli me tangere*
- Three Marys at the Tomb

The Passion
- Crucifixion
- Judgment of Jesus by Pilate

Infancy of Jesus
- Presentation of Jesus in the Temple
- Adoration of the Magi

Mary's Child
- Nativity
- Annunciation

10–14 • BRONZE DOORS OF BISHOP BERNWARD
Made for the abbey church of St. Michael, Hildesheim, Germany. 1015.
Bronze, height 16′ 6″ (5 m).

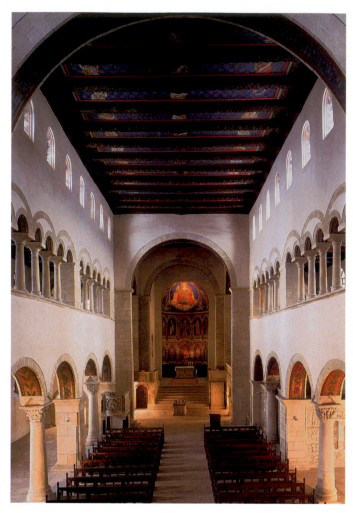

10–15 • NAVE, CHURCH OF ST. CYRIAKUS
Gernrode, Germany. Begun 961, consecrated 973.

ST. CYRIAKUS in Gernrode in 961 (FIG. 10–15), he made his widowed daughter-in-law its first abbess. The church was designed as a basilica, with a nave flanked by side aisles. But the design of the three-level wall elevation—nave arcade, gallery, and clerestory—creates a rhythmic effect distinct from the uniformity that had characterized earlier basilicas (e.g., FIG. 7–8). Rectangular piers alternate with round columns in the two levels of arcades at gallery level; pairs of openings are framed by larger arches and then grouped in threes. The central rectangular piers, aligned on the two levels, bisect the walls vertically into two units, each composed of two broad arches of the nave arcade surmounted by three pairs of arches at the gallery level. This seemingly simple design, with its rhythmic alternation of heavy and light supports, its balance of rectangular and rounded forms, and its combination of horizontal and vertical movements, seems to prefigure the aesthetic exploration of wall design that will characterize the Romanesque architecture of the succeeding two centuries.

Like their Carolingian predecessors, Ottonian monks and nuns created richly illuminated manuscripts, often funded by secular rulers. Styles varied from place to place, depending on the traditions of the particular scriptorium, the models available in its library, and the creativity of its artists.

The **PRESENTATION PAGE** of a Gospel book made in the early eleventh century for Abbess Hitda (d. 1041) of Meschede, near Cologne (FIG. 10–16), represents one of the most distinctive local styles. The abbess herself appears here, offering the book to St. Walpurga, her convent's patron saint. The artist has angled the buildings of the sprawling convent in the background to frame the figures and draw attention to their interaction. The foreground setting—a rocky, undulating strip of landscape—is meant to be understood as holy ground, separated from the rest of the world by golden trees and the huge arch-shaped aura that silhouettes St. Walpurga. The energetic spontaneity of the painting style suffuses the scene with a sense of religious fervor appropriate to the visionary encounter.

The **GOSPELS OF OTTO III** (FIG. 10–17), made in a German monastery near Reichenau about 1000, shows another Ottonian painting style, in this case inspired by Byzantine art in the use of sharply outlined drawing and lavish fields of gold. Backed by a more controlled and balanced architectural canopy than that sheltering Hitda and St. Walpurga, these tall, slender men gesture dramatically with long, thin fingers. The scene captures the moment when Jesus washes the feet of his disciples during their final meal together (John 13:1–17). Peter, who had tried to stop his Lord from performing this ancient ritual

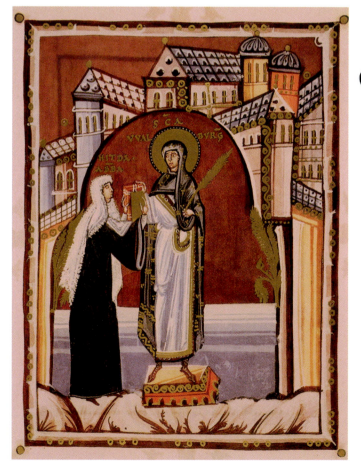

10–16 • PRESENTATION PAGE WITH ABBESS HITDA AND ST. WALPURGA, HITDA GOSPELS
Early 11th century. Ink and colors on vellum, 11⅜″ × 5⅝″ (29 × 14.2 cm). Hessische Landes- und Hochschulbibliothek, Darmstadt, Germany.

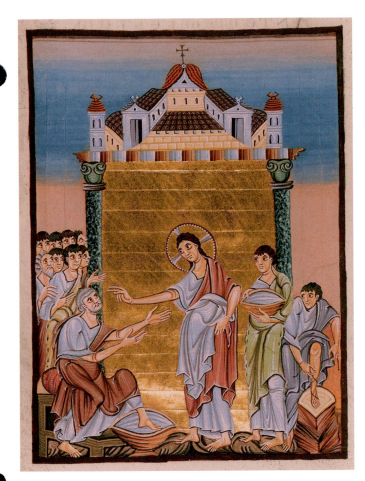

10–17 • CHRIST WASHING THE FEET OF HIS DISCIPLES
From the *Gospels of Otto III*. c. 1000. Ink, gold, and colors on vellum, page size 13⅛″ × 9½″ (33.4 × 24.2 cm). Bayerische Staatsbibliothek Munich (Clm 4453, fol. 237r).

of hospitality, appears at left, one leg reluctantly poised over the basin while a centrally silhouetted and slightly overscaled Jesus gestures emphatically to underscore the necessity and significance of the act. Another disciple at far right enthusiastically raises his leg to untie his sandals so he can be next in line. Selective stylization has allowed the artist of this picture to transform the received Classical tradition into a style of stunning expressiveness and narrative power, features that will also characterize the figural styles associated with the Romanesque.

Romanesque Art

What new features define the art and architecture of the Romanesque period?

During the eleventh century, although Europe remained an agricultural society, with land the primary source of wealth and power for a hereditary aristocracy, towns and cities with artisans and merchants grew in importance. More efficient farming facilitated population growth, and people began to move from agricultural villages into burgeoning urban areas. By the twelfth century, popular movements such as the crusades and pilgrimages began to end European isolation. Although the crusades were brutal military failures, the Western crusaders' encounters

with the sophisticated Byzantine and Islamic cultures introduced new technology and ideas into Europe. People from all levels of society traveled together on pilgrimages to the three holiest places of Christendom: Jerusalem, Rome, and the shrine of St. James in Santiago de Compostela. Travel and trade led to the rise of an increasingly knowledgeable and urbane society, and foreign contacts helped to nourish a period of rich intellectual and artistic development.

Art historians have called the art produced from the mid eleventh through the twelfth century *Romanesque* ("Roman-like"). Early nineteenth-century scholars first used the word with a pejorative edge to describe architecture that had the solid masonry walls, rounded arches, and vaulting characteristic of ancient Roman building but was not quite up to Classical standards. Today, we admire the remarkable vitality and variety of art and architecture that developed during the "Romanesque" period, drawing on many artistic traditions—not only Roman—as it blended various local styles and practices to form a new style. Many consider Romanesque to be the first truly trans-European movement in the history of art.

Architecture

The eleventh and twelfth centuries were a period of great building activity in Europe. The need to provide for personal security in a period of constant local warfare and political upheaval, as well as the desire to glorify the house of the Lord and his saints, meant that construction was focused on castles and churches. Castles had to be imposing masonry structures that would not only signify the importance of local rulers, but also defend him and the community that grew up around him from military assault. The house of God needed to be equally powerful and impressive. As one medieval monk put it, the Christian faithful were so relieved to have passed through the apocalyptic anxiety that had gripped their world at the millennial change around the year 1000, that in gratitude Europe was "clothed everywhere in a white garment of churches" (Radulphus Glaber, cited in *A Documentary History of Art*, vol. I, p. 18). There was a veritable building boom.

Romanesque churches, like their early medieval predecessors, are often based on the basilican plan, but since designs varied from region to region, place to place, there is no such thing as a typical Romanesque church. Although timber remained a common building material, especially in northern Europe, Romanesque builders used masonry when conditions permitted. It was stronger and more durable, and masonry vaults enhanced the acoustical effect of the Gregorian chants sung inside. Stone barrel vaults or four-part groin vaults (see "Arch and Vault," p. 137) reinforced by powerful supporting arches called ribs—a medieval innovation—covered aisles and even naves. **Buttresses** (thick masses of masonry) reinforced walls at critical points and made taller buildings possible. Towers emphasized both the **crossing** (where the nave and transept intersect) and the west façade, which usually contained the principal entrance to the church, often an elaborate portal encrusted with ornamental and figural sculpture.

The plans of Romanesque churches developed in response to the need for more altars for services as congregations increased in size. Additional chapels were also needed to house

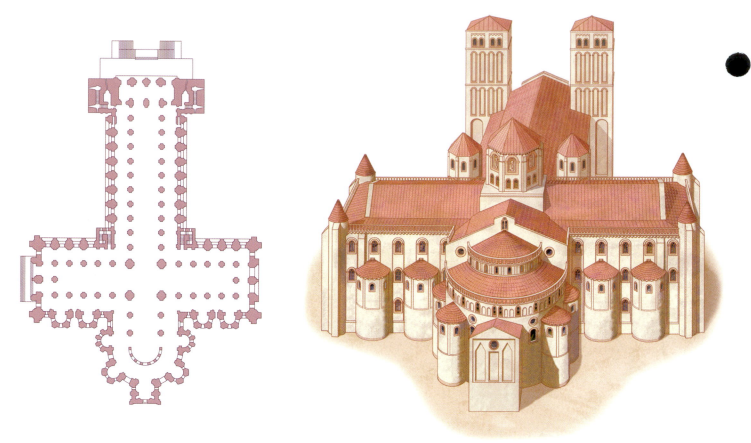

10–18 • PLAN AND RECONSTRUCTION DRAWING OF THE CATHEDRAL OF ST. JAMES
Santiago de Compostela, Galicia, Spain. c. 1078–1122, with later additions.

👁 **Watch** a video about the cathedral of St. James, Santiago de Compostela, on **MyArtsLab**

ever-growing collections of relics. Large interior spaces were necessary to accommodate the crowds of pilgrims who visited churches to venerate these relics, and the visitors needed to be able to move easily from shrine to shrine. Romanesque builders solved these growing demands by increasing the number of chapels on the east side of a wide transept and by adding an ambulatory, or walkway, around the apse, encircled by chapels housing additional altars and relics (**FIG. 10–18**). This permitted pilgrims to circulate freely from chapel to chapel without disrupting regular church services in the main apse.

On entering a Romanesque church like Santiago de Compostela, the viewer's attention is focused forward on the principal altar but is also drawn upward. Barrel vaults, whose strongly expressed transverse arches continue the vertical line of the piers, cover the high spaces of both nave and transepts (**FIG. 10–19**). Groin vaults cover the aisles, and in the upper-level galleries, **half-barrel vaults** (also called **quadrant vaults**) strengthen the building by countering the outward thrust of the high vaults and transferring it to the outer walls and buttresses. Above the church's square crossing, a windowed, octagonal **lantern** tower admits daylight as a beacon, directing the worshipers' attention toward the altar and spotlighting the glittering gold and jewel shrine of the principal **relic**—the body of St. James the Apostle. Throughout the church, half-columns

are attached to all four sides of the piers (for this reason they are known as **compound piers**). Working in concert with the transverse arches that punctuate the vaults, the compound piers divide the building into modular spatial units or bays. And the sculptural quality they give to church interiors emphasizes the stability and monumentality of Romanesque architecture.

Although Romanesque was an architectural style that encompassed the entire breadth of Europe, distinctive local features and traditions distinguished buildings from region to region. In Italy, architects looked to Roman and Early Christian architecture for inspiration. Classical influence was especially strong in the maritime city of Pisa, on the west coast of Tuscany. In 1063, after a decisive victory over the Muslims, the jubilant Pisans began an imposing new cathedral, designed by master builder Busketos as a **cruciform** basilica (**FIG. 10–20**). A long nave with double side aisles (probably an homage to Old St. Peter's) is crossed by projecting transepts, and a dome covers their intersection at the crossing. Unlike early Christian basilicas, the exterior of this cathedral is richly decorated with marble, both the veneer and the attached arcades.

The cathedral was part of an architectural complex at Pisa that also included a circular **baptistery**, begun in 1153, and a campanile, begun in 1174 by master builder Bonanno Pisano. Since this free-standing, cylindrical bell tower was built on

10-19 • INTERIOR OF THE CATHEDRAL OF ST. JAMES

Looking down the nave toward the crossing and choir, Santiago de Compostela. c. 1078–1122.

📖 **Read** the document related to the cathedral of St. James, Santiago de Compostela, on **MyArtsLab**

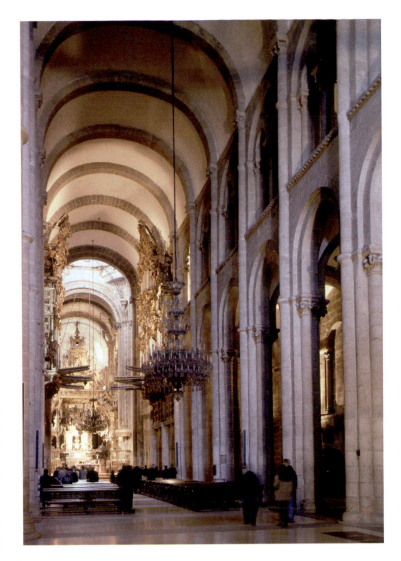

inadequate foundations, it began to lean almost immediately after it was completed and is now famous as "the Leaning Tower of Pisa." Like the cathedral and the baptistery, it is encased in the tiers of the marble arcades that typify Tuscan Romanesque.

Far north of Pisa, builders working in Durham (FIG. **10–21**) made what proved to be very significant advances in the Romanesque structural system. Strategically located on England's northern frontier with Scotland, Durham grew after Duke William of Normandy's conquest of England in 1066 into a fortified complex with a castle, cathedral, monastery, and village, over which the count-bishop held both secular and religious power. His cathedral is one of the most impressive of all medieval buildings as well as one of the most original.

Between 1093 and 1133, the Durham builders developed a new system of vaulting that was carried back to the Norman homeland in France. Massive compound piers alternate with robust columnar piers to support the nave arcade, gallery, clerestory openings, and vaults. The columnar piers are carved with **chevrons** (zigzagging *Vs*), spiral fluting, and diamond patterns, and some have scalloped, cushion-shaped capitals. The ornamental effect was originally enhanced by painting. Above these sculptural nave walls, the masons modified the Romanesque groin-vaulting

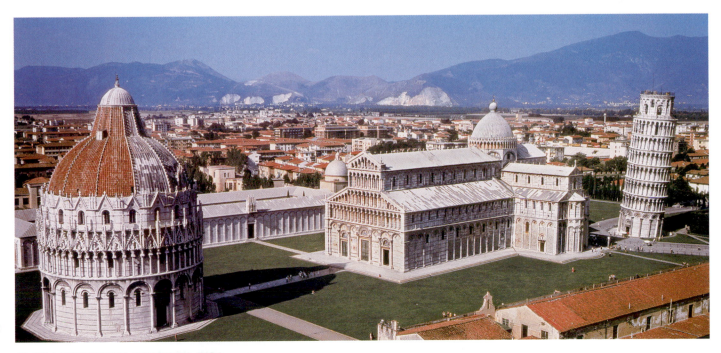

10-20 • CATHEDRAL COMPLEX, PISA

Tuscany, Italy. Cathedral begun 1063; baptistery begun 1153; campanile begun 1174.

EARLY MEDIEVAL AND ROMANESQUE ART **CHAPTER 10 249** ▪

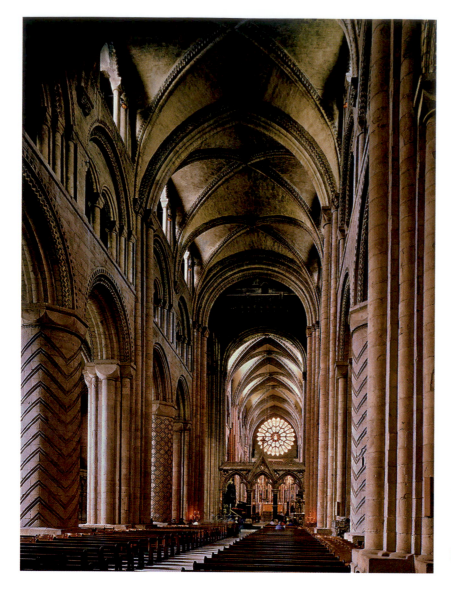

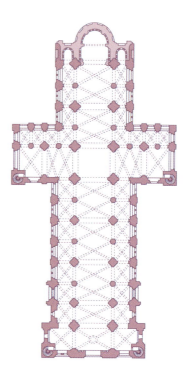

10-21 • INTERIOR VIEW FROM THE WEST AND PLAN OF DURHAM CATHEDRAL
1087–1133. Plan shows original choir, which was replaced in 1242–c. 1280. Vault height about 73′ (22.2 m).

✳ **Explore** the architectural panoramas of Durham Cathedral on **MyArtsLab**

system by applying two pairs of crisscrossing ribs within each long bay. The diagonal ribs create a complex but unifying pattern along the length of the nave, while the boldly projecting transverse arches that separate bay from bay continue the punctuation initiated below by the projecting half-columns of the compound piers. This new system of ribbed groin vaulting would become a hallmark of Gothic architecture, though there it will create a very different aesthetic effect.

Architectural Sculpture and Painting

Architecture dominated the arts in the Romanesque period, not only because it required the material and human resources of entire communities, but because it provided the physical context for a revival of the art of monumental stone sculpture, an art that had been almost dormant in Europe for 500 years. Sculptors provided many Romanesque churches with "speaking" façades, whose richly carved portals are among the greatest artistic achievements of Romanesque art, taking the central messages of the Christian Church out of the sanctuary and into the public spaces of medieval towns. And figural sculpture appeared not only at entrances, but on the capitals of interior as

well as exterior piers and columns, and occasionally spread all over the building in friezes, on corbels, even peeking around cornices or from behind moldings. There was plenty of work for stone sculptors on Romanesque building sites.

At Saint-Pierre in Moissac—a major stop in southwest France on the pilgrimage route to Santiago de Compostela—Abbot Roger (1115–1131) launched an ambitious building campaign that included an imposing portal and projecting porch, encrusted with sculpture (**FIG. 10–22**). A powerful, iconic image of Christ in Majesty dominates the huge **tympanum** (arched half-circle), visualizing a description of his Second Coming in chapters 4 and 5 of the book of Revelation. Although Christ is stable, even static, in this apocalyptic appearance, the figures around him twist with excitement to catch a glimpse of his majestic arrival. Foliate and geometric ornament covers every surface surrounding this tableau, and scalloped profiles of the jambs, as well as the precarious stack of animals on the trumeau (central portal pier) give a sense of instability to the lower part of the portal, as if to underline the ability of the stable figure of Christ in Majesty to provide his own means of support.

Portal sculpture (located around and above the main entrances) was one of the most notable features of Romanesque architecture. The most important carving was located on the lintel, the **tympanum** (the semicircular area above the door lintel), the **archivolts** (the moldings or blocks that follow the contour of the arch), the **trumeau** (the central supporting post), and **jambs** (side posts) of the door.

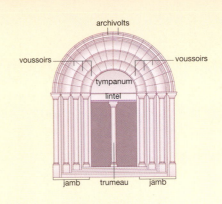

Watch an architectural simulation of a Romanesque church portal on **MyArtsLab**

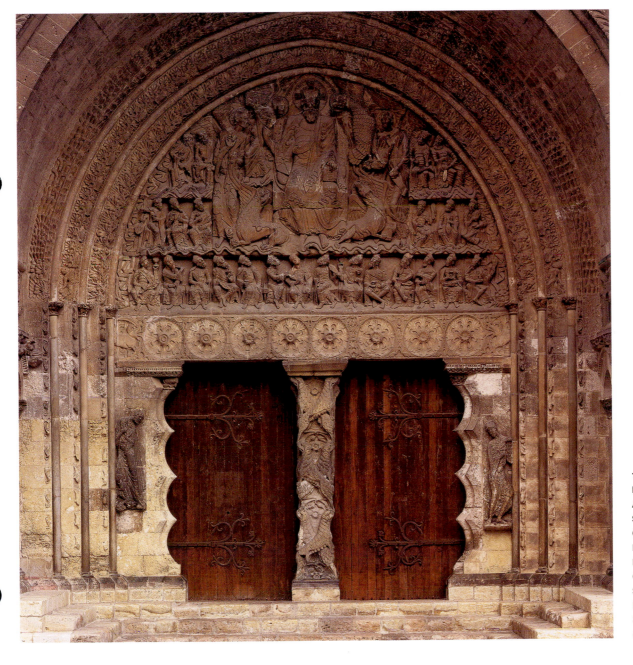

10–22 • SOUTH PORTAL AND PORCH, SHOWING CHRIST IN MAJESTY, PRIORY CHURCH OF SAINT-PIERRE, MOISSAC
Southwest France. c. 1115.

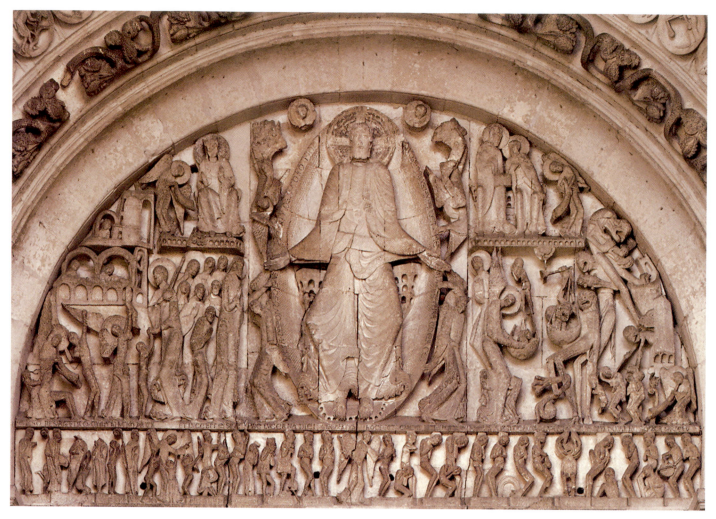

10–23 • Gislebertus (?) THE LAST JUDGMENT, WEST PORTAL, CATHEDRAL (ORIGINALLY ABBEY CHURCH) OF SAINT-LAZARE, AUTUN
Burgundy, France. c. 1120–1130 or 1130–1145.

An inscription just under the feet of the large figure of Christ at the center of this portal proclaims *"Gislebertus hoc fecit"* ("Gislebertus made this"). Traditionally, art historians have seen this as a rare instance of a twelfth-century artist's signature, assigning this façade and related sculpture to an individual named Gislebertus, who was at the head of a large workshop of sculptors. Recently, however, art historian Linda Seidel has challenged this reading of the inscription, arguing that Gislebertus was actually a late Carolingian count who had made significant donations to local churches. Like the names inscribed on many academic buildings of American universities, this legendary donor's name would have been evoked here as a reminder of the rich and long history of secular financial support in Autun, and perhaps also as a challenge to those currently in power to respect and continue that venerable tradition of patronage themselves.

View the Closer Look for the Last Judgment tympanum at Autun on **MyArtsLab**

At the west portal of the Burgundian church of Saint-Lazare at Autun visitors were greeted with a gripping portrayal of the Last Judgment on the tympanum (FIG. 10–23). A monumental Christ, enclosed in a **mandorla** (body halo) held by two svelte angels, presides in judgment over the cowering, naked figures of the resurrected humans at his feet. To worshipers entering the church, the message is clear. The damned writhe in torment on Christ's left (our right) while the saved reach toward an architectural vision of heaven on Christ's right (our left). Since the scene is filled with human interest, viewers can easily project themselves into what is going on. On the lintel, angels physically assist those rising from their sarcophagi, while a pair of giant, pincer-like hands descends aggressively at the right to snatch one of the damned directly into hell. Above these hands, the archangel Michael competes with devils for the souls of those weighed on the scales of good and evil. By far the most riveting players in this drama are the wild, grotesque, screaming demons who grab and torment the damned and even try, in vain, to cheat by yanking the scales to favor damnation. But no vignette is more endearing than the scene at far left, where an angel hoists one of the saved up through an open archway and into the glorious, architectural vision of paradise.

The creation of lively narrative scenes within the geometric confines of capitals (called **historiated capitals**) was an important innovation in Romanesque architectural sculpture. The same sculptors who worked on the Autun tympanum carved historiated capitals for pier pilasters inside the church (**FIG. 10–24**). Several depict scenes from the childhood of Jesus, including one whose charming, doll-like figures enact the scene of Joseph, Mary, and Jesus journeying to Egypt. They are fleeing the paranoid King Herod's order to murder all young boys and eliminate the young royal rival he had learned about from the journeying Magi (Matthew 2:13–16).

The spirit of ancient Rome influenced the work of Italian Romanesque sculptors much as it infused contemporary architecture. The late eleventh-century sculptor Wiligelmo must have been inspired by Roman sarcophagi when he carved the horizontal bands of relief across the west façade of Modena cathedral (**FIG. 10–25**). Wiligelmo took his subjects from the book of Genesis, focusing on events from the Creation to the Flood. This panel shows the **CREATION AND FALL OF ADAM AND EVE**. On the far left, in a mandorla supported by angels, God appears in two persons as both creator and Christ (indicated by the cruciform halo). Following this iconic image, the narrative develops in three scenes from left to right: God creates Adam, then brings Eve from Adam's side, and finally Adam and Eve cover themselves in shame as they greedily eat fruit from the forbidden tree, around which the wily serpent

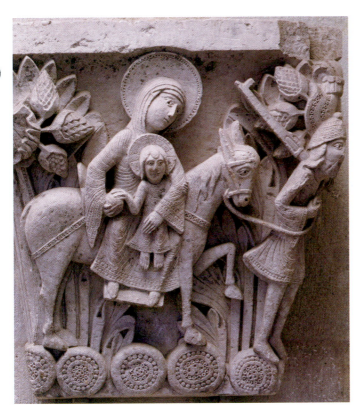

10–24 • THE FLIGHT INTO EGYPT
Capital from the choir pier pilasters, cathedral of Saint-Lazare, Autun. c. 1125.

The decorative wheel forms that appear under the feet of the donkey are probably a reference to the rolling wooden statues used as props in liturgical dramas that were performed in Romanesque churches.

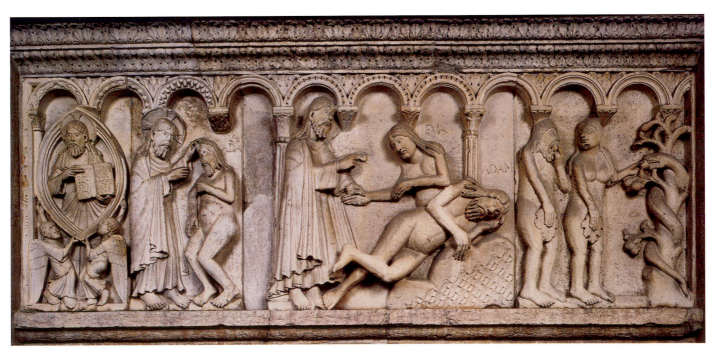

10–25 • Wiligelmo CREATION AND FALL OF ADAM AND EVE
West façade Modena Cathedral. c. 1099. Height about 3′ (92 cm).

A CLOSER LOOK

Bishop Odo Blessing the Feast ▶

From the Bayeux Embroidery, Norman–Anglo-Saxon embroidery from England or France. c. 1066–1082. Linen with wool, height 20″ (50.8 cm). Centre Guillaume le Conquérant, Bayeux, France.

Cooks prepare a feast for the Norman army of Duke William, which has crossed the Channel and assembled on the English coast to wage war against Harold.

The embroiderers, probably Anglo-Saxon women, stitched their designs onto a neutral-colored linen cloth with tightly twisted wool thread, dyed in eight colors. They used only two types of stitches: the quick, overlapping stem stitch which produced a slightly jagged line, and the time-consuming laid-and-couch work used to form the blocks of color that fill the stem-stitched outlines.

Bishop Odo of Bayeux faces forward at the center of the table, hand raised to offer a blessing over the feast laid out before him. Odo's half-brother, Duke William of Normandy (soon to be the Conqueror), sits to his right, while the diner at Odo's left points away from the feast to direct viewers to the next episode.

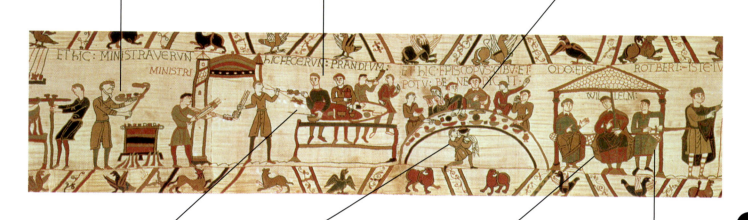

Attendants carry roasted birds on skewers and place them on a makeshift table made of shields resting on trestles. Behind this sideboard, a horn is blown, calling diners to assemble at a curved table laden with food and drink.

A kneeling servant offers a basin and towel so the assembled diners can wash their hands before eating.

Here, William, rather than Odo, takes center stage, his importance underlined by his larger size and the bold embroidery of his name at head level. Those of his companions appear outside the building, above the roof. They have gathered to pin down plans for the next day's battle.

Bishop Odo is engaged in conversation with William, while at right, a man labeled Robert—probably Robert of Mortain, another of William's half-brothers—seems ready to fight, not talk. As he pulls out his sword, its scabbard points viewers onward to the continuation of the story, in a manner similar to the gesturing figure in the previous scene, and the horn blower before that.

🔍 **View** the Closer Look for Bishop Odo Blessing the Feast on **MyArtsLab**

---

twists. Deft modeling and undercutting give these figures a strong three-dimensionality. The framing arcade establishes a stagelike setting, with rock and tree serving as scenery. Wiligelmo's figures exude life and personality. They convey the emotional depth of the narrative they enact, and bright paint, now almost totally lost, must have increased their impact.

Romanesque churches were colorful not only outside but also inside, where frescos, mosaics, or textiles enlivened interior space with religious stories and symbols. The painter of the apse of San Climent in Taull (FIG. 10–26), in the Catalunyan Pyrenees of northern Spain, has almost re-created a Byzantine image of Christ as ruler of the world. Byzantine features include the modeling of forms through the use of repeated colored lines of varying width and shades, and such iconographical features

as the alpha and omega (the first and last letters of the Greek alphabet) flanking Christ and the book he holds in his hands, inscribed in Latin, "*Ego sum lux mundi*" ("I am the light of the world"—John 8:12). But the painter adapted the Byzantine style to the Catalan taste for geometry and ornamental form, turning facial features and draperies into elegant patterns and using wide stripes of color for the background, recalling earlier Spanish Beatus manuscripts (SEE FIG. 10–12).

Manuscripts, Textiles, and Wood Carving

Artists in the eleventh and twelfth centuries were still often monks and nuns. They labored within monastic scriptoria as calligraphers and painters to produce books, and as metalworkers to craft the enamel- and jewel-encrusted items used in

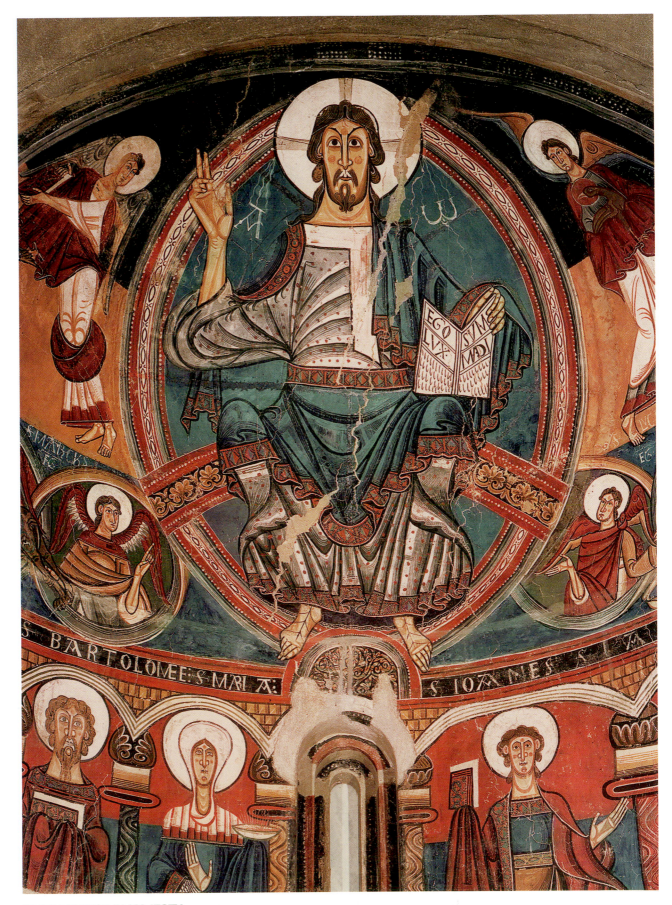

10–26 • CHRIST IN MAJESTY
Detail of apse painting from the church of San Climent, Taull, Catalunya, Spain. c. 1123.
Museu Nacional d'Art de Catalunya, Barcelona.

liturgical services. And they embroidered the vestments, altar coverings, and wall hangings that clothed both celebrants and settings in the Mass. Increasingly, however, secular urban workshops supplied the aristocratic and royal courts with textiles, tableware, books, and weapons, as well as making occasional donations to religious institutions.

Elaborate textiles enhanced a noble's status when hung on the walls of castles and palaces. The Bayeux Embroidery is one of the earliest examples to have survived. (Although traditionally referred to as the Bayeux Tapestry, it actually is an embroidery. In **tapestry**, the colored threads that form patterns or pictures are woven in during the process of making the fabric itself; **embroidery** consists of stitches applied on top of an already-woven fabric ground.) This narrative strip—an astonishing 230 feet long, and containing more than 600 human figures and 700 animals—chronicles the events leading to Duke William of Normandy's conquest of England in 1066, with a clear Norman bias in the telling of the story, even though it may have been Anglo-Saxons who did the actual embroidery (see "A Closer Look," p. 254). Works such as this could be rolled up and transported from residence to residence as the noble Norman owner traveled throughout his domain, and some have speculated that it may have been the backdrop at banquets for stories sung by professional performers who could have received their cues from the identifying inscriptions that accompany most scenes.

Another Romanesque chronicle is the earliest known illustrated history book: the **WORCESTER CHRONICLE** (**FIG. 10–27**), produced in the twelfth century by a monk named John. The pages shown here concern Henry I (ruled 1100–1135), the second son of William the Conqueror to sit on the English throne. The text relates a series of dreams, in which the king's subjects demanded tax relief, and the artist has portrayed these dreams with energetic directness. On the first night, angry farmers (those who work) confront the sleeping king; on the second, armed knights (those who fight) surround his bed; and on the third, monks, abbots, and bishops (those who pray) present their case. In the fourth illustration, the king travels in a storm-tossed ship, saving himself by promising God that he will rescind the tax increase for seven years. The author of the *Worcester Chronicle* assured his readers that this story came from a reliable source—the royal physician Grimbald, who appears in the margins next to the dream scenes. The angry farmers capture our attention today because we seldom see working men with their equipment and simple clothing depicted in painting from this time.

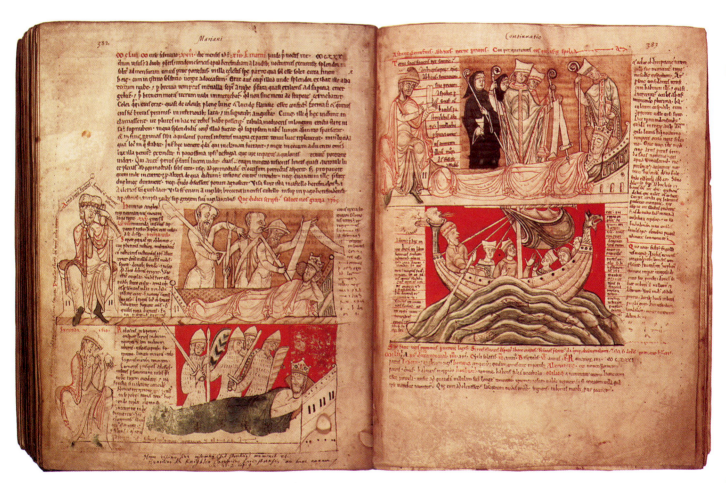

10–27 • John of Worcester **PAGES WITH DREAM OF HENRY I, WORCESTER CHRONICLE**
From Worcester, England. c. 1140. Ink and tempera on vellum, each page 12¾" × 9⅜" (32.5 × 23.7 cm). Corpus Christi College, Oxford (MS 157, pages 382–383).

Hildegard of Bingen

We might expect women to have had a subordinate position in the hierarchical and militaristic society of the twelfth century. On the contrary, aristocratic women took responsibility for managing estates during their male relatives' frequent absences during wars or while serving at court. And women also achieved positions of authority and influence as the heads of religious communities. Notable among them was Hildegard of Bingen (1098–1179). Born into an aristocratic German family, Hildegard became the leader of her convent in 1136, and about 1147 she founded a new convent near Bingen. Hildegard also wrote important treatises on medicine and natural science, invented an alternative alphabet, and was one of the most gifted and innovative composers of her age, writing not only motets and liturgical settings, but also a musical drama that is considered by many to be the first opera. Clearly a major, multitalented figure in the intellectual and artistic life of her time—comparison with the later Leonardo da Vinci comes to mind—she also corresponded with emperors, popes, and powerful abbots.

Following a command she received from God in 1141, and with the assistance of her nuns and the monk Volmar, Hildegard began to record the mystical visions she had been experiencing since she was 5 years old. The resulting book, called the *Scivias* (from the Latin *scite vias lucis*, "know the ways of the light"), is filled not only with words but with striking images of the strange and wonderful visions themselves (FIG. 10–28). The opening page shows Hildegard receiving a flash of divine insight, represented by the tongues of flame encircling her head—she wrote, "a fiery light, flashing intensely, came from the open vault of heaven and poured through my whole brain"—while her scribe Volmar writes to her dictation (FIG. 10–29). But was she also responsible for the arresting pictures of visions that accompany the text in this book? Art historian Madeline Caviness thinks so. Perhaps Hildegard is using the large stylus to sketch on the wax tablets in her lap the pictures of her visions that were meant to accompany the verbal descriptions she dictates to Volmar, who sits at the right with a book in his hand, ready to write them down.

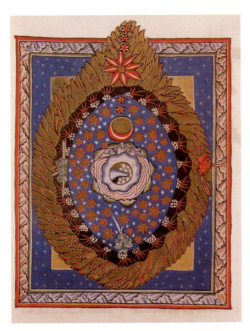

10–28 • Hildegard of Bingen THE UNIVERSE
Facsimile of Part I, Vision 3, of the *Liber Scivias* of Hildegard of Bingen. 1927–1933. Original, 1150–1175.

Hildegard begins her description of this vision with these words: "After this I saw a vast instrument, round and shadowed, in the shape of an egg, small at the top, large in the middle, and narrowed at the bottom; outside it, surrounding its circumference, there was a bright fire with, as it were, a shadowy zone under it. And in that fire there was a globe of sparkling flame so great that the whole instrument was illuminated by it."

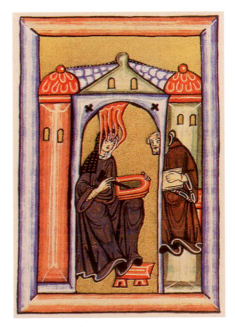

10–29 • HILDEGARD AND VOLMAR
From a facsimile of the frontispiece of the lost *Liber Scivias* of Hildegard of Bingen. Original c. 1150–1175.

This author portrait was once part of a manuscript of Hildegard's *Scivias* that many believe was made during her own lifetime, but it was lost during World War II. Today we can study its images only from black-and-white photographs or from a full-color facsimile copy that was lovingly hand-painted by the nuns of the abbey of St. Hildegard in Eigingen between 1927 and 1933, the source of the figure reproduced here.

In the Romanesque period, as earlier in the Middle Ages, women were involved in the production of books as authors, scribes, painters, and patrons. A Spanish nun named Ende signed a tenth-century manuscript of Beatus's commentaries on the Apocalypse with the words "painter and servant of God." As we have seen, the eleventh-century Abbess Hitda (SEE FIG. 10–16) was an important patron. Working in the early twelfth century, the nun Guda, from Westphalia, was both scribe and painter. In a book of homilies (sermons), she inserted her self-portrait into the letter D and signed the image "Guda, a sinful woman, wrote and illuminated this book" (FIG. 10–30). Guda and her monastic sisters (see "Hildegard of Bingen," p. 257) played an important role in the production of medieval books, and this image is the earliest signed self-portrait by a woman in western Europe.

Since only the wealthiest churches could afford works in precious metals and jewels, wooden sculpture often satisfied the need for devotional images. Statues of the Virgin Mary holding the Christ Child on her lap, a type known as the Throne of Wisdom, were especially popular (FIG. 10–31). Here, Mary is seated on a bench symbolizing the throne of Solomon, the biblical king who embodied wisdom. Posed frontally and rigidly, she supports Jesus securely with both hands. He once held a book—scriptural wisdom—in his left hand and raised his right hand in blessing. For the medieval believer, the wisdom of God became human in Christ; in the medieval scholar's language, he is the Word incarnate. Mary represented the Church, as well as the earthly mother who gave Jesus his human nature and the throne on which he sits in majesty.

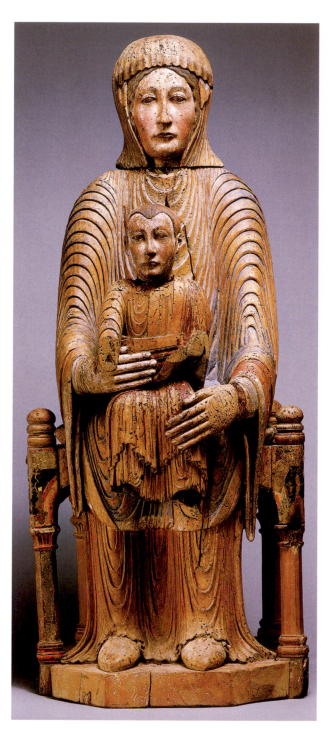

10–30 • SELF-PORTRAIT OF GUDA
From a *Book of Homilies*, Westphalia, Germany. Early 12th century. Ink and color on parchment. Universitätsbibliothek Johann Christian Senckenberg Frankfurt am Main, Germany (MS Barth. 42, fol. 110v).

10–31 • VIRGIN AND CHILD
From Auvergne region, France. Late 12th century. Oak with polychromy, height 31″ (78.7 cm). The Metropolitan Museum of Art, New York. Gift of J. Pierpont Morgan, 1916 (16.32.194).

As the political order of the Western Roman Empire disintegrated, the Christian Church assumed a growing social and intellectual, as well as spiritual, role in Western Europe. Popes and bishops wielded political power; monasteries became sites of learning and art; and the idea of imperial Rome remained strong. When Charlemagne expanded his power and founded a Frankish dynasty in alliance with the pope, he proclaimed his newly acquired status as emperor by emulating Roman art and architecture. At the same time, the artistic abstractions of the former Celtic and Germanic barbarians inspired new artistic traditions in the British Isles.

Christians had long used art to glorify God and convey religious ideas and ideals. During the Romanesque period, the practice blossomed into monumental sculpture and painting integrated into buildings of conspicuous scale and daring structural experimentation. And eleventh- and twelfth-century artists employed a variety of media, developing ever new forms of artistic expression. Their works may have been made for religious contexts, but their focus was on human beings, their stories and struggles, their fears and beliefs. In doing so they were not only satisfying the desires of patrons and viewers of their own time; they were also laying the groundwork for the Gothic art that was to follow.

THINK ABOUT IT

10.1 What aspects of contemporary metalworking traditions are reflected in the representation of Matthew's symbol in FIGURE. 10–3?

10.2 Explain the reference to ancient Roman tradition in the small bronze portrait of a Carolingian ruler in FIGURE 10–6.

10.3 Discuss the subject matter of the bronze doors that Bishop Bernward commissioned for the abbey church of Hildesheim. Why is it appropriate for the entrance to a church?

10.4 Discuss the type of sculpture that was integrated into Romanesque buildings. Where was it located? Why was it there? What sorts of messages did it convey to medieval viewers?

| CROSSCURRENTS |

FIG. 6–32   FIG. 10–6

The equestrian portrait on the right consciously emulates the Roman tradition represented by the work on the left. For the early Middle Ages, this sort of creative appropriation was common artistic practice. Discuss what it tells us about the political pretensions of the Carolingians, grounding your answer in a discussion of these two works.

✓ **Study** and **Review** on **MyArtsLab**

IN PERSPECTIVE

500

St. Patrick in Ireland c. 433–461
Rule of St. Benedict c. 530

600

Visigoths in Spain Adopt
Christianity c. 589

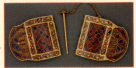

Hinged Clasp, Sutton Hoo
first half of the 7th century

700

Islamic Conquest of Spain 711

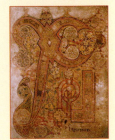

**Chi Rho Page,
Book of Kells**
c. 800

800

Viking Raids Begin 793
Charlemagne Crowned Emperor
by the Pope in Rome
800 (empire lasts until 887)

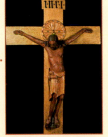

Gero Crucifix
c. 970

900

Ottonian Empire
c. 919–1024

1000

Viking Settlement in
North America 1000

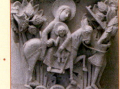

The Flight into Egypt, Autun
c. 1125

William of Normandy
Invades England 1066

First Crusade 1095–1099

1100

Hildegard of Bingen Writes and
Illustrates *Scivias* c. 1141–1151
Second Crusade 1147–1149

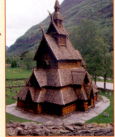

1200

Stave Church, Norway
c. 1125–1150

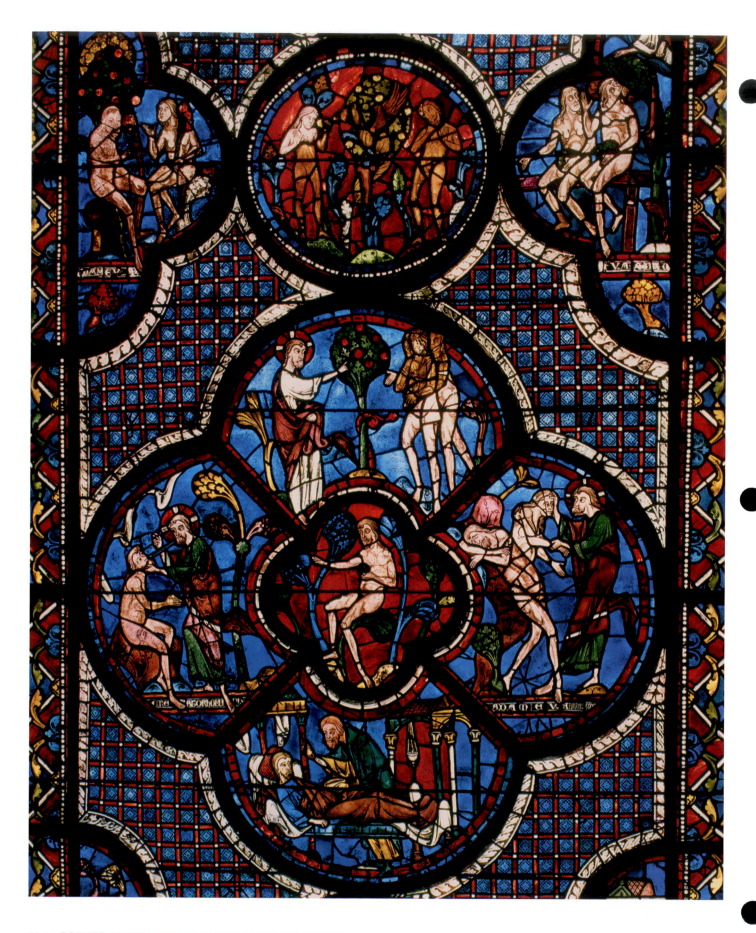

11–1 • SCENES FROM GENESIS IN THE GOOD SAMARITAN WINDOW
Nave aisle, cathedral of Notre-Dame, Chartres, France. c. 1200–1210. Stained and painted glass.

GOTHIC ART

LOOKING FORWARD ▶

The Gothic style dominated much of European art and architecture for 400 years. By the mid twelfth century, advances in building technology, increasing material resources, and new intellectual and spiritual aspirations led to the development of a new art and architecture that expressed the religious and political values of the powerful northern French monasteries where the style was developed. Soon bishops, as well as abbots, were vying to build the largest and most elaborate churches. Just as residents of twentieth-century American cities raced to erect higher and higher skyscrapers, so too the patrons of western Europe competed in the Middle Ages to build cathedrals and churches with ever taller naves and towers, diaphanous walls of glowing glass, and breathtaking interiors that seemed to open up in all directions.

The light captured in stained-glass windows created luminous pictures that must have captivated a faithful population whose everyday existence included little color, outside the glories of the natural world. And the filtered light that passed through these windows transformed interior spaces into a many-colored haze. Truly, Gothic churches became the glorious jeweled houses of God, evocations of the Heavenly Jerusalem. They were also glowing manifestations of Christian doctrine, and invitations to faithful living, encouraging worshipers to follow in the footsteps of the saints whose lives were frequently featured in the windows. Stained glass soon became the major medium of monumental painting.

This detail from the **GOOD SAMARITAN WINDOW** at Chartres Cathedral (**FIG. 11–1**), created in the early years of the thirteenth century, includes scenes from Genesis portraying the creation of Adam and Eve, as well as their subsequent temptation, fall into sin, and expulsion from the paradise of the Garden of Eden to lead a life of work and woe. Adam and Eve's story is used here to interpret the meaning of the parable of the Good Samaritan for medieval viewers, reminding us that stained-glass windows were more than glowing walls activated by color and light. They were also luminous sermons, preaching with pictures rather than with words, and directed at a diverse audience of worshipers drawn from a broad spectrum of medieval society, who derived multiple meanings from such gloriously complicated works of art.

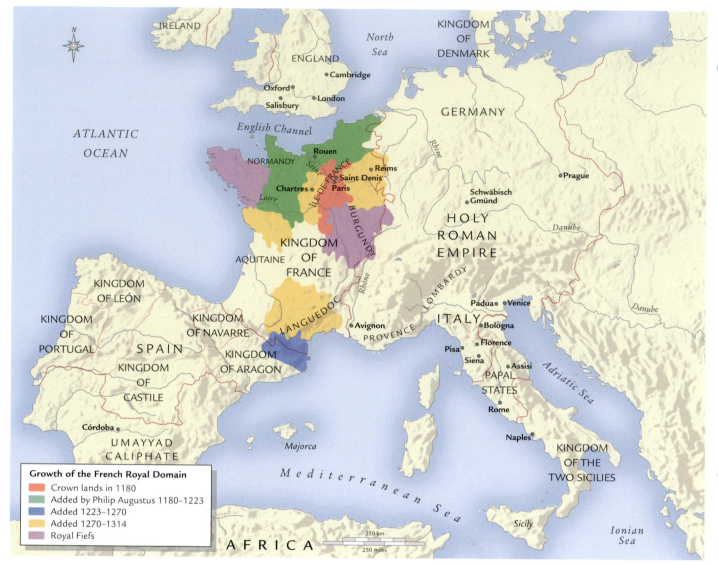

MAP 11–1 • GOTHIC EUROPE AROUND 1200

The color changes on this map chart the gradual expansion of the territory ruled by the king of France during the period when Gothic was developing in the French royal domain.

In the middle of the twelfth century, a distinctive new architecture known today as Gothic emerged in the Île-de-France, the French king's domain around Paris, coincident with the growing power of the French monarchy itself. Within 100 years an estimated 2,700 Gothic churches, shimmering with stained glass and encrusted with sculpture, were built in the Île-de-France region alone. Advances in building technology allowed progressively larger windows and ever loftier vaults supported by streamlined skeletal buttressing. From the capital of Paris, the Gothic style spread throughout Europe and prevailed until about 1400, lingering even longer in some regions (MAP 11–1).

The term "Gothic" was introduced in the sixteenth century by the Italian artist and historian Giorgio Vasari, who disparagingly attributed the by-then-old-fashioned style to the Goths, the Germanic invaders who had "destroyed" the Classical civilization of the Roman Empire that he preferred.

In its own day the Gothic style was simply called "modern art" or the "French style." As it spread from the Île-de-France, it took on regional characteristics and was adapted to all types of structures, including town halls, residences, and synagogues, as well as churches.

During the first flowering of the Gothic style in the twelfth and thirteenth centuries, Europe enjoyed a period of vigorous growth and prosperity. Towns grew into important centers of artistic and intellectual life, while urban universities—first in Bologna, and later in Paris and Oxford—supplanted monastic and cathedral schools as centers of learning. Two new religious orders arose to serve the expanding urban populations, the Franciscans and the Dominicans, whose friars, as these monks were called, wandered the world preaching and ministering to those in need, rather than living a secluded existence in the monastic complex.

Crusades and pilgrimages continued, and increasing contact with the Byzantine and Islamic worlds brought greater access to learned works from Classical antiquity. These writings, particularly those of Aristotle, promoted rational inquiry rather than unquestioning faith as the path to truth, but the thirteenth-century scholar Thomas Aquinas was able to integrate faith and reason in Scholastic philosophy. Artists and master builders of the time, like the Scholastic thinkers, saw divine harmony in rational geometric relationships and expressed these in their art. Unlike their more freewheeling Romanesque predecessors, who used stylization and distortion to achieve emotional impact, thirteenth-century sculptors created more lifelike forms even though they were increasingly suffused with courtly affectation. As in Romanesque, Gothic religious imagery embodied Christian belief, but its effects are more subtle and cerebral, and it incorporates an even wider range of subjects drawn from the natural world. But above all, in Gothic cathedrals medieval worshipers experienced the earthly church as the embodiment of the Heavenly Jerusalem, a celestial city radiant with divine light.

The Origins of Gothic at Saint-Denis

What were the important features of the Gothic style as it appeared at the twelfth-century abbey church of Saint-Denis?

The first Gothic building was the abbey church of Saint-Denis, just north of Paris. This monastery had been founded in the fifth century over the tomb of St. Denis, the early Christian martyr who had been sent from Rome to convert the local pagan population. As early as the seventh century, the monastery had also developed royal significance. Saint-Denis housed the tombs of French kings, the regalia used in royal coronations, and the relics of this patron saint of France.

Construction began on a new church in the 1130s under the supervision of Abbot Suger (abbot 1122–1151), who argued in a written account of his administration that the older building was inadequate to accommodate the crowds of pilgrims who arrived on feast days to venerate the body of St. Denis and too modest to express the importance of the saint himself. In working with builders to conceive a radically new church design, he turned for inspiration to texts that were attributed erroneously to a follower of St. Paul named Dionysius (the Greek form of Denis), who considered radiant light a physical manifestation of God. Through the centuries, this Neoplatonic philosopher also became identified with the martyred Denis whose body was venerated at the abbey, so Suger was adapting what he believed was the patron saint's concept of divine luminosity in designing the new abbey church with walls composed largely of stained-glass windows. In inscriptions he composed for the bronze doors (now lost), he was specific about his motivations for the church's new architectural style: "Bright is the noble work; but being nobly bright, the work should lighten the minds, so that they may travel through the true lights, to the True Light where Christ is the true door" (Panofsky, p. 49).

The **PLAN OF THE CHOIR** (FIG. 11–2, top), built 1140–1144, retains key features of the Romanesque pilgrimage church (SEE FIG. 10–18): a semicircular apse surrounded by an ambulatory, around which radiate seven chapels of uniform size. And the structural elements of the choir had already appeared in Romanesque buildings, including pointed arches, ribbed groin vaults, and external buttressing that relieves stress on tall walls. The dramatic achievement of Suger's builders was the coordinated use of these features to create an architectural whole that emphasized open, flowing space, enclosed by non-load-bearing walls of colorful, glowing stained glass (FIG. 11–2, bottom). As Suger himself put it, the church becomes "a circular string of chapels by virtue of which the whole would shine with the wonderful and uninterrupted light of most luminous windows, pervading the interior beauty" (Panofsky, p. 101).

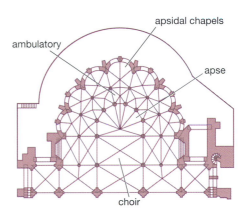

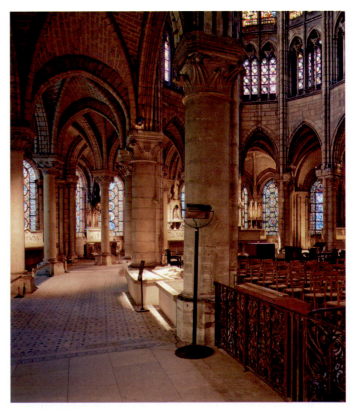

11–2 • **PLAN AND INTERIOR VIEW OF THE CHOIR OF THE ABBEY CHURCH OF SAINT-DENIS**
France. 1140–1144.

📖 **Read** the document related to Abbot Suger on **MyArtsLab**

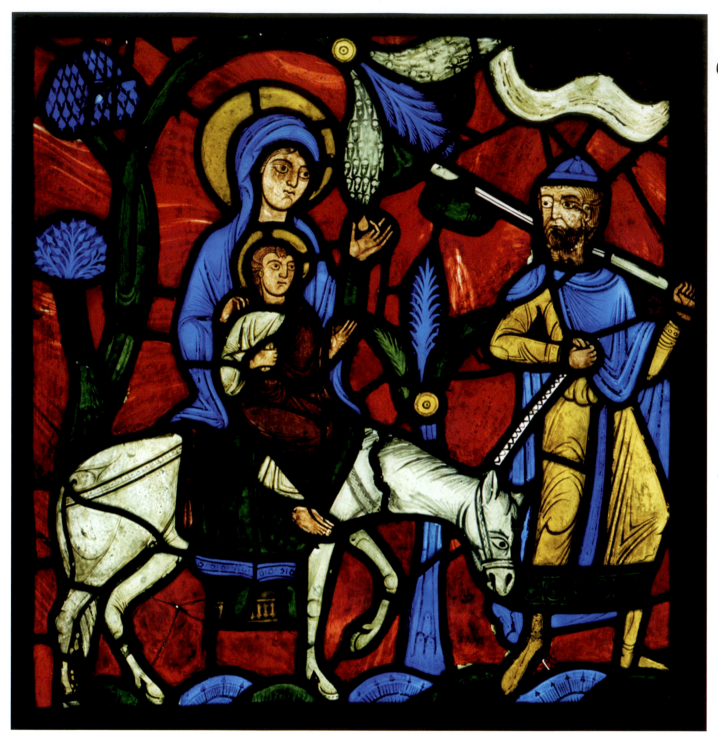

11–3 • FLIGHT INTO EGYPT, FROM THE INFANCY OF CHRIST WINDOW
From the axial choir chapel, abbey church of Saint-Denis. c. 1140–1144. Stained and painted glass,
20½″ × 19¾″ (52 × 50 cm). The Glencairn Museum, Bryn Athyn, Pennsylvania.

And since Suger saw the contemplation of light as a means of illuminating the soul and uniting it with God, he was providing his monks with an environment especially conducive to their primary vocation of prayer and meditation. (For the chalice that Suger designed for use in his new choir at Saint-Denis, SEE FIG. INTRO–10.)

The ground-breaking stained-glass windows of Suger's Saint-Denis were almost lost in the wake of the French Revolution, when this royal abbey represented everything the new leaders were intent on suppressing. Thanks to an enterprising antiquarian named Alexandre Lenoir (1761–1839), however, some twelfth-century windows, though removed from their

The "wonderful and uninterrupted light" that Suger sought in the reconstruction of the choir of Saint-Denis in the 1140s was provided by stained-glass artists who—as he tells us—he called in from many nations to create glowing walls for the radiating chapels, perhaps the clerestory as well. As a result of their exquisite work, this influential building program not only constituted a new architectural style; it catapulted what had been a minor curiosity among pictorial techniques into the major medium of monumental European painting. For several centuries, stained glass would be integral to architectural design, not decoration added subsequently to a completed building. Windows were produced while masons were building walls and carving capitals and moldings.

Our knowledge about the medieval art of stained glass is based on a twelfth-century text, *De diversis artibus* (*On the Various Arts*), written by a German monk who called himself Theophilus Presbyter. In fact, the basic procedure for producing stained-glass windows has changed little since the Middle Ages. It is not a lost art, but it is a complex and costly process. The glass itself was made by bringing sand and ash to the molten state under intense heat, and "staining" it with color through the addition of metallic oxides. This molten material was then blown and flattened into sheets. Using a **cartoon** (full-scale drawing) painted on a whitewashed board as a guide, the

glass painter would cut from these sheets the individual shapes of color that would make up a figural scene or ornamental passage. This was done with a hot iron that would crack the glass into a rough approximation that could be refined by chipping away at the edges carefully with an iron tool—a process called grozing—to achieve the precise shape needed in the final composition.

The artists used a vitreous paint (made, Theophilus tells us, of iron filings and ground glass suspended in wine or urine) at full strength to block light and delineate features such as facial expressions or drapery folds. It could also be diluted to create modeling washes. Once painted, the pieces of glass would be fired in a kiln to fuse the painting with the glass surface. Only then did the artists assemble these shapes of color—like pieces of a complex compositional puzzle—with strips of lead (called **cames**), and subsequently affix a series of these individual panels on an iron framework within the architectural opening to form an ensemble we call a stained-glass window. Lead was used in the assembly process because it was strong enough to hold the glass pieces together but flexible enough to bend around their complex shapes and—perhaps more critically—to absorb the impact from gusts of wind and prevent the glass itself from cracking under pressure.

View the Closer Look on the technique of stained glass on **MyArtsLab**

---

architectural setting, were saved from destruction. During the nineteenth century, parts of them were returned to the abbey, but many panels are now in museums. One of the best-preserved, from a window that narrated Jesus's childhood, portrays the **FLIGHT INTO EGYPT** (FIG. 11–3). The crisp elegance of the delineation of faces, foliage, and drapery—painted with vitreous enamel on the vibrantly colored pieces of glass that make up the panel (see "Stained-Glass Windows," above)—is almost as clear today as it was when the windows were new. One unusual detail—the Virgin reaching out to pick a date from a palm tree that has bent down at the infant Jesus's command to accommodate her hungry grasp—is based on an apocryphal Gospel that was not included in the canonical Christian Scriptures but remained a popular source for twelfth-century artists.

Gothic Art in France

How did Gothic art and architecture develop in France from the twelfth through the fourteenth centuries?

The abbey church of Saint-Denis became the prototype for a new architecture of space and light based on a highly adaptable skeletal framework that supported **rib vaulting** on the points of slender piers—rather than along massive Romanesque walls—reinforced by external buttressing systems. It initiated a period of competitive experimentation in France that resulted

in ever-larger churches enclosing ever-taller interior spaces, walled with ever-greater expanses of stained glass.

At the cathedral of Notre-Dame in Chartres, southwest of Paris, masons built on the concepts pioneered at Saint-Denis. Constructed in several stages beginning in the mid twelfth century and extending into the mid thirteenth, Chartres is an amalgam of early and mature Gothic style. The west façade contains a sculptural program contemporary with the reconstruction of Saint-Denis. Surrounding these three doors—the so-called **ROYAL PORTAL** (FIG. 11–4)—high-relief figures calmly and comfortably fill their architectural settings. On the central tympanum Christ is enthroned in majesty, returning at the end of time. On the right tympanum are scenes from his infancy (representing the Incarnation, his first earthly appearance), and on the left is the Ascension (Jesus's return from earth to heaven). Flanking the three doorway openings are serenely calm **JAMB STATUES** (FIG. 11–5), whose elegantly elongated proportions and linear but lifelike drapery echo the cylindrical shafts behind them. Their meticulously carved, idealized heads radiate a sense of spiritual serenity. The prominence of kings and queens among these jamb statues—presumably representing Christ's royal ancestry in the Hebrew Bible—has given the Royal Portal its name.

The bulk of Chartres Cathedral was constructed after a fire in 1194 destroyed an earlier Romanesque church. Its builders

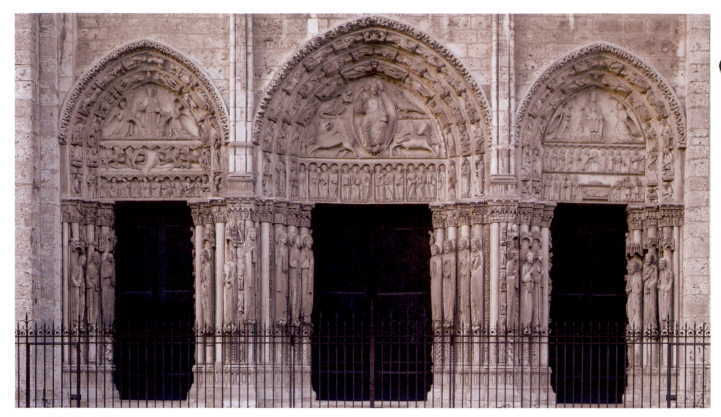

11–4 • ROYAL PORTAL
West façade, Chartres Cathedral. c. 1145–1155.

codified what were to become the typical Gothic structural devices: pointed arches and ribbed groin vaults rising from compound piers over rectangular bays, supported by exterior **flying buttresses** (FIGS. 11–6, 11–7). This system permitted masons to reserve huge high openings for stained-glass windows and reduce the area between clerestory and nave arcade to a short **triforium** (mid-level wall passageway with an arcaded screen), rather than an expanse of flat wall (SEE FIG. 7–8) or a full gallery (SEE FIG. 10–19). This elegant glass-and-masonry shell encloses an enormous open space, with vaults rising 118–120 feet above the floor. In Romanesque churches, worshipers are mainly drawn forward toward the spotlighted apse; at Chartres there is a strong pull upward, to the clerestory windows illuminating the soaring vaults overhead.

Chartres is distinctive among French Gothic buildings in that most of its stained-glass windows have survived, comprising about 22,000 square feet of stained glass installed between 1200 and 1250. The Good Samaritan Window in the nave aisle—visible and legible to viewers, both medieval and modern—illustrates the complexity of Gothic narrative art with a learned allegory on sin and salvation (SEE FIG. 11–1). The principal subject is a parable Jesus told his followers to teach a moral truth (Luke 10:25–37). The protagonist is a traveling Samaritan who cares for a stranger, beaten, robbed, and left for dead by thieves on the side of a road. Jesus's parable is interpreted here as an allegory for his imminent redemption of humanity's sins, since within this window a story from Genesis is juxtaposed with the parable to underscore such an association. Adam and Eve's fall introduced

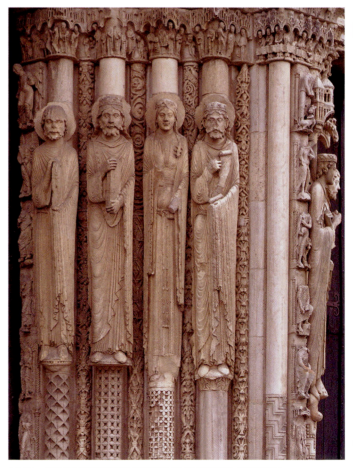

11–5 • JAMB STATUES FROM THE ROYAL PORTAL
Right side of central west door, Chartres Cathedral. c. 1145–1155.

An important innovation of Romanesque and Gothic builders was rib vaulting. Rib vaults are a form of groin vault (see "Arch and Vault," p. 137), in which the diagonal ridges (groins) rest on and are covered by curved, projecting moldings, called ribs. The ribs were constructed first, being supported themselves by timber scaffolding, and when their mortar was set, they in turn supported the forms necessary to build the webbing of the vault. When all the temporary forms were removed, the ribs may have provided strength at the intersections of the webbing to channel load and thrust outward and downward to the foundations; they certainly add visual interest. Ribs developed over time into intricate masonry "skeletons" filled with increasingly lightweight masonry "skins."

👁 **Watch** an architectural simulation about rib vaulting on **MyArtsLab**

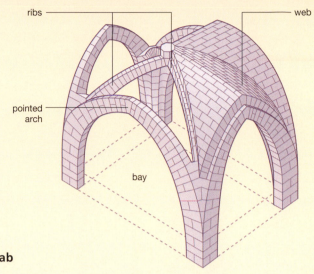

11–6 • **PLAN AND INTERIOR VIEW LOOKING EAST, CHARTRES CATHEDRAL**
c. 1194–1220.

❇ **Explore** the architectural panoramas of Chartres Cathedral on **MyArtsLab**

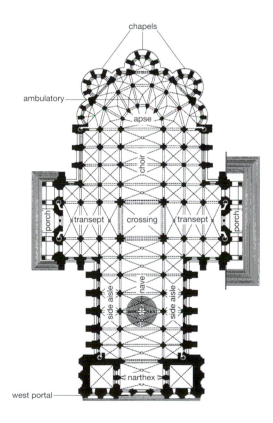

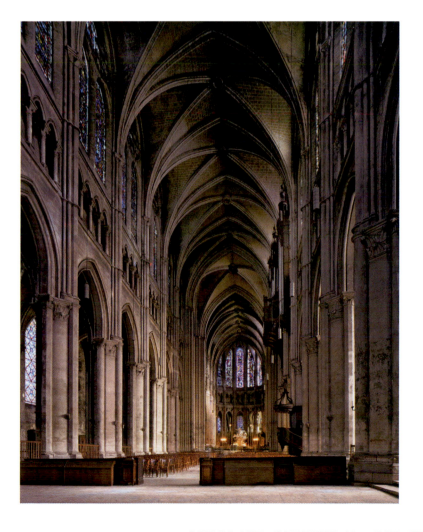

Most large Gothic churches in western Europe were built on the Latin-cross plan, with a projecting transept marking the transition from nave to choir, an arrangement that derives ultimately from the fourth-century Constantinian basilica of Old St. Peter's (SEE FIG. 7–6). The main entrance portal—and sometimes also a narthex—was generally to the west, with the choir and its apse to the east. An ambulatory with radiating chapels circled the apse and facilitated the movement of worshipers through the church.

Many churches have a three-story elevation, with a triforium sandwiched between the nave arcade and a glazed clerestory. Rib vaulting usually covered all spaces. **Flying buttresses** helped support the soaring nave vaults by transferring their outward thrust over the aisles to massive, free-standing, upright external buttresses. Church walls were decorated inside and out with arcades, engaged columns and **colonnettes**, an applied filigree of tracery, and horizontal moldings called **stringcourses**. The pitched roofs above the vaults—necessary to evacuate rainwater from the building—were supported by wooden frameworks. A spire or crossing tower above the junction of the transept and nave was usually planned, though often never finished. Portal façades were also customarily marked by high, flanking towers or gabled porches ornamented with **pinnacles** and finials. Architectural sculpture proliferated on each portal's tympanum, **archivolts**, and **jambs**, and in France a magnificent **rose window** typically formed the centerpiece of façades.

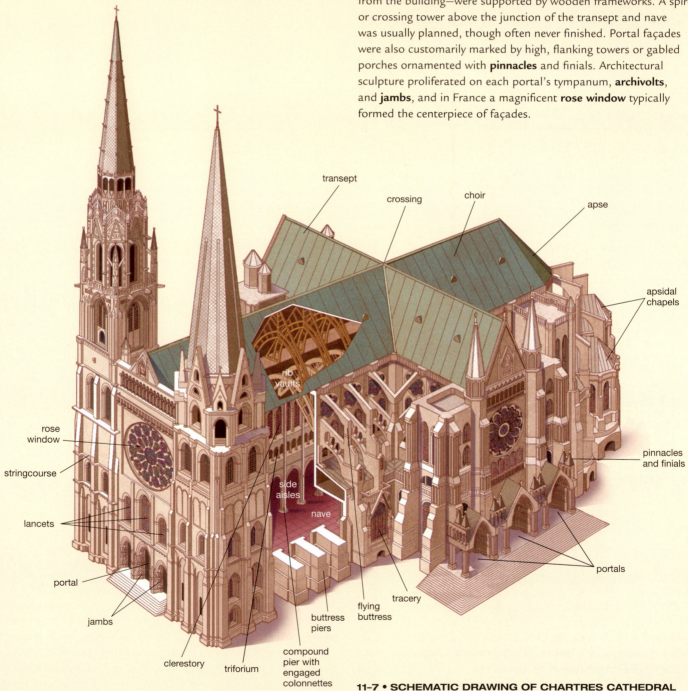

11–7 • SCHEMATIC DRAWING OF CHARTRES CATHEDRAL

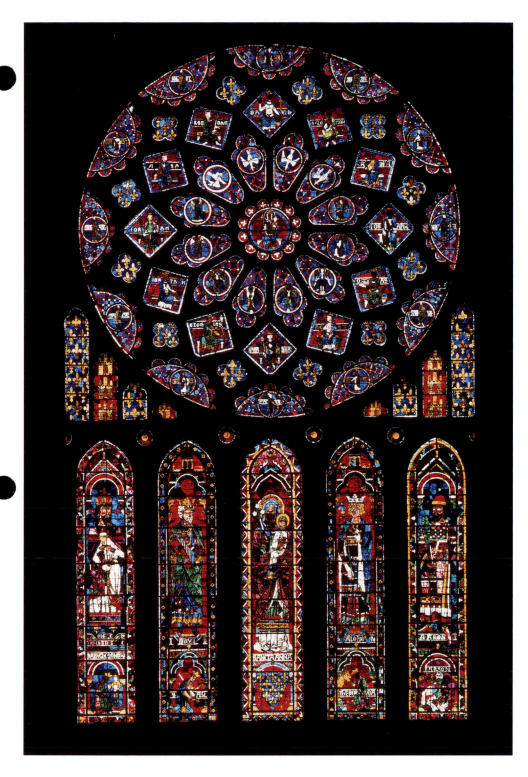

11–8 • ROSE WINDOW AND LANCETS, NORTH TRANSEPT, CHARTRES CATHEDRAL
c. 1230–1235. Stained and painted glass.

View the Closer Look for the rose window and lancets from Chartres on **MyArtsLab**

sin into the world, but Christ (the Good Samaritan) rescues humanity (the traveler) from sin (the thieves) and ministers to them within the Church, just as the Good Samaritan takes the wounded traveler to an inn (bottom scene, FIG. 11–1). Stylistically, these willowy, expressive figures avoid the classicizing stockiness in Wiligelmo's folksy Romanesque rendering of the Genesis narrative at Modena (SEE FIG. 10–25). Instead they adopt the dance-like postures that will come to characterize Gothic figures as the style spreads across Europe in ensuing centuries.

Other windows tell similarly moralizing tales of saints and holy heroes, providing the faithful with role models for a life well lived. But not all windows at Chartres are narrative. Monumental iconic ensembles were easier to "read" in lofty openings more removed from viewers, such as the huge north transept rose floating above five slender lancets (FIG. 11–8), an ensemble proclaiming the Virgin Mary's royal and priestly heritage. In the central lancet, St. Anne holds her daughter, the baby Mary, flanked left to right by statuesque figures of Melchizedek, David, Solomon, and Aaron. Above, in the very center of the rose itself,

Notre-Dame de Paris

The soaring cathedral church of Notre-Dame (Our Lady) of Paris that we see today (FIG. 11–9) began as an early Gothic building bridging the period between Abbot Suger's abbey church of Saint-Denis and the thirteenth-century cathedral of Chartres. Begun in 1163, construction on the choir of Notre-Dame was far enough along for the altar to be consecrated 20 years later. The nave, rising to 115 feet, dates to 1180–1200. The west façade, erected between 1200 and 1250, incorporated an earlier portal made for the twelfth-century church.

After 1225, a new master mason modernized and lightened the building by transforming the clerestory into the large double-**lancet** and rose windows we see today. Notre-Dame may have had the first true flying buttresses (experts are still arguing) although those seen at the right of the photograph, rising dramatically to support the high vault of the choir, result from later remodeling. The 290-foot spire over the crossing is the work of the nineteenth-century architect Eugène Emmanuel Viollet-le-Duc (1814–1879).

Notre-Dame barely survived the French Revolution. Revolutionary zealots decapitated the statues associated with deposed nobility and their "superstitious" religion, and transformed the cathedral into a secular "Temple of Reason" (1793–1795). But it would not be long until Notre-Dame was returned to religious use. Napoleon crowned himself emperor at its altar in 1804, and Parisians gathered there to celebrate the liberation of Paris from the Nazis in August, 1944. Today, boats filled with tourists glide under bridges that link the island where the cathedral stands with the Left Bank, the traditional students' and artists' quarter. Notre-Dame so resonates with life and history that it has become more than a house of worship and work of art; it is a symbol of Paris itself.

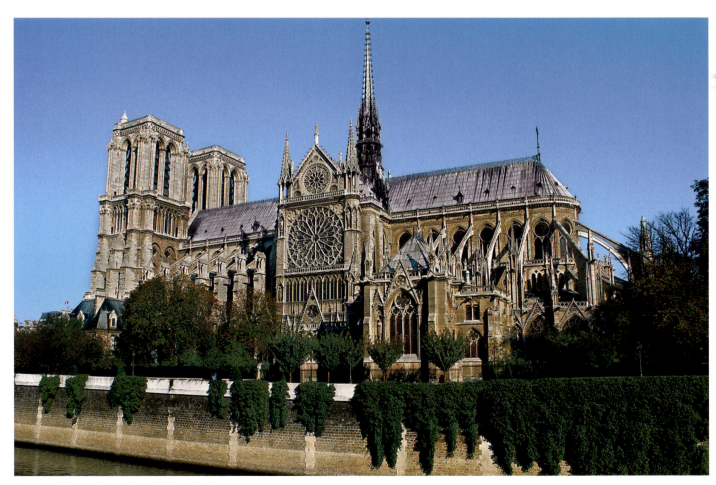

11–9 • CATHEDRAL OF NOTRE-DAME
Seen from the southeast. Paris, France. Begun 1163.

Mary and Jesus are enthroned, surrounded directly by a radiating array of doves and angels, and further out by kings and prophets from the Hebrew Bible. This window was a gift from the young King Louis IX (ruled 1226–1270), probably arranged by his powerful mother Queen Blanche of Castile (1188–1252), who ruled as regent during Louis's minority (1226–1234). Royal heraldic emblems secure the window's association with the king. The arms of France—golden *fleurs-de-lis* on a blue ground—fill a shield, centered under St. Anne. *Fleurs-de-lis* also appear in a series of radiating quatrefoils within the rose and in the graduated lancets bracketing the base of the rose, alternating here with the Castilian device of golden castles on a red ground, a reference to the royal lineage of Louis's powerful mother. Light radiating from the deep blues and reds creates a hazy purple atmosphere in the soft light of the north side of the building. On a sunny day the masonry may seem to dissolve in color, but the theological and political messages of the rose window shine clear.

Important cathedrals were also under construction in Paris (see "Notre-Dame de Paris," p. 270) and Reims (**FIG. 11–10**), the coronation church of French kings. A technique known as **bar tracery**, perfected at Reims, made possible even more expansive walls of glass. In bar tracery, thin stone bars, called **mullions**, form a lacy framework for the glass, replacing the older practice called **plate tracery** in which glass was inserted directly into openings reserved when constructing the wall itself (AS IN FIG. 11–8).

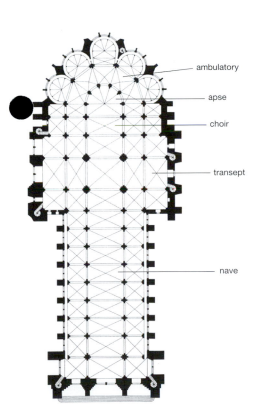

ambulatory

apse

choir

transept

nave

11–10 • PLAN AND WEST FAÇADE, CATHEDRAL OF NOTRE-DAME, REIMS

1220s–1260; towers mid 15th century.

The towers were later additions to this massive cathedral front, as was the row of statues (the so-called Kings' Gallery) stretching across the façade at the base of the towers. The spires were never completed.

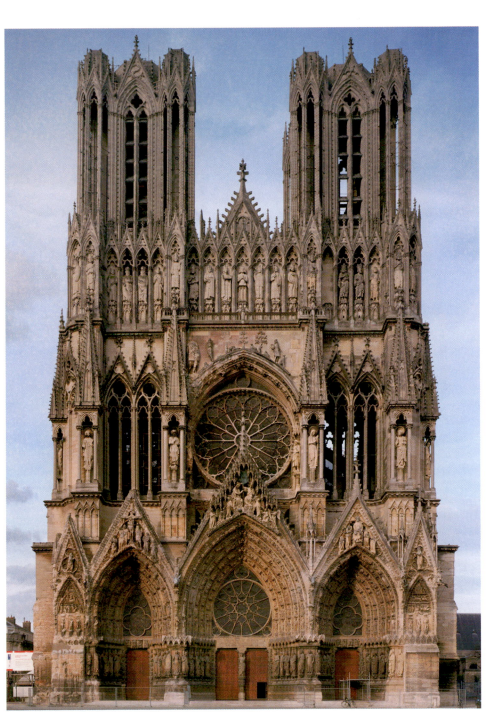

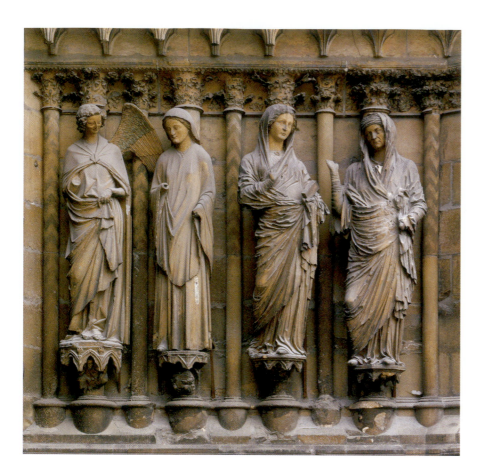

Reims is especially famous for the quantity and quality of its sculpture, which not only encrusts the entire perimeter of the exterior, but even appears on the interior surface of the western wall, where stories enacted by Hebrew Bible prophets and ancestors of Christ served as moral guides for monarchs who faced them when leaving the church after coronation.

The magnificent west façade at Reims has massive gabled portals with soaring peaks sheltering tympana filled with stained-glass windows rather than sculpture. The sheer magnitude of sculpture envisioned for this elaborate cathedral front required the skills of many sculptors, working in an impressive variety of styles over several decades. Four figures from the right jamb of the central portal illustrate this rich stylistic diversity (FIG. 11–11). The pair on the right portrays the Visitation, in which Mary (left), pregnant with Jesus, visits her older cousin, Elizabeth (right), pregnant with St. John the Baptist. The sculptor of these figures, active in Reims about 1230–1235, drew heavily on ancient Roman sources. This is most noticeable in the solidity of the bulky, heavily draped bodies (compare FIG. 6–9). But the women's full faces, wavy hair, and heavy mantles also recall Roman statues, even in their use of the two imperial facial ideals of unblemished youth (Mary) and aged accomplishment (Elizabeth) (compare FIGS. 6–29, 6–30), and they shift their weight to one leg in *contrapposto* as they turn toward each other in conversation.

The pair to the left of the Visitation enacts the Annunciation, in which the archangel Gabriel announces to Mary that she will bear Jesus. This Mary's slight body, broad planes of simple drapery, restrained gesture, inward focus, and delicate features, contrast markedly with the bold tangibility of Mary in the Visitation next to her. She is clearly the work of another sculptor. The angel Gabriel (at far left) represents a third artist, active at the middle of the century. This sculptor created tall, gracefully swaying figures with small, fine-featured heads, whose precious expressions, carefully crafted hairdos, and mannered poses of aristocratic refinement grew increasingly to characterize the figural arts in later Gothic sculpture and painting, becoming the basis for what is called the International Gothic Style, fashionable across Europe well into the fifteenth century.

By the middle of the thirteenth century, builders had thoroughly mastered the design principles and building technology of Gothic architecture and began to focus attention on elaborating and refining the visual elements of the style. They enlarged windows, disguised walls behind carved tracery and bundles of moldings and shafts, and experimented with the linear quality that ribs gave to vaulting. The builders of a new royal chapel in Paris, called the Sainte-Chapelle, pushed the use of stained glass to its limit, almost completely obliterating any sense of a stone wall.

Constructed in 1239–1248 to house King Louis IX's prized collection of relics, the **SAINTE-CHAPELLE** resembles a giant reliquary made of painted stone and glass instead of gold and gems, but turned inside out so that we experience it from within. A ground-level chapel was accessible from the palace courtyard, but the focus here is on a larger upper chapel, used primarily by the royal family. Entering it is like emerging into a glowing jewel box (FIG. 11–12), but this arresting visual impression is only part of the story. The stained-glass windows present extensive narrative **cycles** related to the special function of this chapel. Since they are painted in a bold, energetic style, the stories are easily legible, in spite of their breadth and complexity. Around the sanctuary's **hemicycle** (semicircular space surrounding the altar) are standard themes, such as the Infancy and Passion of Christ, relating to the celebration of the Mass. But along the straight side walls are broader, four-lancet windows whose narrative expanse is dominated by the exploits of the kings and queens of Judah as outlined in the Hebrew Bible, heroes Louis claimed as his own royal ancestors. Above the recessed niche where Louis himself sat at Mass was a window filled with biblical kings, whereas above the corresponding niche on the other

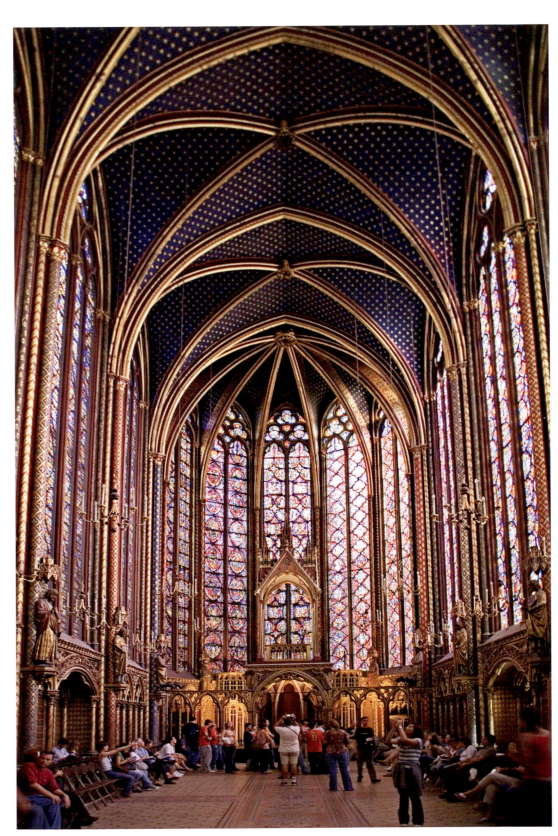

11–12 • INTERIOR, UPPER CHAPEL, SAINTE-CHAPELLE
Paris. 1239–1248.

The direct inspiration for Louis IX's construction of this new royal chapel was the acquisition in 1239 of the regal relic of Christ's crown of thorns, purchased from Baldwin II, Latin ruler of Constantinople. In the charter of 1244 that established services in the Sainte-Chapelle, Pope Innocent IV claimed that Christ had crowned Louis with his own crown, strong confirmation for Louis's own sense of the sacred underpinnings of his kingship.

View the Closer Look for the Sainte-Chapelle on **MyArtsLab**

side of the chapel where his mother, Queen Blanche of Castile, and his wife, Queen Marguerite of Provence, sat, were windows devoted to the lives of Judith and Esther, seen as appropriate role models for medieval queens. Everywhere we look we see kings being crowned, leading soldiers into holy warfare, or performing various royal duties, all framed with heraldic references to Louis and the French royal house. There is even a window that includes scenes from the life of Louis IX himself.

Paris gained renown in the thirteenth century not only for Gothic architecture, stained glass, and sculpture, but also for the production of illustrated books such as small Bibles used by university students, and extravagant devotional and theological works filled with exquisite miniatures for the use of wealthy patrons. One sumptuous example is a three-volume **MORALIZED BIBLE** from around 1230, in which selected scriptural passages are paired with allegorical, or moralized, interpretations, using pictures as well as words to convey the message. The dedication page (**FIG. 11–13**, below left) shows the teenage

King Louis IX and his mother, Queen Blanche of Castile, who served as regent of France until he came of age. The royal pair—emphasized by their elaborate thrones and slightly oversized heads—sits against a solid gold-leaf background under a multicolored architectural framework. Below them, a clerical scholar (left) dictates to a scribe, who seems to be working on a page from this very manuscript, with a column of roundels already outlined for paintings.

This design of stacked **medallions**, forming the layout for each page of this monumental manuscript (**FIG. 11–13**, below right), clearly derives from stained-glass lancets with their columns of superimposed images (SEE FIG. 11–12). But here the schema combines pictures with words. Each page has two vertical strips of painted scenes set against a mosaic-like repeated pattern and filled out by half-quatrefoils in the interstices—the standard format of mid-thirteenth-century windows. Adjacent to each medallion is an excerpt of text, either a summary of a scriptural passage or a terse contemporary interpretation or

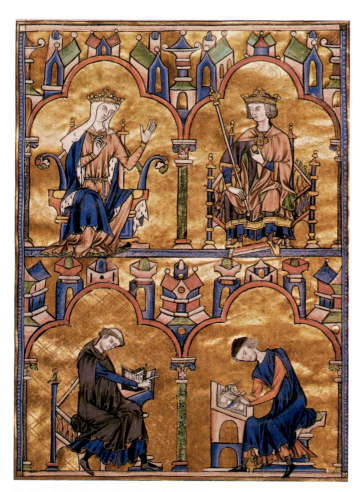

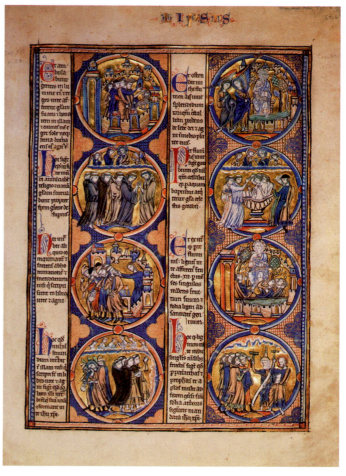

11–13 • TWO PAGES FROM A MORALIZED BIBLE: LOUIS IX AND QUEEN BLANCHE OF CASTILE AND SCENES FROM AND MORALIZATIONS ON THE APOCALYPSE

From Paris. c. 1227–1234. Ink, tempera, and gold leaf on vellum, each page 15″ × 10½″ (38 × 26.6 cm). The Pierpont Morgan Library, New York (MS M240, fol. 8r and 6r).

This three-volume book of biblical commentary in pictures and words seems to have been commissioned by Louis and Blanche as a gift for the cathedral of Toledo in Spain, where most of it still resides. These two illustrations are from eight leaves of the manuscript that somehow made their way out of Toledo and into the art collection of American financier J. Pierpont Morgan (1837–1913).

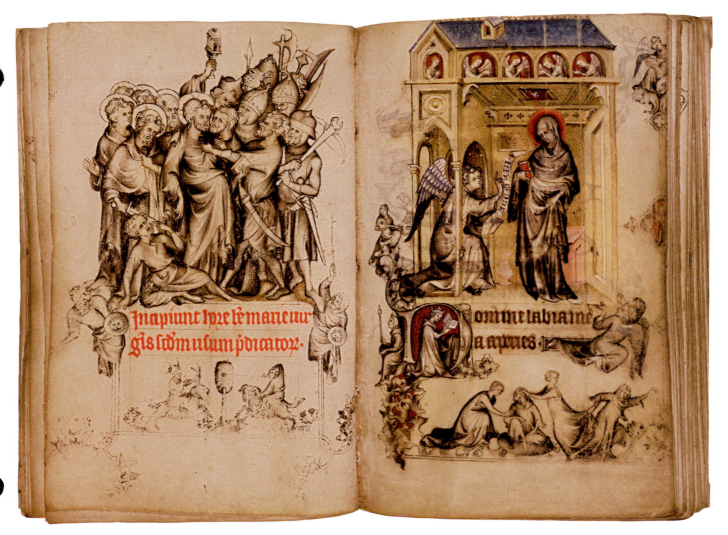

11-14 • Jean Pucelle **TWO-PAGE OPENING WITH THE KISS OF JUDAS AND THE ANNUNCIATION FROM THE HOURS OF JEANNE D'EVREUX**

From Paris. c. 1325–1328. Grisaille and color on vellum, each page 3½″ × 2¼″ (8.2 × 5.6 cm). The Metropolitan Museum of Art, New York. The Cloisters Collection (54.1.2, fols. 15v–16r).

In this opening Pucelle juxtaposes complementary scenes drawn from the Infancy and Passion of Christ, placed on opposing pages, in a scheme known as the Joys and Sorrows of the Virgin. The "joy" of the Annunciation on the right is paired with the "sorrow" of the betrayal and arrest of Christ on the left.

allegory. Both pictures and texts alternate between scriptural summaries and their moralizing explications, outlined in words and visualized with pictures. This adds up to a very learned and complicated compilation, perhaps devised by clerical scholars at the University of Paris, and certainly painted by some of the most important professional artists in Paris.

By the late thirteenth century, private prayer books were becoming popular among wealthy patrons. Called **Books of Hours** because they contain special prayers to be recited at the eight canonical devotional "hours" between morning and night, these books included everything a lay person needed for pious practice—psalms, offices of the Virgin and other saints, a calendar of feast days, and prayers for the dead. They were often personalized for individual patrons by including prayers to favorite or patron saints or by focusing on a personal devotional practice. Sometimes they record important

events in the patron's life, for example marriage or the birth and baptisms of children.

A tiny, exquisite Book of Hours given by King Charles IV of France (ruled 1322–1328) to his young wife, Queen Jeanne d'Evreux, around the time of their marriage in 1325, is the work of renowned painter Jean Pucelle (**FIG. 11–14**). Abandoning the intense colors used by earlier illuminators, Pucelle worked in **grisaille** (paintings executed only in shades of gray), adding only delicate touches of color. In the Annunciation, to the right on this two-page opening, an elegantly swaying Mary receives the archangel Gabriel in a room that seems to project outward from the page toward the viewer. Queen Jeanne herself appears in the initial "D" below the Annunciation, kneeling before a lectern and reading from her Book of Hours, perhaps beginning her private devotions with the very words written on this page: "*Domine labia mea aperies*" ("O Lord open thou my

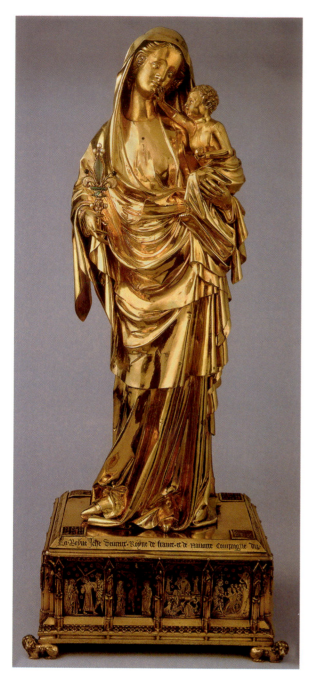

lips"—Psalm 51:15). This inclusion of the praying patron's portrait, a practice that continued in monumental painting and sculpture through the fifteenth century (SEE FIGS. 12–3, 12–7), conveyed the idea that these pictures were not scenes illustrating a continuing story, but personal "visions" inspired by meditation. In the Kiss of Judas on the left page, the traitorous disciple Judas Iscariot embraces Jesus, betraying him to soldiers who have come to seize him and setting in motion the events that lead to the Crucifixion. The spoof of military training sketched below, showing "knights" riding goats and jousting at a barrel stuck on a pole, may be a commentary on the lack of valor shown by the soldiers assaulting Jesus.

These paintings show Pucelle's debt to the sculptural and painting style associated with the French court. Softly modeled, voluminous draperies are gathered loosely, falling in projecting diagonal folds around tall, elegantly posed figures with carefully arranged curly hair and broad foreheads. Jesus on the left and Mary on the right stand in the swaying S-curve pose typical of French art since the middle of the thirteenth century (SEE FIG. 11–11, leftmost figure), accepting their destiny with courtly decorum.

During the fourteenth century religious subjects became more emotionally expressive, especially in small, precious objects that demanded close scrutiny from viewers. A silver-gilt image of a standing **VIRGIN AND CHILD** (FIG. 11–15) is a rare survivor that verifies the acclaim that was accorded Parisian goldsmiths. An inscription on the base documents the statue's donation to the abbey of Saint-Denis in 1339 by Queen Jeanne d'Evreux, whose Book of Hours we already know. The Virgin cradles her son in her left arm, and supports her weight on her left leg, creating the graceful S-curve pose that was a stylistic signature of the period. Jesus's tender gesture, lightly caressing his mother's chin, gives the regal rendering a distinctly human touch.

Not all Gothic art was made for churches or portrayed religious themes. Among the most sumptuous and sought-after Parisian luxury products were small chests assembled from carved ivory plaques that were used by wealthy women to store jewelry or other personal treasures. The entirely secular subject matter of these chests was romantic love. Indeed, they seem to have been courtship gifts by smitten men to desired women, or wedding presents offered by grooms to their brides.

On the lid of one ivory box, jousting is the theme (FIG. 11–16). Spread over the central two panels, a single scene catches two

11–15 • VIRGIN AND CHILD
From the abbey church of Saint-Denis.
c. 1324–1339. Silver gilt and enamel,
height 27⅛" (69 cm).
Musée du Louvre, Paris.

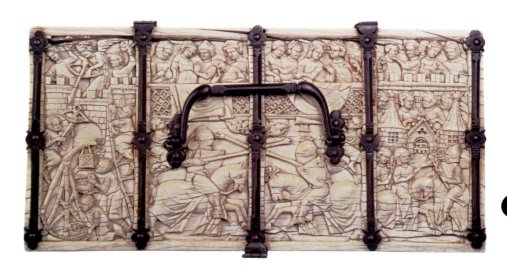

11–16 • JOUSTING AND ATTACK ON THE CASTLE OF LOVE
Top of an ivory chest. From Paris. c. 1330–1350. Elephant ivory with modern iron mounts, 4⅞" × 9¹¹⁄₁₆" (12.4 × 24.6 cm). The Walters Art Museum, Baltimore.

charging knights in the heat of a tournament, while trumpeting heralds call the attention of spectators, lined up above in a gallery to observe this public display of virility. The panel at right mocks the very ritual showcased in the middle panels by pitting a woman against a knight, battling not with lances but with a long-stemmed rose (symbolizing sexual surrender) and an oak bough (symbolizing fertility). Instead of observing these silly goings-on, however, the spectators tucked into the upper architecture pursue their own flirtations. Finally, in the scene on the left, knights use crossbows and a catapult to hurl roses at the Castle of Love, while Cupid returns fire with his seductive arrows. The miniature fortifications that form the backgrounds—with their crenellated walls and symmetrical towers—remain even now symbols of the aristocratic castles of the Middle Ages.

Gothic Art in England and Germanic Lands

How does the thirteenth- and fourteenth-century Gothic art and architecture of England and Germanic lands compare with the foundational monuments in France?

As the Gothic style spread outside France, it not only became an international style in Europe but—in the thirteenth and fourteenth centuries—also took on innovative regional forms. In England, for instance, there was less emphasis on height than in France. English churches have long, broad naves and screenlike façades. Walls, even if they retained a Romanesque sense of solidity and horizontal continuity, were enlivened by an elaborate, linear profusion of arch moldings and by clusters of applied colonnettes often in contrasting colors of stone.

The thirteenth-century **CATHEDRAL OF SALISBURY** (1220–1258) is an excellent example of English Gothic architecture (**FIG. 11–17**). Typically English is the park-like setting (the cathedral close, or precinct) and attached cloister and chapter house for the cathedral clergy. Many English churches were completed with splendid towers and spires in the fourteenth century, and at Salisbury, about 1320–1330, Master Richard of

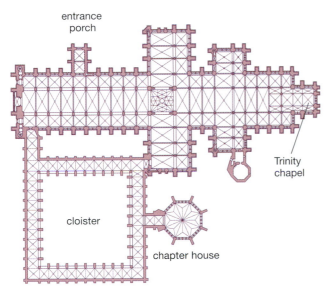

11–17 • PLAN AND VIEW FROM ABOVE, SALISBURY CATHEDRAL
England. 1220–1258; cloister and chapter house 1263–1284.

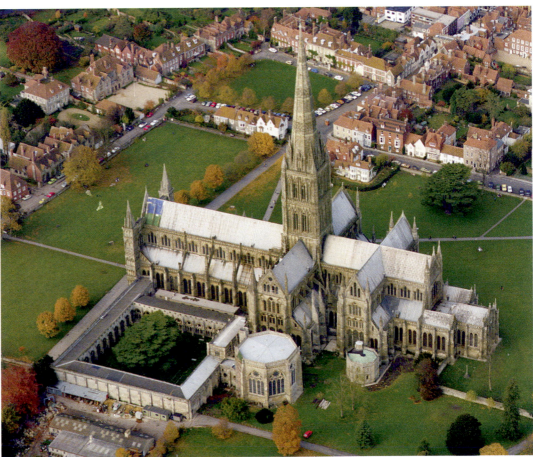

Farleigh built a crossing tower with a spire rising to the extraordinary height of 400 feet. Taller than anything visualized by the original builders, the spire required extra buttressing, so the builders added flying buttresses.

Typical of English cathedrals, **SALISBURY** has wide projecting transepts (double transepts, in this case), a square east end, with a spacious sanctuary. The interior **(FIG. 11–18)** reflects enduring Norman traditions (SEE FIG. 10–21), with its heavy walls and tall nave arcade surmounted by a gallery and a clerestory with simple lancet windows, but the effect is quite different. A strong emphasis on the horizontal movement of the arcades, unbroken by any continuous vertical projections from the compound piers, directs attention forward to the altar,

rather than upward into the vaults. The shafts supporting the four-part rib vaults are made of a darker stone called Purbeck marble that contrasts with the lighter stone of the rest of the interior. The original painting and gilding of the stonework would have enhanced the effect.

Like the French, the English made richly decorated books. The dazzling artistry and delight in ambiguity and contradiction that had marked early medieval manuscripts in the British Isles (SEE FIG. 10–1) survives into the Gothic period in the *Windmill Psalter* of about 1270–1280. The letter *B*—the first letter of Psalm 1, which begins with the words "*Beatus vir qui non abit in consilio impiorum*" ("Happy are those who do not follow the advice of the wicked")—fills the entire left page of this

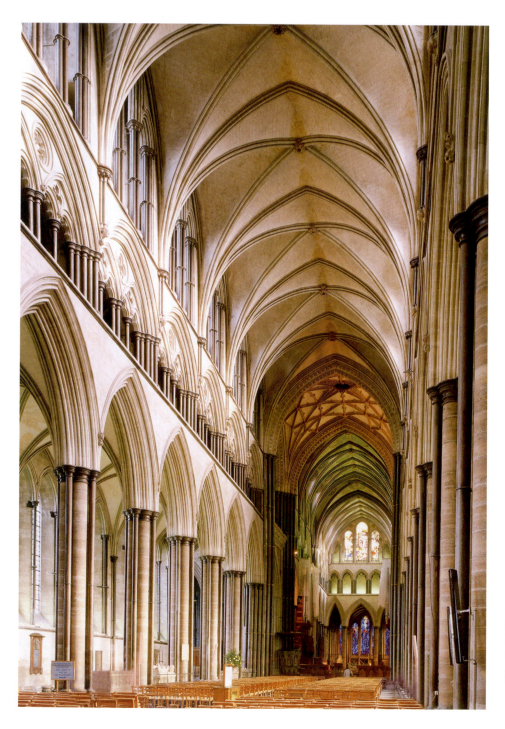

11–18 • NAVE, SALISBURY CATHEDRAL
Looking east toward the high altar. 1220–1258.

✳ **Explore** the architectural panoramas of Salisbury Cathedral on **MyArtsLab**

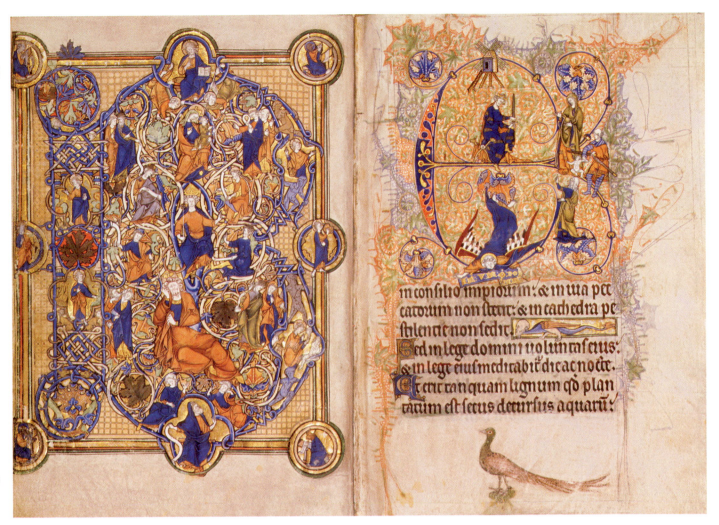

11–19 • TWO-PAGE OPENING WITH PSALM 1 FROM THE WINDMILL PSALTER
From London. c. 1270–1280. Ink, pigments, and gold on vellum, each page 12¾″ × 8¾″
(32.3 × 22.2 cm). The Pierpont Morgan Library, New York (M. 102, fols. 1v-2r).

View the Closer Look for the two-page opening with Psalm 1
from the *Windmill Psalter* on **MyArtsLab**

opening and outlines a densely interlaced thicket of tendrils and figures **(FIG. 11–19)**. This is a Tree of Jesse, a genealogical diagram of Jesus's royal and spiritual ancestors in the Hebrew Bible based on a prophecy in Isaiah 11:1–3. An oversized, reclining figure of Jesse, father of King David, appears sheathed in a red mantle, with the blue trunk of a vinelike tree emerging from his side. Above him is his majestically enthroned royal son, who, as an ancestor of Mary just above him, is also an ancestor of Jesus, who appears at the top of the sequence. In the circling foliage flanking this sacred royal family tree are a series of prophets, representing Jesus's spiritual heritage.

E, the second letter of the psalm's first word, only appears at the top of the right page and is formed from large tendrils emerging from delicate background vegetation to support the figures of characters in the story of the Judgment of Solomon portrayed within it (I Kings 3:16–27). Two women (one above the other at the right) claiming the same baby appear before King Solomon (enthroned on the crossbar) to settle their dispute. The king's

judgment is to order a guard to slice the baby in half with his sword and give each woman her share. This trick exposed the real mother, who hastened to give up her claim in order to save the baby's life. The rest of the psalm's opening words appear on a banner carried by an angel who swoops down at the bottom of the *E*.

Surprising images proliferate among the pages' foliage; many are visual puns on the text. For example, the large windmill (that gives the Psalter its name) at the top of the initial *E* evokes the statement in the psalm that the wicked would not survive Judgment but would become "like chaff driven by the wind" (Psalm 1:4). Such imagery would have stimulated the user's contemplation of the inner meanings of the text's familiar messages.

The English were also renowned for pictorial needlework, using colored silk and gold thread to create images as detailed as the painters produced in manuscripts. Popular throughout Europe, this art came to be called *opus anglicanum*

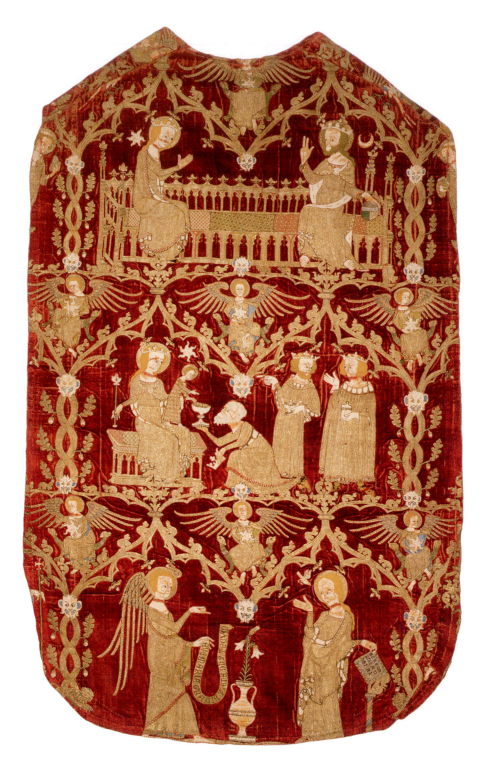

11–20 • SCENES FROM THE LIFE OF THE VIRGIN, BACK OF THE CHICHESTER-CONSTABLE CHASUBLE
From a set of vestments embroidered in *opus anglicanum* in southern England. c. 1330–1350. Red velvet with silk, metallic thread, and seed pearls; length 4′ 3″ (1.29 m), width 30″ (76 cm). The Metropolitan Museum of Art, New York. Fletcher Fund, 1927 (2.7 162.1).

(English work). The names of several prominent embroiderers are known, but in her own day no one surpassed Mabel of Bury St. Edmunds, who created both religious and secular work for King Henry III (ruled 1216–1272). None of Mabel's work has been identified, but perhaps it resembled the embroidery on the **CHICHESTER-CONSTABLE CHASUBLE (FIG. 11–20)**—a vestment worn by priests celebrating the Mass with images formed by subtle gradations of colored silk. The Annunciation, the Adoration of the Magi, and the Coronation of the Virgin are arranged in three registers framed by cusped, crocketed arches, supported on animal heads and twisting branches sprouting

oak leaves with seed-pearl acorns. As the priest moved, the vestment would have glinted in the candlelight. So heavy did such gold and bejeweled garments become that their wearers often needed help to move.

Germanic Lands

East of England and France, in the Germanic lands of the Holy Roman Empire, a new type of Gothic architecture developed in the thirteenth century in response to the increasing importance of sermons within church services. These so-called **hall churches** featured a nave and side aisles with vaults of equal height, creating a spacious and open interior that could accommodate the large crowds drawn by charismatic preachers.

The flexible design of the hall church made it widely adaptable. Built in the third quarter of the thirteenth century using the hall church design, Prague's **OLD-NEW SYNAGOGUE (ALTNEUSCHUL)** is the oldest functioning synagogue in Europe (**FIG. 11-21**). Like a hall church, the vaults of the synagogue are all the same height. But unlike a basilican church, with its division into nave and side aisles, the Altneuschul has two aisles, each with three bays of four-part rib vaulting, supported by the walls and two octagonal piers. A nonfunctional fifth rib has been added to each vault, perhaps to undermine the cross form made by the intersecting diagonal ribs.

The synagogue has two focal points, the *aron*, or shrine for the Torah scrolls, located on the east wall, toward Jerusalem, and a central raised reading platform called the *bimah*, here straddling the two central bays. The interior of the Altneuschul was originally richly adorned with murals.

In the fourteenth century, architects of the famous Parler family also experimented with the form of the hall church. Heinrich Parler designed and began the **CHURCH OF THE HOLY CROSS** in Schwäbisch Gmünd, Swabia, in 1317 (**FIG. 11-22**). In 1351, his son Peter (c. 1330–1399), the most

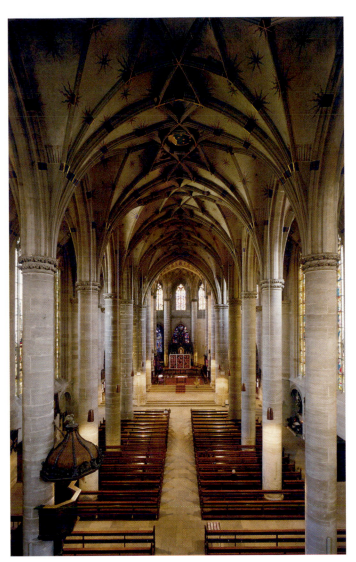

11-22 • Heinrich and Peter Parler
CHURCH OF THE HOLY CROSS
Schwäbisch Gmünd, Germany. Begun 1317; choir 1351; vaulting completed 16th century.

brilliant architect of this talented family, joined the workshop. He designed the choir as a vast hall church whose triple-aisled form was enlarged by a ring of deep chapels between the buttresses. The unity of the entire space was enhanced by the complex web vault that distracted from the division of the interior space into bays. Charles IV of Bohemia (ruled 1346–1375) recognized Peter's talent and in 1353 called on him to build the cathedral of Prague, Charles's capital city. Henceforth Peter Parler and his heirs were the most influential architects in the Holy Roman Empire.

Late Medieval Art in Italy

What are the important developments in Italian sculpture and painting during the late Middle Ages?

The thirteenth century was a period of political division and economic expansion for the Italian peninsula. The papacy had emerged from a conflict with the Holy Roman Empire as a

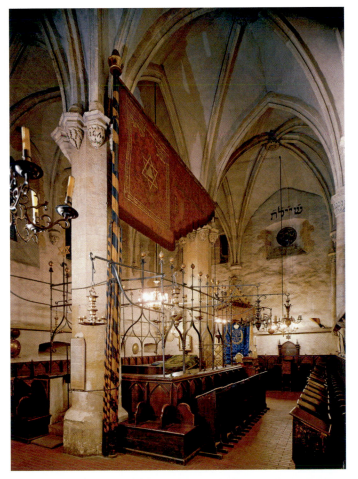

11-21 • INTERIOR, OLD-NEW SYNAGOGUE (ALTNEUSCHUL)
Prague, Bohemia (Czech Republic). c. late 13th century; *bimah* after 1483.

Effects of Good Government in the City and in the Country ▶

Ambrogio Lorenzetti, fresco in the Sala della Pace, Palazzo Pubblico, Siena, Italy. 1338–1340. Total length of fresco c. 46′ (14 m).

Ambrogio paid tribute to his patrons by discreetly tucking into this corner of the fresco an idealized portrait of Siena, identified by the inclusion of the dome of the cathedral and its distinctively striped campanile.

Featured in the foreground next to a shoemaker's shop is a sinuous string of dancers holding hands—probably a professional troupe of male entertainers masquerading as women as part of a spring festival. One figure stands behind, singing and playing a tambourine to provide the musical accompaniment.

High on the rooftops, a team of masons stand on exterior scaffolding constructing the wall of a new building—a sure sign of urban prosperity and a rare glimpse of medieval laborers at work.

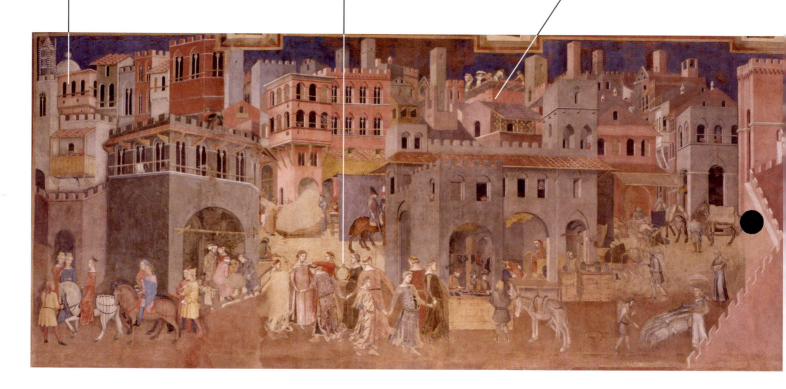

📷 **View** the Closer Look for *Effects of Good Government in the City and in the Country* on **MyArtsLab**

significant international force, but its temporal success weakened its spiritual authority and brought it into conflict with the growing power of the kings of France and England. In 1309, after the election of a French pope, the papal court moved from Rome to Avignon, in southern France. During the Great Schism of 1378 to 1417, there were two rival lines of popes, one in Rome and one in Avignon, each claiming legitimacy.

A growing sense of individualism promoted patronage of the arts, and artists began to emerge as independent agents. Their ambitiousness and their sense of stylistic individualism reflected their economic and social freedom. Although their

methods and working conditions remained largely unchanged, they now formed powerful urban **guilds** and contracted freely with wealthy townspeople and nobles as well as with civic and religious institutions.

For example, in 1338, the city council of Siena commissioned Ambrogio Lorenzetti to paint murals in a room called the Sala della Pace (Chamber of Peace) in the city hall. The theme was to be the contrast between the effects of good and bad government on people's lives (see "A Closer Look," above). For the *Effects of Good Government in the City*, Ambrogio portrayed a vibrant urban scene filled with the bustling activity of

Hovering above the gate that separates city and country life is a woman clad in a wisp of transparent drapery, a scroll in one hand and a miniature gallows complete with a hanged man in the other. She represents Security, and her scroll bids those coming into the city to enter without fear because she has taken away the power of the guilty who would harm them.

Two aristocrats on horseback ride out into the country to go hawking, passing by a line of peasants bringing pigs and produce up the hill in the opposite direction into town.

Ambrogio's agricultural panorama shows activities of all seasons simultaneously: sowing, hoeing, and harvesting.

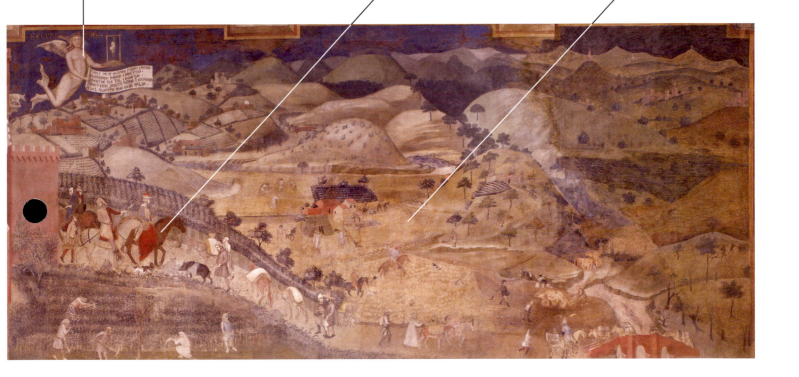

productive citizens, who also have time for leisurely diversions. He shows the city from shifting viewpoints so we can see as much as possible, and renders its inhabitants larger in scale than the buildings around them so as to highlight their activity. *Effects of Good Government in the Country* is a panoramic landscape, showing a natural world marked by agricultural activity and harmonious coexistence, with little regard to class distinctions. Ambrogio's vision is of an orderly society, urban as well as rural, marked by peace and plenty. Sadly, famine, poverty, and the horrible epidemic of the Black Death overtook Siena just a few years after this work was completed.

Sculpture

In the first half of the thirteenth century, Holy Roman Emperor Frederick II had fostered a Classical revival at his southern Italian court, a revival that inspired artists to turn to Roman sculpture for inspiration. Nicola Pisano (active c. 1258–1278), who moved from the south to Tuscany at mid-century, brought this classicizing initiative with him. An inscription on a freestanding marble pulpit in the Pisa Cathedral baptistery identifies Nicola as a supremely self-confident sculptor: "In the year 1260 Nicola Pisano carved this noble work. May so gifted a hand be praised as it deserves." The rectangular panels forming the

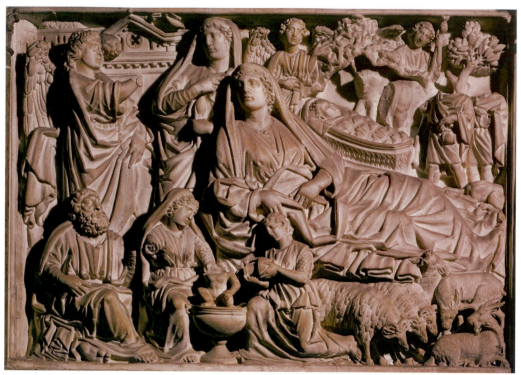

11–23 • Nicola Pisano
ANNUNCIATION, NATIVITY, AND ADORATION OF THE SHEPHERDS
Panel from the baptistery pulpit, Pisa. 1260. Marble, 33½″ × 44½″ (85 × 113 cm).

pulpit's enclosure illustrate New Testament subjects, each containing several scenes framed as an independent composition.

One combines the **ANNUNCIATION, NATIVITY, AND ADORATION OF THE SHEPHERDS (FIG. 11–23)**. The Virgin reclines in the middle of the composition after having given birth to Jesus, who below receives his first bath from midwives. The upper left-hand corner holds the Annunciation—the moment of Christ's conception, as announced by the archangel Gabriel. The scene in the upper right combines the Annunciation to the Shepherds with their Adoration of the Child. The viewer's attention moves from group to group within the shallow space, always returning to the regally detached mother of God in the center. The format, style, and technique of Roman sarcophagus reliefs—readily accessible in the burial ground near the baptistery—may have provided Nicola's models for this carving. The sculptural treatment of the deeply cut, full-bodied forms is certainly Classical in inspiration, as are the heavy, placid faces.

Painting in Siena and Florence

Two very important centers of Italian Gothic painting developed in Siena and Florence, rivals in this as in so much else. Siena's foremost painter was Duccio di Buoninsegna (active 1278–1318). He transformed the tradition in which he worked by synthesizing the softened figure style of Late Byzantine art and the linear grace and easy relationship between figures and their settings that characterizes French Gothic. Between 1308 and 1311, Duccio and his workshop painted a huge **altarpiece** commissioned by Siena Cathedral and known as the **MAESTÀ** (*Majesty*) **(FIG. 11–24)**. Creating this altarpiece—assembled from many wood panels bonded together before painting—was an arduous undertaking. The work was not only large (the central panel alone was 7 by 13 feet) but it had to be painted on both sides since it could be seen from all directions when installed on the main altar at the center of the sanctuary.

Because the *Maestà* was dismantled in 1771, its power and beauty can only be imagined from scattered parts, some still in Siena but others elsewhere. FIGURE 11–24 is a reconstruction of how the front of the original altarpiece might have looked. It was dominated by a huge *Virgin and Child in Majesty* (hence its title *Maestà*), flanked by 20 angels and ten saints. Above and below were smaller-scale narrative scenes from the Life of the Virgin and the Infancy of Christ.

On the back were episodes from the later life of Christ, focusing on his Passion. Characteristic of Duccio's narrative style is the scene of the **RAISING OF LAZARUS (FIG. 11–25)**. Lyrical figures enact the event with graceful decorum, but their highly charged glances and expressive gestures—especially the bold reach of Christ—convey a strong sense of dramatic urgency. The shading of drapery and the modeling of faces faithfully describe the figures' three-dimensionality, but the crisp outlines of the jewel-colored shapes created by their drapery, as well as the sinuous continuity of folds and gestures, generate rhythmic patterns across the surface. Experimentation with the portrayal of space extends from the receding rocks of the mountainous landscape to carefully studied interiors,

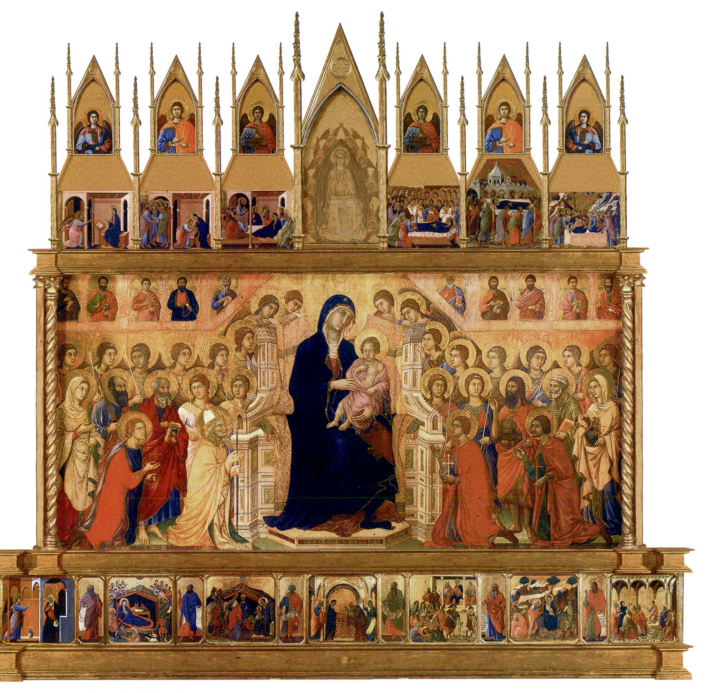

11-24 • Duccio di Buoninsegna
CONJECTURAL RECONSTRUCTION OF THE FRONT OF THE MAESTÀ ALTARPIECE
Made for Siena Cathedral. 1308–1311. Tempera and gold on wood, main panel 7′ × 13′ (2.13 × 4.12 m).

The inscription running around the base of the majestic throne of the Virgin includes the artist's signature: "Holy Mother of God, be thou the cause of peace for Siena and life to Duccio because he painted thee thus." Duccio had in 1288 designed a splendid stained-glass window portraying the Death, Assumption, and Coronation of the Virgin for the huge circular opening in the east wall of the sanctuary. It would have hovered over the installed *Maestà* when it was placed on the altar in 1311.

📖 **Read** the document related to Duccio's *Maestà* on **MyArtsLab**

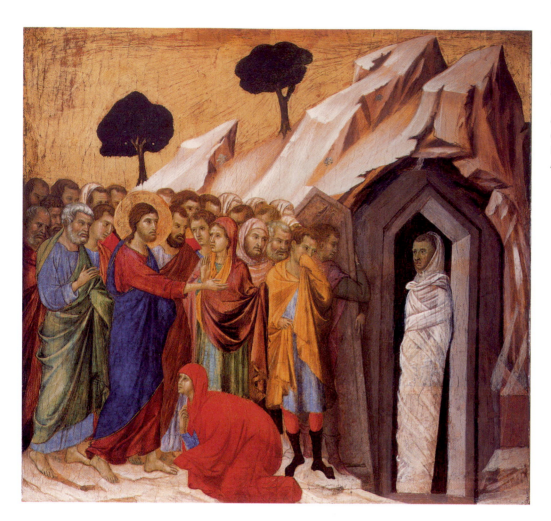

11–25 • Duccio di Buoninsegna **RAISING OF LAZARUS**
From the back of the *Maestà* altarpiece, Siena Cathedral. 1308–1311. Tempera and gold on wood, 17⅛″ × 18¼″ (43.5 × 46.4 cm). Kimbell Art Museum, Fort Worth, Texas. APX (1975.01).

here the tomb of Lazarus whose heavy door was removed by the straining hug of a bystander to reveal the shrouded figure of Jesus's about-to-be-resurrected friend, leaning against the door jamb.

The enthusiasm with which the citizens of a city greeted a great painting or altarpiece like the *Maestà* demonstrates the power of images as well as the association of the magnificent work with the glory of the city itself. We are fortunate to have a contemporary account of the day Duccio's completed altarpiece for Siena Cathedral was carried from his workshop on December 20, 1311, in a joyous procession:

> On the day that it was carried to the [cathedral] the shops were shut, and the bishop conducted a great and devout company of priests and friars in solemn procession, accompanied by…all the officers of the commune, and all the people, and one after another the worthiest with lighted candles in their hands took places near the picture, and behind came the women and children with great devotion. And they accompanied the said picture up to the [cathedral], making the procession around the campo [square], as is the custom, all the bells ringing joyously, out of reverence for so noble a picture as is this.
> (*A Documentary History of Art*, p. 135)

Artists in Florence were moving toward the portrayal of a more lifelike world somewhat earlier than in Siena. Duccio's Florentine counterpart was an older painter named Cenni di Pepi (active c. 1272–1302), better known by his nickname, Cimabue. Cimabue probably painted the **VIRGIN AND CHILD ENTHRONED (FIG. 11–26)** in about 1280 for the main altar of the church of the Sta. Trinità (Holy Trinity) in Florence. At over 12 feet high, this enormous panel painting set a new precedent for monumental altarpieces. Cimabue surrounds the hierarchically scaled Virgin and Child with angels and places a row of prophets beneath them. Looking out at viewers while holding the infant Jesus in her lap, Mary gestures toward her son, recalling a formula popular in early Byzantine art (SEE FIG. 7–20).

Cimabue also follows Byzantine practice in creating highlights on the draperies of holy figures with thin lines of gold, as if to capture their divine radiance. Mary's huge throne, painted to represent gold with inset enamels and gems, provides an architectural framework for the composition. The viewer seems suspended in space in front of the image, simultaneously looking down on the projecting elements of the throne and Mary's lap, while looking straight ahead at the prophets at the base of the throne and the angels to each side. These spatial ambiguities, as well as subtle asymmetries throughout the centralized composition, the Virgin's engaging gaze, and the individualized faces of the old men, give the picture a sense of life and the figures a sense of presence.

According to the sixteenth-century chronicler Giorgio Vasari, Cimabue discovered a talented shepherd boy, Giotto di Bondone, and taught him how to paint. Then, "Giotto obscured the fame of Cimabue, as a great light outshines a lesser." Vasari explains that Giotto (active c. 1300–1337) "became such an excellent imitator of nature that he completely banished that crude Greek [i.e., Byzantine] style and revived the modern and excellent art of painting, introducing good drawing from live natural models, something which had not been done for more than two hundred years" (Vasari, trans. Bondanella and Bondanella, p. 16).

Giotto's 1305–1310 painting of the **VIRGIN AND CHILD ENTHRONED** (**FIG. 11–27**) for the church of Ognissanti (All Saints) in Florence reflects Cimabue's influence in the positioning of figures within a largely symmetrical composition. Gone, however, are the Virgin's modestly inclined head and the delicate gold folds in her drapery. Instead, light and shadow play gently across her stocky form, and her action—holding her child's leg instead of pointing him out to us—seems less contrived. This colossal Mary overwhelms her slender Gothic tabernacle of a throne. Despite Giotto's retention of the hierarchically scaled and formal, enthroned image type, set against

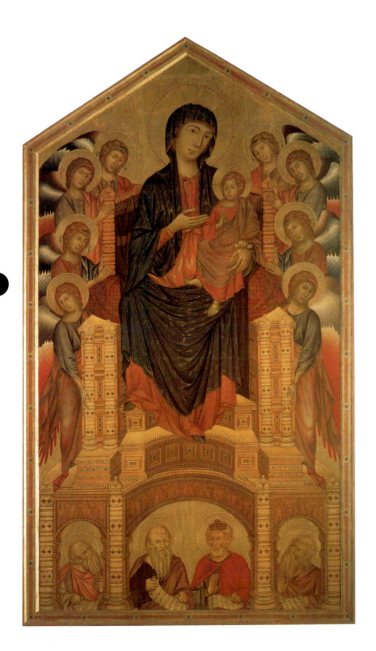

11-26 • Cimabue VIRGIN AND CHILD ENTHRONED
Probably painted for the high altar of the church of Sta. Trinità, Florence. c. 1280. Tempera and gold on wood, 12′ 7″ × 7′ 4″ (3.53 × 2.2 m). Galleria degli Uffizi, Florence.

👁 **Watch** a video about the egg tempera process on **MyArtsLab**

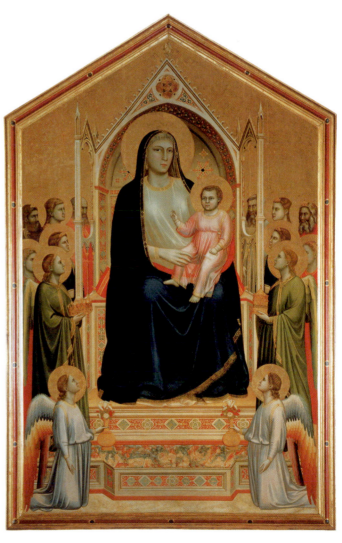

11-27 • Giotto di Bondone VIRGIN AND CHILD ENTHRONED
Probably painted for the high altar of the church of Ognissanti, Florence. 1305–1310. Tempera and gold on wood, 10′ 8″ × 6′ 8¼″ (3.53 × 2.05 m). Galleria degli Uffizi, Florence.

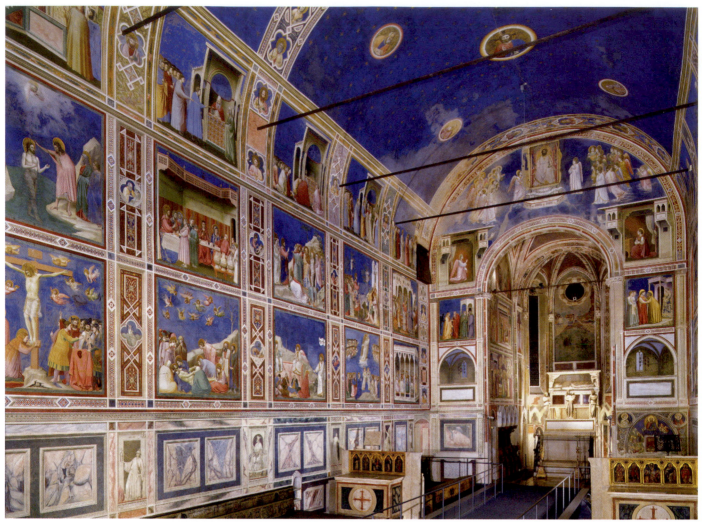

11–28 • Giotto di Bondone SCROVEGNI (ARENA) CHAPEL
View toward the north and east walls with frescos. Padua. 1305–1306.

a flat, gold background, he has created the sense that these are fully three-dimensional beings, whose plainly draped, bulky bodies inhabit real space.

Giotto's masterpiece is the frescoed interior of the **SCROVEGNI CHAPEL** in Padua, painted about 1305 (**FIG. 11–28**). The frescos were commissioned by Enrico Scrovegni, whose family fortune was made through the practice of usury— which at this time meant charging interest when loaning money, a sin so grave that it resulted in exclusion from the Christian sacraments. The building of this chapel next to his new pala- tial residence seems to have been conceived at least in part as a penitential act, part of his campaign to seek absolution for his own and his father's sins.

Architecturally, the chapel (also known as the Arena Chapel because of its location near an ancient Roman arena) is a simple, barrel-vaulted room that provides broad walls and a boxlike space to showcase the paintings. Giotto covered the entrance wall with the Last Judgment (not visible here) and the sanctuary wall with highlighted scenes from the Life of Christ, notably the Annunciation spread over the two painted architectural frameworks on either side of the high arched

opening into the sanctuary itself. He subdivided the side walls into framed pictures. At the bottom is a dado of allegorical grisaille paintings of Virtues and Vices, from which rise ver- tical bands containing quatrefoil portraits that span the vault, crossing a star-spangled sky in which large portrait disks float like glowing moons. Set into this framework are rectangular scenes aligned in three horizontal bands of narrative, por- traying the life of the Virgin and her parents at the top and the life of Jesus along the middle and lower registers. Both the individual scenes and the overall program display Giotto's genius for distilling complex stories into a series of compelling moments. He concentrates on the human dimensions of the unfolding drama—from touches of anecdotal humor to expres- sions of profound anguish—rather than on its symbolic or theological weight.

Giotto's prodigious narrative skills are apparent in four pictures on the north wall (**FIG. 11–29**). At top left Jesus per- forms his first miracle, changing water into wine at the wedding feast at Cana. The wine steward—looking very much like the jars of new wine himself—sips the results. To the right is the Raising of Lazarus. The basic elements of the scene are familiar

Cennino Cennini's *Il Libro dell'Arte* (*The Handbook of the Crafts*), a compendium of Florentine painting techniques from about 1400, includes step-by-step instructions for making panel paintings, a process also used at this time in Siena.

The wood for the panels, he explains, should be fine-grained, free of blemishes, and thoroughly seasoned by slow drying. To prepare such a panel for painting, first the surface was covered with clean white linen strips soaked in a **gesso** made from gypsum, a task best done on a dry, windy day. Gesso provided a ground, or surface, on which to paint, and Cennini specified that at least nine layers should be applied, and the surface then be burnished until it resembled ivory. Only then could the artist sketch the composition of the work with charcoal made from burned willow twigs. At this point, advised Cennini, "When you have finished drawing your figure, especially if it is in a very valuable [altarpiece], so that you are counting on profit and reputation from it, leave it alone for a few days, going back to it now and then to look it over and improve it wherever it still needs something...(and bear in mind that you may copy and examine things done by other good masters; that it is no shame to you)" (Cennini, p. 75). When finalized, he directed, the design should be inked in with a fine squirrel-hair brush. Gold leaf was affixed next. On a humid day, the tissue-thin gold sheets were carefully glued down with a mixture of fine powdered clay and egg white over a reddish clay ground called bole, then burnished with a gemstone or the tooth of a carnivorous animal. **Punched** and incised patterning would be added later.

Italian painters at this time worked principally in **tempera** paint—powdered pigments mixed most often with egg yolk, a little water, and an occasional touch of glue. Apprentices were kept busy grinding pigments and mixing paints according to their masters' recipes, setting them out for more senior painters in wooden bowls or shell dishes.

Cennini outlined a highly formulaic painting process. Faces, for example, were always to be done last, with flesh tones applied over two coats of a light greenish pigment and highlighted with touches of red and white. The finished painting was given a layer of varnish to protect it and intensify its colors.

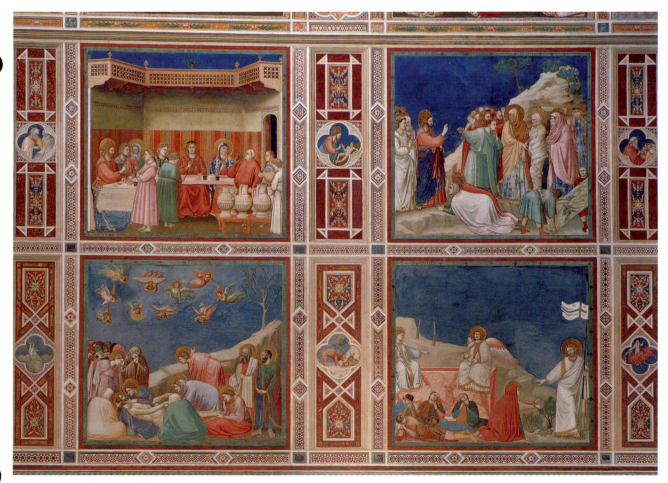

11–29 • Giotto di Bondone MARRIAGE AT CANA, RAISING OF LAZARUS, LAMENTATION, AND RESURRECTION (NOLI ME TANGERE)
Frescos from north wall of the Scrovegni (Arena) Chapel, Padua. 1305–1306.

The two techniques used in mural painting are *buon* ("true") *fresco* ("fresh"), in which color is applied with water-based paints on wet plaster, and *fresco secco* ("dry"), in which paint is applied to a dry plastered wall.

The advantage of *buon fresco* is its durability. As the painted plaster dries, a chemical reaction bonds the pigments into the wall surface. In *fresco secco*, by contrast, the color does not become part of the plaster wall and tends to flake off over time. The chief disadvantage of *buon fresco* is that it must be done quickly, without mistakes. The painter plasters and paints only as much as can be completed in a day, which explains the Italian term for each of the sections: *giornata*, or day's work. The size of a *giornata* varies according to the complexity of the painting within it. A face, for instance, might take an entire day, whereas large areas of sky can be painted quite rapidly. In Giotto's Scrovegni Chapel scholars have identified 852 separate *giornate*, some worked on concurrently within a single day by assistants in Giotto's workshop.

In medieval and Renaissance Italy, a wall to be frescoed was first prepared with a rough, thick undercoat of plaster (the *arriccio*). When this was dry, assistants copied the master painter's composition onto it with charcoal, at times corrected by the master. These drawings, known as *sinopia*, have an immediacy and freshness lost in the finished painting. Work proceeded in irregularly shaped *giornate* conforming to the contours of major figures and objects. Assistants covered one section at a time with a fresh, thin coat of very fine plaster (the *intonaco*) over the *sinopia*, and when this was

"set" but not dry, artists painted it with pigments mixed with water, working from the top down so that drips fell on unfinished portions. Some areas requiring pigments such as ultramarine blue (which was unstable in *buon fresco*), as well as areas requiring gilding, would be added after the wall was dry, using the *fresco secco* technique.

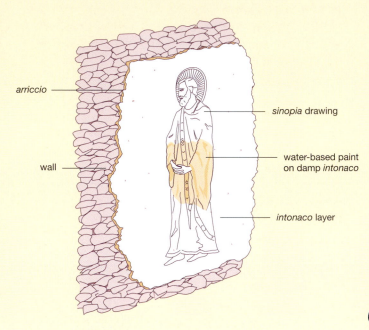

arriccio

sinopia drawing

water-based paint on damp *intonaco*

wall

intonaco layer

View the Closer Look on the technique of fresco on **MyArtsLab**

---

from Duccio's rendering (SEE FIG. 11–25), but the comparison highlights with real clarity the distinctiveness of Giotto's narrative and pictorial style. He has sacrificed the elegantly cut and jewel-toned pattern of silhouettes within a solid figural mass in order to emphasize the bold modeling of individualized, solid figures. They twist in space, using postures and gestures to react to the human drama by pleading for Jesus's help and by expressing astonishment at the miracle or revulsion at the smell of death. Jesus is separated from the crowd. His transforming gesture is highlighted against the dark blue of the background, his profile face locked in communication with the similarly isolated Lazarus, whose eyes, still fixed in death, let us know that the miracle is just about to happen. On the lower register, Jesus's grief-stricken followers lament over his corpse with palpable suffering. The stricken Virgin pulls her dead son close, communing with mute intensity, while the red-cloaked John flings his arms back in convulsive despair. This mourning gives way on the right to the Resurrection, indicated by the weighty

angels flanking the empty tomb and by Jesus's own sense of movement—he seems almost ready to leave the earthly stage by walking out of the picture.

The theological importance of these moments in Jesus's life is not completely eclipsed by Giotto's stirring attention to the human condition. Educated worshipers would also see in Jesus's miracle at Cana a prefiguration of the miraculous transubstantiation of bread and wine into Jesus's body and blood in the Mass. And the resurrection of the ghoulish Lazarus prefigures Jesus's own Resurrection, placed just below to encourage the comparison. These are traditional medieval associations. What is new here is the way Giotto draws his viewers into the experience of these events, imagining them in relation to their own life experiences. Giotto's approach embodied a new Franciscan value on personal piety rooted in empathetic responses to sacred stories—medieval artistic and devotional practices that helped set the stage for the development of the Italian Renaissance.

LOOKING BACK ◀

The art and architecture of Gothic France experienced a rich and rapid evolution, and achieved a growing international impact, as it emerged from Abbot Suger's vision of light-saturated monastic spirituality in the 1140s, through the great cathedral projects of the first half of the thirteenth century, and into King Louis IX's Parisian jewel-box Sainte-Chapelle of the 1240s. To enhance the desired effects of light and color, architects made buildings taller, walls lighter, and windows larger.

The fourteenth century saw regional architectural variations in centers throughout Europe, and the strong impact of Gothic painting in Italy, notable in the elegant, graceful figures that enact sacred stories in Duccio's Sienese *Maestà* of the early 1300s. But even if Sienese painting was a key contributor to the development of mainstream European Gothic art, it was Florentine painting, in the style championed by Giotto and kept alive by his pupils and their followers, that would most inspire Italian artists over the next two centuries.

THINK ABOUT IT

11.1 Explain what you think are the most important innovations—structural and stylistic—that earned the abbey church at Saint-Denis the reputation as the first Gothic church.

11.2 Identify the three works of art in this chapter that were commissioned by French king Louis IX. Discuss their relationships to his political life and aspirations.

11.3 How is the illumination of the *Windmill Psalter* (FIG. 11–19) used to convey complex theological ideas and/or teach moral lessons?

11.4 Compare and contrast Duccio's and Giotto's renderings of the biblical story of Christ's Raising of Lazarus (FIGS. 11–25, 11–29). In what ways are these paintings representative of Sienese and Florentine art at the beginning of the fourteenth century?

| CROSSCURRENTS |

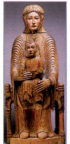 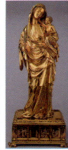

Depictions of the Virgin Mary holding the infant Jesus represent a continuing theme in the history of European Christian art, developed early on, and continuing to this day. Describe the relationship between mother and child in each. Characterize the difference in artistic style. How does the choice of medium contribute to the distinction between them?

FIG. 10–31   FIG. 11–15

✓ **Study** and **Review** on **MyArtsLab**

IN PERSPECTIVE

1100

1150

1200

1250

1300

1350

1400

Suger, Abbot of Saint-Denis
abbot 1122–1151

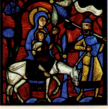

**Flight into Egypt,
St. Denis**
c. 1140–1144

Second Crusade 1147–1149

Plantagenet Dynasty in England
1154–1485

Third Crusade 1188–1192
Queen Blanche of Castile
1188–1252

Fourth Crusade Takes
Constantinople 1204
Franciscan Order
Founded 1209

Louis IX (St. Louis),
King of France
ruled 1226–1270

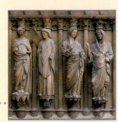

**Jamb Statues,
Reims Cathedral**
c. 1230–1250

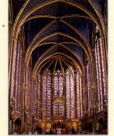

Sainte-Chapelle, Paris
1239–1248

Western Control of Constantinople
Ends 1261
Thomas Aquinas Begins Writing
Summa Theologica 1266

Papacy Resides in Avignon
1309–1377
Queen Jeanne d'Evreux
1310–1371

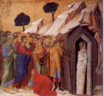

DUCCIO, Raising of Lazarus
1308–1311

Hundred Years' War
1337–1453

Black Death Begins/Boccaccio
Begins Writing *The Decameron*
1348

Great Schism 1378–1417

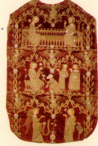

**Chichester-Constable
Chasuble**
c. 1330–1350

Chaucer Starts Work on
The Canterbury Tales 1387

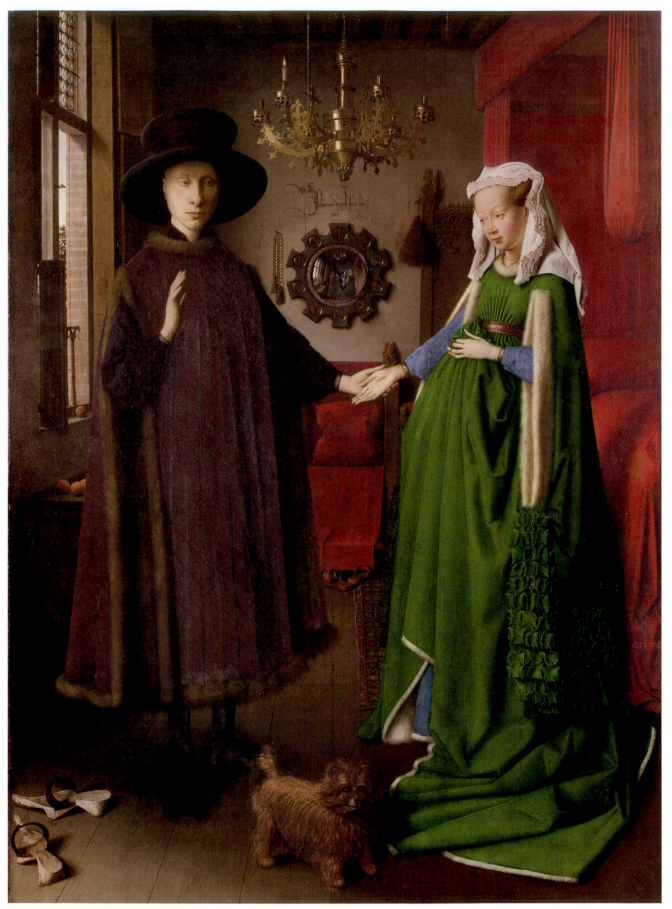

12-1 • Jan van Eyck DOUBLE PORTRAIT OF GIOVANNI ARNOLFINI AND HIS WIFE
1434. Oil on wood panel, 33″ × 22½″ (83.8 × 57.2 cm). The National Gallery, London.

EARLY RENAISSANCE ART

12.1 Define the nature of the Northern Renaissance in Flanders.

12.2 Explain the growth of printmaking in fifteenth-century Europe.

12.3 Discuss the development of Italian Renaissance art and architecture in Florence.

12.4 Trace the spread of the Renaissance from Florence to other Italian cities.

LOOKING FORWARD ▶

Fifteenth-century Europe saw the emergence of wealthy merchants whose rise to power was fueled by individual accomplishment, rather than hereditary succession within noble families. Certainly Giovanni Arnolfini—the pasty gentleman with the extravagant hat in this **DOUBLE PORTRAIT** (FIG. **12–1**)—earned, rather than inherited, the right to have himself and his wife recorded by renowned artist Jan van Eyck. It was the wealth and connections he made as an Italian cloth merchant providing luxury fabrics to the Burgundian court that put him in the position to commission such a precious picture, in which both patron and painter are identified with conspicuous clarity. Giovanni's face looks more like a personal likeness than anything we have seen since ancient Rome, and not only did Jan van Eyck inscribe his name above the convex mirror ("Jan van Eyck was here 1434"); his personal painting style also carries the stamp of authorship. The doll-like face of the woman standing next to Giovanni is less individualized. Has she lifted her skirt over her belly so she can follow Giovanni who has taken her by the hand? Or are most modern observers correct in assuming that she is pregnant? This painting is full of mysteries.

The precise identity of the couple is still open to scholarly debate. And is this a wedding, a betrothal, or perhaps security for a shady financial deal? Recently it has been interpreted as a memorial to a beloved wife lost to death, perhaps in childbirth. Only the wealth of the couple is beyond dispute. They are surrounded by luxury objects: lavish bed hangings, sumptuous chandelier, precious Oriental carpet, rare oranges, not to mention their extravagant clothing. The man wears a fur-lined, silk velvet *heuque* (sleeveless over-garment). The woman's gown not only employs more costly wool fabric than necessary to cover her slight body; the elaborate cutwork decoration and white fur lining of her sleeves are conspicuous indicators of cost. In fact, the painting itself—probably hung in the couple's home—was an object of considerable value.

Even within its secular setting, however, the picture resonated with sacred meaning. The Church still provided spiritual grounding for men and women of the Renaissance. The crystal prayer beads hanging next to the convex mirror imply the couple's piety, and the mirror itself, a symbol of the all-seeing eye of God, is framed with a circular cycle of scenes from Christ's Passion. A figure of St. Margaret, protector of women in childbirth, is carved at the top of a post of the high-backed chair beside the bed, and the perky *affenpinscher* in the foreground may be more than a pet. Dogs served as symbols of fidelity and also have funerary associations, and choosing a rare, ornamental breed like this may have been yet another opportunity to express wealth.

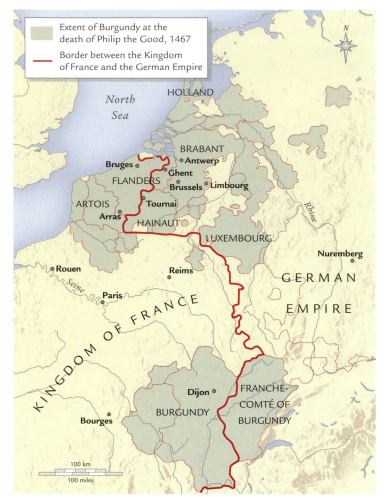

MAP 12–1 • CENTERS OF NORTHERN EUROPEAN ART DURING THE FIFTEENTH CENTURY

The dukes of Burgundy—whose territory is shaded green on this map—became major cultural and political leaders in Northern Europe during the fifteenth century.

Fascinated by what they saw around them, fifteenth-century artists sought to observe and represent the variety of textures, shapes, and spaces they experienced in their world. They carefully described with paint the colors and textures of surfaces, and they developed intellectual systems, such as linear perspective, for pictorial simulations of three-dimensional forms arranged in space. They and their patrons were guided by a new emphasis on Humanist thinking, which placed great value on science, reason, and the individual, while never abandoning a steadfast religious faith.

Though the actual term "Renaissance" (French for "rebirth") was applied to this period by later historians, its origins lie in the thought of Petrarch and other fourteenth-century scholars, who believed in the power and potential of human beings for great individual accomplishment. These Italian Humanists also looked back at the 1,000 years extending from the disintegration of the Western Roman Empire to their own day and determined that the human achievements of the Classical world were followed by a period of decline—a "middle" or "dark" age. They saw their own era as a third age characterized by a revival,

rebirth, or renaissance, when humanity began to emerge from what they saw as intellectual and cultural stagnation and to appreciate once more the achievement of the ancients and the value of rational, scientific investigation. Clearly new things were happening in art as well as in intellectual life during the fifteenth century, and not only in Italy but also in Northern Europe. We will find, however, that northern and Italian artists will take somewhat divergent paths as they explore new ways of representing the natural world and the social and spiritual systems that sustained it.

Northern Renaissance Art

What features define the Northern Renaissance art of Flanders?

In Northern Europe (MAP 12–1), where the Gothic style originated and first flourished, artists came to the Renaissance by way of an intense curiosity about the natural world. Gothic artists in France, the Germanic lands, and the Low Countries (present-day Belgium, the Netherlands, and Luxembourg) had already captured the visual appearance of birds, plants, and animals with breathtaking virtuosity in manuscript painting, textiles, and sculpture. They enlarged on these interests in the fourteenth century by highlighting such effects as reflections on water, steamy breath on a cold winter's day, and the sheen of metal basins. In the fifteenth century, they worked to incorporate these details within scenes that seem to replicate their actual material world. Similarly, fifteenth-century portraits appear astonishingly lifelike, and even in religious paintings, saints and angels have distinct personalities, as if based on specific human models.

The Limbourg Brothers

Among the finest painters in Northern Europe at the beginning of the fifteenth century were three brothers, Pol, Herman,

and Jean Limbourg—their "last" name referring to their home region. At the time, people generally did not have family names in the modern sense, but were known instead by their first names, often followed by a reference to their place of origin, parentage, or occupation. For instance, the name Jan van Eyck (SEE FIG. 12–1) means "Jan from [the town of] Eyck."

About 1404, the Limbourg brothers entered the service of Duke Jean of Berry, for whom they produced their most famous surviving work, the so-called **TRÈS RICHES HEURES** (*Very Sumptuous Hours*), between 1411 and 1416. This Book of Hours included a monthly calendar of holy days with full-page paintings. The subjects alternated between the peasants' labors and the aristocrats' diversions that were common each month. On the February page (**FIG. 12–2**), farm folks relax before a blazing fire. Although many country people at this time lived in hovels,

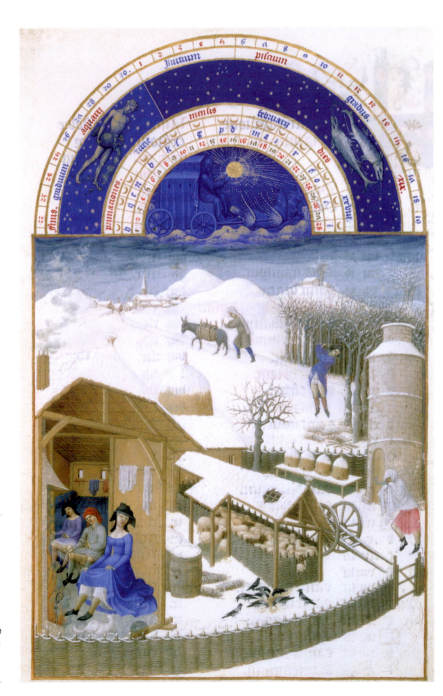

12-2 • Pol, Herman, and Jean Limbourg
FEBRUARY, TRÈS RICHES HEURES OF JEAN, DUC DE BERRY
1411–1416. Colors and ink on parchment, 11⅜″ × 8¼″ (29 × 21 cm). Musée Condé, Chantilly, France.

Although all figures in this scene are lower in social standing than the aristocratic patron of this book, not all are of the same class. Largest in scale and most elegantly dressed is the woman closest to us at lower left, perhaps the owner of the farm, who carefully lifts her over-garment and balances it daintily with both hands as she warms herself. She shares her fire with a lower-class couple, smaller because farther in the background, who wear less expensive clothing and are considerably less well behaved, especially the uncouth man, who exposes himself as he lifts his clothing to take advantage of the fire's warmth.

Women Artists in the Late Middle Ages and the Renaissance

Since most formal apprenticeships were not open to them, medieval and Renaissance women artists typically learned to paint from their husbands and fathers. Noblewomen, who were often educated in convents, also learned to draw, paint, and embroider. One of the earliest examples of a signed work by a woman is in a tenth-century Spanish manuscript of Beatus's commentary on the Apocalypse illustrated by an artist named Ende, who describes herself as "painter and servant of God." We have already seen the self-portrait of a twelfth-century German nun named Guda (SEE FIG. 10–30).

Examples proliferate during the later Middle Ages. In the fourteenth century, Jeanne de Montbaston and her husband, Richart, worked together as book illuminators under the auspices of the University of Paris. After Richart's death,

Jeanne maintained the workshop and, following the custom of the time, was sworn in as a *libraire* (publisher) by the university in 1353. Bourgot, the daughter of the miniaturist Jean le Noir, illuminated books for King Charles V of France and Duke Jean of Berry. In the fifteenth century, women could be admitted to guilds in the Flemish towns of Ghent, Bruges, and Antwerp.

The position of women artists in Italy was not as strong as in Flanders. The Humanists' emphasis on academic study rather than apprenticeship for artists, the tie between mathematics and the new linear perspective, and the emphasis on anatomical study—forbidden to women—and figure drawing from models prevented women from following careers in painting. Some women nevertheless learned from their fathers or husbands and participated in the family business.

---

this farm looks comfortable and well maintained, with timber-frame buildings, a row of beehives, a sheepfold, and woven wattle fences. Most remarkably, the details of the painting convey the feeling of the cold winter weather: the leaden sky, the bare trees, the soft snow, the steamy breath of the bundled-up worker blowing on his hands, and the comforting smoke curling up from the farmhouse chimney.

The painting clearly maintains several Gothic conventions common in Northern Renaissance art well into the first half of the fifteenth century. These include the cutaway view of the house showing both interior and exterior (SEE FIG. 11–14), the special attention to anecdotal detail, and the high placement of the **horizon line**. But scale relationships seem more consistent with our experience in the natural world since as the landscape recedes, the size of figures and buildings diminishes progressively in stages from foreground to middle ground to background.

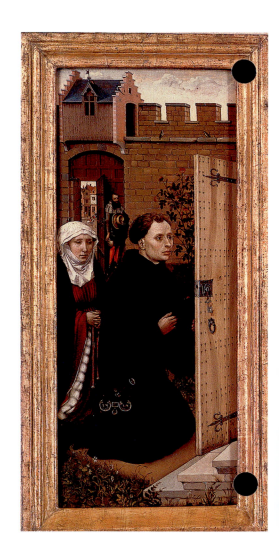

12-3 • Workshop of the Master of Flémalle MÉRODE ALTARPIECE **(TRIPTYCH OF THE ANNUNCIATION) (OPEN)**

c. 1425–1430s. Oil on wood panel, center 25¼″ × 24⅞″ (64.1 × 63.2 cm), each wing approx. 25⅜″ × 10⅞″ (64.5 × 27.6 cm). The Metropolitan Museum of Art, New York. The Cloisters Collection, 1956 (56.70).

In the late nineteenth century, this **triptych** was associated with a group of stylistically related works and assigned to an artist called the Master of Flémalle, who was subsequently identified by some art historians as a documented artist named Robert Campin. Recently, however, experts have questioned this association and proposed that the triptych we now see was the work of several artists working within the workshop that created the stylistic cluster. Current opinion holds that the Annunciation was initially created as an independent panel, and a short time later expanded into a triptych with the addition of the side panels under the patronage of the donor in the foreground at left. Finally, some time later in the 1430s, the figure of his wife was added behind him, presumably on the occasion of his marriage.

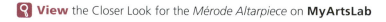

View the Closer Look for the *Mérode Altarpiece* on **MyArtsLab**

Painting in Flanders

During the fifteenth century, Flanders—roughly equivalent to the present-day lands of western Belgium, the southwestern Netherlands, and a small area of northern France—was the commercial center of Northern Europe, attracting an international cadre of ambitious bankers and merchants like Giovanni Arnolfini from Lucca, whose portrait we have already explored (SEE FIG. 12–1). Supported by such wealthy patrons, Flemish painters developed a new style of meticulous detail and spiritual power. Their works were greatly admired across Europe, and their influence spread even into Italy.

Workshop of the Master of Flémalle. Some of the earliest and most outstanding artists in the new Flemish style painted in the workshop of an artist known as the Master of Flémalle, identified by some art historians as Robert Campin (active 1406–1444). Between about 1425 and the 1430s they painted the triptych now known as the **MÉRODE ALTARPIECE** (FIG. 12–3) after its later owners. Its relatively small size (slightly more than 2 feet tall and about 4 feet wide with the **wings** open) suggests that it was made for a small private chapel. The Annunciation of the central panel is set in a contemporary Flemish home and incorporates common household objects, many invested with religious meaning. The lilies on the table, for example, often appear in Annunciations to symbolize Mary's virginity. The hanging water pot in the background niche also refers to Mary's purity and her role as the vessel for the Incarnation of God in Christ. What seems at first to be a towel hung over the prominent, hinged rack next to the niche may be a tallis (Jewish prayer shawl). Some art historians have referred to these objects as "hidden" or "disguised" symbols because they are treated as a normal part of the setting, but their religious meanings would have been obvious to the intended audience.

In the left wing of the triptych, the people who commissioned it—presumably a married couple—kneel in a garden before the open door of the house where the Annunciation is taking place. Their oddly unfocused eyes are directed not outward but inward, implying that the central scene is a vision brought on by their devotional meditations. Such presentations, popular with Flemish patrons, allowed those who commissioned a religious work to appear in the same space and time, and often on the same scale, as the religious figures represented. On the right wing, Joseph is working in his carpentry shop, his window opening onto an exquisitely detailed rendering of a bustling Flemish street scene. Even here there is symbolism. The mousetraps on the workbench and extended windowsill refer to

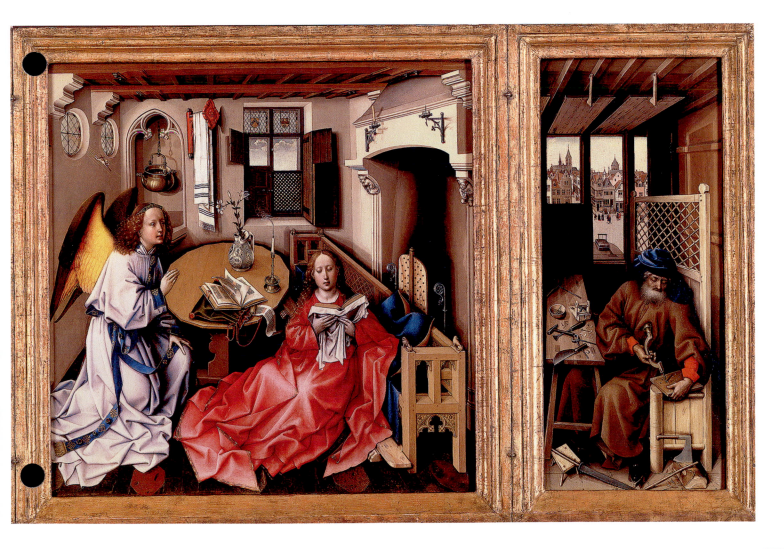

Whereas Italian artists favored tempera, and used it almost exclusively for panel painting until the end of the fifteenth century (see "Cennini on Panel Painting," p. 289), Flemish artists preferred oil paints, which are created by suspending powdered pigments in linseed—and occasionally walnut—oil. They exploited the potential of this medium throughout the fifteenth century with a virtuosity that has never been surpassed.

Tempera had to be applied in a very precise manner because it dried almost as quickly as it was laid down. Shading was restricted to careful overlying strokes in graded tones ranging from white and gray to dark brown and black. Because tempera is opaque, light striking its surface does not penetrate to lower layers of color and reflect back, so the resulting surface is **matte**, or dull, taking on a sheen only with an overlay of varnish.

On the other hand, oil paint is a viscous medium which takes much longer to dry, and while it is still wet, changes can easily be made. Once applied, the paint has time to smooth out during the drying process, erasing traces of individual brushstrokes. Perhaps even more importantly, oil paint is translucent when applied in very thin layers, called **glazes**. Light striking a surface built up of glazes penetrates to the lower layers and is reflected back, creating the appearance of an interior glow. These luminous effects enabled artists to capture jewel-like colors and the varying effects of light on changing textures, enhancing the illusion that viewers are looking at real objects rather than their painted imitation.

So brilliant was Jan van Eyck's use of oil paint that he was credited by Giorgio Vasari with inventing the medium. Actually, it had been in use at least since the twelfth century.

👁 **Watch** the videos about the process of oil painting and grinding oil paint on **MyArtsLab**

Christ as the bait in a trap set by God to catch Satan. Joseph is drilling holes in a small plank used as a drainboard in wine-making, calling to mind the Eucharist and Christ's passion.

The complex and consistent treatment of light in the central panel of the *Mérode Altarpiece* represents a major preoccupation of Flemish painters. The strongest illumination comes from an unseen source at the upper left in front of the **picture plane** (corresponding with the picture's surface), as if sunlight were entering through the opened front of the room through which we look. More light comes from the rear windows, and a few painted, linear rays come from the round window at left, a symbolic vehicle for the Christ Child's descent. Jesus seems to slide down the rays of light linking God with Mary, carrying the cross of human salvation over his shoulder. The light falling on the Virgin's lap emphasizes this connection, and the transmission of the symbolic light through a transparent panel of glass (which remains intact) recalls the virginal nature of Jesus's conception.

Jan van Eyck. Jan van Eyck (active 1420s–1441), a contemporary of the Master of Flémalle, became court painter to Duke Philip the Good of Burgundy (ruled 1419–1467), who was the uncle of the king of France and one of the wealthiest and most sophisticated men in Europe. He made Jan one of his confidential employees and even sent him on a diplomatic mission

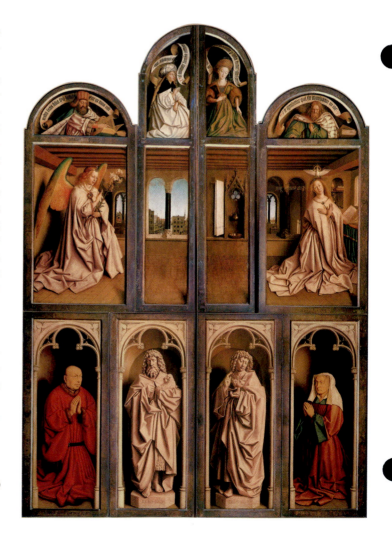

12–4 • Jan and Hubert (?) van Eyck
GHENT ALTARPIECE: ANNUNCIATION WITH DONORS (CLOSED) AND ADORATION OF THE MYSTIC LAMB (OPEN)
Cathedral of St. Bavo, Ghent. Completed 1432. Oil on panel, height 11′ 5¾″ (3.5 m), width when open 15′ 1½″ (4.6 m).

to Portugal. In a letter of 1434–1435, Duke Philip confessed that he could find no other painter equal to his taste or so excellent in art and science. But the duke was not Jan's only patron. In the Low Countries—where cities were largely independent of the landed nobility—civic leaders, town councils, and rich merchants were also important art patrons.

In his lifetime, one of the most famous works of Jan van Eyck was a huge polyptych with a very complicated and learned theological program that he (perhaps in collaboration with his brother Hubert) painted for a chapel in what is now the cathedral of St. Bavo in Ghent (FIG. 12–4). The wealthy patrons who funded this pious donation as a part of the refurbishing of their family chapel—Jodocus Vijde and his wife Isabella Borluut—appear in vibrant colors on the otherwise sober painting on the outside of the polyptych's shutters, visible only when the altarpiece is closed. When it was opened on Sundays and feast days the effect was no longer muted but rich and colorful. Dominating the tableau by size, central placement, and vibrancy of color is an enthroned figure of God, flanked by the Virgin Mary and John the Baptist, then by angelic musical ensembles, and finally at the outside Adam and Eve, represented as startlingly lifelike nudes. The five lower panels present a unified landscape field of meadows and woods, with cities in the distance, all against a continuous horizon. A diverse array of saints—apostles, martyrs, confessors, virgins, hermits, pilgrims, warriors, judges—assemble to adore the Lamb of God at the end of time as described in the book of Revelation.

The three-dimensional mass of the figures, the voluminous draperies as well as their remarkable surface realism, and the scrupulous attention to the luminous details of textures as variable as jewels and human flesh, are magnificent examples of Jan's artistic wizardry. He has carefully controlled the lighting within this multi-panel ensemble to make it appear that the objects represented are illuminated by sunlight coming through the window of the very chapel where it was meant to be installed. Jan's painting is firmly grounded in the terrestrial world even when he is rendering a visionary subject.

Jan's best-known painting today is a distinctive double portrait of a couple identified as a Giovanni Arnolfini and his wife (SEE FIG. 12–1). Early interpreters saw this fascinating work as representing a wedding or betrothal. Above the mirror on the back wall, the artist inscribed the words: *Johannes de eyck fuit hic 1434* ("Jan van Eyck was here 1434"). More normal for a signature would have been, "Jan van Eyck made this," so the words

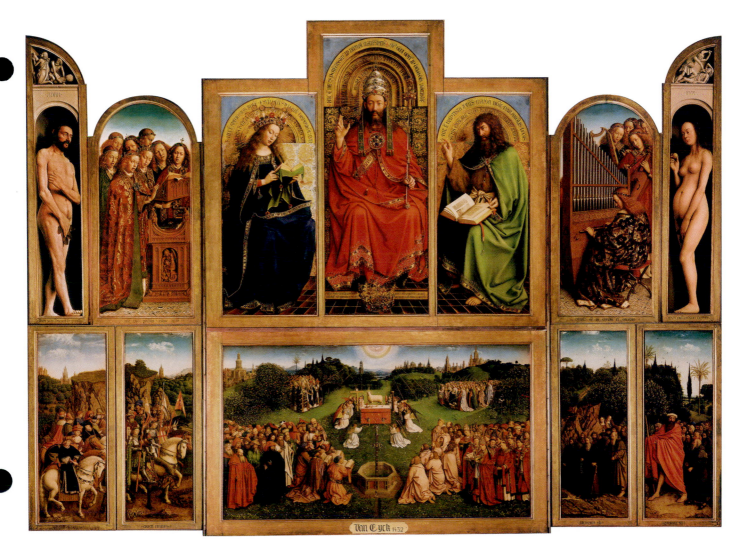

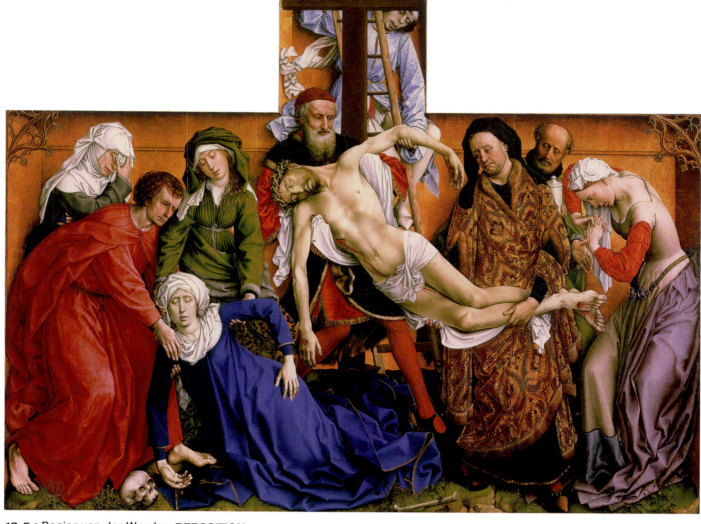

12–5 • Rogier van der Weyden DEPOSITION
From an altarpiece commissioned by the Crossbowmen's Guild, Louvain, Belgium. Before 1443 (possibly
c. 1435–1438). Oil on wood panel, 7′ 2⅝″ × 8′ 7⅛″ (2.2 × 2.62 m). Museo del Prado, Madrid.

"was here" have suggested to some that Jan served as a witness to a matrimonial episode portrayed in the painting. And he is not the only witness recorded here. The convex mirror between the figures reflects not only the back of the couple but a front view of two visitors standing in the doorway, entering the room. Perhaps one of them is the artist himself.

New research has complicated the developing interpretation of this painting by acknowledging that the Giovanni Arnolfini traditionally identified with the man in the painting only married his wife Giovanna Cenami in 1447, long after the date on the wall and Jan van Eyck's own death. Art historian Linda Seidel has proposed that the picture is actually a prospective portrait of Giovanni and Giovanna's marriage in the future, painted in 1434 to secure the early transfer of the dowry from her father to her future husband, and other scholars have offered other reinterpretations by opening up the identity of the pair represented here. Lorne Campbell has suggested that the man is actually a different Giovanni Arnolfini, accompanied by his putative second wife; Margaret Koster has most recently

interpreted this as a memorial portrait of this same Giovanni's first wife, Costanza Trenta, who died the year before this picture was painted, perhaps in childbirth. The true meaning of this fascinating masterpiece may remain a mystery, but it is doubtful that art historians will stop trying to solve it.

Rogier van der Weyden. Rogier van der Weyden (c. 1399–1464), an artist slightly younger than Jan, maintained a large workshop in Brussels—where he was official city painter—attracting apprentices and assistants from as far away as Italy. Nevertheless, not a single existing work of art bears his signature. To establish the stylistic character of Rogier's art, scholars have turned to a large painting of the **DEPOSITION (FIG. 12–5)**, likely the central panel of an altarpiece, commissioned by the Louvain Crossbowmen's Guild sometime before 1443.

The Deposition—the removal of Christ's body from the cross—was a popular theme in the fifteenth century because of its potential for a dramatic, personally engaging portrayal. Rogier sets the scene on the shallow stage of a gilt wooden box, just like the case of a carved and painted altarpiece. The ten solid, three-dimensional figures, however, are not simulations of polychromed wood carving, but near life-size renderings of actual human figures who seem to press forward into the viewer's space, allowing them no escape from the forceful expressions of heartrending grief. Jesus's friends seem palpably real, with their portrait-like faces and scrupulously described contemporary dress, as they tenderly and sorrowfully remove his body from the cross for burial. Jesus's corpse dominates the center of the composition, drooping in a languid curve, framed by jarringly thin, angular arms. His pose is echoed by the rhyming form of the swooning Virgin. It is as if mother and son share in the redemptive passion of his death on the cross, encouraging viewers to identify with them both, or join their assembled companions in mourning their fate. Although united by their sorrow, the mourning figures react in personal ways, from the intensity of Mary Magdalen at far right, wringing her hands in anguish, to John the Evangelist's blank stare at left, lost in grief as he reaches to support the collapsing Virgin. The anguish of the woman behind him, mopping her tear-soaked eyes with the edge of her veil, is almost unbearably poignant.

Second-Generation Painters

The extraordinary achievements of the Master of Flémalle, Jan van Eyck, and Rogier van der Weyden attracted many followers. They were active throughout the second half of the fifteenth century, and their patrons often extended beyond Flanders.

Petrus Christus. Petrus Christus (documented from 1444; d. c. 1475), who worked in Bruges, was among the most interesting painters in this second generation. His 1449 painting **A GOLDSMITH IN HIS SHOP** (FIG. 12–6), once thought to represent St. Eligius, patron saint of metalworkers, is now seen as a secular vocational portrait of an actual goldsmith. Both finished products and raw materials of the jeweler's trade sit on the shelves behind him: containers, rings, brooches, a belt buckle, a string of beads, coral, and crystal cylinders. He is in the process of weighing a ring to determine its value,

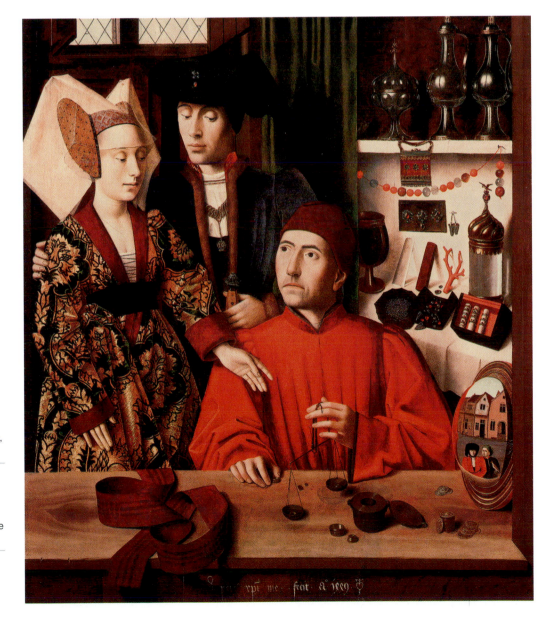

12–6 • Petrus Christus
A GOLDSMITH IN HIS SHOP
1449. Oil on oak panel, 38⅝″ × 33½″ (98 × 85 cm). The Metropolitan Museum of Art, New York. Robert Lehman Collection, 1975 (1975.1.110).

The artist signed and dated his work in a bold inscription that appears just under the tabletop at the bottom of the painting: "Master Petrus' Christus made me in the year 1449."

🔍 **View** the Closer Look for Christus's *A Goldsmith in His Shop* on **MyArtsLab**

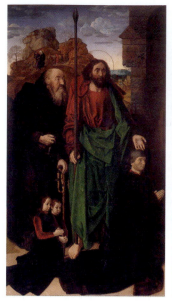
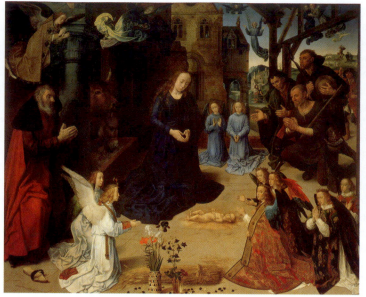
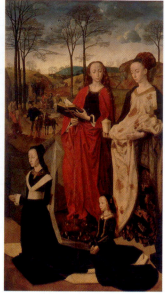

12–7 • Hugo van der Goes PORTINARI ALTARPIECE (OPEN)
c. 1474–1476. Tempera and oil on wood panel, center 8′ 3½″ × 10′ (2.53 × 3.01 m);
wings each 8′ 3½″ × 4′ 7½″ (2.53 × 1.41 m). Galleria degli Uffizi, Florence.

as a handsome couple—dressed in the height of Burgundian court fashion—look on. A betrothal belt curls across the counter, suggesting that the couple may be in the process of acquiring rings for their upcoming marriage. As in Jan van Eyck's double portrait (SEE FIG. 12–1), a convex mirror extends the viewer's field of vision in front of the picture plane, in this case showing two men on the street outside the window through which we ourselves view the interior of this shop. Whether or not the reflected image has symbolic or narrative meaning, within a shop it would have had a practical value, allowing the goldsmith to observe the approach of potential customers.

Hugo van der Goes. Hugo van der Goes (c. 1440–1482), dean of the painters' guild in Ghent from 1468 to1475, united the intellectual prowess of Jan van Eyck with the emotional sensitivity of Rogier van der Weyden to create an entirely new personal style. Hugo's major work was an exceptionally large altarpiece, more than 8 feet tall, commissioned by Tommaso Portinari for the family chapel in Florence and probably painted between 1474 and 1476 (**FIG. 12–7**). Portinari, a Florentine living in Bruges, was the local manager of the bank owned by the powerful Medici family. He and his wife, Maria Baroncelli, are seen kneeling with their three eldest children, accompanied by patron saints, on the interiors of the hinged side panels. The central panel represents the Adoration of the newborn Jesus by Mary and Joseph, a host of angels, and a few shepherds who have rushed in from the fields. The monumental figures of Joseph, Mary, and the shepherds are the same size as the patron saints on the wings; the Portinari family and the angels are small in comparison.

In the center, the Christ Child rests naked and vulnerable on the ground with rays of light emanating from his body. This image was based on the visionary writing of the medieval Swedish mystic St. Bridget, who described Mary kneeling to adore the Child immediately after giving birth. Aspects of the setting are infused with symbolic meaning. The wheat sheaf in the foreground refers both to the location of the event in Bethlehem (in Hebrew "house of bread") and to the Eucharistic host which represented the body of Christ. The **majolica** (glazed earthenware) *albarello*, or drug jar, a luxury ceramic imported from Spain, is decorated with vines and grapes, alluding to the Eucharistic wine that represented Christ's blood. It holds three irises—white for purity and purple for Christ's royal ancestry—and a red lily, another symbol of the blood of Christ. But Hugo's artistic vision goes far beyond formal religious symbolism. The shepherds who crouch in unaffected awe before the miraculous event are among the most sympathetically rendered images of common people to be found in the art of this, or any, period, and the portraits of the Portinari children are unusually sensitive renderings of the delicate features of youthful faces.

The work of these Northern Renaissance painters presents a stark contrast to what we will discover in contemporary Florentine art. During the sixteenth century, Michelangelo sharply criticized the detailed realism of Flemish art in an often-quoted assessment:

> In Flanders they paint with a view to external exactness or such things as may cheer you and of which you cannot speak ill, as for example saints and prophets. They paint stuffs and masonry and the green grass of the fields and the shadows of trees, and rivers and bridges, which they call landscapes, with many figures on this side and many figures on that, and all this, though it pleases some persons, is done without reason or art, without symmetry or proportion, without skillful choice of boldness and, finally, without substance or vigor.
> (Snyder, p. 88)

This was a minority viewpoint from someone who championed alternative values. In fact, Flemish art was so admired in the fifteenth century that many artists visited Flanders to study the work. Only at the end of the century did European patrons begin to favor the new styles of art and architecture developing in Italy.

Tapestries

Equally—perhaps even more—admired than northern paintings were Flemish textiles, among the most treasured luxury arts of the Renaissance. Major weaving centers arose in Brussels, Tournai, Arras, and in the Loire Valley, where Flemish and French artists produced outstanding tapestries. They provided both insulation and sumptuous decoration for the stone walls of castle halls, churches, and municipal buildings, and because they were much more expensive than wall or panel paintings, they also showed off the owners' wealth. Since they were portable, many were included among aristocratic baggage as courts moved from residence to residence.

One of the finest examples of Renaissance tapestry is a series known as the *Hunt of the Unicorn* from around 1500, including the well-preserved **UNICORN IS FOUND (FIG. 12–8)**. Its fine condition and the technical virtuosity of its weaver allow us to appreciate the rich colors of fabric and foliage,

and the subtle modeling of human faces and animal fur. The subject concerns the unicorn, a mythical horselike beast with a single horn said to be supernaturally swift; it could be captured only by a virgin, to whom it came willingly. The animal became both a symbol of the Incarnation (Christ is the unicorn captured by the Virgin Mary) and also a metaphor for romantic love and a suitable subject for wedding tapestries. The unicorn's horn was believed to be an antidote for poison; the unicorn here dips its horn into the stream to purify the water from the fountain.

The natural world portrayed with such splendor in this tapestry also has potential for symbolic meaning. Lions, for instance, represent valor, faith, mercy, and—because they were thought to breathe life into their cubs—the Resurrection of Christ. The stag is another Resurrection symbol (it sheds and grows its antlers, and it represents the urgent spiritual quest of the soul for God—especially in its lunge for the fountain, recalling an image in Psalm 42:1: "As a deer longs for flowing streams of water, so my soul longs for you, O God." Even today we still associate rabbits with fertility and dogs with fidelity. Many of the identifiable plants, described with botanical precision, carry religious and secular meaning: the strawberry stands for sexual love, the pansy for remembrance, the oak for fidelity, the holly for protection, and the orange for fertility.

12–8 • THE UNICORN IS FOUND

From the *Hunt of the Unicorn* tapestry series. c. 1495–1505. Wool, silk, and metal threads (13–21 warp threads per inch), 12′ 1″ × 12′ 5″ (3.68 × 3.78 m). The Metropolitan Museum of Art, New York. Gift of John D. Rockefeller, Jr. The Cloisters Collection, 1937 (37.8.2).

The price of a tapestry depended on the materials used. Rarely was a fine, commissioned series woven only with wool; instead tapestry producers enhanced it to varying degrees with colored silk and silver and gold threads. The richest kind of tapestry was one made entirely of silk and gold. Because the silver and gold threads used silk wrapped with real metal, people later burned many tapestries in order to retrieve the precious materials. As a result of this practice, few French royal tapestries have survived. Many existing works show obvious signs that the metallic threads were painstakingly pulled out in order to get the gold but preserve the tapestries.

View the Closer Look for the technique of tapestry on **MyArtsLab**

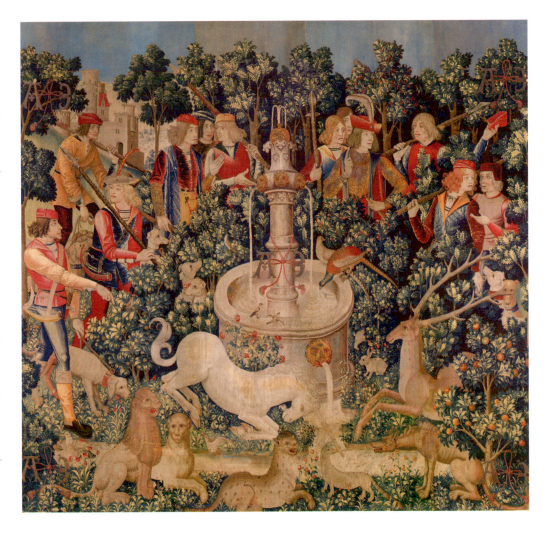

The Graphic Arts

How did printmaking emerge as a popular art form in fifteenth-century Europe?

Printmaking flourished in Europe with the wider availability of paper and the development of printing presses at the end of the fourteenth century. The techniques used by fifteenth-century printmakers were woodcut and engraving (see "Woodcuts and Engraving," p. 306).

During the fifteenth century, the use of woodcuts to print books on paper in multiple copies began to replace the copying of books individually by hand. The publication of the *Nuremberg Chronicle* by prosperous Nuremberg printer Anton Koberger is a landmark in this development. Published in 1493 in an **edition** of 2,500, artists Michael Wolgemut and Wilhelm Pleydenwurff furnished woodcuts for the 1,809 illustrations dispersed throughout the book—spread across the width of whole pages or tucked into the text along either margin. Those interested in purchasing the book could obtain it in Latin or German, on parchment or on paper, bound or unbound, as it came from the press or tinted with color. It seems fitting that

the only instance of a double-page picture—filling the entire expanse of an opening with text restricted to headings and labels—is a panoramic view of **THE CITY OF NUREMBERG** where this collaborative enterprise was centered (**FIG. 12–9**). Illustrated here is a view of this expansive cityscape in a copy of the book that was originally owned by a bibliophile who could afford to have the woodcuts painted by hand with color to enhance the appearance of this proud Renaissance city's portrait.

The technique of engraving, which allows finer lines and sharper details than woodcutting, may have developed from the highly skilled metalworking techniques used by goldsmiths and armorers who recorded their work by rubbing lampblack into the engraved lines and pressing paper over the plate. German artist Martin Schongauer (c. 1435–1491), who learned engraving from his goldsmith father, was an immensely skillful printmaker who excelled both in drawing and in the difficult technique of shading from deep black to faintest grays using only lines. In his **TEMPTATION OF ST. ANTHONY**, engraved about 1470–1475 (**FIG. 12–10**), Schongauer illustrated the original biblical meaning of temptation as a physical assault

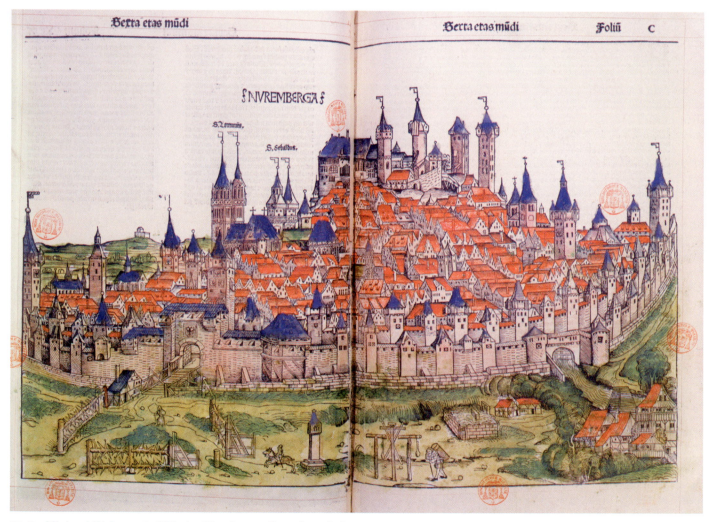

12–9 • Michael Wolgemut, Wilhelm Pleydenwurff, and workshop
THE CITY OF NUREMBERG, FROM THE NUREMBERG CHRONICLE
Published by Anton Koberger in 1493. Woodcut within a printed book, hand-colored after printing, each page 18½″ × 12¾″ (47 × 32.4 cm). Bibliothèque Mazarine, Paris.

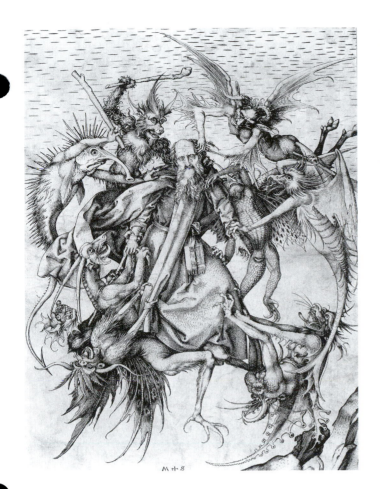

12–10 • Martin Schongauer TEMPTATION OF ST. ANTHONY
c. 1470–1475. Engraving, 12¼″ × 9″ (31.1 × 22.9 cm). The
Metropolitan Museum of Art, New York. Rogers Fund, 1920 (20.5.2).

rather than a subtle inducement. Wildly acrobatic slithery, spiky demons lift Anthony off the ground to torment and terrify him in midair. The engraver intensified the horror of the moment by condensing the action into a swirling vortex of figures beating, scratching, poking, tugging, and no doubt shrieking at the stoical saint, who remains impervious to all their torments because of his power to focus inwardly on his private meditations.

In Italy, the new Renaissance interest in Classical sculpture and anatomical research inspired an engraving by the Florentine goldsmith and sculptor Antonio del Pollaiuolo (c. 1432–1498): **BATTLE OF THE NUDES** (FIG. 12–11). Pollaiuolo may have intended this, his only known—but highly influential—print, as a study of the human figure in action. The naked men, fighting against each other ferociously against a tapestry-like background of foliage, seem to represent the same individual in a variety of poses, many of which are taken from Classical sources. Much of the engraving's fascination lies in how Pollaiuolo depicts muscles of the male body reacting under tension. Like their Flemish counterparts, Italian artists moved gradually toward a greater precision in rendering the illusion of physical reality. But as we shall see, Italians studied the figure more analytically than Flemish artists, with the goal of achieving perfected but generic figures set within a rationally ordered, rather than a visually described space.

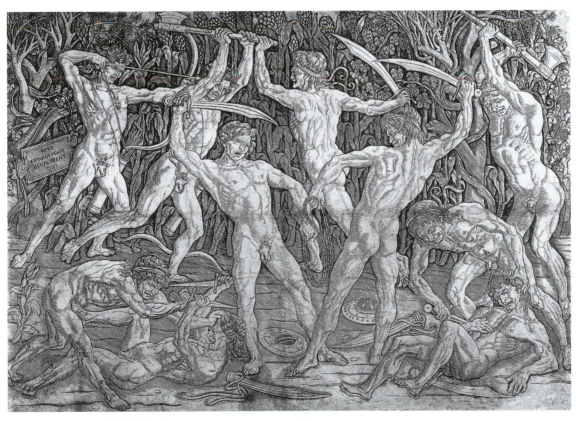

12–11 • Antonio del Pollaiuolo BATTLE OF THE NUDES
c. 1490. Engraving, 15¾″ × 22¹³⁄₁₆″ (40 × 58 cm). Yale University Art Gallery, New Haven, Connecticut.
Maitland F. Griggs, B.A. 1896, Fund 1951.9.18.

An artist making a **woodcut** draws a design on a smooth block of fine-grained wood, then cuts away all the areas around the lines with a sharp tool called a gouge, leaving them in high relief. When the block's surface is inked and a piece of paper pressed down hard on it, the ink on the relief areas is transferred to the paper to create a reverse image.

Engraving on metal, in contrast, requires a technique called **intaglio**, in which lines are **incised** (cut into) the plate with tools called gravers or **burins**. Ink is applied over the whole plate and forced down into the lines, after which the surface of the plate is carefully wiped clean. The ink in the recessed lines transfers to a sheet of paper pressed hard against the plate with the aid of a press.

Whichever technique is used, the great advantage of printmaking is that woodblocks and metal plates can be used repeatedly to make nearly identical images.

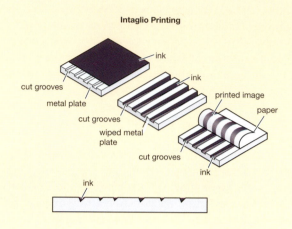

Intaglio Printing

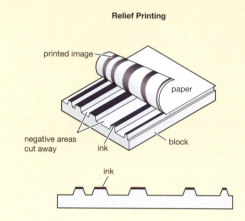

Relief Printing

👁 **Watch** a video about the process of intaglio on **MyArtsLab**

Italian Renaissance Art in Florence

How did Italian Renaissance art and architecture develop in Florence?

By the end of the Middle Ages, the most important Italian cultural centers were north of Rome at Florence, Milan, Venice, and the smaller duchies of Mantua, Ferrara, and Urbino (**MAP 12–2**). Much of the power was in the hands of wealthy families: the Medici in Florence, the Visconti and Sforza in Milan, the Gonzaga in Mantua, the Este in Ferrara, and the Montefeltro in Urbino. Cities grew in wealth and independence as people moved to them from the countryside in unprecedented numbers. As in Northern Europe, commerce became increasingly important. Money conferred status, and a shrewd business or political leader could become very powerful. Patronage of the arts was an important public activity with political overtones. One Florentine merchant, Giovanni Rucellai, succinctly noted that he supported the arts "because they serve the glory of God, the honour of the city, and the commemoration of myself" (Baxandall, p. 2).

Beginning around 1400, Italian painters and sculptors, like their Flemish counterparts, increasingly focused their attention on rendering the illusion of physical reality, building on the achievements of their great Florentine forebear Giotto. However, rather than seeking to replicate the detailed visual appearance of nature, as the Flemings did, Italian artists aimed at achieving lifelike but idealized figures—perfected, generic types—portrayed as weighty, three-dimensional forms set within a rationally configured space organized through the use of linear perspective. At the same time, Italian architects began to use mathematically derived design principles and the Classical architectural orders to create buildings conforming to ideals of symmetry and restraint.

The towering pioneers of early Renaissance art—the architect Brunelleschi, the sculptor Donatello, and the painter Masaccio—all came from Florence, the birthplace of the ideas that blossomed into the Italian Renaissance.

Architecture

Filippo Brunelleschi (1377–1446), a young sculptor-turned-architect (see "The Competition Reliefs," p. 308), was one of the principal pioneers of Florentine Renaissance architecture. His design for the vast **DOME OF FLORENCE CATHEDRAL** (**FIG. 12–12**) was a revolutionary feat of engineering. The dome is essentially a Gothic construction based on the pointed arch, using internal ribs to support the vault. It has an octagonal outer shell and a lower inner shell connected through a system of arches and horizontal sandstone rings. Brunelleschi invented an ingenious structural system—more efficient, less costly, and safer than earlier systems—by which each portion of the dome reinforced the next one as it was built up layer by layer. When completed, this self-buttressed unit required no external support. To this day, the dome remains the source of immense local pride.

MAP 12–2 •
FIFTEENTH-CENTURY ITALY

Powerful families divided the Italian peninsula into city-states: the Medici in Florence, the Sforza in Milan, the Montefeltro in Urbino, and the Gonzaga in Mantua. After 1420, the popes ruled Rome, while in the south Naples and Sicily were French and then Spanish territories. Venice maintained its independence as a republic.

12–12 • Filippo Brunelleschi
DOME OF FLORENCE CATHEDRAL

1420–1436; lantern completed 1471.

The cathedral of Florence has a long and complex history. Arnolfo di Cambio's original plan was approved in 1294, but political unrest in the 1330s brought construction to a halt until 1357. Most of the building we see today was constructed between 1357 and 1378, but Brunelleschi's great dome—now the dominant architectural feature—was only begun in 1420. This dome was a source of immense local pride from the moment of its completion. Renaissance architect and theorist Leon Battista Alberti described it as rising "above the skies, large enough to cover all the peoples of Tuscany with its shadow" (Goldwater and Treves, p. 33).

◉ **Watch** an architectural simulation of the dome of Florence Cathedral on **MyArtsLab**

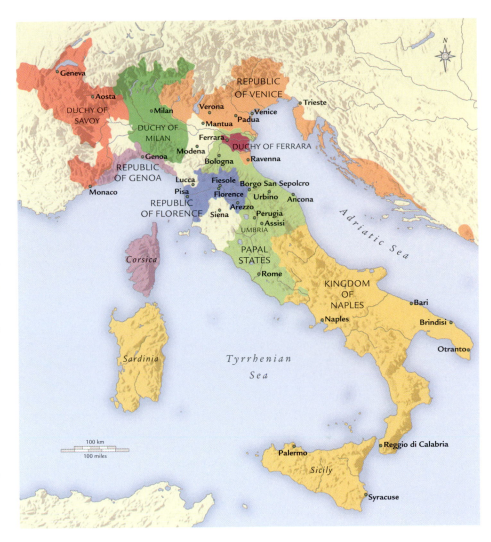

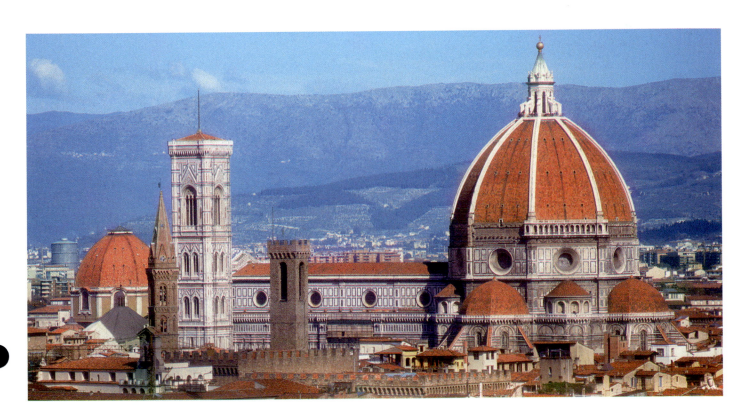

The Competition Reliefs

In 1401, the building supervisors of the baptistery of Florence Cathedral decided to commission a new pair of bronze doors, funded by the powerful wool merchants' guild. Instead of choosing a well-established sculptor, they announced a competition for the commission. This prestigious project would be awarded to the artist who demonstrated the greatest talent and skill in executing a trial piece: a bronze relief representing Abraham's sacrifice of Isaac (Genesis 22:1–13) composed within the same Gothic quatrefoil framework used in Andrea Pisano's first set of bronze doors for the baptistery, made in the 1330s. The narrative subject was full of dramatic potential: Abraham, commanded by God to slay his beloved son Isaac as a burnt offering, has traveled to the mountains for the sacrifice, but just as he is about to slaughter Isaac, an angel appears, commanding him to release his son and substitute a ram tangled in the bushes behind him.

Two competition panels have survived, those submitted by the presumed finalists: Filippo Brunelleschi and Lorenzo Ghiberti, both young artists in their early twenties. Brunelleschi's composition (FIG. 12–13) is rugged and explosive, marked by raw dramatic intensity. At the right, Abraham lunges forward, grabbing his son by the neck, while the angel swoops energetically to stay his hand just as the knife is about to strike. Isaac's awkward pose embodies his fear and struggle. Ghiberti's version

(FIG. 12–14) is quite different—suave and graceful rather than powerful and dramatic. Poses are controlled and choreographed; the harmonious pairing of son and father contrasts sharply with the wrenching struggle in Brunelleschi's rendering. And Ghiberti's Isaac is not a stretched, scrawny youth, but a fully idealized Classical figure, exuding calm composure.

Brunelleschi's biographer, Antonio di Tuccio Manetti, claimed that the competition ended in a tie, and that when the committee decided to split the commission between the two young artists, Brunelleschi withdrew. It is possible, however, that the cloth merchants chose Ghiberti. Perhaps they preferred the suave elegance of his figural composition. Perhaps they preferred the prominence of elegantly disposed swags of cloth, reminders of the source of their patronage and prosperity. But they also may have been swayed by the technical superiority of Ghiberti's relief. Unlike Brunelleschi, Ghiberti cast background and figures mostly as a single piece, making his bronze stronger, lighter, and less expensive to produce. The finished doors, installed in the baptistery in 1424, were so successful that Ghiberti was commissioned to create a third set (SEE FIG. 12–21), his most famous work, hailed by Michelangelo as the "Gates of Paradise." Brunelleschi would refocus his career on buildings rather than bronzes, becoming one of the most important architects of the Italian Renaissance (SEE FIGS. 12–12, 12–15).

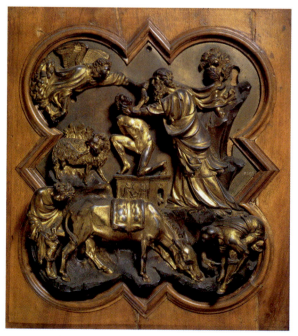

12–13 • Filippo Brunelleschi SACRIFICE OF ISAAC
1401–1402. Bronze with gilding, 21″ × 17½″ (53 × 44 cm) inside molding. Museo Nazionale del Bargello, Florence.

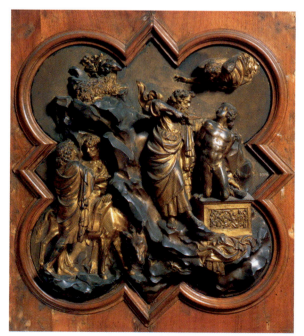

12–14 • Lorenzo Ghiberti SACRIFICE OF ISAAC
1401–1402. Bronze with gilding, 21″ × 17½″ (53 × 44 cm) inside molding. Museo Nazionale del Bargello, Florence.

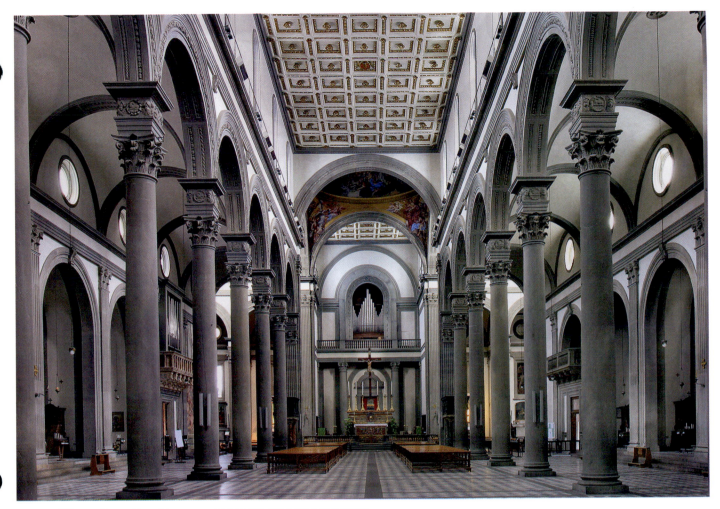

12–15 • Filippo Brunelleschi NAVE, CHURCH OF SAN LORENZO
Florence. Choir and transept begun c. 1425; nave constructed 1442–c. 1470.

Cosimo de' Medici funded the reconstruction of this church with an initial gift of 40,000 florins, in exchange for the right to be buried in front of the main altar.

✳ **Explore** the architectural panoramas of the church of San Lorenzo on **MyArtsLab**

Brunelleschi also produced remarkably innovative plans for smaller projects in Florence. In 1425, he was called in to take charge of a reconstruction of the Medici family's parish **CHURCH OF SAN LORENZO (FIG. 12–15)** that had begun in 1421. Brunelleschi's interior features Classically inspired moldings and pilasters of pietra serena (a gray stone) set against white walls to emphasize the mathematical basis of his design. Like many Romanesque and Gothic builders before him, he worked out his church plans using a module, or basic unit of measure, that could be multiplied or divided to generate every element of the design. The result was a series of clear, rational interior spaces in harmony with one another and full of Classical details.

The church of San Lorenzo is an austere basilica with a long nave flanked by single side aisles and covered with a flat ceiling inset with coffers, like a Roman basilica. A hemispherical dome on pendentives covers the crossing. Each nave arch springs from an **impost block**, or section of entablature, resting on slender Corinthian columns. With this arrangement, Brunelleschi managed to bend, without exactly breaking, the rules of Classical architecture, in which piers, rather than columns, supported arches, and columns only supported entablatures. The church of San Lorenzo was an experimental building combining old and new elements, but Brunelleschi's rational approach, unique sense of order, and innovative incorporation of Classical motifs inspired later Renaissance architects, many of whom learned from his work firsthand by completing his unfinished projects.

Brunelleschi's role in the Medici palace in Florence (now known as the **PALAZZO MEDICI-RICCARDI**), begun in 1446, is unclear **(FIG. 12–16)**. According to Giorgio Vasari, the sixteenth-century artist and theorist who wrote what some consider the first modern history of art, Brunelleschi's model for the *palazzo* (any large house was called a *palazzo*, or palace) was rejected as too grand by Cosimo de' Medici the Elder. Many now attribute the design of the building to Michelozzo di Bartolomeo. Private homes were supposed to be limited to a dozen rooms, but Cosimo actually acquired and demolished 20 small houses to provide the site for his imposing new

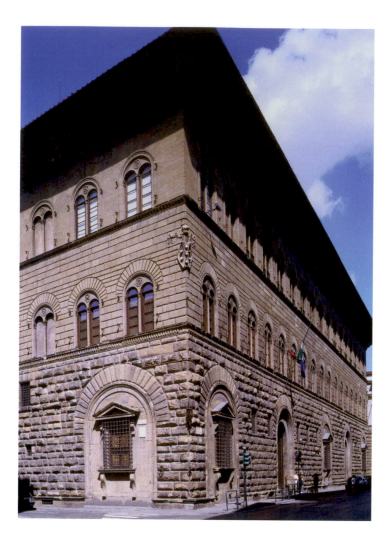

Cosimo de' Medici did not decide to build a new palace just to provide more living space for his family. He also incorporated into the plans offices and storage rooms for conducting his business affairs. For the palace site, he chose the Via de' Gori at the corner of the Via Larga, the widest city street at that time. Despite his practical reasons for constructing a large residence and the fact that he chose simplicity and austerity over grandeur in the exterior design, his detractors commented and gossiped. As one exaggerated: "[Cosimo] has begun a palace which throws even the Colosseum at Rome into the shade."

residence, each story over 20 feet in height. In Florence the house was not only a dwelling place; it symbolized the family and established its proper place in the Florentine social hierarchy.

Though huge in size, this *palazzo* is marked by fine proportions and elegant, Classically inspired detail. On one side, the ground floor originally opened through large, round arches onto the street, providing space for the family business. These arches were walled up in the sixteenth century and given windows designed by Michelangelo. The large **rusticated** stone blocks—that is, blocks with their outer faces left rough—facing the lower story clearly set it off from the two upper levels. In fact, all three stories are distinguished by stone surfaces that vary from sculptural at the ground level to almost smooth on the third floor.

Inside, the *palazzo* conforms to the time-honored tradition of placing rooms around a central courtyard. Unlike

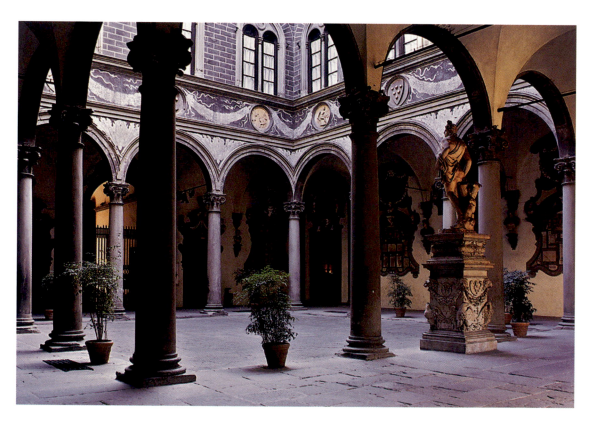

12–17 • COURTYARD WITH SGRAFFITO DECORATION, PALAZZO MEDICI-RICCARDI
Florence. Begun 1446.

irregular medieval plans, the Medici palace **COURTYARD** is square with rooms arranged symmetrically (**FIG. 12–17**). Round arches on slender columns form a continuous arcade under an enclosed second story. Tall windows in the second story match the exterior windows on this same level. Disks bearing the Medici arms surmount each arch in a frieze decorated with swags in **sgraffito** (decoration produced by scratching through a layer of darker plaster or glaze). Such classicizing elements, inspired by the study of Roman ruins, gave the great house an aura of dignity and stability that enhanced the status of its owners. The Medici palace inaugurated a new fashion for monumentality and regularity in residential Florentine architecture. Wealthy Florentine families soon emulated it in their own houses.

Sculpture

The new architectural language inspired by ancient Classical forms was paralleled by a similar impetus in sculpture. One of the leaders in this field was Donatello, born Donato di Niccolò Bardi (c. 1386–1466), perhaps the most influential and innovative sculptor of the early Italian Renaissance. He approached each commission as an opportunity for a new experiment. For example, his rendition of the biblical hero **DAVID**, who slew the giant Goliath with a stone from his slingshot, is the earliest known life-size, free-standing bronze nude in European art since antiquity (**FIG. 12–18**). Exactly when Donatello made the statue is unknown, but it was first recorded in 1469 in the courtyard of the Medici palace in Florence, mounted on a base engraved with an inscription extolling Florentine heroism and virtue. Although the work clearly draws on the Classical tradition of heroic nudity, the meaning of this sensuous prepubescent boy in a jaunty hat and boots, standing on his enemy's severed head, has long piqued art-historical interest. Some have interpreted David's angular pose, dreamy expression, and underdeveloped torso as Donatello's attempt to heighten the spectacular heroism of this child who takes on the adult responsibility of challenging and defeating a giant enemy warrior. Others have seen overt homoeroticism, pointing to the openly effeminate conception of David and the way a wing from the helmet on Goliath's severed head caresses the young hero's inner thigh.

In 1443, Donatello was probably called to Padua to execute an equestrian statue (**FIG. 12–19**) commemorating the Paduan general of the Venetian army, **ERASMO DA NARNI**, nicknamed *Gattamelata* ("Honeyed Cat"). His sources for this statue were surviving Roman bronze equestrian portraits, notably the famous image of the emperor Marcus Aurelius (**SEE FIG. 6–32**), which the sculptor certainly knew from a visit to Rome. The completed *Gattamelata*, installed on a high base in front of the church of St. Anthony of Padua, was the first life-size bronze equestrian statue since antiquity. Viewed from a distance, Donatello's man-animal juggernaut seems capable of thrusting forward at the first threat. Seen up close, however, the man's sunken cheeks, sagging jaw, ropey neck, and stern but sad expression suggest a warrior grown old and tired at the end of a distinguished military career.

While Donatello was working in Padua, his rival Lorenzo Ghiberti (1378–1455) labored on the prestigious commission in Florence for a third set of gilded bronze doors to be installed in the baptistery facing the cathedral's west façade (see "The

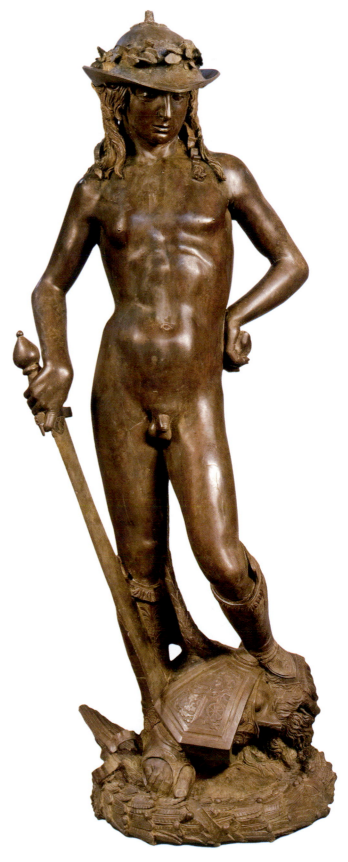

12-18 • Donatello DAVID
c. 1446–1460 (?). Bronze, height 5′ 2¼″ (1.58 m). Museo Nazionale del Bargello, Florence.

⊙ **Watch** a video about the process of lost-wax casting on **MyArtsLab**

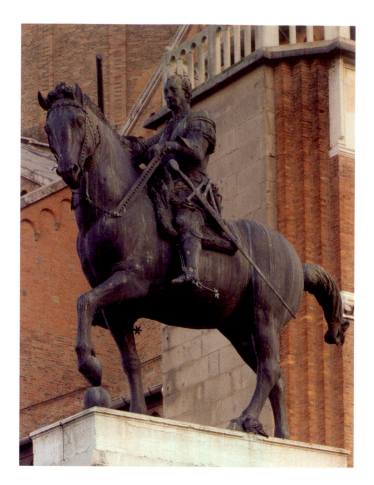

12–19 • Donatello EQUESTRIAN MONUMENT OF ERASMO DA NARNI (GATTAMELATA)
Piazza del Santo, Padua. 1443–1453. Bronze, height approx. 12′ 2″ (3.71 m).

Competition Reliefs," p. 308, for Ghiberti's choice for the second set). These doors (**FIGS. 12–20, 12–21**), installed in 1452, were reportedly said by Michelangelo to be worthy of the "**GATES OF PARADISE**," a name by which they are still known. Overall gilding unifies the ten large, square reliefs. Ghiberti organized the space depicted within each panel either by a system of linear perspective—approximating the one described by theorist Leon Battista Alberti (1404–1472) in his 1436 treatise on painting (see "Linear Perspective," p. 314)—or by a series of arches, rocks, or trees that chart a step-by-step path into the distance. Foreground figures are grouped in the lower third of each panel, while the other figures decrease gradually in size to map their positioning in receding space. The clear differentiation between foreground and background provided clearly separated settings for the sequence of unfolding events, separated by narrative time, within a single pictorial frame.

The story of Jacob and Esau (Genesis 25 and 27) fills the center panel of the left door. Ghiberti creates a coherent and measurable space peopled by graceful, idealized figures (SEE FIG. 12–20). He pays careful attention to **one-point perspective** in laying out the architectural setting. Squares in the pavement establish the receding lines of the orthogonals that converge

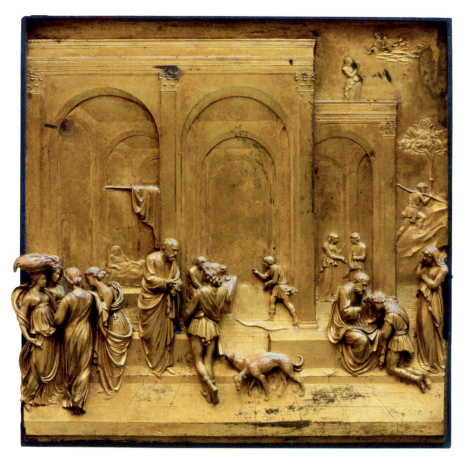

12–20 • Lorenzo Ghiberti JACOB AND ESAU
Panel from the Gates of Paradise (East Doors), formerly on the baptistery of San Giovanni, Florence. c. 1435. Gilded bronze, 31¼″ (79 cm) square. Museo dell'Opera del Duomo, Florence.

12–21 • Lorenzo Ghiberti
GATES OF PARADISE
(East Doors), baptistery of San Giovanni, Florence. 1425–1452. Gilded bronze, height 15′ (4.57 m). Museo dell'Opera del Duomo, Florence.

The door panels, commissioned by the wool manufacturers' guild, depict ten scenes from the Hebrew Bible, beginning with the Creation in the upper left panel. The murder of Abel by his brother, Cain, follows in the upper right panel, succeeded in the same left-right paired order by the Flood and the drunkenness of Noah, Abraham sacrificing Isaac, the story of Jacob and Esau, Joseph sold into slavery by his brothers, Moses receiving the Tablets of the Law, Joshua and the fall of Jericho, David and Goliath, and finally Solomon and the Queen of Sheba. Ghiberti placed his own portrait in the frame beside the Jacob and Esau panel. He wrote in his *Commentaries* (c. 1450–1455): "I strove to imitate nature as clearly as I could, and with all the perspective I could produce, to have excellent compositions with many figures."

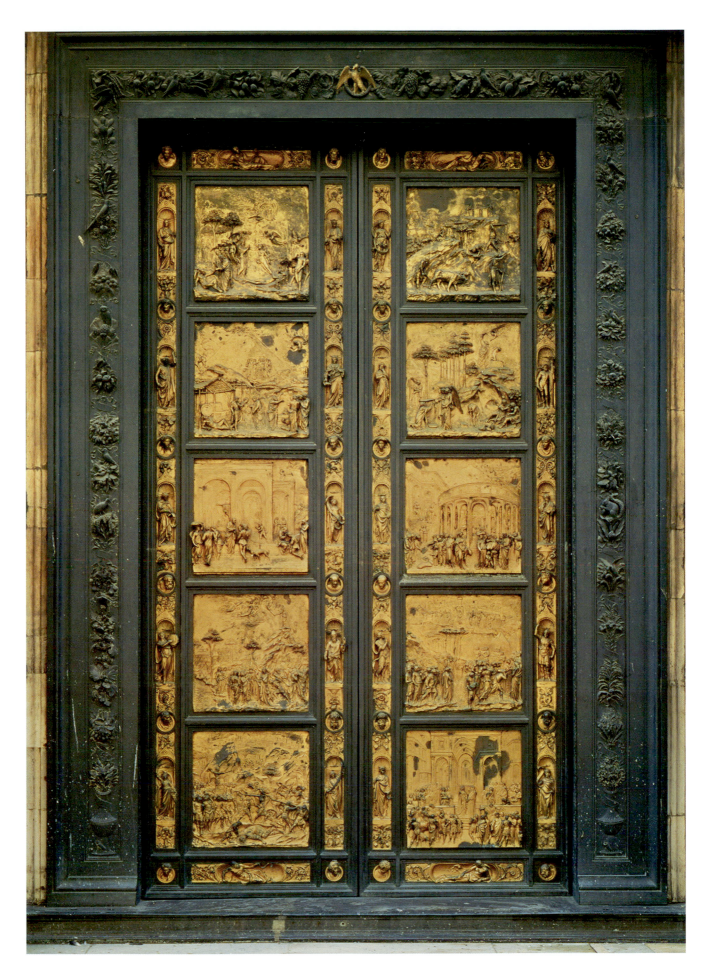

Fifteenth-century Italian artists developed a system known as **linear**, or **mathematical**, **perspective** that enabled them to represent three dimensions on a two-dimensional surface, simulating the recession of space in the visible world pictorially in a way they found convincing. The sculptor and architect Filippo Brunelleschi first demonstrated the system about 1420, and the theorist and architect Leon Battista Alberti codified it in 1436 in his treatise *Della Pittura* (*On Painting*).

For Alberti, a picture's surface was conceived as a flat plane that intersected the viewer's field of vision at right angles. This highly artificial concept presumed a viewer standing dead center at a prescribed distance from a work of art. From this single fixed vantage point, everything would appear to recede into the distance at the same rate, following imaginary lines called **orthogonals** that met at a single **vanishing point** on the horizon. By using orthogonals in concert with controlled diminution of scale as forms move back toward the vanishing point, artists could replicate the optical illusion that things appear to grow smaller, rise higher, and come closer together as they get farther away from us. Linear perspective makes pictorial spaces seem almost like extensions of the viewer's real space, creating a compelling, even exaggerated sense of depth.

Perugino's *Delivery of the Keys to St. Peter* (FIG. 12–22) is a remarkable study in linear perspective. The clear demarcation of the paving stones of the piazza provides a geometric grid of orthogonal and horizontal lines against which the figures stand like chess pieces on the squares. People and buildings are scaled to size according to their distance from the picture plane and modeled by a consistent light source from the upper left. Horizontally, the composition is divided between the foreground frieze of figures and the widely spaced background buildings, vertically by the open space at the center between Christ and Peter and by the symmetrical architectural forms on either side of this central axis.

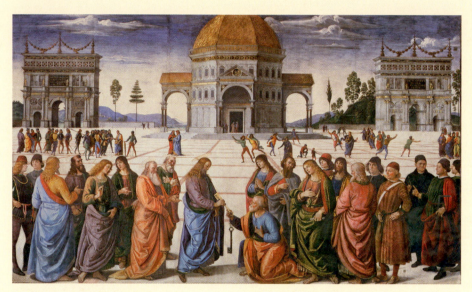

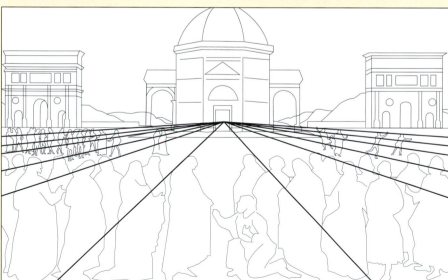

12–22 • Perugino
DELIVERY OF THE KEYS TO ST. PETER WITH A SCHEMATIC DRAWING SHOWING ORTHOGONALS AND VANISHING POINT
Sistine Chapel, Vatican, Rome. 1481. Fresco, 11′ 5½″ × 18′ 8½″ (3.48 × 5.7 m).

Perugino's painting is, among other things, a representation of Alberti's description of an ideal city which had a "temple" (that is, a church) at the very center of a great open space raised on a dais and separate from any other buildings so that it would always be visible.

to a vanishing point under the **loggia**, while towering arches overlap and gradually diminish in size from foreground to background to define the receding space above the high-relief figures. The story unfolds in a sequence of individual episodes, beginning in the background. On the rooftop (upper right) Rebecca stands, listening as God warns of her unborn sons' future conflict; under the left-hand arch she gives birth to the twins. The adult Esau sells his rights as oldest son to his brother Jacob, and when he goes hunting (center right), Rebecca and Jacob plot against him. Finally, in the right foreground, Jacob receives Isaac's blessing, while in the center, Esau faces his father. Ghiberti's portrayal of this scene relates closely to parallel developments in Florentine painting.

Painting

One of the major achievements of Italian Renaissance artists was the consistently scaled integration of human figures into rationally receding architectural settings using linear perspective. This was accomplished early on in the works of the Florentine painter Tommaso di Ser Giovanni di Mone Cassai (1401–1428), nicknamed Masaccio ("Big Tom"). In his short but brilliant career of less than a decade, Masaccio established a new direction in Florentine painting, much as Giotto had done a century earlier. The exact chronology of his works is uncertain, but his fresco of the **TRINITY** in the church of Sta. Maria Novella in Florence falls sometime between 1425 and 1428 (**FIG. 12–23**).

This fresco was meant to give the illusion of a stone funerary monument and altar table set in a deep **aedicula** (framed niche) in the wall. The effect of looking up into a barrel-vaulted niche was made plausible through precisely rendered linear perspective. The eye level of an adult viewer standing in the church determined the horizon line on which the vanishing point was centered, just below the kneeling figures above the altar. The niche itself resembles the classicizing Renaissance architecture of San Lorenzo (SEE FIG. 12–15). A consistent illumination, whose "source" seems to lie behind the viewer, models the figures and casts reflections on the painted coffers (recessed panels) of the vault.

The figures are organized in a measured progression into space. At the back, a looming figure of God the Father holds the cross on which Jesus hangs, while the dove of the Holy Spirit seems poised in downward flight between Jesus's tilted halo and the Father's

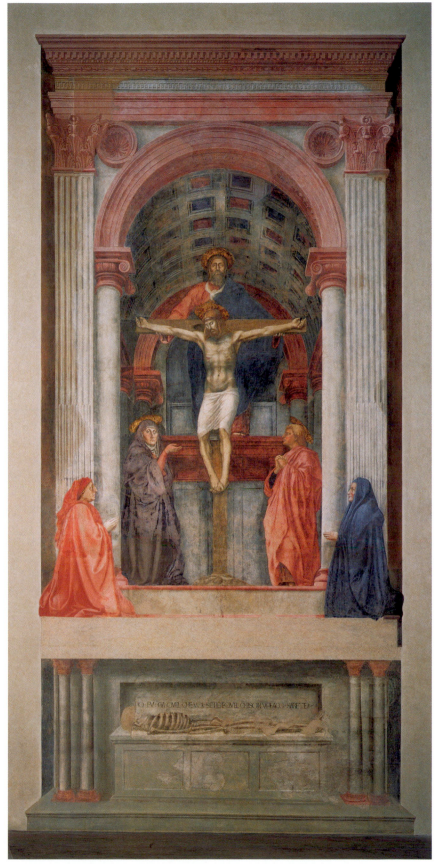

12–23 • Masaccio
TRINITY WITH THE VIRGIN, ST. JOHN THE EVANGELIST, AND DONORS
Church of Sta. Maria Novella, Florence. c. 1425–1428. Fresco, 21′ × 10′ 5″ (6.4 × 3.2 m).

👁 **Watch** a video about Masaccio's *Trinity* on **MyArtsLab**

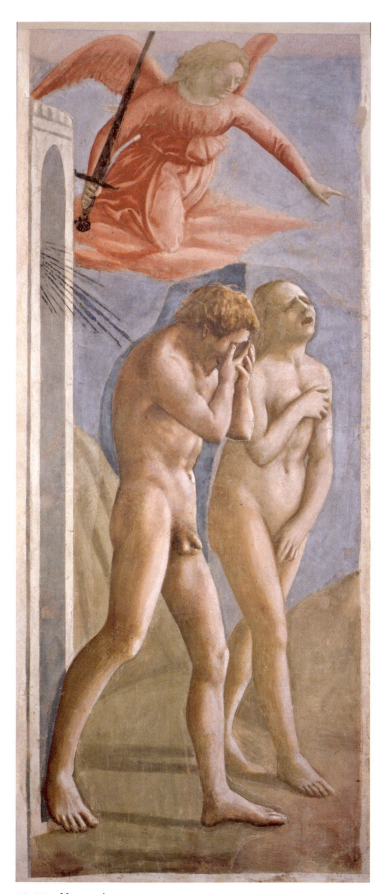

12–24 • Masaccio
THE EXPULSION OF ADAM AND EVE FROM PARADISE
Brancacci Chapel, church of Sta. Maria del Carmine, Florence. c. 1427.
Fresco, 7′ × 2′ 11″ (214 × 90 cm).

head. Mary and St. John the Evangelist stand at the foot of the cross. Mary gazes calmly out at us, her raised hand gesturing toward the Trinity. Outside and in front of the niche the donors—members of the Lenzi family—kneel in prayer closer to us than the Crucifixion. Below, in an open sarcophagus, a skeleton provides a grim reminder of the Christian belief that since death awaits us all, our only hope is redemption and the promise of life in the hereafter, rooted in Christ's sacrifice on the cross. The inscription above the skeleton reads: "I was once that which you are, and what I am you also will be."

Masaccio's brief career culminated in the frescos he painted on the walls of the Brancacci Chapel in the church of Sta. Maria del Carmine in Florence. Reproduced here are the two best-known scenes: **THE EXPULSION OF ADAM AND EVE FROM PARADISE** (FIG. 12–24) and **THE TRIBUTE MONEY** (FIG. 12–25). Adam and Eve are represented as monumental nude figures, combining Masaccio's study of the human figure with his knowledge of ancient Roman sculpture. The mass of their bodies reveals the underlying structure of bone and muscle, and a single light source emphasizes their tangibility with modeling and cast shadows. Departing from earlier interpretations that emphasized wrongdoing and original sin when representing this event, Masaccio stresses the psychological impact of shame of these first humans, who have been cast out of Paradise mourning and protesting, thrown naked and unprepared into the world.

In *The Tribute Money*, Masaccio portrays an incident from the Life of Jesus (Matthew 17:24–27) that highlights St. Peter, to whom this chapel was originally dedicated. In the central scene, a tax collector (dressed in a short red tunic and seen from behind) asks Peter (in the left foreground with the short gray beard) if Jesus pays the Jewish temple tax (the "tribute money" of the title). Set against the stable backdrop of a semicircular grouping of the apostles, a masterful sequence of dynamic diagonals in the postures and gestures of the three main figures interlocks them in a compositional system that charges their interaction with a sense of tension, calling out for resolution. Jesus instructs Peter to "go to the sea and cast a hook; take the first fish that comes up," which Peter does at the far left. In the fish's mouth, Peter finds a coin which he gives with another diagonal gesture to the tax collector at the far right, whose slanting cane prevents our eyes from venturing further to signal the conclusion of this multi-scene narrative episode.

The Tribute Money is particularly remarkable for its early use of both linear and atmospheric perspective to integrate figures, architecture, and landscape into a consistent whole. The group of disciples around Jesus forms a clear central focus, behind which the landscape seems to recede logically into the far distance. To foster this illusion, Masaccio used linear perspective in the depiction of the house, and then reinforced it by diminishing the sizes of the barren trees and reducing the size of the crouching Peter at far left. At the central vanishing point established by the orthogonals of the house is the head of Jesus. A

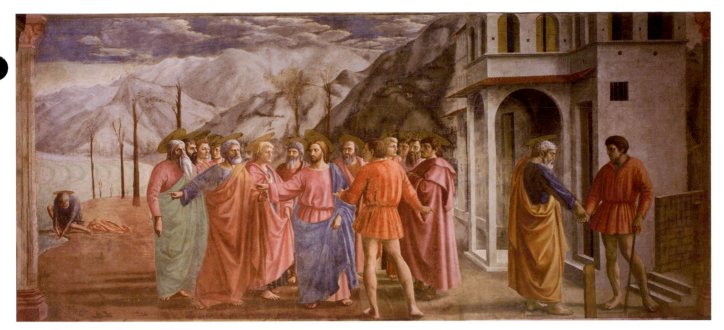

12-25 • Masaccio THE TRIBUTE MONEY
Brancacci Chapel, church of Sta. Maria del Carmine, Florence. c. 1427. Fresco, 8′ 1″ × 19′ 7″ (2.46 × 6 m).

Much valuable new information about the Brancacci Chapel frescos was discovered during the course of a cleaning and restoration carried out between 1981 and 1991. Art historians now have a more accurate picture of how the frescos were done and in what sequence.

second vanishing point determines the position of the steps and stone rail at the right. The cleaning of the fresco during the 1980s—which revealed that it was painted in 32 *giornate* (a *giornata* is a section of fresh plaster that could be prepared and painted in one day)—uncovered Mascaccio's subtle use of color to create atmospheric perspective in the distant landscape. The mountains fade from grayish green to grayish white and the houses and trees on their slopes are more sketchy, to simulate the lack of clear definition when viewing things in the distance through haze.

As with *The Expulsion of Adam and Eve from Paradise*, Masaccio models figures here with bold highlights and long shadows, giving a strong sense of volumetric solidity and implying a light source at the far right, as if the scene were lit by the actual window in the rear wall of the chapel. Not only does the lighting give the forms sculptural definition, but the colors vary in **tone** according to the strength of the illumination. Masaccio used a wide range of hues—pale pink, mauve, gold, seafoam-green, apple-green, and peach—and a sophisticated shading technique using contrasting colors, as in St. Andrew's green mantle, shaded with red instead of darker green. The figures of Jesus and the apostles originally had gold-leaf haloes, several of which have flaked off. But rather than silhouette the heads against consistently flat gold circles in the medieval manner (compare FIGS. 11–25 through 11–27), Masaccio conceived of haloes as gold disks hovering in space above each head that moved with the heads as they moved, and he foreshortened them in relation to the angle from which each is seen.

Masaccio's figures exhibit his debt to Roman sculpture and also to the painting of Giotto and his followers, which he could have seen around him in fifteenth-century Florence. But some stylistic innovations take time to be fully accepted, and Masaccio's innovative depictions of volumetric solidity, consistent lighting, and spatial integration were best appreciated by a later generation of painters. Many important sixteenth-century Italian artists, including Michelangelo (see Chapter 13), studied and sketched Masaccio's Brancacci Chapel frescos, as they did Giotto's Scrovegni Chapel frescos (see Chapter 11).

In the meantime, the tradition of covering walls with paintings in fresco continued uninterrupted through the fifteenth century. Between 1435 and 1445 the decoration of the Dominican monastery of San Marco in Florence, where Fra Angelico served as the prior, was one of the most important projects. Born Guido di Pietro da Mugello (c. 1395/1400–1455), Fra Angelico ("Angelic Brother") earned his nickname through his piety as well as his painting. He is first documented painting in Florence in 1417–1418, and he remained an active painter after taking vows as a Dominican monk in nearby Fiesole between 1418 and 1421.

In the monastery of San Marco, Fra Angelico and his assistants created paintings to inspire meditation in each monk's cell (44 in all), in the chapter house (meeting room), and even in the corridors. At the top of the stairs in the north corridor, where the monks would pass on their way to their individual cells, Fra Angelico painted a serene picture of the **ANNUNCIATION (FIG. 12–26)**. To describe the quiet, measured space where the demure archangel greets the unassuming, youthful Mary, Fra Angelico used linear perspective with consummate skill, extending the monks' stairway and corridor outward into an imagined portico and garden beside the Virgin's house.

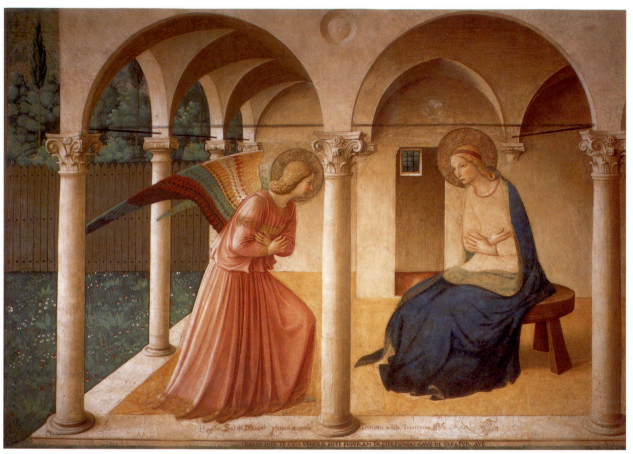

12–26 • Fra Angelico **ANNUNCIATION**
North corridor, monastery of San Marco, Florence. c. 1438–1445. Fresco, 7′ 1″ × 10′ 6″ (2.2 × 3.2 m).

The slender, graceful figures, wearing quietly flowing draperies, assume modest poses. Natural light falling from the left models their forms gently, casting an almost supernatural radiance over their faces and hands. The scene is a sacred vision rendered in a contemporary setting, welcoming the monks to the most intimate areas of the monastery and preparing them for their private meditations.

While Fra Angelico was still painting his radiant visions of Mary and Jesus in the monastery of San Marco, a new generation of artists emerged. Thoroughly conversant with the theories of Brunelleschi and Alberti, they had mastered the techniques (and tricks) of depicting figures in a constructed architectural space. Some artists became specialists. The eccentric painter Paolo di Dono (c. 1397–1475), called Paolo Uccello ("Paul Bird"), devoted himself with particular fervor to the study of linear perspective. In his biographies of Italian artists, Vasari described Uccello as "solitary, eccentric, melancholy, and impoverished" (Vasari, trans. Bondanella and Bondanella, p. 79), a man so obsessed with the science of perspective that he neglected his painting, his family, and even his pet birds (his *uccelli*). According to Vasari, Uccello's wife complained that he sat up drawing all night and when she called to him to come to bed he would say, "Oh, what a sweet thing this perspective is!" (p. 83). His overriding interest in the rendering of perspective and experimenting with the geometry of form and volume transforms the battle scenes he created to decorate the house of a wealthy Florentine patron into bloodless tableaus of frozen knights, rather than heated moments in the height of hectic military engagements (see "A Closer Look," p. 319).

Contrasting sharply with Uccello's scientific obsession is the fascination of the Florentine painter Sandro Botticelli (1445–1510) with fluid, linear, graceful figures resembling dancers. Among Botticelli's best-known works are paintings of mythological subjects, among them the **BIRTH OF VENUS** (**FIG. 12–27**). This painting was probably made around 1484–1486 for the private collection of Lorenzo de' Medici ("the Magnificent"; 1449–1492), who had become ruler of Florence in 1469. The central image, a type known as the "modest Venus," ultimately derives from a Classical Greek statue that was widely copied by the Romans (SEE FIG. INTRO–6). Botticelli's Classical goddess of love and beauty, born of seafoam, averts her eyes from our gaze as she floats ashore on a scallop shell, carefully arranging her hands and hair to hide—or draw attention to—her sexuality. Blown by the wind god Zephyr (with his love, the nymph Chloris), and welcomed on the right by a devotee who offers her a garment embroidered with flowers, Venus arrives at her earthly home. The circumstances of the commission are uncertain, but since it is painted on canvas, it may have been a banner or a painted tapestry-like wall hanging.

The Battle of San Romano ▶

Paolo Uccello. 1438–1440. Tempera on wood panel, 6′ × 10′ 7″ (1.83 × 3.23 m). The National Gallery, London.

Hedges of oranges, roses, and pomegranates form a tapestry-like backdrop for the battle. These fruits are ancient fertility symbols, suggesting that the patron may have commissioned the series of paintings to which this picture belongs on the occasion of his wedding in 1438.

Florentine general Niccolò da Tolentino leads his army to victory against the Sienese at the Battle of San Romano on June 1, 1432. Niccolò holds aloft his baton of command, which, with his white horse and fashionable crimson-and-gold damask hat, ensures that he dominates the scene.

Lionardo Bartolini Salimbeni (1409–1479), who headed Florence's governing Council of Ten during the war against Lucca and Siena, commemorated here, probably commissioned this painting c. 1438 as part of a set of three for his home. By 1492, however, they had been removed and hung in Lorenzo de' Medici's private chamber in the Medici palace.

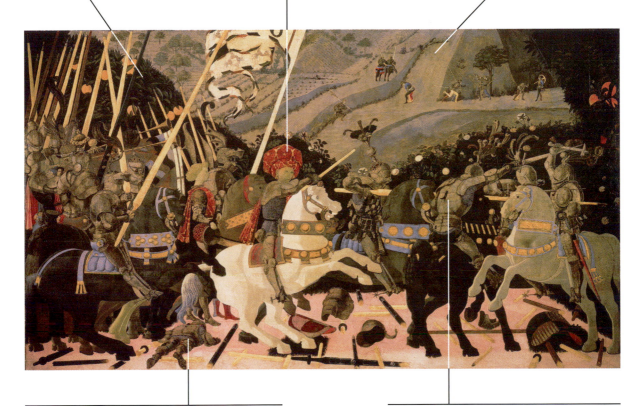

This fallen soldier—like many of the broken lances on the ground around him—creates an implied orthogonal of the linear perspective system, as if he had magically snapped into place on an unseen grid when he hit the ground.

Originally the splendor of this painting depended in part on the silver leaf that covered the armor of these soldiers, an effect that can only be imagined since the silver is now tarnished to a dull gray.

🔎 **View** the Closer Look for Uccello's *The Battle of San Romano* on **MyArtsLab**

Urbino, Mantua, Venice, and Rome

How did the Renaissance spread from Florence to other Italian cities?

In the second half of the fifteenth century, the ideas and ideals of Florentine Renaissance artists like Brunelleschi, Donatello, and Masaccio began to spread from Florence to the rest of Italy as artists who had trained or worked in Florence traveled to other cities to work, carrying the Renaissance style with them. Northern Italy embraced the new Classical ideas swiftly, especially in the ducal courts at Urbino and Mantua, and Venice and Rome also emerged as innovative art centers.

Urbino

Under Federico da Montefeltro, Urbino developed into a thriving artistic center. A new palace was under construction from the 1450s into the 1470s, and promising architects and artists were brought in to make the new princely residence and the court that occupied it a showcase of ducal splendor.

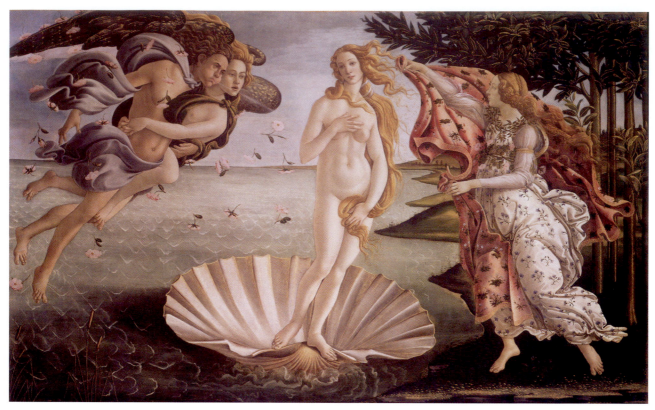

12–27 • Sandro Botticelli BIRTH OF VENUS
c. 1484–1486. Tempera and gold on canvas, 5′ 8⅞″ × 9′ 1⅞″ (1.8 × 2.8 m). Galleria degli Uffizi, Florence.

Prominent among those who came to work for the duke was painter Piero della Francesca (c. 1415–1492). Born in the small Tuscan town of Borgo San Sepulcro, Piero worked in Florence in the 1430s. He knew current art theory and art practice, including Brunelleschi's system of spatial illusion and linear perspective, Masaccio's powerful modeling of forms and use of atmospheric perspective, and Alberti's theoretical treatises. He was also an accomplished mathematician, generally credited with the modern rediscovery of Euclid. Piero was one of the few practicing artists who also wrote his own theories of art.

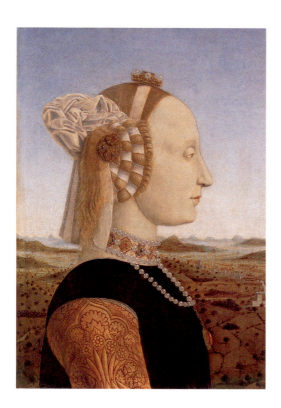

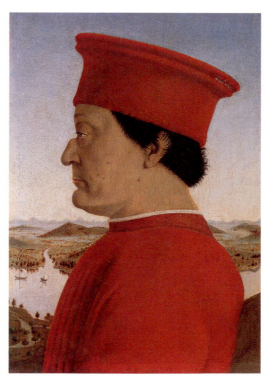

12–28 • Piero della Francesca **BATTISTA SFORZA (LEFT) AND FEDERICO DA MONTEFELTRO (RIGHT)**
c. 1474. Oil on wood panel, each 18½″ × 13″ (47 × 33 cm). Galleria degli Uffizi, Florence.

Battista Sforza died in 1472 at age 26, shortly after the birth of her ninth child, a son who would one day be duke. We are told that Federico was disconsolate. Some arranged aristocratic marriage alliances blossomed into loving partnerships, and it seems that one such was memorialized in this double portrait.

Not surprisingly, in his treatises on mathematics and perspective he emphasized the geometry and the volumetric construction of forms and spaces that were so apparent in his own paintings. In fact, the organizing geometry of Piero's pictures was related to a mathematical skill called gaging, used by the very merchants who commissioned many of his paintings to estimate the volume and value of the commodities in which they traded. This link between the intellectual and commercial practices of painters and their patrons indicates the strong integration of Italian Renaissance art with the culture within which it developed.

Around 1474, during his sojourn at Federico da Montefeltro's court in Urbino, Piero painted a pair of companion portraits of Federico and his recently deceased wife, **BATTISTA SFORZA** (**FIG. 12–28**). The small panels resemble Flemish painting in their detail and luminosity, their record of surfaces and textures, and their vast landscapes. But in traditional Italian fashion, figures are portrayed in strict profile, disengaged psychologically from the viewer. The profile format also allowed for an accurate recording of Federico's likeness without emphasizing two disfiguring scars—the loss of his right eye from a lance blow and his broken nose. His good left eye is shown, and the angular profile of his nose might easily be merely a distinctive family trait. Typically, Piero emphasized the underlying geometry of the forms. Dressed in the most elegant fashion (Federico wears his red ducal robe and Battista's jewels are meticulously recorded), they are silhouetted against a panoramic landscape. These are the hills around Urbino, seemingly dissolving into infinity through an atmospheric perspective as subtle and luminous as in any Flemish panel painting. Piero would have had contact in Urbino with the Flemish artists who were also working there.

Mantua

North of Urbino and the Montefeltro court, the Renaissance also appeared in Mantua, where Andrea Mantegna (1431–1506) was called to the court of Ludovico Gonzaga in 1460 and worked there for the rest of his life. Between 1465 and 1474, Mantegna painted frescos in the **CAMERA PICTA** (Painted Room) of the ducal palace (**FIG. 12–29**). On the vaulted ceiling, Mantegna painted a *tour-de-force* of perspective and foreshortening,

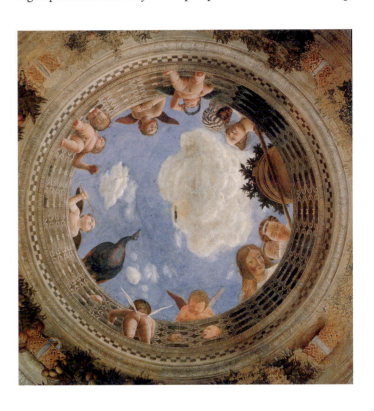

12–29 • Andrea Mantegna
TWO VIEWS OF
THE CAMERA PICTA
Ducal palace, Mantua.
1465–1474. Fresco, diameter
of false oculus 8′ 9″ (2.7 m),
room 26′ 6″ (8 m) square.

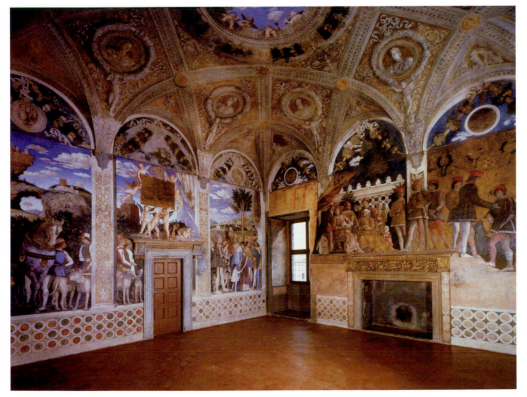

creating a viewpoint called *di sotto in sù* (seen directly from below), which began a long tradition of illusionistic ceiling painting. The room appears to be open to a cloud-filled sky through a large oculus in a simulated marble-and-mosaic-covered vault. On each side of a precariously balanced planter, three young women and an exotically turbaned African man peer at us over a marble parapet. A fourth young woman in a veil looks dreamily upward. Joined by a large peacock, several **putti** (a *putto* is a little boy, often shown naked and winged) play around the **balustrade**, three standing on the interior ledge of the cornice, unprotected by the balustrade barrier, toes projecting into space but seemingly oblivious to the danger of their perch. Mantegna completed the decoration of the room with murals featuring portraits of members of the Gonzaga family—each seemingly identified in a portrait likeness—welcoming the return of Ludovico's son, Cardinal Francesco Gonzaga.

Venice

In the last quarter of the fifteenth century, Venice emerged as a major Renaissance art center. Ruled as an oligarchy (government by a select few) with an elected duke (*doge* in the Venetian dialect), Venice had turned marshes into a commercial seaport, and they depended on naval power and on the natural defense of their lagoons rather than city walls for protection. In addition to its long history of painting and sculpture, Venice excelled in the arts of textiles and jewelry, gold and enamel, glass and mosaic, fine printing and bookbinding.

The most important Venetian painters of this period were two brothers: Gentile (c. 1429–1507) and Giovanni (c. 1430–1516) Bellini. Giovanni's painting of **ST. FRANCIS IN ECSTASY (FIG. 12–30)**, also from around the 1470s, recalls Flemish art in the fine detail with which he rendered the natural world. The saint stands bathed in early morning sunlight, his outspread hands displaying his stigmata. Francis had moved to a cave in the barren wilderness in his search for communion with God, but in the world Giovanni creates for him, the fields blossom and flocks of animals graze. The grape arbor over his desk adds to the atmosphere of sylvan delight. Like most of the fifteenth-century religious art we have seen, however, Bellini presents viewers with a natural world saturated in symbolism. Here a relationship between St. Francis and Moses is outlined. The tree symbolizes the burning bush; the stream, the miraculous spring brought forth by Moses. The crane and donkey represent the monastic virtue of patience. The detailed description, luminous palette, and symbolic surroundings suggest Flemish art, but the golden light suffusing the painting is unmistakably Venetian.

Rome

Late in the fifteenth century, the city of Rome became a magnet for Renaissance artists. Pope Sixtus IV summoned a group of young Florentine and Umbrian painters to decorate the walls of his newly built Sistine Chapel (SEE FIG. 13–10), among them Pietro Vannucci, called Perugino (c. 1445–1523), who, though active in Florence, came from near the town of Perugia in Umbria. In 1482, he painted the *Delivery of the Keys to St. Peter* (SEE FIG. 12–22), an event not actually described in the Bible but suggested in Matthew 16:19. The event came to signify the supremacy of papal authority: Christ is shown giving the keys to the kingdom of heaven to the apostle Peter, who, as the first bishop of Rome, was also considered the first pope. As Perugino and other Florentine artists were called to the Vatican to fulfill papal commissions, the center of Italian art began to shift from Florence to Rome.

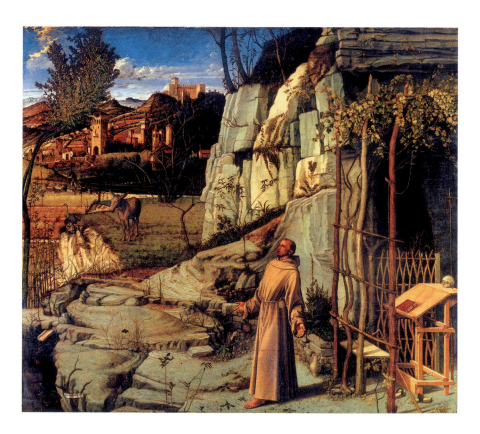

12–30 • Giovanni Bellini
ST. FRANCIS IN ECSTASY
c. 1470s. Oil and tempera on wood panel, 49″ × 55⅞″ (125 × 142 cm). The Frick Collection, New York.

LOOKING BACK ◄

Fifteenth-century European art embodies the values and worldview of a new intellectual and social order. The kind of logical discourse formerly reserved for theology was now applied to the material world. Individuals gained importance, not only as inquiring minds but as the subject of inquiry. Artists, too, began to be recognized as individual personalities with distinct talents and distinguishable styles.

Because patrons wanted to see themselves depicted as they actually looked, portraits take on an arrestingly lifelike quality rooted in careful description. And this desire for faithfully observed representations extended to portrayals of the natural and constructed environment. Artists gave patrons identifiable views of the buildings and countryside where they worked and played, offering paintings that adopted new and rationalized ways of representing space and organizing pictures with linear perspective. By the end of the fifteenth century, the artistic mastery of the material world through careful observation and scientific compositional systems must have seemed complete. During the next century, however, High Renaissance artists will employ these same techniques to explore new subjects in new ways.

THINK ABOUT IT

12.1 Discuss the symbolic meanings that fifteenth-century viewers would have comprehended in the objects contained in the domestic environments of either the *Mérode Altarpiece* (FIG. 12–3) or the Arnolfini double portrait (FIG. 12–1). How have the artists made these objects look so real?

12.2 Describe the difference between woodcuts and engravings. Why would an artist choose one over the other?

12.3 Define linear perspective. Choose a work in this chapter that clearly demonstrates its use and discuss how the artist employs this technique. Does perspective affect the way the story is told or the meaning that it conveys?

12.4 Choose one wealthy patron discussed in this chapter and explain how his patronage fostered the emergence of the Renaissance in fifteenth-century Italy.

| CROSSCURRENTS |

 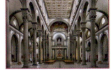

FIG. 7–8   FIG. 12–15

Since the reign of the emperor Constantine in the fourth century CE, Christians have used the Roman basilica plan in designing churches. Look carefully at these two interiors and discuss what aspects of the early plan stay constant and what features have changed in the Renaissance example.

IN PERSPECTIVE

1400

Great Schism Ends 1417

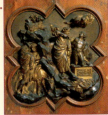

GHIBERTI, *Sacrifice of Isaac* 1401–1402

1425

Alberti Publishes *Della Pittura* (*On Painting*) 1436

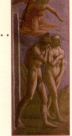

MASSACCIO, The Expulsion of Adam and Eve from Paradise c. 1427

1450

Ghiberti Writes *Commentaries* c. 1450–1455
Habsburgs Begin Rule of Holy Roman Empire 1452
Hundred Years' War Ends 1453
Gutenberg Prints Bible 1455

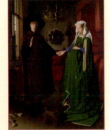

VAN EYCK, Giovanni Arnolfini and His Wife 1434

Lorenzo de' Medici Rules Florence 1469–1492

1475

William Caxton Establishes First English Printing House 1476

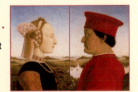

PIERO DELLA FRANCESCA, Double Portrait c. 1474

Columbus Reaches the West Indies 1492

Savonarola Executed 1498

1500

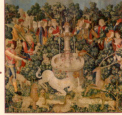

Tapestry from the Unicorn Series c. 1495–1505

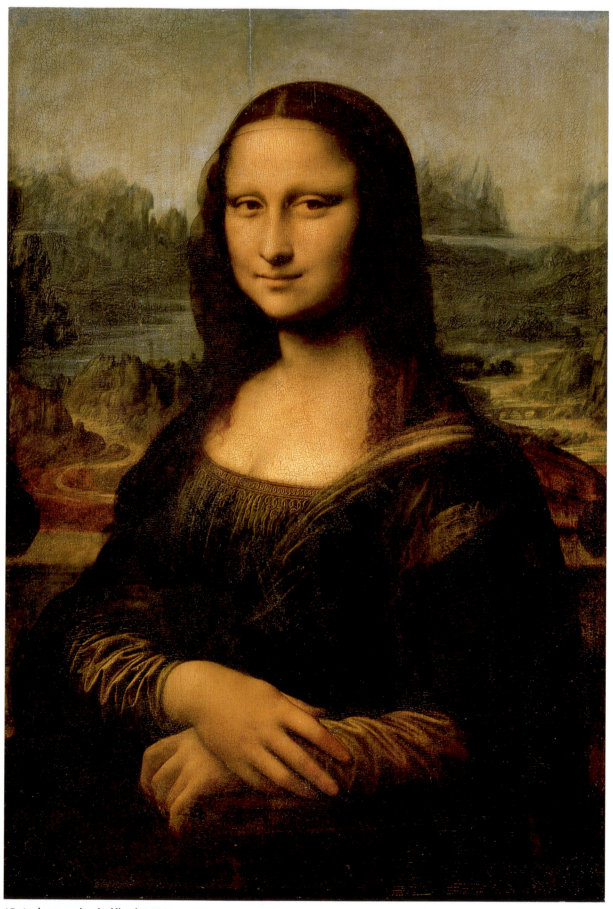

13–1 • Leonardo da Vinci **MONA LISA**
c. 1503–1506. Oil on wood panel, 30¼″ × 21″ (76.8 × 53.3 cm). Musée du Louvre, Paris.

ART OF THE HIGH RENAISSANCE AND REFORMATION

LEARNING OBJECTIVES

13.1 Characterize the High Renaissance art of Italy.

13.2 Summarize the development of Mannerism in Italy and France.

13.3 Distinguish several styles of sixteenth-century art in Germany.

13.4 Describe the distinctive trends in the sixteenth-century art of the Netherlands and Spain.

LOOKING FORWARD ▶

Is it Mona Lisa's "smile" that grabs us? Is it the sense of mystery created by the smoky haze that envelops both her and the weird landscape behind her? Are we captivated by the way she turns to confront us directly with such stunning self-confidence? What is it that has made this painting so compelling to centuries of art lovers? It may be the world's most famous painting.

Actually the **MONA LISA (FIG. 13–1)** is not especially mysterious. No secret code needs to be cracked. Leonardo da Vinci, one of the most famous painters and most fertile minds of the Italian Renaissance, painted this portrait between 1503 and 1506, while he was living in Florence. Although there is lingering uncertainty, most art historians agree with sixteenth-century Italian biographer Giorgio Vasari, who claimed that the *Mona Lisa* portrays Lisa di Antonio Maria Gherardini, wife of Florentine merchant Francesco del Giocondo. ("Mona" is a term of respect, a contraction of "Madonna," meaning "my lady"). Lisa married Francesco in 1495, when she was 16, so Leonardo painted her during her mid-twenties. But he never delivered the painting. He kept it with him for the rest of his life, continuing to tinker with it, probably working on it while he was in Rome after 1513, and taking it with him in 1516 when he moved to France at the invitation of Francis I. After Leonardo's death in 1519,

the king purchased the *Mona Lisa* for Fontainebleau. Louis XIV moved it to Versailles, and Napoleon hung it in his bedroom in the Tuileries Palace. It now hangs at the Louvre. It is one of the most popular destinations for tourists visiting Paris.

This was an unusual portrait for its time. Leonardo abandoned the long-standing Italian tradition of painting wealthy wives in profile view, wearing the jewelry that signified their status and proclaimed their husbands' wealth (SEE FIG. 12–28). Mona Lisa seems to be the likeness of a specific woman who turns with calm assurance to engage viewers, hands relaxed in her lap. Her expression has been called "enigmatic." It hides rather than reveals her thoughts and personality. It lacks the warmth one expects to see in her eyes, which have shifted to the side to look straight out at us. The psychological complexity Leonardo has given to this face may explain the spell it has cast over viewers.

One thing is clear. This portrait embodies many of the hallmarks of the High Renaissance style that will solidify in Rome during the first two decades of the sixteenth century—the blend of naturalistic description and classicizing idealism, and the clarity and balanced structure of the pyramidal composition that gives utter stability to the monumentally sculptural human form.

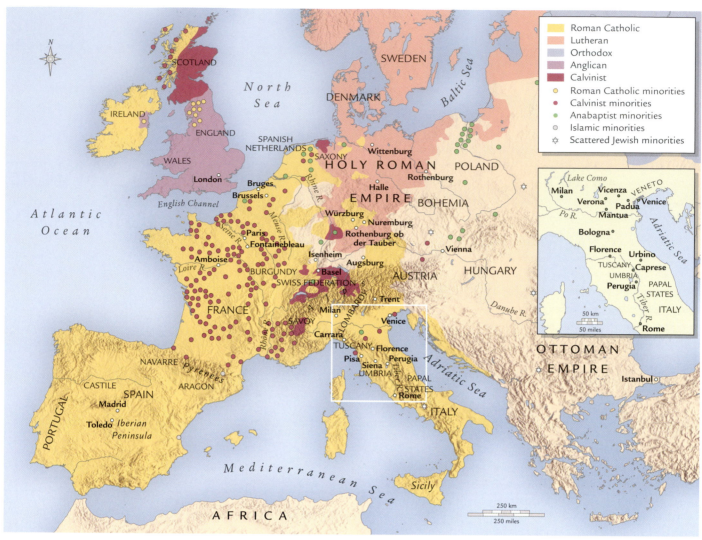

MAP 13-1 • RENAISSANCE EUROPE

Sixteenth-century Europe remained largely Roman Catholic, except in Switzerland and the far north, where the impact of the Protestant Reformation was strongest.

During the sixteenth century, early Renaissance Humanism underwent a radical shift. Its medieval roots and often uncritical acceptance of the authority of Classical texts slowly gave way to a critical exploration of new ideas, the natural world, and distant lands in Africa, Asia, and the Americas. The authority of the pope was even questioned in the movement known as the Reformation. The influential writings and leadership of important reformers, such as Martin Luther (1483–1546) in Germany, led to the establishment of Protestant churches in Northern Europe. And, at the Council of Trent (1545–1563), the Roman Catholic hierarchy responded with a program to counter the Reformation.

During this period, travel in Europe became easier and safer. Since artists journeyed from city to city, even country to country, styles and techniques became less regional and more international (**MAP 13–1**). The materials artists worked with changed, too. Although fresco painting was still common, more and more artists painted with oil on canvas, producing oil paintings in their studios and transporting and installing them

elsewhere. Artists became sought-after international celebrities, and their social status rose as painting, sculpture, and architecture came to be seen as liberal rather than manual arts, requiring intellectual activity, not simply technical skill.

Italian Art of the High Renaissance

How can we explain the High Renaissance art of Italy?

Early sixteenth-century Italian art reflects a self-confident Humanism, an abiding admiration for Classical forms, and a dominating sense of stability and order. These qualities characterize the work of four towering figures of the Italian Renaissance: Leonardo, Raphael, Michelangelo, and Titian. The achievements of these artists are so remarkable that nineteenth-century scholars called the period in Italy from about 1495 until the death of Raphael in 1520 the "High" Renaissance, a term that encapsulates an art-historical claim that what happened in Rome at this time represents a pinnacle of achievement within a longer artistic movement—that it set standards for the future.

The Vitruvian Man

Artists throughout history have turned to geometric shapes and mathematical proportions to seek the ideal representation of the human form. Leonardo, and before him the first-century BCE Roman architect and engineer Vitruvius, equated the ideal man with both circle and square. In his ten-volume *De architectura* (*On Architecture*), Vitruvius wrote:

> For if a man be placed flat on his back, with his hands and feet extended, and a pair of compasses centered at his navel, the fingers and toes of his two hands and feet will touch the circumference of a circle described therefrom. And just as the human body yields a circular outline, so too a square figure may be found from it. For if we measure the distance from the soles of the feet to the top of the head, and then apply that measure to the outstretched arms, the breadth will be found to be the same as the height.
> (Book III, Chapter 1, Section 2)

Vitruvius determined that the ideal body should be eight heads high. Leonardo added his own observations—in the reversed writing he always used for his notebooks—when he created his well-known diagram for the ideal male figure, called the **VITRUVIAN MAN** (**FIG. 13–2**).

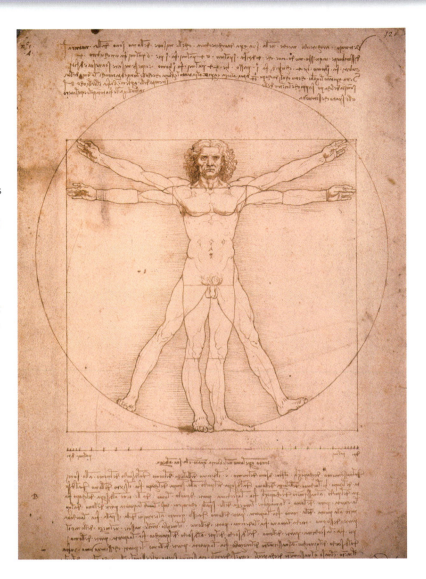

13–2 • Leonardo da Vinci VITRUVIAN MAN
c. 1490. Ink, approx. 13½″ × 9⅝″ (34.3 × 24.5 cm). Galleria dell'Accademia, Venice.

📖 **Read** the document related to Leonardo da Vinci on **MyArtsLab**

Leonardo da Vinci

Leonardo da Vinci (1452–1519) received his training in the workshop of the painter and sculptor Andrea del Verrocchio in Florence, where his family had moved from the village of Vinci when Leonardo was 12 or 13. His artistic fame rests on only a few known works of art, for his fertile mind jumped restlessly from one project to another. His passion was not restricted to painting, but included mathematics, science, and engineering. He compiled volumes of detailed drawings and notes on anatomy, botany, geology, meteorology, architectural design, and mechanics (see "The Vitruvian Man," above). He worked at the court of Duke Ludovico Sforza of Milan from 1481 until 1498, spending much of his time on military and civil-engineering projects. But at Ludovico's request, Leonardo also created one of the defining monuments of Renaissance art: an image of

THE LAST SUPPER painted on the wall of the refectory (dining room) in the monastery of Sta. Maria delle Grazie in Milan between 1495 and 1498 (**FIGS. 13–3** and **INTRO–17**).

On one level, Leonardo painted a scene from a life story, capturing the moment when Jesus tells his companions during their last *seder* meal that one of them will betray him. They react individually, with shock, disbelief, or horror, presenting a study of human emotions. On another level, the *Last Supper* is a symbolic evocation of Jesus's coming sacrifice for the salvation of humankind, the foundation of the institution of the Mass, even a prefiguration of the gathering of this local monastic community in this room for its communal meals. Leonardo has arranged the disciples in four groups of three flanking the stable, pyramidal form of Jesus, who sits calmly in the middle of the general commotion. Leonardo placed Judas in the first triad to the left of Jesus, along with the young John the Evangelist and the elderly Peter. Judas, Peter, and John were each to play essential roles in Jesus's mission: Judas, to set in motion the events leading to the Crucifixion; Peter, to lead the Church after Jesus's death; and John, the visionary, to foretell the Second Coming of Christ and the Last Judgment in the Apocalypse.

The scene is set in a stage-like recession that extends the space of the refectory itself with a careful geometry. The one-point linear perspective is emphasized by the tapestries on the side walls. Orthogonals converge on the head of Jesus at mathematical center, behind which three windows form a natural—rather than symbolic—halo of light. Leonardo

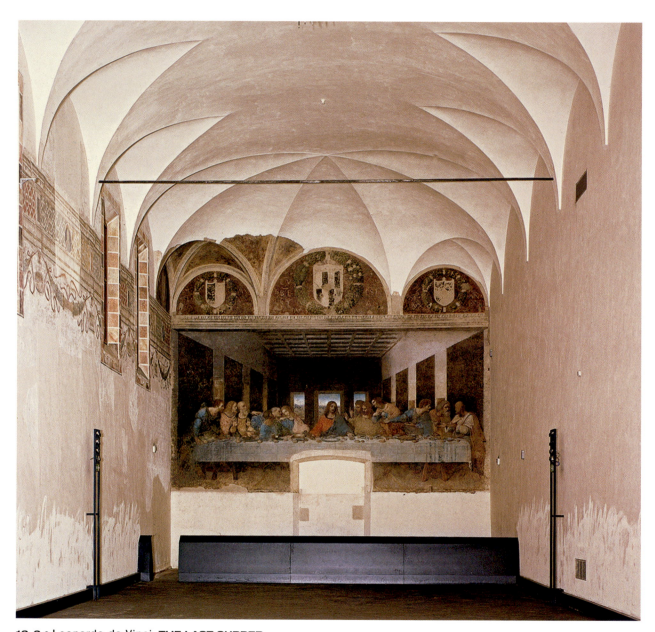

13–3 • Leonardo da Vinci THE LAST SUPPER
Wall painting in the refectory, monastery of Sta. Maria delle Grazie, Milan. 1495–1498. Tempera and oil on plaster, 15′ 2″ × 28′ 10″ (4.6 × 8.8 m). (SEE ALSO FIG. INTRO–17.)

Instead of painting in fresco, Leonardo devised an experimental technique for this mural. Hoping to achieve the freedom and flexibility of painting on panel, he worked directly on dry *intonaco* (a thin layer of smooth plaster) with an oil tempera paint whose formula is unknown. The result was disastrous. Within a short time, the painting began to deteriorate, and by the middle of the sixteenth century its figures could be seen only with difficulty. In the seventeenth century, the monks saw no harm in cutting a doorway through the lower center of the composition. Since then the work has barely survived, despite many attempts to halt its deterioration and restore its original appearance. The painting narrowly escaped complete destruction in World War II, when the refectory was bombed to rubble around its heavily sandbagged wall. The most recent restoration was completed in May 1999. The coats of arms at the top are those of patron Ludovico Sforza (ruled 1494–1499) and his wife Beatrice.

modeled the figures in a rich **chiaroscuro** (an Italian word combining "*chiaro*" ["light"] and "*scuro*" ["dark"], used to describe the gradual transition from highlight to shadow, creating the illusion of three-dimensional form), which over time had been obscured by the deterioration of his experimental medium of oil paint on plaster, but is now more visible after restoration in the 1990s.

Leonardo returned to Florence in 1500, where he painted perhaps his most famous work, *Mona Lisa* (SEE FIG. 13–1), between about 1503 and 1506. The subject of this portrait may have been 24-year-old Lisa Gherardini del Giocondo, wife of a prominent Florentine merchant. The solid, pyramidal form of her half-length figure is silhouetted against distant, hazy mountains that give the painting a sense of mystery. To achieve this atmosphere and to help unify his compositions, Leonardo partly covered his paintings with a thin, lightly tinted varnish, which helped create the effect of an overall smoky haze, or *sfumato*. Because early evening light is likely to produce a similar effect naturally, he recommended that painters set up their studios in a courtyard with black walls and a linen sheet stretched overhead to reproduce the effects of twilight. The implied challenge of Mona Lisa's direct stare, contrasting with her apparent serenity, has made the *Mona Lisa* one of the most studied and written about, indeed perhaps the best-known paintings in the history of art.

Leonardo returned to Milan in 1508 and stayed until 1513. He was later called to the Vatican by Pope Leo X, although there is no evidence that he produced any works of art during his stay there. In 1516, he accepted the French King Francis I's invitation to relocate to France, taking the *Mona Lisa* with him. He died there in 1519.

Raphael

About 1505—while Leonardo was working on the *Mona Lisa*—Raphael (Raffaello Santi or Sanzio, 1483–1520) arrived in Florence from his native Urbino after studying in Perugia with the leading artist of that city, Perugino (SEE FIG. 12–22). Raphael's paintings of the Virgin and Child, such as **THE MADONNA OF THE GOLDFINCH** of 1506 (**FIG. 13–4**), quickly brought him fame and attracted patrons. The monumental, pyramidal

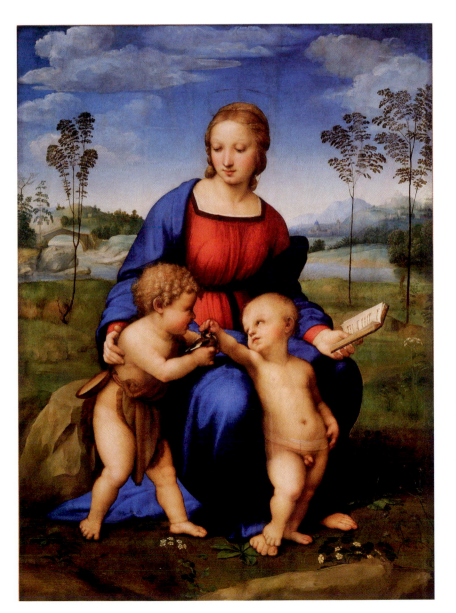

13–4 • Raphael THE MADONNA OF THE GOLDFINCH (MADONNA DEL CARDELLINO)
1506. Oil on wood panel, 42″ × 29½″ (106.7 × 74.9 cm). Galleria degli Uffizi, Florence.

The vibrant colors of this painting were revealed over the course of a careful, ten-year restoration, completed only in 2008.

🔍 **View** the Closer Look for Raphael's *The Madonna of the Goldfinch* on **MyArtsLab** form of the three-figure composition—the Virgin Mary and the infant Christ (right) and John the Baptist (left)—and the carefully modeled draperies reveal the impact of the work of Leonardo. However, the clear, even light contrasts with the hazy *sfumato* favored by Leonardo, reflecting instead the atmospheric clarity, solid modeling, and brilliant colors, as well as the courtly and playful poses of Perugino's paintings. The goldfinch that John the Baptist holds in his hand was a symbol of Christ's death on the cross, an allegorical meaning that makes the skittish Christ Child's retreat into secure contact with his mother understandable.

Raphael's greatest achievements came during a dozen years in Rome, where he arrived around 1508. As the fortunes of the ruling families of Florence and Milan fluctuated sharply because of political struggles, Rome was becoming the artistic and intellectual center of Italy, and Pope Julius II began a campaign to rebuild the Vatican. He put Raphael to work almost immediately decorating the papal apartments. In the pope's library (FIG. 13–5), Raphael painted the four branches of knowledge as conceived in the sixteenth century: theology (the *Disputa*, discussions concerning the true presence of Christ in the Eucharistic Host), philosophy (*School of Athens*), poetry and the arts (*Parnassus*, home of the Muses), and law, or jurisprudence (the *Cardinal Virtues under Justice*).

Raphael's most influential achievement in these rooms was the **SCHOOL OF ATHENS** (FIG. 13–6), painted during 1510–1511. The painting summarizes the ideals of the Renaissance papacy in its grand conception of harmoniously arranged

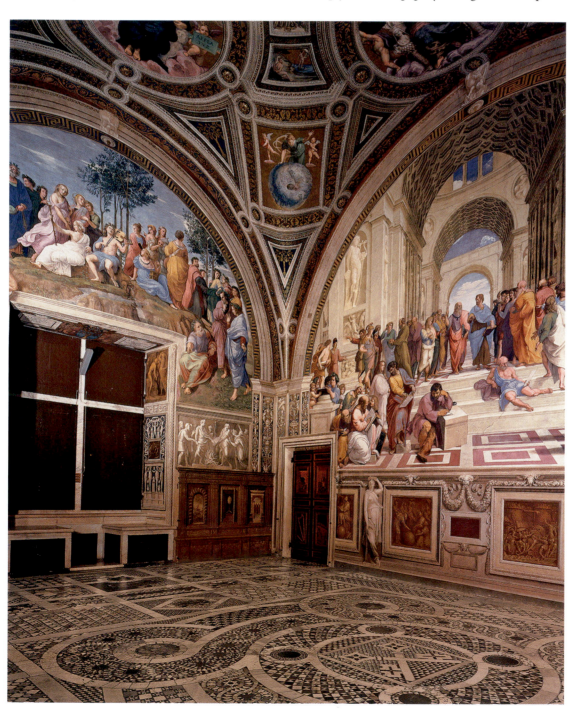

13–5 • Raphael
STANZA DELLA SEGNATURA
Vatican, Rome. Right: Philosophy or the *School of Athens*; left (over the window): Poetry or *Parnassus*. 1510–1511. Fresco.

forms and rational space, as well as the calm dignity of its figures. The shape of the walls and vault of the room itself inspired the composition. The viewer gazes at the scene through an illusionistic arch. The Classical Greek philosophers Plato (left) and Aristotle (right) command center stage—placed on either side of the vanishing point, silhouetted against the sky, and framed under three successive barrel vaults. Plato gestures toward the heavens as the ultimate source of his philosophy, while Aristotle, his outstretched hand palm down, emphasizes the importance of gathering scientific knowledge empirically by observing the natural world. Looking down from niches in the walls are Minerva (on the right), the Roman goddess of wisdom, and Apollo (holding a lyre), the Greek and Roman god of the sun, rationality, poetry, and music. Surrounding Plato and Aristotle are mathematicians, naturalists, astronomers, geographers, and other philosophers, debating and demonstrating their theories. For all their serene idealism, the figures within the painting break Classical conventions in their dynamically foreshortened *contrapposto* poses. Flooded with light from a single source, the scene takes place in an immense barrel-vaulted interior seemingly inspired by the architect Donato Bramante's new design for St. Peter's, which was under construction next door at the time. The grandeur of the building is matched by the monumental dignity of the philosophers themselves, each of whom has a distinct physical and intellectual presence. The sweeping arcs of the composition are activated by the variety and energy of their poses, creating a dynamic unity that is characteristic of High Renaissance art.

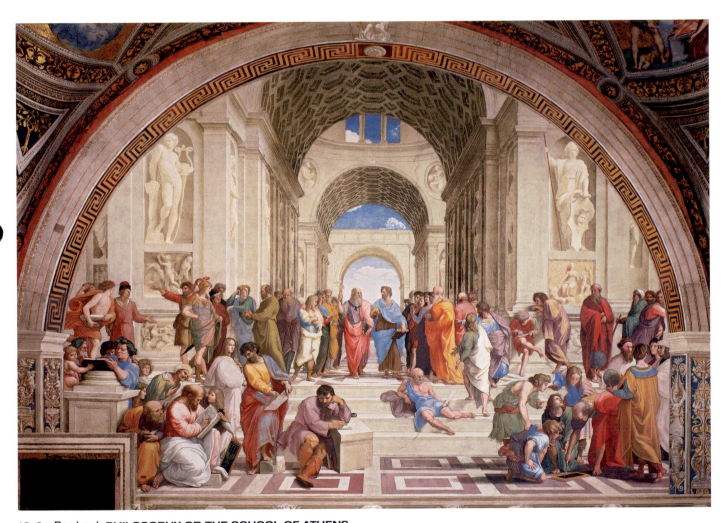

13–6 • Raphael PHILOSOPHY OR THE SCHOOL OF ATHENS
Stanza della Segnatura, Vatican, Rome. 1510–1511. Fresco, 19′ × 27′ (5.79 × 8.24 m).

Raphael gave many of the figures in his imaginary gathering of philosophers the features of his friends and colleagues. Plato, standing immediately to the left of the central axis and pointing to the sky, was said to have been modeled after Leonardo da Vinci; Euclid, shown inscribing a slate with a compass at the lower right, was a portrait of Raphael's friend, the architect Donato Bramante. Michelangelo, who was at work on the Sistine Chapel ceiling only steps away from the room where Raphael was painting this fresco, is shown as the solitary figure at the lower left center, leaning on a block of marble and sketching, in a pose reminiscent of the figures of sibyls and prophets on his great ceiling. Raphael's own features appear on the overlapped second figure in the front group at the far right, as the face of a young man listening to a discourse by the astronomer Ptolemy.

View the Closer Look for Raphael's *School of Athens* on **MyArtsLab**

In 1515, Raphael was commissioned by Julius II's successor, Pope Leo X (pontificate 1513–1521), to provide **cartoons** (paintings to serve as models for works in another medium) on themes from the Acts of the Apostles to be woven in Brussels into tapestries—the most prestigious and expensive kind of wall decoration—for the walls below the fifteenth-century frescos of the Sistine Chapel (SEE FIG. 13–10). Raphael and his assistants made charcoal drawings, then painted over them with color for the weavers to match. First in the series was the **MIRACULOUS DRAFT OF FISHES** (John 21:1–11) (**FIG. 13–7**), showing the apostle Peter kneeling before the seated Christ, an important motif since the pope claimed absolute authority as Peter's successor. The monumental, muscle-bound, straining figures in this composition show the impact of Michelangelo's influence on Raphael's art; his Sistine ceiling had been completed only three years earlier. The three cranes in the foreground symbolized for sixteenth-century viewers the ever-alert and watchful pope, a topical reference because when the tapestries were first displayed in the Sistine Chapel on December 26, 1519, papal authority was already being challenged by reformers including Martin Luther.

In 1520, after a brief illness, Raphael died at age 37. After a state funeral, he was buried in the ancient Roman Pantheon, originally a Classical temple to the gods of Rome, but at that time a Christian church dedicated to the Virgin Mary (SEE FIGS. 6–27, 6–28).

Michelangelo

Michelangelo Buonarroti (1475–1564) was born in the Tuscan town of Caprese, but he grew up in Florence, and spent his long career working there and in Rome. At age 13, he was apprenticed to the painter Domenico Ghirlandaio. He soon joined the household of Lorenzo de' Medici ("the Magnificent"; 1449–1492), where he studied sculpture with Bertoldo di Giovanni, a pupil of Donatello.

While living in the Medici household, Michelangelo also came in contact with Neoplatonic philosophers who were part of Lorenzo the Magnificent's circle, continuing a long tradition of Medici patronage of Classical and Neoplatonic scholars. Neoplatonism takes various forms at different times and places, but basically it is characterized by a sharp opposition of the spiritual (the ideal or idea) and the physical (carnal matter that can be overcome by severe discipline and aversion to the world of the senses). Within discussions in the Medici academy, the perfectibility of the sculptural form was seen as a metaphor for the human ability to strive for perfection in a virtuous life. The sculptor's ability to release artistic form from a stone block was seen as equivalent to discovering and expressing the moral truth of the soul within the physical form of a human being. Such powerful ideas had a formative impact on the young Michelangelo, who was just coming into his own as a sculptor.

Michelangelo's major early work—at the turn of the century and well after his departure from the Medici household

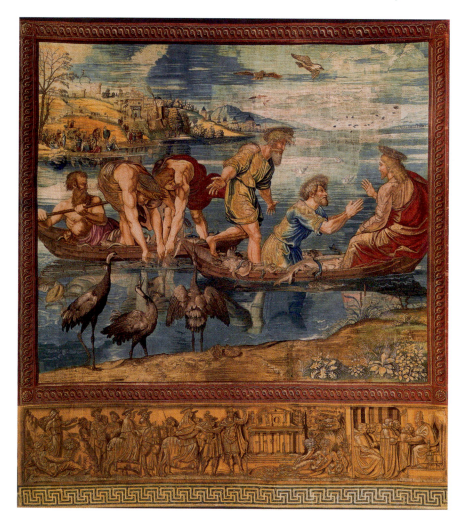

13–7 • Shop of Pieter van Aelst, Brussels, after cartoons by Raphael and assistants MIRACULOUS DRAFT OF FISHES ON THE SEA OF GALILEE

From the nine-piece *Acts of the Apostles* series; lower border, two incidents from the life of Giovanni de' Medici, later Pope Leo X. Designed 1515–1516; woven 1517; installed in the Sistine Chapel 1519. Wool and silk with silver-gilt wrapped threads, 16′ 1″ × 21′ (5.9 × 6.4 m). Musei Vaticani, Pinacoteca, Rome.

following Lorenzo's death in 1492—was a marble **PIETÀ**, commissioned by a French cardinal and installed as a tomb monument in Old St. Peter's (**FIG. 13–8**). Michelangelo traveled to the marble quarries at Carrara in central Italy to select the block from which to make this large work, a practice he would follow for nearly all his sculpture. The choice of the stone was important to him because, following the Neoplatonic metaphor, he envisioned his sculpture as already existing within the marble, needing only his tools to "set it free."

The **pietà**—a representation of the Virgin supporting and mourning the dead Jesus—had long been a popular subject in Northern Europe, but was rare in Italian art at the time. Italians generally preferred the Lamentation, a narrative tableau including many of Christ's followers (SEE FIG. 11–29, lower left).

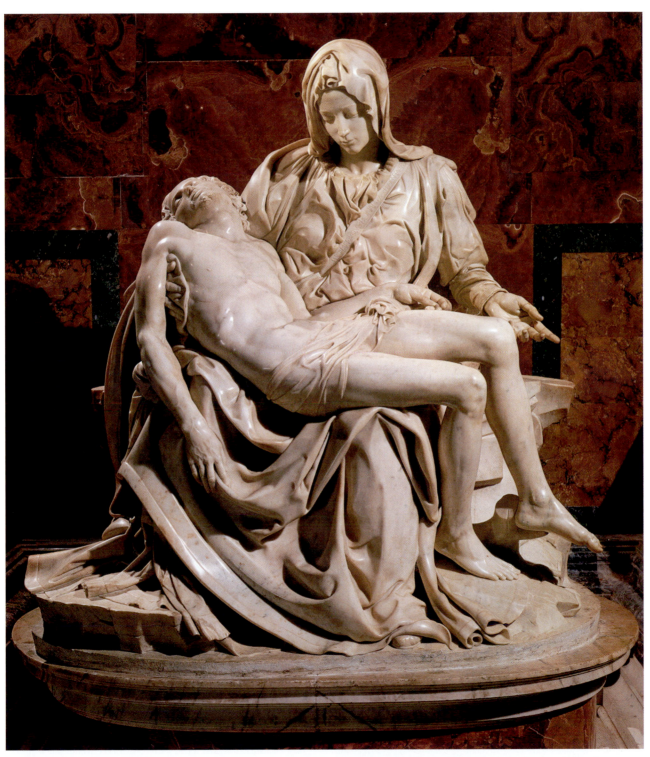

13–8 • Michelangelo PIETÀ
From Old St. Peter's. c. 1500. Marble, height 5′ 8½″ (1.74 m). St. Peter's, Vatican, Rome.

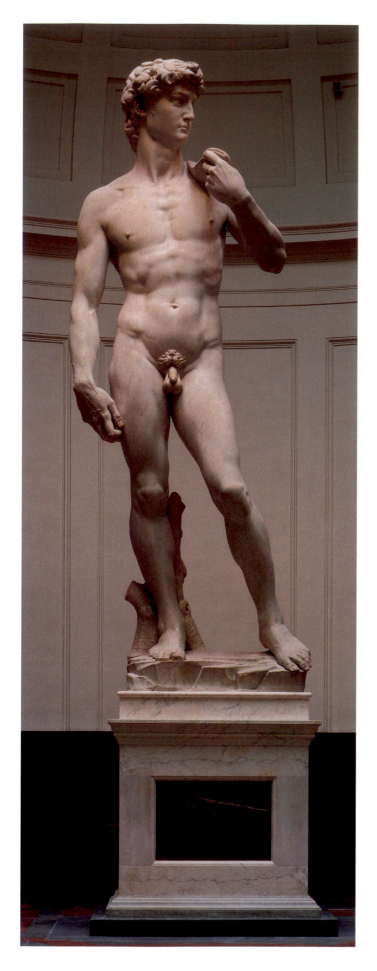

Michelangelo's Virgin looks startlingly young—her youthfulness perhaps an outward manifestation of her inner virtue. She is heroic in stature, effortlessly holding the unnaturally smaller, lifeless body of her grown son. Inconsistencies in scale and age are forgotten, however, when contemplating the sweetness of expression, technical virtuosity of the carving, and the smooth modeling of the luscious forms. The work was meant to be seen up close, at the statue's own level, so that the viewer can look into the compelling beauty of Jesus's face. The 25-year-old Michelangelo is said to have slipped into the church at night to sign the statue on a strap across the Virgin's breast, answering directly questions that had come up about the identity of its creator.

In 1501, Michelangelo accepted a Florentine commission for a statue of the biblical hero **DAVID** (FIG. 13–9) for placement high atop a buttress of the cathedral. But when it was finished in 1504, the *David* was so admired that the city council claimed it for the principal city square, next to the Palazzo della Signoria, home of the city's government. Although the statue embodies the antique ideal of the athletic male nude, the emotional power of the facial expression and concentrated gaze is new. Unlike Donatello's bronze *David* (SEE FIG. 12–18), this is not a triumphant hero with the head of the giant Goliath already under his feet. Slingshot over his shoulder and a rock in his right hand, Michelangelo's *David* knits his brow and stares into space, seemingly preparing himself psychologically for the danger ahead. No match for his opponent in experience, weaponry, or physical strength, Michelangelo's powerful *David* stands for the supremacy of right over might—a perfect symbol for the Florentines, who had recently fought the forces of Milan, Siena, and Pisa, and still faced political and military pressure.

Michelangelo had a contract to make other statues for the cathedral, but in 1505 Pope Julius II arranged for him to come to Rome to work on the pope's spectacular tomb, envisioned for the center of the new St. Peter's. In 1506, Julius set this commission aside, and ordered Michelangelo to paint the ceiling of his private chapel in the Vatican, known as the **SISTINE CHAPEL** (FIG. 13–10). At first Julius wanted simple *trompe l'oeil* coffers; later he asked for the Twelve Apostles. According to Michelangelo, when the artist objected to the limitations of Julius's plan, the pope told him to paint whatever he liked. This Michelangelo presumably did, although he surely had a theological advisor.

Michelangelo's design for the **SISTINE CEILING** consists of an illusionistic architectural structure, filled with individual figures and narrative scenes. Running completely around the ceiling is a painted cornice with projections supported by

13–9 • Michelangelo DAVID
1501–1504. Marble, height 17′ (5.18 m). Galleria dell'Accademia, Florence.

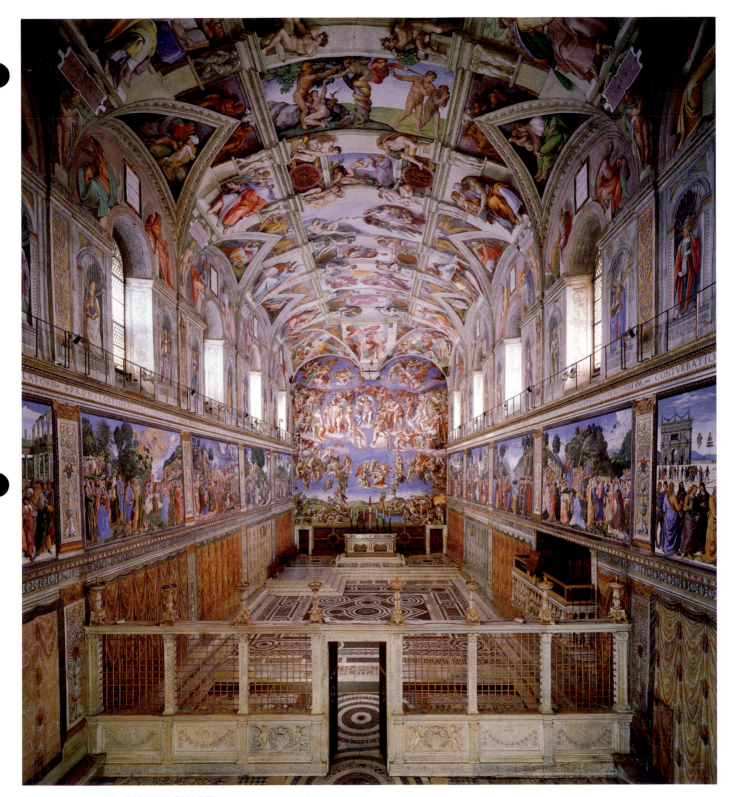

13–10 • INTERIOR, SISTINE CHAPEL

Vatican, Rome. Built 1475–1481. Wall frescos 1481–1483; ceiling painted 1508–1512; wall behind altar painted 1536–1541. The ceiling measures 45′ × 128′ (13.75 × 39 m).

Named after its builder, Pope Sixtus IV, the chapel is slightly more than 130 feet long and about 43½ feet wide, approximately the same measurements recorded in the Hebrew Bible for the Temple of Solomon. The floor mosaic was recut from stones used in the floor of an earlier papal chapel. The side walls were painted in fresco between 1481 and 1483 with scenes from the life of Moses and the life of Christ by Perugino, Botticelli, Ghirlandaio, and others. (The left side of Perugino's painting [SEE FIG. 12–22] can be seen at the right edge of the photograph.) Below these are *trompe l'oeil* painted draperies, where Raphael's tapestries illustrating the Acts of the Apostles once hung. Michelangelo's famous ceiling frescos begin with the lunette scenes above the window arches (SEE FIG. 13–11). On the end above the altar is his *Last Judgment*, finished in 1541 (SEE FIG. 13–13).

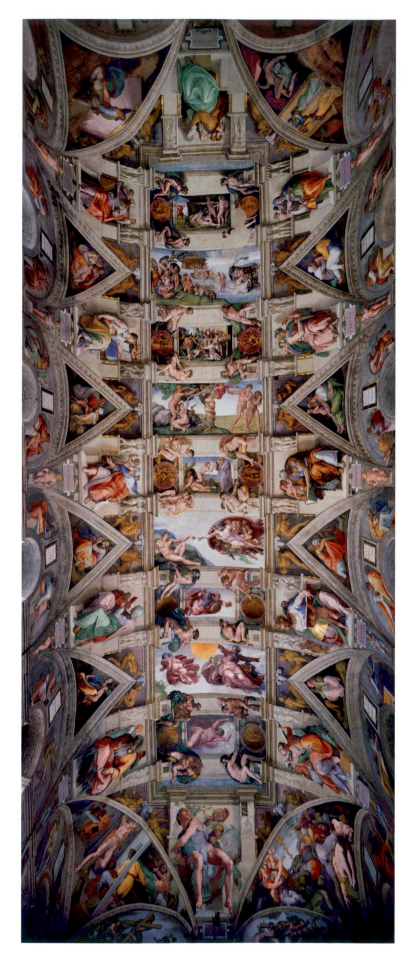

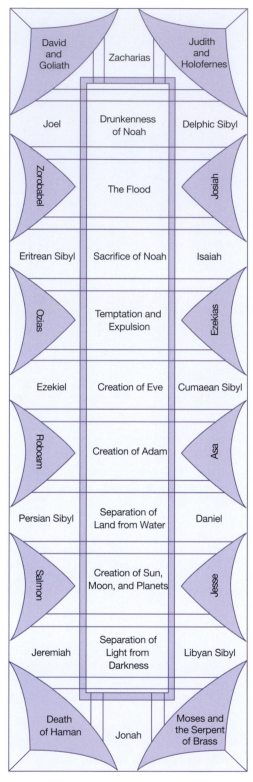

David and Goliath	Zacharias	Judith and Holofernes
Joel	Drunkenness of Noah	Delphic Sibyl
Zorobabel	The Flood	Josiah
Eritrean Sibyl	Sacrifice of Noah	Isaiah
Ozias	Temptation and Expulsion	Ezekias
Ezekiel	Creation of Eve	Cumaean Sibyl
Roboam	Creation of Adam	Asa
Persian Sibyl	Separation of Land from Water	Daniel
Salmon	Creation of Sun, Moon, and Planets	Jesse
Jeremiah	Separation of Light from Darkness	Libyan Sibyl
Death of Haman	Jonah	Moses and the Serpent of Brass

ALTAR

13–11 • Michelangelo OVERALL VIEW OF THE CEILING AND SCHEMATIC DRAWING IDENTIFYING ITS SUBJECTS, SISTINE CHAPEL
1508–1512. Fresco.

✳ **Explore** the architectural panoramas of the Sistine Chapel on **MyArtsLab**

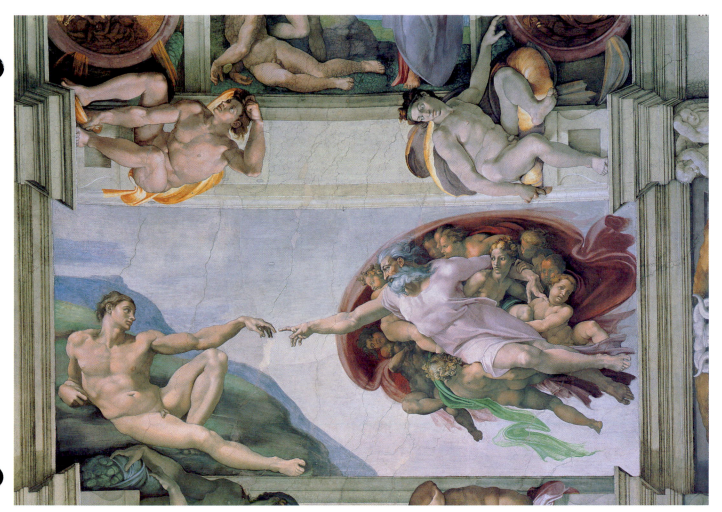

13-12 • Michelangelo CREATION OF ADAM
Sistine Chapel ceiling. 1511–1512. Fresco, 9′ 2″ × 18′ 8″ (2.8 × 5.7 m).

pilasters decorated with sculptured *putti* (**FIG. 13–11**). Between the pilasters are prophets from the Hebrew Bible and Classical sibyls (female seers) who were believed to have foretold Jesus's birth. Figures of nude young men (*ignudi*) sit in a variety of poses on pedestals above the fictive cornice. Behind the youths, shallow bands of painted stone **molding** divide the vault into nine compartments framing successive scenes from Genesis—the Creation, the Fall, and the Flood. Eight triangular compartments over the windows contain the ancestors of Jesus.

Perhaps the most familiar scene is near the ceiling's center—the **CREATION OF ADAM** (**FIG. 13–12**), in which Michelangelo captures the moment when God charges the languorous Adam with the spark of life. As if to echo the biblical text, Adam's heroic body, outstretched arm, and profile almost mirror those of God, in whose image he has been created. Emerging under God's other arm, and looking across him in the direction of her future companion, is the robust and energetic figure of Eve before her creation.

A quarter of a century after finishing the ceiling, Michelangelo again went to work in the Sistine Chapel, this time on the **LAST JUDGMENT**, painted some time between 1536 and 1541 on the large end wall behind the altar (**FIG. 13–13**). Michelangelo,

now entering his sixties, had complained for years of feeling old, yet he accepted this important and demanding task, which took him two years to finish. He painted a writhing swarm of resurrected humanity, with the saved dragged from their graves and pushed up into a vortex of figures around Christ. Despite the efforts of several saints to save them at the last minute, the damned plunge toward hell on the right. Just under Christ's feet at right is St. Bartholomew, who was martyred by being skinned alive. In his left hand he holds his flayed skin, the distorted face of which is painted with Michelangelo's own features. On the lowest level of the mural, directly above the altar, the demonic boatman Charon propels his craft on the River Styx toward the gaping, fiery mouth of hell, a grim and constant reminder to the celebrants of the Mass—the pope and his cardinals—that they too will face stern judgment at the end of time.

In addition to his success as a sculptor and painter, Michelangelo was also an influential architect. After completing the *Last Judgment*, he took on his most important building commission: the rebuilding of St. Peter's in Rome. The project had begun in 1506, when Pope Julius II made the astonishing decision to demolish the venerable but crumbling Constantinian basilica over St. Peter's tomb (SEE FIG. 7–6). To design and build

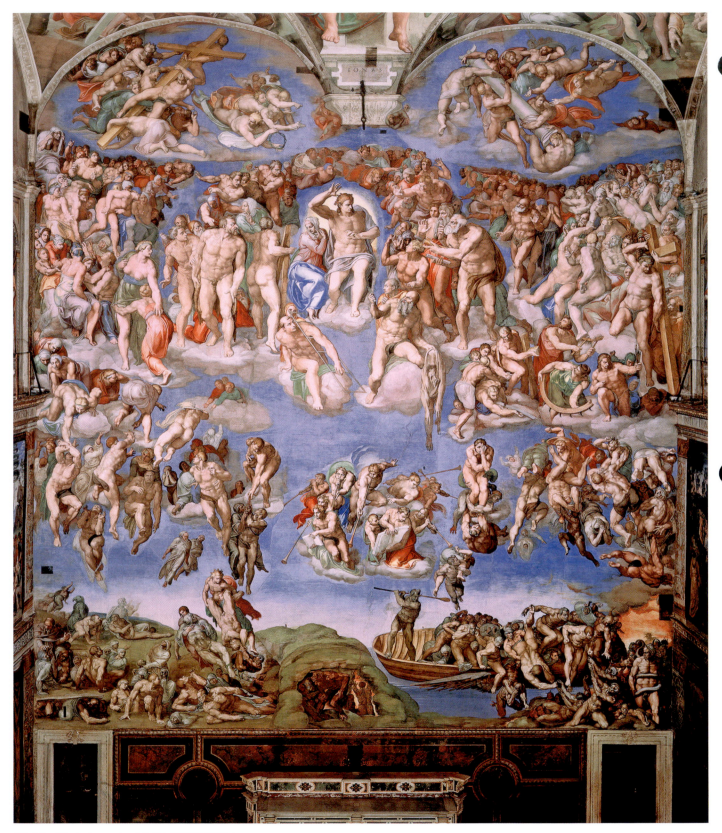

13–13 • Michelangelo LAST JUDGMENT
Sistine Chapel. 1536–1541. Fresco, 48′ × 44′ (14.6 × 13.4 m), encompassing approx. 2,100 square feet (190 square meters) of surface.

Conservative clergy criticized this painting because of its frank nudity, and after Michelangelo's death they ordered bits of drapery to be painted by artist Daniele da Volterra to censor the offending passages, earning Daniele the unfortunate nickname Il Braghettone ("breeches painter").

📖 **Read** the document related to Michelangelo's poetry on **MyArtsLab**

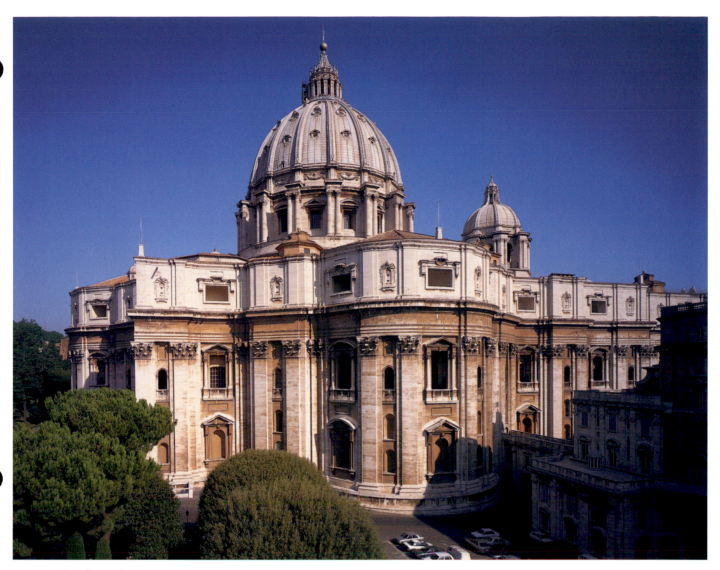

13-14 • Michelangelo ST. PETER'S BASILICA
View from the southwest. Vatican, Rome. c. 1546–1564 (dome completed 1590 by Giacomo della Porta;
lantern 1590–1593).

the magnificent new church, the pope appointed the architect Donato Bramante (1443/4–1514), like Raphael a native of Urbino. Bramante envisioned the new St. Peter's as a central-plan building, a Greek cross with four arms of equal length, crowned with an enormous dome over the central square crossing (see "St. Peter's Basilica," p. 340). His design may refer to the early Christian tradition of **martyria** (central-plan churches over martyrs' tombs; see "Longitudinal-Plan and Central-Plan Churches," p. 166), and in Renaissance thinking, the central plan and dome also symbolized the perfection of God.

Ultimately, Michelangelo transformed the church into a building of magnificent proportions and superhuman scale (**FIG. 13–14**). Seventeenth-century additions and renovations dramatically changed the original and the appearance of the interior (SEE FIGS. 14–2, 14–3), but Michelangelo's St. Peter's can still be seen in the contrasting forms of the flat and angled exterior walls and the three surviving **hemicycles** (semicircular projections). Colossal pilasters (flat, engaged column-like elements extending through two or more stories), **blind windows**

(frames without openings), and niches surround the sanctuary of the church. How Michelangelo would have built the great dome is not known; most scholars believe that it would have been hemispherical. The current dome, erected by Giacomo della Porta in 1588–1590, has a steeper profile but retains Michelangelo's basic design: segmented with regularly spaced ribs, seated on a high drum with pedimented windows between paired columns, and surmounted by a tall lantern shaped like a circular temple.

Michelangelo—often described by his contemporaries as difficult, even arrogant—alternated between periods of depression and frenzied activity. Yet he was devoted to his friends and helpful to young artists. He believed his art was divinely inspired, and later in life he became deeply absorbed in religion and dedicated himself chiefly to religious works—many left unfinished—that subverted Renaissance ideals of human perfectibility and denied his own youthful idealism. In the process he pioneered new stylistic directions that would inspire succeeding generations of artists.

The original church of St. Peter's was built in the fourth century CE by Constantine, the first Christian Roman emperor, to mark the grave of the apostle Peter, first bishop of Rome and therefore the first pope. Constantine's architect erected an imperial Roman basilica with a nave, two flanking side aisles set off by colonnades, and an apse. To accommodate the large numbers of pilgrims visiting the shrine, he also added a transept. The nave and aisles were, in effect, a covered cemetery, carpeted with the tombs of believers wishing to be buried near the apostle's tomb. When it was built, Constantine's basilica was one of the largest buildings in the world (368 feet long and 190 feet wide). For over a thousand years it was the most important pilgrimage site in Europe.

That anyone, even a pope, would pull down such a venerated building is an indication of the extraordinary self-assurance both of the Renaissance and Pope Julius II himself. The deaths of the pope and the architect Bramante in 1513–1514 put a temporary halt to the project, designed with a central plan crowned by an enormous dome. Successive plans by Raphael and others altered the central plan to provide the church with a nave. However, when Michelangelo was appointed architect in 1546, he returned to the Greek-cross plan and simplified Bramante's design to create a single, unified space. The dome was finally completed (1588–1590) some years after Michelangelo's death by Giacomo della Porta, who gave the dome a taller and slimmer profile and changed the shape of its openings.

During the Counter-Reformation, the Church emphasized congregational worship, and more space was needed for people and processions. Moreover, it was felt that the new church should more closely resemble Old St. Peter's and should extend over roughly the same area, including the ground covered by the original atrium. In 1606, Pope Paul V commissioned the architect Carlo Maderno to change Michelangelo's central plan back once again to a longitudinal plan, building a nave of slightly more than 636 feet and adding a Baroque façade (SEE FIG. 14–3), thus completing St. Peter's as we see it today. Later in the seventeenth century, the sculptor and architect Gianlorenzo Bernini added a new approach to the basilica, an enormous plaza surrounded by a great colonnade, like a huge set of arms extended to embrace the faithful who approached the principal church of Western Christendom.

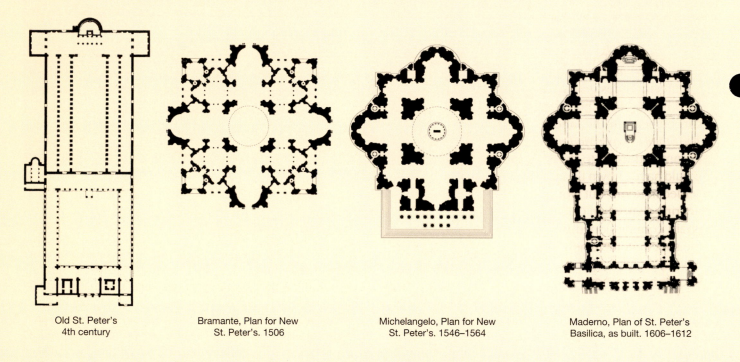

Old St. Peter's
4th century

Bramante, Plan for New
St. Peter's. 1506

Michelangelo, Plan for New
St. Peter's. 1546–1564

Maderno, Plan of St. Peter's
Basilica, as built. 1606–1612

👁 **Watch** an architectural simulation about the plans for St. Peter's Basilica on **MyArtsLab**

Properzia de' Rossi

In this age of artistic giants, very few women had the opportunity or inclination to become sculptors. Properzia de' Rossi (c. 1490–1529/30), who lived in Bologna, was an exception. She mastered many arts, including engraving, and was famous for her miniature sculptures, carving an entire Last Supper on a peach pit. She created this marble relief of **JOSEPH AND**

POTIPHAR'S WIFE (FIG. 13–15) for the cathedral of San Petronio in Bologna, showing the biblical hero fleeing to escape the partially clad seductress, who snatches at his cloak. Properzia is the only woman whom sixteenth-century historian Vasari included in the 1550 edition of his *Lives of the Artists*, where he reports that a rival male sculptor prevented her from being paid fairly and from securing additional commissions.

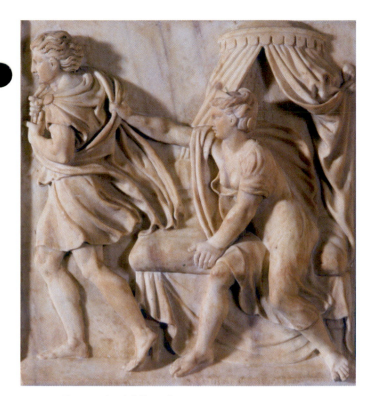

**13–15 • Properzia de' Rossi
JOSEPH AND POTIPHAR'S WIFE**
Cathedral of San Petronio, Bologna.
1525–1526. Marble, 1′ 9″ × 1′ 11″
(54 × 58 cm). Museo de San Petronio,
Bologna.

Venice and the Veneto

In the last quarter of the fifteenth century, Venice emerged as a major artistic center. Venetian painters had embraced the oil medium from the late 1470s, earlier than Italian artists elsewhere, because the use of oil glazes permitted the brilliant color and lighting effect desired by Venice's most famous Renaissance painters: Giorgione, Titian, Tintoretto, and Veronese. By the sixteenth century, Venetians did not see themselves as rivals of Florence and Rome, but rather as superiors.

Giorgione. The career of Giorgione (Giorgio da Castelfranco; c. 1475–1510) was brief—he died from the plague—and most scholars accept fewer than ten paintings as entirely by his hand. But his importance to Venetian painting is critical. He introduced new, enigmatic pastoral themes, known as *poesie* (or "painted poems"), that were inspired by the contemporary literary revival of ancient pastoral poetry. He is significant for his sensuous nude figures, and, above all, for his appreciation of nature in landscape painting, which played an increasingly important role in sixteenth-century art. Giorgione's early life and training are undocumented, but Leonardo's subtle lighting system and mysterious, intensely observed landscapes clearly inspired him.

One of Giorgione's most compelling works, today called **THE TEMPEST** (FIG. 13–16), was painted shortly before his

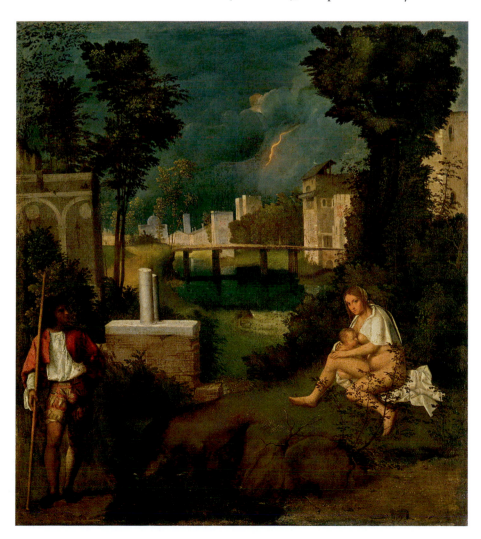

13–16 • Giorgione THE TEMPEST
c. 1506. Oil on canvas, 32″ × 28¾″ (82 × 73 cm).
Galleria dell'Accademia, Venice.

X-rays of this painting show that Giorgione altered his composition while he was still at work on it—the soldier replaces a second nude woman initially planned on the left.

View the Closer Look for Giorgione's *The Tempest* on **MyArtsLab**

death. Simply trying to understand what is happening in the picture piques our interest. At the right, a woman is seated on the ground, nude except for the end of a long white cloth thrown over her shoulders. Her nudity seems maternal, her sensuality generative rather than erotic as she nurses the baby, protectively and lovingly embraced at her side. On the other side of the painting stands a mysterious man, perhaps wearing the uniform of a German mercenary soldier. His shadowed head turns toward the woman, but his body faces the viewer. Inexplicably, a spring gushes forth between the figures, feeding a lake surrounded by substantial houses, and in the far distance a bolt of lightning splits the darkening sky. The artist's attention seems focused on the landscape and the unruly elements of nature as much as on the figures.

Titian. In 1507, Giorgione took on a new assistant, Tiziano Vecellio, better known today as Titian (c. 1488–1576). The painting called **PASTORAL CONCERT** (FIG. 13–17) has been attributed to both of them. Perhaps Giorgione began the painting and Titian completed it after Giorgione's death, or Titian, inspired by Giorgione, may have painted it alone. As in *The Tempest*, the idyllic, verdant landscape is one of the principal subjects of the painting. In this mythic world, two young men—an aristocratic musician and a barefoot peasant—turn toward each other, seemingly oblivious to the two naked women beside them. While the meaning of this juxtaposition of nude and clothed figures is obscure, in a general sense this outdoor concert evokes the romantic ideal of a lost golden age, some misty time in remote antiquity when people led a carefree pastoral life, a theme much loved by Classical and early Renaissance poets. In fact, the painting is now interpreted as an allegory on the invention of poetry. Titian showcases here his renowned talent for painting sensuous female nudes whose swelling flesh seems to glow with an incandescent light, inspired by flesh-and-blood beauty as much as any source from poetry or art.

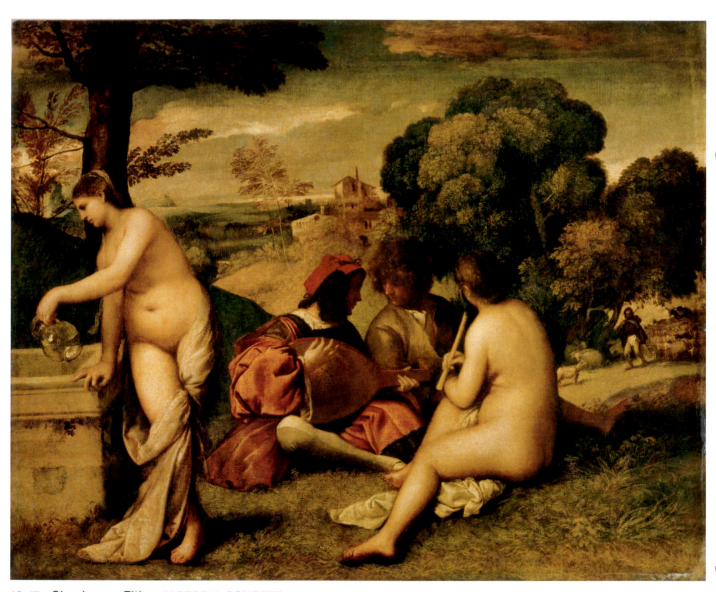

13–17 • Giorgione or Titian PASTORAL CONCERT
c. 1510. Oil on canvas, 41¼″ × 54⅜″ (105 × 139 cm). Musée du Louvre, Paris.

Women Patrons of the Arts

In the sixteenth century, many wealthy women—both from aristocratic and bourgeois families—were enthusiastic patrons of the arts. Two English queens—the Tudor half-sisters Mary I and Elizabeth I—glorified their reigns with art, and the Habsburg princesses Margaret of Austria and Mary of Hungary presided over brilliant Humanist courts when they were regents. The Marchesa of Mantua, Isabella d'Este (1474–1539) (FIG. 13–18), became a major patron of painters, musicians, composers, and writers. Married to Francesco II Gonzaga at age 15, she had great beauty, great wealth, and a brilliant mind that made her a successful diplomat and administrator. She was a true Renaissance woman, her motto the epitome of rational thinking: "Neither through Hope nor Fear." An avid collector of manuscripts and books, she sponsored the publication of an edition of Virgil while still in her twenties. She also collected ancient art and objects, as well as works by contemporary Italian artists including Mantegna, Leonardo, Perugino, Correggio, and Titian. Her study was a veritable museum. Mantegna painted the walls above the storage and display cabinets, and the ceiling was covered with mottoes and visual references to Isabella's impressive literary interests.

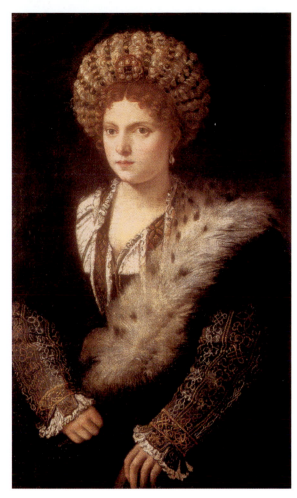

13–18 • Titian ISABELLA D'ESTE
1534–1536. Oil on canvas, 40⅛″ × 25¼″ (102 × 64.1 cm).
Kunsthistorisches Museum, Vienna.

This great Humanist and patron of the arts was 60 years old when Titian painted her portrait, but he had studied an earlier portrait of her in order to capture her youthful beauty.

In 1516, Titian became official painter to the Republic of Venice. Three years later, the powerful Pesaro family commissioned him to paint an altarpiece for the Franciscan church of Sta. Maria Gloriosa dei Frari in Venice—a Madonna and Child surrounded by members of the Pesaro family (FIG. 13–19). In the left foreground, Jacopo Pesaro, bishop of Paphos, kneels directly in front of the Virgin. No doubt he merited this honored spot because he had led the papal army to victory over the Turks in 1502. A turbaned Turkish captive stands behind him, and a knight holds a banner displaying the arms of Pope Alexander VI. St. Peter, a monumental seated figure with his keys at his feet, looks approvingly at Jacopo, while St. Francis, at right, gazes upward at the Christ Child.

The grandeur of the scene, with its massive columns and marble staircase, proclaims the power and glory of the Pesaros. No photograph can convey the vibrancy of the paint surfaces, which Titian built up in layers of pure colors, chiefly red, white, yellow, and black. The powerful intersecting diagonals of the composition reach from Jacopo Pesaro to the Virgin (innovatively placed off-center), and from the family at the lower right to the tilting banner at the upper left. The arresting visage of the youth who turns to meet our gaze at lower right guarantees our engagement.

Paintings of nude reclining women became especially popular in sophisticated court circles, where male patrons could enjoy "Venuses" under the cloak of respectable Classical

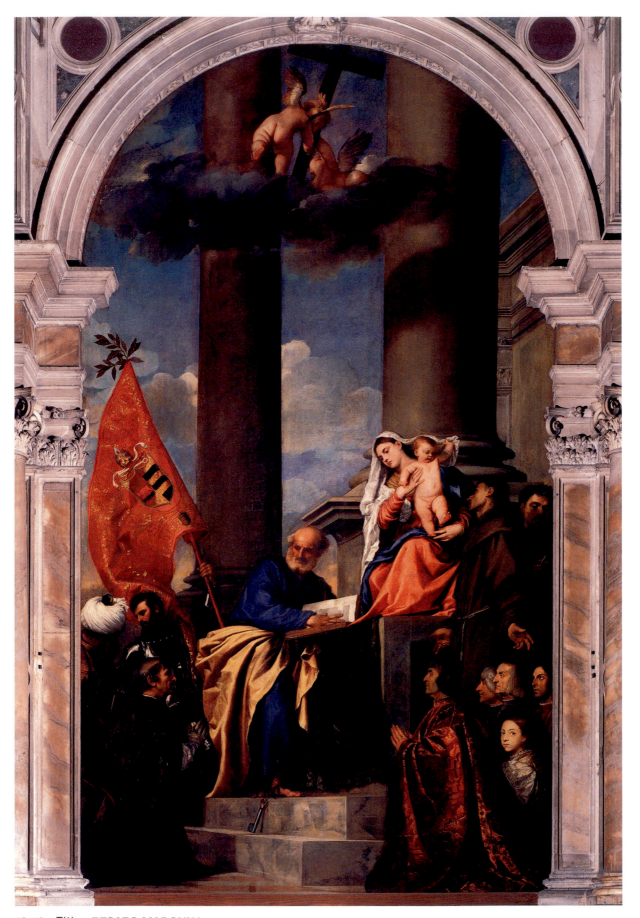

13–19 • Titian PESARO MADONNA
Pesaro Chapel, Sta. Maria Gloriosa dei Frari, Venice. 1519–1526. Oil on canvas, 16′ × 8′ 10″ (4.9 × 2.7 m).

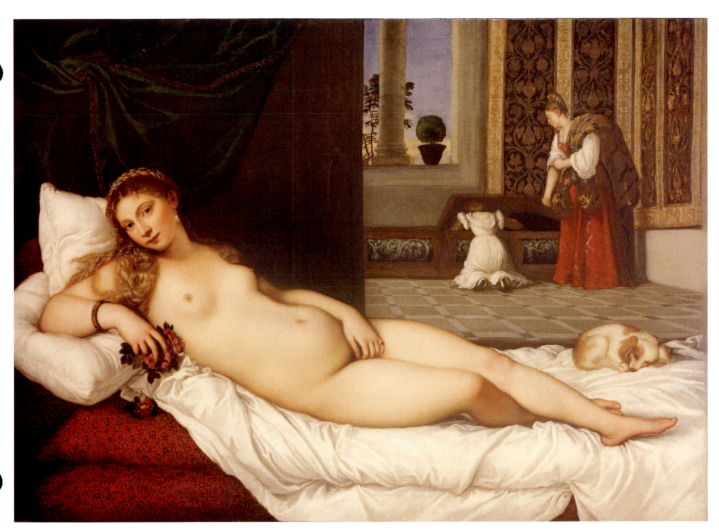

13–20 • Titian "VENUS" OF URBINO
c. 1538. Oil on canvas, 3′ 11″ × 5′ 5″ (1.19 × 1.65 m). Galleria degli Uffizi, Florence.

mythology. Seemingly typical of such paintings is the **"VENUS"** that Titian delivered to Guidobaldo della Rovere (duke of Urbino, 1538–1574) in spring 1538 (**FIG. 13–20**). Here, we seem to see a beautiful Venetian courtesan with deliberately provocative gestures, stretching languidly on her couch in a spacious palace, her glowing flesh and golden hair set off by white sheets and pillows. But for its original audience, art historian Rona Goffen has argued, the painting was more about marriage than mythology or seductiveness. The multiple matrimonial references in this work include the pair of *cassoni* (marriage or trousseau storage chests) in the background, where servants are removing or storing the woman's clothing, the bridal associations of the myrtle and roses she holds in her hand, and even the spaniel snoozing at her feet—a traditional symbol of fidelity and domesticity, especially when sleeping so peacefully. Titian's picture might be associated with Guidobaldo's marriage in 1534 to the 10-year-old Giulia Verano. Four years later, when this painting arrived, she would have been considered an adult rather than a child bride. Could this painting represent neither a Roman goddess

nor a Venetian courtesan, but a faithful wife welcoming her husband into their lavish home?

Veronese. Paolo Caliari (1528–1588), called Veronese after his hometown of Verona, is nearly synonymous today with the popular image of Venetian splendor and pageantry. Like Titian, Veronese employed elaborate architectural settings and costumes for religious images, but he also added still lifes, anecdotal vignettes, and other details unconnected with the main subject that proved immensely appealing to Venetian patrons. One of Veronese's most famous works is the painting now called **FEAST IN THE HOUSE OF LEVI** (**FIG. 13–21**), created for the Dominican monastery of SS. Giovanni e Paolo. At first glance the true subject of this painting seems to be architecture; the inhabitants of the space are only secondary. Beyond the enormous loggia, entered through colossal triumphal arches, an imaginary city of white marble gleams in the distance. The size of the canvas allowed Veronese to make his figures realistically proportional to the architectural setting without losing their substance.

Veronese Is Called before the Inquisition

According to the New Testament, Jesus revealed his impending death to his disciples during a *seder* meal celebrating the Jewish festival of Passover. Known to Christians as the Last Supper, situated in the Gospels on the evening before the Crucifixion, this was a popular subject in sixteenth-century European art. But in 1573, when the painter Veronese delivered an enormous *Last Supper* to fulfill a commission (**FIG. 13–21**), the patrons were shocked, not only by its grandiose pageantry but by the "impiety" of surrounding Jesus with a man picking his teeth, scruffy dogs, and foreign soldiers. As a result of the furor, Veronese was called before the Inquisition. There he justified himself first by asserting that the picture actually depicted not the Last Supper,

but rather the Feast in the House of Simon, a small dinner held shortly before Jesus's final entry into Jerusalem. He also noted that artists customarily invent details in their pictures and that he had received a commission to paint the piece "as I saw fit." His argument fell on unsympathetic ears—he was ordered to change the painting. Later he sidestepped the issue by changing its title to that of another banquet, one given by the tax collector Levi, whom Jesus had called to follow him (Luke 5:27–32). Perhaps with this change of subject, Veronese took modest revenge on the Inquisitors. When Jesus himself was criticized for associating with such unsavory people at this meal, he replied, "I have not come to call the righteous to repentance but sinners" (Luke 5:32).

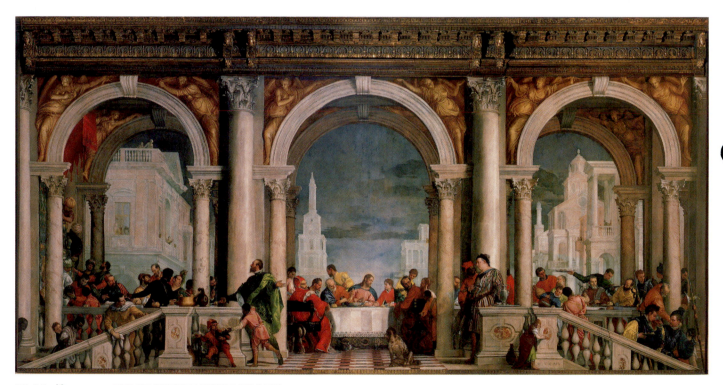

13–21 • Veronese FEAST IN THE HOUSE OF LEVI
From the refectory of the monastery of SS. Giovanni e Paolo, Venice. 1573. Oil on canvas, 18′ 3″ × 42′
(5.56 × 12.8 m). Galleria dell'Accademia, Venice.

📖 **Read** the document related to Veronese on **MyArtsLab**

Tintoretto. Jacopo Robusti (1518–1594), called Tintoretto ("little dyer") after his father's trade, carried Venetian Renaissance painting in another direction. A sign in his studio proclaimed his artistic goal as combining Titian's color with the drawing of Michelangelo. The speed with which Tintoretto drew and painted was the subject of comment in his own time

and of legends thereafter. Perhaps he seemed to paint so rapidly because he employed a large workshop, which included other members of his family. Of his eight children, four became artists. His oldest child, Marietta Robusti, worked with him as a portrait painter, and two or perhaps three of his sons also joined the shop. Another daughter, famous for her needlework,

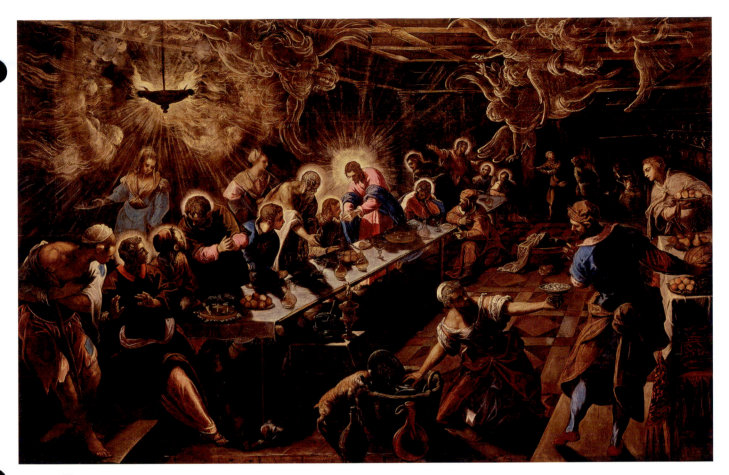

13–22 • Tintoretto THE LAST SUPPER
Church of San Giorgio Maggiore, Venice. 1592–1594. Oil on canvas, 12′ × 18′ 8″ (3.7 × 5.7 m).

became a nun. Marietta, in spite of her fame and many commissions, stayed in her father's shop until she died, at age 30. So skillfully did she capture her father's style and technique that today art historians cannot be certain which paintings are hers.

Tintoretto often developed a composition by creating a small-scale model like a miniature stage set, which he populated with wax figures. He then adjusted the positions of the figures and the lighting until he was satisfied with the entire scene. Using a grid of horizontal and vertical threads placed in front of this model, he could easily sketch the composition onto squared paper for his assistants to recopy onto a large canvas. Assistants also primed the canvas and blocked in the areas of dark and light. The artist himself finished the painting, concentrating his attention on the more difficult passages.

With his dynamic technique, strong colors, and bright highlights, Tintoretto created a pictorial mood of intense spirituality. **THE LAST SUPPER** (FIG. 13–22), one of his last paintings, is filled with the kind of everyday details that Veronese also included, such as a servant kneeling by a basket of provisions, which is inspected by a curious cat. But these realistic elements are transformed by the plunging, off-center perspective and by the brilliant, otherworldly light emanating from Jesus and the disciples, which takes the place of traditional haloes. Bands of angels swoop in from above as the supernatural and secular worlds become one. Compared with the

timeless, rigorous geometry of Leonardo da Vinci's *Last Supper* (SEE FIG. INTRO–17), Tintoretto's composition—seen from the corner rather than head on—is sweeping motion and twisting, gesturing figures. The spectator is drawn irresistibly inward, caught up in the sacred drama. And the narrative emphasis has shifted from Leonardo's study of personal betrayal to Tintoretto's reference to the institution of the Eucharist. Jesus offers bread and wine to a disciple in the manner of a priest administering the sacrament.

Palladio. Andrea Palladio (Andrea di Pietro; 1508–1580) was the most important architect of this period in Venice. He began his career as a stonecutter in Padua, but after moving to Vicenza (in a region ruled by Venice), he became the protégé of a Humanist scholar and amateur architect, Giangiorgio Trissino, with whom he made three trips to Rome, studying and drawing ancient Roman remains. From this background, he developed into a scholar and an architectural theorist as well as a designer of buildings. His famous and influential *I quattro libri dell'architettura* (*Four Books of Architecture*), published in 1570, provided ideal plans for country estates, using proportions derived from ancient Roman structures. Despite their theoretical bent, Palladio's books were more practical than earlier treatises. Perhaps his early experience as a stonemason provided him with the knowledge and self-confidence to approach technical problems and discuss them as clearly

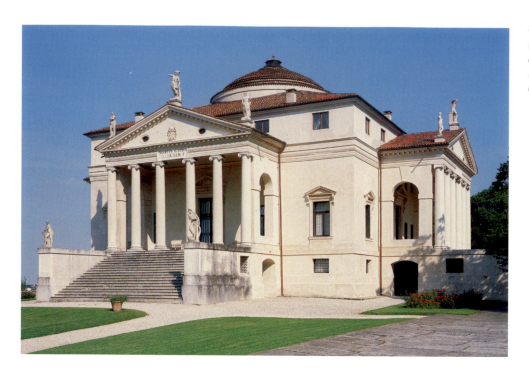

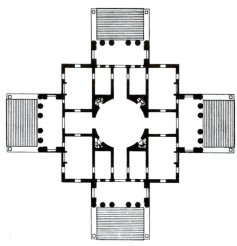

as he did theories of ideal proportion and uses of the Classical orders. The early eighteenth century witnessed an important Palladian revival, and Palladio's *Four Books of Architecture* became a standard work in the libraries of the educated. Thomas Jefferson had one of the first copies in America.

Palladio's versatility is already apparent in numerous **villas** (country houses on large estates) built early in his career. His famous **VILLA ROTONDA**, just outside Vicenza (**FIG. 13–23**), was completed in 1569. Although the term "villa" implies a working farm, Palladio designed this one as a retreat for relaxation, literally a party house. To maximize vistas of the countryside, he placed a porch elevated at the top of a wide staircase on each face of the building. Called the Villa Rotonda because it had been inspired by another round building, the Roman Pantheon (**SEE FIG. 6–28**), it was renamed Villa Capra after the family that purchased it in 1591. The plan shows the geometrical clarity of Palladio's design: a circle inscribed in a square inside a larger square, with symmetrical rectangular rooms and identical rectangular porticoes and staircases projecting from each of its faces.

The use of a central dome on the Villa Rotunda was a daring innovation that effectively secularized the dome and initiated a long tradition of domed country houses, particularly in England and the United States, including Monticello, Thomas Jefferson's country house in Virginia (**SEE FIG. 17–18**).

Mannerism

What characterizes the development of Mannerism in Italy and France?

A new style developed in Florence and Rome in the 1520s that art historians have associated with the death of Raphael and labeled "Mannerism," a word deriving from the Italian *maniera* (meaning "style"). Mannerism developed into an anti-Classical movement in which artificiality, grace, and elegance took priority over the ordered balance and lifelike references that were hallmarks of High Renaissance art. Patrons favored esoteric subjects, displays of extraordinary technical virtuosity, and the pursuit of beauty for its own sake. Artists fearlessly manipulated and distorted accepted formal conventions, creating contrived compositions, irrational spatial environments, and figures with elongated proportions, complicated artificial poses, enigmatic gestures, and dreamy expressions. Painters quoted from ancient and modern works of art in much the same manner as contemporary poets and authors were quoting from ancient and modern literary classics. Mannerist sculpture—often small and made from precious metals—also stylizes body forms and foregrounds displays of technical skill. Mannerist architects designed buildings that defy uniformity and balance and used Classical orders in unconventional, even playful, ways.

The altarpiece created by Jacopo Carucci da Pontormo (1494–1557) between 1525 and 1528 for the Capponi Chapel in the church of Sta. Felicità in Florence is a dreamlike rendering of the **DEPOSITION** that bears the principal hallmarks of Mannerist style (**FIG. 13–24**). Its ambiguous composition enhances its visionary quality. Shadowy ground and cloudy sky

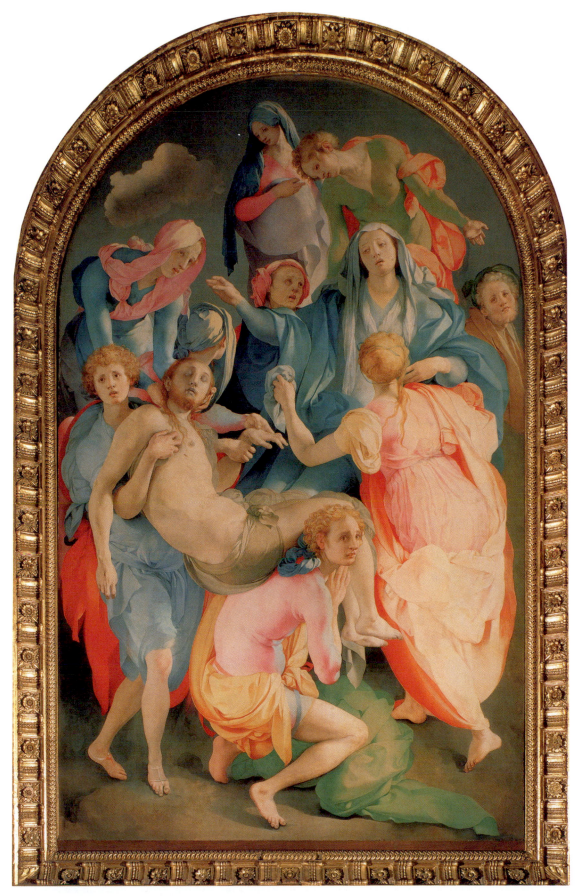

13-24 • Jacopo Carucci da Pontormo DEPOSITION
Capponi Chapel, church of Sta. Felicità, Florence. 1525–1528. Oil and tempera on wood panel,
10′ 3″ × 6′ 4″ (3.12 × 1.93 m).

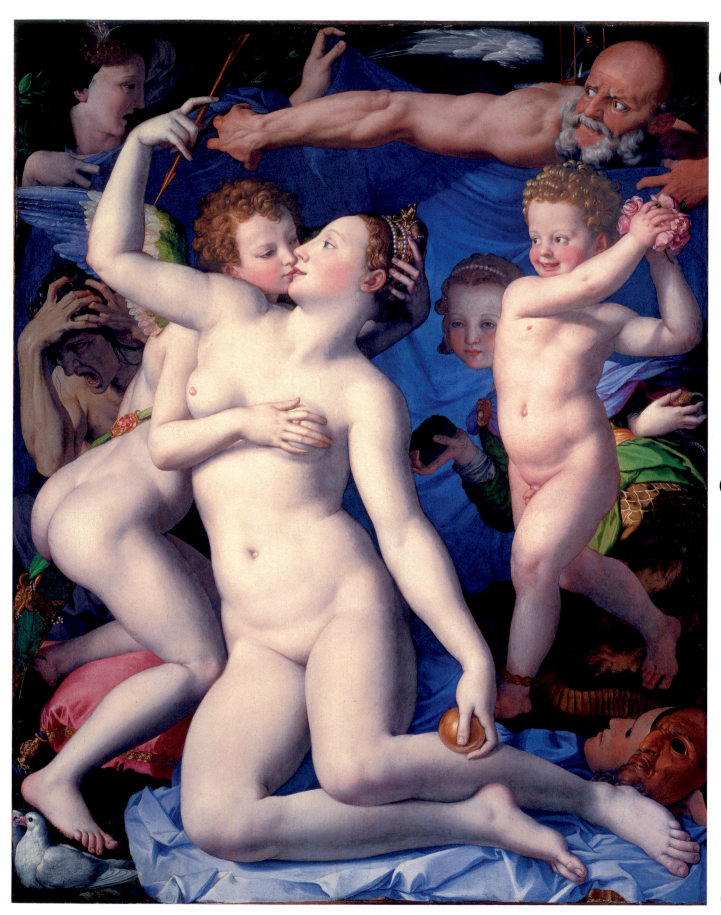

13–25 • Bronzino ALLEGORY WITH VENUS AND CUPID
Mid-1540s. Oil on wood panel, 57½″ × 46″ (2.16 × 1.32 m). The National Gallery, London.

give little sense of a specific location. Some figures press forward into the viewer's space, while others seem to levitate or stand precariously on tiptoe. Pontormo chose a moment just after the removal of Jesus's body from the cross, when the youths who have lowered him pause to regain their hold on the corpse, which intentionally recalls Michelangelo's Vatican *Pietà* (SEE FIG. 13–8). Odd poses and drastic shifts in scale charge the scene emotionally, but perhaps most striking is the use of weird colors in odd juxtapositions—baby blue and pink with accents of olive green, yellow, and scarlet. The overall tone of the picture is set by the unstable youth crouching in the foreground, whose skintight bright pink shirt is shaded in iridescent, pale gray-green, and whose anxious expression is projected out of the painting, directly at the viewer.

Pontormo's assistant at this time was Agnolo di Cosimo (1503–1572), whose nickname "Bronzino" means "copper-colored" (just as we might call someone "Red"). In 1530, he established his own workshop, and by 1540 he was court painter to the Medici. His **ALLEGORY WITH VENUS AND CUPID** is one of the strangest paintings of the sixteenth century (**FIG. 13–25**). It contains all the formal, iconographical, and psychological characteristics of Mannerist art. Seven figures, three masks, and a dove interweave in an intricate, claustrophobic formal composition pressed breathlessly into the foreground plane. Taken as individual images, they display Mannerism's exaggerated poses, graceful forms, polished surfaces, and delicate colors. But a closer look uncovers disturbing erotic attachments and bizarre irregularities. The painting's complex allegory and relentless ambiguity probably delighted mid-sixteenth-century courtiers who enjoyed equally sophisticated wordplay and esoteric Classical references, but for us it defies easy explanation. Nothing is quite what it seems.

Venus and her son Cupid engage in an unsettlingly lascivious dalliance, encouraged by a *putto* sauntering in from the right—representing Folly, Jest, or Playfulness—who is about to throw pink roses at them while stepping on a thorny branch that draws blood from his foot. Cupid gently kisses his mother and pinches her erect nipple while Venus snatches an arrow from his quiver. An old man, Time or Chronos, assisted by Truth or Night, pulls back a curtain to expose the couple. Lurking just behind Venus a monstrous serpent—which has the upper body and head of a beautiful young girl and the legs and claws of a lion—crosses her hands to hold a honeycomb and the stinger at the end of her tail. This strange hybrid has been interpreted both as Fraud and Pleasure.

In the shadows to the left, a pale man who screams and tears at his hair has recently been identified as a victim of syphilis, which raged as an epidemic during this period. The painting could, therefore, be a warning of the dangers of this disease, believed in the sixteenth century to be spread principally by coitus, kissing, and breast feeding, all of which are alluded to in the intertwined Cupid and Venus. But the complexity of the painting makes room for multiple meanings, and deciphering them would be typical of the sorts of games enjoyed by sixteenth-century intellectuals. Perhaps the allegory tells of the impossibility of constant love and the folly of lovers, which becomes apparent across time. Or perhaps it is an allegorical warning of the dangers of illicit sexual liaisons, including the

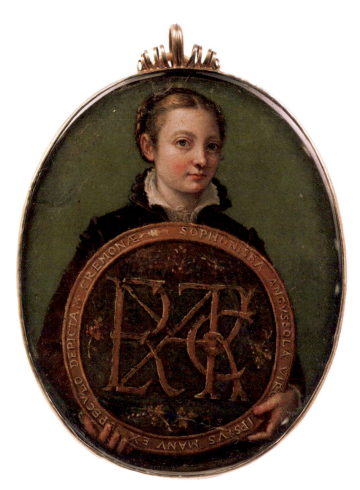

13–26 • Sofonisba Anguissola SELF-PORTRAIT
c. 1556. Oil on parchment on cardboard, 3¼″ × 2½″ (8.3 × 6.4 cm). Museum of Fine Arts, Boston. Photograph © 2015 Museum of Fine Arts, Boston. Emma F. Munroe Fund (60.155).

Sofonisba was not the only talented Anguissola daughter. Her sisters Elena, Lucia, Minerva, Europa, and Anna were all painters, too. Only their brother, Asdrubale, evidently lacked the family talent, but as a member of the city council of Cremona he focused on his political career.

pain, hair loss, and disfiguration of venereal disease. It could be both, and even more. Duke Cosimo de' Medici ordered the painting himself, and presented it as a diplomatic gift to French King Francis I, who would doubtless have relished its overt eroticism and flawless execution.

Many sixteenth-century Italian artists continued to draw inspiration from the great leaders of the earlier generation, especially Raphael and Michelangelo. In 1557, the father of Sofonisba Anguissola (c. 1532–1625), a gifted portrait painter from Cremona, consulted Michelangelo about his daughter's artistic talents. He asked for a drawing that she might copy and hoped the master would critique her work. Michelangelo obliged.

Sofonisba was a skilled miniaturist, an important kind of painting in the sixteenth century, when people had few means of recording the features of a lover, friend, or family member. She painted her own miniature portrait holding a medallion, the border of which spells out her name and hometown (**FIG. 13–26**). The interlaced letters at the center of the medallion are a riddle; they seem to form a monogram with the first letters of her sisters' names: Minerva, Europa, Elena—names that reflect the enthusiasm for the Classical world in Renaissance Italy.

In 1560, Sofonisba accepted the invitation of the queen of Spain to become a lady in waiting and court painter, a post she held for 20 years. Unfortunately, most of her Spanish works were lost in a seventeenth-century palace fire. After her years at court, she retired to Sicily (then a Spanish territory), where she died at age 92. Anthony van Dyck met Sofonisba in Palermo in 1624, where he sketched her and claimed that she was then 96 years old. He wrote that she advised him on positioning the lights for her portrait, asking that the light not be placed too high because the strong shadows would bring out her wrinkles.

Bologna was especially hospitable to accomplished women at this time. It boasted some two dozen women painters as well as a number of women scholars who lectured at the university. Lavinia Fontana (1552–1614) learned to paint from her father, a Bolognese follower of Raphael. By the 1570s, her success was so well rewarded that her husband, the painter Gian Paolo Zappi, gave up his own career to care for their large family and help his wife by building frames for her paintings. In 1603, she moved to Rome as an official painter to the papal court, and the Habsburgs became major patrons of her work.

In 1581, while still in her twenties, Lavinia Fontana painted a **NOLI ME TANGERE** (FIG. 13–27), where Christ reveals himself for the first time to Mary Magdalen following his Resurrection (John 20:17), greeting her with the words "Do not touch me" (in Latin, "*Noli me tangere*"), explaining to her that he now existed in a new form somewhere between physical and spiritual. The biblical account claims that Mary Magdalen at first

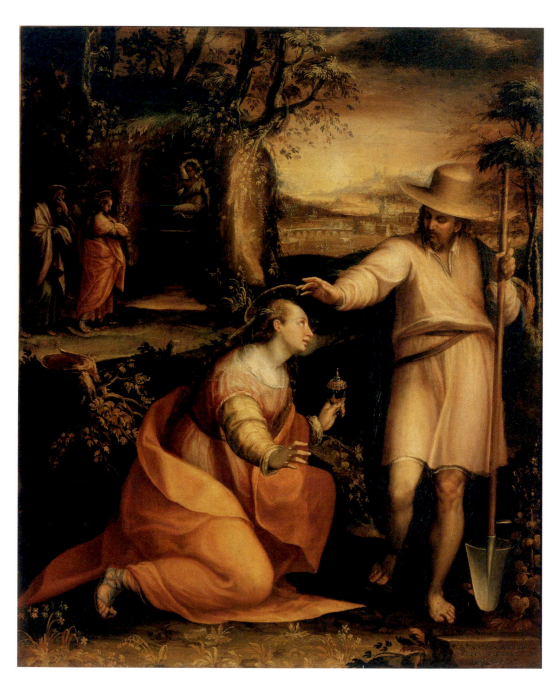

13–27 • Lavinia Fontana
NOLI ME TANGERE
1581. Oil on canvas,
47⅜″ × 36⅝″ (120.3 × 93 cm).
Galleria degli Uffizi, Florence.

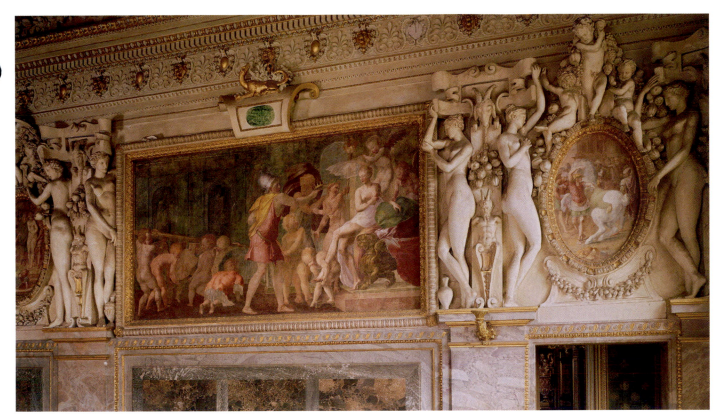

13-28 • Primaticcio STUCCO AND WALL PAINTING
Chamber of the duchess of Étampes, Château of Fontainebleau. 1540s.

This was originally the bedroom of Francis I's mistress, the duchess of Étampes, but in 1749 Louis XV had the space transformed as part of a new grand staircase providing access to his apartments.

mistook Christ for a gardener, so Fontana represents him with a broad-brimmed hat and spade. In the middle ground, Fontana portrays a second version of the Resurrection, where other women followers of Christ discover an angel in his empty tomb. This secondary scene's unsettling diagonal plunge into depth and temporal disconnect is a typical feature of late Mannerist painting in Italy, as are the affected pose of the foregrounded Christ and the elongated proportions of the Magdalen.

France

Painters from Italy carried the Mannerist style to France, where King Francis I (ruled 1515–1547) was an important patron of the arts and an enthusiastic devotee of the Italian Renaissance. Francis even persuaded Leonardo to join him in 1516 at the French royal château at Amboise, where the artist spent the last two years of his life, offering advice on architectural projects and, as the king said, providing the pleasure of his conversation.

Eventually choosing a medieval hunting lodge at Fontainebleau as his primary residence, Francis began transforming it in 1526 into a grand country palace, or **château**. In 1530, he imported a Florentine artist, the Mannerist painter Rosso Fiorentino (1495–1540), to direct the project. After Rosso died, he was succeeded by his Italian colleague Francesco Primaticcio (1504–1570), who spent the rest of his career at Fontainebleau working on the decoration of the château from 1532 until his

death. During that time, he also commissioned and imported a large number of copies and casts made from original Roman sculpture, including the *Apollo Belvedere* in the Vatican gardens, the newly discovered *Laocoön* (SEE FIG. INTRO–20), and even the relief decoration on the Column of Trajan. These works provided an invaluable visual resource for the artists employed on the project.

Among Primaticcio's first projects at Fontainebleau was the redecoration, in the 1540s, of the chambers of the king's official mistress, Anne, duchess of Étampes (FIG. 13–28). The artist combined the arts of woodworking, stucco relief, and fresco painting in his complex but lighthearted and graceful interior design. The lithe figures of his stucco nymphs recall Pontormo's painting style (SEE FIG. 13–24), with their elongated bodies and small heads. Their spiraling postures and teasing bits of clinging drapery charge the work with a playful eroticism. Garlands, mythological figures, and Roman architectural ornament almost overwhelm the walls with lavish visual enrichment. This first School of Fontainebleau established an Italianate tradition of Mannerist painting and interior design that spread to other centers in France and the Netherlands.

But not all the artists working at the court of **FRANCIS I** were Italian. The Flemish artist Jean Clouet (c. 1485–c. 1540) found great favor at the royal court. At about the same time as he became principal court painter in 1527, he produced an official

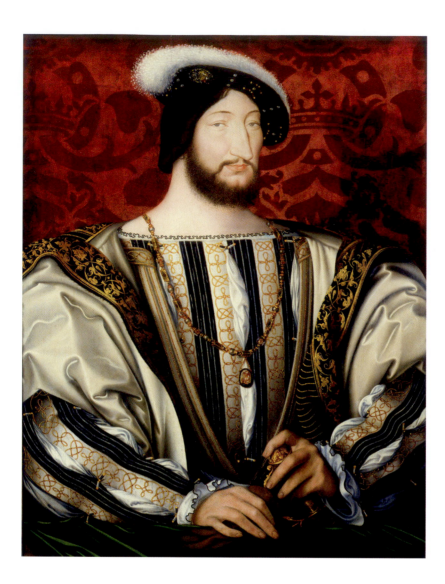

13–29 • Jean Clouet **FRANCIS I**
1525–1530. Oil and tempera on wood
panel, 37¾″ × 29⅛″ (95.9 × 74 cm).
Musée du Louvre, Paris.

portrait of the king (**FIG. 13–29**). Clouet created a flattering image of pure power, modulating Francis's distinctive features with soft shading and highlighting the nervous activity of his fingers. Elaborate, puffy sleeves broadened the king's shoulders to fill the entire width of the panel, much as Renaissance parade armor turned scrawny men into giants. The detailed rendering of the delicately worked costume of silk, satin, velvet, jewels, and gold embroidery could be painted separately from the portrait itself. Royal clothing was often loaned to the artist or modeled by a servant to spare the "sitter" the boredom of posing. In creating such official portraits, the artist sketched the subject, then painted a prototype that, upon approval, became the model for numerous replicas made for diplomatic and family purposes.

German Art

How can we distinguish among several styles of sixteenth-century art in Germany?

Early sixteenth-century painting in Germany was dominated by two artists of very different temperament and ambition— Matthias Gothardt, known as Matthias Grünewald (c. 1470/75– 1528), and Albrecht Dürer (1471–1528). Grünewald continued indigenous currents of medieval mysticism and emotional spirituality in his extraordinarily moving paintings. Dürer, on the other hand, used intense observation of the world to render lifelike representations of nature, linear perspective to create convincing illusions of space, and a reasoned new canon of proportions to standardize depictions of the human figure after Classical ideals.

Grünewald

Grünewald is best known today for the wings he painted between about 1510 and 1515 for an altarpiece carved around 1500 by Nikolaus Hagenauer for the Community of St. Anthony in Isenheim, whose hospital specialized in diseases of the skin, including the plague and leprosy. The completed **ISENHEIM ALTARPIECE** (**FIG. 13–30**)—impressive in size

13–30 • Nikolaus Hagenauer and Matthias Grünewald **ISENHEIM ALTARPIECE**
Closed (top) and open (bottom), from the Community of St. Anthony, Isenheim, France. Sculpture c. 1500, painting c. 1510–1515. Painted and gilt limewood, oil on panel; center painted panels 9′ 9″ × 10′ 9″ (2.97 × 3.28 m); each wing 8′ 2″ × 3′ ½″ (2.49 × 0.93 m); predella 2′ 5½″ × 11′ 2″ (0.75 × 3.4 m). Musée d'Unterlinden, Colmar, France.

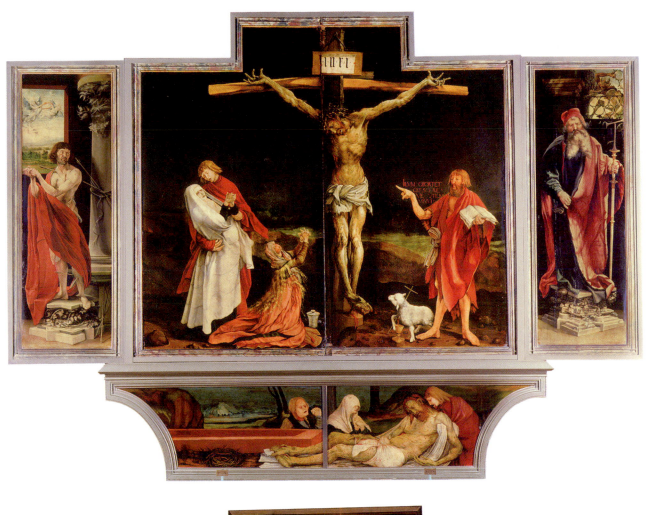

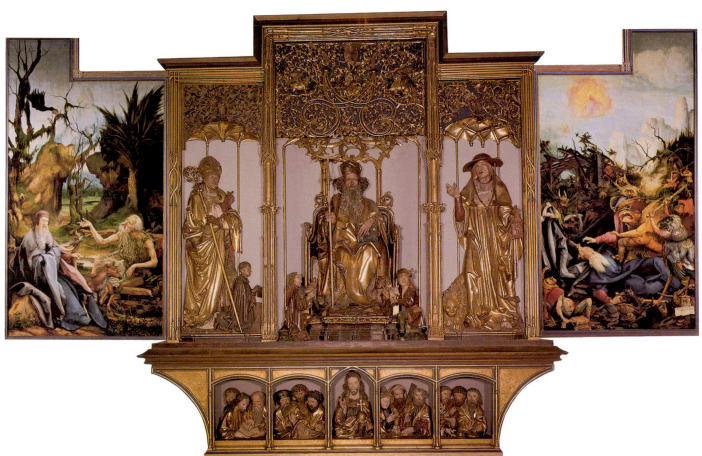

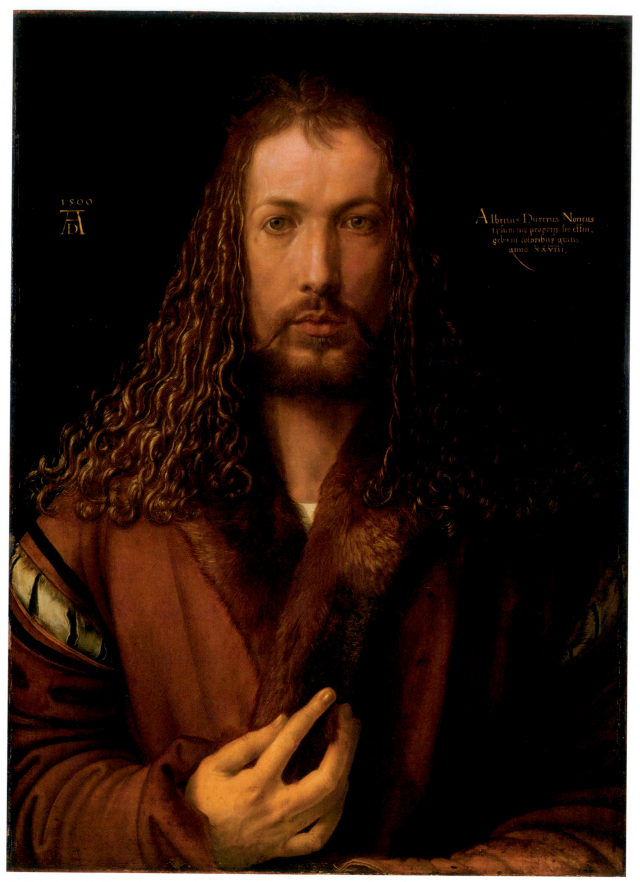

1500

Ạ͞D

Albertus Durerus Noricus
ipsum me proprijs sic effin,
gebam coloribus ætatis
anno XXVIII.

13–31 • Albrecht Dürer SELF-PORTRAIT
1500. Oil on wood panel, 26¼″ × 19¼″ (66.3 × 49 cm). Alte Pinakothek, Munich.

📖 **Read** the document related to Albrecht Dürer on **MyArtsLab**

and complexity—was thought to have healing properties itself, and viewing it was part of the treatment given to patients who entered the hospital. Made with multiple wings, the altarpiece was displayed in different configurations depending upon the Church calendar. On normal weekdays, when it was closed (FIG. 13–30, top), viewers saw a grisly portrayal of the Crucifixion in a darkened landscape, flanked on the wings by life-size figures of SS. Sebastian and Anthony Abbot, standing like statues on *trompe l'oeil* pedestals. The tortured body of Jesus is described in horrific detail, covered with gashes and pierced by the thorns used to crown his head. Not only does his ashen color, clotted blood, open mouth, and blue lips indicate that he is dead—he appears already to be decaying, an effect enhanced by the palette of putrescent greens, yellows, and purplish red. An immaculately garbed Virgin Mary has collapsed into the arms of a ghostlike John the Evangelist, and Mary Magdalen has fallen in anguish to her knees. Her clasped hands with exaggerated fingers echo Jesus's claw-like fingers, cramped in rigor mortis, as well as the emphatically pointing finger of John the Baptist to the right. Below, in the predella, or supporting platform, Jesus's bereaved mother and friends prepare his racked body for burial, a scene that must have been familiar in the abbey's hospital.

When the altarpiece was completely opened —only for the special festivals of St. Anthony— Hagenauer's sculpture was the focus (FIG. 13–30, bottom). Grünewald's paintings were restricted to the wings: at right St. Anthony attacked by horrible demons, perhaps inspired by the horrors of the diseased patients, and on the left the meeting of St. Anthony with the hermit St. Paul in a wilderness landscape full of the medicinal plants used in the hospital's therapy. Grünewald painted the face of Paul with his own self-portrait, while Anthony is a portrait of the donor and administrator of the hospital, the Italian Guido Guersi, whose coat of arms Grünewald painted on the rock next to him.

Grünewald's paintings display conspicuous virtuosity and expressive power, but it was Albrecht Dürer who became the foremost artist of the German Renaissance. Studious, analytical, meticulous, and as self-confident as Michelangelo, Dürer was the son of a Nuremberg goldsmith and served apprenticeships in painting, stained-glass design, and printmaking. He encountered the latest developments in Italian Renaissance art during two trips to the Italian peninsula, in 1494–1495 and 1505–1506. He seems to have resolved to reform German art by publishing theoretical writings and manuals that discussed Renaissance problems of perspective, ideal human proportions, and the techniques of painting.

Dürer

During Dürer's first trip to Italy he absorbed both the idealism associated with Italian art and the concept of the artist as an independent creative genius. In his SELF-PORTRAIT of 1500 (FIG. 13–31), he represents himself as an idealized, even Christlike, figure in a severely frontal pose, meeting the viewer's eyes like an icon. His rich, fur-lined robes and flowing locks of curly hair create a monumental equilateral triangle, a timeless symbol of unity. Ultimately, what is showcased here are Dürer's awesome gifts of hand as much as his intellectual gifts of mind, two aspects of his distinction as an artist, emblematized by the brightly illuminated head and hand that align on a vertical axis to dominate this arresting self-portrait.

Dürer's early interest in Italian art and his theoretical investigations continued in his 1504 engraving of ADAM AND EVE (FIG. 13–32). These figures represent his first documented use of an ideal of human proportions based on Classical sculpture, probably known to him through contemporary prints or drawings. But behind his idealized figures, he recorded the flora and fauna of their setting with typically Northern descriptive detail. Embedded in the landscape are symbols of the four humors, referencing the belief that after Adam and Eve disobeyed God, they and their descendants became vulnerable to imbalances in body fluids that altered human temperament.

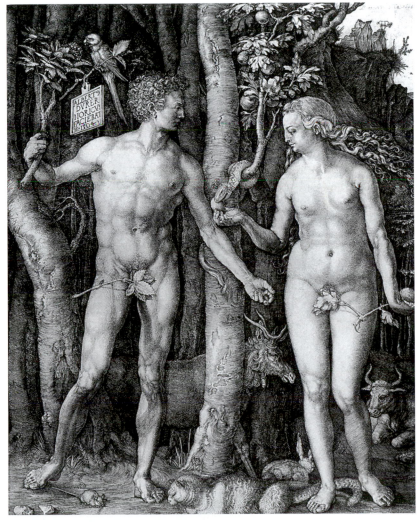

13–32 • Albrecht Dürer **ADAM AND EVE**
1504. Engraving, 9⅞″ × 7⅝″ (25.1 × 19.4 cm).
Yale University Art Gallery, New Haven, Connecticut.

An excess of black bile from the liver produced melancholy, despair, and greed; yellow bile caused anger, pride, and impatience; phlegm in the lungs resulted in lethargy, disinterest, and a lack of emotion; and an excess of blood made a person unusually optimistic but also compulsively interested in the pleasures of the flesh. These four human temperaments are symbolized here by the melancholy elk, the choleric cat, the phlegmatic ox, and the sensual rabbit. The scurrying mouse is an emblem of Satan; the parrot may symbolize false wisdom, since it can only repeat mindlessly what it hears. Dürer's pride in his engraving can be seen in the prominence of his signature—a placard bearing his full name and date hanging on a branch next to Adam.

The Reformation and the Arts

Against a backdrop of broad dissatisfaction with financial abuses and decadent lifestyles among the clergy, religious reformers within the Catholic Church began to challenge its specific practices and beliefs, especially the sale of indulgences (guarantees of relief from the punishment required after death for forgiven sins). From their protests, the reformers came to be called Protestants, and their insistence on church reform gave rise to a movement called the Reformation. Two of the most important early reformers were themselves Catholic priests and trained theologians: Desiderius Erasmus of Rotterdam (1466?–1536), and Martin Luther (1483–1546). They questioned official Church teachings and the pope's supremacy; they emphasized individual faith and saw ultimate religious authority in the Bible. Failing in their attempt to reform practices from within the Catholic Church, Protestants broke away from Rome. Rome launched a Counter-Reformation. At the Council of Trent (1545–1563), the Roman Catholic hierarchy formulated a program that included the Inquisition, with its special tribunals to root out heresy.

The effects of the Reformation on art were significant and at times destructive. Some Protestants considered religious

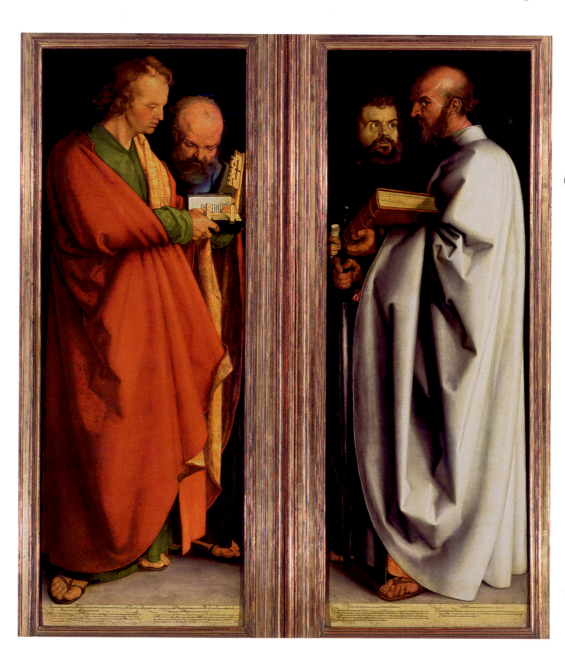

13–33 • Albrecht Dürer FOUR APOSTLES
1526. Oil on wood panel, each panel 7′ ½″ × 2′ 6″ (2.15 × 0.76 m). Alte Pinakothek, Munich.

A long inscription on the frame warns the viewer not to be led astray by "false prophets" but to heed the words of the New Testament as recorded by these "four excellent men." Below each figure are excerpts from their letters and from the Gospel of Mark warning against those who do not understand the true word of God. In the inscriptions, Dürer used Luther's German translation of the New Testament.

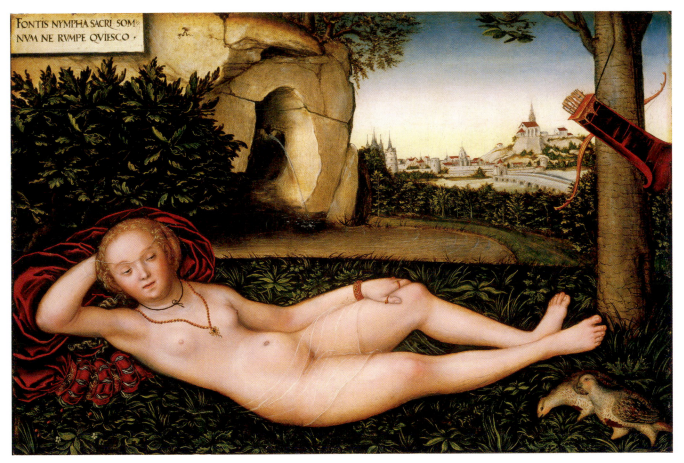

13–34 • Lucas Cranach the Elder NYMPH OF THE SPRING
c. 1537. Oil on panel, 19″ × 28½″ (48.5 × 72.9 cm). National Gallery of Art, Washington, D.C.

imagery idolatrous; in some areas religious art was destroyed and church interiors whitewashed in fits of iconoclasm. As a result, many artists turned to portraiture and other secular subjects to make their livings. In Catholic regions, people still venerated traditional images of Christ and the saints, but officials from the Church scrutinized works of art for heretical or profane subject matter.

Martin Luther, himself, never supported the destruction of religious art, and Dürer, who admired Luther's writings, may have painted a pair of large panels commonly known as the **FOUR APOSTLES (FIG. 13–33)** in order to demonstrate that Protestant imagery was possible. The paintings depict SS. John, Peter, Paul, and Mark. On the left panel, the elderly St. Peter seems to shrink behind the young St. John, Luther's favorite evangelist. On the right panel, the evangelist Mark is nearly hidden behind St. Paul, whose teachings and epistles were greatly admired by the Protestants. Dürer presented the panels, painted in 1526, to the city of Nuremberg, which had already adopted Lutheranism (then almost synonymous with Protestantism) as its official religion. Dürer wrote, "For a Christian would no more be led to superstition by a picture or effigy than an honest man to commit murder because he carries a weapon by his side. He must indeed be an unthinking man who would worship picture, wood, or stone. A picture therefore brings more good than harm, when it is honorably, artistically, and well made" (cited in Snyder, p. 333).

Martin Luther's favorite painter, Lucas Cranach the Elder (1472–1553) was court painter to Frederick the Wise of Saxony, for whom he made woodcuts, painted altarpieces, and portraits. Just how far the German artists' style and conception of figure could differ from Italian Renaissance ideals is easily seen in Cranach's **NYMPH OF THE SPRING (FIG. 13–34)**, especially when compared with Titian's *"Venus" of Urbino* (SEE FIG. 13–20). Cranach's source was a fifteenth-century inscription on a fountain beside the Danube, cited in the upper left corner of the painting: "I am the nymph of the sacred font. Do not interrupt my sleep for I am at peace."

Cranach records the Danube landscape with characteristic Northern attention to detail and turns his nymph into a provocative young woman, who glances slyly out at the viewer through half-closed eyes. She has cast aside a fashionable red velvet gown, but still wears her jewelry, which together with her transparent veil enhances rather than conceals her nudity—especially those coral beads that fall between her breasts, outlining their contours. Unlike other artists working for Protestant patrons, many of whom looked on earthly beauty as a sinful vanity, Cranach seems delighted by earthly things: the lush foliage that provides the nymph's couch, the pair of partridges (symbols of Venus and married love), and Cupid's bow and quiver of arrows hanging on the tree. Could this nymph be a living beauty in the Wittenburg court? She is surely not an idealized embodiment of a Classical Venus.

The French Ambassadors ▶

Hans Holbein the Younger. 1533. Oil on wood panel, 81⅛″ × 82⅝″ (2.07 × 2.1 m). The National Gallery, London.

Embossing on the sheath of the dagger tells us that de Dinteville is 28, while an inscription on the edge of the book (Bible?) under de Selve's arm records that he is 24.

These objects on the top shelf were used to observe natural heavenly phenomena and chart the passage of time. The items displayed on the lower shelf relate more to terrestrial concerns.

Music is a common symbol of harmony in this period, and the broken string on this lute has been understood as an allusion to the discord created by the sweep of Protestant reform across Europe.

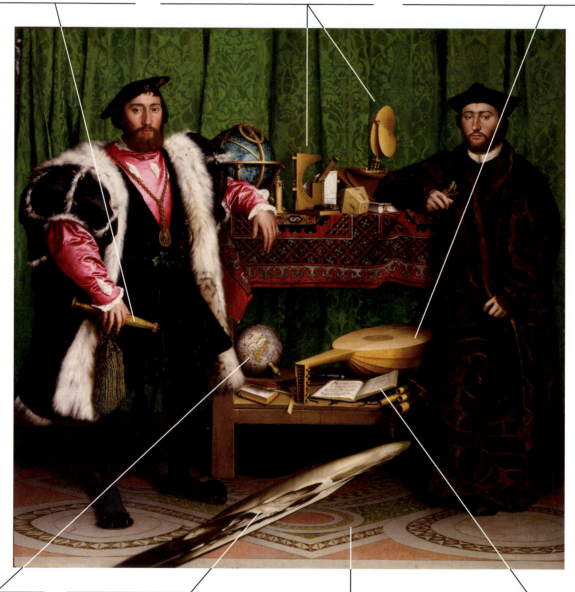

This globe has Polisy, the de Dinteville family estate, marked at the center. It was here that this painting was hung when the ambassador returned to France at the end of 1533.

This bizarre, but prominently placed skull—as well as the skull badge that appears on de Dinteville's cap—reminded viewers of their own mortality. The foreground skull is distorted by **anamorphosis**, in which images are stretched horizontally with the use of a trapezoidal grid so that they must be viewed from the side to appear correctly proportioned.

This pavement—known as "Cosmati work" after the thirteenth-century Italian family that specialized in it—is copied from the floor in Westminster Abbey and may proclaim the ambassadors' involvement in a holy enterprise of reconciliation. The artist signed the painting on the left edge of the floor: "Johannes Holbein pingebat, 1533."

This is a Lutheran hymnal published in 1527, open at one of Luther's best-known compositions: "Come, Holy Ghost, our souls inspire." Neither man was a Protestant, but some of de Selve's contemporaries saw him as sympathetic to the cause of the reformers.

View the Closer Look for Holbein's *The French Ambassadors* on **MyArtsLab**

Holbein

In the context of the volatile German religious and political climate, some artists left their homes to seek patronage abroad. Hans Holbein the Younger (1497–1543), born in Augsburg, spent much of his early career in Basel, Switzerland, but worked in Antwerp and London from 1526 to 1528 to escape religious turmoil. Although he had converted to Protestantism by 1532, harassment from reformers sent him once again to England, where he served as court painter to the Tudor monarch Henry VIII (ruled 1509–1547).

During the 1530s, Holbein created a spectacular series of portraits of nobles and diplomats associated with the Tudor court, whose international climate is embodied in a work of 1533 (see "A Closer Look," p. 360)—a German painter's rendering in England of two French diplomats, one of them representing the court of Francis I in the Vatican. *The French Ambassadors* foregrounds Holbein's virtuosity as a painter and constructs rich characterizations of Jean de Dinteville, French ambassador to England, and his friend Georges de Selve, bishop of Lavaur and ambassador to the Vatican. With a loving detail that recalls the work of Jan van Eyck, Holbein describes the surface textures and luminosity of the objects gathered in the painting to reflect the intellectual gifts and symbolize the political accomplishments of these two men. References to the conflicts between European states, and within the Catholic Church itself, imply that these bright and confident young ambassadors will apply their considerable diplomatic skills to finding a resolution.

Netherlandish and Spanish Art

What were the distinctive trends in the sixteenth-century art of the Netherlands and Spain?

Politically, the Netherlands (at this time, Holland and Belgium) and Spain were united under the Habsburg Empire, but their art was far from unified. Some artists continued the styles of the late fifteenth century; others looked back to earlier Flemish painters for models. Some became Mannerists in the Italian mode. A few, such as the Netherlandish artist Hieronymus Bosch and Cretan expatriate painter El Greco working in Spain, were so individualistic that they defy neat characterization.

Hieronymus Bosch (c. 1450–1516) created a world of fantastic and unsettling imagery in paintings such as the **GARDEN OF EARTHLY DELIGHTS** (FIG. 13–35). There are many interpretations of this triptych. The subject seems rooted in the Christian belief in humanity's natural state of sinfulness, but it was not painted for a church. It was probably commissioned by Count Hendrick III of Nassau for his Brussels townhouse, and the artist's choice of a triptych format, which evokes an

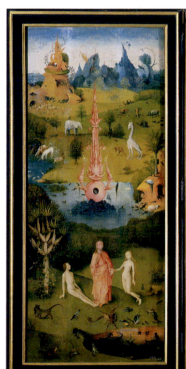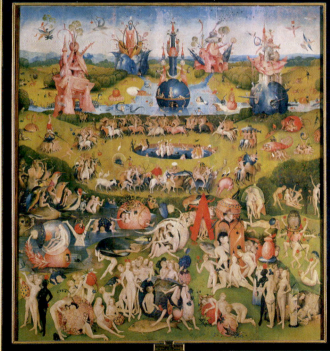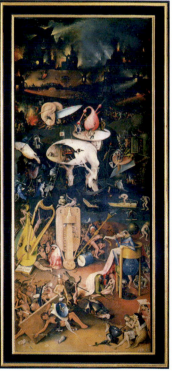

13–35 • Hieronymus Bosch GARDEN OF EARTHLY DELIGHTS (OPEN)
c. 1505–1515. Oil on wood panel, center panel 7′ 2½″ × 6′ 4¾″ (2.2 × 1.95 m), each wing 7′ 2½″ × 3′ 2″ (2.2 × 0.97 m). Museo del Prado, Madrid.

Despite—or perhaps because of—its bizarre subject matter, the triptych was copied in 1566 in tapestry versions, one (now in El Escorial, Madrid) for a cardinal and another for Francis I. At least one painted copy was made as well. Bosch's original triptych was sold at the outbreak of the Netherlands' revolt and sent in 1568 to Spain, where it entered the collection of Philip II.

📖 **Read** the document related to Hieronymus Bosch on **MyArtsLab**

altarpiece, may have been an understated irony. In a private home the painting surely inspired lively discussion, much as it does today in the Prado museum.

The imagery begins with the Creation of Adam and Eve on the left wing, and ends with the Last Judgment on the right. Only the damned—not the saved—are shown in the Judgment scene, perhaps warning that damnation is the natural outcome of a life lived in ignorance and folly, that humans ensure their own damnation through the self-centered pursuit of the pleasures of the flesh. The central panel illustrates just such activities with graphic abandon. Seemingly harmless diversions such as games, romance, and music turn into sins such as lust, gluttony, and sloth. Luscious fruits—strawberries, cherries, grapes, and pomegranates—appear everywhere in the *Garden*, serving as food, as shelter, and in one instance even as a boat. Herbalists believed these fruits enhanced sexual desire. Fruits also suggest that life is as fleeting and insubstantial as the taste of a strawberry.

The works of Bosch were so popular that, nearly a half century after his death, the painter Pieter Bruegel the Elder (c. 1525–1569) began his career by imitating them. Bruegel soon developed his own style and themes, producing artfully composed works that reflected contemporary social, political, and religious conditions, working first in Antwerp and then in Brussels. Between 1551 and 1554, Bruegel traveled across the Alps and through Italy, all the way to Sicily. Unlike many Renaissance artists, he did not record the ruins of ancient Rome or the wonders of Italian cities. Instead he was fascinated by the landscape, particularly the formidable jagged rocks and sweeping panoramic views of Alpine valleys, which he recorded in detailed drawings. Back home in his studio, he painted the flat and rolling lands of Flanders as broad panoramas, but added imaginary mountains on the horizon.

Cycles, or series, of paintings on a single allegorical subject such as the Times of Day, the Seasons, or the Five Senses became popular decorations in Flemish upper-class homes. Bruegel's **RETURN OF THE HUNTERS** (**FIG. 13–36**) of 1565 is one of a cycle of six panels, each representing a pair of months. Here Bruegel describes November and December with the bleak atmosphere of early nightfall during a damp, cold

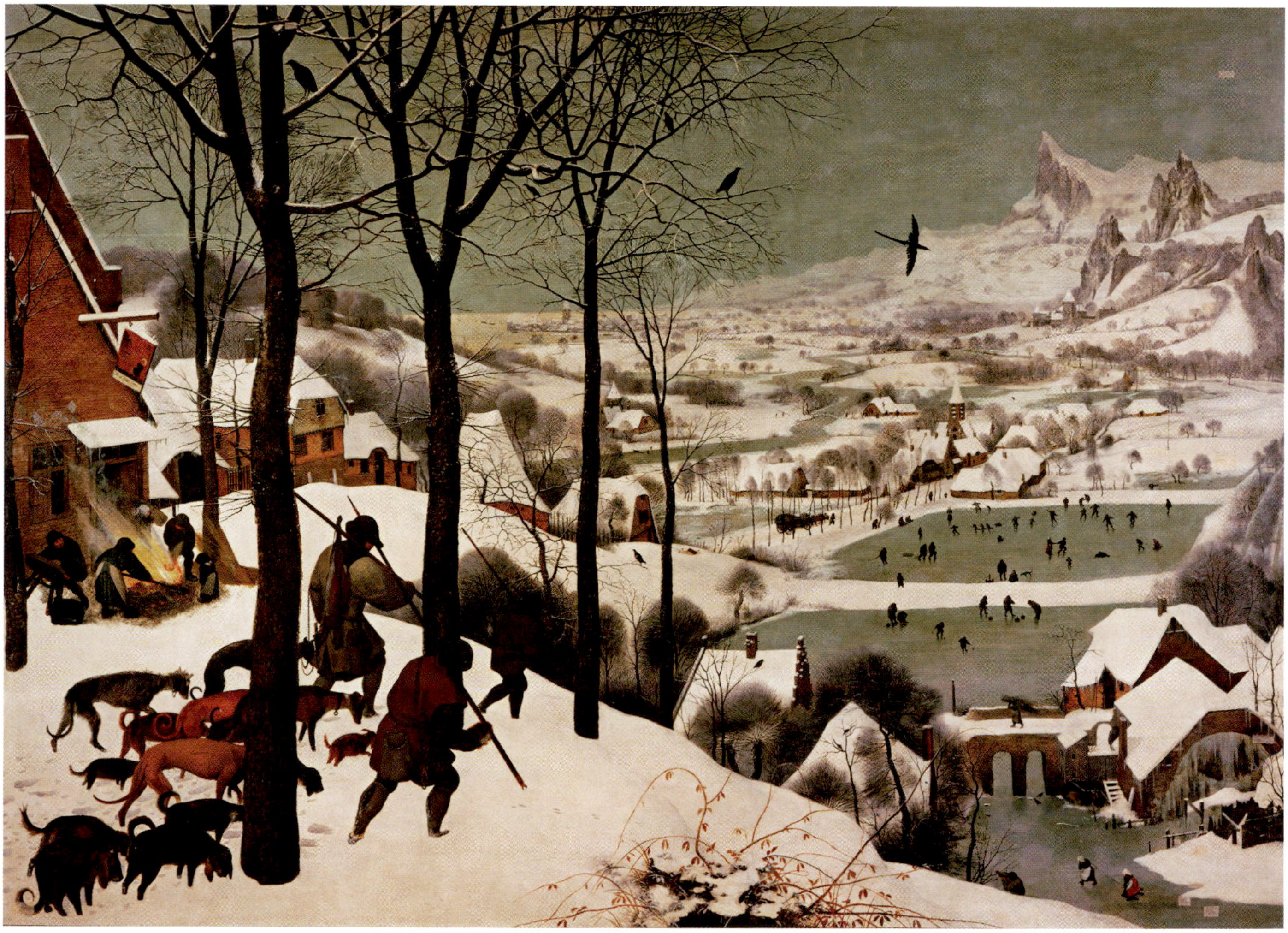

13–36 • Pieter Bruegel the Elder **RETURN OF THE HUNTERS**
1565. Oil on wood panel, 3′ 10½″ × 5′ 3¾″ (1.18 × 1.61 m). Kunsthistorisches Museum, Vienna.

View the Closer Look for Bruegel's *Return of the Hunters* on **MyArtsLab**

winter with a freshness that recalls the much earlier paintings of his compatriots the Limbourgs (SEE FIG. 12–2). The hunters are foregrounded on the verge of a sharp plunge into space, slogging stoically by, trailed by their dogs, while workers at an inn singe a pig in a fire. A row of trees forms a receding set, consistently diminishing in scale, to draw us back into the picture's distant panorama. The stark contrast of light and dark highlights the playful movement of ice skaters on frozen fields under the snow-covered fantasy of an alpine background.

With religious art declining in the face of Protestant disapproval, portraits became a major source of work for artists. Antwerp painter Caterina van Hemessen (1528–1587), who learned to paint from her father, developed an international reputation as a portraitist. To maintain interest on her foreground subjects, she painted them against even, dark-colored backgrounds, on which she identified the sitter by name and age, signing and dating each work. The inscription on her **SELF-PORTRAIT (FIG. 13–37)** reads: "I Caterina van Hemessen painted myself in 1548. Her age 20." In delineating her own features, van Hemessen presented a serious young person

who looks up to acknowledge us, interrupting her work on a portrait of a woman client. Between 1548 and 1552, she painted ten signed and dated portraits of women, seemingly her specialty. She became a favored court artist to Mary of Hungary, sister of Emperor Charles V and regent of the Netherlands, for whom she painted not only portraits but religious works, and whom she followed back to Spain when Mary ceased to be regent in 1556.

Philip II of Spain (ruled 1556–1598) was a great patron of Titian and collected the work of Bosch, but he did not like the works of the man who in the twentieth century became one of Spain's most famous painters: Kyriakos (Domenikos) Theotokopoulos (1541–1614), who arrived in Spain in 1577 after working for ten years in Italy. El Greco ("the Greek"), as he was called, began his career as a Byzantine icon painter in his native Crete. He entered Titian's studio in Venice around 1566, but about 1570 he moved to Rome. His mature style combined the intense emotionalism of late Byzantine art (SEE FIGS. 7–24, 7–25) with rich color and loose brushwork reminiscent of Tintoretto. This distinctive pictorial vision equipped him well

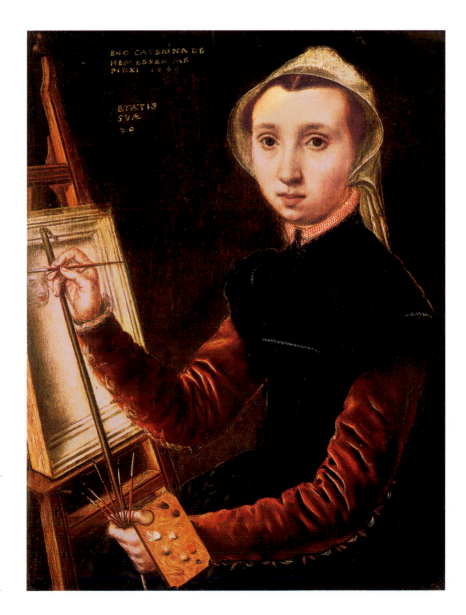

13–37 • Caterina van Hemessen SELF-PORTRAIT AT THE EASEL
1548. Oil on panel, 12¼″ × 9¼″ (31.1 × 23.5 cm). Öffentliche Kunstsammlung, Basel, Switzerland. Permanent loan from the Prof. J.J. Bachofen-Burckhardt Foundation, 1921 (1361).

This self-portrait of the artist at work provides a glimpse into an artist's studio and working methods. The panel on the easel already has its frame, against which the painter leans her mahlstick—an essential painter's tool used to steady the hand while doing fine, detailed work.

to express in paint the intense spirituality of a fervent religious revival in late sixteenth-century Spain.

In 1586, the artist was commissioned by the Orgaz family to honor an illustrious ancestor who had been a great benefactor of the Church. At his funeral in 1323, SS. Augustine and Stephen were said to have appeared to lower this Count Orgaz's body into his tomb, while his soul was seen ascending to heaven. In El Greco's **BURIAL OF COUNT ORGAZ** (FIG. 13–38), an angel in the center lifts Orgaz's tiny ghostly soul along the central axis toward the enthroned Christ at the apex of the canvas, while the miraculous burial takes place below. Portraits of local aristocrats and religious notables fill the background. Following Italian Mannerist practice, there is no reference to a specific setting (SEE FIG. 13–24). El Greco placed his own 8-year-old son at the lower left next to St. Stephen and signed the painting on the boy's white kerchief. He may have put his own features on the man above Saint Stephen's head, who, like the child, looks straight out at the viewer.

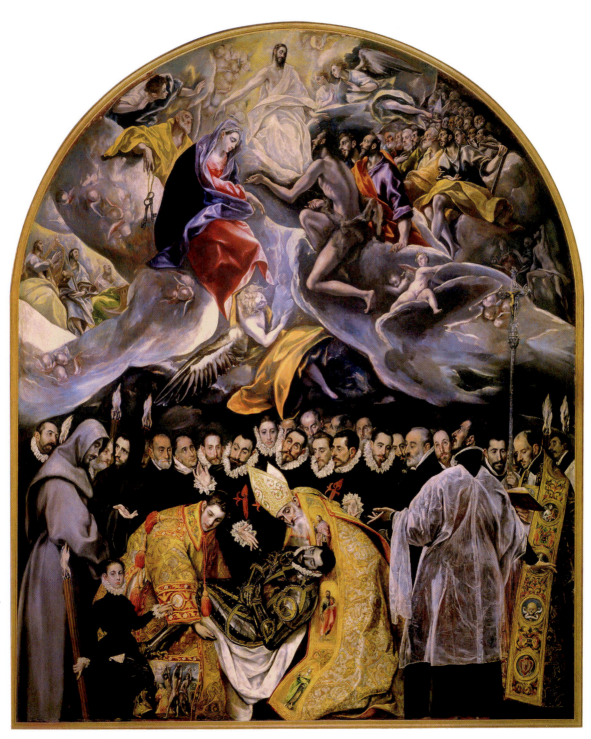

13-38 • El Greco BURIAL OF COUNT ORGAZ
Church of Santo Tomé, Toledo, Spain. 1586. Oil on canvas, 16′ × 11′ 10″ (4.88 × 3.61 m).

LOOKING BACK ◄

In the fifteenth and sixteenth centuries in Europe, artists and scholars began to explore the natural world with the kind of intensity that their medieval predecessors had devoted to heaven and hell. They continued theological debates, but they also studied human and animal anatomy, botany and geology, astronomy and mathematics. Italian artists followed a conceptual and imaginative bent, while Flemish and French artists followed a more perceptual approach in describing the appearance of their world. Painting, sculpture, and architecture began to be seen as liberal—rather than manual—arts since they required a liberal education as well as technical training.

The Protestants carried on the tradition of using the visual arts to promote a cause, to profess beliefs, and to glorify—just as the Catholic Church had over the centuries used great church buildings and religious art for their theological as well as aesthetic value. The effects of the Reformation and the Counter-Reformation would continue to reverberate in the arts of the following century throughout Europe and, across the Atlantic, in America.

THINK ABOUT IT

13.1 Discuss Julius II's efforts to use art and architecture to create a new golden age of the papacy. Your answer should focus on two specific works he commissioned.

13.2 Select either Pontormo's *Deposition* or Bronzino's *Allegory* and explain the ways in which the painting is characteristic of Mannerist art and its anti-Classical objectives.

13.3 Explore the impact of Italian art and ideas on the work and self-image of German artist Albrecht Dürer. Focus your answer on one specific work, discussing its Italianate features but also the ways it maintains key aspects of the Northern tradition.

13.4 Distinguish between two of the various styles produced in sixteenth-century art of the Habsburg Empire by comparing specific works by two of the following artists: Bosch, Bruegel, or El Greco.

| CROSSCURRENTS |

FIG. INTRO–13

FIG. 13–31

Throughout the history of European art, many artists have painted portraits of themselves that captured their self-image and how it relates to their role as artists within the culture in which they lived. Assess the way these two artists present themselves and their craft in these two self-portraits.

1500

IN PERSPECTIVE

• Pope Julius II papacy 1503–1513

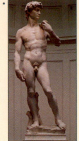
MICHELANGELO,
David
1501–1504

• Henry VIII, King of England
  ruled 1509–1547

• Francis I, King of France
  ruled 1515–1547
• Luther Officially Protests Church's
  Sale of Indulgences 1517
• Death of Leonardo at the Court of
  French King Francis I 1519
• Charles V, Holy Roman Emperor
  ruled 1519–1556

1520
• Death of Raphael 1520
• First Circumnavigation of
  Earth 1522
• Peasants' War 1524–1526

• Charles V Orders Sack
  of Rome 1527

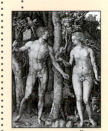
DÜRER,
Adam and Eve
1504

1540
• Jesuit Order Confirmed 1540

• Pope Paul III Institutes
  Inquisition 1542

• Council of Trent 1545–1563

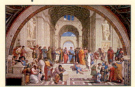
RAPHAEL,
School of Athens
1510–1511

• Vasari's *Lives* Published 1550

• Philip II, King of Spain ruled 1556–1598

• Elizabeth I, Queen of England
  ruled 1558–1603

1560

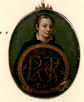
ANGUISSOLA,
Self-Portrait
c. 1556

• Death of Michelangelo 1564

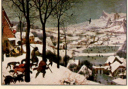
BRUEGEL,
Return of the Hunters
1565

• Veronese Appears before
  the Inquisition 1573

1580

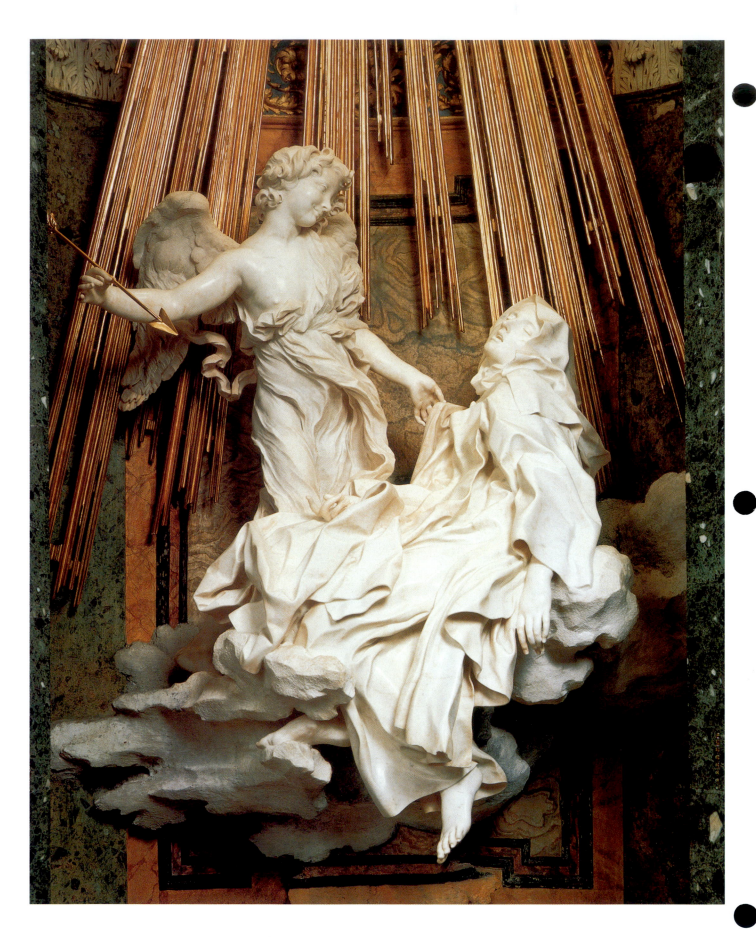

14–1 • Gianlorenzo Bernini ST. TERESA OF ÁVILA IN ECSTASY
Cornaro Chapel, church of Sta. Maria della Vittoria, Rome. 1645–1652. Marble, height of the group 11′ 6″ (3.5 m).

SEVENTEENTH-CENTURY ART IN EUROPE

14.1 Explain the establishment of the Baroque style in Rome.

14.2 Characterize the "Golden Age" of painting in Spain.

14.3 Recognize new developments in Flemish art that took place in the workshop of Peter Paul Rubens.

14.4 Discuss the distinctive styles and subjects preferred in the Protestant Netherlands.

14.5 Differentiate the royal and Neoclassical art of France from developments elsewhere in Europe.

LOOKING FORWARD ▶

In the church of Sta. Maria della Vittoria in Rome, the sixteenth-century Spanish mystic St. Teresa of Ávila (1515–1582, canonized 1622) swoons in ecstasy on a bank of billowing marble clouds (FIG. 14–1). A puckish angel tugs open her robe, aiming a gilded arrow at her body. Gilded bronze rays of supernatural light descend, even as actual light illuminates the figures from a hidden window above. This dramatic scene, created by Gianlorenzo Bernini (1598–1680) between 1645 and 1652, represents a famous vision described with startling, physical clarity by Teresa, in which an angel pierced her repeatedly with an arrow, transporting her to a state of ecstatic oneness with God, charged with erotic associations.

The sculpture is an exquisite example of the emotional, theatrical style perfected by Bernini in response to the religious and political climate in Rome during the period of spiritual renewal known as the Counter-Reformation. Many had seen the Protestant Reformation of the previous century as an outgrowth of Renaissance Humanism with its emphasis on rationality and independent thinking. In response, the Catholic Church took a reactionary, authoritarian position, supported by the new Society of Jesus founded by Ignatius Loyola (1491–1556, canonized 1622). In the "spiritual exercises" (1522–1523)

initiated by St. Ignatius, Christians were enjoined to use all their senses to transport themselves emotionally as they imagined the events on which they were meditating. They were to feel the burning fires of hell or the bliss of heaven, the lashing of the whips, and the flesh-piercing crown of thorns. Art became an instrument of propaganda and also a means of leading the spectator to a reinvigorated Christian practice and belief.

Of course, the arts had long been used to convince or inspire, but nowhere more effectively than by the Catholic Church in the seventeenth century. To serve the educational and evangelical mission of the revitalized and conservative Church, paintings and sculpture had to depict events and people accurately and clearly, following guidelines established by religious leaders. Throughout Catholic Europe, painters such as Peter Paul Rubens and Michelangelo Merisi da Caravaggio created brilliant religious art under official Church sponsorship. And although today some viewers find this sculpture of St. Teresa uncomfortably charged with sexuality, the Church approved of the depictions of such sensational and supernatural mystical visions. They helped worshipers achieve the emotional state of religious ecstasy that was the goal of the Counter-Reformation.

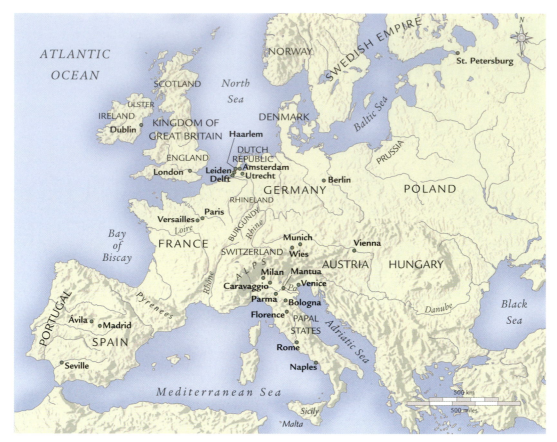

MAP 14–1 • SEVENTEENTH-CENTURY EUROPE

During the seventeenth century, Protestantism remained dominant primarily in the north (Great Britain, the Dutch Republic, and Germany), while in the south (France, Spain, and Italy), Catholicism was strengthened by the Counter-Reformation.

The intellectual and political forces set in motion by the Renaissance and Reformation of the fifteenth and sixteenth centuries intensified in the seventeenth century. Religious wars continued, although gradually the Protestant forces gained control in the north, where Spain recognized the independence of the Dutch Republic in 1648. In Rome an energized papacy, aided by the new Jesuit Order, maintained the primacy of Catholicism in southern Europe, the Holy Roman Empire, and France (MAP 14–1). As rulers' economic strength began to slip away, artists found patrons in the Church and the secular state, as well as in the newly confident and prosperous urban middle class. What evolved was a style that art historians have called "the Baroque." The label may be related to the Italian word *barocco*, a jeweler's term for an irregularly shaped pearl—something beautiful, fascinating, and strange.

Baroque art deliberately evokes intense emotional responses from viewers. Dramatically lit, theatrical compositions often combine several media within a single work as artists foreground their technical virtuosity. But the seventeenth century also saw its own version of Classicism, a more moving and dramatic variant of Renaissance ideals and principles featuring idealization based on observation of the material world; balanced (though often asymmetrical) compositions; diagonal movement in space; rich, harmonious colors; and

the inclusion of visual references to ancient Greece and Rome. Many seventeenth-century artists sought lifelike depiction of their world in portraiture, **genre paintings** (scenes from everyday life), **still lifes** (paintings of inanimate objects such as food, fruit, or flowers), and religious scenes enacted by ordinary people in ordinary settings. Intense emotional involvement, lifelike renderings, and Classical references may exist in the same work, and are all part of the stylistic complexion of seventeenth-century Europe.

Rome

How was the Baroque style established in Rome?

The patronage of the Church and aristocratic Roman families allied with the papacy—such as the Borghese, the Barberini, and the Farnese—dominated Italian art from the late sixteenth to the late seventeenth century. Following the directives of the Counter-Reformation, splendid religious architecture was embellished with painting and sculpture aimed at helping convince the faithful of the power of traditional religion. In Rome, the Borghese Pope Paul V (pontificate 1605–1621) ordered the expansion and modernization of the new St. Peter's Basilica. In 1606, he commissioned the architect Carlo Maderno (1556–1629) to add a longitudinal nave and a new façade to

Michelangelo's central-plan building, only a half century old (see "St. Peter's Basilica," p. 340).

When Maffeo Barberini was elected pope as Urban VIII (pontificate 1623–1644), he gave the young Bernini the daunting task of designing an enormous bronze **baldachin**, or canopy, over the main altar of St. Peter's. The **BALDACCHINO** (**FIG. 14–2**), completed in 1633, stands about 100 feet high and exemplifies the Baroque taste for dramatic, multimedia extravaganzas. The twisting form of the gigantic bronze columns at the corners copies columns from the altar shrine of Old St. Peter's that were believed to come from Solomon's Temple in Jerusalem. The winding grapevines that encircle them are an ancient symbol of the wine of the Eucharist. Bernini's columns thus combine symbolism from Judaism and Christianity, conforming to the view of Christian scholars that Solomon's Temple supports the Christian Church just as the Hebrew Bible is the foundation of the New Testament. Crowning the structure is an orb and a cross representing universal dominion of Christ. The

angels and *putti*, as well as the tasseled panels imitating textiles on the entablature, are all cast in bronze. The *Baldacchino* marks the high altar and the sacred site of the tomb of St. Peter, but it also celebrates Urban VIII and his family, the Barberini, whose emblems—honeybees, suns, and laurel leaves—are prominently displayed.

Visible through the *Baldacchino*'s columns is a huge bronze reliquary containing an ancient wooden throne thought to have belonged to St. Peter as the first bishop of Rome. The Chair of St. Peter symbolizes the direct descent of Christian authority from this apostle to the reigning pope, a belief rejected by Protestants and therefore deliberately emphasized in Counter-Reformation Catholicism. The chair is lifted upward by four theologians amid a surge of gilded clouds toward an explosion of angels, *putti*, and gilded rays of glory, surrounding a stained-glass window depicting the dove of the Holy Spirit. The actual sunlight and the flickering candles, reflected and multiplied by the gilded bronze, are meant to be part of the dazzling effect.

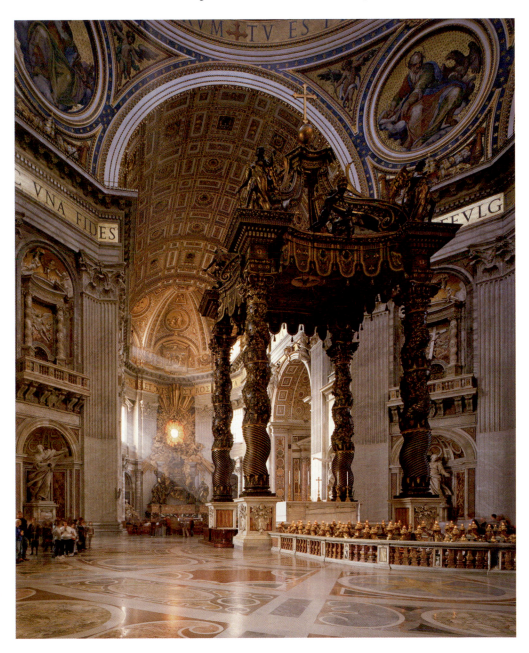

14–2 • Gianlorenzo Bernini
BALDACCHINO
In the crossing of St. Peter's Basilica, Vatican, Rome. 1624–1633. Gilt bronze, height 100′ (30.48 m). Chair of St. Peter (visible at the back) 1657–1666, gilt bronze, marble, stucco, and glass. Pier decorations 1627–1641, gilt bronze and marble.

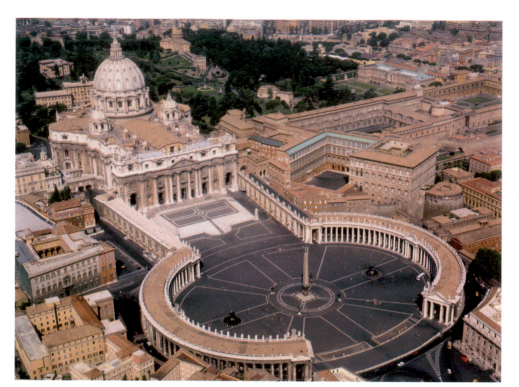

14–3 • Gianlorenzo Bernini
**ST. PETER'S BASILICA
AND SQUARE**
Vatican, Rome. Carlo Maderno, façade
1607–1615; Bernini, piazza designed
c. 1656–1657.

Perhaps only a Baroque artist of
Bernini's talents could have unified
the many styles that come together in
St. Peter's. The visitor today does not
see a piecing together of parts made
by different builders at different times,
starting with Bramante's original design
for the building in the sixteenth century,
but rather a triumphal unity of all the
parts in one coherent whole.

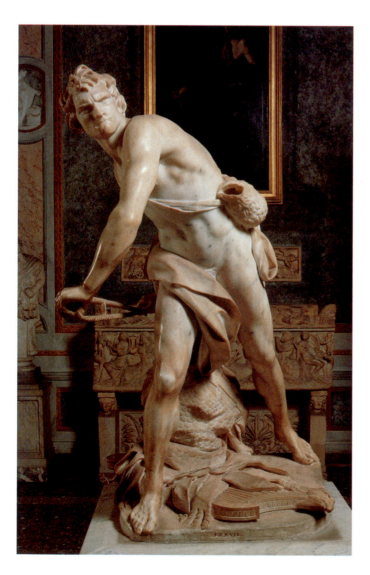

While he was working on the Chair of St. Peter, Bernini also designed and supervised the building of a colonnade to enclose a huge double piazza in front of the church (FIG. 14–3). The space at Bernini's disposal was irregular and already contained an Egyptian **obelisk** (moved there in 1586) and a fountain (to the right, made by Maderno in 1613), which had to be incorporated into the overall plan. In a remarkable design, Bernini framed the oval open space with two enormous, curved covered walkways using giant Tuscan columns. These connect with two straight but diverging porticoes that lead up a slight incline to the two ends of Maderno's church façade.

Bernini characterized his design as the "motherly arms of the church" reaching out to the world. He intended to build a third section of the colonnade closing the open side so that only after pilgrims had crossed the Tiber River bridge and made their way through narrow streets would they encounter the enormous open space before the imposing church. This element of surprise would have made the basilica and its setting an even more awe-inspiring sight. The approach today—along the grand avenue of the Via della Conciliazione running from the Tiber to the basilica—was conceived by Benito Mussolini in 1936 as part of his master plan to transform Rome into a grand fascist capital.

Bernini began his career as a sculptor, not as an architect, and he continued to sculpt throughout his career, both for the papacy and for private clients. His **DAVID** (FIG. 14–4), made for the nephew of Pope Paul V in 1623, introduced a new type of three-dimensional composition that intrudes forcefully into

14–4 • Gianlorenzo Bernini DAVID
1623. Marble, height 5' 7" (1.7 m). Galleria Borghese, Rome.

14–5 • Gianlorenzo Bernini
CORNARO CHAPEL
Church of Sta. Maria della Vittoria, Rome.
1642–1652.

👁 **Watch** an architectural
simulation about the Cornaro
Chapel on **MyArtsLab**

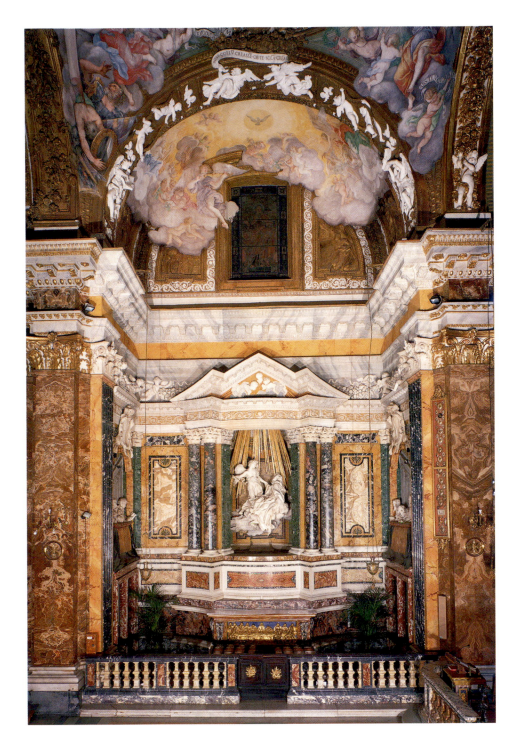

the viewer's space. The hero bends at the waist and twists far to one side, ready to launch the fatal rock at Goliath. Unlike Donatello's already victorious, introspective boy (SEE FIG. 12–18), or Michelangelo's pensive young man, contemplating the task ahead (SEE FIG. 13–9), Bernini's more mature David, with his lean, sinewy body, clenched mouth, and straining muscles, is all tension, action, and determination. By creating a twisting figure caught in movement, Bernini incorporates the surrounding space within his composition, implying the presence of the unseen adversary somewhere behind the viewer, who stands in the midst of the action, rather than to the side as a dispassionate observer.

Even after Bernini's appointment as Vatican architect in 1629, his large workshop enabled him to accept outside commissions. From 1642 until 1652, Bernini worked on the decoration of the funerary chapel of Cardinal Federigo Cornaro (FIG. 14–5) in the Roman church of Sta. Maria della Vittoria, designed by Maderno earlier in the century. Bernini covered the walls of the tall, shallow chapel with colored marble panels and created a sculptural tableau of *St. Teresa of Ávila in Ecstasy* (SEE FIG. 14–1) above the altar. On the chapel's high back wall, the curved ceiling surrounding the window appears to dissolve into a painted vision of clouds and angels, and on the side walls, kneeling against what appear to be balconies,

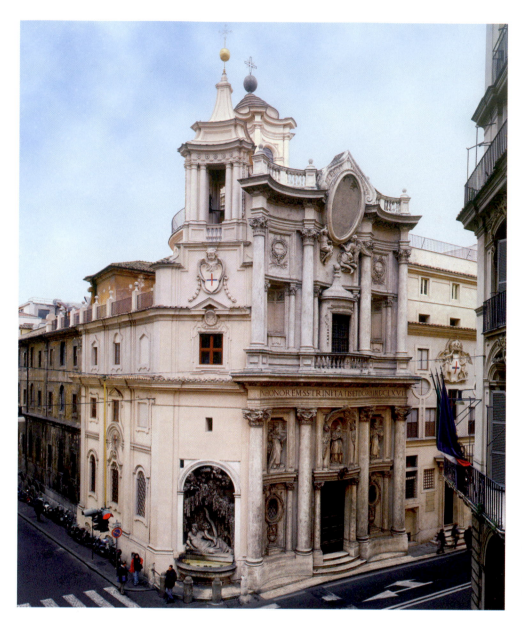

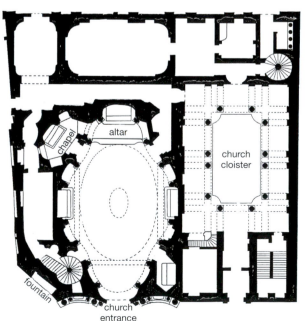

14–6 • Francesco Borromini
EXTERIOR VIEW AND PLAN OF THE CHURCH OF SAN CARLO ALLE QUATTRO FONTANE
Rome. 1638–1667.

are portrait statues of members of the Cornaro family. Two are reading from their prayer books; others converse; and one leans out from his seat, apparently to look at someone entering the chapel. Bernini's complex, theatrical interplay of audience and spectacle, set within several levels of illusion, was imitated by sculptors throughout Europe.

Francesco Borromini (1599–1667), a nephew of Carlo Maderno, began his career in his uncle's workshop and later worked with Bernini at St. Peter's, but he soon emerged as one of the preeminent Baroque architects in Rome. His first independent commission was the **CHURCH OF SAN CARLO ALLE QUATTRO FONTANE** (St. Charles at the Four Fountains), designed on an irregular plot of land at the intersection of two wide avenues with fountains marking the corners of the crossing (**FIG. 14–6**). Undulating walls define the elongated interior space, above which floats an oval dome, supported on pendentives (**FIG. 14–7**). Recessed coffers form an eccentric honeycomb of crosses, elongated hexagons and octagons that decrease sharply in size as they approach the lantern, which

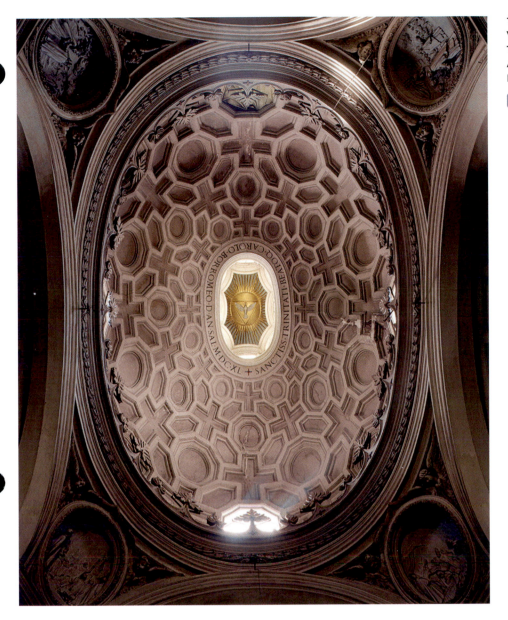

14-7 • Francesco Borromini
**VIEW INTO THE DOME OF
THE CHURCH OF SAN CARLO
ALLE QUATTRO FONTANE**
Rome. 1638–1667.

✷ **Explore** the architectural
panoramas of the church of
San Carlo alle Quattro Fontane
on **MyArtsLab**

frames a hovering rendering of the dove of the Holy Spirit. The dome appears to be shimmering and inflating—almost floating up and away—thanks to the light sources in the lower coffers and lantern.

It is difficult today to appreciate how audacious Borromini's design for this small church was. In it he abandoned the modular, additive system of planning taken for granted by every architect since Brunelleschi. He worked instead from an overriding geometrical scheme, as a Gothic architect might, subdividing modular units to obtain more complex, rational shapes. For example, the elongated, octagonal plan of San Carlo is composed of two triangles set base to base along the short axis of the plan (SEE FIG. 14–6). This diamond shape is then subdivided into secondary triangular units made by calculating the distances between what will become the concave centers of the four major and five minor niches. Yet Borromini's conception of the whole is not medieval. The chapel is dominated horizontally by a Classical entablature that breaks any surge upward toward the dome. Borromini's treatment of the architectural elements as if they were malleable was also unprecedented. His contemporaries understood immediately what an extraordinary innovation the church represented; the Trinitarian monks who had commissioned it received requests for plans from visitors from all over Europe. Although Borromini's innovative work had little impact on the architecture of Classically minded Rome, it was widely imitated in northern Italy and beyond the Alps.

Borromini designed the building's façade as an undulating, sculpture-filled screen punctuated with large columns and deep concave and convex niches that create dramatic effects of light and shadow. He gave a strong vertical thrust to the center by placing over the tall doorway a statue-filled niche, then a windowed niche covered with a canopy, then a giant, forward-leaning **cartouche** held up by angels carved in such high relief that they appear to hover in front of the wall. The entire composition is crowned with a balustrade broken by the sharply pointed frame of the cartouche. As with the design of the interior, Borromini's façade was enthusiastically imitated.

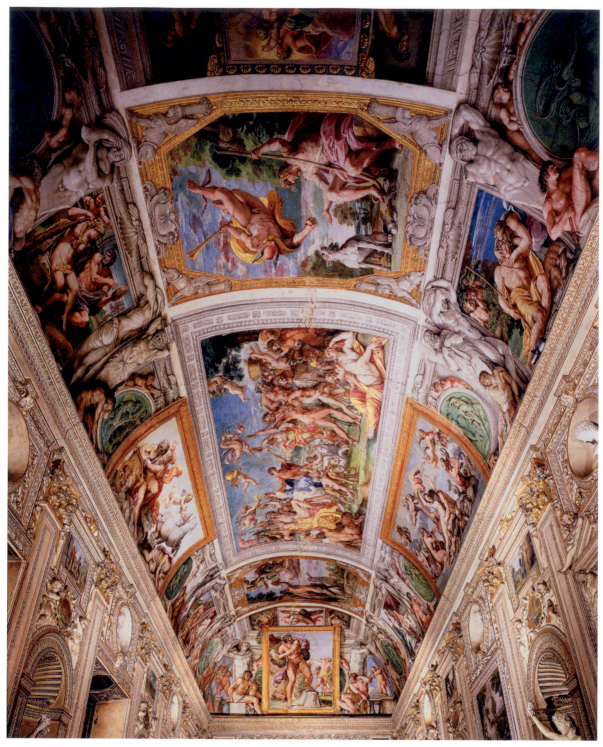

14–8 • Annibale Carracci CEILING OF GALLERY, PALAZZO FARNESE
Rome. 1597–1601. Fresco, approx. 68′ × 21′ (20.7 × 6.4 m).

Roman Baroque illusionism reached its peak in ceiling decorations for churches, civic buildings, palaces, and villas. Many were covered entirely by *trompe l'oeil* painting, but some were complex constructions combining architecture, painting, and stucco sculpture. A ceiling painted by Annibale Carracci (1560–1609) in the Roman palace of the powerful Farnese family is considered the major monument of early Baroque Classicism. Commissioned to celebrate the wedding of Duke Ranuccio Farnese of Parma to the pope's niece, it presents an exuberant mythological tribute to earthly love **(FIG. 14–8)**. Annibale, co-founder with his family of an art **academy** in Bologna, was assisted by his brother Agostino (1557–1602) on this spectacular project, painted at the turn of the century (1597–1601). The ceiling painting creates the illusion of framed

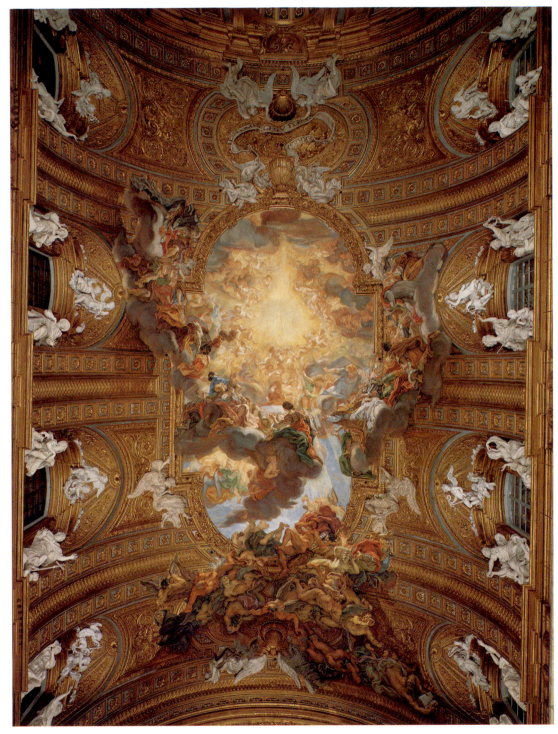

14–9 • Giovanni Battista Gaulli
THE TRIUMPH OF THE NAME OF JESUS AND THE FALL OF THE DAMNED
Vault of the church of Il Gesù, Rome. 1672–1685. Fresco with stucco figures.

paintings, stone sculpture, bronze medallions, and nude youths in an architectural framework, and was clearly inspired by Michelangelo's Sistine Chapel ceiling (SEE FIGS. 13–10, 13–11). But instead of Michelangelo's cool illumination and intellectual detachment, the Farnese ceiling glows with a warm light that recalls the work of the Venetian painters Titian and Veronese. The ceiling became famous almost immediately, and since the

Farnese family, proud of the gallery, generously allowed young artists to sketch there, Annibale's great work influenced Italian art well into the seventeenth century.

Closer in spirit and style to Bernini's art is **THE TRIUMPH OF THE NAME OF JESUS** (FIG. 14–9), which fills the nave vault of the church of Il Gesù, mother church of the Society of Jesus (the Jesuits), in Rome. The vault was originally unpainted,

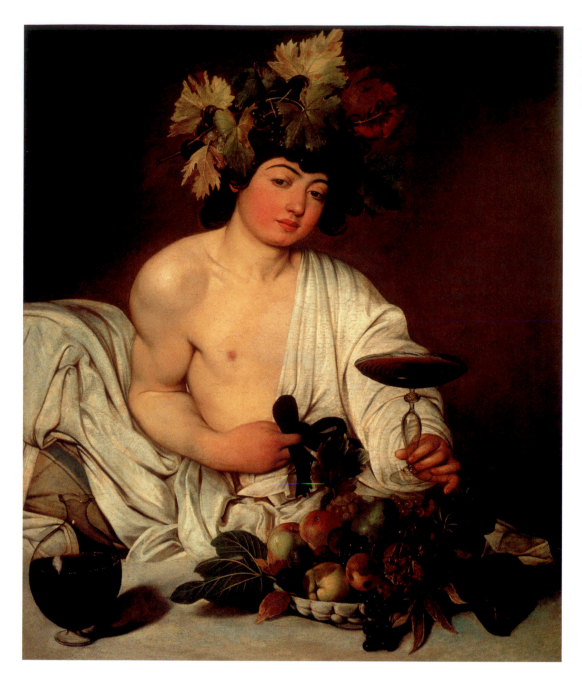

14–10 • Caravaggio
BACCHUS
1595–1596. Oil on canvas,
37″ × 33½″ (94 × 85 cm).
Galleria degli Uffizi,
Florence.

but Giovanni Battista Gaulli (1639–1709) created the ceiling we see today between 1672 and 1685. He had worked during his youth for Bernini, from whom he absorbed a Baroque taste for drama and multimedia spectacle. But this astonishing creation went beyond anything that had preceded it. Architecture, sculpture, and painting combine to produce the illusion that clouds and angels have floated down through an opening at the top of the church. The focus, off-center, is the brilliant golden aura surrounding the letters IHS (barely visible in FIG. 14–9), the monogram of Jesus and the insignia of the Jesuits. The subject is the Last Judgment, with the elect rising toward the sacred name and the damned plummeting through the ceiling toward the nave floor. The sweeping extension of the work into the nave space, the powerful appeal to the viewers' emotions, and the near-total unity of the multimedia visual effect—all hallmarks of Italian Baroque—were never surpassed.

But not all Roman Baroque art was meant to overwhelm the viewer by sheer spectacle. Michelangelo Merisi (1571–1610), known as Caravaggio after his birthplace in northern Italy, introduced a powerfully frank realism and dramatic, theatrical lighting and gesture to Italian Baroque art. After his arrival in Rome in 1592, Caravaggio at first painted for a small sophisticated circle associated with the household of art patron Cardinal del Monte, where the artist was invited to reside. His subjects from the 1590s include still lifes and scenes featuring fortune-tellers, cardsharps, and glamorous young men dressed as musicians or mythological figures. The **BACCHUS** of 1595–1596 (**FIG. 14–10**) is among the most polished of these early works. Caravaggio seems to have painted exactly what he saw, reproducing the "farmers' tan" of those parts of this partially dressed youth—hands and face—that have been exposed to the sun, as well as the dirt under his fingernails. The figure himself is strikingly androgynous. Made up with painted lips and smoothly arching eyebrows, he seems to offer the viewer the gorgeous glass goblet of wine held delicately in his left hand, while fingering the black bow that holds his loose clothing together at the waist. Is this a provocative invitation to an erotic encounter or a young actor outfitted for the role of Bacchus, god of wine? Does the juxtaposition of the youth's invitation with a still life of rotting fruit transform this into an image about the transitory nature of sensual pleasure, either admonishing viewers to avoid sins of the flesh or encouraging them to enjoy life's pleasures while they can? The ambiguity seems to make the painting even more provocative.

Most of Caravaggio's commissions after 1600 were for religious art, and reactions to these paintings were mixed. On occasion, patrons rejected his powerful, sometimes brutal, naturalism as unsuitable to the elevated subject matter. However, this very realism recalls Counter-Reformation ideas of spirituality, as put forward in the meditations, or *Spiritual Exercises*, of St. Ignatius Loyola, the founder of the Jesuit Order. It was also connected to the populist theology of the preacher Filippo de' Neri (1515–1595, canonized 1622), who consciously strove to make Christian history and doctrine understandable and meaningful to common people.

One of Caravaggio's earliest religious commissions was the 1599–1600 decorative program of the private chapel of the Cointrel family (Contarelli in Italian) in the French community's church in Rome (FIG. 14–11). Unlike in the Renaissance, when frescos were applied directly to the walls, Caravaggio produced three huge oil paintings on canvas in his studio, only later installing them within the chapel as a coordinated ensemble: two scenes from the life of St. Matthew on the side walls, and the saint's portrait as Gospel writer over the altar.

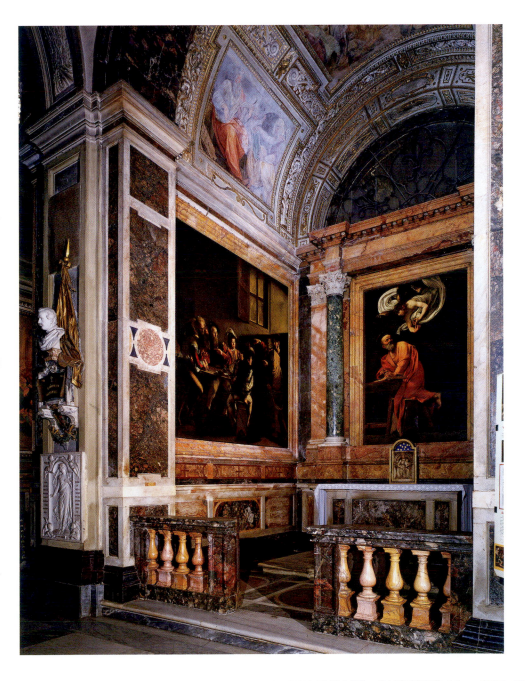

14–11 • CONTARELLI CHAPEL
Church of San Luigi dei Francesi, Rome.

Whereas Caravaggio was commissioned in 1599 for the paintings on the side walls of this chapel—*The Calling of St. Matthew* (visible at left) and across from it *The Martyrdom of St. Matthew* (not visible here)—it was only in 1602 that he was contracted to paint the portrait of Matthew writing his Gospel to hang over the altar. He delivered the painting in that same year, but it was rejected because the saint looked too crude and common to satisfy clerical taste, and the fleshiness of the angel, who sidles up to Matthew with striking coziness, was considered inappropriately risqué. Caravaggio painted a second, more decorous version, seen here, with a nobler Matthew and more distant angel, and the rejected version was snapped up by the Roman collector Vincenzo Giustiniani, who actually paid for the replacement in order to acquire the more sensational original. Unfortunately, this first painting was destroyed in the Allied bombing of Berlin during World War II.

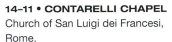

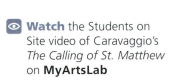 **Watch** the Students on Site video of Caravaggio's *The Calling of St. Matthew* on **MyArtsLab**

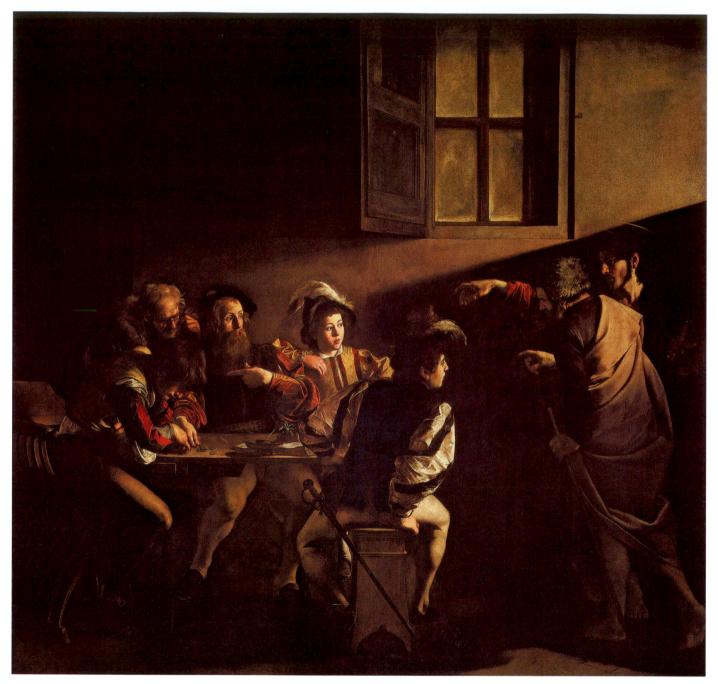

14–12 • Caravaggio THE CALLING OF ST. MATTHEW
Contarelli Chapel, church of San Luigi dei Francesi, Rome. 1599–1600. Oil on canvas,
10′ 7½″ × 11′ 2″ (3.24 × 3.4 m).

🔍 **View** the Closer Look for Caravaggio's *The Calling of St. Matthew* on **MyArtsLab**

THE CALLING OF ST. MATTHEW (FIG. 14–12) depicts the moment when Jesus chooses the tax collector Levi to become one of his apostles (Mark 2:14, Matthew 9:9). Levi—who will become St. Matthew—sits at a table counting or collecting money, surrounded by elegant young men in plumed hats, velvet doublets, and satin shirts. Nearly hidden behind the back of the beckoning St. Peter, the gaunt-faced Jesus points dramatically at Levi with a gesture that is repeated in the tax collector's own surprised response, pointing to himself as if to say, "Who? Me?" An intense raking light enters the painting from upper right, as if it were coming from the chapel's actual window above the altar to spotlight the important features of this darkened scene. Viewers, encountering the painting obliquely across the empty space of the chapel interior, seem to be

14–13 • Artemisia Gentileschi
JUDITH AND HER MAIDSERVANT WITH THE HEAD OF HOLOFERNES
c. 1625. Oil on canvas, 72½″ × 55¾″ (184.2 × 141.6 cm). The Detroit Institute of Arts, Detroit, Michigan. Gift of Leslie H. Green.

The beautiful Jewish widow Judith saved her people from the Assyrian army by entering the enemy camp and enticing the general Holofernes to eat and drink until he fell into a stupor. Then she cut off his head and escaped, carrying the trophy as evidence of her heroic act.

Read the document related to Artemisia Gentileschi on **MyArtsLab**

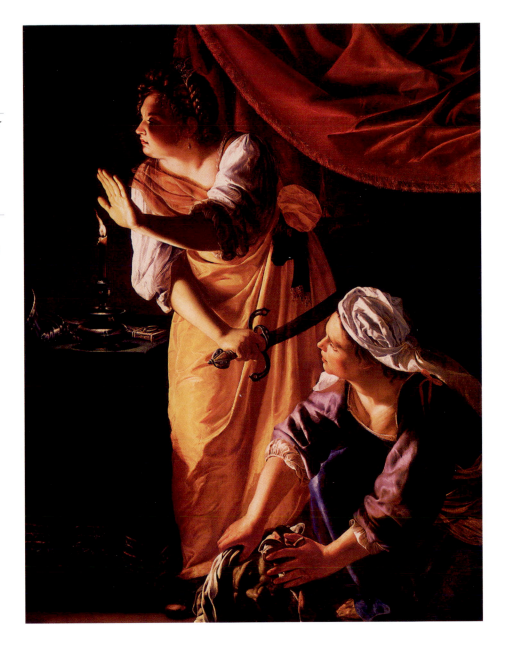

witnessing the scene as it is occurring, elevated on a recessed stage opening through the wall before them.

Despite the esteem in which Caravaggio was held as an artist, his violent temper repeatedly got him into trouble. During the last decade of his life, he was frequently arrested, initially for minor offenses—throwing a plate of artichokes at a waiter, carrying arms illegally, or street brawling—but in May 1606 he killed a man in a duel fought over a disputed tennis match and had to flee from Rome as a fugitive under a death sentence. He supported himself on the run by painting in Naples, Malta, and Sicily, before dying on July 18, 1610, just short of his 39th birthday, of a fever contracted during a journey back to Rome where he expected to be pardoned for his capital offense.

Caravaggio's unvarnished realism and **tenebrism** (an exaggerated and theatrical type of *chiaroscuro* where selected forms emerge strongly highlighted from a pervasively dark background) inspired an entire generation of painters. One of his most gifted Italian followers was Artemisia Gentileschi

(1593–c. 1652), whose international reputation helped spread the Caravaggesque style beyond Rome. Artemisia first studied and worked under her father, an early follower of Caravaggio. In 1616, she moved to Florence, where she was elected at age 23 to the Florentine Academy of Design. In one of several versions of the Jewish heroine Judith's triumph over the Assyrian general Holofernes (**FIG. 14–13**), Artemisia uses Baroque naturalism and tenebrist effects, dramatically spotlighting Judith still holding the bloody sword and shielding the candle's light, as her maid stuffs the general's head into a sack. Throughout her life, Artemisia painted many such images of heroic biblical women, which art historians have interpreted in relation to Artemisia's own struggle to claim her rightful place within an art world dominated by overpowering men. She declares her professional accomplishment clearly and confidently in a self-portrait of 1630 (SEE FIG. INTRO–13), presenting herself in the guise of a personification of the art of painting itself.

Spain

What constitutes the "Golden Age" of painting in Spain?

With the growth of nation-states and absolute monarchies in seventeenth-century Europe, kings and nobles realized that impressive buildings and splendid portraits could secure and enhance their status by surrounding them with an aura of power. Spain's Habsburg kings Philip II, Philip III, Philip IV, and Charles II saw the political and economic decline of the Spanish part of their empire. What had seemed an endless flow of gold and silver from the Americas diminished, and Protestant England and the Dutch Republic were an increasingly serious threat to Spanish trade and colonial possessions. Agriculture, industry, and trade all suffered, and there were repeated local rebellions, culminating in 1640, when Portugal re-established its independence.

In spite of economic decline, during the seventeenth century Spanish artists and writers created a "Golden Age," which included one of the most brilliant painters of any age: Diego Rodriguez de Silva y Velázquez (1599–1660). Velázquez entered the painters' guild of Seville in 1617. Like many artists in Spain and Spanish-ruled Naples in the early seventeenth century, at the beginning of his career he was profoundly influenced by Caravaggio. He worked from life, painting tavern, market, and kitchen scenes of ordinary people amid still lifes of foods and kitchen utensils. The model for the **WATER CARRIER OF SEVILLE** (FIG. 14–14), painted about 1619, was a well-known character in that city. The objects and figures in the painting, arranged with mathematical rigor, allowed the artist to exhibit his virtuosity in rendering sculptural volumes and contrasting textures such as pottery, glass, and fabrics. Selected elements in the picture are illuminated by dramatic splashes of natural light—Velázquez's version of Caravaggio's tenebrism.

In 1623, Velázquez moved to Madrid, where he became a courtier and the official painter to the young Philip IV (ruled 1621–1665), a powerful position that he held until his death in 1660. Visits to Italy in 1629–1631 and again in 1649–1651, where Velázquez studied narrative paintings with complex figural compositions, influenced the evolution of his style.

Perhaps Velázquez's most striking, certainly his most enigmatic work is the enormous multiple portrait known as **LAS MENINAS**, or *The Maids of Honor*, painted in 1656, near the end

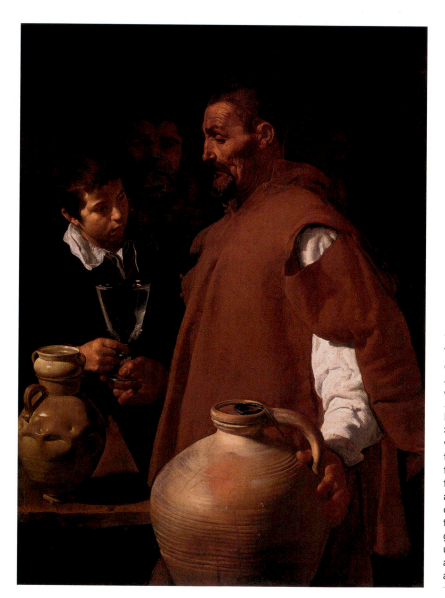

14–14 • Diego Velázquez
WATER CARRIER OF SEVILLE
c. 1619. Oil on canvas,
41½″ × 31½″ (105.3 × 80 cm).
Wellington Museum, London.

In the oppressively hot climate of Seville, Spain, where this painting was made, water vendors walked the streets selling their cool liquid from large clay jars like the one in the foreground. In this scene, the clarity and purity of the water are proudly demonstrated by its seller, who offers the customer a sample poured into a glass goblet. The jug's contents were usually sweetened by the addition of a piece of fresh fruit or a sprinkle of aromatic herbs.

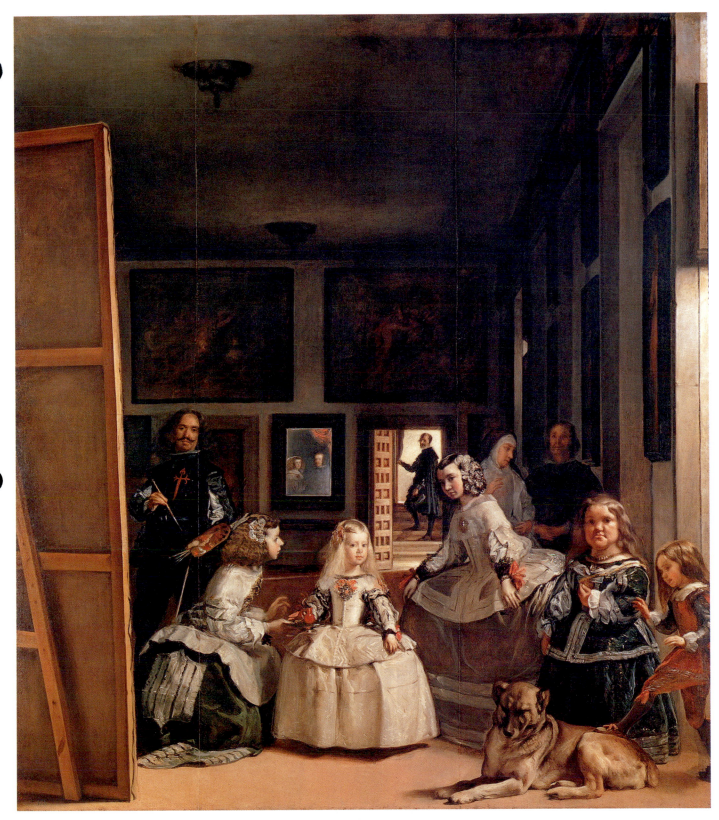

14–15 • Diego Velázquez LAS MENINAS (THE MAIDS OF HONOR)
1656. Oil on canvas, 10′ 5″ × 9′ ½″ (3.18 × 2.76 m). Museo del Prado, Madrid.

View the Closer Look for Velázquez's *Las Meninas* on **MyArtsLab**

of his life (**FIG. 14–15**). Velázquez draws viewers directly into the scene. In one interpretation, the viewer stands in the very space occupied by King Philip and his queen, whose reflections can be seen in the large mirror on the back wall, perhaps a clever reference to Jan van Eyck's Arnolfini double portrait (SEE FIG. 12–1), which was part of the Spanish royal collection at this time. Echoing pictorially the claim made in Jan's signature, Velázquez himself is also present, brushes and palette in hand, beside a huge canvas. However, the central focus of the painting is neither the artist nor the royal couple but their brilliantly illuminated 5-year-old daughter, the Infanta (princess) Margarita, who is surrounded by attendants, most of whom are identifiable portraits. In his characteristic bravura style of painting, Velázquez built up his forms with layers of loosely applied paint and finished off the surfaces with dashing highlights in white, lemon yellow, and pale orange. His technique captures the appearance of light reflecting from surfaces, while on close inspection his forms dissolve into a complex maze of individual strokes of paint.

No consensus exists today on the precise meaning of this monumental painting. It is a royal portrait; it is also a self-portrait of Velázquez standing at his easel. But fundamentally, *Las Meninas* is a personal artistic statement. Throughout his life, Velázquez had sought respect and acclaim for himself and for the art of painting. Here, dressed as a courtier, the Order of Santiago covering his chest (added later) and the keys of the palace tucked into his sash, Velázquez proclaims the dignity and importance of painting as one of the liberal arts.

Velázquez's contemporary, Francisco de Zurbarán (1598–1664), also emerged from the Caravaggesque school of painting in Seville. He painted, however, not for royalty, but mainly for the powerful monasteries of the Spanish church. In an arresting painting of 1628, he portrayed the martyred **ST. SERAPION** (**FIG. 14–16**), member of the thirteenth-century Mercedarians—a Spanish order founded to rescue Christian prisoners of the Moors—who sacrificed himself in exchange for the release of Christian captives. The dead man's pallor, his rough hands, and the coarse ropes contrast with the off-white of his creased monastic habit, its folds carefully arranged in a pattern of highlights and varying depths of shadow. The only colors are the red and gold of the insignia. This timelessly immobile composition

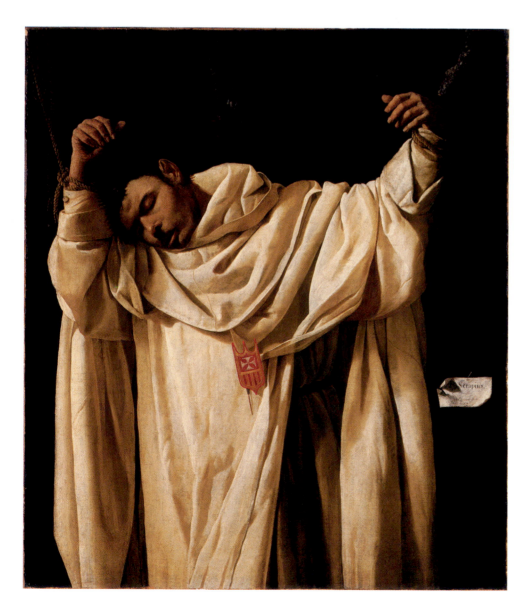

14–16 • Francisco de Zurbarán
ST. SERAPION
1628. Oil on canvas, 47½″ × 40¾″ (1.21 × 1.04 m). Wadsworth Atheneum, Hartford, Connecticut.

is like a tragic still life, a study of fabric and flesh become inanimate, silent, and at rest.

Seville declined after an outbreak of the plague in 1649, but it remained a center for trade with the Spanish colonies, where the work of Bartolomé Estebán Murillo (1617–1682) had a profound influence on art and religious iconography. Many patrons wanted images of the Virgin Mary and especially of the Immaculate Conception, and the Counter-Reformation had provided specific instructions for artists painting this theme: Mary was to be dressed in blue and white, her hands folded in prayer, as she is carried upward by angels. She may be surrounded by an unearthly light ("clothed in the sun") and may stand on a crescent moon in reference to the woman of the Apocalypse (SEE FIG. 10–12). Angels often carry palms and symbols of the Virgin, such as a mirror, a fountain, roses, and lilies. The Catholic Church exported to the New World many paintings faithful to these orthodox guidelines by Murillo, Zurbarán, and others. When the indigenous population began to visualize the Christian story, paintings such as Murillo's **THE IMMACULATE CONCEPTION** (**FIG. 14–17**) guided their imagining.

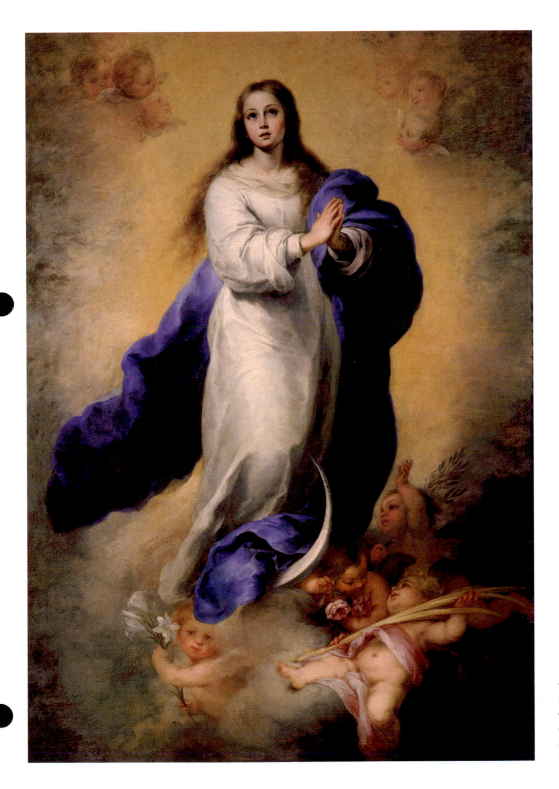

14–17 • Bartolomé Estebán Murillo **THE IMMACULATE CONCEPTION**
c. 1660–1665. Oil on canvas, 81⅛″ × 56⅝″ (2.06 × 1.44 m). Museo del Prado, Madrid.

Flanders

What new developments took place in the Antwerp workshop of Peter Paul Rubens?

Flanders was part of the Spanish Habsburg domain during most of the seventeenth century. After a period of relative autonomy under Habsburg regents from 1598 to 1633, the region came under direct and often oppressive Spanish rule. In spite of the shifting political climate, however, artists of great talent flourished in the cultural center of Antwerp, where the Spanish were enthusiastic patrons of the arts.

The art of Peter Paul Rubens (1577–1640) has become nearly synonymous with the Flemish Baroque style. Rubens was accepted into the Antwerp painters' guild at age 21, and shortly thereafter, in 1600, he left for Italy, where he obtained a post with the duke of Mantua. Other than designs for court entertainment and occasional portraits, the duke never acquired an original painting by Rubens. Instead, he had him copy famous paintings in collections all over Italy to enlarge the ducal collection, thus providing the young painter with an excellent education.

In 1608, Rubens returned to Antwerp, where he accepted a position as court painter to the Habsburg regents of Flanders, the Spanish princess Isabella Clara Eugenia (daughter of Philip II) and her husband, Archduke Albert. His first major commission was a large canvas triptych for the main altar of the church of St. Walpurga, **THE RAISING OF THE CROSS (FIG. 14–18)**, painted in 1610–1611. Unlike many earlier triptychs, in which the wings contain related but independent images—as seen, for example, in Grünewald's *Isenheim Altarpiece* (SEE FIG. 13–30)—Rubens extended the action and landscape of the central scene across all three panels. At the center, Herculean figures strain to haul upright the wooden cross with Jesus already stretched upon it. The followers of Jesus mourn at left, while soldiers on the right supervise the execution. In his paintings Rubens merges the drama and intense emotion of Caravaggio with the virtuoso technique of Annibale Carracci, but he transforms these qualities into a distinctive personal style. The heroic nude figures, dramatic lighting effects, dynamic diagonal composition, and intense emotions show the artist's debt to Italian art, but the rich colors and the careful description of surface textures reflect his native Flemish tradition.

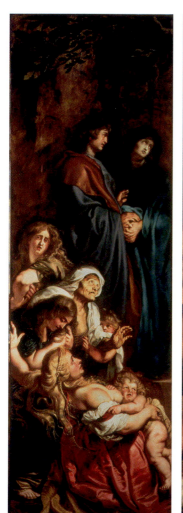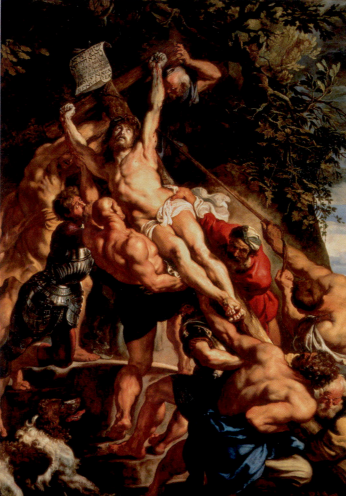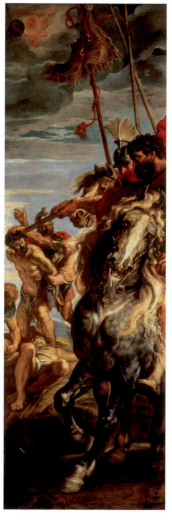

14–18 • Peter Paul Rubens **THE RAISING OF THE CROSS**
Painted for the church of St. Walpurga, Antwerp, Belgium. 1610–1611. Oil on canvas, center panel 15′ 1⅞″ × 11′ 1½″ (4.62 × 3.39 m), each wing 15′ 1⅞″ × 4′ 11⅞″ (4.62 × 1.52 m). Cathedral of Our Lady, Antwerp.

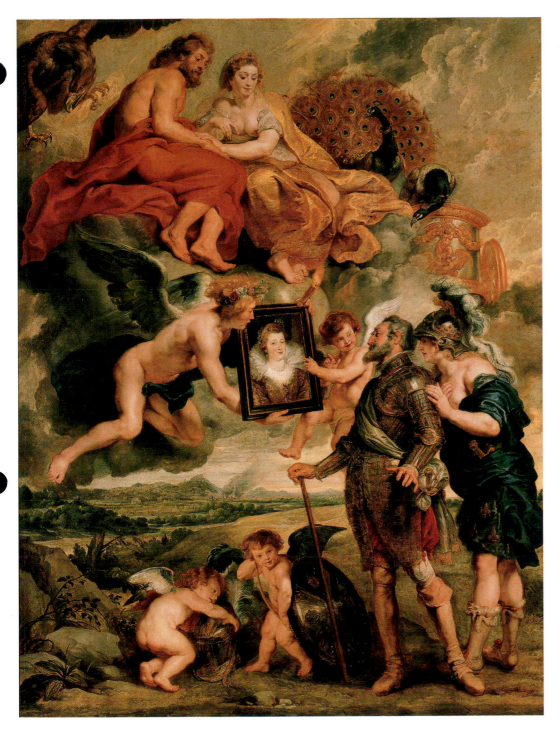

14–19 • Peter Paul Rubens
HENRY IV RECEIVING THE PORTRAIT OF MARIE DE' MEDICI
1621–1625. Oil on canvas, 12′ 11⅛″ × 9′ 8⅛″ (3.94 × 2.95 m). Musée du Louvre, Paris.

📖 **Read** the document related to Peter Paul Rubens on **MyArtsLab**

Rubens's intelligence, courtly manners, and personal charm made him a valuable and trusted courtier to royal patrons, including Philip IV of Spain, Marie de' Medici of France, and Charles I of England. In fact, he became the first international superstar of the European art world. In 1621, Marie de' Medici, widow of the French king Henry IV and regent for her young son, Louis XIII, asked Rubens to paint the story of her life. In 24 paintings, Rubens glorified her role in ruling France and also commemorated the founding of the Bourbon dynasty, which began with Henry IV. The lives and political careers of Marie and Henry appear as one continuous triumph overseen by ancient Roman gods. In the painting depicting the royal engagement

(FIG. 14–19), Henry IV falls in love with Marie as he gazes at her portrait, shown to him—at the exact center of the composition—by Cupid and the god of marriage, Hymen. The supreme Roman god, Jupiter, and his wife, Juno, look down approvingly from the clouds. A personification of France encourages Henry, outfitted with steel breastplate and silhouetted against a landscape in which the smoke of battle lingers in the distance, to abandon war for love, as *putti* frolic below with pieces of his armor. The ripe colors, lavish textures, and dramatic diagonals give sustained visual excitement to these enormous canvases, making them not only important works of art but political propaganda of the highest order.

Rubens accepted commissions from all over Europe and employed dozens of assistants as specialists in the painting of portraits, textiles, landscapes, even fruits and flowers. Using workshop assistants was standard practice among major artists, but Rubens was particularly efficient and created something close to a painting factory. Some of his most spectacular paintings were collaborations. Frans Snyders (1579–1657), a specialist in painting animals and flowers, was brought in by Rubens to paint the enormous eagle who devours the liver of the mythical hero in **PROMETHEUS BOUND** (see "A Closer Look," p. 387), begun in 1611–1612 and perhaps worked on as late as 1618. The dramatic lighting, dynamic composition, and loose, energetic brushwork of this painting—which the artist kept for a while in his own personal collection—were clearly Rubens's own, while Snyders's tight and detailed technique sets up a telling representational contrast between the massive predator and its writhing, muscular victim.

Another of Rubens's collaborators, Anthony van Dyck (1599–1641), had an illustrious independent career as a portraitist. A precocious student at age 10, he had his own studio and a roster of pupils at age 16, although he did not become a member of the Antwerp painters' guild until 1618, the year after he began his association with Rubens as a specialist in painting heads. Later in his career, Van Dyck became court painter to Charles I of England, by whom he was knighted and given a studio, a large salary, and a summer home.

In **CHARLES I AT THE HUNT** (FIG. 14–20) of 1635, Van Dyck was able, by clever manipulation of the setting, to portray the king truthfully and still present him as an imposing figure. Dressed casually for the hunt and standing on a bluff overlooking a distant view, Charles, who was in fact very short, appears here taller than his pages and even than his horse, since its head is down and its heavy body is partly off the canvas. The viewer's gaze is directed to the king's pleasant features, framed by his

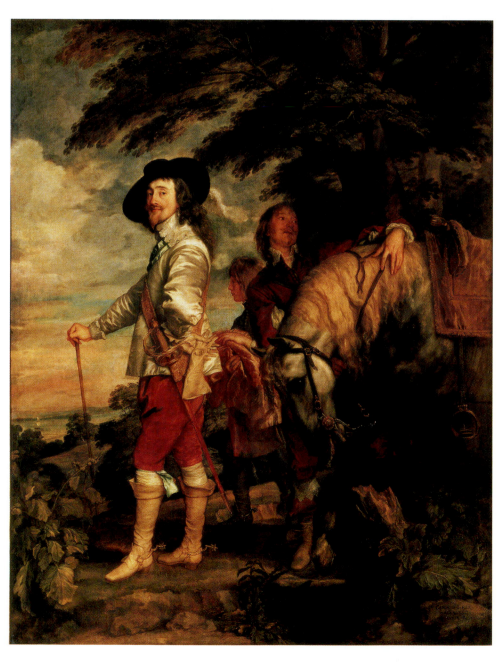

14–20 • Anthony van Dyck
CHARLES I AT THE HUNT
1635. Oil on canvas, 9′ × 7′ (2.75 × 2.14 m). Musée du Louvre, Paris.

Prometheus Bound ▶

Peter Paul Rubens and Frans Snyders. c. 1611–1618. Oil on canvas, 95½″ × 82½″ (2.43 × 2.1 m). Philadelphia Museum of Art. Purchased with the W. P. Wilstach Fund, 1950.

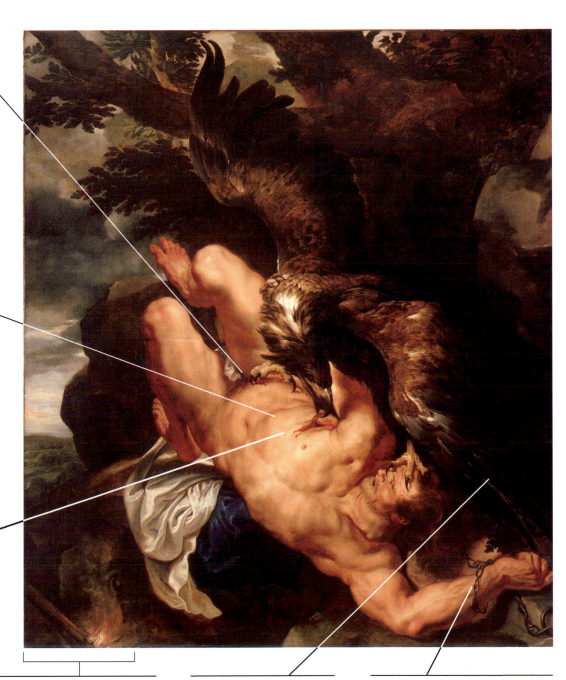

The talons of the eagle are poised to dig into sensitive areas of the groin, and the struggling hero's face underlines the excruciating nature of his pain.

During the seventeenth century, the struggle between Prometheus and the eagle was sometimes interpreted allegorically as the struggle involved in artistic creativity, or as the heroism involved in enduring suffering of body or soul. Some saw in Prometheus a prototype of the Christ of the Crucifixion, an association furthered here by the placement of the gash on Prometheus's side.

The eagle has pierced Prometheus's side to devour his liver, an action that identifies the subject. This hero of Greek myth was chained to Mount Caucasus and sentenced to this sensational punishment because, in direct defiance of Zeus's command, he stole fire from Mount Olympus and sneaked it to earth so humankind would no longer be confined to cold and darkness. And since Prometheus's liver regenerated each night, his fate was to have it plucked out again and again, day after day.

After the main composition was complete, Rubens added a 17½-inch strip of canvas to the left side of the painting in order to provide a more expansive space for the dramatic action. Its insertion allows for the inclusion of the fire that got Prometheus into trouble (at lower left), as well as the bright light on the horizon. Some have interpreted the latter as a touch of optimism to counteract the enduring punishment enacted in the foreground.

The eagle in this picture was painted by Frans Snyders, a specialist in painting animals and flowers whom Rubens brought in to render the detailed feathers and powerful posture of this bird of prey.

These small chains that confine Prometheus to the rock hardly seem adequate to confine the powerfully muscular hero, as Rubens conceives him, leading some to speculate that the artist wanted his incarceration to seem more psychological than physical.

View the Closer Look for Rubens and Snyders's *Prometheus Bound* on **MyArtsLab**

jauntily cocked hat. As if in decorous homage, the tree branches bow gracefully toward him, echoing the curving lines of the hat and the graceful cascade of his hair.

Religious and political tensions, particularly a conflict between Charles and the religious reformers known as Puritans, resulted in a series of civil wars, beginning in 1642. Charles lost his throne, and his head, in 1649. Once in power, the Puritans, led by Oliver Cromwell as lord protector, stifled artistic expression, but in 1660 the restoration of the Stuart dynasty under Charles II brought renewed patronage of foreign artists, especially portrait painters.

The Dutch Republic

What styles and subjects were preferred in the Protestant Netherlands?

Spain recognized the sovereignty of the northern Netherlands in 1648. Even before this official recognition, the Dutch Republic—as the United Northern Provinces of the Low Countries was officially known—managed not only to maintain its hard-won freedom but also to prosper. Dutch artists found many eager patrons among the prosperous middle-class citizens of Amsterdam, Leiden, Haarlem, Delft, and Utrecht. Portraiture was especially popular and took many forms, ranging from pictures of single individuals in sparse settings to allegorical depictions in elaborate costumes set in symbolic contexts. Group portraiture that documented the membership of corporate

organizations became a Dutch specialty. These large canvases, filled with many individuals who shared the cost of the commission, challenged painters to present a coherent, interesting composition that also gave equal attention to each individual portrait.

Frans Hals (c. 1581/85–1666), the leading painter of Haarlem, developed a distinctive personal style grounded in the Netherlandish love of description. Like Velázquez, he tried to re-create the optical effects of light on the shapes and textures of objects, and he painted loosely and boldly, with slashing strokes and angular patches of paint. Only when seen at a distance do the colors merge into solid forms over which a flickering light seems to move. In Hals's hands, this seemingly effortless, spontaneous technique suggests an infectious joy in life.

In his double portrait of **ISAAC MASSA AND BEATRIX VAN DER LAEN** (FIG. 14–21)—probably painted on the occasion of their marriage in 1622—Hals has captured the warmth and affection of this prosperous couple, whose welcoming expressions beckon viewers to join them in their lavish garden of love. Massa—a noted geographer and prosperous fur merchant—cedes the center of the picture to his blushing bride, whose extravagant white ruff frames her coy glance out at the viewer. The wedding ring on her finger—conspicuously displayed between their two faces—as well as the vines of ivy clinging to the tree trunk—a symbol of faithfulness in love—secure the association of the painting with the theme of marriage. And although their stylish and expensive

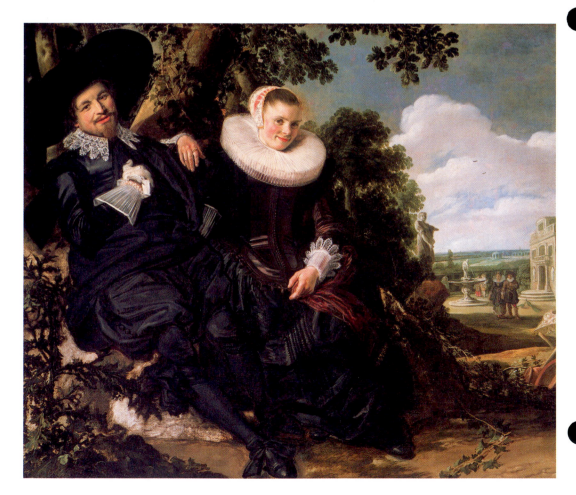

14–21 • Frans Hals
ISAAC MASSA AND BEATRIX VAN DER LAEN
c. 1622. Oil on canvas, 55″ × 65½″ (140 × 166.5 cm). Rijksmuseum, Amsterdam.

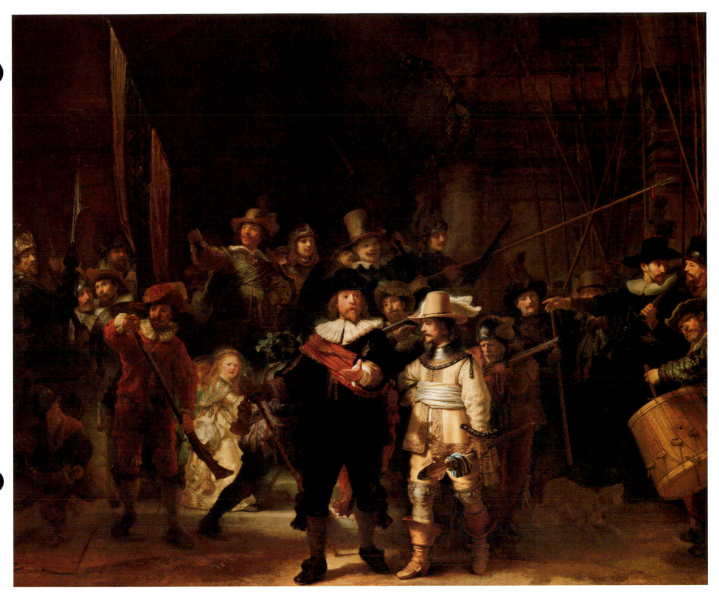

14–22 • Rembrandt van Rijn THE COMPANY OF CAPTAIN FRANS BANNING COCQ (THE NIGHT WATCH)
1642. Oil on canvas, 11′ 11″ × 14′ 4″ (3.63 × 4.37 m) (cut down from the original size). Rijksmuseum, Amsterdam.

clothing identifies them as members of the upper class, their relaxed postures and friendly faces create a strong rapport with a broad audience.

The most important painter working in the Netherlands in the seventeenth century was Rembrandt van Rijn (1606–1669). After studying painting in Amsterdam and Leiden and working as an artist in both cities, Rembrandt established a busy studio in Amsterdam, producing both paintings and etchings of mythological subjects, religious scenes, and landscapes. Like many Dutch artists of the time, however, his primary source of income was from portraiture.

In 1640, a civic guard company commissioned Rembrandt to create a large group portrait of its members for its new meeting hall. **THE COMPANY OF CAPTAIN FRANS BANNING COCQ (FIG. 14–22)** transforms a group portrait into a dramatic event. The painting has become known as *The Night Watch* because a layer of dirt and old varnish had so obscured its colors by the nineteenth century that viewers thought the scene took place at night. Since its cleaning and restoration during the 1970s, however, the painting glows with a golden light that ignites its palette of rich colors—browns, blues, olive green, orange, and red—around a central core of lemon yellow. As the company takes up its ranks, a crowd, including children, mills around. The surprising, highlighted image in the left middle ground of a girl carrying a chicken with prominent claws (*klauw* in Dutch) may be a pun on the name of the guns (*klover*) that gave the name "The Kloveniers" to this company. The complex interactions of the figures and the vivid, individualized likenesses of the militiamen make this painting one of the greatest group portraits in the Dutch tradition.

Rembrandt was the first artist to popularize **etching** as a major form of artistic expression. In the etching process, a metal plate is coated on both sides with an acid-resistant resin that dries hard without being brittle. Then, instead of laboriously cutting the lines of the desired image directly into the plate as in an engraving (see "Woodcuts and Engravings," p. 306), the artist draws through the resin with a sharp needle to expose the metal. The plate is then immersed in acid, which eats into the metal exposed by the drawn lines. By controlling the time the acid stays on different parts of the plate, the artist can make fine, shallow lines or heavy, deep ones. After the resin covering is removed from the surface of the plate, an impression is taken. If changes need to be made, lines can be "erased" with a sharp metal scraper. Not surprisingly, a complex image with a wide range of tones requires many steps.

Another technique for registering images with incised lines on a metal plate is called **drypoint**, in which a sharp needle is used to scratch lines directly into the metal. In drypoint, however, the burr (metal pushed up by the needle), is left in place. Unlike engraving, in which the burr is scraped off, here both the burr and the groove hold the ink. This creates a printed line with a rich black appearance that is impossible to achieve with engraving or etching alone. Unfortunately, drypoint burr is fragile, and no more than a dozen prints can be made before it flattens and loses its character. Rembrandt's earliest prints were entirely etched, but later he added drypoint to develop tonal richness.

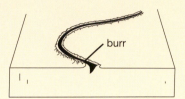

Rembrandt's etchings and drypoints (see "Etching and Drypoint," above) were sought after, widely collected, and brought high prices even during his lifetime. His deep speculations on the meaning of the life of Christ evolved in a series of prints, **THE THREE CROSSES**, in which he sought to capture the moment during the Crucifixion when Jesus cried out, "Father, into your hands I commend my spirit" (Luke 23:46). We can follow Rembrandt's creative process through four successive stages of this print, from the relatively anecdotal depiction of the crosses and the surrounding crowd in the first state (FIG. 14–23) to the haunting blackness that characterizes the fourth and final state. As Jesus cries out, a mystical light, beyond rational explanation, illuminates the darkened scene. The "realism" here is spiritual, conveying inner meaning not surface details. The eternal battle of dark and light, doom and salvation, evil and good, all seem to be waged anew.

Rembrandt painted many self-portraits, and as the artist aged, these personal images became more searching and, like many of his paintings, expressed an internalized spirituality and psychological honesty new in the history of art. In a **SELF-PORTRAIT** of 1658 (FIG. 14–24), the artist assumes an almost regal pose, at ease, with arms and legs spread, holding a staff as if it were a baton of authority. Yet his face and eyes seem weary and introspective, and we know that he had reason to worry.

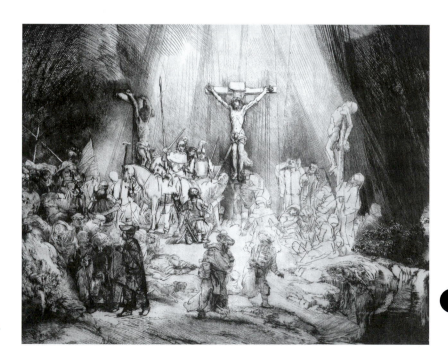

14–23 • Rembrandt van Rijn
THE THREE CROSSES (FIRST STATE)
1653. Drypoint, 15⅛" × 17¾" (38.5 × 45 cm).
Rijksmuseum, Amsterdam.

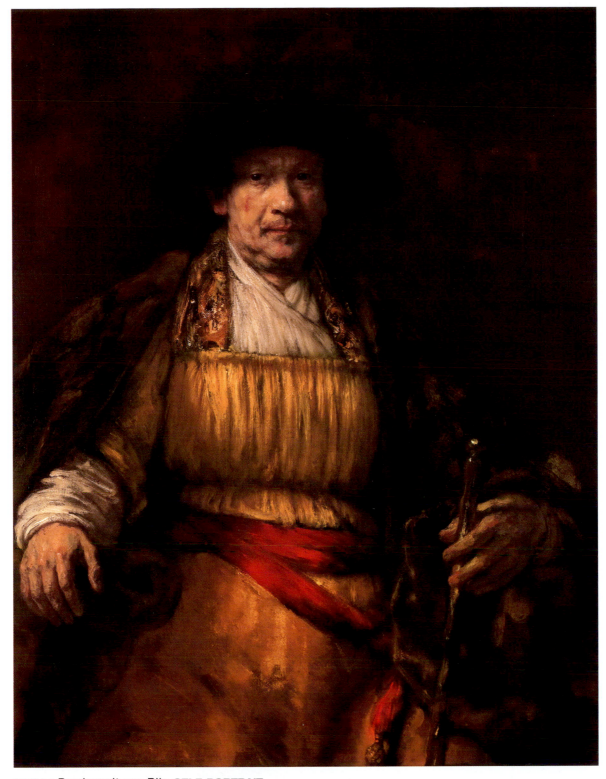

14-24 • Rembrandt van Rijn SELF-PORTRAIT
1658. Oil on canvas, 52⅝″ × 40⅞″ (133.6 × 103.8 cm). The Frick Collection, New York.

He had declared bankruptcy in 1656, and over the two-year period between that moment and this self-portrait, Rembrandt had sold his private art collection and even his house to cover his debts. It is possible to relate the stress of this situation with the way he represents himself here. A few well-placed brushstrokes are sufficient to capture the tension in the fingers and the weariness in the deep-set eyes, half in shadow. Mercilessly analytical, the portrait depicts the furrowed brow, sagging flesh, and aging face of one who has suffered pitfalls but managed to survive, retaining his dignity.

More typical of Dutch painters, Judith Leyster (c. 1609–1660) painted boisterous genre scenes categorized in their own time by descriptive titles such as "merry company" or "garden party." In her lively **SELF-PORTRAIT** (FIG. 14–25), Leyster displays on her easel the type of work on which her popularity was based. The subject, a man playing a violin, may also be a visual pun on the painter's instruments, the palette and brush. To let the viewer immediately see the difference between her painted portrait and the painted painting, she varied her technique, executing the image on her easel more loosely. The narrow range of colors sensitively dispersed in the composition and the warm spotlighting are typical of Leyster's mature style.

The art produced in the Netherlands during the seventeenth century shows that the Dutch delighted in depictions not only of themselves, but also of their country's landscape, cities, and scenes of daily life, known as genre paintings (SEE FIG. INTRO–16). Perhaps the most evocative painter of contemporary Dutch life was Johannes Vermeer of Delft (1632–1675). Vermeer produced few works, and most concentrate on enigmatic scenes of women in their homes, occupied with some cultivated activity such as writing, reading letters, or making music. These are quiet interior scenes, low-key in color, asymmetrical but strongly geometric in organization. An even, pearly light from a window gives solidity to the figures and objects in the room. Emotion is subdued, evoking the stillness of meditation.

The brushwork is so controlled that it becomes invisible, except where he paints his characteristic pools of reflected light as tiny, pearl-like droplets of color.

In **WOMAN HOLDING A BALANCE** (FIG. 14–26), painted about 1664, perfect compositional equilibrium creates a moment of supreme stillness. The woman contemplates the balance in her right hand, drawing our attention to the act of weighing and judging. Hung on the wall behind her is a painting of the Last Judgment, highlighting the figure of Christ the Judge directly over her head. The juxtaposition seems to turn Vermeer's genre scene into a metaphor for eternal judgment, a sobering religious reference that may reflect the artist's own position as a Catholic living in a Protestant country. The woman's moment of quiet introspection in front of the gold and pearls displayed on the table before her, shimmering with reflected light from the window, also evokes the *vanitas* theme of the transience of earthly life, inspiring spiritual reflections on the fleeting nature of beauty, youth, and riches.

Another type of genre painting that achieved great popularity in the Netherlands is the architectural interior. Buildings seem to have been painted for their own special beauty, just like landscapes, cities, and harbors. Emanuel de Witte (1617–1692) specialized in architectural painting, and many of his

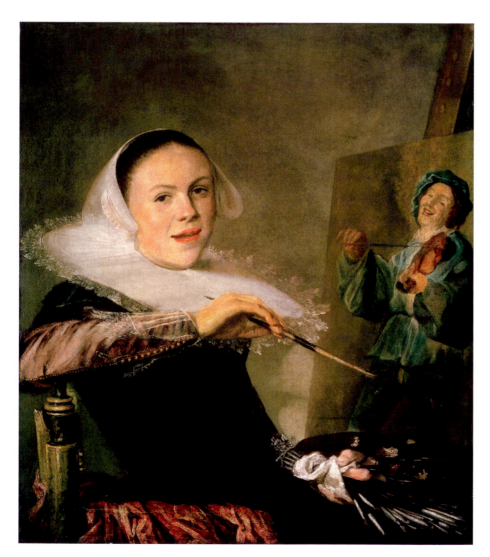

14–25 • Judith Leyster SELF-PORTRAIT
1635. Oil on canvas, 29⅜″ × 25⅝″
(74.6 × 65.1 cm). National Gallery of Art, Washington, D.C. Gift of Mr. and Mrs. Robert Woods Bliss.

View the Closer Look for Leyster's *Self-Portrait* on **MyArtsLab**

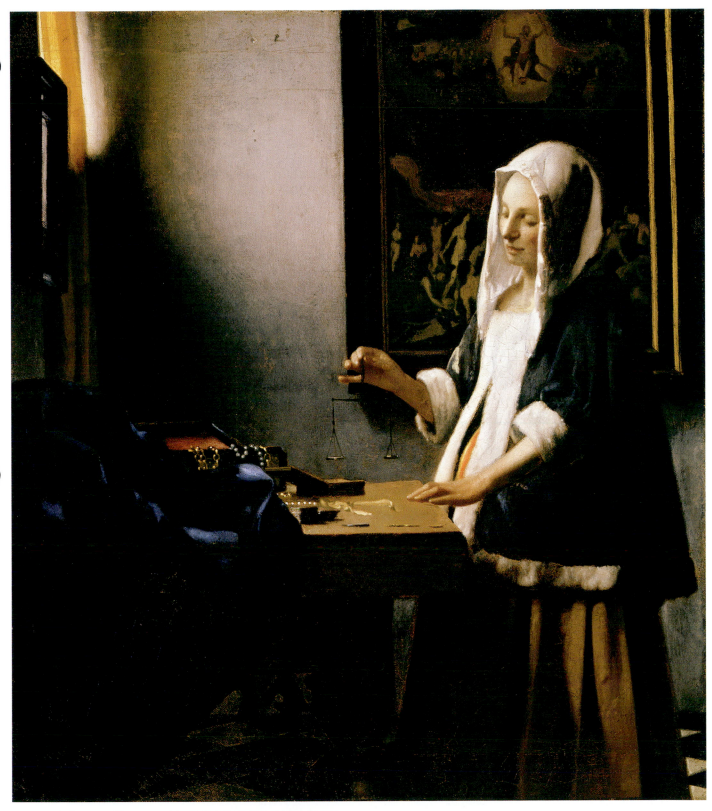

14–26 • Johannes Vermeer WOMAN HOLDING A BALANCE
c. 1664. Oil on canvas, 15⅝″ × 14″ (39.7 × 35.5 cm). National Gallery of Art, Washington, D.C.

👁 **Watch** a video about Vermeer's *Woman Holding a Balance* on **MyArtsLab**

interiors depict actual buildings, such as his **PORTUGUESE SYNAGOGUE, AMSTERDAM** (FIG. 14–27). The synagogue is shown as a rectangular hall with women's galleries on both sides, roofed by three wooden barrel vaults and lit by large glass windows. Standing within this space, the elegant couple in the foreground, the crowd behind them, and the dogs in the foreground provide a sense of scale and add human interest.

Today, this painting is interesting not only as a work of art, but also as a record of seventeenth-century synagogue architecture, documenting religious tolerance in an age when Jews were often persecuted. Expelled from Spain and Portugal beginning in the late fifteenth century, many Jews had settled in Amsterdam, where there was at this time a community of about 2,300, most of whom were well-to-do merchants. Fund-raising for a new synagogue began in 1670, and in 1671 Elias Bouman and Daniel Stalpaert won the building competition. With its classical architecture, Brazilian jacaranda-wood furniture, and 26 brass chandeliers, this was considered one of the most impressive buildings in Amsterdam. The synagogue was spared by the Nazis during World War II because the Germans planned to turn it into a museum of Jewish culture.

The Dutch loved the landscapes and vast skies of their country. Jacob van Ruisdael's **VIEW OF HAARLEM WITH BLEACHING GROUNDS** (FIG. 14–28), painted about 1670,

celebrates the flatlands outside Haarlem that had been reclaimed from the sea as part of a massive landfill project that the Dutch compared with God's restoration of the earth after Noah's flood. Such a religious interpretation may be referenced here in the prominent Gothic church of St. Bavo, looming on the horizon. Devoting almost three-fourths of this painting to a glorious rendering of the powerfully cloudy sky gives it a spectacular monumentality, dwarfing the labor of the tiny humans spotlighted below, caught in the process of spreading white linen across the broad fields to bleach in the sun. This glorification of the industriousness of citizens engaged in one of Haarlem's principal industries must have made the painting particularly appealing to the patriotic local market.

The Dutch love of nature is also apparent in still-life paintings of artfully arranged everyday objects or flowers. The latter were more than straightforward depictions of actual fresh flowers. Artists made color sketches of prime examples of each type of flower and studied scientifically accurate color illustrations in botanical publications (see "Science and the Changing Worldview," p. 396). Once in the studio, they would use their sketches and notebooks to compose imaginary bouquets of perfect specimens, juxtaposing within their arrangements flowers that did not bloom at the same time. *Flower Piece with Curtain* by Adriaen van der Spelt and Frans van Mieris

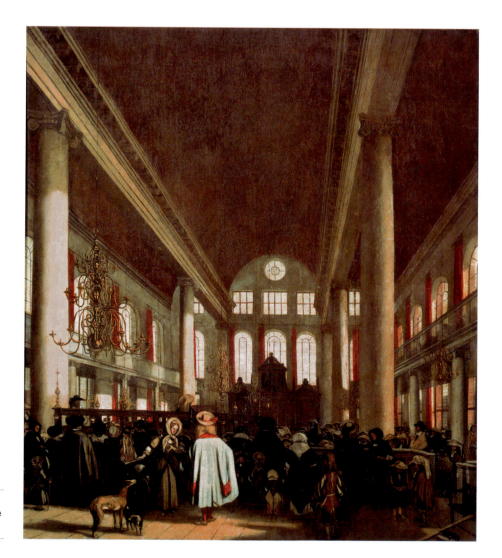

14–27 • Emanuel de Witte
PORTUGUESE SYNAGOGUE, AMSTERDAM
1680. Oil on canvas, 43½″ × 39″ (110.5 × 99.1 cm). Rijksmuseum, Amsterdam.

Architects Daniel Stalpaert and Elias Bourman built the synagogue in 1671–1675.

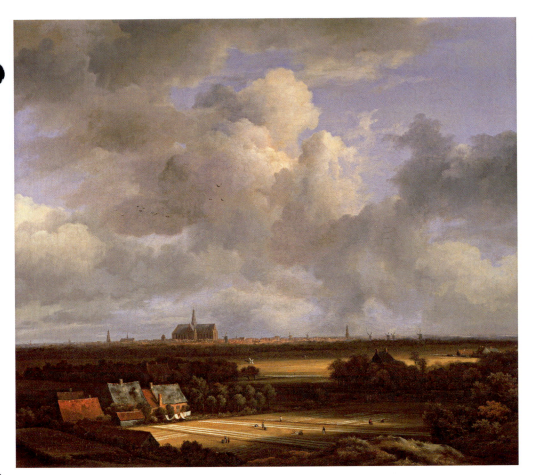

(SEE FIG. INTRO–2) is a playful, but learned, example. The stunning still-life paintings of Clara Peeters contain not only arranged flowers, but fruits, nuts, and precious objects, many of them the luxury imports that were prized possessions of wealthy Dutch merchants (see "A Closer Look," p. 7).

Rachel Ruysch (1663–1750) was one of the most sought-after and highest-paid flower painters in Amsterdam. During her 70-year career, her works were highly prized for their sensitive, free-form floral arrangements and their unusual and beautiful color harmonies (FIG. 14–30). Perhaps less daring than some of her peers, she was more "scientific" in outlook, transforming each flower in her still lifes into a botanical study. Ruysch had learned botany as a girl from her father, a professor of anatomy and botany in Amsterdam. Although married with 10 children, Ruysch never stopped painting. She achieved such fame in her lifetime that her paintings often brought higher prices than works by Rembrandt. Frequently she enlivened her compositions with reptiles or insects—in this case, two snail shells and a large gray moth—that lend an unsettling feeling to her paintings since such predators pose a potential threat to the fragile beauty of the flowers. And besides appreciating the sumptuousness of the natural world and the virtuosity with which it is captured by Ruysch, viewers may have also recognized the singularly expensive flaming tulip as a warning against the vanity of pride and greed, just as the short life of the cut flowers may have reminded them of the fleeting nature of beauty and human life. In the Protestant Netherlands, even art informed by science could carry a moral message.

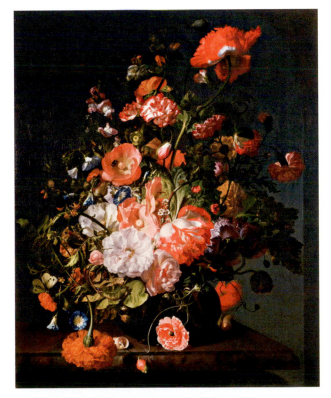

14–30 • Rachel Ruysch **FLOWER STILL LIFE**
After 1700. Oil on canvas, 30″ × 24″ (76.2 × 61 cm). The Toledo Museum of Art, Ohio. Purchased with funds from the Libbey Endowment. Gift of Edward Drummond Libbey.

Science and the Changing Worldview

From the mid sixteenth through the eighteenth centuries, new discoveries about the natural world brought a sense of both the grand scale and the microscopic detail of the universe. To publish their theories and research, early scientists learned to draw or depended on artists to draw what they discovered in the world around them. This practice would continue until the invention of photography in the nineteenth century.

Artist and scientist were seldom the same person, but Anna Maria Sibylla Merian (1647–1717) contributed to botany and entomology both as a researcher and as an artist. German by birth and Dutch by training, Merian was once described by a Dutch contemporary as a painter of worms, flies, mosquitoes, spiders, "and other filth." In 1699, the city of Amsterdam subsidized Merian's research on plants and insects in the Dutch colony of Surinam in South America, where she spent two years exploring the jungle and recording insects. On her return to the Dutch Republic, she published the results of her research as *Metamorphosis of Insects in Surinam*, illustrated with 72 large plates engraved after her watercolors **(FIG. 14–29)**. For all her meticulous scientific accuracy, Merian also took care to arrange her depictions of exotic insects and elegant fruits and flowers into skillful and harmonious compositions.

But interest in scientific exploration was not limited to the Netherlands. The writings of philosophers Francis Bacon (1561–1626) in England and René Descartes (1596–1650) in France helped establish a new method of studying the world by insisting on scrupulous objectivity and logical reasoning. Bacon argued that the facts be established from observation and tested by controlled experiments. Descartes, who was also a mathematician, is credited with inventing analytic geometry and the modern scientific method.

In 1543, the Polish scholar Nicolaus Copernicus (1473–1543) published *On the Revolutions of the Heavenly Spheres*, which contradicted the long-held view that Earth is the center of the universe (the Ptolemaic theory) by arguing instead that Earth and other planets revolve around the Sun. The Church viewed Copernican theory as a challenge to its doctrines, and in 1616 put Copernicus's work on its Index of Prohibited Books, but Johannes Kepler (1571–1630), court mathematician and astronomer to Holy Roman Emperor Rudolf II, continued demonstrating that the planets revolve around the Sun in elliptical orbits, believing that the overall design of the universe was an expression of divine order. Galileo Galilei (1564–1642), an astronomer, philosopher, and physicist, developed the telescope as a tool for observing the heavens and provided further confirmation of Copernican theory. After the Church prohibited the teaching of that theory, Galileo was tried for

heresy by the Inquisition and forced to recant his views, although at the end of his trial, according to legend, he muttered, "*Eppur si muove!*" ("Nevertheless it [Earth] does move").

The new seventeenth-century science turned to the study of the very small as well as to the vast reaches of space. This included the refinement of the microscope by the Dutch lens-maker and amateur scientist Anton van Leeuwenhoek (1632–1723). Leeuwenhoek perfected grinding techniques and increased the power of magnification in his lenses far beyond the requirements of a simple magnifying glass. Ultimately, he was able to study the inner workings of plants and animals and even see micro-organisms.

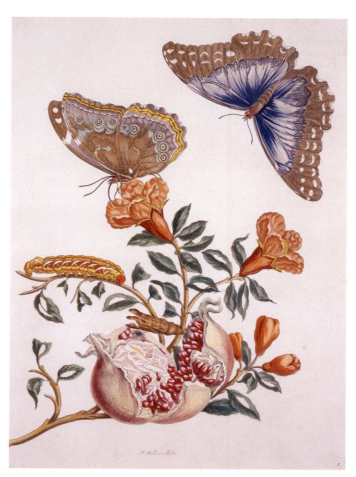

14–29 • Anna Maria Sibylla Merian PLATE 9 FROM METAMORPHOSIS OF INSECTS IN SURINAM
1719 (printed posthumously). Bound volume of 72 hand-colored engravings (second edition), 18⅞″ × 13″ (47.9 × 33 cm). National Museum of Women in the Arts, Washington, D.C. Gift of Wallace and Wilhelmina Holladay (1956.57).

France

How does the royal and Neoclassical art of France differ from developments elsewhere in Europe?

Absolute monarchs were expected to be patrons of the arts in seventeenth-century Europe. Many emulated the example of the French king Louis XIV (ruled 1643–1715), striving to match his court at Versailles by building and rebuilding their own palaces, planting vast gardens dotted with richly sculptured fountains, and spending fortunes on paintings and the decorative arts. However, the early seventeenth century had actually been a difficult period in France, marked by almost continuous foreign and civil wars. King Henry IV was assassinated in 1610, and the country endured the prolonged regency of Queen Marie de' Medici for their 9-year-old son, Louis XIII (ruled 1610–1643).

Louis XIV also came to the throne as a youth, and began his personal rule only in 1661. His autocratic reign was the longest in European history. He became known as *le Roi Soleil* ("the Sun King") and was sometimes glorified in art through identification with the sun god, Apollo. In a 1701 portrait by the French court painter Hyacinthe Rigaud (1659–1743), the richly costumed monarch is framed by a lavish, billowing curtain (**FIG. 14–31**). Proudly showing off his elegant legs, the 63-year-old **LOUIS XIV** poses in a blue robe of state, trimmed with gold *fleurs-de-lis* and lined with white ermine. He wears the high-heeled shoes he devised to compensate for his shortness. Despite his pompous pose and magnificent surroundings, the directness of the king's gaze and the frankness of his aging face make him appear surprisingly human.

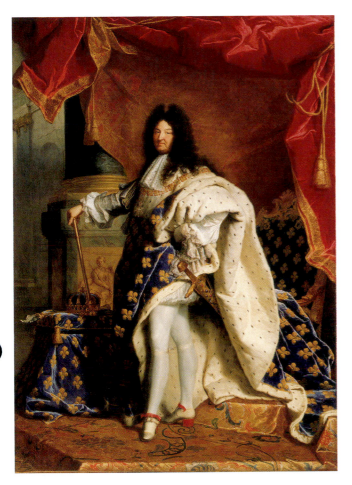

14-31 • Hyacinthe Rigaud LOUIS XIV
1701. Oil on canvas, 9′ 2″ × 7′ 10½″ (2.79 × 2.4 m).
Musée du Louvre, Paris.

Louis XIV had ordered this portrait as a gift for his grandson, the future Philip V of Spain (ruled 1700–1746), but when Rigaud finished the painting, Louis liked it too much to give it away and only three years later he ordered a copy from Rigaud to give to his grandson. The request for copies of royal portraits was not unusual since the aristocratic families of Europe were linked through marriage. Paintings made appropriate gifts and at the same time memorialized important political alliances by recording them in visual form.

👁 **View** the Closer Look for Rigaud's *Louis XIV* on **MyArtsLab**

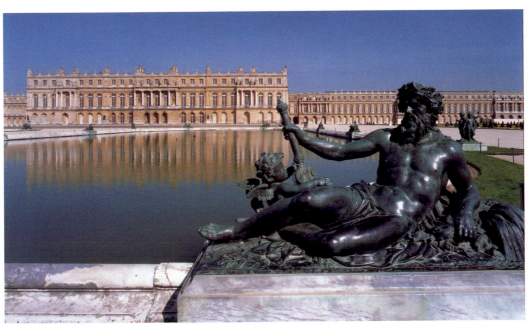

14-32 • Jean-Baptiste Tuby **NEPTUNE, BRONZE STATUE BY A REFLECTING POOL IN FRONT OF** Louis Le Vau and Jules Hardouin-Mansart **GARDEN FAÇADE, PALAIS DE VERSAILLES**
France, 1668–1685.

👁 **Watch** a video about Versailles on **MyArtsLab**

Under Louis XIV's lavish patronage of the arts, the French court became the cultural center of Europe. The Royal Academy of Painting and Sculpture, founded in 1648, maintained strict control over the arts, and membership ensured an artist lucrative royal and civic commissions. Although it was not the first European arts academy, none before it had exerted such dictatorial authority—an authority that lasted in France until the late nineteenth century (see "Grading the Old Masters," below). Classicism enjoyed particular favor in the academy and permeated French seventeenth-century painting, sculpture, and architecture. When the corresponding Royal Academy of Architecture was founded in 1671, its members developed guidelines for architectural design based on the belief that mathematics was the true basis of beauty, with Vitruvius and Palladio as their models.

In 1668, Louis XIV turned his attention to transforming a small hunting château at Versailles, built by his father Louis XIII, into the seat of his spectacular court of 5,000 aristocrats, supported by 14,000 resident soldiers and servants. This vast royal project consumed the energy of France's greatest painters, sculptors, designers, and architects for decades. The new architectural complex went up around the original château under the direction first of Louis Le Vau (1612–1670), beginning in 1668, and then after his death, of Jules Hardouin-Mansart (1646–1708) (FIG. 14–32). The three-story garden façade has a lightly rusticated ground floor, a grand first or main floor (we would call it the second floor) lined with enormous arched windows separated by Ionic columns or pilasters, and a less lofty attic level with rectangular windows. The overall design is a sensitive balance of horizontals and verticals relieved by a restrained overlay of regularly spaced projecting blocks with open, colonnaded porches.

Concurrently, André Le Nôtre (1613–1700), who planned the gardens, turned the terrain around the palace into an extraordinary work of art, destined to have a powerful influence on urban as well as garden design (FIG. 14–33). Neatly contained expanses of lawn and broad, straight vistas seem to stretch to the horizon, while the formal gardens, pools, fountains, and sculpture immediately behind the palace are an exercise in precise geometry. From these gardens, terraces descend to shaped, wooded areas and the mile-long Grand Canal. Classically harmonious and restful in their symmetrical, geometric design, the vast Versailles gardens extend into the surrounding countryside.

Residents and visitors to the château originally admired the gardens from an arcaded rear terrace, but in his renovations, Hardouin-Mansart enclosed this previously open space, turning it into an immense gallery known as the **HALL OF MIRRORS** (FIG. 14–34). He lit the 240-foot-long hall with 17 immense arched windows, lining the opposite wall with Venetian glass

ART AND ITS CONTEXTS

Grading the Old Masters

The members of the French Royal Academy of Painting and Sculpture considered ancient Classical art the standard by which contemporary art should be judged. By the 1680s, however, younger artists began to argue that modern art might equal and even surpass the art of the ancients. A related debate arose over the relative merits of drawing and color in painting. Conservatives argued that drawing was superior because it appealed to the mind, while color appealed to the senses. They saw the work of Nicolas Poussin as the perfect embodiment of Classical principles. But younger artists preferred the vivid colors of Titian, Veronese, and Rubens, claiming that painting should deceive the eye, and since color achieves this deception more convincingly than drawing, color should be valued over drawing. The two factions were called *poussinistes* (in honor of Poussin) and *rubénistes* (for Rubens).

The portrait painter and critic Roger de Piles (1635–1709) took up the cause of the *rubénistes* in a series of published pamphlets.

In *The Principles of Painting*, he evaluated painters on a scale of 0 to 20. He gave no score higher than 18, since no mortal could possibly achieve perfection. Caravaggio received the lowest grade, a 0 in expression and 6 in drawing, while Michelangelo and Leonardo both got a 4 in color and Rembrandt a 6 in drawing. Top grades (18) went to Titian for color, Rubens for composition, and Raphael for drawing and expression.

If we work out the "grades" using the traditional scale of 90% = A, 80% = B, and so forth, many important painters don't do very well. Raphael and Rubens get A's, but no one seems to get a B, although Van Dyck is close with a C+. Poussin and Titian earn solid C's, while Rembrandt slips by with a C–. Leonardo gets a D, but Michelangelo, Dürer, and Caravaggio are resounding failures in de Piles's view. Tastes change. Someday our ideas may seem just as misguided as those of the **academicians**.

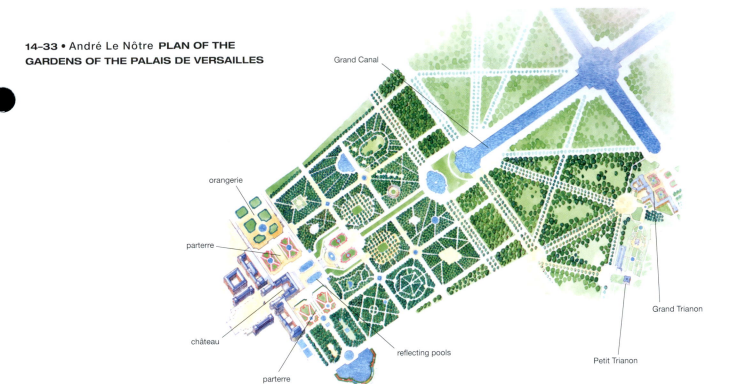

14–33 • André Le Nôtre PLAN OF THE GARDENS OF THE PALAIS DE VERSAILLES

Grand Canal

orangerie

parterre

château

parterre

reflecting pools

Grand Trianon

Petit Trianon

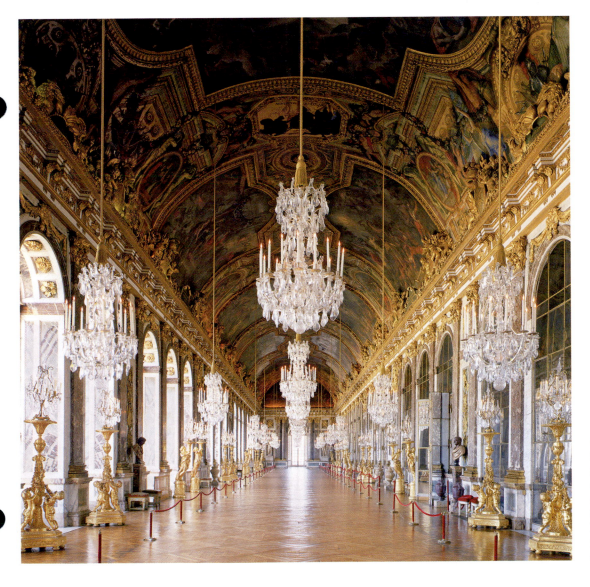

14–34 • Jules Hardouin-Mansart (ARCHITECTURE) AND Charles Le Brun (PAINTING) HALL OF MIRRORS
Palais de Versailles. Begun 1678. Length approx. 240′ (73 m).

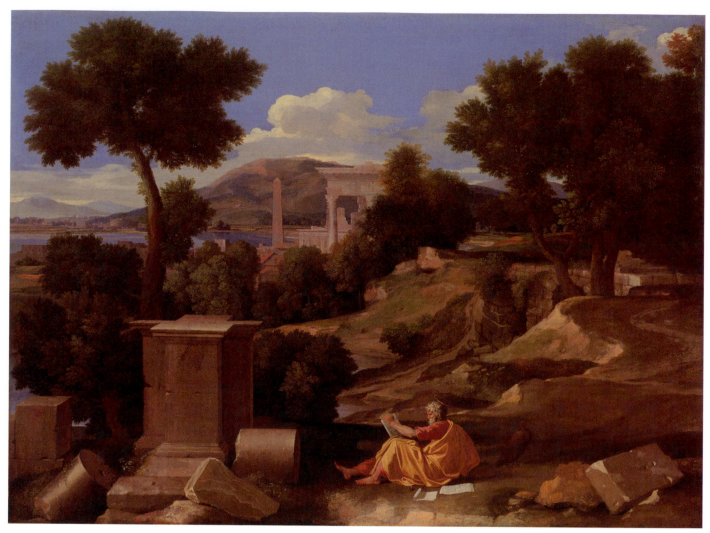

14–35 • Nicolas Poussin LANDSCAPE WITH ST. JOHN ON PATMOS
1640. Oil on canvas, 39½″ × 53¾″ (100.3 × 136.4 cm). The Art Institute of Chicago.
A. A. Munger Collection, 1930.500.

mirrors—enormously expensive in the seventeenth century—of exactly the same size and shape. They reflect the natural light from the windows and give the impression of an even larger space. In a tribute to Annibale Carracci's Farnese ceiling (SEE FIG. 14–8), the painter Charles Le Brun (1619–1690), a founding member of the Royal Academy of Painting and Sculpture, decorated the vaulted ceiling with paintings glorifying the reign of Louis XIV and his military triumphs, assisted by Classical gods.

As in the Netherlands, seventeenth-century painting in France was much affected by developments in Italian art. French painter Nicolas Poussin (1594–1665) actually pursued his career in Italy. As a dedicated Classicist, he did not paint landscapes as he saw them but instead reorganized nature,

buildings, and figures into carefully ordered compositions such as his **LANDSCAPE WITH ST. JOHN ON PATMOS (FIG. 14–35)**, from 1640. The artist devised a consistently organized progression from the picture plane to the horizon through a clearly defined foreground, middle ground, and background. Receding zones are marked by alternating sunlight and shade, as well as by the placement of Classical architectural elements. In the middle distance behind St. John are an imaginary ruined temple and obelisk, while across the lake on the left the round building is Hadrian's tomb from Rome. Precisely placed trees, hills, mountains, water, and even clouds have an almost architectural formal solidity. The true subject of Poussin's painting is not the writing figure of St. John, but the balance and order of nature.

During a period when political and religious factions attacked each other with lethal fanaticism, works of art often played an important role in capturing the imagination and swaying the emotions of viewers. Spectacular visions, brilliant political portraits, and ostentatious buildings proclaimed the power of Church and State. Some artists became international superstars; the Antwerp artist Rubens enjoyed the patronage of the kings of Spain, France, and England. Other artists, such as Caravaggio, played the role of disruptive outsiders, even when they sought the patronage of the establishment. Patronage even began to extend into the newly affluent middle class, especially in the Dutch Republic.

Many artists abandoned Renaissance ideals of beauty and grace. Seeking a new relationship with the natural world and influenced by the scientific interests of the day, they addressed new subjects, including landscape, still life, and scenes of daily life. Others, like today's Postmodernists, delighted in self-conscious references to the past, often turning to the art and architecture of ancient Rome for grand themes or decorative details. Meanwhile, the ancient world provided the historical context of works of art and "critical theory" for the education of artists in official academies.

THINK ABOUT IT

14.1 Explain how Bernini and Caravaggio established the Baroque style in sculpture and painting respectively, focusing on one specific work by each artist.

14.2 Discuss the complicated portrayal of space in Velázquez's *Las Meninas*. How does this painter differentiate foreground and background? How does he suggest the extension of pictorial space to include the area in front of the picture plane?

14.3 Do you consider the art of Peter Paul Rubens to be "Baroque"? In what ways are his paintings similar to and different from the work of Caravaggio?

14.4 Discuss the development of portraiture, still life, and genre painting in the Dutch Republic during the seventeenth century. What accounts for the increased importance of these subjects at this time?

14.5 Why is Poussin's landscape in FIGURE 14–35 considered an example of seventeenth-century Classicism?

| CROSSCURRENTS |

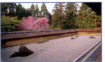

FIG. 9–24

FIG. 14–33

Garden design weaves its way through the history of art during most periods and places. These two distinguished examples were produced for two very different architectural complexes. Assess the way these two gardens were used and discuss how their form is related to their function. How are they representative of their cultural context?

☑ **Study** and **Review** on **MyArtsLab**

IN PERSPECTIVE

1600

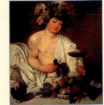

CARAVAGGIO,
Bacchus
1595–1596

• Mayflower Lands in
North America **1620**

1625

• Galileo Forced to Recant **1633**

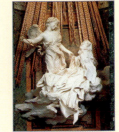

• Louis XIV, King of France
ruled **1643–1715**

BERNINI,
St. Teresa in Ecstasy
1645–1652

• Spanish Habsburgs Recognize
Independence of Dutch Republic/
Founding of French Royal Academy
of Painting and Sculpture **1648**

1650

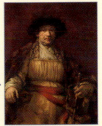

REMBRANDT,
Self-Portrait
1658

• Founding of French
Royal Academy of
Architecture **1671**

1675

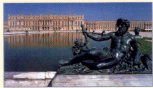

Palais de Versailles
1668–1685

• Newton Publishes His Laws of Gravity **1687**

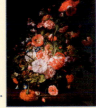

• Steam Engine Invented **1698**

1700

RUYSCH,
Flower Still Life
after 1700

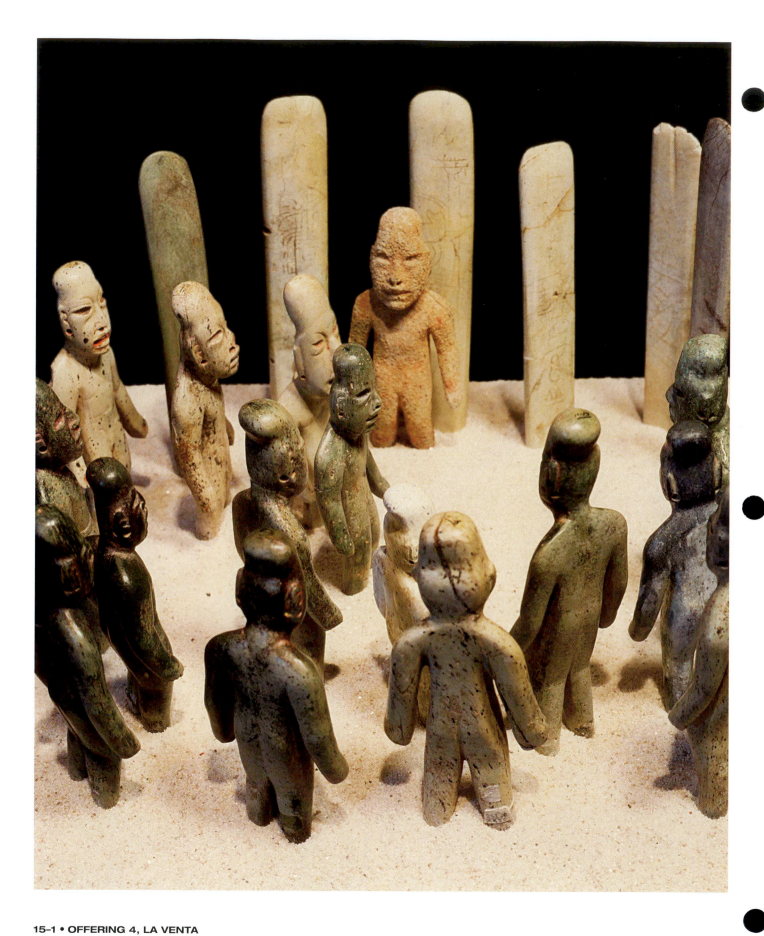

15-1 • OFFERING 4, LA VENTA
Mexico. Olmec culture, c. 900–400 BCE. Jade, greenstone, granite, and sandstone, height of figures 6¼″–7″ (16–18 cm).
Museo Nacional de Antropología, Mexico City.

ART OF THE AMERICAS

LEARNING OBJECTIVES

15.1 Differentiate the art and architecture of a series of cultures in Mesoamerica.

15.2 Summarize the development of art and architecture in Peru over a period of more than 1,000 years.

15.3 Describe the effect of the Spanish conquest on the cultures of Mesoamerica and South America.

15.4 Distinguish among various styles and functions of art and architecture from cultures across North America.

LOOKING FORWARD ▶

The scene hints at a story in progress (FIG. 15–1). Fifteen figures of precious greenstone converge on a single figure made of a baser, more porous stone. The tall oblong stones in the background evoke an architectural space, perhaps a location within the Olmec center of La Venta (Mexico), where this tableau was created sometime between 900 and 400 BCE. The figures have the slouching bodies, elongated heads, almond-shaped eyes, and downturned mouths characteristic of Olmec art. Holes for earrings and the simple lines of the bodies suggest that these sculptures may originally have been dressed and adorned with perishable materials. The poses of the figures, with their knees slightly bent and their arms flexed at their sides, lend a sense of arrested movement—but what is going on? Is it a council? A trial? An initiation? Are the greenstone figures marching in front of the reddish granite figure as he reviews them, or moving to confront him? With no texts to explain the scene, the specific tale it tells may never be known, but it is clear that this offering commemorates an important event.

And it was remembered. This tableau was set up in earth and buried underneath a plaza at La Venta, one of a number of offerings of works of art and precious materials beneath the surface of the city. Colored sand and floors covered the offerings, each colored floor signifying a successive renovation of the plaza. Over a century after these sculptures were buried, a hole was dug directly over the offering and it was viewed once more. Pieces of the later floors fell into the hole, but the figures themselves were not disturbed. After this, the scene was buried once again. The precision of this later excavation suggests that the exact location of the tableau was remembered and that this work of art, although hidden, still exerted tremendous power.

This extraordinary find demonstrates the importance of scientific archaeological excavations for understanding ancient art. Had these objects been torn out of the ground by looters and sold piecemeal on the black market, we would never have known how Olmec sculptures were used to create narrative installations or imagined that buried art could be remembered for so long. Instead, this discovery provides a context for isolated greenstone figures that have been found throughout Mesoamerica (modern Mexico, Guatemala, and Honduras). It provides evidence that these scattered sculptures were made by the Olmec, Mesoamerica's first great civilization, and suggests that originally these objects might have once been assembled in meaningful ensembles like the offering excavated at La Venta.

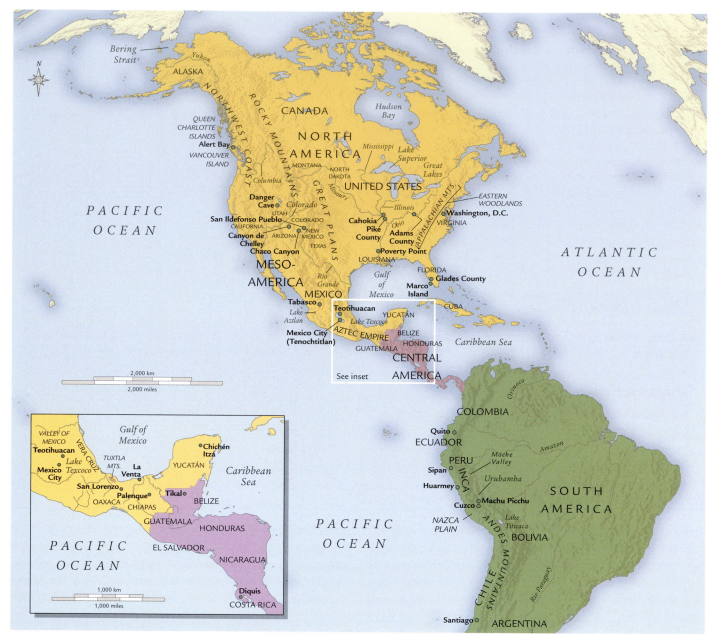

MAP 15–1 • THE AMERICAS

Diverse indigenous cultures were spread across the Americas, each shaping a distinct artistic and architectural tradition.

I n recent years, the question of the original settlement of the Americas has become a topic of debate. The traditional view had been that human beings first arrived in North and South America from Asia during the last Ice Age, when glaciers trapped enough of the world's water to lower the level of the oceans and expose a land bridge across the Bering Strait. Perhaps as early as 20,000 to 30,000 years ago, Paleolithic hunter-gatherers would have crossed over this corridor and begun to spread out into two vast, uninhabited continents.

This view is now challenged by the early dates of some new archaeological finds and by evidence suggesting the possibility of connections with Europe as well, perhaps along the Arctic coast of the North Atlantic. Recently, some have suggested that Pacific Islanders could have sailed to the coast of Chile and

spread out from there. In any event, between 10,000 and 12,000 years ago, bands of hunters roamed throughout the Americas. After the ice had retreated and rising oceans had flooded the Bering Strait, the people of the Western Hemisphere were essentially cut off from those of Africa and Eurasia until they were overrun by European invaders beginning in the late fifteenth century CE (**MAP 15–1**).

In this isolation, the people of the Americas experienced transformations similar to those that followed the end of the Paleolithic era elsewhere. In most regions, they developed an agricultural way of life. A trio of native plants—corn, beans, and squash—was especially important, but people also cultivated potatoes, tobacco, cacao (chocolate), tomatoes, and avocados. As elsewhere, the shift to agriculture in the Americas was accompanied by population growth and, in some places, the rise of hierarchical societies and the appearance of ceremonial centers and towns with monumental architecture and the development of the arts. The people of Mesoamerica—the region that extends from central Mexico well into Central America—developed writing, a complex and accurate calendar, and a sophisticated system of mathematics. Central and South American peoples had an advanced metallurgy and produced exquisite work in gold, silver, and copper. The inhabitants of the American Southwest built multistoried, apartment-like villages and cliff dwellings, as well as elaborate irrigation systems with canals. Basketry and weaving became major art forms across the Americas.

The sudden incursion of Europeans from the fifteenth century onward had a dramatic and lasting impact on Native American people and their art. In some areas, highly advanced civilizations, such as those of the Aztec and Inca, were destroyed. In other regions, such as the North American plains, indigenous groups lost much of their land and saw their populations decimated by newly introduced diseases, yet they retained their traditions and still exist as distinct cultural entities today.

Mesoamerica

What differentiates the art and architecture of a series of cultures in Mesoamerica?

Ancient Mesoamerica encompassed the area from north of the Valley of Mexico (the location of Mexico City) to present-day Belize, Honduras, and western Nicaragua in Central America. The people of this environmentally diverse region, which included tropical rainforests and semiarid mountains, were linked by cultural similarities and trade. Among the shared features were a ritual ballgame with religious and political significance, aspects of monumental building construction, and a complex system of multiple calendars including a 260-day divinatory cycle and a 365-day ritual and agricultural cycle. Mesoamerican society was also sharply divided into elite and commoner classes.

Archaeologists have traditionally divided Mesoamerican civilizations into three broad periods: Formative or Preclassic (1500 BCE–250 CE), Classic (250–900 CE), and Postclassic (900–1521 CE). The Classic period brackets the time during which the Maya erected dated stone monuments. As with the study of ancient Greek art, the term "Classic" reflects the view of early scholars that the this period was a kind of golden age, equivalent to the Classical period in ancient Greece (see Chapter 5). Although this view is no longer current—and the periods are only roughly applicable to other parts of Mesoamerica—the terminology has endured.

The Olmecs

The first major Mesoamerican art, that of the Olmec, emerged around 1500 BCE during the Formative/Preclassic period. In the fertile, swampy coastal areas of the modern Mexican states of Veracruz and Tabasco, the Olmec raised massive earth mounds on which they constructed ceremonial centers that included large, open plazas. And as we have already seen (SEE FIG. 15–1),

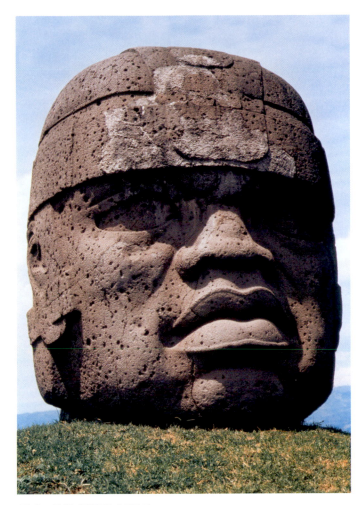

15–2 • COLOSSAL HEAD
San Lorenzo, Mexico. Olmec culture, c. 1200–900 BCE. Basalt, height 7′ 5″ (2.26 m).

The colossal heads found at La Venta and San Lorenzo were carved from basalt boulders that were transported to the Gulf Coast from the Tuxtla Mountains, more than 60 miles inland.

what was buried beneath their surface may have been as important as what was aboveground.

They also created monumental and exposed works of basalt sculpture, including **COLOSSAL HEADS (FIG. 15–2)**, altars, and seated figures. The huge basalt blocks for the large sculptures were quarried at distant sites and transported to San Lorenzo, La Venta, and other centers. The colossal heads range in height from 5 to 12 feet and weigh from 5 to more than 20 tons. They portray adult males wearing close-fitting caps with chin straps and large, round earspools (cylindrical earrings that pierce the earlobe). The fleshy faces have almond-shaped eyes, flat, broad noses, thick protruding lips, and downturned mouths. Since each face is different, they may represent specific individuals. Ten colossal heads were found at San Lorenzo. Many had been mutilated and buried about 900 BCE when the site went into decline. At La Venta, 102 basalt monuments have been found. Olmec artists also made smaller, more portable objects in ceramic and jade (which was imported from the area of present-day Guatemala), and Olmec objects were exported widely.

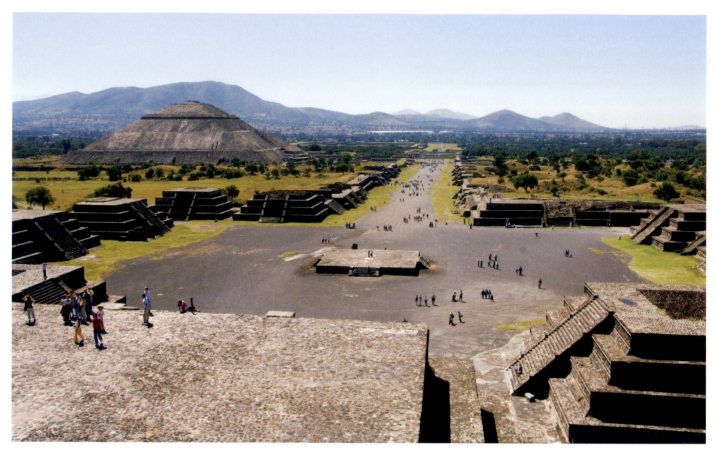

15-3 • OVERALL VIEW AS SEEN FROM THE PYRAMID OF THE MOON AND PLAN OF THE CEREMONIAL CENTER OF THE CITY OF TEOTIHUACAN
Mexico. Teotihuacan culture, c. 100–650 CE.

👁 **Watch** a video about Teotihuacan on **MyArtsLab**

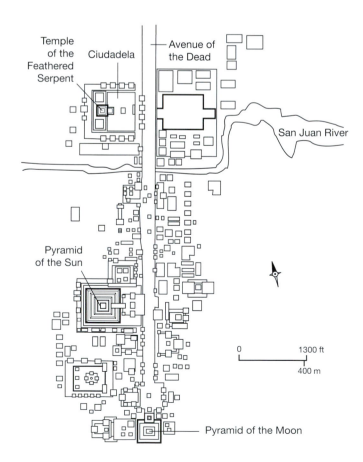

By 200 CE, forests and swamps began to reclaim Olmec sites, but Olmec civilization had spread throughout Mesoamerica and was to have an enduring influence on its successors. As the Olmec centers of the Gulf Coast faded, the great Classic-period centers at Teotihuacan in the Valley of Mexico as well as in the Maya region were beginning their ascendancy.

Teotihuacan

Located some 30 miles northeast of present-day Mexico City, the city of Teotihuacan experienced a period of rapid growth early in the first millennium CE. By 200 CE, it had emerged as Mesoamerica's first truly urban settlement, a significant center of commerce and manufacturing. At its height, between 300 and 650 CE, Teotihuacan covered nearly 9 square miles and had a population of at least 125,000, making it the largest city in the Americas and one of the largest in the world at that time (**FIG. 15–3**). One reason for its dominance was its control of the market for high-quality obsidian. This volcanic stone, made into tools and vessels, was traded for luxury items such as the green feathers of the quetzal bird, used for priestly headdresses, and the spotted fur of the jaguar, used for ceremonial garments.

The people of Teotihuacan worshiped many deities that were recognizably similar to those worshiped by later Mesoamerican people, including the Aztecs, who dominated central

Mexico at the time of the Spanish conquest. Among these are the Rain or Storm God (god of fertility, war, and sacrifice), known to the Aztecs as Tlaloc, and the Feathered Serpent, known to the Maya as Kukulcan and to the Aztecs as Quetzalcoatl.

Teotihuacan's principal monuments include the Pyramid of the Sun, the Pyramid of the Moon, and the Ciudadela (Spanish for fortified city center), a vast sunken plaza surrounded by temple platforms. The city's principal religious and political center, the Ciudadela could accommodate an assembly of more than 60,000 people. Its focal point was the pyramidal Temple of the Feathered Serpent. This seven-tiered structure exhibits the *talud-tablero* construction that is a hallmark of the Teotihuacan architectural style. The sloping base, or *talud*, of each platform supports a vertical *tablero*, or entablature, which is surrounded by a frame and filled with sculptural decoration. The **TEMPLE OF THE FEATHERED SERPENT** was enlarged several times, and—as was characteristic of Mesoamerican pyramids—each enlargement completely enclosed the previous structure, like the layers of an onion. Archaeological excavations of this temple's earlier-phase *tableros* (**FIG. 15–4**) and a stairway balustrade have revealed painted heads of the Feathered Serpent, the goggle-eyed Storm God associated with warfare, and reliefs of aquatic shells and snails. The flat, angular, abstract style, typical of Teotihuacan art, is in marked contrast to the curvilinear style of Olmec art. The Storm God features a squarish, stylized head or headdress with protruding upper jaw, huge, round eyes originally inlaid with obsidian, and large,

circular earspools. The fanged serpent heads, perhaps composites of snakes and other creatures, emerge from an aureole of stylized feathers. The Storm God and the Feathered Serpent may be symbols of regeneration and cyclical renewal, perhaps representing the alternating wet and dry seasons.

Sometime in the early seventh century disaster struck Teotihuacan. The ceremonial center burned, and the city went into a permanent decline. Nevertheless, its influence continued as other centers throughout Mesoamerica, as far south as the highlands of Guatemala, borrowed and transformed its imagery over the next several centuries. And the site remained a legendary pilgrimage center, especially dear to the much later Aztec people (c. 1300–1525 CE), who believed it to be the place where the gods created the sun and the moon. In fact, Teotihuacan, a word indicating a place of divinity, is the Aztec name for the city.

The Maya

The homeland of the Maya people is in southern Mesoamerica, which includes the Yucatán peninsula and the lands of several present-day countries, including Guatemala, Belize, and the western parts of Honduras and El Salvador. The Maya built imposing pyramids, temples, palaces, and administrative structures in densely populated cities. They developed the most advanced hieroglyphic writing in Mesoamerica and the most sophisticated version of the Mesoamerican calendrical system. In addition, they studied astronomy and the natural cycles of plants and animals, and they used sophisticated mathematical concepts like zero and place value.

An increasingly detailed picture of the Maya has been emerging from recent archaeological research and from advances in deciphering their writing. It shows a society divided into competing city-states in a near constant state of war with each other. A hereditary ruler and an elite class of nobles and priests governed each city-state, supported by a large group of farmer-commoners. Rulers established their legitimacy, maintained links with their divine ancestors, and sustained the gods through elaborate rituals, including ballgames, bloodletting ceremonies, and human sacrifice. A complex pantheon of deities presided over the Maya universe.

Maya civilization emerged during the Late Preclassic period (400 BCE–250 CE), reached its peak in the southern lowlands of Mexico and Guatemala during the Classic period (250–900 CE), and shifted to northern Yucatán during the Postclassic period (900–1521 CE). In Palenque, a prominent city of the Classic period, the major buildings are grouped on high ground. A central group of structures includes the so-called **PALACE** (an administrative center as well as a royal residence), the **TEMPLE OF THE INSCRIPTIONS**, and two other temples (**FIG. 15–5**). Most of the structures in the four building complexes were commissioned by a powerful ruler, Pakal the Great (*pakal* is Mayan for "shield"), who ruled from 615 to 683 CE, and his two sons, who succeeded him.

The Temple of the Inscriptions is a nine-level pyramid that rises to a height of about 75 feet. Priests would climb the steep stone staircase on the exterior to reach the temple on top, topped with a crest known as a **roof comb**. Its façade still retains much of its stucco sculpture. The inscriptions that give

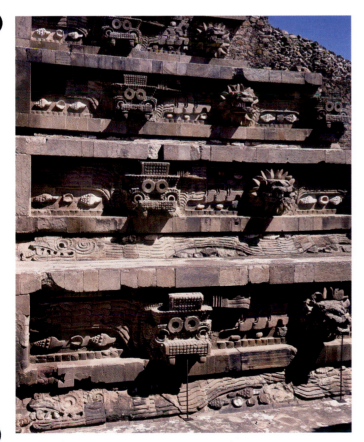

15-4 • TEMPLE OF THE FEATHERED SERPENT, THE CIUDADELA

Teotihuacan, Mexico. Teotihuacan culture, c. 200 CE.

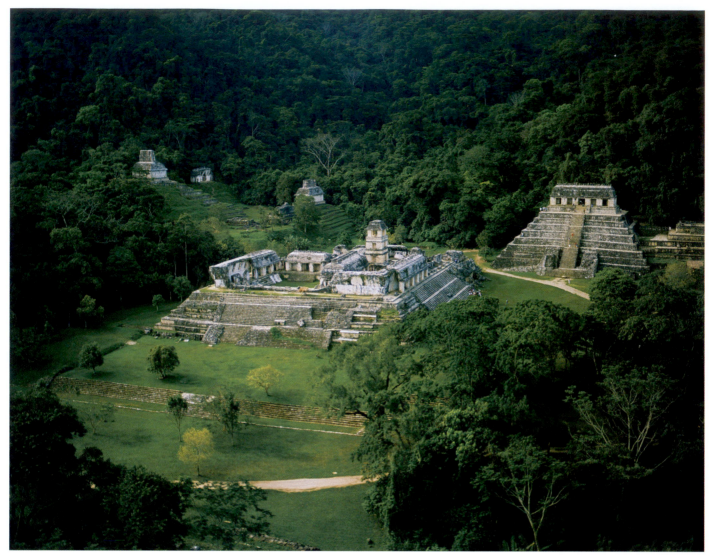

15–5 • PALACE (FOREGROUND) AND TEMPLE OF THE INSCRIPTIONS (TOMB-PYRAMID OF PAKAL THE GREAT)
Palenque, Mexico. Maya culture. Palace, 5th–8th century CE; Temple of the Inscriptions, c. 683 CE.

🔖 **Read** the document related to the Maya civilization on **MyArtsLab**

the temple its name line the back wall of the outer chamber, and link the accomplishments of Pakal to the mythical history of the city.

In 1948, a Mexican archaeologist cleared the rear chamber of the summit shrine and entered the corbel-vaulted stairwell that zigzagged 80 feet down to the tomb of Pakal the Great. After four years of work, the undisturbed tomb of the ruler was revealed. Covered in jade ornaments, he lay in a monolithic carved sarcophagus that represented him balanced between the underworld and the earth. A stucco portrait found underneath the sarcophagus depicts the ruler in the guise of the Maize God, with a headband of maize flowers and upswept hair that recall the leaves of the plant (FIG. 15–6). His features—sloping forehead and elongated skull (babies' heads were bound to produce this shape), large curved nose (enhanced by an ornamental bridge), full lips, and open mouth—are characteristic of the Maya ideal of beauty, also associated with the youthful Maize God, who represented—among other things—the cycle

of death and rebirth, as in the constant cycle of planting and harvesting life-sustaining food. Pakal's long, narrow face and jaw, however, are individual characteristics that carry a sense of personal likeness into this symbolic portrait. Traces of pigment indicate that, like much Maya sculpture, this stucco head was once colorfully painted.

Elite men and women, rather than gods, were the usual subjects of Maya relief sculpture, and most works show rulers performing religious rituals in elaborate costumes and headdresses. One of the most outstanding examples is one of a series of carved lintels from a temple in the city of Yaxchilan, dedicated in 726 CE by Lady Xok, the principal wife and queen of the ruler nicknamed "Shield Jaguar the Great." The ritual portrays an event when Shield Jaguar (ruled 681–742 CE) became the ruler of Yaxchilan in 681 CE: Lady Xok pulls a rope of thorns through her perforated tongue in a bloodletting ritual, and her husband stands with a torch to illuminate the scene (see "A Closer Look," p. 410). The relief—originally

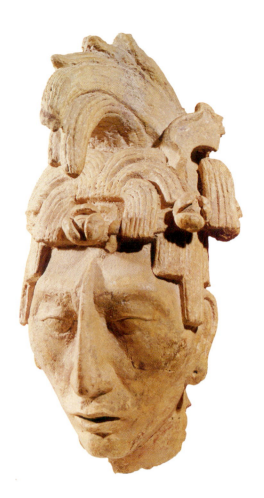

15–6 • PORTRAIT HEAD OF PAKAL THE GREAT
From his tomb, Temple of the Inscriptions, Palenque, Mexico. Maya culture, mid-7th century CE. Stucco and red paint, height 16⅞″ (43 cm). Museo Nacional de Antropología, Mexico City.

brightly painted—is unusually high, giving the sculptor ample opportunity to display a virtuoso carving technique, which can be seen in Lady Xok's garments and jewelry. That the queen figures so prominently on the temple's lintels is an indication of her importance at court, and of the status that elite Maya women could attain. They were important actors in the rituals that assured the power of Maya rulers and the survival of their subjects.

As the focus of Maya civilization shifted northward in the Postclassic period, a northern Maya group called the Itzá rose to prominence. Their principal center, Chichén Itzá, which means "at the mouth of the well of the Itzá," flourished from the ninth to the thirteenth century CE, eventually covering about 6 square miles.

One of Chichén Itzá's most conspicuous structures is a massive, nine-level pyramid in the center of a large plaza with a stairway on each side leading to a square temple on the pyramid's summit (**FIG. 15–7**). Sculpture at Chichén Itzá, including half-reclining figures known as **chacmools**, has the sturdy forms, proportions, and angularity of architecture, rather than the curving complexity and subtle modeling of Classic Maya sculpture. The *chacmool*s may represent fallen warriors and were used to receive sacrificial offerings.

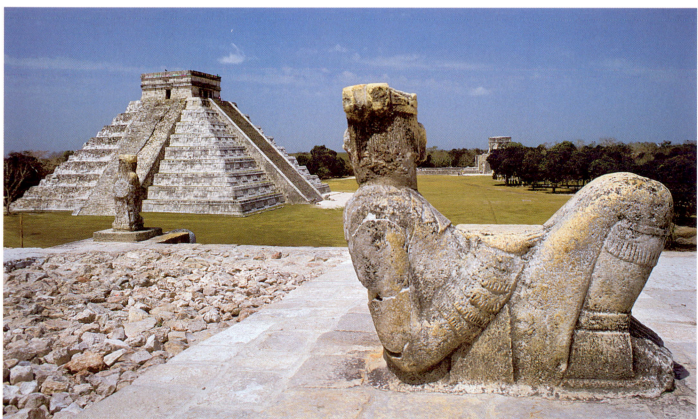

15–7 • PYRAMID ("EL CASTILLO") WITH CHACMOOL IN FOREGROUND
Chichén Itzá, Yucatán, Mexico. Maya culture, 9th–12th century CE.

Shield Jaguar and Lady Xoc ▶

Lintel 24, Yaxchilan, Mexico. Maya culture, 725 CE. Limestone, 43½″ × 31¾″ (110.5 × 80.6 cm). British Museum, London.

The sharply outlined subjects, as well as the way they project forward from a deeply recessed, blank background, focus viewers' attentions on the bodies of Shield Jaguar and his kneeling wife, Lady Xoc.

Shield Jaguar holds a huge torch, indicating that this ritual took place within a dark room or at night.

Shield Jaguar's elaborate headgear includes the shrunken head of a sacrificial victim, proclaiming his past piety in another ritual pleasing to the gods.

The two inscriptions—almost acting as an internal frame for the standing figure—record the date and the nature of the ritual portrayed: bloodletting on October 28, 709 CE. It also identifies the standing king as Shield Jaguar and the kneeling woman as Lady Xoc.

Tasseled headdresses are associated with bloodletting rituals.

Lady Xoc pulls a rope of thorns through her perforated tongue, while spiraling dotted lines show the blood she is sacrificing to the gods. The spiny rope falls into a basket with blood-spotted paper and a stingray spine, also sometimes used for bloodletting. This ritual of self-mutilation was required of royalty as it was believed to gain favor with the gods, and thus maintain royal rule and continuation of human life within the kingdom.

Lady Xoc is lavishly dressed in a garment made of patterned fabric, edged with a fringe. The mosaics on her cuffs and collar could be made of jade or shell.

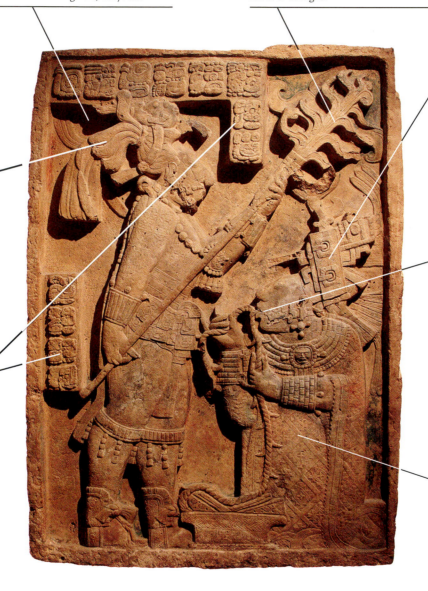

View the Closer Look for Shield Jaguar and Lady Xoc on **MyArtsLab**

The Aztecs

Maya civilization was in decline by the beginning of the Spanish conquest in 1519. Already by the end of the fifteenth century, a people known as the Aztecs controlled much of Mexico. Their rise to power had been recent and swift. Only 400 years earlier, according to their own legends, they had been a nomadic people living on the shores of a mythical island called Aztlan (from which the word "Aztec" derives) somewhere to the northwest of the Basin of Mexico, where present-day Mexico City is located. They called themselves the Mexica, hence the name "Mexico."

After a period of migration, the Aztecs arrived in the Basin of Mexico in the thirteenth century. There they eventually settled on an island in Lake Texcoco, where they had seen an eagle perching on a prickly pear cactus (*nochtli*) growing out of a stone (*tetl*), a sign that the god Huitzilopochtli (the solar god of Mexico) told them would mark the end of their wandering. They called the place Tenochtitlan (meaning "the prickly pear cactus on a stone"). The city was situated on a collection of islands linked by human-made canals.

In the fifteenth century, the Aztecs, joined by allies in a triple alliance, began an aggressive campaign of expansion. The tribute they exacted from all over central Mexico transformed Tenochtitlan into a glittering capital. As the Spanish conquistador Hernán Cortés approached Tenochtitlan in November 1519, he and his soldiers marveled at the stone buildings, towers, and temples that seemed from a distance to rise from the water like a mirage.

Most Aztec books were destroyed in the wake of the Spanish invasion, but the work of Aztec scribes appears in several manuscripts created after the conquest. The first page of the **CODEX MENDOZA**, prepared for the Spanish viceroy in the 1540s, portrays an idealized representation of the city of Tenochtitlan (**FIG. 15–8**). An eagle perched on a prickly pear cactus growing from a stone—the symbol of the city—fills the center of the page. Waterways divide the city into four quarters and indicate the lake surrounding it. Early leaders are seated in the quadrants, and the victorious warriors at the bottom of the page represent early Aztec conquests of nearby cities.

At the center of Tenochtitlan was a walled, sacred precinct, whose focal point was the **TEMPLO MAYOR** (Great Temple) (**FIG. 15–9**), a 130-foot-high stepped pyramid with dual temples

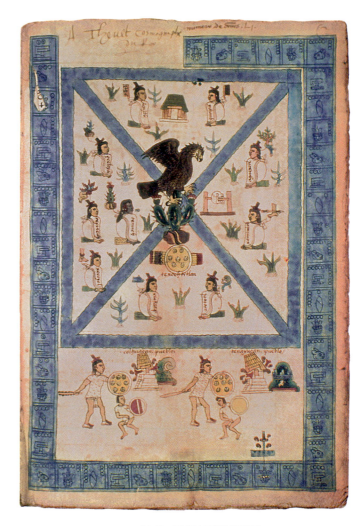

15–8 • THE FOUNDING OF TENOCHTITLAN
Page from *Codex Mendoza*. Aztec, 1545 CE. Ink and color on paper, 8⁷⁄₁₆″ × 12³⁄₈″ (21.5 × 31.5 cm). The Bodleian Library, Oxford (MS. Arch Selden. A.1.fol. 2r).

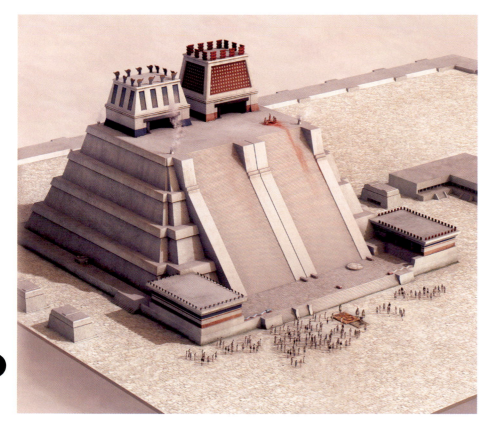

15–9 • RECONSTUCTION OF THE GREAT AZTEC PYRAMID (TEMPLO MAYOR) OF TENOCHTITLAN IN c. 1500 CE

on top, one of which was dedicated to Huitzilopochtli (the solar god of the Mexica) and the other to Tlaloc (an ancient rain god tracing back to Teotihuacan). During the winter rainy season the sun rose behind the temple of Tlaloc, and during the dry season it rose behind the temple of Huitzilopochtli. The double temples thus united two natural forces, sun and rain, or fire and water. At the spring and summer equinoxes, the sun rose between the two temples.

Sacrificial victims climbed stairs on the exterior of the great pyramid to the temple of Huitzilopochtli at the summit, where priests threw them over a stone, quickly cut open their chests, and pulled out their still-throbbing hearts, a sacrifice that ensured the survival of the sun, the gods, and the Aztecs. The bodies were then rolled down the stairs and dismembered. Thousands of severed heads were said to have been kept on a skull rack in the plaza of the sacred precinct, represented in FIGURE 15–8 by the rack with a single skull to the right of the eagle.

Aztec sculpture was monumental, powerful, and often unsettling. A particularly striking example is an imposing statue of **THE GODDESS COATLICUE**, mother of Huitzilopochtli (**FIG. 15–10**). Coatlicue means "she of the serpent skirt," and this broad-shouldered figure with clawed feet wears a skirt

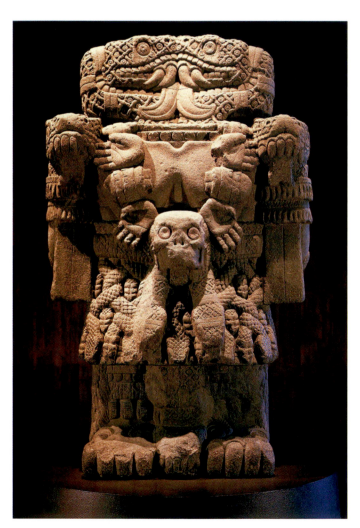

15–10 • THE GODDESS COATLICUE
Mexico. Aztec, c. 1500 CE. Basalt, height 8′ 6″ (2.65 m). Museo Nacional de Antropología, Mexico City.

of twisted snakes. The sculpture may allude to the moment of Huitzilopochtli's birth. When Coatlicue conceived Huitzilopochtli by placing a ball of hummingbird feathers (the soul of a fallen warrior) in her bosom, her other children—the stars and moon—jealously conspired to kill her. As they attacked, Huitzilopochtli emerged from his mother's body fully grown and armed, drove off his half-brothers, and destroyed his half-sister, the moon goddess Coyolxauhqui. Coatlicue herself, however, did not survive the encounter. In this sculpture, she has been decapitated, and a pair of serpents, symbols of gushing blood, rise from her neck to form her head. In the confronting profiles, their eyes are her eyes, their fangs her tusks. Around her stump of a neck hangs a necklace of sacrificial offerings—human hands, hearts, and a dangling skull. Despite its surface intricacy, the statue's massive form creates an impression of commanding solidity, and the whole sculpture leans forward, looming over the viewer. The colors with which it was originally painted would no doubt have heightened its dramatic impact.

South America: The Central Andes

How did art and architecture develop in Peru over a period of over 1,000 years?

Like Mesoamerica, the central Andes of South America—primarily present-day Peru and Bolivia—saw the development of complex hierarchical societies with rich and varied artistic traditions. The area is one of dramatic contrasts. The narrow coastal plain, bordered by the Pacific Ocean on the west and the soaring Andes Mountains on the east, is one of the driest deserts in the world. Life here depends on the rich marine resources of the Pacific and the oases formed by rivers that descend from the Andes. The Andes themselves are a region of snowcapped peaks, fertile river valleys, and high grasslands, home to llamas, alpacas, vicuñas, and guanacos. The lush eastern slopes of the Andes descend to the tropical rainforest of the Amazon Basin.

In the central Andes, the earliest evidence of monumental architecture dates to the third millennium BCE. Sites with ceremonial mounds and plazas were discovered near the sea, while early centers in the highlands consisted of multiroomed, stone-walled structures with sunken central fire pits for burning ritual offerings. Large, U-shaped ceremonial complexes with circular sunken plazas were built from the second millennium BCE. Some of the most enigmatic monumental constructions in Peru are the colossal earthworks, or **geoglyphs**, first created by the people of the Nazca culture, who dominated portions of the south coast of Peru during the first seven centuries CE. On great stretches of desert, the people literally drew in the earth, creating images that can only be seen fully from the air, dwarfing even the most ambitious modern environmental sculpture. By removing a layer of dark, oxidized stones, they exposed the lighter underlying stones. In this way, they created gigantic images—including a **HUMMINGBIRD** with a beak 120 feet long (**FIG. 15–11**), a killer whale, a monkey, a spider, a duck, and other birds—similar to those they used to decorate their pottery. They also made abstract patterns and groups of straight, parallel lines that extend for up to 12 miles. The purpose and meaning of these geoglyphs remain a mystery, but the "lines" of stone are wide enough to be used as ceremonial pathways.

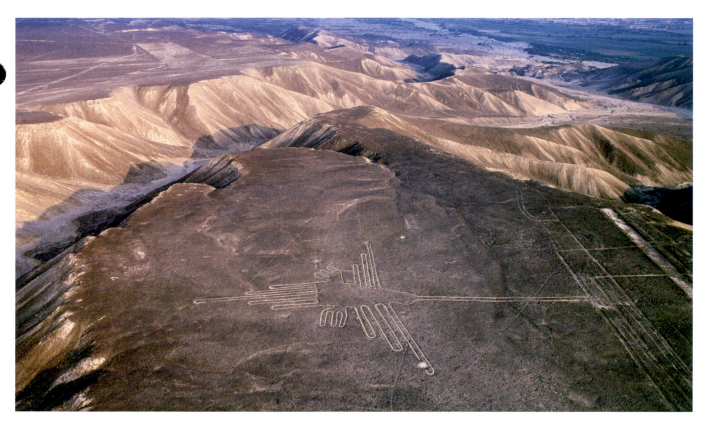

15–11 • GEOGLYPH (EARTH DRAWING) OF A HUMMINGBIRD
Nazca Plain, southwest Peru. Nazca culture, c. 1–700 CE. Length approx. 450′ (137 m); wingspan approx. 220′ (60.9 m).

👁 **Watch** a video about the earth drawings on the Nazca Plain on **MyArtsLab**

The Moche Culture

The Moche culture dominated the north coast of what is now Peru, from the Piura Valley to the Huarmey Valley—a distance of some 370 miles—between about 100 BCE and 700 CE. Moche lords ruled each valley in this region from a ceremonial-administrative center. The largest of these, in the Moche Valley (from which the culture takes its name), contained the so-called Pyramids of the Sun and the Moon, both built entirely of **adobe** bricks. The Pyramid of the Sun, one of the largest ancient structures in South America, was originally 1,000 feet long by 500 feet wide, rising in a series of terraces to a height of 59 feet. This site had been thought to be the capital of the entire Moche realm, but accumulating evidence indicates that the Moche maintained a decentralized social network.

The Moche were exceptional potters and metalsmiths. They developed ceramic molds that allowed them to mass-produce forms. Some vessels were made in the shapes of human beings, animals, and architectural structures. The ceramic vessel in FIGURE 15–12 shows a **MOCHE LORD** sitting in a throne-like

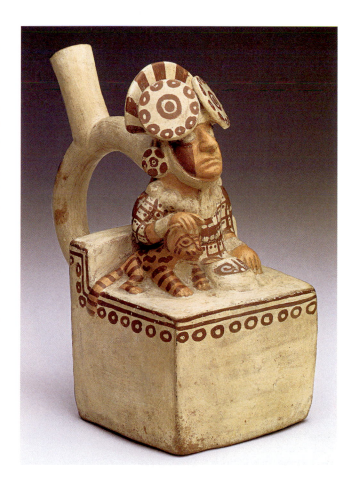

15–12 • MOCHE LORD WITH A FELINE
From Moche Valley, Peru. Moche culture, c. 100 BCE–500 CE.
Painted ceramic, height 7½″ (19 cm). The Art Institute of Chicago.
Buckingham Fund (1955–2281).

Behind the figure is the distinctive stirrup-shaped handle and spout. Vessels of this kind, used in Moche rituals, were also treasured as special luxury items and were buried with individuals of high status.

15–13 • EARSPOOL

From Sipán, Peru. Moche culture, c. 300 CE. Gold, turquoise, quartz, and shell, diameter c. 3″ (9.4 cm). Bruning Archaeological Museum, Lambayeque, Peru.

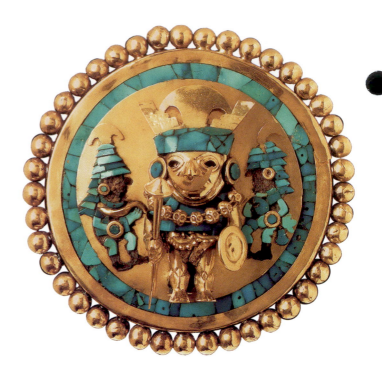

structure associated with high office. He wears an elaborate headdress and large earspools and strokes a cat or perhaps a jaguar cub. Other vessels have portrait likenesses or record in intricate fine-line painting mythological narratives and ritual scenes similar to those painted on the walls of temples and administrative buildings. Moche metalsmiths, the most sophisticated in the central Andes, developed several innovative metal alloys.

A central theme in Moche iconography is the ceremony in which prisoners captured in battle are sacrificed and elaborately dressed figures drink their blood. Archaeologists have labeled the principal figure in this ceremony as the Warrior Priest and other important figures as the Bird Priest and the Priestess. The recent discovery of a number of spectacularly rich Moche tombs indicates that the sacrifice ceremony was an

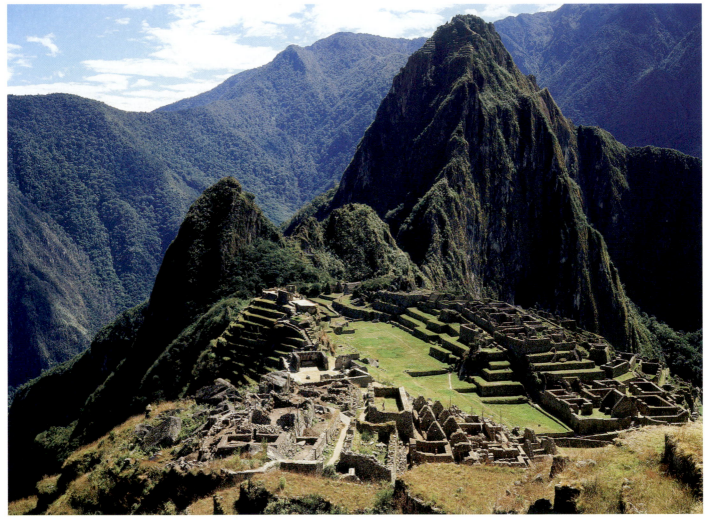

15–14 • MACHU PICCHU, PERU

Inca, 1450–1530 CE.

👁 **Watch** a video about Machu Picchu on **MyArtsLab**

actual Moche ritual performed by Moche lords and ladies. The occupant of a tomb at Sipán was buried with the regalia of a warrior priest. Among the riches accompanying him was a pair of exquisite gold-and-turquoise **EARSPOOL**s, each of which depicts three Moche warriors (**FIG. 15–13**). The central, frontal figure bursts into three dimensions, while his profile companions are presented in flat inlay. All three are adorned with tiny gold-and-turquoise earspools, simpler versions of the objects they themselves adorn. They wear gold-and-turquoise headdresses topped with delicate sheets of gold that resemble the crescent-shaped knives used in sacrifices. The central figure has a crescent-shaped nose ornament and carries a gold club and shield. A necklace of owl's-head beads strung with gold thread hangs around his shoulders—similar objects have been found in other tombs at Sipán.

The Inca Empire

At the beginning of the sixteenth century, the Inca Empire was one of the largest states in the world. It extended for more than 2,600 miles along western South America, encompassing most of present-day Ecuador, Peru, Bolivia, northern Chile, and part of Argentina. The Inca called their empire the Land of the Four Quarters. At its center was their capital, Cuzco, "the navel of the world," located high in the Andes Mountains. The early history of the Inca people is obscure, but in the fifteenth century, the Inca, like the Aztecs in the Basin of Mexico, began to expand, suddenly and rapidly. Through conquest, alliance, and intimidation, they subdued most of their vast domain by 1500. To hold this linguistically and ethnically diverse empire together, the Inca relied on religion, an efficient bureaucracy, and various forms of labor taxation, satisfied by a set amount of time spent performing tasks for the state. To speed transport and communication, the Inca built more than 23,000 miles of roads, along which storehouses and lodgings—more than 1,000 have been found—were spaced a day's journey apart. A relay system of runners could carry messages between Cuzco and the farthest reaches of the empire in about a week.

Inca builders created stonework structures of great refinement and durability (see "Inca Masonry," below). The most spectacular surviving example is **MACHU PICCHU** (**FIG. 15–14**). At 9,000 feet above sea level, the site straddles a ridge between two high peaks in the eastern slopes of the Andes. Machu Picchu, located near the eastern limits of the empire, was the ruler's summer home. Its temples and sacred stones imply it may also have had an important religious function.

The production of textiles is an ancient art in the Andes. Among the Incas, cloths of cotton and camelid fibers (llama, alpaca, and vicuña) were a primary form of wealth. Both men and women worked as weavers for the central government, paying their labor taxes by producing textiles. And cloth was deemed a fitting offering for the gods, so fine garments were draped around statues, and even burned as sacrificial offerings.

ELEMENTS OF ARCHITECTURE | Inca Masonry

Working with the simplest of tools—mainly heavy stone hammers—and using no mortar, Inca builders created superb stonework, built terraces for growing crops, and made structures both simple and elaborate, including roads that linked the empire together. At a few Inca sites, the stones were boulder-size—up to 27 feet tall.

At Machu Picchu (SEE FIG. 15–14), all buildings and terraces were made of granite, the hard stone occurring at the site. Commoners' houses and some walls were constructed of irregular stones that were carefully fitted together, while fine smoothed stones laid in even rows distinguished temples and palaces.

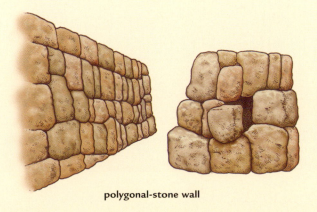

polygonal-stone wall

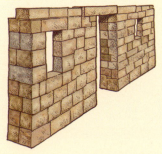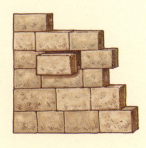

smooth-surfaced wall

👁 **Watch** an architectural simulation about Inca masonry on **MyArtsLab**

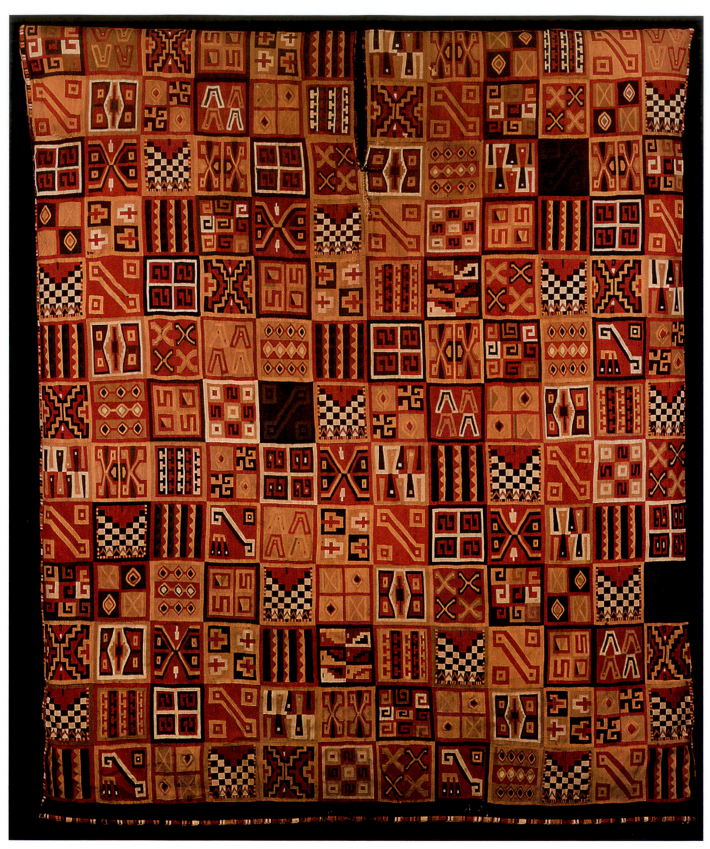

15–15 • TUNIC
From Peru. Inca, c. 1500 CE. Camelid fiber and cotton, 35⅞″ × 30″ (91 × 76.5 cm).
Dumbarton Oaks Research Library and Collection, Washington, D.C.

The patterns on garments carried symbolic messages, including indications of a person's ethnic identity and social rank. In the elaborate **TUNIC** in FIGURE 15–15, each square represents a miniature tunic with a different pattern and meaning. For example, the checkerboard pattern designated military officers and royal escorts, and the four-part motifs may refer to the empire as the Land of the Four Quarters. While we may not be sure what was meant in every case, patterns and colors seem to have been standardized like uniforms in order to convey information at a glance. Perhaps an exquisite tunic such as this, containing patterns associated with multiple ranks and statuses, was woven as a royal garment.

The Aftermath of the Spanish Conquest

What effect did the Spanish conquest have on the cultures of Mesoamerica and South America?

Hernán Cortés arrived off the eastern coast of Mexico from the Spanish colony in Cuba in 1519. He forged alliances with the Aztecs' enemies and, within two years, took control of Tenochtitlan. Over the next several years, Spanish forces subdued much of the rest of what is today Mexico and established it as a Spanish colony. In 1532, Francisco Pizarro, following Cortés's example, led an expedition to South America. He and his men seized the Inca ruler, Atahualpa, held him for a huge ransom in gold, and then treacherously strangled him. They marched on to Cuzco and seized it in 1533. The Spanish conquerors were obsessed with amassing gold and silver. They melted down whatever they could find to enrich themselves and the royal coffers of Spain, destroying in the process much of the art of the indigenous cultures.

Native American populations in Mexico and Peru declined sharply after the conquest because of the exploitative policies of the conquerors and the ravages of smallpox and other European diseases, against which the indigenous people had no immunity. This demographic collapse meant that the population of the Americas declined by as much as 90 percent in the century after contact with Europe. European missionaries suppressed local beliefs and practices and worked to spread Christianity throughout the Americas. Although increasing numbers of Europeans began to settle and dominate the land, the production of art did not end with the Spanish conquest. Traditional media, including fine weaving, continue to this day, transforming and remaining vital as indigenous people adjust to a changing world.

North America

How did the style and function of art and architecture differ among cultures across North America?

In America north of Mexico, from the upper reaches of Canada and Alaska to the southern tip of Florida, there existed many different peoples with widely varying cultures. In previous times their artworks—often small, portable, fragile, and impermanent—were collected as anthropological artifacts or curiosities rather than works of art. As a consequence, anthropology and natural history museums often have large collections of indigenous art. That this attitude has changed is signaled by the establishment of such prestigious institutions as the National Museum of the American Indian in Washington, D.C. And works of an increasing number of young Native American artists can be seen alongside Euro-American artists in mainstream art galleries.

Early Cultures of the East

The early history of the indigenous cultures of eastern North America is only beginning to be understood. Archaeologists have shown that as early as 3400–3000 BCE people lived in communities formed around a central earthen mound—a platform that probably supported a chief's house, the shrines of ancestors, and a place for a sacred fire, tended by special guardians.

In 1895, excavators working in submerged mud and shell mounds off Key Marco on the west coast of Florida made a remarkable discovery from what has been named the Florida Glades culture. Painted wooden animal and bird heads, a human mask, and the figure of a kneeling cat-human were found in circumstances that suggested a ruined shrine. Recently, carbon-14 dating of these items has confirmed a date of about 1000 CE. The sculptors show a remarkable power of observation in reproducing the creatures they saw around them, such as the **PELICAN** in FIGURE 15–16. The surviving head, neck, and breast are made of carved wood painted black, white, and gray (other pieces also included pink and blue). The bird's outstretched wings were discovered nearby, but the wood shrank and disintegrated as it dried. Carved wooden wolf and deer

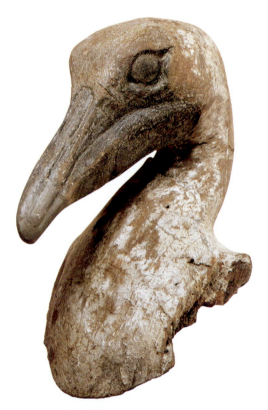

15–16 • PELICAN FIGUREHEAD
From Key Marco, Florida. Glades culture, c. 1000 CE. Wood and paint, 4⅜″ × 2⅜″ × 3⅛″ (11.2 × 6 × 8 cm). The University of Pennsylvania Museum of Archaeology and Anthropology, Philadelphia.

15–17 • BEAVER EFFIGY PLATFORM PIPE

From Bedford Mound, Pike County, Illinois. Hopewell culture, c. 100–400 CE. Pipestone, river pearls, and bone, 4⁹⁄₁₆″ × 1⁷⁄₈″ × 2″ (11.6 × 4.76 × 5.1 cm). Gilcrease Museum, Tulsa, Oklahoma.

Pipes like this may have been used for smoking hallucinatory plants, perhaps during rituals involving the animal carved on the pipe bowl. Could the beaver's shining pearl eyes suggest an association with the spirit world?

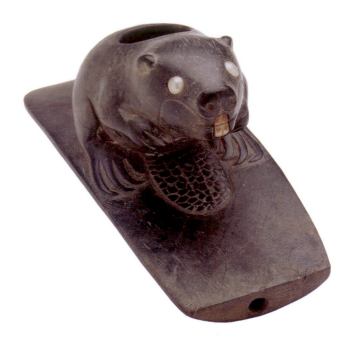

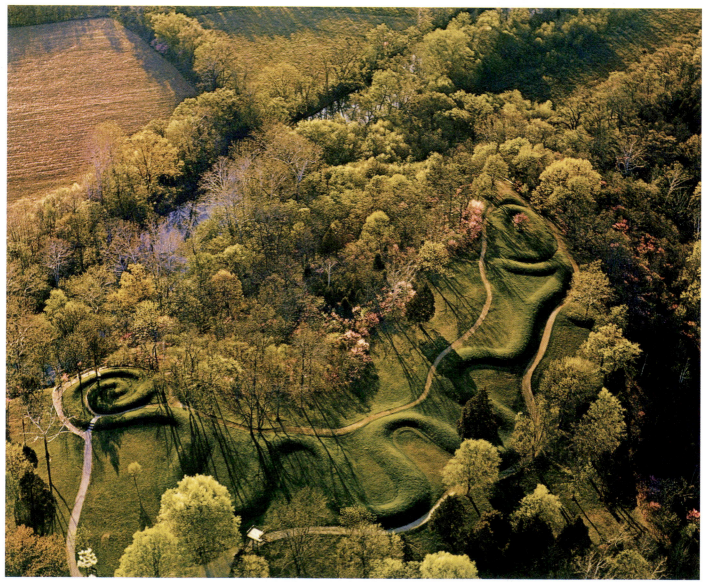

15–18 • GREAT SERPENT MOUND

Adams County, Ohio. c. 1070 CE. Length 1,254′ (328.2 m).

heads were also found. Archaeologists think the heads might have been attached to ceremonial furniture or posts. Some see evidence here of a bird and animal cult or perhaps the use of birds and animals as clan symbols.

In the fertile lands near the Ohio, Illinois, Mississippi, and Missouri rivers, the people of the Adena, Hopewell, and Mississippian cultures cultivated maize (corn) and other crops. Sometime before 1000 BCE, they began building monumental earthworks and burying their leaders with valuable grave goods. Objects discovered in these burials show that the people of the Mississippi and Ohio valleys traded widely with other regions. For example, burials of the mound-building Adena (c. 1100 BCE–200 CE) and Hopewell (c. 100 BCE–550 CE) cultures contained objects made with copper imported from the Upper Peninsula of present-day Michigan and silhouettes cut in sheets of mica from the Appalachian Mountains.

The Hopewell people also made pipes of fine-grain pipestone carved with lifelike representations of forest animals and birds, sometimes with inlaid eyes and teeth of freshwater pearls and bone. A pearl-eyed beaver crouching on a platform forms the bowl of a **PIPE** found in present-day Illinois (**FIG. 15–17**). As in a modern pipe, the bowl—a hole in the beaver's back—could be filled with tobacco or other dried leaves, the leaves lighted, and smoke drawn through the hole in the stem. Using the pipe this way, the smoker would be face to face with the beaver, whose shining pearl eyes may suggest an association with the spirit world.

The people of the Mississippian culture (700–1550 CE) continued the mound-building tradition of the Adena, Hopewell, and other early eastern cultures. One of the most impressive Mississippian-period earthworks is the **GREAT SERPENT MOUND**, nearly a quarter of a mile long, in present-day Ohio (**FIG. 15–18**). Carbon-14 dating of wood charcoal samples from the mound suggests that the earthwork was built about 1070 CE. There have been many interpretations of the twisting snake form, especially the "head" at the highest point, an oval enclosure that some see as the serpent opening its jaws to swallow a huge egg. Perhaps the people who built it were responding to the spectacular astronomical display of Halley's comet in 1066.

Mississippian peoples built a major urban center known as **CAHOKIA** near the juncture of the Illinois, Missouri, and Mississippi rivers (now East St. Louis, Illinois). Although the site may have been inhabited as early as about 3000 BCE, most monumental construction at Cahokia took place between about 1000 and 1300 CE. At its height, the city had a population of about 15,000 people, with another 10,000 in the surrounding countryside (**FIG. 15–19**).

The most prominent feature of Cahokia is an enormous earth mound called Monk's Mound, covering 15 acres and originally 100 feet high. A small, rounded platform on its summit initially supported a wooden fence and a rectangular building, aligned with the sun at the equinox. Smaller rectangular and conical mounds in front of the principal mound surrounded a large, roughly rectangular plaza. The city's entire ceremonial center was protected by a stockade, or fence, of upright wooden posts—a sign of increasing insecurity or warfare. In all, the walled enclosure contained more than 500 mounds, platforms, wooden enclosures, and houses. The various earthworks functioned as tombs and as bases for palaces and temples, and also to make astronomical observations.

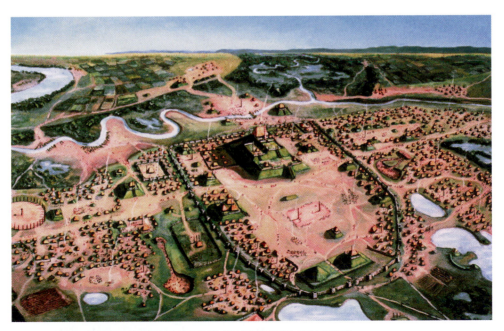

15–19 • RECONSTRUCTION DRAWING OF CENTRAL CAHOKIA AS IT WOULD HAVE APPEARED AROUND 1150 CE
Collinsville, Illinois. Mississippian culture, c. 1000–1350 CE. Earth mounds and wooden structures; east–west length approx. 3 miles (4.82 km), north–south length approx. 2¼ miles (3.62 km); base of great mound, 1,037′ × 790′ (316 × 240.8 m), height approx. 100′ (30.5 m).
Painting by William R. Iseminger. Courtesy of Cahokia Mounds State Historic Site.

The Southwest

Farming cultures were slower to arise in the arid Southwest, which became home to three major early cultures. The Hohokam culture, centered in the central and southern parts of present-day Arizona, emerged around 200 BCE and endured until sometime after 1300 CE. The Hohokam built large-scale irrigation systems, multistoried residences, and ballcourts that demonstrate ties with Mesoamerica.

The Mimbres/Mogollon culture flourished from about 200 to 1250 CE in the mountains of south- and west-central New Mexico and east-central Arizona. The potters of the Mimbres River valley in southwest New Mexico produced deep bowls painted with lively, imaginative, and sometimes complex scenes of humans and animals (FIG. 15–20). Much of our knowledge of this ceramic tradition is based on examples excavated in burials under the floors of Mimbres dwellings, where food bowls—most of them intentionally punctured before burial—were inverted and placed over the head of the deceased. Some scholars believe these perforated bowls could have represented the dome of the sky and embodied ideas about the transport of the dead from the earth into the spirit world.

The Ancestral Puebloans (formerly called Anasazi), emerged somewhat later, around 550 CE, in the Four Corners region where Colorado, Utah, Arizona, and New Mexico meet. They also found artistic expression in the production of painted pottery. They adopted the irrigation technology of the Hohokam to produce food for settled communities, and began building elaborate, multistoried, apartment-like "great houses" with many rooms for specialized purposes, including communal food storage and rituals.

The largest known great house is **PUEBLO BONITO IN CHACO CANYON**, New Mexico, which was built between about 830 and 1250 CE (FIG. 15–21). This remarkable, D-shaped structure, one of nine great houses in Chaco Canyon, covered more than 3 acres and eventually contained over 800 rooms in four or five stories and 30 **kivas** (subterranean circular rooms used as ceremonial centers), arranged in a D shape. The sandstone masonry walls on the ground floor were 4 feet thick, and trunks of ponderosa pines transported from 50 miles away were used for roof beams. Amazingly, all aspects of construction, including quarrying, timber cutting, and transport, were done without draft animals, wheeled vehicles, or metal tools. The size of this complex has led some to speculate that it may have provided temporary housing for people on pilgrimage to a sacred site, especially since it sits at the center of a network of wide, straight roads, discovered through aerial photography.

The village-dwelling Pueblo people of the contemporary Southwest—descendants of the earlier cultures in the area—still make fine ceramics that are traditional in both technique and design. One of the best-known twentieth-century Pueblo

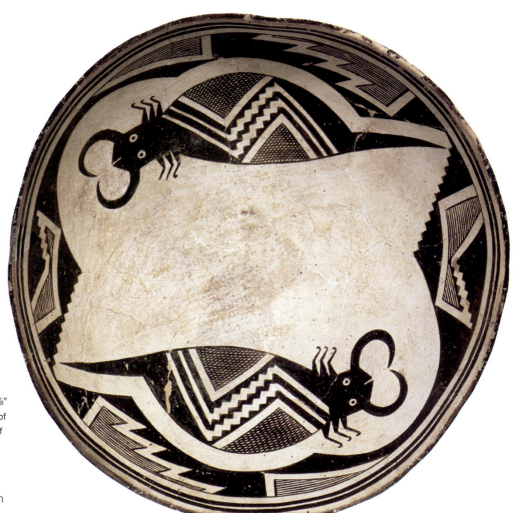

15–20 • BOWL WITH SCORPIONS

From Swarts Ruin, southwest New Mexico. Mimbres culture, c. 1000–1150 CE. Earthenware, white slip, and black paint, height 4¾″ (12 cm), diameter 11⅝″ (29.5 cm). © President and Fellows of Harvard College, Peabody Museum of Archaeology and Ethnology, Harvard University, PM# 24–15–10/94585.

View the Closer Look for the Bowl with Scorpions on **MyArtsLab**

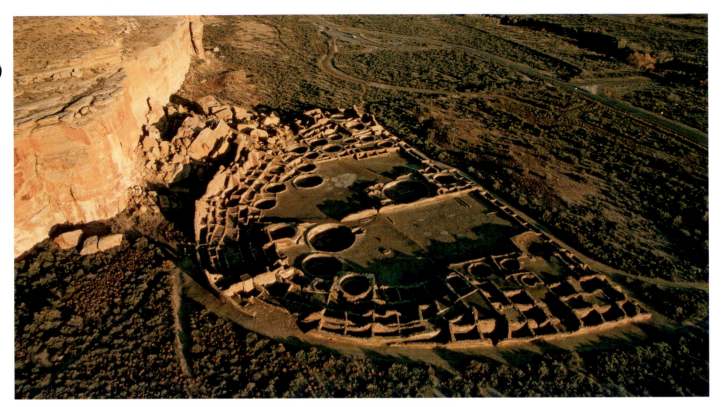

15-21 • PUEBLO BONITO, CHACO CANYON
New Mexico. Ancestral Puebloan culture, 830–1250 CE.

potters was Maria Montoya Martinez (1887–1980) of the San Ildefonso Pueblo in New Mexico. Inspired by prehistoric pottery that was unearthed at nearby archaeological excavations and the then-fashionable Euro-American Art Deco, she and her husband, Julian Martinez (1885–1943), developed a distinctive **BLACKWARE** ceramic style, notable for its elegant forms and subtle textures (**FIG. 15–22**). Maria made pots covered with slip that was then burnished, and Julian, using additional slip, painted the designs. After firing, the burnished ground became a lustrous black while the slip painting retained its matte surface.

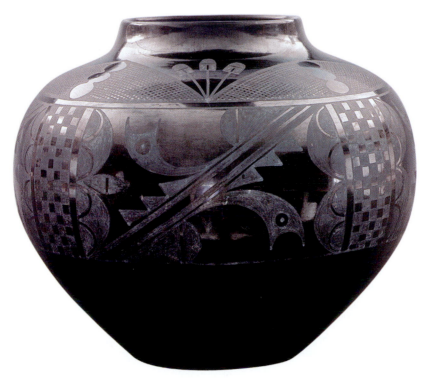

15-22 • Maria Montoya Martinez and Julian Martinez BLACKWARE STORAGE JAR
From San Ildefonso Pueblo, New Mexico. c. 1942 CE. Coil-built ceramic with black slip, height 18¾″ (47.6 cm), diameter 22½″ (57.1 cm). Museum of Indian Arts and Culture/Laboratory of Anthropology, Museum of New Mexico, Santa Fe.

Basketry involves weaving reeds, grasses, or other materials to form containers. The three principal basket-making techniques are **coiling** (sewing together a spiraling foundation of rods with some other material); **twining** (sewing together a vertical warp of rods); and **plaiting** (weaving strips over and under each other). In North America the earliest evidence of basketwork, found in Danger Cave, Utah, dates to as early as 8400 BCE. Over the subsequent centuries basket-makers developed their craft into an art form that combined utility with great beauty.

The coiled basket shown here (**FIG. 15–23**) was made by a Pomo woman in California. According to Pomo legend, the earth was dark until their ancestral hero stole the sun and brought it to earth in a basket. He hung the basket first just over the horizon, but, dissatisfied with the light it gave, he kept suspending it in different places across the dome of the sky. He repeats this process every day, which is why the sun moves across the sky from east to west. In the Pomo basket, the structure of coiled willow and bracken fern root produces a spiral surface into which the artist worked sparkling pieces of clamshell, trade beads, and the soft tufts of woodpecker and quail feathers. Such exquisite baskets were treasured possessions, often cremated with their owners at death.

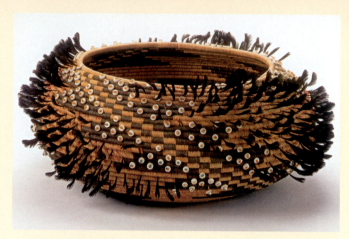

15–23 • FEATHERED BOWL
Pomo, c. 1877 CE. Willow, bulrush, fern, feathers, shells, glass beads, height 6″ (15.2 cm), diameter 13″ (33 cm). Philbrook Museum, Tulsa, Oklahoma. Gift of Clark Field (1948.39.37).

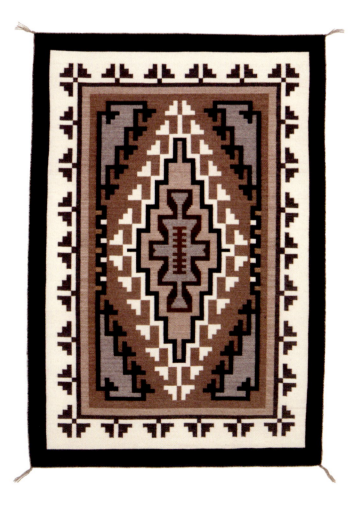

Sometime between 1100 and 1500 CE, the Navajo migrated to the Southwest and developed a semisedentary way of life based on agriculture and (after the introduction of sheep by the Spaniards) shepherding. Using the wool of their sheep, Navajo women became renowned for their skill as weavers, both among fellow Native Americans and also Euro-American collectors. According to Navajo mythology, the universe itself is a weaving, its fibers spun by Spider Woman out of sacred cosmic materials. Spider Woman taught the art of weaving to Changing Woman (a Mother Earth figure), and she in turn taught it to Navajo women, who continue to keep this art vital, seeing its continuation as a sacred act. Earliest Navajo blankets had simple horizontal stripes, but over time, weavers have introduced more intricate patterns. The **TAPESTRY WEAVING** in **FIGURE 15–24**—designed in the Two Gray Hills style that developed during the early twentieth century around a trading post of that name in northwest New Mexico—was created in 2003 by Julia Jumbo (1928–2007). This artist, who learned her art as a child and used her weaving to support her family, is renowned for the clarity of her traditional designs and the technical perfection of her fine weave. She has restricted herself here to the natural colors of the handspun wool.

15–24 • Julia Jumbo TWO GRAY HILLS TAPESTRY WEAVING
Navajo, 2003 CE. Handspun wool, 36″ × 24½″ (91.2 × 62.1 cm). Wheelwright Museum of the American Indian, Santa Fe, New Mexico.

The Eastern Woodlands and the Great Plains

When European settlement began in earnest in North America around the late 1500s to early 1600s CE, forests stretched from Hudson Bay to the Gulf of Mexico and from the Atlantic coast to the Mississippi River and Missouri River watersheds. Between this Eastern Woodlands region and the Rocky Mountains to the west lay an area of prairie grasslands now known as the Great Plains.

In the Eastern Woodlands, most Native American peoples lived in stable villages and supported themselves by a combination of hunting and agriculture. They used waterproof birchbark to construct their homes and to make the watercraft known as the canoe. As European settlers on the eastern seaboard began to turn forests into farms, they put increasing pressure on the Eastern Woodlands peoples, seizing their lands and forcing them westward. The resulting interaction of Eastern Woodlands artists with one another and with Plains artists led to the emergence of a Prairie style among numerous groups.

Woodlands art focused on personal adornment—tattoos, body paint, elaborate dress—and fragile arts such as **quillwork**. Quillwork involved dyeing porcupine and bird quills with a variety of natural dyes, soaking the quills to soften them, and then working them into rectilinear, ornamental surface patterns on deerskin clothing and on birchbark items like baskets and boxes. A Sioux legend recounts how a mythical ancestor, Doublewoman ("double" because she was both beautiful and ugly, benign and dangerous), appeared to a woman in a dream and taught her the art of quillwork. As the legend suggests, quillwork, like basketry (see "Basketry," p. 422), was a woman's art form. The Sioux **BABY CARRIER** in FIGURE 15–25 is richly decorated with quillwork symbols of protection and well-being, including bands of antelopes in profile and thunderbirds flying with their heads turned and tails outspread. The thunderbird was an especially beneficent symbol, thought to be capable of protecting against both human and supernatural adversaries.

On the Great Plains, two differing ways of life developed, one traditional, agricultural, and sedentary, and the other (relatively recent and short-lived, 1700–1870) nomadic and dependent on the region's great migrating herds of buffalo for food, clothing, and shelter. Horses—introduced by Spanish explorers in the sixteenth century—and later firearms, made buffalo hunting vastly more efficient, increasing the appeal of the nomadic way of life. The nomadic Plains peoples developed a light, portable dwelling known as a **tipi** (formerly spelled "teepee") (FIG. 15–26), which was sturdily constructed to withstand the wind, dust, and storms of the prairies. Buffalo hides (later, canvas) covered a framework of poles to form an almost conical structure that leaned slightly in the direction of the prevailing wind. The flap-covered door and smoke hole (the opening at the top above the central hearth) usually faced away from the wind. Designed and built by women, the tipis required 20 to 40 buffalo hides, depending on their size. An inner lining covered the lower part of the walls and part of the floor to protect the

15–25 • BABY CARRIER
From Upper Missouri River area. Eastern Sioux, 19th century CE. Wooden board, buckskin, and porcupine quill, length 31″ (78.7 cm). Department of Anthropology, Smithsonian Institution. CAT#73311/NEG 77-13301.

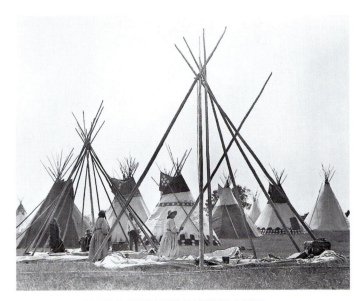

15–26 • BLACKFOOT WOMEN RAISING A TIPI
Photographed c. 1900 CE. Montana Historical Society, Helena.

When packed to be dragged by a horse, the tipi served as a platform for transporting other possessions as well. Tipis were the property and responsibility of women. Blackfoot women could set up their tipis in less than an hour.

occupants from drafts. Women painted, embroidered, quilled, and beaded tipi linings, backrests, clothing, and equipment. Plains men recorded their exploits in symbolic and narrative form in paintings on tipi linings and covers and also on buffalo-hide robes.

The earliest known painted buffalo-hide robe illustrates a battle fought in 1797 by the Mandan (of what is now North Dakota) and their allies against the Sioux (**FIG. 15–27**). The painter, trying to capture the full extent of a conflict in which five nations took part, shows a party of warriors in 22 separate episodes. The party is led by a man with a pipe and an elaborate eagle-feather headdress, and the warriors are armed with bows and arrows, lances, clubs, and flintlock rifles. The figures stand out clearly against the light-colored background of the buffalo hide. The painter pressed lines into the hide, then filled in with black, red, green, yellow, and brown pigments. A strip of colored porcupine quills runs down the "spine." The robe would have been worn draped over the shoulders of the powerful warrior whose deeds it commemorates. As he moved, the painted horses and warriors would appear to come alive, transforming him into a living representation of his exploits.

Life and art on the Plains changed abruptly in 1869, when the Euro-Americans finished the transcontinental railway, bringing increasing numbers of settlers into Native American lands. By 1890 these new settlers had killed off most of the buffalo while farmers and ranchers took over more and more of the land, thereby destroying the Native American way of life on the Great Plains.

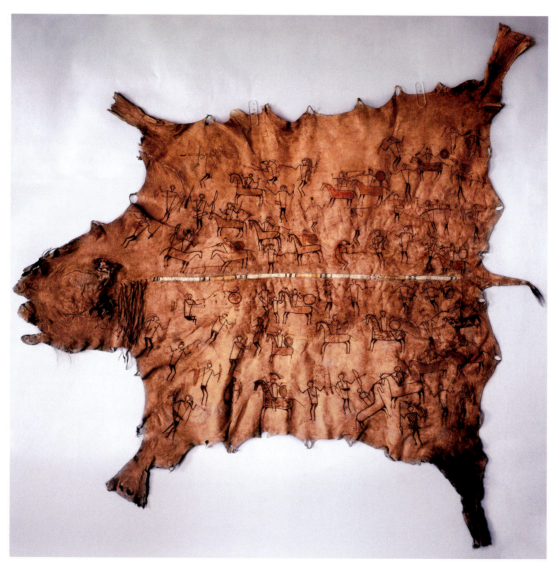

15–27 • BATTLE SCENE, HIDE PAINTING

From North Dakota. Mandan, 1797–1800 CE. Tanned buffalo hide, dyed porcupine quills, and black, red, green, yellow, and brown pigment, 7′ 10″ × 8′ 6″ (2.44 × 2.65 m). © President and Fellows of Harvard College, Peabody Museum of Archaeology and Ethnology, Harvard University, PM# 99–12–10/53121.

This painted hide robe was collected in 1804 by Meriwether Lewis and William Clark on their 1804–1806 expedition into western lands acquired by the United States in the Louisiana Purchase. It is the earliest documented example of Plains painting. Lewis and Clark presented it to President Thomas Jefferson, who displayed the robe in the entrance hall of Monticello, his home in Virginia (SEE FIG. 17–18).

Hamatsa Masks

During the harsh winter season, when spirits are thought to be most powerful, many Northwest Coast peoples seek spiritual renewal through their ancient rituals—including the potlatch (ceremonial gift-giving) and the initiation of new members into the prestigious Hamatsa society. With snapping beaks and cries of "*Hap! Hap! Hap!*" ("Eat! Eat! Eat!"), Hamatsa, the people-eating spirit of the north, and his three assistants—horrible monster birds—begin their wild ritual dance (**FIG. 15–28**). The dancing birds threaten and even attack the Kwakwaka'wakw (Kwakiutl) people who gather for the Winter Ceremony. At this time, youths are captured, taught the Hamatsa lore, and then—in a spectacular theater-dance performance—are "tamed" and brought back into civilized life.

Then, the masked bird dancers appear—first Raven-of-the-North-End-of-the-World, then Crooked-Beak-of-the-End-of-the-World, and finally the untranslatable Huxshukw, who cracks open skulls with its beak and eats the brains of its victims. Snapping their beaks, these masters of illusion enter the room backward, their masks pointed up as though the birds were looking skyward. They move slowly counterclockwise around the floor. At each change in the music they crouch, snap their beaks, and let out wild cries of "*Hap! Hap! Hap!*" Essential to the ritual dances are the huge carved and painted wooden masks, operated by strings worked by the dancers. Among the finest masks are those by Willie Seaweed (1873–1967), a Kwakwaka'wakw chief (**FIG. 15–29**). Their brilliant colors and exuberantly decorative carving style determined the direction of twentieth-century Kwakwaka'wakw sculpture.

The Canadian government, abetted by missionaries, outlawed the Winter Ceremony and potlatches in 1885, claiming the event was injurious to health, encouraged prostitution, endangered children's education, damaged the economy, and was cannibalistic. But the Kwakwaka'wakw refused to give up their "oldest and best" festival, one that spoke powerfully to them in many ways, establishing social rank and playing an important role in arranging marriages. By 1936, the government and the missionaries, who called the Kwakwaka'wakw "incorrigible," gave up. But not until 1951 could the Kwakwaka'wakw people gather openly for Winter Ceremonies, including the initiation rites of the Hamatsa society.

The photographer Edward S. Curtis (1868–1952) devoted 30 years to documenting the lives of Native Americans and First Nations peoples. The 1914 photograph in FIGURE 15–28 shows participants in a film he made about the Kwakwaka'wakw. For the film, his assistant, Richard Hunt (a member of the Kwakwaka'wakw), borrowed family heirlooms and commissioned many new pieces from the finest Kwakwaka'wakw artists. Most of the pieces are now in museum collections. The photograph shows carved and painted posts, masked dancers (including those representing people-eating birds), a chief at the left (holding a speaker's staff and wearing a cedar neck ring), and spectators at the far right.

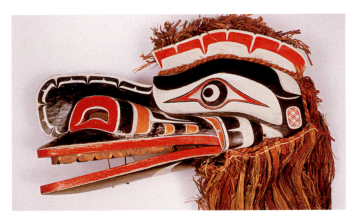

15-29 • Attributed to Willie Seaweed
KWAKWAKA'WAKW (KWAKIUTL) BIRD MASK
From Alert Bay, Vancouver Island, Canada. Prior to 1951 CE. Cedar wood, cedar bark, feathers, and fiber, 10″ × 72″ × 15″ (25.4 × 183 × 38.1 cm). Collection of UBC Museum of Anthropology, Vancouver, Canada.

The name "Seaweed" is an Anglicization of the Kwakwaka'wakw name Siwid, meaning "Paddling Canoe," "Recipient of Paddling," or "Paddled to"—referring to a great chief whose potlatch guests paddled from afar. Willie Seaweed was not only the chief of his clan, but a great orator, singer, and tribal historian who kept the tradition of the potlatch alive during years of government repression.

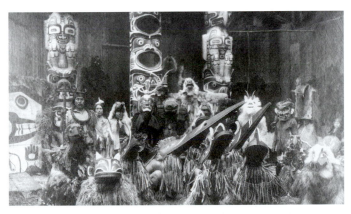

15-28 • Edward S. Curtis
KWAKWAKA'WAKW (KWAKIUTL) HAMATSA DANCERS
Canada. Photographed in 1914 CE.

The Northwest Coast

Before the arrival of European explorers, the Native American peoples composing the First Nations of the Northwest Coast—among them the Tlingit (of southern Alaska), the Haida (of southern Alaska and the Queen Charlotte Islands), and the Kwakwaka'wakw (formerly spelled Kwakiutl, of the central Canadian coast and Alert Bay)—lived on the Pacific coast of North America from what is today southern Alaska to as far south as what is today northern California. Their major food source was salmon from the region's many rivers. Harvested and dried, the fish could sustain large populations throughout the year.

People lived in extended family groups or clans in large, elaborately decorated communal houses made of massive timbers and thick planks. Clans claimed descent from a mythic animal or animal-human ancestor. Chiefs, who were in the most direct line of descent from the ancestor, validated their status and garnered prestige for themselves and their families by holding ritual feasts known as potlatches during which they gave valuable gifts to their guests. Shamans, both male and female, mediated between the human and spirit worlds.

The participants who danced in the Winter Ceremony of the Kwakwaka'wakw wore striking costumes and gigantic carved and painted masks (see "Hamatsa Masks," p. 425). Among the most elaborate masks were those used by the elite Hamatsa society in their dances. Transformed into supernatural creatures, the dancers searched for "victims." By using strings inside the masks, they could snap the beaks open and shut with spectacular effect. Even when seen outside the context of performance, the bold forms and color schemes of these masks retain power and meaning that activate the viewer's imagination.

Textile blankets produced collaboratively by the men and women of the Chilkat Tlingit (on the southeast coast of Alaska and adjacent British Columbia) had great prestige among Northwest Coast peoples (FIG. 15–30). Men drew the patterns on boards, and women wove them into the BLANKETs, using shredded cedar bark and mountain-goat wool. The weavers did not use looms; instead, they hung cedar warp threads from a rod and twined colored goat wool back and forth through them to make the pattern, which in this technique can be defined by curving lines. The ends of the warp form the fringe at the bottom of the blanket.

The popular design used here is known as the diving whale—the central panel shows the downward facing whale(s), while the panels to the sides have been interpreted as this animal's body or seated ravens seen in profile. Precise identifications and meanings have not been established. Characteristic of Northwest painting and weaving, the images are composed of two basic elements: the ovoid, a slightly bent rectangle with rounded corners, and the formline, a continuous, shape-defining line. Here, subtly swelling black formlines define gently curving ovoids and C shapes. When the blanket was worn, its two-dimensional shapes would have become three-dimensional, with the dramatic central figure curving over the wearer's back and the intricate side panels crossing over his shoulders and chest. As with many works by native North American makers, when we encounter this blanket—or the mask in FIGURE 15–29, the hide painting in FIGURE 15–27, even the baby carrier in FIGURE 15–25—isolated in a museum case as "art," it loses the vivacity it would have had within social life or communal activity. These works were created for a dynamic display of ritual and performance, not for detached observation, aesthetic contemplation, or art-historical analysis.

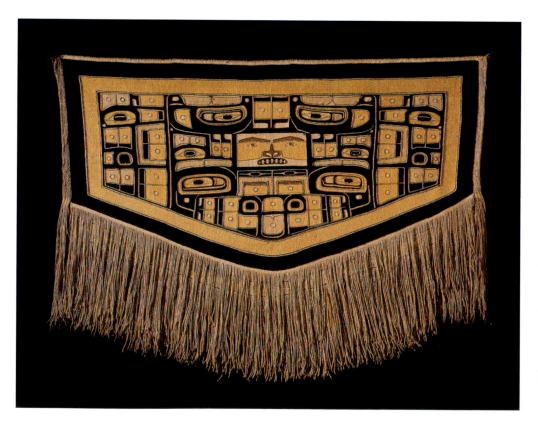

15–30 • CHILKAT BLANKET
From southeast Alaska. Tlingit people, c. 1850 CE. Mountain-goat wool, yellow cedar bark, linen thread, approx. 51″ × 72″ (1.3 × 1.83 m). Thaw Collection, Fenimore Art Museum, Cooperstown, New York.

View the Closer Look for the Chilkat Blanket on **MyArtsLab**

LOOKING BACK ◄

Although works of visual and symbolic power were central to the lives of indigenous peoples in the Americas, they were not considered "works of art." We have given their material culture that label. In Mesoamerica, monumental sculpture covered buildings, where gods and goddesses loomed over the devotees. In North American river valleys people shaped the earth itself into huge serpents, bears, and eagles, while in the Nazca Plain in Peru images of birds and insects were engraved into the earth's surface. Native American art could be small and fragile, as well as large and enduring. Inca textiles have been preserved in the desert climate, while in North America only relatively modern basketry, quillwork, weavings, and hide paintings remain. In some instances, only ceramics survive.

Valued first as anthropological "curiosities" in natural history museums, and subsequently produced on a large scale as tourist souvenirs or "exotic" decorative objects, the arts of the indigenous peoples of the Americas have now been recognized for their distinctive visual and symbolic power, just as contemporary Native American artists are claiming their proper place within the mainstream of an international art world.

THINK ABOUT IT

15.1 Explain the original function of an ancient building from Mesoamerica by situating it within its broader sociocultural context.

15.2 Distinguish the characteristic styles and techniques associated with two different Peruvian cultures, focusing your discussion on one specific work from each.

15.3 Discuss two works of art within this chapter that exhibit influence from European culture. How have the indigenous artists adapted the foreign forms or materials?

15.4 Choose a native North American work that was made to be used in social life or ritual. Explain the difference between its form and meaning while in use and while observed in the context of a museum installation.

| CROSSCURRENTS |

These two portraits were made for the tombs of the two men they represent. What characteristics of these rulers are emphasized in these likenesses? How do these works, and the way they were used, embody the priorities and politics of the two cultures that produced them?

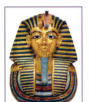 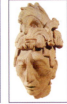

FIG. 3–1   FIG. 15–6

☑ **Study** and **Review** on **MyArtsLab**

IN PERSPECTIVE

1200 BCE

● Olmec Culture in Mexico
c. 1500 BCE–200 CE

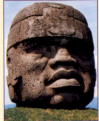

Olmec Colossal Head
c. 1200–900 BCE

500

● Maya Culture in Southern Mesoamerica c. 250 BCE–1521 CE
● Hohokam Culture in Southwest North America c. 200 BCE–1300 CE
● Moche Culture in Peru c. 100 BCE–700 CE
● Hopewell Culture in Central North America c. 100 BCE–550 CE
● Teotihuacan Culture in Mexico c. 1–750 CE

1 CE

● Mimbres/Mogollon Culture c. 200–1250 CE

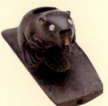

Hopewell Platform Pipe
c. 100–400 CE

500

● Ancestral Puebloan Culture in Southwest North America c. 550–1250 CE
● Diquis in Costa Rica/Mississippian Culture of Central North America 700–1550 CE

1000

● Navajo People Migrate to Southwest North America 1100–1500 CE

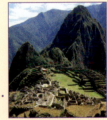

Machu Picchu, Peru
1450–1530 CE

● Aztec Empire in Mexico at Its Height c. 1400–1519 CE
● Inca Empire in the Andes at Its Height 1438–1532 CE

1500

● Cortés Conquers Aztecs 1519–1524 CE
● Pizarro Conquers Incas 1532 CE

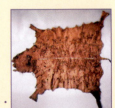

Battle Scene, Hide Painting
1797–1800 CE

1700

● Plains Nomadic Culture in North America 1700–1870 CE

● Louisiana Purchase 1803 CE

● Transcontinental United States Railroad Completed 1869 CE
● Kwakwaka'wakw Winter Ceremony Outlawed 1885–1951 CE

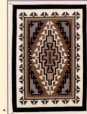

2000

● Opening of the National Museum of the American Indian in Washington, D.C. 2004 CE

Navajo Tapestry Weaving
2003 CE

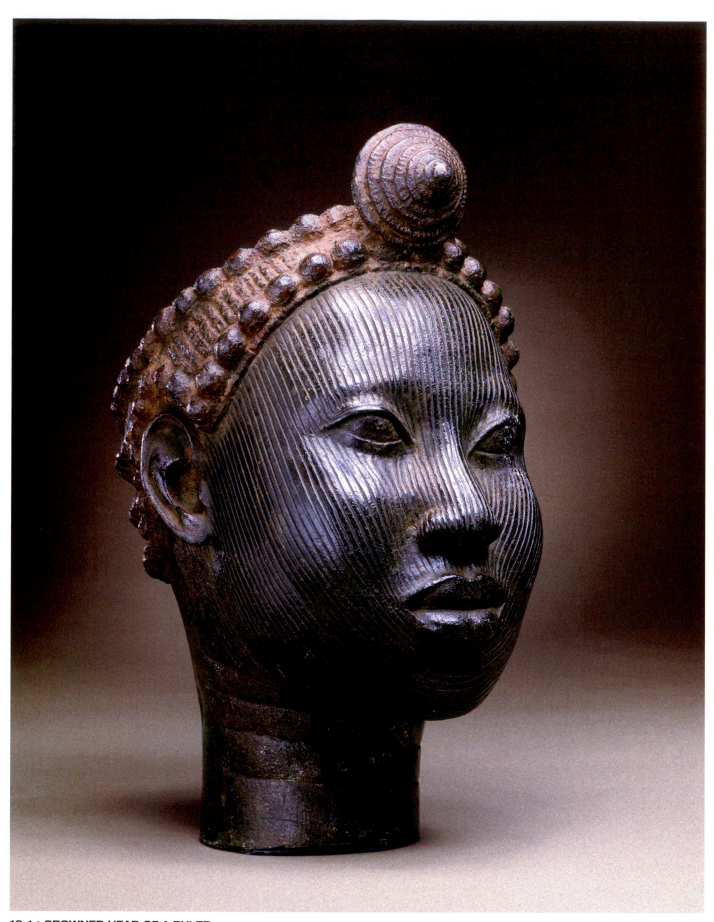

16–1 • CROWNED HEAD OF A RULER
From Ife. Yoruba culture, 12th–15th century CE. Bronze, height 9⁷⁄₁₆″ (24 cm). Private Collection.

AFRICAN ART

16.1 Discuss the relationship of early art and architecture in Africa to the series of cultures that produced it.

16.2 Explain the connection between later African art and the major transitions of human life and death.

16.3 Recognize the ways that later African art relates to beliefs about a spirit world.

16.4 Identify the link between later African art and the power of the political leaders who often commissioned it.

LOOKING FORWARD ▶

The Yoruba people of southwestern Nigeria regard the city of Ife (also known as Ile-Ife) as the "navel of the world," the site of creation, the place where Ife's first ruler—the *oni* (king) Oduduwa—came down from heaven to create Earth and then to populate it. By the eleventh century CE, Ife was a lively metropolis, and even today, every Yoruba city claims "descent" from it. Ife was, and remains, the sacred city of the Yoruba people.

A sculptural tradition of casting lifelike human heads, using the lost-wax process, began in Ife about 1050 CE and flourished over four centuries. Although the ancestral line of the Ife *oni* has continued unbroken since that time, knowledge of the precise purpose of these arresting works has been lost. The cast-bronze head in FIGURE **16–1** demonstrates the extraordinary artistry that produced them. The modeling of the flesh—covered with thin, parallel **scarification** patterns (decorations made by scarring)—is remarkably sensitive, especially the subtle transitions around the nose and mouth. The full, delicate lips and expressive eyes bulge organically outward in ways that are strikingly similar to the faces of some modern Yoruba, underlining its strong sense of an individual likeness.

The head was cast with a crown; its size and delicate features suggest it may represent a female *oni*. Although its precise use is not known, similar life-size heads have large holes in the neck, suggesting they may have been attached to wooden

figures, and mannequins with naturalistic facial features have been documented at memorial services for deceased individuals among contemporary Yoruba peoples. This Ife mannequin would have been dressed in the *oni*'s robes. But the head could also have been used to display a crown during annual purification and renewal rites.

The question of whether such Ife heads are true portraits has been debated, and their lifelikeness certainly gives an impression that they could be. They all, however, seem to represent individuals of the same age and embody a similar concept of physical perfection, suggesting they are idealized images representing both physical beauty and moral character. As we have seen in the portraits of other cultures, however, idealization does not preclude the possibility that these faces describe the distinguishing characteristics of a specific human being's individual face.

The superb naturalism of Ife sculpture contradicted everything Europeans thought they knew about African art. The German scholar, Leo Frobenius, who "discovered" Ife sculpture in 1910 suggested that it was created not by Africans but by survivors from the legendary lost island of Atlantis. Later, there was speculation that influence from ancient Greece or Renaissance Europe must have reached Ife. Scientific study, however, finally put such prejudiced proposals to rest.

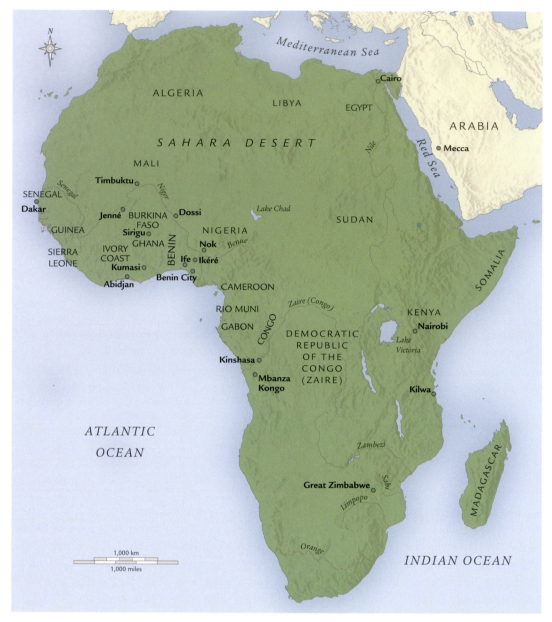

MAP 16–1 • AFRICA

The vast continent of Africa is home to a variety of geographical and climatic habitats—broad prairies, mountains, lush forests, deserts—which supported innumerable cultures.

Africa is a continent of enormous diversity (MAP 16–1). Geographically, it ranges from vast deserts to tropical rainforests, from flat grasslands to spectacular mountains and dramatic rift valleys. Human diversity is equally impressive. More than 1,000 major languages have been identified, representing a vast variety of cultures, each with its own history, customs, and art forms. Africa is the site of one of the great ancient civilizations, that of Egypt (see Chapter 3), and North Africa later contributed to the development of Islamic art and culture (see Chapter 8).

Early African Art

How does the early art and architecture of Africa express the series of cultures that produced it?

The history of African art begins in the Paleolithic era. Like prehistoric people around the world, early Africans painted and inscribed an abundance of images on the walls of caves and rock shelters. The mountains of the central Sahara have especially fascinating examples of rock art, with the earliest images dating from at least 8000 BCE. At that time, the Sahara was a great grassy plain, perhaps much like the game-park areas of present-day East Africa. Vivid images of hippopotamuses, elephants, giraffes, antelope, and other animals incised into rock surfaces testify to the abundant wildlife that roamed the region.

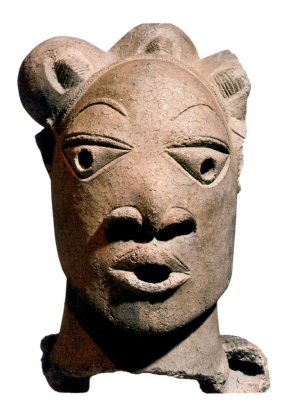

16–2 • HEAD
From Nigeria. Nok culture, c. 500 BCE–200 CE. Terra cotta, height 14 3/16″ (36 cm). National Museum, Lagos, Nigeria.

By 4000 BCE, hunting had given way to herding as the Saharan climate became more arid. Remarkably lifelike paintings on rock surfaces from the herding period show scenes of cattle and the people who tended them. The desiccation of the Sahara coincided with the rise of Egyptian civilization along the Nile Valley to the east. As the Saharan grasslands dried up, some of their inhabitants may have migrated to the Nile Valley region in search of arable land and pasture. Perhaps this migration, by greatly expanding the population of the valley, contributed to the tensions that resulted in the emergence of complex forms of social organization there.

Saharan people presumably migrated southward as well, into the Sudan, the broad belt of grassland that stretches across Africa south of the Sahara Desert, bringing with them knowledge of agriculture and animal husbandry. Agriculture reached the Sudan by at least 3000 BCE, and knowledge of iron-working spread across the area toward the middle of the first millennium BCE.

Nok

Some of the earliest evidence of iron technology in sub-Saharan Africa comes from the so-called Nok culture, which arose in the western Sudan (present-day Nigeria), as early as 500 BCE. The Nok people were farmers who grew grain and oil-bearing seeds; they were also smelters, using the technology for refining ore. In addition, they created the earliest known sculpture in sub-Saharan Africa, producing accomplished terra-cotta figures of human and animal subjects between about 500 BCE and 200 CE.

The Nok **HEAD** shown here (**FIG. 16–2**), slightly larger than life-size, originally formed part of a complete figure. The

triangular or D-shaped eyes are characteristic of Nok style and appear also on sculptures of animals. Each large knot of the elaborate hairstyle is pierced with a hole that may have held ornamental feathers. Other Nok figures have beaded necklaces and other prestige ornaments. Since the original context for these pieces is unknown—none of these sculptures was excavated by archaeologists—it is difficult to speculate on their original meaning and function.

Ife and Benin

The city of Ife, a sacred site for the Yoruba people, had arisen in the southern, forested part of present-day Nigeria by about 800 CE, several centuries after the last Nok terra cottas were produced. Lifelike sculpted heads, created by the artists of this sacred city between about 1050 CE and 1400 CE are among the most remarkable works in the history of art (SEE FIG. 16–1).

Ife was probably the artistic parent of the great city-state of Benin, which arose 150 miles to the southeast. According to oral histories, the earliest kings of Benin belonged to the Ogiso, or Skyking, dynasty. After a long period of misrule, however, the Edo people of Benin asked the *oni* of Ife for a new ruler. The *oni* sent Prince Oranmiyan, who founded a new dynasty in 1170 CE. Two centuries later, the fourth king, or *oba*, of Benin decided to start a tradition of memorial sculpture like that of Ife (**FIG. 16–3**). He sent to Ife for master metal-casters, and the practice of casting **MEMORIAL HEAD**s for the shrines of the royal ancestors of Benin is still in the hands of their descendants to this day.

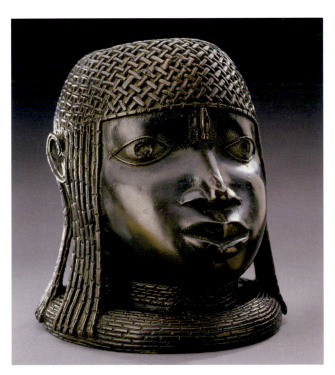

16–3 • MEMORIAL HEAD OF AN OBA (KING)
From Benin, Nigeria. c. 16th century CE. Brass, height 9″ (23 cm). The Nelson-Atkins Museum of Art, Kansas City, Missouri.

This head belongs to a small group of rare early Benin sculptures called "rolled-collar" heads that are distinguished by the roll collar that serves as a firm base for the exquisitely rendered head.

The lost-wax process begins with a core on which the sculptor models an image in wax. A mold is then formed of heat-resistant clay covering the wax model. Next the wax is melted and replaced with molten metal. When the metal solidifies, the mold is broken away and the cast image is finished and polished. The usual metal used in this casting process was bronze, an alloy of copper and tin, although sometimes casters used brass, an alloy of copper and zinc.

The sequence of drawings here shows the steps used by the Benin sculptors of Africa. A heat-resistant "core" of clay approximating the shape of the sculpture-to-be (and eventually becoming the hollow inside the sculpture) was covered by a layer of wax having the thickness

of the final sculpture. The sculptor carved or modeled the details in the wax. Rods and a pouring cup made of wax were attached to the model. A thin layer of fine, damp sand was pressed very firmly into the surface of the wax model, and then model, rods, and cup were encased in thick layers of clay. When the clay was completely dry, the mold was heated to melt out the wax. The mold was then placed upside down in the ground, ready to receive the molten metal. When the metal was completely cool, the outside clay cast and the inside core were broken up and removed, leaving the cast-metal sculpture. Details were polished to finish the piece, which could not be duplicated because the mold had been destroyed in the process.

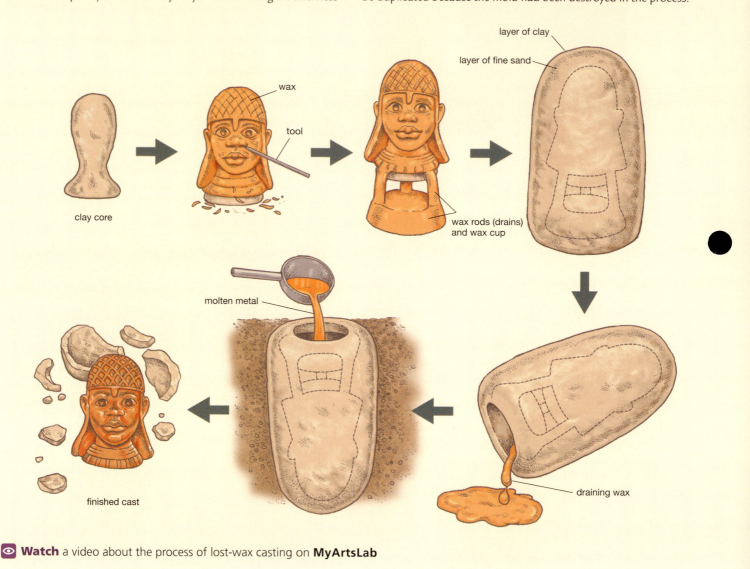

clay core — wax — tool — layer of clay — layer of fine sand — wax rods (drains) and wax cup — molten metal — draining wax — finished cast

👁 **Watch** a video about the process of lost-wax casting on **MyArtsLab**

The Benin kings also commissioned important works in ivory. One example is a beautiful ornamental **HIP PENDANT** (**FIG. 16–4**) that represents an *iyoba* ("queen mother"—the *oba*'s mother), the senior female member of the royal court. The mask was carved as a belt ornament worn at the *oba*'s hip. Its pupils were originally inlaid with iron, as were the scarification

patterns on the forehead. This particular belt ornament may represent Idia, who was the mother of Esigie, a powerful *oba* who ruled from 1504 to 1550. Idia is particularly remembered for raising an army and using magical powers to help her son defeat his enemies. Like Idia, the Portuguese helped Esigie expand his kingdom. The necklace represents heads of

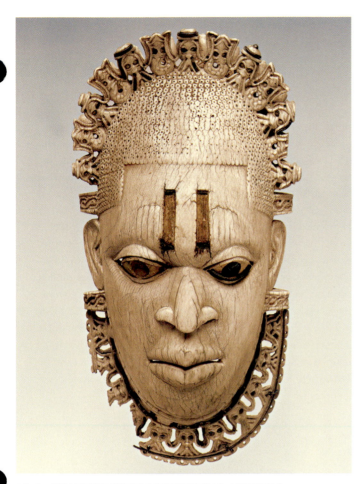

lids, and a long straight nose. He wears short pants and a helmet with a chin strap, and his horse has an ornate bridle. Such elaborate military equipment suggests that the horseman could be a guardian figure, hero, or even a deified ancestor. Similar figures have been found in sanctuaries. Over time, urban life declined, and so did the arts. In the fifteenth and sixteenth centuries, when rivals began to raid these African cities, the long tradition of ceramic sculpture came to an end.

When Koi Konboro, the twenty-sixth king of Jenné, converted to Islam in the thirteenth century, he transformed his palace into the first of three successive mosques in the city. Like the two that followed, the first mosque was built of adobe (a sun-dried mixture of clay and straw). With its great surrounding wall and tall towers, it was said to have been more beautiful and more lavishly decorated than the Kaaba, the central shrine of Islam, at Mecca. In the early nineteenth century, the mosque was razed by more austere Muslim rulers who considered it inappropriately sumptuous. A humbler structure was built on another site to replace it. This second mosque was in turn replaced by the current grand mosque, constructed between 1906 and 1907 on the ancient site and in the style of the original.

16–4 • HIP PENDANT REPRESENTING AN IYOBA ("QUEEN MOTHER")
From Benin City, Nigeria. c. 1550 CE. Ivory, iron, and copper, height 9¼″ (23.4 cm). The Metropolitan Museum of Art, New York. The Michael C. Rockefeller Memorial Collection, Gift of Nelson A. Rockefeller, 1972 (1978.412.323).

🔎 **View** the Closer Look for the Hip Pendant on **MyArtsLab**

Portuguese soldiers with beards and flowing hair. In the crown, more Portuguese heads alternate with figures of mudfish, which symbolize Olokun, the Lord of the Great Waters. Mudfish live near riverbanks, mediating between water and land, just as the *oba*, who is viewed as semidivine, mediates between the human world and the supernatural world of Olokun.

Jenné and Great Zimbabwe

Ife and Benin were only two of the many cities that arose in ancient Africa. At a site near Jenné, known as Jenné-Jeno or Old Jenné, excavations (by both archaeologists and looters) have uncovered hundreds of terra-cotta figures dating from the thirteenth to the sixteenth centuries CE. The figures were polished, covered with a red clay slip, and fired at a low temperature. A **HORSEMAN**, armed with quiver and arrows and a dagger, is an impressive example (**FIG. 16–5**). Man and horse are formed of rolls of clay on which details of faces, clothing, and harness are carved, engraved, and painted. The rider has a long oval head and jutting chin, pointed oval eyes set in multiple framing

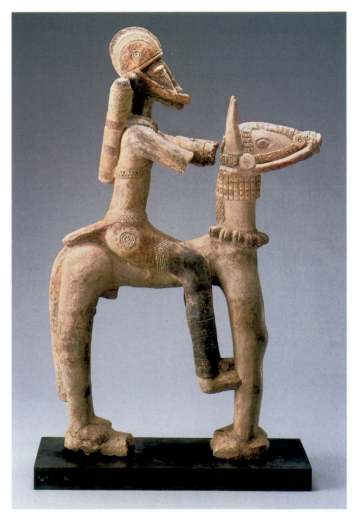

16–5 • HORSEMAN
From Old Jenné, Mali. 13th–15th century CE. Terra cotta, height 27¾″ (70.5 cm). The National Museum of African Art, Smithsonian Institution, Washington, D.C. Museum Purchase (86–12–2).

ART AND ITS CONTEXTS

The Myth of "Primitive" Art

The word "primitive" was once used by Western art historians to lump together the art of Africa, the Pacific Islands, and the indigenous art of the Americas. The term itself means "early," but its use was meant to imply that these civilizations were crude, simple, and backward, stuck in an early stage of development.

The use of the term "primitive" was rooted in racism and colonialism. Criteria used to label a people primitive included the use of so-called Stone Age technology, the absence of written histories, and the failure to build "great" cities. Such attitudes were extended to the creations of these cultures, and "primitive" art became the dominant label for their cultural products. Yet the accomplishments of the people of Africa strongly belie such categorization: Africans south of the Sahara have smelted and forged iron since at least 500 BCE, and Africans in many areas made and used high-quality steel for weapons and tools. Many African people have recorded their histories in Arabic since at least the tenth century. The first European visitors to Africa admired politically and economically sophisticated urban centers such as Benin, Kilwa, Jenné, Great Zimbabwe, and Mbanza Kongo.

Until quite recently, Westerners tended to see Africa as a single country and not as an immense continent of vastly diverse cultures. Moreover, they perceived artists working in Africa as craftworkers bound to styles and images dictated by village elders and producing art that was anonymous and interchangeable. Over the past several decades, however, these misconceptions have crumbled. Art historians and anthropologists have now identified numerous African cultures and artists and compiled catalogs of their work. Certainly we will never know the names of the vast majority of African artists of the past, just as we do not know the names of the sculptors responsible for the portrait busts of ancient Rome or the monumental reliefs of the Hindu temples of South Asia. But, as elsewhere, the greatest artists in Africa were famous and sought after, while innumerable others labored honorably and not at all anonymously.

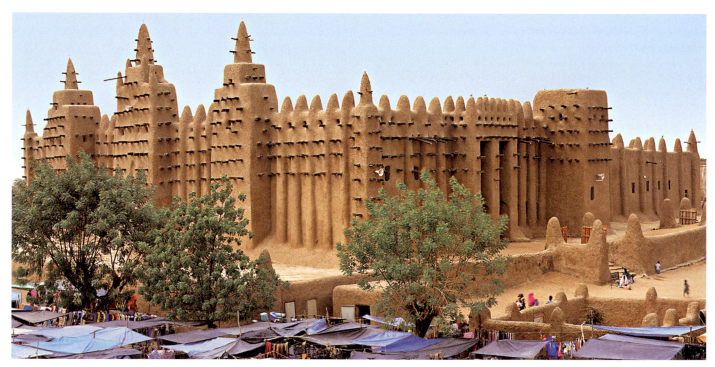

16–6 • GREAT FRIDAY MOSQUE

Jenné, Mali, showing the eastern and northern façades. Rebuilding of 1907 in the style of 13th-century CE original.

The plan of the mosque is not quite rectangular. Inside, nine rows of heavy adobe columns, 33 feet tall and linked by pointed arches, support a flat ceiling of palm logs. An open courtyard on the west side (not seen here) is enclosed by a great double wall only slightly lower than the walls of the mosque itself. The main entrances to the prayer hall are in the north wall (to the right in the photograph).

👁 **Watch** an architectural simulation explaining adobe-brick construction on **MyArtsLab**

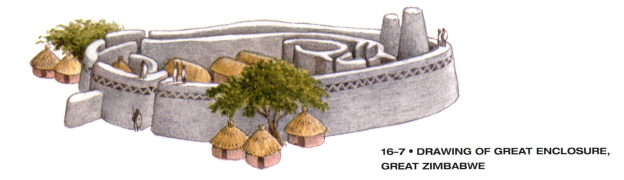

16-7 • DRAWING OF GREAT ENCLOSURE, GREAT ZIMBABWE

The mosque's eastern, or "marketplace," façade (FIG. 16–6) boasts three tall towers, the central one containing the *mihrab*. The finials, or crowning ornaments, at the top of each tower bear ostrich eggs, symbols of fertility and purity. The walls of the mosque are distinguished by tall, narrow, engaged columns, which act as buttresses. These columns are characteristic of West African mosque architecture, and their cumulative rhythmic effect is one of great verticality and grandeur. The most unusual features of West African mosques are the torons, wooden beams projecting from the walls. Torons provide permanent supports for the scaffolding erected each year so that the exterior of the mosque can be replastered.

Thousands of miles from Jenné in southeastern Africa, the city of Great Zimbabwe was home to the Shona people. Zimbabwe was part of an extensive trade network along the Zambezi, Limpopo, and Sabi rivers. It funneled gold, ivory, and exotic skins to coastal trading towns built by Arabs and Swahili-speaking Africans, and between 1000 and 1500 CE, it was controlled from Great Zimbabwe. It is estimated that at the height of its power in the fourteenth century, Great Zimbabwe and its environs housed a population of more than 10,000 people. A large cache of goods found there containing items such as Portuguese medallions, Persian pottery, and Chinese porcelain testifies to the extent of trade at Great Zimbabwe.

The word "Zimbabwe" derives from the Shona term for "venerated houses" or "houses of stone," and, indeed, much of Great Zimbabwe consisted of stone structures built by the ancestors of the present-day Shona people, who still live in the region. Masons used the enormous boulders abundant in the vicinity—and the uniform granite blocks that split naturally from them—to build a series of tall enclosing walls. As the artisans grew more skillful, they used dressed, or smoothly finished, stones and laid them in fine, level courses. Each enclosure defined a family's living space and contained dwellings made of adobe with conical thatched roofs.

The largest building complex at Great Zimbabwe is located in a broad valley below the hilltop enclosures. Known today as Imba Huru, or the Big House, it was probably a royal residence as well as a religious center. It is ringed by a massive masonry wall—more than 800 feet long, 32 feet high, and 17 feet thick at the base—constructed without mortar. Inside the outer wall are numerous smaller stone enclosures and adobe platforms (FIG. 16–7). A fascinating structure known simply as the CONICAL TOWER (FIG. 16–8) is 18 feet in diameter and 30 feet high, and

16-8 • CONICAL TOWER, GREAT ENCLOSURE, GREAT ZIMBABWE
Shona, Zimbabwe. c. 1350–1450 CE. Stone, height of tower 30′ (9.1 m).

View the Closer Look for Great Zimbabwe on **MyArtsLab**

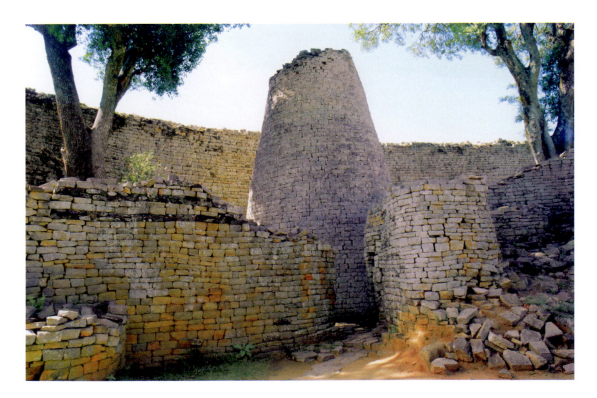

the tower was originally capped with three courses of ornamental stonework. Resembling a large version of a present-day Shona granary, it may have represented the good harvest and prosperity believed to result from allegiance to the ruler of Great Zimbabwe.

During the twentieth century, African sculptures—wood carvings of astonishing formal inventiveness and power—found admirers around the world. Wood decays rapidly, however, and little wood sculpture from lands south of the Sahara remains from before the nineteenth century. As a result, much of ancient Africa's artistic heritage has been irretrievably lost. Yet the beauty of ancient African creations in such durable materials as terra cotta, stone, and bronze bear eloquent witness to the skill of ancient African artists and the splendor of the civilizations in which they worked.

Later African Art in Life and Death

How does African art of the modern era relate to the major transitions of human life and death?

European exploration and subsequent colonization of the African continent brought Africa's flourishing and diverse societies into sudden and traumatic contact with the "modern" world that Europe had largely created. European ships first visited sub-Saharan Africa in the fifteenth century CE, and for the next several hundred years, European contact with Africa was almost entirely limited to coastal areas, where trade, including the tragic slave trade, was carried out. Between the sixteenth and nineteenth centuries, over 10 million slaves were taken from Africa to colonies in the Western Hemisphere in an Atlantic slave trade sponsored by countries such as Great Britain, Portugal, France, Spain, Denmark, Holland, and the United States.

During the nineteenth century, as the slave trade was gradually eliminated, European explorers and Christian missionaries began to investigate the unmapped African interior. Drawn by the potential wealth of Africa's natural resources, European governments began to seek territorial concessions from African rulers. Diplomacy soon gave way to force, and, toward the end of the century, competition among rival European powers fueled the so-called Scramble for Africa, when European leaders raced to lay claim to whatever portion of the continent they were powerful enough to seize. By 1914, virtually all of Africa was under colonial rule. In the years following World War I, nationalistic movements arose across the continent; from the 1950s through the mid-1970s, one colony after another gained its independence.

Art and Domestic Life

Shelter is a basic human concern, yet, as we have seen, different cultures approach its design and construction in different ways—differences that often help us understand cultural values and priorities. The farming communities of the Nankani people in the West African border area between Burkina Faso and Ghana developed a distinctive painted architecture. The earthen buildings of their walled compounds are low and single-storied with either conical roofs or flat roofs that form terraces. Some buildings are used only by men, others by women. The Nankani men control the ancestral shrine by the entrance, the corral for cattle, and the granary; they have rectangular houses. The inner courtyards, outdoor kitchen, and round houses are the women's areas (**FIG. 16–9**). Men build the compound; women paint the buildings inside and out.

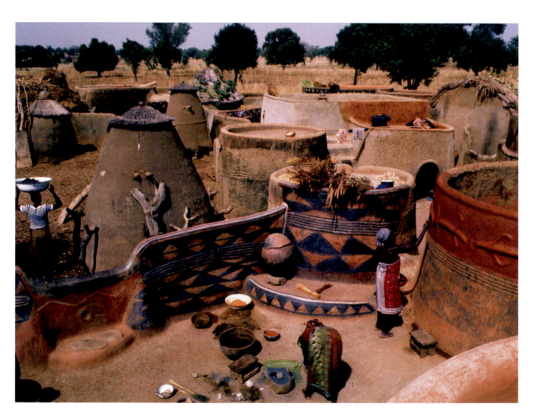

16–9 • NANKANI COMPOUND
Sirigu, Ghana. 1972 CE.

Among the Nankani people, creating living areas is a cooperative but gender-specific project. Men build the structures, women decorate the surfaces. The structures themselves are also gender-specific. The round dwellings shown here are women's houses located in an interior courtyard; men occupy rectangular flat-roofed houses. The bisected lozenge design on the dwelling to the left is called *zalanga*, the name for the braided sling that holds a woman's gourds and most treasured possessions.

Mande Pots

In many West African cultures, fired ceramics are made exclusively by women. Among the Mande-speaking people of Mali, Burkina Faso, Guinea, and Ivory Coast, potters are *numumusow*, female members of *numu* lineages. Their husbands, fathers, and sons are the sculptors and blacksmiths of the Mande.

Numumusow make a wide selection of vessels whose shapes reflect their intended use: wide bowls and cooking pots, narrow-necked water bottles, small eating dishes, and huge storage jars (FIG. 16–10). The *numumusow* form the soft and sticky clay by coiling and modeling with their fingers. They decorate their vessels by burnishing (polishing), engraving, adding pellets or coils of clay, or coloring with slip (diluted colored clay). The vessels are fired at low temperatures in a shallow pit or in the open; this produces a ware that can be used to cook over an open fire without breaking.

Even though most urban Africans use metal and plastic dishes and cookware today, large earthenware jars still keep water cool and clean in areas where refrigeration is expensive. In the past, water-storage jars were public display pieces, standing near the entrance to the house, where a guest would be offered a drink of cool water as an essential part of hospitality. Mande vessels for drinking water are often decorated with incised lines and molded ridges. In this example, the raised images of lizards may refer to Mande myths or philosophical concepts.

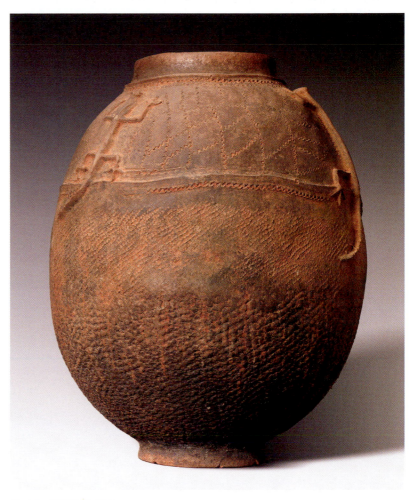

16–10 • WATER JAR
From Mali (Bamana people). Mande culture, 20th century CE. Earthenware, 23½″ × 18¾″ (59.7 × 47.6 cm). The Nelson-Atkins Museum of Art, Kansas City, Missouri. Purchase: William Rockhill Nelson Trust through the George H. and Elizabeth O. Davis Fund (96-36/1). Photo: John Lamberton.

The women decorate the walls with horizontal molded ridges called *yidoor* ("rows in a cultivated field") and "long eye" (long life) to express good wishes for the family. They paint the walls with rectangles and squares divided diagonally to create triangular patterns that contrast with the curvature of the walls. The painted patterns are called "braided sling," "broken pottery," and "broken gourd," and sometimes, since the triangular motifs can be seen as pointing up or down, they are called "filed teeth." The same geometric motifs are used on pottery and baskets, and for scarification of the skin. When people decorate themselves, their homes, and their possessions with the same patterns, art serves to enhance cultural identity.

Art and Initiation

Among the best-known works of African art are masks, central components in ritual performances that mark seasonal changes or major transitions in human life. The Bwa people of central Burkina Faso use masks when young Bwa men and women are initiated into adulthood following the onset of puberty. The initiates are first separated from younger playmates by older relatives who "kidnap" them, though their disappearance is explained in the community by saying that they have been devoured by wild beasts. The initiates remove their clothing and sleep on the ground without blankets. Isolated from the community, they are instructed about the world of nature spirits and the masks that represent them. They learn of the spirit each mask represents, and they memorize the story of each spirit's encounter with the founding ancestors of the clan. They also learn how to construct the costumes worn with the masks, and they learn the songs that accompany them in performance. Returning to the community, the initiates display their new knowledge in a public ceremony. Each boy performs with one of the masks, in a dance that expresses the character and personality that the mask represents. The girls, who are not allowed to wear the masks, sing the accompanying songs. At the end of the masquerade, the young men and women rejoin their families as adults, ready to marry, start farms, and begin families of their own.

Most Bwa **MASKS** depict spirits that take human or animal forms. Among the most spectacular masks, however, are those that represent spirits that have taken neither human nor animal form. Crowned with a tall, narrow plank, they are covered with abstract patterns that are easily recognized by the initiates (**FIG. 16–11**). The white crescent at the top represents the quarter-moon, under which initiations are held, and the white triangles underneath them represent bull roarers—sacred sound-makers that are swung around the head on a long cord to re-create spirit voices. The large central X represents the scar that every initiated Bwa wears as a mark of devotion. The horizontal zigzags at the bottom represent the path of ancestors and symbolize adherence to ancestral ways, their form conveying the difficulty of following this path. The curving red hook that projects above the face is said to represent the beak of the hornbill, a bird associated with the supernatural world and believed to be an intermediary between the living and the dead.

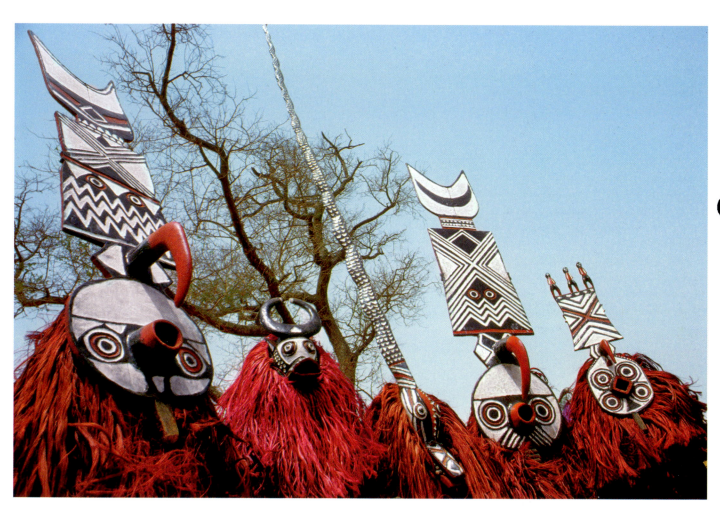

16–11 • FIVE MASKS IN PERFORMANCE
From Dossi, Burkina Faso. Bwa culture, 1984 CE. Wood, mineral pigments, and fiber, height approx. 7′ (2.13 m).

The Bwa have been making and using such masks since well before Burkina Faso achieved its independence in 1960. We might assume their use is centuries old, but in this case, the masks are a comparatively recent innovation. The elders of the Bwa family who own these masks state that they, like all Bwa, once followed the cult of the spirit of Do, who is represented by masks made of leaves. In the last quarter of the nineteenth century, the Bwa were the targets of slave raiders from the north and east. Their response to this new danger was to acquire wooden masks from their neighbors, for such masks seemed a more effective and powerful way of communicating with spirits who could help them. Thus, faced with a new form of adversity, the Bwa sought a new tradition to cope with it.

◉ **Watch** a video of the Bwa masks in a performance on **MyArtsLab**

Kuba Funerary Masks

The Kuba people of the Democratic Republic of Congo perform funerary masquerades to honor deceased members of the men's initiation society and high-ranking individuals who belonged to the community council of elders. In the southern Kuba region, funeral rites for initiated men are often accompanied by the appearance of one or more masquerade figures on the day of interment of the deceased. On these occasions initiation society members, family, and friends of the deceased celebrate the departed's life while mourning his death. In part, funeral rites are elaborate because of the belief that the spirit of the recently deceased (*mwendu*) may bring harm to his family or community if his achievements and status in life are not acknowledged at the funeral. The *mwendu* may be angered for a variety of reasons. Perhaps outstanding debts were not paid and the money or other goods were kept by a family member. Or the deceased had asked for something to be buried with him and this request was not honored. Disrespect is most often shown if the deceased is not given a proper burial, one equal to his rank in life. For an initiated man, a funeral masquerade is mandatory in this region, and members of the community-based men's initiation society show their solidarity with the deceased and his spirit by performing a masquerade at his funeral.

Among the most spectacular masks is that of *Ngady mwaash* (FIG. 16–12)—the name means literally "female mask." The faces of the masks are carved from wood and covered with an exuberant blend of bold geometric patterns composed of contrasting areas of triangles and parallel lines. A triangular-shaped hat, identical to that worn by female diviners, is attached to the mask, signifying that *Ngady mwaash* embodies the power of nature spirits (*ngesh*) to whom Kuba diviners attribute their extraordinary powers. The costume for *Ngady mwaash* is composed of a shirt and leggings, often extensively decorated with painted black-and-white triangles. Small wooden dowels attached to the front of the shirt represent breasts. Although wearing a woman's long embroidered skirt, *Ngady mwaash* is always performed by a man. Costume accessories include strands of beaded and shell-laden bandoliers that crisscross the chest and decorated leg- and armbands.

The funeral masquerade performance is held near the residence of the man who has died, just prior to burial. The perimeter of the dance ground is lined with family, friends, and onlookers who watch *Ngady mwaash* taking turns performing with another masked figure designated as male, such as the masked figure *Bwoom*, who carries a short sword and exudes power and restrained aggression. The *Bwoom* dancer employs lunging movements and quick short jabs with his sword, causing onlookers to suspect that he may suddenly lose control and harm someone. This feeling of apprehension is a constituent part of the performance, and is a principal reason why community members look forward to the masquerade with such anticipation. In contrast, the performance style of *Ngady mwaash* is decidedly nonthreatening, with graceful movements as the dancer's body, legs, arms, and hands move in fluid gestures. The differences in the performance styles of male and female masquerade figures parallel the difference in the dance styles of men and women in Kuba culture.

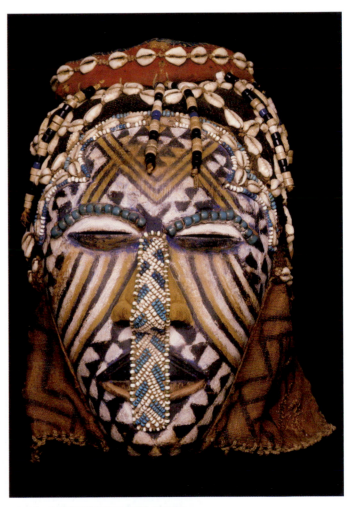

16–12 • NGADY MWAASH MASK
From Democratic Republic of Congo. Kuba peoples, late 19th–mid-20th century CE. Wood, pigment, glass beads, cowrie shells, fabric, and thread, height 12½″ (31.8 cm). The Art Institute of Chicago (1982.1505).

Art and Death

In the view of many African peoples, death is not an end but a transition—the leaving behind of one phase of life and the beginning of another. Just as ceremonies mark the initiation of young men and women into the community of adults, so too they mark the initiation of the newly dead into the community of spirits. The living preserve and honor the memory of the deceased—often appealing to their spirits to intercede on their behalf with nature spirits—in special dances involving masks to help the community mourn distinguished adults (see "Kuba Funerary Masks," p. 439). There are also special practices to mourn the particularly traumatic death of a child.

The Yoruba people of Nigeria have one of the highest rates of twin births in the world, and the birth of twins is a joyful occasion. But since twins are more delicate than single babies, occasionally one or both may die. When a Yoruba twin dies, parents often consult a diviner, who may tell them that an image of a **TWIN (ERE IBEJI)** must be carved to serve as a dwelling place for the deceased twin's spirit (**FIG. 16–13**). When the image is finished the mother brings the artist gifts. Then she dances home, carrying the figure as she would a living child, accompanied by the singing of neighborhood women. She places the figure in a shrine in her bedroom and lavishes care upon it, feeding it, dressing it richly, and anointing it with cosmetic oils. The Yoruba believe that the spirit of a dead twin thus honored will be appeased and will look with favor on surviving family members.

The female twins in FIGURE 16–13 may be the work of the Yoruba artist Akiode (d. 1936). Their beautiful, glossy surfaces and ample forms suggest that they are healthy and well fed. Full breasts, elaborate hairstyles, and scarification patterns signal the mature adulthood that they might one day have achieved. They represent hope for the future, for survival, and for prosperity.

Later African Art and the Spirit World

How does later African art relate to beliefs about a spirit world?

Much traditional African art is devoted to dealings with a spirit world that controls success or failure in life. Spirits are believed to inhabit the fields that produce crops, the rivers that provide fish, the forests that are home to game, or the land that must be cleared in order to build a new village. Families, too, may acknowledge the existence of ancestral spirits. To communicate with these all-important spirits, many African societies rely on a specialist, such as a diviner who opens the lines of communication between the supernatural and human worlds, using techniques such as prayer, sacrifice, offerings, ritual performance, divination, and sometimes the creation of images that give visible identity and personality to what is imaginary and intangible.

Minkisi (the plural form of *Nkisi*, a Kikongo word that means "container") are objects harnessing spirit forces or powers that are were made by the Kongo and Songye peoples of the Democratic Republic of Congo. *Minkisi* were produced

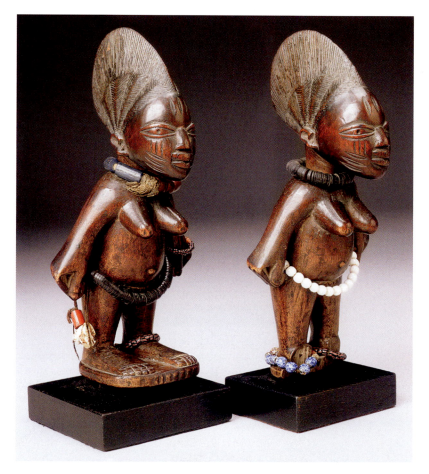

16–13 • TWIN FIGURES (ERE IBEJI)
From Nigeria. Yoruba culture,
20th century CE. Wood, height 7⅞" (20 cm).
The University of Iowa Museum
of Art, Iowa City. The Stanley Collection.

As with other African sculpture, patterns of use result in particular signs of wear. The facial features of *ere ibeji* are often worn down or even obliterated by repeated feedings and washings. Camwood powder applied as a cosmetic builds to a thick crust in areas that are rarely handled, and the blue indigo dye regularly applied to the hair eventually builds to a thin layer.

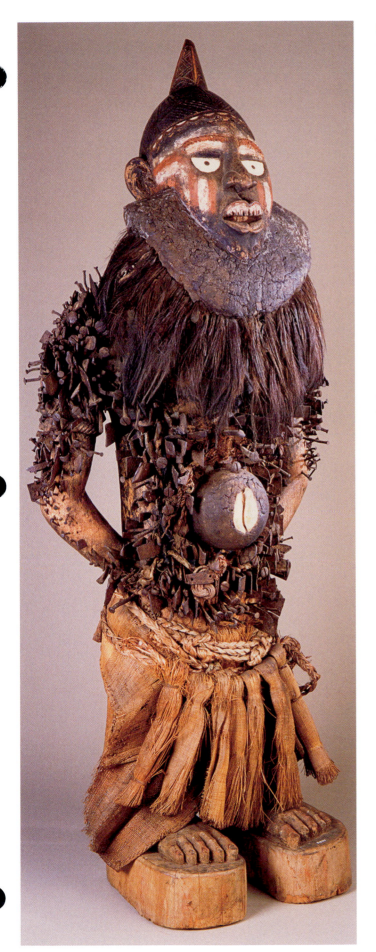

primarily during the nineteenth and early to mid twentieth centuries CE to alleviate illness, protect vulnerable individuals such as children, and provide success in hunting, trade, and other endeavors. A subset of the *Minkisi* group is the more specialized *Nkisi Nkonde*, which served a divinatory and judicial function to seek out wrongdoers and punish them for their misdeeds (FIG. 16–14). An *Nkisi Nkonde* began as an unadorned wooden figure, often in human or animal form. It was purchased from a carver at a market or commissioned by a diviner or chief on behalf of his society.

The diviner prescribes the attachment of medicinal ingredients or *bilongo*, to the figure. Taken from the plant, animal, and material worlds, they can be suspended in a packet from the figure's neck, placed into its beard, or inserted into a body cavity within its belly. The *bilongo* activates the object with potent earthly and supernatural powers, even allowing it to hunt down criminals and punish them according to the severity of their crime. A *Nkisi Nkonde*, therefore, served an important public function as an impartial arbiter of justice. In smaller villages, where European colonial rule had removed local judicial authorities and consolidated them within the capital city, this was particularly important. Two rural warring communities, for example, might agree to end their conflict by swearing an oath of peace and then driving a nail into the *Nkisi Nkonde* to seal the agreement. Should either party break the oath, it was believed that the *Nkisi Nkonde*, as arbiter of the agreement, would avenge the wronged party by meting out an appropriate punishment to the offender.

Some African people believe the spirit world is a parallel realm in which spirits may have families, live in villages, and possess personalities complete with faults and virtues. The Baule people of the Ivory Coast believe that each of us lived in such a spirit world before we were born. While there, we had a spirit spouse, whom we left behind when we entered this life. When someone has difficulty assuming his or her gender-specific role as an adult Baule—a man who has not married, for example, or a woman who has not borne children—and dreams of his or her spirit spouse, a diviner may prescribe the commissioning of an

16–14 • POWER FIGURE (NKISI NKONDE)
From the Democratic Republic of Congo. Kongo culture, 19th century CE. Wood, nails, pins, blades, and other materials, height 44″ (111.7 cm). The Field Museum, Chicago (# A109979Ac).

This sculpture provides a dramatic example of the ways in which works of African art are transformed by use. When first carved, the figure is "neutral," with no particular significance or use. Magical materials applied by a diviner transform the figure into a powerful being, at the same time modifying its form. While the object is empowered, nails may also be added as part of a healing or oath-taking process. And when the figure's particular powers are no longer needed, then additions may all be stripped away to be replaced with different magical materials that give the same figure a new function. There is no single artist; many creators played a role in forming the *Nkisi Nkonde* we see in a museum. In their hands the figure becomes a visual document of the history of the conflicts and afflictions that have threatened the community.

🔍 **View** the Closer Look for the Power Figure (*Nkisi Nkonde*) on **MyArtsLab**

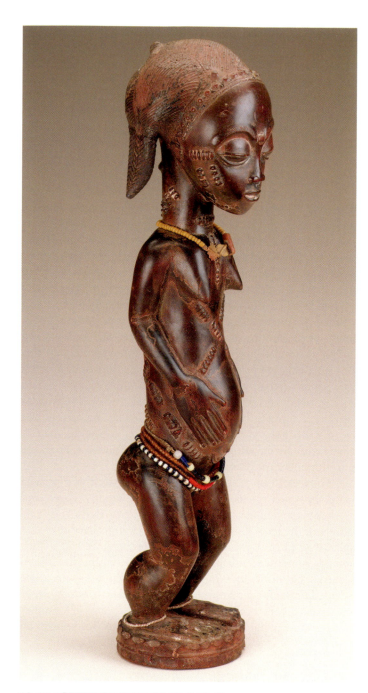

16–15 • SPIRIT SPOUSE (BLOLO BLA)
From Ivory Coast. Baule culture, early–mid-20th century CE.
Wood, glass beads, gold hollow beads, plant fiber, white pigment,
and encrustation, height 19¼″ (48.9 cm). The Pennsylvania University
Museum of Archaeology and Anthropology, Philadelphia.

Later African Art and Political Power

*What is the relationship between later African art
and the political leaders who often commissioned it?*

As in societies throughout the world, art in Africa is used to
identify those who hold power in this world as well as in the
spirit world. Among the Ashanti peoples of Ghana, for example, the ruler's spokesperson carried a special staff to identify
him as a leader and royal advisor. The finial of one **STAFF (FIG.
16–16)** is an allegorical carving of a man holding an egg. Political power is like an egg, states an Ashanti proverb—grasp it too
tightly and it will shatter in your hand, but hold it too loosely
and it will slip from your fingers. This staff was probably made
in the 1960s or 1970s CE by Kojo Bonsu—son of famous carver
Osei Bonsu (1900–1976)—who lives in the Ashanti city of
Kumasi and continues to carve prolifically. He embellished the
staff with gold leaf to signal its importance. Gold was a major
source of power for the Ashanti, who traded it for centuries,
first across the Sahara to the Mediterranean world, and then
directly to Europeans on the West African coast.

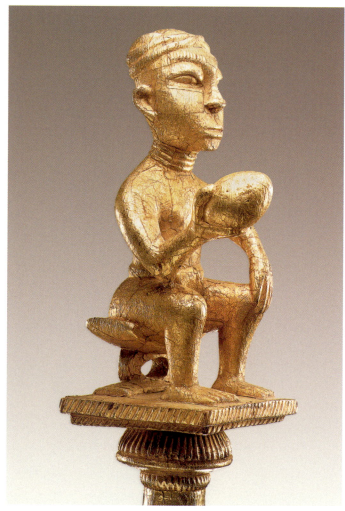

16–16 • Attributed to Kojo Bonsu
FINIAL OF A SPOKESPERSON'S STAFF (OKYEAME POMA)
From Ghana. Ashanti culture, 1960s–1970s CE. Wood and gold,
height 11¼″ (28.57 cm). The Gold of Africa Barbier-Mueller Collection.

image of the **SPIRIT SPOUSE (FIG. 16–15)**—either a female
figure (*blolo bla*) for a man or a male figure (*blolo bian*) for a
woman. The figures display the most admired and desirable
marks of beauty so that the spirit spouses may be encouraged
to enter and inhabit them. The owner keeps the figure in his
or her room, dressing it in beautiful textiles and jewelry, washing it, anointing it with oil, feeding it, and caressing it. The
Baule hope that by caring for and pleasing their spirit spouse a
balance may be restored that will free the individual's human
life to unfold smoothly.

A CLOSER LOOK

● **A Palace Door** ▶ Olowe of Ise. From Yoruba royal palace in Ikéré, Nigeria. Yoruba culture, c. 1925 CE.
Wood and pigment, height 72″ (1.9 m). The Detroit Institute of the Arts. Gift of Bethea and Irwin Green.

Musicians performing for the royalty below.

The carvings on this side of the door focus on divination. This man stands with a sacrificial animal and a display of palm nuts that will be used in reading oracles to foretell the future.

The diviner sits here with his divination board and a ceremonial cup for palm nuts.

These two columns of heads could represent members of the royal court, royal ancestors, or even enemies taken in battle.

The *oni* is represented here as a seated crowned figure flanked on the left by a guard and on the right by two royal wives. The principal wife nurses a child and wears a European top hat, a symbol of her power.

The group of wives seems to be dancing to the music played in the top scene. The two at the right lift their breasts in a gesture of generosity and affection associated with elder women.

Farm workers carrying their bounty.

A pair of wrestlers, perhaps also a part of the royal entertainment.

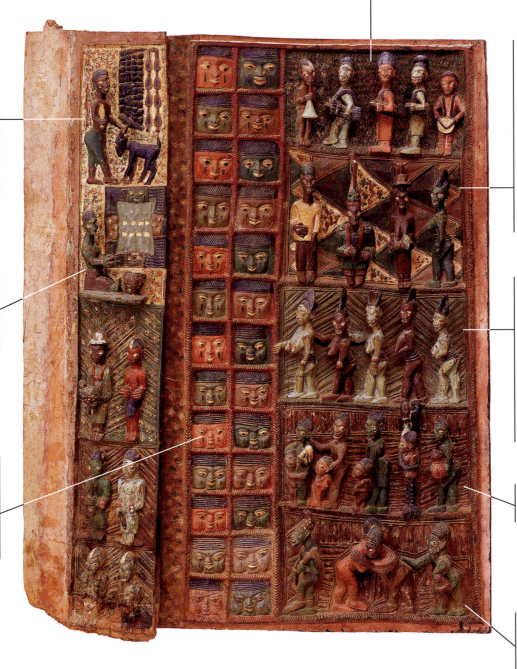

 View the Closer Look for a Palace Door on **MyArtsLab**

Yoruba kings manifested their power through large and lavish palaces. In the traditional plan, the principal rooms opened onto a veranda, where elaborately figured posts supported the roof, and dense, highly descriptive figure carvings covered the doors, often encrusted with elaborate carvings. Olowe of Ise—among the most important modern Yoruba artists—carved posts and entranceways in wood for the palaces of the Ekiti-Yoruba kingdoms in southwestern Nigeria. The palace door in Ikéré (see "A Closer Look," p. 443) is a magnificent example of his work. Its asymmetrical composition combines narrative and symbolic scenes in horizontal, rectangular panels. Figures with tall bodies, elongated necks, and elaborate hairstyles face out toward viewers. They are carved in such high relief that their upper portions are actually carved in the round. Art historian Philip Allison wrote of meeting Olowe and watching him work, and (echoing the praises of the Yoruba themselves) described Olowe carving the iron-hard African oak "as easily as [he would] a calabash [gourd]." (For an offering bowl carved by Olowe, SEE FIG. INTRO–11.)

Woven textiles, called **kente**, still signal status among the Ashanti in Ghana (**FIG. 16–17**) and have become popular globally as an expression of African cultural heritage. Originally, kente cloth was associated with royalty and produced under royal control. Some patterns were only worn by the Ashanti king. And even though its use is now more widespread, kente cloth is primarily reserved for festive attire worn at special occasions. The pattern shown here is *Oyokoman Adweneasa*, characterized by wide gold and green stripes set on deep red grounds. *Oyokoman* refers to the powerful Oyoka clan, and *Adweneasa* means "my skill is exhausted," a reference to the way the artist has woven elaborate patterns into every available area to the very edge of the fabric ensemble until running out of space.

Kente cloth is made on small, light, horizontal looms that produce long, narrow strips of fabric that are subsequently sewn together to form large rectangles of finished cloth. Ashanti weavers begin by laying out the long warp threads in a brightly colored pattern. Today the threads are likely to be rayon. Formerly, however, they were cotton, and later silk, which the Ashanti produced by unraveling Chinese cloth obtained through European trade. Weft threads are woven through the warp to produce complex patterns. This example belongs to a type known as *faprenu*, with a dense double weave consisting of twice as many weft threads as warp threads.

Many African artists today have come of age in a post-colonial culture that mingles elements of American, European, and African traditions. Drawing on these diverse influences, they have established a place in the international art scene along with their European, American, and Asian counterparts, and their work is shown as readily in Paris, Tokyo, and Los Angeles as it is in the African cities of Abidjan, Kinshasa, and Dakar.

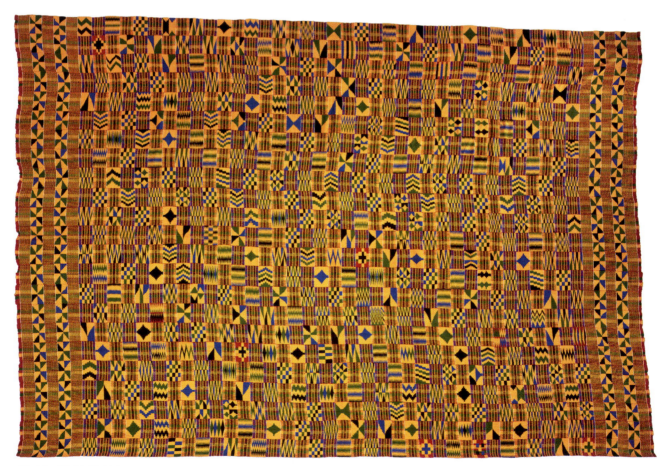

16–17 • KENTE CLOTH

From Ghana. Ashanti culture, c. 1980 CE. Rayon, 10′ 3½″ × 7′ 1½″ (3.1 × 1.3 m). Fowler Museum of Cultural History, University of California in Los Angeles.

LOOKING BACK ◄

In many cultures, distinctions between "fine art" and "craft" do not exist. Also absent is the Western academic hierarchy of materials, in which marble, bronze, oils, and fresco are valued over terra cotta, wood, watercolor, and stained glass. The hierarchy of subjects that privileges **history painting** is equally irrelevant outside the European tradition. As in the Americas, the indigenous peoples of Africa did not produce ritual or political objects as works of art, but as expressions of cultural values, often invested with great spiritual power. They were prized for their effectiveness in social ceremony. Such qualities and expectations cannot be fully comprehended or appreciated when such works are encased in glass boxes within museums. We must imagine them "living" within the societies that made and originally used them. How powerfully might our minds and emotions be engaged if we saw Kwakwaka'wakw or Bwa masks (SEE FIGS. 15–29, 16–11) participating in religious ritual, transforming not only the outward appearance, but also the very essence of performers and observers alike.

THINK ABOUT IT

16.1 Explain how the ivory in FIGURE 16–4 was originally used. How could a museum exhibition help viewers understand this important aspect of its meaning?

16.2 Explain the role of masquerade in African art by discussing the use of masks in two rites of passage: the initiation rites of the Bwa culture and the Kuba funeral ceremony.

16.3 How did the spirit spouse in FIGURE 16–15 connect its owner with the spirit world?

16.4 Choose a work in this chapter that was made for a political leader and discuss how its form and meaning relate to the political aspirations of its patron.

| CROSSCURRENTS |

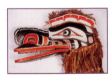

FIG. 15–29

FIG. 16–12

Neither of these works was meant to be exhibited in a museum case for an art-loving public seeking a cultural experience. Both took on their primary meaning in the process of the performance of a cultural ritual. Discuss the ways in which an understanding of the ritual context of each is necessary if we are to grasp their cultural meanings for those who made them and saw them in use. How did they end up in museums?

IN PERSPECTIVE

500 BCE

0

500 CE

1000

1500

2000

Nok Culture c. 500 BCE–200 CE

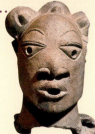

Nok Head
c. 500 BCE–200 CE

Ife c. 800 CE–present

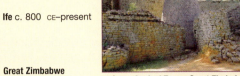

Conical Tower, Great Zimbabwe
c. 1350–1400 CE

Great Zimbabwe
c. 1000–1500 CE

Benin c. 1170 CE–present

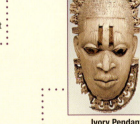

Ivory Pendant, Benin City
c. 1550 CE

Europeans Establish Contact with Coastal Sub-Saharan Africa c. 1400 CE

Portuguese First Encounter Kongo Culture 1482 CE

Cordial Relations Established between Benin and Portugal 1485 CE

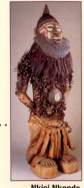

Nkisi Nkonde, Kongo Culture
19th century CE

Most of Africa Brought under Colonial Rule c. 1800–1914 CE

British Sack and Burn Benin Royal Palace 1897 CE

Oba of Benin Returns from Exile c. 1914 CE

African Colonies Gain Independence 1950s–1980s CE

Yoruba Palace Door
c. 1925 CE

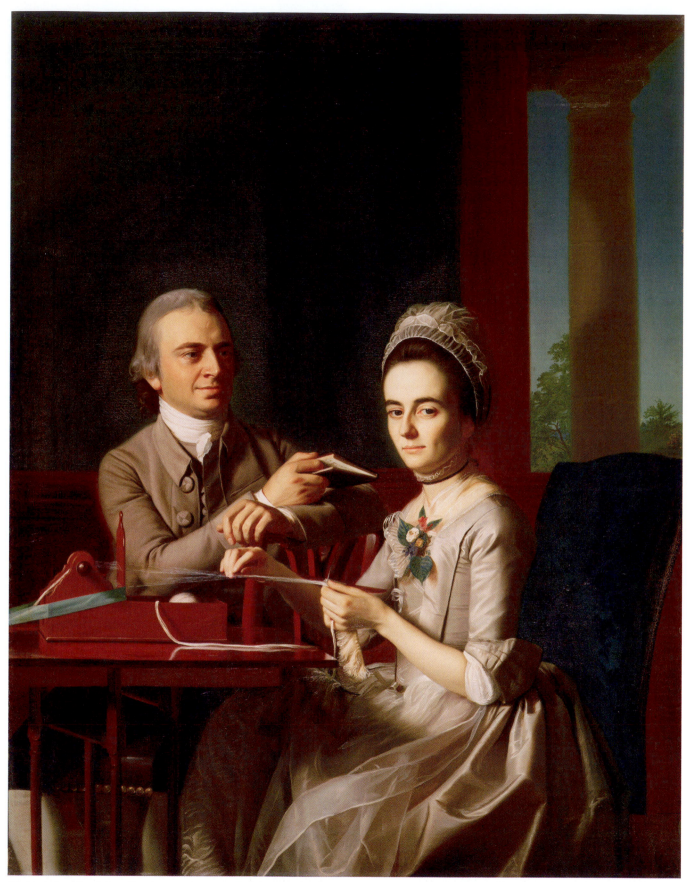

17-1 • John Singleton Copley **THOMAS MIFFLIN AND SARAH MORRIS (MR. AND MRS. MIFFLIN)**
1773. Oil on canvas, 61⅝″ × 48″ (156.5 × 121.9 cm). Philadelphia Museum of Art. Bequest of Mrs Esther F. Wistar
to the Historical Society Of Pennsylvania in 1900 and acquired by mutual agreement with the society through the generosity of
Mr. and Mrs. Fitz Eugene Dixon, Jr.

EUROPEAN AND AMERICAN ART, 1715–1840

17.1 Explain how the ornate style of the Rococo era reflected salon life among the aristocracy in eighteenth-century France.

17.2 Distinguish English and French eighteenth-century paintings of moralizing narratives and portraits from contemporary Rococo art.

17.3 Compare Neoclassicism and Romanticism as two cultural expressions of mid-eighteenth- to mid-nineteenth-century Europe.

17.4 Identify aspects of Romanticism in nineteenth-century English, American, and German landscape painting.

LOOKING FORWARD ▶

Our encounter with the Philadelphia couple portrayed in this arresting double portrait (**FIG. 17–1**) of 1773 by Boston painter John Singleton Copley (1738–1815) is very different from our experience of looking at the Arnolfinis in Jan van Eyck's signature work painted almost three and a half centuries earlier (SEE FIG. 12–1). Here it is the spotlighted woman, Sarah Morris, who most commands our attention. She turns to meet our gaze, and she is the focus not only for us, but for her husband, ardent patriot Thomas Mifflin. He is content to sit in the background of this picture, interrupting his reading to look admiringly at his beloved Sarah.

The couple was visiting Boston for a family funeral when they commissioned Copley to paint their portrait in 1773, the same year that American colonists protested against the British tax on tea by staging the Boston Tea Party. Thomas, a Quaker, had already established himself as a successful merchant. In 1775, he would be commissioned as a general in George Washington's army, and would eventually become a framer of the Constitution and the first governor of Pennsylvania. His intelligent and accomplished partner Sarah shared his conviction for the cause of American independence. Her political persuasions are emphasized in the painting by what she is doing: weaving

a homespun fringe on a portable loom to support the Colonial boycott on British imports. This double portrait's record of an affectionate marriage that was also an equal partnership seems curiously modern. But its veracity is confirmed by the historical record, and such unions were not unusual in the upper social echelons of eighteenth-century American society.

In 1773, Copley was Boston's preeminent portrait painter and a wealthy man. His reputation rested on his remarkably clear, sharp, precise painting style that seemed to reveal not only every minute detail of his sitter's physical appearance and personality, but also the gorgeous satins, silks, and laces of the women's dresses and the expensive polished furniture that were the signs of their wealth and status. Although his father-in-law was the Boston representative of the East India Company (whose tea was dumped into the harbor), Copley was nonetheless sympathetic to the revolutionary cause and tried unsuccessfully to mediate the crisis in Boston. This portrait of Sarah Morris and Thomas Mifflin was painted when Copley himself was ambivalent about the political future of America—he would flee the unsettled climate of the colonies the following year to begin a second career in London—but his sitters reveal only their own sober commitment to the cause.

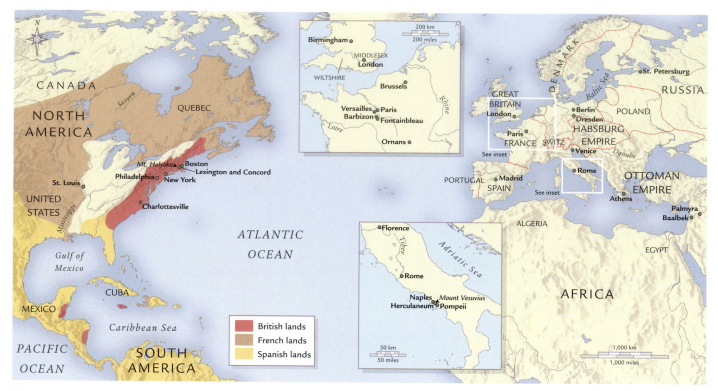

MAP 17–1 • EIGHTEENTH-CENTURY EUROPE AND NORTH AMERICA

Between 1715 and 1840, three major artistic styles—Rococo, Neoclassicism, and Romanticism—flourished in Europe and North America.

The American War of Independence was just one of many revolutions to shake the established order during the eighteenth and early nineteenth centuries. This was an age of radical change in society, thought, and politics, and while these transformations were felt especially in England, France, and the United States, they had consequences throughout the West and, eventually, the world.

Cultural historians call the eighteenth century the Age of Enlightenment or the Age of Reason. Reason certainly became the touchstone for evaluating nearly every civilized endeavor, including philosophy and politics, as well as art and architecture (MAP 17–1). An optimistic, even reverential attitude toward scientific inquiry developed, and this enthusiasm extended to historical and archaeological studies, as well as to investigations of the natural world. Nature, which was thought to embody reason, was invoked to corroborate the correctness—and goodness—of everything from political systems to architectural designs.

Rococo

How did the ornate style of the Rococo era reflect salon life among the aristocracy in eighteenth-century France?

In the modern age, the shift from art produced at the behest of individual or institutional patrons—the monarchy, aristocracy, Church, as well as wealthy merchants—to art produced as a commodity sold to the industrial rich, and even the emerging middle classes, had its roots in the Rococo, when the court culture of Versailles changed to salon culture in Paris. The term "Rococo" combines the Italian word *barocco* (an irregularly shaped pearl, possibly the source of the word "baroque") and the French *rocaille* (a popular form of garden or interior ornamentation using shells and pebbles). It describes the refined and fanciful style that became fashionable in parts of Europe during the eighteenth century. Rococo represents a reaction against the **Grand Manner** of Baroque art, identified with the formality and rigidity of seventeenth-century court life. Rococo is characterized by pastel colors, delicately curving forms, dainty figures, and lightheartedness. The style began in French architectural decoration at the end of Louis XIV's reign and quickly spread across Europe.

The duke of Orléans, regent for the boy-king Louis XV (ruled 1715–1774), made his home in Paris, and the royal court—delighted to escape Versailles—followed him there, building elegant townhouses (in French, *hôtels*), in whose small rooms the Rococo style flourished. The **SALON DE LA PRINCESSE** in the Hôtel de Soubise in Paris (FIG. 17–2), designed by Germain Boffrand and begun in 1732, is typical. The glitter of silver or gold against expanses of white or pastel color, the visual confusion of mirror reflections, delicate ornament in sculpted stucco, carved wood panels called *boiseries*, and inlaid wood designs on furniture and floors were all part

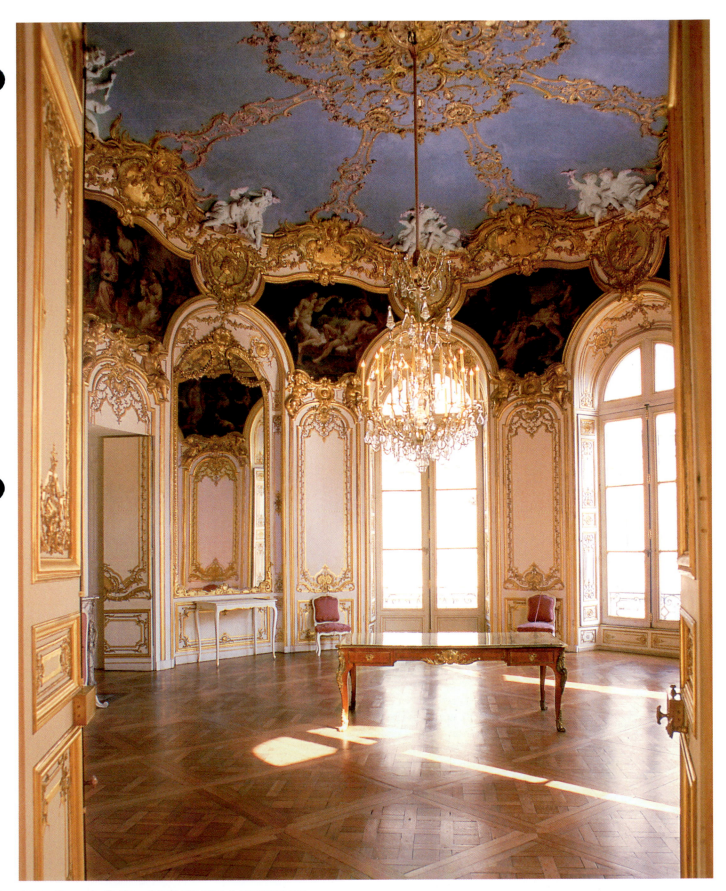

17–2 • Germain Boffrand SALON DE LA PRINCESSE
Hôtel de Soubise, Paris. Begun 1732.

of the new look. In residential settings, pictorial themes were often taken from Classical love stories, and sculpted ornaments were typically filled with *putti*, cupids, and clouds. In these elegant rooms, Parisian intellectuals gathered for conversation and entertainments presided over by accomplished, educated women of the upper class.

In painting, the Rococo style emerged with the career of the French artist Jean-Antoine Watteau (1684–1721). Watteau worked for a time as a decorator of interiors. In 1717, he was elected to membership of the Royal Academy of Painting and Sculpture on the basis of a painting he submitted to secure his admission: **THE PILGRIMAGE TO CYTHERA** (**FIG. 17–3**). There was no established category for such a painting, so the academicians created a new classification for it: the *fête galante*, or elegant outdoor entertainment. Watteau depicts a dreamworld in which beautifully dressed couples—accompanied by *putti*—depart for, or perhaps take their leave from, dalliance on the mythical island of love. The lush landscape has no more reality than a painted theater backdrop. It would never soil the characters' shimmering satins and plush velvets, nor would a summer shower threaten their charmed reverie. Watteau's idyllic vision, with its overtones of wistful melancholy, had a powerful

attraction in early eighteenth-century Paris and soon charmed most of Europe.

Tragically, Watteau died from tuberculosis while still in his thirties, but he left many followers, including Jean-Honoré Fragonard (1732–1806), who carried Watteau's French Rococo fantasies into the second half of the eighteenth century. In 1767, Fragonard created a small jewel of a painting seeped in sensuality. **THE SWING** (**FIG. 17–4**) shows a pretty young woman, suspended on a swing, her movement created by an elderly bishop obscured by the shadow of the bushes on the right, who pulls her with a rope. On the left, the girl's blushing lover hides in the bushes, swooning with anticipation. As the swing approaches, he is rewarded with an unobstructed view up her skirt, lifted on his behalf by her extended leg. The young man reaches out toward her with his hat as if to make a mockingly useless attempt to conceal the view, while she glances down, seductively tossing one of her shoes toward him. The playful abandon of the lovers, the complicity of the sculpture of Cupid on the left, his shushing gesture assuring that he will not tell, the *putti* with a dolphin beneath the swing who seem to urge the young woman on, and the poor duped bishop to the right, all work together to create an image that bursts with anticipation and desire, but also maintains a robust sense of humor.

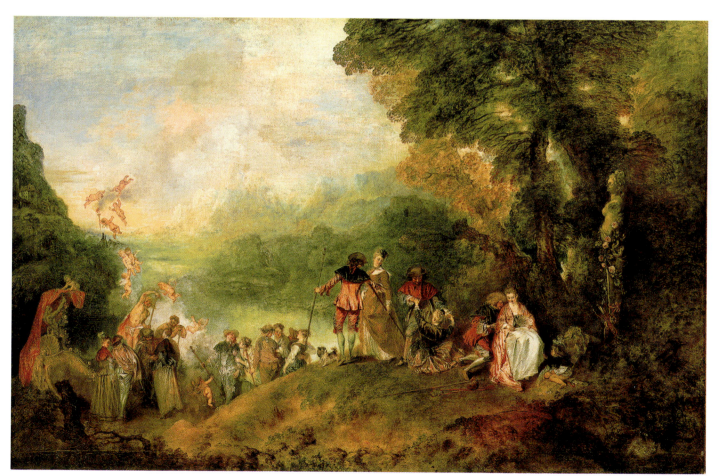

17–3 • Jean-Antoine Watteau THE PILGRIMAGE TO CYTHERA
1717. Oil on canvas, 4′ 3″ × 6′ 4½″ (1.3 × 1.9 m). Musée du Louvre, Paris.

Read the document related to Jean-Antoine Watteau on **MyArtsLab**

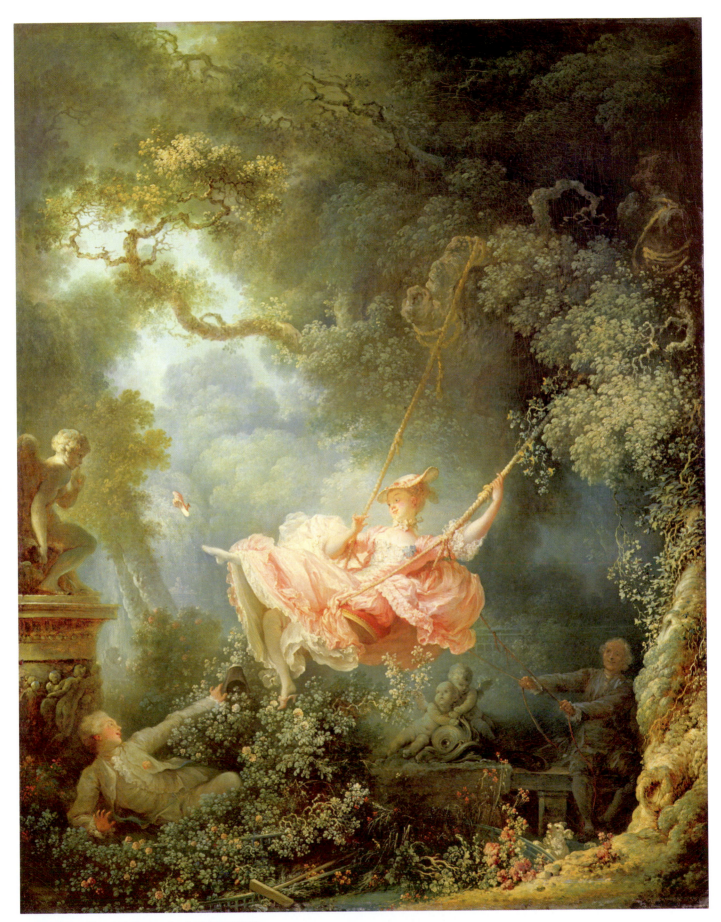

17–4 • Jean-Honoré Fragonard THE SWING
1767. Oil on canvas, 31⅞″ × 25¼″ (81 × 64.2 cm). The Wallace Collection, London.

Moralizing Narratives and Portraits

How are eighteenth-century English and French paintings of moralizing narratives and portraits different from contemporary Rococo art?

Not all eighteenth-century paintings were so playfully risqué. Members of the growing English middle class—newly prosperous merchants and professionals—helped fuel a market for paintings portraying satires, genre scenes, or episodes drawn from history or literature that drove home a moral lesson. Many reflected Enlightenment values, including an interest in promoting public virtue and social progress, a love of natural beauty, and a faith in reason and science.

British patrons tended to favor amusing and easily understandable satirical and moralizing scenes over high-minded history paintings with subjects drawn from mythology, the Bible, or Classical literature. By doing so, they challenged art theorists of their time and earlier, who had long considered history painting the highest form of artistic endeavor. Following the discontinuation of government censorship in 1695, there had emerged in Britain a flourishing culture of literary satire, directed at a variety of political and social targets. Inspired by the work of these novelists and essayists, painter William Hogarth (1697–1764) believed that art should contribute to the improvement of society. About 1730 he began illustrating moralizing tales of his own invention in sequences comprised of four to six paintings. He then reproduced the canvases as prints, to be sold as sets to the public, both maximizing his profits and disseminating his message as broadly as possible.

Hogarth's *Marriage à la Mode* series (1743–1745) was inspired by Joseph Addison's 1712 essay promoting the concept of marriage based on love. The opening scene, **THE MARRIAGE CONTRACT** (FIG. 17–5), shows the gout-ridden Lord Squanderfield pointing proudly to his family tree as he arranges for his son to marry the daughter of a wealthy merchant. The merchant will be securing his family's entry into the aristocracy, while the lord gains the money he needs to complete his Palladian house, visible through the window. Sitting back to back are the loveless couple, who will be sacrificed for their fathers' pride and greed. The young Squanderfield admires himself in the mirror, while the lawyer Silvertongue whispers to the unhappy fiancée. The five subsequent scenes show the progressively disastrous results of such a union, culminating in murder and suicide. Stylistically, Hogarth's paintings combine the accumulated detail characterizing seventeenth-century Dutch genre painting (SEE FIG. INTRO–16) with the casual elegance of Rococo. His work became so popular that in 1745 he was able to devote himself fully to moralizing satires, even giving up portrait painting—an art he deplored as a form of vanity.

AN EXPERIMENT ON A BIRD IN THE AIR-PUMP (FIG. 17–7) by English painter Joseph Wright of Derby (1734–1797) comes out of an Enlightenment fascination with the drama and romance of science. Wright belonged to the Lunar Society, a group of industrialists (including Josiah Wedgwood), merchants, traders, and progressive aristocrats who met monthly in or near Birmingham to exchange ideas about science and technology. As part of the society's attempts to popularize science, Wright painted a series of "entertaining" scenes of scientific

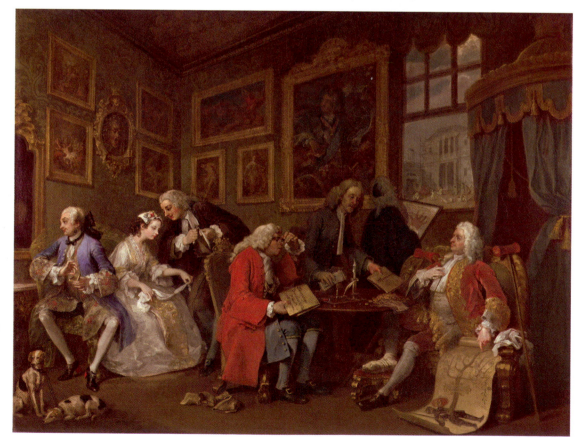

17–5 • William Hogarth THE MARRIAGE CONTRACT
From *Marriage à la Mode.* 1743–1745. Oil on canvas, 27½″ × 35¾″ (69.9 × 90.8 cm). The National Gallery, London.

"Am I Not a Man and a Brother?"

For two centuries the name Wedgwood has been—and still remains—synonymous with fine English ceramics, especially tableware. But Josiah Wedgwood was also active in the international effort to abolish slavery. To publicize the abolitionist cause, he commissioned the sculptor William Hackwood to design an emblem for the British Committee to Abolish the Slave Trade, formed in 1787. In the compelling image created by Hackwood (FIG. 17–6), the legend, "Am I Not a Man and a Brother?" surrounds an African man kneeling in chains. Wedgwood sent copies of the medallion to Benjamin Franklin, then president of the Philadelphia Abolition Society, and to others in the movement. In the nineteenth century, the women's suffrage movement in the United States adapted the image by representing a woman in chains with the motto, "Am I Not a Woman and a Sister?"

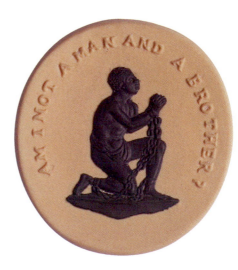

17–6 • William Hackwood, for Josiah Wedgwood **"AM I NOT A MAN AND A BROTHER?"** 1787. Black-and-white jasperware, 1⅜″ × 1⅜″ (3.5 × 3.5 cm). Image courtesy of the Wedgwood Museum, Barlaston, Staffordshire, UK.

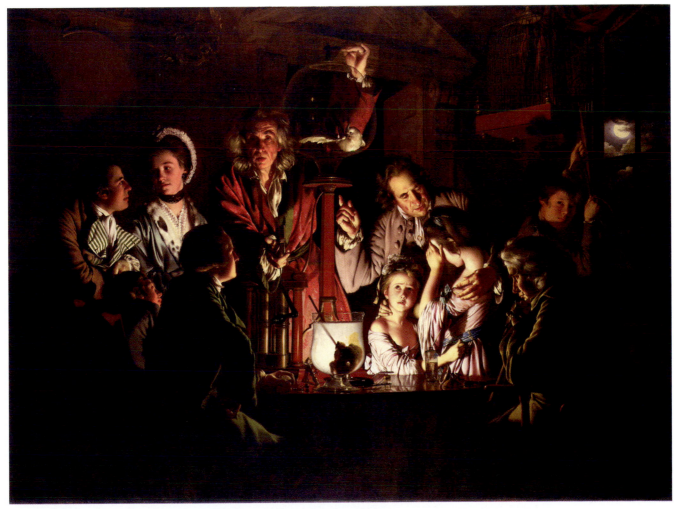

17–7 • Joseph Wright AN EXPERIMENT ON A BIRD IN THE AIR-PUMP
1768. Oil on canvas, 6′ × 8′ (1.83 × 2.44 m). The National Gallery, London.

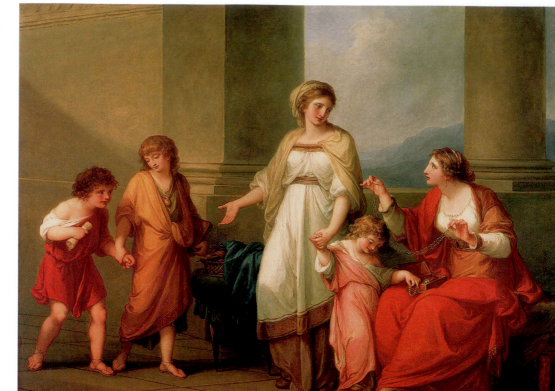

experiments. In the experiment shown here, air was pumped out of the large glass bowl until the small creature inside, a bird, collapsed from lack of oxygen; before the animal died, air was reintroduced by a simple mechanism at the top of the bowl. In front of an audience of adults and children, the shadowy figure of the scientist is on the verge of reintroducing air into the glass receiver. Near the window at the right—through which a full moon alludes to the Lunar Society—a boy stands ready to lower a cage when the bird revives. By delaying the reintroduction of air, the scientist has created considerable suspense, as the reactions of the two girls indicate. Their father attempts to dispel their fears with an instructive voice of reason.

The Italian-trained Swiss artist Angelica Kauffmann (1741–1807), a renowned history painter, was invited to Britain in 1766 by a wealthy client, and by 1768 she was one of only two women artists named among the founding members of the Royal Academy in London (see "Art Academies in the Eighteenth Century," p. 455). In her painting **CORNELIA POINTING TO HER CHILDREN AS HER TREASURES (FIG. 17–8)**, Kauffmann illustrated both an incident from ancient Republican Rome and a moral lesson. A woman visitor, who has been showing Cornelia her jewels, requests to see those of her hostess. In response, Cornelia gestures to her children, saying, "These are my jewels." The setting is ordered and simple, and the figures are based loosely on ancient Roman paintings. The sentiment, however—the glorification and idealization of the "good mother"—belongs unmistakably to the eighteenth century.

Portraiture

The eighteenth century witnessed a flourishing of the art of portraiture as wealthy patrons commissioned paintings to showcase their wealth and proclaim their virtue and high status. In fact, British patrons preferred pictures of themselves to grand scenes of Classical or religious history, and Thomas Gainsborough (1727–1788) grew into one of England's greatest portraitists by catering to the tastes of the rich and famous. The emphasis on setting in his early portrait of **ROBERT ANDREWS AND FRANCES CARTER (FIG. 17–9)** almost turns this work into a landscape painting, and the shimmering satin of Mrs. Andrews's skirt, the bench on which she sits, as well as the fluttering lyricism of the countryside and the casual elegance of the couple's poses recall the Rococo of Watteau. But essentially this work is about the connection of the landed gentry with the estates that signaled their identity and provided their wealth and power. Andrews's land-holdings had just expanded as a result of his marriage, and the hunting rifle tucked casually under his arm is a clear sign of his dominion over the expansive landscape.

In Colonial America, self-taught portraitist John Singleton Copley (1738–1815) developed into what one art historian has called "America's First Old Master." Copley's training and experience were limited, but he was already drawing attention as a painter by the time he was 15. Copley's clients, who included notable patriots Sam Adams and Paul Revere, valued not only his technical skill, but also his ability to dignify them while recording their features with unflinching accuracy.

Art Academies in the Eighteenth Century

During the seventeenth century, the French king had founded royal academies to instruct and encourage artists, architects, writers, scientists, musicians, and dancers. In 1667, the Royal Academy of Painting and Sculpture began occasionally to exhibit members' recent work and these came to be known as "**Salons**" because they were held in the Salon Carré in the Louvre Palace. From 1737, Salons were mounted every other year, with a jury of members selecting the works that would be shown. As the only public art exhibitions of any importance in Paris, the Salons were enormously influential in establishing officially approved styles and in molding public taste.

In England, the Royal Academy of Arts, founded in 1768, was significantly different. Since it was a private institution, it was independent of any interference from the Crown. It served only two functions: to operate an art school and to hold two annual exhibitions, one displaying art of the past and the other presenting contemporary art, open to any exhibitor on the basis of merit alone. The Royal Academy continues to function in this way today.

Besides the influential French and British academies, other art academies, public and private, sprang up throughout Europe in the eighteenth century. All primarily welcomed male artists. Some restricted the number of women members, while others welcomed women only as honorary members. In France, only seven women were admitted to full membership between 1648 and 1706. In 1770, when four women were members of the French Royal Academy, because the men worried that women members would become "too numerous," the academy declared that four women would be the limit at any one time. Women were not admitted to the academy's school nor allowed to compete for academy prizes, both of which were nearly indispensable for professional success. Women fared even worse at the British Royal Academy in London. After the Swiss painters Angelica Kauffmann and Mary Moser were named founding members in 1768, no other women were elected until 1922, and even then only as associates.

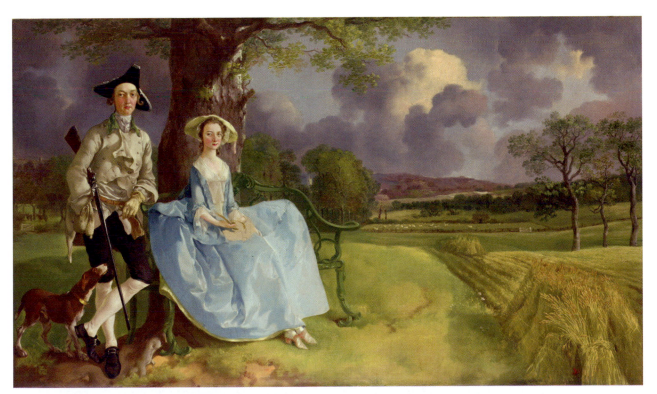

17–9 • Thomas Gainsborough ROBERT ANDREWS AND FRANCES CARTER (MR. AND MRS. ANDREWS) c. 1748–1750. Oil on canvas, 27½″ × 47″ (69.7 × 119.3 cm). The National Gallery, London.

Gainsborough was engaged to paint this couple's portrait shortly after the 20-year-old Robert Andrews married 16-year-old Frances Carter in November 1748. An area of painting in Frances's lap has been left unfinished, perhaps anticipating the later addition of a child for her to hold.

The austere seriousness of his *Thomas Mifflin and Sarah Morris* (SEE FIG. 17–1)—preoccupied as they both are with politics, leaving little leisure for noble diversions such as hunting—sharply contrasts with Gainsborough's lighthearted and pretty rendering of *Robert Andrews and Frances Carter* (SEE FIG. 17–9). Copley seems to capture something significant here about the nature of the Colonial American experience, soon to ignite in revolution. By that time, however, Copley himself would already be pursuing a second career as a history painter in London, where he moved in 1774 to escape political unrest in the colonies and was elected to the Royal Academy in 1779.

In France, a reaction against Rococo solidified during the 1760s, and many French portraitists began to work in a more restrained style. Marie-Louise-Élisabeth Vigée-Lebrun's **PORTRAIT OF MARIE ANTOINETTE WITH HER CHILDREN** falls into this mode (**FIG. 17–10**). Painted two years before the outbreak of the French Revolution, this work by the queen's favorite painter is a flagrant piece of royal propaganda. The court had hoped that the queen's depiction as the "good mother"—a theme already seen in Angelica Kauffmann's painting of Cornelia (SEE FIG. 17–8)—would counter her public image as immoral, extravagant, and conniving. Marie Antoinette's youngest son squirms on her lap, and her daughter leans affectionately against her. In a poignant touch, the older son points to the empty cradle of a recently deceased sibling. The image of Marie Antoinette as a loving mother surrounded by her children represented the ideal expounded by Enlightenment philosophers, especially the influential French-Swiss theorist Jean-Jacques Rousseau (1712–1778), who concluded that men and women should conform to the roles assigned to them by nature (i.e., biology), with women tending to the home and raising children, and men practicing learned professions, governing the state, and taking other active roles in public life.

In 1783, Vigée-Lebrun (1755–1842) was elected to one of the four places in the French Academy available to women (see "Art Academies in the Eighteenth Century," p. 455). Also elected in that year was Adélaïde Labille-Guiard (1749–1803), who in 1790 successfully petitioned to end the restriction on entry for women. Her commitment to increasing the number of women painters in France is reflected in a monumental but engaging **SELF-PORTRAIT WITH TWO PUPILS (FIG. 17–11)** that she submitted to the Salon of 1785. This image of the artist at her easel, although it flatters her conventional feminine charms in a manner derived from the Rococo tradition, was also meant to answer sexist rumors that her paintings and those by Vigée-Lebrun had actually been painted by men. In a witty role reversal, the only male to be seen is her father, and he is there only in a sculpted portrait bust at her side.

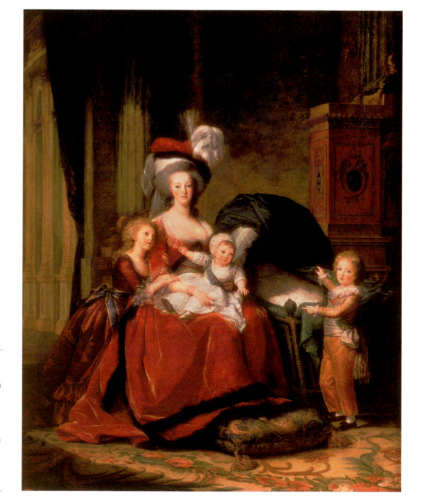

17–10 • Marie-Louise-Élisabeth Vigée-Lebrun PORTRAIT OF MARIE ANTOINETTE WITH HER CHILDREN
1787. Oil on canvas, 9′ ½″ × 7′ ⅝″ (2.75 × 2.15 m). Musée Nationale du Château de Versailles.

As the favorite painter of the queen, Vigée-Lebrun escaped from Paris with her daughter on the eve of the Revolution in 1789 and fled to Rome. After a very successful self-exile working in Italy, Austria, Russia, and England, the artist finally resettled in Paris in 1805 and again became popular with Parisian art patrons. Over her long career, she painted about 800 portraits in a style that changed very little over the decades.

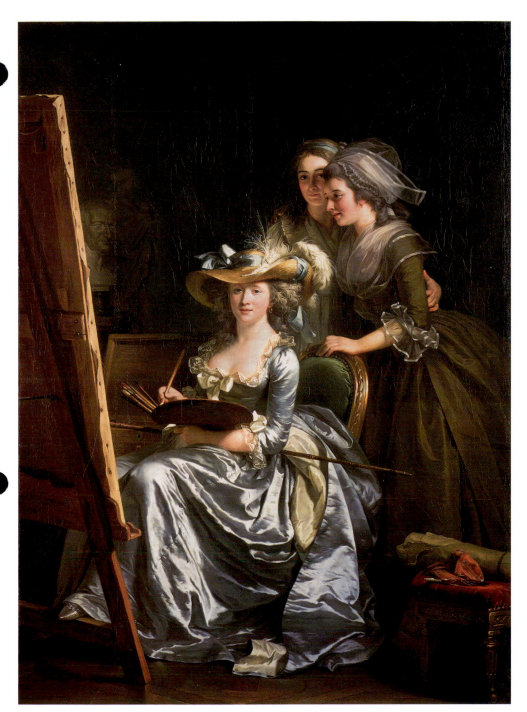

**17-11 • Adélaïde Labille-Guiard
SELF-PORTRAIT WITH TWO
PUPILS, MADEMOISELLE MARIE
GABRIELLE CAPET (1761–1818)
AND MADEMOISELLE
CARREAUX DE ROSEMOND
(D. 1788)**
1785. Oil on canvas, 6′ 11″ × 4′ 11½″
(2.11 × 1.51 m). The Metropolitan
Museum of Art, New York.
Gift of Julia A. Berwind (53.2255).

Neoclassicism and Romanticism

*How do Neoclassicism and Romanticism differ
as two cultural expressions of mid-eighteenth- to
mid-nineteenth-century Europe?*

The period between the mid eighteenth and the mid nineteenth
century in Europe, and its cultural extension in America (SEE
MAP 17–1), is characterized by a marked increase in stylistic
variety in the visual arts. Art historians have focused their principal attention on two trends they have named Neoclassicism
and Romanticism.

Neoclassicism, rooted in stylistic sources from ancient
Greek or Roman art, is defined by heroic nudity in sculpture

and sometimes painting, by Classical orders in architecture, by
the dominance of drawing over **painterly** effects in the visual
arts, and by a general emphasis on what were perceived to be
noble and serious modes of expression that often manifested
themselves in subjects highlighting moral incorruptibility,
patriotism, and courage. In paintings, brushstrokes are tightly
controlled, compositions are ordered and balanced, figures are
idealized beyond blemish, emotions are kept to a minimum.

Many see Italy—its wealth of antique ruins enhanced in
1748 by the archaeological discovery of the ancient city of Pompeii—as the birthplace of eighteenth-century Neoclassicism,
led by Antonio Canova (1757–1822), the foremost Neoclassical sculptor in Europe. Born into a family of stonemasons near

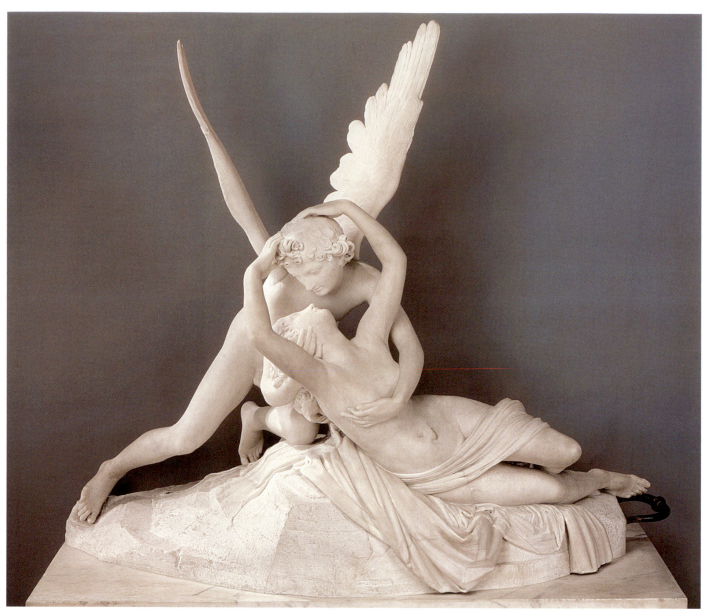

17–12 • Antonio Canova CUPID AND PSYCHE
1787–1793. Marble, 61″ × 68″ (1.55 × 1.73 cm). Musée du Louvre, Paris.

Venice, Canova settled in Rome in 1781, rapidly achieving accolades that compared him with Michelangelo. One of Canova's most admired works depicts the erotically charged mythological subject **CUPID AND PSYCHE** (**FIG. 17–12**) in a way that recalls the ancient Classical sculpture that attracted artists and scholars to Rome. Condemned to a death-like sleep by a jealous Venus, Psyche revives at Cupid's kiss. His projecting wings offset the rounded forms of the two linked bodies and balance the downward diagonal extensions of the figures' legs. The lustrous finish of their marble skin shines against the contrasting textures of drapery and rocks. Although carved fully in the round, the work is meant to be experienced frontally, as a symmetrically stable composition of interlocking triangles and ovals. The effect is ordered, decorous, and calming, if still titillating.

The mode of expression that art historians label Romanticism features loose, fluid brushwork, strong colors, dramatic contrasts of light and dark, complex compositions, and expressive poses and gestures, all reminiscent of the more dramatic aspects of the Baroque. Paintings and sculptures were often based on literary fantasies set in remote times or exotic places and infused with a spirit of sensationalism or melancholy. Romanticism was an imaginative approach to art, centered in the strong feelings of artists and their attempts to inspire those same feelings in viewers. The Enlightenment's faith in reason and empirical knowledge was strongly challenged by Romanticism's celebration of the emotions and subjectivity.

Characteristic of this trend is the work of Swiss painter John Henry Fuseli (1741–1825), who glorified the irrational side of human nature that the Enlightenment sought to deny. Fuseli was raised in an intellectual household that celebrated originality, freedom of expression, and the imaginative power of the irrational. After studying in Rome (1770–1778), where he was drawn to Michelangelo rather than to Classical art, Fuseli settled permanently in London. By the early 1780s, with works such as **THE NIGHTMARE (FIG. 17–13)**, he developed a reputation as a painter of the irrational and the erotic. Fuseli depicts a sleeping woman, sprawled across a divan, oppressed by an erotic dream brought on by the gruesome demon sitting on her chest. In comparison to Canova's calming configuration, the asymmetry of the heroine's offset position is particularly unsettling. The phosphorescent eyes of the horse which thrusts its head into the scene from the murky background at left heightens the frightening effect. And since Romantic art is often personally charged and subjectively felt, it is hardly surprising that Fuseli's *Nightmare* may be autobiographical. On the back of the painting, he sketched a portrait of Anna Landolt, a woman he loved and lost, and whom he confessed he often encountered in erotic dreams.

Art historians at times think of Neoclassicism and Romanticism as successive stylistic movements. Perhaps they have been overly influenced by the progression these two tendencies followed in French painting, moving from David and his followers from the 1780s onward to Géricault and Delacroix by the 1820s. But surveying the broader European landscape, we will discover that stylistic progression, even crisp stylistic differentiation, is not so tidy. The contrasting works of Canova and Fuseli, for example, are essentially contemporary, and by the end of the eighteenth century, many works of art combine elements of both Neoclassicism and Romanticism, though they still sometimes also draw from Rococo, or even Baroque. By the middle of the nineteenth century, as we will see in Chapter 18, new interests in styles and subjects that more faithfully evoke ordinary life and reproduce its frank visual appearance will mount a challenge to all these by-then-traditional artistic tendencies, rooted in past styles or escapist fantasies.

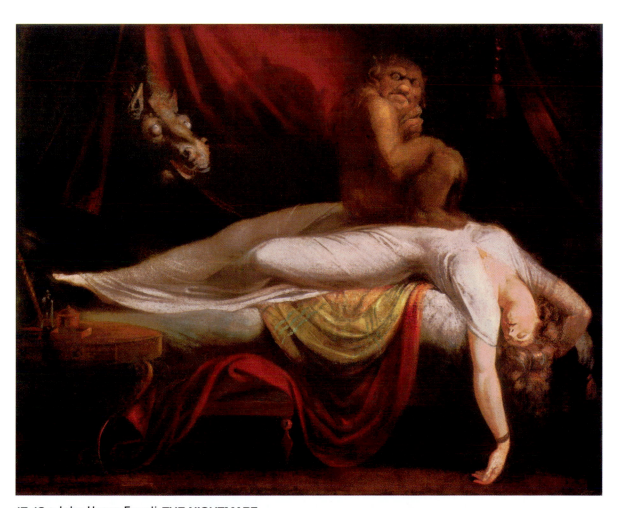

17–13 • John Henry Fuseli THE NIGHTMARE
1781. Oil on canvas, 39¾″ × 49½″ (101 × 127 cm). The Detroit Institute of Arts. Founders Society Purchase with funds from Mr. and Mrs. Bert L. Smokler and Mr. and Mrs. Lawrence A. Fleischmann.

Fuseli was not popular with the English critics. One writer said that his 1780 entry in the London Royal Academy exhibition "ought to be destroyed," and Horace Walpole called another painting in 1785 "shockingly mad, mad, mad, madder than ever." Even after achieving the highest official acknowledgment of his talents, Fuseli was called "the Wild Swiss" and "Painter to the Devil." But the public appreciated his work, and *The Nightmare*, exhibited at the Royal Academy in 1782, was repeated in at least three more versions and its imagery was disseminated through prints published by commercial engravers. One of these prints would later hang in the office of the Austrian psychoanalyst Sigmund Freud, who believed that dreams were manifestations of the dreamer's repressed desires.

Neoclassical Painting in France

The most important French Neoclassical painter was Jacques-Louis David (1748–1825), who dominated French art for over 20 years during the French Revolution and the subsequent reign of Napoleon. In 1774, David won the Prix de Rome, a competitive scholarship for study in Italy awarded to the top graduating students from the French Academy's art school. During six years in Rome, David studied the art of Raphael and Michelangelo, the Baroque Classicism of Poussin and the Carracci, and above all, ancient Roman sculpture and frescos. After his return to Paris, he produced a series of severe Classical paintings that extolled the antique virtues of stoicism, courage, masculinity, and patriotism. Perhaps the most significant of these works, painted as a royal commission, was the **OATH OF THE HORATII** of 1784–1785 (**FIG. 17–14**).

The subject was inspired by Pierre Corneille's seventeenth-century drama *Horace*, that was itself based on ancient Roman history. David invented for his painting, however, an incident that is not found in the play nor in any ancient text—the Horatii taking an oath to fight to the death for Rome. The young men's father, Horace, standing at the center, administers the oath to his sons. To the right, Horace's daughter-in-law Sabina

(from an enemy family) and his daughter Camilla (betrothed to Sabina's brother) both weep, knowing that whatever the outcome of the battle, they will inevitably lose someone dear to them. The tense, energetic young men with prominent glittering swords strike a powerful contrast to the limp swooning of the women, already mourning the tragedy to come, but the entire figural composition is stabilized by the interlocking of classical pyramidal groupings, coordinated with the measured rhythm of repeated arches in the background. The painting's moral message—valuing patriotic duty above personal interests and even family obligations—is expressed with such clarity and power that it created a sensation when David exhibited it in Rome and Paris in early 1785.

David's *Oath* became an emblem of the French Revolution of 1789, which, ironically, precipitated the downfall of the monarchy that had commissioned the work. Its harsh lesson in republican citizenship effectively captured the mood of the new leaders of the French Republic established in 1792—especially the Jacobins, egalitarian democrats who presided over the Reign of Terror in 1793–1794, unprecedented in its appetite for murderous vengeance. The initial French Republic ended in 1799 when the government was reorganized under Napoleon

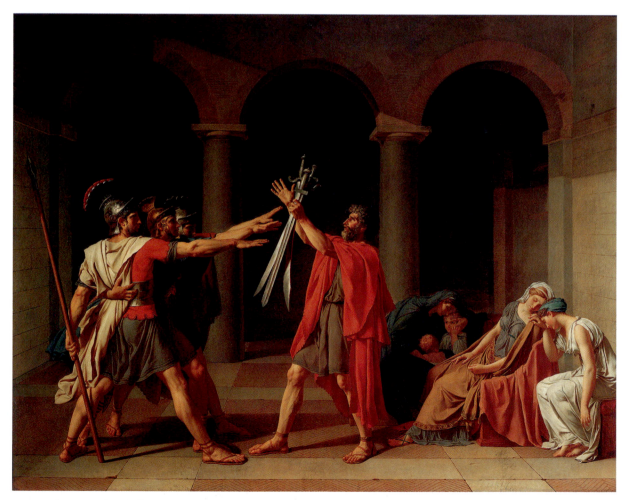

17–14 • Jacques-Louis David **OATH OF THE HORATII**
1784–1785. Oil on canvas, 10′ 8⅜″ × 14′ (3.26 × 4.27 m). Musée du Louvre, Paris.

🔎 **View** the Closer Look for David's *Oath of the Horatii* on **MyArtsLab**

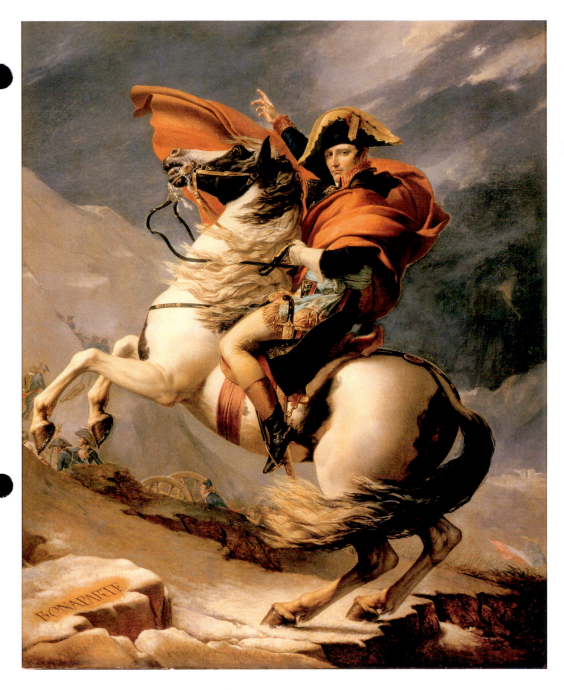

17–15 • Jacques-Louis
David **NAPOLEON
CROSSING THE
SAINT-BERNARD**
1800–1801. Oil on canvas,
8′ 11″ × 7′ 7″ (2.7 × 2.3 m).
Musée National du Château
de Versailles, Versailles.

📖 **Read** the document
related to Jacques-Louis
David on **MyArtsLab**

Bonaparte, a popular and successful general. After Napoleon was named emperor in 1804, David became his court painter.

Even before that time, David had produced canvases that turned Napoleon into an iconic, larger-than-life figure. **NAPOLEON CROSSING THE SAINT-BERNARD (FIG. 17–15)**, painted during 1800–1801, is an idealized vision of the future emperor leading his troops across the Alps into Italy. Although Napoleon actually made the crossing on a donkey, here he charges up the mountain on a rearing horse, past rocks incised with his name and the names of his heroic predecessors, Hannibal and Charlemagne. While strongly Neoclassical in its firm drawing and crisp delineation of individual forms, the painting's sweeping diagonals and flowing draperies recall the idealized Grand Manner of the Baroque. David's career had become so closely linked with Napoleon that when Napoleon fell from

power in 1814, David went into exile in Brussels, where he died in 1825.

As the leading force in French painting during the Revolutionary and Napoleonic eras, David trained many young artists, among them the highly talented Jean-Auguste-Dominique Ingres (1780–1867). Ingres thoroughly absorbed his teacher's Neoclassicism, and interpreted it in a new manner. Being inspired more by the works of Raphael than by antique art, Ingres emulated the Renaissance artist's graceful lyricism, precise drawing, and idealized forms. Ingres won the Prix de Rome and lived in Italy from 1806 to 1824, ultimately returning in 1835 to serve as director of the French Academy in Rome until 1841.

Ingres's most famous paintings were sultry portraits of aristocratic women and exotic, Orientalizing fantasies featuring nude odalisques (female slaves or concubines living in a Turkish

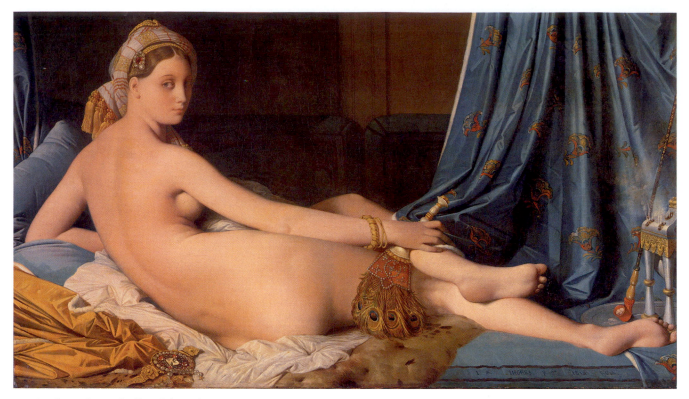

17–16 • Jean-Auguste-Dominique Ingres LARGE ODALISQUE
1814. Oil on canvas, approx. 35″ × 64″ (88.9 × 162.5 cm). Musée du Louvre, Paris.

During Napoleon's campaigns against the British in North Africa, the French discovered the exotic Near East.
Upper-middle-class men were particularly attracted to the institution of the harem, perhaps partly as a reaction
against the egalitarian demands of women of their own class that had been unleashed by the French Revolution.

sultan's harem). In the **LARGE ODALISQUE** (FIG. **17–16**) of 1814, the cool gaze that the woman levels at her master, while turning her naked body away from what we assume is his gaze, makes her simultaneously erotic and aloof. The cool blues of the couch and the curtain heighten the effect of the woman's warm skin, while the tight angularity of the crumpled sheets accentuates the languid, sensual contours of her body. Ingres's virtuosity in defining form and differentiating surface textures is so dazzling that we are hardly aware of the physical medium of paint that has brought them into being.

Although Ingres's commitment to fluid line and elegant postures was grounded in his Neoclassical training, he treated a number of fantasy themes, such as the odalisque, in a highly personal fashion that suggests Romanticism. Note the elongation of the woman's back (she seems to have several extra vertebrae); the widening of her hip; and her tiny, seemingly boneless feet. They may be anatomically incorrect, but his audience found them aesthetically compelling. As a teacher and theorist, Ingres established the taste of a generation and helped ensure the dominance of Neoclassicism over a strong subcurrent of Romanticism in French painting well into the nineteenth century.

Neoclassical Architecture in England and the United States

Neoclassicism was not restricted to painting. While Rococo remained popular on the Continent, a group of British architects

and wealthy amateurs advocated a return to the Classical austerity and simplicity they saw in the architecture of Andrea Palladio, traveling to Italy to see it and then returning home to build magnificent Palladian villas set in extensive gardens on country estates.

In the art of garden design, the British could claim true originality. They created layouts that contrasted sharply not only with the rigid formality of seventeenth-century French gardens but also with the Classicism of English stately homes. Known throughout Europe as the English landscape garden, the sweeping lawns, winding paths, irregularly shaped pools and streams, and asymmetrically placed groves of trees imitated the appearance of the natural rural landscape, carefully and discreetly "improved" by human intelligence and skill.

An especially innovative British Neoclassical designer was the Scottish architect Robert Adam (1728–1792). When he made the Grand Tour (a trip through Europe with an extended stay in Rome) in 1754–1758, Adam largely ignored the great Roman civic architecture and focused instead on the applied ornament of Roman domestic buildings. When he returned to London to set up an architectural firm with his two younger brothers, he brought with him drawings and prints that provided a complete inventory of ancient decorative motifs, which he then modified to formulate his own elegant style. His designs proved ideally suited both to the evolving taste of wealthy clients and to the imperial aspirations of the new British king, George III, whose reign began in 1760.

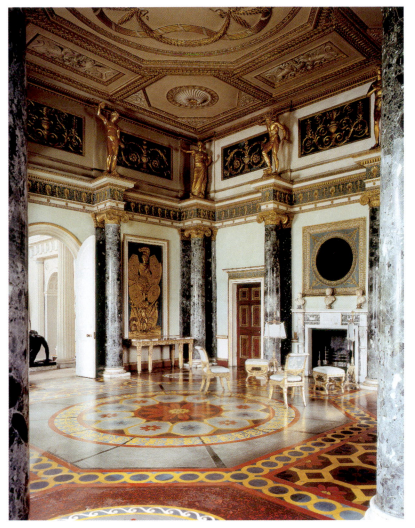

17–17 • Robert Adam ANTEROOM, SYON HOUSE
London, England. 1760–1769.

Adam's conviction that it was acceptable to modify details of the Classical orders was generally opposed by the British architectural establishment. As a result of that opposition, Adam was never elected to the Royal Academy.

Adam achieved wide renown for his interior designs, such as the renovations he carried out between 1760 and 1769 for the duke of Northumberland at his country estate, **SYON HOUSE**, near London. The opulent colored marbles, gilded relief panels, Classical statues, spirals, garlands, rosettes, and gilded moldings are luxuriously profuse, yet restrained by the strong geometric order imposed on them (**FIG. 17–17**). Adam's preference for bright pastel colors and small-scale decorative elements derives both from Rococo and the recently uncovered ruins of Pompeii (see Chapter 6). Such interiors were designed partly as settings for the art collections of British aristocrats, which included antiquities as well as a range of Neoclassical painting, sculpture, and decorative arts, including fine silver (see "A Closer Look," p. 464).

Neoclassicism continued as the dominant architectural style in the United States during the Federal period (1783–1830) that followed the colonies' victory in their War of Independence. Thomas Jefferson (1743–1826), an enthusiastic amateur architect, had in the 1770s designed his Virginia residence, Monticello, in a style influenced by ancient Roman architecture and British Palladian villas, with direction from Palladio's *Four Books of Architecture*. But when Jefferson went to Paris as the American ambassador to France from 1785 to 1789, he discovered an elegant domestic architecture that made his home seem provincial. When he returned to **MONTICELLO** in 1793, he completely redesigned the house, using French doors and tall narrow windows (**FIG. 17–18**), placing a balustrade above the unifying cornice to mask the second floor. Despite these French elements and his stated rejection of the British Palladian mode, the building's simplicity and combination of temple front and dome remain closer to English than to French buildings.

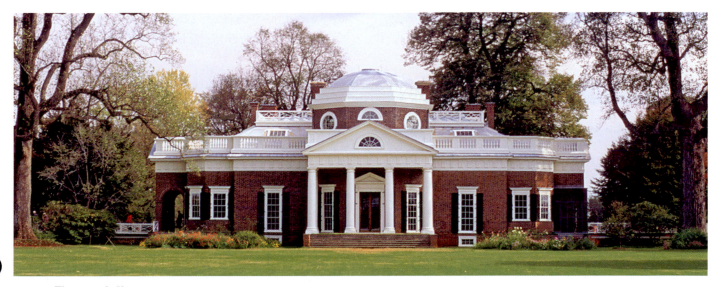

17–18 • Thomas Jefferson MONTICELLO
Near Charlottesville, Virginia. 1769–1782, 1796–1809.

A CLOSER LOOK

Georgian Silver ▶

Elizabeth Morley. George III toddy ladle, 1802; Alice and George Burrows. George III snuffbox, 1802; Elizabeth Cooke. George III salver, 1767; Ann and Peter Bateman. George III goblet, 1797; Hester Bateman. George III double beaker, 1790. National Museum of Women in the Arts, Washington, D.C. Silver Collection assembled by Nancy Valentine, purchased with funds donated by Mr. and Mrs. Oliver Grace and family.

During the Georgian period—the years from 1714 to 1830, when Great Britain was ruled by four successive kings named George—wealthy British families filled their homes with objects made of fine silver. The utensils and vessels they collected were not simply practical articles; they signified high social status. All of the objects shown here bear the marks of silver shops run either wholly or partly by women, who played a significant role in the production of silver at this time.

This goblet was used for drinking punch, a potent alcoholic beverage enjoyed by British high society. The gilded interior protected the silver from the acid in alcoholic drinks.

This box contained snuff, a pulverized tobacco inhaled by both men and women of the upper class. This snuffbox has curved sides for easy insertion into the pocket of a gentleman's tight-fitting trousers.

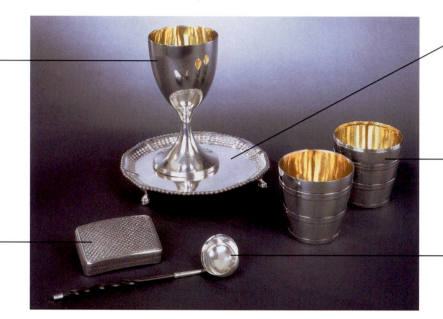

The filled goblets would have been served on a flat salver.

These "double beaker" cups are also for drinking punch. The smaller size made them convenient for use when traveling.

This ladle was used to pour punch from a bowl into a goblet. Its twisted whalebone handle floats, making it easy to retrieve from the bowl.

View the Closer Look for Georgian Silver on **MyArtsLab**

Romantic Painting and Printmaking in France and Spain

Romanticism, already anticipated in French painting during Napoleon's reign, did not gain wide public acceptance until after 1830. Artists who painted in this style began to draw on new literary sources; they also added a new dimension of social criticism. Their dramatic presentations, especially the work of Théodore Géricault (1791–1824) and Eugène Delacroix (1798–1863), were intended to stir public emotions.

After a brief stay in Rome between 1816 and 1817, Géricault returned to Paris determined to make a great painting of a contemporary event, and he settled on the scandalous and sensational shipwreck of the **MEDUSA** for his subject (**FIG. 17–19**). In 1816, a ship carrying colonists headed for Madagascar ran aground near its destination; its captain was an incompetent aristocrat appointed by the newly restored monarchy for political reasons. Because there were insufficient lifeboats for all on board, the captain reserved them for himself and his officers, consigning the 152 passengers and crew to a hastily built raft, which tossed about on stormy seas for nearly two weeks

before it was found. The 15 passengers who had managed to survive over this period had subsisted for the last days of their horrific voyage on human flesh. Géricault decided to show the moment when they first spotted their rescue ship, their survival not yet assured.

The artist's academic training underlies the painting's careful organization, constructed as a series of interlocking triangular figural groups. The outstretched arms of the victims lead viewers' eyes to the upper right, where the climactic figure of Jean Charles, an African survivor, is held aloft, waving a red cloth to attract the attention of a ship that is still only a speck on the stormy horizon. By placing a black man at the top of the pyramid of survivors and giving him the power to save his comrades by signaling the rescue ship, Géricault suggests that freedom for all will occur only when the most oppressed member of society is emancipated.

At the Salon of 1819, Géricault showed this painting under the neutral title *A Shipwreck Scene*, perhaps to downplay its contemporary political critique and deflect attention to a larger philosophical theme—the eternal struggle of humanity

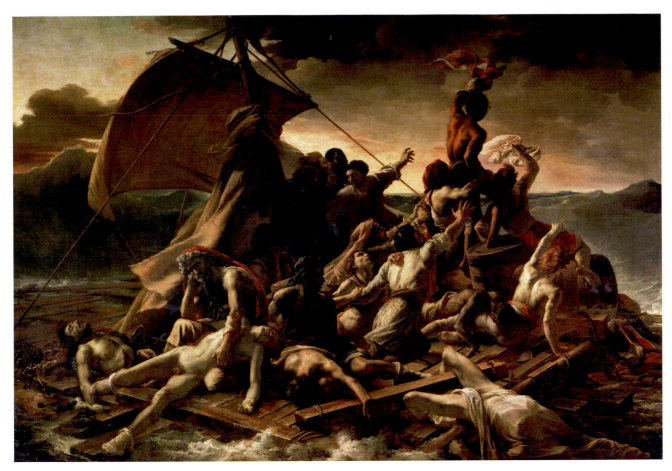

17–19 • Théodore Géricault **THE RAFT OF THE "MEDUSA"**
1818–1819. Oil on canvas, 16′ 1″ × 23′ 6″ (4.9 × 7.16 m). Musée du Louvre, Paris.

View the Closer Look for Géricault's *The Raft of the "Medusa"* on **MyArtsLab**

against the elements. Most contemporary French critics, however, were not fooled, and interpreted the painting as a political commentary. Liberals praised it for exposing the scandal, and royalists condemned it as sensationalist journalism rather than art. Because the monarchy refused to buy it, Géricault exhibited *The Raft of the "Medusa"* commercially on a two-year tour of Ireland and England, where the London exhibition attracted more than 50,000 paying visitors. Today, the work remains a masterful illustration of human tragedy, revealing the injustice that often causes it and inspiring responses of indignant compassion.

Eugène Delacroix, who modeled for one of the nude victims on Géricault's raft, soon succeeded him as the inspirational leader of the Romantic movement. **LIBERTY LEADING THE PEOPLE: JULY 28, 1830 (FIG. 17–20)**—his most famous work, now as well as then—summarized for many the destiny of France after the fall of Napoleon in 1815. The new constitutional monarchy undid many reforms instituted after the Revolution, including the reinstatement of press censorship, the return of education to Church control, and the limitation of voting rights. Public resentment ignited in a massive uprising in July 1830, and Delacroix's painting memorialized this revolt a few months after it took place. An allegorical figure of Liberty leads the revolutionaries—a motley crew of students, laborers, children, and top-hatted lawyers—into the heat of battle. This

is not the record of an actual event but an imaginative artistic re-creation, faithful to the emotional climate of the moment as the artist himself felt it.

Honoré Daumier (1808–1879) worked in the more popular print medium of **lithography** (see "Lithography," p. 467), publishing his first lithograph in 1829, at age 21, in the weekly satirical magazine *La Silhouette*. In the wake of the 1830 revolution in Paris, Daumier began supplying pictures to *La Caricature*, an anti-monarchist, pro-republican magazine, and the equally partisan *Le Charivari*, the first daily newspaper illustrated with lithographs. In 1834, Daumier made a lithographic print of the atrocities on **RUE TRANSNONAIN (FIG. 17–21)**. A government guard had been shot and killed on this street during a demonstration by workers, and in response the riot squad killed everyone in the building where they believed the marksman was hiding. Daumier shows the bloody aftermath of the event, an innocent family disturbed from their sleep and then murdered. The wife lies in the shadows to the left, her husband in the center of the room, and an elderly man to the right. It takes a few moments for viewers to realize that under the central figure's back there are also the bloody head and arms of a murdered child. Daumier was known for his biting caricatures and social commentary in print form, but this image is one of his most powerful.

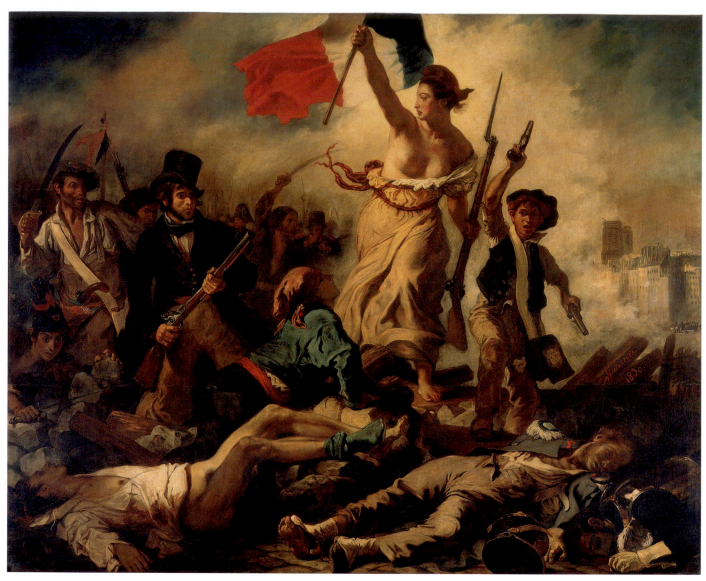

17–20 • Eugène Delacroix LIBERTY LEADING THE PEOPLE: JULY 28, 1830
1830. Oil on canvas, 8′ 6½″ × 10′ 8″ (2.6 × 3.25 m). Musée du Louvre, Paris.

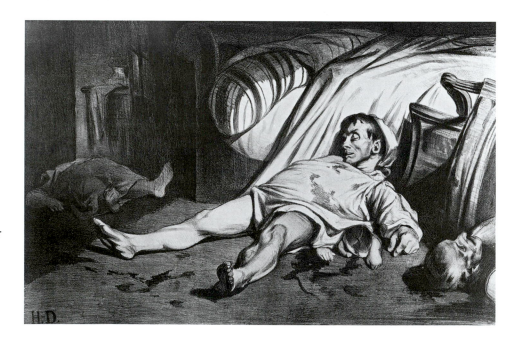

17–21 • Honoré Daumier RUE TRANSNONAIN, LE 15 AVRIL 1834
1834. Lithograph, 11″ × 17⅜″ (28 × 44 cm). Bibliothèque Nationale, Paris.

TECHNIQUE | Lithography

Aloys Senefelder invented **lithography** in Bavaria, Germany, in 1796 and registered for an exclusive right to the process the following year. Lithography is a planographic process—that is, the printing is done from a flat surface. It was the first wholly new printing process to be introduced since the fifteenth century, when the intaglio, or **incising**, process was developed (see "Woodcuts and Engravings," p. 306).

Lithography, still popular today, is based on the natural antagonism between oil and water. Artists draw on a flat surface—traditionally, fine-grained stone—with a greasy crayon. The stone's surface is flooded with water, over which an oil-based ink is rolled. The ink adheres to the greasy areas but not to the damp ones. Then a sheet of paper is placed face-down on the inked stone, and the stone and paper, covered by a blanket for protection, are passed through a flatbed press. A scraper applies light pressure from above as the stone and paper pass under it, transferring ink from stone to paper. This makes lithography

a direct method of creating a printed image. Goya, Géricault, Delacroix, Daumier, and Toulouse-Lautrec (see Chapter 18) exploited the medium to great effect. By the end of the nineteenth century, inexpensive lithographs were in every house and owned by people at every level of society.

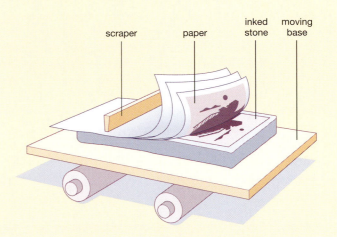

scraper   paper   inked stone   moving base

● **Watch** a video about the process of lithography on **MyArtsLab**

In Spain, Francisco Goya y Lucientes (1746–1828) became the major figure in the Romantic movement, famous as both painter and printmaker. In 1799, he published *Los Caprichos* (*The Caprices*), the first of several suites of etchings he created during his career. Setting the tone for the series of 80 etchings is **THE SLEEP OF REASON PRODUCES MONSTERS (FIG. 17–22)**. Although the text published with the print sounds a hopeful note ("Imagination abandoned by reason produces impossible monsters; united with her, she is the mother of the arts and the source of their wonders"), the images are an angry attack on contemporary Spanish manners and morals that make Hogarth's satire (SEE FIG. 17–5) seem tame. This print shows a slumbering personification of Reason, behind whom lurk dark creatures of the night—owls, bats, and a cat—that are let loose when Reason sleeps. The following prints enumerate specific

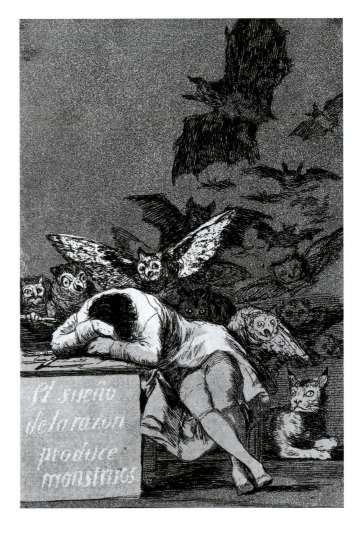

17-22 • Francisco Goya THE SLEEP OF REASON PRODUCES MONSTERS NO. 43
From *Los Caprichos* (*The Caprices*). 1796–1798; published 1799. Etching and aquatint, 8½″ × 6″ (21.6 × 15.2 cm). Courtesy of The Hispanic Society of America, New York.

Goya offered 300 sets of this series for sale in 1799 but withdrew them two days later without explanation. He was probably responding to a Church warning that if he did not, he might be called to appear before the Inquisition because of the unflattering portrayal of the Church in some of the etchings. In 1803, Goya donated the plates to the Royal Printing Office.

● **View** the Closer Look for Goya's *The Sleep of Reason Produces Monsters* on **MyArtsLab**

follies of Spanish life. Goya hoped they would alert Spanish people to the errors of their foolish ways and reawaken them to reason. The premise may be hopeful, but Goya's portrait of human folly and cruelty is bitter and disturbing. Far from Enlightenment faith in the inherent rationality and goodness of humanity, Goya believed that the violence, greed, and foolishness of his society had to be examined mercilessly if it were to be changed in any way.

This theme continues in Goya's painting of the **THIRD OF MAY, 1808** (FIG. 17–23). In 1808, Napoleon conquered Spain and placed his brother Joseph Bonaparte on its throne. Many Spaniards, including Goya, at first welcomed the French because they brought political reform, but the new government soon turned despotic. On May 2, 1808, a rumor spread through Madrid that the French planned to kill the royal family. The populace rose up, and a day of bloody street fighting ensued. Hundreds of Spanish people were arrested, herded into a convent, and executed by a French firing squad before dawn on May 3rd. In Goya's impassioned memorial to that slaughter, the broad gestures of the defenseless rebels and the mechanical efficiency of the firing squad create a nightmarish tableau. A spotlighted victim in a brilliant white shirt confronts his faceless killers with outstretched arms, recalling the crucified Jesus, an image of searing pathos. This powerful work encapsulates the essence of Romanticism: the sensationalizing of a current event, the loose brushwork, the unbalanced composition, and the theatrical lighting. This painting is not a cool, didactic representation of civic sacrifice, like David's *Oath of the Horatii* (SEE FIG. 17–14); it is an image of conspicuous horror and blind terror. When asked why he painted such a brutal scene, Goya responded, "To warn men never to do it again."

The Art of the Americas under Spain

The sixteenth-century Spanish conquest of Central and South America had led to the suppression of indigenous religions and the forced conversion of native peoples to Roman Catholicism. The Christian iconography of the conquerors mixed with the symbolism of indigenous beliefs, and even the Virgin Mary took on a Mesoamerican inflection after she was believed to have appeared in Mexico. In 1531, a Mexican peasant named

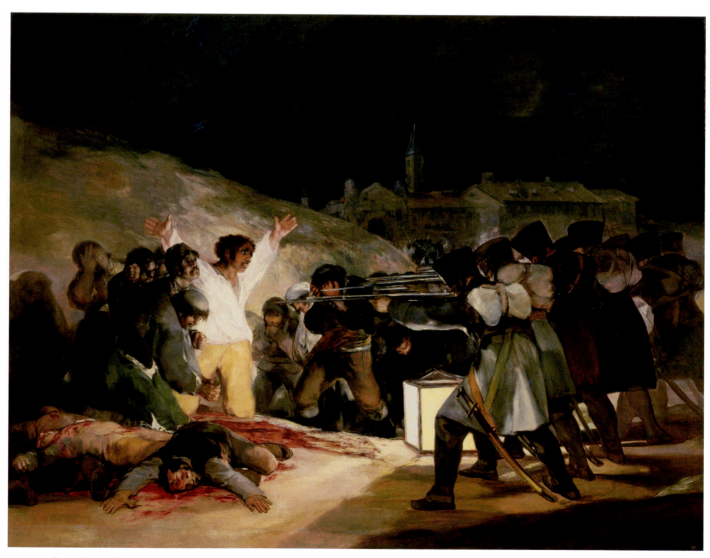

17–23 • Francisco Goya THIRD OF MAY, 1808
1814–1815. Oil on canvas, 8′ 9″ × 13′ 4″ (2.67 × 4.06 m). Museo del Prado, Madrid.

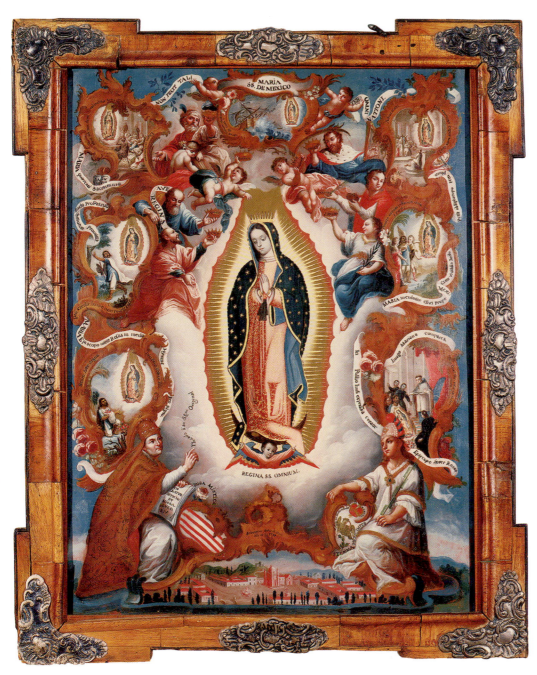

17–24 • Sebastian Salcedo
VIRGIN OF GUADALUPE
1779. Oil on panel and copper,
25″ × 19″ (63.5 × 48.3 cm).
Denver Art Museum.

At the bottom right is the
female personification of New
Spain (Mexico) and at the left is
Pope Benedict XIV (pontificate
1740–1758), who in 1754
declared the Virgin of Guadalupe
to be the patroness of the
Americas. Between the figures,
the sanctuary of Guadalupe
in Mexico can be seen in the
distance. The four small scenes
circling the Virgin represent the
story of Juan Diego, and at the
top, three scenes depict Mary's
miracles. The six figures above
the Virgin represent prophets
and patriarchs from the Hebrew
Bible and apostles and saints
from the New Testament.

Juan Diego claimed that the Virgin Mary visited him and, in
his native Nahuatl language, told him to build a church on a
hill where an Aztec goddess had once been worshiped—subsequently causing flowers to bloom so that Juan Diego could show
them to the archbishop as proof of his vision. When Juan Diego
opened his bundle of flowers, the cloak he had used to wrap
them in is said to have borne the image of a Mexican Mary, presented in a composition quite popular in Spain, portraying the
Virgin of the Immaculate Conception (SEE FIG. 14–17). The site
of Juan Diego's vision was renamed Guadalupe, after Our Lady
of Guadalupe in Spain, and it became a venerated pilgrimage
center. In 1754, Pope Benedict XIV declared the Virgin of Guadalupe, as depicted here in a 1779 work by Sebastian Salcedo,
the patron saint of the Americas (FIG. 17–24).

Romantic Landscape Painting

*What aspects of Romanticism are found in
nineteenth-century English, American, and German
landscape painting?*

Romanticism in England flourished in landscape painting.
It took two forms—the tranquil and the dramatic. The tranquil style entailed closely observed representations of nature,
meant to communicate reverence for the landscape as a spiritual precinct and to counteract the effects of industrialization
and urbanization that were rapidly transforming it. In contrast,
dramatic landscape painting emphasized turbulent or fantastic
natural scenery, often shaken by natural disasters such as storms
and avalanches, and aimed to stir viewers' emotions and arouse

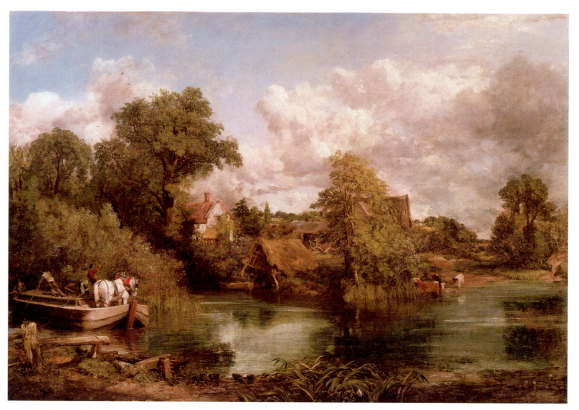

17–25 • John Constable THE WHITE HORSE
1819. Oil on canvas, 4′ 3¾″ × 6′ 2⅛″ (1.31 × 1.88 m). The Frick Collection, New York.

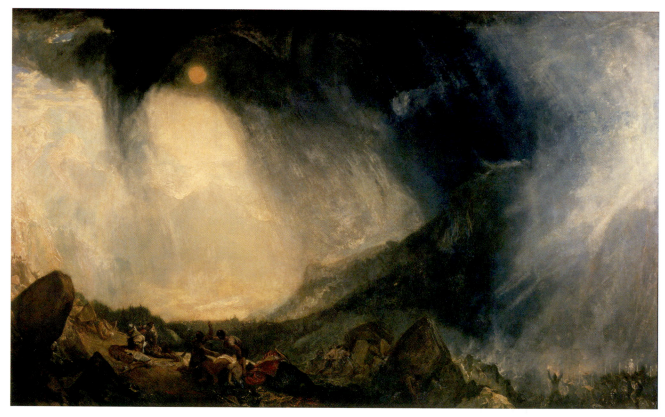

17–26 • Joseph Mallord William Turner SNOWSTORM: HANNIBAL AND HIS ARMY CROSSING THE ALPS
1812. Oil on canvas, 4′ 9″ × 7′ 9″ (1.46 × 2.39 m). Tate, London.

Watch a video about Joseph Mallord William Turner on **MyArtsLab**

a feeling of awe. John Constable (1776–1837) specialized in carefully observed scenes of rural tranquility, while Joseph Mallord William Turner (1775–1851) focused on loosely painted studies of mood and drama.

Constable claimed that the landscape of his youth in southern England had made him a painter before he ever picked up a brush. In spite of his training at the Royal Academy, where landscape was considered an inferior subject for art, he was captivated by the landscapes of seventeenth-century Dutch artists, and decided to follow in their footsteps. **THE WHITE HORSE** (**FIG. 17–25**) of 1819 draws on Constable's determination to base his work on careful studies of nature. Although he composed his paintings in his studio, he used sketches recorded on walking tours, insisting that art should be an objective record of things actually seen. His goal was to capture the time of day, the humidity in the air, the smell of wet earth. In this painting, a storm passes away to the right, while a farmer and his helpers ferry a workhorse across a river. Sunlight glistens off the water and foliage, an effect Constable achieved through tiny dabs of pure white paint. The painting is deeply nostalgic, harking back to an agrarian past that was fast disappearing in industrial England.

Turner, Constable's contemporary, won public acclaim at an early age. By age 27, he was elected to full membership of the Royal Academy, eventually becoming a professor at the Royal Academy school. In his mature paintings, the phenomena of colored light and misty atmosphere became his true subject. To academicians, his works increasingly looked like sketches or preliminary underpaintings of unfinished canvases, but to his admirers, including Constable, they were "golden visions, glorious and beautiful," painted with "tinted steam."

His **SNOWSTORM: HANNIBAL AND HIS ARMY CROSSING THE ALPS** (**FIG. 17–26**) epitomized Romanticism's view of the awesomeness of nature. An enormous vortex of wind, mist, and snow masks the sun and threatens to annihilate the soldiers marching below it. Barely discernible in the distance is the figure of Hannibal, mounted on an elephant to lead his troops through the Alps to meet the Roman army in 218 BCE. Turner probably meant his painting as an allegory of the Napoleonic Wars. Napoleon himself had crossed the Alps, an event celebrated by David in a laudatory portrait (SEE FIG. 17–15). But while David's painting, which Turner saw in Paris in 1802, conceived Napoleon as a powerful figure, commanding not only his troops but nature itself, Turner reduced Hannibal to a speck on the horizon, threatened with his troops by natural disaster, as if foretelling their eventual defeat.

Turner's paintings also evoke notions of the **sublime**, an aesthetic category outlined by British writer Edmund Burke in an essay of 1756 that strongly influenced Romantic artists.

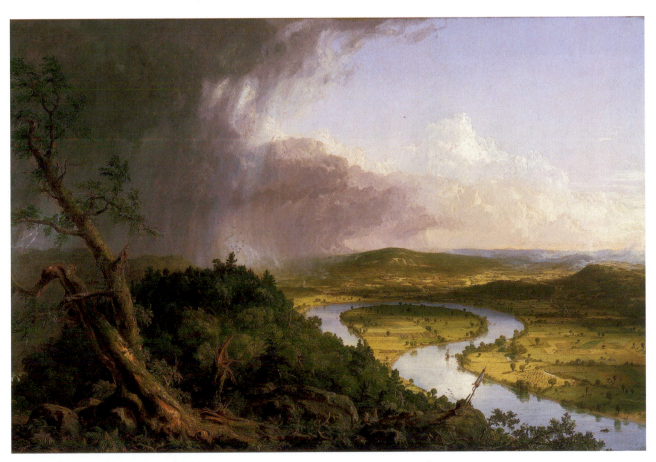

17–27 • Thomas Cole THE OXBOW
1836. Oil on canvas, 51½″ × 76″ (1.31 × 1.94 cm). The Metropolitan Museum of Art, New York. Gift of Mrs. Russell Sage, 1908 (08.228).

View the Closer Look for Cole's *The Oxbow* on **MyArtsLab**

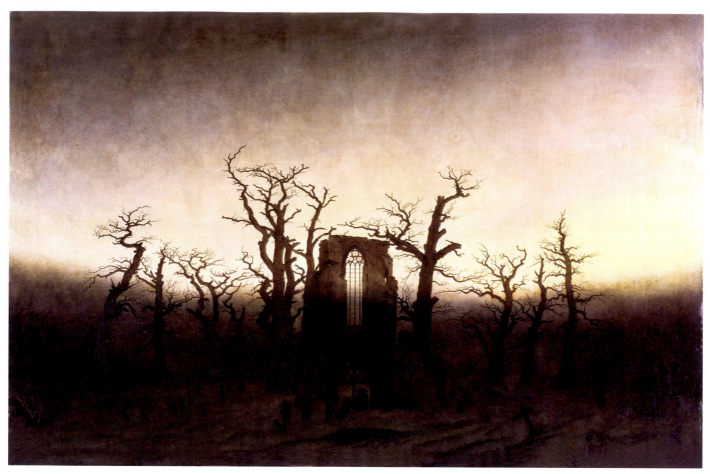

17–28 • Caspar David Friedrich ABBEY IN AN OAK FOREST
1809–1810. Oil on canvas, 44″ × 68½″ (111.8 × 174 cm). Berlin, Nationalgalerie, Staatliche Museen zu Berlin.

According to Burke, when we witness something that instills fascination mixed with fear, or when we stand in the presence of something far larger than ourselves, our feelings will transcend those we encounter in normal life. The awe-inspiring aspect of savage grandeur, uncontrollable by mere humans, evokes the transcendent power of God. Turner translated this concept of the sublime into powerful paintings of turbulence in the natural world.

If we place English Romantic landscape painters in a sequence, with those favoring imagination and drama at one end (Turner) and partisans of down-to-earth idylls on the other (Constable), we will find the middle ground occupied by American painters such as Thomas Cole (1801–1848). Cole emigrated from England to the United States at age 17 and by 1820 was working as an itinerant portrait painter. On trips around New York State, he sketched and painted the landscape, which quickly became his chief interest as he launched what became known as the Hudson River School. Cole painted **THE OXBOW** (**FIG. 17–27**) for exhibition at the National Academy of Design in New York. The monumental scale suits the dramatic view from the top of Mount Holyoke in western Massachusetts across a spectacular oxbow bend in the Connecticut River. To Cole, such ancient geological formations constituted America's "antiquities." Along a great sweeping arc produced by the departing dark clouds and the edge of the mountain, Cole

contrasts two sides of the American landscape: dense, stormy wilderness and congenial, pastoral valleys. The fading storm perhaps suggests that the wild will eventually give way to the bountiful, yielding its fruits to civilization.

In Germany, the Romantic landscape painter Caspar David Friedrich (1774–1840) considered landscape as a vehicle through which to achieve spiritual revelation. As a young man, he was influenced by the writings and teachings of Gotthard Kosegarten, a local Lutheran pastor and poet who taught that the divine was visible through a deep personal connection with nature. Kosegarten argued that just as the Bible was God's book, the landscape was God's "Book of Nature." Friedrich studied at the Copenhagen Academy before settling in Dresden, where the poet Johann Wolfgang von Goethe encouraged him to make landscape the principal subject of his art. He sketched from nature but painted in the studio, synthesizing his sketches with his memories of and feelings about nature. Through the foggy atmosphere of Friedrich's **ABBEY IN AN OAK FOREST** (**FIG. 17–28**), a funeral procession of monks in the lower foreground is barely visible through the gloom settling on the snow-covered world of human habitation. Most prominent are the boldly silhouetted trunks and bare branches of a grove of oak trees, and nestled among them is the ruin of a Gothic wall, a formal juxtaposition that creates a natural cathedral from this cold and mysterious landscape.

The eighteenth century marks a great divide. When it opened, a few wealthy aristocrats controlled the land worked by the largest and poorest class. By the century's end revolutions were wrenching power away from this aristocracy, and new sources of wealth expanded the affluent middle class. The peasants continued to suffer. Such political and economic developments manifested a broader philosophical revolution known as the Enlightenment, characterized by an optimistic view that humanity and its institutions could be reformed, if not perfected. Philosophers insisted that humans were here not to serve God or the ruling class, but to pursue their own happiness and fulfillment.

Three artistic styles are surveyed in this chapter: Rococo, Neoclassicism, and Romanticism. Severe and serious, Neoclassicism arose in Enlightenment reaction to the playful and sensuous Rococo style that dominated the early century. In many ways Neoclassicism's antithesis, Romanticism foregrounded imagination and emotions, forming a subjective reaction to an Enlightenment focus on rationality. No longer the privileged preserve of aristocrats, art begins to engage with the complexities of a real world in transition, and it will blossom near the middle of the nineteenth century in a new attention to the actual conditions of that real world, often using art to challenge and critique it.

THINK ABOUT IT

17.1 Summarize some of the key stylistic traits of French Rococo art and architecture, and explain how these traits relate to the social context of salon life. Then analyze one Rococo work from the chapter and explain how it is typical of the period style.

17.2 What moralizing theme is shared by Angelica Kauffmann's history painting of Corneila and Marie-Louise-Élisabeth Vigée-Lebrun's portrait of Marie Antoinette? How is it expressed by these artists in two very different types of painting?

17.3 Explain the relationship of David's *Oath of the Horatii* to Enlightenment thought and Classical art.

17.4 What features of Romanticism characterize Turner's *Snowstorm: Hannibal and His Army Crossing the Alps*?

| CROSSCURRENTS |

FIG. 12–1   FIG. 17–1

Double portraits of couples are common in the history of European art. Assess the ways in which these two examples portray the nature of the marital relationship of these men and women. How do the portrayals reflect the social structures and concerns of the cultural situations in which these couples lived?

✓ **Study** and **Review** on **MyArtsLab**

IN PERSPECTIVE

1700

1720

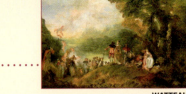

WATTEAU,
The Pilgrimage to Cythera
1717

1740

● Discovery of Pompeii 1748

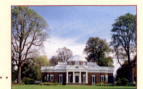

JEFFERSON, Monticello
1769–1809

● Seven Years' War
1756–1763

1760

● English Royal Academy
of Arts Founded 1768

● Louis XV, King of France
ruled 1715–1774

● Louis XVI, King of France
ruled 1774–1792

● American Revolution
Begins 1776

1780

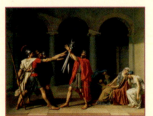

DAVID, Oath of the Horatii
1784–1785

● Thomas Jefferson in France as American Ambassador
1785–1789

● French Revolution Begins 1789

1800

● Napoleon, Emperor
of France
ruled 1804–1814

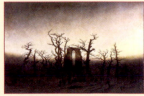

FRIEDRICH, Abbey in an Oak
Forest 1809–1810

1820

DELACROIX,
Liberty Leading the People
1830

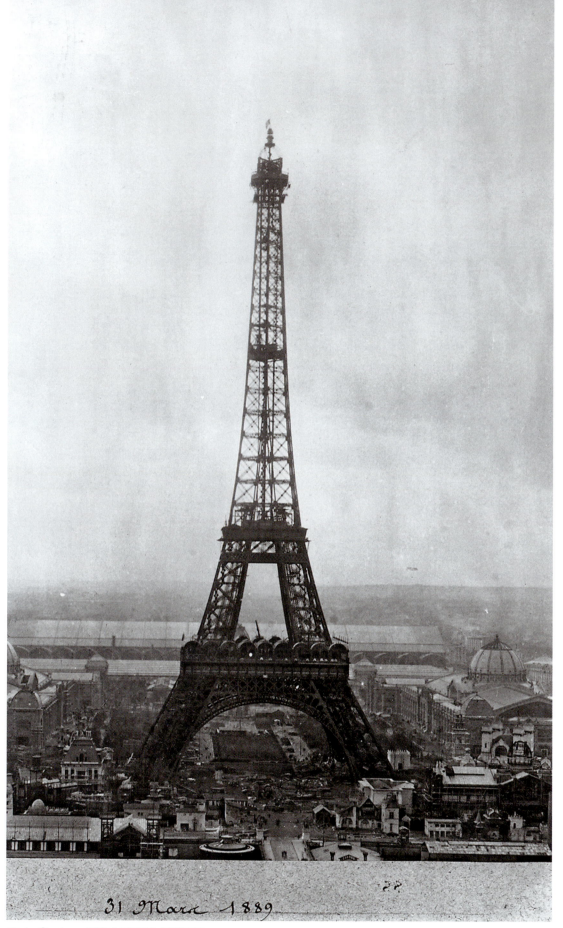

31 Mars 1889

18–1 • Gustave Eiffel EIFFEL TOWER
Paris. 1887–1889. Photographed in March, 1889. Height 984′ (300 m).

👁 **Watch** the Students on Site video of the Eiffel Tower on **MyArtsLab**

EUROPEAN AND AMERICAN ART, 1840–1910

18.1 Describe the impact of historicism and a new interest in structural innovation in late nineteenth-century architecture.

18.2 Explain the continuation of academic Neoclassical standards, as well as movements that worked to reject them, in late nineteenth-century art and architecture.

18.3 Identify the early experiments that led to the emergence of photography as a new art form.

18.4 Discuss the ways in which the movement toward Realism in art reflected the social and political concerns of the nineteenth century.

18.5 Summarize the origins, nature, and content of Impressionism.

18.6 Distinguish among the several manifestations of Post-Impressionism.

LOOKING FORWARD ▶

The world-famous **EIFFEL TOWER** (FIG. **18–1**) is a proud reminder of the nineteenth-century French belief in the progress and ultimate perfectibility of civilization through science and technology. Structural engineer Gustave Eiffel (1832–1923) designed and constructed the tower to serve as a monumental approach to the 1889 Universal Exposition in Paris. When completed, it stood 984 feet high and was the tallest structure in the world, taller than the Egyptian pyramids or Gothic cathedrals. The Eiffel Tower was the main attraction of the Universal Exposition, one of more than 20 such international fairs staged throughout Europe and the United States in the second half of the nineteenth century. These events showcased and compared international industry, science, and the applied, decorative, and fine arts. An object of pride for the French nation, the Eiffel Tower was intended to demonstrate France's superior engineering, technological and industrial knowledge, and power. Although originally conceived as a temporary structure, it still stands today.

The initial response to the Eiffel Tower was mixed. In 1887, a group of 47 writers, musicians, and artists wrote to *Le*

Temps protesting "the erection…of the useless and monstrous Eiffel Tower," which they described as "a black and gigantic factory chimney." Gustave Eiffel, however, said, "I believe the tower will have its own beauty," and that it "will show that we [the French] are not simply an amusing people, but also the country of engineers." Indeed, when completed, the Eiffel Tower quickly became an international symbol of advanced thought and modernity among artists, and was admired by the public as a wondrous spectacle. Today it is the symbol of Paris itself.

The tower was one of the city's most photographed structures in 1889, its immensity dwarfing the tiny buildings below. Thousands of tourists to the Exposition bought souvenir photographs taken by professional and commercial photographers. This one, dating from late March 1889, shows the tower almost complete. A close look at the bottom two tiers with the fairgrounds below betrays evidence of rapid last-minute construction in preparation for the May 6th opening of the Exposition.

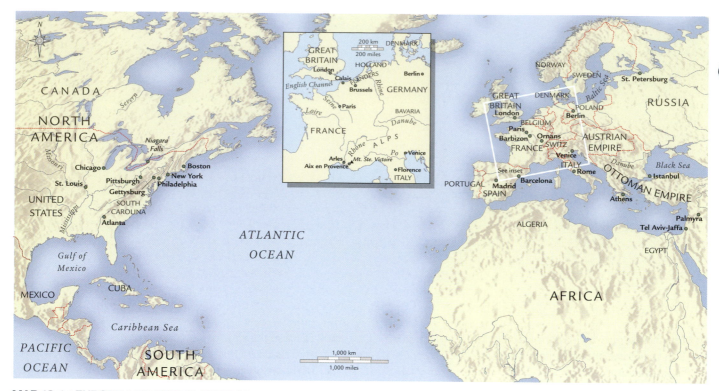

MAP 18-1 • EUROPE AND NORTH AMERICA IN 1848

By the mid nineteenth century social and technological changes were transforming Europe and the United States and were contributing to the rapid growth of the urban centers.

The Enlightenment set in motion powerful forces that would dramatically transform life in Europe and the United States during the nineteenth century (**MAP 18-1**). Great advances in manufacturing, transportation, and communications created new products for consumers and new wealth for entrepreneurs, fueling the rise of urban centers and improving living conditions for many. Animating these developments was the widespread belief in "progress" and the ultimate perfectibility of human civilization—a belief rooted deeply in Enlightenment thought. But this so-called Industrial Revolution also condemned masses of workers to poverty and catalyzed new political movements that sought to reform society.

Technological developments in agriculture and manufacturing displaced many owners of small farms and cottage industries—as well as their employees—forcing people to move to new factory and mining towns in search of employment. Increasing numbers of industrial laborers suffered miserable working and living conditions. In response, socialist movements condemned the exploitation of laborers by capitalist factory owners and advocated communal or state ownership of the means of production and distribution. The most radical of these movements was communism, which called for the abolition of private property. In 1848, Karl Marx and Friedrich Engels published the *Communist Manifesto*, which predicted the violent overthrow of the property-holding bourgeoisie (middle class) by the proletariat (working class) and the creation of a classless society.

Also in 1848, the Americans Lucretia Mott and Elizabeth Cady Stanton held the country's first women's rights convention, in Seneca Falls, New York. In their fight to improve the status of women, they called for the equality of women and men before the law, property rights for married women, the acceptance of women into institutions of higher education, the admission of women to all trades and professions, equal pay for equal work, and women's suffrage (achieved only in 1920).

American suffragists were also active in the abolitionist movement, which sought to end slavery, but slavery in the United States was only finally eliminated as a result of the devastating Civil War (1861–1865). After this battle between the states, the United States became a major industrial power, and the American Northeast underwent rapid urbanization, fueled by millions of immigrants from Europe seeking economic opportunities.

The second half of the nineteenth century has been called the "positivist age" because of widespread faith in the affirmative consequences of rational thought and scientific progress. This was the period that brought us the telephone and radio, vaccines and disinfectant, steel and electrical lighting. But some scientific discoveries challenged traditional religious beliefs and affected social philosophy. Geologists claimed that the earth was far older than the 6,000 years claimed by biblical fundamentalists, and Charles Darwin challenged the literal acceptance of the biblical account of Creation, proposing that all life evolved from a common ancestor and changed through genetic mutation and natural selection. Religious conservatives attacked Darwin's account of evolution, which they saw as a denial of the divine creation of humans and even of the existence of God.

These developments parallel transformations in the visual arts. There was widespread rejection of Romanticism in favor of visualizing the ordinary, observable world, at times seeking scientific accuracy. There is a positivist component across the full range of artistic developments after 1850—from photography's ability to record certain aspects of the world with unprecedented accuracy, to Impressionism's quasi-scientific emphasis on the optical properties of light and color. In architecture, the application of new technologies also led gradually to the abandonment of the fashion for facing buildings with historicizing ornamentation in favor of allowing structural systems and materials to emerge and create expressive qualities on their own.

But the emphasis on science, technology, and the modern world did not go unchallenged. Later in the nineteenth century, some artists began to turn to radically new abstract ways of expressing their personal feelings about their subjects or evoking affective states of mystery or spirituality. Like the Romantic artists before them, they shunned the depiction of the ordinary or the heroic in favor of exploring the realms of myth, fantasy, and imagination.

Architecture

What was the impact of historicism and a new interest in structural innovation on late nineteenth-century architecture?

Major works of public architecture in the nineteenth century were decorated, inside and out, with motifs drawn from historic models—a practice called **historicism**. The conventions of historicism were taught at the architecture school of the École des Beaux-Arts (School of Fine Arts) in Paris, which became an important training ground for European and American architects. A spectacular example of historicizing architecture is the Paris **OPÉRA** (opera house) (FIG. 18–2), designed by Charles Garnier (1825–1898). The underlying cast-iron frame of the building is concealed by a lavish overlay of nonstructural "neo-Baroque" decoration, employed here to recall an earlier period of French greatness. The opulence is consistent with the building's primary function as the site of entertainment, showcasing the dedication to wealth and pleasure that characterized the period. Gilded decoration, exuberant sculpture, and a lavish mix of expensive, polychrome materials cover the foyer (entrance hall or lobby), where the great, sweeping staircase (FIG. 18–3) served as a stage—rivaling the one inside where the operatic spectacles were performed—on which members of the Parisian elite—nobility and newly wealthy bourgeois—could

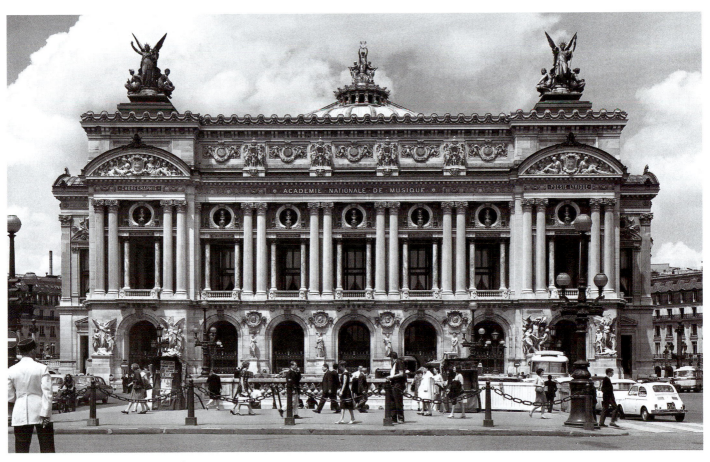

18–2 • Charles Garnier THE OPÉRA
Paris. 1861–1874.

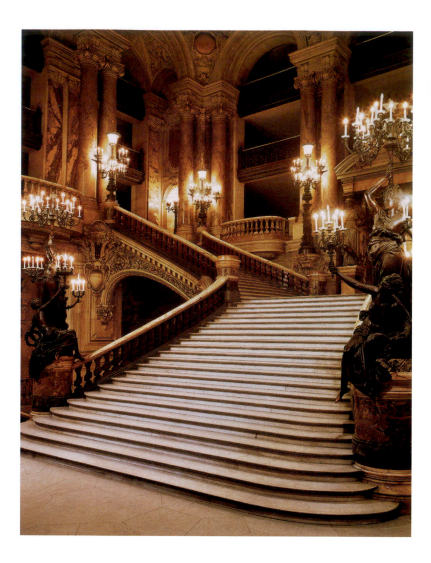

18-3 • Charles Garnier
GRAND STARCASE, THE OPÉRA
Paris. 1861–1874.

✻ **Explore** the architectural panoramas of the interior of the Opéra, Paris, on **MyArtsLab**

display themselves. As Garnier himself said, the purpose of the Opéra was to fulfill the most basic of human desires: to hear, to see, and to be seen.

While historicism and revival styles were popular, modern conditions and materials had an increasing impact on architecture. Building techniques introduced in the late eighteenth and first half of the nineteenth centuries ultimately led to an emphasis on structure and the abandonment of any historicizing decorative overlay. It was engineers rather than architects who had pioneered the use of the most important new building materials: cast iron, wrought iron, and steel. They sought with these new materials to create skeletal structures—recalling those achieved in stone by builders of the Gothic period—that transformed the pure qualities of light, space, and movement into the aesthetic components of architectural design. The Eiffel Tower (SEE FIG. 18–1) is a prime example of this new design direction, dominating the skyline of modern Paris just as the towers of Notre-Dame had been the focus of the medieval city.

Iron-framed buildings, however, have a fatal susceptibility to fire. Exposed to intense heat, iron will warp, buckle, collapse, even melt. The immediate solution was to encase internal iron supports in fireproof materials and return to masonry sheathing. In the early 1860s, the perfection of a technique for making inexpensive steel (an alloy of iron and carbon) introduced new architectural possibilities. Steel is lighter and stronger than iron, making taller buildings feasible, as did the introduction of passenger elevators, the first of which was installed in the United States in 1857.

Steel was first used for building in 1884 by a group of young Midwestern architects now known as the "Chicago School." Equipped with the new technologies and eager to escape from Beaux-Arts historicism, they produced a new kind of building: the skyscraper. An early example of their work, and evidence of its rapid spread throughout the Midwest, is the **WAINWRIGHT BUILDING** in St. Louis, Missouri (**FIG. 18–4**), built by Louis Sullivan (1856–1924). Sullivan adapted the formal vocabulary and basic compositional rules of the Beaux-Arts tradition, dividing the ten-story office building into three parts—base, body, and crowning cornice—but he gave the building an entirely new vertical emphasis. The Wainwright Building is taller than it is wide, and its design emphasizes this; corner piers rise in uninterrupted lines to the cornice, their verticality echoed and reinforced between the windows by small piers, designed to suggest the steel framing beneath them. The Chicago School had found an American alternative to the Beaux-Arts tradition—an end to historicism and the invention of a new architectural style emphasizing scale and structural advances that was immanently appropriate to the modern age.

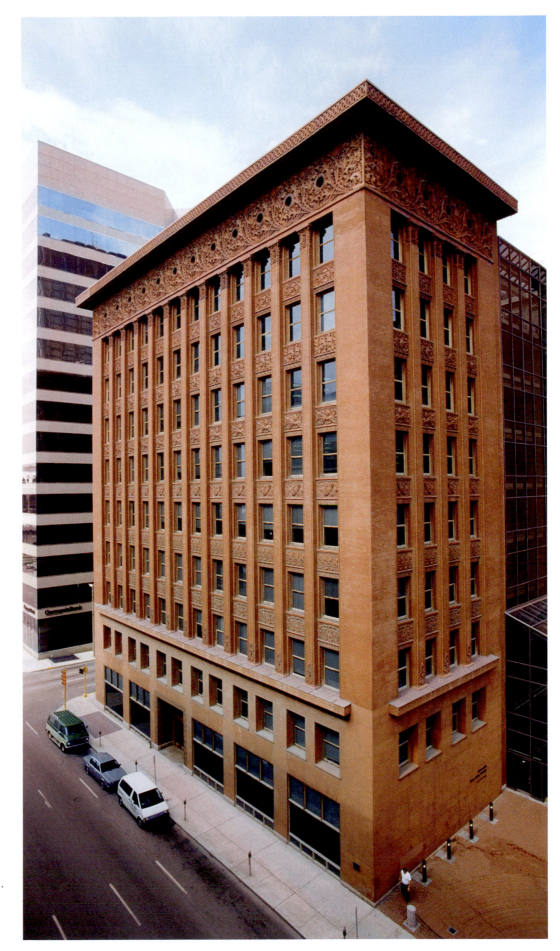

18–4 • Louis Sullivan
WAINWRIGHT BUILDING
St. Louis, Missouri. 1890–1891.

View the Closer Look
for the Wainwright
Building on **MyArtsLab**

Orientalism

In **THE SNAKE CHARMER (FIG. 18–5)**, French academic painter Jean-León Gérôme (1824–1904) luxuriates in the nineteenth-century fantasy of the Middle East—an example of **Orientalism** in art. A young boy, entirely naked, handles a python, while an older man beside him plays a fipple flute, and a huddled audience sits in the background shadows. The setting is a large blue-tiled room, painted with an almost photographic clarity and attention to detail, leading us to think that this is an accurate representation of a specific event in an actual place. Gérôme traveled to the Middle East several times, and was praised by critics of the 1855 Salon for his ethnographic accuracy, but his *Snake Charmer* is a complete fiction, mixing Egyptian, Turkish, and Indian cultures together in a fantasized pastiche.

The French fascination with Middle Eastern cultures dates to Napoleon's 1798 invasion of Egypt and his wanton looting of objects from the country for the Louvre Museum, which he opened in 1804. In the 1840s and 1850s, photographic studios were established by British, French, and Italian photographers at major tourist sites in the Middle East in order to provide photographs for European visitors and armchair tourists at home, thus satisfying and fueling a popular interest in the region.

Orientalism is found in both academic and avant-garde modern art; we have already encountered it in the Neoclassicism of Ingres (SEE FIG. 17–16). The scholar Edward Said described Orientalism as the colonial gaze in which the colonizer gazes upon the colonized Orient (the Middle East rather than Asia) as something to possess, as a "primitive" or "exotic" playground for the "civilized" European visitor, in which "native" men are savage and despotic and "native" women—and here boys—are sensuously described and sexually alluring.

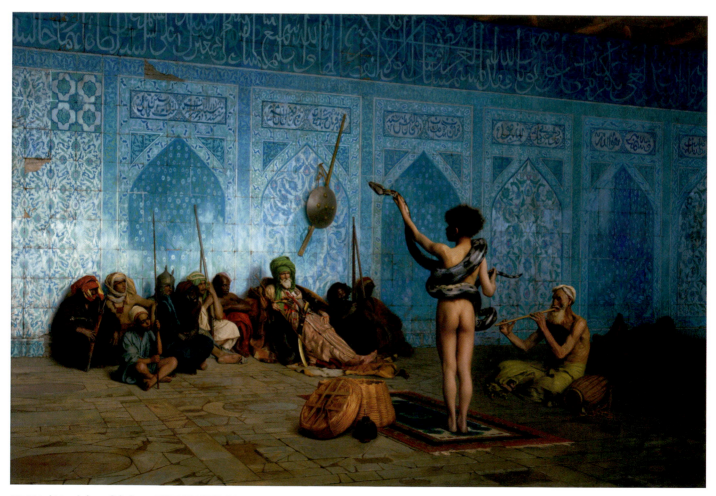

18–5 • Jean-Léon Gérôme THE SNAKE CHARMER
c. 1870. Oil on canvas, 33″ × 48⅛″ (83.8 × 122.1 cm). Clark Art Institute, Williamstown, Massachusetts.
Acquired by Sterling and Francine Clark, 1942. 1955.51.

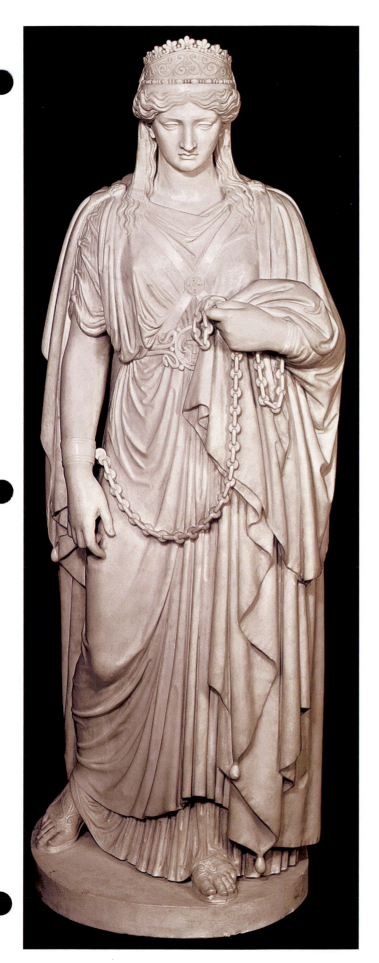

Academic and Anti-Academic Art

How did academic Neoclassical standards survive in the late nineteenth century and what were the movements that worked to reject them?

Historicism in nineteenth-century architecture had its counterpart in academic painting and sculpture conforming to the conservative principles of the French Academy, which continued to exert enormous international influence throughout the century. Students at the École des Beaux-Arts and comparable academic institutions began their training by copying prints and plaster casts of Classical and Renaissance sculpture; then they studied live models posed like Classical sculpture. When, in the opinion of their teachers, they had developed sufficient technical skill and detailed knowledge of the human form to make actual paintings or sculptures, they were expected to recall their earlier immersion in Classical art and "correct" ordinary nature, emulating higher Classical ideals. The works they produced depended on motifs drawn from historical models, often combining allusions to several different periods in a single work. Some academic artists used their classicizing skills to create smoothly painted Orientalist fantasies that catered to the public taste for exotic scenes with erotic overtones (see "Orientalism," p. 480).

As a sequel to study at the Academy, or sometimes as an alternative to it, young artists, and sculptors in particular, often visited or settled in Italy. Italy remained the wellspring of inspiration for artists. For sculptors it was also the source of the materials and skilled workers needed to work in fine white marble, the material associated with Classical sculpture. By the second half of the nineteenth century bustling artists' colonies in Rome and Florence even included women, whom the American author Henry James dubbed the "white, marmorean [marble] flock."

The most prominent of these women, Harriet Hosmer (1830–1908), had moved to Rome in 1852, rapidly mastering the Neoclassical mode and producing major exhibition pieces such as **ZENOBIA IN CHAINS** (FIG. 18–6). Neoclassical in form but Romantic in content, the sculpture represents an exotic historical subject calculated to appeal to viewers' emotions. Zenobia, the heroic third-century queen of Palmyra, was defeated by the Romans and forced to march through the streets of Rome in chains. Hosmer presents her as a noble figure, resolute even in defeat. "I have tried to make her too proud to exhibit passion or emotion of any kind," wrote Hosmer of Zenobia, "not subdued, though a prisoner; but calm, grand, and strong within herself." Zenobia embodies an ideal of womanhood strikingly modern in its defiance of Victorian conventions of female submissiveness.

18–6 • Harriet Hosmer ZENOBIA IN CHAINS
1859. Marble, height 4′ (1.21 m). Wadsworth Atheneum, Hartford, Connecticut. Gift of Mrs. Josephine M. J. Dodge.

Reactions against the Academy

In England, reaction against academic art began building at mid century as seven young artists formed the Pre-Raphaelite Brotherhood in 1848 to counter what they considered the misguided practices of contemporary British art. Instead of the idealized Raphaelesque conventions taught at the Royal Academy, they looked back to the Middle Ages and Early Renaissance ("pre-Raphael") for the gentle beauty, descriptive naturalism, and moralizing spirituality that they found lacking in the art of their own time.

Dante Gabriel Rossetti (1828–1882) was a leading member of the Pre-Raphaelite Brotherhood. His painting **LA PIA DE' TOLOMEI** (**FIG. 18–7**), illustrating a story from Dante's *Purgatory*, is saturated with symbolism. La Pia (the Pious One), wrongly accused of infidelity and locked up by her husband in a castle, is dying. The rosary and prayer book at her side refer

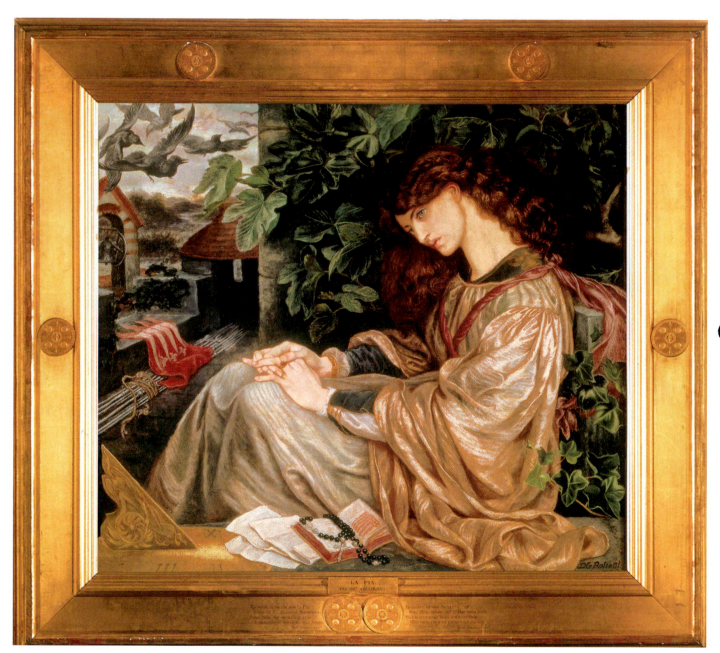

18–7 • Dante Gabriel Rossetti LA PIA DE' TOLOMEI
1868–1869. Oil on canvas, 41½″ × 47½″ (105.4 × 119.4 cm). Spencer Museum of Art, The University of Kansas, Lawrence. Museum purchase: State funds (1956.0031).

The massive gilded frame Rossetti designed for *La Pia de' Tolomei* features simple moldings on either side of broad, sloping boards, into which are set a few large roundels. The title of the painting is inscribed above the paired roundels at the lower center. On either side of them appear four lines from Dante's *Purgatory* spoken by the spirit of La Pia, in Italian at the left and in Rossetti's English translation at the right: "Remember me who am La Pia,—me/ From Siena sprung and by Maremma dead./This in his inmost heart well knoweth he/With whose fair jewel I was ringed and wed."

to the piety signaled by her name, while the sundial and ravens symbolize the passage of time and her impending death. La Pia's continuing love for her husband, whose letters lie under her prayer book, is also symbolized by the evergreen ivy behind her. The luxuriant fig leaves that surround her are traditionally associated with lust and original sin. They have no source in Dante's tale, but they had personal relevance for the artist. Jane Burden, Rossetti's model for this and many other paintings, was the wife of his friend William Morris, but she had become Rossetti's lover. By fingering her wedding ring, La Pia/Jane suggests she is a captive not so much of her husband as of her marriage. In the context of the artist's personal history, this becomes a metaphor for Rossetti's own unhappy situation.

William Morris (1834–1896) was less interested in painting than in domestic design. His interest developed in the context of a widespread reaction against gaudy and shoddy industrially produced goods, and he sought to provide handcrafted alternatives to them, inspired by the medieval art he so revered. When he married Jane Burden in 1859, Morris set out to decorate their new home by designing and producing their furniture himself, eventually founding a decorating firm to produce a full range of domestic products. Although many of the furnishings offered by Morris & Company were expensive, one-of-a-kind items, others, such as the rush-seated **CHAIR** illustrated here (**FIG. 18–8**), were relatively affordable. Concerned with creating a "total" environment in which architecture and décor were styled in harmony, Morris and his colleagues designed not only furniture but also stained glass, tiles, wallpaper, and fabrics such as the Peacock and Dragon curtain seen here behind the Sussex chair.

Morris was a socialist who saw the pre-industrial era as a model for both economic and social reform. He sought to eliminate industrialization not only because he found factory-made products ugly, but also to ameliorate the deadening impact of factory life on industrial workers. He argued that when laborers made handcrafted objects, they had the satisfaction of being involved in the entire process of creation and thus produced honest and beautiful things. Morris's work and ideas inspired what became known as the Arts and Crafts Movement.

Not all those who reacted against official academic art were motivated by a commitment to improving the conditions of modern life. Many, including the American expatriate James Abbott McNeill Whistler (1834–1903), simply saw the Arts and Crafts Movement as a means to satisfy his elitist taste for pure beauty, something he found lacking in the art of his time. Whistler collected Japanese art when it became available in curio shops in London and Paris after the 1853 reopening of that nation to the West, and in 1864, he exhibited three paintings that signaled a new direction influenced by the pure aesthetic delight he saw in Japanese art. One of them, *Rose and Silver: The Princess from the Land of Porcelain* (SEE FIG. INTRO–19, left wall), shows a European woman dressed in a Japanese robe and surrounded by a collection of Asian artifacts, Whistler's answer to the medieval costumes and environments favored by the Pre-Raphaelites. Whistler's growing commitment to an art of purely aesthetic values, derived from Asian sensibilities, culminated in the dining-room decoration he created for a wealthy English patron—*Harmony in Blue and Gold: The Peacock Room*, a

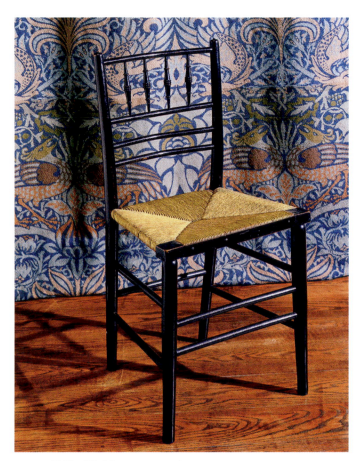

18–8 • Philip Webb SINGLE CHAIR FROM THE SUSSEX RANGE
(Foreground in photo) In production from c. 1865. Ebonized wood with rush seat, 32⅝″ × 19⅜″ (83.8 × 35.6 cm). Manufactured by Morris & Company. William Morris Gallery (London Borough of Waltham Forest).

William Morris PEACOCK AND DRAGON CURTAIN
(Background in photo) 1878. Handloomed jacquard-woven woolen twill, 12′ 10½″ × 11′ 5⅛″ (3.96 × 3.53 m). Manufactured at Queen Square and later at Merton Abbey.

Morris and his principal furniture designer, Philip Webb (1831–1915), adapted the Sussex range from traditional rush-seated chairs of the Sussex region. The handwoven curtain in the background is typical of Morris's fabric designs in its use of flat patterning that affirms the two-dimensional character of the textile medium. The pattern's prolific organic motifs and soothing blue and green hues—the decorative counterpart to those of naturalistic landscape painting—were meant to provide relief from the stresses of modern urban existence.

showcase for *Rose and Silver* (discussed in the Introduction, SEE FIG. INTRO–19).

In 1877, Whistler exhibited in London several nighttime landscapes, including **NOCTURNE IN BLACK AND GOLD, THE FALLING ROCKET** (**FIG. 18–9**), depicting a fireworks show viewed over a lake by several observers dimly recognizable in the foreground. The exhibition inspired a vitriolic review from England's leading art critic, John Ruskin, a devotee of Pre-Raphaelite art. He found Whistler's work disturbingly unfinished and devoid of moral purpose, asking in print how the artist could demand such high prices "for flinging a pot of paint in the public's face." Whistler sued Ruskin for

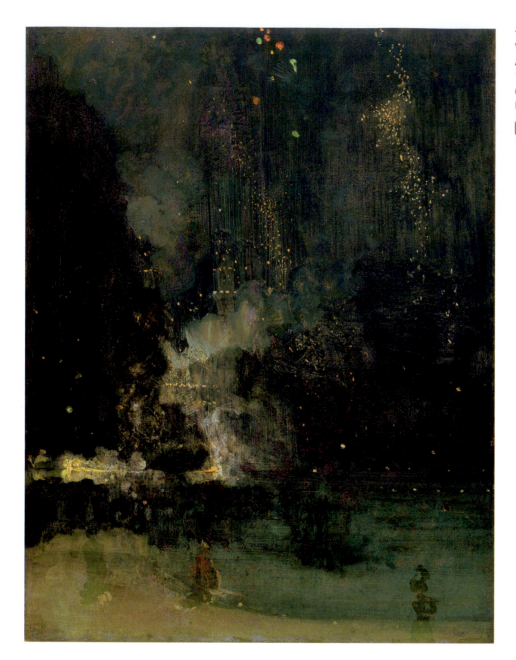

18–9 • James Abbott McNeill Whistler **NOCTURNE IN BLACK AND GOLD, THE FALLING ROCKET**

1875. Oil on panel, 23¾″ × 18⅜″ (60.2 × 46.7 cm). Detroit Institute of Arts, Michigan. Gift of Dexter M. Ferry, Jr.

Read the document related to Whistler's *Nocturne in Black and Gold, The Falling Rocket* on **MyArtsLab**

libel, defending on the witness stand his view that art has no higher purpose than creating visual delight, that it needed no identifiable subject matter to be successful, and that the prices he charged for his pictures compensated him not just for the two days it took to paint them but also for "knowledge gained through a lifetime." The trial was decided in Whistler's favor, but he was awarded only a farthing (a quarter of a penny) in damages, and his considerable legal expenses bankrupted him. While Whistler himself never made a completely abstract painting, his theories became important for justifying abstract art in the next century.

Art Nouveau

Whistler's commitment to promoting art as a means to pure visual delight anticipated a popular style known as Art Nouveau (literally "New Art"). Practitioners of Art Nouveau such as Belgian architect Victor Horta (1861–1947) rejected the

values of modern industrial society and works such as the Eiffel Tower (SEE FIG. 18–1) that showcased exposed structure as architectural style. They sought new aesthetic forms that would recapture a pre-industrial sense of beauty, creating a stylistic vision that permeated European art in many media at the end of the nineteenth century. They applied fluid linear arabesques and stylized organic forms to all aspects of design, drawing inspiration from ancient Celtic art and from nature—vines, snakes, flowers, and winged insects—whose delicate and sinuous forms were the basis for their graceful and attenuated curvilinear designs. They sought to interrelate all aspects of design into a harmonized system, comparable to the organic harmony they saw in nature itself. In 1892, Horta received his first independent commission, to design **TASSEL HOUSE**, a private residence in Brussels (**FIG. 18–10**). The result, especially the house's entry hall and staircase, was strikingly original. Horta laid out the wall decoration, floor mosaic, and ironwork (used instead of stone or wood) as an intricate series of long, graceful curves, integrating interior design and architectural forms into an exquisite and unified whole.

Almost ten years before Horta's decorative ironwork at Tassel House, the Catalan architect Antoní Gaudí (1852–1926) was already designing Art Nouveau buildings in Barcelona. His brilliantly creative **CASA BATLLÒ** (FIG. 18–11), draws on indigenous Islamic, Gothic, and Baroque traditions as well as Art Nouveau aesthetic principles in a dynamic design, free from right angles. In 1904, wealthy industrialist Josep Batllò commissioned Gaudí to replace a nondescript building of the 1870s with a distinctive private residence to rival and surpass the lavish houses of other prominent local families. Gaudí convinced his patron to maintain the underlying structure of the existing building, but to reface it and reorganize its interior spaces. The resulting façade is a dreamlike fantasy of undulating sandstone sculpture and surfaces sheathed by multicolor glass and tile mosaic. The gaping lower-story windows brought the building the nickname "house of yawns," while the use of giant human tibia for upright supports led others to call it "house of bones." The roof resembles a recumbent dragon, with overlapping tiles as scales. A fanciful turret surfaces through its edge, recalling the sword of St. George—patron of Catalunya—plunged into the back of his legendary foe. Gaudí's highly personal alternative to academic historicism and modern industrialization in urban buildings such as this reflects his affinity for Iberian traditions as well as his concern to provide organic and fanciful surroundings to enrich the lives of city dwellers.

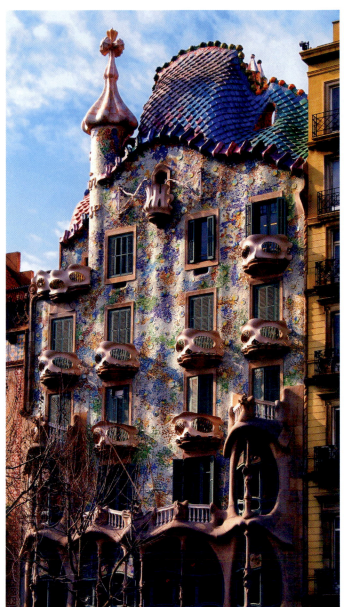

18–11 • Antoní Gaudí **CASA BATLLÒ**
43 Passeig de Gràcia, Barcelona. 1904–1907.

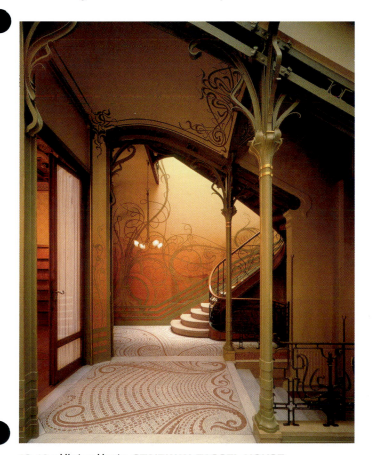

18–10 • Victor Horta **STAIRWAY, TASSEL HOUSE**
Brussels. 1892–1893.

Early Photography

What were the early experiments that led to the emergence of photography as a new art form?

The development of photography was a prime manifestation of the new, positivist interest in descriptive accuracy. Since the Renaissance, Westerners had been seeking a mechanical method for recording what they saw. One early device was the *camera obscura* (Latin for "dark chamber"). It consisted of a darkened room or box with a lens on one side through which light passed, projecting onto the opposite wall (or box side) an upside-down image of the scene, which an artist could then trace. Photography was developed as a way to "fix"—that is, to make permanent—the visual impressions produced by a *camera obscura* (later called simply a "camera") on light-sensitive material.

A camera is essentially a lightproof box with a hole, called the aperture (a), which is usually adjustable in size and regulates the amount of light that strikes the film (b). The aperture is covered with a lens (c), which focuses (d) the image on the film, and a shutter (e), a kind of door that opens for a controlled amount of time to regulate the length of time that the film is exposed to light—usually a small fraction of a second. In the example illustrated, the shutter is open, exposing the film to light. Modern cameras with viewfinders (f) and small single-lens reflex cameras are generally used at eye level, permitting the photographer to see virtually the same image that the film will capture.

In modern black-and-white photography, silver halide crystals (silver combined with iodine, chlorine, or other halogens) are suspended in a gelatin base to make an emulsion that coats the film (in early photography, before the invention of plastic, a glass plate was coated with a variety of emulsions). Later, when the film is placed in a chemical bath (developed), the silver deposits turn black, as if tarnishing. The more light the film receives, the denser the black tone created. A positive image is created from the negative in a darkroom, where the film negative is placed over a sheet of paper that, like the film, has been treated to be light-sensitive, and light is directed through the negative onto the paper. Through this process, a multiple number of positive prints can be generated from a single negative.

Today this chemical has been largely replaced by digital photography, which records images as digital information files that can be manipulated on computers rather than in darkrooms. The artistic potential of the new photographic medium is being exploited in contemporary art, though some artists continue to use chemical photography in their work.

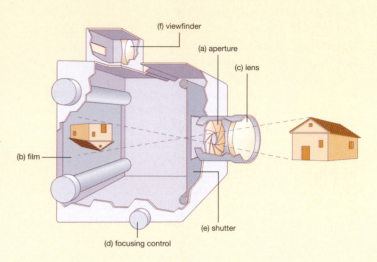

The first person to "fix" a photographic image in France was painter Louis-Jacques-Mandé Daguerre (1787–1851), who discovered that exposure to light for 20 to 30 minutes would produce a latent image on a silver-coated metal plate treated with iodine fumes, which could then be made visible when subsequently exposed to mercury vapor. By 1837, he had developed a method of fixing the image by bathing the plate in a strong solution of common salt after exposure. Daguerre's first picture of this type (**daguerreotype**), a still life of plaster casts and a framed drawing (**FIG. 18–12**), already stakes a claim for photography as art through its specifically "artistic" subject matter.

The 1839 announcement of Daguerre's invention prompted the English scientist William Henry Fox Talbot (1800–1877) to publish the results of his own work on what he called the **calotype** (from the Greek term for "beautiful image"). Beginning in the mid-1830s, Fox Talbot had made negative copies of engravings, pieces of lace, and leaves by placing them on paper impregnated with silver chloride and exposing them to light. By the summer of 1835, he was using this chemically treated paper in both large and small cameras. Then, in 1840, he discovered, independently of Daguerre, that latent images resulting from exposure to the sun for short periods of time could be developed chemically. Applying the technique he had earlier used with engravings and leaves, Fox Talbot was able to make positive prints from the calotype negatives. Thus unlike daguerreotypes—which created a single, positive image—Talbot's calotype process produced a

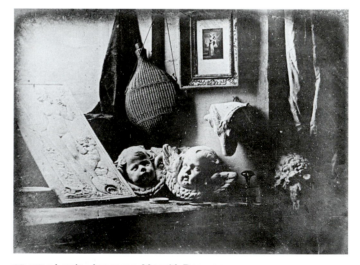

18–12 • Louis-Jacques-Mandé Daguerre
THE ARTIST'S STUDIO
1837. Daguerreotype, 6½″ × 8½″ (16.5 × 21.6 cm).

negative image from which an unlimited number of positives, or prints, could be made.

Between 1844 and 1846, Fox Talbot published a book in six parts entitled *The Pencil of Nature*, illustrated entirely with calotypes. The subjects were often rural scenes or still lifes. In **THE OPEN DOOR** (**FIG. 18–13**) the photographer evoked

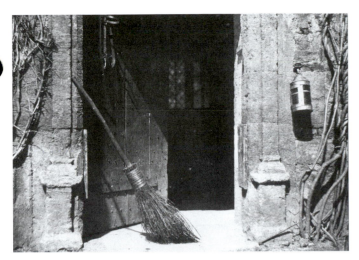

18-13 • William Henry Fox Talbot **THE OPEN DOOR**
1843. Salt-paper print from a calotype negative, 5⅝″ × 7¹¹⁄₁₆″
(14.3 × 19.5 cm). Science Museum, London. Fox Talbot Collection.

an agrarian way of life that was fast disappearing. A traditional, handcrafted broom of a type that mass production was beginning to make obsolete rests against the doorway of a timeworn cottage, paralleling the diagonal lines of shadows on the upper right of the door.

In 1851, Frederick Scott Archer, a British sculptor and photographer, took a major step in the development of early photography. Archer found that silver nitrate would adhere to glass if it was mixed with collodion, a combination of guncotton, ether, and alcohol used in medicinal bandages. When wet, this collodion–silver nitrate mixture needed only a few seconds'

exposure to light to create an image. The result was a glass negative, from which countless positive proofs with great tonal subtleties could be made.

American photographers used this newly refined process to document the momentous events of the Civil War (1861–1865) in artfully composed pictures. At the beginning of the conflict, Alexander Gardner (1821–1882) was a "camera operator" on Mathew Brady's (1822–1896) project to document the war, and, working with his assistant, Timothy O'Sullivan (c. 1840–1882), he made war photographs that were widely distributed. **THE HOME OF THE REBEL SHARPSHOOTER (FIG. 18–14)** was taken after the Battle of Gettysburg in July 1863. In the field, the technical difficulties were considerable. Glass plates had to be kept wet, and if dust contaminated the plate, the image would also be ruined. Since long exposure times made action photographs impossible, early war photographs were taken in camp or in the aftermath of battle.

Gardner's image seems to show a rebel sharpshooter who has been killed in his look-out. But this rock formation was in the middle of the battlefield, and had neither the height nor the view needed for a sharpshooter. In fact, the photographers dragged the dead body to the site and posed it; and the rifle propped against the wall was theirs. The staging of this photograph raises questions about visual fact and fiction. Like a painting, a photograph is composed to create a picture, but photography promises a kind of factuality that we do not expect from painting. Interestingly, the manipulation of this photograph did not concern nineteenth-century viewers, who understood clearly photography's inability to record the visual world without bias.

One of the most creative early photographers was Julia Margaret Cameron (1815–1879), who received her first camera

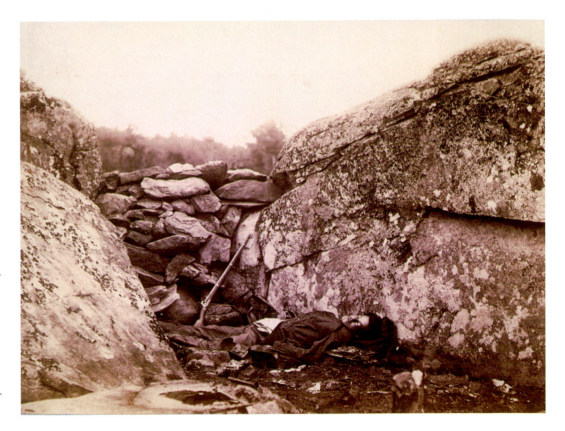

18-14 • Alexander Gardner **THE HOME OF THE REBEL SHARPSHOOTER: BATTLE FIELD AT GETTYSBURG**
1863. Albumen print, 7″ × 9″ (18 × 23 cm). Library of Congress, Washington, D.C.

Ⓡ **View** the Closer Look for Gardner's *The Home of the Rebel Sharpshooter* on **MyArtsLab**

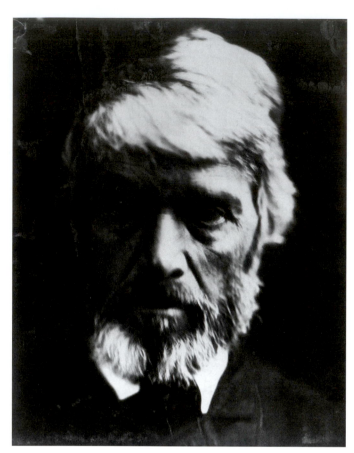

18–15 • Julia Margaret Cameron
PORTRAIT OF THOMAS CARLYLE
1867. Silver print, 10″ × 8″ (25.4 × 20.3 cm). The Royal Photographic Society, London.

In her autobiography Cameron said, "When I have had such men before my camera my whole soul has endeavored to do its duty towards them in recording faithfully the greatness of the inner as well as the features of the outer man."

as a gift from her daughters when she was 49. Her principal subjects became the great men of British arts, letters, and sciences, many of whom had long been family friends. Like many of Cameron's portraits, her likeness of famous British historian **THOMAS CARLYLE** is slightly out of focus on purpose (**FIG. 18–15**). By blurring details Cameron sought to call attention to the light that suffused her subjects—an artistic metaphor for creative genius. Carlyle's concentrated expression is so intense that the dramatic lighting of his hair, face, and beard almost seems to emanate from within. With regard to her medium Cameron said, "My aspirations are to ennoble Photography and to secure for it the character and uses of High Art by combining the real and ideal."

Realism

How did the movement toward Realism in art reflect the social and political concerns of the nineteenth century?

Toward the middle of the nineteenth century, both Neoclassicism and Romanticism were challenged by a new movement that art historians have labeled Realism. To a certain extent this new direction was motivated by a positivist rejection of Romantic subjectivism and imaginativeness on the one hand, and Neoclassical idealism and balance on the other, in favor of the accurate and seemingly unmitigated description of the ordinary, observable world, showcasing its "unvarnished truth." Some have related this allegiance to factual accuracy in recording visual appearance to the advent of photography and its development into a new artistic medium. But at its inception, Realism carried a social critique, and often a political message; it was less of a style than a commitment to paint the modern world honestly, without turning away from the brutal truths of life for all people, the poor as well as the privileged. It is this new trend—encompassing new motivations, new subjects, and new modes of representing them—that propels the history of art forward toward Modernism.

Early French Realist Painters

A defining moment in French Realism was the Revolution of 1848. In February of that year, an uneasy Parisian coalition of socialists, anarchists, and workers overthrew the monarchy and established the Second Republic (1848–1851), whose founders' socialist goals, including collective ownership of the means of production and distribution, were abandoned when conservative factions won the elections that summer.

Painter Gustave Courbet (1819–1877) was inspired and radicalized by the events of 1848 to turn his attention to portraying poor and ordinary people. Born and raised in the town of Ornans near the Swiss border and largely self-taught as an artist, he moved to Paris in 1839, where he proclaimed his political commitment in three large paintings he submitted to the Salon of 1850–1851. One of these, **A BURIAL AT ORNANS** (**FIG. 18–16**), is a monumental canvas commemorating (but not actually recording) the funeral of Courbet's grandfather Oudot, who had died in 1847. A crush of people line up in rows across the picture plane. Through the work's grand scale, the artist accords the ordinary citizens aligned here the respect conventionally reserved for participants in major historical, religious, or mythological events. And the genuine sorrow of some mourners is contrasted with the apparent indifference of the two Church officials dressed in red behind the officiating priest. Conservative critics hated the work for its focus on common people, its disrespect for traditional standards of order and beauty. Critics also decried the absence of any suggestion of an afterlife; here death and burial are simply physical facts. Courbet relished the controversy.

Similar accusations of political radicalism were leveled against Jean-François Millet (1814–1875). This artist grew up on a farm and, despite living in Paris between 1837 and 1848, never felt comfortable with urban life. After the Revolution of 1848, Millet began to focus on paintings of peasant life, and a state commission allowed him to move from Paris to the village of Barbizon where he could be a closer observer of the difficulties and simple pleasures of rural life. Among his best-known works is **THE GLEANERS** (**FIG. 18–17**), showing three women gathering stray, left-over grain after harvest. The warm colors and hazy atmosphere initially seem soothing, but the scene is one of extreme poverty; gleaning was a form of relief offered to the rural poor, requiring hours of backbreaking work to collect enough wheat to make a single loaf of bread. When the painting

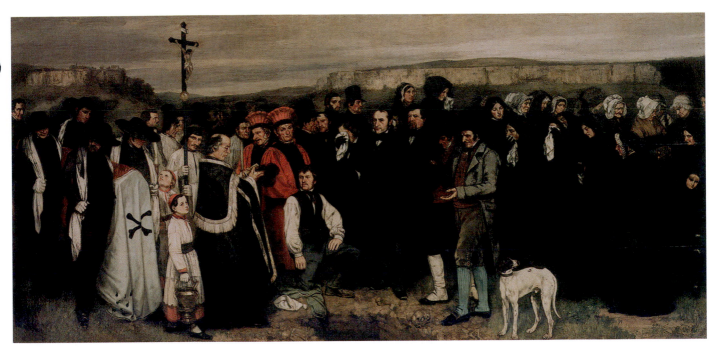

18–16 • Gustave Courbet A BURIAL AT ORNANS
1849. Oil on canvas, 10′ 3½″ × 21′ 9″ (3.1 × 6.6 m). Musée d'Orsay, Paris.

A Burial at Ornans was inspired by the 1848 funeral of Courbet's maternal grandfather, Jean-Antoine Oudot, a veteran of the Revolution of 1789. The painting is not meant as a record of that particular funeral, however, since Oudot is shown alive in profile at the extreme left of the canvas, his image adapted by Courbet from an earlier portrait. The two men to the right of the open grave, dressed not in contemporary but in late eighteenth-century clothing, are also revolutionaries of Oudot's generation, and their proximity to the grave suggests that one of their peers is being buried. Perhaps Courbet's picture links the revolutions of 1789 and 1848, both of which sought to advance the cause of democracy in France.

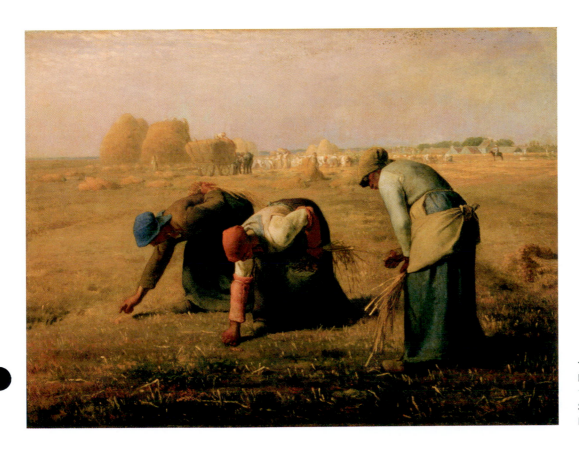

18–17 • Jean-François Millet **THE GLEANERS**
1857. Oil on canvas, 33″ × 44″ (83.8 × 111.8 cm). Musée d'Orsay, Paris.

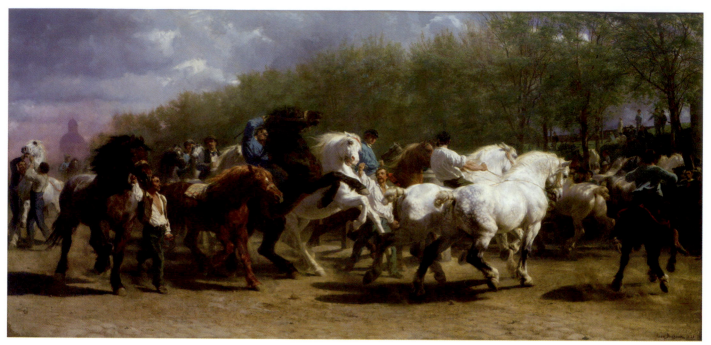

18–18 • Rosa Bonheur THE HORSE FAIR
1853–1855. Oil on canvas, 8′ ¼″ × 16′ 7½″ (2.44 × 5 m). The Metropolitan Museum of Art, New York.
Gift of Cornelius Vanderbilt, 1887 (87.25).

📖 **Read** the document related to Rosa Bonheur on **MyArtsLab**

was shown in 1857, critics noted its implicit social criticism and labeled it "Realist." Millet denied the accusations, but his paintings contradict him.

Rosa Bonheur (1822–1899) was among the most popular French painters of farm life. Her success in what was then a male domain owed much to the socialist convictions of her parents, who belonged to a radical utopian sect that believed in the equality of women. In order to achieve accurate depictions of her beloved farm animals, she read zoology books and made detailed studies in stockyards and slaughterhouses. In fact, to gain access to these all-male preserves, Bonheur had to obtain police permission to dress in men's clothing. Her professional breakthrough came in the Salon of 1848, where she showed eight paintings and won a first-class medal.

Bonheur's **THE HORSE FAIR** (FIG. 18–18), painted between 1853 and 1855, portrays splendid Percheron horses and their grooms at the Paris horse market. Some have interpreted the painting as a commentary on the lack of rights for women in the 1850s, but it was not read that way at the time. Although unusually monumental for a painting of farm animals, it was highly praised at the 1853 Salon. It later toured Britain and the United States, where members of the public paid to see it, and it was widely disseminated in print form on both sides of the Atlantic. In 1887, it was purchased by Cornelius Vanderbilt, who donated it to the new Metropolitan Museum of Art in New York. Bonheur became so famous that in 1865 she received France's highest award, membership in the Legion of Honor, becoming the first woman to be awarded its Grand Cross.

"The Painter of Modern Life"

By the mid-1860s Parisian painter Édouard Manet (1832–1883) had become the unofficial leader of a group of progressive artists and writers who gathered at the Café Guerbois in the Montmartre district of Paris. These artists, who matured around 1870, pushed the French Realist tradition into new territory. Instead of continuing themes that had engaged Courbet, Millet, and Bonheur—the working classes and rural life—they generally moved to what they thought were more modern subjects: the city, the bourgeois (upper middle class), and leisure. And although many of them also painted the countryside, their point of view was usually that of a city dweller on holiday.

Frustration among progressive artists with the exclusionary practices of the juries that decided which painting would hang in grand, official Salon exhibitions reached a fever pitch in 1863 when the jury turned down nearly 3,000 submitted works. A storm of protest erupted, prompting French emperor Napoleon III to order an exhibition of the rejected work called the "*Salon des Refusés*" ("Salon of the Rejected"). Featured in it was Manet's **LE DÉJEUNER SUR L'HERBE (THE LUNCHEON ON THE GRASS)** (FIG. 18–19), which scandalized viewers and helped establish Manet as a radical artist by provoking a critical avalanche that mixed shock with bewilderment.

Manet's strong commitment to Realism was fueled by his friendship with poet Charles Baudelaire. In his 1863 article "The Painter of Modern Life," Baudelaire called for an artist to be the painter of contemporary manners, "the painter of the

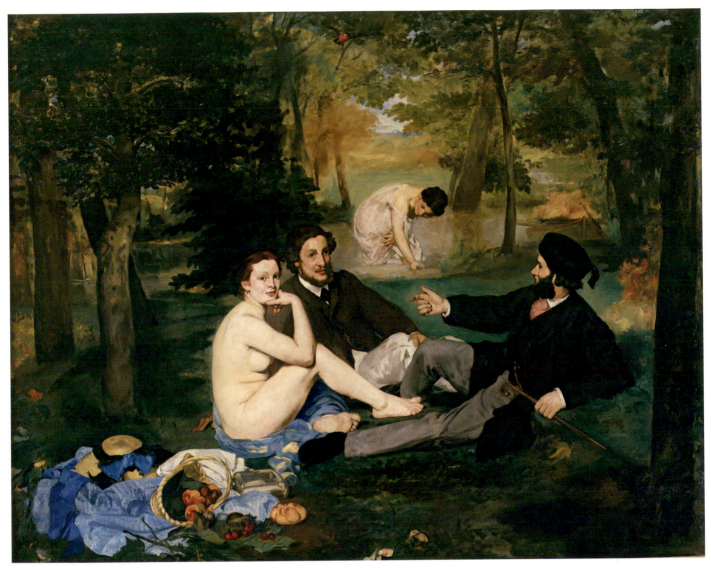

18–19 • Édouard Manet LE DÉJEUNER SUR L'HERBE (THE LUNCHEON ON THE GRASS)
1863. Oil on canvas, 7' × 8' 8" (2.13 × 2.64 m). Musée d'Orsay, Paris.

passing moment and of all the suggestions of eternity that it contains." In *Le Déjeuner sur l'herbe* Manet rose to that challenge. To viewers accustomed to the traditional use of controlled gradations of shadow to model smoothly rounded forms, which were then nestled within spaces logically mapped by illusionistic perspective, this painting seemed a jarring rejection of the basic tenets of painting. Manet offered flat, sharply outlined, and starkly lit figures who, rather than being integrated with their natural setting, seem to stand out sharply against it, like silhouetted cut-outs propped up before a painted backdrop. The fact that Manet based his composition on Renaissance works, such as Titian's *Pastoral Concert* (SEE FIG. 13–17), a copy of which was hanging in his studio, and an engraving of a deeply Classical work by Raphael—the source for the pose of the naked woman's right arm as well as the broad gesture of the reclining man on the right—only made Manet's painting more unsettling by underlining his subversiveness.

Most disturbing to contemporary viewers, however, was the "immorality" of Manet's subject: a suburban picnic featuring a scantily clad bathing woman in the background and—even worse—in the foreground, a completely naked woman seated alongside two fully clothed bourgeois men. Manet's scandalized audience assumed that these women were prostitutes and the well-dressed men their clients. But what was fundamentally shocking was the work's modernity, presenting frank nudity not as part of historical or mythological narrative, but within the context of contemporary life. The underlying meanings of this radical painting are still the subject of art-historical debate. Some see it as a commentary on the alienation of modern life, for the figures do not connect with one another psychologically. Even if the man on the right gestures toward his companions, the other man looks off absently, while the nude turns her attention boldly toward the viewer, making us quite aware of our own estrangement from what is going on in the painting.

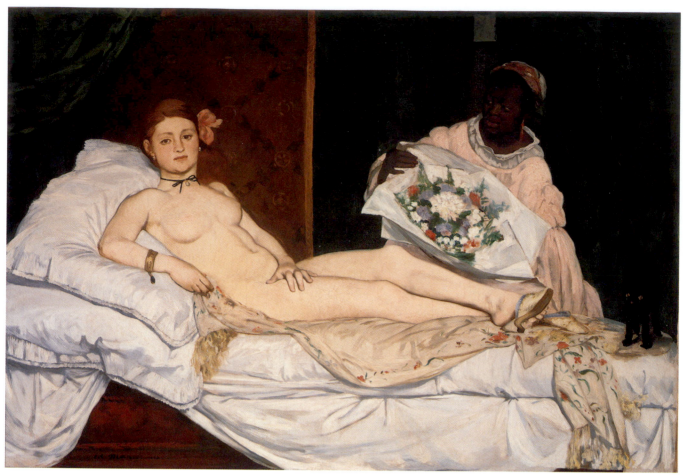

18–20 • Édouard Manet OLYMPIA
1863. Oil on canvas, 4′ 3″ × 6′ 2¼″ (1.31 × 1.91 m). Musée d'Orsay, Paris.

🔍 **View** the Closer Look for Manet's *Olympia* on **MyArtsLab**

Shortly after completing *Le Déjeuner sur l'herbe*, Manet painted **OLYMPIA** (**FIG. 18–20**), the title of which alluded to a socially ambitious prostitute of the same name in a novel and play by Alexandre Dumas *fils* ("the son," that is "the younger"). Like *Le Déjeuner sur l'herbe*, *Olympia* was based on a painting by Titian, the *"Venus" of Urbino* (SEE FIG. 13–20). At first glance, Manet appears to pay homage to Titian in subject (at that time believed to be a Venetian courtesan) and composition, but Manet has made his modern counterpart the very antithesis of Titian's reclining nude. Whereas Titian's woman is curvaceous and softly rounded, Manet's is angular and flattened. Whereas Titian's looks lovingly at the male spectator, Olympia appears coldly indifferent, if not downright defiant. Our relationship with Olympia is underscored by the reaction of her cat, who—unlike the sleeping dog in Titan's painting—arches its back at us. Manet has subverted the entire tradition of the accommodating female nude, for Olympia stares down on us, indicating that she is in the position of power. Despite our offering of flowers, presented by her Caribbean servant arriving from the background, she may not surrender to our advances, a point underscored by the protective placement of her tensed left hand (compare FIG. 13–20). Not surprisingly, conservative critics heaped scorn on the painting when it was displayed at the Salon of 1865.

A Continuing American Tradition

Although Neoclassicism prevailed in sculpture, Realism (though the term was not used in the United States) was an unbroken tradition in American painting stretching back to Colonial portrait painters (SEE FIG. 17–1). Advocates had long considered it distinctly American and democratic, and as we have already seen, the Civil War (1861–1865) brought increasing attention to that most exactly descriptive medium—photography—in the work of Alexander Gardner (SEE FIG. 18–14).

Another artist who made his name recording images of the Civil War was Winslow Homer (1836–1910). In his role as both reporter and illustrator for *Harper's Weekly*, Homer produced works that are considered to be among the finest pictorial reporting of the Civil War. In 1867, after a ten-month sojourn in France, Homer returned to paint nostalgic visions of the rural scenes that had figured in his magazine illustrations. Following a visit during 1881–1882 to a tiny English fishing village on the rugged North Sea coast, however, Homer developed a commitment to depicting the working poor. Moved by the hard lives and strength of character of the people he encountered there, he set aside idyllic subjects for themes of heroic struggles against natural adversity. In England, he had been particularly impressed by the "breeches buoy," a mechanical

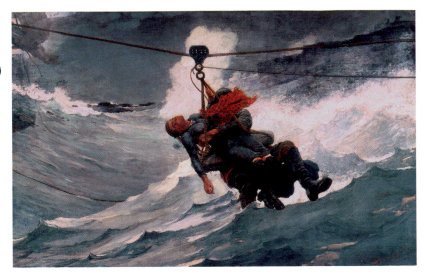

18–21 • Winslow Homer THE LIFE LINE
1884. Oil on canvas, 28¾″ × 44⅝″ (73 × 113.3 cm). Philadelphia Museum of Art. The George W. Elkins Collection, 1924.

apparatus used for rescues at sea. During the summer of 1883, he made sketches of one imported by the lifesaving crew in Atlantic City, New Jersey. The following year he painted **THE LIFE LINE** (**FIG. 18–21**), which depicts a coast guard saving a shipwrecked woman with the use of a breeches buoy—a testament not simply to valor but also to human ingenuity.

The most uncompromising American Realist was Philadelphia artist Thomas Eakins (1844–1916). Following academic training at the Pennsylvania Academy of the Fine Arts and anatomical study at the nearby Jefferson Medical College, supplemented by a stint at the École des Beaux-Arts in Paris, Eakins spent six months in Spain, where he encountered the highly descriptive works of Diego Velázquez (SEE FIG. 14–14). Returning to Philadelphia in 1870, Eakins specialized in frank portraits, often in everyday settings, whose lack of conventional charm generated little popular interest. But he was a charismatic teacher and was soon appointed director of the Pennsylvania Academy.

THE GROSS CLINIC (**FIG. 18–22**) was one of Eakins's most controversial paintings. Although created specifically for the 1876 Philadelphia Centennial Exhibition, it was rejected from the fine arts exhibition—the jury did not consider surgery a fit subject for art—and relegated to the scientific and medical display. The monumental painting shows Dr. Samuel David Gross performing an operation in the surgical amphitheater of Jefferson Medical College, assisted by famous associates

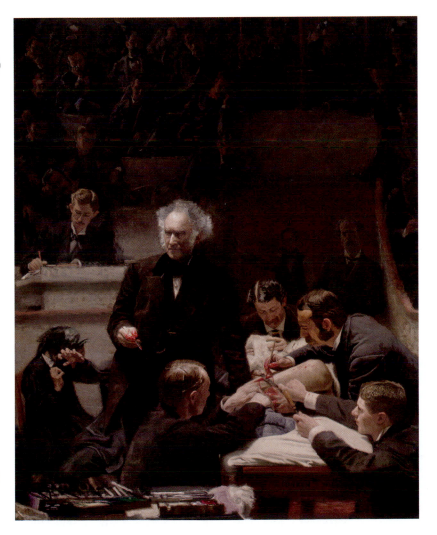

18–22 • Thomas Eakins
THE GROSS CLINIC (PORTRAIT OF DR. SAMUEL D. GROSS)
1875. Oil on canvas, 8′ × 6′ 6″ (2.43 × 1.98 m). Pennsylvania Academy of the Fine Arts and Philadelphia Museum of Art. Gift of the Alumni Association to Jefferson Medical College in 1878 and purchased by the Pennsylvania Academy of the Fine Arts and the Philadelphia Museum of Art in 2007 with the generous support of more than 3,600 donors.

Eakins's career as a Realist artist developed in relationship to his association with the Pennsylvania Academy of the Fine Arts in Philadelphia, where he started teaching the year after he painted this work and was named director in 1882. But in 1886, when he removed the loincloth from a male model in a class where women were present, the scandalized Academy board offered him the choice of changing his teaching methods or resigning. He resigned.

and observed by young medical students in the background, as well as by Eakins himself, who included his portrait along the painting's right edge. A woman at left, presumably a relative of the patient, cringes in horror at the bloody spectacle. But the surgeon is portrayed as a heroic figure, spotlighted by beams of light on his forehead and bloodied right hand with glinting scalpel. Principal illumination, however, is reserved for the patient, presented here not as an entire body but a dehumanized jumble of thigh, buttock, socked feet, and bunches of cloth. Eakins used light not to stir emotions but to make a point: amid the darkness of ignorance and fear, modern science is the light of knowledge. The procedure showcased here, in fact, was an innovative surgery that allowed Dr. Gross to save a patient's leg that heretofore would have been routinely amputated.

Among Eakins's students at the Pennsylvania Academy of Fine Arts were women and African Americans, groups often excluded from art schools. One of his star pupils was Henry Ossawa Tanner (1859–1937) who, from 1879 to 1885, absorbed Eakins's lessons of truthful representation and his focus on real-life subjects. In 1891, after working as a photographer and teacher in Atlanta, Tanner moved to Paris where his painting received favorable critical attention. In the 1890s, he painted scenes from African-American and rural French life in a style

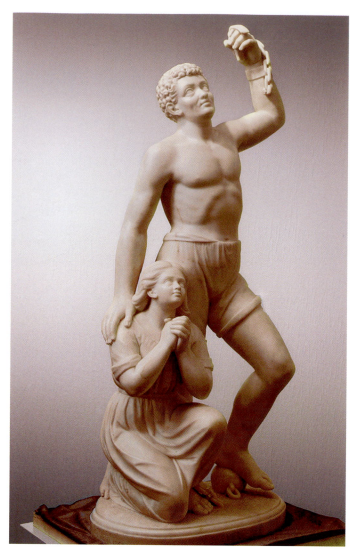

18-24 • Edmonia Lewis FOREVER FREE
1867. Marble, 41¼″ × 22″ × 17″ (104.8 × 55 × 43.2 cm). Howard University Art Gallery, Washington, D.C.

This sculpture not only celebrates emancipation, but also subtly reflects white attitudes toward women and people of color. Lewis's female is less radicalized and more submissive than her male counterpart, aligning her with the contemporary ideal of womanhood and making her more appealing to white audiences.

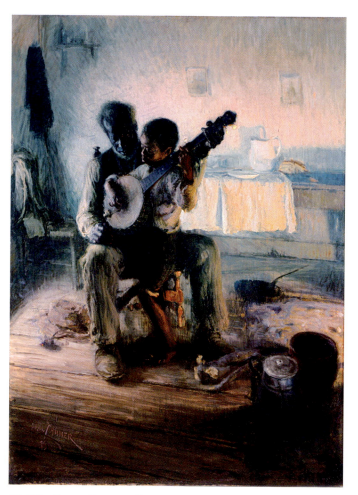

18-23 • Henry Ossawa Tanner THE BANJO LESSON
1893. Oil on canvas, 49″ × 35½″ (124.4 × 90 cm). Hampton University Museum, Hampton, Virginia.

that combined Eakins's Realism with the delicate brushwork he had learned in France. With strongly felt, humanizing images like the **THE BANJO LESSON (FIG. 18–23)**, he sought to counter caricatures of African-American life created by other artists. An elderly man is teaching a young boy seated on his lap, and as their seriousness and concentration connect them, their poverty seems to fade. The use of the banjo here is especially significant since it had become identified with images of minstrels—just the sort of derogatory caricatures that Tanner sought to replace with his sympathetic genre scenes focused on the intimate interactions that brought dignity and pride to family life. After a trip to Palestine in 1897, Tanner turned to religious subjects, believing that Bible stories could illustrate the struggles and hopes of contemporary African Americans.

Edmonia Lewis (c. 1845–after 1911), born in New York State to a Chippewa mother and an African-American father, was orphaned at age 4 and raised by her mother's family. With the help of abolitionists, she attended Oberlin College, the first college in the United States to grant degrees to women, and then moved to Boston. Her highly successful busts and medallions of abolitionist leaders and Civil War heroes financed her move to Rome in 1867, where she was welcomed into the sculpture circle of Harriet Hosmer (SEE FIG. 18–6), using Neoclassicism to address modern, Realist issues. Still inspired by the struggle of the recently freed slaves for equality, her **FOREVER FREE (FIG. 18–24)** commemorates the Emancipation Proclamation (1862–1863). A woman kneels in grateful prayer, while her male companion boosts himself up on the ball that once bound his ankle, raising his broken shackles in a gesture of triumphant liberation. Lewis's enthusiasm outran her financial abilities, so that she had to borrow money to pay for the marble for this work. She shipped it from Rome back to Boston hoping that a subscription drive among abolitionists would redeem her loan. The effort was only partially successful, but her steady income from the sale of commemorative medallions eventually paid it off.

Impressionism

What are the origins, nature, and content of Impressionist painting?

Among the artists who frequented the Café Guerbois with Manet were Claude Monet, Edgar Degas, and Pierre-Auguste Renoir. With the exception of Degas—who, like Manet, remained a studio painter—they began to paint outdoors, *en plein air* ("in the open air"), in an effort to record directly the fleeting effects of light and atmosphere. *Plein-air* painting was greatly facilitated by the invention in 1841 of tin tubes for oil paint, which artists could conveniently pack and take with them.

In April 1874, Monet, Degas, and Renoir, joined by Berthe Morisot, Camille Pissarro, Paul Cézanne, and others, exhibited together in Paris as the *Société Anonyme des Artistes Peintres, Sculpteurs, Graveurs, etc.* (Corporation of Artists Painters, Sculptors, Engravers, etc.). While the exhibition received some positive reviews, Louis Leroy, writing for the satirical journal *Charivari*, seized upon the title of Monet's painting **IMPRESSION, SUNRISE (FIG. 18–25)** and dubbed the entire exhibition "impressionist." Leroy was ridiculing the fast, open brushstrokes and unfinished look of some of the paintings, but Monet and

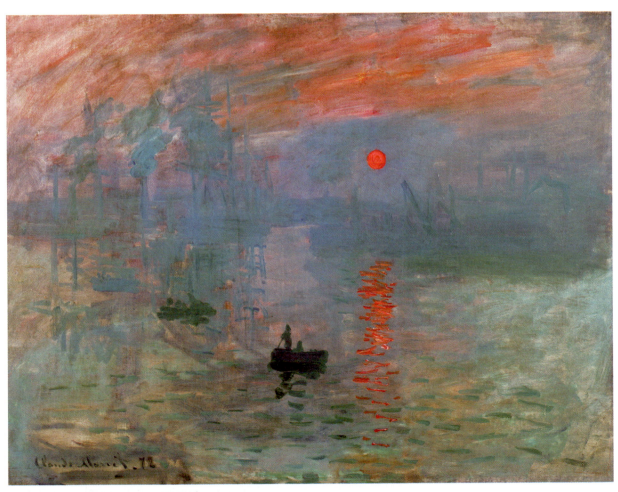

18-25 • Claude Monet IMPRESSION, SUNRISE
1872. Oil on canvas, 19½″ × 25½″ (49.5 × 64.7 cm). Musée Marmottan, Paris.

📖 **Read** the document related to Claude Monet on **MyArtsLab** his colleagues liked the name because it aptly described their aim to render in paint an instantaneous impression of a fleeting moment. Seven more Impressionist exhibitions followed between 1876 and 1886, with the roster of painters varying slightly on each occasion. By the end of the century, such independent exhibitions effectively ended the French Academy's Salon system and its centuries-old stranglehold on determining artistic standards.

Claude Monet (1840–1926) developed his own technique of applying paint with strokes and touches of pure color, intended to describe flowers, leaves, waves, figures, and buildings, but also to register simply as marks of paint on the surface of the canvas. Monet's fully Impressionist pictures of the 1870s and 1880s—such as *Impression, Sunrise* and **BOULEVARD DES CAPUCINES, PARIS** (FIG. 18–26)—are made up almost entirely of flecks of color (Leroy sneeringly called them "tongue-lickings"). Using these discrete marks of paint, Monet recorded the shifting play of light on the surface of objects and the effect of that light on the eye, rather than the physical substance of the objects or the spatial volume they occupied.

The American painter Lilla Cabot Perry (1848–1933) recalled Monet telling her, "When you go out to paint, try to forget what objects you have before you—a tree, a house, a field, or whatever. Merely think, here is a little square of blue, here an oblong of pink, here a streak of yellow, and paint it just as it looks to you, the exact color and shape, until it gives your own

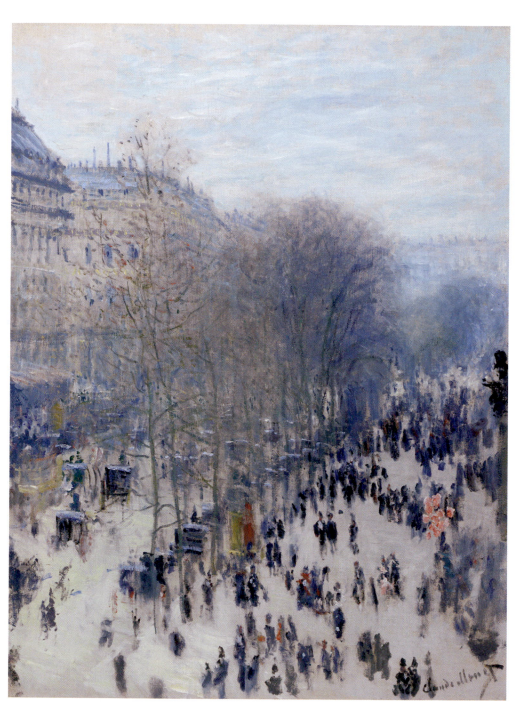

18–26 • Claude Monet
BOULEVARD DES CAPUCINES, PARIS
1873–1874. Oil on canvas, 31¼″ × 23¼″ (79.4 × 59.1 cm). The Nelson-Atkins Museum of Art, Kansas City, Missouri. Purchase: The Kenneth A. and Helen F. Spencer Foundation Acquisition Fund (F72–35). Photo: Jamison Miller.

Monet painted this picture from the balcony of the studio of Parisian photographer Nadar at 35 Boulevard des Capucines, the site of the first Impressionist exhibition. In an appreciative review, critic Ernest Chesnau wrote: "The extraordinary animation of the public street, the crowd swarming on the sidewalks, the carriages on the roadway, and the boulevard's trees waving in the dust and light—never has movement's elusive, fugitive, instantaneous quality been captured and fixed in all its tremendous fluidity as it has in this extraordinary, marvelous sketch."

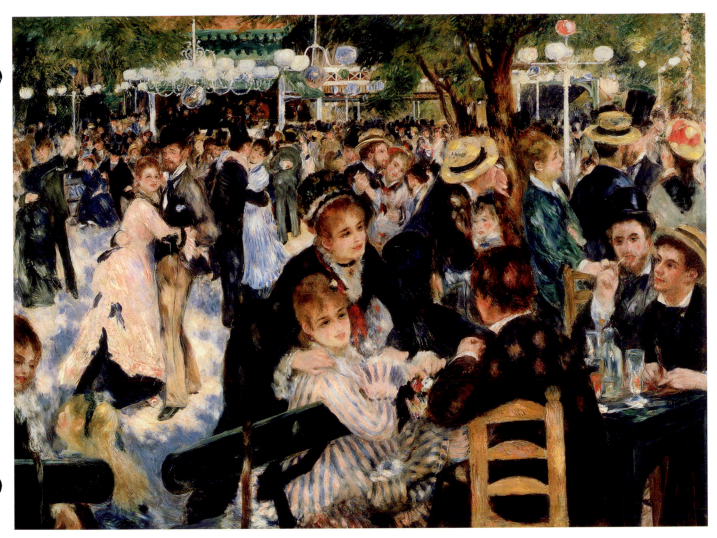

18–27 • Pierre-Auguste Renoir MOULIN DE LA GALETTE
1876. Oil on canvas, 4′ 3½″ × 5′ 9″ (1.31 × 1.75 m). Musée d'Orsay, Paris.

naïve impression of the scene before you." Two important ideas are expressed here: a quickly painted oil sketch provides the most accurate record of what is seen, and artists have a special—perhaps unique—ability to see the world freshly, untainted by intellectual preconceptions or socially imposed patterns. In this way Monet creates the intensity of a spontaneous, first sketch, but presents these fresh impressions as finished works of art. In academic training, sketches had been considered merely part of the preparation for the final work. As a result, many viewers did not see Monet's paintings as "finished."

Impressionist painter Pierre-Auguste Renoir (1841–1919) focused most of his attention on figure painting, producing images of the upper middle class at leisure. When he met Monet at the École des Beaux-Arts in 1862, he was in fact working as a figure painter. Monet encouraged him to lighten his palette and to paint outdoors, and by the mid-1870s Renoir was combining a spontaneous handling of natural light with animated figural compositions. In **MOULIN DE LA GALETTE (FIG. 18–27)**, for example, Renoir depicts a convivial crowd relaxing on a Sunday afternoon at an old-fashioned dance hall—the Moulin de la Galette ("Pancake Mill")—in the Montmartre

area of Paris, which opened its outdoor courtyard during good weather. Renoir glamorizes the working-class clientele by placing his attractive, bourgeois artist friends and their models in their midst, striking poses of relaxed congeniality, smiling, dancing, and chatting. The overall mood is knit together by the dappled sunlight falling through the trees and Renoir's soft brushwork weaving blues and purples through the crowd and around the canvas. This naïve image of a carefree life of innocent leisure—a kind of bourgeois paradise removed from the real world—encapsulates Renoir's idea of the essence of art: "For me a picture should be a pleasant thing, joyful and pretty—yes pretty! There are quite enough unpleasant things in life without the need for us to manufacture more." As we have seen, not everyone painting at this time agreed with him.

Berthe Morisot (1841–1895), who participated in seven of the Impressionists' eight exhibitions, married Manet's brother, Eugène, in 1874, and unlike most married women painters of the time, who gave up their art to devote themselves to domestic duties, Morisot continued painting even after the birth of their daughter in 1879. She dedicated her art to the lives of bourgeois women, whom she depicted in a style that became increasingly

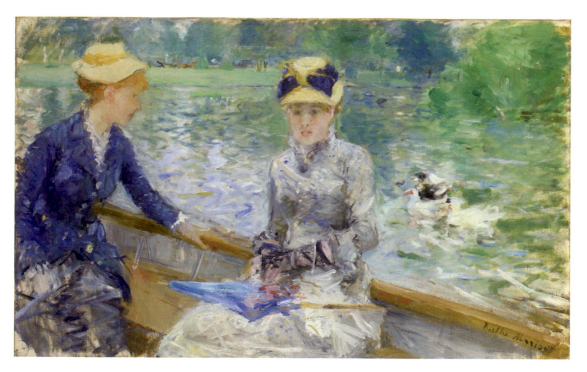

18-28 •
Berthe Morisot
SUMMER'S DAY
1879. Oil on canvas,
17^{13}/$_{16}$" × 29^{5}/$_{16}$"
(45.7 × 75.2 cm).
The National Gallery,
London.

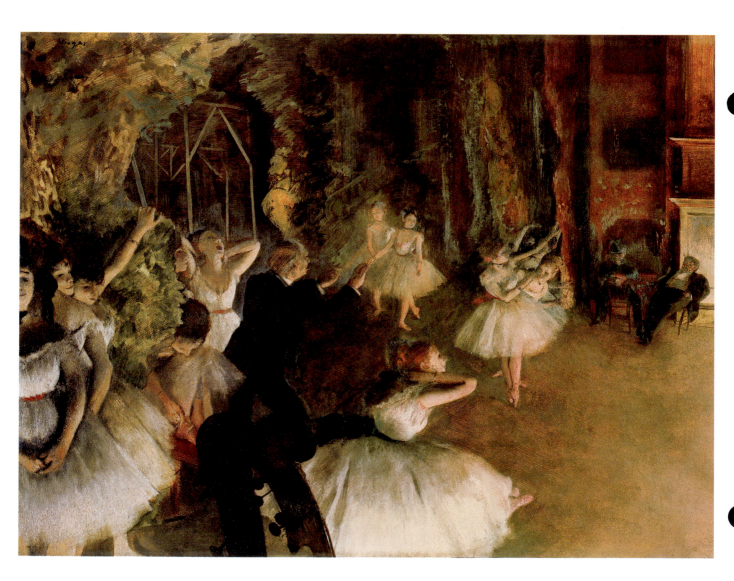

loose and painterly over the course of the 1870s. In **SUMMER'S DAY** of 1879 (**FIG. 18–28**), Morisot adopts the "sketch aesthetics" of Impressionism, dissolving forms into a flurry of feathery brushstrokes. In her paintings, Morisot sought an equality for women that she felt men refused to cede. Late in life she commented, "I don't think there has ever been a man who treated a woman as an equal, and that's all I would have asked, for I know I'm worth as much as they" (Higonnet, p. 19).

Unlike Morisot, not every painter who exhibited with the Impressionists truly worked in an Impressionist style. The artist whose work most severely tests the Impressionist label is Edgar Degas (1834–1917). His friendship with Manet, whom he met in 1862, and with the Realist critics in his circle, led him gradually away from the constrictions of his rigorous academic training and toward frank portrayals of contemporary life—in other words Realism. After a period of painting psychologically probing portraits of friends and relatives, Degas turned in the 1870s to such Paris amusements as the music hall, opera, ballet, circus, and racetrack.

Degas was especially drawn to the ballet. From carefully observed studies of rehearsals and performances, and from dancers hired as models, he arranged his own visual choreography. **THE REHEARSAL OF THE BALLET ON STAGE** (**FIG. 18–29**) is not a factual record of something seen but a careful contrivance calculated to delight the eye but also to refocus the mind on the stern realities of modern life. Several of the dancers look bored or exhausted; others stretch, perhaps to mitigate the toll this physical work took on their bodies. In the right background slouch two well-dressed, middle-aged men, each probably a "protector" of one of the dancers. Because ballerinas generally came from lower-class families and exhibited their scantily clad bodies in public—something that "respectable" bourgeois women did not do—they were widely assumed to be sexually available, and they often attracted the attentions of wealthy men willing to support them in exchange for sexual favors.

The rehearsal is viewed as if from an opera box close to the stage, creating an abrupt foreshortening of the scene, emphasized by the dark scrolls of the bass viols that jut up from the lower left. Degas's work shows two new important influences. The angular viewpoint from above in this and many of his other works may derive from Japanese prints, which he collected, and the seemingly arbitrary cropping of figures, seen here in the ballerina at far left, shows the influence of photography, which he also practiced.

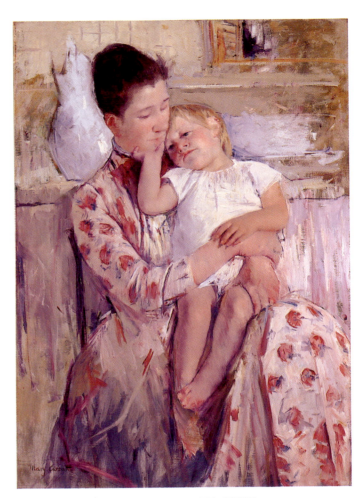

18–30 • Mary Cassatt MOTHER AND CHILD
c. 1890. Oil on canvas, 35½″ × 25⅜″ (90.2 × 64.5 cm). The Roland P. Murdock Collection, Wichita Art Museum, Wichita, Kansas.

Another artist who exhibited with the Impressionists but whose art soon diverged from them in both style and technique—conditioned in part by her contact with Degas—was American expatriate Mary Cassatt (1844–1926). Born near Pittsburgh, raised in the cosmopolitan world of Philadelphia, and studying during the early 1860s at the Pennsylvania Academy of the Fine Arts, she moved to Paris in 1865 to further her academic training and lived there for most of the rest of her life. Cassatt focused her paintings on the world to which she had best access: the domestic and social life of bourgeois women. She is known for extraordinarily sensitive paintings of mothers with children, which, like the genre paintings of expatriate artist Henry Ossawa Tanner (SEE FIG. 18–23), sought to counteract the clichéd conceptions of her age. In a painting of this theme from about 1890 (**FIG. 18–30**) she uses a contrast between the loosely painted, Impressionist treatment of clothing and setting and the solidly modeled forms of faces and hands to rivet viewers' attention on the tender connection between mother and child. And because the structured composition and traditional subject recall much earlier portrayals of the Virgin and Child (e.g., SEE FIGS. 11–15, 13–4), she elevates this vignette of modern life to the level of heroic dialogue with the history of art.

18–29 • Edgar Degas
THE REHEARSAL OF THE BALLET ON STAGE
c. 1874. Pastel over brush-and-ink drawing on thin, cream-colored woven paper, laid on Bristol board, mounted on canvas, 21⅜″ × 28¾″ (54.3 × 73 cm). The Metropolitan Museum of Art, New York. Bequest of Mrs. H. O. Havemeyer Collection, Gift of Horace Havemeyer, 1929 (29.160.26).

View the Closer Look for Degas's *The Rehearsal of the Ballet on Stage* on **MyArtsLab**

Japonisme

Japan was forcibly opened by the U.S. Navy to Western trade and diplomacy in 1853. Two years later, when France, England, Russia, and the United States signed trade agreements that permitted regular exchange of goods, Japanese art became available to European and American artists. One of the first works that engaged the attention of Modern painters was a sketchbook called *Manga* by Katsushika Hokusai (1760–1849), which several Parisian artists eagerly passed around.

The Paris International Exposition of 1867 hosted the first exhibition of Japanese prints in Europe, and soon, Japanese lacquers, fans, bronzes, hanging scrolls, kimonos, ceramics, illustrated books, and *ukiyo-e* (prints of the "floating world," the realm of geishas and popular entertainment) began to appear for sale in specialty shops, art galleries, and even some department stores. Soon it became fashionable for those in the art world to collect Japanese objects for their homes. The French obsession with Japan and its arts reached such proportions by 1872 that the art critic Philippe Burty gave it a name: *japonisme*.

Japanese art had a profound impact on Western painting and printmaking, eventually also on architecture, but the influence was extraordinarily diverse. What individual artists took depended on their own interests. Whistler found encouragement for his purely aesthetic conception of art, liberated from Renaissance rules of representation and perspective. Edgar Degas discovered realistic subjects; complex, diagonal compositional arrangements; and elevated viewpoints. Those interested in the reform of late nineteenth-century industrial design found in Japanese objects both the fine craft and honest elegance they thought lacking in the West.

Mary Cassatt not only admired Japanese art, but directly emulated the compositions, designs, and colors of *ukiyo-e* after multiple visits to an influential 1890 exhibition of 725 woodblock prints mounted at the École des Beaux-Arts in Paris. This art appealed to Cassatt because its concentration on the private lives of women (FIG. 18–31) coordinated well with her own preferred subject matter (SEE FIG. 18–30), and she also felt a connection to the stylistic character of these prints—their cropped, diagonally structured, and often asymmetrical compositions; their use of broad, flat, unmodulated areas of color or tone; their emphasis on outline and pattern over form and space; and their oblique vantage points. This exhibition inspired Cassatt to create her own portfolio of 10 prints (FIG. 18–32), emulating not the woodblock technique of the Japanese printmakers she so admired, but using the more timely medium of aquatint and drypoint to create a pictorial homage to them. The exhibition of these prints in 1891 was her first solo show, and her work was acclaimed by her fellow artists. Cassatt's friend and mentor Edgar Degas was dumbfounded—"I do not admit that a woman can draw like that."

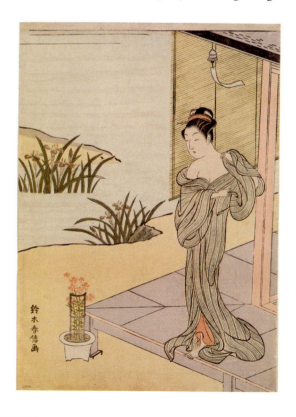

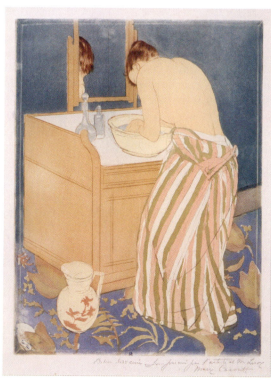

18–31 • Suzuki Harunobu **YOUNG WOMAN LOOKING AT A POT OF PINKS** c. 1767. Woodblock print, 10⅝″ × 7½″ (27 × 19.2 cm). The Cleveland Museum of Art. The Kelvin Smith Collection, given by Mrs. Kelvin Smith 1985.304.

18–32 • Mary Cassatt **WOMAN BATHING** 1890–1891. Color drypoint and aquatint, 16⅝″ × 12″ (42.3 × 30.5 cm). National Gallery of Art, Washington, D.C. Chester Dale Collection 1963.10.253.

Post-Impressionism

What distinguishes the several manifestations of Post-Impressionism?

Realist and Impressionist artists continued to create innovative and significant works until late in the nineteenth century, but by the mid-1880s, they had relinquished their dominance to a younger generation of innovative painters, who experimented with new visual languages tailored to new expressive subjects. The English critic Roger Fry coined the term "Post-Impressionism" in 1910 to identify these diverse new trends, some rooted in reactions against Impressionism. Art historians number among the principal artists united under this term Paul Cézanne, Georges Seurat, Paul Gauguin, Vincent van Gogh, and Henri de Toulouse-Lautrec. Each of these painters moved through an Impressionist phase and continued to use bright Impressionist palettes. But each also came to reject Impressionism's emphasis on the spontaneous recording of light and color and instead sought to create art with a greater degree of formal order and structure. This goal led the Post-Impressionists to develop more abstract and expressive styles that would prove highly influential for the development of Modernist painting in the early twentieth century.

Some Post-Impressionists saw art as a force for social commentary, even as a way to promote social change. The name that came into general use to describe such art was **avant-garde**. Originally a military term for an advance unit, it was used in 1825 by a French socialist, the comte de Saint-Simon, to refer to those artists whose visual expression would prepare people to accept the social changes he and his colleagues envisioned. The idea of producing a socially revolutionary art had already attracted such Realist artists as Courbet and Millet, but the widespread popularity of this notion dates from the Post-Impressionist era. Eventually the term came to stand for the forward-looking aspect of Modern art conceived more broadly, the belief that Modernist artists are working ahead of the public's ability to comprehend developments within the art world. This promoted a sense on the part of artists that they stood in an elite and progressive position as harbingers of change and prophets of progress, set against the mundane preoccupations of the world around them.

Georges Seurat (1859–1891) was among the first in his generation to think of himself as an avant-garde artist. He devoted his energies to "correcting" Impressionism, which he found too intellectually shallow and too improvisational. Seurat belonged to a group of artists, intellectuals, and amateur scientists who were studying theories of vision, light, and color, and he applied their theories to his painting by juxtaposing small strokes of pure, unblended color in an almost abstract arrangement, a technique known as "divisionism" or "pointillism."

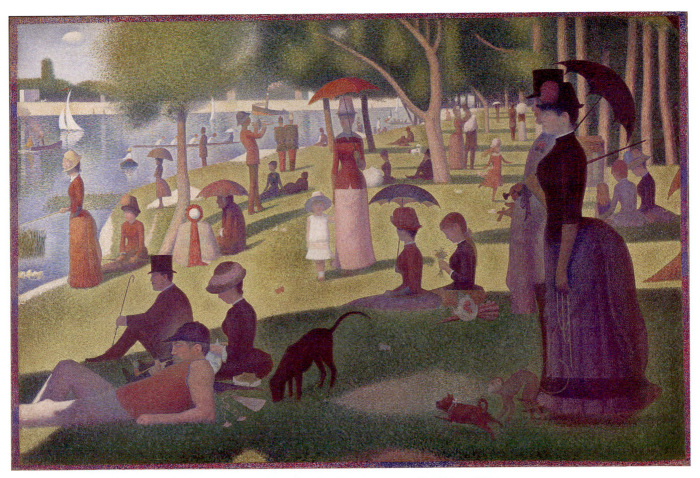

18–33 • Georges Seurat A SUNDAY AFTERNOON ON THE ISLAND OF LA GRANDE JATTE
1884–1886. Oil on canvas, 6′ 9½″ × 10′ 1¼″ (2.07 × 3.08 m). The Art Institute of Chicago. Helen Birch Bartlett Memorial Collection (1926.224).

The work that became the centerpiece of this style and made Seurat's reputation was **A SUNDAY AFTERNOON ON THE ISLAND OF LA GRANDE JATTE** (FIG. 18–33), which Seurat first exhibited at the eighth and final Impressionist exhibition in 1886. The theme of weekend leisure is typically Impressionist, but the rigorous technique, the stiff formality of the figures, and the highly calculated geometry of the composition produce a solemn, abstract effect quite at odds with the casual naturalism of earlier Impressionism. Seurat painted the entire canvas using only 11 colors in three values. When seen from a distance of about 9 feet the picture reads as figures in a park, but when viewed at closer range, from a distance of about 3 feet,

A CLOSER LOOK

Mahana no atua (Day of the God) ▶ **Paul Gauguin. 1894.** Oil on canvas, 27⅜″ × 35⅝″ (69.5 × 90.5 cm). The Art Institute of Chicago. Helen Birch Bartlett Memorial Collection (1926.198).

Gauguin divided the painting into three horizontal zones, progressively abstract from top to bottom. The upper zone, painted in the most lifelike manner, centers on the statue of a god set in a beach landscape populated by Tahitians.

As was his practice in many of his Tahitian paintings, Gauguin did not base this sculpted idol on a statue he saw in Tahiti, but rather on pictures he owned of the Buddhist temple complex at Borobudur (SEE FIG. 4–11).

This middle zone contains three figures posed on an unnaturally pink beach. The green, arched form behind the central woman links her visually to the idol immediately above her.

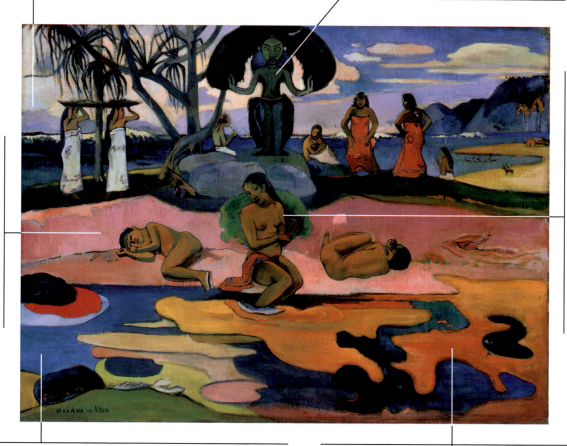

The central female bather dips her feet in the water and looks coyly out at viewers, while on either side of her two androgynous figures recline in fetus-like postures. Their poses perhaps symbolize — left to right — birth, life, and death.

Filling the bottom third of the painting is a striking pool of water, abstracted into a dazzling array of bright colors arranged in a puzzle-like pattern of flat, curvilinear shapes. The left half of this pool seems rooted in natural description, evoking spatial recession. But on the right it becomes flatter and more stylized.

By reflecting a strange and unexpected reality exactly where we expect to see a mirror image of the familiar world, this magic pool seems the perfect symbol of Gauguin's desire to evoke "the mysterious centers of thought." His aim was symbolic rather than descriptive works of art.

View the Closer Look for Gauguin's *Mahana no atua (Day of the God)* on **MyArtsLab**

the individual marks of color become more distinct and the formerly recognizable forms begin to dissolve into abstraction.

From its first appearance, the painting has been the subject of a number of conflicting interpretations. Contemporary accounts of the island indicate that on Sundays—the newly designated official day off for French working families to spend time together—it was noisy, littered, and chaotic. By painting the island the way he did, Seurat may have intended to represent an ideal image of working-class and middle-class life and leisure—a model of how tranquil the island, and perhaps life, *should* be in this fantasy of a harmonious blending of the classes. But some art historians see Seurat satirizing here the sterile habits and rigid attitudes of the growing Parisian middle class, not to mention their domineering presence within this working-class preserve. Or is he simply engaged in an intellectual exercise on the nature of form and color in works of art?

For one Post-Impressionist artist, the desire to escape modern life in Paris was a clear goal; Paul Gauguin (1848–1903) fled first to Brittany and then to Panama. At age 37, he had given up his conventional life as a Paris stockbroker and abandoned his wife and five children to pursue a full-time painting career. In 1888, he spent two months with Van Gogh in Arles, and sailed for Tahiti in the South Pacific in 1891. Before Gauguin left for the South Pacific, he had already found inspiration in the simplified drawing, flattened space, and super-naturalistic color of medieval stained glass, Breton folk art, and Japanese prints. He rejected Impressionism (although he had exhibited in the last four Impressionist exhibitions, 1880–1886) because it neglected subjective feelings. Gauguin called his own style *synthetism*, because it synthesized observation of the subject in nature with the artist's feelings about that subject, expressed through abstracted line, shape, space, and color. In his own words, "Don't paint from nature too much. Art is abstraction. Derive this abstraction from nature while dreaming before it, and think more of the creation that will result."

Very much a product of such synthesis is *Mahana no atua* (*Day of the God*) (see "A Closer Look," p. 502), which, despite its Tahitian subject, was painted in France during Gauguin's brief return visit after two years in the South Pacific. Gauguin had gone to Tahiti hoping to find an unspoiled, pre-industrial paradise. He had imagined the Tahitians to be childlike and close to nature, but what he discovered, instead, was a thoroughly colonized country whose native culture was rapidly disappearing under the pressures of Westernization. In his paintings, Gauguin chose to ignore this reality and to depict the Edenic ideal of his own imagination.

Among the artists in Gauguin's circle before his departure for Tahiti was the Dutch painter Vincent van Gogh (1853–1890). Van Gogh had moved to Paris in 1886, where at first he came under the influence of the Impressionists. He quickly adapted Seurat's divisionist technique to his own use—rather than laying down his paint regularly in dots, he applied it freely in multidirectional dashes of **impasto** (thickly applied pigment), giving his pictures a sense of physical energy and a palpable surface texture. Van Gogh shared Gauguin's desire for a simple, pre-industrial life, and the two planned to move to the south of France and establish a commune of like-minded artists. When Gauguin finally joined Van Gogh, their constant quarrels soon led to violent confrontation and Gauguin's departure. Only a few close friends and his brother Theo stood by Van Gogh to the end. After a series of psychological crises that led to his hospitalization, Van Gogh shot himself in July 1890.

The paintings Van Gogh produced during the last year and a half of his life testify to his heightened emotional state. At the same time, they contributed significantly to the emergence of a new tradition of **expressionism** (art that exaggerates aspects of form to evoke subjective emotions rather than a reasoned response), in which the intensity of an artist's feelings overrides any desire for fidelity to the actual appearance of things. A prime example is **THE STARRY NIGHT** (**FIG. 18–34**), which Van Gogh completed near the asylum of Saint-Rémy, where the

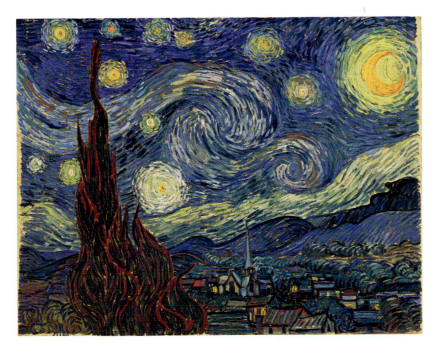

18-34 • Vincent van Gogh **THE STARRY NIGHT** 1889. Oil on canvas, 28¾″ × 36¼″ (73 × 92 cm). The Museum of Modern Art, New York. Acquired through the Lillie P. Bliss Bequest (472.1941).

artist spent his last years. The sky, blazing with exploding stars high above the quiet town, is clearly more a record of what Van Gogh felt than what he saw. Contemplating life and death in a letter, he wrote, "Just as we take the train to get to Tarascon or Rouen, we take death to reach a star." This idea seems rendered visible in the painting by the cypress tree, a traditional symbol of both death and eternal life, which rises dramatically to link the terrestrial world with the heavens.

A more frightening image of the night sky can be seen in the most famous painting of the Norwegian Edvard Munch (1863–1944). **THE SCREAM** (FIG. 18–35) is an unforgettable image of modern alienation that radiates expressionist intensity of feeling. It is the stuff of nightmares. Munch recorded the painting's genesis in his diary: "one evening I was walking along a path; the city was on one side, and the fjord below. I was tired and ill.…I sensed a shriek passing through nature.… I painted this picture, painted the clouds as actual blood." The overwhelming anxiety that sought release in this primal scream was a dread of death, as the sky and the figure's skull-like head suggest, but the setting of the picture also suggests a fear of open spaces. The expressive abstraction of form and color in the painting reflects the influence of Gauguin and his Scandinavian followers, whose work Munch had encountered shortly before painting *The Scream*.

Henri de Toulouse-Lautrec (1864–1901) sought to communicate the psychological impact of the modern world not with the convulsive distortions of **expressionism**, but by

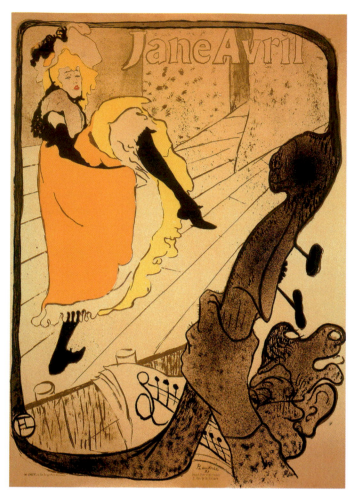

18–36 • Henri de Toulouse-Lautrec **JANE AVRIL**
1893. Lithograph, 50½″ × 37″ (129 × 94 cm). San Diego Museum of Art. The Baldwin M. Baldwin Collection.

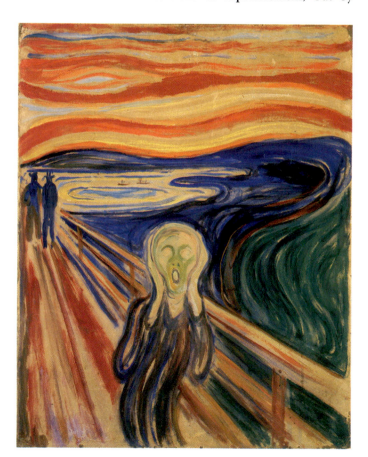

18–35 • Edvard Munch **THE SCREAM**
1910? Tempera and oil on unprimed canvas, 33″ × 26″ (83.5 × 66 cm). Munch Museum, Oslo.

capturing the emotive energy that surrounded him. From the late 1880s—through his designs for lithographic posters used as advertisements for popular night spots and entertainers—Toulouse-Lautrec chronicled life in Montmartre, a section of Paris devoted to entertainment and inhabited by those who lived on the fringes of society. His portrayal of the café dancer **JANE AVRIL** (FIG. 18–36) demonstrates the remarkable artistry that he brought to an essentially commercial project. The composition juxtaposes the dynamic figure of the dancer on a boldly foreshortened stage with the cropped arm of a bass viol player in the immediate foreground, a device we have already seen in the work of Degas (SEE FIG. 18–29). But Toulouse-Lautrec has extended the bass viol's head into a curving frame that surrounds Avril, connecting her visually with her musical accompaniment. The emphasis on outline, suppression of modeling, tipped-up ground, and integration of blank paper into the composition all demonstrate the impact of Japanese woodblock prints (see "Japonisme," p. 500). The emphasis on curving lines and the incorporation of lettering into the total design are reminiscent of Art Nouveau. Ultimately, although they are energetic and colorful, many of Toulouse-Lautrec's images evoke the sad reality behind the festivities at popular dance halls, revealing the artist's sensitivity to a new kind of loneliness: the modern feeling of alienation.

Cézanne

No artist had a greater impact on the next generation of Modern painters than Paul Cézanne (1839–1902). Son of a prosperous banker in the southern French city of Aix-en-Provence, Cézanne began his career painting dark, unsettling Romantic scenes of dramatic conflict and sexual violence—consistently rejected by the Salon—but during the 1870s his style changed under the impact of Impressionism; he adopted a bright palette and loose brushwork and began painting landscapes. Like the Impressionists, with whom he exhibited in 1874 and 1877, Cézanne dedicated himself to objective transcriptions of what he called his "sensations" of nature. Unlike the Impressionists,

however, Cézanne did not seek to capture transitory effects of light and atmosphere. Instead, he created highly structured paintings through a careful and methodical application of color that merged drawing and modeling into a single process. His professed aim was to "make of Impressionism something solid and durable, like the art of the museums."

Cézanne's dedicated pursuit of this goal is evident in a series of paintings of **MONT SAINTE-VICTOIRE**, a mountain near his home in Aix-en-Provence. In this example (**FIG. 18–37**), the mountain rises above the valley, which is dotted with houses and trees and is traversed at the far right by a railroad viaduct. Framing the scene at the left is an evergreen tree,

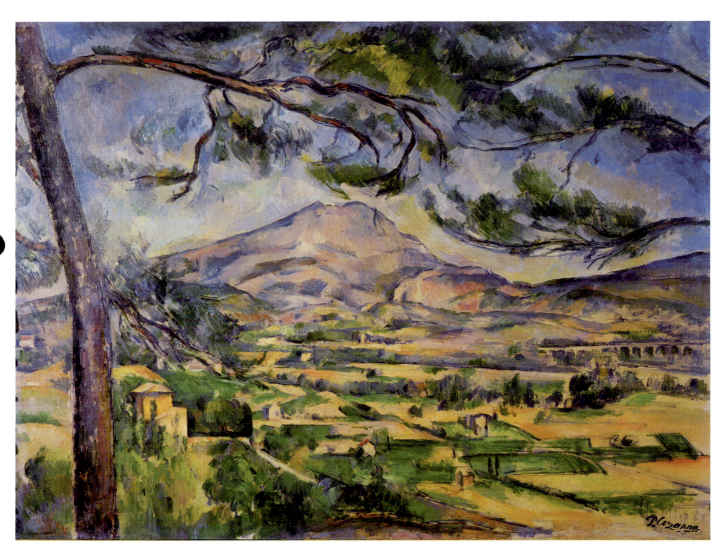

18-37 • Paul Cézanne MONT SAINTE-VICTOIRE
c. 1885–1887. Oil on canvas, 25½″ × 32″ (64.8 × 92.3 cm). Courtauld Gallery, London. © Samuel Courtauld Trust, the Courtauld Gallery, London.

On the one hand, recession into depth is suggested by elements such as the foreground tree that helps draw the eye into the valley, and by the gradual transition from the intense greens and orange-yellows of the foreground to the softer blues and pinks in the distant mountain range, which create an effect of atmospheric perspective. On the other hand, this illusion of consistent recession into depth is challenged by the inclusion of blues, pinks, and reds in the foreground foliage, which relate the foreground forms to the background mountain and sky, and by the tree branches in the sky, which follow the contours of the mountain, making the peak appear nearer and binding it to the foreground plane.

Watch a video about Cézanne's *Mont Sainte-Victoire* on **MyArtsLab**

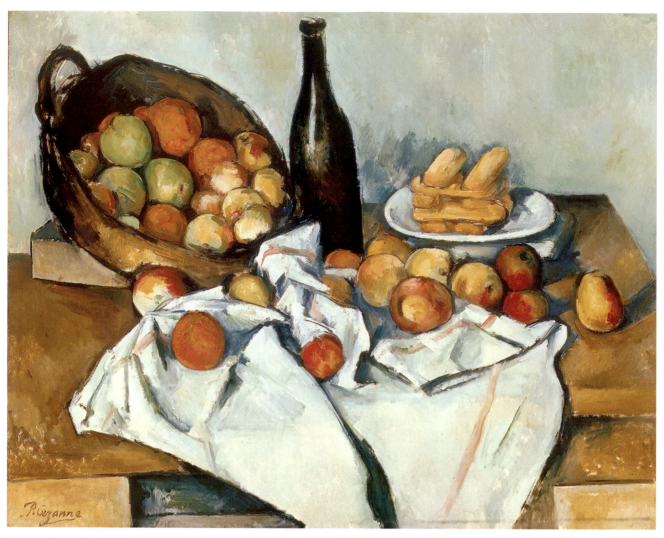

18–38 • Paul Cézanne STILL LIFE WITH BASKET OF APPLES
1890–1894. Oil on canvas, 24⅜″ × 31″ (62.5 × 79.5 cm). The Art Institute of Chicago. Helen Birch Bartlett Memorial Collection 1926.252.

which echoes the contours of the mountain, creating visual harmony between the two principal elements of the composition. The even lighting, still atmosphere, and absence of human activity in the landscape communicate a sense of stasis and timelessness, in contrast to the Impressionists' interest in capturing a personal and momentary aspect of an ever-changing world. Cézanne's handling of paint is more deliberate and controlled than the Impressionists' spontaneous and loose brushwork. His brushstrokes, which vary from short **cross-hatchings** to sketchy lines to broader swaths of flat color, weave together the elements of the painting into a unified but flattened pictorial design. This surface organization vies with the clear sense of receding space, generating tension between the illusion of three dimensions within the picture and the physical reality and chromatic delight of its two-dimensional surface. Photographs of the landscape Cézanne painted here show that rather than reproducing the details as they are, he reorganized what he saw into a personal harmony that he thought the scene demanded. His commitment to the painting as a work of art, which he called "something other than reality"—not a representation of nature

but "a construction after nature"—was a crucial step toward the modern art of the next century.

Spatial ambiguities of a different sort appear in Cézanne's late still lifes, in which many of the objects may seem, at first glance, to be incorrectly drawn. In **STILL LIFE WITH BASKET OF APPLES (FIG. 18–38)**, for example, the right side of the table is higher than the left, the wine bottle has two different silhouettes, and the pastries on the table next to it are tilted upward toward the viewer, while the apples below seem to be seen head on. Such shifting viewpoints are not evidence of incompetence, however, but of Cézanne's willful rejection of the rules of traditional perspective. Although **scientific perspective** mandates that the eye of the artist (and hence the viewer) occupy a fixed point relative to the scene being observed (see "Linear Perspective," p. 314), Cézanne presents the objects in his still lifes from a variety of different positions just as we might move around or turn our heads to take everything in. The composition as a whole, assembled from multiple sightings, is more complex and dynamic. Instead of a faithful reproduction of static objects from a stable vantage point, Cézanne was re-creating, or reconstructing, our experience of them through time.

Sculpture

Europe's most successful and influential sculptor during the Post-Impressionist era was Auguste Rodin (1840–1917). Rodin failed on three occasions to gain entrance to the École des Beaux-Arts and as a result spent the first 20 years of his career assisting other sculptors and decorators. After a trip to Italy in 1875, where he saw the works of Donatello and Michelangelo, Rodin began to develop a style of vigorously modeled figures in unconventional poses, which was simultaneously scorned by critics and adored by the general public. His status as a major sculptor was confirmed in 1884, when he won the competition for the **BURGHERS OF CALAIS** (**FIG. 18–39**), a monument commissioned by the city of Calais to commemorate an event from the Hundred Years' War. In 1347, King Edward III of England offered to spare the besieged city of Calais if six leading

citizens (burghers) would surrender themselves for execution. Rodin shows the six volunteers—dressed in sackcloth with rope halters and carrying the keys to the city—marching out to what they assume will be their deaths. Though it is unknown to them at this point, the king would be so impressed by their courage that he would spare them.

The Calais commissioners were not pleased with Rodin's conception of the event. Instead of calm, idealized heroes, Rodin presented ordinary-looking men in various attitudes of resignation and despair. He exaggerated their facial expressions, lengthened their arms, greatly enlarged their hands and feet, and swathed them in heavy fabric, showing not only how they may have looked but also how they must have felt as they forced themselves to take one difficult step after another. Rodin's willingness to stylize the human body for expressive purposes

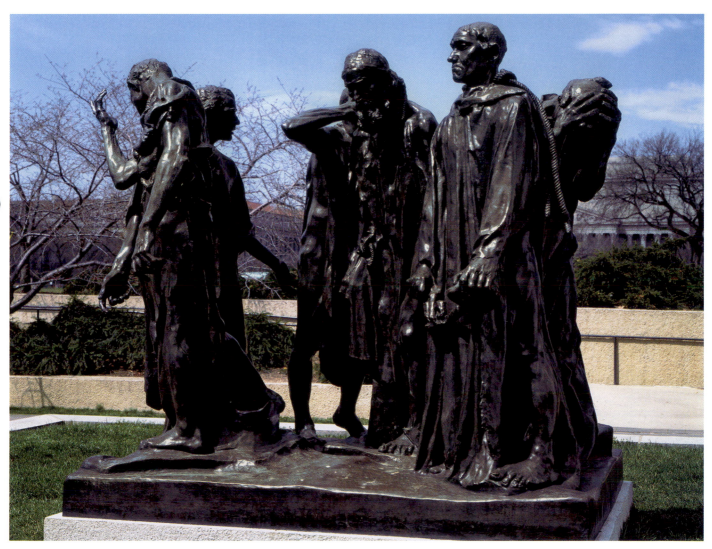

18–39 • Auguste Rodin BURGHERS OF CALAIS
1884–1889. Bronze, 6′ 10½″ × 7′ 11″ × 6′ 6″ (2.1 × 2.4 × 2 m). Hirshhorn Museum and Sculpture Garden, Smithsonian Institution, Washington, D.C. Gift of Joseph H. Hirshhorn, 1966.

Rodin's relocation of public sculpture from a high pedestal to a low base will lead, in the twentieth century, to the elimination of the pedestal itself and to the presentation of sculpture in the "real" space of the viewer.

View the Closer Look for Rodin's *Burghers of Calais* on **MyArtsLab**

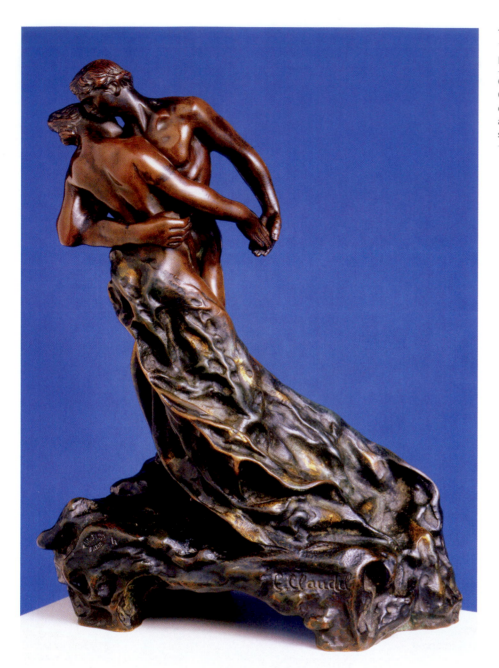

18–40 • Camille Claudel THE WALTZ
1892–1905. Bronze, height 9⅞" (25 cm).
Neue Pinakothek, Munich.

Claudel's close friend, French composer
Claude Debussy, whose innovative musical
compositions were often influenced by
art and literature, displayed a cast of this
sculpture on his piano.

opened the way for subsequent sculptural abstractions. Nor were the commissioners pleased with Rodin's plan to display the figures on a low base, almost at street level, to suggest to viewers that ordinary people like themselves were capable of noble acts. Rodin's removal of public sculpture from a high pedestal to a low base would lead, in the twentieth century, to the elimination of the pedestal itself and to the presentation of sculpture in the "real" space of the viewer.

Camille Claudel (1864–1943), who was Rodin's assistant while he worked on the *Burghers of Calais*, was herself an accomplished sculptor whose work was long overshadowed by the dramatic story of her life. Claudel formally began to study sculpture in 1879 and became Rodin's pupil four years later. After she started working in his studio, she also became his mistress, and their often stormy relationship lasted 15 years.

Both during and after her association with Rodin, Claudel enjoyed independent professional success, but she also suffered from psychological problems that eventually overtook her, and she spent the last 30 years of her life in a mental asylum.

Among Claudel's most celebrated works is **THE WALTZ** (**FIG. 18–40**). The sculpture depicts a dancing couple, both nude, although the woman's lower body is enveloped with long, flowing drapery. In Claudel's original conception, both figures were entirely naked, but she had to add drapery to the female figure after a government inspector declared their sensuality indecent. The swirling drapery and sinuous, intertwined lines of their poses—which recall the fluid lines of Art Nouveau, fashionable at this time—convey an illusion of fluent motion as the dancing partners whirl in space, nearly losing their balance.

In the early nineteenth century, Neoclassicism and Romanticism dominated European art, the former championed in the academies, the latter manifested in landscapes, literary themes, or dramatic current events, rendered in dynamic, unbalanced compositions and loose, painterly brushwork. Emerging in the 1840s, Realists challenged both stylistic currents in scenes of modern life—both in the country and the city—cultivating accurate descriptions of visual appearance and galvanizing the call for social and political change.

The Impressionists during the 1870s reacted against all three of these stylistic movements, rejecting traditional rules and techniques, painting landscapes and city life in pure colors and loose brushstrokes to capture the fleeting play of light in an instantaneous "impression." By the mid-1880s artists began to explore several new directions. Post-Impressionists introduced more structured formal organization and deeper personal expression. Symbolists took refuge from the changing world in the creative realm of imagination. Expressionists sought to picture emotional states. Artists sought to become part of a cultural avant-garde, to innovate, to be different, to be modern.

THINK ABOUT IT

18.1 What nineteenth-century technical innovations made the construction of taller buildings possible?

18.2 How did the Pre-Raphaelite artists in England rebel against the standards and expectations of academic art?

18.3 Discuss the contributions of Daguerre and Fox Talbot to the emergence of photography as a new artistic medium.

18.4 Evaluate Gustave Coubet's Realist painting *A Burial at Ornans* in relation to the social and political issues of its time and place.

18.5 Characterize the style and content of one Impressionist painting, focusing on how it differs from traditional European painting.

18.6 Compare and contrast two Post-Impressionist paintings by two different artists discussed in this chapter. Explain how each offers an alternative to Impressionism.

| CROSSCURRENTS |

FIG. 13–20   FIG. 18–20

European artists often include reflections of art from the past in works that address concerns of the present. This is certainly the case here, where Manet's painting recalls aspects of the composition and subject of a famous painting by Titian that was hung in the Louvre. But the messages are very different. Analyze the meanings of these two paintings. Do they express the concerns of artist, patron, society, or some mixture of the three?

✓ **Study** and **Review** on **MyArtsLab**

IN PERSPECTIVE

1830

1840

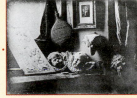

Beginnings of Modern Photography c. 1840

DAGUERRE, The Artist's Studio 1837

1850

Pre-Raphaelite Brotherhood Founded 1848

United States Forcibly Opens Japan to Western Trade and Diplomacy 1853

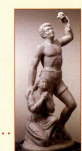

LEWIS, Forever Free 1867

1860

American Civil War 1861–1865
Emancipation Proclamation 1862–1863
"Salon des Refusés" 1863

WHISTLER, Nocturne in Black and Gold 1875

1870

First Impressionist Exhibition of the *Société Anonyme* 1874

Artist James Abbott McNeill Whistler Sues the Critic John Ruskin for Libel 1877

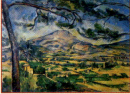

CÉZANNE, Mont Sainte-Victoire c. 1885–1887

1880

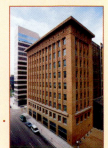

Paris Universal Exposition 1889

1890

SULLIVAN, Wainwright Building 1890–1891

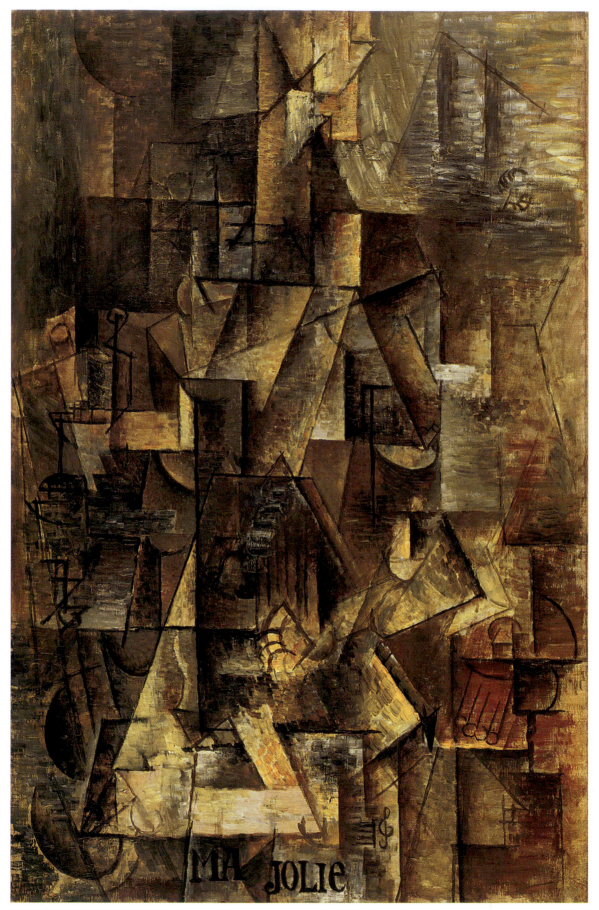

19–1 • Pablo Picasso **MA JOLIE**
1911–1912. Oil on canvas, 39⅜″ × 25¾″ (100 × 65.4 cm). The Museum of Modern Art, New York.

MODERN ART IN EUROPE AND THE AMERICAS, 1900–1945

LEARNING OBJECTIVES

19.1 Trace the spread of Modernism across Europe in the early twentieth century.

19.2 Characterize the arrival of Modernism in the United States.

19.3 Summarize the new developments in Modern art and architecture in Europe between World Wars I and II.

19.4 Compare the assimilation of and the resistance to European Modernism in American art and architecture between World Wars I and II.

LOOKING FORWARD ▶

Pablo Picasso (1881–1973) was a towering presence at the center of the Parisian art world throughout much of the twentieth century, continually transforming the form, meaning, and conceptual framework of his art as his style developed in relation to many factors at play in the world around him. Early in the century in his great Cubist work **MA JOLIE (FIG. 19–1)** of 1911–1912, Picasso challenged his viewers to think about the very nature of communication through painting. Remnants of the subjects Picasso worked from are evident throughout, but any attempt to reconstruct the "subject"—a woman with a stringed instrument—poses difficulties for the viewer. *Ma Jolie* ("My Pretty One") is in some sense a portrait, though hardly a traditional one. Picasso makes us work to see and to understand the figure. We can discover several things about Ma Jolie from the painting; we can see parts of her head, her shoulders, and the curve of her body, a hand, or a foot. But in Paris in 1911, "Ma Jolie" was also the title of a popular song, so the inclusion of writing and a musical staff in the painting may also suggest other meanings. Our first impulse might be to wonder what exactly is pictured on the canvas. To that question, Picasso provided the sarcastic answer, "It's My Pretty One!"

On the other hand, it might be argued that the human subject provided only the raw material for a formal, abstract arrangement. A subtle tension between order and disorder is maintained throughout this painting. For example, the shifting effect of the surface—a delicately patterned texture of grays and browns—is unified through the persistent use of short, horizontal brushstrokes. Similarly, with the linear elements, strict horizontals and verticals dominate, although irregular curves and angles break up their regularity. The combination of horizontal brushwork and right angles firmly establishes a grid that effectively counteracts the surface flux. Moreover, the repetition of certain diagonals and the relative lack of details in the upper left and upper right create a dominant pyramidal shape reminiscent of Classical systems of compositional stability (SEE FIG. 13–1). Thus, what at first may seem a chaotic composition of lines and muted colors turns out to be a carefully organized design. For many, the aesthetic satisfaction of such a work depends on the way chaos seems to resolve itself into order.

In 1923, Picasso said, "Cubism is no different from any other school of painting. The same principles and the same elements are common to all. The fact that for a long time Cubism has not been understood…means nothing. I do not read English, [but] this does not mean that the English language does not exist, and why should I blame anyone…but myself if I cannot understand [it]?"

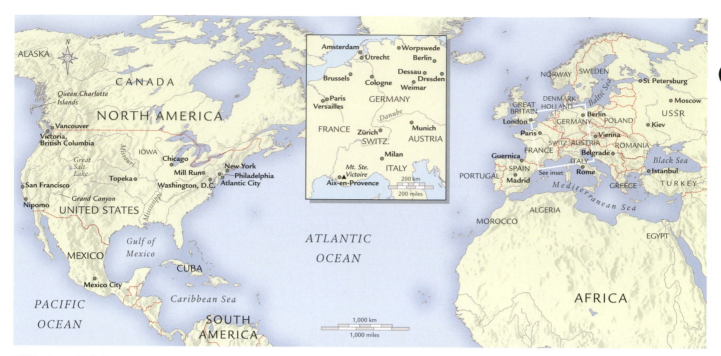

MAP 19–1 • EUROPE AND NORTH AMERICA IN THE 1920S AND 1930S

During the first half of the twentieth century, European avant-garde art movements in France and Germany—especially in Paris and Berlin—influenced the development of Modern art across Europe and North America.

The backdrop of politics, war, and technological change is critical to understanding twentieth-century art. As the century dawned, many Europeans and Americans believed optimistically that human society would "advance" through the spread of democracy, capitalism, and technological innovation. However, the competitive nature of colonialism, nationalism, and capitalism created great instability in Europe, and countries joined together in rival political alliances (**MAP 19–1**).

World War I erupted in August 1914, initially pitting Britain, France, and Russia (the Allies) against Germany and Austria (the Central Powers). The United States entered the war with the Allies in 1917 and contributed to an Allied victory the following year. World War I significantly transformed European politics, economics, and culture, especially in Russia, which became the world's first Communist nation in 1917, when a popular revolution brought the Bolshevik (meaning "Majority") Communist party of Vladimir Lenin to power. In 1922, the Soviet Union (U.S.S.R.), a Communist state encompassing Russia and neighboring states, was created.

American and Western European economies soon recovered from the war (with the exception of Germany, whose economy was weakened by reparations that the Allies demanded), but the 1929 New York stock-market crash plunged much of the world into the Great Depression. In 1933, U.S. President Franklin D. Roosevelt responded with the New Deal, an ambitious welfare program meant to provide jobs and stimulate the American economy. Britain and France instituted state welfare policies during the 1930s as well. Elsewhere in Europe, the economic crisis brought to power right-wing totalitarian regimes: Benito Mussolini in Italy,

Adolf Hitler in Germany, and General Francisco Franco in Spain. Meanwhile, in the Soviet Union, Joseph Stalin succeeded Lenin in 1924.

German aggression toward Poland in 1939 led to the outbreak of World War II, the most destructive war in history. World War II claimed the lives of millions of soldiers and civilians from Asia, North America, and Europe, including 6 million European Jews who perished in the Nazi Holocaust. It ended in Europe in May 1945 and in the Pacific that August.

During the two great wars of the twentieth century, technological innovations resulted in such deadly devices as the fighter bomber and the atom bomb. Yet dramatic scientific developments and improvements in medicine, agriculture, communications, and transportation also transformed the daily life of millions of people, especially in Europe and North America. The first analog and digital computers, designed to process huge amounts of data and perform advanced calculations, were also introduced in the 1930s, though they were not widely used until after World War II.

Accompanying the momentous changes in politics, economics, and science were equally revolutionary developments in art and culture, which scholars have gathered under the label of "Modernism." Although the word "modern" simply means "up-to-date," the term "Modernism" (or "Modern," with a capital M) connotes a specific movement in the history of art, focused on a rejection of conventions and a commitment to radical innovation. Like scientists and inventors, Modern artists engaged in a process of experimentation and discovery, exploring new possibilities of creativity and expression in a rapidly changing world.

Early Modernism in Europe

How did Modernism spread across Europe in the early twentieth century?

As the twentieth century progressed, the pace of artistic innovation within Modernism increased, producing a dizzying succession of movements, or "isms," including Fauvism, Cubism, Futurism, Dadaism, and Surrealism. Each movement had a charismatic leader or group who promoted a defining philosophy, often through written declarations of principles called manifestos. Although Modernism is characterized by tremendous diversity, several broad tendencies mark many Modernist artists across the boundaries created by the "isms." Foremost is a tendency toward abstraction, at times going as far as **nonrepresentational** art, which communicates exclusively through such formal means as line, shape, color, and texture, avoiding any reference to the natural world or to narrative subject matter. A second aspect of Modernism is a tendency to emphasize the physical process of artistic creation, for example, by highlighting the visibility of brushstrokes or chisel marks. A third feature is Modernism's continual questioning of the nature of art itself through the adoption of new techniques and ordinary materials that break down distinctions between art and everyday life.

The rise and spread of Modernism in the early twentieth century was driven by such exhibitions as the 1905 "Salon d'Automne" ("Autumn Exhibition") in Paris, which launched the Fauve movement; the first *Der Blaue Reiter* exhibition in Munich in 1911; and the 1913 New York Armory Show, the first large-scale introduction of European Modernism to American audiences. The Museum of Modern Art opened in New York in 1929, and state-supported museums dedicated to Modern art also appeared in major European capitals, such as Paris, Rome, and Brussels, signaling the transformation of Modernism from an embattled fringe movement to an officially recognized vanguard of "high culture."

Les Fauves

The Salon system still operated in France, but the ranks of artists dissatisfied with its conservative precepts were swelling. Early in the century, these malcontents launched the "*Salon d'Automne*" in opposition to the official Salon in the spring. Reviewing the exhibition in 1905, critic Louis Vauxcelles referred to some of the young painters contemptuously as *fauves* ("wild beasts"), a term that captured the sense of forceful color and impulsive brushwork in their paintings, which conveyed a new intensity of visual experience—"like sticks of dynamite," as *fauve* painter André Derain remarked. Vauxcelles's derogatory characterization seemed more than fitting to those who admired these paintings, and art historians now group them under the label Fauvism.

LE BONHEUR DE VIVRE (THE JOY OF LIFE) (FIG. 19–2), painted by one of Fauvism's leading painters Henri Matisse (1869–1954), transforms hedonistic pursuits within a pastoral landscape into a vibrant arrangement of luscious colors. Naked revelers dance, make love, commune with nature, or simply lounge in their idyllic, seaside glade. Freed from naturalistic constraints, colors contribute as much to the joyous mood as the uninhibited figures themselves. The long, flowing curves of the trees and the sinuous contours of the nude

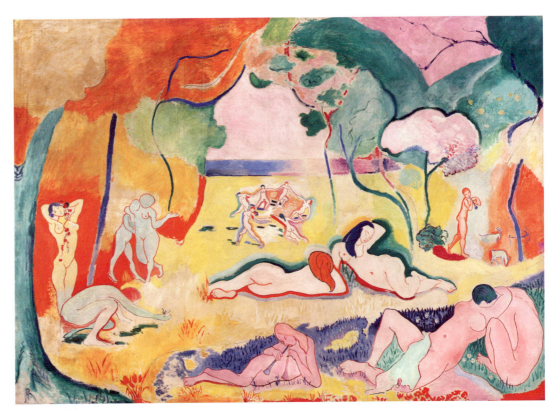

19–2 • Henri Matisse
LE BONHEUR DE VIVRE (THE JOY OF LIFE)
1905–1906. Oil on canvas, 5′ 8½″ × 7′ 9¾″ (1.74 × 2.38 m). The Barnes Foundation, Philadelphia, Pennsylvania.
© 2014 Succession H. Matisse / Artists Rights Society (ARS), New York, NY.

The Joy of Life was originally owned by the brother and sister Leo and Gertrude Stein, important American patrons of European avant-garde art in the early twentieth century. They hung their collection in their Paris apartment, where they hosted an informal salon that attracted leading literary, musical, and artistic figures, including Matisse and Picasso. In 1913, Leo moved to Italy while Gertrude remained in Paris, pursuing a career as a Modernist writer and continuing to host a salon with her partner, Alice B. Toklas.

bodies animate the composition with continual movement and at the same time establish a quality of "serenity, relief from the stress of modern life," as Matisse characterized his work from this period. He wrote, "The whole arrangement of my picture is expressive. The place occupied by figures or objects, the empty spaces around them, the proportions, everything plays a part….The chief aim of color should be to serve expression as well as possible."

"The Bridge" and Expressionism

The German counterpart to Fauvism was *Die Brücke* (The Bridge). In 1905, a group of radical German artists, including Ernst Ludwig Kirchner (1880–1938), came together in Dresden to form what they called a brotherhood, rooted in their shared admiration for the writings of German philosopher Friederich Nietzsche. In *Thus Spoke Zarathustra*, Nietzsche used the metaphor of the bridge to explain how civilization is precariously balanced between two contradictory states of being in the evolutionary process: progress and degeneration, or modernity (the future) and barbarism (the past). With Nietzsche, these artists perceived possibilities for rebirth and renewal in "primitive" states such as childhood or in animal instincts, and they believed that both Modernity (as symbolized by the metropolis) and the "primitive" held connotations for regeneration, but that both could also signify and lead to regression. They associated large urban centers with fresh creativity and new beginnings, yet also acknowledged how the modern metropolis tended to breed a competitive climate that inspired a Darwinian struggle for the survival of the fittest. Seeing just below the surface of polite society

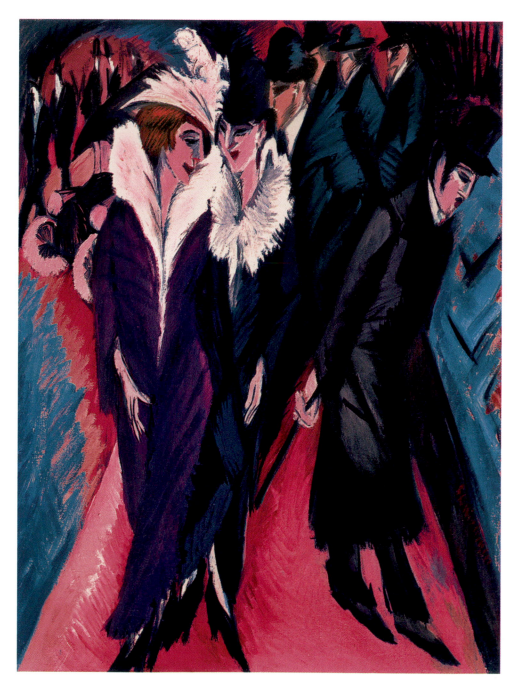

19–3 • Ernst Ludwig Kirchner STREET, BERLIN
1913. Oil on canvas, 47½" × 37⅞" (120.6 × 91 cm). The Museum of Modern Art, New York. Purchase (274.39).

View the Closer Look for Kirchner's *Street, Berlin* on **MyArtsLab**

a seething barbarism on the verge of being unleashed, *Die Brücke* artists were both excited by and wary of this precarious balance.

Kirchner's **STREET, BERLIN** (**FIG. 19–3**) captures this dynamic paradox in a sharp critique of urban life. Dominating the left half of the painting are two prostitutes—their profession advertised by their lavish feathered hats and fur-trimmed coats—strutting past well-dressed bourgeois men, their potential clients. The immediacy of their hurried movement is conveyed through Kirchner's slashing brushstrokes. Although crowded together physically, the figures seem isolated from one another psychologically—artificial and dehumanized mannequins, with masklike faces and stiff gestures, victims of modern urban alienation. The harsh, raw colors, tilted perspective, and angular, brutal brushstrokes register Kirchner's expressionistic response to a metropolis where savagery can be masked by seemingly civilized behaviors.

Käthe Kollwitz (1867–1945) was even more deeply involved with the ills of society, especially the plight of the working class. Raised in a socialist household, she studied at the Berlin School of Art for Women and at a similar school in Munich. Art for her was a political tool, and to reach as many people as possible, she became a printmaker. Between 1902 and 1908, she produced a series of seven etchings in a stark graphic style devoted to the sixteenth-century rebellion known as the Peasants' War. In **THE OUTBREAK** (**FIG. 19–4**), Kollwitz takes full advantage of etching techniques to express the peasants' emotive energy exploding against their oppressors, creating a passionate picture of political revolt. Raw and jagged lines scratched into the plate communicate the peasants' built-up fury from years of mistreatment. In the front, with her back to us, arms silhouetted against the sky, is the leader, Black Anna, modeled after the figure of the artist herself.

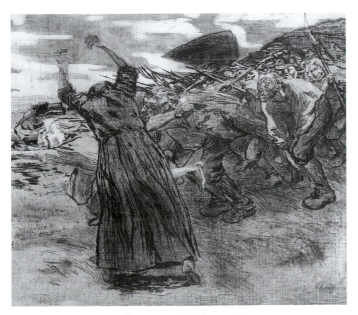

19–4 • Käthe Kollwitz THE OUTBREAK
From the *Peasants' War* series. 1903. Etching, 20″ × 23⅓″ (50.7 × 59.2 cm). Staatliche Museen zu Berlin, Preussischer Kulturbesitz, Kupferstichkabinett.

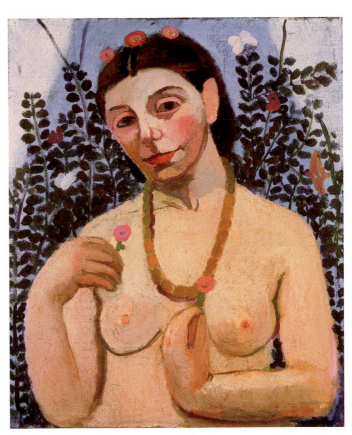

19–5 • Paula Modersohn-Becker
SELF-PORTRAIT WITH AN AMBER NECKLACE
1906. Oil on canvas, 24″ × 19¾″ (61 × 50 cm). Öffentliche Kunstsammlung, Kunstmuseum, Basel, Switzerland (1748).

Paula Modersohn-Becker (1876–1907) also trained at the Berlin School of Art for Women, before moving in 1898 to Worpswede, an artist's colony in rural northern Germany. Dissatisfied with the local artists' naturalistic style, she made four trips to Paris between 1900 and her death in 1907 to see the latest developments in art and was particularly drawn to the work of Gauguin (see "A Closer Look," p. 502). His influence is evident in her 1906 **SELF-PORTRAIT WITH AN AMBER NECKLACE** (**FIG. 19–5**). The basic shapes and simple outlines of her figure—with its prominent eyes as well as its nudity, her body decorated only with flowers and a necklace—suggest that she may have seen African sculpture as well as Post-Impressionist painting in Paris. By presenting herself against a screen of flowering plants and tenderly holding flowers that echo the shape and color of her breasts, she shows herself as a natural being at one with nature, but she also has a powerful, human presence. Modersohn-Becker looks out of the canvas directly at us to return our gaze, an artist of strong independent ideas and a woman of sharp intelligence.

"The Blue Rider"

In 1911, an expressionist group of nine painters—sharing an interest in the power of color—formed in Munich around the Russian artist Vasily Kandinsky (1866–1944). They adopted the name *Der Blaue Reiter* (The Blue Rider or The Blue Knight), based on a popular Russian image of St. George, mounted on

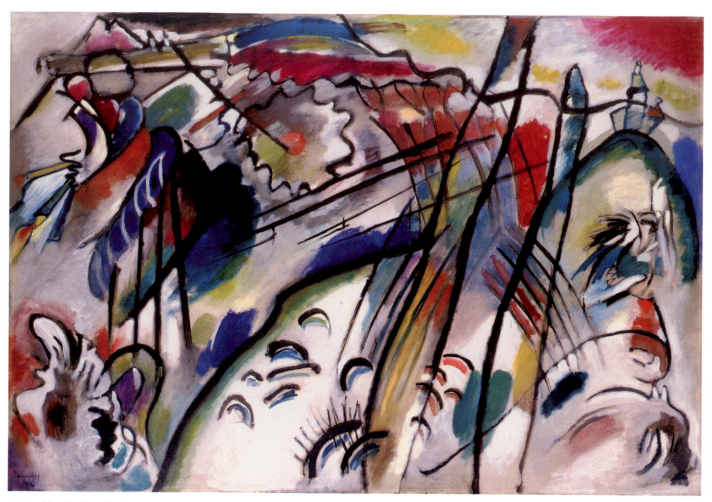

19–6 • Vasily Kandinsky IMPROVISATION 28 (SECOND VERSION)
1912. Oil on canvas, 43⅞″ × 63⅞″ (111.5 × 162.3 cm). Guggenheim Museum, New York.
Solomon R. Guggenheim Founding Collection. By Gift 37.239.

Kandinsky explained the musical analogies evoked in paintings like this in a short book about his own working methods called *Concerning the Spiritual in Art*: "Color directly influences the soul. Color is the keyboard, the eyes are the hammers, the soul is the piano with many strings. The artist is the hand that plays, touching one key or another purposely, to cause vibrations in the soul."

📖 **Read** the document related to Vasily Kandinsky on **MyArtsLab**

a horse and slaying a dragon that appeared on the Moscow city emblem. Kandinsky considered the color blue symbolic of spirituality and the male principle.

Born into a wealthy Moscow family, Kandinsky initially trained as a lawyer, but after visiting Modern art exhibitions and taking private art lessons, he gave up the legal profession, moved to Munich, and established himself as an artist. Studying Whistler (SEE FIG. 18–9) convinced him of a strong relationship between the arts of painting and music, and his musical explorations led him to the work of Austrian composer Arnold Schoenberg, who in the years around 1910 was taking a momentous step in musical history. Since antiquity, Western music had been grounded in the use of scales or modes to create the "tonal center" of a musical composition. Schoenberg, however, treated all notes equally, denying listeners any sense of repose and prolonging tension indefinitely.

After contacting the composer, Kandinsky wondered, if music can do without a tonal center, can painting do without subject matter? Sometime in 1910, Kandinsky painted his first completely abstract work. Typical of the paintings that followed is **IMPROVISATION 28** (FIG. 19–6), the title itself indicative of the impact of musical thought on the evolution of his work. There is a vestige of landscape in this work; Kandinsky found references to the natural world the trickiest to transcend. But if we see buildings or faces here, we may be seeing the painting in an old-fashioned way, looking for correspondences between it and the world where none is intended. Kandinsky would have us look at his painting as if we were listening to a symphony, responding instinctively and freely to this or that passage, and then to the total experience, energized by dynamic linearity and enriched by vibrant patches of sensual color.

Cubism

Of all the Modernist "isms" of early twentieth-century art, Cubism was probably the most influential. The joint invention of Pablo Picasso (1881–1973) and Georges Braque (1882–1963)—who worked side by side in Paris, the undisputed capital of the art world before 1950—Cubism proved a fruitful launching pad for both artists, allowing them to comment on modern life and investigate the ways in which artists perceive and represent the world around them.

Picasso was born in Spain and educated in art academies in Madrid and Barcelona, but he moved to Paris in 1904 and would live in France for the rest of his life. Initially drawn to the socially conscious tradition in French painting that included artists such as Daumier (SEE FIG. 17–21) and Toulouse-Lautrec

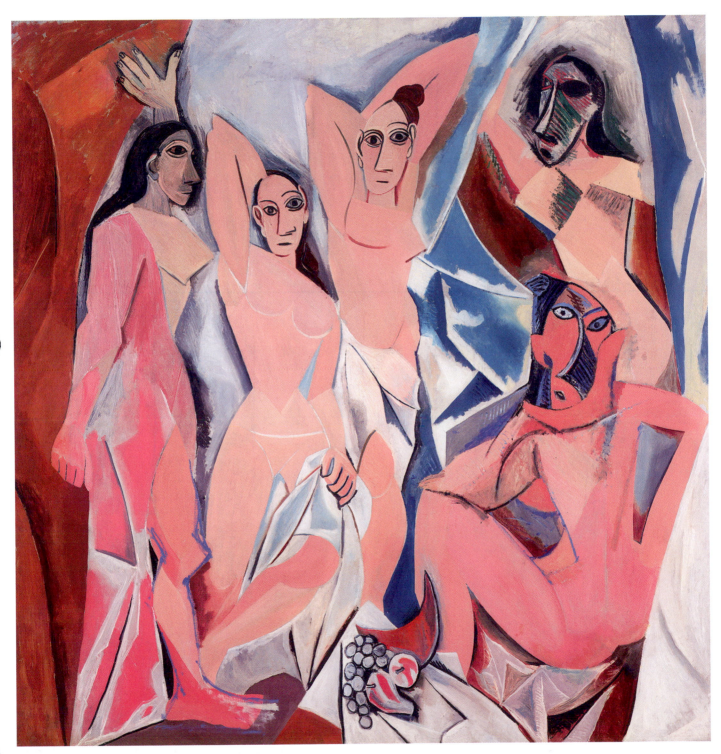

19–7 • Pablo Picasso LES DEMOISELLES D'AVIGNON
1907. Oil on canvas, 8′ × 7′ 8″ (2.43 × 2.33 m). The Museum of Modern Art, New York. Acquired through the Lillie P. Bliss Bequest (333.1939).

View the Closer Look for Picasso's *Les Demoiselles d'Avignon* on **MyArtsLab**

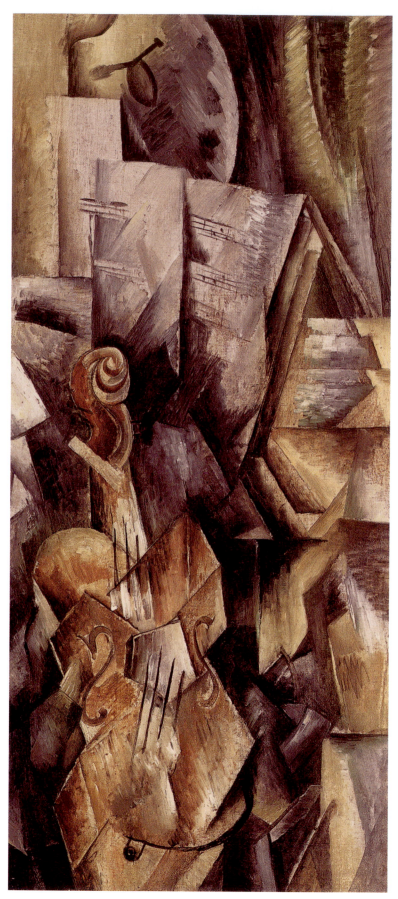

19–8 • Georges Braque VIOLIN AND PALETTE
1909–1910. Oil on canvas, 36⅛″ × 16⅞″ (91.8 × 42.9 cm).
Solomon R. Guggenheim Museum, New York (54.1412).

(SEE FIG. 18–36), Picasso went through an extraordinary and complex transformation between early 1905 and the winter of 1906–1907. In 1906, the Louvre installed a newly acquired collection of sculpture from Iberia (Spain and Portugal) that dated to the sixth and fifth centuries BCE, and these archaic figures became a powerful influence on his work over the next year. Even more influential were his repeated visits to the ethnographic museum where African art brought back from France's colonies was displayed. Picasso greatly admired the expressive power and unfamiliar formal qualities of African masks, and he bought several pieces and kept them in his studio.

Picasso's wide-ranging studies culminated in 1907 in **LES DEMOISELLES D'AVIGNON** (FIG. 19–7), one of the most radical and complex paintings of the twentieth century. The simplified features and wide, almond-shaped eyes of the three figures on the left reflect the Iberian influence, while the two figures at the right were inspired by African masks. Given contemporary condescending attitudes toward what were considered "primitive" cultures, Picasso's wholesale adoption and adaptation of Iberian and African art in a large, multifigure painting was an act of cultural rebellion. The painting might be viewed as Picasso's response to Matisse's *Le Bonheur de Vivre* (SEE FIG. 19–2), exhibited the year before, or more broadly to the French Neoclassical tradition as embodied in Ingres's paintings of odalisques (SEE FIG. 17–16). Picasso, however, substituted a brothel for a harem. The term *demoiselles* (meaning "young ladies") was a euphemism for prostitutes, and "Avignon" refers not to the French town but to a street in the red-light district of Barcelona.

Picasso makes viewers looking at this painting uneasy. The women are shielded by masks, flattened and fractured into sharp angular shapes. The space they inhabit is incoherent and convulsive. The women pose for, and some look directly at, us—conventional cues of accessibility that are contradicted by their hard, piercing gazes and tight mouths, and what one art historian has called "a tidal wave of aggression." Even the fruit in the foreground, symbols of female sexuality, seems hard and dangerous. Women, Picasso suggests, are not the gentle and passive creatures men would like them to be. This viewpoint contradicts an enduring tradition, prevalent at least since the Renaissance, of portraying sexual availability in the female nude, just as strongly as Picasso's treatment of space shatters the reliance on ordered linear perspective, equally standard since the Renaissance.

Most of Picasso's friends were horrified by his new work. Matisse, for example, accused Picasso of making a joke of modern art and threatened to break off their friendship. But one artist, Georges Braque, responded positively—he saw in *Les Demoiselles d'Avignon* a potential for new visual experiments. Picasso has used broken and distorted forms expressionistically to convey his view of women, which some feminists have branded misogynistic. But what secured his place in the Parisian avant-garde was the revolution in form this painting inaugurated. Braque responded eagerly to Picasso's formal innovations and set out, alongside Picasso, to develop them by flattening pictorial space, by incorporating multiple perspectives within a single picture plane, and by fracturing form, all features that these artists had admired in Cézanne's late paintings.

Braque carried the formal experiment further during 1908. In his landscape painting, he reduced nature's complexity to its essential colors and basic geometric shapes, but his works were rejected that year from the Autumn Salon. Matisse dismissively referred to Braque's "little cubes." The critic Louis Vauxcelles picked up the phrase, claiming that Braque "reduced everything to cubes," thus giving birth to the art-historical category of Cubism. Braque's painting also pointed Picasso in a new direction, and soon the two artists began an intimate working relationship that lasted until Braque went off to war in 1914. "We were like two mountain climbers roped together," Braque would later say.

The move toward abstraction and simplification continued in a series of still-life paintings Braque and Picasso produced over the next two and a half years. In Braque's **VIOLIN AND PALETTE** (FIG. 19–8), the gradual abstraction of deep space and recognizable subject matter is well under way.

The still-life items here are not arranged in a measured recession from foreground to background but are pushed close to the picture plane, compressed into a shallow space. Braque knit the various elements—a violin, an artist's palette, and some sheet music—together into a single shifting surface of forms and colors. In some areas of the painting, formal elements lose not only their natural spatial relations but their coherent shapes as well. Where representational motifs remain—the violin, for example—Braque fragments them to facilitate their integration into the compositional whole. Such paintings of 1909–1910 initiate what art historians call Analytic Cubism because of the way the artists broke objects into parts as if to analyze them.

Picasso and Braque's Analytic Cubist works of 1911 and early 1912 reflect a different approach to the breaking up of forms and the flattening of pictorial space. Instead of simply fracturing objects visually, they pick them apart and rearrange their component parts. In this way, Analytic Cubism replicates the actual process of perception, during which we examine objects from various points of view and then reassemble our glances into a whole object in our brain. Only Picasso and Braque reassemble their shattered subjects not according to our process of perception but conforming to principles of artistic composition, to communicate meaning rather than to represent observed reality. For example, remnants of the subject are evident throughout Picasso's *Ma Jolie* (SEE FIG. 19–1), but any attempt to reconstruct from them the image of a woman with a stringed instrument would be misguided since the subject provided only the raw material for a formal composition. *Ma Jolie* is not a representation of a woman, a place, or an event; it is simply a painting.

Works like *Ma Jolie* brought Picasso and Braque to the brink of nonrepresentation, but in the spring of 1912 they pulled back and began to create works that suggested more clearly discernible subjects. This second major phase of Cubism is known as Synthetic Cubism because of the way the artists created motifs by combining simpler elements, as in a chemical synthesis. Picasso's **LA BOUTEILLE DE SUZE** (FIG. 19–9), like many of the works he and Braque created between 1912 and 1914, is a **collage** (from the French *coller*, meaning "to glue"), a work composed of separate elements pasted together. At the center, assembled newsprint and construction paper suggest a tray or round table supporting a glass and a bottle of liquor with an actual label. Around this arrangement Picasso pasted larger pieces of newspaper and wallpaper. As in earlier Cubism, multiple perspectives are offered. We see the top of the blue table, tilted to face us, and simultaneously the side of the glass. The bottle stands on the table, its label facing us, while we can also see the round profile of its opening, as well as the top of the cork that plugs it. The elements together evoke not only a place—a bar—but also an activity: the viewer alone with a newspaper, enjoying a quiet drink. The newspaper clippings glued to this picture, however, disrupt the quiet mood. They refer to the First Balkan War of 1912–1913, which contributed to the outbreak of World War I. Did Picasso want to underline the disorder in his art by comparing it with the disorder building in the world around him, or was he warning his viewers not to sit complacently and sip Suze while political events threatened to shatter the peaceful pleasures this work evokes?

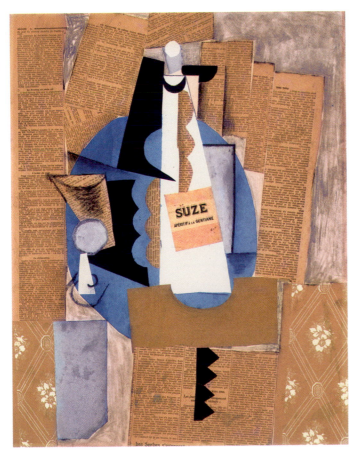

19–9 • Pablo Picasso
LA BOUTEILLE DE SUZE (BOTTLE OF SUZE)
1912. Pasted paper, gouache, and charcoal, 25¾″ × 19¾″ (65.4 × 50.2 cm). Mildred Lane Kemper Art Museum, Washington University, St. Louis, Missouri. University Purchase, Kende Sale Fund, 1946.

Responses to Cubism

As Cubism evolved and emerged from the studios of Braque and Picasso, the world of art was altered irrevocably. The radical innovations may have upset the general public and many critics, but members of the avant-garde saw in them the future of Modern art. Cubism's way of viewing the world resonated with artists in many countries. They interpreted Cubism in personal ways, significantly broadening and extending its visual message beyond the ideas and images envisioned by Picasso and Braque.

France. Robert Delaunay (1885–1941) and his wife, the Ukranian-born Sonia Delaunay-Terk (1885–1979), took the relatively monochromatic and static Analytic Cubism into a new direction by fusing it with Fauvist color in works celebrating the modern city and modern technology. The critic and poet Guillaume Apollinaire labeled the style "Orphism" (from Orpheus, the legendary Greek musician), implying an analogy between their painting and music. The Delaunays preferred to think of their work in terms of "simultaneity," a complicated concept connoting the collapse of spatial distance and temporal sequence into a simultaneous "here and now," and the creation of harmonic unity out of seemingly discordant elements.

Delaunay-Terk became an important textile and clothing designer. Her greatest critical success came at the International Exposition of Modern Decorative and Industrial Arts in 1925, for which she decorated a **CITROËN** sports car to match one of her fashion ensembles (**FIG. 19–10**). Her bold geometric patterns seem to express the new modernity of the automobile age. The small three-seater Citroën was specifically designed to appeal to the "new woman," who, like Delaunay-Terk, was more mobile, less tied to home and family, and less dependent on men than her predecessors. Sadly, there are only black-and-white photographs of these designs.

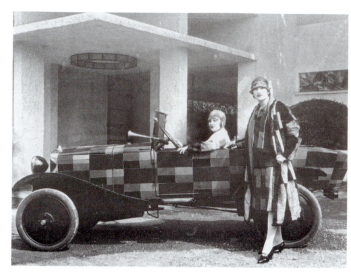

19–10 • Sonia Delaunay-Terk
CLOTHES AND CUSTOMIZED CITROËN B-12
From *Maison de la Mode*, 1925.

Similarly fascinated by technology was Fernand Léger (1881–1955), who developed a version of Cubism based on machine forms. His artistic development was affected by his wartime experience. Drafted into the French army, he was almost killed by poison gas in 1916, and this experience led him to see more beauty in everyday objects, even those made by machines. **THREE WOMEN** (**FIG. 19–11**) is a machine-age version of the French academic subject of the reclining nude (SEE FIG. 17–16). The picture space is shallow and compressed but less radically shattered than in Analytic Cubism. The women, arranged within a geometric grid, stare out blankly at us with Classical calmness. They have identical faces, and their

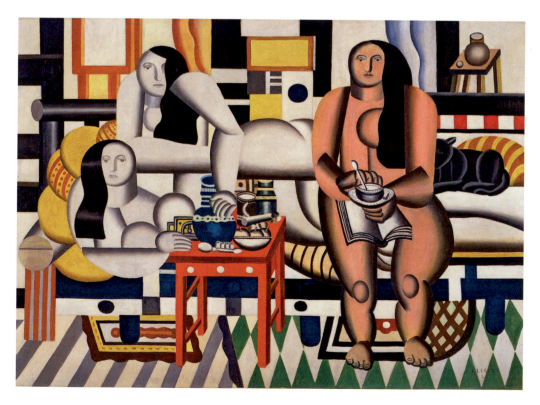

19–11 • Fernand Léger THREE WOMEN
1921. Oil on canvas, 6′ ½″ × 8′ 3″ (1.84 × 2.52 m). The Museum of Modern Art, New York. Mrs. Simon Guggenheim Fund (189.1942).

Cubist figure studies, which Boccioni saw in Paris in 1911, inspired the exaggerated muscular curves and counter-curves of this powerful sculpture, the stretched and inflated forms which express the figure's force and speed. The work personifies the new Italian man envisioned by the Futurists, a strong figure rushing headlong into the brave new world. In keeping with his Futurist ideals, Boccioni celebrated Italy's entry into World War I by enlisting and was killed in combat.

Russia. Since the time of Peter the Great (ruled 1682–1725), the Russian upper classes had turned to Western Europe for cultural models. Natalia Goncharova (1881–1962) was one of many Russian artists who adopted avant-garde French styles with some ambivalence. Among her creations were costumes and sets that she designed—merging abstraction with Russian folk art—for the impresario Sergei Diaghilev's famed Ballets Russes, including the performances of *Le Coq d'or* (1914), *Night on Bald Mountain* (1923), and the 1926 revival of Igor Stravinsky's *Firebird*.

Goncharova and her lifelong companion, Mikhail Larionov (1881–1964), were torn between the desire to develop a native, characteristically Russian art and the wish to keep up with the developments of Western Modernism. They created a new Russian style known as Rayonism. In her **ELECTRIC LIGHT** (**FIG. 19–13**), Goncharova combines two styles: simplified

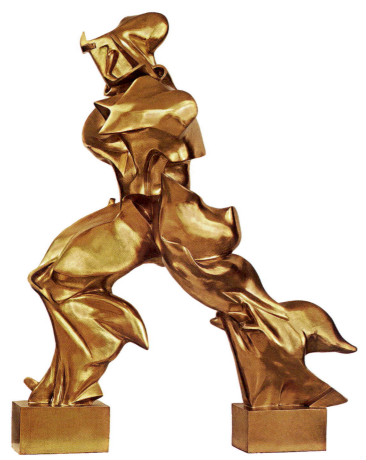

19–12 • Umberto Boccioni
UNIQUE FORMS OF CONTINUITY IN SPACE
1913. Bronze, 43⅞″ × 34⅞″ × 15¾″ (111.4 × 88.6 × 40 cm).
The Museum of Modern Art, New York. Acquired through the
Lillie P. Bliss Bequest (231.1948).

Boccioni and the Futurist architect Antonio Sant'Elia were both killed in World War I. The Futurists had ardently promoted Italian entry into the war on the side of France and England. After the war Marinetti's movement, still committed to nationalism and militarism, supported the rise of fascism under Benito Mussolini, although a number of the original members of the group rejected this direction.

---

bodies seem assembled from standardized, interchangeable metal parts. The bright, exuberant colors and patterns that surround them, however, suggest an orderly industrial society in which everything has a place.

Italy. In Italy, Cubism led to Futurism, which emerged on February 20, 1909, when a Milanese literary magazine editor, Filippo Marinetti, published his "Foundation and Manifesto of Futurism" on the front page of a Parisian newspaper. Marinetti's manifesto attacked everything old, dull, "feminine," and safe, and proposed to shake Italy free of its past by embracing an exhilarating, "masculine," "futuristic," and even dangerous world based on the thrill, speed, energy, and power of modern urban life.

Among the artists and poets who gathered around Marinetti was Umberto Boccioni (1882–1916), whose major sculptural work, **UNIQUE FORMS OF CONTINUITY IN SPACE** (**FIG. 19–12**), seems to epitomize a revitalized Italy.

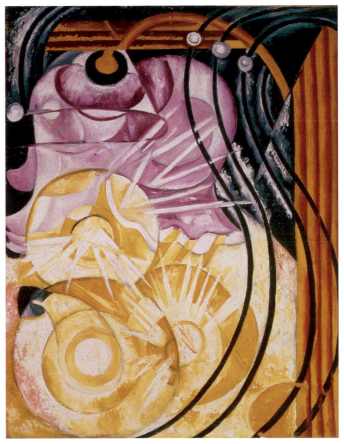

19–13 • Natalia Goncharova ELECTRIC LIGHT
1913. Oil on canvas, 41½″ × 32″ (105.5 × 81.3 cm).
Musée National d'Art Moderne. Centre National d'Art et de Culture Georges Pompidou.

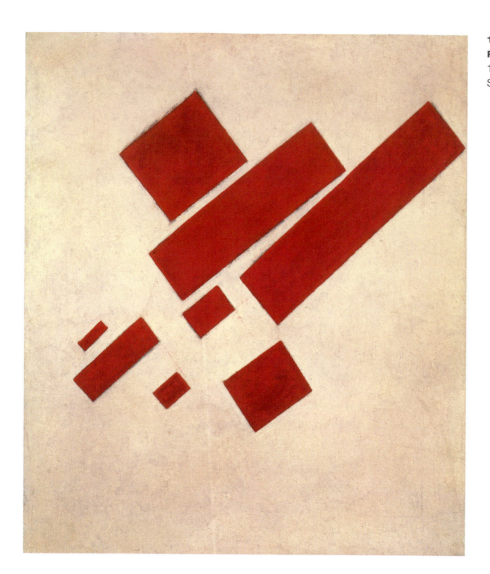

Cubist shapes and a dynamic Futurist composition. Brilliant electric light bulbs almost explode into yellow disks and rays, energized by their swinging, snake-like cords and switches. The painting is at the same time a study in contrasting enhanced colors and a potent symbol of technological advance—of Russia's modernity.

After Goncharova and Larionov left for Paris in 1915, their colleague Kazimir Malevich (1878–1935) emerged as the leading figure of the Moscow avant-garde, and he is recognized as the first Modern artist to produce a truly nonrepresentational work of art. According to his later reminiscences, "in the year 1913, in my desperate attempt to free art from the burden of the object, I took refuge in the square form and exhibited a picture which consisted of nothing more than a black square on a white field." Malevich exhibited 39 works in this radically new mode in St. Petersburg in the winter of 1915–1916. One, **SUPREMATIST PAINTING (EIGHT RED RECTANGLES)** (**FIG. 19–14**), consists simply of rectangles arranged diagonally on a white painted ground. Malevich called this art "Suprematism," short for "the supremacy of pure feeling in creative art." By eliminating traditional subject matter and focusing entirely on formal issues, Malevich intended to "liberate" the essential beauty of all great art.

This Russian avant-garde enthusiastically supported the Revolution that broke out in 1917, thinking that their radical new form of art was appropriate for the new Russia that would emerge from the ashes of the tsarist dictatorship. Into the 1920s it was. But eventually avant-garde art was branded "bourgeois" and "decadent" by the Soviet government, and a highly representational and heroic style called Socialist Realism became state policy in 1932 under dictator Joseph Stalin.

Dada

The Dada movement, which began with the opening of the Cabaret Voltaire in Zürich, Switzerland, on February 5, 1916, was a remarkable manifestation of the disillusioned mood of its time, as World War I, which had begun in 1914, spiraled out of control and settled into a stalemate during which the latest technologies for killing were piling up human casualties of unprecedented proportions. Witnessing how thoughtlessly life was discarded in the trenches, Dada mocked the senselessness of rational thought and even the foundations of modern society. The cabaret's founders, the German actor and artist Hugo Ball (1886–1927) and his companion, Emmy Hennings, a nightclub singer, attracted a circle of avant-garde writers and artists who shared in Ball's and Hennings's disgust with the political culture that had visited such brutality on their world.

Ball's performance while **RECITING THE SOUND POEM, "KARAWANE"** (FIG. 19–15), reflects the spirit of the cabaret. Ball encased his legs and body in blue cardboard tubes, and wore on his head a white-and-blue "witch-doctor's hat," as he called it. The huge gold-painted cardboard collar over his shoulders flapped when he moved his arms. Dressed in this manner, he slowly and solemnly recited the poem, which consisted entirely of nonsense sounds. By retreating into sound alone, he avoided language, which he believed had been spoiled by the lies and excesses of journalism and advertising. But his goals were not all political and intellectual. Ball also wanted to introduce the healthy play of children back into restricted adult lives. The flexibility of interpretation inherent in Dada extended to its name, which, according to one account, was chosen at random from a dictionary. In German, "dada" signifies "baby talk"; in French, it means "hobbyhorse"; and in Russian, "yes, yes." The name, and the movement, could be defined as the individual wished.

Dada first spread from Zürich to New York and Barcelona, and then to Berlin (1918), Cologne, and Paris. The leading figure in New York was French artist Marcel Duchamp (1887–1968), who had moved to New York in 1915. Duchamp and his friends maintained that art should appeal to the mind rather than to the senses. This cerebral approach is exemplified in Duchamp's **readymades**—ordinary manufactured objects transformed into artworks simply through their selection by the artist. The most notorious readymade was **FOUNTAIN** (FIG. 19–16), a porcelain urinal turned through 90 degrees and signed with the pseudonym "R. Mutt," a play on the name of the fixture's manufacturer. Duchamp submitted *Fountain* anonymously in 1917 to the first exhibition of the American

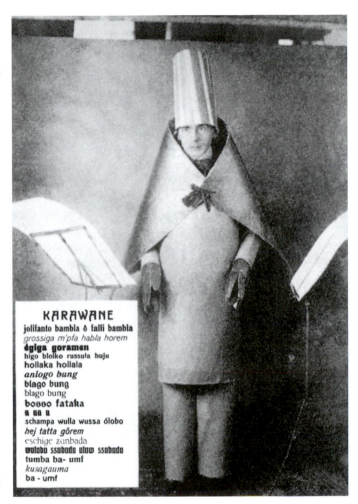

19–15 • HUGO BALL RECITING THE SOUND POEM "KARAWANE"
Photographed at the Cabaret Voltaire, Zürich, 1916. Kunsthaus Zürich Dada-Archive. © 2014 Kunsthaus Zürich. All rights reserved.

19–16 • Marcel Duchamp FOUNTAIN
1917. Porcelain urinal and enamel paint. Photograph by Alfred Stieglitz. Philadelphia Museum of Art, The Louis and Walter Arensberg Collection 1950.

Stieglitz's photograph is the only known image of Duchamp's original *Fountain*, which mysteriously disappeared after it was rejected by the jury of the American Society of Independent Artists exhibition. In 1950, Duchamp produced several replicas of the lost original simply by buying more urinals and signing them "R. Mutt/1917." One of these replicas sold at auction in 1999 for $1.76 million, setting a record for a work by Duchamp.

👁 **Watch** a video about Marcel Duchamp on **MyArtsLab**

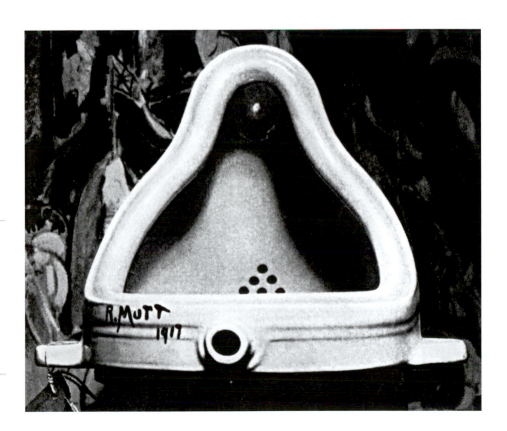

Society of Independent Artists, open to anyone who paid a $6 entry fee. Duchamp, a founding member of the society, entered the found object partly as a test. A majority of the society's directors declared that *Fountain* was not a work of art, and, moreover, was indecent, so the piece was refused. Duchamp immediately resigned from the society in mock horror. He wrote, "The only works of art America has given are her plumbing and bridges." In a more serious vein, he added: "Whether Mr. Mutt with his own hands made the fountain or not has no importance. He CHOSE it. He took an ordinary article of life, placed it so that its useful significance disappeared under the new title and point of view—created a new thought for that object." Duchamp's philosophy of the readymade, succinctly expressed in these words, had a tremendous impact on later twentieth-century artists.

A major figure in Berlin Dada, Hannah Höch (1889–1978) concentrated on pointed political commentary in the medium of photomontage (photographic collage). Between 1916 and 1926 she designed decorative patterns and wrote articles on crafts for a women's magazine. She disapproved of contemporary mass-media representations of women and had to fight for her place as the sole woman among the Berlin Dada group, one of whom described her contribution disparagingly as merely conjuring up beer and sandwiches. In **CUT WITH THE DADA KNIFE THROUGH THE LAST WEIMAR BEER-BELLY CULTURAL EPOCH IN GERMANY (FIG. 19–17)**, Höch collages images and words from the popular press, political posters, and photographs to create a complex and angry critique of the Weimar Republic in 1919. She shows women physically cutting apart the beer-bloated German establishment in this photomontage and includes portraits of androgynous Dada characters, such as herself and several other Berlin Dada artists, along with Marx and Lenin. It is tempting to wonder which side she really thinks her fellow Dadaists stand on.

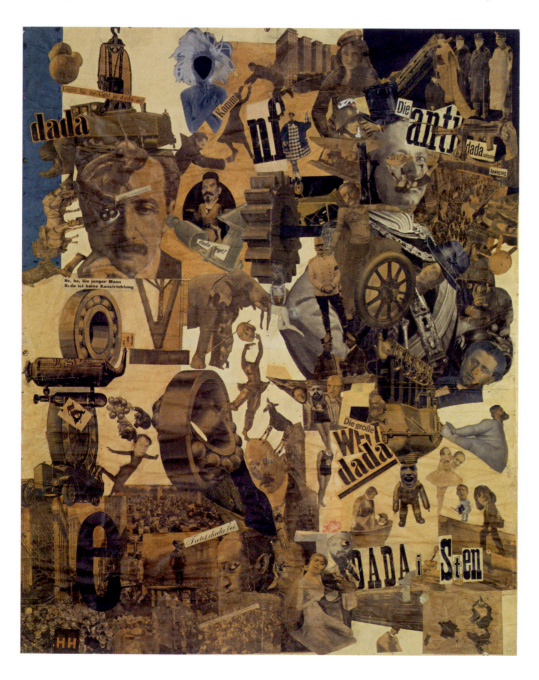

**19–17 • Hannah Höch
CUT WITH THE DADA KITCHEN KNIFE THROUGH THE LAST WEIMAR BEER-BELLY CULTURAL EPOCH IN GERMANY**
1919. Collage, 44⅞″ × 35⅜″ (114 × 90 cm). Nationalgalerie, Staatliche Museen zu Berlin.

Read the document related to Hannah Höch on **MyArtsLab**

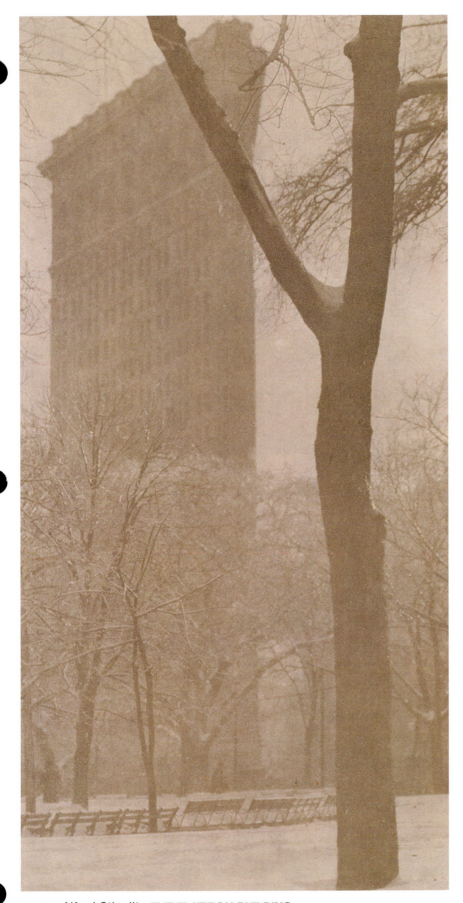

Modern Art Comes to the United States

How and when did Modernism arrive in the United States?

At the end of the nineteenth century, American artists, led by artist-teacher Robert Henri (1865–1929), sought a purely "American" style, as free from Impressionism as it was from European academic conventions. Henri told his students, "Paint what you see. Paint what is real to you." In 1908, he organized an exhibition of paintings by artists who came to be called "The Eight," five of whom became known as members of the Ashcan School because of their interest in depicting scenes of gritty urban life in New York City.

An outspoken opponent of the Ashcan School was the photographer Alfred Stieglitz (1864–1946), who chose a different approach in photographing the quintessentially modern city of New York in poetic images of romanticized urban scenes (**FIG. 19–18**). In 1905, Stieglitz opened a New York gallery where he exhibited contemporary art and photography, hoping to break down the artificial barrier between the two. Located at 291 Fifth Avenue, the Little Galleries of the Photo-Secession was soon simply called 291. In collaboration with another American photographer, Edward Steichen (1879–1973), who then lived in Paris, Stieglitz arranged exhibitions unlike any seen before in the United States, showing works by Cézanne, Toulouse-Lautrec, Rodin, Picasso, Braque, Matisse, and the Romanian sculptor Constantin Brancusi. He also gave shows—sometimes their first—to American Modernists such as Arthur Dove, John Marin, and Georgia O'Keeffe.

The event that climaxed Stieglitz's pioneering efforts on behalf of European Modernism (although he himself did not arrange it) was the so-called Armory Show, an "International Exhibition of Modern Art," which was held in 1913 in the drill hall of the 69th Regiment Armory in New York City. The aim of the exhibition was to call attention both to the outmoded views of the National Academy of Design and to the by then old-fashioned Realist tradition perpetuated by the Ashcan School.

Of the more than 1,600 works in the show, only about a quarter were by Europeans, but it was to these works that primary attention was paid. Critics claimed that Matisse, Kandinsky, Braque, and others were the agents of "universal anarchy." The American academic painter Kenyon Cox called them "savages." When a selection of works from the show traveled on

19–18 • Alfred Stieglitz THE FLATIRON BUILDING
1903. Photogravure, 6¹¹⁄₁₆″ × 3⁵⁄₁₆″ (17 × 8.4 cm). The Metropolitan Museum of Art, New York. Gift of J. B. Neumann, 1958 (58.577.37).

Portrait of a German Officer ▶

Marsden Hartley. 1914. Oil on canvas, 68¼″ × 41⅜″ (178 × 105 cm). The Metropolitan Museum of Art, New York. The Alfred Stieglitz Collection, 1949 (49.70.42).

While living in Berlin in 1914, Hartley fell in love with a young Prussian lieutenant, Karl von Freyburg, whom Hartley later described in a letter to Alfred Stieglitz as, "in every way a perfect being—physically, spiritually and mentally, beautifully balanced—24 years young...." Freyburg's death in combat during October 1914 devastated the artist, and he memorialized his fallen lover in this symbolic portrait.

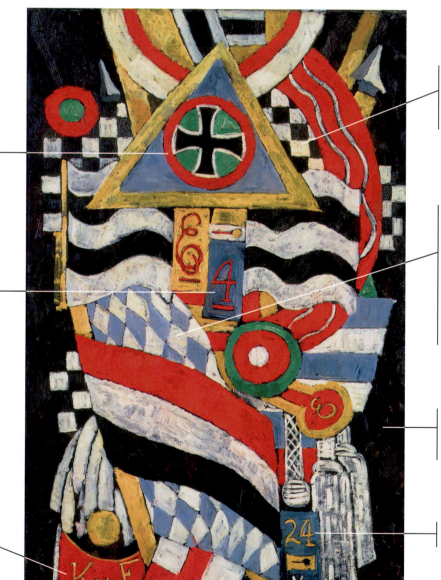

Symbolic references to Freyburg include epaulettes, lance tips, and the Iron Cross he was awarded the day before he was killed.

Freyburg's regiment number ("4") is shown at the center of the abstracted chest along with a red cursive "E," for "Edmund" (Hartley's given name), placed near Freyburg's heart.

Hartley identifies his subject with his initials: "Kv.F."

The black-and-white checkerboard patterns evoke Freyburg's love of chess, a poignant personal reference.

The blue-and-white diamond pattern comes from the Bavarian flag; the red, white, and black bands constitute the flag of the German Empire, adopted in 1871; and the black-and-white stripes are those of the historic flag of Prussia.

The funereal black background heightens the intensity of the foreground colors.

"24" was Freyburg's age at his death.

🔍 **View** the Closer Look for Hartley's *Portrait of a German Officer* on **MyArtsLab**

to Chicago, civic leaders there called for an investigation by a morals commission. Faculty and students at the School of the Art Institute were so enraged that they hanged Matisse in effigy.

A number of younger artists, however, responded positively. For example, Marsden Hartley (1877–1943), who had been a regular exhibitor at Stieglitz's gallery, and whose works were included in the Armory Show, showed every sign of becoming a pioneer of American Modernism (see "A Closer Look," p. 526). During an extended stay in Europe between 1912 and 1915, Hartley discovered Cubism in Gertrude Stein's circle in Paris and was drawn to Kandinsky's expressionism in Berlin. But as a gay man seeking a place within an America marked by little tolerance for diversity, he spent most of his career wandering around Europe and North America, seeking a spiritual and cultural home, and restlessly moving between European Modernism and the American Realist traditions.

Georgia O'Keeffe (1887–1986), another pioneering American Modernist, was born in rural Wisconsin and "discovered" by Stieglitz when a New York friend showed him her work. In 1916, she was included in a group show at 291 and Stieglitz mounted a solo show for her the following year. Critics described O'Keeffe's famous flower paintings (SEE FIG. INTRO–4) as essentially feminine, vaginal forms, and Stieglitz did little to dissuade this reading of her art; in fact, he promoted it. But O'Keeffe objected strenuously to this critical caricature, demanding that she was an artist, not a "woman artist."

After O'Keeffe moved to New York in 1918—marrying Stieglitz in 1924—she began painting New York skyscrapers, seen at that time as embodiments of American inventiveness and energy. But paintings such as **CITY NIGHT** (FIG. 19–19) are not unambiguous celebrations of lofty buildings. O'Keeffe frequently portrayed her architectural subjects from a low vantage

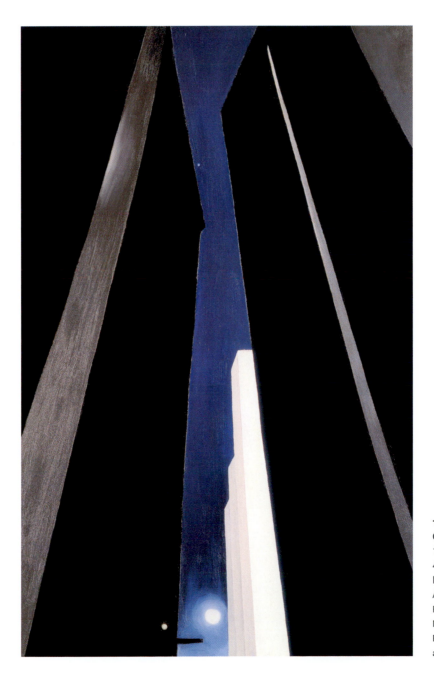

19–19 • Georgia O'Keeffe **CITY NIGHT**
1926. Oil on canvas, 48 × 30″ (123 × 76.9 cm). Minneapolis Institute of Arts. Gift of funds from the Regis Corporation, Mr. and Mrs. W. John Driscoll, the Beim Foundation, the Larsen Fund, and by public subscription.

point so that they appear to loom ominously over the viewer. Here, for instance, the dark tonalities, stark forms, and exaggerated perspective produce a sense of menace that also appears in the art of other American Modernists. In 1929, O'Keeffe began spending her summers in New Mexico and moved permanently to a ranch north of Santa Fe in the 1940s, dedicating her art to evocative representations of the local landscape and culture.

European Art Between the Wars

What were the new developments in Modern art and architecture in Europe between World Wars I and II?

The "Great War," as World War I was then known, had a devastating effect on Europe's artists and architects. Many responded to the destruction and loss of a generation of young men by criticizing European traditions; others focused on rebuilding. Members of artists' groups such as the Dutch de Stijl and the German Bauhaus sought the basis for a new society in severely rational beauty and order. The Surrealists, in contrast, celebrated subjectivity, intuition, and chance.

Constructivism

In Russia, the most dynamic artistic achievements of the period immediately following World War I came from avant-garde artists who enthusiastically supported the Russian Revolution of 1917, during which the tsar was overthrown, and the Bolsheviks (radical Socialists) rose to power under Vladimir Lenin. Among these artists were Constructivists, who were committed to the notion that artists should leave the studio and "go into the factory, where the real body of life is made." They envisioned politically engaged artists devoted to creating useful objects and promoting the aims of collective society.

One member of this socially visionary movement was engineer El Lissitzky (1890–1941). After the revolution, he taught architecture and graphic arts and soon came under the influence of Malevich, who was a fellow professor. By 1919, El Lissitzky was using Malevich's formal vocabulary for propaganda posters and for artworks he called "*Prouns*" (pronounced "pro-oon"), an acronym for "Project for the Affirmation of the New." Most **PROUN**s were paintings or prints, but a few were early examples of **installation art** (FIG. **19–20**)—artworks

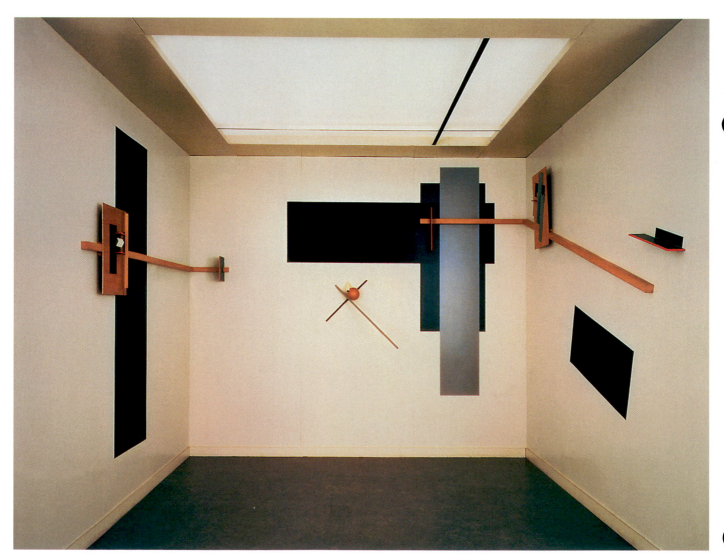

19–20 • El Lissitzky PROUN SPACE, CREATED FOR THE GREAT BERLIN ART EXHIBITION
1923, reconstruction 1971. Van Abbemuseum, Eindhoven, The Netherlands.

created for a specific site, arranged to create a total environment. Lissitzky thought that painting was too personal and imprecise, preferring to "construct" *Prouns* using the exacting instruments of mechanical drawing and industrial technology.

De Stijl

In the Netherlands, the counterpart to El Lissitzky's Constructivism was de Stijl ("The Style"), a movement led by Piet Mondrian (1872–1944). De Stijl was grounded in the conviction that there are two kinds of beauty: a sensual or subjective one and a higher, rational, objective, "universal" kind. In his mature works, Mondrian sought the essence of universal beauty, eliminating representational elements because of their subjective associations and curves because of their sensual appeal.

From about 1920, in paintings such as **COMPOSITION WITH YELLOW, RED, AND BLUE (FIG. 19–21)**, he restricted his formal vocabulary to the three **primary colors** (red, yellow, and blue), the three neutrals (black, gray, and white), and horizontal and vertical lines. The two linear directions are meant to symbolize the harmony of a series of opposites, including male versus female, individual versus society, and spiritual versus material. For Mondrian, the essence of higher beauty was resolved conflict or what he called "dynamic equilibrium." Here, in a typical composition, Mondrian achieved this equilibrium through the precise arrangement of color areas of different size, shape, and "weight," asymmetrically grouped around the edges of a canvas whose center is dominated by a large area of white. The ultimate purpose of such a painting is to demonstrate a universal style with applications beyond the realm of art. Mondrian hoped to be the world's last artist, believing that if art provided us with the beauty that was lacking in our world and inspired the incorporation of beauty into every aspect of daily life, there would be no need for artists to create special objects labeled "art."

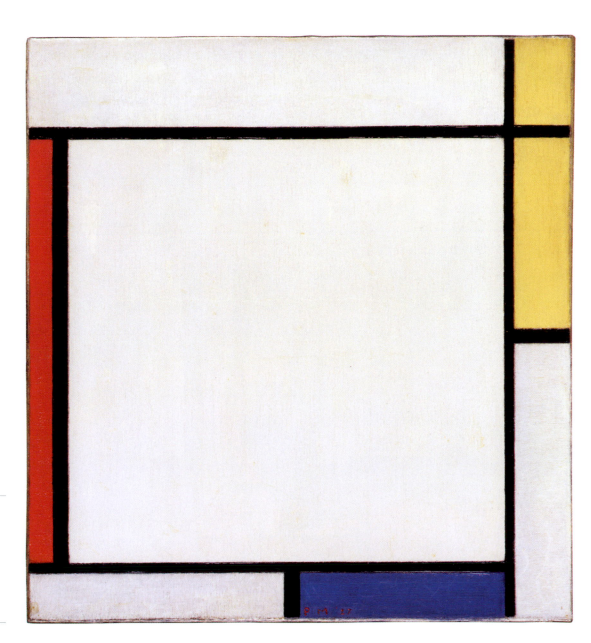

19–21 • Piet Mondrian
COMPOSITION WITH YELLOW, RED, AND BLUE
1927. Oil on canvas, 14⅞" × 13¾" (37.8 × 34.9 cm). The Menil Collection, Houston.
© 2014 Mondrian/Holtzman Trust c/o HCR International Washington, D.C.

Mondrian so disliked the sight of nature, whose irregularities he held largely accountable for humanity's problems, that when seated at a restaurant table with a view of the outdoors, he would ask to be moved.

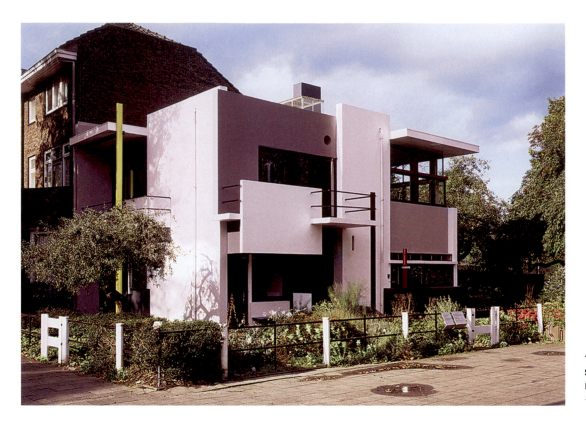

19–22 • Gerrit Rietveld
SCHRÖDER HOUSE
Utrecht, The Netherlands.
1925.

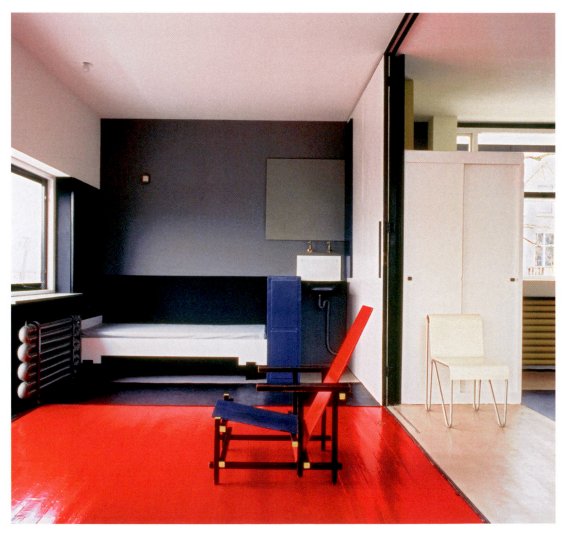

19–23 • Gerrit Rietveld
**INTERIOR, SCHRÖDER
HOUSE, WITH
"RED-BLUE" CHAIR**
1925.

Given this perspective, it is hardly surprising that de Stijl developed in architectural design as well as painting. Architect and designer Gerrit Rietveld (1888–1964) took the lead with his design of the **SCHRÖDER HOUSE** in Utrecht (**FIG. 19–22**), a seminal monument in the development of the Modern architectural movement known as the International Style (see "The International Style," p. 532). Rietveld applied Mondrian's principle of dynamic equilibrium to the whole house. The radically asymmetrical exterior is composed of interlocking gray and white planes of varying sizes, combined with horizontal and vertical accents in primary colors and black. His famous **"RED-BLUE" CHAIR** is shown here in the bedroom (**FIG. 19–23**), where his patron, Truus Schröder-Schräder, wanted sliding partitions to allow modifications in the spaces used for sleeping, working, and entertaining. She desired a home that suggested an elegant austerity, with the basic necessities sleekly integrated into a balanced and restrained whole.

Architectural Purism

Like the Dutch proponents of de Stijl, followers of a French movement known as Purism firmly believed in the power of art to change the world. The leading Purist figure was the Swiss-born Charles-Édouard Jeanneret (1887–1965), a largely self-taught architect and designer who moved to Paris in 1917. Three years later, Jeanneret, partly to demonstrate his faith in the ability of individuals to remake themselves, renamed himself Le Corbusier, a play on the French word for crow (*corbeau*).

Le Corbusier's **VILLA SAVOYE** (**FIG. 19–24**) has become an icon of the International Style. This weekend retreat house near Versailles is the purest embodiment of his domino construction system, first elaborated in 1914, in which seemingly floating slabs of concrete reinforced with steel bars were positioned on free-standing steel posts. This elevation of the house allowed the owners, arriving from Paris, to drive right underneath it and into a three-car garage. The incorporation of flat-roof terraces, partition walls slotted between supports on the interior, and **curtain walls** on the exterior with ribbon windows running along their entire length all became hallmarks of Modern architecture. Le Corbusier referred to this building as a "machine for living," meaning that it was as rationally designed as an automobile or an appliance.

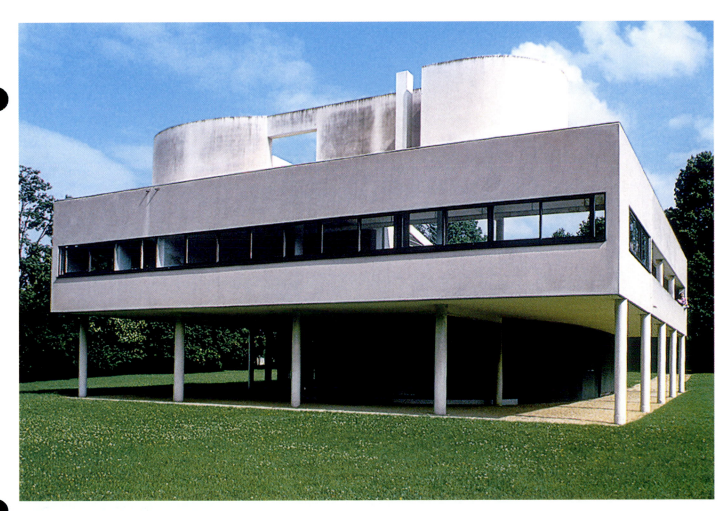

19-24 • Le Corbusier VILLA SAVOYE
Poissy-sur-Seine, France. 1929–1930.

✳ **Explore** the architectural panoramas of the Villa Savoye on **MyArtsLab**

After World War I, increased exchanges between Modern architects led to the development of a common formal language, transcending national boundaries, which came to be known as the International Style. The term gained wide currency as a result of a 1932 exhibition at the Museum of Modern Art in New York, "The International Style: Architecture Since 1922," organized by the architectural historian Henry-Russell Hitchcock and the architect and curator Philip Johnson. Hitchcock and Johnson identified three fundamental principles of the style.

The first principle was "the conception of architecture as volume rather than mass." The use of a structural skeleton of steel and ferroconcrete made it possible to eliminate load-bearing walls. The building could then be wrapped in a skin of glass, metal, or masonry, creating the effect of enclosed space (volume) rather than dense material (mass). And interiors could feature open, free-flowing plans providing maximum flexibility in the use of space.

The second principle was "regularity rather than symmetry as the chief means of ordering design." Regular distribution of structural supports and the use of standard building parts promoted rectangular regularity rather than the balanced axial symmetry of Classical architecture. The avoidance of Classical balance also encouraged an asymmetrical disposition of the building's components.

The third principle was the rejection of "arbitrary applied decoration." The new architecture depended upon the intrinsic elegance of its materials and the formal arrangement of its elements to produce harmonious aesthetic effects.

Pioneered in France, Germany, and the Netherlands, and spreading by the 1920s into other industrialized countries, the International Style remained influential in architectural design until the 1970s. It was particularly important in United States, where numerous architects sought refuge as they fled Germany during the 1930s, notably Walter Gropius and Mies van der Rohe.

The Bauhaus

The German counterpart to the total, rational planning envisioned by de Stijl and Le Corbusier was carried out at a school called the Bauhaus (loosely translated as "House of Building"). The Bauhaus (1919–1933) was the brainchild of Walter Gropius (1883–1969), another founder of Modern architecture. Gropius, who belonged to several utopian groups, admired the spirit of the medieval building guilds, or *Bauhütten*, that had erected the great German cathedrals. He sought to revive their collaborative spirit and bring together modern art and industry by combining the schools of art and craft in the German city of Weimar into this single institution.

At first the Bauhaus had no formal training program in architecture. Gropius felt that students needed to demonstrate proficiency in workshop courses before going on to study architecture. The workshops—which included classes in pottery, metalwork, textiles, stained glass, furniture making, carving, and wall painting—were intended to teach both specific technical skills and basic design principles. Learning was rooted in doing. Since Gropius believed that art should serve a socially useful function, in 1922 the Bauhaus implemented a new emphasis on industrial design.

The next year the Hungarian-born László Moholy-Nagy (1895–1946) reoriented the Bauhaus workshops toward the creation of sleek, functional designs suitable for mass production. The elegant **TEA AND COFFEE SERVICE** by Marianne Brandt (1893–1983), for example (**FIG. 19–25**), though handcrafted in silver, was a prototype for mass production in a

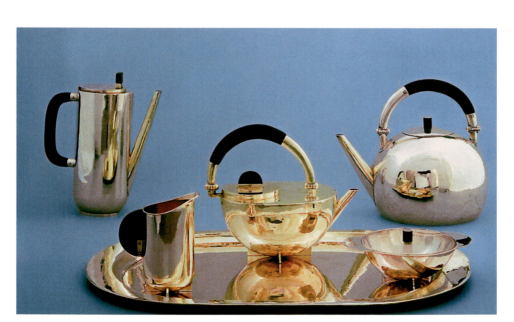

19–25 • Marianne Brandt
TEA AND COFFEE SERVICE
1924. Silver and ebony, with Plexiglas cover for sugar bowl. Bauhaus Archiv, Berlin.

The lid of Marianne Brandt's sugar bowl is made of Plexiglas, reflecting the Bauhaus's interest in incorporating the latest advances in materials and technology into the manufacture of utilitarian objects.

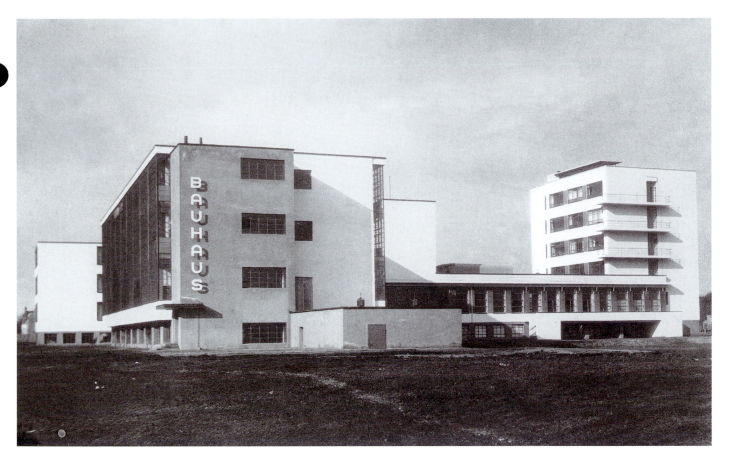

19–26 • Walter Gropius BAUHAUS BUILDING
View from northwest. Dessau, Germany. 1925–1926.

One of the enduring contributions of the Bauhaus was graphic design. The sans-serif letters of the building's sign not only harmonize with the architecture's clean lines but also communicate the Bauhaus commitment to modernity. Sans-serif typography (that is, a typeface without serifs, the short lines at the end of the stroke of a letter) had been used since the early nineteenth century, but many new sans-serif typefaces were created in the 1920s.

cheaper metal such as nickel silver. Several of Brandt's designs went into mass production, earning much-needed revenue for the school. After Gropius and Moholy-Nagy left the Bauhaus in 1928, Brandt directed the metal workshop. As a woman holding her own in the otherwise all-male metal workshop, she was exceptional at the Bauhaus. Although women were admitted to the school on an equal basis with men, Gropius opposed their education as architects and channeled them into pottery and textile workshops, which he deemed more appropriate for them.

When the Bauhaus moved to the German city of Dessau in 1925, Gropius designed the new building, built in 1925–1926 (**FIG. 19–26**). Since Gropius made no attempt to cover or decorate his building materials, the structure frankly acknowledges the reinforced concrete, steel, and glass of which it is built. Modern engineering methods made it possible to eliminate the need for walls to be structural supports and to replace them with glass panels to create light, airy interior spaces. Even the sans-serif (without serifs) letters of the Bauhaus sign proclaim its sleek, functional ideals.

From 1930 on, the Bauhaus was directed by the architect Ludwig Mies van der Rohe (1886–1969). Mies had a passion

for realizing the subtle perfection of structure, proportion, and detail, using sumptuous materials such as travertine, richly veined marbles, tinted glass, and bronze. After moving to Berlin in 1932, the school remained under his direction, but in 1933 the new German chancellor, Adolf Hitler, forced its closure (see "Suppression of the Avant-Garde in Germany," p. 534). Hitler opposed Modern art on two grounds: first, it was cosmopolitan rather than nationalistic; second, he believed it to be overly influenced by Jews. The first was a matter of opinion; the second was patently untrue.

Surrealism

The intellectual successor to Dada was Surrealism, a movement founded by French writer André Breton (1896–1966). Breton sought to free human behavior from the constrictions of reason and bourgeois morality. In 1924, he published his *Manifesto of Surrealism*, outlining his own view of the theory of Austrian psychiatrist Sigmund Freud (1856–1939) that the human psyche is a battleground where the rational forces of the conscious mind struggle against the irrational, instinctual urges of the unconscious. Breton and his followers employed a number of

Suppression of the Avant-Garde in Germany

The 1930s in Germany witnessed a serious political reaction against avant-garde art and, eventually, a concerted effort to suppress it. One of the principal targets was the Bauhaus, the art and design school founded in 1919 by Gropius, where Mies van der Rohe, Paul Klee, Kandinsky, Josef Albers, and many other luminaries taught. Through much of the 1920s, the Bauhaus had struggled against an increasingly hostile and reactionary political climate. As early as 1924, conservatives had considered it not only educationally unsound but also politically subversive. To avoid having the school shut down, Gropius accepted the invitation of the liberal mayor of Dessau to move it there in 1925, but he left soon after the relocation. Gropius's successors faced increasing political pressure, and this prime center of Modernist practice was again forced to move in 1932, this time to Berlin.

After Adolf Hitler came to power in 1933, the Nazi party mounted an aggressive campaign against Modern art. In his youth Hitler himself had been a mediocre academic painter, and he had developed an intense hatred of Modernism and the avant-garde. During the first year of his regime, the Bauhaus was forced to close for good. A number of the artists, designers, and architects who had been on its faculty, including Gropius, Mies, and Albers, fled to the United States.

The Nazis also attacked Modernist painters, whose often intense depictions of German soldiers defeated in World War I and the economic depression following the war were considered unpatriotic.

Most of all, the expressionistic exaggeration of human forms and facial features was deemed offensive. The works of these and other artists were removed from museums, while the artists were subjected to public ridicule and often forbidden to buy canvas or paint.

As a final move against the avant-garde, the Nazi leadership organized in 1937 a notorious exhibition of banned works. The "Degenerate Art" exhibition was intended to erase Modernism once and for all from the artistic life of the nation. Seeking to brand all the advanced movements of art as sick and degenerate, it presented confiscated Modern artworks as specimens of human pathology; the organizers printed derisive slogans and comments to that effect on the gallery walls (FIG. 19–27). Ironically, the 650 paintings, sculptures, prints, and books confiscated from German public museums were viewed by 2 million people in the four months the exhibition was on view in Munich and by another million during its subsequent three-year tour of German cities.

By the time World War II broke out, the German authorities had confiscated countless "subversive" works from all over the country. Most were publicly burned, though the Nazi officials sold much of the looted art at public auction in Switzerland to obtain foreign currency. The ownership of much of the surviving art is still in question. Many artists fled to neighboring countries or the United States, but some, such as Ernst Ludwig Kirchner, whose *Street, Berlin* (SEE FIG. 19–3) was included in the "Degenerate Art" exhibit, were driven to suicide by their loss.

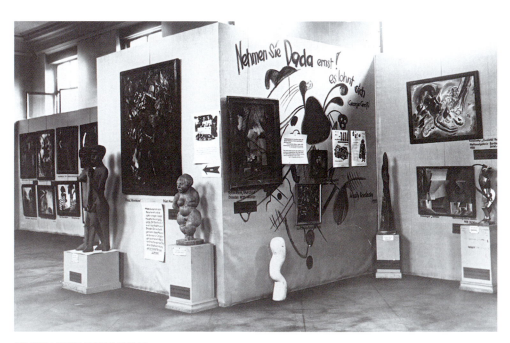

19–27 • THE DADA WALL
In Room 3 of the "Degenerate Art" ("*Entartete Kunst*") Exhibition, Munich. 1937.

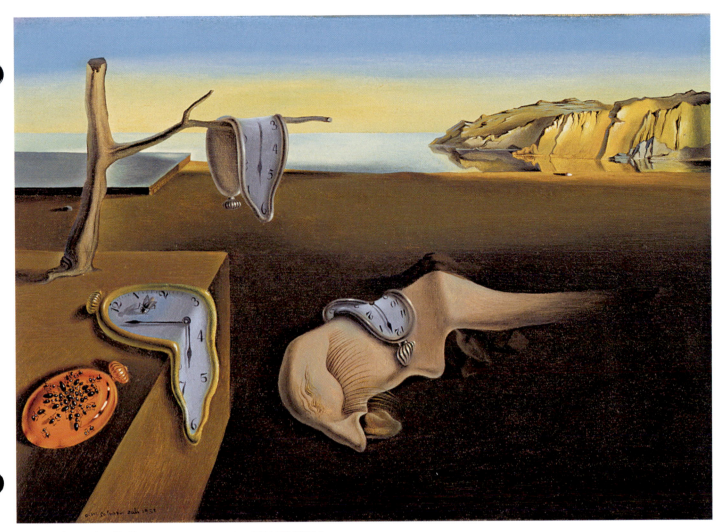

19–28 • Salvador Dalí THE PERSISTENCE OF MEMORY
1931. Oil on canvas, 9½″ × 13″ (24.1 × 33 cm). The Museum of Modern Art, New York. Given anonymously (162.1934).

techniques for liberating the individual unconscious, including dream analysis, free association, *automatic writing*, word games, and hypnotic trances. Their aim was to help people discover the more intense reality, or "surreality," that lay beyond rational constraint.

Among the writers and artists around Breton was the Spanish painter and printmaker Salvador Dalí (1904–1989). Dalí contributed the "paranoid-critical method" to Surrealist practice. In this approach, sane artists cultivate the ability of the paranoid to misread ordinary appearances in order to free themselves from the shackles of conventional thought. Dalí demonstrated his method in **THE PERSISTENCE OF MEMORY (FIG. 19–28)** by placing limp timepieces in a very realistic view of the Bay of Rosas near his birthplace in Catalunya.

According to Dalí, the idea of the soft watches came to him one evening after dinner while he was meditating on a plate of ripe Camembert cheese. One of the limp watches drapes over an amoeba-like human head, its shape inspired by a large rock on the coast. This head, which Dalí identified as a self-portrait, appeared in several paintings and, in combination with the limp watches, may express the anxiety Dalí felt concerning his own sexuality. Another image of anxiety in the work is the ant-covered watchcase at the lower left, inspired by Dalí's childhood memories of seeing dead animals swarming with ants. The absurd yet compelling image of ants feeding on a metallic watch typifies the Surrealist interest in unexpected juxtapositions of disparate realities. Dalí's choice of a meticulously descriptive style makes his irrational world seem more convincing, thus more unsettling.

Building on Duchamp's earlier readymades, the Swiss artist Meret Oppenheim (1913–1985), one of the few women invited to participate in the Surrealist movement, produced disquieting assemblages such as **OBJECT (LE DÉJEUNER EN FOURRURE) (FIG. 19–29)**. Consisting of a cup, saucer, and spoon covered with the fur of a Chinese gazelle, Oppenheim's work transforms implements normally used for drinking tea into a hairy ensemble that simultaneously attracts and repels the viewer.

In contrast, a more benign and playful spirit animates the painting of Catalan artist Joan Miró (1893–1983), who exhibited on numerous occasions with the Surrealists, but who never officially joined the group or shared its theoretical interests. In **COMPOSITION** of 1933 (**FIG. 19–30**), he silhouettes shapes

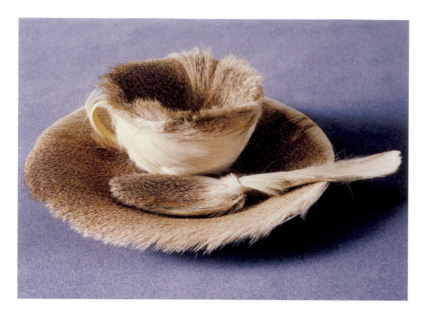

19–29 • Meret Oppenheim
OBJECT (LE DÉJEUNER EN FOURRURE/ LUNCHEON IN FUR)
1936. Fur-covered cup, diameter 4⅜″ (10.9 cm); fur-covered saucer, diameter 9⅜″ (23.7 cm); fur-covered spoon, length 8″ (20.2 cm); overall height 2⅞″ (7.3 cm). The Museum of Modern Art, New York (130.1946A-C).

Oppenheim's *Object* was inspired by a café conversation with Picasso about her designs for jewelry made of fur-lined metal tubing. When Picasso remarked that one could cover just about anything with fur, Oppenheim replied, "Even this cup and saucer."

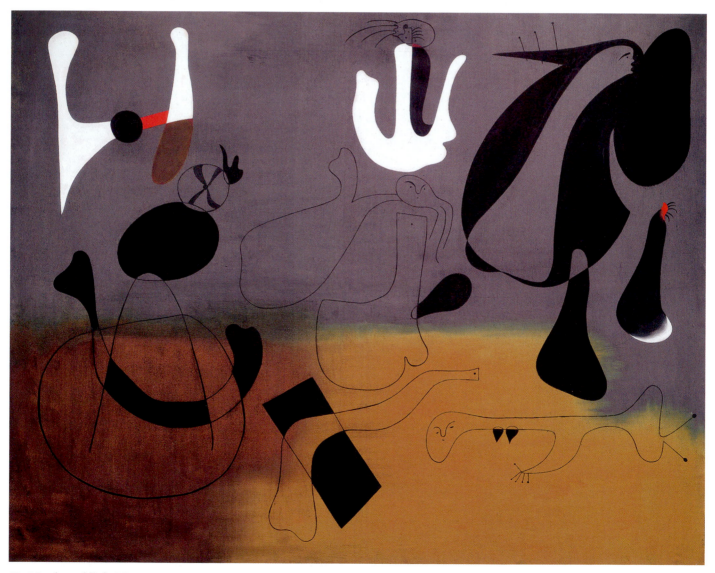

19–30 • Joan Miró COMPOSITION
1933. Oil on canvas, 51¼″ × 63½″ (130.2 × 161.3 cm). Wadsworth Atheneum, Hartford, Connecticut.

Guernica

On April 26, 1937, during the Spanish Civil War, German bombers flying for Spanish fascist leader General Francisco Franco targeted the Basque city of Guernica. This inhuman act, the world's first intentional mass bombing of civilians, killed more than 1,600 people and shocked the world. Pablo Picasso, living in Paris at the time, reacted to the massacre by painting *Guernica* (FIG. **19–31**), a stark, hallucinatory nightmare that became as powerful a symbol of the brutality of war for the twentieth century as Goya's *Third of May, 1808* (SEE FIG. 17–23) had been for the nineteenth.

Focusing on the victims—frozen in mid-movement as if caught by the flashbulb or a reporter's camera—Picasso restricted his palette to black, gray, and white—the stark tones of the newspaper photographs that publicized the atrocity. Expressively distorted women, one holding a dead child and another trapped in a burning house, wail in desolation at the carnage. Some have interpreted the screaming horse as an image of betrayed innocence, representing the suffering Spanish Republic. The bull could symbolize either Franco or Spain. But Picasso refused to provide interpretations of the layered symbolism, claiming *Guernica* was about massacred people and animals—beyond that, its meaning is fluid.

The work excited widespread admiration when exhibited later that year in the Spanish Republic's pavilion at the International Exposition in Paris because the artist used the language of Modern art to comment in a heartfelt manner on what seemed an international scandal. Picasso spent World War II in Paris, and when a Nazi officer showed him a reproduction of *Guernica* and asked, "Is it you who did that?" Picasso is said to have replied, "No, it is you." Unfortunately, the tactic of bombing civilians became a common strategy employed by all sides in this brutal international war that left such a strong imprint on the developing history of Modern art.

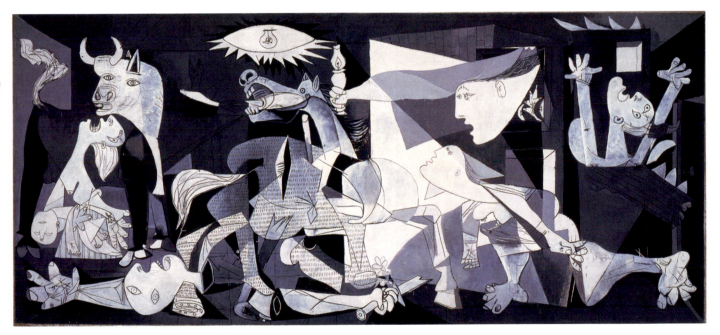

19–31 • Pablo Picasso GUERNICA
1937. Oil on canvas, 11′ 6″ × 25′ 8″ (3.5 × 7.8 m). Museo Nacional Centro de Arte Reina Sofia, Madrid.
On permanent loan from the Museo del Prado, Madrid.

View the Closer Look for Picasso's *Guernica* on **MyArtsLab**

so sharply against a hazy background that the picture takes on the feeling of the collage Miró made as a preparatory study. The **biomorphic**, curving contours evoke organic forms—many rooted in features that recall human figures—that seem to be taking shape before our eyes. Their identity is in flux just as our thought process is always in flux. Are they ancestral spirits or menacing ghosts? Do they tell a story, express a struggle, embody an emotion? Although at its core this is an abstract composition commanded by a high degree of formal control, it seems at the same time evocative of primal or mythic meaning.

Sculpture

Constantin Brancusi (1876–1957) took a different approach to portraying "the essence of things." He arrived in Paris from his native Romania in 1904, and by 1907 was an assistant to Rodin. Soon, however, he became more captivated by the "primitive" works of the Parisian avant-garde. In **TORSO OF A YOUNG MAN** (FIG. 19–32), he emphasized formal and conceptual simplicity, distilling his subject into smooth and purified forms. He has turned this male human trunk into three cylinders, precariously balanced on two cubes and two trapezoids. Brancusi was motivated by his interest in the ancient Greek philosophy of Plato, who held that all natural forms are imperfect imitations of their perfect ideas, which exist only in the mind. He wrote, "What is real is not the external form but the essence of things. Starting from this truth it is impossible for anyone to express anything essentially real by imitating its exterior surface."

During the 1920s and 1930s, British sculptor Henry Moore (1898–1986) engaged in his own pursuit of an ideal of "truth to material." Moore's art developed in a series of massive, simplified reclining female figures, inspired by the *chacmools* of Toltec and Maya art (SEE FIG. 15–7). **RECUMBENT FIGURE** (FIG. 19–33) of 1938 reveals Moore's sensitivity to the inherent qualities of the stone, whose natural striations harmonize with the sinuous surfaces of the design. While certain elements of the body, such as the head, breasts, supporting elbow, and raised knee, are clearly defined, other parts flow together into an undulating mass more suggestive of a hilly landscape than of a human body. An open cavity penetrates the torso, emphasizing the relationship of solid and void fundamental to Moore's art. The sculptor wrote in 1937, "A hole can itself have as much shape-meaning as a solid mass."

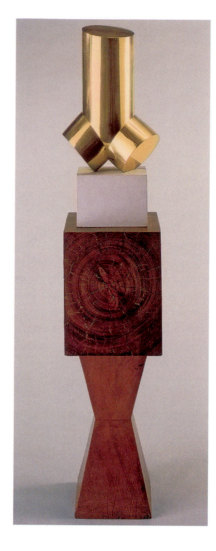

19–32 • Constantin Brancusi TORSO OF A YOUNG MAN
1924. Bronze on stone and wood bases; combined figure and bases 40⅜″ × 20″ × 18¼″ (102.4 × 50.5 × 46.1 cm). Hirshhorn Museum and Sculpture Garden, Smithsonian Institution, Washington, D.C. Gift of Joseph H. Hirshhorn, 1966.

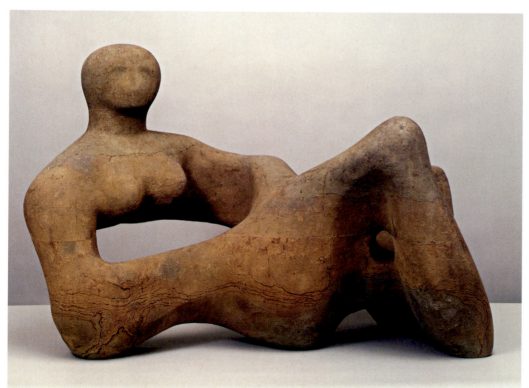

19–33 • Henry Moore RECUMBENT FIGURE
1938. Green Hornton stone, 35″ × 52″ × 29″ (88.9 × 132.7 × 73.7 cm). Tate, London.

Originally carved for the garden of the architect Serge Chermayeff in Sussex, Moore's sculpture was situated next to a low-lying Modernist building with an open view of the gently rolling landscape. "My figure looked out across a great sweep of the Downs, and her gaze gathered at the horizon," Moore later recalled. "The sculpture had no specific relationship to the architecture. It had its own identity and did not *need* to be on Chermayeff's terrace, but it so to speak *enjoyed* being there, and I think it introduced a humanizing element; it became a mediator between modern house and ageless land."

American Art between the Wars

How did American artists and architects both assimilate and resist the tenets of European Modernism between World Wars I and II?

The Armory Show of 1913 had marked an important turning point in American art, as artists began to assimilate the most recent developments of the European avant-garde. But many artists soon retreated from this imported Modernism, returning their focus to the American scene, chronicling the life and landscape of their own world. Only in the late 1930s and 1940s did artists and architects fleeing Hitler's Europe renew American interest in nonrepresentational art.

The United States

The American sculptor and engineer Alexander Calder (1898–1976) made contact with members of the Dada and Surrealist groups on visits to Paris in the 1920s and 1930s. He also visited Mondrian's studio, where he was impressed by the rectangles of colored paper that Mondrian had tacked up everywhere on the walls. What would it be like, he wondered, if the flat shapes were moving freely in space, interacting in not just two but three dimensions? The experience inspired Calder to begin creating mobiles, sculptures like his **LOBSTER TRAP AND FISH TAIL** (**FIG. 19–34**) in which the individual parts float and bob in response to shifting currents of air. The term "mobile," which in French means both "moving body" and "motive," or "driving force," came from Calder's friend Marcel Duchamp, who no doubt relished the double meaning of the word.

But not all American art between the wars derived from avant-garde developments in Paris. During the Great Depression, artists across the country documented the lives and circumstances of the American people and the American landscape, painting in styles that derived from native Realist

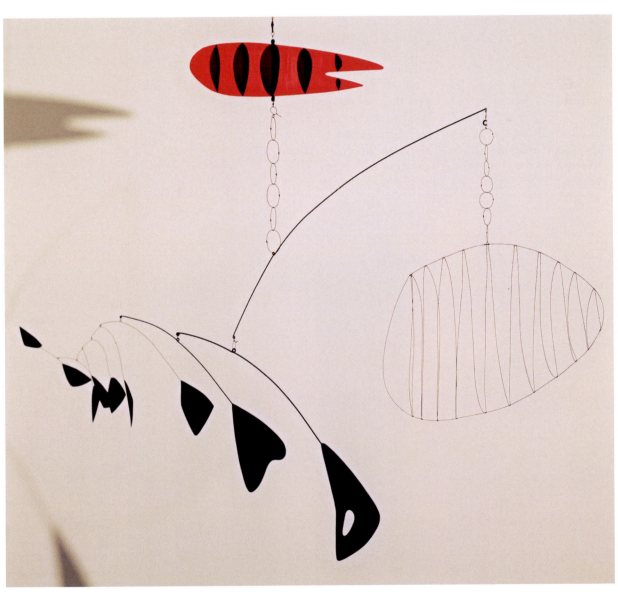

19–34 • Alexander Calder LOBSTER TRAP AND FISH TAIL
1939. Hanging mobile of painted steel wire and sheet aluminum, height 8′ 6″ (2.6 m). The Museum of Modern Art, New York. Commissioned by the Advisory Committee for the stairwell of the Museum (590.1939.A–D).

traditions. Art historians refer to this movement as American Scene Painting. One group of painters from the Midwest, called Regionalists, took generally sympathetic attitudes toward their subjects. Their leader was Iowa painter Grant Wood (1891–1942), who focused on the farms and small-town life of the American heartland. His **AMERICAN GOTHIC (FIG. 19–35)** is usually mistaken for a picture of a husband and wife, but it was actually meant to show an aging Iowa farmer and his unmarried daughter (Wood's dentist and sister were the models). The stony-faced pair stands in front of their house, built in a Victorian style known as "Carpenter Gothic," which suggests the importance of religion in their lives. The farmer's pitchfork signifies his occupation while giving him a somewhat menacing air. The woman is associated with potted plants, seen behind her right shoulder, which symbolize traditionally feminine domestic and horticultural skills. Wood considered the painting to be a sincerely affectionate portrayal of the small-town

Iowans he had grown up with—conservative, provincial, religious Midwesterners, descendants of the pioneers.

In spite of the largely optimistic visions of the Regionalists, the economic hardships of the Great Depression meant that many farmers faced bankruptcy, and rural regions suffered great poverty. In 1935, a newly established government agency, the Farm Securities Administration (FSA), began to hire photographers to document the problems of farmers and migrant workers. Dorothea Lange (1895–1965) played a major role in the formation of the FSA photography program. As a freelance photographer in San Francisco, Lange was touched by the struggles of the city's poor and unemployed, and she began to photograph their plight. In 1934, she collaborated on a report on migrant farm laborers in California, which helped persuade state officials to build migrant labor camps. Her photographs influenced the federal government to include a photographic unit in the FSA, and in 1935 Lange was hired as one of the

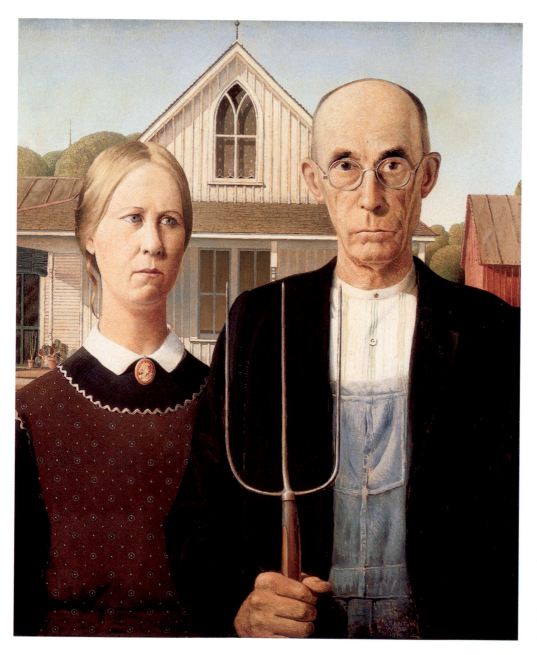

19–35 • Grant Wood
AMERICAN GOTHIC
1930. Oil on beaverboard, 29⅞″ × 24⅞″ (74.3 × 62.4 cm). The Art Institute of Chicago. Friends of American Art Collection. 1930.934. Art © Figge Art Museum, successors to the Estate of Nan Wood Graham/Licensed by VAGA, New York, NY.

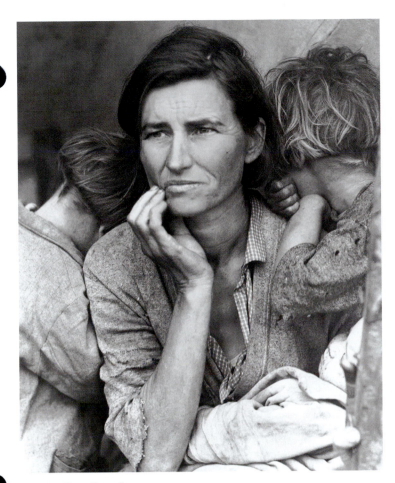

unit's first photographers. Her most famous photograph is **MIGRANT MOTHER, NIPOMO, CALIFORNIA** (FIG. 19–36). The woman in the picture is Florence Thompson, a 32-year-old mother of ten children. Drawn and prematurely aged, she gazes past the viewer into an uncertain future. The fears of all disenfranchised people, perpetually shunted to the margins of society, seem crystallized in her worried face.

The Harlem Renaissance

During the 1930s, hundreds of thousands of African Americans migrated from the rural, mostly agricultural South to the urban, industrialized North, fleeing racial oppression and seeking greater social and economic opportunity. This Great Migration prompted the formation of the so-called "New Negro" movement, which encouraged African Americans to become politically progressive and racially conscious. It also stimulated a flowering of art and culture known as the Harlem Renaissance, which encouraged the work of musicians like Duke Ellington and poets like Langston Hughes. The intellectual leader of the movement was Alain Locke (1886–1954), a critic and philosophy professor who encouraged black artists and writers to seek their artistic roots in the traditional arts of Africa, rather than assimilate within mainstream American or European artistic traditions.

Aaron Douglas (1898–1979)—a native of Topeka, Kansas, who moved to New York City in 1925—answered Locke's call and rapidly developed an abstract style of schematic, silhouetted figures influenced by African art. Douglas limited his palette to a few subtle hues, varying in **value** from light to dark and sometimes organized abstractly into concentric bands that suggest musical rhythms or spiritual emanations. In **ASPECTS OF NEGRO LIFE: FROM SLAVERY THROUGH RECONSTRUCTION** (FIG. 19–37), painted

19–36 • Dorothea Lange
MIGRANT MOTHER, NIPOMO, CALIFORNIA
February 1936. Gelatin-silver print. Library of Congress, Washington, D.C.

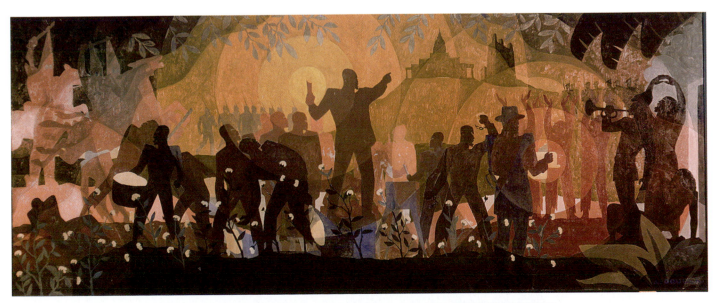

19–37 • Aaron Douglas ASPECTS OF NEGRO LIFE: FROM SLAVERY THROUGH RECONSTRUCTION
1934. Oil on canvas, 5′ × 11′ 7″ (1.5 × 3.5 m). Schomburg Center for Research in Black Culture, New York Public Library.

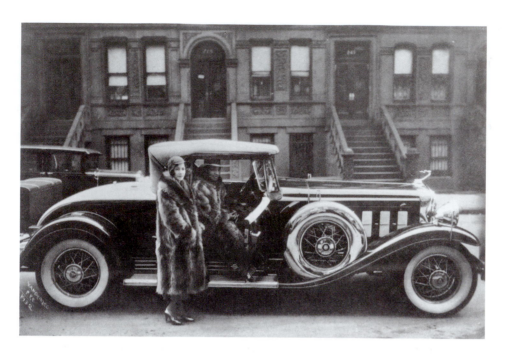

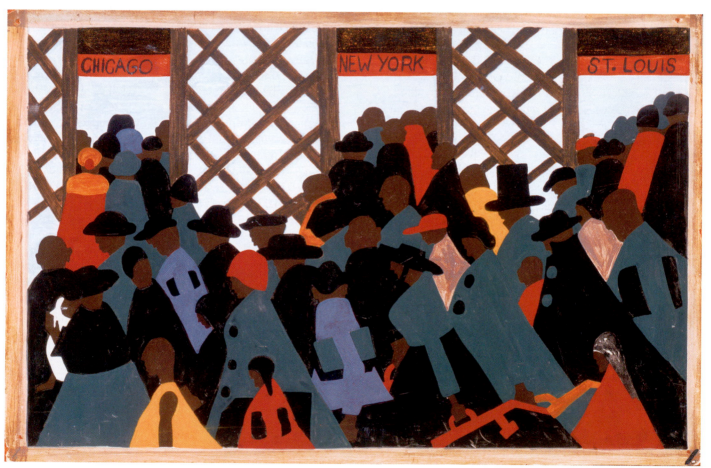

19–39 • Jacob Lawrence THE MIGRATION SERIES, PANEL 1 (DURING WORLD WAR THERE WAS A GREAT MIGRATION NORTH BY SOUTHERN AFRICAN-AMERICANS)
1940–1941. Tempera on Masonite, 12″ × 18″ (30.5 × 45.7 cm). The Phillips Collection, Washington, D.C. Acquired 1942.

This is the first image in Lawrence's 60-panel cycle that tells the story of the migration of Southern African Americans to the industrialized North in the decades between the two world wars. Edith Halpert exhibited the entire series in 1941 at her Downtown Gallery. Thus, at age 23, Lawrence became the first African-American artist to gain acclaim in the segregated New York art world. The next year, *The Migration Series* was jointly acquired by the Phillips Collection in Washington, D.C., and the Museum of Modern Art in New York, each of which purchased 30 paintings.

for the Harlem branch of the New York Public Library under the sponsorship of the federal Public Works of Art Project, Douglas intended to awaken in African Americans a sense of their place in history. At the right, they celebrate the Emancipation Proclamation of 1862–1863, which freed the slaves. Concentric circles issue from the Proclamation, which is read by a figure in the foreground. At the center of the composition, an orator, symbolizing black leaders of the Reconstruction era, urges black freedmen, some still picking cotton, to cast their ballots, while he points to a silhouette of the U.S. Capitol on a distant hill. Concentric circles highlight the ballot in his hand. In the background, the fearsome Ku Klux Klan, hooded and on horseback, invades from the left while at the right the arts— a jazz trumpeter and a dancer—herald freedom. The heroic orator at the center of Douglas's panel remains the focus of the composition, inspiring contemporary viewers to continue the struggle for equality.

Like Douglas, photographer James VanDerZee (1886–1983) created positive, non-stereotypical images of African Americans that proclaimed the racial pride and social empowerment promoted by the "New Negro" movement. The largely self-taught VanDerZee maintained a studio in Harlem for nearly 50 years, specializing in portraits of the neighborhood's upper-middle-class residents. **COUPLE WEARING RACCOON COATS WITH A CADILLAC, TAKEN ON WEST 127TH STREET, HARLEM, NEW YORK (FIG. 19–38)** depicts the ideal "New Negro" man and woman: prosperous, confident, and cosmopolitan, thriving and living glamorously, even in the midst of the Depression.

Influenced by Aaron Douglas, the younger Harlem artist Jacob Lawrence (1917–2000) devoted much of his early work to chronicling black history, in carefully researched groups of small paintings conceived as cycles. From 1940 to 1941, Lawrence created his best-known cycle, **THE MIGRATION SERIES**.

Sixty panels narrate the great twentieth-century exodus of African Americans from the rural South to the urban North, an exodus that had brought Lawrence's own parents from South Carolina to Atlantic City, New Jersey, where he was born. The first panel (**FIG. 19–39**) depicts a train station filled with black migrants who stream through portals labeled with the names of Northern and Midwestern destinations. The boldly abstracted style, with its simple shapes and bright colors, is based on Lawrence's own study of the African art that also influenced Cubist painters.

Mexico

Artists in Mexico also focused on local scenes and concerns as they fulfilled government commissions to decorate public buildings with murals celebrating the history, life, and work of the Mexican people. Prominent in the new Mexican mural movement of the 1930s initiated by this public patronage, was Diego Rivera (1886–1957). Rivera had lived in Paris, painting in the Synthetic Cubist style, and between 1920 and 1921 he traveled to Italy to study the great frescos of the Renaissance. On his return to Mexico, he fulfilled government commissions for a series of monumental murals, inspired by both Italian Renaissance art and the indigenous art of Mexico. In 1932, the Rockefeller family commissioned Rivera to paint a mural for the lobby of the RCA Building in Rockefeller Center in New York City on the theme "Man at the Crossroads Looking with Hope and High Vision to the Choosing of a New and Better Future." When Rivera, a Communist, provocatively included a portrait of Lenin in the mural, the Rockefellers canceled his commission, paid him his fee, and had the unfinished mural destroyed. In response to what he called an "act of cultural vandalism," Rivera re-created the mural in the Palacio de Bellas Artes in Mexico City, under the new title **MAN, CONTROLLER OF THE UNIVERSE (FIG. 19–40)**.

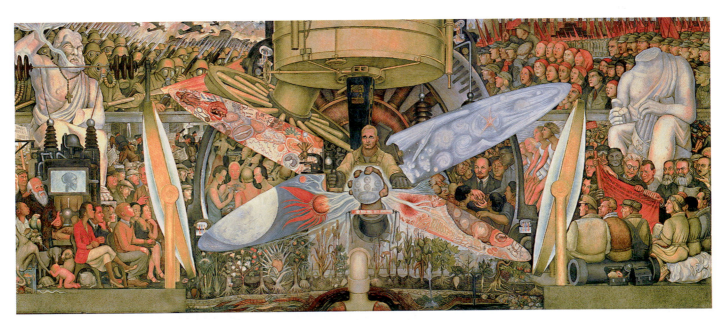

19–40 • Diego Rivera MAN, CONTROLLER OF THE UNIVERSE
1934. Fresco, 15' 9⅛" × 37' 2½" (4.85 × 11.45 m). Museo del Palacio de Bellas Artes, Mexico City.

👁 **Watch** a video about Diego Rivera's fresco technique on **MyArtsLab**

At the center of the mural, a figure in overalls represents Man, who symbolically controls the universe through his manipulation of technology. Crossing behind him are two great ellipses that represent, respectively, the microcosm of living organisms as seen through the microscope at Man's right hand, and the macrocosm of outer space as viewed through the giant telescope above his head. Below, fruits and vegetables rise from the earth as a result of his agricultural efforts. To the viewer's right, Lenin joins the hands of several workers of different races; at the left, decadent capitalists debauch themselves in a nightclub. Rivera vengefully included in this section a portrait of the bespectacled John D. Rockefeller, Jr. At the sides of the

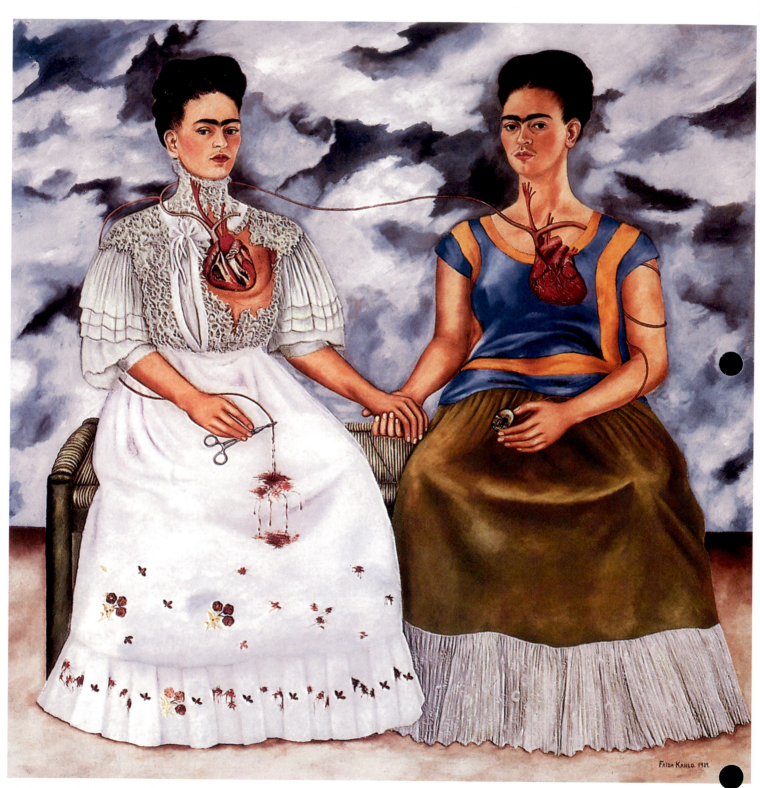

19–41 • Frida Kahlo THE TWO FRIDAS
1939. Oil on canvas, 5′ 8½″ × 5′ 8½″ (1.74 × 1.74 m). Museo de Arte Moderno, Instituto Nacional de Bellas Artes, Mexico City.

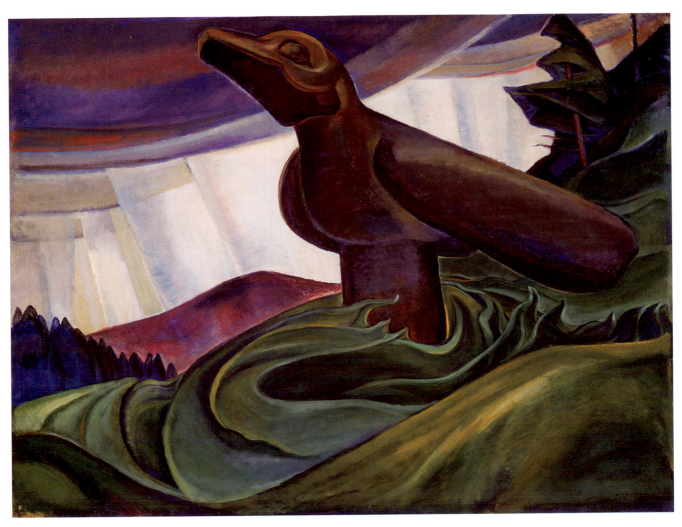

19–42 • Emily Carr **BIG RAVEN**
1931. Oil on canvas, 34¼″ × 44⅞″ (87 × 114 cm). The Vancouver Art Gallery, Canada. Emily Carr Trust.

mural, Rivera contrasts the peaceful socialist workers at right with the militarism and labor unrest of the capitalist world to the left.

While the muralists painted public messages, other Mexican artists made more private, introspective statements in easel paintings. André Breton claimed Frida Kahlo (1910–1954) to be a natural Surrealist, although she herself said: "I never painted dreams. I painted my own reality." That reality included her mixed German and Mexican ancestry. In **THE TWO FRIDAS (FIG. 19–41)**, Kahlo presented an identity split into two ethnic selves: the European one, in a Victorian dress; and the Mexican one, wearing traditional Mexican clothing. The painting also reflects her stormy relationship with Diego Rivera, whom she married in 1929 but was divorcing in 1939 when she was painting this picture. She told an art historian at the time that the Mexican image was the Frida whom Diego loved, and the European image was the Frida he did not. The two Fridas join hands and the artery running between them begins at a miniature portrait of Rivera as a boy held by the Mexican Frida, travels through the exposed hearts of both Fridas, and ends in the lap of the Europeanized Frida, who attempts without success to stem the flow of blood.

Canada

Emily Carr (1871–1945) taught art in Vancouver, British Columbia, where she became a founding member of the British Columbia Society of Art. On a 1907 trip to Alaska, she first encountered the monumental carved poles of Northwest Coast Native Americans and resolved to document these "real art treasures of a passing race." Over the next 23 years Carr visited more than 30 villages across British Columbia, making drawings and watercolors, which became the basis for oil paintings. **BIG RAVEN (FIG. 19–42)**, painted in 1931 in a dramatic and powerful sculptural style full of dark and brooding energy, derives from a watercolor she made in 1912 in an abandoned village in the Queen Charlotte Islands. She had discovered a carved raven raised on a pole, the surviving member of a pair that had marked a mortuary house. In her autobiography Carr described the raven as "old and rotting," but in her painting the bird appears strong and majestic, thrusting dynamically above the swirling vegetation, a symbol of enduring spiritual power. Through its focus on a Native American artifact set in a recognizably northwestern Canadian landscape, Carr's *Big Raven* asserts a national pride comparable to the paintings of the Mexican muralists and the Harlem Renaissance.

Architecture

After 1900, New York had assumed the lead over Chicago in the development of the skyscraper, whose soaring height was made possible by the steel-frame support skeleton (see "The Skyscraper," p. 547). New York clients, however, rejected the innovative style pioneered in Chicago by Louis Sullivan (SEE FIG. 18–4), preferring the historicizing approach still popular on the east coast, as exemplified by the **WOOLWORTH BUILDING** of 1911–1913 (**FIG. 19–43**). When it was completed at 792 feet and 55 floors, it was the world's tallest building. In the 1930s it would be surpassed by an even more famous skyscraper, the Empire State Building, whose structure is likewise covered by a veneer of applied ornamental panels. With the arrival of European Modernism, however, the International Style became the architectural movement embraced by American business leaders. It seemed to epitomize the efficiency, standardization, and impersonality that had become synonymous with the modern corporation itself.

Other architects and critics, however, called for an American architecture that would provide spiritual nourishment to those starved by the severity of the International Style. As early as 1900, Frank Lloyd Wright (1867–1959) advocated an "organic" approach that integrated architecture with nature. The best-known expression of Wright's conviction that buildings ought to be not only on the landscape, but *in* it, is **FALLING-WATER**, in rural Pennsylvania (**FIG. 19–44**), commissioned by Edgar Kaufmann, a Pittsburgh department-store owner, to replace a family summer cottage on a site that featured a waterfall into a pool where the Kaufmann children played. Wright decided to build the house into the cliff over the pool, allowing the water to flow around and under the house. In a daring engineering move, he **cantilevered** a series of broad concrete terraces out from the house, echoing the great slabs of natural rock. The rocks on which the family had once sunbathed by the waterfall became the hearthstone of their fireplace. Long bands of windows and glass doors offer spectacular views, uniting woods, water, and house. Such houses do not simply testify to the ideal of living in harmony with nature; they declare war on the modern industrial city. When asked what could be done to improve the city, Wright responded bluntly, "Tear it down."

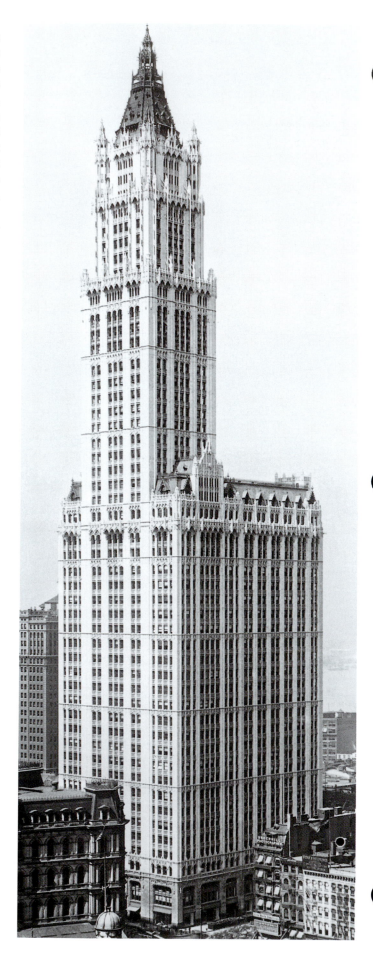

19–43 • Cass Gilbert WOOLWORTH BUILDING
New York. 1911–1913.

The development of the skyscraper design and aesthetic depended on several things: metal beams and girders for the structural-support skeleton; the separation of the building-support structure from the enclosing wall layer (the cladding); fireproofing materials and measures; elevators; and plumbing, central heating, artificial lighting, and ventilation systems. First-generation skyscrapers, built between about 1880 and 1900, were concentrated in the Midwest, especially Chicago. Second-generation skyscrapers, with more than 20 stories, date from after 1895 and are found more frequently in New York.

The first tall buildings were free-standing towers, sometimes with a base, like the Woolworth Building of 1911–1913 (SEE FIG. 19–43). But New York City's Building Zone Resolution of 1916 introduced mandatory setbacks—recessions from the ground-level building line—to ensure light and ventilation of adjacent sites. Built in 1931, the 1,250-foot setback form of the Empire State Building, diagrammed here, presents a streamlined design with exterior cladding that conceals the great complexity of the internal structure and mechanisms that make its height possible.

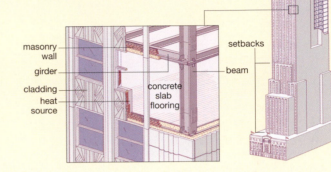

elevator shafts (layer two)

stairwells (layer one)

masonry wall

girder

cladding

heat source

concrete slab flooring

setbacks

beam

Watch an architectural simulation about skyscraper construction on **MyArtsLab**

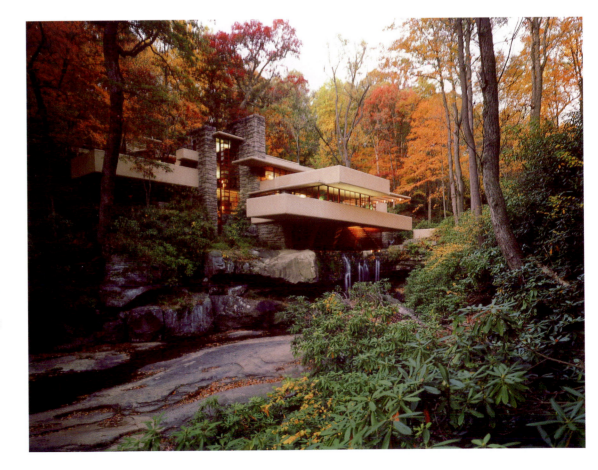

19–44 • Frank Lloyd Wright EDGAR KAUFMANN HOUSE (FALLINGWATER) Mill Run, Pennsylvania. 1937.

Explore the architectural panoramas of Fallingwater on **MyArtsLab**

An even stronger connection to the landscape, combined with a dose of Modernism's devotion to the integrity of building materials, is evident in the architecture of Mary Colter (1869–1958), which developed concurrently and separately from that of Wright. Born in Pittsburgh and educated in San Francisco, she spent most of her career designing for the Fred Harvey Company, a firm in the American Southwest that catered to the tourist trade. Colter was an avid student of Native American arts, and her buildings quote liberally from the traditions of the Puebloan peoples. She designed several visitor facilities at Grand Canyon National Park, of which the most dramatic is the **LOOKOUT STUDIO** (**FIG. 19–45**). Built on the edge of the canyon's south rim, the building's foundation is in natural rock, and the walls are built of local stone, making it seem an extension of the sheer natural wall beneath. The sole concession to Modernism is the liberal use of glass and the flat cement floor. Colter's designs for hotels and railway stations throughout the Southwest helped establish an enduring architectural identity for that region as distinct as the skyscraper which stood for the faraway metropolis of New York.

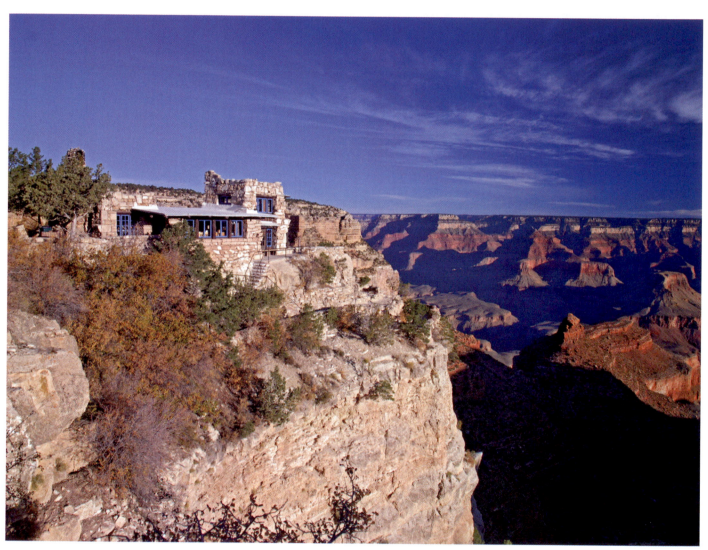

19–45 • Mary Colter LOOKOUT STUDIO
Grand Canyon National Park, Arizona. 1914.

The story of twentieth-century art recalls the title of Aldous Huxley's 1928 novel *Point Counter Point*. Artists and art movements reacted to each other with accelerating speed and vigor, as artistic innovation and public taste swung back and forth—as it had earlier between the poles of Rococo and Neoclassicism, Romanticism and Realism. This point–counterpoint relationship even appears on a personal level, as between Braque and Picasso, two artists who challenged and inspired each other to create Cubist paintings, prints, and collages. Their relationship exemplifies the way in which individual artists often propose, test, and revise their ideas within a broader artistic community.

Rapidly developing technology had a profound impact on how people made and saw art. Futurism sought to capture the energy of the Modern age, while Dada mocked and denied the very validity of the work of art itself. Surrealist artists turned inward as they explored a symbolic dreamworld, while other artists glorified external appearances and celebrated their local heritage. Decades of technological innovation blossomed in amazing achievements in architecture as engineering and aesthetic practice combined to allow new building forms, from skyscrapers to private homes, pitting city streamliners against regional naturalists—yet another point–counterpoint within the restless creativity characterizing twentieth-century culture.

THINK ABOUT IT

19.1 Discuss the impact that Cubism had on subsequent avant-garde art styles in the early part of the twentieth century by analyzing two works from the chapter.

19.2 Characterize the effect of the appearance of European Modernism in the United States at the Armory Show of 1913 by focusing on one painting discussed in this chapter.

19.3 Explain how both Dada and Surrealism changed the form, content, and concept of art.

19.4 Evaluate Frank Lloyd Wright's Fallingwater as a reaction against the International Style of European Modern architecture.

| CROSSCURRENTS |

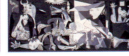

FIG. 17–23   FIG. 19–31

The horrific violence of war and political oppression has been eloquently expressed by many artists throughout the history of art. Discuss the political circumstances that led to the creation of these two examples, and assess how they relate to the styles of the artists and their time. Who was the audience for these works?

IN PERSPECTIVE

1900

• Wright Brothers' First Flight 1903

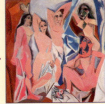

PICASSO,
Les Demoiselles d'Avignon
1907

1910

• First Flight across English Channel 1909
• Mexican Revolution 1910–1917

• First Balkan War 1912–1913
• Armory Show 1913
• World War I 1914–1918 ·······

• Russian Revolution 1917

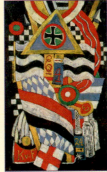

HARTLEY,
Portrait of a German Officer
1914

1920

• Soviet Union Formed 1922

• Stalin Comes to Power 1924

1930

• Museum of Modern Art (MoMA) in New York Opens/Great Depression Begins 1929

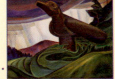

CARR, Big Raven
1931

• New Deal in the United States/ Hitler Comes to Power in Germany 1933
• First Analog Computer 1935
• Spanish Civil War 1936–1939

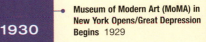

• First Digital Computer 1939
• World War II 1939–1945

1940

MIRÓ, Composition
1933

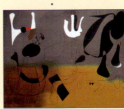

• Atomic Bomb Dropped on Hiroshima and Nagasaki 1945

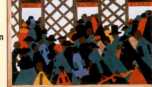

LAWRENCE, The Migration Series
1940–1941

1950

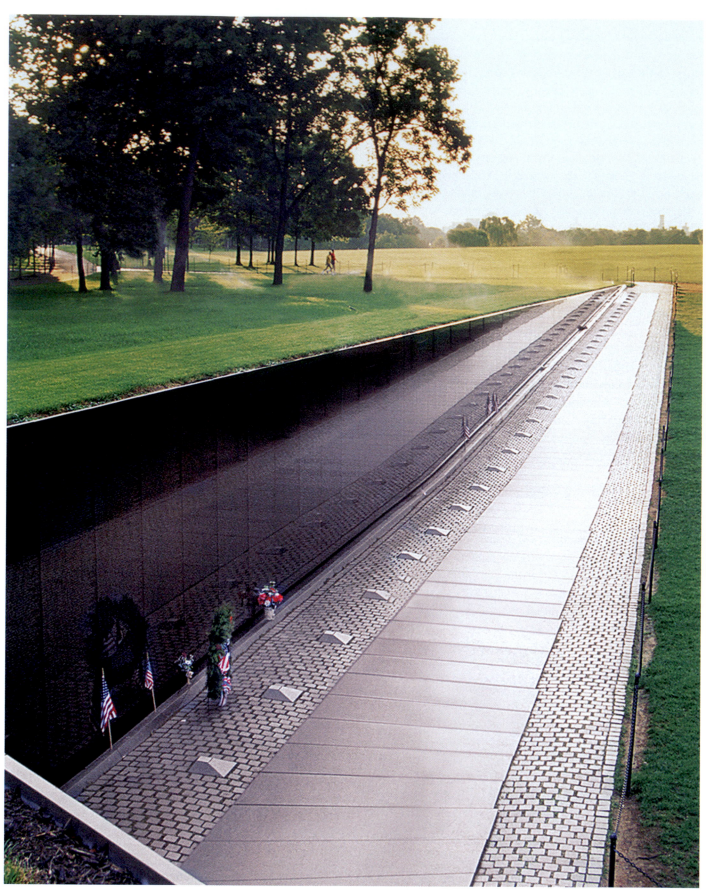

20–1 • Maya Ying Lin VIETNAM VETERANS' MEMORIAL
1981–1983. Black granite, length 500′ (152 m). The Mall, Washington, D.C.

👁 **Watch** an Art21 video about Maya Lin on **MyArtsLab**

ART SINCE 1945

20.1 Describe how and why Abstract Expressionism transformed painting after 1945.

20.2 Characterize the variety of artistic movements that followed the height of Abstract Expressionism.

20.3 Distinguish Late Modernism from the styles and subjects associated with Postmodernism.

20.4 Summarize new developments in architecture and public memorials during the late twentieth and early twenty-first centuries.

LOOKING FORWARD ▶

Flat, polished stone walls inscribed with thousands of names reflect back the images of the living as they contemplate the **MEMORIAL** to the dead and missing veterans of the war in Vietnam (1955–1975) **(FIG. 20–1)**. The design is brilliant in its simplicity. The artist, Maya Ying Lin (b. 1960), combined two basic ideas: the minimal grandeur of long and sleek, black granite walls and row upon row of engraved names—the abstract and the intimate conjoined. The power of Lin's memorial lies in its understatement. It is a statement of loss, sorrow, and the futility of war; the names are so numerous that they lose individuality and become a surface texture. It is a timeless monument to suffering humanity, faceless in sacrifice, observed by viewers who must themselves descend into the earth to survey it. Maya Ying Lin said, "The point is to see yourself reflected in the names."

The walls also reflect more than visitors. One wall faces and reflects the George Washington Monument (constructed 1848–1884). Robert Mills, the architect of many public build-

ings at the beginning of the nineteenth century, chose the obelisk, a time-honored Egyptian sun symbol, for his monument commemorating the nation's founder. The other wall leads the eye to the Neoclassical-style Lincoln Memorial. By subtly incorporating the Washington and Lincoln memorials into its design, Lin's Vietnam Veterans' Memorial is incorporated into the nation's unfolding history, perhaps recalling earlier sacrifices in times of war.

Until the modern era, most public art celebrated and commemorated political and social leaders and certain consequences of war in large, free-standing monuments, sometimes motivated by patriotism and a sincere desire to honor heroes, at other times presenting political propaganda or seeking social intimidation. Lin's memorial in Washington, D.C., to the American men and women who died in or never returned from the Vietnam War was unique. Perhaps that is one reason it remains among the most visited works of public art and certainly among the most affecting war memorials ever conceived.

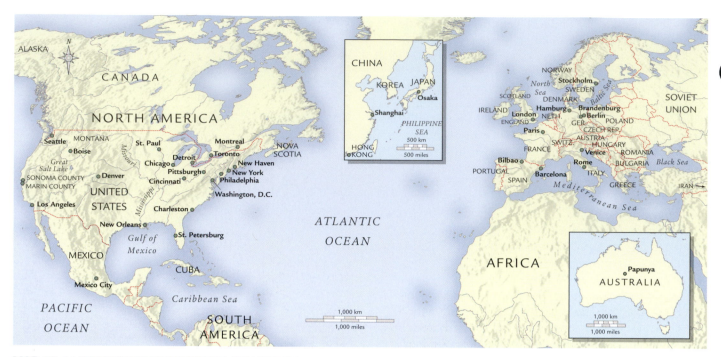

MAP 20–1 • CONTEMPORARY EUROPE AND NORTH AMERICA

The contemporary art world is global, incorporating artistic developments in Asia, Africa, and Australia, as well as Europe and the Americas.

The year 1945 brought the end of World War II (1939–1945). Its horrors had surpassed even those of World War I. The human loss was almost too profound and grotesque to comprehend. More than 30 million people died. The unimaginable horror of the concentration camps and the awful impact of the dropping of nuclear bombs shook humanity to its core. Art—indeed the world—would never be the same.

The political and economic shifts brought by the end of the war meant that the United States and the Soviet Union emerged as the world's most powerful nations and soon were engaged in the Cold War (**MAP 20–1**). The Soviets set up Communist governments in Eastern Europe and supported the development of communism elsewhere. Meanwhile, the United States, through financial aid and political support, sought to contain communism's global spread. A second huge Communist nation emerged in 1949 when Mao Zedong established the People's Republic of China. The United States tried to prevent the further spread of communism in Asia, intervening in the Korean War (1950–1953) and the Vietnam War (1955–1975). The United States and the Soviet Union built massive nuclear arsenals aimed at each other, effectively deterring either from aggression for fear of an apocalyptic retaliation. Meanwhile, the old European states gave up their empires. The British led the way by withdrawing from India in 1947. Other European nations gradually granted independence to colonies in Asia and Africa.

The United States' stature after World War II as the most powerful and wealthy democratic nation was soon reflected in the arts. American artists and architects led in artistic innovation, and by the late 1950s the dominance of their work was acknowledged across the Atlantic, even in Paris. This dominance lasted until around 1970, when the belief in the existence of an identifiable mainstream, or single dominant line of artistic development, began to wane (see "Clement Greenberg and the Idea of the Mainstream," p. 554).

Although Realism had dominated American art in the period between the two world wars, some artists of the period had maintained an interest in abstract and nonrepresentational styles of art. America's living link with the European Modernist tradition was Hans Hofmann (1880–1966), a German-born teacher and painter who had come to the United States before World War II. The rise of fascism in Europe and the outbreak of World War II stranded people like Hofmann and led a number of prominent European artists and writers to flee to the United States. By 1940 André Breton, Salvador Dalí, and Piet Mondrian were all living in New York, where they altered the character and artistic concerns of the art scene.

Abstract Expressionism

How and why did Abstract Expressionism transform painting after 1945?

Deeply affected by the ideas of Surrealism and the teaching of Hans Hofmann, New York artists of the 1940s began working in a style collectively called Abstract Expressionism. This term designates not an organized movement but the work of a wide range of loosely affiliated artists active in the 1940s and 1950s bound by a common purpose: expressing their profound social alienation in the wake of World War II and making art that was both moral and universal. Two major approaches emerged: **Action Painting**, characterized by active paint handling; and **Color Field Painting**, distinguished by broad sweeping expanses of color. Some art historians prefer to refer to the work of these artists simply as the New York School.

The Abstract Expressionists took from the Surrealists both a commitment to examining the unconscious and techniques for doing so, but whereas the European Surrealists had derived their notion of the unconscious from Sigmund Freud, many of the Americans subscribed to the thinking of Swiss psychoanalyst Carl Jung (1875–1961). His theory of the "collective unconscious" holds that beneath one's private memories is a storehouse of feelings and symbolic associations common to all humans.

A leading Jung-inspired Abstract Expressionist was the action painter Jackson Pollock (1912–1956). Undergoing Jungian analysis between 1939 and 1941, the alcoholic and self-destructive artist made little progress with his personal problems, but the sessions greatly affected his work, giving him a new vocabulary of signs and symbols and a belief in the therapeutic role of art in society. In the mid-1940s, Pollock began to employ enamel house paints along with conventional oils, and in the winter of 1946 to 1947, using sticks and brushes, he dripped them in a variety of fluid movements onto large canvases spread out on the floor (**FIG. 20–2**). In 1947, influential critic Clement Greenberg described Pollock as "the most powerful painter in North America," and in 1950, *Time* magazine described him as "Jack the Dripper."

Over the next four years Pollock produced a series of graceful linear abstractions such as **AUTUMN RHYTHM**

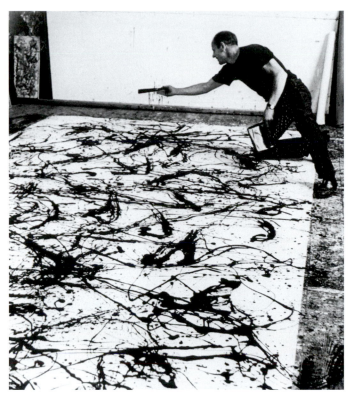

20–2 • Rudolph Burckhardt
JACKSON POLLOCK PAINTING
1950.

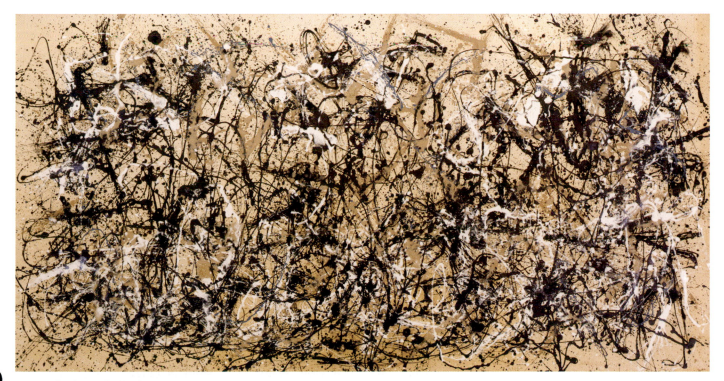

20–3 • Jackson Pollock AUTUMN RHYTHM (NUMBER 30)
1950. Oil on canvas, 8′ 9″ × 17′ 3″ (2.66 × 5.25 m). The Metropolitan Museum of Art, New York. George A. Hearn Fund, 1957 (57.92).

Watch a video of Jackson Pollock painting on **MyArtsLab**

Clement Greenberg and the Idea of the Mainstream

A central conviction of Modernist artists, critics, and art historians has been the existence of an artistic mainstream, the notion that some artworks are more important than others because they are central to the progressive unfolding of some larger historical pattern associated with what is considered "high culture." According to this view, position in the overall evolutionary pattern confers value; any art outside this "mainstream," regardless of its appeal, can be ignored (see "'High' and 'Low' Culture in the Myth of the Modernism," p. 562).

The first significant discussions of the Modernist mainstream emerged after World War II, shaped by the critical writings of Clement Greenberg (1909–1994). Greenberg argued that beginning with Realist painter Édouard Manet (see Chapter 18), Modern art progressively eliminated narrative, figuration, and pictorial space from painting because art itself was undergoing a "process of self-purification" in reaction to a deteriorating civilization.

Greenberg identified and championed Abstract Expressionism as the dominant style of the late 1940s and 1950s—in other words as art's mainstream. Inspired in part by Hofmann's teaching, Greenberg demanded close analysis of the work of art and critical judgments based on visual perception alone—a method called **formalism**.

Belief in the concept of the mainstream gradually eroded, however, and a reaction against Greenberg's ideas set in during the 1970s. Because Greenbergian formalism omitted so much of the history of recent art, observers began questioning whether a single, dominant mainstream had ever existed. The extraordinary proliferation of art styles and trends after the 1960s fueled those doubts.

(NUMBER 30) (FIG. 20–3). Delicate skeins of paint effortlessly loop over and under one another in a mesmerizing pattern that spreads across the vast surface of the canvas. As the title of this and other Pollock paintings suggest, the artist seems to have felt that in the free, unself-conscious act of painting he was giving vent to primal, natural forces. Pollock said that he was creating for "the age of the airplane, the atom bomb, and the radio," and the works do seem to embody something of the tensions of the Cold War period, as each side silently threatened the other with instant annihilation.

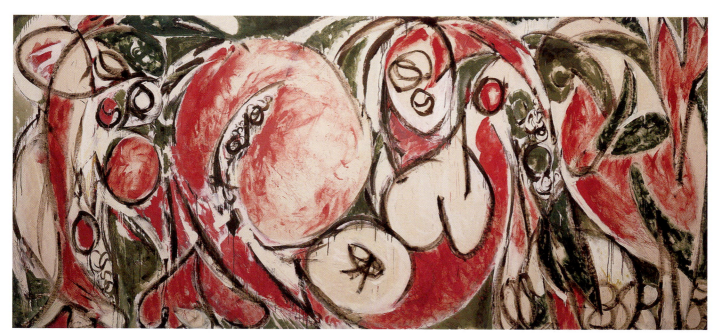

20–4 • Lee Krasner THE SEASONS
1957. Oil on canvas, 7' 8¾" × 16' 11¾" (2.36 × 5.18 m). Whitney Museum of Art, New York.
© Whitney Museum of Art, New York. Purchased with funds from Frances and Sydney Lewis (by exchange), the Mrs. Percy Uris Purchase Fund, and the Painting and Sculpture Committee (87.7).

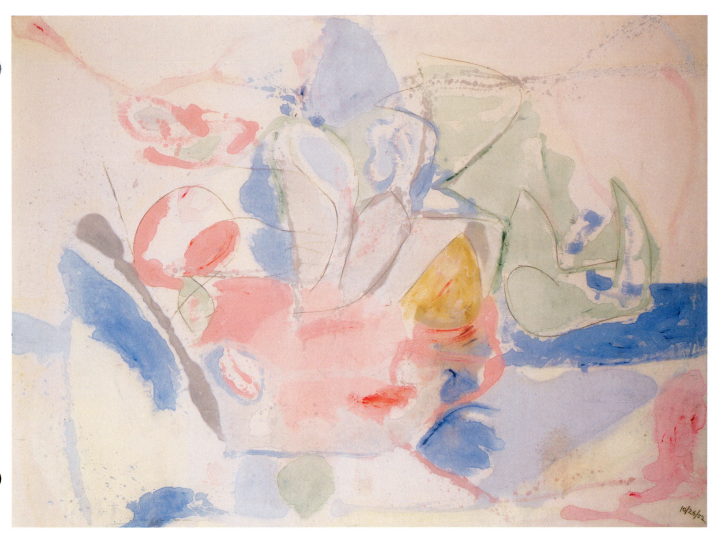

20–5 • Helen Frankenthaler MOUNTAINS AND SEA
1952. Oil and charcoal on canvas, 7′ 2¾″ × 9′ 8¼″ (2.2 × 2.95 m). Collection: Helen Frankenthaler
Foundation, Inc. (on extended loan to the National Gallery of Art, Washington, D.C.)

In 1945, Pollock married Lee Krasner (1908–1984), a student of Hofmann who produced fully nonrepresentational work several years before Pollock. When Krasner moved in with Pollock in 1942, she virtually stopped painting in order to devote herself to the conventional role of a supportive wife. But she soon resumed her art, and despite the problems that developed in their marriage—exacerbated by Pollock's alcoholism—she continued to paint. After Pollock's death in an automobile crash in 1956, Krasner took over his studio and during the next year and a half produced a dazzling group of monumental, dazzling gestural paintings (**FIG. 20–4**), painted in bold sweeping curves that express not only her grief but also her identification with the forces of nature suggested by the bursting, rounded forms and spring-like colors. "Painting, for me, when it really 'happens' is as miraculous as any natural phenomenon," she said, suggesting an attitude similar to that of Pollock, who found "pure harmony" in the act of painting.

Helen Frankenthaler (1928–2011), after a visit to Pollock's studio in 1951, painted more lyrical versions of Action Painting that had a strong impact on later artists. Like Pollock,

she worked on the floor, drawn to what she described as Pollock's "dancelike use of arms and legs." But rather than flinging or dripping full-strength paint, as Pollock did, Frankenthaler poured her thinned oil paints so that they soaked into the raw canvas, producing an effect in **MOUNTAINS AND SEA** (**FIG. 20–5**) that resembles watercolor. A few delicate contour lines suggest not only the mountains of Nova Scotia referenced in the painting's title, but also less translatable, dream-inspired Surrealistic forms.

In contrast, Willem de Kooning (1904–1997) insisted, "Art never seems to make me peaceful or pure," and remarked, "I work out of doubt." Immigrating from his native Netherlands to the United States in 1926, he initially painted nonrepresentationally, but he shocked the New York art world in the early 1950s by returning to the figure with a series of paintings of women. The first, **WOMAN I** (**FIG. 20–6**), took him almost two years to finish. De Kooning's wife, the artist Elaine de Kooning (1918–1989), said that he painted it, scraped it, and repainted it about 200 times. Part of De Kooning's dissatisfaction stemmed from the way his subject, a figure inspired by conventionally

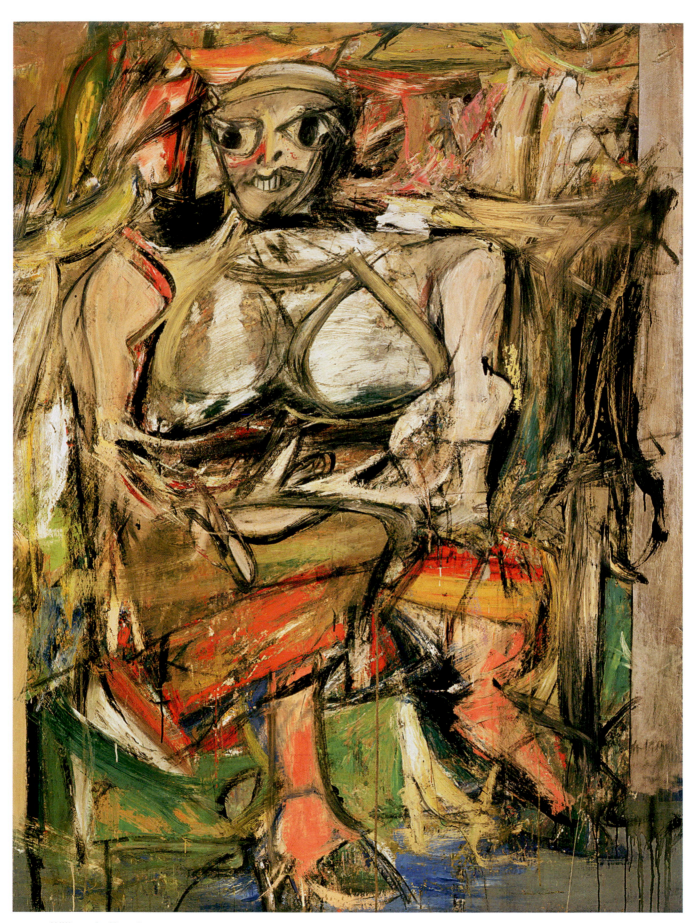

20-6 • Willem de Kooning **WOMAN I**
1950–1952. Oil on canvas, 6′ 3⅞″ × 4′ 10″ (1.93 × 1.47 m). The Museum of Modern Art, New York (478.1953).

pretty images of women seen in American advertising, kept veering away from those models. What emerges in *Woman I* is not the elegant companion of advertising fantasy but a powerful adversary, more dangerous than alluring. The prettiness of the soft pastel colors and the luxuriousness of the painted surface are nearly lost in the furious slashing of his brush. The image is powerfully sexual, full of implied violence, and intensely passionate, like a great fertility goddess. But on another level it connects with the coloristic tradition of artists such as Titian and Rubens, who superbly transformed female flesh into luscious layers of paint.

During the 1950s, De Kooning dominated the avant-garde in New York. Among the handful of Modernist painters who resisted his influence was Mark Rothko (1903–1970). By 1940, with little formal art training, Rothko was already producing paintings in the manner of the European Surrealists informed by Jung's archetypal imagery. By the mid-1940s, he began to paint very large canvases with rectangular shapes arranged in a vertical format in which he allowed his colors to bleed into one another. These paintings, such as **UNTITLED (ROTHKO NUMBER 5068.49) (FIG. 20–7)**, are neither simple arrangements of flat geometric shapes on a canvas nor atmospheric, archetypical landscapes. Rothko thought of his shapes as fundamental "ideas" expressed in rectangular form, unmediated by a recognizable subject, which sit in front of a painted field (hence the name "Color Field Painting"). He preferred to show

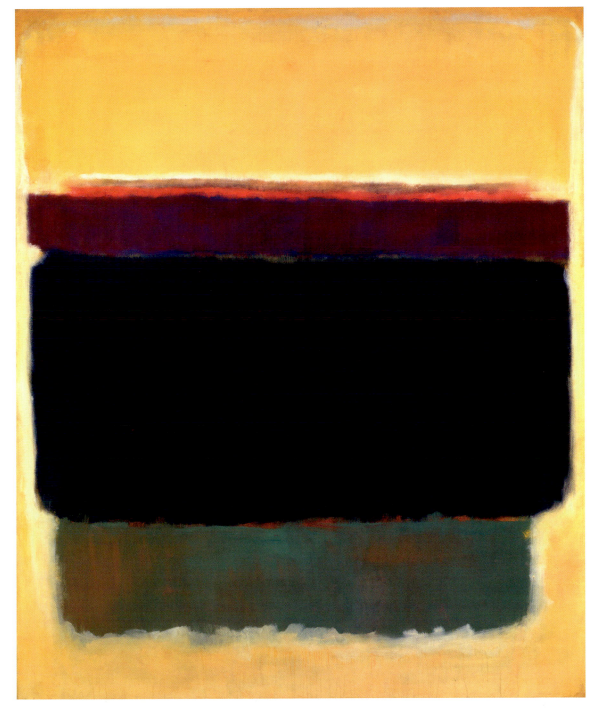

20-7 • Mark Rothko UNTITLED (ROTHKO NUMBER 5068.49)
1949. Oil on canvas, 6′ 9⅜″ × 5′ 6⅜″ (2.1 × 1.7 m). National Gallery of Art, Washington, D.C.
© 1997 Christopher Rothko and Kate Rothko Prizel. Gift of the Mark Rothko Foundation, Inc.

his paintings together in series or rows and illuminated indirectly to evoke moods of transcendental meditation.

The New York School also included talented sculptors such as David Smith (1906–1965), who learned metalworking as a welder and riveter at an automobile plant in his native Indiana; avoiding the precious materials of traditional sculpture, he created his works out of standard industrial materials. After World War II, Smith began to weld horizontally formatted, open-form sculptures that were like drawings in space. The forms of the vertical *Cubi* series (SEE FIG. INTRO–5) were actually determined by standardized, precut sizes of stainless-steel sheets. In photographs they sometimes look coldly industrial, but when observed outdoors as Smith intended, their highly burnished surfaces show the gestural marks of the sculptor's tools upon them, and reflect and refract the sun in different ways depending on the time of day, weather conditions, and distance from which they are viewed. Vaguely anthropomorphic, like giant totemic figures, the sculptures are surprisingly organic when seen at close range.

After Abstract Expressionism

What series of major artistic movements followed the height of Abstract Expressionism?

The generation of artists who began to make art in the 1950s moved beyond Abstract Expressionism and increasingly addressed the real world, acknowledging its fragmentation, its relativism, and its messy relation to popular culture.

Assemblage

One alternative path was **assemblage**—combining disparate elements to construct a work of art. By 1950, Louise Nevelson (1899–1988) had developed an Analytic Cubist-inspired version of assemblage. Prowling the streets of downtown Manhattan, she collected discarded packing boxes in which she would carefully arrange chair legs, broom handles, cabinet doors, spindles, and other wooden refuse. She painted her assemblages a matte black to obscure the identity of the individual elements, to integrate them formally, and to provide an air of mystery.

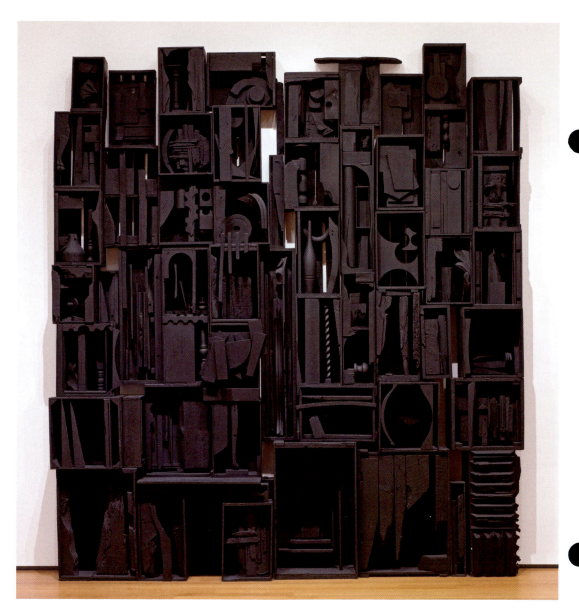

20–8 • Louise Nevelson
SKY CATHEDRAL
1958. Assemblage of wood construction painted black, 11′ 3½″ × 10′ ¼″ × 18″ (3.44 × 3.05 × 4.57 m). The Museum of Modern Art, New York. Gift of Mr. and Mrs. Ben Mildwoff (136.1958.1-57).

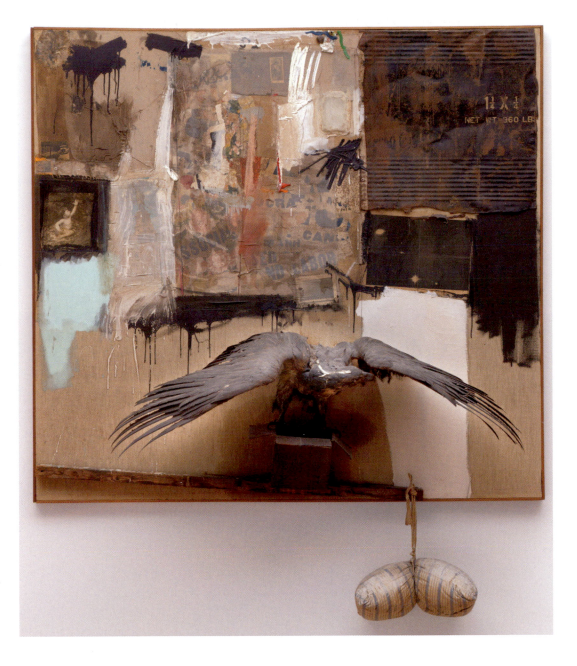

Avant-garde critics were
not bothered by the fact that
much of Rauschenberg's
materials were drawn from
popular culture. Many of
the early twentieth-century
collagists, including Picasso
and Braque, had worked
with similar materials.
However, critics such as
Hilton Kramer (at the *New
York Times*) and Thomas
Hess (at *ARTnews*) pointed
out that whereas earlier
artists had aesthetically
coordinated such elements,
transforming the crude
materials of life into the finer
ones of art, Rauschenberg
and his associates left them
in their raw, "unpurified"
condition. In their view, such
works were not art at all.

After stacking several of these boxes together against a studio wall, Nevelson realized that the accumulated effect was more powerful than viewing them individually. One of her first monumental wall assemblages was **SKY CATHEDRAL (FIG. 20–8)**. What she particularly liked about the new schema was the way it could transform ordinary space just as the prosaic elements she worked with had themselves been transformed into a work of art. To add a further poetic dimension, Nevelson first displayed *Sky Cathedral* bathed in soft blue light, recalling moonlight.

Robert Rauschenberg (1925–2008) developed a distinctive style of assemblage in artworks he called "combines"—combinations of painting, collage, and sculpture using non-traditional materials. **CANYON (FIG. 20–9)** incorporates an assortment of old family photographs, public imagery (the Statue of Liberty), fragments of political posters (in the center), and various objects purchased or salvaged from the trash (the flattened

steel drum at upper right), and projecting three-dimensional forms such as a stuffed eagle (donated by a friend) perched on a box and a dirty pillow tied with cord and suspended from a piece of wood. The rich disorder, enhanced by the seemingly sloppy application of paint, challenges viewers to make sense of what they see. In fact, Rauschenberg meant his work to be open to various readings, so he assembled material that each viewer might interpret differently. Cheerfully accepting the chaos and unpredictability of modern urban experience, he tried to find artistic metaphors for it. "I only consider myself successful," he said, "when I do something that resembles the lack of order I sense."

When the Museum of Modern Art organized an exhibition titled "The Art of Assemblage" in 1961, Rauschenberg was one of two major American artists included in the show; the other was his fellow southerner, close friend, and at times lover, Jasper Johns (b. 1930). Inspired by the example of Marcel Duchamp

(SEE FIG. 19–16), Johns produced more controlled, cerebral, and puzzling works that addressed directly issues raised in contemporary art. For instance, art critics had praised the evenly dispersed, "non-hierarchical" quality of Abstract Expressionist painting—particularly Pollock's—and Johns mocks and undoes this esteemed aspect of New York School painting. In **TARGET WITH PLASTER CASTS** (FIG. 20–10)—neither a painting nor a sculpture but both—plaster casts of human body parts are lined up in boxes with hinged lids along the top of the work, parodying the nonhierarchical manner of Abstract Expressionism, but the target below is emphatically hierarchical.

Target has a psychological dimension that may stem from the artist's own anxieties and fears. The casts above the target fragment a human body without any sense of the organic whole that bound them, rendering them blank and empty as the target itself. The viewer can complete the process of depersonalization by closing some, or just a few, of the hinged flaps over the closet-like boxes that contain them, obliterating all or part of the human presence. This juxtaposition of fragmented and partially hidden body parts and the sharply defined target takes on richer meaning in the context of Johns's position as a gay artist in the restrictive, often paranoid, climate of Cold War America.

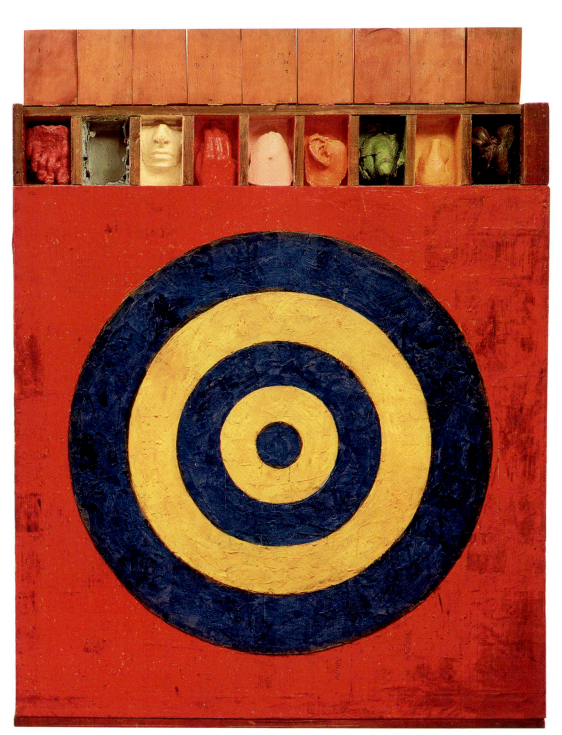

20–10 • Jasper Johns TARGET WITH PLASTER CASTS
1955. Assemblage of encaustic and collage on canvas, with plaster objects in wooden boxes with hinged lids, 51″ × 44″ (129.5 × 111.8 cm). Collection of Mr. and Mrs. Leo Castelli.

View the Closer Look for Johns's *Target with Plaster Casts* on **MyArtsLab**

Homage to New York

On the evening of March 17, 1960, a distinguished group of guests, including Governor Nelson Rockefeller of New York, gathered in the sculpture garden of New York's Museum of Modern Art. Awaiting them was an unlikely construction: HOMAGE TO NEW YORK (FIG. 20–11) by the Swiss-born artist Jean Tinguely (1925–1991). The work was assembled from yards of metal tubing, several dozen bicycle and baby-carriage wheels, a washing-machine drum, an upright piano, a radio, several electric fans, a noisy old Addressograph machine, a bassinet, numerous small motors, two motor-driven devices that produced abstract paintings by the yard, several bottles of chemical inks, and assorted noisemakers. White paint covered everything except the crowning element—an inflated orange meteorological balloon.

The machine, designed to destroy itself when activated, was plugged in as the expectant guests watched. Smoke poured out of the machinery and covered the crowd. Parts of the contraption broke free and scuttled off in various directions, sometimes threatening onlookers. A device meant to douse the burning piano—which repeatedly played three notes—failed to work, and firefighters had to be called in. The firefighters extinguished the blaze and finished the work's destruction to boos from the crowd, which, with the exception of the museum officials, had been delighted by the spectacle. The artist said the event was better than any he could have planned.

This new kind of art, dramatic but transitory, prefigured a question and answer raised by musician and philosopher John Cage (see p. 567). Surveying art and music in 1961, he asked, "Where do we go from here," and his answer was, "Towards theater."

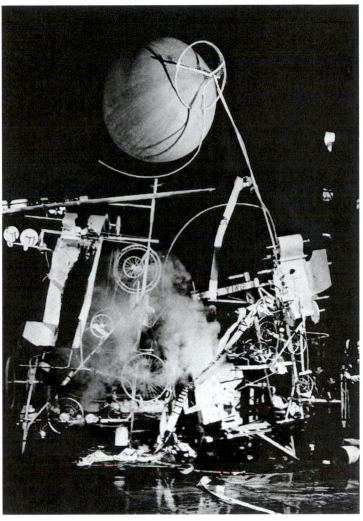

20–11 • Jean Tinguely
FRAGMENT FROM HOMAGE TO NEW YORK
1960. Painted metal, wood, and cloth, 6′ 8¼″ × 29⅝″ × 7′ 3⅞″ (203.7 × 75.1 × 223.2 cm). Self-destroying sculpture in the garden of the Museum of Modern Art, New York. Gift of the artist (227.1968).

Steadfastly silent but boldly present, in this painting personal identity remains elusive, selectively masked, removed from the center, and safely off target.

The work of Johns had a powerful effect on the artists who matured around 1960, and Johns's interest in Duchamp helped elevate that artist to a place of importance previously reserved for Picasso. And not since Dada had the art world seen sensationalism to compare with the kinetic sculptures of Jean Tinguely (1925–1991). In his *Homage to New York* (see "*Homage to New York*," p. 561), this anarchist wanted to free the machine, to let it play. "Art hasn't been fun for a long time," Tinguely said. Like the creations of his Dada forebears, Tinguely's work was implicitly critical of an overly restrained and practical bourgeois mentality.

Pop Art

Pop art, as its name suggests, took its style and subject matter from popular culture: its sources were comic books, advertisements, movies, and television. Many critics were alarmed by Pop, fearful that open acknowledgment of already powerful commercial culture would threaten the survival of both Modernist art and "high culture"—meaning a civilization's most sophisticated, not its most representative, products (see "'High' and 'Low' Culture in the Myth of Modernism," p. 562).

Pop art originated in London in the work of the Independent Group (IG), formed in 1952 by a few members of London's Institute of Contemporary Art (ICA). One of the IG's most prominent figures was artist Richard Hamilton (1922–2011)

"High" and "Low" Culture in the Myth of Modernism

One of the prevailing ideals of the Modernist avant-garde was to distance itself intellectually and aesthetically from the banalities of everyday, middle-class life—what was referred to as "lowbrow" culture.

"Lowbrow" and "kitsch" are labels applied to the habits, tastes, artifacts (mostly mass-produced), and amusements of ordinary, popular culture, that is, any cultural expression that falls outside the parameters of what was considered elite, or "high" culture (see "Clement Greenberg and the Idea of the Mainstream," p. 554). The term "kitsch" derives from the German word *verkitschen* (to make cheap). Mass-produced consumer goods have generally been given this label—

a categorization that often has a pejorative sense when such goods are compared to "high," or fine, art. Kitsch has taken on a further connotation of vulgarity—cheap or uneducated "bad taste."

Boundaries between "high" and "low," "good" and "bad," began to blur when the Pop artists of the early 1960s appropriated imagery culled from "low" popular culture for incorporation into "high" art—similar to what Marcel Duchamp did when he exhibited a urinal as a work of art in 1917 (SEE FIG. 19–16). Postmodern artists continue to question and obscure distinctions between "high" and "low" as a way of repudiating what they see as the smugness of Modernism.

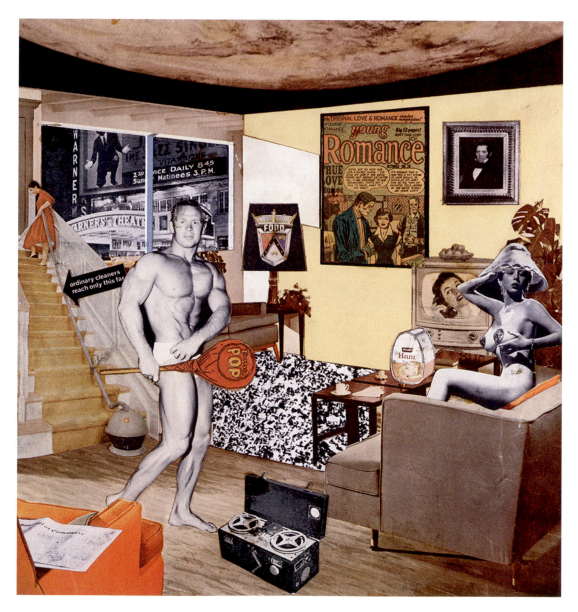

20–12 • Richard Hamilton JUST WHAT IS IT THAT MAKES TODAY'S HOMES SO DIFFERENT, SO APPEALING? 1956. Collage, 10¼″ × 9¾″ (26 × 24.8 cm). Kunsthalle, Tübingen, Germany.

👁 **Watch** a podcast about Richard Hamilton's work on **MyArtsLab**

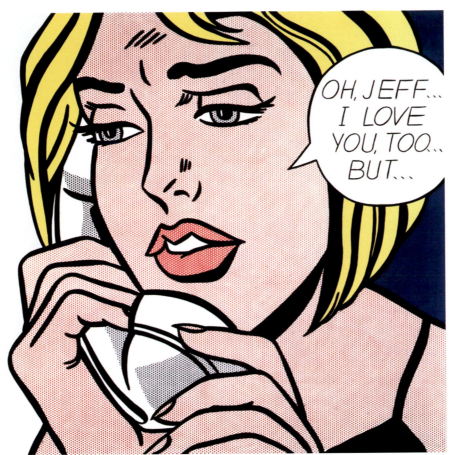

20-13 • Roy Lichtenstein
OH, JEFF...I LOVE YOU,
TOO...BUT...
1964. Oil on Magna on canvas,
4′ × 4′ (1.22 × 1.22 m).
Private collection. © Estate of
Roy Lichtenstein.

whose 1956 collage, **JUST WHAT IS IT THAT MAKES TODAY'S HOMES SO DIFFERENT, SO APPEALING?** (**FIG. 20–12**), satirizes modern life and especially American materialism by mocking its marketing strategies. American advertisements, whose utopian vision of a future of contented people with ample leisure time to enjoy cheap and plentiful material goods, was very appealing to people living amid the austerity of postwar Britain. Products of the American mass media and commercial culture—including Hollywood movies, Madison Avenue advertising, science fiction, and pop music—soon became the central subject matter of British Pop art.

American Pop artist Roy Lichtenstein (1923–1997) based his art on imagery he found in cartoons and advertisements, even adopting the print medium's heavy outlines and the **Benday dots** used in offset printing. Although many people assume that he merely copied from the comics, in fact he made numerous subtle, important formal adjustments that tightened, clarified, and strengthened the final image. **OH, JEFF...I LOVE YOU, TOO...BUT...** (**FIG. 20–13**) compresses a popular romance story line that temporarily threatens a love relationship into a single frame. But Lichtenstein plays ironic games by pitting illusion against reality. We know that comic-book emotions are unrealistically melodramatic, yet he presents this overblown episode vividly, almost reverently, enshrined in a work of high art. The issue of what is real and what is unreal in media culture, of its superficiality and its ability to

manipulate, was a topic of concern and discussion in the early 1960s, as it still is today.

From the 1960s, Pop art was dominated by artistic giant Andy Warhol (1928–1987), heir to Duchamp's ideals about the nature of art and the role of artists in art making. A successful commercial illustrator in New York City during the 1950s, Warhol decided in 1960 to pursue a career as an artist, and from that time until his death in 1987, he created an immense body of work, including prints, paintings, sculptures, and films. Warhol knew advertising culture well, and he began to take as his subjects popular consumer items such as Brillo boxes, Campbell's Soup cans, and Coca-Cola bottles, reproducing them using the cheap industrial print method of **silkscreen** (in which a fine mesh silk screen is used as a printing stencil). Warhol argued that past art demanded thought and understanding, whereas advertising and celebrity culture demanded only immediate attention, very quickly becoming uninteresting and boring. In keeping with this position, he suggested that art should be like movie stars, interesting for 15 minutes.

Warhol's **MARILYN DIPTYCH** (**FIG. 20–14**) is one of a series of silkscreens that Warhol made immediately after the actress's death, an apparent suicide, in 1962. He memorializes Monroe, using a famous publicity photograph transferred directly onto silkscreen (see "Appropriation and the 'Death of the Author,'" p. 565), thus rendering it flat and bland so that Monroe's signature features—her bleach-blond hair, her ruby lips, and her sultry, blue-shadowed eyes—stand out as

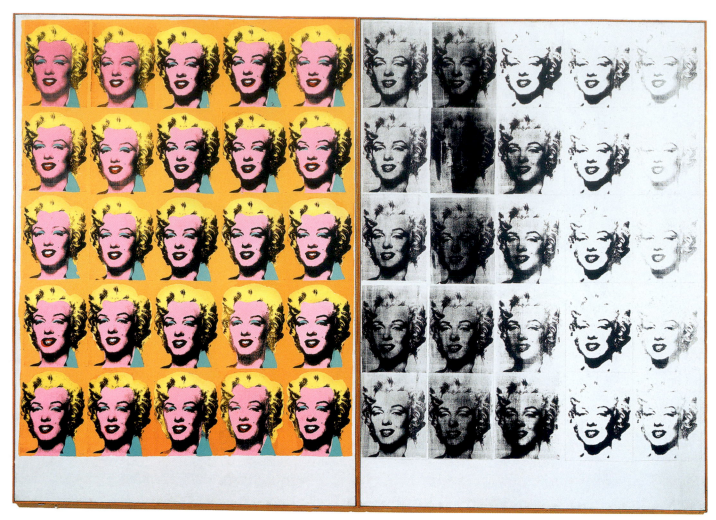

20–14 • Andy Warhol MARILYN DIPTYCH
1962. Oil, acrylic, and silkscreen on enamel on canvas, two panels, each 6′ 10″ × 4′ 9″ (2.05 × 1.44 m). Tate, London.

Warhol assumed that all Pop artists shared his affirmative view of ordinary culture. In his account of the beginnings of the Pop movement, he wrote: "The Pop artists did images that anybody walking down Broadway could recognize in a split second—comics, picnic tables, men's trousers, celebrities, shower curtains, refrigerators, Coke bottles—all the great modern things that the Abstract Expressionists tried so hard not to notice at all."

👁 **Watch** a video about the silkscreen process on **MyArtsLab**

a caricature of the actress. The face portrayed is not that of Norma Jeane (Monroe's real name) but of Monroe the celluloid sex symbol as made over by the movie industry. Warhol made multiple prints from this screen, aided by a host of assistants working with assembly-line efficiency. (In 1965, Warhol even—ironically—named his studio "The Factory," further mocking the commercial aspect of his art by suggesting he was only in it for the profit.) The diptych format recalls the conventions of religious art, perhaps suggesting that Marilyn was a martyr in the pantheon of departed movie stars. By symbolically treating the famous actress as a saint, Warhol shed light on his own fascination with fame.

Unlike Warhol and Lichtenstein, Swedish-born Claes Oldenburg (b. 1929) took a more critical, and also more humorous,

attitude toward consumer culture. Oldenburg's humor is evident in such large-scale public projects as his 1969 **LIPSTICK (ASCENDING) ON CATERPILLAR TRACKS** for his alma mater, Yale University (**FIG. 20–15**). The late 1960s were marked by student demonstrations against the Vietnam War. By mounting a giant lipstick tube on tracks from a Caterpillar tractor, Oldenburg suggested a missile rising from a tank and simultaneously subverted the warlike reference by casting the missile in the eroticized form of a feminine cosmetic with blatant phallic associations. Oldenburg thus urged his audience, in the vocabulary of the time, to "make love, not war." The university, offended by the work's irreverent humor, made Oldenburg remove it. In 1974, he reworked the sculpture in fiber-glass, aluminum, and steel and donated it to Yale, which this time accepted it.

Appropriation and the "Death of the Author"

During the late 1970s and 1980s, **appropriation** (the incorporation of a preexisting image into a new creation) became popular among American and European Postmodern artists. Artists borrowing figures or compositions, of course, has been standard practice throughout the history of art, but traditionally these borrowings had been adapted or personalized by the borrower. Straightforward reuse was not considered legitimate until Marcel Duchamp changed the rules with his readymades (SEE FIG. 19–16), insisting that the essence of an artwork was not inventive formal realization but underlying concepts or ideas. Duchamp's appropriations inspired Pop artists like Lichtenstein and Warhol (SEE FIGS. 20–13, 20–14) to reuse imagery from popular culture, high art, ordinary commerce, and even tabloids, and they, in turn, paved the way for the Postmodern artists who came after them.

Appropriation is grounded in the ideas of Post-Structuralist French literary criticism. In his essay "The Death of the Author" (1968), for example, Roland Barthes (1915–1980) argued that the meaning of a work of art depends not on its author's intent but on its reader's understanding. Barthes questioned the Modernist notion of originality, rooted in the idea of authors as individual creators of new meaning, proposing instead that authors recycle meanings from other sources.

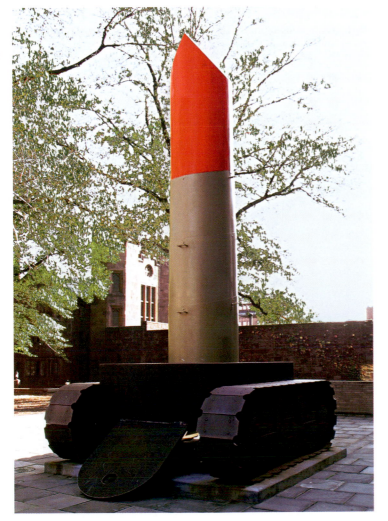

20–15 • Claes Oldenburg
LIPSTICK (ASCENDING) ON CATERPILLAR TRACKS
1969, reworked 1974. Cor-Ten steel, aluminum; coated with resin and painted with polyurethane enamel, 23′ 6″ × 24′ 10½″ × 10′ 11″ (7.16 × 7.58 × 3.33 m). Installed at Beinicke Plaza, Yale University, New Haven, Connecticut. Yale University Art Gallery. Gift of Colossal Keepsake Corporation. © 1969 Claes Oldenburg.

Minimalism and Process Art

In striking contrast to the emphasis on image-based content in Pop art, other styles that emerged in the wake of Abstract Expressionism focused on stripping all external references from artworks and reducing them to technical essentials. Sculptor Donald Judd (1928–1994) turned to a style known as Minimalism. Convinced that Abstract Expressionism had deteriorated into a set of techniques for faking both the subjective and the transcendent, around 1960 Judd began to search for an art free of falsehood. He decided that sculpture offered a better medium than painting for creating such matter-of-fact art. Rather than *depicting* shapes, which Judd thought smacked of illusionism and therefore fakery, he produced *actual* shapes. Seeking simplicity and clarity, he soon evolved a formal vocabulary reduced to identical rectangular units arranged in rows and constructed of industrial materials (**FIG. 20–16**). The objects are aggressively themselves, with neither a base below or a case around them. Judd provides the viewer with a set of clear, self-contained visual facts, setting the conceptual clarity and physical perfection of his art against the messy complexity of the real world.

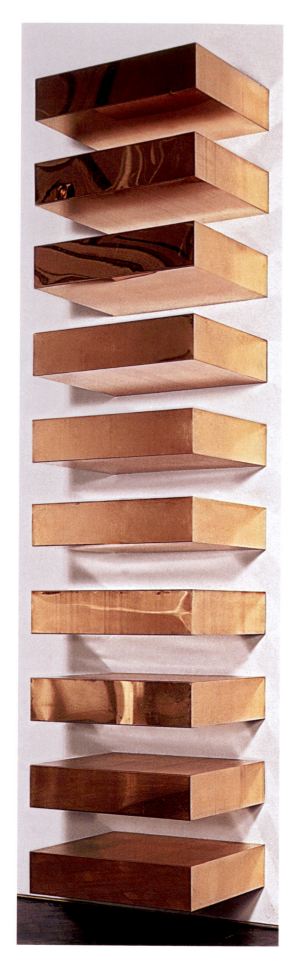

Although Judd passionately protested against the Vietnam War, he wanted his art to deal only with aesthetic issues, not personal convictions. Some artists disagreed. For Eva Hesse (1936–1970), personal history was a central influence in artistic creation. Born in Hamburg, Germany, to Jewish parents, Hesse narrowly escaped the Nazi Holocaust when her family emigrated to New York City in 1939. Initially painting darkly Expressionistic self-portraits that reflected the emotional turbulence of her life, in 1964 she turned to abstract sculpture and adapted the vocabulary of Minimalism to her own, more self-expressive purpose in what art historians have labeled Process Art. "For me…," said Hesse, "art and life are inseparable. If I can name the content…it's the total absurdity of life." The "absurdity" that Hesse pursued in her last works was the complete denial of fixed form and scale, so vital to Minimalists like Judd. Her **NO TITLE** (FIG. 20–17), for example, takes on a different shape and size each time it is installed. The work consists of several sections of rope, which Hesse and her assistant dipped in latex, knotted and tangled, and then hung from wires attached to the ceiling. The resulting linear web or "drawing in space" resembles a three-dimensional version of a dripped action painting by Jackson Pollock, and, like Pollock's work, it achieves a sense of structure despite its chaotic appearance. The Minimal art of Judd is tightly controlled by the artist, but Hesse allowed the natural force of gravity and the serendipity of installation a larger role.

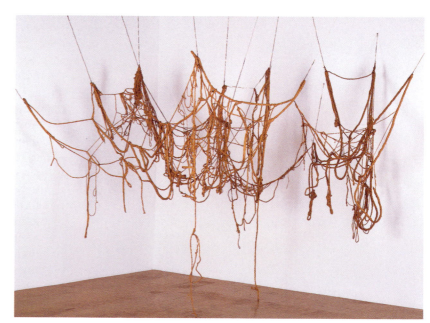

20–17 • Eva Hesse NO TITLE
1970. Latex, rope, string, wire, 96″ × 216″ × 36″ (175.3 × 548.6 × 91.4 cm) (variable).
Whitney Museum of American Art, New York, purchased with funds from Eli and Edythe L. Broad, the Mrs. Percy Uris Purchase Fund, and the Painting and Sculpture Committee, April 1988. © The Estate of Eva Hesse. Courtesy Hauser & Wirth.

📖 **Read** the document related to Eva Hesse on **MyArtsLab**

Conceptual and Performance Art

While Judd and Hesse seemed radical, at least they were making things. The artists who came to be known as Conceptualists pushed Minimalism and Process Art to their logical extreme, often by eliminating the art object itself. The ultimate root of Conceptual art is in Marcel Duchamp and his assertion that making art should be a mental, not a physical, activity.

The most prominent American Conceptual artist, Joseph Kosuth (b. 1945), abandoned painting in 1965 to examine the intersection of language and vision, the abstract idea, and concrete imagery. His early work was indebted to Duchamp and the linguistic philosophy of Ludwig Wittgenstein (1889–1951). His work is about the imperfect possibilities of communication, either visual or verbal. In **ONE AND THREE CHAIRS** (FIG. 20–18) there is an actual chair, a photograph of a chair, and a dictionary definition of "chair"—that is an object, an imperfect visual representation or idea of the object, and a verbal abstraction of the object. The title tells us that we can read this work as one chair represented three different ways or as three different chairs. Either way, Kosuth demonstrates the impossibility of precise representation and communication of an idea, leaving us to ponder the question: Which is the "real" chair?

Many Conceptual artists used their own bodies as a medium and engaged in activities or performances that they considered works of art. Some had fallen under the spell of composer and philosopher John Cage (1912–1992) during the 1950s. Cage incorporated everyday experience and pure

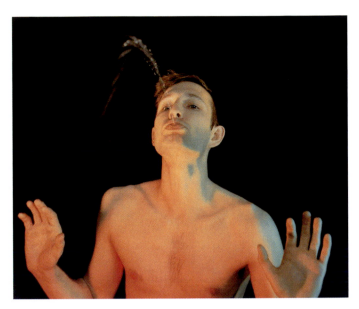

20–19 • Bruce Nauman **SELF-PORTRAIT AS A FOUNTAIN**
1966–1967. Color photograph, 19¾″ × 23¾″ (50.1 × 60.3 cm).
Courtesy Leo Castelli Gallery, New York.

chance in his musical compositions. He advocated the unity of the arts—including theater, music, and dance as well as the visual arts. Under Cage's influence, Allan Kaprow (1927–2006) gave up painting for loosely scripted, multimedia **Happenings**. Meanwhile in Japan, the Gutai group of artists produced dramatic displays they called **Performance Art**. In *Hurling Colors* of 1956, they smashed bottles of paint on a canvas laid on the floor. In Paris, Yves Klein (1928–1962)—who after 1957 worked only in blue, which he considered the most spiritual color—produced *Anthropometries of the Blue Period* in 1960. He covered three nude female models with blue paint and directed them to press their bodies against large sheets of paper covering the floor. Klein's *Monotone Symphony*—20 minutes of single notes followed by 20 minutes of silence—accompanied the performance. In part, this was a satire on the pretentiousness of Pollock's Action Painting (SEE FIG. 20–2). In contrast, Klein's work was created by a sensuous and diverting display, without even touching it himself. "I dislike artists who empty themselves into their paintings," he wrote. "They spit out every rotten complexity as if relieving themselves, putting the burden on their viewers."

From 1966 to 1967, the American artist Bruce Nauman (b. 1941) made a series of 11 color photographs based on word-play and visual puns. In **SELF-PORTRAIT AS A FOUNTAIN** (FIG. 20–19), for example, the bare-chested artist tips his head back, spurts water into the air, and, in the spirit of Duchamp, designates himself a work of art, even naming himself *Fountain*, the title of Duchamp's famous urinal (SEE FIG. 19–16). Nauman, like Kosuth, leaves us with the question: Which is the "real" fountain? Is it our abstracted idea of a fountain alluded to in the title (conceptual) or Nauman's claim to be a fountain (visual)? Could it be his sly reference to Duchamp's *Fountain* (art historical)?

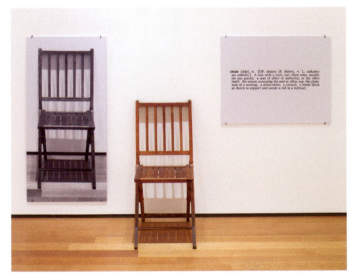

20–18 • Joseph Kosuth **ONE AND THREE CHAIRS**
1965. Wood folding chair, photograph of chair, and photographic enlargement of dictionary definition of chair; chair, 32⅜″ × 14⅞″ × 20⅞″ (82.2 × 37.8 × 53 cm); photo panel 36″ × 24⅛″ (91.4 × 61.3 cm); text panel 24⅛″ × 24½″ (61.3 × 62.2 cm). The Museum of Modern Art, New York. Larry Aldrich Foundation (393.1970A-C).

Earthwork and Site-Specific Art

Conceptual and Performance artists seemed to have taken art to its limits, but most of their events happened in art galleries or museums. Some artists in the late 1960s and 1970s wondered if art could do without such traditional settings. Perhaps artists in the present—like some in the past (e.g., SEE FIGS. INTRO–1, 1–8, 15–18)—could take the earth itself as a medium and shape a site or do something on it. Sculptors began to work outdoors, using what they found at the site to fashion **earthworks**. They also experimented with a category of art called **site-specific sculpture**, designed for a specific outdoor location.

Robert Smithson (1938–1973) sought to illustrate what he called the "ongoing dialectic" in nature between the constructive forces that build and shape form and the destructive forces that destroy it. **SPIRAL JETTY (FIG. 20–20)**, a 1,500-foot stone and earth platform spiraling into the Great Salt Lake in Utah, reflects these ideas. To Smithson, the salty water and the algae of the lake suggested the primordial ocean where life began,

and the abandoned oil rigs dotting the lake shore brought to mind both prehistoric dinosaur skeletons and the abandoned remains of a vanished civilization. He used the spiral because it is an archetypal shape that appears throughout the natural world—from galaxies to seashells—and has been used in human art for millennia. Unlike Modernist squares and circles, it is a "dialectical" shape, one that opens and closes, curls and uncurls endlessly, suggesting to Smithson the perpetual "coming and going of things." He hoped that the algae living in the lake would turn the water into a display of ephemeral colors, and that eventually the action of the water would cause the earthwork to erode and disappear. It is now covered with crystallized salt and can be seen on Google Earth.

Surely the most visible site-specific sculptors were Christo and Jeanne-Claude. Christo Javacheff (b. 1935) emigrated from his native Bulgaria to Paris in 1958, where he met Jeanne-Claude de Guillebon (1935–2009), and in 1964, they immigrated to New York. Their artistic collaboration began in

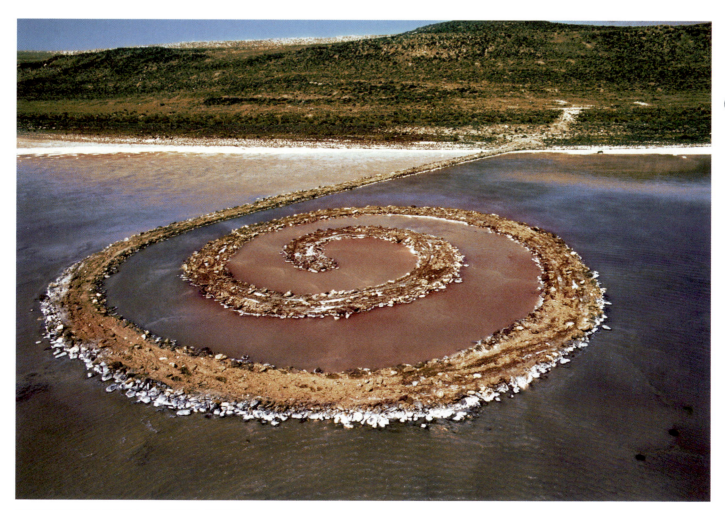

20–20 • Robert Smithson SPIRAL JETTY
1969–1970. Black rock, salt crystal, and earth spiral, length 1,500′ (457 m). Great Salt Lake, Utah.
© Estate of Robert Smithson / Licensed by VAGA, New York

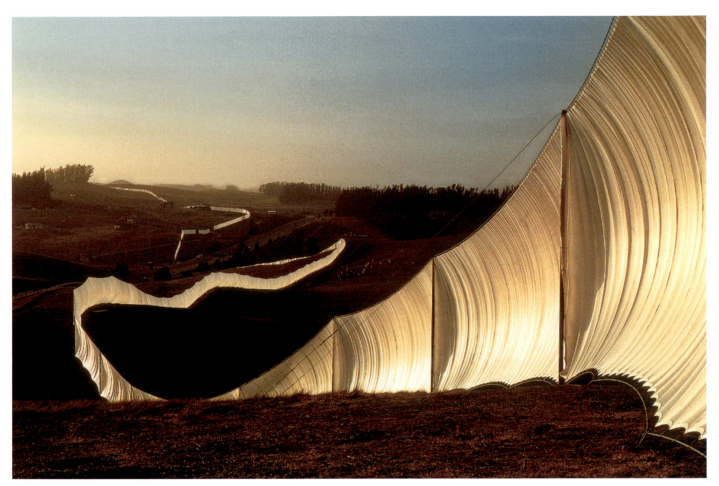

20–21 • Christo and Jeanne-Claude
RUNNING FENCE, SONOMA AND MARIN COUNTIES, CALIFORNIA, 1972–76
Nylon fence, height 18′ (5.5 m), length 24½ miles (40 km). Photo: Jeanne-Claude.

1961 with *Stacked Oil Barrels and Dockside Packages, Cologne Harbor, 1961*. One of their best-known works from the 1970s, **RUNNING FENCE, SONOMA AND MARIN COUNTIES, CALIFORNIA, 1972–76 (FIG. 20–21)** consisted of a 24½-mile-long, 18-foot-high nylon curtain that crossed two counties in northern California. The artists chose the location in Sonoma and Marin counties because they found it beautiful, as well as to call attention to the link between urban, suburban, rural spaces, and the ocean. At the same time, given the nature of their work, their conflict and collaboration with various social groups opened the workings of the political system to scrutiny, investing their work with a sense of social space. They spent 42 months overcoming the resistance of county commissioners, as well as local residents. To realize their massive projects, Christo and Jeanne-Claude usually rely on a diverse and devoted community of supporters and workers, including college students, ranchers, lawyers, and fellow artists. In a way this *Fence* broke down barriers that frequently separate social groups. The work remained in place for two weeks and then was taken down.

Feminist Art

The late 1960s and early 1970s also saw the rise of the feminist movement in the United States. Through Modernism, feminists challenged one of the major unacknowledged assumptions in the history of art—that great art was made by men—and discovered that women had contributed to most of the movements of Western art but were rarely even mentioned in accounts of its history. Feminists attacked the traditional Western hierarchy that valued the "fine arts"—easel- and wall painting, sculpture, and architecture—over "the crafts"—such as ceramics and textiles—and in the process relegated women's achievements to second-class status.

But the inequities were not restricted to art's past. In August 1970 (the fiftieth anniversary of the adoption of the Nineteenth Amendment to the Constitution, which guaranteed women the right to vote), women assessed their progress in various fields since 1920. They were disappointed by what they found. In the arts, women constituted about half the nation's practicing artists, but only 18 percent of commercial New York galleries carried any work by women. And of the 143 artists whose works were in the 1969 Whitney Annual (now Biennial)—one of the country's most important exhibitions of the work of living artists—only eight were women. Few women served as museum directors, and few achieved the rank of full professor in art history departments. To focus more attention on women in the arts, feminist artists began organizing women's cooperative galleries, while feminist art historians wrote about women artists. In 1971, Miriam Schapiro (b. 1923) and Judy Chicago (b. 1939) established the Feminist Art Program, dedicated to training women artists, at the California Institute of the Arts (CalArts).

Schapiro championed the theory that women have a distinct artistic sensibility that can be distinguished from that of men, and hence they have a specifically feminine aesthetic.

During the late 1950s and 1960s she made explicitly female versions of the dominant Modernist styles, including reductive, hard-edged abstractions of the female form: large X-shapes with openings at their centers. In 1973, she created **PERSONAL APPEARANCE #3** (FIG. 20–22), using underlying hard-edged rectangles and overlaying them with a collage of fabric and paper, materials associated with women's craftwork. She called her new technique *fem mage* (from *female* and *collage*), saying, "I dovetail my feminism with decoration" (cited in Gouma-Peterson, p. 29). The formal and emotional richness of her work were meant to counter the Minimalist aesthetic of the 1960s, which Schapiro and other feminists considered typically male.

Judy Chicago's work **THE DINNER PARTY** (FIG. 20–23) is perhaps the best-known work of feminist art from the 1970s.

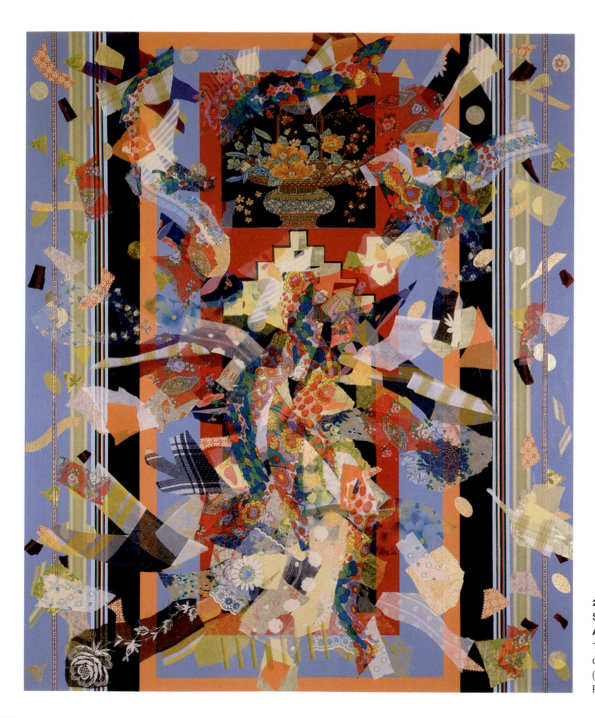

20–22 • Miriam Schapiro **PERSONAL APPEARANCE #3**
1973. Acrylic and fabric on canvas, 60″ × 50″ (152.4 × 127 cm). Private collection.

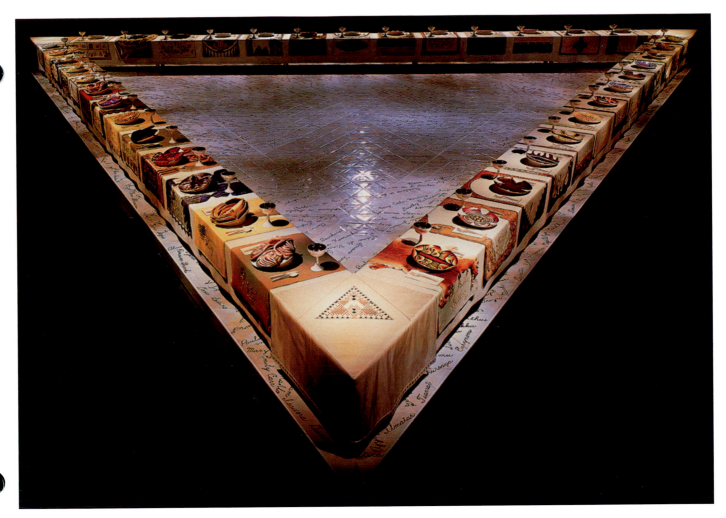

20–23 • Judy Chicago THE DINNER PARTY
Overall installation view. 1974–1979. White tile floor inscribed in gold with 999 women's names; triangular table
with painted porcelain, sculpted porcelain plates, and needlework. Mixed media, 48′ × 42′ × 3′ (14.6 × 12.8 × 1 m).
Collection of The Brooklyn Museum of Art. Gift of The Elizabeth A. Sackler Foundation Through the Flower, NM.

In 1970, she had adopted the surname Chicago (the city of her birth) to free herself from "all names imposed upon her through male social dominance." At CalArts, Chicago and Schapiro led a collective of 21 women students in the creation of *Womanhouse* (1971–1972), a collaborative art environment. From *Womanhouse* emerged *The Dinner Party* (1974–1979), a complex, mixed-media installation that fills an entire room with powerful proclamations of the accomplishments of women throughout history. Five years of collaborative effort went into the creation of the work, involving hundreds of women and several men who volunteered their talents as ceramists, needleworkers, and china painters to realize Chicago's designs.

The Dinner Party is composed of a large, triangular table, each side stretching 48 feet, which rests on a triangular platform covered with 2,300 triangular porcelain tiles. Chicago saw the equilateral triangle as a symbol of the equalized world sought by feminism and also identified it as one of the earliest symbols of the feminine. The porcelain "Heritage Floor" bears the names of 999 notable women from myth, legend, and history. Along each side of the table, 13 place settings each represent a famous woman. The 39 women thus honored include some that we

have encountered in this book, including the ancient Egyptian pharaoh Hatshepsut (SEE FIG. 3–12); the Renaissance art patron Isabella d'Este (SEE FIG. 13–18); and the painters Artemisia Gentileschi (SEE FIGS. INTRO–13, 14–13) and Georgia O'Keeffe (SEE FIGS. INTRO–4, 19–19). Chicago emphasized china painting and needlework in *The Dinner Party* to celebrate craft media traditionally practiced by women and to argue for their consideration as "high" art forms equivalent to easel-painting and sculpture. Most of the plates feature abstract designs based on female genitalia because, as Chicago said, "that is all [these women] had in common....They were from different periods, classes, ethnicities, geographies, experiences, but what kept them within the same confined historical space" was their biological sex.

In the early 1970s, African-American artist Faith Ringgold (b. 1930) began to paint on soft fabrics rather than stretched canvases and to frame her images with decorative quilted borders. In 1977, Ringgold began writing an autobiography, and, unable immediately to find a publisher, she decided to tell her story on quilts. Ringgold's story quilts are always narrated by women, and usually address themes related to women's lives.

A splendid example is **TAR BEACH** (FIG. 20–24) based on the artist's childhood memories of growing up in Harlem. The "Tar Beach" of the title is the roof of the apartment building where Ringgold's family slept on hot summer nights. The little girl, Cassie, describes sleeping on Tar Beach as a magical experience.

She dreams that she can fly and that she owns everything she passes over. Ringgold's colorful painting in the center of the quilt shows Cassie and her brother lying on a blanket at the lower right while their parents and two neighbors play cards at a table at center. Directly above the adults appears a second

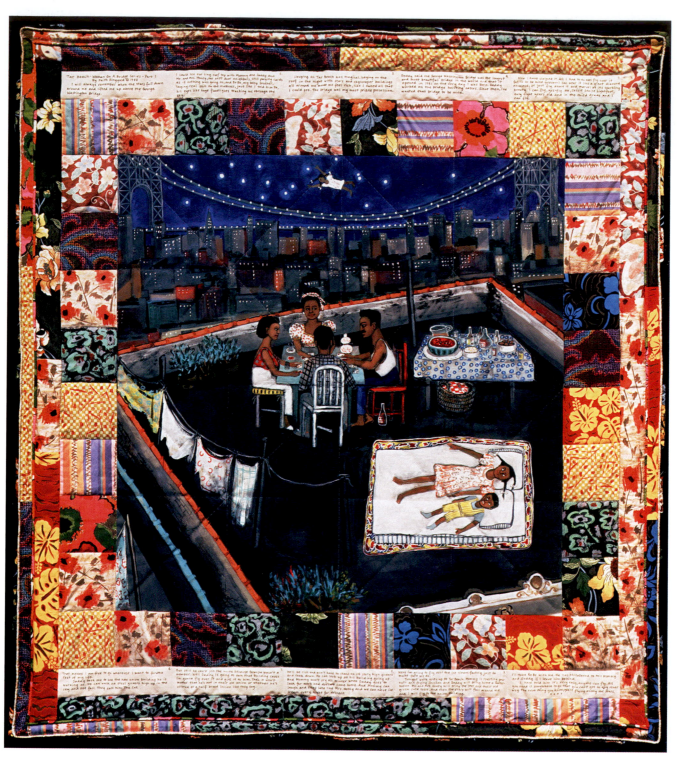

20–24 • Faith Ringgold TAR BEACH
Part I from the *Woman on a Bridge* series. 1988. Acrylic on canvas, bordered with printed, painted, quilted, and pieced cloth, 74⅝″ × 68½″ (190.5 × 174 cm). Solomon R. Guggenheim Museum, New York.
Photo © Faith Ringgold 1988.

View the Closer Look for Ringgold's *Tar Beach* on **MyArtsLab**

Modernist art and "low" popular culture, combining Cubist-style fragmentation, Fauvist color, Surrealist biomorphism, and the gestural brushstrokes of Abstract Expressionism, while also drawing inspiration from cartoons and animated films.

The influence of American and European Modernism spread around the world during the second half of the twentieth century. In Australia, for example, Aboriginal artists adopted canvas and acrylic paint for rendering traditional imagery once associated with more ephemeral media such as bark, sand, and body painting. In 1971, native experts in sand painting—an ancient ritual art form that involves creating large colored designs on the ground—formed an art cooperative in Papunya, in central Australia, and painting soon became an economic mainstay in the region. After a 1988 exhibition of his paintings, Clifford Possum Tjapaltjarri (c. 1932–2002), one of the cooperative's founders, gained an international reputation. Following the traditions of sand painting, he worked with his canvas on the floor, painting traditional patterns, principally in the traditional red and yellow colors. His work may at first seem nonrepresentational, but it tells stories rooted in complex myths, traditions, and social rules. Any formal resemblance to Modernist Western painting is accidental, but such stylistic similarities certainly contributed to the international interest in Possum Tjapaltjarri's art.

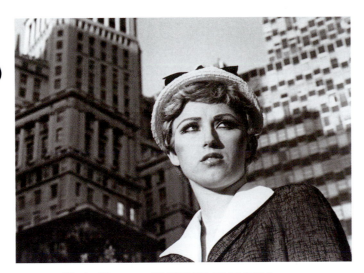

20–25 • Cindy Sherman **UNTITLED FILM STILL**
1978. Gelatin silver print, 8″ × 10″ (20.3 × 25.4 cm).
Courtesy of the artist and Metro Pictures, New York.

📖 **Read** the document related to Cindy Sherman
on **MyArtsLab**

Cassie, flying over the George Washington Bridge against a star-dotted sky. Cassie's childish fantasy of achieving the impossible is charming but also delivers a serious message by reminding viewers of the real social and economic limitations that African Americans have faced throughout American history.

In 1977, Cindy Sherman (b. 1954), began work on a series of black-and-white photographs of herself in various assumed roles, modeled on publicity stills from B-movies of the mid twentieth century to examine the roles that popular culture assigns to women. In one of these photographs, Sherman plays a small-town "girl" recently arrived in the big city, its buildings looming threateningly behind her (**FIG. 20–25**). The image suggests a host of films in which a similar character is overwhelmed by dangerous forces and is rescued by a hero. Critics have discussed these images as questioning the culturally constructed roles played by women in society, and as a critique of the male gaze. In these photographs, Sherman is both the photographer and the photographed. By assuming both roles, she complicates the relationship between the person looking and the person being looked at, and she subverts the way in which photographs of women communicate stereotypes.

Late Modernism and Postmodernism

How is Late Modernism distinct from the styles and subjects associated with Postmodernism?

By the 1970s, artists and critics alike were proclaiming the death of Modernism, but many artists remained committed to its central tenets: formal innovation and personal expression. Elizabeth Murray (1940–2007), was just such a late Modernist painter, whose artistic breakthrough came in the late 1970s, when she began to work on irregularly shaped canvases. **CHAOTIC LIP** (**FIG. 20–26**) is an enormous, organically shaped canvas with rounded lobes that radiate out in several directions. Murray's bold and colorful style is inspired simultaneously by "high"

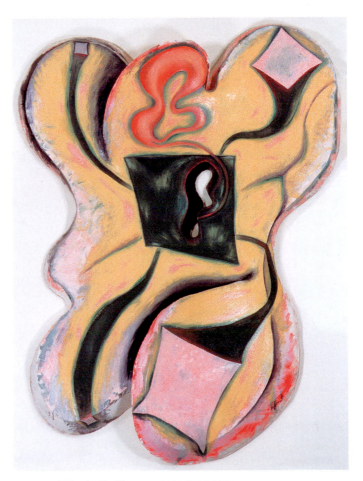

20–26 • Elizabeth Murray **CHAOTIC LIP**
1986. Oil on canvas, 9′ 9½″ × 7′ 2½″ × 1′ (3.01 × 2.22 × 0.31 m).
Spencer Museum of Art, The University of Kansas, Lawrence.

Man's Love Story ▶

Clifford Possum Tjapaltjarri. Papunya, Northern Territory, Australia, 1978.
Synthetic polymer paint on canvas, 6′ 11¾″ × 8′ 4¼″ (2.13 × 2.55 m). Art Gallery of South Australia, Adelaide. Visual Arts Board of the Australia Council Contemporary Art Purchase Grant, 1980.

As throughout the history of art, motifs in this painting have multiple meanings. The circle represents an ant hole here, but can also be a hole where the ancestral spirit beings exited and entered the earth, a person as viewed from above, or a campfire.

Honey ants are a sweet delicacy. A digging stick is used to open up the nest, exposing the ant colony for removal.

Hair is spun, using a spindle rotated across the thigh, to produce a surprisingly strong string, used for utilitarian and ceremonial purposes.

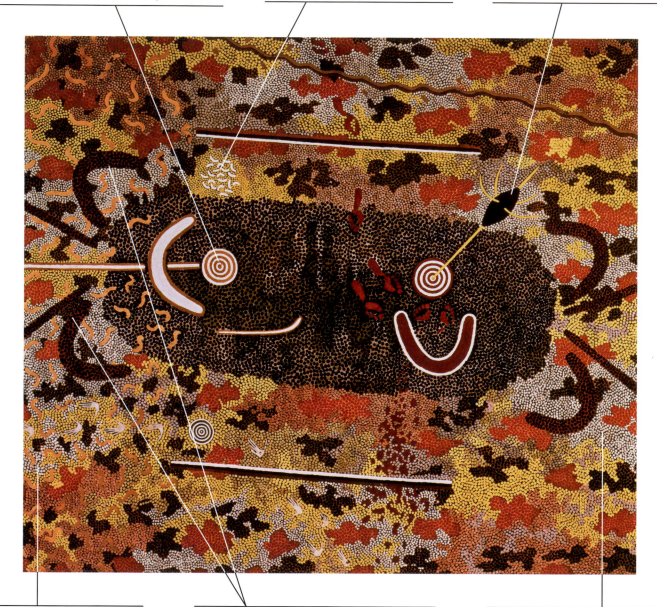

Synthetic polymer, or acrylic, paint replaces the earth-toned ochers used in the original sand paintings of this pictorial tradition.

Women are important figures in Australian mythic narratives, which are known as "Dreaming Stories," and are represented here in several places. Indigenous women paint their own stories, too, which usually center on food and food gathering.

The dots are made using a stick with a round, flat end that is dipped into the paint. Several people can work at the same time to fill in dotted areas.

🔎 **View** the Closer Look for Tjapaltjarri's *Man's Love Story* on **MyArtsLab**

Man's Love Story (see "A Closer Look," p. 574) involves two mythical ancestors. One came to Papunya in search of honey ants. He is the white U-shape on the left, seated in front of a water hole with an ants' nest, represented by concentric circles. His digging stick lies to his right. The straight white "journey line" represents his trek from the west. The second ancestor, represented by the brown-and-white U-shaped form, came from the north, leaving footprints, and sat down by another water hole nearby. He began to spin a string made of human hair on a spindle (the form leaning toward the upper right of the painting), but was distracted by thoughts of the woman he loved, who belonged to a kinship group into which he could not marry. When she approached, he let his hair string blow away (represented by the brown flecks below him) and lost all his work. Four women (the dark, dotted U-shapes) came at night, surrounding the camp to guard the lovers. What seems to be a richly decorative surface pattern is in fact a visual record of the ephemeral impressions left on the earth by the mythical figures—their tracks, direction lines, and the U-shaped marks they left when sitting.

Postmodernism

Artists inspired by the theories of art critics such as Greenberg (see "Clement Greenberg and the Idea of the Mainstream," p. 554), believed that art was a pure realm that belonged outside ordinary existence and that the history of art has followed a coherent, progressive trajectory culminating in Modernism. To the generation of artists and critics that grew to maturity around 1970, by contrast, concepts of artistic purity and notions of a unified mainstream development seemed naïve and misguided, even disingenuously arrogant. They accepted and fostered artistic **pluralism** (a simultaneous variety of artistic trends and styles) as a manifestation of their culturally heterogeneous age.

The decline of Modernism and rise of pluralism was neither uniform nor sudden. Its gradual erosion occurred over a long period and was the result of many individual transformations. The variety of approaches to art that emerged has been characterized by the umbrella term "Postmodernism."

Neo-Expressionism. Much contemporary art from around 1970 to the present implicitly acknowledges the exhaustion of the old Modernist promotion of innovation—and what it implied about the "progressive" development of art history—by reviving older styles. The names assigned to these Postmodern strategies often begin with the prefix "Neo," denoting a new form of something that already existed, a practice we have already encountered in the eighteenth century with "Neoclassicism." Neo-Expressionism was one of the first of these revival styles. German Neo-Expressionist Anselm Kiefer was born in 1945, during the last weeks of World War II, and his paintings revisit his country's Nazi past and the events of the war. The burned and barren landscape in **MÄRKISCHE HEIDE** (The Heath of the Brandenburg March) (FIG. 20–27) evokes the ravages of war experienced in the Brandenburg area, near Berlin. The road that lures us into the landscape—a standard device used since the seventeenth century—invites us into the region's dark past. Kiefer's works compel viewers to ponder troubling historical and social realities, "in order," he said, "to understand the madness."

In the United States, the tragically short-lived Jean-Michel Basquiat (1960–1988) painted Neo-Expressionist canvases that grew out of graffiti art. The Brooklyn-born Basquiat was raised in middle-class comfort but rebelled by quitting high school and leaving home to become a street artist. In 1980, Basquiat participated in the highly publicized "Times Square Show" which showcased the raw and aggressive styles of subway and

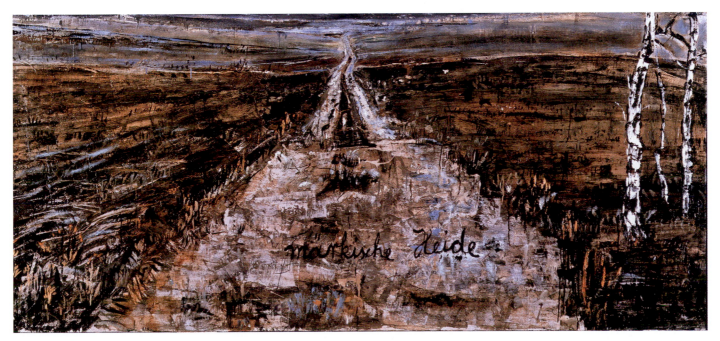

20–27 • Anselm Kiefer MÄRKISCHE HEIDE
1974. Oil, acrylic, and shellac on burlap, 3′ 10½″ × 8′ 4″ (1.18 × 2.54 m). Van Abbemuseum, Eindhoven, the Netherlands. © Anselm Kiefer.

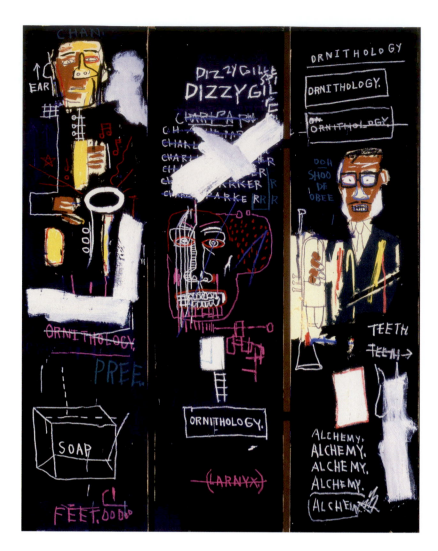

20-28 • Jean-Michel Basquiat HORN PLAYERS
1983. Acrylic and oil paintstick on canvas, three panels, overall 8′ × 6′ 5″ (2.44 × 1.91 m). Broad Art Foundation, Santa Monica, California.

graffiti artists. Basquiat said he wanted to make "paintings that look as if they were made by a child," but in reality his work is a sophisticated mix of appropriated imagery from Modern art combined with blunt references to race and the street. The strongly emotional **HORN PLAYERS (FIG. 20–28)** of 1983 portrays legendary jazz musicians Charlie Parker (upper left) and Dizzy Gillespie (center right), using urgent paint application and hurried lettering to convey Basquiat's dedication to jazz, as well as his passionate determination to foreground African-American subjects in an unsentimental way. He said: "Black people are never portrayed realistically, not even portrayed, in Modern art, and I'm glad to do that." Basquiat died from a heroin overdose at age 27.

Social Commentary and Moral Activism. As a major form of cultural communication, the visual arts have always been used to drive home ideas, and Postmodern artists often use their art to underline their own political and moral convictions. Roger Shimomura (b. 1939) turned painting and prints into personal political statements in a series based on his grandmother's diary. His 1978 painting *Diary* (SEE FIG. INTRO–12) visualizes his grandmother's account of the family's experience in an internment camp in Idaho, where U.S. citizens of Japanese ancestry were forcibly confined during World War II. Shimomura shows

his grandmother writing while he (the toddler) and his mother stand by an open door that reveals a barbed-wire-enclosed compound. Shimomura melded two formal traditions—the Japanese art of color woodblock prints (SEE FIGS. INTRO–7, 9–27, 9–28) and American Pop art—into a personal style that expresses his own dual heritage at the same time as it presents a nuanced social commentary.

Chicana artist Judith F. Baca (b. 1946) followed Postmodern revivalist tendencies when she emulated the style of the Mexican mural movement of the early twentieth century (SEE FIG. 19–40) to recount from a new perspective the history of California **(FIG. 20–29)**. The resulting **GREAT WALL OF LOS ANGELES**, begun in 1976, extends almost 2,500 feet along a flood drainage canal, making it the world's longest mural. Baca's history of California emphasizes the role of ethnic minorities, including the deportation of Mexican Americans during the Great Depression and the internment of Japanese-American citizens during World War II, but it concludes with more positive evocations of the opportunities gained during the 1960s. Like Judy Chicago's *Dinner Party* (SEE FIG. 20–23), Baca's *Great Wall of Los Angeles* was a collaborative effort, involving professional artists and hundreds of young people, all of whom shared its painted execution under the artist's direction.

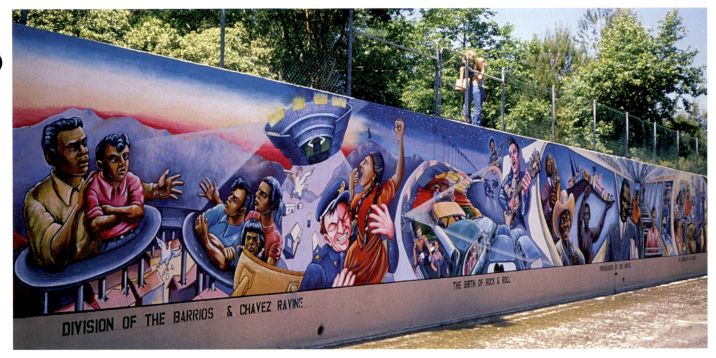

20-29 • Judith F. Baca THE DIVISION OF THE BARRIOS (DETAIL FROM THE GREAT WALL OF LOS ANGELES)
1976–1983 (section shown painted summer 1983). Acrylic on cast concrete, height 13′ (4 m), overall length of mural 2,500′ (762 m).
San Fernando Valley Tujunga Wash, Van Nuys, California. © SPARC www.sparcmurals.org.

The African-American painter Kerry James Marshall (b. 1955) updated the pre-Modern genre of history paintings for his Postmodern social commentary. In **MANY MANSIONS** (FIG. 20–30), he painted a visual essay on life in public housing projects, like those in Alabama and California where he grew up.

In the background we see the huge buildings of Stateway Gardens in Chicago, one of America's largest and worst maintained housing projects (demolished in 2007), and three well-dressed black men in the foreground plant a garden in order to help create a sense of community. They are arrayed in an off-center

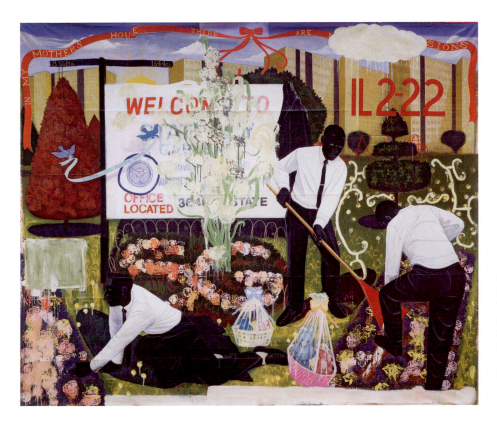

20-30 • Kerry James Marshall MANY MANSIONS
1994. Acrylic on paper mounted on canvas, 114¼″ × 135⅛″ (2.9 × 3.43 m). The Art Institute of Chicago. Max V. Kohnstamm Fund 1995.147.

⊙ **Watch** an Art21 video about Kerry James Marshall on **MyArtsLab**

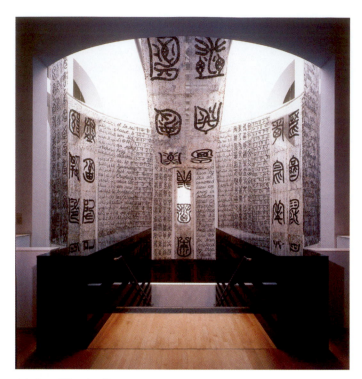

20–31 • Wenda Gu
UNITED NATIONS—BABEL OF THE MILLENNIUM
1999. Hair, glue, and rope, dimensions variable; height 75′ (22.9 m), diameter 34′ (10.4 m). San Francisco Museum of Modern Art. Gift of Viki and Kent Logan. © Wenda Gu.

triangle that Marshall based on Théodore Géricault's *Raft of the "Medusa"* (SEE FIG. 17–19). He told an interviewer from the PBS television network, "That whole genre of history painting, that grand narrative style of painting, was something that I really wanted to position my work in relation to." But overlying this weighty historical reference are touches of sentimentality, such as the red ribbon across the top with the adapted biblical quotation: "In my mother's house there are many mansions." Two bluebirds fly along at the left bearing another ribbon in their beaks. Such overtly cute features, juxtaposed with an impossibly florid garden, lend the work a strong sense of irony.

Shanghai-born Wenda Gu (b. 1955) has dedicated his art to bringing people together. He creates metaphors for the mixture of races that he predicts will eventually unite humanity into "a brave new racial identity." In 1993, he began his *United Nations* series, consisting of installations made of human hair pressed or woven into bricks, carpets, and curtains. Many of his "monuments," such as **UNITED NATIONS—BABEL OF THE MILLENNIUM (FIG. 20–31)**, incorporate invented scripts that, by frustrating viewers' ability to read them, "evoke the limitations of human knowledge" and help prepare them for entry into an "unknown world."

Identity, Race, and Ethnicity

Many Postmodern artists have explored their racial, ethnic, and gender identities in works of art that, like those we have just examined, aim to provoke social change. The photographs of Shigeyuki Kihara (b. 1975)—a multimedia and performance artist of Samoan and Japanese descent who lives in New

Zealand—challenge us to rethink our perceptions in relation to distorting stereotypes. She explores issues of culture, identity, stereotypes, authenticity, representation, and gender roles by appropriating nineteenth- and early twentieth-century colonial photographs that depicted Pacific Island men and women, both alone and in couples, as bare-breasted and sexualized "dusky maidens" and emasculated "noble savages." Kihara confronts these stereotypes in carefully restaged, sepia-toned photographs that directly challenge viewers' perceptions of gender and gender roles.

In **ULUGAL'I SAMOA: SAMOAN COUPLE (FIG. 20–32)** the photographed couple is clothed as they might have been in the nineteenth century, wearing large pieces of Samoan bark cloth, and holding traditional Samoan status objects. Kihara herself poses as the native woman, but has also superimposed her own face, with wig and mustache, onto the body of the male figure. This is one of a series of photographs entitled "*Fa'a fafine*: In a Manner of a Woman." *Fa'a fafine* is the Samoan word for a biological male who lives as a woman, the "third gender" socially accepted historically throughout much of Polynesia. Kihara is, herself, *fa'a fafine*, and in this photograph, like others in the series, she blurs notions of who or what is male or female, original or copy, reality or perception.

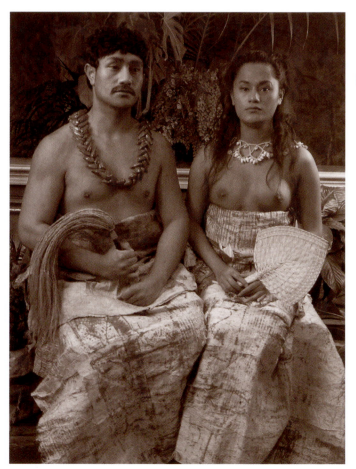

20–32 • Shigeyuki Kihara
ULUGAL'I SAMOA: SAMOAN COUPLE
2004–2005. C-type photograph, edition 5, 31½″ × 23⅜″ (80 × 60 cm). The Metropolitan Museum of Art, New York. Gift of Shigeyuki Kihara, 2009.

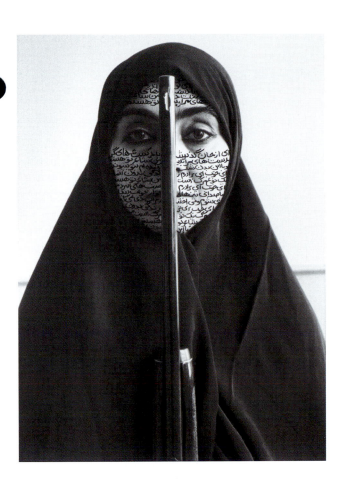

20–33 • Shirin Neshat **REBELLIOUS SILENCE**
1994. Black-and-white RC print and ink (photo taken by C. Preston), 11″ × 14″ (27.9 × 35.6 cm). © Shirin Neshat. Courtesy Gladstone Gallery.

Photography is the chosen medium for a similarly challenging commentary on identity in the work of Iranian artist Shirin Neshat (b. 1957). Exploring how Iranian women are stereotyped in the West, she asserts that Islamic women's identities are more varied and complex than is frequently perceived. In **REBELLIOUS SILENCE** (**FIG. 20–33**), from her 1994 *Women of Allah* series, the woman wears a traditional chador, but her face is visible, written over with calligraphy and bisected by a rifle barrel. The text and weapon seem to protect her from the viewer, but they also create a sense of incomprehensibility or foreignness that prompts us to try to categorize her. But the woman looks directly and defiantly out of the photograph at us, meeting our gaze and returning it. She challenges us to acknowledge her presence as an individual, but to do so, we have to look through, and beyond, the stereotype of an Iranian woman masked by a chador, Farsi text, and an instrument of war.

The art of Kara Walker (b. 1969) aims to hit raw nerves, to shock, at times to horrify. Walker cuts large-scale silhouettes of figures out of black construction paper, waxing them to the walls of galleries, and illuminating them with projected light. In **DARKYTOWN REBELLION** (**FIG. 20–34**), she shows a slave revolt and massacre in an unfolding tale of horror that belies the delicacy of its stylistic presentation. The room swirls with incongruously beautifully

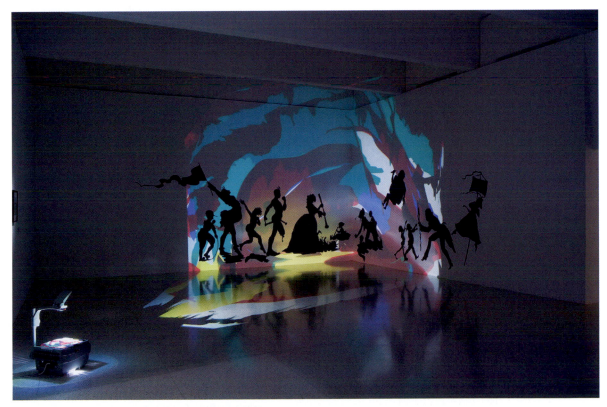

20–34 • Kara Walker **DARKYTOWN REBELLION**
2001. Cut paper and projection on wall, 14′ × 37′ (4.3 × 11.3 m) overall. Musée d'Art Moderne Grand-Duc Jean, Luxembourg. Artwork © 2001 Kara Walker, courtesy of Sikkema Jenkins & Co.

👁 **Watch** an Art21 video about Kara Walker on **MyArtsLab**

Controversies over Public Funding of the Arts

Should public money support art that some taxpayers believe to be offensive and indecent? This question ignited a political firestorm in 1989–1990 after controversial works of art by Robert Mapplethorpe (1946–1989) and Andres Serrano (b. 1950) went on public display in exhibitions funded in part by the National Endowment for the Arts (NEA), an agency of the U.S. government. The ensuing debate pitted artists and museums against political and religious leaders in what is now referred to as the "Culture Wars."

Serrano's 1989 work *Piss Christ*—a photograph of a plastic crucifix submerged in the artist's urine—was at the center of the debate. Serrano did not create this work with federal funding, but the museum that exhibited it had received NEA funds. The Reverend Donald Wildmon, leader of the American Family Association, described *Piss Christ* as "hate-filled, bigoted, anti-Christian, and obscene," and told his followers to flood Congress and the NEA with letters protesting the misuse of public funds. Several high-profile conservative Republican politicians swiftly joined his attack.

At the same time, a traveling retrospective of the work of photographer Mapplethorpe, who had recently died from AIDS, was canceled by the Corcoran Gallery of Art in Washington, D.C., for fear that the show's content might cause offense or threaten the museum's government funding. The exhibition was NEA-funded, and included several homoerotic and sadomasochistic images, including very provocative self-portraits of the artist. When it was shown in Cincinnati, the museum director was arrested, and Congress slashed NEA funding by $45,000, the amount of money that had supported the exhibitions of works by Serrano and Mapplethorpe. Additionally, in 1990 the NEA rescinded the grants awarded to four artists—Karen Finley, John Fleck, Holly Hughes, and Tim Miller—because they made lesbian, gay, or radical feminist art. The "NEA Four" sued and won back their grants in 1993, but a so-called "obscenity clause" was added to NEA regulations, requiring adherence to "general standards of decency and respect for the diverse beliefs and values of the American public" when granting awards. During the next five years, the NEA was largely restructured by the Republican-controlled House of Representatives, some of whose members wanted to eliminate the agency altogether, and in 1996, Congress cut its budget by 40 percent.

But controversies over public funding continued. In 1999, the Brooklyn Museum of Art exhibited "Sensation: Young British Artists from the Saatchi Collection," causing another major controversy over public funding and "offensive" art. Mayor Rudolph Giuliani threatened to eliminate city funding and evict the museum from its city-owned building if it persisted in showing art that he considered "sick" and "disgusting." Giuliani and Catholic leaders took particular offense at Chris Ofili's **THE HOLY VIRGIN MARY** (FIG. 20–35). When the Brooklyn Museum of Art refused to cancel the show, Giuliani withheld the city's monthly maintenance payment and filed a suit in the state court to revoke the museum's lease. In response, the museum filed and was granted an injunction against Giuliani's actions in federal court on the grounds that they violated the First Amendment. Guiliani had argued that Ofili's art fostered religious intolerance, but the court ruled that the government has "no legitimate interest in protecting any or all religions from views distasteful to them," adding that taxpayers "subsidize all manner of views with which they do not agree" and even those "they abhor."

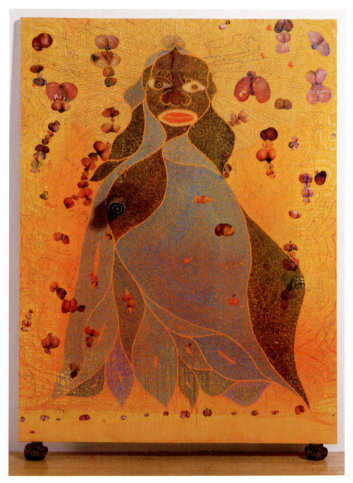

20–35 • Chris Ofili THE HOLY VIRGIN MARY
1996. Acrylic, oil paint, polyester resin, paper collage, glitter, map pins, and elephant dung on linen, 7′ 11″ × 5′ 11⁵⁄₁₆″ (2.44 × 1.83 m). Collection Museum of Old and New Art (MONA), Hobart, Australia.
© Chris Ofili.

white, black, pink, green, blue, and yellow projected lights and shadows that dance over the walls. As we walk around the space looking at the figures, we step in front of the projector, casting our own shadows on the walls and placing us uncomfortably close to, or actually within, the narrative itself. Walker blends fiction and fact to evoke a history of oppression and terrible violence. She contrasts the tight, cramped features of her white characters with the stereotypical black features of her African Americans. As silhouettes, all these figures are black; we cannot sort them racially by skin color. In order to read the narrative, we must look for other visual markers of race, making us draw upon an entire history of ugly stereotypes in the process. In this way Walker catches us in the act of being racist, making it clear that racism is neither theoretical nor a thing of the past. As Walker has said: "It's interesting that as soon as you start telling the story of racism you start reliving it." Kara Walker's art is not meant to be pleasant; it seeks to change us by altering our perception of the world in which we live.

Installation: Electronic and Video Art. The renewed realization of art's potential as an instrument of social change and the desire to make art meaningful to a larger and more diverse public took on a new prominence approaching the 1990s. Artists experimented with new media like video to connect with their media-saturated culture. Jenny Holzer (b. 1950) turned to some of advertising's more pervasive tools, including electronic signage, to reach out to people who do not usually go to galleries and museums. For example, using the Spectacolor board then in use in New York City's Times Square, she flashed a series of short, provocative messages—one-liners suited to the reading habits of Americans raised on advertising soundbites.

In a spectacular installation of 1989–1990, Holzer wrapped her signboards in a continuous loop around the multilevel spiraling interior of Frank Lloyd Wright's Guggenheim Museum (**FIG. 20–36**). The words moved and flashed in red, green, and yellow colored lights, challenging the visitor with unsettling declarations ("You are a victim of the rules you live by") and disturbing commands ("Scorn Hope," "Forget Truths," and "Don't Try to Make Me Feel Nice"). The installation also included, on the ground floor and in a side gallery, spotlighted granite benches carved with more of Holzer's texts. The juxtaposition of moving works as lights in motion with the static, hand-carved inscriptions on benches, evocative of antiquity and mortality, was particularly striking.

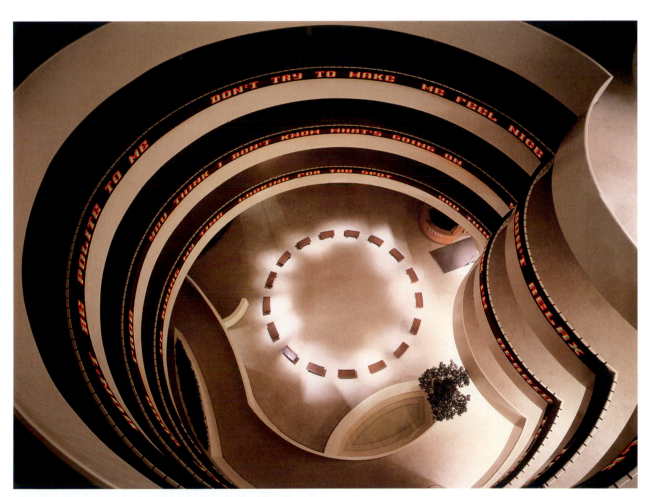

20–36 • Jenny Holzer UNTITLED (SELECTIONS FROM TRUISMS, INFLAMMATORY ESSAYS, THE LIVING SERIES, THE SURVIVAL SERIES, UNDER A ROCK, LAMENTS, AND MOTHER AND CHILD TEXT)
Installation within the Guggenheim Museum, 1989. Extended helical tricolor LED electronic-display signboard; site-specific dimensions, 16½″ × 162′ × 6″ (41.9 × 4,900 × 15.2 cm). Solomon R. Guggenheim Museum, New York (89.326). Partial gift of the artist, 1989.

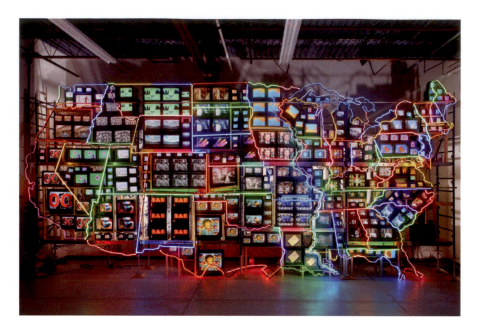

A number of contemporary artists create installations with video, either using the video monitor itself as a visible part of their work or projecting video imagery onto walls, screens, or other surfaces. Korean-born Nam June Paik (1931–2006) was a pioneer in this medium. He proclaimed that just "as collage technique replaced oil paint, the cathode ray [television] tube will replace the canvas." He began working with modified television sets in 1963 and bought his first video camera in 1965. Paik worked with live, recorded, and computer-generated images displayed on video monitors of varying sizes, which

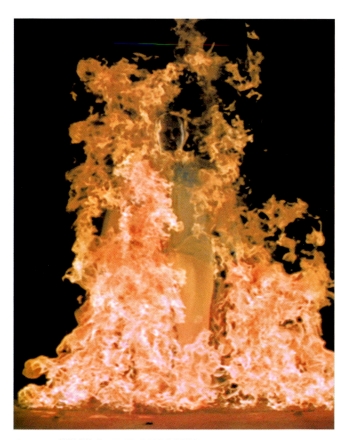

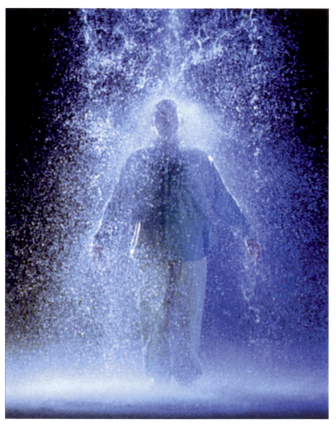

20–38 • Bill Viola **THE CROSSING**
1996. Two channels of color video projections from opposite sides of a large, dark gallery onto two back to back screens suspended from the ceiling and mounted on the floor; four channels of amplified stereo sound; four speakers; height 16′ (4.88 m). Private collection.

he often combined into ensembles such as **ELECTRONIC SUPERHIGHWAY: CONTINENTAL U.S.** (FIG. 20–37), a site-specific sculpture created for the Holly Soloman Gallery in New York. It featured a neon-outlined map of the continental United States (Alaska and Hawaii on side walls) set against a wall of video monitors displaying rapidly changing, soundtracked images reflecting each state's culture and history. New York State was the only exception. There monitors displayed live, closed-circuit images of the gallery visitors, placing them in the artwork and transforming them from passive spectators into active participants.

In 1996, the California video artist Bill Viola (b. 1951) created **THE CROSSING** (FIG. 20–38)—a double projection of two brilliantly colored videos on opposite sides of a tall screen. On one side, a man is seen slowly walking toward the camera from a great distance and stops close to the camera. A drop of water falls on his head. The drops increase, building to a deluge that washes him away. On the reverse screen, a similar scenario unfolds, except that this time tiny flames lick at his feet, eventually growing into a wild conflagration that finally engulfs him as the sound of the fire grows in intensity. But Viola is interested in the way vision informs perception; there is in fact only one sound track—we simply perceive it differently according to which image we are watching. Viola's video is not only sensory, but meditative; its elemental symbolism is informed by Viola's spirituality and intense study of world religions.

New Ideas in Traditional Materials. Only since the Renaissance has there been a strict distinction between the so-called "high" or "fine" arts—architecture, sculpture, painting, prints, and, more recently, photography—and the so-called "minor" or "decorative" arts such as ceramics, textiles, glass, metalwork, furniture, and jewelry, which some see compromised by a practical or an ornamental function. In the postwar decades of the twentieth century, however, a number of artists took up an initiative begun during the nineteenth-century Arts and Crafts Movement (SEE FIG. 18–8) to push the so-called "crafts" toward acceptance as "high" art. Ceramics, wood, and glass became media for the production of sculpture.

A major innovator in clay was the Montana-born Peter Voulkos (1924–2002), who came under the influence of De Kooning and other gestural painters in 1953. The radical American break from European and Asian traditions, sometimes called the "Clay Revolution," began with the ruggedly sculptural ceramic works Voulkos produced in the mid-1950s. By the late 1950s Voulkos had abandoned the pot form altogether and was making large ceramic works spontaneously assembled from numerous wheel-thrown and slab-built elements, their surfaces often covered with bright, freely applied glazes or epoxy paint. In the early 1960s, Voulkos returned to traditional ceramic forms but rendered them nonfunctional by tearing, gouging, and piercing them in the gestural fashion derived from Abstract Expressionism (FIG. 20–39).

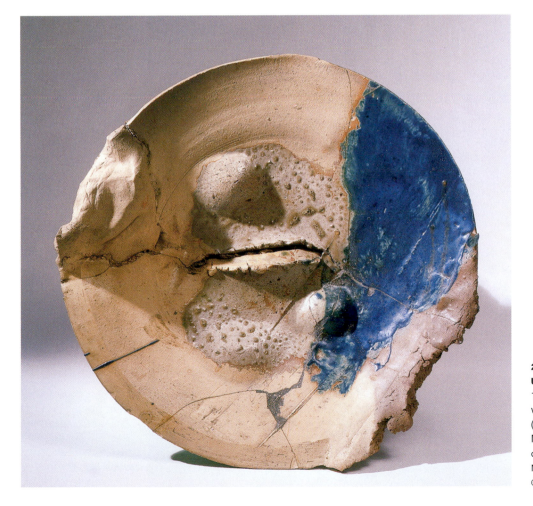

20–39 • Peter Voulkos
UNTITLED PLATE
1962. Gas-fired stoneware with glaze, diameter 16¼″ (41.3 cm). The Oakland Museum of California. Gift of the Art Guild of The Oakland Museum Association (62.87.4). © The Voulkos Family Trust.

A comparable revolution in using glass as a "high" art medium was initiated by Harvey Littleton (1922–2013), who in 1963 established America's first studio program in glass at the University of Wisconsin. Other glass programs soon sprang up around the country, many of them led by Littleton's former students, including Dale Chihuly (b. 1941) who established the famous Pilchuck Glass School in Seattle in 1971. Chihuly has become well known for glass sculptures that draw on the natural forms of plants and sea life, some small enough to hold in the hand, but others covering entire ceilings or standing in the open landscape, large as trees. THE SUN (FIG. 20–40) is a multi-part blown-glass sculpture, showcasing the artist's virtuosity in glassmaking. Created for installation in the Desert Botanical Garden in Phoenix, the work bursts forth in a multitude of twisting, wriggling, spiraling forms. Brilliantly liquid, visually thrilling, and broadly accessible, Chihuly's technologically innovative sculptures suggest a deep connection with nature, inviting contemplation, meditation, and an awareness of global environmentalism.

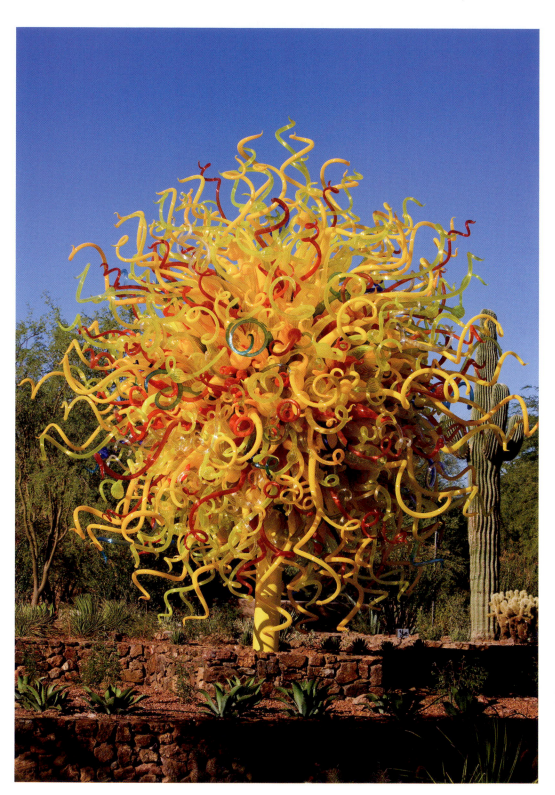

20–40 • Dale Chihuly
THE SUN
Desert Botanical Garden, Phoenix, Arizona. 2008. Installed November 22, 2008–May 31, 2009. Diameter 14′ (4.26 m).

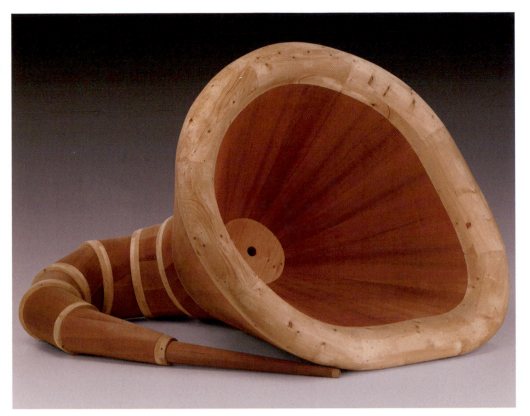

As with ceramics and glass, artists' use of traditional woodworking techniques also broke down barriers between decorative and fine arts. Martin Puryear (b. 1941) is a contemporary sculptor whose medium happens to be wood. Perhaps it was an early interest in biology that shaped Puryear's mature aesthetic, but his skills as a wood sculptor were certainly shaped by his experiences working with local carpenters as a Peace Corps volunteer in Sierra Leone and subsequently with cabinet makers in Sweden. His **PLENTY'S BOAST (FIG. 20–41)**, while hardly representational, suggests any number of things, including a strange sea creature or a fantastic musical instrument. Perhaps the most obvious reference is to the horn of plenty evoked in the sculpture's title. But the cone is empty, implying an "empty boast"—another phrase suggested by the title. The richness of the sculpture lies not only in its multiple metaphorical references (a common Postmodern trait), but also in its superbly crafted, idiosyncratic yet elegant form. As if clinging to his relationship to early twentieth-century Modernism, Puryear has said, "The task of any artist is to discover his own individuality at its deepest."

Japanese-born artist Hiroyuki Hamada (b. 1968), who moved to the United States when he was 18, also creates highly individualized and powerfully elegant abstract forms. But his chosen medium is more complicated, and his fastidiously textured surfaces more intricate. Over a substructure of wood and foam, he applies a layer of plaster, which he refines and finishes over several years. In **#55 (FIG. 20–42)**, Hamada used drill bits to give the upper half of the form an intricately patterned surface, before staining it with resin and tar to add a complementary contrast in color. There is an archetypal quality to his

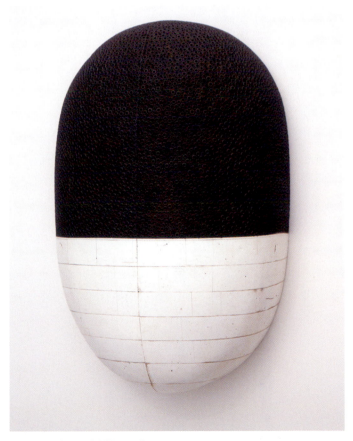

20-42 • Hiroyuki Hamada #55
2005–2008. Enamel, oil, plaster, tar, and resin, over a wood and foam core, 44″ × 24″ × 12½″ (112 × 61 × 32 cm). Collection of Bodo Vincent Andrin.

elemental sculptural forms. They seem strange but at the same time hauntingly familiar, remaining open to a variety of viewer associations. Is this a fragment of a spacecraft, an ancient cocoon, an exotic fruit, or a barnacled buoy? Hamada prefers to leave the question of meaning open, naming his sculptures after their numerical position within a creative sequence. "A title would tell people how to interpret the work," he has said, "and I don't want that."

Postwar Architecture and Public Memorials

What were some new developments in architecture and public memorials during the late twentieth and early twenty-first centuries?

The stripped-down, rectilinear, industrial vocabulary pioneered by such Modernist architects as Gropius (SEE FIG. 19–26) and

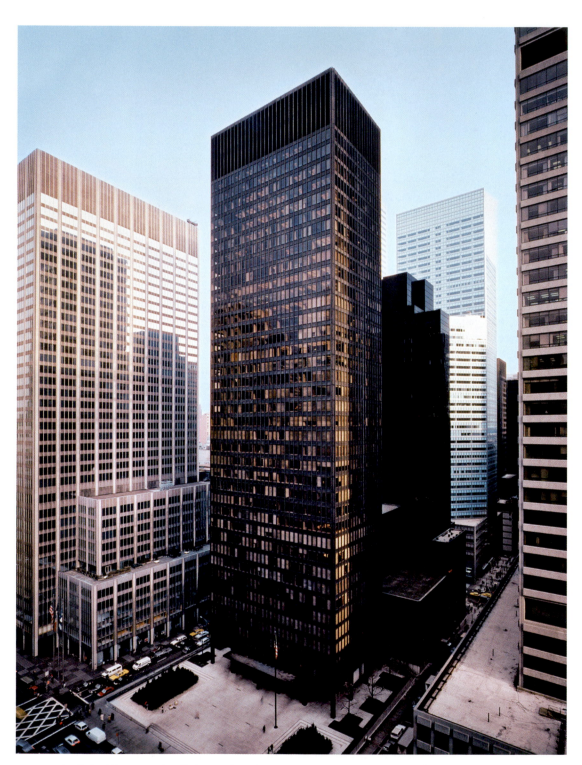

20–43 • Ludwig Mies van der Rohe and Philip Johnson **SEAGRAM BUILDING**
New York. 1954–1958.

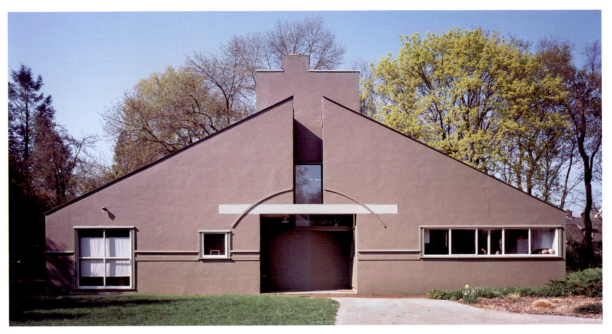

20–44 • Robert Venturi VANNA VENTURI HOUSE
Chestnut Hill, Philadelphia, Pennsylvania. 1961–1964.

Le Corbusier (SEE FIG. 19–24) and known as the International Style dominated urban construction in much of the world after World War II (see "The International Style," p. 532). Many of the finest examples were built in the United States by Bauhaus architects—including Ludwig Mies van der Rohe (1886–1969)—who escaped Nazi Germany and assumed prestigious positions at American schools of architecture and design.

Whether designing housing, schools, or office buildings, Mies used the same sleek, rectilinear system that came to signify the efficient culture of postwar capitalism. His buildings differ only in details. Because he had a large budget for the **SEAGRAM BUILDING** in New York City (**FIG. 20–43**), which he designed with Philip Johnson (1906–2005), he used custom-made bronze instead of standardized steel on the exterior. Mies would have preferred to leave the internal steel structure visible, but building codes required him to encase them in concrete, so the exterior bronze beams are only ornamental stand-ins for the functional girders inside. Tall, narrow windows with discreet dark glass emphasize the skyscraper's height and give it—and the Seagram Company that commissioned it—a discreet and dignified image. The straight lines and clean design seemed to embody the qualities of efficiency and practicality that postwar business was eager to project, and this is perhaps one of the reasons this particular Modernist style dominated corporate architecture after World War II.

Postmodernism manifested itself first in the work of Philadelphia architect Robert Venturi (b. 1925), who rejected the abstract purity of the International Style by incorporating design elements drawn from vernacular (meaning ordinary or popular) buildings. Parodying Mies's famous aphorism "Less is more," Venturi claimed that "Less is a bore" in his pioneering 1966 book *Complexity and Contradiction in Architecture.*

He argued that the problem with International Style architects was their impractical unwillingness to accept the modern city for what it is: a complex, contradictory, and heterogeneous collection of "high" and "low" architectural forms. Taking these ideas further in the book *Learning from Las Vegas* (1972), he suggested that rather than turning their backs in disdain on ordinary commercial buildings, architects should get in "the habit of looking nonjudgmentally" at them. "Main Street is almost all right," Venturi observed.

While writing *Complexity and Contradiction in Architecture*, Venturi designed a house for his mother (**FIG. 20–44** and plan on p. xvii) that put many of his new ideas into practice. The shape of the façade returns to the archetypal "house" shape that Modernists (SEE FIGS. 19–22, 19–24) had rejected because of its clichéd historical associations. Venturi's vocabulary of triangles and squares is arranged in a playful asymmetry that skews the staid harmonies of Modernist design, while the rounded moldings over the door are a purely decorative flourish—heretical in the strict tenets of the International Style. But the most disruptive element of the façade is the deep cleavage over the door, which opens to reveal a mysterious upper wall and chimney top. The interior is equally complex and contradictory.

Another reaction to mid-century Modernism in architecture is known as High Tech, characterized by the expressive use of exposed building materials, technology, equipment, and components. Among the most spectacular examples is the **HONG KONG & SHANGHAI BANK** (**FIG. 20–45**) by English architect Norman Foster (b. 1935). Invited by his client to design the most beautiful bank in the world, Foster spared no expense in the creation of this futuristic 47-story skyscraper. The rectangular plan features service towers at the east and west ends, eliminating the central service core typical of International

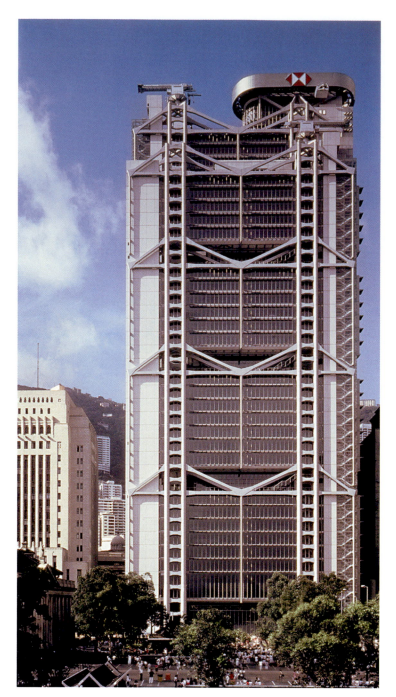

20–45 • Norman Foster
HONG KONG &
SHANGHAI BANK
Hong Kong. 1979–1986.
Foster + Partners. Photo: Ian Lambot.

👁 **Watch** an architectural
simulation about the steel
skeleton of the Hong Kong
& Shanghai Bank on
MyArtsLab

Style skyscrapers. The load-bearing steel skeleton, composed of giant masts and girders, is on the exterior. The individual stories hang from this structure, allowing for uninterrupted façades and open working areas filled with natural light.

More recently, a tendency to disturb even further traditional architectural values of harmony, unity, and stability by using skewed, distorted, and dynamic geometry has been labeled Deconstructivist architecture because of its perceived relationship with the theories of French philosopher Jacques Derrida (see "Appropriation and the 'Death of the Author,'" p. 565). The Toronto-born, California-based architect Frank Gehry (b. 1929) is one of the best-known proponents. In the 1990s, Gehry developed a powerfully organic, sculptural style,

exemplified in his dramatic **GUGGENHEIM MUSEUM** in the Basque city of Bilbao, Spain (**FIG. 20–46**), where he reconciled the client's needs for a museum and civic monument with his own interest in sculptural form. Gehry covered the building's complex steel skeleton with a thin skin of silvery titanium that shimmers gold or silver depending on the light. Seen from the north, the building resembles a giant ship, a reference to the shipbuilding and port facilities so important to the economy of Bilbao. This building initiated a trend of adventurous designs for art museums—such as the jagged projections of Daniel Libeskind's 2006 museum extension in Denver—that continues today. "Artists want to be in great buildings," Gehry claimed.

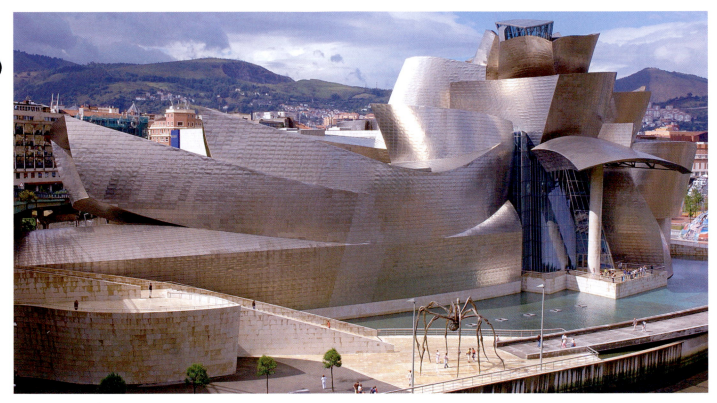

20–46 • Frank Gehry GUGGENHEIM MUSEUM
Bilbao, Spain. 1993–1997. Sculpture of a spider in the foreground: Louise Bourgeois (1911–2010), *Maman*, 1999.

Public Memory

Public memorials often engage our intellect, reminding us of important events in history, claiming their enduring significance. But they can also appeal to our emotions, inspiring personal responses as well as encapsulating a collective consciousness. In recent years, art designed for public spaces—rather than for museum walls or private collectors—has provoked sensational controversies surrounding public funding, censorship, and individual rights.

The Vietnam Veterans' Memorial (SEE FIG. 20–1), now widely admired as a fitting and moving testament to the Americans lost in that conflict, was originally a lightning rod for contention. The request for design proposals for this monument stipulated that it be without political or military content, that it be reflective in character, that it harmonize with its surroundings, and that it include the names of the more than 58,000 dead and missing. In 1981, the Vietnam Veterans' Memorial Fund awarded the commission to Maya Ying Lin, then an undergraduate in the architecture department at Yale University. Her Minimalist-inspired design called for two 200-foot-long walls (later expanded to almost 250 feet), sunk into rising ground. The names of the dead were to be incised into the walls in the order in which they died.

It seems somehow fitting that the Cold War ended in 1980, just before this memorial was erected. Soviet leader Mikhail Gorbachev's economic and political reforms, known as "*glasnost*," ultimately led to the dissolution of the Soviet Union, giving rise to a cluster of independent republics that turned to capitalism, many instituting democratic reforms on social, economic, and political levels. Global capitalism increased the economic interdependence among nations, and wealthy countries like the United States saw increasing prosperity. Thanks to remarkable advances in transportation and communication, including the Internet, the world has begun to seem smaller. And with enhanced global communication has come increased awareness of the grave problems that confront human beings in the twenty-first century. The devastating terrorist attacks on the United States at the World Trade Center in New York and the Pentagon in Washington, D.C., on September 11, 2001, only escalated tension around the globe.

Soon after the World Trade Center was destroyed, artists, architects, government officials, and ordinary citizens sought to create a meaningful testament that would serve as a global statement against the horrors of terrorism. Conceived and executed during the Cold War, the Modernist World Trade Center reflected the United States' self-confidence as a global power. The Twin Towers stood 110 stories tall, dominating the Manhattan skyline. Their sheer size left all in awe of this major engineering accomplishment.

Most felt the World Trade Center site had to be rebuilt: as a memorial, as a symbol, and as a functional group of buildings. In February 2003, the Polish-born American architect Daniel Libeskind (b. 1946) won an international competition to design the site. Libeskind's plans are centered around a sunken

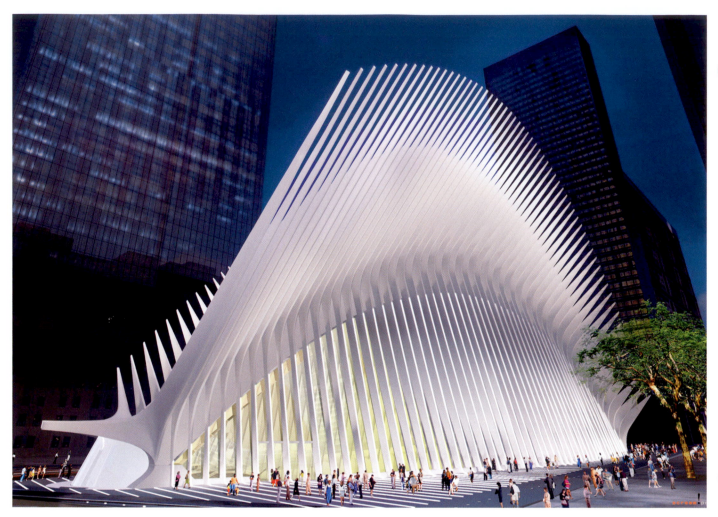

20–47 • Santiago Calatrava **THE WORLD TRADE CENTER, TRANSPORTATION HUB, NEW YORK**
2006–2009. Digital three-dimensional model.

field incorporating the foundations of the destroyed towers and the concrete slurry wall that prevented the Hudson River from flooding the site—Libeskind's metaphor of tenacity and survival. This area also includes a memorial to the more than 2,500 people who died there. A skyscraper soaring to the patriotic height of 1,776 feet would contain gardens which Libeskind calls "a constant affirmation of life." Libeskind sees the tower rising triumphant from the disaster of September 11 as "an affirmation of vitality in the face of danger, an affirmation of life in the aftermath of tragedy."

As part of the World Trade Center site, Spanish architect Santiago Calatrava (b. 1951) designed a subway and train station (**FIG. 20–47**). The steel-and-glass terminal would comfortably handle 80,000 travelers a day. Calatrava has conceived a light, airy structure. Hinged wings of a retractable roof were originally intended to open each year on the anniversary of the attack, and Calatrava carefully positioned the terminal on the site to coordinate with the place of the sun at the time of the tragedy. This image of hope—Calatrava has described it as the hands of a child releasing a bird—built on the site of unfathomable loss charts new domains for communal commemorations in the twenty-first century. It continues the fundamental quest of artists throughout history to extend the boundaries of human perception, feeling, and thought in ways that express our deepest hopes and give form to our most powerful dreams.

LOOKING BACK ◄

During the 1950s, Modernist artists made assault after assault on traditions that dated back to the Renaissance. As in the earlier twentieth century, movements followed each other in quick succession, each claiming to be more radical than the last. Abstract Expressionists eliminated representation and narrative. Minimal artists eliminated personal feeling and social reference. Conceptual artists eliminated the art object itself. Performance artists refused to produce anything permanent. Feminists assaulted the unspoken tradition of male dominance.

By the 1970s there seemed to be no traditional rules of art left to break, and the avant-garde all but ceased to exist as a group separate from society at large. Postmodern artists ceased focusing on formal innovation and began looking both inside—exploring ethnic and racial identities—and outside—reflecting on the state of their larger world. Both foci opened new possibilities for interaction with their audiences and with the history of art. As we, as members of those audiences, become increasingly aware of the art of the past, we will enrich our own ability to appreciate the as-yet-unimagined varieties of creativity that await us in the future.

THINK ABOUT IT

20.1 Discuss the goals and interests of the painters associated with Abstract Expressionism. What role did Surrealism and other earlier twentieth-century art movements play in the formation of this postwar movement?

20.2 Explain the emergence of Pop art in the 1950s and 1960s. How and why did Pop react to Abstract Expressionism? Who were the major figures in the movement?

20.3 Analyze how contemporary American artists have used their art to address social and political issues surrounding race.

20.4 Discuss the major characteristics that separate Postmodern architecture from the Modernism of the International Style.

| CROSSCURRENTS |

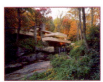 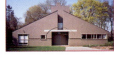

FIG. 19–44   FIG. 20–44

Distinguished modern architects have designed private homes as well as large commercial, religious, or public buildings. Discuss the circumstances that led to the creation of these two famous modern houses. How do these works fit into the career of their architects and engage with the larger concerns of architectural design at the moment when they were built? How is their physical context related to their design?

☑ **Study** and **Review** on **MyArtsLab**

IN PERSPECTIVE

1940

World War II Ends 1945

Britain Withdraws from India 1947
Israel Declares Independence 1948
People's Republic of China Established 1949

1950

Korean War 1950–1953

Civil Rights Movement Begins in United States 1954
U.S. Military Aid to South Vietnam Begins 1955
U.S.S.R. Launches First Satellite, Sputnik I 1957

BURCKHARDT, Jackson Pollock Painting 1950

1960

Soviet Yuri Gagarin Is the First Human in Space 1961
President John F. Kennedy Assassinated 1963
Escalation of U.S. Military Involvement in Vietnam 1965
Martin Luther King, Jr., Assassinated 1968
Apollo 11 Lands First Humans on the Moon 1969

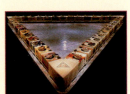

CHICAGO, The Dinner Party 1974–1979

1970

Stephen Hawking Proposes Black Hole Theory 1974
End of U.S. Military Involvement in Vietnam 1975

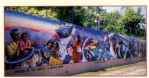

BACA, Great Wall of Los Angeles Begun 1976

1980

Tiananmen Square Protests in China 1989
U.S.S.R. Dissolved/Nelson Mandela Released from Prison, Signaling the End of Apartheid in South Africa/ Germany Reunited 1990
Advent of World Wide Web early 1990s

VIOLA, The Crossing 1996

1990

First Cloned Mammal, Dolly the Sheep 1996

2000

Human Genome Sequence Decoded 2000

World Trade Center Attack 2001

U.S. War in Iraq Begins 2003

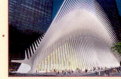

Barack Obama Elected President of United States 2008

2010

CALATRAVA, Transportation Hub 2006–2009

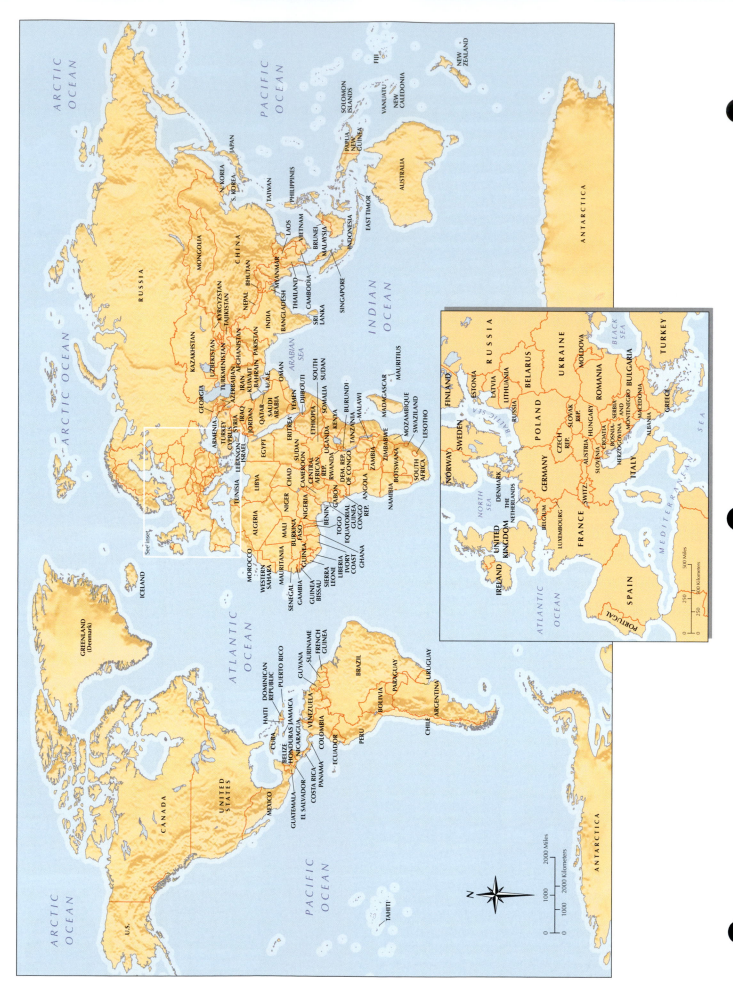

ARCTIC OCEAN

PACIFIC OCEAN

FIJI

NEW ZEALAND

SOLOMON ISLANDS

VANUATU

NEW CALEDONIA

PAPUA NEW GUINEA

AUSTRALIA

EAST TIMOR

ANTARCTICA

RUSSIA

MONGOLIA

N. KOREA

S. KOREA

JAPAN

TAIWAN

CHINA

KYRGYZSTAN

TAJIKISTAN

NEPAL

BHUTAN

MYANMAR

LAOS

VIETNAM

THAILAND

CAMBODIA

BRUNEI

MALAYSIA

PHILIPPINES

INDONESIA

KAZAKHSTAN

UZBEKISTAN

TURKMENISTAN

AZERBAIJAN

IRAN

AFGHANISTAN

PAKISTAN

INDIA

BANGLADESH

SRI LANKA

SINGAPORE

INDIAN OCEAN

ARABIAN SEA

KUWAIT

BAHRAIN

U.A.E.

OMAN

GEORGIA

ARMENIA

TURKEY

CYPRUS

SYRIA

LEBANON

ISRAEL

JORDAN

IRAQ

QATAR

SAUDI ARABIA

YEMEN

DJIBOUTI

ERITREA

ETHIOPIA

SOUTH SUDAN

SUDAN

EGYPT

LIBYA

CHAD

NIGER

CENTRAL AFRICAN REP.

CAMEROON

NIGERIA

UGANDA

KENYA

SOMALIA

RWANDA

BURUNDI

DEM. REP. OF CONGO

TANZANIA

MALAWI

ZAMBIA

ZIMBABWE

MOZAMBIQUE

MADAGASCAR

MAURITIUS

SWAZILAND

LESOTHO

SOUTH AFRICA

BOTSWANA

NAMIBIA

ANGOLA

CONGO REP.

GABON

EQUATORIAL GUINEA

TOGO

BENIN

GHANA

IVORY COAST

LIBERIA

SIERRA LEONE

GUINEA

GUINEA BISSAU

GAMBIA

SENEGAL

BURKINA FASO

MALI

MAURITANIA

WESTERN SAHARA

MOROCCO

ALGERIA

TUNISIA

See inset

ICELAND

GREENLAND (Denmark)

ATLANTIC OCEAN

CANADA

UNITED STATES

U.S.

MEXICO

GUATEMALA

EL SALVADOR

BELIZE

HONDURAS

NICARAGUA

COSTA RICA

PANAMA

CUBA

HAITI

DOMINICAN REPUBLIC

PUERTO RICO

JAMAICA

GUYANA

SURINAME

FRENCH GUIANA

VENEZUELA

COLOMBIA

ECUADOR

PERU

BRAZIL

BOLIVIA

PARAGUAY

URUGUAY

ARGENTINA

CHILE

PACIFIC OCEAN

TAHITI

ARCTIC OCEAN

ANTARCTICA

Inset

NORWAY

SWEDEN

FINLAND

RUSSIA

ESTONIA

LATVIA

LITHUANIA

RUSSIA

BELARUS

UKRAINE

MOLDOVA

POLAND

ROMANIA

BULGARIA

BLACK SEA

TURKEY

GREECE

MACEDONIA

ALBANIA

SERBIA

MONTENEGRO

BOSNIA AND HERZEGOVINA

CROATIA

SLOVENIA

HUNGARY

AUSTRIA

SLOVAK REP.

CZECH REP.

GERMANY

SWITZ.

ITALY

FRANCE

LUXEMBOURG

BELGIUM

THE NETHERLANDS

DENMARK

NORTH SEA

UNITED KINGDOM

IRELAND

ATLANTIC OCEAN

SPAIN

PORTUGAL

MEDITERRANEAN SEA

BALTIC SEA

500 Miles
800 Kilometers
250
250
0
0

2000 Miles
2000 Kilometers
1000
1000
0

N

GLOSSARY

abacus The flat slab at the top of a capital, directly under the entablature.
abstract Art that does not attempt to describe the appearance of visible forms but rather to transform them into stylized patterns or to alter them in conformity to ideals.
academy, academician An institution established for the training of artists. Academies date from the Renaissance and after; they were particularly powerful, state-run institutions in the seventeenth and eighteenth centuries. In general, academies replaced guilds as the venue where students learned the craft of art and were also provided with a complete education, including art theory and artistic rules. The academies helped artists to be seen as trained specialists, rather than as craftsworkers, and promoted the change in the social status of the artist. An academician is an official academy-trained artist.
acanthus A leafy Mediterranean plant whose leaves are reproduced in Classical architectural ornament used on moldings, friezes, and capitals.
Action Painting Using broad gestures to drip or pour paint onto a pictorial surface. Associated with mid-twentieth-century American Abstract Expressionists, such as Jackson Pollock.
adobe Sun-baked blocks made of clay mixed with straw. Also: the buildings made with this material.
aedicula (aediculae) A decorative architectural frame, usually found around a niche, door, or window. An aedicula is made up of a pediment and entablature supported by columns or pilasters.
aisle Passage or open corridor of a church, hall, or other building that parallels the main space, usually on both sides, and is delineated by a row, or arcade, of columns or piers. Called side aisles when they flank the nave of a church.
akropolis The citadel of an ancient Greek city, located at its highest point and housing temples, a treasury, and sometimes a royal palace. Most famous is the Acropolis in Athens, which includes the ruins of the Parthenon.
alabaster A soft, fine, translucent, white stone.
album A book consisting of a series of paintings or prints (album leaves).
allegory In a work of art, an image (or images) that symbolizes an idea, concept, or principle, often suggesting a deeper meaning or moral message.
altar A tablelike structure where religious rites are performed. In Christian churches, the altar is the site of the rite of the Eucharist.
altarpiece A painted or carved panel or ensemble of panels placed at the back of or behind and above an altar. Contains religious imagery, often specific to the place of worship for which it was made, that viewers can look at during liturgical ceremonies (especially the **Eucharist**) or personal devotions.
ambulatory The passage (walkway) around the apse in a basilican church or around the central space in a central-plan building.
amphora An ancient Greek jar for storing oil or wine, with an egg-shaped body and two curved handles.
animal style or interlace A type of imagery used in Europe and western Asia during the ancient and medieval periods, characterized by animals or animal-like forms arranged in intricate patterns or combats.
apotheosis Deification of a person or thing. In art, often shown as an ascent to heaven or glory, borne by an eagle, angels, or ***putti***.
apprentice A student artist or craftsperson in training. In a traditional system of art and craft training established under the guilds and still in use today, master artists took on apprentices (students) for a specific number of years. The apprentice was taught every aspect of the artist's craft, and he or she participated in the master's workshop or atelier.
appropriation Term used to describe the practice of some Postmodern artists of adopting images in their entirety from other works of art or from visual culture for use in their own art. The act of recontextualizing the appropriated image allows the artist to critique both it and the time and place in which it was created.
apse, apsidal A large semicircular or polygonal (and usually vaulted) niche protruding from the end wall of a building. In a Christian church, it contains the altar. Apsidal is an adjective describing the condition of having such a semicircular or polygonal space.
aquatint A type of intaglio printmaking developed in the eighteenth century that produces an area of even tone without laborious cross-hatching. The aquatint is made by using a porous resin coating on a metal plate, which, when immersed in acid, allows an even, all-over biting of the plate. The resulting printed image has a granular, textural effect.
aqueduct A trough to carry flowing water supported, if necessary, by arches.
arabesque European term for a type of linear surface decoration based on foliage and calligraphic forms, usually characterized by flowing lines and swirling shapes.
arcade A series of arches, carried by columns or piers and supporting a common wall or lintel. In a blind arcade, the arches and supports are engaged (attached to the background wall) and have a purely decorative function.
arch In architecture, a curved structural element that spans an open space. Built from wedge-shaped stone blocks called voussoirs, which, when placed together and held at the top by a trapezoidal keystone, form an effective weight-bearing unit. Requires buttresses at either side to contain outward thrust caused by the weight of the structure. Corbel arch: arch or vault formed by courses of stones, each of which projects beyond the lower course until the space is enclosed; usually finished with a capstone. Horseshoe arch: an arch of more than a half-circle, often used in western Islamic architecture. Relieving arch: an arch built into a heavy wall just above a post-and-lintel structure (such as a gate, door, or window) to help support the wall above, relieving some of the weight on the lintel by transferring the load to the side walls.
Archaic smile The curved lips of an ancient Greek statue from the period c. 600–480 BCE, usually interpreted as a way of animating facial features.
architrave The bottom element of an entablature, beneath the frieze and the cornice.
archivolt A band of molding framing an arch, or a series of stone blocks that form an arch resting directly on flanking columns or piers.
ashlar See **dressed stone**.
assemblage An artwork created by gathering and manipulating two- and/or three-dimensional found objects.
atelier The studio or workshop of a master artist or craftsperson, often including junior associates and apprentices.
atmospheric perspective See perspective.
atrium An unroofed interior courtyard in a Roman house, sometimes having a pool. Also: the open courtyard in front of a Christian church, or an entrance area in modern architecture.
attic story The top story of a building. In Classical architecture, the level above the entablature often decorated or carrying an inscription.
attribute The symbolic object or objects that identify a particular deity, saint, or personification in art.
automatic writing, automatism A technique in which artists abandon the usual intellectual control over their brush or pencil. The artist's aim is to allow the subconscious to create the artwork without rational interference.
avant-garde A term derived from the French military word meaning "before the group," or "vanguard." Avant-garde denotes those artists or concepts of a strikingly new, experimental, or radical nature for the time.
axis mundi A concept of an "axis of the world," which marks sacred sites and denotes a link between the human and celestial realms. For example, in Buddhist art, the *axis mundi* can be marked by monumental freestanding decorated pillars.
baldachin A canopy (whether suspended from the ceiling, projecting from a wall, or supported by columns) placed over an honorific or sacred space such as a throne or church altar.
balustrade A low barrier consisting of a series of short, usually round posts (called balusters), with a rail on top.
baptistery A building used for the Christian ritual of baptism. It is usually separate from the main church and often octagonal or circular in shape.
bar tracery See tracery.
barbarian A term used by the ancient Greeks and Romans to label all foreigners outside their cultural orbit (e.g., Celts, Goths, Vikings).
barrel vault See vault.
bas relief Another name for low relief ("bas" is the French word for "low"). See relief sculpture.
basilica A large rectangular building. Often built with a clerestory, side aisles separated from the center nave by colonnades, and an apse at one or both ends. Roman centers for administration, later adapted to Christian church use.
bay A unit of space defined by architectural elements such as columns, piers, and walls.
beehive tomb A corbel-vaulted tomb, conical in shape like a beehive, and covered by an earthen mound.
Benday dots In modern printing and typesetting, the dots that make up lettering and images. Often machine- or computer-generated, the dots are very small and closely spaced to give the effect of density and richness of tone.
biomorphic Adjective used to describe forms that resemble shapes found in nature.
bird's-eye view A view from above.
black-figure A technique of ancient Greek pottery in which black figures are painted on a red clay ground.
blackware A ceramic technique that produces pottery with a primarily black surface. Blackware has both matte and glossy patterns on the surface of the wares.
blind window Frames attached to the surface of a wall without openings.
block printing A printed image, such as a woodcut or wood engraving, made from a carved wooden block.
bodhisattva Sacred beings on the brink of buddhahood who have achieved enlightenment but choose to remain on earth to help others attain emancipation from the world (*nirvana*).
Book of Hours A private prayer book, having a calendar, services for the canonical hours, and, sometimes, special prayers.
bracket, bracketing An architectural element that projects from a wall and that often helps support a horizontal part of a building, such as beams or the eaves of a roof.
bronze A metal made from copper alloy, usually mixed with tin. Also: any sculpture or object made from this substance.
burin A metal instrument used in engraving to cut lines into the metal plate. The sharp end of the burin is trimmed to give a diamond-shaped cutting point, while the other end is finished with a wooden handle that fits into the engraver's palm.
buttress, buttressing An architectural support of projecting masonry built against an exterior wall to brace the wall and counter the thrust of the vaults. Flying buttress: An arch built on the exterior of a building that transfers the thrust of the roof vaults at important stress points through the wall to a detached buttress pier.
cairn A pile of stones or earth and stones that served both as a prehistoric burial site and as a marker of underground tombs.
calligraphy Handwriting as an art form.
calotype The first photographic process utilizing negatives and paper positives. It was invented by William Henry Fox Talbot in the late 1830s.
came (cames) A lead strip used in the making of leaded or stained-glass windows. Cames have an indented vertical groove on the sides into which the separate pieces of glass are fitted to make the overall design.
cameo A low-relief carving on a semiprecious stone or gemstone.
camera obscura An early cameralike device used in the Renaissance and later for recording images of nature. Made from a dark box (or room) with a hole in one side (sometimes fitted with a lens), the *camera obscura* operates when bright light shines through the hole, casting an upside-down image of an object outside onto the inside wall of the box.

canon Established rules or standards.

canon of proportions A set of ideal mathematical ratios in art based on measurements, as in the proportional relationships among the basic elements of the human body.

cantilever A beam or structure that is anchored at one end and projects horizontally beyond its vertical support, such as a wall or column. It can carry loads throughout the rest of its unsupported length.

capital The sculpted block that tops a column. According to the conventions of the Classical **orders**, capitals include specific decorative elements. A **historiated capital** is one displaying human figures or narrative scenes.

capstone The final, topmost stone in a corbel arch or vault, which joins the sides and completes the structure.

cartoon A full-scale drawing of a design that will be executed in another medium, such as wall painting, tapestry, or stained glass.

cartouche A frame for a hieroglyphic inscription formed by a rope design surrounding an oval space and signifying a sacred or honored name. Also: in architecture, a decorative device or plaque used for inscriptions or epitaphs.

caryatid A sculpture of a draped female figure acting as a column supporting an **entablature**.

catacomb An underground cemetery consisting of tunnels on different levels, having niches for burials, urns, and sarcophagi, and often incorporating rooms (*cubicula*).

cathedral The principal Christian church in a diocese, built in the bishop's administrative center and housing his throne (*cathedra*).

cella The principal interior room in a Greek or Roman temple within which the cult statue was usually housed. Also called the naos.

centering A temporary structure that supports a masonry arch, vault, or dome during construction until the mortar is fully dried and the masonry is self-sustaining.

central-plan building Any structure designed with a primary central space surrounded by symmetrical areas on each side. For example, a **rotunda**.

ceramics Wares made of baked clay.

chacmool In Mayan sculpture, a half-reclining figure probably representing an offering-bearer.

château (châteaux) A French country house or residential castle. A *château fort* is a military castle incorporating defensive works such as towers and battlements.

cherub (cherubim) The second-highest order of angels. Popularly, an idealized small child, usually depicted naked and with wings.

chevron A decorative motif made up of repeated inverted Vs; a zigzag pattern.

chiaroscuro An Italian word designating the contrast of dark and light in a painting, drawing, or print. *Chiaroscuro* creates spatial depth and volumetric forms through gradations in the intensity of light and shadow.

choir The section of a Christian church reserved for the clergy, monks, or nuns, either between the transept crossing and the apse or extending into the nave—separated from the rest of the church by screens or walls and fitted with stalls (seats).

cista (cistae) Cylindrical containers used by wealthy Etruscan and Roman women as cases for toiletry articles.

Classical A term referring to the art and architecture of ancient Greece and Rome.

classical, classicism Any aspect of later art or architecture reminiscent of the rules, canons, and examples of the art of ancient Greece and Rome. Also: in general, any art aspiring to the qualities of restraint, balance, and rational order exemplified by the ancients. Also: the peak of perfection in any period.

clerestory The topmost zone of a wall with windows in a basilica, extending above the aisle roofs. Provides direct light into the central interior space (the nave).

cloister An enclosed space, open to the sky, at the heart of a monastery, surrounded by an arcaded walkway, often having a fountain and garden. Since the most important monastic buildings (e.g., dormitory, refectory, church) open off the cloister, it represents the center of the monastic world.

codex (codices) A book, or a group of manuscript pages (**folios**), held together by stitching or other binding on one side.

coffer A recessed decorative panel that is used to reduce the weight of and to decorate ceilings or vaults. The use of coffers is called coffering.

coiling A technique in basketry. In coiled baskets a spiraling structure is held in place by another material.

collage A technique in which cutout paper forms (often painted or printed), and/or found materials, are pasted onto another surface. Also: an image created using this technique.

colonnade A row of columns, supporting a straight lintel (as in a porch or portico) or a series of arches (an arcade).

colonnette A small column, often attached to a pier or wall.

colophon The data placed at the end of a book listing the book's author, publisher, illuminator, and other information related to its production.

Color Field Painting A type of Abstract Expressionist painting in the 1950s and 1960s characterized by broad abstract sweeps of solid color that emphasize the surface of the **picture plane** and de-emphasize gestural brushstrokes.

column An architectural element used for support and/or decoration. Consists of a rounded vertical shaft placed on a base topped by a decorative capital. May follow the rules of one of the Classical orders. Although usually free-standing, columns can be attached to a wall (engaged).

complementary color The primary and secondary colors across from each other on the color wheel (red and green, blue and orange, yellow and purple). When juxtaposed, the intensity of both colors increases.

Composite order See order.

composition The overall arrangement, organizing design, or structure of a work of art.

compound pier A pier or large column with shafts, pilasters, or colonnettes attached to it on one or more sides.

conch A half-dome.

concrete A building material developed by the ancient Romans, made primarily from lime, sand, cement, and rubble mixed with water. Concrete is easily poured or molded when wet and hardens into a particularly strong and durable stonelike substance.

connoisseurship A term derived from the French word *connoisseur,* meaning "an expert," and signifying the study and evaluation of art based on formal, visual, and stylistic analysis. A connoisseur studies the style and technique of an object to deduce its relative quality and identify its maker and/or place of production through visual comparisons with other works of secure authorship and provenance.

content When discussing a work of art, the term can include all of the following: its subject matter; the ideas contained in the work; the artist's intention; or its meaning for the beholder.

contextualism An interpretive approach in art history that focuses on the cultural context of an art object, using the literature, history, economics, and social developments (among other things) of a period, to explain the work's meaning.

contrapposto An Italian term meaning "set against," used to describe the Classical convention of representing human figures with opposing alternations of tension and relaxation on either side of a central axis to imbue figures with a sense of the potential for movement.

convention A traditional way of representing forms.

corbel, corbeling A roofing and arching technique in which each course of stone projects inward and slightly beyond the previous layer (a corbel) until the uppermost corbels meet, creating a nearly pointed arch or vault. Also: brackets that project from a wall.

corbel arch See arch.

corbeled vault See vault.

Corinthian order See order.

cornice The uppermost section of a Classical entablature. More generally, a horizontally projecting element found at the top of a building wall or pedestal. A raking cornice is formed by the junction of two slanted cornices, most often found in pediments.

cross-hatching A technique primarily used in printmaking and drawing, in which a set of parallel lines (hatching) is drawn across a previous set, but from a differing (usually right) angle. Cross-hatching gives a great density of tone and allows the artist to create the illusion of shadows efficiently.

crossing The intersection of the nave and the transept in a church, often marked on the exterior by a tower or dome.

cruciform A term describing anything that is cross-shaped, as in the cruciform plan of a church.

cubiculum (cubicula) A small private room for burials in the catacombs.

cuneiform writing An early form of writing with wedge-shaped marks impressed into wet clay with a stylus; used primarily by ancient Mesopotamians.

curtain wall A wall in a building that does not support any of the weight of the structure.

cycle A series of images depicting a story or theme intended to be displayed together.

cyclopean construction A method of building utilizing huge blocks of rough-hewn stone. Any large-scale, monumental building project that impresses by sheer size. Named after one-eyed giants of legendary strength from Greek myth.

cylinder seal A small cylindrical stone decorated with incised patterns. When rolled across soft clay or wax, the resulting raised pattern or design (relief) served as an identifying signature.

dado (dadoes) The lower part of a wall, differentiated in some way (by a molding or decoration) from the upper section.

daguerreotype An early photographic process named for Louis-Jacques-Mandé Daguerre. A daguerreotype was a positive print made on a light-sensitized copper plate.

Daoism A Chinese philosophy that emphasizes the close relationship of humans and nature.

diptych Two panels of equal size, usually decorated with paintings or reliefs, and hinged together.

dolmen A prehistoric structure made up of two or more large (often upright) stones supporting a large, flat, horizontal slab or slabs.

dome A rounded vault, usually over a circular space. Consists of curved masonry and can vary in shape from hemispherical to bulbous to ovoidal. May use a supporting vertical wall (drum), from which the vault springs, and may be crowned by an open space (oculus) and/or an exterior lantern. When a dome is built over a square space, an intermediate element is required to make the transition to a circular drum. There are two systems: A dome on pendentives incorporates arched, sloping intermediate sections of wall that carry the weight and thrust of the dome to heavily buttressed supporting piers. A dome on squinches uses an arch built into the wall (squinch) in the upper corners of the space to carry the weight of the dome across the corners of the square space below. A half-dome or **conch** may cover a semicircular space.

Doric order See order.

dressed stone Highly finished, precisely cut blocks of stone laid in even courses, creating a uniform face with fine joints. Often used as a facing on the visible exterior of a building, especially as a veneer for the façade. Also called ashlar.

drillwork The technique of using a drill for the creation of certain effects in sculpture.

drum The circular wall that supports a dome. Also: a segment of the circular shaft of a column.

drypoint An intaglio printmaking process by which a metal (usually copper) plate is directly inscribed by means of a pointed instrument (**stylus**). The resulting design of scratched lines is inked, wiped, and printed. Also: the print made by this process.

earthworks Artwork and/or sculpture, usually on a large scale, created by manipulating the natural environment. Also: the earth walls of a fort. See also **geoglyph**.

echinus A cushion-like circular element found below the abacus of a Doric capital.

edition A single printing of a book or print. An edition includes only what is printed at a particular moment, usually pulled from the same press by the same publisher.

elevation The arrangement, proportions, and details of any vertical side or face of a building. Also: an architectural drawing showing an exterior or interior wall of a building.

embroidery The technique in needlework of decorating fabric by stitching designs and figures with threads. Also: the material produced by this technique.

en plein air A French term meaning "in the open air," describing the Impressionist practice of painting outdoors so artists could have direct access to the fleeting effects of light and atmosphere while working.

enamel A technique in which powdered glass is applied to a metal surface in a decorative design. After firing, the glass forms an opaque or transparent substance that is fixed to the metal background. Also: an object created with enamel technique.

encaustic A painting medium using pigment suspended in hot wax.

engaged column See column.

engraving An intaglio printmaking process of inscribing an image, design, or letters onto a metal or wood surface from which a print is made. An engraving is usually drawn with a sharp implement (burin) directly onto the surface of the plate. Also: the print made from this process.

entablature In the Classical orders, the horizontal elements above the columns and capitals. The entablature consists of, from top to bottom, a cornice, frieze, and architrave.

entasis A slight swelling of the shaft of a Greek column that gives the building a sense of energy and upward lift.

etching An intaglio printmaking process in which a metal plate is coated with acid-resistant resin and then inscribed with a stylus in a design, revealing the plate below. The plate is then immersed in acid, and the design of exposed metal is eaten away by the acid. The resin is removed, leaving the design etched permanently into the metal and the plate ready to be inked, wiped, and printed.

Eucharist The central rite of the Christian Church, from the Greek word for "thanksgiving." Also known as the Mass or Holy Communion, it re-enacts Christ's sacrifice on the cross and commemorates Christ's Last Supper with his apostles. According to traditional Catholic Christian belief, consecrated bread and wine become the body and blood of Christ; in Protestant belief, bread and wine symbolize the body and blood.

exedra (*exedrae*) In architecture, a semicircular niche. On a small scale, often used as decoration, whereas larger exedrae can form interior spaces.

expressionism Styles in which aspects of a work of art are exaggerated to evoke subjective responses rather than to portray objective reality or seek a rational response.

façade The face or front wall of a building.

fête galante A subject in painting depicting well-dressed people at leisure in a park or country setting. It is most often associated with eighteenth-century French Rococo painting.

fillet The flat ridges separating the carved-out **flutes** on the **shaft** of a **column**.

finial A knoblike architectural decoration usually found at the top point of a spire, pinnacle, canopy, or gable. Also found on furniture and ceremonial staffs.

fluting, fluted Shallow concave grooves running vertically on the **shaft** of a **column**, **pilaster**, or other surface.

flying buttress See buttress.

flying gallop A non-naturalistic pose in which animals are depicted hovering above the ground with legs fully extended backward and forward to signify that they are running.

foreground Within the depicted space of an artwork, the area that is closest to the picture plane.

foreshortening The illusion created on a flat surface in which figures and objects appear to recede or project sharply into space. Accomplished according to the rules of perspective.

form In speaking of a work of art or architecture, the term refers to purely visual components: line, color, shape, texture, mass, spatial qualities, and composition—all of which are called "formal elements" and are explored through formal analysis.

formalism, formalist An approach to the understanding, appreciation, and valuation of art based almost solely on considerations of form. This approach tends to regard an artwork as independent of its time and place of making.

forum A Roman town center; site of temples and administrative buildings and used as a market or public gathering area.

fresco A painting technique in which water-based pigments are applied to a surface of wet plaster and are absorbed into it, becoming part of the wall itself (called *buon fresco*). *Fresco secco* is created by painting on dried plaster, and the color can flake off. Murals made by both these techniques are called frescos.

frieze The middle element of an entablature, between the architrave and the cornice. Usually decorated with sculpture, painting, or moldings. Also: any continuous flat band with relief sculpture or painted decorations.

fusuma Sliding doors covered with paper, used in traditional Japanese construction. *Fusuma* are often highly decorated with paintings and colored backgrounds.

gable The triangular wall space found on the end wall of a building between the two sides of a pitched roof. Also: a triangular decorative panel that has a gablelike shape.

gallery In church architecture, the story found above the side aisles or ambulatory, or across the width at the end of the nave or transepts, usually open to and overlooking the main interior space. Also: a building or hall in which art is displayed or sold.

genre A type or category of artistic form, subject, technique, style, or medium.

genre painting A painting depicting a scene of everyday life, including (among others) domestic interiors and street scenes.

geoglyphs Earthwork designs on a colossal scale, often created in a landscape as if to be seen from an aerial viewpoint.

Geometric Style of art characterized by patterns of rectangles, squares, and other abstract shapes, as in ancient Greek art in the period c. 900–700 BCE.

gesso A substance made from glue, gypsum, and/or chalk forming the ground or the priming layer of a wood panel or canvas. Provides a smooth surface for painting.

gilding The application of paper-thin **gold leaf** or gold pigment to an object made from another medium (for example, a sculpture or painting). Usually used as a decorative finishing detail.

giornata (*giornate*) Adopted from the Italian term meaning "a day's work," a *giornata* is the section of a fresco plastered and painted in a single day.

glazing In ceramics, an outermost layer of vitreous liquid (glaze) that, upon firing, renders ceramics waterproof, and forms a decorative surface. In painting, a technique particularly used with oil media in which a transparent layer of paint (glaze) is laid over another, usually lighter, painted or glazed area. In architecture, the process and technique of filling openings in a building with windows of clear **stained glass**.

gold leaf Paper-thin sheets of hammered gold that are used in gilding.

Grand Manner An elevated style of painting popular in the eighteenth century in which the artist looked to the ancients and to the Renaissance for inspiration.

granulation A technique for decorating gold in which tiny balls of the precious metal are fused to the main surface in a pattern.

graphic arts A term referring to those arts that are drawn or printed and that utilize paper as primary support.

grid A system of regularly spaced horizontally and vertically crossed lines that gives regularity to an architectural plan or in the composition of a work of art. Also: in painting, a grid enables designs to be enlarged or transferred easily.

grisaille A style of monochromatic painting executed primarily in shades of gray. Also: a painting in this style.

groin vault See vault.

ground line The solid baseline that indicates the ground plane on which the figure stands. In ancient representations, such as those of the Egyptians, the figures and the objects are placed on a series of groundlines to indicate depth (space in **registers**).

guild An association of artists or craftsworkers. Medieval and Renaissance guilds had great economic power, as they controlled the selling and marketing of its members' products, and provided economic protection, political solidarity, and training in the craft to its members. The painters' guild was usually dedicated to St. Luke, their patron saint.

half-barrel vault See vault.

hall church A building with nave and side aisles of equal height, creating a spacious and open interior especially suited for preaching.

halo A circle of light that surrounds and frames the heads of emperors and Christian saints to signify power and/or sanctity. Also known as a nimbus.

handscroll A long, narrow, horizontal painting and/or text common in Chinese and Japanese art and intended for individual use. A handscroll is stored wrapped tightly around a wooden pin and is unrolled for viewing or reading.

hanging scroll In Chinese and Japanese art, a vertically oriented painting or text mounted within sections of silk. At the top is a semicircular rod; at the bottom is a round dowel. Hanging scrolls are kept rolled and tied except for special occasions, when they are hung for display, contemplation, or commemoration.

haniwa Pottery forms (cylinders, buildings, and human figures) that were placed on top of Japanese tombs or burial mounds in the Kofun period.

Happening An art form developed in the 1960s incorporating performance, theater, and visual images. A Happening was organized without a specific narrative or intent; with audience participation, the event proceeded according to chance and individual improvisation.

hemicycle A semicircular interior space or structure.

henge A circular area enclosed by stones or wood posts set up by Neolithic peoples. It is usually bounded by a ditch and raised embankment.

hierarchic scale The use of differences in size to indicate relative importance. For example, with human figures, the larger the figure, the greater his or her importance.

hieroglyphs Picture writing; words and ideas rendered in the form of pictorial symbols.

high relief See relief sculpture.

historiated capital See capital.

historicism The strong consciousness of and attention to the institutions, themes, styles, and forms of the past, made accessible by historical research, textual study, and archaeology.

history painting Paintings based on historical, mythological, or biblical narratives. Once considered the noblest form of art, history paintings generally convey a high moral or intellectual idea and are often painted in a grand pictorial style.

horizon line A horizontal "line" formed by the implied meeting point of earth and sky. In linear perspective, the vanishing point or points are located on this "line."

horseshoe arch See arch.

hue Pure color. The saturation or intensity of the hue depends on the purity of the color. Its value depends on its lightness or darkness.

hypostyle hall A large interior room characterized by many closely spaced columns that support its roof.

icon An image representing a sacred figure or event in the Byzantine (later the Orthodox) Church. Icons were venerated by the faithful, who believed their prayers were transmitted through them to God.

iconic image A picture that expresses or embodies an intangible concept or idea.

iconoclasm The banning and/or destruction of icons and religious images. Iconoclasm in eighth- and ninth-century Byzantium and sixteenth- and seventeenth-century Protestant territories arose from differing beliefs about the power, meaning, function, and purpose of imagery in religion.

iconography Identifying and studying the subject matter and conventional symbols in works of art.

iconostasis A screen covered with **icons** that separates the **sanctuary** (where the altar is located) from the congregational space in an Orthodox church.

idealization A process in art through which artists strive to make their forms and figures attain perfection, based on pervading cultural values and/or their own personal ideals.

illumination A painting on paper or parchment used as illustration and/or decoration for manuscripts or albums. The illustrators are referred to as illuminators. Also: the technique of decorating manuscripts with such paintings.

illusionism, illusionistic Art that attempts faithful description of the appearance of the real world, using pictorial devices such as perspective and foreshortening.

impasto Thickly applied paint that gives the quality of a three-dimensional surface to a painting.

impost, impost block A block imposed between the top of a pier or above the capital of a column in order to provide extra support at the springing of an arch.

impression A single print. Each and every impression of a print is by nature different, given the possibilities for variation inherent in the printing process, which requires the plate to be inked and wiped between every impression.

incising A technique in which a design or inscription is cut into a hard surface with a sharp instrument.

ink painting A monochromatic style of painting developed in China using black ink with gray washes.

inlay A decorative process in which pieces of one material are set into the surface of an object fashioned from a different material.

installation art A term coined in the 1960s and 1970s to refer to works created for a specific site and arranged (usually temporarily) to create a total environment.

intaglio Term used for a technique in which the design is carved out of the surface of an object, such as an engraved seal stone. In the graphic arts, intaglio includes engraving, etching, and drypoint—all processes in which ink transfers to paper from incised, ink-filled lines cut into a metal plate.

intarsia Technique of **inlay** decoration using variously colored woods.

interlace A type of linear decoration in which ribbonlike bands are illusionistically depicted as if woven under and over one another.

intuitive perspective See perspective.

Ionic order See order.

iwan A large, vaulted chamber with a monumental arched opening on one side.

jamb In architecture, the vertical element found on both sides of a door or an opening in a wall, often supporting an arch or lintel.

japonisme A style in nineteenth-century French and American art that was highly influenced by Japanese art.

joined-block sculpture A method of constructing large-scale wooden sculpture developed in Japan. The entire work is constructed from smaller hollow blocks, each individually carved and assembled when complete. The joined-wood technique allowed the production of larger sculpture, as the multiple joints alleviate the problems of drying and cracking found with sculpture carved from a single block.

kente A woven cloth made by the Ashanti peoples of Africa. Kente cloth is woven in long, narrow pieces in complex and colorful patterns, which are then sewn together.

key block A key block is the master block in the production of a colored woodcut, which requires different blocks for each color. The key block is a flat piece of wood with the entire design carved or drawn on its surface. From this, other blocks with partial drawings are made for printing the areas of different colors.

keystone The topmost voussoir at the center of an arch, and the last block to be placed. The pressure of this block holds the arch together. Often of a larger size than the other voussoirs and/or decorated.

kiln An oven designed to produce the high temperature necessary for the baking, or firing, of clay; the melting of the glass used in enamel work; and the fixing of vitreous paint on stained glass.

kiva A subterranean, circular room used as a ceremonial center in some Native American cultures.

***kore* (*korai*)** An archaic Greek statue of a young woman or girl.

***kouros* (*kouroi*)** An archaic Greek statue of a young man or boy.

lacquer A type of hard, glossy surface varnish, originally developed for use on objects in East Asian cultures, made from the sap of the Asian sumac or from shellac, a resinous secretion from the lac insect. Lacquer can be layered and manipulated or combined with pigments and other materials for various decorative effects.

lancet A tall, narrow window crowned by a sharply pointed arch, typically found in Gothic architecture.

lantern A turretlike structure situated on a roof, vault, or dome, with windows that allow light into the space below.

linear, linearity An emphasis on line.

linear perspective See perspective.

lintel A horizontal element of any material carried by two or more vertical supports to form an opening.

literati painting A style of painting that reflects the taste of the educated class of East Asian intellectuals and scholars. Aspects include an appreciation for the antique, small scale, and an intimate connection between maker and audience.

lithograph A print made from a design drawn on a flat stone block with greasy crayon. Oil-based ink is applied to a wet stone and, when printed, adheres only to the greasy areas of the design.

loggia Italian term for a roofed structure with one or more of its sides open to the air. Often used as a corridor between buildings or around a courtyard, loggias usually have arcades or colonnades.

longitudinal-plan building Any structure designed with a rectangular shape and a longitudinal axis. If a cross-shaped building, the main arm of the building would be longer than any arms that cross it. For example, **basilicas**.

lost-wax casting A method of casting metal, such as bronze, by a process in which a wax mold is covered with clay and plaster, then fired, melting the wax and leaving a hollow form. Molten metal is then poured into the hollow space and slowly cooled. When the hardened clay and plaster exterior shell is removed, a solid metal form remains to be smoothed and polished.

low-relief See relief sculpture.

lunette A semicircular wall area, framed by an arch over a door or window. Can be either plain or decorated.

madrasa An Islamic institution of higher learning, where teaching is focused on theology and law.

majolica Pottery painted with a tin glaze that, when fired, gives a lustrous and colorful surface.

mandorla An almond-shaped area in which a sacred figure, such as Christ, is represented.

Mannerism, Mannerist A sophisticated, elegant sixteenth-century European style characterized by elongated forms, irrational spatial relationships, unusual colors and lighting effects, and exquisite craft.

manuscript A handwritten book or document.

maqsura An enclosure for rulers or dignitaries in front of the ***mihrab*** of a **mosque**.

martyrium (martyria) In Christian architecture, a church, chapel, or shrine built over the grave of a martyr.

mastaba A flat-topped, one-story building with slanted walls over an ancient Egyptian underground tomb.

mathematical perspective See perspective.

matte A smooth surface without shine or luster.

mausoleum A monumental building used as a tomb. Named after the tomb of Mausolos erected at Halikarnassos around 350 BCE.

medallion Any round ornament or decoration. Also: a large medal.

medium (media) The materials from which a work of art is made.

megaron A "great room" or large audience hall in a Mycenaean Greek ruler's residence.

menorah A Jewish lamp-stand with seven or nine branches; the nine-branched menorah is used during the celebration of Hanukkah. Representations of the seven-branched menorah, once used in the Temple of Jerusalem, became a symbol of Judaism.

metope The carved, painted, or plain rectangular spaces between the triglyphs of a Doric frieze.

middle ground Within the depicted space of an artwork, the area that takes up the middle distance of the image. See also foreground.

mihrab A recess or niche that distinguishes the wall oriented toward Mecca (*qibla* wall) in a **mosque**.

millefiori A term derived from the Italian for "a thousand flowers" that refers to a glass-making technique in which rods of differently colored glass are fused in a long bundle that is subsequently sliced to produce disks or beads with small-scale, multicolor patterns.

minaret A tall, slender tower on the exterior of a **mosque** from which believers are called to prayer.

minbar A high platform or pulpit in a **mosque**.

modeling In painting, the process of creating the illusion of three-dimensionality on a two-dimensional surface by the use of light and shade. In sculpture, the process of molding a three-dimensional form out of a malleable substance.

module A basic unit of construction.

molding A shaped or sculpted strip with varying contours and patterns. Used as decoration on architecture, furniture, frames, and other objects.

monumental A term used to designate a project or object that, whatever its physical size, gives an impression of grandeur.

mosaic Images formed by small colored stone or glass pieces (**tesserae**) affixed to a hard, stable surface.

mosque A building used for communal Muslim worship.

motif Any recurring element of a design or composition. Also: a recurring theme or subject in artwork.

Mozarabic An eclectic style practiced in Christian medieval Spain while much of the Iberian peninsula was ruled by Muslim dynasties.

mudra A symbolic hand gesture in Buddhist art that denotes certain behaviors, actions, or feelings.

mullion A slender straight or curving bar that divides a window into subsidiary sections to create **tracery**.

muqarnas In Islamic architecture, the niche-like cells that mark the transition between decorative flat and rounded surfaces; often found on or under the vault of a dome.

mural Literally, "wall-like." A large painting or decoration, created either directly on the wall, or created separately and affixed to the wall.

naos The principal room in a temple or church. In ancient architecture, known as the cella. In a church, known as the nave and sanctuary.

narrative image A picture that recounts an event drawn from a story, either factual (e.g., biographical) or fictional. In continuous narrative, multiple scenes from the same story appear within a single compositional frame.

narthex The vestibule or entrance porch of a church.

naturalism, naturalistic A **style** of depiction in which the physical appearance of the rendered image in nature seems to be accurately described.

nave The central aisle of a basilica, two or three stories high, flanked by aisles, and defined by the nave arcade or nave colonnade.

necropolis A large cemetery or burial area, literally "city of the dead."

niche A hollow or recess in a wall or other solid architectural element. Niches can be of varying size and shape, and may be intended for many different uses, from display of objects to housing of a tomb.

niello A metal technique in which a black sulfur alloy is rubbed into fine lines engraved into a metal (usually gold or silver). When heated, the alloy becomes fused with the surrounding metal and provides contrasting detail.

nimbus Another term for **halo**. A figure whose head is surrounded by a nimbus is referred to as nimbed.

nonrepresentational art Art that does not attempt to reproduce the appearance of objects, figures, or scenes in the natural world. Also called nonobjective art.

obelisk A tall, four-sided stone shaft, hewn from a single block, that tapers at the top and is completed by a pyramidion. A sun symbol erected by the ancient Egyptians in ceremonial spaces (such as entrances to temple complexes). Today used as a commemorative monument.

oculus (oculi) In architecture, a circular opening. Oculi are usually found either as windows or at the apex of a dome. When at the top of a dome, an oculus is either open to the sky or covered by a decorative exterior lantern.

oil painting Any painting executed with the pigments suspended in a medium of oil. Oil paint has particular properties that allow for greater ease of working (among others, a slow drying time, which allows for corrections, and a great range of relative opaqueness of paint layers, which permits a high degree of detail and luminescence).

one-point perspective See perspective.

oratory A small chapel.

order A system of proportions in Classical architecture developed by the ancient Greeks that includes every aspect of the building's plan, elevation, and decorative system. Composite: a combination of the Ionic and the Corinthian orders. The capital combines acanthus leaves with volute scrolls. Corinthian: the most ornate of the orders, the Corinthian includes a base, a **fluted** column shaft with a capital elaborately decorated with acanthus-leaf carvings. Its entablature consists of an architrave decorated with moldings, a frieze often containing sculptured reliefs, and a cornice with dentils. Doric: the column shaft of the Doric order can be **fluted** or smooth-surfaced and has no base. The Doric capital consists of an undecorated echinus and abacus. The Doric entablature has a plain architrave, a frieze with metopes and triglyphs, and a simple cornice. Ionic: the column of the Ionic order has a base, a **fluted** shaft, and a capital decorated with volutes. The Ionic entablature consists of an architrave of three panels and moldings, a frieze usually containing sculpted relief ornament, and a cornice with dentils. Tuscan: a Roman variation on Doric characterized by a smooth-surfaced column shaft with a base, a plain architrave, and an undecorated frieze. A colossal order is any of the above built on a large scale, rising through several stories in height and often raised from the ground by a pedestal.

orientalism A fascination with Middle Eastern cultures that inspired eclectic nineteenth-century European fantasies of exotic life that often formed the subject of paintings.

orthogonal Any line running back into the represented space of a picture perpendicular to the imagined picture plane. In linear perspective, all orthogonals converge at a single vanishing point in the picture and are the basis for a grid that maps out the internal space of the image. An orthogonal plan is any plan for a building or city that is based exclusively on right angles, such as the grid plan of many modern cities.

pagoda An East Asian reliquary tower built with successively smaller, repeated stories. Each story is usually marked by an elaborate, projecting roof.

painterly A style of painting which emphasizes the techniques and surface effects of brushwork (also color, light, and shade).

palazzo Italian term for palace, used for any large urban dwelling.

palette A handheld support used by artists for arranging colors and mixing paint during the process of painting. Also: the choice of a range of colors used by an artist in a particular work, or typical of his or her style. In ancient Egypt, a flat stone used to grind and prepare makeup.

palmette A fan-shaped petal design used as decoration on Classical Greek vases.

panel painting Any painting executed on a wood support. The wood is usually planed to provide a smooth surface. A panel can consist of several boards joined together.

parchment A writing surface made from treated skins of animals. Very fine parchment is known as vellum.

passage grave A prehistoric tomb under a cairn, reached by a long, narrow, slab-lined access passage or passageways.

patron The institution or person who commissions or finances a work of art.

pedestal A platform or base supporting a sculpture or other monument. Also: the block found below the base of a Classical column (or colonnade), serving to raise the entire element off the ground.

pediment A triangular gable found over major architectural elements such as Classical Greek porticoes, windows, or doors. Formed by an entablature and the ends of a sloping roof or a raking cornice. A similar architectural element is often used decoratively above a door or window, sometimes with a curved upper molding. A broken pediment is a variation on the traditional pediment, with an open space at the center of the topmost angle and/or the horizontal cornice.

pendentive The concave triangular section of a vault that forms the transition between a square or polygonal space and the circular base of a dome.

Performance Art A contemporary artwork based on a live, sometimes theatrical performance by the artist.

peristyle A surrounding colonnade in Greek architecture. A peristyle building is surrounded on the exterior by a colonnade. Also: a peristyle court is an open colonnaded courtyard, often having a pool and garden.

perspective A system for representing three-dimensional space on a two-dimensional surface. Atmospheric perspective: A method of rendering the effect of spatial distance by subtle variations in color and clarity of representation. Intuitive perspective: A method of giving the impression of recession by visual instinct, not by the use of an overall system or program. Oblique perspective: An intuitive spatial system in which a building or room is placed with one corner in the picture plane, and the other parts of the structure recede to an imaginary vanishing point on its other side. One-point and multiple-point perspective (also called linear, scientific, or mathematical perspective): A method of creating the illusion of three-dimensional space on a two-dimensional surface by delineating a horizon line and multiple orthogonal lines. These recede to meet at one or more points on the horizon (called vanishing points), giving the appearance of spatial depth. Called scientific or mathematical because its use requires some knowledge of geometry and mathematics, as well as optics. Reverse perspective: A Byzantine perspective theory in which the orthogonals or rays of sight do not converge on a vanishing point in the picture, but are thought to originate in the viewer's eye in front of the picture. Thus, in reverse perspective the image is constructed with orthogonals that diverge, giving a slightly tipped aspect to objects.

pictograph A highly stylized and simplified depiction serving as a symbol for a person or object.

picture plane The theoretical spatial plane corresponding with the actual surface of a painting.

pier A masonry support made up of many stones, or rubble and concrete (in contrast to a column shaft, which is formed by a single stone or a series of drums), often square or rectangular in plan and capable of carrying very heavy architectural loads. See also compound pier.

pietà A devotional subject in Christian religious art showing the dead body of Jesus laid across the lap of his grieving mother, Mary. When others are present, the subject is called the Lamentation.

pilaster An engaged **column**-like element that is rectangular in format and used for decoration in architecture.

pinnacle The highest point.

plaiting In basketry, the technique of weaving strips of fabric or other flexible substances under and over each other.

plan A graphic convention for representing the arrangement of the parts of a building.

plate tracery See **tracery**.

plein air See ***en plein air***.

plinth The slablike base or pedestal of a **column**, statue, wall, building, or piece of furniture.

pluralism A social structure or goal that allows members of diverse ethnic, racial, or other groups to exist within society while continuing to practice the customs of their own divergent cultures. Also: an adjective describing the state of having many valid contemporary styles available at the same time to artists.

podium A raised platform that acts as the foundation for a building, or as a platform for a speaker.

polychrome, polychromy The multicolored decoration applied to any part of a building, sculpture, or piece of furniture. This can be accomplished with paint or through the use of multicolored materials.

porcelain A type of extremely hard and fine white ceramic first made by Chinese potters in the eighth century CE. Made from a mixture of kaolin and petuntze, porcelain is fired at a very high temperature, and the final product has a translucent surface.

portal A grand entrance, door, or gate, usually to an important public building, and often decorated with sculpture.

portico A projecting roof or porch supported by columns, often marking an entrance.

post-and-lintel construction An architectural system of construction with two or more vertical elements (posts) supporting a horizontal element (**lintel**).

predella The lower zone, or base, of an altarpiece, decorated with painting or sculpture related to the main iconographic theme of the altarpiece.

primary colors (or hues) Blue, red, and yellow, the three colors from which all others are derived.

primitivism The borrowing of subjects or forms usually from non-European or prehistoric sources by Western artists, in an attempt to infuse their work with the expressive qualities they attributed to other cultures, especially colonized cultures.

pronaos The enclosed vestibule of a Greek or Roman temple, found in front of the **cella** and marked by a row of columns at the entrance.

proscenium The stage of an ancient Greek or Roman theater. In modern theater, the area of the stage in front of the curtain. Also: the framing arch that separates a stage from the audience.

punch A handheld metal instrument used to stamp decorative designs onto a surface, such as metal or leather.

putto (putti) A plump, naked little boy, often winged. In Classical art, called a cupid; in Christian art, a cherub.

pylon A massive gateway formed by a pair of tapering walls of oblong shape. Erected by ancient Egyptians to mark the entrance to a temple complex.

qibla The direction of Mecca. In a **mosque**, the *qibla* wall (containing the ***mihrab***) is oriented toward Mecca.

quadrant vault See vault.

quillwork A Native American decorative craft technique in which the quills of porcupines and bird feathers are dyed and attached to material in patterns.

raku A type of ceramic pottery made by hand, coated with a thick, dark glaze, and fired at a low heat. The resulting vessels are irregularly shaped and glazed and are highly prized for use in the Japanese tea ceremony.

readymade An object from popular or material culture presented without further manipulation as an artwork by the artist.

realism, realistic Lifelike description of the appearance of objects, people, and the natural world. When capitalized as Realism, refers to a specific movement in European art during the mid nineteenth century that associates realism with a social or political message.

red-figure A technique of ancient Greek ceramic painting in the sixth and fifth centuries BCE. Characterized by red-clay-colored figures reserved on a black background.

register A device used in systems of spatial definition. In painting, a register indicates the use of differing ground lines to differentiate layers of space within an image. In sculpture, the placement of self-contained bands of reliefs in a vertical arrangement. In printmaking, the marks at the edges used to align the print correctly on the page, especially in multiple-block color printing.

relic Venerated objects or body parts associated with a holy figure, such as a saint, often housed in **reliquaries**.

relief sculpture A sculpted image or design whose flat background surface is carved away to a certain depth, setting off the figure(s). Called high or low (bas) relief depending upon the extent of projection of the image from the background. Called sunken relief when the image is modeled below the original surface of the background, which is not cut away.

relieving arch See arch.

reliquary A container, often made of precious materials, used as a repository for sacred relics.

repoussé A technique of pushing or hammering metal from the back to create a protruding image. Elaborate reliefs are created by pressing or hammering metal sheets against carved wooden forms.

representational Any art that attempts to depict an aspect of the external, natural world in a visually understandable way.

rib vault See vault.

roof comb In a Mayan building, a masonry wall along the apex of a roof that is built above the level of the roof proper. Roof combs support the highly decorated false façades that rise above the height of the building at the front.

rose window A round window, often filled with stained glass set into tracery patterns in the form of wheel spokes, common on the façades of the naves and transepts of Gothic cathedrals.

rosette A round or oval ornament resembling a rose.

rotunda Any building (or part thereof) constructed in a circular (or sometimes polygonal) shape, usually producing a large open space crowned by a dome.

rustication, rusticated In building, the rough, irregular, and unfinished effect deliberately given to the exterior facing of a stone edifice. Rusticated stones are often large and used for decorative emphasis around doors or windows or across the entire lower floors of a building.

sacristy In a Christian church, the room, usually close to the **sanctuary**, in which the priest's robes and the sacred vessels are housed.

Salon The annual display of art by French artists in Paris during the eighteenth and nineteenth centuries. Established in the seventeenth century as a venue to show the work of members of the French Academy, the Salon and its judges established the accepted official style of the time.

sanctuary A sacred or holy enclosure used for worship. In ancient Greece and Rome, consists of one or more temples and an altar. In Christian architecture, the space around the altar in a church.

sarcophagus (sarcophagi) A rectangular stone coffin. Often decorated with relief **sculpture**.

scarification Controlled scarring of the human body for aesthetic and/or cultural reasons.

scientific perspective See perspective.

scriptorium (scriptoria) A room in a monastery housing a workshop for writing or copying manuscripts.

sculpture in the round Three-dimensional sculpture that is carved free of any background or block.

sfumato In painting, the effect of haze in an image. Resembling the color of the atmosphere at dusk, *sfumato* gives a smoky effect.

sgraffito A decoration produced by scratching through darker plaster or glaze.

shade Any area of an artwork that is shown through various technical means to be in shadow. The technique for making this effect is "shading."

shaft The main vertical section of a column between the capital and the base, usually circular in cross section.

shikhara In the architecture of northern India, a conical (or pyramidal) structure creating the vertical focus of a Hindu temple.

silkscreen A printing process in which a fine mesh silk screen is used as a stencil to reproduce a design in multiple copies.

site-specific sculpture A sculpture commissioned and designed for a particular spot.

slip A mixture of clay and water applied to a ceramic object as a final decorative coat. Also: a solution that binds different parts of a vessel together, such as the handle and the main body.

spandrel The area of wall adjoining the exterior curve of an arch between its springing and the keystone, or the area between two arches, as in an arcade.

squinch An arch or lintel built over the upper corners of a square space, allowing a circular or polygonal dome to be more securely set on top of the walls.

stained glass Molten glass stained with color using metallic oxides. Stained glass is most often used in windows, for which small pieces of different colors are precisely cut and assembled into a design, held together by lead cames. Additional painted details may be added with vitreous paint.

stave church A Scandanavian wooden structure with four huge timbers (staves) at its core.

stele (stelae), also stela (stelae) An upright stone slab decorated with inscriptions or reliefs. Used as a grave marker or commemorative monument.

stereobate The series of steep steps that form a platform for Greek temples.

still life A type of painting that has as its subject inanimate objects (such as food and dishes) or fruit and flowers taken out of their natural contexts.

stringcourse A continuous horizontal band, such as a molding, decorating the face of a wall.

stucco A mixture of lime, sand, and other ingredients made into a material that can be easily **molded** or **modeled**. When dry, produces a durable surface used for covering walls or for architectural sculpture and decoration.

stupa In Buddhist architecture, a bell-shaped or pyramidal religious monument, made of piled earth or stone and containing sacred relics.

style A particular manner, form, or character of representation, construction, or expression that is typical of an individual artist or of a certain place or period.

stylization, stylized A manner of representation that conforms to an intellectual or artistic idea rather than to a lifelike description of natural appearance.

stylobate In Classical architecture, the stone platform on which a temple stands.

stylus An instrument with a pointed end (used for writing and printmaking), which makes a delicate line or scratch. Also: a special writing tool for cuneiform **writing** with one pointed end and one triangular wedge end.

sublime A concept, thing, or state of exceptional and awe-inspiring beauty and moral or intellectual expression. The sublime was a goal to which many nineteenth-century artists aspired in their artworks.

sunken relief See relief sculpture.

swag A decorative device in architecture or interior ornament (and in paintings) in which a loosely hanging garland is made to look like flowers or gathered fabric.

talud tablero A design characteristic of Mayan architecture at Teotihuacan in which a sloping *talud* supports a wall-like *tablero,* where ornamental painting and sculpture are usually placed.

tapestry A pictorial textile in which the colored **weft** threads that form the pattern or pictures are woven into an un-dyed **warp** during the process of making the fabric itself.

technique The process that transforms **media** into works of art.

tempera A painting medium made by blending egg or egg yolks with water, pigments, and occasionally other materials, such as glue.

tenebrism The use of strong *chiaroscuro* and artificially illuminated areas to create a dramatic contrast of light and dark in painting.

tipi (formerly spelled tepee) A portable dwelling constructed from hides (later canvas) stretched on a structure of poles set in a circle at the base and leaning against one another at the top. Tipis were typically found among the nomadic Native Americans of the North American plains.

terra cotta A medium made from clay fired over a low heat and sometimes left unglazed. Also: the orange-brown color typical of this medium.

tessera (tesserae) Small pieces of stone, glass, or other material that are assembled to create a mosaic.

tholos tomb Circular, vaulted structure used as a burial place in Mycenaean culture.

tint The dominant color in an object, image, or pigment.

tone The overall degree of brightness or darkness in an artwork. Also: saturation, intensity, or value of color and its effect.

torana In Indian architecture, an ornamented gateway, usually leading to a stupa.

torc A circular neck ring worn by Celtic warriors.

tracery Linear networks within a window opening or applied to a flat surface that often create elaborate decorative patterns. In **plate tracery** a series of openings are cut through the wall, while in **bar tracery** they are formed by bars of stone or wood called **mullions** inserted within large openings in the wall.

transept The arm of a cruciform church, perpendicular to the nave. The point where the nave and transept intersect is called the crossing. Beyond the crossing lies the sanctuary, whether apse, choir, or chevet.

triforium The element of the interior elevation of a church found directly below the clerestory and consisting of a series of arched openings in front of a passageway within the thickness of the wall.

triglyph Rectangular blocks between the metopes of a Doric frieze. Identified by the three carved vertical grooves, which approximate the appearance of the ends of wooden beams.

triptych An artwork made up of three panels. The panels may be hinged together so the side segments (wings) fold over the central area.

triumphal arch A freestanding, massive stone gateway with a large central arch, built as urban ornament and/or to celebrate military victories (as by the Romans).

trompe l'oeil A manner of representation in which artists faithfully describe the appearance of natural space and forms with the express intention of fooling the eye of the viewer, who may be convinced or fooled momentarily that the painted subject actually exists as three-dimensional reality.

trumeau A column, pier, or post found at the center of a large portal or doorway, supporting the lintel.

tugra Imperial cipher developed into a calligraphic art form by the Ottomans.

Tuscan order See order.

twining A basketry technique in which short rods are sewn together vertically. The panels are then joined together to form a vessel.

tympanum In medieval and later architecture, the area over a door enclosed by an arch and a lintel, often decorated with sculpture or mosaic.

ukiyo-e A Japanese term for a type of popular art that flourished from the sixteenth century, particularly in the form of color woodblock prints. *Ukiyo-e* prints often depicted the world of courtesans and actors, as well as landscapes and myths.

undercutting A technique in sculpture by which the material is cut back under the edges so that the remaining form projects strongly forward, casting deep shadows.

underglaze Color or decoration applied to a ceramic piece before glazing.

value The darkness (low value) or lightness (high value) of a color (**hue**).

vanishing point In a perspective system, the point on the horizon line at which orthogonals meet. A complex system can have multiple vanishing points.

vanitas An image, especially popular in Europe during the seventeenth century, in which all the objects symbolize the transience of life. *Vanitas* paintings are usually of still lifes or genre subjects.

vault An arched masonry structure that spans an interior space. Barrel or tunnel vault: an elongated or continuous semicircular vault, shaped like a half-cylinder. Groin or cross vault: a vault created by the intersection of two barrel vaults of equal size which creates four side compartments of identical size and shape. Quadrant or half-barrel vault: as the name suggests, a half-barrel vault. Rib vault: ribs (extra masonry) demark the junctions of a groin vault. Ribs may function to reinforce the groins or may be purely decorative. Corbeled vault: a vault made by projecting courses of stone. See also corbeling.

vellum A fine animal skin prepared for writing and painting. See also parchment.

veneer In architecture, the exterior facing of a building, often in decorative patterns of fine stone or brick. In decorative arts, a thin exterior layer of finer material (such as rare wood, ivory, metal, and semiprecious stones) laid over less valuable material.

verism A style in which artists concern themselves with describing the exterior likeness of an object or person, usually by rendering its visible details in a finely executed, meticulous manner.

villa A country house, usually on a large estate.

volumetric A term indicating the concern for rendering the impression of three-dimensional volumes in painting, usually achieved through modeling and the manipulation of light and shadow (*chiaroscuro*).

volute A spiral scroll, as seen on an Ionic capital.

votive figure An image created as a devotional offering to a god or other deity.

voussoirs The oblong, wedge-shaped stone blocks used to build an arch. The topmost voussoir is called a keystone.

wall painting See mural.

warp The vertical threads in a weaver's loom. Warp threads make up a fixed framework that provides the structure for the entire piece of cloth, and are thus often thicker than weft threads. See also weft.

wash A diluted watercolor or ink. Washes may be applied to drawings or prints to add tone or touches of color.

watercolor A painting technique in which pigments suspended in water are applied to absorbent paper, creating an image that cannot be corrected or reworked.

weft The horizontal threads in a woven piece of cloth. Weft threads are woven at right angles to and through the warp threads to make up the bulk of the decorative pattern. In carpets, the weft is often completely covered or formed by the rows of trimmed knots that form the carpet's soft surface. See also warp.

westwork The monumental, west-facing entrance block of a Carolingian, Ottonian, or Romanesque church. The exterior consists of multiple stories between two towers; the interior includes an entrance vestibule, a chapel, and often a series of galleries overlooking the nave.

wing A side panel of a triptych or polyptych (usually found in pairs), which was hinged to fold over the central panel. Wings often held the depiction of the donors and/or subsidiary scenes relating to the central image.

woodblock print A print made from one or more carved wooden blocks. In Japan, woodblock prints were made using multiple blocks carved in relief, usually with a block for each color in the finished print. See also woodcut.

woodcut A type of print made by carving a design into a wooden block. Ink is applied to the block with a roller. As the ink only touches the surface areas and lines remaining between the curved-away parts of the block, it is these areas and lines that make the print when paper is pressed against the inked block, leaving the carved-away parts of the design to appear blank. Also: the process by which the woodcut is made.

ziggurat In Mesopotamia, a tall stepped pyramidal structure of earthen materials, often supporting a shrine.

BIBLIOGRAPHY

General

30,000 Years of Art: The Story of Human Creativity Across Time and Space. London; New York: Phaidon, 2007.

Adams, Laurie Schneider. *Art across Time*. 3rd ed. New York: McGraw-Hill, 2007.

Andrews, Malcolm. *Landscape and Western Art*. Oxford History of Art. Oxford: Oxford Univ. Pr., 1999.

The Art Atlas. Ed. John Onians. New York: Abbeville, 2008.

Ball, Philip. *Bright Earth: Art and the Invention of Color*. Chicago: Univ. of Chicago Pr., 2003.

Bearden, Romare. *A History of African American Artists: From 1792 to the Present*. New York: Pantheon, 1993.

Bell, Julian. *Mirror of the World: A New History of Art*. London: Thames & Hudson, 2007.

Berlo, Janet Catherine, and Lee Ann Wilson. *Arts of Africa, Oceania, and the Americas: Selected Readings*. Englewood Cliffs, N.J.: Prentice Hall, 1993.

Breward, Christopher. *Fashion*. Oxford History of Art. Oxford; New York: Oxford Univ. Pr., 2003.

The Bulfinch Guide to Art History: A Comprehensive Survey and Dictionary of Western Art and Architecture. Ed. Shearer West. Boston: Little, Brown, 1996.

Büttner, Nils. *Landscape Painting: A History*. New York: Abbeville, 2006.

Chadwick, Whitney. *Women, Art, and Society*. 4th ed. New York: Thames & Hudson, 2007.

A Concise History of Architecture Styles. Ed. Emily Clark. London: A & C Black, 2003.

Conway, Hazel. *Understanding Architecture: An Introduction to Architecture and Architectural History*. 2nd ed. London; New York: Routledge, 2005.

Davies, Penelope J.E. et al. *Janson's History of Art: the Western Tradition*. 8th ed. Upper Saddle River, NJ: Pearson/Prentice Hall, 2010.

The Dictionary of Art. Ed. Jane Turner. 34 vols. New York: Grove's Dictionaries, 1996.

Dictionary of Women Artists. Ed. Delia Gaze. London; Chicago: Fitzroy Dearborn, 1997.

A Documentary History of Art. Ed. Elizabeth G. Holt. 3 vols. New Haven: Yale Univ. Pr., 1986.

Encounters: The Meeting of Asia and Europe, 1500–1800. Eds. Anna Jackson and Amin Jaffer. London: Victoria and Albert Museum; New York: Abrams, 2004.

Encyclopedia of Comparative Iconography: Themes Depicted in Works of Art. Ed. Helene Roberts. 2 vols. Chicago: Fitzroy Dearborn, 1998.

Encyclopedia of Gardens: History and Design. Ed. Candice Shoemaker. Chicago: Fitzroy Dearborn, 2001.

Encyclopedia of World Art. 17 vols. New York: McGraw-Hill, 1972–87.

Fazio, Michael W. *A World History of Architecture*. 2nd ed. Boston: McGraw-Hill, 2008.

Gascoigne, Bamber. *How to Identify Prints: A Complete Guide to Manual and Mechanical Processes From Woodcut to Inkjet*. 2nd ed. New York: Thames & Hudson, 2004.

Gardner, Helen. *Gardner's Art through the Ages*. 12th ed. Eds. F. Kleiner and C. Mamiya. Fort Worth: Harcourt Brace College, 2005.

Griffiths, Antony. *Prints and Printmaking: An Introduction to the History and Techniques*. 2nd ed. London: British Museum, 1996.

Hall, James. *Dictionary of Subjects and Symbols in Art*. 2nd ed. Boulder: Westview, 2008.

Heller, Nancy G. *Women Artists: An Illustrated History*. 4th ed. New York: Abbeville, 2003.

Honour, Hugh. *The Visual Arts: A History*. 7th ed. Upper Saddle River, NJ: Pearson/Prentice Hall, 2005.

Hughes, Robert. *American Visions: The Epic History of Art in America*. New York: Knopf, 1997.

Hults, Linda C. *The Print in the Western World: An Introductory History*. Madison: Univ. of Wisconsin Pr., 1996.

Johnson, Paul. *Art: A New History*. New York: HarperCollins, 2003.

Kemp, Martin. *The Oxford History of Western Art*. Oxford: Oxford Univ. Pr., 2000.

Kostof, Spiro. *A History of Architecture: Settings and Rituals*. 2nd ed. New York: Oxford Univ. Pr., 1995.

Langmuir, Erika. *Yale Dictionary of Art and Artists*. New Haven: Yale Univ. Pr., 2000.

Marien, Mary W. *Photography: A Cultural History*. 3rd ed. Upper Saddle River, NJ: Pearson/Prentice Hall, 2010.

McConkey, Wilfred J. *Klee as in Clay: A Pronunciation Guide*. 3rd ed. Lantham, MD: Madison Books, 1992.

Morgan, Ann Lee. *The Oxford Dictionary of American Art and Artists*. ed. Bruce M. Metzger and Roland E. Murphy. New revised standard version. New York: Oxford Univ. Pr., 1991.

The New Oxford Annotated Bible with Apocrypha/Deutero-canonical Books. Oxford; New York: Oxford Univ. Pr., 2007.

Ochoa, George, and Melinda Corey. *The Wilson Chronology of the Arts*. New York: H. W. Wilson, 1998.

The Oxford Companion to Western Art. Ed. Hugh Brigstocke. Oxford; New York: Oxford Univ. Pr., 2001.

The Oxford Dictionary of Art. 4th ed. Ed. Ian Chilvers. New York: Oxford Univ. Press, 2009.

Patton, Sharon F. *African-American Art*. Oxford; New York: Oxford Univ. Pr., 1998.

The Penguin Dictionary of Architecture and Landscape Architecture. John Fleming et al. 5th ed. New York: Penguin, 1998.

Pohl, Frances. *Framing America: A Social History of American Art*. 2nd ed. New York: Thames & Hudson, 2008.

Rosenblum, Naomi. *A World History of Photography*. 4th ed. New York: Abbeville, 2007.

Roth, Leland M. *Understanding Architecture: Its Elements, History, and Meaning*. New York: Icon Editions, 1993.

Shepherd, Rowena. *1000 Symbols*. New York: Thames & Hudson, 2002.

Slatkin, Wendy. *Women Artists in History: From Antiquity to the Present*. 4th ed. Upper Saddle River, NJ: Prentice Hall, 2001.

St. James Guide to Black Artists. Pref. H. Dodson. Detroit: St. James Pr., 1997.

Stokstad, Marilyn. *Art History*. 3rd ed. Upper Saddle River, NJ: Pearson/Prentice Hall, 2008.

Sutton, Ian. *Western Architecture: From Ancient Greece to the Present*. World of Art. New York: Thames & Hudson, 1999.

Trachtenberg, Marvin, and Isabelle Hyman. *Architecture, from Prehistory to Postmodernity*. 2nd ed. New York: Abrams, 2002.

Watkin, David. *A History of Western Architecture*. 4th ed. New York: Watson-Guptill, 2005.

Wilkins, David, et al. *Art Past/Art Present*. 6th ed. Upper Saddle River, NJ: Pearson/Prentice Hall, 2009.

Women Artists: The National Museum of Women in the Arts. Ed. Susan F. Sterling. New York: Abbeville, 1995.

Introduction

Acton, Mary. *Learning to Look at Paintings*. 2nd ed. New York: Routledge, 2009.

The Architecture Reader: Essential Writings from Vitruvius to the Present. Ed. A. Krista Sykes. New York: Braziller, 2007.

Arnold, Dana. *Art History: A Very Short Introduction*. Oxford; New York: Oxford Univ. Pr., 2004.

Art and History: Images and Their Meaning. Eds. Robert Rothberg and Theodore Rabb. Cambridge: Cambridge Univ. Pr., 1988.

Art in Theory 1648–1815: An Anthology of Changing Ideas. Eds. Charles Harrison et al. Oxford; Malden, MA: Blackwell, 2001.

Art in Theory, 1815–1900: An Anthology of Changing Ideas. Eds. Charles Harrison et al. Malden, MA: Blackwell, 1998.

The Art of Art History: A Critical Anthology. Ed. Donald Preziosi. Oxford; New York: Oxford Univ. Pr., 1998.

Baxandall, Michael. *Patterns of Intention: On the Historical Explanation of Pictures*. New Haven: Yale Univ. Pr., 1985.

A Companion to Art Theory. Eds. Paul Smith and Carolyn Wilde. Oxford: Blackwell, 2002.

Critical Terms for Art History. Eds. Robert S. Nelson and Richard Shiff. 2nd ed. Chicago: Univ. of Chicago Pr., 2003.

Freeland, Cynthia A. *Art Theory: A Very Short Introduction*. Oxford; New York: Oxford Univ. Pr., 2003.

Geertz, Clifford. "Art as a Cultural System." *Modern Language Notes* 91, 1976, pp. 1473–1499.

Glancey, Jonathan. *Architecture*. New York: DK Pub., 2006.

Langer, Suzanne. *Feeling and Form*. Upper Saddle River, NJ: Prentice Hall, 1978.

Leppert, Richard D. *The Nude: The Cultural Rhetoric of the Body in the Art of Western Modernity*. Boulder, CO: Westview, 2007.

MacGregor, Arthur. *Curiosity and Enlightenment: Collectors and Collections From the 16th to the 19th Century*. New Haven; London: Yale Univ. Pr., 2007.

Minor, Vernon Hyde. *Art History's History*. Upper Saddle River, NJ: Prentice Hall, 2001.

Panofsky, Erwin. *Meaning in the Visual Arts*. Phoenix ed. Chicago: Univ. of Chicago Pr., 1982, 1955.

Preble, Duane. *Artforms: An Introduction to the Visual Arts*. 8th ed. Upper Saddle River, NJ: Pearson/Prentice Hall, 2008.

Recht, Roland, et al. *The Great Workshop: Pathways of Art in Europe, 5th to 18th Centuries*. Brussels: Mercatorfonds; Ithaca: Cornell Univ. Pr., 2007.

Sowers, Robert. *Rethinking the Forms of Visual Expression*. Berkeley: Univ. of California Pr., 1990.

Taylor, Joshua. *Learning to Look: A Handbook for the Visual Arts*. Chicago: Chicago Univ. Pr., 1981.

Williams, Robert. *Art Theory: An Historical Introduction*. Malden, MA: Blackwell, 2004.

Chapter 1 Prehistoric Art in Europe

Bahn, Paul G. *The Cambridge Illustrated History of Prehistoric Art*. Cambridge: Cambridge Univ. Pr., 1998.

Bataille, Georges. *The Cradle of Humanity: Prehistoric Art and Culture*. Ed. Stuart Kendall. New York: Zone Books; Cambridge, MA: MIT Pr., 2005.

Boardman, John. *The World of Ancient Art*. London; New York: Thames & Hudson, 2006.

Chippindale, Christopher. *Stonehenge Complete*. New and exp. ed. New York: Thames & Hudson, 2004.

Clottes, Jean. *Cave Art*. London; New York: Phaidon, 2008.

———. *World Rock Art*. Los Angeles: Getty Conservation Institute, 2002.

Guthrie, R. Dale. *The Nature of Paleolithic Art*. Chicago: Univ. of Chicago Press, 2005.

Hill, Rosemary. *Stonehenge*. Cambridge, MA: Harvard Univ. Pr., 2008.

McCarter, Susan Foster. *Neolithic*. New York; London: Routledge, 2007.

The Oxford Illustrated History of Prehistoric Europe. Ed. Barry W. Cunliffe. New York: Oxford Univ. Press, 2001.

Price, T. Douglas. *Images of the Past*. 5th ed. Boston: McGraw-Hill, 2008.

Runnels, Curtis Neil. *Greece Before History: An Archaeological Companion and Guide*. Stanford, CA: Stanford Univ. Pr., 2001.

Sandars, N. K. *Prehistoric Art in Europe*. 2nd ed. Pelican History of Art. New Haven: Yale Univ. Pr., 1995.

Sura Ramos, Pedro A. *The Cave of Altamira*. New York: Abrams, 1999.

White, Randall. *Prehistoric Art: The Symbolic Journey of Mankind*. New York: Abrams, 2003.

Chapter 2 Art of the Ancient Near East

Beyond Babylon: Art, Trade, and Diplomacy in the Second Millennium B.C. Ed. Joan Aruz et al. New York: Metropolitan Museum of Art; New Haven: Yale Univ. Pr., 2008.

Black, Jeremy A. *Gods, Demons and Symbols of Ancient Mesopotamia: An Illustrated Dictionary*. London: British Museum, 1992.

Bottéro, Jean. *Ancestor of the West: Writing, Reasoning, and Religion in Mesopotamia, Elam, and Greece*. Chicago: Univ. of Chicago Pr., 2000.

Collon, Dominique. *Ancient Near Eastern Art*. Berkeley: Univ. of California Pr., 1995.

Curatola, Giovanni, et al. *The Art and Architecture of Mesopotamia*. New York: Abbeville, 2007.

———. *The Art and Architecture of Persia*. New York: Abbeville, 2007.

Curtis, John. *Ancient Persia*. Cambridge, MA: Harvard Univ. Pr., 1989.

Errington, Elizabeth. *From Persepolis to the Punjab: Exploring Ancient Iran, Afghanistan and Pakistan*. London: British Museum, 2007.

Fildes, Alan. *Alexander the Great: Son of the Gods*. Los Angeles: J. Paul Getty Museum, 2002.

Forgotten Empire: The World of Ancient Persia. Eds. John Curtis and Nigel Tallis. Berkeley: Univ. of California Pr., 2005.

Frankfort, Henri. *The Art and Architecture of the Ancient Orient*. 5th ed. Pelican History of Art. New Haven: Yale Univ. Pr., 1996.

Haywood, John. *Ancient Civilizations of the Near East and the Mediterranean*. London: Cassell, 1997.

Leick, Gwendolyn. *A Dictionary of Ancient Near Eastern Architecture*. London; New York: Routledge, 1988.

Roaf, Michael. *Cultural Atlas of Mesopotamia and the Ancient Near East*. New York: Facts on File, 1990.

Roux, Georges. *Ancient Iraq*. 3rd ed. London: Penguin, 1992.

Saggs, H. W. F. *Babylonians*. London: British Museum, 1995.

———. *Civilization before Greece and Rome*. New Haven: Yale Univ. Pr., 1989.

Treasures from the Royal Tombs of Ur. Eds. Richard L. Zettler and Lee Horne. Philadelphia: Univ. of Pennsylvania, Museum of Archaeology and Anthropology, 1998.
Winter, Irene. "Sex, Rhetoric and the Public Monument: The Alluring Body of the Male Ruler in Mesopotamia." In *Sexuality in Ancient Art*. Eds. N. B. Kampen et al. Cambridge and New York: Cambridge Univ. Pr., 1996, pp. 11–26.

Chapter 3 Art of Ancient Egypt

Aldred, Cyril. *The Egyptians*. 3rd ed. rev. and updated by Aidan Dodson. London: Thames & Hudson, 1998.
Arnold, Dieter. *The Encyclopedia of Ancient Egyptian Architecture*. Princeton: Princeton Univ. Pr., 2003.
Brier, Bob. *Daily Life of the Ancient Egyptians*. 2nd ed. Westport, CT: Greenwood, 2008.
Egyptian Art in the Age of the Pyramids. New York: Metropolitan Museum of Art, 1999.
Egyptian Treasures from the Egyptian Museum in Cairo. Ed. Francesco Tiarditti. New York: Abrams, 1999.
Foster, John L., trans. *Love Songs of the New Kingdom*. New York: Charles Scribner's Sons, 1974.
Hawass, Zahi A. *Tutankhamun and the Golden Age of the Pharaohs*. Washington, D.C.: National Geographic, 2005.
Hellum, Jennifer. *The Pyramids*. Westport, CT: Greenwood, 2007.
Kozloff, Arielle P. *Egypt's Dazzling Sun: Amenhotep III and His World*. Cleveland: Cleveland Museum of Art, 1992.
Lehner, Mar. *The Complete Pyramids*. New York: Thames & Hudson, 1997.
Malek, Jaromir. *Egypt: 4,000 Years of Art*. London: Phaidon, 2003.
_____. *Egyptian Art*. Art & Ideas. London: Phaidon, 1999.
Menu, Bernadette. *Ramesses II: Greatest of the Pharaohs*. Discoveries. New York: Abrams, 1999.
Montet, Pierre. *Everyday Life in Egypt in the Days of Ramesses the Great*. Trans. A. R. Maxwell-Hyslop and Margaret S. Drower. Philadelphia: Univ. of Pennsylvania Pr., 1981.
The Pharaohs. Ed. Cristiane Ziegler. New York: Rizzoli, 2002.
Pharaohs of the Sun: Akhenaten, Nefertiti, Tutankhamen. Eds. Rita E. Freed, Yvonne J. Markowitz and Sue H. D'Auria. Boston: Museum of Fine Arts; Little, Brown, 1999.
Reeves, C.N. *The Complete Tutankhamun: The King, the Tomb, the Royal Treasure*. London: Thames & Hudson,1990.
_____. *The Complete Valley of the Kings: Tombs and Treasures of Egypt's Greatest Pharaohs*. London: Thames & Hudson, 1996.
Robins, Gay. *The Art of Ancient Egypt*. Rev. ed. Cambridge, MA: Harvard Univ. Pr., 2008.
Roehrig, Catharine H., Renee Dreyfus, and Cathleen A. Keller. *Hatshepsut, from Queen to Pharaoh*. New York: Metropolitan Museum of Art, 2005.
Russmann, Edna R. *Civilization before Greece and Rome*. New Haven: Yale Univ. Pr., 1989.
_____. *Temples and Tombs: Treasures of Egyptian Art from the British Museum*. New York: American Federation of Arts; Seattle: Univ. of Washington Pr., 2006.
Smith, Craig B. *How the Great Pyramid Was Built*. Washington, D.C.: Smithsonian Books, 2004.
Walker, Susan. *Ancient Faces: Mummy Portraits from Roman Egypt*. 2nd ed. London: British Museum, 2000.
Wilkinson, Richard H. *Reading Egyptian Art: A Hieroglyphic Guide to Ancient Egyptian Painting and Sculpture*. London: Thames & Hudson, 1992.
Winstone, H. V. F. *Howard Carter and the Discovery of the Tomb of Tutankhamun*. Rev. ed. Manchester: Barzan, 2006.

Chapter 4 Early Asian Art

Ancient Sichuan: Treasures From a Lost Civilization. Ed. Robert Bagley. Seattle: Seattle Art Museum; Princeton: Princeton Univ. Pr., 2001.
Barnhart, Richard M. *Three Thousand Years of Chinese Painting*. New Haven: Yale Univ. Pr., 1997.
Behl, Benoy K. *The Ajanta Caves: Artistic Wonder of Ancient Buddhist India*. New York: Abrams, 1998.
Berkson, Carmel. *The Life of Form in Indian Sculpture*. New Delhi: Abhinav, 2000.
Brand, Michael. *The Vision of Kings: Art and Experience in India*. Canberra: National Gallery of Australia; New York: Thames & Hudson, 1995.
Clunas, Craig. *Art in China*. Oxford History of Art. Oxford: Oxford Univ. Pr., 1997.
Craven, Roy C. *Indian Art: A Concise History*. Rev. ed. World of Art. New York: Thames & Hudson, 1997.
The Crossroads of Asia: Transformation in Image and Symbol in the Art of Ancient Afghanistan and Pakistan. Ed. Elizabeth Errington. Cambridge: Ancient India and Iran Trust, 1992.
Dehejia, Vidya. *Indian Art*. Art & Ideas. London: Phaidon, 1997.
Ebrey, Patricia B. *The Cambridge Illustrated History of China*. 2nd ed. Cambridge: Cambridge Univ. Pr., 2010.
Eck, Diana L. *Darsan: Seeing the Divine Image in India*. 3rd ed. Chambersburg, PA: Anima, 1998.
Elisseeff, Danielle, and Vadime Elisseeff. *Art of Japan*. New York: Abrams, 1985.
Fang, Jing Pei. *Symbols and Rebuses in Chinese Art: Figures, Bugs, Beasts, and Flowers*. Berkeley, CA: Ten Speed Pr., 2004.
Frampton, Kenneth. *Japanese Building Practice: From Ancient Times to the Meiji Period*. New York: Van Nostrand Reinhold, 1997.
The Glory of the Silk Road: Art From Ancient China. Ed. Li Jian. Dayton, Ohio: Dayton Art Institute, 2003.
Harle, James C. *The Art and Architecture of the Indian Subcontinent*. 2nd ed. Pelican History of Art. New Haven: Yale Univ. Pr., 1994.
Heller, Amy. *Early Himalayan Art*. Oxford: Ashmolean Museum, 2008.
Khanna, Balraj. *Human and Divine: 2000 Years of Indian Sculpture*. London: Hayward Gallery; Berkeley, CA: Univ. of California Pr., 2000.
Lee, Sherman E. *China, 5,000 Years: Innovation and Transformation in the Arts*. New York: Solomon R. Guggenheim Museum, 1998.
_____. *A History of Far Eastern Art*. 5th ed. New York: Abrams, 1994.
Mason, Penelope. *History of Japanese Art*. 2nd ed. rev. by Donald Dinwiddie. Upper Saddle River, NJ: Pearson/Prentice Hall, 2005.
Michell, George. *Elephanta*. Bombay: India Book House, 2002.
Mitter, Partha. *Indian Art*. Oxford; New York: Oxford Univ. Pr., 2001.
Owyoung, Steven D. *Ancient Chinese Bronzes in the Saint Louis Art Museum*. St. Louis, MO: St. Louis Art Museum, 1997.
Paine, Robert Treat. *Art and Architecture of Japan*. 3rd ed. Pelican History of Art. Harmondsworth, UK: Penguin, 1981.
Pearson, Richard. *Ancient Japan*. Washington, DC: Sackler Gallery, 1992.
Possessing the Past: Treasures From the National Palace Museum. New York: Metropolitan Museum of Art; Taipei: National Palace Museum, 1996.
Rhie, Marylin M. *Early Buddhist Art of China and Central Asia*. 2 vols. in 3. Leiden; Boston: Brill, 1999–2002.
Shinto: The Sacred Art of Ancient Japan. Ed. Victor Harris. London: British Museum, 2001.
Stanley-Baker, Joan. *Japanese Art*. Rev. and exp. ed. World of Art. New York: Thames & Hudson, 2000.
Sullivan, Michael. *The Arts of China*. 4th ed. exp. and rev. Berkeley: Univ. of California Pr., 1999.
Thorp, Robert L. *Chinese Art and Culture*. New York: Abrams, 2001.
Tregear, Mary. *Chinese Art*. Rev. ed. World of Art. New York: Thames & Hudson, 1997.
Watson, William. *The Arts of China to AD 900*. Pelican History of Art. New Haven: Yale Univ. Pr., 1995.
Welch, Patricia B. *Chinese Art: A Guide to Motifs and Visual Imagery*. North Clarendon, VT: Tuttle, 2008.
Whitfield, Roderick, and Anne Farrer. *Caves of the Thousand Buddhas: Chinese Art from the Silk Route*. London: British Museum, 1990.

Chapter 5 Art of Ancient Greece and the Aegean World

Ashmole, Bernard. *Architect and Sculptor in Classical Greece*. Wrightsman Lectures. New York: New York Univ. Pr., 1972.
Barletta, Barbara A. *The Origins of the Greek Architectural Orders*. Cambridge; New York: Cambridge Univ. Pr., 2001.
Beard, Mary. *Classical Art: From Greece to Rome*. Oxford History of Art. Oxford: Oxford Univ. Pr., 2001.
Biers, William. *The Archaeology of Greece: An Introduction*. 2nd ed. Ithaca: Cornell Univ. Pr., 1996.
Boardman, John. *Greek Art*. 4th ed. rev. and exp. World of Art. London: Thames & Hudson, 1997.
_____. *Greek Sculpture: The Archaic Period, A Handbook*. World of Art. New York: Oxford Univ. Pr., 1991.
_____. *Greek Sculpture: The Classical Period, A Handbook*. London: Thames & Hudson, 1985.
_____. *The Greeks Overseas: Their Early Colonies and Trade*. Rev. ed. London: Thames & Hudson, 1999.
Burn, Lucilla. *Hellenistic Art: From Alexander the Great to Augustus*. Los Angeles: J. Paul Getty Museum, 2004.
The Cambridge Companion to Archaic Greece. Ed. H. A. Shapiro. Cambridge; New York: Cambridge Univ. Pr., 2007.
The Cambridge Companion to the Aegean Bronze Age. Ed. Cynthia W. Shelmerdine. Cambridge; New York: Cambridge Univ. Pr., 2008.
The Cambridge Illustrated History of Ancient Greece. Ed. Paul Cartledge. Cambridge Illustrated History. Cambridge: Cambridge Univ. Pr., 1998.
Curl, James S. *Classical Architecture: An Introduction to its Vocabulary and Essentials*. New York: Norton, 2003.
Fitton, J. Lesley. *Cycladic Art*. 2nd ed. London: British Museum, 1999.
Fullerton, Mark D. *Greek Art*. Cambridge: Cambridge Univ. Pr., 2000.
Grant, Michael. *Atlas of Classical History*. 5th ed. New York: Oxford Univ. Pr., 1994.
_____. *Myths of the Greeks and Romans*. New York: Meridian, 1995.
Great Moments in Greek Archaeology. Athens: Kapon Editions, 2007.
Greek Sculpture: Function, Materials, and Techniques in the Archaic and Classical Periods. Ed. Olga Palagia. New York: Cambridge Univ. Pr., 2006.
Hard, Robin. *The Routledge Handbook of Greek Mythology: Based on H. J. Rose's "Handbook of Greek Mythology."* London; New York: Routledge, 2004.
Higgins, Reynold. *Minoan and Mycenean Art*. Rev. ed. World of Art. New York: Thames & Hudson, 1997.
Hurwit, Jeffrey M. *The Acropolis in the Age of Pericles*. Cambridge; New York: Cambridge Univ. Pr., 2004.
Jenkins, Ian. *The Parthenon Sculptures*. Cambridge: Harvard Univ. Pr., 2007.
Kunze, Max. *The Pergamon Altar: Its Rediscovery, History, and Reconstruction*. Berlin: Staatliche Museen zu Berlin, Antikensammlung, 1991.
Lawrence, A. W. *Greek Architecture*. Rev. by R. A. Tomlinson. 5th ed. Pelican History of Art. New Haven: Yale Univ. Pr., 1996.
Neils, Jenifer. *The British Museum Concise Introduction to Ancient Greece*. Ann Arbor, MI: Univ. of Michigan Pr., 2008.
Osborne, Robin. *Archaic and Classical Greek Art*. Oxford History of Art. Oxford: Oxford Univ. Pr., 1998.
The Parthenon: From Antiquity to the Present. Ed. Jenifer Neils. Cambridge; New York: Cambridge Univ. Pr., 2005.
Pedley, John Griffiths. *Greek Art and Archaeology*. 4th ed. Upper Saddle River, NJ: Pearson/Prentice Hall, 2007.
Pollitt, J. J. *Art and Experience in Classical Greece*. Cambridge: Cambridge Univ. Pr., 1972.
_____. *Art in the Hellenistic Age*. Cambridge: Cambridge Univ. Pr., 1986.
_____. *The Art of Ancient Greece: Sources and Documents*. Cambridge; New York: Cambridge Univ. Pr., 1990.
Preziosi, Donald, and Louise Hitchcock. *Aegean Art and Architecture*. Oxford History of Art. Oxford: Oxford Univ. Pr., 1999.
Smith, R. R. R. *Hellenistic Sculpture: A Handbook*. World of Art. New York: Thames & Hudson, 1991.
Spivey, Nigel. *Greek Art*. Art & Ideas. London: Phaidon, 1997.
Stewart, Andrew F. *Greek Sculpture: An Exploration*. 2 vols. New Haven: Yale Univ. Pr., 1990.

Chapter 6 Etruscan and Roman Art

Allan, Tony. *Life, Myth and Art in Ancient Rome*. Los Angeles: J. Paul Getty Museum, 2005.
Art of the Classical World in the Metropolitan Museum of Art: Greece, Cyprus, Etruria, Rome. New York: Metropolitan Museum of Art; New Haven: Yale Univ. Pr., 2007.
Balsdon, J. P. V. D. *Roman Women*. London: The Bodley Head, 1962.
Borrelli, Federica. *The Etruscans: Art, Architecture, and History*. Los Angeles: J. Paul Getty Museum, 2004.
Brendel, Otto J. *Etruscan Art*. 2nd ed. Pelican History of Art. New Haven: Yale Univ. Pr., 1995.
_____. *Prolegomena to the Study of Roman Art*. New Haven, Yale Univ. Pr., 1979.
Brown, Peter. *The World of Late Antiquity: A.D. 150–750*. New York: Norton, 1989.
D'Ambra, Eve. *Roman Art*. Cambridge: Cambridge Univ. Pr., 1998.
Dunabin, Katherine M. D. *Mosaics of the Greek and Roman World*. Cambridge: Cambridge Univ. Pr., 1999.
Elsner, Jas. *Imperial Rome and Christian Triumph: The Art of the Roman Empire, A.D. 100–450*. Oxford History of Art. Oxford: Oxford Univ. Pr., 1998.
Gabucci, Ada. *Ancient Rome: Art, Architecture, and History*. Los Angeles: J. Paul Getty Museum, 2002.
_____. *Rome*. Berkeley: Univ. of California Pr., 2006.

Haynes, Sybille. *Etruscan Civilization: A Cultural History*. London: British Museum, 2000.

Holloway, R. Ross. *Constantine and Rome*. New Haven: Yale Univ. Press, 2004.

Hopkins, Keith. *The Colosseum*. London: Profile Books, 2005.

Kamm, Antony. *The Romans: An Introduction*. 2nd ed. London; New York: Routledge, 2008.

Kleiner, Fred S. *A History of Roman Art*. Australia: Thomson/Wadsworth, 2007.

Ling, Roger. *Ancient Mosaics*. Princeton: Princeton Univ. Pr., 1998.

MacDonald, William L. *The Architecture of the Roman Empire: An Introductory Study*. Rev. ed. 2 vols. Yale Publications in the History of Art. New Haven: Yale Univ. Pr., 1982.

_____. *The Pantheon: Design, Meaning, and Progeny*. With a new foreword by John Pinto. Cambridge, MA: Harvard Univ. Pr., 2002.

Mattusch, Carol C. *Pompeii and the Roman Villa: Art and Culture around the Bay of Naples*. Washington, D.C.: National Gallery of Art, 2008.

Mazzoleni, Donatella. *Domus: Wall Painting in the Roman House*. Los Angeles: J. Paul Getty Museum, 2004.

Packer, James E. *The Forum of Trajan in Rome: A Study of the Monuments in Brief*. Berkeley: Univ. of California Pr., 2001.

Pollitt, J. J. *The Art of Rome, c. 753 B.C.–337 A.D.: Sources and Documents*. Englewood Cliffs, NJ: Prentice Hall, 1966.

Polybius. *The Histories*. Trans. W. R. Paton. 6 vols. Loeb Classical Library. Cambridge, MA: Harvard Univ. Pr., 1998.

Ramage, Nancy H. *The British Museum Concise Introduction to Ancient Rome*. Ann Arbor, MI: Univ. of Michigan Pr., 2008.

Ramage, Nancy H., and Andrew Ramage. *Roman Art: Romulus to Constantine*. 4th ed. Upper Saddle River, NJ: Pearson/Prentice Hall, 2005.

Sear, Frank. *Roman Architecture*. London: Routledge, 1998.

Spivey, Nigel. *Etruscan Art*. World of Art. New York: Thames & Hudson, 1997.

Stewart, Peter. *Roman Art*. Oxford: Oxford Univ. Pr., 2004.

_____. *The Social History of Roman Art*. Cambridge; New York: Cambridge Univ. Pr., 2008.

Strong, Donald. *Roman Art*. 2nd. rev. and annotated ed. Pelican History of Art. New Haven: Yale Univ. Pr., 1995.

Vitruvius, Pollio. *Vitruvius on Architecture*. Ed. Thomas G. Smith. New York: Monacelli, 2003.

Ward-Perkins, J. B. *Roman Imperial Architecture*. Pelican History of Art. New Haven: Yale Univ. Pr., 1994, 1981.

Chapter 7 Jewish, Early Christian, and Byzantine Art

Age of Spirituality: Late Antique and Early Christian Art, Third to Seventh Century. New York: Metropolitan Museum of Art, 1979.

Byzantium, 330–1453. Eds. Robin Cormack and Maria Vassilaki. London: Royal Academy of Arts; New York: Abrams, 2008.

Byzantium: Faith and Power (1261–1557). Ed. Helen C. Evans. New York: Metropolitan Museum of Art; New Haven: Yale Univ. Pr., 2004.

Cormack, Robin. *Byzantine Art*. Oxford History of Art. Oxford: Oxford Univ. Pr., 2000.

Cutler, Anthony. *The Hand of the Master: Craftsmanship, Ivory, and Society in Byzantium, 9th–11th Centuries*. Princeton: Princeton Univ. Pr., 1994.

Demus, Otto. *Mosaic Decoration of San Marco, Venice*. Chicago: Univ. of Chicago Pr., 1988.

Fine, Steven. *Art and Judaism in the Greco-Roman World: Toward a New Jewish Archaeology*. Cambridge; New York: Cambridge Univ. Pr., 2005.

Freely, John. *Byzantine Monuments of Istanbul*. Cambridge: New York: Cambridge Univ. Pr., 2004.

The Glory of Byzantium. Eds. Helen C. Evans and William D. Wixon. New York: Abrams, 1997.

Grant, Michael. *From Rome to Byzantium: The Fifth Century A.D*. London; New York: Routledge, 1998.

Interpreting Late Antiquity: Essays on the Post-Classical World. Ed. G. W. Bowersock et al. Harvard University Press Reference Library. Cambridge, MA: Belknap Press of Harvard Univ. Pr., 2001.

Kitzinger, Ernst. *The Art of Byzantium and the Medieval West: Selected Studies*. Bloomington: Indiana Univ. Pr., 1976.

_____. *Byzantine Art in the Making: Main Lines of Stylistic Development in Mediterranean Art 3rd to 7th Century*. Cambridge, MA: Harvard Univ. Pr., 1977.

Kleinbauer, W. Eugene. *Hagia Sophia*. London: Scala; Istanbul: Archaeology & Art Publications, 2004.

Koch, Guntram. *Early Christian Art and Architecture: An Introduction*. London: SCM Pr., 1996.

Krautheimer, Richard. *Early Christian and Byzantine Architecture*. 4th ed. Pelican History of Art. Harmondsworth: Penguin, 1986.

Lowden, John. *Early Christian and Byzantine Art*. Art & Ideas. London: Phaidon, 1997.

Mainstone, R. J. *Hagia Sophia: Architecture, Structure and Liturgy of Justinian's Great Church*. London: Thames & Hudson, 1988.

Mark, Robert, and Ahmet S. Cakmak. *Hagia Sophia from the Age of Justinian to the Present*. Cambridge: Cambridge Univ. Pr., 1992.

Mathews, Thomas F. *Byzantium: From Antiquity to the Renaissance*. New York: Abrams, 1998.

_____. *The Clash of Gods: A Reinterpretation of Early Christian Art*. Princeton: Princeton Univ. Pr., 1999.

The Oxford History of Byzantium. Ed. Cyril Mango. Oxford; New York: Oxford Univ. Pr., 2002.

Olin, Margaret. *The Nation without Art: Examining Modern Discourses on Jewish Art*. Lincoln: Univ. of Nebraska Pr., 2001.

Ousterhout, Robert. *Master Builders of Byzantium*. Princeton: Princeton Univ. Pr., 1999.

Picturing the Bible: The Earliest Christian Art. Ed. Jeffrey Spier. New Haven: Yale Univ. Pr., 2007.

Rutgers, Leonard V. *Subterranean Rome: In Search of the Roots of Christianity in the Catacombs of the Eternal City*. Leuven: Peeters, 2000.

Sed-Rajna, Gabrielle. *Jewish Art*. New York: Abrams, 1997.

Tree of Paradise: Jewish Mosaics From the Roman Empire. Ed. Edward Bleiberg. Brooklyn: Brooklyn Museum, 2005.

Vio, Ettore, and Eunio Concina. *The Basilica of St. Mark in Venice*. New York: Riverside Pr., 1999.

Webb, Matilda. *The Churches and Catacombs of Early Christian Rome: A Comprehensive Guide*. Brighton: Sussex Academic Pr., 2001.

Weitzmann, Kurt. *Late Antique and Early Christian Book Illumination*. New York: Braziller, 1977.

Chapter 8 Islamic Art

Al-Andalus: The Art of Islamic Spain. Ed. Jerrilynn D. Dodds. New York: Metropolitan Museum of Art, 1992.

Atil, Esin. *The Age of Sultan Suleyman the Magnificent*. Washington, D.C.: National Gallery of Art, 1987.

Blair, Sheila. *Islamic Calligraphy*. Edinburgh: Edinburgh Univ. Pr., 2006.

Blair, Sheila S., and Jonathan M. Brown. *The Art and Architecture of Islam 1250–1800*. New Haven: Yale Univ. Pr., 1994.

Brend, Barbara. *Islamic Art*. Cambridge, MA: Harvard Univ. Pr., 1991.

Canby, Sheila R. *Islamic Art in Detail*. London: British Museum, 2005.

Dodds, Jerrilyn D., ed. *Al Andalus: The Art of Islamic Spain*. New York: Metropolitan Museum of Art, 1992.

Ettinghausen, Richard. *Islamic Art and Architecture, 650–1250*. 2nd ed. Pelican History of Art. New Haven: Yale Univ. Pr., 2001.

Frishman, Martin, and Hasan-Uddin Khan. *The Mosque: History, Architectural Development and Regional Diversity*. London: Thames & Hudson, 1994.

Grabar, Oleg. *The Alhambra*. Cambridge, MA: Harvard Univ. Pr., 1978.

_____. *The Dome of the Rock*. Cambridge, MA: Harvard Univ. Pr., 2006.

_____. *The Formation of Islamic Art*. New Haven: Yale Univ. Pr., 1987.

_____. *Islamic Visual Culture, 1100–1800*. Constructing the Study of Islamic Art, Vol. 2. Aldershot, UK; Burlington, VT: Ashgate/Variorum, 2006.

_____. *Mostly Miniatures: An Introduction to Persian Painting*. Princeton: Princeton Univ. Pr., 2000.

_____, and Richard Ettinghausen. *The Art and Architecture of Islam, 650–1250*. Penguin History of Art. New Haven: Yale Univ. Pr., 2001.

Hillenbrand, Robert. *Islamic Art and Architecture*. London: Thames & Hudson, 1999.

Irwin, Robert. *The Alhambra*. Cambridge, MA: Harvard Univ. Pr., 2004.

_____. *Islamic Art in Context: Art, Architecture, and the Literary World*. Perspectives. New York: Abrams, 1997.

The Koran: With a Parallel Arabic Text. Trans. with notes by N. J. Dawood. London; New York: Penguin Books, 2000.

Necipoglu, Gülru. *The Age of Sinan: Architectural Culture in the Ottoman Empire*. London: Reaktion, 2005.

Palace and Mosque: Islamic Art from the Near East. Ed. Tim Stanley. London: Victoria and Albert Museum, 2004.

Sims, Eleanor. *Peerless Images: Persian Painting and Its Sources*. New Haven; London: Yale Univ. Pr., 2002.

Welch, Stuart C. *From Mind, Heart, and Hand: Persian, Turkish, and Indian Drawings From the Stuart Cary Welch Collection*. New Haven: Yale Univ. Pr.; Cambridge, MA: Harvard Univ. Art Museums, 2004.

Chapter 9 Later Asian Art

Addiss, Stephen. *77 Dances: Japanese Calligraphy by Poets, Monks, and Scholars, 1568–1868*. Boston: Weatherhill, 2006.

_____. *How to Look at Japanese Art*. New York: Abrams, 1996.

Andrews, Julia F. *A Century in Crisis: Modernity and Tradition in the Art of Twentieth-Century China*. New York: Guggenheim Museum, 1998.

Asher, Catherine B. *Architecture of Mughal India*. New York: Cambridge Univ. Pr., 1992.

Awakenings: Zen Figure Painting in Medieval Japan. Eds. Naomi N. Richard and Melanie B. D. Klein. New York: Japan Society; New Haven: Yale Univ. Pr., 2007.

Barnhart, Richard M., et al. *Three Thousand Years of Chinese Painting*. The Culture & Civilization of China. New Haven: Yale Univ. Pr.; Beijing: Foreign Languages Pr., 1997.

Beach, Milo Cleveland. *Mughal and Rajput Painting*. New York: Cambridge Univ. Pr., 1992.

Blurton, T. Richard. *Hindu Art*. Cambridge, MA: Harvard Univ. Pr., 1993.

Calza, Gian Carlo. *Hokusai*. London; New York: Phaidon, 2003.

Chinese Architecture. Ed. and exp. by Nancy Steinhardt. New Haven: Yale Univ. Pr.; Beijing: New World Pr., 2002.

Clunas, Craig. *Empire of Great Brightness: Visual and Material Cultures of Ming China, 1368–1644*. Honolulu: Univ. of Hawaii Pr., 2007.

Eight Dynasties of Chinese Painting: The Collections of the Nelson Gallery-Atkins Museum, Kansas City, and the Cleveland Museum of Art. Cleveland: Cleveland Museum of Art; Bloomington: Indiana Univ. Pr., 1980.

Fang, Jing Pei. *Treasures of the Chinese Scholar: Form, Function, and Symbolism*. New York: Weatherhill, 1997.

Fisher, Robert E. *Buddhist Art and Architecture*. World of Art. New York: Thames & Hudson, 1993.

Fong, Wen. *Landscapes Clear and Radiant: The Art of Wang Hui (1632–1717)*. New York: Metropolitan Museum of Art; New Haven: Yale Univ. Pr., 2008.

Guth, Christine. *Art of Edo Japan: The Artist and the City, 1615–1868*. Perspectives. New York: Abrams, 1996.

Hearn, Maxwell K. *How to Read Chinese Paintings*. New York: Metropolitan Museum of Art; New Haven: Yale Univ. Pr., 2008.

Hickman, Money L. *Japan's Golden Age: Momoyama*. New Haven: Yale Univ. Pr., 1996.

Holdsworth, May. *The Forbidden City*. Hong Kong; New York: Oxford Univ. Pr., 1998.

Karetzky, Patricia E. *Chinese Buddhist Art*. New York: Oxford Univ. Pr., 2002.

Khanna, Balraj and Aziz Kurtha. *Art of Modern India*. London: Thames & Hudson, 1998.

Koch, Ebba. *The Complete Taj Mahal and the Riverfront Gardens of Agra*. London: Thames & Hudson, 2006.

Kossak, Steven. *Indian Court Painting, 16th–19th Century*. New York: Metropolitan Museum of Art, 1997.

Latter Days of the Law: Images of Chinese Buddhism, 850–1850. Ed. Marsha Weidner. Lawrence, KS: Spencer Museum of Art, 1994.

Losty, Jeremiah P. *The Art of the Book in India*. London: British Library, 1982.

Merritt, Helen, and Nanako Yamada. *Guide to Modern Japanese Woodblock Prints, 1900–1975*. Honolulu: Univ. of Honolulu Pr., 1995.

Michell, George. *Hindu Art and Architecture*. New York: Thames & Hudson, 2000.

_____. *The Majesty of Mughal Decoration: The Art and Architecture of Islamic India*. London: Thames & Hudson, 2007.

_____. *The Royal Palaces of India*. London: Thames & Hudson, 1994.

Munroe, Alexandra. *Japanese Art after 1945: Scream Against the Sky*. New York: Abrams, 1994.

Murase, Miyeko. *Iconography of the Tale of Genji: Genji Monogatari Ekotoba*. New York: Weatherhill, 1983.

_____. *Masterpieces of Japanese Screen Painting: The American Collections*. New York: Braziller, 1990.

Ng, So Kam. *Brushstrokes: Styles and Techniques of Chinese Painting*. San Francisco: Asian Art Museum of San Francisco, 1993.

Plutschow, Herbert E. *Rediscovering Rikyu and the Beginnings of the Japanese Tea Ceremony*. Folkestone, UK: Global Oriental, 2003.

Possessing the Past: Treasures From the National Palace Museum. New York: Metropolitan Museum of Art; Taipei: National Palace Museum, 1996.

Rowland, Benjamin. *Art and Architecture of India: Buddhist, Hindu, Jain*. Pelican History of Art. Harmondsworth, UK: Penguin, 1977.

Seo, Audrey Yoshiko. *The Art of Twentieth-Century Zen: Paintings and Calligraphy by Japanese Masters*. Boston: Shambhala, 1998.

Singer, Jane C. *Divine Presence: Arts of India and the Himalayas*. Barcelona: Casa Asia; Milan: 5 Continents, 2003.

Sullivan, Michael. *Art and Artists of Twentieth-Century China*. Berkeley: Univ. of California Pr., 1996.

Thompson, Sarah E. *Undercurrents in the Floating World: Censorship and Japanese Prints*. New York: Asia Society, 1992.

Tillotson, G. H. R. *The Rajput Palaces: The Development of an Architectural Style, 1450–1750*. New York: Oxford Univ. Pr. 1999.

Tregear, Mary. *Chinese Art*. Rev. ed. New York: Thames & Hudson, 1997.

Vainker, S. J. *Chinese Paintings in the Ashmolean Museum*. Oxford: Ashmolean Museum, 2000.

———. *Chinese Pottery and Porcelain: From Prehistory to the Present*. London: British Museum, 1991.

Verma, Som Prakash. *Painting the Mughal Experience*. New Delhi; New York: Oxford Univ. Pr., 2005.

Watson, William. *The Arts of China, 900–1620*. Pelican History of Art. New Haven: Yale Univ. Pr., 2000.

———. *The Arts of China after 1620*. Pelican History of Art. New Haven: Yale Univ. Pr., 2007.

Zhongshi, Ouyang, et al. *Chinese Calligraphy*. New Haven: Yale Univ. Pr.; Beijing: Foreign Languages Pr., 2008.

Chapter 10 Early Medieval and Romanesque Art

Alexander, J. J. G. *Medieval Illuminators and Their Methods of Work*. New Haven: Yale Univ. Pr., 1992.

Backhouse, Janet. *The Golden Age of Anglo-Saxon Art, 966–1066*. Bloomington: Indiana Univ. Pr., 1984.

Bandmann, Günter. *Early Medieval Architecture as Bearer of Meaning*. New York: Columbia Univ. Pr., 2005.

Benton, Janetta R. *Art of the Middle Ages*. World of Art. New York: Thames & Hudson, 2002.

Braunfels, Wolfgang. *Monasteries of Western Europe: The Architecture of the Orders*. New York: Thames & Hudson, 1993.

Brown, Michelle. *Understanding Illuminated Manuscripts: A Guide to Technical Terms*. Malibu, CA: J. Paul Getty Museum and the British Library, 1994.

Calkins, Robert C. *Illuminated Books of the Middle Ages*. Ithaca, NY: Cornell Univ. Pr., 1983.

———. *Medieval Architecture in Western Europe: From A.D. 300–1500*. New York: Oxford Univ. Pr., 1998.

———. *Monuments of Medieval Art*. New York: Dutton, 1979.

Caviness, Madeline H. "Hildegard as Designer of the Illustrations to her Works." In *Hildegard of Bingen: The Context of her Thought and Art*. Eds. Charles Burnett and Peter Dronke. London: Warburg Institute, 1998, pp. 29–63.

Coldstream, Nicola. *Masons and Sculptors*. Toronto; Buffalo: Univ. of Toronto Pr., 1991.

A Companion to Medieval Art. Ed. Conrad Rudolph. Blackwell Companions to Art History. Oxford: Blackwell, 2006.

Conant, Kenneth J. *Carolingian and Romanesque Architecture, 800–1200*. 4th ed. Pelican History of Art. New Haven: Yale Univ. Pr., 1993.

Diebold, William J. *Word and Image: An Introduction to Early Medieval Art*. Boulder, CO: Westview, 2000.

A Documentary History of Art. Ed. Elizabeth G. Holt. Vol. 1. New Haven: Yale Univ. Pr., 1986.

Dodwell, C. R. *Pictorial Arts of the West, 800–1200*. Pelican History of Art. New Haven: Yale Univ. Pr., 1993.

Evans, Angela Care. *The Sutton Hoo Ship Burial*. Rev. ed. London: British Museum, 1994.

Farr, Carol. *The Book of Kells: Its Function and Audience*. British Library Studies in Medieval Culture. London: British Library, 1997.

Forsyth, Ilene H. *The Throne of Wisdom: Wood Sculptures of the Madonna in Romanesque France*. Princeton: Princeton Univ. Pr., 1972.

From Attila to Charlemagne: Arts of the Early Medieval Period in the Metropolitan Museum of Art. Ed. Katharine R. Brown et al. New York: Metropolitan Museum of Art; New Haven: Yale Univ. Pr., 2000.

Harbison, Peter. *The Golden Age of Irish Art: The Medieval Achievement, 600–1200*. London: Thames & Hudson, 1999.

Hearn, M. F. *Romanesque Sculpture: The Revival of Monumental Stone Sculptures in the Eleventh and Twelfth Centuries*. Ithaca, NY: Cornell Univ. Pr., 1981.

Horn, Walter W., and Ernest Born. *Plan of Saint Gall: A Study of the Architecture and Economy of, and Life in a Paradigmatic Carolingian Monastery*. California Studies in the History of Art, 19. 3 vols. Berkeley: Univ. of California Pr., 1979.

Kubach, Hans E. *Romanesque Architecture*. History of World Architecture. New York: Electa/Rizzoli, 1988.

Laing, Lloyd. *Art of the Celts*. World of Art. New York: Thames & Hudson, 1992.

Lasko, Peter. *Ars Sacra, 800–1200*. 2nd ed. Pelican History of Art. New Haven: Yale Univ. Pr., 1994.

Lepage, Jean-Denis. *Castles and Fortifed Cities of Medieval Europe: An Illustrated History*. Jefferson, NC: McFarland, 2002. *Making Medieval Art*. Ed. Phillip Lindley. Donington, UK: Shaun Tyas, 2003.

The Making of England: Anglo-Saxon Art and Culture, AD 600–900. Eds. Leslie Webster and Janet Backhouse. London: British Museum, 1991.

Megaw, Ruth. *Celtic Art: From Its Beginnings to the Book of Kells*. Rev. and exp. ed. New York: Thames & Hudson, 2001.

Mentre, Mirelle. *Illuminated Manuscripts of Medieval Spain*. New York: Thames & Hudson, 1996.

Musset, Lucien. *The Bayeux Tapestry*. New ed. Woodbridge, UK; Rochester, NY: Boydell Pr., 2005.

Myer-Harting, Henry. *Ottonian Book Illumination: An Historical Study*. 2nd rev. ed. 2 vols. London: Harvey Miller, 1999.

Nees, Lawrence. *Early Medieval Art*. Oxford History of Art. Oxford: Oxford Univ. Pr., 2003.

Schapiro, Meyer. *Language of Forms: Lectures on Insular Manuscript Art*. Ed. Jane Rosenthal. New York: Pierpont Morgan Library, 2006.

———. *Romanesque Architectural Sculpture*. Ed. Linda Seidel. Chicago: Univ. of Chicago Pr., 2006.

———. *Romanesque Art*. New York: George Braziller, 1977.

Seidel, Linda. *Legends in Limestone: Lazarus, Gislebertus, and the Cathedral of Autun*. Chicago: Chicago Univ. Pr., 1999.

Sekules, Veronica. *Medieval Art*. Oxford History of Art. Oxford: Oxford Univ. Pr., 2001.

Shahar, Shulamith. *The Fourth Estate: A History of Women in the Middle Ages*. Rev. ed. London; New York: Routledge, 2003.

Snyder, James. *Art of the Middle Ages*. 2nd ed. Upper Saddle River, NJ: Pearson/Prentice Hall, 2006.

Stalley, R. A. *Early Medieval Architecture*. Oxford History of Art. Oxford: Oxford Univ. Pr., 1999.

Stokstad, Marilyn. *Medieval Art*. 2nd ed. Boulder, CO: Westview Pr., 2004.

Vikings: The North Atlantic Saga. Eds. William Fitzhugh and Elisabeth Ward. Washington, D.C.: Smithsonian Institution Pr., 2000.

Williams, John. *The Illustrated Beatus: Corpus of the Illumination of the Commentary on the Apocalypse*. 5 vols. London: Harvey Miller, 1994–2003.

Wilson, David M. *The Bayeux Tapestry: The Complete Tapestry in Color*. New York: Random House, 1985.

Wilson, David M., and Ole Klindt-Jensen. *Viking Art*. 2nd ed. Minneapolis: Univ. of Minnesota Pr., 1980.

Wolf, Norbert. *Romanesque Art*. Basic Genre. Köln: Taschen, 2007.

Chapter 11 Gothic Art

Bellosi, Luciano. *Cimabue*. New York: Abbeville, 1998.

Bony, Jean. *French Gothic Architecture of the 12th and 13th Centuries*. California Studies in the History of Art 20. Berkeley: Univ. of California Pr., 1983.

Branner, Robert. *Gothic Architecture*. New York: George Braziller, 1961.

The Cambridge Companion to Giotto. Eds. Anne Derbes and Mark Sandona. Cambridge; New York: Cambridge Univ. Pr., 2004.

Camille, Michael. *Gothic Art: Glorious Visions*. Perspectives. New York: Abrams, 1996.

Cennini, Cennino d'Andrea. *The Craftsman's Handbook*. Trans. Daniel V. Thompson, Jr. New York: Dover Publications, 1960.

Coldstream, Nicola. *Masons and Sculptors*. Toronto; Buffalo: Univ. of Toronto Pr., 1991.

———. *Medieval Architecture*. Oxford History of Art. Oxford: Oxford Univ. Pr., 2002.

Clark, William W. *The Medieval Cathedrals*. Westport, CT: Greenwood, 2005.

Cole, Bruce. *Giotto: The Scrovegni Chapel, Padua*. New York: Braziller, 1993.

Crosby, Sumner M. *The Royal Abbey of Saint-Denis from Its Beginnings to the Death of Suger, 475–1151*. Yale Publications in the History of Art. New Haven: Yale Univ. Pr., 1987.

A Documentary History of Art. Vol. 1. Ed. Elizabeth G. Holt. New Haven: Yale Univ. Pr., 1986.

Erlande Brandenburg, Alain. *Notre-Dame de Paris*. New York: Abrams, 1998.

Frankl, Paul. *Gothic Architecture*. Rev. ed. New Haven: Yale Univ. Pr., 2000.

Gothic: Art for England 1400–1547. Eds. Richard Marks and Paul Williamson. London: Victoria and Albert Museum; New York: Abrams, 2003.

Grodecki, Louis, and Catherine Brisac. *Gothic Stained Glass, 1200–1300*. Ithaca, NY: Cornell Univ. Pr., 1985.

Grössinger, Christa. *Picturing Women in Late Medieval and Renaissance Art*. New York: St. Martin's, 1997.

Hyman, Timothy. *Sienese Painting: The Art of a City-Republic (1278–1477)*. New York: Thames & Hudson, 2003.

Jordan, Alyce. *Visualizing Kingship in the Windows of the Sainte-Chapelle*. Turnhout: Brepols, 2002.

Maginnis, Hayden B. J. *The World of the Early Sienese Painter*. University Park: Pennsylvania State Univ. Pr., 2001.

Moskowitz, Anita Fiderer. *Italian Gothic Sculpture: c. 1250–c. 1400*. New York: Cambridge Univ. Pr., 2001.

Nussbaum, Norbert. *German Gothic Church Architecture*. Trans. Scott Kleager. New Haven: Yale Univ. Pr., 2000.

Panofsky, Erwin. *Abbot Suger on the Abbey Church of St. Denis and Its Art Treasures*. 2nd ed. Princeton, NJ: Princeton Univ. Pr., 1979.

Poeschke, Joachim. *Italian Frescoes, the Age of Giotto, 1280–1400*. New York: Abbeville, 2005.

Pope-Hennessy, John W. *An Introduction to Italian Sculpture*. 4th ed. 3 vols. Vol. 1: *Italian Gothic Sculpture*. London: Phaidon, 1996.

Sauerlander, Willibald. *Gothic Sculpture in France, 1140–1270*. London: Thames & Hudson, 1972.

Scott, Robert A. *The Gothic Enterprise: A Guide to Understanding the Medieval Cathedral*. Berkeley: Univ. of California Pr., 2003.

Simson, Otto Georg von. *The Gothic Cathedral: Origins of Gothic Architecture and the Medieval Concept of Order*. 3rd ed. Bollingen Series. Princeton: Princeton Univ. Pr., 1988.

Vasari, Giorgio. *The Lives of the Artists*. Trans. Julia and Peter Bondanella. New York: Oxford Univ. Pr., 1991.

White, John. *Art and Architecture in Italy, 1250 to 1400*. 3rd ed. Pelican History of Art. Harmondsworth: Penguin, 1993.

Wieck, Roger S. *Painted Prayers: The Book of Hours in Medieval and Renaissance Art*. New York: Braziller in assoc. with the Pierpont Morgan Library, 1997.

Williamson, Paul. *Gothic Sculpture, 1140–1300*. Pelican History of Art. New Haven: Yale Univ. Pr., 1995.

Wilson, Christopher. *The Gothic Cathedral: The Architecture of the Great Church, 1130–1530*. Repr. with revisions. New York: Thames & Hudson, 2000.

Chapter 12 Early Renaissance Art

Adams, Laurie. *Italian Renaissance Art*. Boulder, CO: Westview Pr., 2001.

Ames, Lewis F. *The Intellectual Life of the Early Renaissance Artist*. New Haven: Yale Univ. Pr., 2000.

Baxandall, Michael. *Painting and Experience in Fifteenth-Century Italy: A Primer in the Social History of Pictorial Style*. 2nd ed. Oxford; New York: Oxford Univ. Pr., 1988.

Black, C. F. *Cultural Atlas of the Renaissance*. New York: Prentice Hall, 1993.

Borchert, Till-Holger. *Jan van Eyck: Renaissance Realist*. Köln: Taschen, 2008.

The Cambridge Companion to Masaccio. Ed. Diana C. Ahl. New York: Cambridge Univ. Pr., 2002.

Campbell, Lorne. *National Gallery of Art Catalogues: The Fifteenth Century Netherlandish Schools*. London: National Gallery, 1998.

Cavallo, Adolph S. *The Unicorn Tapestries at the Metropolitan Museum of Art*. New York: The Metropolitan Museum of Art; Abrams, 1998.

Christine de Pizan. *The Book of the City of Ladies*. Trans. Earl J. Richards. New York: Persea Books, 1982.

Cole, Bruce. *Studies in the History of Italian Art, 1250–1550*. London: Pindar, 1996.

The Gates of Paradise: Lorenzo Ghiberti's Renaissance Masterpiece. Ed. G. M. Radke. Atlanta: High Museum of Art, 2007.

Goldwater, Robert, and Marco Treves. *Artists on Art from the XIV to the XX Century*. New York: Pantheon Books, 1945.

Grössinger, Christa. *Picturing Women in late Medieval and Renaissance Art*. Manchester: New York: Manchester Univ. Pr. and St. Martin's, 1997.

Hartt, Frederick, and David G. Wilkins. *History of Italian Renaissance Art: Painting, Sculpture, Architecture*. 6th ed. Upper Saddle River, NJ: Pearson/Prentice Hall, 2007.

Heydenreich, Ludwig Heinrich. *Architecture in Italy, 1400 to 1500*. Rev. by P. Davies. Pelican History of Art. New Haven: Yale Univ. Pr., 1996.

Huizinga, Johan. *The Autumn of the Middle Ages*. Chicago: Univ. of Chicago Pr., 1996.

Koster, Margaret L. "The *Arnolfini Double Portrait*: A Simple Solution." *Apollo* 157 (September 2003), pp. 3–14.

Limentani Virdis, Caterina. *Great Altarpieces: Gothic and Renaissance*. New York: Vendome and Rizzoli, 2002.

Lincoln, Evelyn. *The Invention of the Italian Renaissance Printmaker*. New Haven: Yale Univ. Pr., 2000.

Lubbock, Jules. *Storytelling in Christian Art from Giotto to Donatello*. New Haven; London: Yale Univ. Pr., 2006.

Making Renaissance Art. Ed. Kim Woods. New Haven: Yale Univ. Pr. and The Open University, 2007.

Nevola, Fabrizio. *Siena: Constructing the Renaissance City*. New Haven: Yale Univ. Pr., 2007.

Norman, Diana. *Painting in Late Medieval and Renaissance Siena (1260–1555)*. New Haven: Yale Univ. Pr., 2003.

Pacht, Otto. *Early Netherlandish Painting: From Rogier van der Weyden to Gerard David*. London: Harvey Miller, 1997.

_____. *Van Eyck and the Founders of Early Netherlandish Painting*. London: Harvey Miller, 1994.

Pope-Hennessy, John W. *An Introduction to Italian Sculpture*. 4th ed. 3 vols. Vol. 2: *Italian Renaissance Sculpture*. London: Phaidon, 1996.

Saalman, Howard. *Filippo Brunelleschi: The Buildings*. University Park: Pennsylvania State Univ. Pr., 1993.

Seidel, Linda. *Jan van Eyck's Arnolfini Portrait: Stories of an Icon*. New York: Cambridge Univ. Pr., 1993.

Smith, Jeffrey C. *The Northern Renaissance*. London; New York: Phaidon, 2004.

Snyder, James. *Northern Renaissance Art: Painting, Sculpture, and the Graphic Arts from 1350 to 1575*. 2nd ed. Upper Saddle River, NJ: Pearson/Prentice Hall, 2005.

Vasari, Giorgio. *The Lives of the Artists*. Trans. Julia and Peter Bondanella. New York: Oxford Univ. Pr., 1991.

Welch, Evelyn S. *Art and Society in Italy, 1350–1500*. New ed. Oxford History of Art. Oxford: Oxford Univ. Pr., 2000, 1997.

Chapter 13 Art of the High Renaissance and Reformation

Bambach, Carmen. *Drawing and Painting in the Italian Renaissance Workshop: Theory and Practice, 1300–1600*. Cambridge: Cambridge Univ. Pr., 1999.

Baxandall, Michael. *The Limewood Sculptors of Renaissance Germany*. New Haven: Yale Univ. Pr., 1980.

Black, C. F. *Cultural Atlas of the Renaissance*. New York: Prentice Hall, 1993.

Blunt, Anthony. *Art and Architecture in France: 1500–1700*. 5th ed. Pelican History of Art. New Haven: Yale Univ. Pr., 1999.

Boucher, Bruce. *Andrea Palladio: The Architect in His Time*. 2nd ed. New York: Abbeville, 2007.

Brambilla Barcilon, Pinin. *Leonardo: The Last Supper*. Chicago: Univ. of Chicago Pr., 2001.

Brown, Jonathan. *Painting in Spain, 1500–1700*. Pelican History of Art. New Haven: Yale Univ. Pr., 1998.

Brown, Patricia F. *Art and Life in Renaissance Venice*. Perspectives. New York: Abrams, 1997.

Burke, Peter. *The Italian Renaissance: Culture and Society in Italy*. 2nd ed. Princeton: Princeton Univ. Pr., 1999.

The Cambridge Companion to Raphael. Ed. Marcia B. Hall. Cambridge; New York: Cambridge Univ. Pr., 2008.

Chastel, Andre. *French Art*. 4 vols. Vol. 2: *The Renaissance, 1430–1620*. Paris: Flammarion, 1995.

Cole, Alison. *Virtue and Magnificence: Art of the Italian Renaissance Courts*. Perspectives. New York: Abrams, 1995.

Dixon, Laurinda. *Bosch*. Art & Ideas. New York: Phaidon Pr., 2003.

Farago, Claire J. *Reframing the Renaissance: Visual Culture in Europe and Latin America, 1450–1650*. New Haven: Yale Univ. Pr., 1995.

Ferino Pagden, Sylvia. *Sofonisba Anguissola: A Renaissance Woman*. Washington, D.C.: National Museum of Women in the Arts, 1995.

Field, Judith V. *The Invention of Infinity: Mathematics and Art in the Renaissance*. Oxford: Oxford Univ. Pr., 1997.

Foister, Susan. *Holbein and England*. New Haven: Published for Paul Mellon Centre for Studies in British Art by Yale Univ. Pr., 2004.

Franklin, David. *Painting in Renaissance Florence, 1500–1550*. New Haven: Yale Univ. Pr., 2001.

Freedberg, S. J. *Painting in Italy, 1500 to 1600*. 3rd ed. Pelican History of Art. New Haven: Yale Univ. Pr., 1993.

The Genius of Venice, 1500–1600. Eds. Jane Martineau and Charles Hope. New York: Abrams, 1984.

Goffen, Rona. *Renaissance Rivals: Michelangelo, Leonardo, Raphael, Titian*. New Haven: Yale Univ. Pr., 2002.

———. *Titian's Venus of Urbino*. Masterpieces of Western Painting. Cambridge, UK: Cambridge Univ. Pr., 1997.

———. *Titian's Women*. New Haven: Yale Univ. Pr., 1997.

Graham-Dixon, Andrew. *Renaissance*. Berkeley: Univ. of California Pr., 1999.

Hall, Marcia B. *After Raphael: Painting in Central Italy in the Sixteenth Century*. Cambridge; New York: Cambridge Univ. Pr., 1999.

Harbison, Craig. *The Mirror of the Artist: Northern Renaissance Art in Its Historical Context*. Perspectives. New York: Abrams, 1995.

Hopkins, Andrew. *Italian Architecture: from Michelangelo to Borromini*. London; New York: Thames & Hudson, 2002.

The Image of the Individual: Portraits in the Renaissance. Eds. Nicolas Mann and Luke Syson. London: British Museum Pr., 1998.

Italian Women Artists: From Renaissance to Baroque. Ed. Elizabeth S. G. Nicholson et al. Milan: Skira; New York: Rizzoli, 2007.

Koerner, Joseph L. *The Reformation of the Image*. Chicago: Univ. of Chicago Pr., 2004.

Landau, David, and Peter Parshall. *The Renaissance Print: 1470–1550*. New Haven: Yale Univ. Pr., 1994.

Leonardo da Vinci, Michelangelo, and the Renaissance in Florence. Ed. David Franklin. Ottawa: National Gallery of Canada, 2005.

Looking at Italian Renaissance Sculpture. Ed. Sarah B. McHam. Cambridge: Cambridge Univ. Pr., 1998.

Lotz, Wolfgang. *Architecture in Italy, 1500–1600*. Pelican History of Art. New Haven: Yale Univ. Pr., 1995.

Markschies, Alexander. *Icons of Renaissance Architecture*. Munich; New York: Prestel, 2003.

Murray, Linda. *The High Renaissance and Mannerism: Italy, the North, and Spain, 1500–1600*. World of Art. London: Thames & Hudson, 1995.

Nash, Susie. *Northern Renaissance Art*. New York: Oxford Univ. Pr., 2008.

Paoletti, John T., and Gary M. Radke. *Art in Renaissance Italy*. 3rd ed. Upper Saddle River, NJ: Pearson/Prentice Hall, 2005.

Partridge, Loren W. *The Art of Renaissance Rome, 1400–1600*. Perspectives. New York: Abrams, 1996.

_____. *Michelangelo, the Last Judgment: A Glorious Restoration*. New York: Abrams, 1997.

Picturing Women in Renaissance and Baroque Italy. Eds. Geraldine A. Johnson and Sara F. M. Grieco. Cambridge; New York: Cambridge Univ. Pr., 1997.

Pope-Hennessy, John W. *An Introduction to Italian Sculpture*. 4th ed. 3 vols. Vol. 3: *Italian High Renaissance and Baroque Sculpture*. London: Phaidon Pr., 1996.

Renaissance Florence: A Social History. Eds. Roger J. Crum and John T. Paoletti. New York: Cambridge Univ. Pr., 2006.

Renaissance Venice and the North: Crosscurrents in the Time of Bellini, Dürer, and Titian. Eds. Bernard Aikema and Beverly Brown. New York: Rizzoli, 2000.

Richter, Gottfried. *The Isenheim Altar: Suffering and Salv-ation in the Art of Grünewald*. Edinburgh: Floris Books, 1998.

Rosand, David. *Painting in Cinquecento Venice: Titian, Veronese, Tintoretto*. Rev. ed. Cambridge: Cambridge Univ. Pr., 1997.

Rowland, Ingrid D. *The Culture of the High Renaissance: Ancients and Moderns in Sixteenth-Century Rome*. Cambridge: Cambridge Univ. Pr., 1998.

The Sistine Chapel: A Glorious Restoration. Eds. Pierluigi de Vecchi et al. New York: Abrams, 1994.

Sixteenth-Century Italian Art. Ed. Michael W. Cole. Malden, MA; Oxford: Blackwell, 2006.

Smith, Jeffrey Chipps. *The Northern Renaissance*. London; New York: Phaidon, 2004.

Snyder, James. *Northern Renaissance Art: Painting, Sculpture, and the Graphic Arts from 1350 to 1575*. 2nd ed. Upper Saddle River, NJ: Pearson/Prentice Hall, 2005.

Titian to Tiepolo: Three Centuries of Italian Art. Ed. Gilberto Algranti. New York: Rizzoli/St. Martin's, 2002.

Turner, Richard. *Renaissance Florence: The Invention of a New Art*. Perspectives. New York: Abrams, 1997.

Vasari, Giorgio. *The Lives of the Artists*. Trans. Julia and Peter Bondanella. New York: Oxford Univ. Pr., 1991.

Wohl, Hellmut. *The Aesthetics of Italian Renaissance Art: A Reconsideration of Style*. Cambridge: Cambridge Univ. Pr., 1999.

Women Who Ruled: Queens, Goddesses, Amazons in Renaissance and Baroque Art. Ed. Annette Dixon. London: Merrell; Ann Arbor: Univ. of Michigan Museum of Art, 2002.

Wundram, Manfred. *Andrea Palladio, 1508–1580: Architect Between the Renaissance and Baroque*. Köln; Los Angeles: Taschen, 2004.

Zerner, Henri. *Renaissance Art in France: The Invention of Classicism*. Paris: Flammarion; London: Thames & Hudson, 2003.

Chapter 14 Seventeenth-Century Art in Europe

Alpers, Svetlana. *The Art of Describing: Dutch Art in the Seventeenth Century*. Chicago: Chicago Univ. Pr., 1983.

_____. *The Making of Rubens*. New Haven: Yale Univ. Pr., 1995.

Baroque Architecture, Sculpture, Painting. Ed. Rolf Toman. Köln: Könemann, 1998.

Blunt, Anthony. *Roman Baroque*. London: Pallas Athene, 2001.

Boucher, Bruce. *Italian Baroque Sculpture*. World of Art. New York: Thames & Hudson, 1998.

Brown, Jonathan. *Painting in Spain, 1500–1700*. Pelican History of Art. New Haven: Yale Univ. Pr., 1998.

Brown, Jonathan, and Carmen Garrido. *Velasquez: The Technique of Genius*. New Haven: Yale Univ. Pr., 1998.

The Cambridge Companion to Velázquez. Ed. Suzanne L. Stratton-Pruitt. Cambridge; New York: Cambridge Univ. Pr., 2002.

The Cambridge Companion to Vermeer. Ed. Wayne E. Franits. Cambridge: Cambridge Univ. Pr., 2001.

Chapman, H. Perry. *Rembrandt's Self-Portraits: a Study in 17th-Century Identity*. Princeton: Princeton Univ. Pr., 1990.

Chastel, Andre. *French Art*. 4 vols. Vol. 3: *The Ancien Régime, 1620–1775*. Paris: Flammarion, 1995.

Earls, Irene. *Baroque Art: A Topical Dictionary*. Westport, CT: Greenwood, 1996.

Franits, Wayne E. *Dutch Seventeenth-Century Genre Painting: Its Stylistic and Thematic Evolution*. New Haven: Yale Univ. Pr., 2004.

The Genius of Rome, 1592–1623. Ed. Beverly L. Brown. London: Royal Academy of Arts; New York: Abrams, 2001.

Italian Women Artists: From Renaissance to Baroque. Ed. Elizabeth S. G. Nicholson et al. Milan: Skira; New York: Rizzoli, 2007.

Judith Leyster: A Dutch Master and Her World. Eds. James Welu and Pieter Biesboer. New Haven: Yale Univ. Pr., 1993.

Keazor, Henry. *Nicolas Poussin, 1594–1665*. Köln; London: Taschen, 2007.

Kiers, Judikje. *Golden Age of Dutch Art: Painting, Sculpture, and Decorative Art*. London: Thames & Hudson, 2000.

Lagerlof, Margaretha R. *Ideal Landscape: Annibale Caracci, Nicolas Poussin, and Claude Lorrain*. New Haven: Yale Univ. Pr., 1990.

Lemerle, Frédérique. *Baroque Architecture 1600–1750*. Paris: Flammarion, 2008.

Liedtke, Walter. *Vermeer and the Delft School*. New York: Metropolitan Museum of Art, 2001.

Minor, Vernon H. *Baroque and Rococo: Art & Culture*. New York: Abrams, 1999.

Olson, Todd. *Poussin and France: Painting, Humanism, and the Politics of Style*. New Haven: Yale Univ. Pr., 2002.

Pérouse de Montclos, Jean-Marie. *Versailles*. New York: Abbeville, 1991.

Picturing Women in Renaissance and Baroque Italy. Eds. Geraldine A. Johnson and Sara F. M. Grieco. Cambridge; New York: Cambridge Univ. Pr., 1997.

Pope-Hennessy, John W. *An Introduction to Italian Sculpture*. 4th ed. 3 vols. Vol. 2: *Italian Renaissance Sculpture*; Vol. 3: *Italian High Renaissance and Baroque Sculpture*. London: Phaidon, 1996.

Rand, Richard. *Claude Lorrain, the Painter as Draftsman: Drawings from the British Museum*. New Haven: Yale Univ. Pr.; Williamstown, MA: Clark Art Institute, 2006.

Saints & Sinners: Caravaggio & the Baroque Image. Ed. Franco Mormando. Boston: McMullen Museum of Art and Univ. of Chicago Pr., 1999.

Slive, Seymour. *Dutch Painting 1600–1800*. Pelican History of Art. New Haven: Yale Univ. Pr., 1995.

Sutton, Peter. *The Age of Rubens*. Boston: Museum of Fine Arts, 1993.

Tomlinson, Janis. *From El Greco to Goya: Painting in Spain, 1561–1828*. Perspectives. New York: Abrams, 1997.

The Triumph of the Baroque: Architecture in Europe, 1600–1750. Ed. Henry A. Millon. New York: Rizzoli, 1999.

Varriano, John. *Caravaggio: The Art of Realism*. University Park, PA: The Pennsylvania State Univ. Pr., 2006.

Vlieghe, Hans. *Flemish Art and Architecture, 1585–1700*. Pelican History of Art. New Haven: Yale Univ. Pr., 1998.

Westermann, Mariët. *Art and Home: Dutch Interiors in the Age of Rembrandt*. Denver, CO: Denver Art Museum; Netherlands: Waanders, 2001.

_____. *A Worldly Art: The Dutch Republic, 1585–1718*. Perspectives. New York: Abrams, 1996.
White, Christopher. *Rembrandt as an Etcher: A Study of the Artist at Work*. 2nd ed. New Haven: Yale Univ. Pr., 1999.
Wittkower, Rudolf. *Art and Architecture in Italy, 1600 to 1750*. 6th rev. ed. 3 vols. Pelican History of Art. New Haven: Yale Univ. Pr., 1999.

Chapter 15 Art of the Americas

Art of the North American Indians: The Thaw Collection. Ed. Gilbert T. Vincent et al. Cooperstown, NY: Fenimore Art Museum and Univ. of Washington Pr., 2000.
Auger, Emily E. *The Way of Inuit Art: Aesthetics and History In and Beyond the Arctic*. Jefferson, NC: McFarland, 2005.
Berlo, Janet C., and Ruth B. Phillips. *Native North American Art*. Oxford History of Art. Oxford: Oxford Univ. Pr., 1998.
Broder, Patricia Janis. *Earth Songs, Moon Dreams: Paintings by American Indian Women*. New York: St. Martin's Pr., 1999.
Changing Hands: Art Without Reservation. Eds. David McFadden and Ellen Taubman. 2 vols. London: Merrell; New York: American Craft Museum, 2002.
Coe, Michael D. *The Maya*. 7th ed. fully rev. and exp. Ancient Peoples and Places. New York: Thames & Hudson, 2005.
______. *Mexico: From the Olmecs to the Aztecs*. 6th ed. rev. and exp. London: Thames & Hudson, 2008.
Donnan, Christopher. *Moche Portraits from Ancient Peru*. Austin: Univ. of Texas Pr., 2003.
Fagan, Brian M. *Chaco Canyon: Archeologists Explore the Lives of an Ancient Society*. New York: Oxford Univ. Pr., 2005.
First American Art: The Charles and Valerie Diker Collection of American Indian Art. Eds. Bruce Bernstein and Gerald McMaster. Washington, D.C.: National Museum of the American Indian, 2004.
Frank, Larry. *Historic Pottery of the Pueblo Indians, 1600–1880*. 2nd ed. West Chester, PA: Schiffer, 1990.
Hawthorn, Audrey. *Kwakiutl Art*. Seattle: Univ. of Washington Pr.; Vancouver: Douglas & McIntyre, 1994.
Herring, Adam. *Art and Writing in the Maya Cities, A.D. 600–800: A Poetics of Line*. Cambridge: Cambridge Univ. Press, 2005.
Horse Capture, Joseph D., and George P. *Beauty, Honor and Tradition: The Legacy of Plains Indian Shirts*. Washington, D.C.: National Museum of the American Indian; Minneapolis, MN: Univ. of Minnesota Pr., 2001.
Jonaitis, Aldona. *Art of the Northwest Coast*. Seattle: Univ. of Washington Pr.; Vancouver: Douglas & McIntyre, 2006.
Kubler, George. *The Art and Architecture of Ancient America: The Mexican, Maya, and Andean Peoples*. 3rd ed. Pelican History of Art. New Haven: Yale Univ. Pr., 1990.
McQuiston, Don. *Visions of the North: Native Art of the Northwest Coast*. San Francisco: Chronicle Books, 1995.
Master of the Americas: In Praise of the Pre-Columbian Artists: The Dora and Paul Janssen Collection. Ed. Geneviève Le Fort. Brussels: Mercatofonds; Milan: 5 Continents, 2005.
Mexico: Splendors of Thirty Centuries. New York: Metropolitan Museum of Art, 1990.
Miller, Mary Ellen. *The Art of Mesoamerica: from Olmec to Aztec*. 4th ed. World of Art. London: Thames & Hudson, 2006.
———. *Maya Art and Architecture*. World of Art. London: Thames & Hudson, 1999.
———, and Simon Martin. *Courtly Art of the Ancient Maya*. San Francisco: Fine Arts Museums of San Francisco, 2004.
———, and Karl Taube. *The Gods and Symbols of Ancient Mexico and the Maya: An Illustrated Dictionary of Mesoamerican Religion*. London: Thames & Hudson, 1993.
Monroe, Dan L., et al. *Gifts of the Spirit: Works of Nineteenth-Century and Contemporary Native American Artists*. Salem, MA: Peabody Essex Museum, 1996.
Noble, David Grant. *In Search of Chaco: New Approaches to an Archaeological Enigma*. Santa Fe, NM: School of American Research Pr., 2004.
Olmec Art of Ancient Mexico. Eds. Elizabeth P. Benson and Beatriz de la Fuente. Washington, DC: National Gallery of Art, 1996.
Pasztory, Esther. *Pre-Columbian Art*. New York: Cambridge Univ. Pr., 1998.
Penney, David W. *North American Indian Art*. World of Art. London: Thames & Hudson, 2004.
Phillips, Charles. *The Art & Architecture of the Aztec & Maya: An Illustrated Encyclopedia of the Buildings, Sculptures and Art of the Peoples of Mesoamerica*. London: Southwater, 2007.
Power, Susan C. *Early Art of the Southeastern Indians: Feathered Serpents & Winged Beings*. Athens: Univ. of Georgia Pr., 2004.
Raven Travelling: Two Centuries of Haida Art. Ed. Daina Augaitis et al. Vancouver: Vancouver Art Gallery, 2006.
Schobinger, Juan. *The Ancient Americans: A Reference Guide to the Art, Culture, and History of Pre-Columbian North and South America*. Armonk, NY: Sharp Reference, 2001.
Stone-Miller, Rebecca. *Art of the Andes: From Chavin to Inca*. 2nd ed. World of Art. New York: Thames & Hudson, 2002.
Taíno: Pre-Columbian Art and Culture From the Caribbean. Ed. Fatima Bercht et al. New York: El Museo del Barrio: Monacelli, 1997.
Trimble, Stephen. *Talking With the Clay: The Art of Pueblo Pottery in the 21st Century*. 20th Anniversary rev. ed. Santa Fe, NM: School for Advanced Research Pr., 2007.
Uncommon Legacies: Native American Art from the Peabody Essex Museum. Ed. John B Grimes et al. New York: American Federation and the Univ. of Washington Pr., 2002.
Wyatt, Gary. *Mythic Beings: Spirit Art of the Northwest Coast*. Vancouver: Douglas & McIntyre; Seattle: Univ. of Washington Pr., 1999.

Chapter 16 African Art

Africa, Arts and Cultures. Ed. John Mark. London: British Museum, 2000.
African Costumes and Textiles from the Berbers to the Zulus: The Zaira and Marcel Mis Collection. Anne-Marie Bouttiaux et al. Milan: 5 Continents, 2008.
African Seats. Ed. Sandro Bocola. Munich; New York: Prestel, 1995.
Art of the Senses: African Masterpieces from the Teel Collection. Ed. Suzanne P. Blier. Boston: MFA Publications; New York: D.A.P./Distributed Art Publishers, 2004.
Asante, Molefi K. *Spear Masters: An Introduction to African Religion*. Lanham, MD: Univ. Pr. of America, 2007.
Astonishment and Power. Washington, D.C.: National Museum of African Art, 1993.
Bacquart, Jean-Baptiste. *The Tribal Arts of Africa*. New York: Thames & Hudson, 1998.
Bargna, Ivan. *African Art*. Milan: Jaca; Wappingers' Falls, NY: Antique Collector's Club, 2000.
Bassani, Ezio. *African Art and Artifacts in European Collections: 1400–1800*. London: British Museum, 2000.
Bassani, Ezio, et al. *Arts of Africa: 7000 Years of African Art*. Milan: Skira; Monaco: Grimaldi Forum, 2005.
______. *The Power of Form: African Art From the Horstmann Collection*. Milan: Skira; New York: Rizzoli, 2002.
Berzock, Kathleen Bickford. *Benin: Royal Arts of a West African Kingdom*. Chicago: Art Institute of Chicago; New Haven; London: Yale Univ. Pr., 2008.
______. *For Hearth and Altar: African Ceramics From the Keith Achepohl Collection*. Chicago: Art Institute of Chicago; New Haven: Yale Univ. Pr., 2005.
Blauer, Ettagale. *African Elegance*. New York: Rizzoli, 1999.
Blier, Suzanne Preston. *Ritual Arts of Africa: The Majesty of Form*. Perspectives. New York: Abrams, 1998.
Cameron, Elisabeth L. *Art of the Lega*. Los Angeles: UCLA Fowler Museum of Cultural History; Seattle: Univ. of Washington Pr., 2001.
Cultural Atlas of Africa. Ed. Jocelyn Murray. New York: Facts on File, 1998.
Drewal, Henry J. *Beads, Body, and Soul: Art and Light in the Yorùbá Universe*. Los Angeles: Fowler Museum of Cultural History, 1998.
Eternal Ancestors: The Art of the Central African Reliquary. Ed. Alisa LaGamma. New York: Metropolitan Museum of Art; New Haven: Yale Univ. Pr., 2007.
Garlake, Peter S. *Early Art and Architecture of Africa*. Oxford History of Art. Oxford: Oxford Univ. Pr., 2002.
_____. *The Hunter's Vision: The Prehistoric Art of Zimbabwe*. Seattle: Univ. of Washington Pr., 1995.
Gillow, John. *African Textiles*. San Francisco: Chronicle Books, 2003.
Hackett, Rosalind I. J. *Art and Religion in Africa*. Religion in the Arts Series. London; New York: Cassell, 1996.
Hair in African Art and Culture. Eds. Roy Sieber and Frank Herreman. New York: Museum for African Art; Munich; New York: Prestel, 2000.
Jenkins, Earnestine. *A Kingly Craft: Art and Leadership in Ethiopia: A Social History of Art and Visual Culture in Pre-Modern Africa*. Lanham, MD: Univ. Pr. of America, 2008.
Kasfir, Sidney L. *Contemporary African Art*. World of Art. London: Thames & Hudson, 2000.
Magnin, André. *African Art Now: Masterpieces from the Jean Pigozzi Collection*. New York: Merrell; Houston: Museum of Fine Arts, 2005.
Maurer, Evan, and Niangi Batulukisi. *Spirits Embodied: Art of the Congo: Selections From the Helmut F. Stern Collection*. Minneapolis, MN: Minneapolis Institute of Arts, 1999.
McClusky, Pamela. *Art from Africa: Long Steps Never Broke a Back*. Seattle: Seattle Art Museum; Princeton: Princeton Univ. Pr., 2002.
Meyer, Laure. *African Forms: Art and Rituals*. New York: Assouline, 2001.
______. *Art and Craft in Africa: Everyday Life, Ritual, and Court Art*. Paris: Terrail, 1995.
Morris, James, and Suzanne P. Blier. *Butabu: Adobe Architecture of West Africa*. New York: Princeton Architectural Pr., 2004.
Okediji, Moyosore B. *African Renaissance: New Forms, Old Images in Yoruba Art*. Boulder: Univ. Pr. of Colorado, 2002.
Perrois, Louis. *Fang*. Visions of Africa. Milan: 5 Continents, 2006.
Phillips, Tom. *Africa: The Art of a Continent*. London: Prestel, 1996.
Prussin, Labelle. *African Nomadic Architecture: Space, Place, and Gender*. Washington, D.C.: Smithsonian Institution; National Museum of African Art, 1995.
Roy, Christopher D. *Clay and Fire: Pottery in Africa*. Iowa Studies in African Art 4. Iowa City: Univ. of Iowa School of Art & Art History, 2000.
Schuster, Carl, and Edmund Carpenter. *Patterns That Connect: Social Symbolism in Ancient & Tribal Art*. New York: Abrams, 1996.
Spring, Christopher. *Angaza Afrika: African Art Now*. London: Laurence King Publishing, 2008.
Stepan, Peter. *Africa*. London: Prestel, 2001.
______. *Spirits Speak: A Celebration of African Masks*. Munich; New York: Prestel, 2005.
Thompson, Robert F. *Face of the Gods: Art and Altars of Africa and the African Americas*. New York: Museum for African Art; Munich: Prestel, 1993.
Visonà, Monica B., et al. *A History of Art in Africa*. Upper Saddle River, NJ: Pearson/Prentice Hall, 2007.
Vogel, Susan Mullin. *Baule: African Art, Western Eyes*. New Haven: Yale Univ. Art Gallery, 1997.
Wheelock, Thomas G. B. *Land of the Flying Masks: Art and Culture in Burkina Faso*. Munich; New York: Prestel, 2007.
Willett, Frank. *African Art: An Introduction*. 3rd ed. World of Art. New York: Thames & Hudson, 2003.

Chapter 17 European and American Art, 1715–1840

Angelica Kauffman: A Woman of Immense Talent. Ed. Tobias Natter. Ostfildern: Hatje Cantz, 2007.
Antoine Watteau: Perspectives on the Artist and the Culture of His Time. Ed. Mary D. Sheriff. Newark: Univ. of Delaware, 2006.
Art and the Academy in the Nineteenth Century. Eds. Rafael Denis and Colin Trodd. New Brunswick, NJ: Rutgers Univ. Pr., 2000.
Bergdoll, Barry. *European Architecture 1750–1890*. Oxford History of Art. New York: Oxford Univ. Pr., 2000.
Boime, Albert. *Art in an Age of Bonapartism, 1800–1815*. Chicago: Univ. of Chicago Pr., 1990.
_____. *Magisterial Gaze: Manifest Destiny and American Landscape Painting*. Washington, D.C.: Smithsonian Institution, 1991.
Brown, David B. *Romanticism*. Arts & Ideas. London: Phaidon, 2001.
The Cambridge Companion to Delacroix. Ed. Beth S. Wright. Cambridge; New York: Cambridge Univ. Pr., 2001.
Chastel, Andre. *French Art*. 4 vols. Vol. 3: *The Ancien Régime, 1620–1775*; Vol. 4: *The Age of Eloquence, 1775–1820*. Paris: Flammarion, 1995.
Clark, T. J. *The Absolute Bourgeois: Artists and Politics in France, 1848–1851*. Berkeley: Univ. of California Pr., 1999.
_____. *Image of the People: Gustave Courbet and the 1848 Revolution*. Berkeley: Univ. of California Pr., 1999.
Cooper, Wendy A. *Classical Taste in America 1800–1840*. Baltimore: Baltimore Museum of Art, 1993.
Denis, Rafael C., and Colin Trodd. *Art and the Academy in the Nineteenth Century*. New Brunswick, NJ: Rutgers Univ. Pr., 2000.
Eisenman, Stephen, and Thomas E. Crow. *Nineteenth-Century Art: A Critical History*. 3rd ed. London; New York: Thames & Hudson, 2007.

Hallett, Mark. *Hogarth.* Art & Ideas. London: Phaidon, 2000.
Handlin, David P. *American Architecture.* 2nd ed. World of Art. London: Thames & Hudson, 2004.
Hemingway, Andrew, and William Vaughn. *Art in Bourgeois Society, 1790–1850.* Cambridge: Cambridge Univ. Pr., 1998.
Hofmann, Werner. *Goya: To Every Story There Belongs Another.* New York: Thames & Hudson, 2003.
Irwin, David. *Neoclassicism.* London: Phaidon, 1997.
Johns, Christopher M. S. *Antonio Canova and the Politics of Patronage in Revolutionary and Napoleonic Europe.* Berkeley: Univ. of California Pr., 1998.
King, David N. *Complete Works of Robert and James Adam and Unbuilt Adam.* Repr. with corrections and additions. Oxford: Architectural Pr., 2001.
Lewis, Michael J. *American Art and Architecture.* World of Art. London; New York: Thames & Hudson, 2006.
Miller, Angela L., et al. *American Encounters: Art, History and Cultural Identity.* Upper Saddle River, NJ: Pearson/Prentice Hall, 2008.
Mitchell, Timothy. *Art and Science in German Landscape Painting, 1770–1840.* New York: Oxford Univ. Pr., 1993.
Monneret, Sophie. *David and Neoclassicism.* Paris: Terrail, 1999.
Neoclassicism and Romanticism: Architecture, Sculpture, Painting, Drawing, 1750–1848. Ed. Rolf Toman. Köln: Könemann, 2000.
Nineteenth-Century Theories of Art. Ed. Joshua C. Taylor. Berkeley: Univ. of California Pr., 1987.
Novotny, Fritz. *Painting and Sculpture in Europe, 1780–1880.* 2nd ed. Pelican History of Art. New Haven: Yale Univ. Pr., 1995.
Porterfield, Todd B. and Susan L. Siegfried. *Staging Empire: Napoleon, Ingres, and David.* University Park: Pennsylvania State Univ. Pr., 2006.
Prettejohn, Elizabeth. *Beauty and Art, 1750–2000.* Oxford History of Art. Oxford; New York: Oxford Univ. Pr., 2005.
Rosenblum, Robert, and H. W. Janson. *19th-Century Art.* Rev. and updated ed. Upper Saddle River, NJ: Pearson/Prentice Hall, 2005.
Shelton, Andrew C. *Ingres.* London; New York: Phaidon, 2008.
Vaughan, William, and Françoise Cachin. *Arts of the 19th Century.* 2 vols. New York: Abrams, 1998.
West, Alison. *From Pigalle to Préault: Neoclassicism and the Sublime in French Sculpture, 1760–1840.* Cambridge: Cambridge Univ. Pr., 1998.
Wintermute, Alan. *Watteau and His World: French Drawing from 1700–1750.* New York: Rizzoli; St. Martin's, 1999.

Chapter 18 European and American Art, 1840–1910

Adams, Steven. *The Barbizon School and the Origins of Impressionism.* London: Phaidon, 1994.
Adler, Kathleen. *Impressionism.* New Haven: Yale Univ. Pr., 1999.
Adler, Kathleen, et al. *Americans in Paris, 1860–1900.* London: National Gallery, 2006.
Art and the Academy in the Nineteenth Century. Eds. Rafael Denis and Colin Trodd. New Brunswick, NJ: Rutgers Univ. Pr., 2000.
Art, Culture, and National Identity in Fin-de-Siècle Europe. Eds. Michelle Facos and Sharon L. Hirsh. Cambridge; New York: Cambridge Univ. Pr., 2003.
Barger, M. Susan, and William B. White. *The Daguerreotype: Nineteenth-Century Technology and Modern Science.* Washington, D.C.: Smithsonian Institution, 1991.
Baudelaire, Charles. *The Painter of Modern Life, and Other Essays.* Ed. Jonathan Mayne. 2nd ed. London: Phaidon, 1995.
Blakesley, Rosalind P. *The Arts and Crafts Movement.* London: Phaidon, 2006.
Boime, Albert. *The Academy and French Painting in the Nineteenth Century.* New Haven: Yale Univ. Pr., 1986.
Brettell, Richard R. *Impressionism: Painting Quickly in France, 1860–1890.* New Haven: Yale Univ. Pr. and the Clark Art Institute, 2000.
______. *Modern Art, 1851–1929: Capitalism and Representation.* Oxford History of Art. Oxford: Oxford Univ. Pr., 1999.
Broude, Norma. *Impressionism: A Feminist Reading: The Gendering of Art, Science, and Nature in the Nineteenth Century.* New York: Rizzoli, 1991.
_____. *World Impressionism: The International Movement, 1860–1920.* New York: Abrams, 1990.
Callen, Anthea. *The Art of Impressionism: Painting Technique and the Making of Modernity.* New Haven: Yale Univ. Pr., 2000.
Clark, T. J. *The Painting of Modern Life: Paris in the Time of Manet and His Followers.* Rev. ed. Princeton: Princeton Univ. Pr., 1999.
Clarke, Graham. *The Photograph.* Oxford History of Art. Oxford: Oxford Univ. Pr., 1997.
Conrads, Margaret C. *Winslow Homer and the Critics: Forging a National Art in the 1870s.* Princeton: Princeton Univ. Pr. and the Nelson-Atkins Museum of Art, 2001.
Critical Readings in Impressionism and Post-Impressionism: An Anthology. Ed. Mary T. Lewis. Berkeley: Univ. of California Pr., 2007.
Denvir, Bernard *Post-Impressionism.* World of Art. New York: Thames & Hudson, 1992.
Escritt, Stephen. *Art Nouveau.* Arts & Ideas. London: Phaidon, 2000.
The French Academy: Classicism and Its Antagonists. Ed. June Hargrove. Newark: Univ. of Delaware Pr., 1990.
Gerdts, William H. *American Impressionism.* 2nd ed. New York: Abbeville, 2001.
Gibson, Michael. *Symbolism.* Köln: Taschen, 1995.
Gray, Michael, et al. *First Photographs: William Henry Fox Talbot and the Birth of Photography.* New York: PowerHouse Books; Museum of Photographic Arts, San Diego, 2002.
Hamilton, George H. *Painting and Sculpture in Europe, 1880–1940.* 6th ed. Pelican History of Art. New Haven: Yale Univ. Pr., 1993.
Handlin, David P. *American Architecture.* 2nd ed. World of Art. London: Thames & Hudson, 2004.
Herbert, Robert L. *From Millet to Léger: Essays in Social Art History.* New Haven: Yale Univ. Pr., 2002.
_____. *Seurat: Drawings and Paintings.* New Haven. Yale Univ. Pr., 2001.
Higonnet, Anne. *Berthe Morisot's Images of Women.* Cambridge, MA: Harvard Univ. Pr., 1992.
Hornberg, Cornelia. *Vincent van Gogh and the Painters of the Petit Boulevard.* New York: St. Louis Art Museum; Rizzoli, 2001.
House, John. *Impressionism: Paint and Politics.* New Haven: Yale Univ. Pr., 2004.
Kendall, Richard. *Degas: Beyond Impressionism.* London: National Gallery, 1996.
Lambourne, Lionel. *Japonisme: Cultural Crossings between Japan and the West.* New York: Phaidon, 2005.
Lewer, Debbie. *Post-Impressionism to World War II.* Malden, MA: Blackwell, 2006.
Lewis, Mary T. *Cézanne.* Arts & Ideas. London: Phaidon, 2000.
Lewis, Michael J. *American Art and Architecture.* World of Art. London; New York: Thames & Hudson, 2006.
Lucie-Smith, Edward. *American Realism.* New York: Abrams, 1994.
Machotka, Pavel. *Cezanne: Landscape into Art.* New Haven: Yale Univ. Pr., 1996.
Malpas, James. *Realism.* Cambridge: Cambridge Univ. Pr., 1997.
Masson, Raphaël. *Rodin.* Paris: Flammarion; Paris: Musée Rodin, 2004.
Miller, Angela L., et al. *American Encounters: Art, History, and Cultural Identity.* Upper Saddle River, NJ: Pearson/Prentice Hall, 2008.
Newhall, Beaumont. *The History of Photography: From 1839 to the Present.* Rev. and exp. 5th ed. New York: Museum of Modern Art; Boston: Little, Brown, 1999.
Nochlin, Linda. *Representing Women.* New York: Thames & Hudson, 1999.
Nord, Phillip. *Impressionists and Politics: Art and Democracy in the Nineteenth Century.* London: Routledge, 2000.
Novak, Barbara. *American Painting of the Nineteenth Century: Realism, Idealism, and the American Experience.* 3rd ed., with a new pref. Oxford; New York: Oxford Univ. Pr., 2007.
Orvell, Miles. *American Photography.* Oxford History of Art. Oxford: New York: Oxford Univ. Pr., 2003.
The Oxford Companion to the Photograph. Ed. Robin Lenman. Oxford; New York: Oxford Univ. Pr., 2005.
Post-Impressionism: Cross-currents in European and American Painting, 1880–1906. Washington, D.C.: National Gallery of Art, 1980.
Rapetti, Rodolphe. *Symbolism.* Paris: Flammarion; New York: Rizzoli, 2005.
Roos, Jane Mayo. *Early Impressionism and the French State, 1866–1874.* Cambridge: Cambridge Univ. Pr., 1996.
Rosenblum, Naomi. *A World History of Photography.* 4th ed. New York: Abbeville, 2007.
Rosenblum, Robert, and H.W. Janson. *19th-Century Art.* Rev. and updated ed. Upper Saddle River, NJ: Pearson/Prentice Hall, 2005.
Rubin, James Henry. *Impressionism.* London: Phaidon, 1999.
______. *Impressionism and the Modern Landscape: Productivity, Technology, and Urbanization from Manet to Van Gogh.* Berkeley: Univ. of California Pr., 2008.
Schapiro, Meyer. *Impressionism: Reflections and Perceptions.* New York: George Braziller, 1997.
Sewell, Darrel. *Thomas Eakins.* Philadelphia: Philadelphia Museum of Art, 2001.
Smith, Paul. *Impressionism: Beneath the Surface.* Perspectives. New York: Abrams, 1995.
_____. *Seurat and the Avant-Garde.* New Haven: Yale Univ. Pr., 1997.
Thomson, Belinda. *Impressionism: Origins, Practice, Reception.* New York: Thames & Hudson, 2000.
_____. *Post-Impressionism.* Movements in Modern Art. Cambridge: Cambridge Univ. Pr., 1998.
Todd, Pamela. *Pre-Raphaelites at Home.* New York: Watson-Guptill, 2001.
Treuherz, Julian. *Dante Gabriel Rossetti.* London: Thames & Hudson, 2003.
Van Gogh's Imaginary Museum: Exploring the Artist's Inner World. Amsterdam: Van Gogh Museum; New York: Abrams, 2003.
Werner, Marcia. *Pre-Raphaelite Painting and Nineteenth-Century Realism.* Cambridge; New York: Cambridge Univ. Pr., 2005.
Women in Impressionism: From Mythical Feminine to Modern Woman. Ed. Sidsel M. Søndergaard. Milan: Skira; New York: Rizzoli, 2006.

Chapter 19 Modern Art in Europe and the Americas, 1900–1945

The A-Z of Modern Architecture. Ed. Peter Gössel. Köln; Los Angeles: Taschen, 2007.
American Art in the 20th Century: Painting and Sculpture, 1913–1993. Ed. Christos M. Joachimides and Norman Rosenthal. Munich: Prestel; New York: te Neues, 1993.
Antliff, Mark. *Cubism and Culture.* World of Art. London: Thames & Hudson, 2001.
Arnason, H. H. *History of Modern Art: Painting, Sculpture, Architecture, Photography.* 6th ed. Upper Saddle River, NJ: Pearson/Prentice Hall, 2009.
Art in Theory, 1900–1990: An Anthology of Changing Ideas. Eds. Charles Harrison and Paul Woods. New ed. Cambridge, MA: Blackwell, 2003.
Art of the Forties. Ed. Riva Castleman. New York: Museum of Modern Art, 1991.
Bauhaus Culture: From Weimar to the Cold War. Ed. Kathleen James-Chakraborty. Minneapolis: Univ. of Minnesota Pr., 2006.
Bearden, Romare. *A History of African-American Artists: From 1792 to the Present.* New York: Pantheon, 1993.
Behr, Shulamith. *Expressionism.* New York: Cambridge Univ. Pr., 1999.
Bois, Yves Alain. *Matisse and Picasso.* Paris: Flammarion, 1998.
Brown, Milton W. *The Story of the Armory Show: The 1913 Exhibition That Changed American Art.* 2nd ed. New York: Abbeville, 1988.
Chipp, Herschel B. *Theories of Modern Art: A Source Book by Artists and Critics.* California Studies in the History of Art 11. Berkeley: Univ. of California Pr., 1996.
Colquhoun, Alan. *Modern Architecture.* Oxford History of Art. Oxford; New York: Oxford Univ. Pr., 2002.
Corn, Wanda. *The Great American Thing: Modern Art and National Identity, 1915–1935.* Berkeley: Univ. of California Pr., 1999.
Cowling, Elizabeth, et al. *Matisse, Picasso.* London: Tate; Paris: Réunion des Musées Nationaux; New York: Museum of Modern Art, 2002.
Craven, Wayne. *American Art: History and Culture.* Rev. ed. New York: McGraw Hill, 2003.
Curtis, Penelope. *Sculpture, 1900–1945: After Rodin.* Oxford History of Art. Oxford: Oxford Univ. Pr., 1999.
Dachy, Marc. *Dada: The Revolt of Art.* New York: Abrams, 2006.
Dada. Ed. Rudolf Kuenzli. Themes and Movements. London; New York: Phaidon, 2006.
Davies, Hugh M., et al. *Frida Kahlo, Diego Rivera, and Twentieth-Century Mexican Art: the Jacques and Natasha Gelman Collection.* San Diego: Museum of Contemporary Art, 2000.
Degenerate Art: The Fate of the Avant-Garde in Nazi Germany. Ed. Stephanie Barron. Los Angeles: Los Angeles County Museum of Art, 1991.
Dickerman, Leah. *Dada: Zurich, Berlin, Hannover, Cologne, New York, Paris.* Washington, D.C.: National Gallery of Art and Distributed Art Publishers, 2005.
Droste, Magdalena. *Bauhaus, 1919–1939.* Köln: Taschen, 1990.
Duchamp, Man Ray, Picabia. Ed. Jennifer Mundy. London: Tate, 2008.

Elger, Dietmar. *Expressionism: A Revolution in German Art*. Köln: Taschen, 1998.

Folgarait, Leon. *Mural Painting and Social Revolution in Mexico, 1920–1940: Art of the New Order*. New York: Cambridge Univ. Pr., 1998.

Foster, Hal, et al. *Art Since 1900: Modernism, Antimodernism, Postmodernism*. Vol. 1, *1900–1944*. New York: Thames & Hudson, 2004.

Frampton, Kenneth. *Modern Architecture: A Critical History*. World of Art. 4th ed. London; New York: Thames & Hudson, 2007.

German Expressionism: Art and Society. Eds. Stephanie Barron and Wolf-Dieter Dube. New York: Rizzoli, 1997.

Golding, John. *Paths to the Absolute: Mondrian, Malevich, Kandinsky, Pollock, Newman, Rothko, and Still*. Princeton: Princeton Univ. Pr., 2000.

Gooding, Mel. *Abstract Art*. Movements in Modern Art. Cambridge; New York: Cambridge Univ. Pr., 2001.

Gray, Camilla. *Russian Experiment in Art, 1863–1922*. Rev. and exp. ed. New York: Thames & Hudson, 1986.

Green, Christopher. *Picasso's Les Demoiselles d'Avignon*. Masterpieces of Western Painting. Cambridge: Cambridge Univ. Pr., 2001.

_____. *Art in France, 1900–1940*. Pelican History of Art. New Haven: Yale Univ. Pr., 2000.

Greenough, Sarah, et al. *Modern Art and America: Alfred Stieglitz and His New York Galleries*. Washington, D.C.: National Gallery of Art; New York: Bullfinch, 2000.

Harrison, Charles. *Primitivism, Cubism, Abstraction: The Early Twentieth Century*. New Haven: Yale Univ. Pr., 1993.

Haskell, Barbara. *The American Century: Art and Culture, 1900–1950*. New York: Whitney Museum of American Art, 1999.

Hunter, Sam. *Modern Art: Painting, Sculpture, Architecture*. 3rd ed. rev. and exp. Upper Saddle River, NJ: Pearson/Prentice Hall, 2004.

Julier, Guy. *The Thames & Hudson Dictionary of Design Since 1900*. 2nd ed. London; New York: Thames & Hudson, 2005.

Klingsöhr-Leroy, Cathrin. *Surrealism*. Köln: Taschen, 2004.

Kovtun, E. F. *The Russian Avant-Garde in the 1920s–1930s: Paintings, Graphics, Sculpture, Decorative Arts from the Russian Museum in St. Petersburg*. Schools and Movements. Bournemouth: Parkstone; St. Petersburg: Aurora, 1996.

Levine, Neil. *The Architecture of Frank Lloyd Wright*. Princeton: Princeton Univ. Pr., 1996.

Lewer, Debbie. *Post-Impressionism to World War II*. Malden, MA: Blackwell, 2006.

Lewis, Samella S. *African American Art and Artists*. Rev. and exp. ed. Berkeley: Univ. of California Pr., 2003.

Lloyd, Jill. *German Expressionism: Primitivism and Modernity*. New Haven: Yale Univ. Pr., 1991.

Lupfer, Gilbert. *Walter Gropius, 1883–1969: The Promoter of a New Form*. Köln: Taschen, 2004.

Miller, Angela L., et al. *American Encounters: Art, History, and Cultural Identity*. Upper Saddle River, NJ: Pearson/Prentice Hall, 2008.

Murray, Joan. *Canadian Art of the Twentieth Century*. Toronto: Dundurn, 1999.

Overy, Paul. *De Stijl*. World of Art. New York: Thames & Hudson, 1991.

The Oxford Companion to the Photograph. Ed. Robin Lenman. Oxford; New York: Oxford Univ. Pr., 2005.

Parkinson, Gavin. *The Duchamp Book*. Essential Artists. London: Tate; New York: Abrams, 2008.

Patton, Sharon. *African-American Art*. Oxford History of Art. Oxford: Oxford Univ. Pr., 1998.

Potts, Alex. *The Sculptural Imagination: Figurative, Modernist, Minimalist*. New Haven: Yale Univ. Pr., 2000.

Powell, Richard J. *Black Art: A Cultural History*. 2nd ed. World of Art. London: Thames & Hudson, 2003.

Rickey, George. *Constructivism: Origins and Evolutions*. Rev. ed. New York: Braziller, 1995.

Rosenblum, Robert. *Cubism and Twentieth-Century Art*. Rev. ed. New York: Abrams, 2001.

Rubin, William. *Picasso and Braque: Pioneering Cubism*. New York: Museum of Modern Art, 1989.

The Sources of Surrealism: Art in Context. Ed. Neil Matheson. Aldershot; Burlington, VT: Lund Humphries, 2006.

Surrealist Painters and Poets: An Anthology. Ed. Mary Ann Caws. Cambridge, MA: MIT Pr., 2001.

Udall, Sharyn R. *Carr, O'Keeffe, Kahlo: Places of Their Own*. New Haven: Yale Univ. Pr., 2000.

Weiss, Jeffrey S. *The Popular Culture of Modern Art: Picasso, Duchamp, and Avant-Gardism*. New Haven: Yale Univ. Pr., 1994.

Whitfield, Sarah. *Fauvism*. World of Art. New York: Thames & Hudson, 1996.

Whitford, Frank. *The Bauhaus: Masters and Students by Themselves*. Woodstock, NY: Overlook Pr., 1993.

Women Artists in the 20th and 21st Century. Ed. Uta Grosenick. Köln; New York: Taschen, 2001.

Wright, Alastair. *Matisse and the Subject of Modernism*. Princeton: Princeton Univ. Pr., 2004.

Yablonskaya, Miuda. *Women Artists of Russia's New Age, 1900–1935*. New York: Rizzoli, 1990.

Zafran, Eric, and Paul Paret. *Surrealism and Modernism: From the Collection of the Wadsworth Atheneum*. Hartford, CT: Wadsworth Atheneum, 2003.

Chapter 20 Art Since 1945

American Art in the 20th Century: Painting and Sculpture, 1913–1993. Eds. Christos M. Joachimides and Norman Rosenthal. Munich: Prestel; New York: te Neues, 1993.

Anfam, David. *Abstract Expressionism*. World of Art. New York: Thames & Hudson, 1990.

Archer, Michael. *Art Since 1960*. 2nd ed. New York: Thames & Hudson, 2002.

Art in Theory, 1900–1990: An Anthology of Changing Ideas. Eds. Charles Harrison and Paul Woods. New ed. Cambridge, MA: Blackwell, 2003.

Atkins, Robert. *Artspeak: A Guide to Contemporary Ideas, Movements, and Buzzwords*. 2nd ed. New York: Abbeville, 1997.

Ault, Julie. *Art Matters: How the Culture Wars Changed America*. Ed. Brian Wallis, Marianne Weems, and Philip Yenawine. New York: New York Univ. Pr., 1999.

Beardsley, John. *Earthworks and Beyond: Contemporary Art in the Landscape*. 4th ed. ebook. New York: Abbeville Press, 2006.

Bishop, Claire. *Installation Art: A Critical History*. New York: Routledge, 2005.

Blais, Joline, and Jon Ippolito. *At the Edge of Art*. London: Thames & Hudson, 2006.

Broude, Norma, and Mary D. Garrard. *The Power of Feminist Art: The American Movement of the 1970s, History and Impact*. New York: Abrams, 1994.

Burton, Johanna, et al. *Pop Art: Contemporary Perspectives: Princeton University Art Museum*. Princeton: The Museum; New Haven: Yale Univ. Pr., 2007.

Conceptual Art: A Critical Anthology. Eds. Alexander Alberro and Blake Stimson. Cambridge, MA: MIT Pr., 1999.

Cotton, Charlotte. *The Photograph as Contemporary Art*. World of Art. London; New York: Thames & Hudson, 2004.

Deepwell, Katy. *Women Artists and Modernism*. New York: St. Martin's, 1998.

Discourses: Conversations in Postmodern Art and Culture. Ed. Russell Ferguson. Documentary Sources in Contemporary Art. Cambridge, MA: MIT Pr., 1990.

Fineberg, Jonathan. *Art Since 1940: Strategies of being*. 3rd. ed. Upper Saddle River: Pearson/Prentice Hall, 2011.

Foster, Hal, et al. *Art Since 1900: Modernism, Antimodernism, Postmodernism*. Vol. 2: *1945 to the present*. New York: Thames & Hudson, 2004.

Goldberg, Rose L. *Performance Art: From Futurism to the Present*. Rev. ed. London: Thames & Hudson, 2001.

Gouma-Peterson, Thalia. *Miriam Schapiro*. New York: Abrams, 1999.

Grande, John K. *Art Nature Dialogues: Interviews with Environmental Artists*. Albany: State Univ. of New York Pr., 2004.

Greenberg, Clement. *Clement Greenberg, Late Writings*. Ed. Robert C. Morgan. Minneapolis: Univ. of Minnesota Pr., 2003.

Heartney, Eleanor, et al. *After the Revolution: Women Who Transformed Contemporary Art*. Munich; New York: Prestel, 2007.

Hertz, Richard. *Theories of Contemporary Art*. 2nd ed. Englewood Cliffs, NJ: Prentice Hall, 1993.

Holzer, Jenny. *Jenny Holzer*. Ostfildern, Germany: Hatje Cantz, 2008.

Joselit, David. *American Art Since 1945*. World of Art. London: Thames & Hudson, 2003.

Kingsley, April. *The Turning Point: The Abstract Expressionists and the Transformation of American Art*. New York: Simon & Schuster, 1992.

Lucie-Smith, Edward. *Movements in Art since 1945*. New ed. World of Art. London: Thames & Hudson, 2001.

Madoff, Steven H. *Pop Art: A Critical History*. Berkeley: Univ. of California Pr., 1997.

Martin, Sylvia. *Video Art*. Basic Art Series. Köln; Los Angeles: Taschen, 2006.

Marzona, Daniel. *Conceptual Art*. Köln; Los Angeles: Taschen, 2005.

_____. *Minimal Art*. Köln; Los Angeles: Taschen, 2004.

McCarthy, David. *Pop Art*. New York: Cambridge Univ. Pr., 2000.

Meyer, James. *Minimalism*. Themes and Movements. London: Phaidon, 2000.

Modern Contemporary: Art Since 1980 at MoMA. Eds. Kirk Varnedoe et al. 2nd ed. New York: Museum of Modern Art and Distributed Art Publishers, 2004.

New York, New York: Fifty Years of Art, Architecture, Cinema, Performance, Photography and Video. Eds. Germano Celant and Lisa Dennison. Milan: Skira; Monaco: Grimaldi Forum, 2006.

The Oxford Companion to the Photograph. Ed. Robin Lenman. Oxford; New York: Oxford Univ. Pr., 2005.

Paul, Christiane. *Digital Art*. 2nd ed. World of Art. London: Thames & Hudson, 2008.

Pearlman, Alison. *Unpackaging Art of the 1980s*. Chicago: Univ. of Chicago Pr., 2003.

Phillips, Lisa. *The American Century: Art and Culture, 1950–2000*. New York: Whitney Museum of American Art, 2000.

Pop Art: Contemporary Perspectives. Princeton: Princeton Univ. Art Museum, 2007.

Ratcliff, Carter. *The Fate of a Gesture: Jackson Pollock and Postwar American Art*. New York: Farrar, Straus, Giroux, 1996.

Rexer, Lyle. *How to Look at Outsider Art*. New York: Abrams, 2005.

Robertson, Jean, and Craig McDaniel. *Themes of Contemporary Art: Visual Art after 1980*. 2nd ed. New York: Oxford Univ. Pr., 2010.

Rush, Michael. *New Media in Art*. 2nd ed. World of Art. London: Thames & Hudson, 2005.

_____. *Video Art*. Rev. ed. London: Thames & Hudson, 2007.

Rushing, Jackson W. *Native American Art in the Twentieth Century: Makers, Meanings, and Histories*. London: Routledge, 1999.

Sandler, Irving. *Art of the Postmodern Era: From the Late 1960s to the Early 1990s*. New York: IconEditions, 1996.

_____. *The New York School: The Painters and Sculptors of the Fifties*. New York: Harper & Row, 1978.

Shapiro, David, and Cecile Shapiro. *Abstract Expressionism: A Critical Record*. New York: Cambridge Univ. Pr., 1990.

Sparke, Penny. *An Introduction to Design and Culture: 1900 to the Present*. 2nd ed. London; New York: Routledge, 2004.

Theories and Documents of Contemporary Art: A Sourcebook of Artists' Writings. Eds. Kristine Stiles and Peter Selz. California Studies in the History of Art 35. Berkeley: Univ. of California Pr., 1996.

Varnedoe, Kirk. *Pictures of Nothing: Abstract Art Since Pollock*. Bollingen Series 48. Princeton: Princeton Univ. Pr., 2006.

Wagner, Anne M. *Three Artists (Three Women): Modernism and the Art of Hesse, Krasner, and O'Keeffe*. Berkeley: Univ. of California Pr., 1996.

Waldman, Diane. *Collage, Assemblage, and the Found Object*. New York: Abrams, 1992.

Women Artists in the 20th and 21st Century. Ed. Uta Grosenick. Köln; New York: Taschen, 2001.

Women Making Art: Women in the Visual, Literary, and Performing Arts Since 1960. Eds. Deborah Johnson and Wendy Oliver. Eruptions, Vol. 7. New York: Peter Lang, 2001.

Word as Image: American Art, 1960–1990. Milwaukee: Milwaukee Art Museum, 1990.

CREDITS

Introduction
Intro-01 © Paul M.R. Maeyaert; Intro -02 Photography © The Art Institute of Chicago; Intro-04 © 2014 Georgia O'Keeffe Museum/Artists Rights Society (ARS), New York; Intro-05 Art © Estate of David Smith/Licensed by VAGA, New York, NY; Intro-06 Alinari Archives, Florence – Reproduced with the permission of Ministero per i Beni e le Attività Culturali; Intro-08 Photo: E.G. Schempf; Intro-09Box1 Ashmolean Museum, Oxford, England, UK; Intro-09Box2 Museum purchase in memory of Ellen B. Elliott. Fowler McCormick, Class of 1922, Fund. 2008-345 © 2014 Princeton University Art Museum/Art Resource NY/Scala, Florence. Photo: Bruce M. White; Intro-10 Image courtesy of the Board of Trustees, National Gallery of Art, Washington D.C.; Intro-11 Photograph: Franko Khoury; Intro-13 The Royal Collection © 2014 Her Majesty Queen Elizabeth II/The Bridgeman Art Library; Intro-14 © 2014 Photo Nat. Portrait Gall. Smithsonian/Art Resource/Scala, Florence; Intro-15 Photo ©Achim Bednorz, Köln. © F.L.C./ ADAGP, Paris/Artists Rights Society (ARS), New York 2014; Intro-16 Digital image courtesy of the Getty's Open Content Program; Intro-17 Index Ricerca Iconografica; Intro-18 © 2014 Image copyright The Metropolitan Museum of Art/ Art Resource/Scala, Florence; Intro-20a Hirmer Fotoarchiv; Intro-20b Araldo de Luca/CORBIS; Intro-21 ©V&A Images.

Chapter 1
01-01 © 2014 Scala, Florence/BPK, Bildagentur für Kunst, Kultur und Geschichte, Berlin; 01-02 Photo: Yvonne Mühleis ©Landesamt für Denkmalpflege im RP Stuttgart; 01-03 akg-images/Erich Lessing; 01-04 Jack Unruh/National Geographic Creative; 01-05 Slide n°10 (French Ministry of Culture and Communication, Regional Direction for Cultural Affairs – Rhône-Alpes region – Regional department of archaeology; 01-06 akg-images; 01-07 Yvonne Vertut; 01-08 Sisse Brimberg/National Geographic Creative; 01-09 Yvonne Vertut; 01-09Box Reconstruction by John Swogger, originally published as figure 5.8 in Ian Hodder's The Leopard's Tale; 01-10 The Art Archive/Museum of Anatolian Civilisations Ankara/Gianni Dagli Orti; 01-11a, b akg-images/Erich Lessing; 01-12©National Monuments Service Dept of Arts, Heritage and the Gaeltacht. Photo: Con Brogan; 01-13 Peter Adams/The Image Bank/Getty.

Chapter 2
02-01 © Photo Josse/Leemage; 02-01 Box AP/PA Photos; 02-03a, b © 2014 Photo Scala, Florence/BPK, Bildagentur für Kunst, Kultur und Geschichte, Berlin; 02-05 Courtesy of Penn Museum, object B17694, image 160104; 02-05 © The Trustees of the British Museum; 02-06 Courtesy of Penn Museum, object B16728, image 10872; 02-07 Michael S. Yamashita/Corbis; 02-08 RMN/Arnaudet; 02-09 RMN/ Hervé Lewandowski; 02-10 © 2014 Image copyright The Metropolitan Museum of Art/Art Resource/Scala, Florence; 02-11, 12 © The Trustees of the British Museum; 02-14 © 2014 Photo Scala, Florence/BPK, Bildagentur für Kunst, Kultur und Geschichte, Berlin; 02-15 Kurt and Rosalia Scholz/SuperStock.

Chapter 3
03-01 IAM/akg-images; 03-01Box akg-images/Erich Lessing; 03-02 Iberfoto/Alinari Archives; 03-04 National Geographic/ SuperStock; 03-05 Dorling Kindersley; 03-06 Araldo DeLuca/ Index Ricerca Iconografica; 03-07 ©2015 Museum of Fine Arts, Boston, Harvard University – Boston Museum of Fine Arts Expedition, 11.1738; 03-08 RMN/Franck Raux; 03-09 Araldo de Luca; 03-11 Photo: Jürgen Liepe; 03-12 Image © 2014 The Metropolitan Museum of Art/Art Resource/Scala, Florence; 03-13 Kurt and Rosalia Scholz/SuperStock; 03-16 Yvonne Vertut; 03-17,18 © 2014 Photo Scala, Florence; 03-19, 20 © 2014 Photo Scala, Florence/BPK Bildagentur für Kunst, Kultur und Geschichte, Berlin; 03-21 Araldo de Luca; 03-22, 23 © The Trustees of the British Museum.

Chapter 4
04-01 O. Louis Mazzatenta/National Geographic Creative; 04-02 National Museum of India, New Delhi, India/The Bridgeman Art Library; 04-03 Borromeo/Art Resource, NY; 04-04 © Adam Woolfitt/Robert Harding World Imagery/ Corbis; 04-05 Richard Ashworth/Robert Harding; 04-06 Gift of Mr. and Mrs. Eric Lidow in honor of the museum's twenty-fifth anniversary (M.91.90); 04-07 Rick Asher; 04-08 ACSAA Slide 325; 04-09 Dinodia Photo LLP; 04-10 Luca Tettoni/Robert Harding; 04-11 © Luca Tettoni/Corbis; 04-12 Courtesy of the Institute of History and Philology, Academia Sinica; 04-13 Cultural Relics Publishing House; 04-14Box © 2014 Princeton University Art Museum/Art Resource NY/Scala, Florence. Photo: Bruce M. White; 04-15 Wolfgang Kaehler/Corbis; 04-16 Cultural Relics Publishing House; 04-17 Photograph by John C. Huntington Courtesy of The Huntington Photographic Archive at The Ohio State University; 04-18 The Collection of the National Palace Museum; 04-19 James Caldwell/Alamy; 04-22 Tokyo National Museum DNP Archives.Com Co., Ltd; 04-23 Yoshio Watanabe/Pacific Press Service; 04-24 Getty/DAJ; 04-25 Japan National Tourist Organization.

Chapter 5
05-01 Photo Vatican Museums; 05-02 © 2014 Image copyright The Metropolitan Museum of Art/Art Resource/ Scala, Florence; 05-03 McRae Books Srl; 05-04 © 2014 White Images/Scala, Florence; 05-05, 6 © Craig & Marie Mauzy, Athens; 05-07 Studio Kontos Photostock; 05-08 The Art Archive/National Archaeological Museum Athens/Gianni Dagli Orti; 05-10 © Craig & Marie Mauzy, Athens; 05-12 Photographer: Kein Eintrag, DAI Deutsches Archaologisches Institut, Athens, NEG D-DAI-ATH-Mykene 63; 05-13 © 2014 Photo The Metropolitan Museum of Art/ Art Resource/Scala, FlorenceScala; 05-14b © Craig & Marie Mauzy, Athens; 05-15, 16, 17, 18, 19 Staatliche Antikensammlungen und Glyptothek München, Photograph by Renate Kühling; 05-20, 21 © Craig & Marie Mauzy, Athens; 05-21Box © 2014 Photo Scala, Florence – courtesy of the Ministero Beni e Att. Culturali; 05-22a Craig & Marie Mauzy; 05-22b Studio Kontos Photostock; 05-23 © 2014 Photo Scala, Florence/BPK, Bildagentur für Kunst, Kultur und Geschichte, Berlin; 05-24a, b akg-images/ Nimatallah; 05-26a © Craig & Marie Mauzy, Athens; 05-27, 28 © The Trustees of the British Museum; 05-29 Giraudon/ The Bridgeman Art Library; 05-30 akg-images/Nimatallah; 05-31 Studio Kontos Photostock; 05-32, 33 © Craig & Marie Mauzy, Athens; 05-34 akg-images/Nimatallah; 05-35 Photo Vatican Museums; 05-36 © 2014 Photo Scala, Florence – courtesy of the Ministero Beni e Att. Culturali; 05-37 Canali Photobank, Milan, Italy; 05-38b © Craig & Marie Mauzy, Athens; 05-39 RMN/Hervé Lewandowski; 05-40 © 2014 Image copyright The Metropolitan Museum of Art/Art Resource/Scala, FlorenceScala; 05-42 ©RMN/ Jean-Gilles Berizzi; 05-43 © 2014 Musei Capitolini, Rome/ Photo Scala, Florence; 05-44 © 2014 Photo Scala, Florence/ BPK, Bildagentur für Kunst, Kultur und Geschichte, Berlin; 05-45 © 2014 Photo Scala, Florence/BPK, Bildagentur für Kunst, Kultur und Geschichte, Berlin.

Chapter 6
06-01, 2 © Vincenzo Pirozzi, Rome; 06-03a Image courtesy of Dr Penelope Davies; 06-04 © 2014 Photo Scala, Florence – courtesy of the Ministero Beni e Att. Culturali; 06-05 akg-images/Nimatallah; 06-06 Araldo de Luca/ CORBIS; 06-07 Courtesy of the American Numismatic Society; 06-08 © 2014 Photo Scala, Florence – courtesy of the Ministero Beni e Att. Culturali; 06-09 Araldo de Luca/ CORBIS; 06-10a © Vincenzo Pirozzi, Rome ; 06-11 Danita Delimont Stock Photography; 06-12 Araldo de Luca/CORBIS; 06-13 akg-images Mondadori Portfolio/Andrea Jemolo; 06-14 akg-images/Andrea Jemolo; 06-16 Index Ricerca Iconografica; 06-17 Photo Vatican Museums; 06-18, 19, 20 Canali Photobank, Milan, Italy; 06-21 Index Ricerca Iconografica; 06-22 akg-images/Erich Lessing; 06-23 Lautaro/Alamy; 06-24a Courtesy of Dr James E. Packer; 06-24b Index Ricerca Iconografica; 06-25 © Vincenzo Pirozzi, Rome; 06-26 © 2014 Photo Scala, Florence – courtesy of the Ministero Beni e Att. Culturali; 06-27 Christian Reister/BROKER/Robert Harding; 06-28 © Vincenzo Pirozzi, Rome; 06-29a Araldo de Luca/Corbis; 06-29b Araldo de Luca; 06-30a, b Ikona; 06-31 © Fotografica Foglia, Naples; 06-32 Canali Photobank Milan, Italy; 06-33 Araldo de Luca/ Corbis; 06-34 ©Cameraphoto Arte, Venice; 06-35a Raimund Kutter/BROKER/Robert Harding; 06-36, 37 ©Vincenzo Pirozzi, Rome; 06-38 Ikona.

Chapter 7
07-01 akg-images/Pirozzi; 07-02 Ikona; 07-03 © 2014 Photo Art Resource/Scala, Florence; 07-03Box Zev Radovan/ Bibleland Pictures; 07-04 Yale University Art Gallery, Dura-Europos Collection; 07-08 Index Ricerca Iconografica; 07-09 Canali Photobank, Milan, Italy; 07-10 Cameraphoto Arte, Venice; 07-11 Vasari/Index Ricerca Iconografica; 07-12 Photo: Ayhan Altun; 07-13b Reprinted with the permission of Perspecta, Yale School of Architecture; 07-14 Photo: Ayhan Altun; 07-16 © 2014 Photo Scala, Florence; 07-17, 18 Cameraphoto Arte, Venice; 07-19 Bildarchiv der Osterreichische Nationalbibliothek; 07-20 Studio Kontos Photostock; 07-22b Photo: Bruce White; 07-23 Cameraphoto Arte, Venice; 07-24, 25 Photo: Ayhan Altun; 07-26 ©2014 Photo Scala, Florence.

Chapter 8
08-02a Zoonar GmbH/Alamy; 08-02b Dorling Kindersley; 08-03 The Art Archive/Gianni Dagli Orti; 08-04 Roger Wood/CORBIS; 08-05a akg-images/A.F. Kersting; 08-06 akg-images/Erich Lessing; 08-07 © 2014 The Metropolitan Museum/Scala, Florence; 08-08 RMN/Thierry Ollivier; 08-09a Werner Forman Archive Ltd; 08-10 © 2014 The Metropolitan Museum of Art/Art Resource/Scala, Florence; 08-11 Dr. Wilfried Bahnmuller/BROKER/Robert Harding; 08-12 Peter Sanders Photography; 08-13a Sonia Halliday Photographs; 08-14, Box © 2014 Photo The Metropolitan Museum of Art/ Art Resource/Scala, Florence; 08-15 RMN (Musée du Louvre)/ Franck Raux; 08-17 akg-images/Roland & Sabrina Michaud; 08-18 Image courtesy of the Aga Khan Museum; 08-19 Courtesy of the architect/Aga Khan Trust for Culture.

Chapter 9
09-01 © Peter Adams/Corbis; 09-02 David Cumming; Eye Ubiquitous/CORBIS; 09-06 Museum of Fine Arts, Boston; 09-07 Photo: Katherine Wetzel; 09-08 Dave G. Houser/Corbis; 9-10 Corbis; 09-12 © The Trustees of the British Museum; 09-13 The Collection of the National Palace Museum; 09-14 Photograph Robert Newcombe; 09-16 Robert Harding World Imagery; 09-17 Tokyo National Museum DNP Archives.Com Co., Ltd; 09-20 akg-images/ Nimatallah; 09-21 Japan National Tourist Organization; 09-24 Michael S. Yamashita/Corbis; 09-25 Japan National Tourist Organization; 09-27 © 2014 Photo The Metropolitan Museum of Art/Art Resource/Scala, Florence.

Chapter 9
09-01 Peter Adams/Corbis; 09-02 David Cumming/Eye Ubiquitous/CORBIS; 09-06 Museum of Fine Arts, Boston; 09-07 Photo: Katherine Wetzel; 09-08 Dave G. Houser/ Corbis; 9-10 Corbis; 09-12 © The Trustees of the British Museum; 09-13 The Collection of the National Palace Museum; 09-14 Photograph Robert Newcombe; 09-16 Robert Harding World Imagery; 09-17 Tokyo National Museum DNP Archives.Com Co., Ltd; 09-20 akg-images/ Nimatallah; 09-21 Japan National Tourist Organization; 09-24 Michael S. Yamashita/Corbis; 09-25 Japan National Tourist Organization; 09-27 © 2014 Photo The Metropolitan Museum of Art/Art Resource/Scala, Florence.

Chapter 10
10-01 Trinity College, Dublin; 10-02 © The Trustees of the British Museum; 10-03 Trinity College Library; 10-04 Nationalmuseet Danske Afdeling; 10-05a akg/ Bildarchiv Monheim; 10-06 akg-images/Erich Lessing; 10-07b Achim Bednorz; 10-08a Stiftsbibliotjek, St. Gallen; 10-10 Giraudon/The Bridgeman Art Library; 10-11, 12 © 2014 Photo Pierpont Morgan Library/Art Resource/Scala, Florence; 10-13 © Rheinisches Bildarchiv Köln; 10-14 Foto Marburg, Frank Tomio; 10-15 Achim Bednorz; 10-16 Hessisches Landes- und Hochschulebibliothek; 10-19 Archivo Oronoz; 10-20 Studio Folco Quilici Produzioni Edizioni Srl; 10-21a akg-images/A.F. Kersting; 10-22, 23 © Achim Bednorz, Köln; 10-24 Cathedral Museum of St. Lazare, Autun, Burgundy, France/The Bridgeman Art Library; 10-25 Index Ricerca Iconografica; 10-25Box Musée de la Tapisserie, Bayeux, France/The Bridgeman Art Library; 10-26 Photographic reproduction: MNAC – Museu Nacional d'Art de Catalunya, Barcelona. Photographers: Calveras/Mérida/ Sagristà; 10-27 By permission of the President and Fellows of Corpus Christi College, Oxford; 10-28, 29 akg-images/Erich Lessing; 10-31 © 2014 Photo The Metropolitan Museum of Art/Art Resource/Scala, Florence.

Chapter 11
11-01 Sonia Halliday Photographs; 11-02b © Paul M.R. Maeyaert; 11-04, 5, 6b © Achim Bednorz, Köln; 11-08 Angelo Hornak, London; 11-09 Corbis; 11-10 © Achim Bednorz, Köln; 11-11 Angelo Hornak Photo Library; 11-12 F1 ONLINE/SuperStock; 11-13a © 2014 Photo The Pierpont Morgan Library/Art Resource/Scala Florence; 11-13b © 2014 The Pierpont Morgan Library/Art Resource/ Scala Florence; 11-14 © 2014 The Metropolitan Museum of Art/Art Resource/Scala, Florence; 11-15 RMN/Martine Beck-Coppola; 11-17b Skyscan/Corbis; 11-18 akg-images/ A.F. Kersting; 11-19 © 2014 Photo Pierpont Morgan Library/Art Resource/Scala, Florence; 11-20 © 2014 Photo The Metropolitan Museum of Art/Art Resource/Scala, Florence; 11-21 akg-images/Erich Lessing; 11-22 © Achim Bednorz, Köln; 11-22Box1, 2 © Quattrone, Florence; 11-23 © 2014 Photo Scala, Florence; 11-24 Lew Minter; 11-25 © 2014 Photo Scala, Florence; 11-26, 27 © Quattrone, Florence; 11-28 © 2014 Photo Scala, Florence; 11-29 © Quattrone, Florence.

Chapter 12
12-01 © 2014 Photo The National Gallery, London/Scala, Florence; 12-02 akg-images; 12-03 © 2014 Photo The Metropolitan Museum of Art/Art Resource/Scala, Florence; 12-04a akg-images/Erich Lessing; 12-04b akg-images; 12-05 akg-images/Joseph Martin; 12-06 © 2014 Photo The Metropolitan Museum of Art/Art Resource/Scala, Florence; 12-07 © Quattrone, Florence; 12-08 © 2014 Photo The Metropolitan Museum of Art/Art Resource/Scala, Florence; 12-09 Bibliotheque Mazarine, Paris, France Archives Charmet/The Bridgeman Art Library; 12-10 © 2014 Photo The Metropolitan Museum of Art/Art Resource/Scala, Florence; 12-12 Vanni Archive/Corbis; 12-13, 14, 15

Names in **bold** refer to artists and architects.
Page numbers in *italics* refer to illustrations.